For Reference

Not to be taken from this room

D1591938

WESTERN MOVIE
QUOTATIONS

"I'm glad you decided to drift along with me.
It's kind of lonesome trailing alone."
— as spoken by John Carruthers (John Wayne)
in Robert N. Bradbury's *Blue Steel*
(Lone Star/Monogram, 1934)

"I'd say most of what I'm telling you is true.
And the rest — well, the rest is the West."
— as narrated by Wilford Brimley
in Tad Murphy's *Last of the Dogmen*
(Savory Pictures, 1995)

WESTERN MOVIE QUOTATIONS

Compiled by JIM KANE

McFarland & Company, Inc., Publishers
Jefferson, North Carolina, and London

791.436
K16w

To Vicky, Jennifer, and Michael;
and to the memory of brother Ed Kane —
who never really much cared for westerns,
but nevertheless took me to my first cowboy picture show

Cover: William Demarest and Gary Cooper in *Along Came Jones* (RKO, 1945).

Library of Congress Cataloguing-in-Publication Data

Kane, Jim, 1946–
Western movie quotations / compiled by Jim Kane.
p.   cm.
Includes index.
ISBN 0-7864-0594-5
(illustrated case binding : 50# alkaline paper) ∞
1. Western films — Quotations, maxims, etc.   I. Title
PN1995.9.W4K26   1999
791.43'6278 — dc21
99-24318 CIP

British Library Cataloguing-in-Publication data are available

©1999 Jim Kane. All rights reserved

*No part of this book may be reproduced or transmitted in any form
or by any means, electronic or mechanical, including photocopying
or recording, or by any information storage and retrieval system,
without permission in writing from the publisher.*

Manufactured in the United States of America

*McFarland & Company, Inc., Publishers
Box 611, Jefferson, North Carolina 28640
www.mcfarlandpub.com*

Table of Contents

Introduction   vii

The Quotations (by Topic)

University Libraries
Carnegie Mellon University
Pittsburgh PA 15213-3890

Introduction

Prior to our parents' purchasing a television set, my sister and I arranged to watch Saturday morning westerns at an elderly neighbor's home. The actual negotiations were left to my older sister who at the time was well into her third year of grade school. Beth worked it out so that we would be permitted to come over and watch westerns all morning. The only exception and stipulation was that we were to be "very quiet and still" during the half-hour John Cameron Swayze news show. These terms seemed both reasonable and sensible. As I recall, the sagebrushers started at 6:30 A.M. and we were promptly there at that time watching them. And by the time you could say John Cameron Swayze, we were long gone! But the love of westerns remained.

Westerns are full of colorful characters expressing themselves on a number of subjects. The dialogue takes on meaning and life within the context and the setting in which it is being spoken. And that is what this book is all about.

The characters may be good guys or bad guys, gunfighters or lawmen, cowboys or sodbusters. They may be men or women. The setting may be saloon, cemetery, fort, or ranch. The action may be a showdown, Indian attack, cattle drive, or hanging.

This book is not based upon leading stars or famous movies, but rather characters both small and large and what they had to say, regardless of a movie's importance. The scope is western movies from the 1920s to the present. It includes some silent movies (i.e., title cards) as well as serials.

Western Movie Quotations is a compilation of over 6,000 quotations from more than 1,000 western movies with selected photos from many of these sagebrushers. The book is arranged alphabetically by broad topic. Within each topic, the lines or quotations are arranged alphabetically by movie title. Saddle up — and happy trails!

Acknowledgments

I am indebted to all the motion picture and television actors and actresses, writers, producers, and directors who made this book possible. A special thanks to Bob Wolpert (Charleston) for steering me to McFarland and for the use of many B western movies from his private collection. To Ted Okuda (Chicago) for use of photos from his private collection. To Claire Brandt at Eddie Brandt's Saturday Matinee (North Hollywood) who, on short notice, greatly assisted in the acquisition of the majority of the photos for this project. And to Tom and Jim Goldrup (California) for their very kind photo contributions.

Abbreviations Used in This Book

FOX — Twentieth Century–Fox
HBO — Home Box Office

MGM — Metro Goldwyn Mayer
NGP — National General Picture
PRC — Producer's Releasing Corporation
RKO — RKO Radio
TVW — Television Western
(And please note: "Universal" was used for both Universal and Universal International studios)

Sources Useful in This Compilation

Buscombe, Edward, ed. *The BFI Companion to the Western*. New York: Atheneum, 1988.
Everson, William K. *A Pictorial History of the Western Film*. Secaucus, N.J.: Citadel Press, 1969.
Everson, William K. *The Hollywood Western*. Secaucus, N.J.: Citadel Press, 1992.
Eyes, Allen. *The Western*. London: Tantivy Press, 1975.
Grant, Bruce. *Concise Encyclopedia of the American Indian*. New York: Bonanza Books, 1989.
Hardy, Phil. *The Western*. New York: William Morrow, 1983.
Hyams, Jay. *The Life and Times of the Western Movie*. New York: Gallery Books, 1983.
Lentz, Harris M., III. *Western and Frontier Film and Television Credits 1903–1995*. 2 volumes. Jefferson, N.C.: McFarland, 1996.
Nash, Jay Roberts, and Stanley Ralph Ross. *The Motion Picture Guide*. Chicago: Cinebooks, 1985.
Nye, Douglas E. *Those Six-Gun Heroes*. Spartanburg, S.C.: ETN Endowment of South Carolina, 1982.
Weisser, Thomas. *Spaghetti Westerns — The Good, the Bad and the Violent*. Jefferson, N.C.: McFarland, 1992.

WESTERN MOVIE QUOTATIONS

The arrangement is alphabetical by broad topic;
see the Table of Contents

Bad Guys

See also Holdups; Outlaws, Cattle Rustlers and Horse Thieves

1

Bullwhip: Oh, I have no doubt that you are a scoundrel, Higgins. But you certainly aren't the type who would shoot an unarmed man.

Higgins: Well, that's purely a personal opinion on your part.

Bullwhip Griffin played by Roddy McDowall and Judge Higgins played by Karl Malden: James Neilson's *The Adventures of Bullwhip Griffin* (Buena Vista, 1967).

2

Mrs. Salter: The men look bad to me.

Fred Salter: Well, they ought to feel at home around here.

Mrs. Salter played by Helen Brown and Fred Salter played by Harry Shannon: Ray Nazarro's *Al Jennings of Oklahoma* (Columbia, 1951).

3

Quirt: I thought you weren't allowed to work on Sunday?

Penny: Oh Quirt, there's nothing we're not allowed to do. It's just that we don't believe in doing what we know is wrong.

Quirt: Well, that makes it pretty much each fella's own guess.

Penny: But each fella knows inside.

Quirt: Well, there's a lot of gents I wouldn't want to give that much leeway to.

Quirt Evans played by John Wayne and Prudence "Penny" Worth played by Gail Russell: James Edward Grant's *Angel and the Badman* (Republic, 1947).

4

Peso: Do you like me?

Tom: You're a hero to every kid in the territory. But I never saw much sense in putting a thief on a pedestal.

Peso: I had always hoped that you would follow in my footsteps. But, no, you had to take after your mother …law and order.

Peso played by Gilbert Roland and Tom Herrera played by Robert Horton: Harold Kress' *Apache War Smoke* (MGM, 1952).

5

Miles: You know, Alpheus, the problem with polygamy is that when you've had 27 wives and 56 children, one's just bound to turn out as dirt-stupid and pig-ugly as you.

Miles played by Tom Berenger and Alpheus Young played by Daniel Quinn: Craig R. Baxley's *The*

Avenging Angel (Turner Home Entertainment, 1995).

6

Pop: You see, there things a man ought never do: spit in church, scratch his self in front of his ma, and pick his nose. Yes, that's what my pa learned me and it stood me in good step.

Mace: I don't imagine your pa ever mentioned shooting people, and burning their house down, and stealing, and things like that?

Pop: Well, I'm talking about mannerly things, Mr. Bishop. I ain't talking about making a living.

Pop Chaney played by Will Geer and Mace Bishop played by James Stewart: Andrew McLaglen's *Bandolero!* (20th Century–Fox, 1968).

7

Mace: Why do you ride with men like these?

Dee: Oh, I don't know. I just got used to it, I guess, through the years. You begin to go one way, you keep on going that way, and pretty soon there's no other way.

Mace Bishop played by James Stewart and Dee Bishop played by Dean Martin: Andrew McLaglen's *Bandolero!* (20th Century–Fox, 1968).

8

Maria: I thought he was your friend?

Dee: He is, but that don't make him any less disgusting. As a matter of fact, all my friends are disgusting. You take Pop, for instance. He was due to be shot the day he was born. And that heart of his is nothing more but a festering sore.

Maria Stoner played by Raquel Welch and Dee Bishop played by Dean Martin: Andrew McLaglen's *Bandolero!* (20th Century–Fox, 1968).

9

Jeremy: I don't like that man Cole.

Glyn: Why not?

Jeremy: I heard Grundy say he was a raider on the Missouri border.

Glyn: Well, lots of people used to raid along the border. And some of them decided to change.

Jeremy: That kind can't change. When an apple's rotten, there's nothing you can do except throw it away or it will spoil the whole barrel.

Glyn: Well, there's a difference between apples and men.

Jeremy Baile played by Jay C. Flippen, Emerson Cole Garret played by Arthur Kennedy, Don Grundy played by Frank Ferguson, and Glyn McLyntock played by James Stewart: Anthony Mann's *Bend of the River* (Universal, 1952).

10

Doc: We knew a place where the climate was cool. Way down there between Oklahoma and Texas. A little town of Quinto in the Cimarron sand hills. Badman's Territory they called it. Cherokee Strip where they rigged civil law that carpetbaggers couldn't stick its claws in, and the Army wouldn't waste the powder. Plenty fellas vacationed there. Mostly fast gunhands who didn't like the smell of rope.

Doc Butcher played by Walter Brennan: William D. Russell's *Best of the Badmen* (RKO, 1951).

11

Buck: You want me, Pa?

Rufus: Before you was born I did.

Buck Hannassey played by Chuck Connors and Rufus Hannassey played by Burl Ives: William Wyler's *The Big Country* (United Artists, 1958).

12

Daisy: You stye on the eye of a flea on a thigh of a nit on the neck of a gnat!

Daisy Fisher played by Patrice Wymore: Felix Feist's *The Big Trees* (Warner Bros., 1952).

13

Sheriff: The scum of the whole country is coming west by the wagon-load. We got more criminals than we have citizens.

Brady: Sounds like an up-and-coming country. Looks like we arrived just in time.

Sheriff Gordon played by Lloyd Gough and Jersey Brady played by Percy Kilbride: George Sherman's *Black Bart* (Universal, 1948).

14

Lance: One thing about being a crook: you can spot another crook at fifty paces.

Lance Hardeen played by Jeffrey Lynn: George Sherman's *Black Bart* (Universal, 1948).

15

Hedley: I've decided to launch an attack that will reduce Rock Ridge to ashes.

Taggart: What do you want me to do, sir?

Hedley: I want you to round up every vicious criminal and gunslinger in the west. Take this down. I want rustlers,

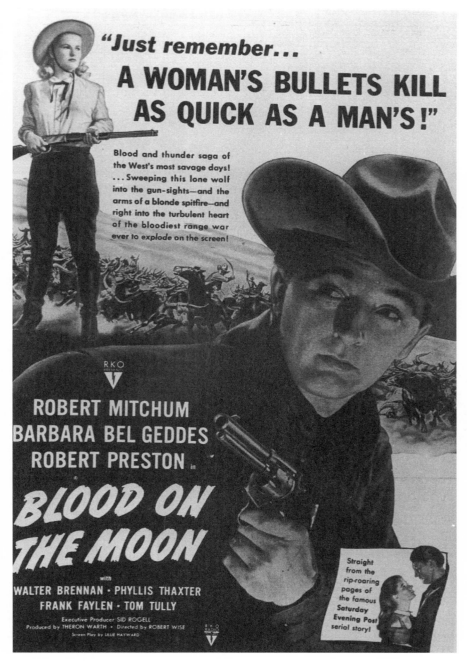

"Just remember...
A WOMAN'S BULLETS KILL
AS QUICK AS A MAN'S!"

Blood and thunder saga of the West's most savage days! ...Sweeping this lone wolf into the gun-sights—and the arms of a blonde spitfire—and right into the turbulent heart of the bloodiest range war ever to explode on the screen!

RKO

ROBERT MITCHUM
BARBARA BEL GEDDES
ROBERT PRESTON in

BLOOD ON THE MOON

with
WALTER BRENNAN · PHYLLIS THAXTER
FRANK FAYLEN · TOM TULLY

Executive Producer SID ROGELL
Produced by THERON WARTH · Directed by ROBERT WISE
Screen Play by LILLIE HAYWARD

Straight from the rip-roaring pages of the famous Saturday Evening Post serial story!

Advertisement for Robert Wise's classic western *Blood on the Moon* (RKO, 1948).

cutthroats, murderers, bounty hunters, desperadoes, mugs, punks, thugs, nitwits, halfwits, dimwits, vipers, snipers, con men, Indian agents, Mexican bandits, muggers, rustlers, bushwhackers, horn swaggerers, horse thieves, bull wits, train robbers, bank robbers, con men, Indian agents, and Methodists!
Taggart: Could you repeat that, sir?
Hedley Lamarr played by Harvey Korman and Taggart played by Slim Pickens: Mel Brooks' *Blazing Saddles* (Warner Bros., 1974).

16
Jim: I've seen dogs that wouldn't claim you for a son, Tate.
Jim Garry played by Robert Mitchum and Tate Riling played by Robert Preston: Robert Wise's *Blood on the Moon* (RKO, 1948).

17
Stage Driver: He's tougher than an old sow's nose!
The Stage Driver played by Hank Bell: Joseph Kane's *The Carson City Kid* (Republic, 1940).

18
John: I suppose you've come to see me about that little thing last night.
Marshal: That wasn't any little thing you did, O'Hanlan. That was a Bannister you shot. I've been wanting to do it for years.
John: You haven't come to arrest me?
Marshal: I've come to warn you. When you kill one Bannister, 500 will come to his funeral.
John: Oh, you mean some of his kin might come here for me, huh?
Marshal: You can chisel it in granite.
John: Well, what am I supposed to do?
Marshal: My advice to you is to grab on to the tail of the first horse you see traveling south.
John: Go back to Texas, you mean?
Marshal: It's still there, ain't it? It makes no difference to me, but them Bannisters are meaner than tiger spit.
John: Can't I count on any help from you?
Marshal: Oh, I have to go to Medicine Bow ...ah ...for a prisoner. But whatever you do, do it like you mean it.
John: Well, how much time do I have?
Marshal: Oh, three days at the most. They live quite a ways out of town. But trouble rides a fast horse!
John O'Hanlan played by James Stewart and Marshal Anderson played by Arch Johnson: Gene Kelly's *The Cheyenne Social Club* (NGP, 1970).

19
Helena: Tell me, Señor, are you as bad as they say?
Chuka: No man is as bad as they say, Señorita.
Helena Chavez played by Angela Dorian/Victoria Vetri and Chuka played by Rod Taylor: Gordon Douglas' *Chuka* (Paramount, 1967).

20
McBain: Now that I can look back on it, I can see how bad it was. That's how come me to give myself up.
Major: Yep, after breaking one ranger's jaw and slicing up two others with a Bowie knife.
McBain: Oh, I feel bad about that. I wasn't using my head.
Major: You used everything else! Feet, fist, and teeth!
McBain: Yes sir. But them rangers sure won me over. If I had just known men like that, I might never have fell in with bad companions.
Ed McBain played by Guinn "Big Boy" Williams and Major Henry played by Bruce Cabot: Michael Curtiz's *The Comancheros* (20th Century–Fox, 1961).

21
Miles: If you expect me to sit around and watch you tear down everything I've

Stagecoach passengers find refuge in a dry wash and fight off Indian attack. Carter Hamilton (John Lund), John Banner (Dale Robertson), Amy Clarke (Linda Darnell), and Senator Blakely (Ward Bond) in *Dakota Incident* (Republic, 1956).

built up, you're crazier than I think. I've worked hard to get where I am ...and done everything a man can do. I've lied, cheated, and stolen. I've even killed to build this set up I've got now. And I'm not going to let any man destroy it. Least of all you.

Younger Miles played by George Macready: Ray Enright's *Coroner Creek* (Columbia, 1948).

22

Duchess: So that ornery varmit finally got what he had comin' to him. Did he talk?

Red Ryder: Well, he couldn't very well seeing how he's dead.

Duchess played by Marin Sais and Red Ryder played by Jim Bannon: Lewis D. Collins' *Cowboy and the Prizefighter* (Eagle-Lion/Equity Pictures, 1950).

23

Blakely: Not all savages paint their faces and wear eagle feathers!

Senator Blakely played by Ward Bond: Lewis R. Foster's *Dakota Incident* (Republic, 1956).

24

Mrs. Cantrell: You're no good, Will.

Cantrell: I've killed a lot of men for saying less than that!

Mrs. Cantrell: You've killed a lot of men for saying nothing at all!

Mrs. Cantrell played by Marjorie Main and William Cantrell played by Walter Pidgeon: Raoul Walsh's *The Dark Command* (Republic, 1940).

25

Cantrell: I know what I'm doing, Ma. I'll be running Kansas yet. I'm going clear

up to the top. But I'm not going for the climb or the view.

William Cantrell played by Walter Pidgeon: Raoul Walsh's *The Dark Command* (Republic, 1940).

26

Sharmon: He spreads evil. He'll not only destroy us, he'll destroy the town.

Sharmon Fulton played by Mara Corday: Harmon Jones' *A Day of Fury* (Universal, 1956).

27

Preacher: That man is a creature of hell. If he stays here, he'll turn this town into a hell.

Marshal: But he can't do it alone. Our problem is to keep him from stampeding us into helping him.

Preacher Jason played by John Dehner and Marshal

Allan Burnett played by Jock Mahoney: Harmon Jones' *A Day of Fury* (Universal, 1956).

28

Jagade: I turned over a rotten log. I didn't create what came crawling out from under.

Jagade played by Dale Robertson: Harmon Jones' *A Day of Fury* (Universal, 1956).

29

Ryan: If you're going to follow somebody, youngster, do a better job of it. This world is full of nervous characters. They'd shoot you in the back first, and then introduce themselves.

Ryan played by Lee Van Cleef: Giulio Petroni's *Death Rides a Horse* (United Artists, 1967).

30

Wes: He's crazy. But then out here it might make him the sanest man around.

Wes Porter played by Buck Taylor: E.W. Swackhamer's *Desperado: The Outlaw Wars* (TVW, 1989).

31

Sheriff: Do you know who I am?
Sikes: I can't say I've had the pleasure.
Sheriff: I'm the man who's gonna see you at the end of a knotted hemp before the month's out.
Sikes: Did I do something to you?
Sheriff: You killed a lady a little while back. Do you remember her?
Sikes: I can't keep track of everybody I meet.

Sheriff Campbell played by Richard Farnsworth and John Sikes played by James Remar: E.W. Swackhamer's *Desperado: The Outlaw Wars* (TVW, 1989).

32

Dooley: I don't mean to pry or nothing, but it's just …I wonder how a man gets such bad enemies.
Cowboy: I never had any good ones.

Dooley played by William Forsythe and the Cowboy played by Emilio Estevez: Gene Quintano's *Dollar for the Dead* (TVW, 1998).

33

Brannon: Now look! You don't have to see a skunk to know he's around.

Sam Brannon played by Walter Brennan: Nathan Juran's *Drums Across the River* (Universal, 1954).

34

Ebenezer: I'll give you some helpful advice: be selfish, be greedy, and trust no one!

Ebenezer Scrooge played by Jack Palance: Ken Jubenvill's *Ebenezer* (TVW, 1997).

35

Teacher: The day began like a thousand other Arizona days. That was …until the cloud came. It began on the horizon. Shadows of dust moving at great speed. And then the pounding of humps of the hard ground. As the whirlwind got closer, you could see into the dust. The shapes of horses and then the riders. Riders with guns on both hips and bandoleers across their chests. They rode hard. They rode with a purpose. As they approached the town, they reined back on their horses. The dust around them settled and you could see their faces. Faces weathered by the Mexican sun. Faces marked by violence.

Teacher Billy Ray Smith played by Anthony Edwards: Peter Markle's *El Diablo* (HBO Pictures, 1990).

36

Spivey: I'll tell you something about this El Diablo. They did find him once. Caught him down in Amos, a little border town north of Laredo. Caught him, tried him, and hanged him all in the same night. But he wouldn't die! He just hanged there by his neck, spitting at the crowd like they disgusted him. Cussed 'em out so bad the women folk had to go home. I was there when they cut him down. And I thank the Lord I left when I did. Three days later, so the story goes, El Diablo returned to Amos with his men and cut out the heart of every man, woman, and child in the whole blessed town. And just left them there to bleach in the sun. Pretty soon, they started to rot and then the buzzards come and started pecking out what was left of the eyeballs…

Spivey Irick played by Jim Beaver: Peter Markle's *El Diablo* (HBO Pictures, 1990).

37

Donner: I see you found yourself a new coat.
Clayton: Yes. A coat of a brave man who died defending the rights of his people. There were two bullet holes in the back of it. You heard of Señor Montez?
Donner: Montez made the mistake of interfering with the law. If you're smart, you won't make the same mistake.
Clayton: If I do, Donner, I'll remember not to turn my back on you.

Burt Donner played by Sterling Hayden and Clayton Fletcher played by John Payne: Lewis Foster's *El Paso* (Paramount, 1949).

38

Evelyn: It's obvious you and your men are hired killers down from the northern range wars.
Larkin: We work in the open. We eat and drink with the ranchers who hire us …and as much respected as anyone in the country.
Evelyn: Don't quibble any fine line with me, Mr. Larkin. You're as dishonest as any common road bandit.
Larkin: I'm not ashamed of the part I play. There's not a territorial border we cross where there's men waiting …hoping I can take them on …waiting to call themselves Larkin men.
Evelyn: You're admitting your only importance is collecting men who don't care whether they live or die …who only live for the moment.
Larkin: It's been a long road to make a name men will follow. You'll get no apology from me.
Evelyn: It won't be long before you'll be running out of borders. You'll come full circle against the law that made you move on.
Larkin: You tie me up pretty good, Evelyn.
Evelyn: Why fight against times changing? Why not join in changing them?
Larkin: Then I'll be like all the rest. Today, I'm one of a few. I lead. That's important to me.

Evelyn played by Inger Stevens and Bob Larkin played by Henry Fonda: Vincent McEveety's *Firecreek* (Warner Bros.–Seven Arts, 1968).

39

Chico: Our orders are to make sure he does not die …but also to make sure he regrets the day he was born.

Chico played by Mario Brega: Sergio Leone's *A Fistful of Dollars* (United Artists, 1964; U.S. 1967).

40

Joe (to friend Zack): You made a mistake. You should have shot out the gun hand.
Matson: It wouldn't have made any difference. Go ahead, shoot it off, and I'll still get you! You shoot out my eyes and I'll still find you! You put a bullet in my heart and I'll make a deal with the devil. I'll trade him for just enough time to come back from hell and kill you. You hear me? I'm gonna kill you!

Joe Jarrett played by Dean Martin, Zack Thomas played by Frank Sinatra, and Matson played by Charles Bronson: Robert Aldrich's *Four for Texas* (Warner Bros., 1964).

41

Ann: Who are those tough looking men?
Brett: The big one leaning against the post is Luke Johnson. They say he is an outlaw.
Ann: Well, why isn't he in prison?
Brett: This isn't Maryland, honey. This is the frontier. The last two marshals that went after Johnson are dead.

Ann Langhorne played by Mary Hart/Lynne Roberts and Brett Langhorne played by Donald Dillaway: Joseph Kane's *Frontier Pony Express* (Republic, 1939).

42

Sieber: There's two dead women there …and two little kids. They scalped them all, all four of 'em. Bounty hunters. The government down here pays 200 pesos a head for the men, 100 for the women, and 50 for those kids. They kill any Indian, and then claim they are Apache. I don't see how any man can sink that low. Must be Texans …the lowest form of white man there is.

Al Sieber played by Robert Duvall: Walter Hill's *Geronimo: An American Legend* (Columbia, 1993).

43

Ruth: Eddie is just a boy. Tom was killed by a hardened criminal.
Ben: Do you think this kid is any less hardened? Since when is a young rattlesnake any less poisonous than an old one?

Ruth Granger played by Maggie Hayes, the Kid (Eddie) played by Robert Vaughn, and Ben Cutler played by Fred MacMurray: Nathan Juran's *Good Day for a Hanging* (Columbia, 1958).

44

Tuco: Who the hell is that? One bastard goes in and another comes out.

Tuco played by Eli Wallach: Sergio Leone's *The Good, the Bad, and the Ugly* (United Artists, 1966; U.S. 1968).

45

Bryant: Now, let's go over what we know or can guess so far. We're faced with a shrewd and ruthless gang of outlaws. Their operation is clever and deadly. They wait until a man with a price on his head is jailed, then spring him and use him as a front man for a series of holdups …making sure he is the only one ever recognized. The reward keeps going up. When it reaches three or four thousand dollars, the man is killed. Somebody is hired to collect the reward.

Michael Bryant, head of the National Detective Agency, was uncredited: Frank McDonald's *Gunfight at Comanche Creek* (Allied Artists, 1964).

46

Spud: You know what you remind me of, Morris? A turd with lips!

Spud Walker played by Ivan Sergei and Jack Morris played by Dave Ward: Larry Ferguson's *Gunfighter's Moon* (Rysher Entertainment, Cabin Fever Entertainment, 1995).

47

Halleck: You don't understand, Devlin. I mean to hire you.
Devlin: I don't like you.
Halleck: Lots of people don't. I still do business with them.
Devlin: I don't like your way of doing.
Halleck: Well, a man can't eat the walnuts unless he cracks a few shells.

Lew Halleck played by Cameron Mitchell and James Devlin played by Steve Forrest: Michael Caffey's *The Hanged Man* (TVW, 1974).

48

Narrator: I don't know who started all this talk about good always being mixed in with the bad, and bad with good. All I know is, when people are alone, when there's no law to see to it that they got to stand inside the bounds, then they're either all good or all bad. And it's a tough thing for a boy to find out that his pa is one of the bad.

Seated: Homer "Wild Horse" Bannon (Melvyn Douglas) and grandson Lon Bannon (Brandon De Wilde). Standing: son Hud Bannon (Paul Newman) with married woman Lily Peters (Yvette Vickers). Hud is a selfish and uncaring person who values and respects nothing. "You keep no check on your appetites at all," says father in *Hud* (Paramount, 1963).

Narration by Noel Hickman (played by Chuck Pierce, Jr. as boy and Charles B. Pierce as old man): Charles B. Pierce's *Hawken's Breed* (Vidmark Entertainment, 1987).

49

Jonas: Where do you hail from?

Beggar: From under a rock. That's where they say we all begin …crawling out from underneath something.

Jonas played by Joseph Cotten and the Beggar played by Al Mulock: Sergio Corbucci's *The Hellbenders* (Embassy Pictures, 1967).

50

Roxanne: He's always looking at the good side of people.

Marcus: Yeah, but while he's looking at their good side, their bad side is gonna finish him.

Roxanne played by Debbie Lytton and Marcus played by Michael Sharrett: Robert Butler's *Hot Lead and Cold Feet* (Buena Vista, 1978).

51

Homer: You don't care about people, Hud. You don't give a damn about 'em. Oh, you got all that charm going for ya. And it makes the youngsters want to be like ya. That's the shame of it because you don't value anything. You don't respect nothing. You keep no check on your appetites at all. You live just for yourself. And that makes you not fit to live with.

Homer Bannon played by Melvyn Douglas and Hud Bannon played by Paul Newman: Martin Ritt's *Hud* (Paramount, 1963).

52

Grey: It concerns honor. Do you know what that is? We're a bunch. We don't mistreat each other, or sell out. We don't steal from each other. We don't throw each other off trains …especially when they're moving. Above all, we don't quit on each other. It also concerns right and wrong. The Creeds did me wrong, and I need to set it right.

General Grey played by Anthony Zerbe: John Patterson's *Independence* (TVW, 1987).

53

Darcy: My mother used to laugh and say: if the good die young, I would live forever.

Luke Darcy played by Jeff Chandler: Melvin Frank's *The Jayhawkers* (Paramount, 1959).

54

Sheriff: Suppose I told you there were a half dozen warrants out for his arrest right now. One for killing a man out in Silver City, Colorado, eight years ago with a knife. Another for killing four Chiricahua Indians.

Kain: Eight years ago? Well, that's ridiculous. That boy couldn't have been more than twelve years old!

Sheriff: You don't judge a rattlesnake by his age. He's a rattler whether he's got one rattler or a dozen.

Sheriff Rand played by Ray Teal and Alexander Kain played by Albert Dekker: Kurt Neumann's *The Kid from Texas* (Universal, 1950).

55

Laigs: All snakes are belly crawlers!

Laigs played by Britt Wood: Lesley Selander's *Knights of the Range* (Paramount, 1940).

56

Renn: A reputation like yours carries an odor all the way from Texas. The only thing you lack is black fur with white stripes.

Renn Frayne played by Russell Hayden: Lesley Selander's *Knights of the Range* (Paramount, 1940).

57

Maria: What have you done?

Joey: I killed a gringo, Mama. I only like gringos when they're dead.

Maria Garza played by Sonia Braga and Joey Garza played by Alexis Cruz: Joseph Sargent's *Larry McMurtry's Streets of Laredo* (Cabin Fever Entertainment, 1995).

58

Blaine: Of all the people I know who ain't worth saving, you're the first one to come to my mind.

Marshal Dan Blaine played by Glenn Ford: Richard Thorpe's *The Last Challenge* (MGM, 1967).

59

Blaine: He was a no good drifter. He'd steal the pennies off a dead man's eyes.

Marshal Dan Blaine played by Glenn Ford: Richard Thorpe's *The Last Challenge* (MGM, 1967).

60

Grat: Those boys are real killers …back-shooters most likely. Listen, they would stand as good a chance against Will Spence as a bunch of worm-eating apples hanging in a high wind.

Grat Dawson played by Richard Jaeckel and Will Spence played by Richard Widmark: Vincent McEveety's *The Last Day* (Paramount, 1975).

61

Doolin: Well, Bob, I'd like for you to explain something to me. Why does it have to be called the Dalton Gang? You explain that to me, please.

Dalton: It's simple, Billy. Gangs is always called after the leader, like the …ah, Jesse and Younger.

Doolin: Well now, I don't see no reason why I can't be the leader.

Dalton: Billy, in the first place, you don't have any leadership qualities …which I do. And in the second place, a Doolin

Gang sounds kind of dumb. I mean, what kind of name is Doolin?

Bill Doolin played by Bo Hopkins and Bob Dalton played by Cliff Potts: Dan Curtis' *Last Ride of the Dalton Gang* (TVW, 1979).

62

Peggy: Your father was a preacher?

Rennie: Kind of a phony evangelist. I tell ya, he was about the meanest man I've ever met in my life. He just naturally liked to beat up on anything that was smaller than him. And of course he could always say he was beating the fear of God into ya.

Peggy: Well, where is he now?

Rennie: Well, I, ah, well I hope I know where he is. You see, he was the first man I ever killed.

Peggy Carter played by Patricia Owens and Rennie played by Henry Silva: John Sturges' *The Law and Jake Wade* (MGM, 1958).

63

McNeely: John Wesley Hardin has made the name of Texas stick in the nostrils of justice.

Captain W.H. McNelly of the Texas Rangers played by Tom Jackson: Raoul Walsh's *The Lawless Breed* (Universal, 1952).

64

Sheriff: You've been a slick, cunning wolf, Zanti, but I finally got ya.

Zanti: You forgot, Señor Sheriff, wolves run in packs. And mine is not far behind.

The Sheriff played by Jack Rockwell and Pandro Zanti played by Earl Dwire: Robert Bradbury's *The Lawless Frontier* (Lone Star/Monogram, 1934).

65

Rhodes: How far down the road do you figure they'll let me get before you have some of your gunmen pop-shot me in the back?

Larry Rhodes played by George O'Brien: David Howard's *Lawless Valley* (RKO, 1938).

66

Ryan: Choctaw is a gunhand. Bronson likes his work. Dekker is a shadow walker. He walks big when he's with Choctaw, but a back-shooter inside.

Marshal Cotton Ryan played by Robert Ryan, Choctaw Lee played by William Watson, Vincent Bronson played by Lee J. Cobb, and Jack Dekker played by Ralph Waite: Michael Winner's *Lawman* (United Artists, 1971).

67

Bruto: What are you doing sitting under my little shade tree?

Blessing: Your shade tree?

Bruto: Yes, my shade tree. Isn't that right, Ignacio?

Blessing: Well, our apologies. We didn't know it was your shade tree.

Bruto: Well, it is too late to say I'm sorry, amigo. Look, you have already used up all the shade. Now there is none left for me.

Bruto Half-Tongue played by Miguel Sandoval, Anthony Blessing played by Chris Cooper, and Ignacio played by Jimmie F. Skaggs: Peter Werner's *Lone Justice* (Academy Entertainment, 1994).

68

Effie: It don't mean nothin' making a bad man do a good thing.

Effie Pettit played by Donzaleigh Abernathy: Jack Bender's *Lone Justice II* (Triboro Entertainment Group, 1995).

69

Dr. Fisher: A man that hates the way you do makes him evil.

Dr. Fisher played by Harry Shannon: Henry Levin's *The Lonely Man* (Paramount, 1957).

70

Roy: What did you find?

Dan: Nothing but his old watch. Damn sodbusters!

Jake: You shot those two men for a watch?

Dan: Shot 'em, now I'm gonna hang 'em.

Eddie: Hang 'em? Dang, you beat all! I've never heard of hanging dead men.

Dan: Shot 'em, now I'm gonna hang 'em, then I'm gonna burn 'em! Damn sodbusters. Can't ever be too dead to suit me.

Roy Suggs played by Jerry Biggs, Dan Suggs played by Gavan O'Herlihy, Jake Spoon played by Robert Urich, and Eddie Suggs played by Sean Hennigan: Simon Wincer's *Lonesome Dove* (TVW, 1989).

Super bad guy Frank (Henry Fonda) has just placed a harmonica in the boy's mouth with these chilling words: "Keep your loving brother happy." The boy (Dino Mele) would grow up and become known as Harmonica Man (Charles Bronson), bent on revenge in the classic epic by Sergio Leone, *Once Upon a Time in the West* (Paramount, 1968).

71

Chris: Tell me everything you know about him. What he likes, how he acts, everything.

Laurie: Well, ah, the first thing you notice about him are …his eyes. They tell you that he is mad. Crazy mad.

Chris played by Lee Van Cleef and Laurie Gunn played by Stefanie Powers: George McGowan's *The Magnificent Seven Ride* (United Artists, 1972).

72

Boldt: Well, you strike me as a man that's looking for something …and willing to pay for it.

Lockhart: Well, that depends upon what the information is and who's selling it.

Boldt: Well, I ain't got no references. But anybody can tell you that Chris Boldt is a man not to be trusted. That means nobody's secrets are sacred with me.

Lockhart: Huh, huh. And just who were you figuring on selling out?

Boldt: You just name 'em!

Chris Boldt played by Jack Elam and Will Lockhart played by James Stewart: Anthony Mann's *The Man from Laramie* (Columbia, 1955).

73

Ferris: You'd take the pennies off your dead mother's eyes!

Ferris played by Norman Rossington: Richard C. Sarafian's *Man in the Wilderness* (Warner Bros., 1971).

74

Link: Don't you talk anymore, Claude? We used to talk, you and me, when we were kids. What happened? Things have kind of gone to hell, haven't they? And you're still at it: stealing and killing and running.

Link Jones played by Gary Cooper and Claude Tobin played by John Dehner: Anthony Mann's *Man of the West* (United Artists, 1958).

75

Don Diego: Why is it that the scoundrels of the world are always remembered, and the well-bred men completely forgotten?

Teresa: Perhaps it's because there is nothing particularly memorial about scented bathtubs.

Don Diego/Zorro played by Frank Langella and Teresa played by Anne Archer: Don McDougall's *The Mark of Zorro* (TVW, 1974).

76

Mason: I know that breed. They don't like to fight unless they have the drop on someone.

Cliff Mason played by George O'Brien: David Howard's *The Marshal of Mesa City* (RKO, 1939).

77

Clair: Do you have to see a rattler strike to know that he's deadly?

Clair Enoch played by Wanda Hendrix: Ray Nazarro's *Montana Territory* (Columbia, 1952).

78

Old Man Clanton: When you pull a gun, kill a man!

Sam Clanton: Yeah, Pa.

Old Man Clanton played by Walter Brennan and Sam Clanton played by Mickey Simpson: John Ford's *My Darling Clementine* (20th Century–Fox, 1946).

79

Chris: Snakes like you usually die of their own poison.

Chris Morrell played by John Wayne: Harry Fraser's *'Neath the Arizona Skies* (Lone Star/Monogram, 1934).

80

Judge: Viciousness in men, Luke, is inside. Deep inside.

Luke: But why? What caused it? I keep wanting to know what makes him tick.

Judge: Well, it's usually a kind of logical progression. A youngster starts running with a gang. Sooner or later they're killed off or sent to prison until he's the only one left. He's gotten away with killing and he keeps going with it …alone. Pretty soon he's everybody's enemy. He can't let himself even like someone because some day he might have to kill them. By then there's no turning back. Even if he wants to throw his gun away, he can't because he knows that just around the bend there's someone that will kill him.

Judge Benson played by Edgar Stehli and Dr. Luke Canfield played by Charles Drake: Jack Arnold's *No Name on the Bullet* (Universal, 1959).

81

Cotton: If you're trying to get on my good side, forget it. I don't have one.

Cotton played by Shaun Cassidy: Burt Kennedy's *Once Upon a Texas Train* (TVW, 1988).

82

Harmonica Man: Your friends have a high mortality rate, Frank.

Harmonica Man played by Charles Bronson and Frank played by Henry Fonda: Sergio Leone's *Once Upon a Time in the West* (Paramount, 1968).

83

Rio: You're a regular one-eyed jack around here, Dad. I've seen the other side of your face.

Rio played by Marlon Brando and Sheriff Dad Longsworth played by Karl Malden: Marlon Brando's *One-Eyed Jacks* (Paramount, 1961).

84

Hickok: I ought to notch your ears for ya. A man like you ought to be marked.

Wild Bill Hickok played by Don Murray: David Lowell Rich's *The Plainsman* (Universal, 1966).

85

Grant: Captain Jesus Raza. Jesus, what a name for the bloodiest cutthroat in Mexico!

J.W. Grant played by Ralph Bellamy and Captain Jesus Raza played by Jack Palance: Richard Brooks' *The Professionals* (Columbia, 1966).

86

Clint: You really work hard at hating, don't you Morrison?

Clint Cooper played by Audie Murphy and Tom Morrison played by Walter Sande: Sidney Salkow's *The Quick Gun* (Columbia, 1964).

87

Zimmerman: Tevis has no respect for the dead.

Vinnie: And he just loves the living?

Zimmerman played by Hugh Marlowe, Vinnie Holt played by Susan Hayward, and Tevis played by Jack Elam: Henry Hathaway's *Rawhide* (20th Century–Fox, 1951).

88

Whitey: If I was smart, I'd shoot you right now. Except I think I'll keep you around for awhile …just to see what makes you work.

Clay: Maybe you're getting soft, Whitey. Maybe you're turning into a human being.

Whitey: If I ever feel that coming on, I'll shoot myself.

Whitey Kincade played by Dan Duryea and Clay O'Mara played by Audie Murphy: Jesse Hibbs' *Ride Clear of Diablo* (Universal, 1954).

89

Clay: Any relation to the Lowery Gang?

Whitey: No relation. This is them!

Clay O'Mara played by Audie Murphy and Whitey Kincade played by Dan Duryea: Jesse Hibbs' *Ride Clear of Diablo* (Universal, 1954).

90

Esqueda: Can you imagine laughter on Barton's face?

Rio: It's the only place where a smile could be ugly.

Jose Esqueda played by Anthony Quinn, Rio played by Robert Taylor, and Barton played by Jack Elam: John Farrow's *Ride, Vaquero!* (MGM, 1953).

91

Roy: Keep an eye on him, Gabby.

Gabby: Get over there, you sidewinder, or I'll let daylight through your hide!

Roy Rogers played himself and Gabby played by George "Gabby" Hayes: Joseph Kane's *Romance on the Range* (Republic, 1942).

92

Eula: I do not fear a skunk. I simply do not care for its odor.

Eula Goodnight played by Katharine Hepburn: Stuart Millar's *Rooster Cogburn* (Universal, 1975).

93

Narrator: For some reason, the bad guy was always a Colonel who had a beautiful young daughter and about a thousand head of cattle which you would hear but never see.

Narration by Peter, the Town Drunk, played by G.W. Bailey: Hugh Wilson's *Rustlers' Rhapsody* (Paramount, 1985).

94

Rex: You're not a good guy at all!
Bob: I'm a lawyer, you idiot!

Rex O'Herlihan played by Tom Berenger and Bob Barber played by Patrick Wayne: Hugh Wilson's *Rustlers' Rhapsody* (Paramount, 1985).

95

Deneen: I know all about the brother and the sickness inside him. He didn't get that from Steve, he was born with it.
Larson: I don't think that Tony ever did get born. I think that somebody just found him wedged into a gun cylinder and shot him out into the world by pressing the trigger.

Mr. Deneen played by Donald Crisp, Brick Larson played by Ray Teal, Steve Sinclair played by Robert Taylor, and Tony Sinclair played by John Cassavetes: Robert Parrish's *Saddle the Wind* (MGM, 1958).

96

Tony: You better open your eyes because I'm not just a kid brother anymore. I'm a full partner and I ride abreast of you. And you're not sitting on me anymore!
Steve: I never sat on you, I never tied you down! I only wanted one thing in my life and that was to see you rise up. You only got up as high as your gunbelt. And that's a low height for a man.

Tony Sinclair played by John Cassavetes and Steve Sinclair played by Robert Taylor: Robert Parrish's *Saddle the Wind* (MGM, 1958).

97

Steve: I tried to bend that kid a certain way. I tried to shape him. He was some kind of tough leather I had to make soft. But he didn't soften any. He wasn't made that way. He was just rotten leather and he came up hard.

Steve Sinclair played by Robert Taylor: Robert Parrish's *Saddle the Wind* (MGM, 1958).

98

Bob: From what you say about this fella, Savin, he must be some man to reckon with.
Lucky: He's not only bad, he's smart …and that's a dangerous combination.

Bob played by Bob Wills and Lucky Randall played by Russell Hayden: William Berke's *Saddles and Sagebrush* (Columbia, 1943).

99

Walsh: I always told Jones that that bird wouldn't make good as a bad man.

Ed Walsh played by Yakima Canutt and Joseph Conlon, alias Bob Jones, played by Lane Chandler: Armand Schaefer's *Sagebrush Trail* (Lone Star/Monogram, 1933).

100

Cyrus: Kit, once when you were about this high, Tex and Windy brought home a wolf cub with a broken back. You nursed it for weeks, but it finally died with his head in your lap. You cried for days. But it was just a wolf cub. And it probably would have grown up to be a killer like its father.

Cyrus Holliday played by Henry O'Neill, "Kit Carson" Holliday played by Olivia de Havilland, Tex Bell played by Guinn "Big Boy" Williams, and Windy Brody played by Alan Hale: Michael Curtiz's *Santa Fe Trail* (Warner Bros., 1940).

101

Ortega: I don't make war on women and children.
Danny: No, you just leave them widows and orphans!

Ortega played by Jose Nieto and Danny Post played by Alex Nicol: Michael Carreras' *The Savage Guns* (MGM, 1961).

102

Flood: You know, you'd make a fair to middling badman if you ever gave yourself half the chance.

Jim Flood played by Barry Sullivan: Harry Keller's *Seven Ways from Sundown* (Universal, 1960).

103

Dell: Was he very bad?
Jason: Well, let's just say that he wasn't in any danger of getting a headache from the weight of all the gold stars on his crown.

Dell Payton played by Shirley MacLaine and Jason Sweet played by Glenn Ford: George Marshall's *The Sheepman* (MGM, 1958).

104

Brown: He was like a tick that grabs onto your skin and sucks the blood; swells red and fat in the good times, and holds on through the bad. And he never lets go until all the blood was gone.

John George "Kootenai" Brown played by Tom Burlinson: Allan Kroeker's *Showdown at Williams Creek* (Republic Pictures Home Video, 1991).

105

Jason: The life we lead! In and out of jail …in and out of trouble. On the verge of being killed all the time.
Quince: Yeah. Well, when you put it that way, it doesn't sound too bad, does it?

Jason O'Rourke played by Lou Gossett and Quince Drew played by Larry Hagman: Burt Kennedy's *Sidekicks* (TVW, 1974).

106

Reeves: It shames me to be the son of a pig.
Eamon: You'll grow out of it. Just thank your stars you weren't born a half-breed like your demon sisters.

Reeves McCree played by Dermot Mulroney and Eamon McCree played by Alan Bates: Sam Shepard's *Silent Tongue* (Trimark Pictures, 1994).

107

Jesse: I got myself a policy: never do an honest day's work unless it's absolutely necessary.

Frank Jesse played by Dan Duryea: Harry Keller's *Six Black Horses* (Universal, 1962).

108

Wes: I was just telling Cathy, I'm pulling out.
Sam: Oh? Well, any particular reason, Wes?
Wes: What happened to Ard out there?
Sam: Oh, well, they'd had strung him up anyway. I did him a favor.
Wes: Well, I'm pulling out before you do me any favor.

Wes Tancred played by Richard Egan, Cathy played by Angie Dickinson, and Sam played by Paul Richards: Charles Marquis Warren's *Tension at Table Rock* (RKO, 1956).

109

Warden: Why do you work at it so hard: proving to yourself you're a son-of-a-bitch?
Pitman: Because I am. It's my profession, and I'm at the top!

Warden Woodward Lopeman played by Henry Fonda and Paris Pitman, Jr., played by Kirk Douglas: Joseph L. Mankiewicz's *There Was a Crooked Man* (Warner Bros., 1970).

110

Adelaide: I wouldn't give him my sweat if he was dying of thirst.

Adelaide Geary played by Rita Hayworth: Robert Rossen's *They Came to Cordura* (Columbia, 1959).

111

Posse Member: A lot of boys stick up stagecoaches and banks and one thing and another. But a man that would dynamite a water hole in this kind of country is downright criminal.

The Posse Member played by Ben Johnson: John Ford's *The 3 Godfathers* (MGM, 1948).

112

Bogardus: Do you know who I am?
Hickman: I didn't ask.
Bogardus: Bogardus is the name. Bart Bogardus. Jamerson was kin of mine.
Hickman: Well, every family has got one black sheep …some of 'em has got two.

Bart Bogardus played by Neville Brand and Morg Hickman played by Henry Fonda: Anthony Mann's *The Tin Star* (Paramount, 1957).

Ranch owner Jeremy Rudock (James Cagney) instructs ranch hand Steve Miller (Don Dubbins) to hobble three caught horse thieves: Lars Peterson (Vic Morrow), McNulty (Stephen McNally), and Barjack (James Griffith) in Robert Wise's *Tribute to a Bad Man* (MGM, 1956).

113

Kimmel: Someday, you're going to have to pay for your way of life, Tom. You're a bad man and I know it. And if I let you talk me out of it, I'll be lost forever. So my adventures in this life won't mean anything because you will have seduced my soul …and drawn me into your world. Goodbye, Tom.

Glendolene Kimmel played by Linda Evans and Tom Horn played by Steve McQueen: William Wiard's *Tom Horn* (Warner Bros., 1980).

114

Wyatt: What makes a man like Ringo, Doc? What makes him do the things he does?

Doc: Well, a man like Ringo, he's got a great empty hole right through the middle of him. He can never kill enough, or steal enough, or inflict enough pain to ever fill it.

Wyatt: What does he need?

Doc: Revenge.

Wyatt: For what?

Doc: Being born.

Wyatt Earp played by Kurt Russell, Doc Holliday played by Val Kilmer, and Johnny Ringo played by Michael Biehn: George P. Cosmatos' *Tombstone* (Buena Vista, 1993).

115

Billy: You think you got some pretty tough fellas over there in Dodge City. I guess you ain't never heard of Dry Gulch Curly, have you? You see, old Brandyhead Jones, he was a United States Marshal too. He done all the hanging over in our neighborhood. And this Dry Gulch Curly I'm telling you about. He was so tough that when old Brandyhead hung

him, his trigger finger kept jerking for two hours after he was dead.

Billy Burns and Brandyhead Jones both played by George "Gabby" Hayes: Ray Enright's *Trail Street* (RKO, 1947).

116

Masterson: What do you want, Carmody?

Carmody: Look here, Bat. These citizens here have elected me spokesman …

Masterson: Listen, fella, there's only two kind of people I allow to call me Bat: good friends and people I like. You don't belong in either group.

Bat Masterson played by Randolph Scott and Carmody played by Billy House: Ray Enright's *Trail Street* (RKO, 1947).

117

Rudock: You know, I ain't got you figured yet, McNulty. You act like a man with a lot of ideas. But all of them second rate …and not one honorable.

Jeremy Rudock played by James Cagney and McNulty played by Stephen McNally: Robert Wise's *Tribute to a Bad Man* (MGM, 1956).

118

Jeb: Is Trace sinking to your level or are you rising to his?

Jeb Mallick and Trace were uncredited: David Lister's *Trigger Fast* (Vidmark, 1994).

119

Mattie: I won't rest until Tom Chaney is barking in hell.

Mattie Ross played by Kim Darby and Tom Chaney played by Jeff Corey: Henry Hathaway's *True Grit* (Paramount, 1969).

120

Marshal: They don't call him "Lucky" Ned Pepper for nothing.

Mattie: That man gave his life for him [Pepper], and he didn't even look back!

Marshal: Looking back is a bad habit.

Marshal Reuben J. "Rooster" Cogburn played by John Wayne and Mattie Ross played by Kim Darby: Henry Hathaway's *True Grit* (Paramount, 1969).

121

Ross: I told you …you fly with jailbirds and you get dirty wings.

Trapper Ross played by Phil Chambers: Nathan Juran's *Tumbleweed* (Universal, 1953).

122

Holden: Captain Ecuyer, Mr. Garth has three indisputable talents: he is a liar, a cheat, and a coward.

Ecuyer: Captain Holden!

Holden: Captain, I bought this girl which makes him a liar. He stole her from me which makes him a cheat. And he won't fight which makes him a coward.

Captain Christopher Holden played by Gary Cooper, Captain Simson Ecuyer played by Victor Varconi, and Martin Garth played by Howard da Silva: Cecil B. DeMille's *Unconquered* (Paramount, 1947).

123

Joe: Too bad you never knew Ace Hanna. He ran a gambling joint back in Laredo. He shot my old man in a stud game when I was still a kid. Ace felt so bad, he gave me a home.

Trane: What's that got to do with my saving your life?

Joe: Ace used to say: don't take any chances you don't have to, don't trust anybody you don't have to trust, and don't do no favors you don't have to. Ace lived long enough to know he was right. He lived thirty seconds after I shot him!

Joe Erin played by Burt Lancaster and Benjamin Trane played by Gary Cooper: Robert Aldrich's *Vera Cruz* (United Artists, 1954).

124

Parrish: Matlock wasn't the kind to have any friends after he was dead.

John Parrish played by Glenn Ford and Wade Matlock played by Richard Jaeckel: Rudolph Mate's *The Violent Men* (Columbia, 1955).

125

Clegg: You boys ever draw on anybody?

Travis: No, sir. Just snakes.

[*and later, after Travis shoots Clegg*]

Elder: I thought you never drew on a man?

Travis: That's right, sir. Only on snakes.

Uncle Shiloh Clegg played by Charles Kemper, Travis Blue played by Ben Johnson, and Elder Wiggs played by Ward Bond: John Ford's *Wagonmaster* (RKO, 1950).

126

Red: I've worked my way up from a common horse thief to a ten-notch man.

Red played by Dick Wessel: Joseph Kane's *West of the Badlands* (a.k.a. *The Border Legion*; Republic, 1940).

127

Clay: I should have known that scum like you could live with anything above yourselves.

Clay Putnam played by Andrew Duggan: Budd Boetticher's *Westbound* (Warner Bros., 1959).

128

Jim Wyatt: It's funny. I always wanted to be a bad man. Even when we were kids. Do you remember? I guess I'm getting what I deserve.

Jim Wyatt played by Frank McGlynn Jr.: Robert Bradbury's *Westward Ho* (Republic, 1935).

129

Indio: I have something very important to tell you. I have just learned the federales have put a price on my head. Ten pesos! Yes, that's right! Ten stinking pesos! I don't know about you, but this makes me very angry. There is a bandit from Durango who has not robbed and killed as near as many innocent people as I have …and the price on his head is 10,000 pesos!

Indio played by Alfonso Arau: Burt Kennedy's *Where the Hell's That Gold?!!!* (a.k.a. *Dynamite & Gold*; TVW, 1988).

130

Charlie: He had found the band of jackals he needed. But as Jack McCall rode through the center of town, he experienced the terrifying certainty that a man faces when he's about to make his own name famous. He lacked both a hero's calm and a coward's resolve to survive at any price.

Charlie Prince played by John Hurt and Jack McCall played by David Arquette: Walter Hill's *Wild Bill* (MGM/United Artists, 1995).

131

Don Jose: We all dream of being a child again …even the worst of us. Perhaps the worst most of all.

Don Jose played by Chano Urueta: Sam Peckin-

pah's *The Wild Bunch* (Warner Bros.–Seven Arts, 1969).

132

Johnny: Well, that's the way it was. The old man sired two sons. One was no good …never was any good. Robbed a bank …stagecoach. Then when he came home and wanted to hide out, the old man wouldn't go for it. So Dutch shot him …in the back.

Johnny "High Spade" Williams played by Millard Mitchell and Dutch Henry Brown played by Stephen McNally: Anthony Mann's *Winchester '73* (Universal, 1950).

133

Behan: How would you boys like to pick up a little extra spending money?

Jesse: I figure as long as it ain't legal.

John Behan played by Jack Kelly and Jesse Boone played by John Carradine: Burt Kennedy's *Young Billy Young* (United Artists, 1969).

134

(Outlaw's comment upon deciding to ride with outlaw gang rather than stay with bride on wedding night)

Charley: It ain't easy having pals.

Charley Bowdre played by Casey Siemaszko: Christopher Cain's *Young Guns* (20th Century–Fox, 1988).

135

Tom: Are you Billy the Kid?

Dave: No, but I'm Arkansas Dave Rudabaugh. You ever hear of me? I've killed 65 men not countin' Mexicans and Indians. You must have heard of me! Come on! Rudabaugh! That's great!

Tom O'Folliard played by Balthazar Getty and Arkansas Dave Rudabaugh played by Christian Slater: Geoff Murphy's *Young Guns II* (20th Century–Fox, 1990).

136

Doc: You're starting to believe what they're writing about ya, aren't ya? Let me tell ya what you really are. You rode a 15 year old boy straight into his grave. And the rest of us, straight to hell …straight to hell! Mr. Bonney, you are not a god!

Bonney: Why don't you pull the trigger and find out.

Doc Scurlock played by Kiefer Sutherland and William H. Bonney, alias Billy the Kid, played by Emilio Estevez: Geoff Murphy's *Young Guns II* (20th Century–Fox, 1990).

137

Tom: What's scum?

Bonney: Well, Tom, that's bad types. Politicans, bankers, cattle kings … scum.

Tom O'Folliard played by Balthazar Getty and

Burying

See also Dying; Killing

Bear Ghost (Jack Holt) in William Wellman's *Across the Wide Missouri* (MGM, 1951).

138

Narrator: Trees lie where they fall, and men were buried where they died.
Narrative by Howard Keel: William Wellman's *Across the Wide Missouri* (MGM, 1951).

139

Escudo: Ah, poor Ballantine. Who died in the moment of our triumph. So artistic! So generous! And the most honest of us all! I weep for him! May his good soul go to heaven and then be greeted by our Lord above. Wait! This now means there's only four of us! So we divide his share between us, huh?
Escudo played by Pedro Sanchez and Ballantine played by Dean Reed: Frank Kramer's *Adios, Sabata* (United Artists, 1971).

140

Brisco: Well, you had one hell of a funeral, Dad. Governors from three states and two territories showed up. I'm sorry I missed it. I'm, ah, I'm sorry I missed a lot of things. But I'm gonna finish the job you started. You can count on that. John Bly has to be caught ...so I hope you're looking out for me up there. I can use all the help I can get.
Brisco County, Jr. played by Bruce Campbell: Bryan Spicer's *Adventures of Brisco County, Jr.* (TVW — Series Premiere, 1993).

141

Frank: When he buried his boy, you know what he put on the marker? "Here a father's heart is buried." A man with no heart makes a bad enemy.
Frank Newcombe played by Hugh Sanders: Raoul Walsh's *Along the Great Divide* (Warner Bros., 1951).

142

Rev.: If I live to bury Joe Madden, I'll say only four words over his grave: this was a man.
The Reverend Griffin played by Arthur Shields and Joe Madden played by Willard Parker: Hugo Fregonese's *Apache Drums* (Universal, 1951).

143

Bill: Fools! Jug-headed fools! Coming out here in Apache country like they was taking a ride down a city street back east. They never learn until they're dead. And then it makes no never mind.
Bill Gibson played by Arthur Hunnicut: R.G. Springsteen's *Apache Uprising* (Paramount, 1966).

144

Tom: I'm sorry about your father.
Nancy: He died the way he was born ...the way he lived.
Tom: No tears?
Nancy: Later.
Tom: He taught you well, Nancy.
Nancy: He taught me without teaching. That's the best way.
Tom Herrera played by Robert Horton and Nancy Dekker played by Barbara Ruick: Harold Kress' *Apache War Smoke* (MGM, 1952).

145

Ramos: It is a grave I have dug for myself. One day when I am tired of living, I will come here for a long visit.

Ramos played by Frank Silvera: Sidney J. Furie's *The Appaloosa* (Universal, 1966).

146

Minister: I guess it's no secret there was bitter conflict between Eli and his younger brother. It was in Eli's final moment that he was able to reconcile those differences. But he did it. He did it with his own blood. No greater love has a man that he lay down his life for a friend.

The Minister played by Les Hart: Lyman Dayton's *The Avenging* (Imperial Entertainment/Silver King Pictures, 1982).

147

Zack: Mr. Gaunt, how do you advise someone when they have to make a difficult decision? They have two choices, and they don't like either one.
Gaunt: I tell them a third choice is always possible.
Zack: Really!
Gaunt: Yes, and that's when I bring out the mahogany caskets. It's pricier than a pine or a walnut, but it's worth it!

Zack Stone played by Richard Joseph Paul and Undertaker Gaunt played by Carel Struycken: Sam Irvin's *Backlash: Oblivion 2* (Full Moon Entertainment, 1966).

148

Cable: I'll live to spit on your grave!

Cable Hogue played by Jason Robards, Jr.: Sam Peckinpah's *The Ballad of Cable Hogue* (Warner Bros., 1970).

149

Klugg: We never could figure out if they was kinfolk come to join in the fight or just strangers passin' through.
Josie: Well, that was awful!
Klugg: Yes, ma'am, it surely was, them being dead thataway. We never could figure out who'd have to bury 'em.

Klugg played by Timothy Scott and Josie Minick played by Doris Day: Andrew V. McLaglen's *Ballad of Josie* (Universal, 1968).

150

Mortician: Mr. Badger!
Badger: Yea, what? What's the matter?
Mortician: It's about Little Jo!
Badger: Well, speak up, man! What about him!
Mortician: He was a woman!

Two outcasts, prostitute Hildy (Stella Stevens) and prospector Cable Hogue (Jason Robards), in Sam Peckinpah's ***The Ballad of Cable Hogue*** (Warner Bros., 1970).

Mortician P.D. Stith played by Dennis McNiven, Frank Badger played by Bo Hopkins, and Little Jo Monaghan played by Suzy Amis: Maggie Greenwald's *The Ballad of Little Jo* (Fine Line Features, 1993).

151

Karl: Are you all right?

Barbarosa: No, I ain't all right! Do I look all right?

Karl: Well, you look better than you did when you was at the bottom of that grave.

Karl played by Gary Busey and Barbarosa played by Willie Nelson: Fred Schepisi's *Barbarosa* (Universal, 1982).

152

Zeb: They ain't deserving of it, but I reckon we better bury 'em.

Zeb Calloway played by Arthur Hunnicutt: Howard Hawks' *The Big Sky* (Winchester/RKO, 1952).

153

Breck: Well, Zeke, old Wendy has gone on another trail.

Breck Coleman played by John Wayne and Zeke played by Tully Marshall: Raoul Walsh's *The Big Trail* (Fox, 1930).

154

Sheriff: We were voted out of a double hanging, Buchanan. Unless you get on that horse and start riding, we'll make up for it with a double bury.

Sheriff Lou Agry played by Barry Kelley and Tom Buchanan played by Randolph Scott: Budd Boetticher's *Buchanan Rides Alone* (Columbia, 1958).

155

Pecos: Lafe, you and me worked for Lou Agry for nearly a year. And though I don't guess we was ever real buddies, I'm sorry it was me that stopped your clock. You had your good side, Lafe. But you had your bad side too. Well, like cheatin' at stud. And emptying my pockets whenever I got drunk. But I ain't holding these things against you, Lafe. And if you're holding a grudge against me, Lafe, just remember that when it come down to choosing between you and Buchanan here …well …I just had to choose Buchanan on account of he's a West Texan. And like I always say, let bygones be bygones. And I hope you're saying the same wherever you are. Well, so long, Lafe. You died real good.

Pecos Bill played by L.Q. Jones, Lafe played by Don C. Harvey, and Tom Buchanan played by Randolph Scott: Budd Boetticher's *Buchanan Rides Alone* (Columbia, 1958).

156

Lightfoot: Give me my $5.00. If you get shot tonight, I disappear. Oh, I'll come back and bury you …and mumble something Christian over your grave.

Cahill: Lightfoot, your kindness overwhelms me.

Lightfoot played by Neville Brand and Marshal J.D. Cahill played by John Wayne: Andrew McLaglen's *Cahill: United States Marshal* (Warner Bros., 1973).

157

Jubal: I don't want to bury him here. It's an empty place …empty …nothing to remember.

Jubal Hooker played by Simon Oakland: Michael Winner's *Chato's Land* (United Artists, 1972).

158

Kearney: Oh, Otto, me boy. You're so damn inconsiderate. Now I have to dig a grave and bury your bloody ass.

Daniel Kearney played by Rick Dean and Otto Nielsen played by Clint Howard: Mark Griffiths' *Cheyenne Warrior* (Concorde — New Horizons Corp., 1994).

159

Billy: I made you a promise, Mr. Tunstall. Now I'm making myself a promise. It says in the Bible: the candle of the wicked shall be put out.

Billy the Kid played by Geoffrey Deuel and Henry Tunstall played by Patrick Knowles: Andrew McLaglen's *Chisum* (Warner Bros., 1970).

160

Yancy: Louis Heffner, as coroner do your official duty and remove the body!

Heffner: Okay, Yancy. It was self-defense and justifiable homicide. This town needs a Boot Hill and I'll start it with this burial.

Yancy: Fellow citizens! Under the circumstances, we will forgo the sermon and conclude this service with a brief word of prayer.

Yancy Cravat played by Richard Dix and Louis Heffner played by Robert McWade: Wesley Ruggles' *Cimarron* (RKO, 1931).

161

Cookie: Lord, we give you Curly. Try not to piss him off.

Cookie played by Tracey Walter and Curly played by Jack Palance: Ron Underwood's *City Slickers* (Columbia, 1991).

162

Mitch: I'm sorry we buried you, but you looked so dead!

Mitch Robbins played by Billy Crystal: Paul Weiland's *City Slickers II: The Legend of Curly's Gold* (Columbia, 1994).

163

Wes: It reminds me of a little heist we planned in west Kansas about five or six years ago. One fella was smooth and slippery. The other was green and gabby. The third was just plain mean, from the top of his head to his boot heel. The next thing we know, there was a boxcar of soldiers coupled on to that train. Too bad we never knew which one sent word to the soldiers. It would have been better for the other two if we had. Their monuments are right outside of Boxville, Kansas. The prettiest little Bone Orchard you've ever seen. Little stone angels watching them.

Wes McQueen played by Joel McCrea: Raoul Walsh's *Colorado Territory* (Warner Bros., 1949).

164

Reece: Anybody know the right words? When something like this happens, people start asking how come it happen. Was it his fault …or somebody else's fault? Well, that isn't for us to say. You see, we don't know all the answers. All we know is a man is dead and that's that. In the long run, I don't think it would have made any difference anyhow. I mean, if it hadn't been a snake that had got him, it would have been a steer, or a Comanche, or it might have even been a …his horse might have stumbled into a prairie dog hole some dark night. He was a good man with cattle, and always did the best he knew how. I hope someone could say the same over me.

Tom Reece played by Glenn Ford: Delmer Daves' *Cowboy* (Columbia, 1958).

165

Cimarron: They didn't even dig him a decent grave.

Anderson: Well, it's not how you're buried. It's how they remember ya.

Cimarron played by A Martinez and Wil Anderson played by John Wayne: Mark Rydell's *The Cowboys* (Warner Bros., 1972).

166

Anderson: Sometimes it's hard to understand the drift of things. This was a good boy. He'd have been a good man. He didn't get his chance. Death can come for ya anyplace …anytime. It's never welcomed. But if you've done all you can do, and it's your best, in a way I guess you're ready for it.

Wil Anderson played by John Wayne: Mark Rydell's *The Cowboys* (Warner Bros., 1972).

167

Nightlinger: This may seem a lonesome place to leave him. But he is not alone.

Because many of his kind rest here with him. The prairie was like a mother to Mr. Anderson. He belonged to her. She cared for him while he lived. And she is nursing him while he sleeps.

Jebediah Nightlinger played by Roscoe Lee Browne and Wil Anderson played by John Wayne: Mark Rydell's *The Cowboys* (Warner Bros., 1972).

168

It does not matter where his body lies; there the grass is growing …but where his Spirit lies; that would be a good place to be.

A quote by Black Elk in the Epilogue: John Irvin's *Crazy Horse* (Turner Pictures, 1996).

169

S. Hawkins
Undertaker's Parlor
Special Party Rates for
Saturday Night Killings

A sign over undertaker's office: Ray Nazarro's *Cripple Creek* (Columbia, 1952).

170

Undertaker: Very sad affair. But it's the best night's business we've had for some time. I can make a very attractive club rate for all six.
Marshal: Where, Silver, you can lock up now. The corpus delicti have been identified, and Hawkins here offers a very good club rate: six coffins, no flowers, no mourners.

Undertaker Hawkins played by Byron Foulger, Marshal John Tetheroe played by Roy Roberts, and Silver Kirby played by William Bishop: Ray Nazarro's *Cripple Creek* (Columbia, 1952).

171

Undertaker: Good afternoon, gentlemen. Am I wrong or are my services again in demand?
Ivers: You get around fast, don't you?
Undertaker: In my profession, it pays to keep one's ear attuned to the mark of a six gun.

Undertaker Hawkins played by Byron Foulger and Bret Ivers played by George Montgomery: Ray Nazarro's *Cripple Creek* (Columbia, 1952).

172

Barnes: Charity case. Nothing but charity cases. Who is gonna pay for this man's burial?
Banner: You'll find $300 in his vest pocket. You take out for his funeral and send the rest to his nearest relatives.
Barnes: Nearest relatives, huh? Nephew [corpse], you just found yourself an uncle!

Mathew Barnes played by William Fawcett and John Banner played by Dale Robertson: Lewis R. Foster's *Dakota Incident* (Republic, 1956).

173

Banner: It's getting hot. He needs burying!

John Banner played by Dale Robertson: Lewis R. Foster's *Dakota Incident* (Republic, 1956).

174

Wade: Well, this is an honor. Probably the first time a corpse has ever been asked to deliver his own funeral oration. I expected to be carried out of Lordsburg, but here I stand on my way to Colorado filled with wind instead of lead. I couldn't include most of you in my will, but I do leave you all the unmined silver in these hills, all the unspilled whiskey, all the unkissed ladies, and all the unfilled straights and flushes. I want to apologize for leaving the party. For me, there never has been, and never will be, another one like it. And finally, I want to apologize to all of those of you who hoped to gain the doubtful distinction of being the man or woman to shoot and kill the notorious Brett Wade.
Rapp: No apologies necessary, Wade. I'm here to oblige you.

Brett Wade played by Rory Calhoun and Jimmy Rapp played by Alex Nicol: George Sherman's *Dawn at Socorro* (Universal, 1954).

175

Ben: Howdy, Bates. How's the undertaking business?
Bates: Oh, this town is too healthy. If something doesn't happen soon, I'll have to vamoose.

Ben played by Reed Howes and Undertaker Bates played by Nelson McDowell: R.N. Bradbury's *The Dawn Rider* (Lone Star/Monogram, 1935).

176

Bill: Josh and Zeke were pards. I don't guess they'll mind bunking together in the hereafter.
Bigfoot: If anybody knows a good scripture, let 'em say it. We got to skedaddle. I don't fancy another fight with Buffalo Hump.
Bill: There's that scripture about them green pastures ….
Bigfoot: So say it then, Bill!
Bill: Well, ….them there's green pastures …. That's all I can recall.

Bill was uncredited and Bigfoot Wallace played by Keith Carradine: Yves Simoneau's *Dead Man's Walk* (Cabin Fever Entertainment, 1996).

177

Undertaker: Needless to say, Mrs. Mills, we all share your grief.
Mrs. Mills: What's the price of your cheapest funeral?

Arch Brandt, the Undertaker, played by Royal Dano and Mrs. Laurie Mills played by Jacqueline

Scott: Allen Smithee's *Death of a Gunfighter* (Universal, 1969).

178

Mrs. Mills: They said it's only right and proper that I should give Luke a good Christian funeral. Fill him with formaldehyde and plaster down his hair so good Christian folk can come and look at him on display like at a wax museum.

Mrs. Laurie Mills played by Jacqueline Scott: Allen Smithee's *Death of a Gunfighter* (Universal, 1969).

179

Tattinger: What's that dog doing?
Kaleb: Get away from there!
Tattinger: Why, he was fixin' to eat that [dead] Indian!
Kaleb: One tried to eat him once.

Tattinger played by Slim Pickens and Captain Viktor Kaleb played by Bekim Fehmiu: Burt Kennedy's *The Deserter* (a.k.a. *Ride to Glory*; Paramount, 1971).

180

Wash: Oh, Tom! Look here! Look at this post! Soaked through and through with the blood of Saw Tooth McGhee. Yea, he objected to a petticoat a neighbor's wife was wearing …and they fit to a draw. Both are buried in the same grave.
Tom: Saw Tooth and the petticoat?
Wash: No! Saw Tooth and the neighbor! And four innocent bystanders!

Sheriff Washington Dimsdale played by Charles Winninger and Tom Destry Jr. played by James Stewart: George Marshall's *Destry Rides Again* (Universal, 1939).

181

Lance: I send You my father to the Land of the Great Mystery. May You ride with him on the North Wind.

Lance Poole played by Robert Taylor: Anthony Mann's *Devil's Doorway* (MGM, 1950).

182

Nathaniel: I sure never thought I'd end up gravedigging and not even getting paid for it either. Anyhow, it's better to be above ground doing that than below ground doing nothing.

Nathaniel was uncredited: Sergio Corbucci's *Django* (B.R.C./Tecisa, 1966).

183

Dooley: I can't say he looks any worse for being dead.

Dooley played by William Forsythe: Gene Quintano's *Dollar for the Dead* (TVW, 1998).

184

Dooley: I reckon we ought to bury him.
Cowboy: You find the head and I'll bury the rest of him.

Scene from the infamous Last Chance Saloon in the town of Bottleneck from the classic western *Destry Rides Again* (Universal, 1939).

Dooley: I guess the buzzards got to eat too.
   Old Colby, he was once a friend.
Cowboy: And once he wasn't.

Dooley played by William Forsythe and the Cowboy played by Emilio Estevez: Gene Quintano's *Dollar for the Dead* (TVW, 1998).

185
   WILDCAT KELLY
   For Wildcat Kelly
   Life Held No Terror
   Forgetting To Duck
   Was His Only Error

Tombstone reading: John English's *Don't Fence Me In* (Republic, 1945).

186
Jack: He was buried in Twin Wells.
Toni: Kind of tough on the drinking
   water, wasn't it?

Jack Chandler played by Robert Livingston and Toni Ames played by Dale Evans: John English's *Don't Fence Me In* (Republic, 1945).

187
Ellen: You're going to kill me.
Chata: No. You will be alive when I bury
   you in the grave of my son.

Ellen Grange played by Bibi Anderson and Chata played by John Hoyt: Ralph Nelson's *Duel at Diablo* (United Artists, 1966).

188
Sin Killer: I don't really know much about
   Sam Pierce, oh Lord. But from what I
   hear, he'd be needing no introduction to
   you. Seeing how Sam was snatched from
   his loved ones' arms before they even
   had time to get a good grip on him, I'm
   counting on you to give him a better
   break up yonder.

The Sin Killer played by Walter Huston and Sam Pierce played by Charles Bickford: King Vidor's *Duel in the Sun* (Selznick Releasing Organization, 1946).

189
Preacher: We are committing this man, Mr.
   Jones …ah …Mr. Shones, to his life in

the hereafter. We would like to take a moment to acknowledge his contributions to our community. During Mr. Shones' short-lived term as Sheriff, he served the public to the best of his abilities. He shot eight men and three women, most of whom were engaged in breaking the law. I'm sure the others were honest mistakes.

The Preacher was uncredited: Peter Markle's *El Diablo* (HBO Pictures, 1990).

190
Roper: When you're in the grave, Beecher,
   it doesn't matter too much how you got
   there.
Beecher: Well, I think it matters. I think it
   does.
Roper: Write the War Department.

Captain Roper played by William Holden and Lieutenant Beecher played by Richard Anderson: John Sturges' *Escape from Fort Bravo* (MGM, 1953).

191

Reverend: Well, they all look alike to the worms.

Reverend Jonathan Rudd played by Robert Mitchum: Henry Hathaway's *Five Card Stud* (Paramount, 1968).

192

Govern: The Yankees came a long way to be buried.

Govern Sturges played by John Lund: Roger Corman's *Five Guns West* (American Releasing Corp., 1955).

193

Johnny: Hankey was a good man. He didn't have any feelings about anything. All he had was loyalty.

Johnny Tallon played by Dane Clark and Hankey played by Slim Hightower: John Rawlins' *Fort Defiance* (United Artists, 1951).

194

Vinson: Collins, that's deep enough. Roll him in and cover him up. Let's move!

McGurney: You mean without reading the Good Book?

Vinson: If he needs our help to make it upstairs, he's in worse shape than he looks.

Sgt. Vinson played by Joel McCrea and McGurney played by Forrest Tucker: Joseph Newman's *Fort Massacre* (United Artists, 1958).

195

Vinson: I need a six-foot hole dug. Any volunteers?

McGurney: Don't look at me, Sergeant. I'm too overcome with grief.

Pendleton: Well, I certainly can't do that!

Collins: All right, I'll be the goat. Half the tobacco?

McGurney: Collins, three feet will be plenty. He was only half a man.

Sgt. Vinson played by Joel McCrea, McGurney played by Forrest Tucker, Pendleton played by George Neise, and Collins played by Denver Pyle: Joseph Newman's *Fort Massacre* (United Artists, 1958).

196

Luke: What is she trying to prove?

Fiske: That one of us is a hero or a fool.

Luke: Well, anyway, it's her funeral. I don't go to any but my own.

Luke Daly played by Cameron Mitchell and Fiske played by Richard Widmark: Henry Hathaway's *Garden of Evil* (20th Century–Fox, 1954).

197

Hooker: A cross isn't a bad thing to see. It can be beautiful. And everybody has one.

Hooker played by Gary Cooper: Henry Hathaway's *Garden of Evil* (20th Century–Fox, 1954).

198

Preacher: The Good Book speaks a lot of words at a time like this. But I don't think Harry Keough knew too many of them. He wasn't old enough …or calmed enough.

The Preacher was uncreditd: Abner Biberman's *Gun for a Coward* (Universal, 1957).

199

Ode: We'll be taking the Bull up to the wild horse country. He'd want to be planted up there where he could hear the sound of them mustang feet just a drummin' on his grave.

Ode played by Royal Dano and Bull played by Edgar Buchanan: Earl Bellamy's *Gunpoint* (Universal, 1966).

200

Rufus: I stole a Bible, Emmett. Do you want to read over Frank?

Emmett: You know damn right well I can't read! The hell with him anyway!

Rufus: You shouldn't have done that, Emmett. You're gonna get God mad at us and he's liable to …

Emmett: Shut your damn mouth!

Rufus: Well, I want to say something over Frank!

Emmett: Well, say it and get it the hell over with!

Rufus: All right …Frank …you're dead! …Frank …damn if I don't miss you already!

Rufus Clemens played by Strother Martin, Emmett Clemens played by Ernest Borgnine, and Frank Clemens played by Jack Elam: Burt Kennedy's *Hannie Caulder* (Paramount, 1971).

201

Recorder: The gunman who brought him in, he didn't leave any money for burial. So if you're prepared …

Noel: Just put him away. No marker, no words, no tears. Just bury him, understand?

Recorder: I still need …

Noel: A deposit?

Recorder: Yes.

Noel: Well, I got one for ya. And if my pa isn't properly buried by dark, I'm gonna deposit a ball of lead a half inch in diameter just under the skull on top of the brain. You got that, mister?

The Burial Recorder played by Steve Lyons and Noel Hickman played by Chuck Pierce, Jr.: Charles B. Pierce's *Hawken's Breed* (Vidmark Entertainment, 1987).

202

Noel: Spirit and I visit his grave regular now. It's more from love than duty. He saved the life of that woman …and he made the life of this man.

Noel Hickman as an Old Man played by Charles

B. Pierce: Charles B. Pierce's *Hawken's Breed* (Vidmark Entertainment, 1987).

203

Beggar: That fella in the coffin …he's better off than me. He's got a roof over his head.

The Beggar played by Al Mulock: Sergio Corbucci's *The Hellbenders* (Embassy Pictures, 1967).

204

Mayor: I don't know if we shouldn't mark the grave somehow. Sam?

Sam: I don't see any need. It ain't likely anybody is gonna cry over them anyhow.

Mayor Jason Hobart played by Stefan Gierasch and Sheriff Sam Shaw played by Walter Barnes: Clint Eastwood's *High Plains Drifter* (Universal, 1973).

205

Jessie: And we got him a marble headstone. It had his name on it. And underneath we had them put, "In The Fullest of His Years." Is that all right with you?

Russell: I'll settle for that. I'm not on the slab.

Jessie: Well, what do you figure yours is gonna read?

Russell: "Shot Dead," probably.

Jessie: Don't people like you, Mr. Russell?

Russell: It only takes one that doesn't.

Jessie played by Diane Cilento and John Russell played by Paul Newman: Martin Ritt's *Hombre* (20th Century–Fox, 1967).

206

Zebulon: Oh Lord, without consulting with Thee, we have sent thy way some souls whose evil ways passeth all understanding. We ask Thee humbly to receive them …whether you want 'em or not! Amen.

Zebulon Prescott played by Karl Malden: John Ford, George Marshall, and Henry Hathaway's *How the West Was Won* (MGM, 1962).

207

King: Why did you bring these bodies here?

Stuart: They're railroaders. I thought somebody in the railroad might be interested.

King: I'm the railroad! And I'm not interested!

Mike King played by Richard Widmark and Jethro Stuart played by Henry Fonda: John Ford, George Marshall, and Henry Hathaway's *How the West Was Won* (MGM, 1962).

208

Hud: You know something, honcho? If you don't look out for yourself, the only

Grimes (Richard Boone) is bully and bandit leader but is outmatched when he comes up against the *Hombre* (20th Century–Fox, 1967).

helping hand you'll ever get is when they lower the box.

Hud Bannon played by Paul Newman: Martin Ritt's *Hud* (Paramount, 1963).

209

Pastor: I know what you're feeling, my boy. Look at it this way: he's gone to a better place.

Lon: I don't think so ...not unless dirt is a better place than air.

The Pastor was uncredited and Lon Bannon played by Brandon de Wilde: Martin Ritt's *Hud* (Paramount, 1963).

210

Barston: You better hope the wind don't shift. Your townsfolk get a whiff of you, they're liable to clear out faster than you can say ...formaldehyde!

Barston played by Bruce Dern: Sam Pillsbury's *Into the Badlands* (TVW, 1991).

211

Narrator [*referring to the Yukon Dog, Buck*]: And he knew that John Thornton was dead. It left a great void in him somewhat akin to hunger ...but a void which ached and ached ...and which food could not fill.

Narration by Richard Dreyfuss: Peter Svatek's *Jack London's The Call of the Wild: Dog of the Yukon* (Hallmark Entertainment, 1997).

212

"I, Hatchet Jack, being of sound mind and broke legs, do hereby leaveth my bear rifle to whatever finds it. Lord, I hope it be a white man. It is a good rifle and killed the bear that killed me. Anyway, I am dead. Yours truly, Hatchet Jack."

Jeremiah Johnson, played by Robert Redford, reading the last will and testament of a mountain man found frozen: Sydney Pollack's *Jeremiah Johnson* (Warner Bros., 1972).

213

Carson: There's more in them graves than just people.

Kit Carson played by Jon Hall: George B. Seitz's *Kit Carson* (United Artists, 1940).

214

Laurie: Whose funeral?

Tinkersley: Why, it's Doobie Plunkert's. She was well-liked in the town. I liked her myself even though I only met her once. That's why I let my whores sing at her funeral. Now, I kept two back for business. They had scratchy voices anyhow.

Laurie/Lorena Parker played by Sissy Spacek, Tinkersley played by Nik Hagler, and Doobie Plunkert played by Emily Courtney: Joseph Sargent's *Larry McMurtry's Streets of Laredo* (Cabin Fever Entertainment, 1995).

215

Blacksmith: Hardin, that boy cost me $50.00. That's $50.00 for the boy and 50 cents for the grave. That's $50.50 you owe me.

John Wesley: Don't stand there talking nonsense to me while I'm working hard at getting drunk. Just drag your man off behind the sand hill and the big pig will eat him, and save you 50 cents.

The Blacksmith was uncredited. John Wesley Hardin played by Randy Quaid: Joseph Sargent's *Larry McMurtry's Streets of Laredo* (Cabin Fever Entertainment, 1995).

216

Frank: Nothing in his life became him like the leaving it.

Frank James played by Johnny Cash: William A. Graham's *The Last Days of Frank and Jesse James* (TVW, 1986).

217

Jesse: Do me that one favor, Buck, before they close the lid on the coffin. Make damn sure you turn me over.

Frank: So everybody can kiss your better side goodbye?

Jesse: The whole world.

Jesse James played by Kris Kristofferson and Frank "Buck" James played by Johnny Cash: William A. Graham's *The Last Days of Frank and Jesse James* (TVW, 1986).

218

Major: What will happen to Chingachgook now?

Hawkeye: It takes the Mohican only minutes to bury his dead ...but many moons to bury his grief. He'll wander the hills alone until he's ready to come down. Then we'll both go back into the forest and try to find what we lost.

Major: What is that?

Hawkeye: Peace. Peace, Major. The most precious thing a man can have. Chingachgook and me, we'll help those who want to see peace grow.

Major Heyward played by Andrew Prine, Hawkeye played by Steve Forrest, and Chingachgook played by Ned Romero: James L. Conway's *Last of the Mohicans* (TVW, 1977).

219

Cora: Why didn't you bury those people?
Hawkeye: Anyone looking for our trail would see it as a sign we passed that way.

Cora Munro played by Madeleine Stowe and Nathaniel Poe/Hawkeye played by Daniel Day-Lewis: Michael Mann's *The Last of the Mohicans* (20th Century–Fox, 1992).

220

Clint: Well, did you say a few words over the boys?
Ortero: Yea …goodbye.
Clint: Very touching.

Clint Hollister played by Richard Widmark and Ortero played by Robert Middleton: John Sturges' *The Law and Jake Wade* (MGM, 1958).

221

Undertaker: Where's the Durango Kid?
Marshal: That's him.
Undertaker: You mean to say you brought him back alive?
Marshal: Well, for the time being.
Undertaker: Now, we've been friends for a long time, Frame. But since you cleaned up this town, I can't hardly make a living. How do you expect me to make any money off of him?
Durango Kid: Don't worry about it, friend, you won't have to wait long.

The Undertaker, Denver Cahoon, played by Chubby Johnson and Marshal Frame Johnson played by Ronald Reagan: Nathan Juran's *Law and Order* (Universal, 1953).

222

John: What are you doing on the trail? Trying to pick up a little stray business?
Chick: I pick up business any place I can find it. Business was good in Abilene. I had a special embalming and burying job on the Durango Kid. And if I do say so myself, when he was laid out, his own wife didn't even know him. She thought he was a stranger asleep in the parlor.

John Clements played by John McIntire and Chick Noonan the Undertaker played by Tom Fadden: Raoul Walsh's *The Lawless Breed* (Universal, 1952),

223

Calem: Men, Cody Clark is buying drinks. He won all bets.
Cody: That's right. Drinks are on the house …and everybody is welcomed!

Calem: You can also take up a collection for burying Dingo. Add this [money] to it.
Cody: That's right nice of you, Calem. Funny how a man softens to another when once he's killed him.
Calem: I don't know about that. I'd do as much if it were your funeral.

Marshal Calem Ware played by Randolph Scott and Cody Clark played by John Emery: Joseph H. Lewis' *A Lawless Street* (Columbia, 1955).

224

Bronson: We buried brother Jacob here. I had a brother Aaron beside him. They had enough of guns and killing. The dead don't have much.

Vincent Bronson played by Lee J. Cobb: Michael Winner's *Lawman* (United Artists, 1971).

225

Lone Ranger: I swear to you, Dan, no matter how long it takes, no matter where they are, I will find them. What Cavendish and men like him owe you, they will pay in full. There will be justice in the west. To this, my brother, I pledge my life.

The Lone Ranger/John Reid played by Klinton Spilsbury and Dan Reid played by John Bennett Perry: William A. Fraker's *The Legend of the Lone Ranger* (Universal, 1981).

226

Rev: What has happened here?
Bean: These men tried to hang me. They have been killed for it.
Rev: How many of 'em are there?
Bean: A lot of 'em.
Rev: Who did the killing?
Bean: I did. They were bad men, and the whores weren't ladies.
Rev: Vengeance is mine sayeth the Lord!
Bean: It was. I'm waiting for the buzzards. They don't deserve burying.
Rev: Maybe they don't, but they ought to be. They are a stench and an abomination! I got a shovel if you don't.

The Reverend LaSalle played by Anthony Perkins and Roy Bean played by Paul Newman: John Huston's *The Life and Times of Judge Roy Bean* (NGP, 1972).

227

Rev: I will read over the dead now. My Bible, please. Mr., uh …
Bean: Bean.
Rev: Bean?
Bean: Roy Bean. Judge Roy Bean. I am the law in this area.
Rev: What has qualified you as such?
Bean: I know the law. And I have spent my entire life in its flagrant disregard. But I had never killed a man before. Oh, I had shot at some …in

self-defense or blind fright, but I never hit anyone. So God must have directed my bullets. Why, he even sent an angel to deliver this weapon [gun].
Rev: Just how do you intend to dispense this law?
Bean: With this [gun] and a rope.
Rev: And will you rely again on the grace of God?
Bean: Well, I intend to [gun] practice and give Him some help. Get on with the reading.

The Reverend LaSalle played by Anthony Perkins and Judge Roy Bean played by Paul Newman: John Huston's *The Life and Times of Judge Roy Bean* (NGP, 1972).

228

Lone Ranger: Only you, Tonto, know I'm alive. To the world, I'll be buried here beside my brother and my friends …forever.
Tonto: You are alone now. Last man. You are lone ranger.
Lone Ranger: Yes, Tonto, I am …the Lone Ranger!

The Lone Ranger played by Clayton Moore and Tonto played by Jay Silverheels: George B. Seitz's *The Lone Ranger* (Television Series, earliest episodes, Sept. 1949).

229

Jacob: Take your dead and git. And don't bury them on my ground!

Jacob Wade played by Jack Palance: Henry Levin's *The Lonely Man* (Paramount, 1957).

230

Clara: Sometimes it seems like grave digging is all we do around here, don't it Cholo? What do you think happens when we die?
Cholo: Not much. You are just dead.
Clara: Maybe it's not as big a change as we think. Maybe you just go back to where you lived or near your family, or wherever you were the happiest. Only you're just a spirit now …and you don't have the troubles the living have.

Clara played by Anjelica Huston and Cholo played by Jack Caffrey: Simon Wincer's *Lonesome Dove* (TVW, 1989).

231

July: It was my fault [they were killed]! Hell, you told me to stay.
Gus: I know I did, son. And I'm sure you wished you had. But yesterday's gone, we can't get it back. Now you go on with your digging.

July Johnson played by Chris Cooper and Gus McCrae played by Robert Duvall: Simon Wincer's *Lonesome Dove* (TVW, 1989).

232

Rixley: The funeral will be in Chicago and the Governor will be there.

Mortician: Well, I'm sure it will cheer their souls just to hear you say that.

Mr. Rixley played by James Whitmore, Jr. and the Mortician played by John Bottoms: Walter Hill's *The Long Riders* (United Artists, 1980).

233

Frank: Mr. Rixley?
Rixley: That's right.
Frank: My name is Frank James. I came here to turn myself in. Here's my gun. I want something in return. I want to be able to bury my brother.
Rixley: Suppose I don't agree to your terms?
Frank: I'll kill ya.

Frank James played by Stacy Keach and Mr. Rixley played by James Whitmore, Jr.: Walter Hill's *The Long Riders* (United Artists, 1980).

234

Chamlee: I'm sorry, friend, but there'll be no funeral.
Henry: What?
Chamlee: Oh, the grave is dug and the defunct there is as ready as the embalmers ought to make him. But there'll be no funeral.
Henry: What's the matter? Didn't I pay you enough?
Chamlee: It's not a question of money. For $20.00, I'd plant anybody with a hoop and a holler. But the funeral is off.
Henry: Now how do you like that. I want him buried, you want him buried. And if he could sit up and talk, he'd second the motion. Now that's as unanimous as you can get.
Chamlee: Friend, you behave like a brother and a Christian, but you just don't …
Henry: Now look! I'm not looking for any praises. I'm a traveling salesman of ladies' corsets. And I'm walking down the street and a man drops dead right in front of me. For two hours people keep stepping over and around him without lifting a finger. I'm just doing what any decent man would.
Robert: Come on, Henry, let's get on …
Henry: No, wait a minute. This man has to be buried. And soon! He's not turning into any nosegay.
Chamlee: I know, I know, I know. I would if I could but, well, there's an element in town that objects.
Henry: Objects? To what?
Chamlee: They say he isn't fit to be buried there.
Robert: What? In Boot Hill?
Henry: There's nothing up there but murderers, cutthroats, and derelict old

If anyone thought the western was dead, they could take it up with two former Texas Rangers: Gus McCrae (Robert Duvall) and Capt. Woodrow F. Call (Tommy Lee Jones) in the television cowboy classic *Lonesome Dove* (TVW, 1989).

barflies. And if they ever felt exclusive, brother, they're past it now.
Chamlee: They happen to be white, friend. And Old Sam? Well, Old Sam was an Indian.
Henry: Well, I be damned! I never knew you had to be anything but a corpse to get into Boot Hill. How long has this been going on?
Chamlee: Since the town got civilized. Oh, it's not my doing, boys. I don't like it, no sir. I've always treated every man the same …just as another future customer.
Henry: Well in that case, get that hearse rolling.
Chamlee: I can't, my driver's quit!
Robert: He's prejudiced too, huh?

Chamlee: Well, when it comes to a chance of getting his head blown off, he's downright bigoted.

Chamlee played by Whit Bissell, Henry played by Val Avery, and Robert played by Bing Russell: John Sturges' *The Magnificent Seven* (United Artists, 1960).

235

Forbes: Well, should we bury 'em?
Chris: The living need us more.

Noah Forbes played by Michael Callan and Chris played by Lee Van Cleef: George McGowan's *The Magnificent Seven Ride* (United Artists, 1972).

236

Rimes: Let the dead past bury its dead.

J.B. Rimes played by Stephen Boyd: Peter Collinson's *The Man Called Noon* (Frontier Films, 1973).

237
Noon: Are you coming?
Rimes: Yea, I figure you might need me …if only to put a marker on your grave.
Noon played by Richard Crenna and J.B. Rimes played by Stephen Boyd: Peter Collinson's *The Man Called Noon* (Frontier Films, 1973).

238
Sheriff: It's your neck, Lockhart. If you want a Christian funeral, you'd better leave some money with the undertaker.
Sheriff Tom Quigley played by James Millican and Will Lockhart played by James Stewart: Anthony Mann's *The Man from Laramie* (Columbia, 1955).

239
Jim: United in death, the minister said.
Spur: Superstition.
Jim: It's a nice thought, Spur.
Spur: It's a great comfort to widows and fools. There's more to life than death, Jim.
Jim Craig played by Tom Burlinson and Spur played by Kirk Douglas: George Miller's *The Man from Snowy River* (20th Century–Fox, 1982).

240
Grace's Mother: There was nothing you could do. It was God's will.
Zachary Bass: I never much agreed with God's will.
Grace's Mother played by Sheila Raynor and Zachary Bass played by Richard Harris: Richard C. Sarafian's *Man in the Wilderness* (Warner Bros., 1971).

241
Marshal: Oh, I suppose somebody ought to say something nice about the deceased.
Annabelle: How do you know he was nice? We don't know anything about him. The only thing he's got in his wallet is a bunch of names of whorehouses.
Marshal Zane Cooper played by James Garner and Annabelle Bransford played by Jodie Foster: Richard Donner's *Maverick* (Warner Bros., 1994).

242
Sheriff: Possum, help the driver put those bodies on the stage. I'm sending them to Bannack.
Landers: Who were they, Sheriff?
Sheriff: Buzzard and Choppy. I ordered them to leave Montana over a month ago.
Possum: It looks like they've left it for good now. That's what comes from not knowing how to prolong your life. Now I always say …
Sheriff: Go on, do as I told ya!
Possum: Should I charge 'em more as passengers or just as death freight?
Sheriff Henry Plummer played by Preston Foster, Bill Landers played by Myron Healey, and Pos-

sum played by Eddy Waller: Ray Nazarro's *Montana Territory* (Columbia, 1952).

243
Wyatt: I've heard a lot about you, too, Doc. You left your mark around in Deadwood, Denver, and places. In fact, a man could almost follow your trail from graveyard to graveyard.
Doc: There's one here too …the biggest graveyard west of the Rockies. Marshals and I usually get along much better when we understand that right away.
Wyatt Earp played by Henry Fonda and Doc Holliday played by Victor Mature: John Ford's *My Darling Clementine* (20th Century–Fox, 1946).

244
Barfly: Squawk Mulligan tells me you buried your wife several years ago.
Twillie: Ah, yes, I had to …she died.
The Barfly was uncredited. Cuthbert J. Twillie played by W.C. Fields and Squawk Mulligan played by James Conlon: Edward F. Cline's *My Little Chickadee* (Universal, 1940).

245
Ben: He was dead and planted when she got there.
Ben Vandergroat played by Robert Ryan: Anthony Mann's *The Naked Spur* (MGM, 1953).

246
[*tombstone reading*]
   Bart
   Maveric
   Shot Dead
   1880
Brett: There's a "k". Maverick is spelled "ck". Couldn't you put something more on there?
Grave Digger: I put what I known. His name, he's dead, it's 1880.
Brett: I can give you the year of his birth.
Grave Digger: He's past counting birthdays.
Brett Maverick played by James Garner and the Grave Digger was uncredited: Hy Averback's *The New Maverick* (TVW, 1978).

247
Mrs. Winslow: How can you be so disrespectful of your father's memory?
Harriet: I'm not being disrespectful, Mother. I'm being honest. From now on, I'm gonna be honest with my father's memory.
Mrs. Winslow played by Anne Pitoniak and Harriet Winslow played by Jane Fonda: Luis Puenzo's *Old Gringo* (Columbia, 1989).

248
Arroyo: Do you want to drink with me?
Bierce: I thought you didn't drink?
Arroyo: Oh, I don't drink with the living. But tonight I come to visit my dead, to

celebrate with them. Do you visit your dead ones, amigo?
Bierce: No, but sometimes they come to visit me.
General Tomas Arroyo played by Jimmy Smits and Ambrose Bierce played by Gregory Peck: Luis Puenzo's *Old Gringo* (Columbia, 1989).

249
Jason: Lead's gonna fly. I can feel it in my bones. If I should catch one, boys, promise me you'll bury me where I fall.
Jason Pitch played by Jack Elam: Burt Kennedy's *Once Upon a Texas Train* (TVW, 1988).

250
Billy: Well, go ahead.
Pat: Go ahead what?
Billy: Aren't you gonna say something over Doc?
Pat: I don't know what to say. I've never said anything over anybody I've killed before.
Billy: I think we ought to say something over Doc.
Pat: You better do it.
Billy: …so long, Doc.
Billy the Kid played by Jack Buetel, Pat Garrett played by Thomas Mitchell, and Doc Holliday played by Walter Huston: Howard Hughes' *The Outlaw* (United Artists, 1943).

251
Jamie: I wish we had time to bury them fellas.
Josey Wales: To hell with them fellas. Buzzards got to eat …same as worms.
Jamie played by Sam Bottoms and Josey Wales played by Clint Eastwood who also directed *The Outlaw Josey Wales* (Warner Bros., 1976).

252
[*putting his dead friend on a horse and sending him to the enemy camp*]
Josey Wales: This boy was brought up in a time of blood and dying …and he never questioned a bit of it. He never turned his back on his folks or his kind. I rode with him. And I got no complaints. The blue bellies will give ya a better burial than I can, boy.
Josey Wales played by Clint Eastwood who also directed *The Outlaw Josey Wales* (Warner Bros., 1976).

253
Nash: And in a way, you know, it's kind of fitting that of all of us, the Kid was the first to go. He, well, he always did like to lead the way.
Nash Crawford played by Walter Brennan and the Baltimore Kid played by Fred Astaire: George McCowan's *The Over-the-Hill Gang Rides Again* (TVW, 1970).

Pete: All right, then stay here and bury him your-self!

Michael Karns played by Peter Hanson, Jacob Karns played by Dennis O'Keefe, Ben Johnson played by Richard Travis, and Pete Black played by John Payne: Lewis R. Foster's *Passage West* (Paramount, 1951).

256

Brodie: By the way, Reverend, I'm the under-taker. The only silk-lined hearse west of Independence. I'm on the way to the cemetery now. I have a little trouble gettin' the pallbearers out of town, ah, on account of the saloon, you know. Once we get 'em

out in the open, I can bury a man real fast.

Undertaker Brodie was uncredited and the Reverend Jacob Karns played by Dennis O'Keefe: Lewis R. Foster's *Passage West* (Paramount, 1951).

257

Garrett: Won't some of you people get him up off the ground and into it?

Pat Garrett played by James Coburn: Sam Peckinpah's *Pat Garrett and Billy the Kid* (MGM, 1973).

258

Borden: Tap, it ain't every man that gets the chance to see his own funeral. I don't know that I rightly like it though. It seems kind of ghostly like. There's my cousin, Pete, all red-eyed …mostly from corn, not from grief. And there's banker Havens sad as can be. But probably wondering will my house bring money enough at auction to cover the mort-gage.

Sam Borden played by George Cleveland: Jospeh Kane's *The Plunderers* (Republic, 1948).

259

Alice: Where is she …your woman?
Amos: I buried her. Had to …she was dead. Yea, I come here one

Top: Josey Wales (Clint Eastwood) says, "Well, are you gonna pull those pistols or whistle Dixie?" *Bottom:* Old Cherokee Indian, Lone Watie (Chief Dan George) says, "They call us civilized because we're easy to sneak up on," in *The Outlaw Josey Wales* (Warner Bros., 1976).

254

Weeks: Well, that's my hotel over there. It's usually full up, but I can take care of you now that Mr. Holly is changing his room.
Granger: Wrong. Holly isn't changing his room. He checked out.
Weeks: No, he'll be occupying the down-stairs rear. You see, I'm also the Oak-town's undertaker. And having my establishment on the premises, well, it saves so many steps.

Weeks played by Phil Chambers and Ross Granger played by Jock Mahoney: Fred F. Sears' *Overland Pacific* (United Artists, 1954).

255

Michael: But Jacob, the grave isn't deep enough!
Ben: It isn't just the rule of our church. It's the law of the open trails. Graves must be six feet deep and heaped with stones to protect it from wild animals. There must be a cross. I can't leave my son like this, Jacob!

After ingesting lead, Sundown Saunders (Tom Tyler) laments, "I guess it just wasn't in the cards for me to stay on." Looking on are Jeff Ferguson/Guadalupe Kid (Bob Steele), Lullaby Joslin (Guinn "Big Boy" Williams), Stony Brooke (Hoot Gibson), Tuscon Smith (Harry Carey), Bud Taggert (Wally Wales, bandage). (*Powdersmoke Range*, RKO, 1935.)

day and she was sittin' at the table deader than a can of corn beef. The poor old woman didn't even have a chance to finish her bowl of prunes. It hit me plenty hard, ma'am. But what come close to shakin' me was after I done finished diggin' her grave. I come in here to get her and she was all stiffen up …harder than a railroad tie! I had to bury her sittin' up! The poor old woman has to sit up straight and proper until judgment day!

Poker Alice Moffit played by Elizabeth Taylor and Amos played by David Wayne: Arthur Allan Seidelman's *Poker Alice* (TVW, 1987).

260

Burt Hogan: There's no point in getting any ice. We'll just bury Burl as soon as you get the box made up.
Undertaker: Being that it's your brother, I guess you'll want it in oak.
Burt Hogan: Birch or pine will do. I'll even things for Burl without paying a lot for a coffin.

Burt Hogan played by Frank Overton, Burl Hogan played by Allan "Rocky" Lane, and the Undertaker was uncredited: Herbert Coleman's *Posse from Hell* (Universal, 1961).

261

Sundown: Oh, you'll get over this hero-

worshiping idea that's got you hog-tied. Why, a year from now you'll even forget where you buried Smith.

Sundown Saunders played by Tom Tyler and Tucson Smith played by Harry Carey: Wallace Fox's *Powdersmoke Range* (RKO, 1935).

262

Fardan: So what else is on your mind besides 100 proof women, 90 proof whiskey, and 14 carat gold?
Dolworth: Amigo, you just wrote my epitaph.

Henry Rico Fardan played by Lee Marvin and Bill Dolworth played by Burt Lancaster: Richard Brooks' *The Professionals* (Columbia, 1966).

263

Dolworth: The cemetery of nameless men. We buried some fine friends there.

Fardan: And some fine enemies.

Dolworth: That was one hell of a fine battle. Out-numbered and out-gunned, and still we held that pass.

Fardan: Yea, but who cares now …or even remembers?

Bill Dolworth played by Burt Lancaster and Henry Rico Fardan played by Lee Marvin: Richard Brooks' *The Professionals* (Columbia, 1966).

264

Townsman: We're gonna have to bury this old man deep. He stinks something awful.

A line from an uncredited Townsman: Sam Raimi's *The Quick and the Dead* (Tristar, 1995).

265

Matthew: How did you know when he was gonna draw?

Dunson: By watching his eyes. Remember that.

Matthew: I will.

Dunson: Get a shovel and my Bible. I'll read over him.

Matthew Garth played by Montgomery Cliff and Tom Dunson played by John Wayne: Howard Hawks' *Red River* (United Artists, 1948).

266

Simms: Plantin' and readin', plantin' and readin'. Fill a man full of lead, stick him in the ground, and then read words at him. Why, when you killed a man, why try to read the Lord in him as a partner on the job?

Simms played by Hank Worden: Howard Hawks' *Red River* (United Artists, 1948).

267

Captain: Don't cover it up. Why should we deprive the vultures of a good meal.

The Mexican Captain played by C. Henry Gordon: Herbert I. Leeds' *The Return of the Cisco Kid* (20th Century–Fox, 1939).

268

Call: A man should leave more behind than an old board hammered in a sorry piece of dirt.

Captain Woodrow F. Call played by Jon Voight: Mike Robe's *Return to Lonesome Dove* (TVW, 1993).

269

Father: Listen to me, Laurie. Forget Clay and save yourself a lot of grief.

Laurie: Why?

Father: I've seen kids like him time and again in every boomtown in the west.

He's out for revenge …and headed straight for Boot Hill.

The Father, Sheriff Fred Kenyon, played by Paul Birch; the daughter, Laurie Kenyon, played by Susan Cabot; and Clay O'Mara played by Audie Murphy: Jesse Hibbs' *Ride Clear of Diablo* (Universal, 1954).

270

Leech: A man with a bounty on him pretty well guarantees himself a Christian burial. No remains …no reward.

Quinton Leech played by Kenny Rogers: Rod Hardy's *Rio Diablo* (TVW, 1993).

271

Station Master: I took him over to Doc Reynolds. The Doc's cuttin' him up to see what made him tick after his clock was stopped.

The Station Master played by Harry Harvey: Lesley Selander's *Rio Grande Patrol* (RKO, 1950).

272

Sheriff: Hank, go get the undertaker.

Hank: Yes, sir.

Sheriff: Never mind. Here he comes.

Undertaker: Nice to see you, Sheriff. Do you need me?

Sheriff: Yes, Ruff. Got a lot of work for ya. One over there, two over here, and one over in the corner.

Sheriff Pat Cronin played by Bill Williams, Hank played by Hank Worden, and the Undertaker Ruff was uncredited: Howard Hawks' *Rio Lobo* (NGP, 1970).

273

Willie: So that's how you got to be an undertaker! Makes sense …create your own business.

Willie Akers played by Scott Claflin: Richard Lloyd Dewey's *Rockwell* (Imperial Entertainment, 1994).

274

Porter: Hell, I reckon they need words said over 'em. [*pause*] …Ah, the hell with 'em!

Porter Rockwell played by Randy Gleave: Richard Lloyd Dewey's *Rockwell* (Imperial Entertainment, 1994).

275

Hawk: Leave him! We ain't got time for digging. Let the buzzards have him!

Hawk played by Richard Jordan: Stuart Millar's *Rooster Cogburn* (Universal, 1975).

276

Flood: You killed him, you bury him!

Alex Flood played by Dean Martin: Arnold Laven's *Rough Night in Jericho* (Universal, 1967).

277

Colonel: Let me just ask you one question. There's just one thing I'm most curious

about. Why bring the body here? My God, this is a home, people live here!

Henchman: Ah, Colonel, we didn't know exactly what to do with him.

Colonel: Bury him! How about that! Don't you think that's a good idea?

Henchman: Oh, yes sir, yes sir, Colonel!

Colonel: I mean, do you think that when somebody dies, they place them permanently on the family couch?

Henchman: No, sir.

Colonel: Gee whiz! Well, I'm …I'm …I'm sorry. I'm a little upset, that's all. The couch is new and Blackie was my best man. Oh, poor Blackie. Always acting so mean. Always shooting people.

Colonel Ticonderoga played by Andy Griffith and Blackie played by Jim Carter: Hugh Wilson's *Rustlers' Rhapsody* (Paramount, 1985).

278

Deneen: I'd rather send a son of mine riding and never see him again …than have to bury him.

Mr. Deneen played by Donald Crisp: Robert Parrish's *Saddle the Wind* (MGM, 1958).

279

Santee: Well, do you want to come along and see to their rights? They'll get a preacher, and a prayer, and a pine box. All at county expenses, if it means anything to you.

Santee played by Glenn Ford: Gary Nelson's *Santee* (Crown International Pictures, 1973).

280

Lieutenant: All right, Skidmore, ten minutes for burial. I know the ground is hard, but get him under it as far as you can.

Lieutenant Thomas Cantrell played by Jeffrey Hunter and Sergeant Matthew Skidmore played by James Pennick: John Ford's *Sergeant Rutledge* (Warner Bros., 1960).

281

Kroomak: Cut him in five pieces and bury him in the five directions.

Kroomak played by Toshiro Mifune: Jacques Dorfmann's *Shadow of the Wolf* (Triumph Releasing, 1993).

282

Marshal: The day they lay you away, what I'll do on your grave won't pass for flowers!

Marshal Thibido played by Harry Morgan: Don Siegel's *The Shootist* (Paramount, 1976).

283

Beckum: Mr. Books?

Books: Yes, sir.

Beckum: I'm Isaguya Beckum, the undertaker.

Books: How do you do?

Beckum: I hope you don't think my stopping by is untimely, sir.

Books: No, I admire a man with get up and go.

Beckum: As the saying goes in our profession: the early worm gets the bird. I admit to having heard unfortunate things. I'd like to express my heartfelt regret.

Books: All right. What's your proposition?

Beckum: Well, I'm prepared to offer you embalming by the most, ah, scientific method. Bronze coffin guaranteed good for a century regardless of the climatic or geological conditions. My best hearse. The minister of your choice. And the presence of at least, ah, two mourners. A headstone of the finest cut-out-of-marble, and about in the size of a patient befitting your status, sir. And perpetual care for the grounds.

Books: How much?

Beckum: Nothing sir. For the privilege …

Books: No, I mean how much are you gonna make on the deal?

Beckum: Sir!

Books: Oh, Beckum, you're gonna do to me what they did to John Wesley Hardin. You're gonna lay me out, let the public come by and gawk at me for fifty cents a head; ten cents for the children. When the curiosity peters out, you're gonna stuff me in a gunnysack and stick me in a hole while you hurry to the bank with your loot.

Beckum: Mr. Books, I assure you …!

Books: Give me a scrap of paper and a pencil! You'll assure me? What good is your assurance when my veins are filled with your damn juice? No, here's what you're gonna do. First, you're gonna give me fifty dollars cash. Then early Monday morning, you're gonna bring me a headstone. I want a small headstone with this written on it. Nothing else. No jabbery, no angels. You got that?

Beckum: Mr. Books, you are a hard man.

Books: I'm alive.

Beckum: Oh, very well. I'll get my stone cutter to work on the inscription immediately.

Beckum played by John Carradine and John Bernard Books played by John Wayne: Don Siegel's *The Shootist* (Paramount, 1976).

Outlaw Jim Dawkins (William Holden) turns Texas Ranger and finds himself in a showdown with former outlaw buddy on the *Streets of Laredo* (Paramount, 1949).

284

Undertaker: Good morning, gentlemen.

Frank: Good morning.

Undertaker: I trust everything meets with your approval.

Frank: Yea, fine.

Undertaker: I, ah, threw in the band.

Frank: It was a nice touch.

Undertaker: That will be fifty dollars.

Frank: Fifty dollars?

Undertaker: Well, you said to see they were covered in a proper grave!

Frank: Yes, but …

Undertaker: I usually charge thirty a head. I'm giving you a special deal.

Frank: That's still a lot of money.

Undertaker: It cost me five dollars a box, fifty cents apiece to dig the holes.

The Undertaker played by Phil Chambers and Frank Jesse played by Dan Duryea: Harry Keller's *Six Black Horses* (Universal, 1962).

285

Woman Dancer: You know, I can look into your eyes and see that you have led a gay, romantic life. If I'm not too personal, what do you do for a living?

Rufus Black: I sell coffins!

The Woman Dancer was uncredited and Rufus Black played by Eddie Parks: Irving Allen's *Slaughter Trail* (RKO, 1951).

286

Clarence: To the likes of Slade Cantrell, this man was just another John Doe. But he had a name. His name was Del. I never got his last name. I didn't think it was important. But I do now. So I scratched out …Del Doe …on his tombstone.

Tom: That was a nice touch, Clarence.

Clarence: I think my wife, Lilac, said it best: one good Del Doe is worth a hundred hired hands. As farmers, we all know what a Del Doe is worth. But it's getting to the point where Del Does are going to be hard to come by. So we got to send a clear message to Slade Cantrell: for every Del Doe he takes away, there's going to be another one sliding right in there to take his place. And with that I say, Amen.

Clarence Gentry played by Fred Willard and Tom Partridge played by Max Gail: Eugene Levy's *Sodbusters* (Atlantis Releasing, 1994).

287

Colonel: [*examining body*] Well, I'd say he looks healthier than the last time I saw him, Junior.

Junior: How can he look healthier when he's dead?

Colonel: It must agree with him.

Colonel Morgan played by Brian Keith and Junior Frisbee played by Denver Pyle: Andrew V. McLaglen's *something big* (NGP, 1971).

288

Colonel: Sergeant, see that poor Bill is underground before dark.

Sergeant: Yes, sir.

Colonel: The flies are getting bad.

Colonel Morgan played by Brian Keith and Sergeant Fitzsimmons played by Merlin Olsen: Andrew V. McLaglen's *something big* (NGP, 1971).

289

Colonel: What about your friend there? Do you want to bury him?

Cobb: No. Maybe something will come out of the hills tonight and drag him off.

Colonel Morgan played by Brian Keith and Johnny Cobb played by Albert Salmi: Andrew V. McLaglen's *something big* (NGP, 1971).

290

Matt: Well, we'll get us …a lamb, a marble lamb!

Tom: How about a horse?

Matt: A horse? For a grave?

Tom: Well, Ma loved horses.

Matt: Well, she didn't love 'em that much. How would you like to have a marble horse on top of you for the rest of eternity?

John: What's happened to all of us?

Tom: Well, you said she'd like a monument.

John: Yea, but not that kind. She wanted one of us …her family, to amount to something.

Tom: Well, she sure drew a flat, blank zero.

John: Not yet she hasn't. Not if Bud goes back to school.

Bud: Oh no, you wait a minute!

John: That's the kind of monument she wanted.

Bud: Well, why should I be the monument? No, why don't you amount to something?

John: It's too late for the rest of us.

Bud: Well, I'll tell ya, I'm not gonna be no monument!

Matt Elder played by Earl Holliman, Tom Elder played by Dean Martin, John Elder played by John Wayne, and Bud Elder played by Michael Anderson, Jr.: Henry Hathaway's *The Sons of Katie Elder* (Paramount, 1965).

291

Carter: He wasn't much of a hand at nothing but a jug. But he was decent enough to me. I sure hope there's plenty of filled-up jugs wherever he's gone.

Rannie Carter played by Mona Freeman: Leslie Fenton's *Streets of Laredo* (Paramount, 1949).

292

Preacher: We are gathered here today to consign the mortal remains of Miller Trymore …or whatever his name really was. I ain't really got a whole lot to say about Miller because he only rode amongst us two days ago, and was promptly struck down by whatever deadly disease it was that struck him down. We can only hope that whatever deadly disease it was, it wasn't particularly contagious. And with that in mind, I suggest we all bow our heads in devout prayer.

Preacher Henry Jackson played by Henry Jones: Burt Kennedy's *Support Your Local Sheriff!* (United Artists, 1969).

293

Preacher: I'd like to remind everyone that we're here to consign the remains of Miller Trymore.

Fred: It's gold, Henry!

Preacher: Gold?

Fred: Down there in the grave!

Preacher: Well, get this coffin out of the way and we'll have a look!

Preacher Henry Jackson played by Henry Jones and Fred Johnson played by Walter Burke: Burt Kennedy's *Support Your Local Sheriff!* (United Artists, 1969).

294

Tennessee: I never even knew his name.

Tennessee played by John Payne: Allan Dwan's *Tennessee's Partner* (RKO, 1955).

295

Lat: Tom, if I die will you bury me under rocks so the wolves won't get me?

Lat Evans played by Don Murray and Tom Ping played by Stuart Whitman: Richard Fleischer's *These Thousand Hills* (20th Century–Fox, 1959).

296

Major: Let this be a reminder, old man. Either you leave this valley or I'll bury you in it. The choice is yours.

Major Harriman played by Farley Granger: E.B. Clucher's (Enzo Barboni) *They Call Me Trinity* (West Film/Avco Embassy, 1970).

297

Bob: Is that all?

Kearney: Them all the words I know, Bob.

Bob: Then …amen.

Robert Marmaduke Hightower played by John Wayne and William Kearney, "The Abilene Kid," played by Harry Carey, Jr.: John Ford's *The 3 Godfathers* (MGM, 1948).

298

Here lies

Lester Moor

Four Sluggs

From a 44

No Les

No More

Tombstone reading in Boot Hill Cemetery: George P. Cosmatos' *Tombstone* (Buena Vista, 1993).

299

Noble: She's buried right out there somewhere.

Noble Adams played by Kris Kristofferson: John Guillermin's *The Tracker* (HBO Pictures, 1988).

300

Dobbs: Well, I guess we better dig a hole for him.

Fred C. Dobbs played by Humphrey Bogart: John Huston's *The Treasure of the Sierra Madre* (Warner Bros., 1948).

301

Rooster: Boots, I got Hayes and some youngster outside with Moon and Quincy. I want you to bury 'em for me. I'm in a hurry.

Boots: They dead?

Rooster: Well, I wouldn't want you to bury 'em if they wasn't!

Marshal Reuben J. "Rooster" Cogburn played by John Wayne, Moon played by Dennis Hopper, Emmett Quincy played by Jeremy Slate, and Captain Boots Finch played by Ron Soble: Henry Hathaway's *True Grit* (Paramount, 1969).

302

Bragg: Let's scratch some sand over him and keep the buzzards from picking him to pieces.

Pete: Pretty soon wind comes some more, blow sand off, and coyotes dig him up just the same.

Bragg: Ain't you got no respect? It's the idea of the thing. Now get to scratching.

Skinner Bill Bragg played by Wallace Beery and Piute Pete played by Leo Carrillo: Richard Thorpe's *20 Mule Team* (MGM, 1940).

303

Sister: Do you have a shovel?

Hogan: Sister, raise your eyes to heaven. Now, are they [buzzards] or are they not God's creatures?

Sister: Well, of course they are.

Hogan: Well, why do you want to rob 'em of all the convenient nourishment?

Sister Sara played by Shirley MacLaine and Hogan played by Clint Eastwood: Don Siegel's *Two Mules for Sister Sara* (Universal, 1970).

304

Sergeant: You! You're supposed to be dead!

McCabe: I'm sorry, Slim. I didn't quite make it.

Sergeant Davis P. Posey played by Andy Devine and Guthrie "Gus" McCabe played by James Stewart: John Ford's *Two Rode Together* (Columbia, 1961).

305

Priest: There's a body right outside your front door.

Jackson: I know, I put it there.

Priest: I don't suppose you'd be interested in helping us with the burial?

Jackson: What do you think? I came here to dig gold, not to dig graves.

Priest: Every time I meet a man like you who's alive and well, I marvel at the patience of God.

The Priest played by Ted Haler and Jackson played by Christopher Boyer: Michael Bohusz's *Uninvited* (Imperial Entertainment, 1993).

306

Charlie: He's being slapped with a spade right now.

Charlie played by Victor Kilian: Fritz Lang's *Western Union* (20th Century–Fox, 1941).

307

Tom: Where's Meo?

Red: Dead. Yep, he just come in here one night and said he was gonna die. The next morning he was dead. So I buried the old chili-eater out back here.

Tom Black Bull played by Frederic Forrest, Red Dillon played by Richard Widmark, and Meo played by Vito Scotti: Stuart Millar's *When the Legends Die* (20th Century–Fox, 1972).

308

Murray: Barney heard you'd been shot up. He asked after ya.

Bill: Yeah, he seemed mighty disappointed when he heard you wasn't buried yet.

Murray Sinclair played by Robert Preston, Barney Rebstock played by Donald Crisp, and Bill Dansing played by William Demarest: Leslie Fenton's *Whispering Smith* (Paramount, 1948).

309

Abel: When you get through planting them two, I got three more customers [bodies] for you inside the coach. And I believe they got enough money to pay for their own box.

Amos: That's right kindly of you, Abel. You better lay them out in the snow until I get back. That will keep 'em fresh.

Abel Pinkney played by Slim Pickens and Amos Bixby played by Douglas V. Fowley: J. Lee Thompson's *The White Buffalo* (United Artists, 1977).

310

Jack: Is there any good reason why we can't just bury him here? I don't think he'll know the difference.

Alex: I gave him my word.

Jack Conroy played by Ethan Hawke and Alex Larson played by Klaus Maria Brandauer: Randal Kleiser's *White Fang* (Buena Vista, 1991).

311

Dutch: I think the boys are right. I'd like to say a few words for the dear dead departed. And maybe a few hymns would be in order …followed by a church supper …with a choir!

Dutch Engstrom played by Ernest Borgnine: Sam

Peckinpah's *The Wild Bunch* (Warner Bros.–Seven Arts, 1969).

312

Jules: It's a crazy cross. But that's all right. He was a crazy man.

Jules Vincent played by Stewart Granger: Andrew Marton's *The Wild North* (MGM, 1952).

313

Catron: Best thing you can do for him, pilgrim, is make him rest easy while he waits till the end. Anything he drinks is on the house. And then you can bury him out back and away from the hogs. And it won't cost much. I'll even carve him a nice head marker. Twenty-five dollars sound about right? The ground is kind of hard this time of year …and the diggin' ain't easy.

Catron played by Clifton James: Tom Gries' *Will Penny* (Paramount, 1968).

314

Sergeant: The Major is in a hurry to get buried on a Montana mountain.

The Sergeant played by Claude Akins and Major Towns played by Rhodes Reason: Gordon Douglas' *Yellowstone Kelly* (Warner Bros., 1959).

315

Kelly: Yea, he said he was gonna cross the Yellowstone and jump the Sioux.

Harper: Will he try a fool thing like that?

Kelly: If he does, the ground is gonna be full of soldiers.

Kelly played by Clint Walker and Anse Harper played by Edward Byrnes: Gordon Douglas' *Yellowstone Kelly* (Warner Bros., 1959).

Cattle

See also Cowboys; Horses; Ranch and Range

316

Marshal: First off, I'm not the sheriff. I'm just town marshal of Abilene.

Hannaberry: I'd have guessed you was closer to the land …cattle maybe.

Marshal Dan Mitchell played by Randolph Scott and Hannaberry played by Eddy Waller: Edwin Marin's *Abilene Town* (United Artists, 1946).

317

Kelly: Now the main thing to remember is …cattle are like women. Sometimes you have to be firm with them. Sometimes you have to be gentle. And sometimes you have to give them a slap on the rump.

Alvarez Kelly played by William Holden: Edward Dmytryk's *Alvarez Kelly* (Columbia, 1966).

318

Laramie: What does Arizona want him for?

Sheriff: Well, nothing yet. But there's a big herd of cattle coming in today and the boys will be here a couple weeks spending their money while the herd rest up.

Laramie: So you're locking Tracks up to keep him out of competition.

Sheriff: Sure, we got to give the local boys a break!

Laramie Nelson played by Larry "Buster" Crabbe, the Sheriff played by Herbert Haywood, and Tracks Williams played by Raymond Hatton: James Hogan's *The Arizona Raiders* (a.k.a. *Bad Men of Arizona*; Paramount, 1936).

319

Jason: You know, it takes money, capital, brains, and sweat to raise cattle. But any idiot with a two-bit dog and a Winchester can raise sheep.

Jason Meredith played by Peter Graves: Andrew V. McLaglen's *Ballad of Josie* (Universal, 1968).

James McKay (Gregory Peck) is about to be gunned down by Buck Hannassey (Chuck Connors) until the father, Rufus Hannassey (Burl Ives), admonishes his son: "You don't shoot an unarmed man …not while I'm around." Schoolmarm Julie Maragon (Jean Simmons) looks on in William Wyler's *The Big Country* (United Artists, 1958).

320

Major Terrill: There's no prettier sight in the world than 10,000 head of cattle …unless it's 50,000.

Major Henry Terrill played by Charles Bickford: William Wyler's *The Big Country* (United Artists, 1958).

321

Hannassey: Why ain't you dead? You let 'em run my cows off and you come back standing up!

Buck: What could we do, pa? There was twenty of them …just a few of us!

Hannassey: Them cows is worth more than the whole lot of ya.

Rufus Hannassey played by Burl Ives and Buck Hannassey played by Chuck Connors: William Wyler's *The Big Country* (United Artists, 1958).

322

Sam: By the time those cattle get through stomping on Matt, nobody is going to notice he was shot.

Sam Mullen played by James Best and Matt Brown played by Audie Murphy: Thomas Carr's *Cast a Long Shadow* (United Artists, 1959).

323

Russell: Our luck has got to change sometime.

Brett: You're like a bunch of dumb cattle. You're stampeded at the sight of trouble, bawl at the first shift in the wind. Our luck ain't going to change until you start acting like men.

Russell played by Leo Gordon and Brett Stanton played by Dale Robertson: Harmon Jones' *City of Bad Men* (20th Century–Fox, 1953).

324

Ed: We're doing great, guys! We're driving them [cattle]!

Phil: Ah, that's perfect! We're lost but we're making good time!

Ed Furillo played by Bruno Kirby and Phil Berquist played by Daniel Stern: Ron Underwood's *City Slickers* (Columbia, 1991).

325

Mitch: Here's your herd.

Clay: I'm telling ya, I'm as happy as a puppy with two peters!

Mitch Robbins played by Billy Crystal and Clay Stone played by Noble Willingham: Ron Underwood's *City Slickers* (Columbia, 1991).

326

Glen: Oh, by the way, there is something wrong with your cow.

Mitch: What?

Glen: Well, I thought I'd help out with the chores, you know. So I figured I'd milk the cow. I reach under there, and I'm pulling and tugging …I'm tugging, I'm pulling …nothing, not a drop!

Mitch: The cow's name is Norman.

Glen: I'm going to wash up.

Glen Robbins played by Jon Lovitz and Mitch Robbins played by Billy Crystal: Paul Weiland's *City Slickers II: The Legend of Curly's Gold* (Columbia, 1994).

327

Pluthner: Well, don't get any ideas you are through with us. You wouldn't last long cut off from the herd, McQueen. You're branded clean to the bone.

Pluthner played by Harry Woods and Wes McQueen played by Joel McCrea: Raoul Walsh's *Colorado Territory* (Warner Bros., 1949).

328

Harris: We rounded up most of the herd …that is, all we could find.
Reece: How many head did we lose?
Harris: Just over 200.
Reece: That's a lot of cows.
Harris: Yea, it is. It's too bad. It's too bad for you.
Reece: What?
Harris: We found all my cows. It seems it was yours that ran off and got lost.

Frank Harris played by Jack Lemmon and Tom Reece played by Glenn Ford: Delmer Daves' *Cowboy* (Columbia, 1958).

329

Wil: You know, trail driving is no Sunday school picnic. You got to figure you're dealing with the dumbest, orneriest critter on God's green earth. The cow is nothing but a lot of trouble tied up in a leather bag. And the horse ain't much better.

Wil Anderson played by John Wayne: Mark Rydell's *The Cowboys* (Warner Bros., 1972).

330

Cattle Annie: I sure wish I was one 'em.
Rose: But you can't be. All you can do is sit here …and hear that tune play …and watch them leave …and wonder if they're going to come back.
Cattle Annie: You're talking about love. I'm talking about cows!

Cattle Annie played by Dona Drake and Rose of Cimarron played by Louise Allbritton: Gordon Douglas' *The Doolins of Oklahoma* (Columbia, 1949).

331

Adarene: Why, Luz, everybody in [this] county knows you'd rather herd cattle than make love.
Luz: Well, there's one thing you got to say for cattle. Boy, you put your brand on one of them, you're gonna know where it's at!

Adarene Clinch played by Mary Ann Edwards and Luz Benedict played by Mercedes McCambridge: George Stevens *Giant* (Warner Bros., 1956).

332

Dave: They're grazing on Barb land, aren't they?
Vic: So they're eating a mouthful of grass! We got plenty growing around here.

Will Lockhart (James Stewart) searches for the man who sold firearms to the Indians which resulted in his brother's demise in Anthony Mann's top-rate western *The Man from Laramie* (Colombia, 1955).

Dave: Alec always says: a steer swallows a blade of Barb grass, it becomes a Barb steer.

Dave Waggoman played by Alex Nicol, Vic Hansbro played by Arthur Kennedy, and Alec Waggoman played by Donald Crisp: Anthony Mann's *The Man from Laramie* (Columbia, 1955).

333

Dempsey: A maverick …a calf with no mother. No brand neither.
Jeff: Why not?
Dempsey: Oh, on account he was missing at roundup time. He outgrew his mother and wandered off. Sort of like you.

Dempsey Rae played by Kirk Douglas and Jeff Jimson played by William Campbell: King Vidor's *Man Without a Star* (Universal, 1955).

334

McLintock: Cuthbert H. Humphrey, Governor of our territory, is a cull. Do you know what a cull is, ma'am? A cull is a specimen that is so worthless that you have to cut him out of the herd. Now, if all the people in the world were put in one herd, Cuthbert is the one I would throw my rope at.

George Washington McLintock played by John Wayne and Governor Cuthbert H. Humphrey played by Robert Lowery: Andrew V. McLaglen's *McLintock!* (United Artists, 1963).

335

Rhys: Why should I drive cattle I don't own across land I can't own?

Rhys Williams played by Patrick Bergin: Strathford

Hamilton's *The Proposition* (Tanmarsh Communications Limited/A-Pix Entertainment/Poly Gram Filmed Entertainment, 1996).

336

Harter: One morning you'll wake up to a train whistle and there won't be any more cattle drives. Yes sir, in a few years it will all be gone. At least-wise, the way we knew it.

Jeff Harter played by Ben Johnson: Andrew V. McLaglen's *The Rare Breed* (Universal, 1966).

337

When the territories of the great west were thrown open, man of all kinds rushed in. Most came to settle peaceably, lured by free land, gold, cattle. A man could begin a herd with a maverick, an un-branded stray on the public range. By putting his brand on it, he owned it. Cattle barons had started their great herds with mavericks. Now they fought each settler who tried to do the same. They fought to keep the settler off the public land, drive them from their homes, destroy their towns. Vast ranges became the battleground of cattle wars. When the Wyoming big ranchers found that guns were not enough, they used the maverick law, a law to which they appointed themselves commissioners with powers to rule on the ownership of every maverick brand. A commissioner's ruling could declare the settler a rustler, outlaw his brand, make his mavericks illegal to sell.

Prologue to Lee Sholem's *The Redhead from Wyoming* (Universal, 1953).

338

Duncan: I'm just warning you. No animal on my property, branded or not, is a stray. Whatever you pick up on the open range is yours. Anything you take from me has lead coming after it.

Reece Duncan played by Alexander Scourby: Lee Sholem's *The Redhead from Wyoming* (Universal, 1953).

339

Narrator: In the old days of the west, the big cattle spreads had spring and fall round-ups. Then the steers to be sold became a trail herd pointed to the nearest railhead often hundreds of miles away. The trail was sometimes tough with rain, wind, and snow.

Narration by John Payne: Joseph Kane's *The Road to Denver* (Republic, 1955).

340

Howdy: That one is wilder than mountain scenery.

Howdy Lewis played by Henry Fonda: Burt Kennedy's *The Rounders* (MGM, 1965).

341

Cutter: There's more brands on this herd than a dog has fleas!

Cutter played by Edmund Cobb: William Berke's *Saddles and Sagebrush* (Columbia, 1943).

342

Angelo: How come you get into the sheep business, boss?
Jason: Well, I'll tell ya, Angelo. You see, it's this way. I just got tired of kicking cows around. You know how dumb they are.
Angelo: And you think sheep are smarter?

Jason: Oh no, no. They're dumber. Only they're easier kicking …and woolier.

Angelo played by Pedro Gonzales-Gonzales and Jason Sweet played by Glenn Ford: George Marshall's *The Sheepman* (MGM, 1958).

343

Guthrie: Did you know we were going to get some cattle with the place?
Laurie: Cattle? How many?
Guthrie: Two. We're going to be cattle barons.

Jim Guthrie played by Dana Andrews and Laurie Mastin played by Donna Reed: Alfred Werker's *Three Hours to Kill* (Columbia, 1954).

344

Judge Bean: Shad Wilkins, you've been tried and found guilty of the most serious crime west of the Pecos. To wit: shooting a steer. Do you got anything to say for yourself before the sentence of the court is executed?
Shad: I told you they shot at me first. I didn't mean to kill that steer on purpose. I was aiming at the man.
Judge Bean: It's your bad luck you missed him. That's the trouble with you sodbusters. You can't shoot straight. Shad, may the Lord have mercy on your soul.

Judge Roy Bean played by Walter Brennan and Shad Wilkins played by Trevor Bardette: William Wyler's *The Westerner* (United Artists, 1940).

345

Rusty: Look, you got to know how to rope a restless steer down. You can't put a brand on a running critter.

Rusty played by Casey Tibbs: Charles Haas' *Wild Heritage* (Universal, 1958).

— Causes, Conflicts, and Civil War —

See also Dying; Fighting; Killing

346

Rita: I don't know whether you joined us or we joined you, but it's good to be together.

Rita played by Ann Dvorak: Edwin Marin's *Abilene Town* (Untied Artists, 1946).

347

Crockett: It was like I was empty. Well, I'm not empty anymore. That's what's important. To feel useful in this old world. To hit a lick against what's wrong or to say a word for what's right even though you get walloped for saying that word. Now I may sound like a Bible beater yelling up a revival at a river

crossing camp meeting, but that don't change the truth none. There's right and there's wrong. You got to do one or the other. You do the one and you're living. You do the other and you may be walking around, but you're dead as a beaver hat.

Colonel David "Davy" Crockett played by John Wayne: John Wayne's *The Alamo* (United Artists, 1960).

348

Crockett: Some words can give ya a feeling that makes your heart warm. Republic is one of those words.

Colonel David "Davy" Crockett played by John

Wayne: John Wayne's *The Alamo* (United Artists, 1960).

349

Santa Anna: History teaches us, gentlemen, that great generals remain generals by never underestimating their opposition.

Santa Anna played by Raul Julia: Burt Kennedy's *The Alamo: Thirteen Days to Glory* (TVW, 1987).

350

Travis: What are you fighting for?
Bowie: More like the old life, I guess. Like it used to be. Like it is in America where the people own the government. You

see, Santa Anna, he thinks he owns the people. Now I don't like being owned. I'm kind of particular about that kind of thing.

Colonel William Travis played by Alec Baldwin, Jim Bowie played by James Arness and Santa Anna played by Raul Julia: Burt Kennedy's *The Alamo: Thirteen Days to Glory* (TVW, 1987).

351

Travis: This is not about land or money ...but the one thing that no man should never be able to take from another man: the freedom to make his own choices about his life, where he'll live, how he'll live, how he'll raise his family.

Colonel William Travis played by Alec Baldwin: Burt Kennedy's *The Alamo: Thirteen Days to Glory* (TVW, 1987).

352

Professor: Men, we've fought and won. But in winning we have lost something. In defending one law, we've come to despise all law. And if you go on like this, we'll destroy the very thing we fight for.

The Professor played by John F. Hamilton: William A. Seiter's *Allegheny Uprising* (RKO, 1939).

353

In every war ...In every age ...The forgotten weapon is ...Food. For to kill, soldiers must live ...to live, they must eat ...And a herd of cattle is as vital as a herd of cannon ...

Prologue: Edward Dmytryk's *Alvarez Kelly* (Columbia, 1966).

354

Charity: You disappoint me, Mr. Kelly. After what happened to your own home, I should think your sympathies would be with us.
Kelly: I have no sympathies, only instincts. And they shy away from losers.

Charity Warwick played by Victoria Shaw and Alvarez Kelly played by William Holden: Edward Dmytryk's *Alvarez Kelly* (Columbia, 1966).

355

Rossiter: You used to have ten fingers. Now you got nine. Tomorrow you'll have eight. You stay stubborn, the day after then you'll have seven. The day after that ...it's up to you. You decide whether you want to end up with a pair of stumps ...or lend us your talent. You decide.

Colonel Tom Rossiter played by Richard Widmark: Edward Dmytryk's *Alvarez Kelly* (Columbia, 1966).

356

McSpadden: And what do you call this little piece of heaven?
Wirz: That? This is Andersonville.

Sergeant McSpadden played by Frederic Forrest and Captain Wirz, the prison commander, played

A scene from *The Alamo* (United Artists, 1960) with the Gambler (Denver Pyle), Col. David Crockett (John Wayne), Beekeeper (Chill Wills), Jocko (John Dierkes), and Blind Nell (Veda Ann Borg).

by Jan Triska: John Frankenheimer's *Andersonville* (Turner Pictures, 1996).

357

Captain: Walker, were you ever in the Army?
Walker: I rode with Hood.
Captain: I had you figured for a Reb.
Walker: But that's all behind us, Captain. I fight no wars to a lost cause.

Captain Gannon played by Richard Arlen and Jim Walker played by Rory Calhoun: R.G. Springsteen's *Apache Uprising* (Paramount, 1966).

358

Narrator: A little known chapter in the history of the old west began during the waning days of the Civil War. While soldiers of the North and South clashed on the battlefield, military prisons on both sides were woefully overcrowded. Men often died by the score, and those that did not generally existed in wallow, stink, and eroding monotony. When informed of these conditions, President Abraham Lincoln granted Confederate prisoners the opportunity to enlist in the Union Army. They were not asked to fight their brothers in the South, but instead were ordered to help settle and patrol the west: fighting Indians, repairing roads, telegraph wire, and in some cases to bring order to a lawless town. One such rebel to accept these terms was Lee Travis — before the war, a Mississippi riverboat gambler and gunfighter. In 1862, he had worn Confederate gray. Two years later, he was captured. And now in 1865, taking advantage of President Lincoln's offer, he wore the blue Yankee uniform and was embarked on a long journey to the untamed frontier town of Colton, Arizona. A town that today did not know Lee Travis was on his way: didn't know, didn't care.

Narrative at beginning of Lesley Selander's *Arizona Bushwhackers* (Paramount, 1968). Lee Travis played by Howard Keel.

359

Editor: Human misery became his livelihood [Quantrill] …and at an early age.

From the Editor of the *Ohio Gazette* (uncredited): William Witney's *Arizona Raiders* (Columbia, 1965).

360

Editor: Because of him [Quantrill], widows wailed, orphans cried, maidens wept …as they lifted the lifeless forms of their loved ones from the bloody fields …who bore them to untimely graves.

From the Editor of the *Ohio Gazette* (uncredited): William Witney's *Arizona Raiders* (Columbia, 1965).

361

Willie: Well, nobody cares much when you're on the losing side.
Captain: I respect a good soldier no matter what the color of his uniform.

Willie Martin played by Ben Cooper and Captain Tom Andrews played by Buster Crabbe: William Witney's *Arizona Raiders* (Columbia, 1965).

362

Lake: Are you looking for a medal?
Slater: No, I got one.
Lake: I bet you would have traded it for a meal after the surrender.
Slater: How'd you guess?
Lake: Oh, I fought against you rebels: all guts and no sense.

Sergeant George Lake played by Barton MacLane and Jim Slater played by Richard Widmark: John Sturges' *Backlash* (Universal, 1956).

363

Duarte: If the revolutionaries had gold, you would be working for them.
Canales: Yes, your Excellency.
Duarte: You are nothing but a bandit.
Canales: Yes, your Excellency.
Duarte: Remember, Canales, when the revolution is over, I promise to hang you.
Canales: Yes, your Excellency.

General Duarte played by Eduardo Fajardo and Canales played by Aldo Sanbrell: Gene Martin's *Bad Man's River* (Scotia International, 1971).

364

Ringo: My father was an engineer during the war …for the North. At first, he was for the South. But they were losing. And, ah, "never stick with a loser," he always said. "It's a matter of principle."

Ringo played by Giuliano Gemma: Duccio Tessari's *Ballad of Death Valley* (a.k.a. *The Return of Ringo*; Mediterranee-Balcazar/Rizzoli Film, 1966).

365

Dee: Hey, Bobby, here's a momma for you. One boy goes with Quantrill, the other goes with Sherman. One helps burn down a town, the other helps burn down a state. The one that burns down the town is the one that done in his momma.
Mace: Sherman was war, Dee. Quantrill was meanness.

Dee Bishop played by Dean Martin and Mace Bishop played by James Stewart: Andrew McLaglen's *Bandolero!* (20th Century–Fox, 1968).

366

Barbarosa: Did you have bad trouble back there?
Karl: Yes, sir.
Barbarosa: Well, the Mexicans got a saying: what cannot be remedied must be endured.

Barbarosa played by Willie Nelson and Karl played by Gary Busey: Fred Schepisi's *Barbarosa* (Universal, 1982).

367

Hallie: Mr. Yankee, there was enough iron in your leg to shoe a horse!

Hallie played by Mae Mercer and the Yankee Soldier, John McBurney, played by Clint Eastwood: Don Siegel's *The Beguiled* (Universal, 1971).

368

McKay: I'm not going to go on living in the middle of a civil war.

Jim McKay played by Gregory Peck: William Wyler's *The Big Country* (United Artists, 1958).

369

Buck: Remember, the Terrills ain't no friends of ours.
Julie: I'll choose my own friends.
Buck: Oh, they won't do. You got to be on one side or the other. You can't have it both ways.

Buck Hannassey played by Chuck Connors and Julie Maragon played by Jean Simmons: William Wyler's *The Big Country* (United Artists, 1958).

370

Hannassey: The Hannasseys will have no peace until the bones of Henry Terrill is bleaching in Blanco Canyon. Now, he started this blood-spilling, and I aim to finish it!

Rufus Hannassey played by Burl Ives and Major Henry Terrill played by Charles Bickford: William Wyler's *The Big Country* (United Artists, 1958).

371

Smith: Perhaps it's time for us to show a different kind of courage …and do something besides being killed for what we believe.

Joseph Smith played by Vincent Price: Henry Hathaway's *Brigham Young* (20th Century–Fox, 1940).

372

Buffalo Bill: My daddy was killed trying to keep slavery out of Kansas.
Dart: How did he do that?
Buffalo Bill: Well, my daddy hated slavery with such a passion that rather than let the coloreds get in to become slaves, he just fought to keep 'em all out of the state.

Buffalo Bill played by Paul Newman and Oswald Dart played by Robert Doqui: Robert Altman's *Buffalo Bill and the Indians, or Sitting Bull's History Lesson* (United Artists, 1976).

373

Cain: You don't want a cause. You want revenge!

Captain Justice Cain played by Scott Brady: Kent Osborne's *Cain's Cutthroats* (a.k.a. *Cain's Way*; M.D.A. Associates/Fanfare, 1969).

374

Cordoba: The revolution has many friends …for a price.

General Cordoba played by Raf Vallone: Paul Wendkos' *Cannon for Cordoba* (United Artists, 1970).

375

Big Jack: Never fight your own battles when you can get somebody else to.

Big Jack Davis played by Raymond Massey: Andre De Toth's *Carson City* (Warner Bros., 1952).

376

Nye: Anyhow, I used to heard it said: you boys who rode with Hood drank five states dry. You could always tell where Hood's Texans had been by the empty bottles and the dead Yankees.

Nye Buell played by Richard Basehart: Michael Winner's *Chato's Land* (United Artists, 1972).

377

Nye: You know, one thing I never could fathom was this: how did them Yankees win?

Quincey: They had more. More men, more guns, more food, more luck. You know, when I look back at it, I know now that it was there for the seeing …except we didn't see it.

Nye Buell played by Richard Basehart and Quincey Whitmore played by Jack Palance: Michael Winner's *Chato's Land* (United Artists, 1972).

378

Quincey: Hell, it was a good war.

Quincey Whitmore played by Jack Palance: Michael Winner's *Chato's Land* (United Artists, 1972).

379

Carl: Oh, Henry. You and I fought together at Gettysburg. You had never even seen a Negro slave. All you ever knew was that they were human beings with the rights of human beings. And it was worth an arm to you.

Secretary of the Interior Carl Schurz played by Edward G. Robinson and Senator Henry played by Denver Pyle: John Ford's *Cheyenne Autumn* (Warner Bros., 1964).

380

Cisco Kid: I don't fight for causes.
Pancho: Well, what do you fight for?

The Cisco Kid played by Jimmy Smits and Pancho played by Cheech Marin: Luis Valdez's *The Cisco Kid* (Turner Pictures, 1994).

381

General Storey: I was told you were a man of intense loyalty …deeply devoted to the cause.

Capt. Whitlock: The cause? Causes may start wars, but they don't win them!

Brigadier General Storey played by Ray Collins and Captain Lee Whitlock played by Robert Sterling: Frederick de Cordova's *Column South* (Universal, 1953).

382

Conagher: Tell me something, Chris. Where do you stand? Are you riding with the brand …or are you running scared?

Conn Conagher played by Sam Elliott and Chris Mahler played by Gavan O'Herlihy: Reynaldo Villalobos' *Conagher* (Turner Pictures, 1991).

383

Clarke: He really believed what he said.
Banner: Enough to die for it.

Amy Clarke played by Linda Darnell and John Banner played by Dale Robertson: Lewis R. Foster's *Dakota Incident* (Republic, 1956).

384

Weatherby: I should have taken you straight to a doctor.

Hollister: That's how you lost Bull Run, Yankee. Letting the enemy know your casualties.

Martin Weatherby played by Leif Erickson and Blayde "Reb" Hollister played by Gary Cooper: Stuart Heisler's *Dallas* (Warner Bros., 1950).

385

Crockett: Well, me and Russell are figuring on heading down Texas way. That ain't no place these days for a riverboat gambler with wobbly legs.

Thimblerig: There are times when cowardice is a virtue, my dear Colonel. It makes choosing a cause so very simple. Now, I know nothing of this Texas of which you speak. But I do know of the fury of the outraged millions of the law. And as a consequence, I fear what lies behind me far more than the unknown which lies ahead.

Davy Crockett played by Fess Parker and Hans Conried played Thimblerig: Norman Foster's *Davy Crockett, King of the Wild Frontier* (Buena Vista, 1955).

386

Bowie: How many men did you bring?
Crockett: Four, including myself.
Bowie: Four? Two acres of wall to defend. It'll take at least a thousand troops to man the garrison adequately. And I got less than two hundred volunteers.
Crockett: Two hundred stubborn men can do a terrible lot of fighting.

Colonel Jim Bowie played by Kenneth Tobey and Davy Crockett played by Fess Parker: Norman Foster's *Davy Crockett, King of the Wild Frontier* (Buena Vista, 1955).

387

Captain: If you had killed me, I would have been martyred. Now I'll merely be disgraced.

Captain Salazar played by Edward James Olmos: Yves Simoneau's *Dead Man's Walk* (Cabin Fever Entertainment, 1996).

388

Captain: I am almost out of ammunition. If you send us back with no horses and no bullets, Gomez will kill all of us.

Major: Ask that priest for a prayer. If he's a good priest, his prayers might be better than bullets and horses.

Captain Salazar played by Edward James Olmos, the Major was uncredited, and Gomez played by Victor Aaron: Yves Simoneau's *Dead Man's Walk* (Cabin Fever Entertainment, 1996).

389

Shadrach: General Lloyd couldn't find Mexico if you tied him to a horse and pointed him south.

Shadrach played by Harry Dean Stanton and General Lloyd played by Bert Roberts: Yves Simoneau's *Dead Man's Walk* (Cabin Fever Entertainment, 1996).

390

Colonel: But I still give the orders here, do you understand?

Bigfoot: Well, give better ones then! I wouldn't waste a fart on your damn orders!

Colonel Caleb Cobb played by F. Murray Abraham and Bigfoot Wallace played by Keith Carradine: Yves Simoneau's *Dead Man's Walk* (Cabin Fever Entertainment, 1996).

391

David: What kind of war do you call this …raping, looting, burning? Have you all gone crazy?

David Galt played by Vince Edwards: Henry Levin's *The Desperados* (Columbia, 1969).

392

Cowboy: Redlegs and regulators …the only thing that came out of the war was new names for killers.

The Cowboy played by Emilio Estevez: Gene Quintano's *Dollar for the Dead* (TVW, 1998).

393

Don Cesar: My father always said: "When you are in the right, fight; when you are in the wrong, acknowledge it."

Don Cesar de Vega played by Douglas Fairbanks: Donald Crisp's silent film, *Don Q, Son of Zorro* (United Artists, 1925).

394

Dr. Thomas: Don't you feel like a murderer?
MacKay: No, sir.
Dr. Thomas: Shouldn't you?
MacKay: I've never shot anybody without cause. My job is to protect the wagon

Advertisement to John Ford's last western, *Cheyenne Autumn* (Warner Bros., 1964), which treated Indians as people rather than "injuns."

train. When somebody shoots at my people, I shoot back.

Dr. Thomas played by Richard Gaines and Johnny MacKay played by Alan Ladd: Delmer Daves' *Drum Beat* (Warner Bros., 1954).

395

Senator: I once fought for that flag. I'll not fire on it.

Senator McCanles played by Lionel Barrymore: King Vidor's *Duel in the Sun* (Selznick Releasing Organization, 1946).

396

Luke: It's too bad a lot of men got to be killed on our account, huh?

Chavez: Wars begin as personal quarrels.

Luke played by Jim Brown and Chavez played by Patrick O'Neal: John Guillermin's *El Condor* (NGP, 1970).

397

Cabot: How did a decrepit old man like you ever get in the war?

Campbell: Because all the smart young men like you was losing it.

Cabot Young played by William Campbell and Campbell played by William Demarest: John Sturges' *Escape from Fort Bravo* (MGM, 1953).

398

Roper: You're a good officer, Marsh. Only you're unlucky. You got in the wrong army.

Marsh: But the right cause.

Roper: They say that's the one that wins.

Captain Roper played by William Holden and Captain John Marsh played by John Forsythe: John Sturges' *Escape from Fort Bravo* (MGM, 1953).

399

Sean: If it's a revolution, it's confusion.

Sean Mallory played by James Coburn: Sergio Leone's *A Fistful of Dynamite* (United Artists, 1971).

400

Desperate for men during the last days of the war between the States, the South found it necessary to offer pardons to outlaws to carry out special assignments. Strange dark figures rode under the flag of the Confederacy.

Prologue: Roger Corman's *Five Guns West* (American Releasing Corp., 1955).

401

Shalee: It's over. Why go on fighting?

Govern: It's kind of like a stampede …not much sense to it, but it has to run itself out.

Shalee: Men get trampled in stampedes.

Govern: Yes, but somebody has got to ride it out.

Shalee played by Dorothy Malone and Govern Sturges played by John Lund: Roger Corman's *Five Guns West* (American Releasing Corp., 1955).

402

Annie: Times are hard, Mr. Murphy. The South didn't get to keep much after the war …not even their dignity. Mr. Lee is dead and the whole struggle seems like a bad dream. All we got now is Frank and Jesse and the Younger boys poking their finger in the North's eyes. It isn't much, but it'll do until something better comes along.

Murphy: Like what?

Annie: Like a real peace …some honor.

Frank: Now I know why I married this woman. She made bank robbery almost seem noble.

Annie played by Dana Wheeler-Nicholson, Zack Murphy played by Sean Patrick Flanery, Frank James played by Bill Paxton, and Jesse James played by Rob Lowe: Robert Boris' *Frank & Jesse* (Vidmark Entertainment, 1995).

403

Cole: Battles are lost in the same way in which they are won.

Cole Younger (reading passage over his dying brother) played by Randy Travis: Robert Boris' *Frank & Jesse* (Vidmark Entertainment, 1995).

404

Johnnie Gray: If you lose this war, don't blame me.

Johnnie Gray played by Buster Keaton who also co-directed with Clyde Bruckman the silent film, *The General* (United Artists, 1927).

405

Chamberlain: This regiment was found last summer in Maine. There were a thousand of us then. There are less than 300 of us now. All of us volunteered to fight for the Union just as you did. Some came mainly because we were bored at home …thought this looked like it might be fun. Some came because we were ashamed not to. Many of us came because it was the right thing to do. And all of us have seen men die. This is a different kind of army. If you look back through history, you'll see men fighting for pay, for women, for some other kind of loot. They fight for land, power, because the King leads them, or just because they like killing. But we are here for something new. This has not happened much in the history of the world. We are an army out to set other men free. America should be free ground …all of it …not divided by a line between slavery state and free …all the way from here to the Pacific Ocean …where no man has to bow …no man born to royalty. Here we judge you by what you do, not by who your father was. Here you can be something. Here is the place to build a home. But it's not the land. There's always more land. It's the idea that we all have value …you and me. What we're fighting for in the end …we're fighting for each other.

Colonel Joshua Lawrence Chamberlain played by Jeff Daniels: Ronald F. Maxwell's *Gettysburg* (Turner Pictures, 1993).

406

Longstreet: I guess we Southerners and you English have at least one thing in common: We'd rather lose the war than admit to the mistake.

Lieutenant General James Longstreet played by Tom Berenger: Ronald F. Maxwell's *Gettysburg* (Turner Pictures, 1993).

407

Longstreet: We Southerners like our men religious and a little bit mad. I suspect that's why the women fall in love with preachers.

Lieutenant General James Longstreet played by Tom Berenger: Ronald F. Maxwell's *Gettysburg* (Turner Pictures, 1993).

408

Longstreet: Gentlemen, I do believe this attack will decide the fate of our country. All the men who have died in the past are with you here today.

Lieutenant General James Longstreet played by Tom Berenger: Ronald F. Maxwell's *Gettysburg* (Turner Pictures, 1993).

409

Chamberlain: Generals can do anything. There's nothing quite so much like a god on earth as a general on a battlefield.

Colonel Joshua Lawrence Chamberlain played by Jeff Daniels: Ronald F. Maxwell's *Gettysburg* (Turner Pictures, 1993).

410

General Lee: Soldiering has one great trap. To be a good soldier, you must love the army. To be a good commander, you must be willing to order the death of the thing you love.

General Robert E. Lee played by Martin Sheen: Ronald F. Maxwell's *Gettysburg* (Turner Pictures, 1993).

411

General Lee: We are adrift here in a sea of blood and I want it to end.

General Robert E. Lee played by Martin Sheen: Ronald F. Maxwell's *Gettysburg* (Turner Pictures, 1993).

412

General Lee: In the fight that is coming, I want you to stay back from the main line. This army has already lost far too many of its veteran commanders. And you, sir, have a very bad habit of moving too far forward.

Longstreet: I can't lead from behind.

General Robert E. Lee played by Martin Sheen and Lieutenant General James Longstreet played by Tom Berenger: Ronald F. Maxwell's *Gettysburg* (Turner Pictures, 1993).

413

Kilrain: You cannot judge a race. Any man who judges by the group is a pea-wit. You take men one at a time.

Sergeant "Buster" Kilrain played by Kevin Conway: Ronald F. Maxwell's *Gettysburg* (Turner Pictures, 1993).

414

Kemper: I got to hand it to you, George. You certainly do have a talent for trivializing the momentous and complicating the obvious.

Brigadier General James L. Kemper played by Royce D. Applegate and Major General George E. Pickett played by Stephen Lang: Ronald F. Maxwell's *Gettysburg* (Turner Pictures, 1993).

415

Meade: Well, gentlemen, I hope to God this is good ground. Is this good ground, General, that this place should have an army?

Major General George G. Meade played by Richard Anderson: Ronald F. Maxwell's *Gettysburg* (Turner Pictures, 1993).

416

Armistead: George, all science trembles before the siren logic of your fiery intellect.

Brigadier General Lewis A. Armistead played by Richard Jordan and Major General George E. Pickett played by Stephen Lang: Ronald F. Maxwell's *Gettysburg* (Turner Pictures, 1993).

417

Hancock: There are times when a corps commander's life does not count.

Major General Winfield Scott Hancock played by Brian Mallon: Ronald F. Maxwell's *Gettysburg* (Turner Pictures, 1993).

418

[*soldier commenting on certain commanding officers*] Bucklin: They ain't fit to pour pee out of a boot with the instructions written under the heel.

Private Bucklin played by John Diehl: Ronald F. Maxwell's *Gettysburg* (Turner Pictures, 1993).

419

Buford: Old Indian saying: Follow the cigar smoke, find the fat man there.

Brigadier General John Buford played by Sam Elliott in Ronald F. Maxwell's *Gettysburg* (Turner Pictures, 1993).

420

[*conversation between black soldier and white officer*] Trip: I mean, what's the point? Ain't nobody gonna win. It's just gonna go on and on.

Shaw: It can't go on forever.

Trip: Yeah, but ain't nobody gonna win, sir.

Shaw: Somebody's gonna win.

Trip: Who? I mean, you ...you get to go on back to Boston ...a big house and all that. What about us? What do we get?

Shaw: Well, you won't get anything if we lose.

Trip played by Denzel Washington and Colonel Robert Gould Shaw played by Matthew Broderick: Edward Zwick's *Glory* (Tri-Star Pictures, 1989).

421

[*conversation between two black soldiers*] Trip: Nigger, you ain't nothing but the white man's dog!

Rawlins: And what are you? You're so full of hate you just want to go out and fight everybody ...because you was whipped and chased by a hound. Well, that might not be living, but it sure as hell ain't dying!

Trip played by Denzel Washington and John Rawlins played by Morgan Freeman: Edward Zwick's *Glory* (Tri-Star Pictures, 1989).

422

Mary: Sometimes it sure does seem like the country does a whole lot more takin' than it does givin'.

Mary Johnson played by Janet Bailey: Steven H. Stern's *Good Men and Bad* (TV miniseries, Cabin Fever Entertainment, 1995).

423

Tuco: God is with us because He hates the Yanks too!

Blondie: God's not on our side because He hates idiots also.

Tuco played by Eli Wallach and Blondie played by Clint Eastwood: Sergio Leone's *The Good, the Bad, and the Ugly* (United Artists, 1966; U.S. 1968).

424

Blondie: I've never seen so many men wasted so badly.

Blondie played by Clint Eastwood: Sergio Leone's *The Good, the Bad, and the Ugly* (United Artists, 1966; U.S. 1968).

425

Commandant: I don't give a goddamn what they do in Andersonville. While I'm in charge here, the prisoners are not to be tortured, or cheated, or murdered.

Sergeant: Is that an accusation?

Commandant: Sergeant, gangrene is eating my leg away, not my eyes.

The Commandant was uncredited and the Sergeant/Angel Eyes played by Lee Van Cleef: Sergio Leone's *The Good, the Bad, and the Ugly* (United Artists, 1966; U.S. 1968).

426

Andrews: They say the slaughter was so fierce on both sides that you could walk across the field on dead bodies like stepping stones.

James J. Andrews played by Fess Parker: Francis Lyon's *The Great Locomotive Chase* (Buena Vista, 1956).

427

Cole: You know, before the war I used to think I'd be a lawyer. Now I guess I'll be a bank robber.

Cole Younger played by Bruce Bennett: Gordon Douglas' *The Great Missouri Raid* (Paramount, 1951).

Blondie/the Man with No Name (Clint Eastwood) discovers that "what goes around, comes around" in Sergio Leone's ***The Good, the Bad, and the Ugly*** (United Artists, 1966).

428

Warren: I still say the war could have been prevented.

Slayton: How?

Warren: By peaceful means: negotiation, compromise, reason.

Slayton: If you stay out in the west, Mr. Warren, you're going to find you can't negotiate with a Bowie knife or reason with a six-shooter.

Ben Warren played by Rock Hudson and Frank Slayton played by Phil Carey: Raoul Walsh's *Gun Fury* (Columbia, 1953).

429

Officer: It seems to me that pretty near everyone still sees things in terms of North and South after four long years of war.

The ex–Confederate Officer played by Martin Sheen in Peter Edwards' *Guns of Honor* (Vidmark, 1994).

430

Dusty: Blue always looks better with a splash of red.

Dusty Fog played by Christopher Atkins: Peter Edwards' *Guns of Honor* (Vidmark, 1994).

431

Mark: I'll say this about the war, Captain. It robbed us ...most of us of any delusions we had about ourselves or each other.

Mark was uncredited: Peter Edwards' *Guns of Honor* (Vidmark, 1994).

432

Thomas: The Yankees gave ya a bad time ...unless you was Abe Lincoln or a whore.

Thomas Luther Price played by Robert Culp: Burt Kennedy's *Hannie Caulder* (Paramount, 1971).

433

Doc: I don't like what I just saw [a killing]. But war affects different men in different ways. Time ...that's what men need when they get back from a war. Time and people standing by that really care about them and believe in them.

Doc Merriam played by Edgar Buchanan: Henry Levin's *The Man from Colorado* (Columbia, 1948).

434

Colonel: Do you believe that men who fought against each other and tried to kill each other can live in peace?

Colonel Crook played by William Bryant: Lee H. Katzin's *Hondo and the Apaches* (TVW, 1967).

435

Reb: This fool war started in the east. What's us westerners doing in it?

Yankee: I don't rightly know anymore. It ain't quite what I expected. There ain't much glory looking at a man with his guts hanging out.

The Reb soldier played by Russ Tamblyn and the Yankee soldier, Zeb Rawlings, played by George Peppard: John Ford, George Marshall, and Henry Hathaway's *How the West Was Won* (MGM, 1962).

436

Narrator: It had been the bloodiest day of the war on the western front. In the morning, it had looked like a Confederate victory. But by nightfall no man cared to use the words win or lose. After Shilo, the South never smiled.

Narration by Spencer Tracy: John Ford, George Marshall, and Henry Hathaway's *How the West Was Won* (MGM, 1962).

437

Howard: You know, I've fought two great men in my lifetime: Robert E. Lee and Chief Joseph. Lee was fighting for the

An epic western with an all-star cast. *How the West Was Won* (MGM, 1962) started with the mountain men and pioneer families such as the Precotts seen here: Zebulon (Karl Malden), Rebecca (Agnes Moorehead), and daughters Lilith (Debbie Reynolds) and Eve (Carroll Baker). To the far left is a Scotsman (Tudor Owen) taking in a tall tale.

wrong cause …slavery. Joseph is fighting for freedom. Well, I guess I'm in Lee's spot now. I'm the general that's fighting for the wrong cause.

General Oliver O. Howard played by James Whitmore: Richard T. Heffron's *I Will Fight No More Forever* (TVW, 1975).

438

Henchman: I swore I'd follow that man to hell. I reckon I made it. I just hope I can get home from here.

One of General Grey's (Anthony Zerbe) henchmen: John Patterson's *Independence* (TVW, 1987).

439

Travis: These men are Texans, Colonel, and they'll speak for themselves. But in my heart, I know the one thing for which I cannot bring myself ever to beg …and that is freedom.

William B. Travis played by Grant Show and Colonel Stephen F. Austin played by Patrick Duffy: Richard Lang's *James A. Michener's Texas* (TVW, 1995).

440

Alamo Resident: I'm too old to fight, and I'm too young to die. But I ain't gonna run!

The Alamo Resident was uncredited: Richard Lang's *James A. Michener's Texas* (TVW, 1995).

441

Houston: You should also take care of yourself. More men die from pneumonia than from a damn bayonet. Do you know that?

Austin: How am I supposed to know that? This is my first damn war!

Sam Houston played by Stacy Keach and Stephen F. Austin played by Patrick Duffy: Richard Lang's *James A. Michener's Texas* (TVW, 1995).

442

Helen: There is some people who'd give their life for liberty. Do you understand that?

Kidd: I guess so if they want something bad enough.

Helen Sanchez played by Stella Garcia and Joe Kidd played by Clint Eastwood: John Sturges' *Joe Kidd* (Universal, 1972).

443

Dancin' Kid: It seems you lost your taste for fighting, Bart.

Bart: It depends on what I'm fighting for.

The Dancin' Kid played by Scott Brady and Bart Lonergan played by Ernest Borgnine: Nicholas Ray's *Johnny Guitar* (Republic, 1954).

444

Roy: I'm going to tell you a story. I've never told anyone about Major Star. It was during the war. I fought side by side with him. I was real close to him. I watched how that man changed. I saw him fight …shoot and kill. And I saw how he enjoyed it. And after the war, he had forgotten how to judge whether a man was an enemy or a friend. Everywhere he went, there was always somebody waiting for him …waiting to get even …waiting to kill Major Star.

Roy played by John Marley: Jorge Fons' *Jory* (Avco Embassy, 1972).

445

Shep: There's only three things on earth worth fighting for: a woman, a full belly, and a roof over your head.

Shep Horgan played by Ernest Borgnine: Delmer Daves' *Jubal* (Columbia, 1956).

446

Smokestack: It looks like we're already in the war everybody keeps talking about.

Nelson: No, this is worse than war. In a war at least you know who you're fighting.

Smokestack played by Harry Shannon and John Nelson played by Sterling Hayden: Ray Nazarro's *Kansas Pacific* (Allied Artists, 1953).

447

For more than four long years, this nation was torn by a Civil War …the bloodiest and most destructive in our history. For it was a war of neighbor against neighbor, family against family, brother against brother, and flag against flag. Nor was the slaughter confined to the armies of the North and South alone. There was a war-bred outlaw army of guerrillas masquerading under the flags of both sides: pillaging, burning, and killing for private gain.

Prologue to Ray Enright's *Kansas Raiders* (Universal, 1950).

448

Jesse: I ain't riding with you, Colonel.

Quantrill: Not riding with us? May I ask why?

Jesse: I've been thinking all night. I've been thinking for three days.

Quantrill: Thinking about what?

Jesse: What I ought to say. And now I got to say it. I came here to fight. I came here straight from my home, or what was left of it three weeks ago. That was the day Frank and me came home, found the house burning, my ma with her arms shot off, and my pa hanging in a tree in the front yard. It was Redlegs …Yankee guerrillas. One of 'em was drunk and was still there. I come here because I wanted to kill every man I could ever find that would do a thing like that. Then we went out on that raid the other day. And I found we was doing the same thing. It was murdering people that didn't have no chance. People just like my ma and pa. Maybe that's strategy, Colonel, and maybe I don't understand it. But you don't need me for what you're going to do tonight.

Anderson: Maybe we don't need you for nothing at all.

Jesse James played by Audie Murphy, Colonel Quantrill played by Brian Donlevy, and Bill Anderson played by Scott Brady: Ray Enright's *Kansas Raiders* (Universal, 1950).

449

Quantrill: Let the North win the battles. We'll win the war.

Jesse: How are we going to do that if they keep licking us all the time?

Quantrill: Because we are only giving ground. The North is giving men. And the manpower of the North is not completely inexhaustible.

Colonel Quantrill played by Brian Donlevy and Jesse James played by Audie Murphy: Ray Enright's *Kansas Raiders* (Universal, 1950).

450

James: That Colonel Quantrill sure chatters like a magpie, don't he? Mighty near give me an ear ache.

Cole: My old pappy used to say that if a man talked long enough and loud enough, somebody is sure to believe him.

James Younger played by Dewey Martin and Cole Younger played by James Best: Ray Enright's *Kansas Raiders* (Universal, 1950).

451

Call: How was General Grant? I've always been curious about the man.

Brookshire: Well, he looked drunk to me. The man won that war and he was drunk the whole time.

Captain Woodrow F. Call played by James Garner and Ned Brookshire played by Charles Martin Smith: Joseph Sargent's *Larry McMurtry's Streets of Laredo* (Cabin Fever Entertainment, 1995).

452

Frank: The further away that war gets, the more glorious it looks to people.

Frank James played by Johnny Cash: William A. Graham's *The Last Days of Frank and Jesse James* (TVW, 1986).

453

Clarence: You don't feel sorry bringing down blue bellies, do you? They were trying to blow you into eternity, weren't they?

Frank: Not half as hard as I was trying to blow them into eternity.

Clarence Hite played by Mac Bennett and Frank James played by Johnny Cash: William A. Graham's *The Last Days of Frank and Jesse James* (TVW, 1986).

454

Colonel: I'll tell you what happened at Shilo, Captain. I lost 1500 men in a single encounter. We were cut to ribbons by enemy artillery. By the time the report got back to Washington, they were calling me the Butcher of Shilo. Yes, they called me the Butcher of Shilo. But reports are cold facts on paper. I took a calculated risk. I dared where cautious men stood still. But victory is not given to the cautious. That's why the war back east still drags on after four years …because our men in command have no daring. If I'd taken the enemy artillery position, it would have turned the tide. But, unfortunately, the War Department does not reward courage …just results.

Colonel Frank Marston played by Robert Preston: Anthony Mann's *The Last Frontier* (Columbia, 1955).

455

Trainor: If there is to be peace, they are the ones that paid for it. And I think they'd like to know what they died for was worthwhile.

Sergeant Matt Trainor played by Broderick Crawford: Andre De Toth's *Last of the Comanches* (Columbia, 1952).

456

Eustis: The Civil War changed everything. Before the Battle of Bull Run, I was a boy; before Gettysburg, I was a man with hope; before Appomattox, I was a soldier. And then came defeat.

Eustis played by Dermot Mulroney: Geoff Murphy's *The Last Outlaw* (HBO Pictures, 1994).

457

Eustis: Graff was my Colonel and I followed him. He kept us moving forward when the pain of looking back was too great.

Eustis played by Dermot Mulroney and Graff played by Mickey Rourke: Geoff Murphy's *The Last Outlaw* (HBO Pictures, 1994).

458

Britten: Don't be frightened, ma'am. Remember our Southern chivalry. We never shoot women or children. Well …anyway women.

Vance Britten played by Ronald Reagan: Lewis R. Foster's *The Last Outpost* (Paramount, 1951).

459

Delacourt: Now there's one way to handle your problem out here. Offer a bounty for every Rebel scalp.

Britten: You think a Rebel scalp is worth good Union money, sir?

Delacourt: At this point, yes. Besides, the taxpayers are paying it.

Mr. Delacourt played by Lloyd Corrigan and Vance Britten, alias Major Thomas Riordan, played by Ronald Reagan: Lewis R. Foster's *The Last Outpost* (Paramount, 1951).

460

Delacourt: Are you criticizing government policy?

Britten: I'm suggesting it's dangerous to pay a bounty for scalps. Now you take my scalp, for example. If an Apache handed it to you, would you be able to tell whether it was blue or gray?

Delacourt: Well, now if there is any more of this copperhead talk, I'd say it was gray.

Britten: Well, gray or blue, I'm quite attached to it.

Mr. Delacourt played by Lloyd Corrigan and Vance Britten, alias Major Thomas Riordan, played by Ronald Reagan: Lewis R. Foster's *The Last Outpost* (Paramount, 1951).

461

Edward: War changed your husband, didn't it? It does all soldiers. I mean, not making any judgments, but it's a fact. See, after a spell, killing gets easier …almost second nature.

Edward Janroe played by David Dukes: Dick Lowry's *Last Stand at Saber River* (Turner Network Television, 1997).

462

Jake: We were in the same outfit in the war. All of us except Rennie. It was a guerrilla unit raiding northern border towns. We would shoot our way in, loot the town, and then shoot our way out. I was doing it as a soldier. Clint did it because …well, it was the same thing he'd always done. The war hadn't changed his life a bit.

Clint: It just made it legal.

Jake Wade played by Robert Taylor, Clint Hollister played by Richard Widmark, and Rennie played by Henry Silva: John Sturges' *The Law and Jake Wade* (MGM, 1958).

463

Jacob: He thought killing the bad part would bring back the good part …the whole South.

Jacob played by Moses Gunn: Virgil W. Vogel's *Law of the Land* (TVW, 1976).

464

John: Why were you doing that?

Book: Oh, you mean that "massa, massa" routine? No uniforms. You see, slave lovers and slave shooters look an awful lot alike to me. That's why those generals back east invented uniforms. Blue for lovers, gray for shooters. I don't have that advantage.

John Golden played by Jeff Osterhage and Joshua "Book" Brown played by Carl Franklin: Alan J. Levi's *The Legend of the Golden Gun* (TVW, 1979).

465

Crecencio: It's better to make a good run than a bad stand.

Crecencio played by Luis Avalos: Jack Bender's *Lone Justice II* (Triboro Entertainment Group, 1995).

466

General: I don't believe it! You're a Texan trying to make a deal when your country's life hangs in the balance. You, a man who fought against the legions of Santa Anna! Or did you fight?

Burke: I fought. And when it was over I was left with a gun, a rope, and a horse to ride …and all over Texas in which to find a living.

General: Does a man need more?

Burke: I didn't ask for more. But I've learned a few things since then, General. If I'm going to risk my neck again, I want to come out of it this time with something more than glory.

General Andrew Jackson played by Lionel Barrymore and Devereaux Burke played by Clark Gable: Vincent Sherman's *Lone Star* (MGM, 1952).

467

Vance: Brent, we didn't steal this money. We took it in battle fair and square. It's what they call spoils of war.

Vance Reno played by Richard Egan and Brent Reno played by William Campbell: Robert D. Webb's *Love Me Tender* (20th Century–Fox, 1956).

468

Timothy: When it comes down to it, Zeb, would you, uh, would you fight?

Zeb: Well, I don't know. You know I would have fought there at the Alamo with Crockett and Bowie if I had heard about it in time. But that was different. That was Texans fighting Mexicans. Now here where you got Americans fighting Americans, and you have to kill one of your own over that slavery issue, I don't know.

Timothy: Well, Missouri and Kansas is feuding. Free staters, abolitionists …cessation. Now there's a word I never heard of until six months ago. I don't know. I just don't understand any of this.

Zeb: The ones that do the fighting and the dying usually don't.

Timothy Macahan played by Richard Kiley and Zeb Macahan played by James Arness: Bernard McEveety's *The Macahans* (TVW, 1976).

469

Anderson: You can't kill me! I'm a ghost of the Confederacy! And I will not die!

Colonel Anderson played by Kurtwood Smith: Geoff Murphy's *The Magnificent Seven: The Series* (TVW, Series Premiere, 1998).

470

Hayes: They say if a tree falls in the forest and no one hears it, there's a question of whether it makes any noise. If none of

Mountain man and frontiersman Zeb Macahan (James Arness) in *The Macahans* (TVW, 1976), a prelude to the television series *How the West Was Won*.

us lives to tell about this, can we be covered in glory?

Andy Hayes played by James B. Sikking: George McGowan's *The Magnificent Seven Ride* (United Artists, 1972).

471

Reverend: Any man with a just cause should travel with the word of God.
Dundee: With all due respect, God has nothing to do with it. I intend to smite the wicked, not save the heathen.

The Reverend Daklstrom played by R.G. Armstrong and Major Amos Charles Dundee played by Charlton Heston: Sam Peckinpah's *Major Dundee* (Columbia, 1965).

472

Louise: Did McLintock give you that black eye?
Katherine: No, nobody gave it to me. I won it!

Louise Warren played by Yvonne De Carlo,
Katherine McLintock played by Maureen O'Hara, and George Washington McLintock played by John Wayne: Andrew V. McLaglen's *McLintock!* (United Artists, 1963).

473

Benjie: Now get off my land!
Russell: Why you're getting mighty uppity, Mr. landowner Benjie. It just could be you gonna find you on the wrong end of a rope. All right, let's go, men! You know, that war of yours didn't change everything out here. Maybe you'll end up on the limb of a tree anyway. It'd teach you a lesson.

Benjie played by Brock Peters and Russell played by L.Q. Jones: Alf Kjellin's *The McMasters* (Jayjen/Chevron, 1970).

474

Carstairs: You know in my line of work, you got to be able either to sing "The Battle Hymn of the Republic" or "Dixie" ...with equal enthusiasm! Depending upon present company.

Sim Carstairs played by William O'Connell: Clint Eastwood's *The Outlaw Josey Wales* (Warner Bros., 1976).

475

Senator: Fletcher, there's an old saying: To the victors belong the spoils.
Fletcher: There's another old saying, Senator: Don't piss down my back and tell me it's raining.

Senator Lane played by Frank Schofield and Fletcher played by John Vernon: Clint Eastwood's *The Outlaw Josey Wales* (Warner Bros., 1976).

476

Josey Wales: I guess we all died a little in that damn war.

Josey Wales played by Clint Eastwood who also
directed *The Outlaw Josey Wales* (Warner Bros., 1976).

477

Jessie Lee: Obobo, I've been fighting over what's been dead for a long time. I think maybe it's time I start fighting for what's still alive.

Jessie Lee played by Mario Van Peebles and Obobo played by Tiny Lister: Mario Van Peebles' *Posse* (Gramercy Pictures, 1993).

478

Morales: We are not bandits! We are liberators!

Chucho Morales played by Fernando Lamas: Douglas Heyes' *Powderkeg* (TVW, 1971).

479

Raza: They died for what they believed.
Dolworth: The revolution? When the shooting stops and the dead are buried, and the politicians take over, it all adds up to one thing: a lost cause.

Captain Jesus Raza played by Jack Palance and Bill Dolworth played by Burt Lancaster: Richard Brooks' *The Professionals* (Columbia, 1966).

480

Raza: Without love, without a cause, we are nothing. We stay because we believe. We leave because we are disillusioned. We come back because we are lost. We die because we are committed.

Captain Jesus Raza played by Jack Palance: Richard Brooks' *The Professionals* (Columbia, 1966).

481

Hickok: The war is over. You got the same rights as any of us. You also got the same responsibilities. It's about time you figured out which is which.

James Butler "Wild Bill" Hickok played by Robert Culp: Herschel Daugherty's *The Raiders* (Universal, 1964).

482

Ballard: No one will tend to the grave of a traitor.

Major Ballard played by Joseph Mitchell: Tonino Valerii's *A Reason to Live, a Reason to Die* (a.k.a. *Massacre at Fort Holman*; Sancrosiap-Terza/Europrodis/Atlantida/Corona, 1972).

483

Narrator: He regarded the wounded soldiers in an envious way. He conceived persons with torn bodies to be peculiarly happy. He wished that he too had a wound ...a red badge of courage.

Narration by James Whitmore: John Huston's *The Red Badge of Courage* (MGM, 1951).

484

Narrator: He had performed his mistakes in the dark, so he was still a man.

Narration by James Whitmore: John Huston's *The Red Badge of Courage* (MGM, 1951).

485

Narrator: So it came to pass that as he trudged from the place of blood and wrath his soul changed.
Narration by James Whitmore: John Huston's *The Red Badge of Courage* (MGM, 1951).

486

Porter: I got holes in my cap, holes in my pants. But there ain't no holes in me except for the ones that was intended.
Bill Porter played by Arthur Hunnicutt: John Huston's *The Red Badge of Courage* (MGM, 1951).

487

The battle had lasted four days. When it was over, 25,000 men had been killed or wounded. The wounded on these fields of battle had all received their red badge of courage. But the youth, Henry Fleming, however, he emerged from his struggles with something else. He knew that he would no more quail before his guide wherever it should point him. He had been to touch the Great Death ...and found out that, after all, it was but the Great Death. He was a man.
Henry Fleming played by Richard Thomas. Narration: Lee Philips' *The Red Badge of Courage* (TVW, 1974).

488

Sherwood: You mean, sir, that you have struck out for yourself? That you no longer consider yourself a Confederate officer?
Quantrill: The Confederacy is dead! We have loyalties only to the living.
Sherwood: When I took my commission, sir, I didn't know my loyalties changed with the fortunes of war.
Captain Brett Sherwood played by Alan Ladd and Quantrill played by John Ireland: William Dieterle's *Red Mountain* (Paramount, 1951).

489

Sherwood: If anyone wants peace, they should listen to General Sherman's boast: If the crow should fly over the Shenandoah Valley ...it would have to carry its own rations. There's nothing left of the South. Most are even without hope.
Captain Brett Sherwood played by Alan Ladd: William Dieterle's *Red Mountain* (Paramount, 1951).

490

Sherwood: I'm a soldier. I do what I'm told. War has nothing to do with chivalry and nobility. Its success is measured by victory.
Captain Brett Sherwood played by Alan Ladd: William Dieterle's *Red Mountain* (Paramount, 1951).

491

Sherwood: One thing war teaches you is to save whatever you can from defeat ...and not throw everything away with one futile sentimental gesture.
Captain Brett Sherwood played by Alan Ladd: William Dieterle's *Red Mountain* (Paramount, 1951).

492

Chris: The war is over, Brett. Lee surrendered at Appomattox.
Sherwood: Lee surrendered?
Chris: Two days ago. We're one country again, Brett. All the bitterness will pass.
Sherwood: A house divided against itself cannot stand. Your president said that ...our president.
Chris played by Lizabeth Scott and Captain Brett Sherwood played by Alan Ladd: William Dieterle's *Red Mountain* (Paramount, 1951).

493

Lancaster: By the time the war was over, well, we decided that not much good come from all the dying.
McCall: Sometimes freedom has a high price.
Lancaster: Too high for me, boy.
Daniel Lancaster played by Billy Dee Wiliams and Duell McCall played by Alex McArthur: E.W. Swackhamer's *The Return of Desperado* (TVW, 1988).

Lassiter (Richard Boone) loves whiskey and hates Indians. He's on a mission to find stolen carbines and whoever is selling them to the Indians in Gordon Douglas' *Rio Conchos* (20th Century–Fox, 1964).

494

Colbee: We got to stand along side of 'em so that someday they can stand alone.

Colbee played by Warren Oates: Burt Kennedy's *Return of the Seven* (United Artists, 1966).

495

Pardee: It was just two years ago tomorrow that Lee surrendered to Grant at Appomattox. With better soldiers, better men, with superior cause, winning all the battles, still we did not win the war. Have you ever asked yourself why, James? Because we were insufficiently ruthless. We allowed our own code of honor to destroy us.

Colonel Theron Pardee played by Edmond O'Brien and James Lassiter played by Richard Boone: Gordon Douglas' *Rio Conchos* (20th Century–Fox, 1964).

496

Pardee: Renegades are always a risk. A man turns his coat once, what's to prevent him from doing it again.

Colonel Theron Pardee played by Edmond O'Brien: Gordon Douglas' *Rio Conchos* (20th Century–Fox, 1964).

497

Helen: I didn't think a man like you would fight for anything good.

Tex: A man like me might even kill for it.

Helen played by Sylvia Findley and Tex played by George Montgomery: Sidney Salkow's *Robbers' Roost* (United Artists, 1955).

498

Following the dark days of the Civil War the South faced a new enemy, the carpet-bagger. Using the cloak of politics to make a travesty of the courts of justice, they plundered a people beaten but unbowed, still eager to fight, unafraid to die for their vanquished land.

Prelude: Joseph Kane's *Robin Hood of the Pecos* (Republic, 1941).

499

Lafe: General Lee dealt the hand. All I can do is play the cards he gave me.

Lafe Barston played by Errol Flynn: William Keighley's *Rocky Mountain* (Warner Bros., 1950).

500

Jonanna: You sound as if you hate the war as much as I do.

Lafe: You don't have to like a war to fight in it. You just have to believe in what you're fighting for ...or against.

Jonanna Carter played by Patrice Wymore and Lafe Barston played by Errol Flynn: William Keighley's *Rocky Mountain* (Warner Bros., 1950).

501

Lafe: Just where do you think you're going to mail that?

Kip: This isn't a letter. It's a diary for my son to read.

Lafe: I didn't know you had one.

Kip: I haven't. But someday after the war and I'm back in Virginia, I'll get married and have a son. Then one day when he's growing up, he'll ask me what I did in the War Between the States, and I'll let him read this.

Lafe: I hope it has a happy ending.

Kip: If it doesn't, it won't matter.

Lafe Barston played by Errol Flynn and Kip Waterson played by Buzz Henry: William Keighley's *Rocky Mountain* (Warner Bros., 1950).

502

Johanna: I'm afraid I don't understand the fine points of war. One minute you're ready to shoot him down in cold blood. And the next minute you're willing to take his word for something ...as if you were all back in your own homes playing some pleasant little game.

Lafe: Doesn't make much sense, does it?

Johanna: It doesn't make any sense.

Lafe: I guess it's all we have to hang onto. A few little customs from the past. It's to remind us that there was a past.

Johanna Carter played by Patrice Wymore and Lafe Barston played by Errol Flynn: William Keighley's *Rocky Mountain* (Warner Bros., 1950).

503

O'Meara: I'm a Reb and I'll die a Reb. Even if the North considers Lee's surrender the death of the South.

Captain: Let's get one thing straight. Lee's surrender was not the death of the South. It was the birth of the United States.

O'Meara played by Rod Steiger and Captain Clark played by Brian Keith: Samuel Fuller's *Run of the Arrow* (RKO, 1957).

504

Orrin: You best have a good reason for not being dead, and not writing.

Tell: I've been on the move since the war. And for not writing ...never learned.

Orrin Sackett played by Tom Selleck and Tell Sackett played by Sam Elliott: Robert Totten's *The Sacketts* (TVW, 1979).

505

Witcher: They call it a civil war. Now you tell me what's civil about a man killing his own kind?

Lum Witcher played by Jack Elam: Charles B. Pierce's *Sacred Ground* (Pacific International Enterprises/Wilderness Family, 1983).

506

Steve: Look, Ellison, don't bring that moth-eaten rag of a uniform out here and expect to win battles with it. There won't be any bugles. Just move out when you see the sun!

Steve Sinclair played by Robert Taylor and Clay Ellison played by Royal Dano: Robert Parrish's *Saddle the Wind* (MGM, 1958).

507

"With malice toward none and charity for all," this great man said at Gettysburg. Yet after four long years of strife and battle between the North and South, the malice still remained ...and the charity was a forgotten word.

Prologue: Irving Pichel's *Santa Fe* (Columbia, 1951).

508

Britt: You got to get this in your minds: we all fought for something we believed in and lost. Now we got to mend our fences. Hate won't help us any.

Britt Canfield played by Randolph Scott: Irving Pichel's *Santa Fe* (Columbia, 1951).

509

Clint: The further you get from the South, the shorter your memory becomes.

Clint Canfield played by John Archer: Irving Pichel's *Santa Fe* (Columbia, 1951).

510

Kit: Jeb, I'm frightened. That boy is crippled for life. And that man on the train, he died for a principle. A man killed for a principle. One of them is wrong, but which one?

Jeb: Who knows the answer to that, Kit. Everybody in America is trying to decide.

Kit: Yes, by words from the east, and by guns from the west. But one day, the words will turn into guns.

"Kit Carson" Holliday played by Olivia de Havilland and Jeb Stuart played by Errol Flynn: Michael Curtiz's *Santa Fe Trail* (Warner Bros., 1940).

511

Kit: Oh, Jeb, what does pride got to do with human lives?

Jeb: Kit, the two things kind of come together down South. You can't pry them apart. Not even with guns.

"Kit Carson" Holliday played by Olivia de Havilland and Jeb Stuart played by Errol Flynn: Michael Curtiz's *Santa Fe Trail* (Warner Bros., 1940).

512

Martin: You know, wars don't make sense. You burn, you kill. And then come peace, you have to rebuild what you burn.

Corporal Martin played by Milburn Stone: George Marshall's *The Savage* (Paramount, 1952).

513

Summers: It's not a very pretty sight to see burning flesh. But I can assure you, the stench of burning flesh is much worse.

Mike Summers played by Don Taylor: Michael Carreras' *The Savage Guns* (MGM, 1961).

514

Jesse: Did pa tell ya what color I was wearin'?

Mac: Blue or gray, it doesn't matter. A man fights for what he believes in. Just be glad it's over.

Dal: Amen to that.

Jesse Traven played by Jeffrey Osterhage, Mac Traven played by Tom Selleck, and Dal Traven played by Sam Elliott: Andrew V. McLaglen's *The Shadow Riders* (TVW, 1982).

515

Hammond: Even down here, Major, we're aware that the war is over.

Major: Not for me, or for my men. That's why I contacted you. We're in the market for arms and ammunition. We plan to go back and kill Yankees.

Hammond: Well, it's a relief to see that you don't hold a grudge, Major.

Holiday Hammond played by Gene Evans and Major Cooper Ashbury played by Geoffrey Lewis: Andrew V. McLaglen's *The Shadow Riders* (TVW, 1982).

516

Major: I'm talking about the South, Ms. Connery, and a way of life that was taken from us.

Connery: What makes you think you can get it back?

Major: Ms. Connery, the rebel yell was first heard at Manassas and at a hundred battles since then from Richmond to Gettysburg. The rebel yell is hard to describe. It's a mixture of fear and anger and exultation. But it inspires men even from defeat. These damn Yankees think they've heard the last of it, but they haven't. And I'm going to get it back anyway I can.

Major Cooper Ashbury played by Geoffrey Lewis and Kate Connery played by Katharine Ross: Andrew V. McLaglen's *The Shadow Riders* (TVW, 1982).

517

Charlie: James, what about you? Do you ever think you might like to own a slave?

James: Well, I guess I never thought about it, pa.

Charlie: Well think about it! Think about it! If you had the money, would you go out and buy a slave?

James: No, sir, I wouldn't.

Charlie: Why not?

James: If I can't do my own work with my own hands, it would never get done.

Charlie: Now, suppose you had a friend that owned slaves. And suppose somebody was going to come and take them away from them. Would you help him fight to keep 'em?

Charlie Anderson played by James Stewart and James Anderson played by Patrick Wayne: Andrew V. McLaglen's *Shenandoah* (Universal, 1965).

518

Lt.: Mr. Anderson, if you sit in the middle of this war and not get touched, I congratulate you.

Lieutenant Johnson played by Tom Simcox and Charlie Anderson played by James Stewart: Andrew V. McLaglen's *Shenandoah* (Universal, 1965).

519

Charlie: What do you do with dead soldiers?

Charlie Anderson played by James Stewart: Andrew V. McLaglen's *Shenandoah* (Universal, 1965).

520

Charlie: So can you give me one good reason why I should send my family, that took me a lifetime to raise, down that road like a bunch of damn fools to do someone else's fighting?

Lt.: The Union needs all of its sons, Mr. Anderson.

Charlie: That might be so, Johnson, but these are my sons. And they don't belong to the State. When they were babies, I never saw the State coming around with a spare tit. We never asked anything of the State and never expected anything. We do our own living and thanks to no man for the right.

Charlie Anderson played by James Stewart and Lieutenant Johnson played by Tom Simcox: Andrew V. McLaglen's *Shenandoah* (Universal, 1965).

521

Jim: The boy I knew in Abilene has grown into a man.

Chip: There's nothing like a war to make someone grow up fast.

Jim Trask played by Jock Mahoney and Chip Tomlin played by Grant Williams: Charles Haas' *Showdown at Abilene* (Universal, 1956).

522

Chip: You know, it's funny what makes a man go fiddle footin' off to a war he can stay out of. Take us, for instance. Neither of us had to go. But you joined up with the Rebs, and I went with the Union. A gray coat and a blue one. And both of us from the same town, the same state.

Jim: Now listen to me, Chip. When you get home, put that coat away and forget it. Forget you ever wore it or what color it was. That's the only way we can all be friends.

Chip Tomlin played by Grant Williams and Jim Trask played by Jock Mahoney: Charles Haas' *Showdown at Abilene* (Universal, 1956).

523

Chip: It's funny. A man has to fight to live in peace.

Chip Tomlin played by Grant Williams: Charles Haas' *Showdown at Abilene* (Universal, 1956).

524

Jack: Say, how did you lose that arm there, boy?

Buck: I woke up in Chickamauga one morning without it.

Jack played by Richard Gere and Buck played by Lanny Flaherty: Jon Amiel's *Sommersby* (Warner Bros., 1993).

525

Beale: You saw what was going on. Why didn't you do something?

Clint: I don't fight other men's quarrels. I just patch them up afterwards.

Beale: What would you fight for?

Clint: The only thing every man fights for: self-preservation.

Edward Beale played by Rod Cameron. Clint Walker, assuming a role as a doctor, played by John Ireland: Ray Nazarro's *Southwest Passage* (United Artists, 1954).

526

Hudson: And after the war, well, bitterness loses its taste. And many things are forgotten.

Kearney: I hope so.

Lt. Colonel John Hudson played by Paul Kelly and Major Lex Kearney played by Gary Cooper: Andre De Toth's *Springfield Rifle* (Warner Bros., 1952).

527

Doc: Geronimo. You know, he and his people are entitled to all this land around here …at least they think they do. They've been here for a thousand years.

Lt.: Whose side are you on?

Doc: I'm on my own side. That's why I'm still alive.

Lt.: You'll excuse me, sir, but you seem like an Indian lover.

Doc: You'll excuse me but I see no virtue in hating a man who's fighting for his country.

Doc Holliday played by Willie Nelson and Lieutenant Blanchard played by Merritt Butrick: Ted Post's *Stagecoach* (TVW, 1986).

528

Connie: You know, Dad, sometimes I wish we had never left Illinois …with all the trouble and fighting all the time.

Dawson: Yes, but anything that is worth having is worth fighting for.

There's plenty of "country and western" action aboard this Overland Stage: Marshal Curly Wilcox (Johnny Cash), Doc Holliday (Willie Nelson), the gambler Hatfield (Waylon Jennings), the outlaw Billy "Ringo" Williams (Kris Kristofferson), and stage driver Buck (John Schneider) in Ted Post's *Stagecoach* (TVW, 1986).

Connie Dawson played by Gale Storm and Mr. Dawson played by Steve Clark: Lesley Selander's *Stampede* (Warner Bros., 1949).

529

Wes: You know when we were with Quantrill, I thought you was the greatest thing that ever came down the pike. I guess that's why I stayed with you afterwards. I didn't have the sense to know the difference between a war hero and a murderer.

Wes Tancred played by Richard Egan: Charles Marquis Warren's *Tension at Table Rock* (RKO, 1956).

530

Colonel: Now gentlemen, let's all pray that God in His goodness will give us this battle.

Colonel Rogers played by Robert Keith: Robert Rossen's *They Came to Cordura* (Columbia, 1959).

531

Private: Lady! Lady, would you look at a fella who had his ear shot off?

Adelaide: Of course I would.

Major: All they'll notice is what you're wearing around your neck. Did you ever see the Medal of Honor?

Private: No, sir.

Major: It's the most beautiful decoration of all, as it should be. I'd trade an ear for one anytime. Two, in fact.

Private: Excuse me, sir, but I would rather have the ear.

Private Renziehausen played by Dick York, Adelaide Geary played by Rita Hayworth, and Major Thomas Thorn played by Gary Cooper: Robert Rossen's *They Came to Cordura* (Columbia, 1959).

532

Charlie: You know, I went home for awhile after the war. Sometimes you just can't go back to the way you were.

Charlie played by Chris Cooper: Nancy Kelly's *Thousand Pieces of Gold* (Greycat Films, 1991).

533

Lt.: I just wanted to say, ma'am, that you mustn't judge the people of the North by those scum …those carpetbaggers. We're not like that. We're not like that at all: those cheap politicians that scurry down here to take advantage of the chaos.

Lieutenant Marr played by Peter Hansen: Rudolph Maté's *Three Violent People* (Paramount, 1956).

534

Colt: Ms. Hunter, General Robert E. Lee signed a formal statement to the effect that I was an officer and a gentleman. Now, please, have dinner with me tonight. Give me a chance to prove he

wasn't guilty of false statements when he signed my commission.

Colt Saunders played by Charlton Heston and Ms. Lorna Hunter played by Anne Baxter: Rudolph Maté's *Three Violent People* (Paramount, 1956).

535

Priest: To be a revolutionary, one must be prepared to be violent.

The Town Priest played by Fernando Rey: Robert Parrish's *A Town Called Hell* (a.k.a. *A Town Called Bastard*; Scotia International, 1971).

536

Lon: We were all right before the war. Maybe we'll be all right again. Anyway, I want to give it a try. I think you should too, Hoby.

Hoby: I can't wait. Hate is splitting my guts and all this poison inside me is bursting out.

Lon: Don't let it, Hoby. It could kill you.

Hoby: A man could be dead and still walk around.

Lon Cordeen played by Gordon Scott and Hoby Cordeen played by James Mitchum: Albert Band's *The Tramplers* (Embassy Picture Release, 1965).

537

Hook: There was once I wanted to live so bad I turned myself into a dog. For a whole month I was a dog. Have you ever heard of Andersonville? The Rebs called it a prison camp. The devil himself couldn't have thought of a worse crawl in hell. All around men dying of scurvy and dysentery; mush and sick bacon all there was to eat and never enough of that. And everything putrid inside and out. Look, maybe you don't want to hear anymore of this.

Cora: You said talking helps.

Hook: There was a man dying of lung fever …just waiting to die. He was out of his head most of the time. He happened to love dogs. And I found if I barked once or twice, he give me some of his rations. That's how it started. Then I used to wake up in the morning planning on being a dog. I even got down on my hands and knees to put on a good show. For a whole month I was a dog. The poor fella died thinking I was one. But I lived. It all depends upon how hard you want to live I guess.

Sergeant Hook played by Joel McCrea and Cora Sutliff played by Barbara Stanwyck: Charles Marquis Warren's *Trooper Hook* (United Artists, 1957).

538

Georgia: Papa told me that there are two kinds of people in the world. There are masters and there are slaves. And the only difference between the two is land. He said if you lose the land, you lose

your freedom. But if you take care of the land, it will take care of you.

Georgia Lawshe played by Angelina Jolie: Karen Arthur's *True Women* (TVW, 1997).

539

Martha: I thought the war was over.

Georgia: It's reconstruction. The Yankees are going to punish us for losing.

Martha played by Salli Richardson and Georgia Lawshe played by Angelina Jolie: Karen Arthur's *True Women* (TVW, 1997).

540

Holland: The thing about being free is …it's awfully easy to take for granted …until someone snatches it away.

Son Holland played by Scott Bairstow: Rod Hardy's *Two for Texas* (Turner Pictures, 1998).

541

Hugh: I figured I'd have to be dead first before I seen hell.

Hugh Allison played by Kris Kristofferson: Rod Hardy's *Two for Texas* (Turner Pictures, 1998).

542

Bowie: Things are different now, Hugh. All that carousing and hell raisin' we done …I'm done with that. This here is the most important place in the country right now. And I'm a part of it. We're all going to be part of history, Hugh. You know the best thing? We're on the right side!

Jim Bowie played by Peter Coyote and Hugh Allison played by Kris Kristofferson: Rod Hardy's *Two for Texas* (Turner Pictures, 1998).

543

Colonel: Major, I just received word that Lee surrendered to Grant three days ago.

Major: Yes, sir.

Colonel: You knew it?

Major: We received the word yesterday.

Colonel: I don't think you understand, Major. The war is over.

Major: No, sir.

Colonel: Are you telling me that you intend to keep fighting?

Major: Haven't we just proved it, sir?

Colonel: But, why?

Major: Because this is our land …and you're on it.

Colonel: We're all Americans.

Major: Yes, sir. That's always been the saddest part of it.

Yankee Colonel John Henry Thomas played by John Wayne and Confederate Major Sanders played by Royal Dano: Andrew McLaglen's *The Undefeated* (20th Century–Fox, 1969).

544

General: Certainly, as Americans you can appreciate our fight for independence.

Ranch owner and Southern gentleman Colt Saunders (Charlton Heston) introduces his wife, Lorna Hunter Saunders (Anne Baxter), to his oldest friend and ranch foreman, Innocencio (Gilbert Roland). Lorna was a prostitute in her past and hopes that secret will remain just that in Rudolph Mate's *Three Violent People* (Paramount, 1956).

We offer you more than money, señor. We offer a cause.

Joe: How about that, Ben? This here is our cause expert. He fought for the South.

General Aguilar played by Morris Ankrum and Joe Erin played by Burt Lancaster: Robert Aldrich's *Vera Cruz* (United Artists, 1954).

545

General: Money! Is that worth risking your life for?

Trane: It comes closer than anything I know.

General: A man's got to have more than that. He needs something to believe in.

Trane: I got that too [*pointing to his rifle*]!

General Aguilar played by Morris Ankrum and Benjamin Trane played by Gary Cooper: Robert Aldrich's *Vera Cruz* (United Artists, 1954).

546

Urbina: Well, it is like this: Our chief let the Coloradoes have their way with the villagers for awhile before we attacked.

Arnold: You mean to say he was here in time to prevent it?

Urbina: Well, it is like this: The villagers, well, they love my chief, and they love Mexico. But they didn't hate our enemies enough to fight. And now they do.

Urbina played by Robert Viharo and Lee Arnold played by Robert Mitchum: Buzz Kulik's *Villa Rides!* (Paramount, 1968).

547

Major: Isn't it less dangerous to face [Pancho] Villa without your army?

General: Do you think it less dangerous to face Villa with my army?

The Major played by Jose Maria Prada, General Huerta played by Herbert Lom, and Pancho Villa played by Yul Brynner: Buzz Kulik's *Villa Rides!* (Paramount, 1968).

548

Pancho: You're getting paid.

Arnold: How much?

Pancho: Twenty-five pesos for every Colorado you kill.

Arnold: It's pretty cheap.

Pancho: Look, gringo, this is a cheap war. Next year, I'll have more money and we'll have a bigger war. All right?

Pancho Villa played by Yul Brynner and Lee Arnold played by Robert Mitchum: Buzz Kulik's *Villa Rides!* (Paramount, 1968).

549

Pancho: Gringo, you never did have anything. You have lived just for yourself. Not for a cause …not even for a woman.

Pancho Villa played by Yul Brynner: Buzz Kulik's *Villa Rides!* (Paramount, 1968).

550

McCloud: You know, Captain, for a moment there I thought you were going to turn out to be real human after all …with a temper and pride and everything.

Parrish: I saw a lot of proud men get themselves killed during the war proving absolutely nothing. And temper is something only the very strong or the very rich can afford.

Jim McCloud played by Warner Anderson and John Parrish played by Glenn Ford: Rudolph Maté's *The Violent Men* (Columbia, 1955).

551

Libby Prison. Richmond, Virginia. The dreaded blackhole of the Confederacy, known to thousands of captives as "The Devil's Warehouse."

Caption: Michael Curtiz's *Virginia City* (Warner Bros., 1940).

552

Julia: Treating friends like strangers and enemies like friends.

Julia Hayne played by Miriam Hopkins: Michael Curtiz's *Virginia City* (Warner Bros., 1940).

553

Captain: By the way, I'm taking these men with me, sir. We always work together.

General: Well, what are their qualifications?
Captain: Well sir, Marblehead there …
Marblehead: Yes, sir!
Captain: He's probably one of the finest horse thieves east of Chicago.
Marblehead: You mean Kansas City, sir.
Captain: Kansas City. And Moose?
Moose: Yes, sir!
Captain: Well, he's had four wives. So he's had to learn how to keep under cover.

Captain Kerry Bradford played by Errol Flynn, General Meade played by Thurston Hall, Marblehead played by Guinn "Big Boy" Williams, and Olaf "Moose" Swenson played by Alan Hale: Michael Curtiz's *Virginia City* (Warner Bros., 1940).

554

Lincoln: Thank God the killing is over. Your General Lee is meeting our General Grant tomorrow at a place called Appomattox Court House to discuss the terms of peace.
Julia: Then …then we've lost.

Lincoln: Not lost …found. They're coming back …back in the Union. Miss Hayne, you came over 2,000 miles to save the life of a man who was once your enemy. I think very likely you're in love with him. Well, to me you two are symbols of what I hope we can do for our country.

Abraham Lincoln played by Victor Kilian and Julia Hayne played by Miriam Hopkins: Michael Curtiz's *Virginia City* (Warner Bros., 1940).

555

Fargo: You see, Judge, the Apaches and the Mexicanos have been at war for over fifty years. They don't steal each other's women. They either keep them or else they sell them.
Judge: Sell them? Sell them to whom?
Fargo: The Americans are their best market. Them gals end up in saloons and dance halls and …
Judge: Why that's slavery! Slavery of the worst kind.

Apache Chief Mangas Coloradas (Lex Barker) says "a forked tongue is an evil thing" with warrior Ponce (Larry Chance), the Mexican captive Riva (Joan Taylor), good guy Luke Fargo (Ben Johnson), and Judge Bolton (Richard Cutting) in attendance in *War Drums* (United Artists, 1957).

Fargo: I know, Judge. Any kind of slavery is bad. We Americans would like to take the Apache land and move them on government reservations. That's slavery. And down South there is another kind of slavery that President Lincoln wants to do something about.

Luke Fargo played by Ben Johnson and Judge Bolton played by Richard Cutting: Reginald LeBorg's *War Drums* (United Artists, 1957).

556

Miller: Some of those people grew up with me and have known me since I was a kid …and yelling at me and calling me names like I was responsible for the war. Even in the lines we never hated the men we were fighting. We believed one thing and they believed something else. They were on one side and we were on another. But why should they hate me here? This ain't even a state yet.

Hayes: In the lines you can hear a man cry when something rips into him. You see him die and it's common pain and misery …no matter which side he's on. People don't understand that who are out of it. They get hurt by seeing friends and kin dying. And it's the other side that did it. It goes both ways.

Rod Miller played by Michael Dante and John Hayes played by Randolph Scott: Budd Boetticher's *Westbound* (Warner Bros., 1959).

557

Boone: If the Confederacy hadn't run out of medals, I bet we would have got one then.

Cross: If they made a hero out of you, you wouldn't be worth a damn, Boone.

Boone: Yea, I guess so …I guess so. I seen it happen to a lot of soldiers.

Boone played by Jack Elam and Cross played by Willie Nelson: Burt Kennedy's *Where the Hell's That Gold?!!!* (a.k.a. *Dynamite & Gold*; TVW, 1988).

558

Captain: But suppose you lose?

Killian: I intend to. Now don't look so shocked, Captain. We're not fighting to the death. We're fighting for his honor, not for mine.

Captain Charring played by Richard Kelton and Killian played by Hugh O'Brian: Don Taylor's *Wild Women* (TVW, 1970).

559

Orozco: Let me tell you this. We're all fighting in the same revolution. It takes all kinds to win a revolution, my friend. The thieves, the saints, and the bandits. Not all good …not all bad …but all for Mexico!

Orozco played by Noah Beery, Jr.: Budd Boetticher's *Wings of the Hawk* (Universal, 1953).

560

Carter: All's fair in love and war, you know.

Claire: We'll keep love out of this if you don't mind, and we'll talk about war.

King Carter played by Harry Woods and Claire Hartford played by Anne Nagel: Ford Beebe and Ray Taylor's *Winners of the West* (Universal serial, Chapter 7: "Thundering Terror," 1940).

561

Tex: Never stop a good fight because you'll never know when you'll see another.

Tex Houston played by Tom Fadden: Ford Beebe's and Ray Taylor's *Winners of the West* (Universal serial, Chapter 8: "The Flaming Arsenal," 1940).

562

Brady: You look after your honor, Captain. I'll look after my skin.

Martin Brady played by Robert Mitchum: Robert Parrish's *The Wonderful Country* (United Artists, 1959).

563

Marshal: Hey, hey, hey, hey! What's going on here? Hold it, kid, hold it! What's this all about?

Andres: He called me a Mexican.

Marshal: He did? It's true, ain't it? Well?

Andres: Si.

Marshal: You can't change that.

Andres: No.

Marshal: Quit complaining, kid, and be proud of what you are. Fighting for is different from fighting against.

Marshal Dave Harmon played by Clint Walker and Andres played by Miguel Alejandro: Ted Post's *Yuma* (TVW, 1971).

Chase

See also Holdups; Showdown

564

Hutch: The world is too small for you to get far enough away from me! I'll find you sooner or later!

Hutch played by Bud Spencer: Giuseppe Colizzi's *Ace High* (Paramount, 1967).

565

Theodore: Why did you tell me those three biddy kids was a posse?

Amos: Well, I thought I saw them down there in the bushes.

Theodore: Oh, you couldn't see through a barb wire fence!

Theodore Ogilvie played by Don Knotts and Amos Tucker played by Tim Conway: Norman Tokar's *The Apple Dumpling Gang* (Buena Vista, 1975).

566

Doc: We better hightail it out of here!

Doc Butcher played by Walter Brennan: William D. Russell's *Best of the Badmen* (RKO, 1951).

567

Autry: You're running away from those guys!

Garland: I'm not walking away!

Gene Autry played himself and James Garland played by Stephen Dunne: Frank McDonald's *The Big Sombrero* (Columbia, 1949).

568

Buffalo Bill: Where were ya?

Halsey: It's the first month of the moon.

Nate: That's not what Buffalo Bill asked ya! Now where in the hell have you been?

Halsey: During the day of the first moon, Sitting Bull visits the sun in the mountains while his squaws move the teepees to the moon path.

Nate: Damn it, Halsey! Stop sunning and mooning us! Now where in the hell have you been?

Buffalo Bill played by Paul Newman, William Halsey played by Will Sampson, Nate Salsbury played by Joel Grey, and Sitting Bull played by Frank Kaquitts: Robert Altman's *Buffalo Bill and the Indians, or Sitting Bull's History Lesson* (United Artists, 1976).

569

Sutton: Well, I always said I could smell a half-breed sooner than he could smell a trail. You lost it again, didn't you?

Lantz: I sure ain't found it. My old man

used to say the art of tracking was the art of finding something out of place. Here's something out of place …a petticoat.

Jack Sutton played by Skip Homeier and Jacob Lantz played by Eduard Franz: Stuart Heisler's *The Burning Hills* (Warner Bros., 1956).

570

Sundance: Which way?
Butch: It doesn't matter. I don't know where we've been and I've just been there.

The Sundance Kid played by Robert Redford and Butch Cassidy played by Paul Newman: George Roy Hill's *Butch Cassidy and the Sundance Kid* (20th Century–Fox, 1969).

571

Butch: Who are those guys?

Butch Cassidy played by Paul Newman: George Roy Hill's *Butch Cassidy and the Sundance Kid* (20th Century–Fox, 1969).

572

Butch: How many of them are following us?
Sundance: All of them!

Butch Cassidy played by Paul Newman and the Sundance Kid played by Robert Redford: George Roy Hill's *Butch Cassidy and the Sundance Kid* (20th Century–Fox, 1969).

573

Preacher: Oh, excuse me, I didn't introduce myself. Sims, Preacher Sims. Servant of the Lord.
Cain: A preacher, huh? With wanted posters?
Preacher: Well, not ordained exactly but close to it …sort of called to the cloth.
Cain: Why the posters?
Preacher: Well, I sort of mix vocations: a shepherd of the flock …a hunter of men.

Preacher Sims played by John Carradine and Captain Justice Cain played by Scott Brady: Kent Osborne's *Cain's Cutthroats* (a.k.a. *Cain's Way*; M.D.A. Associates/Fanfare, 1969).

574

Townsman: I saw a big reward sign go up in Hangtown once. Shucks, they brought in sixteen corpses the first week …and there wasn't any of 'em that even looked like the fella!

The Townsman was uncredited: Joseph Kane's *The Carson City Kid* (Republic, 1940).

575

Lee: We're getting a posse together. We'll stop him before he gets started!

Lee Jessup played by Bob Steele: Joseph Kane's *The Carson City Kid* (Republic, 1940).

576

Cat: Where are you staying?
Jed: On the run, ma'am. Hiding out in a crowd.

Cat Ballou played by Jane Fonda and Jed played by Dwayne Hickman: Elliot Silverstein's *Cat Ballou* (Columbia, 1965).

577

Jones: I don't think I'm gonna run anymore. I have a feeling maybe that this is where I've been running to.

Jones played by John Ireland: Leon Klimovsky's *Challenge of the Mackennas* (Filmar Compagnia Cinematografica — Atlantida/Hemlock Enterprises, 1969).

578

Marshal: Span out and we'll corral him in the Canyon of the Dead. First man that spots him, give the signal: three shots. And we'll tighten the cinch on him.

The U.S. Marshal played by Morris Ankrum: Raoul Walsh's *Colorado Territory* (Warner Bros., 1949).

579

Colorado: We don't want to turn back.
Brother: Then go forward, my children. Follow the trail over the pass …beyond the Canyon of the Dead.

Colorado Carson played by Virginia Mayo and Brother Thomas played by Frank Puglia: Raoul Walsh's *Colorado Territory* (Warner Bros., 1949).

580

Marshal: Now remember, you men. If you flush him, don't try to shoot it out with him. He's quicker than a black-headed snake. Just send up a smoke signal and we'll spot it.

The U.S. Marshal played by Morris Ankrum: Raoul Walsh's *Colorado Territory* (Warner Bros., 1949).

581

Ben: Frank, take a ride up river. See if they crossed ahead of us. If they cut our track, it's gonna put us between a rock and a hard place.

Ben Lane played by Claude Akins and Frank played by Skip Homeier: Budd Boetticher's *Comanche Station* (Columbia, 1960).

582

Banner: You keep riding, Frank. And don't ever let me find you.

John Banner played by Dale Robertson and Frank Banner played by Skip Homeier: Lewis R. Foster's *Dakota Incident* (Republic, 1956).

583

Nobody: You are being followed, William Blake.
Blake: Are you sure? How do you know?
Nobody: Often the evil stench of white man precedes him.

Nobody played by Gary Farmer and William Blake played by Johnny Depp: Jim Jarmusch's *Dead Man* (Miramax Films, 1996).

584

Buck: Did you run into anyone back along on the trail?
Tom: There's a lot of trails leading a lot of places. And a lot of strangers riding them who would like to keep on being strangers.

Buck Creyton played by Lee Van Cleef and Tom Cameron played by James J. Lydon: Thomas Carr's *The Desperado* (Allied Artists, 1954).

585

Josiah: You testify, then, that to the best of your knowledge David Galt had intended to escape.
Jacob: Hell, Pa, I can't say what was in his mind. But I sure didn't act like he was planning to stick around.

Parson Josiah Galt played by Jack Palance, David Galt played by Vince Edwards, and Jacob Galt played by George Maharis: Henry Levin's *The Desperados* (Columbia, 1969).

586

Hawkeye: Many horses come this way [*pointing at tracks*].
Sergeant: Them are our tracks! Damn you, Hawkeye, you done got us lost again!

Hawkeye was uncredited and the Sergeant played by Terry Wilson: Burt Kennedy's *Dirty Dingus Magee* (MGM, 1970).

587

Friend: They were here.
Reager: The place they've just left is about as close as we seem to get.

Reager's Friend played by Bill Pickel and Reager played by Howie Long: Gene Quintano's *Dollar for the Dead* (TVW, 1998).

588

Skinner: They're on a downhill roll to hell!

Colonel Skinner was uncredited: Gene Quintano's *Dollar for the Dead* (TVW, 1998).

589

Marshal: How about joining the posse, Johnny? It would give you a chance to use that shooting iron legal for a change.

The Marshal/Lightning played by Stephen McNally and Johnny Sombrero played by Eugene Iglesias: Don Siegel's *The Duel at Silver Creek* (Universal, 1952).

590

Pike: Any sign of him?
Henry: Not a fart in the wind.

Pike played by Martin Sheen and Henry played by Harvey Keitel: Anthony Harvey's *Eagle's Wings* (Eagle's Wing Productions/Rank, 1979).

591

Cole: The last time I saw you two, you were ten jumps ahead of a posse raising dust for Mexico.

Outlaw Cheyenne Rogers (Glenn Ford) is not too eager for formal introductions with Allison MacLeod (Evelyn Keyes) when riding a stolen horse into a stable in *The Desperadoes* (Columbia, 1943).

Cole Thornton played by John Wayne: Howard Hawks' *El Dorado* (Paramount, 1967).

592

Taylor: Don't you think one posse chasing us is enough?

Taylor Swope played by John Dehner: Russell Rouse's *The Fastest Gun Alive* (MGM, 1956).

593

Govern: How do you want him?
Captain: Alive if possible. Dead if need be.

Govern Sturges played by John Lund and the Confederate Captain played by Larry Thor: Roger Corman's *Five Guns West* (American Releasing Corp., 1955).

594

Pinkerton: You're dealing with a relentless pursuit of justice.

Allan Pinkerton played by William Atherton:

Robert Boris' *Frank & Jesse* (Vidmark Entertainment, 1995).

595

Tommy: What the hell are you doing?
Avram: I don't ride today.
Tommy: What are you talking about?
Avram: Today is Saturday.
Tommy: So?
Avram: I don't ride on Saturday.
Tommy: Well, I know that but don't tell me you ain't gonna ride today!
Avram: I ain't gonna ride today.
Tommy: I asked you not to tell me that!
Avram: That's what I'm telling you.
Tommy: But this ain't no ordinary Saturday!
Avram: Why is this Saturday different from all other Saturdays?
Tommy: Because this Saturday there's a hanging posse chasing us! I promise

you, right now they're doubling back to that stream!
Avram: I don't ride on Saturdays.
Tommy: Jesus, you give me the pea-doodles! There ain't no Jews in that posse, you know. They would just as soon string you up on Saturday as any other day. They don't give a shit for your holidays!

Tommy played by Harrison Ford and Avram Belinsky played by Gene Wilder: Robert Aldrich's *The Frisco Kid* (Warner Bros., 1979).

596

Billy: Either they need to slow down or we need to hurry up. Let's go!

Billy Montana played by Bruce Boxleitner: Dick Lowry's *The Gambler, Part III — The Legend Continues* (TVW, 1987).

597

Deputy Sheriff: I reckon he's down in old Mexico by now.

Pat Garrett: If he's down in hell, I'll still go down and drag him out.

The Deputy Sheriff was uncredited and Pat Garrett played by Duncan Regehr: William A. Graham's *Gore Vidal's Billy the Kid* (Turner Pictures, 1989).

598

Ahab: According to the Psalms, the Lord is a very pleasant help in trouble. This time He gave me a fast horse and a head start.

Ahab Jones played by Peter Whitney: Lloyd Bacon's *The Great Sioux Uprising* (Universal, 1953).

599

Ballard: When are you gonna let me go?
Slayton: When we're out of Arizona.
Ballard: When will that be?
Slayton: Arizonans are like Texans. They say they're never out of Arizona.

Jennifer Ballard played by Donna Reed and Frank Slayton played by Phil Carey: Raoul Walsh's *Gun Fury* (Columbia, 1953).

600

Warren: We could always use some more gunhands. There's a pretty good reward for the men who bring 'em in.
Chuck: What kind of reward do they got for the men who try and don't?

Ben Warren played by Rock Hudson and Chuck was uncredited: Raoul Walsh's *Gun Fury* (Columbia, 1953).

601

Marshal: What's the trouble now, Jimmy? Is somebody after you?
Ringo: Three somebodies.

Marshal Mark Strett played by Millard Mitch-ell and Jimmy Ringo played by Gregory Peck: Henry King's *The Gunfighter* (20th Century–Fox, 1950).

602

Marshal: I don't want 'em to catch up with you here, Jimmy.
Ringo: I don't want 'em to catch up with me anywhere.

Marshal Mark Strett played by Millard Mitchell and Jimmy Ringo played by Gregory Peck: Henry King's *The Gunfighter* (20th Century–Fox, 1950).

603

Bob: What do you want to do? Spend the rest of your life dodgin' the law?
Chito: No, but I would like to spend the rest of my life.

Bob played by Tim Holt and Chito Rafferty played by Richard Martin: Lesley Selander's *Guns of Hate* (RKO, 1948).

Advertisement for Henry King's classic western *The Gunfighter* (20th Century–Fox, 1950). The story of an aging gunfighter, Jimmy Ringo (Gregory Peck), who can't outrun his reputation.

604

Dillon: What you're saying is the only safe way to get to Cripple Creek is by way of Raton Pass?
Blacksmith: It makes a day longer that way, but it's a damn sight better than getting yourself dog dead.

Matt Dillon played by James Arness and the Blacksmith played by Jim Beaver: Jerry Jameson's *Gunsmoke: The Long Ride* (TVW, 1993).

605

Tucson: We're getting nowheres fast.

Tucson Smith played by Ray Corrigan: Joseph Kane's *Gunsmoke Ranch* (Republic, 1937).

606

Frank: Damn, do you think them soldiers are gonna follow us?
Emmett: I know they will. There they are!
Rufus: Let's bushwhack the bastards!
Emmett: Like hell! Let's get out of here!

Frank Clemens played by Jack Elam, Emmett Clemens played by Ernest Borgnine, and Rufus Clemens played by Strother Martin: Burt Kennedy's *Hannie Caulder* (Paramount, 1971).

607

Emmett: I got a plan!

Frank: What are we gonna do? Starve them out?

Rufus: That is a good idea.

Emmett: Shut up! We're moving out!

Frank: That's the plan?

Emmett: That's right!

Rufus: What do we do after we move out?

Emmett: We'll just keep moving. It's called staying alive!

Emmett Clemens played by Ernest Borgnine, Frank Clemens played by Jack Elam, and Rufus Clemens played by Strother Martin: Burt Kennedy's *Hannie Caulder* (Paramount, 1971).

608

Deckett: I'd say them woods would be a lot safer than out here on this road. We'll take that trail.

Clay: Well, how far?

Deckett: That's one thing I've never been able to measure: how far a man has got to run to be safe.

Marshal Harry Deckett played by Stephen Mc-Nally and Clay Santell played by Audie Murphy: George Sherman's *Hell Bent for Leather* (Universal, 1960).

609

Fallon: Get out of here! The Sheriff's comin'!

Dinkey: I think we're on the wrong side.

Dare: This is no time to think!

Fallon played by Nick Lukats, Dinkey Hooley played by Syd Saylor, and Dare Rudd played by John Wayne: Charles Barton's *Hell Town* (a.k.a. *Born to the West*; Paramount, 1937).

610

Jesse: We got to keep moving. The law has a long reach.

Jesse James/John C. Howard played by Clayton Moore: Fred C. Brannon and Thomas Carr's *Jesse James Rides Again* (Republic serial, Chapter 1: "The Black Raiders," 1947).

611

Johnny: A posse isn't people. I've ridden with 'em and I've ridden against 'em. A posse is an animal. It moves like one and thinks like one.

Vienna: They're men with itchy fingers and a coil of rope around their saddle horns looking for somebody to hang. And after riding a few hours, they don't care much who they hang. You haven't told me a thing I don't know.

Johnny: I haven't finished.

Vienna: Finish, but be brief.

Johnny: A posse feels safe because it's big. They only make a big target. I can ride around 'em, pick off a few. The rest of them will lose their guts, turn tail and break up and go home.

Johnny Guitar played by Sterling Hayden and

Vienna played by Joan Crawford: Nicholas Ray's *Johnny Guitar* (Republic, 1954).

612

Wild Bill: Now don't anybody come through that door too soon!

Wild Bill Hickok played by Bill Elliott: Lambert Hillyer's *King of Dodge City* (Columbia, 1941).

613

Daisy: You couldn't find a milk bucket unless you stepped in it.

Ranson: I found you.

Daisy played by Loretta Swit and Ranson Payne played by Morgan Woodward: Vincent Mc-Eveety's *The Last Day* (Paramount, 1975).

614

Sheriff: Larger posses just make for a louder warning.

Sheriff Timberlake played by William Newman: William A. Graham's *The Last Days of Frank and Jesse James* (TVW, 1986).

615

Burgade: You go on back if you have to. I'll go where I have to.

Sheriff: Yea, well, I know where you're going. You're going about six feet under. That's where you're going. Because they got seven guns to your one.

Sam Burgade played by Charlton Heston and Sheriff Noel Nye played by Michael Parks: Andrew V. McLaglen's *The Last Hard Men* (20th Century–Fox, 1976).

616

Burgade: Everybody's got to die. Nobody's got to give up!

Sam Burgade played by Charlton Heston: Andrew V. McLaglen's *The Last Hard Men* (20th Century–Fox, 1976).

617

Grypton: A man's got to ride hard to get this far lost.

Samuel Grypton played by Edward C. Platt: George Sherman's *The Last of the Fast Guns* (Universal, 1958).

618

Sheriff: You still could have ridden around.

Ellison: Once you start circling, you keep looking back …and there's always someone chasing you.

The Sheriff played by Richard Cutting and Brad Ellison played by Jock Mahoney: George Sherman's *The Last of the Fast Guns* (Universal, 1958).

619

Potts: Hey, there ain't nothin' on our ass but hair, Eustis. There ain't a goddamn posse!

Potts played by Ted Levine and Eustis played by Dermot Mulroney: Geoff Murphy's *The Last Outlaw* (HBO Pictures, 1994).

620

Drune: Get the Sheriff down here, Jed. Tell him after he swears the posse in, he can go back to bed.

Sampson Drune played by Charles Bickford and Jed Clayton played by John Derek: Alfred Werker's *The Last Posse* (Columbia, 1953).

621

Clint: Now anybody that don't want to go along is perfectly free to just turn around and start riding back down the canyon. Of course, anybody that does will get a bullet in his back.

Clint Hollister played by Richard Widmark: John Sturges' *The Law and Jake Wade* (MGM, 1958).

622

Blessing: I'd like to stop at Plum Creek on the way through.

Crecencio: Say hello to your papa?

Blessing: It's been almost six years since I've seen him. My God, six years! Can you believe it?

Crecencio: Well, time flies when people is chasing you, amigo.

Ned Blessing played by Brad Johnson and Crecencio played by Luis Avalos: Jack Bender's *Lone Justice II* (Triboro Entertainment Group, 1995).

623

Leola: How are we gonna get Blessing off by himself, Pop?

Verlon: The same way we catch a fish.

Leola: A fish?

Verlon: Hugh Bell, tell Leola how we catch a fish. Bait! We use bait, Hugh Bell! That's how we catch a fish! Remember now? All right then, tell your brother how we're gonna catch Blessing. Go on, Hugh Bell, tell him …he's waiting!

Hugh Bell: He don't know?

Verlon: No, he don't know! You got to tell him. Go on now!

Leola: Go on, I'm waiting, Hugh Bell. How are we gonna catch Blessing?

Hugh Bell: The same way we catch a fish. Ain't that right, Papa? We get us some …. bait.

Verlon: Ha! Ha! Ha! Ha! That's right, Hugh Bell! We got to get us some bait.

Hugh Bell: Worms and grasshoppers.

Leola Borgers played by Gregory Scott Cummins, Verlon Borgers played by Bill McKinney, Hugh Bell Borgers played by Jeremy Roberts, and Ned Blessing played by Brad Johnson: Jack Bender's *Lone Justice II* (Triboro Entertainment Group, 1995).

624

Sheriff: I think we're chasing a ghost. An invisible horse, and an invisible cowboy. Harry, throw me that canteen. I haven't got enough spit left to wet a stick of gum.

Sheriff Johnson played by Walter Matthau and Harry played by William Schallert: David Miller's *Lonely Are the Brave* (Universal, 1962).

625

Bob: How long do you think it will take that posse to get here?
Cole: There won't be one. They'll go about ten miles and get tired and go back and call the Pinkertons.
Bob: Then how come we're standing guard?
Cole: Because every once in awhile I'm wrong.

Bob Younger played by Robert Carradine and Cole Younger played by David Carradine: Walter Hill's *The Long Riders* (United Artists, 1980).

626

You know how when you take a trip, coming back home seems to take half the time it took ya to get there? Well, in this case, it's true. I've never seen the scenery go by so fast.

Roger Miller was the voice of the horse, Jolly Jumper: Terence Hill's *Lucky Luke* (Silvio Berlusconi Communications, 1991).

627

Nadine: Is that all you're running away from …a reputation?
Wes: Well, it can get too big for a man to live with.

Nadine Corrigan played by Mary Murphy and Wes Steele played by Ray Milland: Ray Milland's *A Man Alone* (Republic, 1955).

628

Weston: But before I could get either one to spill anything, the whole gang jumped me …and I had to carve myself a fast walking stick.

John Weston played by John Wayne: Robert Bradbury's *The Man from Utah* (Lone Star/Monogram, 1934).

629

Dutcher: You know, Mr. Isham, when you're hunting a man that can shoot like Owen Merritt …go losing your head and you might lose your head.

Fay Dutcher played by Richard Rober, Will Isham played by Alexander Knox, and Owen Merritt played by Randolph Scott: Andre De Toth's *Man in the Saddle* (Columbia, 1951).

630

Maltese: I'm sorry, Paulo. There was no possible way he could escape. And then the impossible happened.

Maltese played by Victor Campos and Paulo played by Ron O'Neal: Frank Laughlin's *The Master Gunfighter* (Taylor-McLaughlin/Billy Jack, 1975).

631

Mary: Hunting men for a living seems sort of dreadful. Don't you ever wonder how they feel? Having money offered for their lives?
Hogan: Oh, I know how they feel.
Mary: Pardon?
Hogan: Oh, some of the outlaws got together and put a price on my head. Five thousand dollars. Dead. None of them are worth that to me. You know, sometimes I'm tempted to shoot myself and retire on the reward.

Mary Kingman played by Kim Hunter and "Silver" Ward Hogan played by Jock Mahoney: Richard Bartlett's *Money, Women and Guns* (Universal, 1958).

632

Shook: Where are you headed, Roy?
Roy: I don't know exactly, Shook. But I'm gonna put a lot of miles between me and here before daylight.

Shook was uncredited and Roy Rogers played himself: Frank McDonald's *My Pal Trigger* (Republic, 1946).

633

Jonas: Now, I sure can't tell you which way to go. But if you want to catch 'em, you best go where the money is. If they got it, they're gonna head to where they can spend it. And if they ain't got it, they'll go where they can steal it.

Jonas Cord played by Brian Keith: Henry Hathaway's *Nevada Smith* (Paramount, 1966).

634

Bart: Mr. Galt, why did you let him go?
Galt: You learn more by watching a polecat than by keeping him caged up.

Bart played by Jeff Corey and Edward Galt played by George Macready: Gordon Douglas' *The Nevadan* (Columbia, 1950).

635

Nash: Jason, you all right?
Jason: [*with ear to ground*] Wagon headed south. Four outriders. Three empty horses.
Nash: Hey Jason, I take back everything I've ever said against you. You are as good a scout as you ever were. Being able to hear all that by just putting your ear to the ground.
Jason: I didn't hear anything. They just ran over me! Ha! Ha! Ha! Ha! Ha! That's an old Indian joke. Actually, I seen them from above on the ridge there.
Nash: Then what are you doing flat on the ground?

Jason: I fell off my bicycle!

Nash Crawford played by Chuck Connors and Jason Pitch played by Jack Elam: Burt Kennedy's *Once Upon a Texas Train* (TVW, 1988).

636

John Henry: Yeah, Nash Crawford is some kind of man. If he gets on your trail, you better be ready to buy the farm …bull and all.

John Henry Lee played by Willie Nelson and Nash Crawford played by Chuck Connors: Burt Kennedy's *Once Upon a Texas Train* (TVW, 1988).

637

Charlie: Suppose they catch up with us?
John Henry: They won't.
Charlie: But what if they do?
John Henry: You ever hear tell of the story about the lions over in Africa?
Charlie: Lions?
John Henry: When they start getting old, something inside of 'em tells them they ain't long to live. And they start roaming around looking for a fight. Not just any fight, but a good one. One they wouldn't mind too much not walking away from. And if Captain Hayes and his boys catch up to us out here, that's the kind of fight it's gonna be.

Charlie Lee played by Dub Taylor, John Henry Lee played by Willie Nelson, and Oren Hayes played by Richard Widmark: Burt Kennedy's *Once Upon a Texas Train* (TVW, 1988).

638

Nitro: Having you along is like losing two good men.

Nitro Jones played by Royal Dano: Burt Kennedy's *Once Upon a Texas Train* (TVW, 1988). *See also entry 1770.*

639

Terrill: He's not a hard man to track. He leaves dead men wherever he goes.

Captain Terrill played by Bill McKinney: Clint Eastwood's *The Outlaw Josey Wales* (Warner Bros., 1976).

640

Senator: You're going after him after all, Fletcher. I'm giving you a commission. Hound this Wales to kingdom come.
Fletcher: I'll do it, Senator. A man like Wales lives by the feud. As of what you did here today, I got to kill that man.
Senator: Well, he'll have to run for it now. And hell is where he's headed.
Fletcher: He'll be waiting there for us, Senator.

Senator Lane played by Frank Schofield, Fletcher played by John Vernon, and Josey Wales played by

Max Sand/Nevada Smith (Steve McQueen) is out for revenge against those who killed his folks. On his journey, Max comes across a gunsmith, Jonas Cord (Brian Keith), who teaches him: "Handling one of these things [gun] is only half of it; the other part is learning human nature," in Henry Hathaway's *Nevada Smith* (Paramount, 1966).

Clint Eastwood who also directed *The Outlaw Josey Wales* (Warner Bros., 1976).

641

Bryce: I can't believe this! I'm a fugitive!
Lee: Ain't it exciting!

Bryce played by Chad Willett and Lee Walker played by Willie Nelson: Bill Corcoran's *Outlaw Justice* (TVW, 1999).

642

Argo: There is the key to our entire situation.
Queen: Explain yourself, Argo.
Argo: If we can capture Gene Autry, Radio Ranch would soon become deserted. And the entrance to our underground kingdom would remain forever undiscovered.

Queen: We can't allow Murania to become desecrated by the presence of surface people. Our lives are serene, our minds are superior, our accomplishments greater. Gene Autry must be captured!

Lord Argo played by Wheeler Oakman and Queen Tika played by Dorothy Christie: Otto Brower and B. Reeves (Breezy) Eason's *The Phantom Empire* (Mascot serial, Chapter 1: "The Singing Cowboy," 1935).

643

Hickok: If he ever catches you, I hope you're not around.

Wild Bill Hickok played by Forrest Tucker: Jerry Hopper's *Pony Express* (Paramount, 1953).

644

Cole: I still think you ought to quit.

Kern: Banner, I wouldn't tell this to anybody else, but this is the first time in my life that I felt like a man at a man's game. And I ain't gonna let myself down …or you.

Banner Cole played by Audie Murphy and Seymour Kern played by John Saxon: Herbert Coleman's *Posse from Hell* (Universal, 1961).

645

Ike: I'm scared, Will. I'm scared to go on, and I'm scared to go back. Sometimes I don't know what we're running to, or what we're running from.

Ike played by Aron Kincaid and Will Hansen played by Chuck Connors: Ferde Grofé Jr.'s *The Proud and Damned* (Media Trend–Prestige/Columbia, 1972).

646

Blackjack: Any man who can keep up with me, I'll see ya in Chihuahua. The rest of ya, I'll see ya in hell!

Blackjack played by Eric Roberts: Uli Edel's *Purgatory* (TVW, 1999).

647

Quigley: I don't know where we're going, but there's no use being late.

Matthew Quigley played by Tom Selleck: Simon Wincer's *Quigley Down Under* (MGM–United Artists, 1990).

648

Will: You know, amigos …east, west, north, south …it's all the same to me. What I really don't like is getting told where to go.

Will Fernandez played by Gil Ranson: Tonino Valerii's *A Reason to Live, a Reason to Die* (a.k.a. *Massacre at Fort Holman*; Sancrosiap-Terza/Europrodis/Atlantida/Corona, 1972).

649

Vance: I'll get my men [posse] together!
John: You got one together right now!

Vance played by Randolph Scott and John Pettit played by George "Gabby" Hayes: Ray Enright's *Return of the Badmen* (RKO, 1948).

650

Anisa: Is your wounded friend going with us?
Wyatt: He's not my friend. He's one of my misfortunes. No, we're leaving him here. If he dies, they can bury him. If he gets well, they can boot him out of town.

Anisa Domingo played by Ana Martin and Ben Wyatt played by Robert Taylor: James Neilson's *Return of the Gunfighter* (TVW, 1966).

651

Chris: He wants to know if we are going after them tonight or in the morning.
Vin: It's a big country and finding them could take a long time.
Chris: Hell, I haven't been going anywhere for ten years …and neither have you.
Vin: Ain't it the truth.

Chris played by Yul Brynner and Vin played by Robert Fuller: Burt

Kennedy's *Return of the Seven* (United Artists, 1966).

652

Drury: But I'd say that trailing the Hawk is a one-man job.
Clout: That's just what I've been telling the folks around here for the last few months.
Cowboy: Well, why didn't you do it?
Clout: Well, I couldn't get no one to go with me.

John Drury played by John Wayne and Clout played by Harry Gribbon: Fred Allen's *Ride Him, Cowboy* (Warner Bros., 1932).

653

Wes: Do you figure we lost 'em?
Fern: I figure we got to find a place to hide before the sun comes up tomorrow …and this ain't it.
Wes: It would be a shame to do all this walking for nothing.
Fern: You're one day ahead of the game already …better blisters than neck burns.

Wes played by Jack Nicholson and Vern played by Cameron Mitchell: Monte Hellman's *Ride in the Whirlwind* (Jack H. Harris/Proteus Films, 1966).

Bank President John Pettit (George "Gabby" Hayes) is having his grandson, Johnny (Gary Gray), ride shotgun on their buckboard in Ray Enright's *Return of the Badmen* (RKO, 1948).

654

Gil: It looks to me like you've been riding a long time but not getting very far.

Gil Westrum played by Randolph Scott: Sam Peckinpah's *Ride the High Country* (MGM, 1962).

655

Leech: You got two, maybe three choices: You can go for the iron on your hip, you can die with your fingers in your ear, or you can tell me where they went. Which one is it?

Quinton Leech played by Kenny Rogers: Rod Hardy's *Rio Diablo* (TVW, 1993).

656

Hendricks: Spence, you take five men and go out and guard the north road. Warren, you take a few more …leave some on the south road close in. The rest of you go out to the west fork. Stop everybody going out and in. Shoot anybody who tries to get by. Now move!

Sheriff Tom Hendricks played by Mike Henry: Howard Hawks' *Rio Lobo* (NGP, 1970).

657

Narrator: We kept going until we crossed the border into New Mexico. I knew Sheriff Dietrick's reputation. He had a long arm.

Narration by Bill Mayhew who was played by John Payne. The Sheriff played by John Dierkes: Joseph Kane's *The Road to Denver* (Republic, 1955).

658

Gabby: Well, it looks like we shook them, Roy.

Roy: Maybe, but it wouldn't hurt to put a few more miles between us and them.

Gabby played by George "Gabby" Hayes and Roy played by Roy Rogers: Joseph Kane's *Romance on the Range* (Republic, 1942).

659

Eula: There are nine men with him. How can you best them?

Rooster: Well, ma'am, I've got my Navy Colt sidearm, and the Winchester rifle on my saddle, and I packed it full of cartridges.

Eula: And a prayer on your lips, I hope. You will have need of it.

Rooster: And the government has promised me a posse. Which I figure will be long on promise and short on posse.

Eula Goodnight played by Katharine Hepburn and Rooster Cogburn played by John Wayne: Stuart Millar's *Rooster Cogburn* (Universal, 1975).

660

Rose: He feels sure his men will catch Arizona Jack this time.

Lanning: Oh, he couldn't catch flies!

Rose played by Dorothy Sebastian and George

Lanning played by George Meeker: Joseph Kane's *Rough Riders' Round-Up* (Republic, 1939).

661

Jeb: What do you mean trailing us halfway across Kansas?

Tex: Well, we don't want you to get lost. You see, I know every wrinkle of this here country just like my own face.

Jeb: Well, you should. It's just as dirty!

Jeb Stuart played by Errol Flynn and Tex Bell played by Guinn "Big Boy" Williams: Michael Curtiz's *Santa Fe Trail* (Warner Bros., 1940).

662

Custer: They're running! They're getting away!

Stuart: No they're not. We're going after them!

Custer: Hey, wait a minute! They outnumber us three to one!

Stuart: Well, if it makes you nervous, don't count 'em!

George Armstrong Custer played by Ronald Reagan and Jeb Stuart played by Errol Flynn: Michael Curtiz's *Santa Fe Trail* (Warner Bros., 1940).

663

Deaks: We're gonna run for it!

Jody: Run for it? Five of us from one man?

Deaks: From that man!

Deaks played by Robert Wilke and Jody played by Michael Burns: Gary Nelson's *Santee* (Crown International Pictures, 1973).

664

Tally: How do you pick up trails?

Ahern: Well, the prints of the horse tell you about the rider. The soldier's horse is shod, Indians is not. If the prints are deep in the trail, the horse is carrying a heavy load. The spacing of the prints tells you how fast he was going.

Jim Ahern/Warbonnet played by Charlton Heston and Tally Hathersell played by Susan Morrow: George Marshall's *The Savage* (Paramount, 1952).

665

Chris: Well, Bert, we haven't done bad for six months. We lost all our money, guns, and our gear. Now if we don't starve to death before we heal, we ought to make a sudden rise in life.

Chris Foster played by Audie Murphy and Bert Pickett played by Charles Drake: R.G. Springsteen's *Showdown* (Universal, 1963).

666

Billy: Do you like sheriffing?

Chuck: It's a job.

Billy: What kind of salary do you get?

Chuck: No salary, I …

Kate: Oh, he gets $2.00 for serving a warrant, $3.00 for arresting anybody …

Chuck: And 30 cents a mile for chasing idiots …

Kate: Like you.

Billy: Well then, you ought to thank me for doubling back. I let you make a few extra bucks.

Billy Massey played by Dean Martin, Sheriff Chuck Jarvis played by Rock Hudson and Kate Jarvis played by Susan Clark: George Seaton's *Showdown* (Universal, 1973).

667

Prudy: If you guys are really sincere about capturing the Boss and turning him in, don't you think it's about time you got started?

Jason: We want those other two guys, too!

Quince: We might as well use these guys to help us get those guys.

Prudy: Well, supposing that these guys and us manage to get those guys. What then?

Jason: Quince will think of something.

Prudy Jenkins played by Blythe Danner, Jason O'Rourke played by Lou Gossett, and Quince Drew played by Larry Hagman: Burt Kennedy's *Sidekicks* (TVW, 1974).

668

Ballard: I'm not going anywhere.

Dolly: If you don't, you're gonna be a real dead cowboy.

Dan Ballard played by John Payne and Dolly played by Dolores Moran: Allan Dwan's *Silver Lode* (RKO, 1954).

669

Emmett: Me and my partner robbed a bank in Turley and headed out with a posse on our tails. My partner over there caught one a ways back. I think he kicked off while I was looking for this damn canyon. You Dawson, ain't ya? [I'm] Tex LaRue. I used to ride with Ryan Morris. You know him. Well, Andy Simms told me there was a hideout near here so I headed toward it. I hope you don't mind.

Dawson: Mind? You brought a posse to my best hideout and you ask me if I mind! Mister, I don't know any of those names. You're about to die.

Emmett played by Scott Glenn and Dawson played by James Gammon: Lawrence Kasdan's *Silverado* (Columbia, 1985).

670

Lilly: No, Clint, it won't work.

Clint: Why not? Why can't people like us start over again. Honest …clean.

Lilly: Because you can't start a clean life on dirty money. You couldn't even build a home on it that I could live in. Even the planks and nails would be stolen. Everytime the floor would creak, I'd jump up and look around and you'd be reaching for a gun.

Lilly played by Joanne Dru and Clint McDonald played by John Ireland: Ray Nazarro's *Southwest Passage* (United Artists, 1954).

671

Spikes: Well, you boys left the farm and you had some trouble. You've seen some of the world. How do you find it?

Les: We ain't really seen that much of it. We've been chased through it!

Harry Spikes played by Lee Marvin and Les Richter played by Ron Howard: Richard Fleischer's *The Spikes Gang* (United Artists, 1974).

672

Dave: What they just pulled is an old Apache trick called "the rideaway." The enemy leaves and comes back from a different direction. When the chump walks out, they pop, shoot him.

Dave played by Tim Holt: Lew Landers' *Stagecoach Kid* (RKO, 1949).

673

Gabby: It looks like they are going someplace to make something happen.

Gabby Whittaker played by George "Gabby" Hayes: Joseph Kane's *Sunset on the Desert* (Republic, 1942).

674

Bambino: You thinking of selling [out] your own brother?

Trinity: No, that's an insult! I would never do such a thing for only two hundred bucks.

Bambino played by Bud Spencer (Carlo Pedersoli) and Trinity played by Terence Hill (Mario Girotti): E.B. Clucher's (Enzo Barboni) *They Call Me Trinity* (West Film/Avco Embassy, 1970).

675

Alex: Hey! Where are they, huh? Where did they go?

Wade: That way.

Alex: Well, ain't you gonna help catch 'em?

Wade: No, but I wish I could.

Alex: What did they look like?

Wade: Oh, they'll be easy to catch. Three big men on three white horses.

Alex: Three white fellas …on three big horses, huh?

Alex Potter played by Henry Jones and Ben Wade played by Glenn Ford: Delmer Daves' *3:10 to Yuma* (Columbia, 1957).

676

Hickman: Where's your posse?

Sheriff: I left 'em. And don't call 'em mine. They're all following Bogardus.

Hickman: I told you: If a sheriff don't crack down on the first man that disobeys him, a posse turns into a mob.

Morg Hickman played by Henry Fonda and Sheriff Ben Owens played by Anthony Perkins: Anthony Mann's *The Tin Star* (Paramount, 1957).

677

Noble: From here east to New Mexico and north to Utah, there's 15,000 square miles of hard country and bad memories. If we head due east, we have to cut their trail sooner or later.

Tom: It'll be like trying to find a wave in the ocean.

Noble: I'll know it when I see it.

Noble Adams played by Kris Kristofferson and Tom Adams played by Mark Moses: John Guillermin's *The Tracker* (HBO Pictures, 1988).

678

Jesse: Them pallbearers are sure as hell grouped.

Grady: Maybe we ought to jump 'em and thin 'em out a little.

Lane: We better get moving out of here. Cal!

Calhoun: Yes, sir.

Lane: You and Sam hang back. If anybody starts crossing that river before we're out of sight …baptize them!

Wil Jesse played by Ben Johnson, Grady played by Rod Taylor, Lane played by John Wayne, Calhoun played by Christopher George, and Sam Turner played by Jerry Gatlin: Burt Kennedy's *The Train Robbers* (Warner Bros., 1973).

679

Jesse: Lane says this is the closest way out. Besides, we know the ground.

Grady: Yea, we could get buried in it too!

Jesse: Well, a man can't live forever.

Grady: Not around Lane he can't.

Wil Jesse played by Ben Johnson, Grady played by Rod Taylor, and Lane played by John Wayne: Burt Kennedy's *The Train Robbers* (Warner Bros., 1973).

680

Marshal: When was the last time you saw Ned Pepper?

Quincy: I don't remember any Ned Pepper.

Marshal: Short, feisty fella. Nervous and quick …and got a messed up lower lip.

Quincy: That don't bring nobody to mind. A funny lip?

Marshal: It wasn't always like that. I shot him in it.

Quincy: In the lower lip! What was you aiming at?

Marshal: His upper lip!

Marshal Reuben J. "Rooster" Cogburn played by John Wayne and Emmett Quincy played by Jeremy Slate: Henry Hathaway's *True Grit* (Paramount, 1969).

681

La Boeuf: How much is she paying you?

Rooster: Enough.

La Boeuf: Is she paying you $500?

Rooster: No.

La Boeuf: Well, that's what the governor of Texas has put up for this man she calls Chaney. Payable upon conviction.

Rooster: $500?

La Boeuf: Yep.

Rooster: That's very little for a man who killed a senator.

La Boeuf: Bibbs was a little senator.

La Boeuf played by Glen Campbell and Marshal Reuben J. "Rooster" Cogburn played by John Wayne: Henry Hathaway's *True Grit* (Paramount, 1969).

682

Lieutenant: Well, what's the point, Mr. McIntosh, if we can't close the gap?

McIntosh: Remember the rules, Lieutenant. The first one to make a mistake gets to bury some people.

Lieutenant Garnett DeBuin played by Bruce Davison and McIntosh played by Burt Lancaster: Robert Aldrich's *Ulzana's Raid* (Universal, 1972).

683

Lieutenant: So they are on foot!

McIntosh: That's a mighty fair description of men without horses, Lieutenant.

Lieutenant Garnett DeBuin played by Bruce Davison and McIntosh played by Burt Lancaster: Robert Aldrich's *Ulzana's Raid* (Universal, 1972).

684

Pancho: Come on, you're taking me to Madero!

Arnold: What?

Pancho: Hurry up, get your pants on!

Arnold: How?

Pancho: Well, first one leg …then the other.

Pancho Villa played by Yul Brynner, Lee Arnold played by Robert Mitchum, and President Francisco Madero played by Alexander Knox: Buzz Kulik's *Villa Rides!* (Paramount, 1968).

685

Bessie: We got a long way to go and a short time to get there.

Bessie Baxter played by Marjorie Rambeau: Albert S. Rogell's *War of the Wildcats* (Republic, 1943).

686

Wabi: The difficult part is not the hunt …but becoming the hunter.

Wabi Dray played by Allan Musy: Rene Manzor's *Warrior Spirit* (Cinevideo Plus, 1994).

687

Cole: Take off your clothes, Sheriff!

Sheriff: Do what?

Cole: Take off your clothes!

Deputy: You mean you want for us to take off everything that we got on?

Cole: Down to the last single stitch. Put them in a nice neat little pile right there on the floor.

Sheriff: Cole, Cole! Why are you doing this terrible thing to me?

Cole: Well, a naked sheriff makes for a slow posse.

Lewton Cole played by James Coburn, Sheriff John Copperud played by Carroll O'Connor, and

Ex-sheriff and now bounty hunter Morg Hickman (Henry Fonda) instructs young sherriff Ben Owens (Anthony Perkins), "A decent man doesn't want to kill; but if you're gonna shoot, you shoot to kill," in Anthony Mann's *The Tin Star* (Paramount, 1957).

Deputy Tippen played by Bruce Dern: William A. Graham's *Waterhole No. 3* (Paramount, 1967).

688

Deke: We're after men. And I wish to God I was with 'em!

Deke Thornton played by Robert Ryan: Sam Peckinpah's *The Wild Bunch* (Warner Bros.–Seven Arts, 1969).

689

Walter: If the sheriff has to stop, then you keep right on going and bring those cowboys back. You understand?

John: Dead or alive?

Walter: Alive, of course! That is, if they give you that choice.

Walter Buckman played by Karl Malden and John Buckman played by Tom Skerritt: Blake Edwards' *Wild Rovers* (MGM, 1971).

690

Johnny: You're about ready to fall out of that saddle. Why don't we rest up for a little?

Lin: I'm not that tired.

Johnny: Four or five hours ain't gonna make any difference. We have been chasing him since ...since I can't remember.

Johnny "High Spade" Williams played by Millard Mitchell and Lin McAdam played by James Stewart: Anthony Mann's *Winchester '73* (Universal, 1950).

691

Tower: There's a posse following us!

Morrell: They don't look peaceful. We better run for it!

Nicholas Tower played by John Miljan and Morrell played by Hal Taliaferro/Wally Wales: Joseph Kane's *Young Bill Hickok* (Republic, 1940).

Cooks

See also Cowboys; Pioneers, Settlers, and Sodbusters

692

Billy: If she's as good cooking as she's at ambushing, what have we got to lose?

Merrick: Only our lives.

Deputy Billy Shear played by John Agar and United States Marshal Len Merrick played by Kirk Douglas: Raoul Walsh's *Along the Great Divide* (Warner Bros., 1951).

693

Sam: What will you have?

MacReedy: What do you got?

Sam: Chili and beans.

MacReedy: Anything else?

Sam: Chili without beans.

Sam played by Walter Sande and John J. MacReedy played by Spencer Tracy: John Sturges' *Bad Day at Black Rock* (MGM, 1955).

694

Martha: They're very dangerous men. They've already killed ten people …many of them you know …Juan and his family.

Jacob: Tina and the little boy?

Martha: And Moses Brown.

Jacob: Old Mose …lousy cook.

Martha McCandles played by Maureen O'Hara and Jacob McCandles played by John Wayne: George Sherman's *Big Jake* (NGP, 1971).

695

Abe: How's the coffee, Dakota? Is it strong enough yet?

Dakota: Stop rocking it! If it don't shake, it's strong enough.

Abe Jones played by Milburn Stone and Dakota played by Houseley Stevenson: George Sherman's *Calamity Jane and Sam Bass* (Universal, 1949).

696

Jack: You know, it's customary up here, Mrs. Blake, for everyone to pitch in and do their share. You've been with us for two days and up to now done nothing but sit around and look nasty. Can you cook?

Claire: Yes, I'm considered a very excellent cook.

Jack: How about giving these beans the benefit of your talent?

Claire: I'll do nothing to help you! I'm your prisoner, and since you seem to want me with you, you'll take care of me.

Jack: Want you? We just had an attack of insanity and decided to keep you from

committing suicide. A very bad idea come to think of it.

Jack Thornton played by Clark Gable and Claire Blake played by Loretta Young: William Wellman's *The Call of the Wild* (20th Century–Fox, 1935).

697

Constable: He said you were taking along two men. Why, I …I don't suppose you would consider taking me, sir?

Inspector: You?

Constable: Well, yes sir. I could lead the pack horses, stand night guard, cook.

Inspector: You cook?

Constable: No, sir.

Inspector: But you're willing to learn?

Constable: Yes, sir.

Inspector: It could be dangerous.

Constable: Well, I'm not afraid of the Sioux, sir.

Inspector: Not the Sioux. Your cooking.

Constable Springer played by Burt Metcalfe and Inspector Gannon played by Robert Ryan: Burt Kennedy's *The Canadians* (20th Century–Fox, 1961).

698

Inspector: Did you cook this, Springer?

Constable: Well, yes sir.

Inspector: What is it?

Constable: Stew, sir. My mother used to make it.

Inspector: Is your father still living?

Inspector Gannon played by Robert Ryan and Constable Springer played by Burt Metcalfe: Burt Kennedy's *The Canadians* (20th Century–Fox, 1961).

699

Nye: Harvey, I bet that horse tastes better than he rides.

Harvey: Nye, you would have your own mother in a skillet before she got cold.

Nye Buell played by Richard Basehart and Harvey Lansing played by William Watson: Michael Winner's *Chato's Land* (United Artists, 1972).

700

Harley: I've eaten mighty good food in my life, but this weren't part of it.

Cook: Yea, well, I ain't heard no complaints from none of the others.

Harley: Yea, well, they ain't as well bred as I am.

Harley Sullivan played by Henry Fonda and the Cook played by Phil Mead: Gene Kelly's *The Cheyenne Social Club* (NGP, 1970).

701

Barkley: I remember the first time I found out what was in prairie stew I turned as green as spinach myself. But then, you know, it starts to grow on you a little bit. Rattlesnake and prairie dog …some damn good eatin'!

Barkley played by Dan Haggerty: Mark Griffiths' *Cheyenne Warrior* (Concorde–New Horizons Corp., 1994).

702

Brett: Stewpot, you still look as tough as the meat you cook.

Brett Stanton played by Dale Robertson and Stewpot played by Harry Hines: Harmon Jones' *City of Bad Men* (20th Century–Fox, 1953).

703

Mitch: Where have you been?

Phil: Oh, I was watching 'em castrate a horse.

Mitch: Well, I'm hungry! How about you?

Mitch Robbins played by Billy Crystal and Phil Berquist played by Daniel Stern: Ron Underwood's *City Slickers* (Columbia, 1991).

704

Ben: How come they keep calling me Little Mary?

Cook: That's your name, kid. What's the matter? Don't you like it?

Ben: No, I don't. It's a girl's name.

Cook: Well, that's what they call the cook's helper …Little Mary. But I wish you was a girl.

Ben Mockridge played by Gary Grimes and the Cook played by Raymond Guth: Dick Richards' *The Culpepper Cattle Company* (20th Century–Fox, 1972).

705

Carey: There's lots of food, gentlemen. You may want to wash first before you eat.

Bill: Well, ma'am, if there's grub I'm for eating first and washing later.

Lady Carey and Bill were uncredited: Yves Simoneau's *Dead Man's Walk* (Cabin Fever Entertainment, 1996).

706

Bill: If I eat another plate of beans, I'll float back to Austin.

Bill was uncredited: Yves Simoneau's *Dead Man's Walk* (Cabin Fever Entertainment, 1996).

707

Johnny: My old man used to say: Take a pan of water. Put some coffee in it. Boil it. Throw a horseshoe into it. If the horseshoe sinks, add more coffee.

Johnny Ears played by Franco Nero: Paolo Cavara's *Deaf Smith & Johnny Ears* (MGM, 1972).

708

Virgil: You know, that's pretty good stew as stew goes around here. Of course, I wish old Cookie would stay out of it with his feet when he's mixin' it up.

Virgil played by Whit Bissell: Alfred Werker's *Devil's Canyon* (RKO, 1953).

709

Pancho: Mr. Frog, I am ashamed for you to hire me.

Frog: Yea, you told me you was the best cook in all of Mexico.

Pancho: Oh, si! But I am on the wrong side of the border.

Pancho Grande played by Harold Huber and Frog Millhouse played by Smiley Burnette: Joseph Santley's *Down Mexico Way* (Republic, 1941).

710

Lee Bob: Me and my supper are about to part company.

Lee Bob played by Ray McKinnon: Dick Lowry's *The Gambler Returns: The Luck of the Draw* (TVW, 1991).

711

Lee: One thing I learned, Ed, is to never argue with a woman, a mule, or a cook.

Lee Hackett played by Van Heflin and Ed Hackett played by Tab Hunter: Phil Karlson's *Gunman's Walk* (Columbia, 1958).

712

Hewitt: Martin, there's an old saying that an army travels on its stomach. I'm glad we're not going anywhere.

Lieutenant Frank Hewitt played by Audie Murphy and Ann Martin played by Kathryn Grant: George Marshall's *The Guns of Fort Petticoat* (Columbia, 1957).

713

Dinkey: Too bad to waste such good food on just ordinary cowhands. Why, this kind of food is fittin' for human beings.

Cowhand: Well, I ain't human and that ain't fittin'!

Dinkey Hooley played by Syd Saylor and the Cowhand was uncredited: Charles Barton's *Hell Town* (a.k.a. *Born to the West*; Paramount, 1937).

714

Lillian: It's not bad …if you don't mind the taste.

Professor Lillian Stone played by Barbara Hershey: Tab Murphy's *Last of the Dogmen* (Savory Pictures, 1995).

715

Molly: 'Tis not me you love but my cooking.

Calem: Right you are, Molly! But you know what they say: A man's stomach has more sense in it than either his heart or his head.

Molly Higgins played by Ruth Donnelly and Marshal Calem Ware played by Randolph Scott: Joseph H. Lewis' *A Lawless Street* (Columbia, 1955).

716

Calem: A meal fit for a condemned man, Molly.

Locals gather to discuss why a stranger (Spencer Tracy) came to their desert town and what he may unearth. Tim Horn (Dean Jagger), Mr. Hastings (Russell Collins), Reno Smith (Robert Ryan), Coley Trimble (Ernest Borgnine), and Hector David (Lee Marvin) in John Sturges' *Bad Day at Black Rock* (MGM, 1955).

Marshal Calem Ware played by Randolph Scott and Molly Higgins played by Ruth Donnelly: Joseph H. Lewis' *A Lawless Street* (Columbia, 1955).

717

Gabby: Hurry up, Marjorie, the boys are hungry!

Rosie: That means you're hungry.

Gabby Whittaker played by George "Gabby" Hayes, Marjorie Brooks played by Dale Evans, and Rosie McGerk played by Claire DuBrey: Frank McDonad's *Lights of Old Santa Fe* (Republic, 1940).

718

Gus: And another thing, Bol. I want you to quit whackin' that dinner bell for supper. You can whack it at noon if you want to, but let off doing it in the evening. You see, a man with any sense at all can tell when it's sundown without you whackin' that bell.

Bolivar: General Robert E. Lee freed the slaves. I can whack it if I want to.

Gus: It was Abe Lincoln who freed the slaves, Bol …not General Lee.

Pea-Eye: He didn't free Mexicans anyway. It was, ah, Americans that he freed.

Gus: You're in over your head, Pea. It was a bunch of Africans Abe Lincoln freed …no more American than Call here.

Call: I'm American … by God!

Gus: You was born in Scotland as I recall. You was still dragging on the tit when they brought you over here.

Gus McCrae played by Robert Duvall, Bolivar played by Leon Singer, Pea-Eye Parker played by Tim Scott, and Captain Woodrow F.

Estranged couple George Washington McLintock (John Wayne) and Katherine "Kate" McLintock (Maureen O'Hara) are about to become "unestranged" in the comedy western *McLintock!* (United Artists, 1963).

Call played by Tommy Lee Jones: Simon Wincer's *Lonesome Dove* (TVW, 1989).

719

McLintock: Well, you old Cantonese reprobate, how about it?
Ching: You fire me, I kill myself!
McLintock: I'm not talking about firing ya, I'm retiring ya. You've been rustling food for us for 30 years. We're going to put you out to pasture. All you have to do is give advice and be one of the family.
Ching: I'll kill myself!
McLintock: I may save you the trouble.
Drago: Ching, if you kill yourself, I'll cut off your pigtails and you ain't never going to get to heaven.
Ching: I'll be one of the family?
McLintock: I give you my solemn word.
Ching: Pretty crummy family. Drink too much, get in fights, yell all the time.
McLintock: Cut off his pigtails!
Ching: All right, all right! I'll be one of the family!

George Washington McLintock played by John Wayne, Ching played by H.W. Gim, and Drago played by Chill Wills: Andrew V. McLaglen's *McLintock!* (United Artists, 1963).

720

Kingman: Well, what did you think of the whipper-wheel peas, Mr. Hogan?
Hogan: Well, a man doesn't ask for thirds just to be polite. He may take seconds for that reason. But when he takes thirds, it's because he likes them.

Job Kingman played by Nolan Leary and "Silver" Ward Hogan played by Jock Mahoney: Richard Bartlett's *Money, Women and Guns* (Universal, 1958).

721

Hoyce: Her cooking won't plug no bullet holes.

Hoyce Guthrie played by Richard Crenna: William A. Graham's *Montana* (TVW, 1990).

722

Crandall: Give us a hunk of pie!
Happy: I got peach, apple, pumpkin, strawberry, lemon meringue, chocolate meringue, berry huckle, …
Crandall: Huckleberry!
Happy: I didn't make any today. I got some apple.
Crandall: Strawberry!
Happy: Well, they're out of season. I got some apple.
Crandall: All right, make it apple!

Matt Crandall played by Stanley Blystone and Happy played by Syd Saylor: Harry Fraser's *Navajo Kid* (Producer's Releasing Corp., 1945).

723

Dusty: I make the best cup of coffee in the whole state of Texas. You can float a horseshoe in my coffee.

Dusty Rivers played by Gary Cooper: Cecil B. DeMille's *North West Mounted Police* (Paramount, 1940).

724

Sanderson: I've been in that cow camp starving on my own cooking for so long, I don't hardly throw a shadow no more.

Burn Sanderson played by Chuck Connors: Robert Stevenson's *Old Yeller* (Buena Vista, 1957).

725

Josey Wales: You have any food here?
Lone Watie: All I have is a piece of hard rock candy. But it's not for eating. It's just for looking through.

Lone Watie played by Chief Dan George and Josey Wales played by Clint Eastwood who also directed *The Outlaw Josey Wales* (Warner Bros., 1976).

726

Amos: Now ain't that queer! This stew hadn't been heated up for three days and it's still bubblin'.
Collins: Ah, it's not bubblin'. There's something swimmin' in there!

Amos played by David Wayne and Collins played by Tom Skerritt: Arthur Allan Seidelman's *Poker Alice* (TVW, 1987).

727

Sam: Maybe a little more coffee, Mr. Slade?
Slade: Coffee? This stuff taste like burnt corn boiled in trench water!

Sam Todd played by Edgar Buchanan and Slade the Miner played by Max Terhune: Henry Hathaway's *Rawhide* (20th Century–Fox, 1951).

728

Dunson: What are you mumbling about? Where are those store teeth Matt brought you?
Groot: In my pocket.
Dunson: Well, why don't you use 'em?
Groot: Because they whistle and I use 'em for eating.

Tom Dunson played by John Wayne and Groot Nadine played by Walter Brennan: Howard Hawks' *Red River* (United Artists, 1948).

729

Ruggles: You must listen to an Englishman about tea. If it were coffee, I should be your pupil. But we're making tea. And when making tea, always bring the pot to the kettle and never bring the kettle to the pot.

Colonel Marmaduke "Bill" Ruggles played by Charles Laughton: Leo McCarey's *Ruggles of Red Gap* (Paramount, 1935).

730

Ma: There was a Chinaman who tried to run a chop suey joint there and they shot him.

Egbert: He couldn't cook ham and eggs. He was always doing something Chinese to 'em.

Ma Pettingill played by Maude Eburne and Egbert "Sourdough" Floud played by Charles Ruggles: Leo McCarey's *Ruggles of Red Gap* (Paramount, 1935).

731

Boss: There's something fishy about you two. I can feel it right here! Of course, it could be the beans.

The Boss (of the gang) played by Jack Elam: Burt Kennedy's *Sidekicks* (TVW, 1974).

732

Tod: It isn't so bad, really, if you don't get your nose too close.

Tod Hayhew played by Charles Martin Smith: Richard Fleischer's *The Spikes Gang* (United Artists, 1974).

733

Noble: You better start sittin' a little farther from the trough. You're startin' to look like Grover Cleveland.

Noble Adams played by Kris Kristofferson: John Guillermin's *The Tracker* (HBO Pictures, 1988).

734

Hugh: Then we celebrated with a Kentucky breakfast.
Son: What's a Kentucky breakfast?
Hugh: Ah, three pounds of steak, a bottle of whiskey, and a dog.
Son: What's this dog for?
Hugh: To eat the steak!

Hugh Allison played by Kris Kristofferson and Son Holland played by Scott Bairstow: Rod Hardy's *Two for Texas* (Turner Pictures, 1998).

735

John Henry: Is your cooking still as bad as I remember it?
McCartney: You go to hell!
John Henry: You still got that mangy old cat?
McCartney: Hybrid? The finest partner I ever had. He cleans his paws and buries his leavings. That's a lot more than some folks I know.

Colonel John Henry Thomas played by John Wayne and McCartney played by Dub Taylor: Andrew McLaglen's *The Undefeated* (20th Century–Fox, 1969).

736

Short Grub: Hey, McCartney!
McCartney: Mr. McCartney!
Short Grub: There's something crawling in these beans.
McCartney: Well, you can speak to it but don't play with it …or else the others will want one in their beans too.

Short Grub played by Ben Johnson and McCartney played by Dub Taylor: Andrew McLaglen's *The Undefeated* (20th Century–Fox, 1969).

737

Mollie: Here's a bite [of food] so we'll not be dying on an empty stomach.

Mollie Monahan played by Barbara Stanwyck: Cecil B. DeMille's *Union Pacific* (Paramount, 1939).

738

Doc: Can you cook lamb?

Herman: There are nine different ways to cook mutton. And I know them all! Boiled, stewed, fricassee …

Homer: Never mind that! Do you cook it with the hair on?

Herman: I should say not!

Crowd: Hurray!

Homer: Then you're hired!

Doc Murdock played by John Carradine, Herman played by Slim Summerville, and Homer played by Chill Wills: Fritz Lang's *Western Union* (20th Century–Fox, 1941).

739

Wyatt: Hey, Patience! Get some of the women out to collect the tops of the cloves. Cook 'em up. That's what the Indians do, and they don't get the scurvy.

Buck Wyatt played by Robert Taylor and Patience Hawley played by Hope Emerson: William Wellman's *Westward the Women* (MGM, 1952).

740

Cook: Well, if they're [plates] clean enough to stop eating off of, they're clean enough to start eating off of. Slosh it around and give it a swipe on your sleeve.

The cook, Chaco, played by Guy Wilkerson: Charles Haas' *Wild Heritage* (Universal, 1958).

741

Rusty: You know, the worst thing about a trail drive is the beans. Baked one day, fried the next …they always come out burnt.

Rusty played by Casey Tibbs: Charles Haas' *Wild Heritage* (Universal, 1958).

Cowboys

See also Cooks; Good Guys; Pioneers, Settlers and Sodbusters

742

George: Now wait a minute, Melody. You ain't got to be no dumber than necessary.

Melody: That would make me somebody, wouldn't it?

George Fury played by William Demarest and Melody Jones played by Gary Cooper in Stuart Heisler's *Along Came Jones* (RKO, 1945).

743

Goofy: I'd catch those crooks in no time at all.

Casoose: Listen, Goofy, you couldn't even catch your breath!

Goofy played by Snub Pollard and Casoose played by Raymond Hatton: Christy Cabanne's *Back Trail* (Monogram, 1948).

744

July: Yeah, I believe a fella would believe most anything if all he ever saw was the ass end of a cow.

July played by Richard Roundtree: Clyde Ware's *Bad Jim* (RCA/Columbia Home Video, 1990).

745

Cable: If sugar were two cents a barrel, I couldn't afford a pinch of salt and egg to put on it.

Cable Hogue played by Jason Robards, Jr.: Sam Peckinpah's *The Ballad of Cable Hogue* (Warner Bros., 1970).

746

Leech: I don't know that I would wear that hat too long around here, Mr. McKay.

McKay: Oh, why not?

Leech: Oh, one of these wild cowboys might take it into his head to shoot it off ya.

Steve Leech played by Charlton Heston and Jim McKay played by Gregory Peck: William Wyler's *The Big Country* (United Artists, 1958).

747

Morgan: What's the matter?

Jagger: I've been eating so much rabbit, when I sleep at night, I keep dreaming about carrots.

Chad Morgan played by Alan Ladd and Joe Jagger played by Edmond O'Brien: Gordon Douglas' *The Big Land* (Warner Bros., 1957).

748

Jones: I've been around a lot of cowhands one way or another. A cowboy dresses from the top down. The first thing on is his hat. And he undresses from his bottom up. Last thing off …hat. Oh, and another thing: to be a cowpuncher, that don't mean you actually got to go around punching them, you know.

Miss Jones played by Candice Bergen: Richard Brooks' *Bite the Bullet* (Columbia, 1975).

749

Mister: God, what ain't I've tried. Pony Express rider, Overland Stage driver, lawman, gambler, riverman, rancher, rodeo hand, barman, spittoon man …old man. Never much to remember. Of course, there ain't much to forget either. Nobody's got much use for an old man. I can't blame 'em much. That's why I'm going to win me this here newspaper race. When I cross that finish line, I get to be a big man. Top man. A man to remember.

Mister played by Ben Johnson: Richard Brooks' *Bite the Bullet* (Columbia, 1975).

750

Lance: There was something familiar about that kick in the pants I took.

Charles: You must be awfully sensitive to be able to tell one from another.

Lance Hardeen played by Jeffrey Lynn and Charles E. Boles played by Dan Duryea: George Sherman's *Black Bart* (Universal, 1948).

751

Whitaker: If brains were leather, Philo Sandine couldn't saddle a bug.

Cy Whitaker played by Richard Hamilton and Philo Sandine played by Stuart Margolin: Stuart Margolin's *Bret Maverick: The Lazy Ace* (TVW, 1981).

752

Sundance: You just keep thinking, Butch. That's what you're good at.

Butch: Boy, I got vision and the rest of the world wears bifocals.

The Sundance Kid played by Robert Redford and Butch Cassidy played by Paul Newman: George Roy Hill's *Butch Cassidy and the Sundance Kid* (20th Century–Fox, 1969).

753

Bob: Listen, Steve, I've been wanting to talk to you about the crew.

Steve: Well, what about 'em?

Bob: Why didn't you tell me they're all a bunch of gunslingers and outlaws?

Steve: I didn't think it made any difference to you. It doesn't to me as long as they do their job. How did you find out anyway?

The last rail has been laid and the last spike has been driven. And as General Greenville M. Dodge (Francis McDonald) put it, "And so this great nation is united with a wedding ring of iron," in Cecil B. DeMille's epic story of the *Union Pacific* (Paramount, 1939).

Bob: They didn't make any secret of it. I heard them talking about it.

Steve: Oh?

Bob: Listen, I don't trust them. Suppose you got into some kind of trouble …Indians or rustlers?

Steve: If anything like that happened, there is nobody I'd rather have on my side than Lynch and his men. Sure, they are gunmen, but that's the kind of men you need in emergencies.

Bob: If they stick by you.

Steve: They'll stick. They're good men. Now you just forget about the fact that they might once have been outlaws. They're all right.

Bob Andrews played by Peter Graves and Steve Patrick played by George Montgomery: Harmon Jones' *Canyon River* (Allied Artists, 1956). (See *The Longhorn* this section.)

754

Steve: I've done enough walking to last me a long time. I'm sure glad a cowboy can do most of his work sitting down.

Steve Patrick played by George Montgomery: Harmon Jones' *Canyon River* (Allied Artists, 1956).

755

Harley: I remember when I was about twelve years old. My daddy asked me, he says: "What do you want to be when you grow up, Little Harley?" And like a damn fool I said a cowboy. I've been making wrong moves ever since.

Harley Sullivan played by Henry Fonda: Gene Kelly's *The Cheyenne Social Club* (NGP, 1970).

756

John: How much money do you want, Harley?

Harley: Fifteen or twenty dollars ought to do me.

John: What do you need it for?

Harley: Things.

John: Well, what kind of things?

Harley: Just, just things. You know, like a drink of whiskey if I wanted it, or a new shirt or something.

John: You already have two shirts. You don't wear but one of them at a time unless it's winter.

Harley: There you go thinking like a Republican again.

John: Well, you don't bring up politics while you're borrowing money, Harley. It ain't seemly!

John O'Hanlan played by James Stewart and Harley Sullivan played by Henry Fonda: Gene Kelly's *The Cheyenne Social Club* (NGP, 1970).

757

John: When you're out on the range with nobody to talk to most of the time but your horse, you do a lot of dreaming. And I dreamed of being a man of property. But you know ...you know, Mr. Willowby, and I didn't realize it then, but I've always been a man of property. I have my horse, I have my blanket, and I have the whole west to ride in. How could a man own more than that? No, Mr. Willowby, I'm a cowboy. Always have been ...I know now I always will be.

John O'Hanlan played by James Stewart and Jedediah W. Willowby played by Dabbs Greer: Gene Kelly's *The Cheyenne Social Club* (NGP, 1970).

758

Jenny: When I was young, I had all sorts of dreams. There's something awful sad about an old dream.

John: Yeah, I know. When I was a boy down in the panhandle, that was before I slipped my hobbles, I was a real star-gazer. I tell you, Jenny, I dreamed and I planned big things. And then I started drifting ...and I've been drifting ever since.

Jenny played by Shirley Jones and John O'Hanlan played by James Stewart: Gene Kelly's *The Cheyenne Social Club* (NGP, 1970).

759

Curly: A cowboy leads a different kind of life ...when there were cowboys. We're a dyin' breed. It still means something to me though.

Curly played by Jack Palance: Ron Underwood's *City Slickers* (Columbia, 1991).

760

Clay: Un-by-God-believable! A bunch of tenderfeet bringing in the herd like that. Two weeks ago you boys was as worthless as hen shit on a pump handle. And look at ya now!

Clay Stone played by Noble Willingham: Ron Underwood's *City Slickers* (Columbia, 1991).

761

Frank: You want to go to work, do you?
Dobie: Work?
Frank: Making an honest living?
Dobie: Oh, no. I don't think I could do that. I could cowboy some.
Frank: Well, what will that get you? You work yourself to death for somebody and likely they will have to take up a collection to bury you.

Frank played by Skip Homeier and Dobie played by Richard Rust: Budd Boetticher's *Comanche Station* (Columbia, 1960).

762

McCloud: Well, what are you up to, Conagher? Drifting again?
Conagher: I got tumbleweed fever.
McCloud: You too? Half of the cowboys in the country are chasing tumbleweed.

Charlie McCloud played by Barry Corbin and Conn Conagher played by Sam Elliott: Reynaldo Villalobos' *Conagher* (Turner Pictures, 1991).

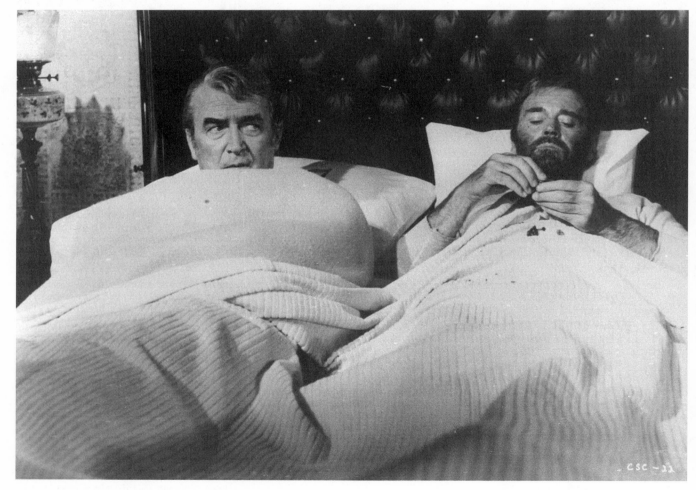

John O'Hanlan (James Stewart) inherits a brothel and brings along his talkative sidekick, Harley Sullivan (Henry Fonda) in *The Cheyenne Social Club* (National General Pictures, 1970).

763

Laban: Who gave you the black eye?

Conagher: No one gave it to me, son. I fought for it.

Laban Teele played by Cody Braun and Conn Conagher played by Sam Elliott: Reynaldo Villalobos' *Conagher* (Turner Pictures, 1991).

764

Reece: Well, what makes you think you'd like to go trail herding?

Harris: Well, ah, all my life I've been dreaming about going into the cattle business. Getting out on the trail and …and I hate Chicago. I'd like to live in the open. You know what I mean?

Reece: Oh yeah, I know what you mean. You mean lying out there under the stars, listening to the boys singing around the campfire. And your faithful old horse standing there grazing at the grass by your side. You do much riding?

Harris: Me? Well I bet I could ride all day and all night.

Reece: Oh, is that a fact? You know, I bet you like horses.

Harris: Yes sir, I sure do.

Reece: Yeah, I thought so. Well, you're an idiot! You're a dreaming idiot, and that's the worst kind. You know what the trail is really like? Dust storms all day, cloud bursts all night. A man has got to be a fool to want that kind of life.

Tom Reece played by Glenn Ford and Frank Harris played by Jack Lemmon: Delmer Daves' *Cowboy* (Columbia, 1958).

765

Slim: Tell the boys about the time you ate them Indians. Huh? Come on!

Joe: Ah, I only ate but one injun in my whole life. And even then it was just a haunch.

[*a little later*]

Curtis: Hey, old Joe would be rather fighting Indians all the time, wouldn't you Joe? Look at him, boss. It makes him hungry just thinking about it.

Joe: Ah, cut it out, will you Curtis? I was near starving to death. In fact, I didn't even know that injun. Anyway, I threw away everything except for one haunch.

Curtis: Which haunch did you keep, Joe?

Joe: Well, the left one of course! The right one is the working haunch. They're always tough.

Slim Barrett played by Buzz Henry, Joe Capper played by King Donovan, and Paul Curtis played by Richard Jaeckel: Delmer Daves' *Cowboy* (Columbia, 1958).

766

Skeeter: Well, cut my legs off and call me Shorty!

Skeeter played by Fuzzy Knight: Ray McCarey's *The Cowboy and the Blonde* (20th Century–Fox, 1941).

767

Ben: I want to go with you, Mr. Culpepper. I ride real good and I can do a lot of things. I mean, I'll work at almost anything, Mr. Culpepper. I really want to go.

Frank: Why?

Ben: Because I want to be a cowboy …more than anything, Mr. Culpepper.

Frank: Well, that's ambition, boy.

Ben Mockridge played by Gary Grimes and Frank Culpepper played by Billy Green Bush: Dick Richards' *The Culpepper Cattle Company* (20th Century–Fox, 1972).

768

Cook: You really got the itch, ain't ya?

Ben: Well, yeah, I do. I guess all I want to do is punch cows and ride and, well, just cowboying. There's nothing better than that. That's all I want.

Cook: Kid, cowboying is something you do when you can't do nothing else.

The Cook played by Raymond Guth and Ben Mockridge played by Gary Grimes: Dick Richards' *The Culpepper Cattle Company* (20th Century–Fox, 1972).

769

Frank: You just like to travel?

Luke: The best part is getting into town or getting out of town. In between is lousy.

Frank Culpepper played by Billy Green Bush and Luke played by Luke Askew: Dick Richards' *The Culpepper Cattle Company* (20th Century–Fox, 1972).

770

Bodeen: You know, Bullock, I believe you're dumber than you think I think you are.

Bodeen/Tom Hatcher played by Keith Coulouris and Bullock played by Tobin Bell: Alan J. Levi's *Dead Man's Revenge* (MCA/Universal Home Video, 1994).

771

Bill: I still wish I had my harmonica. It's dreary out here without no tunes.

Bill was uncredited: Yves Simoneau's *Dead Man's Walk* (Cabin Fever Entertainment, 1996).

772

Call: Well, so far we've been a disgrace in every encounter.

McCrae: Well, we ain't dead. We still got time to learn.

Woodrow F. Call played by Jonny Lee Miller and Augustus McCrae played by David Arquette: Yves Simoneau's *Dead Man's Walk* (Cabin Fever Entertainment, 1996).

773

Kansas: Do you mean to insinuate that I'm dumb?

John: No. Dumber!

Kansas Charlie played by Eddy Chandler and John Scott played by John Wayne: Cullen Lewis' (Lew Collins) *The Desert Trail* (Monogram/Lone Star, 1935).

774

Nora: Look …ah …I'm sorry.

Duell: No, I am a tramp! What can I say?

Nora: Well, you know, one person's tramp is another person's free spirit.

Nora Malloy played by Lise Cutter and Duell McCall played by Alex McArthur: Virgil W. Vogel's *Desperado* (TVW, 1987).

775

Nitro: You ought to knock before you come in here, Countess. Suppose I was taking a bath or something?

Countess: If I ever hear of you taking a bath, I'll start knocking.

Nitro Rankin played by Guinn "Big Boy" Williams and Countess Maletta played by Claire Trevor: Charles Vidor's *The Desperadoes* (Columbia, 1943).

776

Countess: Nitro, did you ever want to live your life over again?

Nitro: Me? No, I couldn't stand the excitement twice in a row.

Countess Maletta played by Claire Trevor and Nitro Rankin played by Guinn "Big Boy" Williams: Charles Vidor's *The Desperadoes* (Columbia, 1943).

777

Clerk: This jacket is made of genuine India rubber. It distracts the rain completely. Wearing one of these is like having a roof over your head.

Sarah: That's fine for folks too stupid to get out of the rain.

The Dry Goods Clerk played by Peter Gregory and Sarah O'Rourke played by Linda Fiorentino: P.J. Pesce's *The Desperate Trail* (Turner Home Entertainment, 1995).

778

Clyde: If your brain would stink, it wouldn't even smell.

Clyde played by Michael Huddleston: P.J. Pesce's *The Desperate Trail* (Turner Home Entertainment, 1995).

779

Dooley: You don't like to talk much, do you?

Cowboy: Nope.

Dooley: Is it me?

Cowboy: It might get to be.

Dooley: And when you're alone, do you ever talk to yourself?

Cowboy: Yep, and I have the good sense to know when to shut up.

Dooley: Well, what do you talk about?

Cowboy: No one else finds me this fascinating. Why you?

Dooley: Well, it ain't that you're so fascinating. It's just that you're the only one here.

Dooley played by William Forsythe and the Cowboy played by Emilio Estevez: Gene Quintano's *Dollar for the Dead* (TVW, 1998).

780

Erica: Do you need spectacles?

Sam: Only for lookin' at distances. But don't tell anyone! Have you ever seen a four-eyed cowboy?

Erica played by Amy Locane and Sam Benson played by Rick Schroder: Ken Jubenvill's *Ebenezer* (TVW, 1997).

781

Cody: It's guts and love and glory
One mortal's chance at fame
His legacy is rodeo
And cowboy is his name.

Cody Lambert (reciting a verse from "Legacy of the Rodeo Man" by Baxter Black) played by Red Mitchell: John G. Avildsen's *8 Seconds* (New Line Cinema, 1994).

782

Tuff: You can't be a cowboy and a nice guy, Lane. It just don't work like that. We got an image to uphold: drinkin', lovin', fightin', cowboyin'.

Tuff Hedeman played by Stephen Baldwin and Lane Frost played by Luke Perry: John G. Avildsen's *8 Seconds* (New Line Cinema, 1994).

783

Wendell: Mama, don't let your babies grow up to be cowboys.

Wendell played by Willie Nelson: Sidney Pollack's *The Electric Horseman* (Columbia/Universal, 1979).

784

Vance: I've always worked my own leather. I'll work it now.

Vance Jeffords played by Barbara Stanwyck: Anthony Mann's *The Furies* (Paramount, 1950).

785

Denise: Where are you from, Billy?

Billy: Wherever this horse and a game of cards takes me.

Denise played by Lenora May and Billy played by Bruce Boxleitner: Dick Lowry's *The Gambler, Part III — The Legend Continues* (TVW, 1987).

786

Eve: How much money you got, Hewey?

Hewey: Well, I reckon if it takes a hundred dollars to get to heaven, I might make it to Fort Worth.

Eve Calloway played by Frances McDormand and Hewey Calloway played by Tommy Lee Jones who also directed *The Good Old Boys* (Turner Pictures, 1995).

787

Hewey: I guess a dollar bill looks as big as a saddle blanket and scarce as rain to you.

Hewey Calloway played by Tommy Lee Jones who also directed *The Good Old Boys* (Turner Pictures, 1995).

788

Eve: You're just like every cowboy I ever saw in my life. If I had a dozen rocking chairs in the room, they'd still squat on the floor.

Eve Calloway played by Frances McDormand: Tommy Lee Jones' *The Good Old Boys* (Turner Pictures, 1995).

789

Eve: The next time I get mad, you just go on out of my sight awhile and give me a little time. You don't have to stay gone two years.

Hewey: I'll try not to make you mad at all. I'll try to keep my mouth shut.

Eve: I wouldn't ask that much of nature.

Eve Calloway played by Frances McDormand and Hewey Calloway played by Tommy Lee Jones who also directed *The Good Old Boys* (Turner Pictures, 1995).

790

Cora: The kind of cowboys we got around here these days, a woman would be better off with a good dog and a hot-water bottle.

Cora Lawdermilk played by Karen Jones: Tommy Lee Jones' *The Good Old Boys* (Turner Pictures, 1995).

791

Loving: Hey, I had a cousin with a name like that one time. "Never-Take-a-Chance" Loving they called him. He got shot though.

Hade: Oh, how is that, Loving?

Loving: Taking a chance. First one he ever took.

Loving played by Chill Wills and Hade Keough played by Dean Stockwell: Abner Biberman's *Gun for a Coward* (Universal, 1957).

792

Jordan: Do you sleep on an ant hill or something?

Old Harry: Huh?

Jordan: Every time I see you, you're scratching yourself.

Old Harry: Yeah, that's right. I was wondering about that, too. I think it's fleas! Yeah, I think I got fleas!

Jordan Yarnell played by David McIlwraith and Old Harry played by Walter Marsh: Larry Ferguson's *Gunfighter's Moon* (Rysher Entertainment/Cabin Fever, 1995).

793

Chad: You shoot almost as good as you talk!

Sheriff Chad Lucas played by Audie Murphy: Earl Bellamy's *Gunpoint* (Universal, 1966).

794

Hewitt: You know, I don't think I'll ever get used to you without gunsmoke in your face.

Lieutenant Frank Hewitt played by Audie Murphy: George Marshall's *The Guns of Fort Petticoat* (Columbia, 1957).

795

Harry: Home is just a place you start from.

Harry Collings played by Peter Fonda who also directed *The Hired Hand* (Universal, 1971).

796

Homer: What can I do with a bunch of rotten oil wells? I can't ride out every day and prowl amongst 'em like I can my cattle. I can't breed 'em or tend 'em or rope 'em or chase 'em or nothing. I can't feel a smidgen of pride in 'em …because they ain't none of my doing.

Homer Bannon played by Melvyn Douglas: Martin Ritt's *Hud* (Paramount, 1963).

797

Kentucky: Keep your shirt on, Cactus, and your mouth closed!

Kentucky played by Ken Maynard and Cactus played by George "Gabby" Hayes: David Howard's *In Old Santa Fe* (Mascot, 1934).

798

Ruth: There never was a horse that couldn't be rode; there never was a cowboy that couldn't be thrown.

Junior: Famous old saying all right.

Ruth Bonner played by Mary Murphy and Junior Bonner played by Steve McQueen: Sam Peckinpah's *Junior Bonner* (CIN, 1972).

799

Missy: What makes you think I'd be disappointed [in cowboys]?

O'Malley: Well, you see cowboys aren't very bright. They're always broke, and generally they're drunk.

Missy Breckenridge played by Carol Lynley and Brendan O'Malley played by Kirk Douglas: Robert Aldrich's *The Last Sunset* (Universal, 1961).

800

Maddox: On the way back, they hit a town called Bannock. They drank their fill, had their women, shot up the town. All just cowboy fun. They killed an old man.

Marshal Jared Maddox played by Burt Lancaster: Michael Winner's *Lawman* (United Artists, 1971).

801

Jerri: Jack, I'm going to tell you something. The world that you and Paul live in doesn't exist. Maybe it never did …out there in the real world. And it's got real borders and real fences. Real laws and

Junior (Steve McQueen) is a rodeo cowboy in a changing west in Sam Peckinpah's *Junior Bonner* (Cinema Releasing Corp., 1972).

real trouble. And either you go by the rules or you lose. You lose everything.
Jack: You can always keep something.

Jerri Bondi played by Gena Rowlands and Jack Burns played by Kirk Douglas: David Miller's *Lonely Are the Brave* (Universal, 1962).

802

Jacob: I'll break you like I'd break any other wild horse. I'll break you or kill you! If you want to run away, I can't stop you. But if you stay here, I'll make a man of you.

Jacob Wade played by Jack Palance: Henry Levin's *The Lonely Man* (Paramount, 1957).

803

Newt: What's the matter with that knife, Bol? It won't hold an edge.
Bol: It is like a wife. Every night you better stroke it.
Gus: If that's the case, your wife over there in Mexico must be getting pretty rusty by now. She don't get sharpened more than, what, twice a year, does she Bol?
Bol: She is old, like you.
Gus: Well, the older the violin, the sweeter the music. You ought to bring her up here to meet me sometime.
Bol: No, I know you. You will try to corrupt her.
Gus: Well then, how about one of your daughters? Hell, you got, what, nine of 'em, ain't ya?

Newt Dobbs played by Ricky Schroder, Bolivar played by Leon Singer, and Gus McCrae played by Robert Duvall: Simon Wincer's *Lonesome Dove* (TVW, 1989).

804

Gus: You ought not be so hard on that boy, Woodrow. Hell, let him sit awhile. The only chance he got at an education is listening to me talk.
Call: What kind of education is that?
Gus: Do you think he'd learn more shoveling horse poop for you?
Call: I've shoveled my share and it ain't hurt me none!

Gus McCrae played by Robert Duvall and Captain Woodrow F. Call played by Tommy Lee Jones: Simon Wincer's *Lonesome Dove* (TVW, 1989).

805

Call: That was the dangedest thing to do, bringing that old sign along. You'll have us the laughing stock of this whole country with that, "We Don't Rent Pigs."
Gus: Well, we don't rent pigs. And I figure it's better to say it right up front.

Bad guy Liberty Valance (Lee Marvin) and good guy Tom Doniphon (John Wayne) are ready to trade lead over who should pick up a steak on the floor when Ransom Stoddard (James Stewart) interrupts: "What's the matter, is everybody in this country kill crazy?" in John Ford's *The Man Who Shot Liberty Valance* (Paramount, 1962).

Because a man that does like to rent pigs is …he's hard to stop.

Call: And if that ain't bad enough, you got all them Greek words on there too.

Gus: I told you, Woodrow, a long time ago. It ain't Greek, it's Latin.

Call: Well, what does it say in Latin?

Gus: Well, it's a motto. It just says itself: Uva Uvam Vivendo Varia Fit.

Call: You don't have no idea what it says. You found that [phrase] in some old book or something. For all you know, it invites people to rob us.

Gus: Well, the first man that comes along that can read Latin is welcome to rob us as far as I'm concerned. I'd like the chance to shoot at an educated man once in my life.

Captain Woodrow F. Call played by Tommy Lee Jones and Gus McCrae played by Robert Duvall: Simon Wincer's *Lonesome Dove* (TVW, 1989).

806

Andy: Jim, I've been wanting to talk to you about the crew.

Jim: What about 'em?

Andy: Why didn't you tell me they were a bunch of gunslingers and outlaws?

Jim: I didn't think it would make any difference to you. It doesn't to me as long as they do their work. How did you find out anyhow?

Andy: They don't make any secret of it. I heard them talking. Listen, Jim, I don't trust them. Suppose you get in some kind of trouble …with injuns or outlaws or something like that?

Jim: Well, if anything like that happens, there is nobody I'd rather have on my side than Purdy and his men. Sure, they are outlaws. But you take it from me, kid, those are the kind of men you need in an emergency.

Andy: Yeah, I know Jim, if they stick by you.

Jim: Well, they'll stick. They're real men. Now you just forget that they were once outlaws. They're not anymore. They're good cowboys.

Andy played by Myron Healey, Jim Kirk played by Wild Bill Elliott, and Purdy played by Lane Bradford: Lewis Collins' *The Longhorn* (Warner Bros., 1951). (See *Canyon River* this section.)

807

Lockhart: We came from Laramie.

Ms. Waggoman: Oh, is that your home?

Lockhart: No ma'am. No, I can't rightly say any place is my home.

Ms. Waggoman: But everybody should have some place to remember and feel like they belong to.

Lockhart: Well, I …I always feel like I belong where I am.

Will Lockhart played by James Stewart and Bar-

bara Waggoman played by Cathy O'Donnell: Anthony Mann's *The Man from Laramie* (Columbia, 1955).

808

Frog: Gene, what's a hydraulic?

Gene: Don't you know? It's a shovel with a handle on both ends.

Frog Millhouse played by Smiley Burnette and Gene played by Gene Autry: Joseph Kane's *Man from Music Mountain* (Republic, 1938).

809

Liberty Valance: I live where I hang my hat.

Liberty Valance played by Lee Marvin: John Ford's *The Man Who Shot Liberty Valance* (Paramount, 1962).

810

Jeff: You still got your saddle.

Dempsey: Never sell that, kid. Sitting in another man's leather is like wearing another man's boots. Never sell your saddle!

Jeff Jimson played by William Campbell and Dempsey Rae played by Kirk Douglas: King Vidor's *Man Without a Star* (Universal, 1955).

811

Jeff: Hey Demps, which way we heading?

Dempsey: Straight north.

Jeff: How did you know?

Dempsey: Just pick a star and follow it. Of course you got to be sure it's the right one.

Jeff: Oh, I guess I'll never learn to pick the right one.

Dempsey: Yes you will. Everybody's got a star to follow.

Jeff: Which one is yours?

Dempsey: I never got around to picking one for myself. I guess I'm sort of like the cattle …drifting north with the grass.

Jeff Jimson played by William Campbell and Dempsey Rae played by Kirk Douglas: King Vidor's *Man Without a Star* (Universal, 1955).

812

Angel: Have you always been gutless?

Bret: Yeah, I think so. Well, for as long as I can remember at any rate. You know, my old pappy always used to say: "He who fights and runs away, can run away another day."

Angel played by Alfred Molina and Bret Maverick played by Mel Gibson: Richard Donner's *Maverick* (Warner Bros., 1994).

813

Hoyce: Clyde, you got nothin' but steer manure for brains!

Hoyce Guthrie played by Richard Crenna and Clyde Guthrie played by Justin Deas: William A. Graham's *Montana* (TVW, 1990).

814

Monte: Martine, was your mother and daddy married?

Martine: Probably. I really don't know.

Monte: How come we never got married?

Martine: You never asked me.

Monte: I never thought of it. Cowboys don't get married …unless they stopped being cowboys.

Martine Bernard played by Jeanne Moreau and Monte Walsh played by Lee Marvin: William A. Fraker's *Monte Walsh* (NGP, 1970).

815

Chet: Mary and I are gonna get married.

Monte: How's that gonna work out?

Chet: What do you mean?

Monte: You being a cowboy.

Chet: Well, I ain't gonna be much longer.

Monte: What are you gonna be?

Chet: Hardware man.

Monte: Oh, you mean you're gonna live in town?

Chet: Look, Monte, do you have any idea how many cowhands there were in this country ten, fifteen years ago? Well, there's a hell of lot fewer now. And pretty soon, there won't be hardly any. The way things are going, it's gonna get tougher.

Monte: Oh come on, Chet! Things aren't that bad!

Chet: Yes they are, Monte.

Monte: You ain't suggesting that I be some hardware man, too, are you?

Chet: Hell no. But nobody gets to be a cowboy forever.

Chet Rollins played by Jack Palance and Monte Walsh played by Lee Marvin: William A. Fraker's *Monte Walsh* (NGP, 1970).

816

Shorty: I wish I knew something besides cowboying.

Shorty Austin played by Mitch Ryan: William A. Fraker's *Monte Walsh* (NGP, 1970).

817

Shorty: Stop babbling about something that ain't anymore. That kind of life you're talking about is dead! The snow buried it last winter.

Monte: It ain't dead! As long as there's one cowboy taking care of one cow, it ain't dead!

Shorty Austin played by Mitch Ryan and Monte Walsh played by Lee Marvin: William A. Fraker's *Monte Walsh* (NGP, 1970).

818

Jesse: Do you know the worst thing about gettin' old?

H.D.: No, sir.

Jesse: Gettin' old.

Jesse Dalton played by Ben Johnson and H.D. Dalton played by Scott Glenn: Stuart Rosenberg's *My*

Heroes Have Always Been Cowboys (Samuel Goldwyn Company, 1991).

819

Jesse: He's gonna ride that damn bull, that's what he's gonna do.

Jud: He hurt his leg. I think it's broke.

Jesse: Most people out there didn't spend their money to watch you walk. They come here to watch you ride that bull. And that's what you're gonna do.

Jesse Dalton played by Ben Johnson and Jud Meadows played by Balthazar Getty: Stuart Rosenberg's *My Heroes Have Always Been Cowboys* (Samuel Goldwyn Company, 1991).

820

Crandall: Say, are you as dumb as you look?

Happy: Oh, no, no! Dumber!

Matt Crandall played by Stanley Blystone and Happy played by Syd Saylor: Harry Fraser's *Navajo Kid* (Producer's Releasing Corp., 1945).

821

Nina: But I don't want to go to school. I want to be a cowboy like you.

Chris: Oh, girls can't be cowboys.

Nina: I can too! I can ride as well as you can.

Chris: But you still can't be a cowboy.

Nina Morrell played by Sarah Jane Rickey and Chris Morrell played by John Wayne: Harry Fraser's *'Neath the Arizona Skies* (Lone Star/Monogram, 1934).

822

April: Oh, Dusty, you're an angel in leather!

Dusty: I'd look funny with leather wings.

April Logan played by Madeleine Carroll and Dusty Rivers played by Gary Cooper: Cecil B. DeMille's *North West Mounted Police* (Paramount, 1940).

823

Calhoun: If you keep looking for trouble as carefully as you have tonight, you're liable to find it.

Captain Webb Calhoun played by Rod Cameron: Joseph Kane's *Oh! Susanna* (Republic, 1951).

824

Will: I don't know what to call you. You ain't pretty enough for a skunk, ain't skinny enough for a snake, too low to be a man, too big to be a mouse. I reckon you're a rat!

Ali: Well, that's logical.

Will Parker played by Gene Nelson and Ali Hakim played by Eddie Albert: Fred Zinnemann's *Oklahoma!* (Magna, 1955).

825

Cotton: We could use some supplies. I'm getting tired of cowboy coffee.

Cotton played by Shaun Cassidy: Burt Kennedy's *Once Upon a Texas Train* (TVW, 1988).

826

Rio: My home is …oh, just any place I throw my saddle down, I guess.

Rio played by Marlon Brando: Marlon Brando's *One-Eyed Jacks* (Paramount, 1961).

827

Clint: Boys, I'll tell ya. I'm getting older. But I still got a few days and nights left if I keep up these drives. But them nights are beginning to bother me. A man's awful alone at night.

Clint Priest played by James Whitmore: Roy Rowland's *The Outriders* (MGM, 1950).

828

Stony: Hey, Lullaby, wake up! It's time to go to sleep!

Stony Brooke played by John Wayne and Lullaby Joslin played by Max Terhune: George Sherman's *Overland Stage Raiders* (Republic, 1938).

829

Jim: Listen, once there was this old man.

Leonard: Yeah?

Jim: Well, that's not the end of the story. There was this old man and he had an old plow, and an old mule, and an old dried-up prune-of-a-wife, and an old shack. And one day that mule just up and died on him. And do you know what he said, Leonard? He said, "Them that has must lose."

Jim Kane played by Paul Newman and Leonard played by Lee Marvin: Stuart Rosenberg's *Pocket Money* (NGP, 1972).

830

Trevor: Puddin, what the devil am I?

Puddin: Well, Mr. Kingman, I figure you already know the answer to that.

Trevor: Huh? What's that?

Puddin: Well, sir, you're just a Texas cowboy.

Trevor Kingman played by Henry Wilcoxon and Puddin played by James Almanzar: Robert Totten's *Pony Express Rider* (Doty-Dayton, 1976).

831

Sundown: Life ain't such a sweet proposition anyway. Just a matter of three squares a day, forty winks, and a lot of powdersmoke.

Sundown Saunders played by Tom Tyler: Wallace Fox's *Powdersmoke Range* (RKO, 1935).

832

Cora: Curt, you're a slow boat to China!

Cora Brown played by Elizabeth Ashley and Curt played by Harry Dean Stanton: Frank Perry's *Rancho Deluxe* (United Artists, 1975).

833

Smith: It's bad luck to sing around dynamite, Mac.

Mr. Smith played by Don S. Davis and Mac played by Jerry O'Connell: *The Ranger, the Cook and a Hole in the Sky* (Hallmark Home Entertainment, 1995).

834

Mac: Red, let me ask you: Have you ever once in your life had one, single, solitary, original thought that didn't bounce off from somewhere else? I mean, have you ever sat down and considered all the available information, weighted it all in your mind, sifted all the possibilities, discarded what you couldn't prove, sorted out what made sense, and came to your own personal, original, Red McBride, opinion?

Red: Why would I go to all that trouble?

Mac played by Jerry O'Connell and Red played by Michael Tayles: John Kent Harrison's *The Ranger, the Cook and a Hole in the Sky* (Hallmark Home Entertainment, 1995).

835

Martha: How dare you hit that man!

Sam: Well, he was going to shoot me!

Martha: Now really, Mr. Burnett. You have a predisposition to violence of which I heartily disapprove.

Sam: Yes, ma'am.

Martha Price played by Maureen O'Hara and Sam Burnett played by James Stewart: Andrew V. McLaglen's *The Rare Breed* (Universal, 1966).

836

Blaine: Drifting is not so bad. A man sees a lot of country.

Kate: Not anything that he can call his own.

Blaine: Why own something if you don't need it?

Stan Blaine played by Alex Nicol and Kate Maxwell played by Maureen O'Hara: Lee Sholem's *The Redhead from Wyoming* (Universal, 1953).

837

McCall: Don't!

Pickett: What?

McCall: Don't be playing that. If there's one thing I can't put up with, it's harmonica music.

Duell McCall played by Alex McArthur and Nathaniel Pickett played by Victor Love: E.W. Swackhamer's *The Return of Desperado* (TVW, 1988).

838

Jasper: Hell, Lippy can't read neither!

Lippy: People who know where they're going don't need a sign to tell them where they got.

Jasper Fant played by Barry Tubb and Lippy played by William Sanderson: Mike Robe's *Return to Lonesome Dove* (TVW, 1993).

839

Gideon: Nothing against your brother, Isom, but I don't want to get caught down wind of him until he gets to a bathhouse.

Gideon Walker played by William Peterson and Isom Pickett played by Louis Gossett, Jr.: Mike Robe's *Return to Lonesome Dove* (TVW, 1993).

840

Steve: If my sleeping bothers you, don't you bother to let me know.

Steve Judd played by Joel McCrea: Sam Peckinpah's *Ride the High Country* (MGM, 1962).

841

Gil: A dandy pair of boots you got here.

Steve: Juan Fernandez made those boots for me in San Antone ...special order. I had a hell of a time getting him to put that hole in there [sole]. A fine craftsman, Juan, but he never understood the principle of ventilation.

Gil Westrum played by Randolph Scott and Steve Judd played by Joel McCrea: Sam Peckinpah's *Ride the High Country* (MGM, 1962).

842

Dude: I'm going to take a bath! I said I would!

Stumpy: Well, Dude, I never had no idea you wouldn't. I was just wondering when.

Dude played by Dean Martin and Stumpy played by Walter Brennan: Howard Hawks' *Rio Bravo* (Warner Bros., 1959).

843

[*two cowboys sharing the same jail cell*]

Guffy: The monotony of this is getting on my nerves.

Gabby: Well, it won't be long now, Guffy. They're executing me this afternoon.

Guffy: But not until five o'clock!

Guffy played by Roscoe Ates and Gabby Hornaday played by George "Gabby" Hayes: Joseph Kane's *Robin Hood of the Pecos* (Republic, 1941).

844

Rooster: Oh, just a minute, sister. I'll put my lariat around your bed. And them night crawlers and snakes will respect it.

Eula: Is that really true? That they won't crawl over a rope?

Rooster: Well, I ain't going to say it's true. And I ain't going to say it ain't. But it's comforting.

Rooster Cogburn played by John Wayne and Eula

Two aging former lawmen, Gil Westrum (Randolph Scott) and Steve Judd (Joel McCrea), team up to transport a shipment of gold. Gil initially takes "the low road" and intends to steal the gold. But circumstances along the journey force both men to reexamine their values and *Ride the High Country* (MGM, 1962). A Sam Peckinpah classic.

Goodnight played by Katharine Hepburn: Stuart Millar's *Rooster Cogburn* (Universal, 1975).

845

Ben: Howdy, do you know what a bronc rider is?

Howdy: What?

Ben: He's a cowboy with his brains kicked out.

Ben Jones played by Glenn Ford and Howdy Lewis played by Henry Fonda: Burt Kennedy's *The Rounders* (MGM, 1965).

846

Rex: May I have my guitar, please? I don't suppose you know that my mother gave me this guitar. And I hold the copyright on that song you were singing?

Peter: No, I didn't.

Rex: This is my campsite! I live here. I'm the one who found the spot. I'm the one who put the rocks in the circle to make a fire!

Rex O'Herlihan played by Tom Berenger and Peter, the Town Drunk, played by G.W. Bailey:

Hugh Wilson's *Rustlers' Rhapsody* (Paramount, 1985).

847

Orrin: You know what my pa used to say?
Tom: What did he say?
Orrin: He used to say, the sorriest fellow in the outfit was always the first one to the water.
Tom: Your pa was right.

Orrin Sackett played by Tom Selleck and Tom Sunday played by Glenn Ford: Robert Totten's *The Sacketts* (TVW, 1979).

848

Orrin: You ain't changed none at all. You're still slower than wet gunpowder.

Orrin Sackett played by Tom Selleck: Robert Totten's *The Sacketts* (TVW, 1979).

849

Seven: And don't call me kid either! My name is Seven.

Flood: What?
Seven: Seven Ways from Sundown Jones.
Flood: Oh. Well, we all have a cross to bear.

Seven Jones played by Audie Murphy and Jim Flood played by Barry Sullivan: Harry Keller's *Seven Ways from Sundown* (Universal, 1960).

850

Siringo: Do you ever shut up?
Powell: Huh?
Siringo: You've been mouthing off ever since we left the agency. Don't you ever stop to draw breath?

Charlie Siringo played by Brad Johnson and Powell played by Chad Lowe: Kevin G. Cremin's *Siringo* (TVW, 1994).

851

Tom: Say, why don't you try gettin' up in the morning?
Frankie: Well, how do I know it's morning until I wake up?

Tom Ownes played by Tom Keene and Frankie

Breen played by David Durand in Lloyd Nosler's *Son of the Border* (RKO, 1933).

852

Parnell: Clint, you're so dumb that even when you get an idea you don't know it.

Parnell played by Robert B. Williams and Clint played by Robert Bray: Lew Landers' *Stagecoach Kid* (RKO, 1949).

853

Jug: You hit that fella from behind?
Latigo: Just as hard as I could!

Jud May played by Jack Elam and Latigo Smith played by James Garner: Burt Kennedy's *Support Your Local Gunfighter* (United Artists, 1971).

854

Martin: I saw you! I saw you strike that poor man!
Rocklin: Yes ma'am. Just as hard as I could.

Miss Martin played by Elizabeth Risdon and Rocklin played by John Wayne: Edwin L. Marin's *Tall in the Saddle* (RKO, 1944).

Cantankerous Dave (George "Gabby" Hayes) has had it with the female hag and nag (not pictured but in adjoining room). "What that old pelican needs is a good spankin'." Agreeing with Dave are Arly Harolday (Ella Raines), Rocklin (John Wayne), and Clara Cardell (Audrey Long) in *Tall in the Saddle* (RKO, 1944).

855

John: Just listen to that rain. Nothing could sound so beautiful.
Nunk: What did you say? Come again?
John: The rain, hear it! A symphony orchestra couldn't make sweeter music than that.
Nunk: What, what say?
John: I said the rain on the roof is lovely to hear!
Nunk: I can't hear a word you're saying on account of the ding-busted rain!

John Phillips played by John Wayne and Dr. Nunk Atterbury played by Spencer Charters: Bernard Vorhaus' *Three Faces West* (Republic, 1940).

856

Rod: Say, how is the old alma mater?
Wabi: Oh, it's kind of quiet now. You know, they haven't found any cows or goats in the dormitory since you left.
Rod: Don't tell me the place has deteriorated into a school of learning!

Rod Drew played by John Wayne and Wabi played by Noah Beery, Jr.: Robert Bradbury's *The Trail Beyond* (Lone Star/Monogram, 1934).

857

Mrs. Lowe: That's all you do, isn't it, Mr. Lane …drift.
Lane: You could say that.
Mrs. Lowe: It doesn't seem like much of a life.
Lane: It's not.
Mrs. Lowe: Then why do you do it?
Lane: It's what I'm good at.

Mrs. Lowe played by Ann-Margret and Lane played by John Wayne: Burt Kennedy's *The Train Robbers* (Warner Bros., 1973).

858

The Kid: Do you ever worry about me?
Dusty: Only when you're behind me.

The Kid played by Todd Jensen and Dusty Fog played by Christopher Atkins: David Lister's *Trigger Fast* (Vidmark, 1994).

859

Ned: Well, I sure do miss my bed.
Will: You said that last night.
Ned: No, last night I said I missed my wife. Tonight, I just miss my goddamn bed.

Ned Logan played by Morgan Freeman and William Bill Munny played by Clint Eastwood who also directed *Unforgiven* (Warner Bros., 1992).

860

Sandy: Hey, gosh, do I hear music? It sounds like music.
Travis: If I'm not loco, so do I.

Sandy: Do ya, do ya suppose it's Navajo?
Elder: I never heard of a Navajo playing a guitar.
Sandy: Come to think of it, neither have I.

Sandy Owens played by Harry Carey, Jr., Travis Blue played by Ben Johnson, and Elder Wiggs played by Ward Bond: John Ford's *Wagonmaster* (RKO, 1950).

861

Sandy: By golly, I bet it's gonna be hotter than …
Mormon: Mind your language!
Sandy: I wasn't cussing!
Mormon: You were gonna say hell!
Sandy: I was gonna say Haiti! But hell ain't cussing! It's geography, the name of a place. Like you might say Abilene or Salt Lake City.

Sandy Owens played by Harry Carey, Jr. and Jackson the Mormon played by Chuck Hayward: John Ford's *Wagonmaster* (RKO, 1950).

862

Desprit: Well, I'm dumber than you think I am, or you're either smarter than I think you are!

Desprit Dan played by George "Gabby" Hayes: Albert S. Rogell's *War of the Wildcats* (Republic, 1943).

863

Hank: Working around the stable like this for so long, I'm getting in a rut. You know, there are so many things to do around a stable, it's …I declare …if you just don't keep going every minute, your work piles up on ya.

Hank York played by Bob Burns: Frank Lloyd's *Wells Fargo* (Paramount, 1937).

864

Cole: If I had to wash dishes, I guess I would give up eating.
Jane-Ellen: What do you do about the dishes when you're home?
Cole: Home? You mean in a house?
Jane-Ellen: Well, you live in a house, don't you?
Cole: No. No, my house is all out there. All one room with a sky for a roof.
Jane-Ellen: Well …big place!
Cole: I got some space to rent.

Cole Hardin played by Gary Cooper and Jane-Ellen Mathews played by Doris Davenport: William Wyler's *The Westerner* (United Artists, 1940).

865

Jane-Ellen: Well, all places aren't just the same. Wouldn't you rather stay a little longer in some places?

Cole: No, they're all the same …beautiful when you leave them. It's …well …it's like the turtle …they carry their homes with them.

Jane-Ellen Mathews played by Doris Davenport and Cole Hardin played by Gary Cooper: William Wyler's *The Westerner* (United Artists, 1940).

866

Lefty: Boss, I never thought of that!
Judson: Nobody expected you to.

Lefty played by Guinn "Big Boy" Williams and Judson Holderness played by David Landau: Henry Hathaway's *When the West Was Young* (a.k.a. *Heritage of the Desert*; Paramount, 1932).

867

Bodine: You show me a young cowboy, or an old cowboy, or an in-between cowboy that's got more than a few dollars in his poke …and I'll show you a cowboy who stopped being a cowboy and started robbing banks.
Post: Well then, let's you and me rob us a bank.
Bodine: That's safer than getting married.

Ross Bodine played by William Holden and Frank Post played by Ryan O'Neal: Blake Edwards' *Wild Rovers* (MGM, 1971).

868

Bodine: If a man had any sense, he'd save his money and get into some other kind of work.
Townsman: Yeah, but where are you going to find a cowboy that's got any sense?

The Townsman was uncredited. Ross Bodine played by William Holden: Blake Edwards' *Wild Rovers* (MGM, 1971).

869

Will: You must need a hand.
Alex: I don't know, old Claude was a pretty good cowpuncher.
Foxy: A mighty good man all the way around.
Will: Well, sure, that's always the way, ain't it?
Alex: What's always the way?
Will: Let a man die and right away he's good old Claude. How was he …before he bucked out?

Will Penny played by Charlton Heston, Alex played by Ben Johnson, and Foxy played by Luke Askew: Tom Gries' *Will Penny* (Paramount, 1968).

870

Catherine: Mr. Penny, how often do you bathe?
Will Penny: What? What?
Catherine: I said, how often do you bathe?
Will Penny: Well, eight or nine times. It, it depends.

Catherine: On what?

Will Penny: Well, on the weather.

Catherine: Eight or nine a month.

Will Penny: Eight or nine times a month? A year!

Catherine: A year?

Will Penny: Well, sure. You have a real good one when you finish the shove up north ...like at the hotel in Alfred. And then one or two in the winter ...and hope you don't catch your death! And a couple in the spring, and then one more good one before you start the shove up again. The rest depends on what kind of water you hit on the drive. Well, what's wrong with that? It's as much as anybody!

Catherine Allen played by Joan Hackett and Will Penny played by Charlton Heston: Tom Gries' *Will Penny* (Paramount, 1968).

871

Vic: Glad to know you, Zeke!

Zeke: That makes it unanimous!

Vic Gordon played by George J. Lewis and Zeke Haydon played by Si Jenks: Spencer Bennet's and Wallace Grissell's *Zorro's Black Whip* (Republic serial, Chapter 6: "Fatal Gold," 1944).

Doctors and Dentists

See also Dying; People

872

Executioner: All right, boys. Old Cuteye has been duly tried by miners' court and found guilty of thievery and sentenced to be hung. However, this one time we got to temper justice with mercy. We are going to let you live long enough to pull this suffering boy's tooth!

The Chief Executioner played by Parley Baer: James Neilson's *The Adventures of Bullwhip Griffin* (Buena Vista, 1967).

873

Doc: But of course if you're determined to watch over him, Penny, you better take a pencil and paper with you. His first conscious words should be recorded. They may be of great interest to history ...or more possibly to a United States Marshal! Who knows what violence is involved with his battered frame and his bullet holes.

Doctor Mangrum played by Tom Powers and Prudence "Penny" Worth played by Gail Russell: James Edward Grant's *Angel and the Badman* (Republic, 1947).

874

Joe: I got a knack at healing. I know something about it.

Sam: Look, you're a great horse doctor, Joe, and ...

Joe: There isn't much difference between a horse and a human. At least I know how to get started. You wouldn't even know that.

Joe Madden played by Willard Parker and Sam Leeds played by Stephen McNally: Hugo Fregonese's *Apache Drums* (Universal, 1951).

875

By These Present Be It Known That
BOSWELL ABERNATHY
Is Authorized To Officiate As:
     Sheriff, Justice of the Peace, Notary
     Public, Veterinarian, Horse Doctor

Wall certificate: James Hogan's *The Arizona Raiders* (a.k.a. *Bad Men of Arizona*; Paramount, 1936).

876

Hodge: Well, Doc?

Doc: I'm afraid he's made his last mistake.

Hodge played by Harry Holman and Doctor Grant played by Andrew Tombes: Tim Whelan's *Badman's Territory* (RKO, 1946).

877

Ringo: It's a matter of principle. I don't operate on a man who wears a gun.

Ringo played by Giuliano Gemma: Duccio Tessari's *Ballad of Death Valley* (a.k.a. *The Return of Ringo*; Mediterranee-Balcazar/Rizzoli Film, 1966).

878

Ringo: You're lucky I came along here. I can fix it up for ya.

Esteban: You?

Ringo: In San Antone I used to work for a barber who was a surgeon on the side. I helped him operate on twelve or thirteen horses.

Esteban: Wait a minute! Listen, I'm not a horse! Understand?

Ringo: And I'm not a doctor. So that makes us even.

Ringo played by Giuliano Gemma and Esteban played by Fernando Sancho: Duccio Tessari's *Ballad of Death Valley* (a.k.a. *The Return of Ringo*; Mediterranee-Balcazar/Rizzoli Film, 1966).

879

Mace: It seems to me you could stand a good scrubbing [bath] yourself.

Attendant: Water washes away a man's protection. It lets miters into his body. And I'm too damn old to take chances.

Mace: Well, if what you're saying is the truth, you must be the best protected man in town.

Attendant: Well, I ain't sick, never been sick, and don't intend to be sick!

Mace Bishop played by James Stewart and the Attendant was Dub Taylor: Andrew McLaglen's *Bandolero!* (20th Century–Fox, 1968).

880

McBurney: I've just been thinking about all the advantages that a one-legged man has. He saves on socks. He doesn't have to worry about trimming as many toenails ...fewer corns and bunions. I've even been contemplating asking her to cut off the other one.

John McBurney played by Clint Eastwood: Don Siegel's *The Beguiled* (Universal, 1971).

881

Hendricks: I got a job for you ...arrow wound.

Captain: Where about?

Glyn: Right up here [*pointing toward shoulder area*]. Part of the [arrow] head is still in it.

Captain: Well, if you can point to it, it ain't serious. Just leave it alone. It will fall out by itself in due time.

Tom Hendricks played by Howard Petrie, Captain Mello played by Chubby Johnson, and Glyn McLyntock played by James Stewart: Anthony Mann's *Bend of the River* (Universal, 1952).

882

Bartender: How he is?

Toby: The Doc wants the shutter that used to carry drunks out.

Sam Rhine the Bartender played by James Kenny, Toby played by Allen Collins, and Doc Scully played by Burgess Meredith: Fielder Cook's *A Big Hand for the Little Lady* (Warner Bros., 1966).

883

Billy: What's wrong with her, Doc? What are those marks on her neck?

Doc: Well if I didn't know better, I'd say it was the work of a vampire.

Billy: Vampire?

Billy the Kid played by Chuck Courtney and Dr.

Gunfighter Quirt Evans (John Wayne) getting reformed by Quaker girl Penny Worth (Gail Russell), in *Angel and the Badman* (Republic 1947).

Henrietta Hull played by Olive Carey: William Beaudine's *Billy the Kid vs. Dracula* (Circle/Embassy Pictures, 1966).

884
Doc: I haven't had a patient in two weeks. The last one I had was dead on arrival. He fell off his horse in front of a stampede and it took the hoofs of a thousand steers to kill him.
Doc Blaine played by Pat O'Malley: Earl Bellamy's *Blackjack Ketchum, Desperado* (Columbia, 1956).

885
Carole: He's sick.
Ridgeway: I know. I've seen this sickness before. It's an old familiar road. Hurt, revenge, hate …all gets twisted in the mind. First thing you know, the mind gets twisted like a hard, hard knot. If there isn't anybody to get it out, it just explodes.
Carole Ridgeway played by Audrey Dalton and

Matthew Ridgeway played by Richard Arlen: Spencer G. Bennet's *The Bounty Killer* (Embassy/Premiere, 1965).

886
Cochise: White Painted Lady, I have old wounds.
Sonseeahray: Yes, but each scar is a mark of love for your people. The path of your people is stretched long behind you. And you are the head. And you are the heart. And you are the blood. Killer of enemies is your father, and you are his son. You will be well.
Cochise played by Jeff Chandler. The White Painted Lady was called Sonseeahray, meaning Morning Star, and played by Debra Paget: Delmer Daves' *Broken Arrow* (20th Century–Fox, 1950).

887
Doc: Billy, my considered diagnosis is that you have the worst ailment known to man …no money!

Dr. Canterbury played by Woodrow Parfrey and Bronco Billy played by Clint Eastwood who also directed *Bronco Billy* (Warner Bros., 1980).

888
Indian Girl: The medicine man will help him. He's trying to restore harmony to his body.
The Delaware Indian Girl played by Carmen Moore: Mark Sobel's *Brothers of the Frontier* (TVW, 1996).

889
Cody: What killed my son?
Doctor: Diphtheria.
Cody: What's that?
Doctor: A germ.
Cody: Where does it come from?
Doctor: Water systems …and sewage. It's a crowd disease. A disease of civilization.
Buffalo Bill Cody played by Joel McCrea and the Doctor played by Edwin Stanley: William Wellman's *Buffalo Bill* (20th Century–Fox, 1944).

890

Billy Joe: You're bleeding again, Pa.
Cahill: Yeah, I guess it goes with the badge. You got a kerchief?
Billy Joe: Yeah.
Cahill: Jam it in this hole. It'll stop the bleeding.

Billy Joe Cahill played by Clay O'Brien and Marshal J.D. Cahill played by John Wayne: Andrew McLaglen's *Cahill: United States Marshal* (Warner Bros., 1973).

891

Murdock: The operation was a success but the patient died.

Murdock played by Harry Woods: Lesley Selander's *Call of the Rockies* (Republic, 1944).

892

Carson: Continue with the operation, Doctor. But remember: If his pulse stops, so will yours!

Sunset Carson played by Sonny "Sunset" Carson: Lesley Selander's *Call of the Rockies* (Republic, 1944).

893

Joshua: If I don't get to a doctor, I'll die!
Elias: It looks that way.

Joshua Everette played by James Whitmore and Elias Hooker played by Ralph Waite: Michael Winner's *Chato's Land* (United Artists, 1972).

894

Wyatt: Say, you're the doctor around here. How come I always have to perform all the complicated operations?
Doc: You know I am a dentist, not a doctor. Wait until somebody shoots him in the teeth.

Wyatt Earp played by James Stewart and Doc Holliday played by Arthur Kennedy: John Ford's *Cheyenne Autumn* (Warner Bros., 1964).

895

Mitch: Sir! El doctor! Hello? Don't sew anything up that's supposed to remain open, ok?

Mitch Robbins played by Billy Crystal: Ron Underwood's *City Slickers* (Columbia, 1991).

896

Bowie: I'll get it [bullet] out as quick and easy as I can.
Seeger: There's no hurry, son. Only don't throw it away. I like to save lead folks take out of me. I got nearly three pounds of it.

James Bowie played by Macdonald Carey and Dan'l Seeger played by Will Geer: George Sherman's *Comanche Territory* (Universal, 1950).

897

Captain: I'm getting out of the Army in seven days.
Martha: As a civilian?
Captain: As a doctor.

Martha: But you're one now.
Captain: Am I? A veterinarian can yank an arrow out of a dead man or a live one. And a blacksmith can cauterize a wound with a hot iron. But neither of 'em can pull a child through diphtheria or pneumonia.

Captain Robert MacClaw played by Guy Madison and Martha played by Joan Weldon: David Butler's *The Command* (Warner Bros., 1953).

898

Palmer: That blow on the head has given him amnesia.
Osborne: How do you know? You're no doctor!
Palmer: Well, you don't have to be to recognize the symptoms.

Palmer played by John Hart and Osborne played by Marshall Reed: Lewis D. Collins' *Cowboy and the Prizefighter* (Eagle-Lion/Equity Pictures, 1950).

899

Doc: That'll be four and a half [dollars]. Two for the tooth, two-and-a-half for the whiskey. You got another swig coming.

Doc Grunch played by George "Gabby" Hayes: Raoul Walsh's *The Dark Command* (Republic, 1940).

900

Judge: Come on, Doc! Your job is pulling teeth out of people's mouths …not putting words in 'em. Let him speak for himself!

Judge Buckner played by Raymond Walburn and Doc Grunch played by George "Gabby" Hayes: Raoul Walsh's *The Dark Command* (Republic, 1940).

901

Doc: You knock 'em loose and I'll pull 'em out. Maybe, I'm just saying maybe, you know, if you was more promiscuous with your punching …we might make a little more money.
Bob: What do you mean …promiscuous?
Doc: Well, ah, you got strange ideas about justice. You don't want to hit nobody unless they deserve it. Now, that's all right. But we're in business. And business is different!

Doc Grunch played by George "Gabby" Hayes and Bob Seton played by John Wayne: Raoul Walsh's *The Dark Command* (Republic, 1940).

902

Wade: All right, what is it?
Doc: Do you know why you have been coughing so much lately? You never gave that wound time to heal properly. It's inflaming the lung.
Wade: Is that a medical opinion or a fact?

Doc: Oh, the way you go at it with whiskey, women, and poker …it's a sucker's game.
Wade: I always figured the game would end with one well-placed bullet.
Doc: Well, it still might! There's a lot of shooting days before Christmas.

Brett Wade played by Rory Calhoun and Doc Jameson played by Roy Roberts: George Sherman's *Dawn at Socorro* (Universal, 1954).

903

Doc: Medically speaking, it's no more than judges-incapacitatus.
Frank: What's that?
Doc: It means the judge won't be handling a gun for a few weeks.

Doc Logan played by James Bell and Frank McLean, the judge's son, was uncredited: Harmon Jones' *A Day of Fury* (Universal, 1956).

904

Doc: It's kind of a range fever. Like most things out here that'll kill ya, it's all our own.

The Doctor played by William Newman: Alan J. Levi's *Dead Man's Revenge* (MCA/Universal Home Video, 1994).

905

Doc: You know, weddings are something like the measles.
Judith: Measles?
Doc: Yeah, you got to have 'em once to get used to 'em.

Doc Belding played by Raymond Hatton and Judith Belding played by Marsha Hunt: James Hogan's *Desert Gold* (Paramount, 1936).

906

Destry: What about the Doc? Is he any good?
Rags: I had a dog once. He got all swelled up. Doc wanted to operate. The next day I had six of the prettiest little puppies you've ever seen.

Destry played by Audie Murphy and Rags Barnaby played by Thomas Mitchell: George Marshall's *Destry* (Universal, 1954).

907

Holland: Oh, just sew me up.
Dr. West: The only thing I ever sewed up was the buttons on my shirt when my wife took off with the traveling preacher.
Holland: What the hell does that mean?
Dr. West: I ain't no doctor.
Holland: Huh?
Dr. West: I'm a dentist.

Handsome Harry H. Holland played by Kirk Douglas and Dr. West played by Stuart Gillard: Steven H. Stern's *Draw!* (TVW, 1984).

A scene from Raoul Walsh's ***The Dark Command*** (Republic, 1940) with three cowboy giants: Fletch McCloud (Roy Rogers), Bob Seton (John Wayne), and Doc Grunch (George "Gabby" Hayes).

908

Duchess: God, oh my God, you're hurt! Is there much pain?

Malloy: It don't even hurt. What did you think? That I'd fall apart with one lousy little bullet?

Duchess: How many times have you been hit by bullets, Malloy?

Malloy: Including this one?

Duchess: Yeah.

Malloy: Once.

Amanda Quaid, alias "Duchess," played by Goldie Hawn and Charlie Malloy played by George Segal: Melvin Frank's *The Duchess and the Dirtwater Fox* (20th Century–Fox, 1976).

909

Cole: Who are you?

Doc: The name's Miller. Some people call me a doctor …and some other things. But I'm the only one in town.

Cole Thornton played by John Wayne and Doc Miller played by Paul Fix: Howard Hawks' *El Dorado* (Paramount, 1967).

910

Mr. Hall: Everything is going to be all right in there, isn't it?

Dulcie: Well, if it isn't, you'll be just about as helpful as that doctor who seems to be on the other side of the county.

Mr. Hall played by John Qualen and Dulcie played by Louise Latham: Vincent McEveety's *Firecreek* (Warner Bros.–Seven Arts, 1968).

911

Evelyn: The amount of blood on that shirt shows you're carrying a bullet. That calls for a doctor.

Larkin: I managed some doctoring last night. The bullet's out.

Evelyn played by Inger Stevens and Bob Larkin played by Henry Fonda: Vincent McEveety's *Firecreek* (Warner Bros.–Seven Arts, 1968).

Wyatt Earp (James Garner) and Doc Holliday (Jason Robards, Jr.) in John Sturges' *Hour of the Gun* (United Artists, 1967). Wyatt is out for revenge and uses his legal warrants as personal hunting licenses.

912

Doc: I'm Doc Fallon. I take care of horses and humans. Sometimes they get well.
Tex: I'm Tex McCloud.
Doc: Well, glad to know you, Tex.
Tex: Do you got a stall for my horse that ain't occupied?
Doc: I sure have. I just keep one special for corpses so I can lay 'em out for burying.

Doc Fallon played by George Cleveland and Tex McCloud played by Sterling Hayden: Ray Enright's *Flaming Feather* (Paramount, 1952).

913

Josh: What does it feel like getting shot?
Gard: Being kicked by a mule.

Josh Birdwell played by Anthony Perkins and Gard Jordan played by Mark Richman: William Wyler's *Friendly Persuasion* (Allied Artists, 1956).

914

Doc: I'm sorry I had to be the one to patch him up. It's hard being the only doctor in town. But the job has its compensation. When they hang him, I'll be the one to pronounce him officially dead.

Doctor Paul Ridgely played by James Drury: Nathan Juran's *Good Day for a Hanging* (Columbia, 1958).

915

Jubal: Sanders! Blake! Hold his shoulders down! Gomez, take his legs!
Rose: Here! Wait! Sterilize the knife with whiskey!
Jubal: Do as she says, Shawnee!
Shawnee: How do you know so blasted much about it?

Jubal Santee played by Neville Brand, Rose Fargo played by Ann Robinson, and Shawnee Jack played by Michael Ansara: Sidney Salkow's *Gun Brothers* (United Artists, 1956).

916

Bat: Are you a doctor?
Doc: No, I am the doctor. And I'm getting a little old to be hauled out of bed every night to sober up drunks and set broken jaws.

Bat Masterson played by Joel McCrea and Doc played by John McIntire: Joseph M. Newman's *The Gunfight at Dodge City* (United Artists, 1959).

917

Saloon Man: Hey Doc, what happens if somebody gets sick?
Doc: They get free medical attention if they're in here. If they're somewhere else, they're out of luck.

Doc played by John McIntire: Joseph M. Newman's *The Gunfight at Dodge City* (United Artists, 1959).

918

Doc: Yeah, well, I never drink during office hours …unless I have the opportunity.

Doc played by John McIntire: Joseph M. Newman's *The Gunfight at Dodge City* (United Artists, 1959).

919

Doc: You're not sorry about losing your badge?
Bat: Yeah, strangely enough I am. You know, Doc, this job was pushed on me. I never wanted it. I never asked for it. But for the first time in my life I really felt good. I don't know how to explain it.
Doc: Well, you don't have to. You've displayed all the symptoms of a man doing something unselfish. It's the only way anyone ever comes down with a case of happiness.

Doc played by John McIntire and Bat Masterson played Joel McCrea: Joseph M. Newman's *The Gunfight at Dodge City* (United Artists, 1959).

920

Doc: There's nothing I'd like better than give you a hand, Jordan. But I take bullets out of people. I don't think I got the spine to put bullets in 'em!

Doc Debney played by Mathew Walker and Jordan Yarnell played by David McIlwraith: Larry Ferguson's *Gunfighter's Moon* (Rysher Entertainment/Cabin Entertainment, 1995).

921

Sheriff: How's Steverts?
Doc: I never will know why so many miracles are wasted on the undeserving.

Sheriff Harry Brill played by Robert F. Simon, the Doc was uncredited, and Jensen Steverts played by Ray Teal: Phil Karlson's *Gunman's Walk* (Columbia, 1958).

922

Doc: My advice to you is to get plenty of rest.

Chad: Plenty of rest? That's your favorite prescription. I bet if I was going on my honeymoon, you'd tell me to get plenty of rest.

Dr. Beardsley played by Roy Barcroft and Sheriff Chad Lucas played by Audie Murphy: Earl Bellamy's *Gunpoint* (Universal, 1966).

923

Doc: Everybody has to travel at their own speed, Chad. I'm afraid you might set a little too fast a pace for most folks here.

Dr. Beardsley played by Roy Barcroft and Sheriff Chad Lucas played by Audie Murphy: Earl Bellamy's *Gunpoint* (Universal, 1966).

924

Mansfield: The doctors are quite concerned.

Mayor: How much time does he have?

Mansfield: According to the doctors, if he doesn't take care of himself, it will be soon.

Denver Kid: And how much time if he does take care of himself?

Bloodshy: They give me at least two days.

Mansfield played by John Williams, Mayor Ragsdale played by Darren McGavin, the Denver Kid played by Don Knotts, and Jasper Bloodshy played by Jim Dale: Robert Butler's *Hot Lead and Cold Feet* (Buena Vista, 1978).

925

Doctor: You know you don't have to get well to please me. I'm used to people dying on me.

Doc: So am I.

The Denver Doctor played by Edward Anhalt and Doc Holliday played by Jason Robards, Jr.: John Sturges' *The Hour of the Gun* (United Artists, 1967).

926

Wood: Now, Mr. Greeter, the apothecary, said two doses a day is all you need for a bullet wound.

Wood Hite played by Peter Bradshaw: William A. Graham's *The Last Days of Frank and Jesse James* (TVW, 1986).

927

Padre: Your friend tells me you're in pain.

Miles: That's right.

Padre: That's good. As long as there's pain that means the body is still fighting.

Padre Jose played by Eduard Franz and Miles Lang played by Gilbert Roland: George Sherman's *The Last of the Fast Guns* (Universal, 1958).

928

Hawkeye: How is he?

Chingachgook: Bad. He's got squaw fever.

Hawkeye played by Randolph Scott and Chingachgook played by Robert Barrat: George B. Seitz's *The Last of the Mohicans* (United Artists, 1936).

929

Gus: I hope you didn't throw my leg away. I may want to make me a walkin' stick out of the bone.

Gus McCrae played by Robert Duvall: Simon Wincer's *Lonesome Dove* (TVW, 1989).

930

Call: What about that trouble up in Arkansas?

Jake: Damn mule skinner threw down on me in a saloon. I shot back at him with a buffalo gun and killed the dentist. It was a pure accident but …but I killed him.

Gus: He was just standing in the wrong place, huh?

Jake: No, actually, he was outside walking down the street. But a plank wall won't stop no fifty caliber bullet.

Gus: But a dentist will?

Jake: Stopped him dandy! It was bad luck all around.

Gus: Well, nobody liked the dentist anyway.

Jake: This one was the mayor. Worse yet, his brother is the sheriff. A young fellow named July Johnson. He was out of town at the time.

Gus: Well, they wouldn't hang you for an accident, not even in Arkansas.

Jake: Seeing how they don't take much shining to gamblers, I wasn't gonna wait around and give them the option.

Captain Woodrow F. Call played by Tommy Lee Jones, Jake Spoon played by Robert Urich, and Gus McCrae played by Robert Duvall: Simon Wincer's *Lonesome Dove* (TVW, 1989).

931

Cole: I sure do feel poorly.

Doc: It ain't no surprise …with eleven bullets [in ya], it must be some kind of record.

Cole Younger played by David Carradine and the Doctor played by Glenn Robards: Walter Hill's *The Long Riders* (United Artists, 1980).

932

Dundee: If you're thinking of cutting that leg off, doctor, don't!

Doctor: I am only concerned to stop the loss of blood …so much of it is alcohol. You should be able to walk in seven days and ride in twelve.

Dundee: I'll walk in two and ride in one more.

Major Amos Charles Dundee played by Charlton Heston and Dr. Aguilar played by Enrique Lucero: Sam Peckinpah's *Major Dundee* (Columbia, 1965).

933

Wyatt: Mac, you and Buck go down and clean up the saloon. Put a couple poker tables together and put some lights around 'em. Doc, you're going to operate.

Wyatt Earp played by Henry Fonda, Mac the bartender played by J. Farrell MacDonald, and Doc Holliday played by Victor Mature: John Ford's *My Darling Clementine* (20th Century–Fox, 1946).

934

Patient: What's that?

Potter: Well, it's laughing gas. That's why they call me Painless Potter. I use it on all my patients.

Patient: Is it safe?

Potter: It's the safest thing in the world. Would you mind paying me now?

The Patient played by Nestor Palva and the Dentist, Painless Peter Potter, played by Bob Hope: Norman Z. McLeod's *The Paleface* (Paramount, 1948).

935

Doctor: He don't need a doctor. He needs a change of underwear!

Scotty: What he needs is a breath of fresh air!

Pancho: I've been busy changing the government, Doctor. No time to change the underwear.

The Doctor played by Carl Rapp, Scotty played by Clint Walker, and Pancho Villa played by Telly Savalas: Eugenio Martin's *Pancho Villa* (Granda/Scotia International, 1975).

936

Dr. Carter: And let me tell you something. That if you got the proper amount of determination …listen …you could overcome any kind of physical handicap with the proper amount of determination. Why, listen! I once knew a man that didn't have a tooth in his head. Yet that man learned to play a bass drum better than anybody I've ever listened to. And that's an absolute fact, friends! I only deal in facts. I'm telling you the truth. I went out in the country. I went out in the great open spaces. And I lived with the Indians. And I was cured by those Indians! I was cured by taking that secret compound of theirs. And let me tell you something …that those Indians, my friends, for generations have been laughing up their sleeves …ah …or at least up their blankets at the doctors. And that's an absolute fact! And I've brought back with me to civilization the secret of that marvelous compound known today as Dr. Carter's Indian Remedy. Now friends, I'm going to give you an opportunity a little bit later to buy a bottle of that remedy for the advertising price of one dollar.

Dr. Carter played by Earle Hodgins: Carl Pierson's *Paradise Canyon* (Monogram, 1935).

937

Doctor: Well, he suffered lacerations, contusions, and concussions. The jugular vein was severed in three places. I counted four broken ribs, and there was a compound fracture of the skull. To put it briefly, he's real dead!

The Doctor was uncredited: Fritz Lang's *Rancho Notorious* (RKO, 1952).

938

Doc: Murder is a serious business. It takes a lot out of a man.

Doc Howe played by Richard Alexander: Al Herman's *Renfrew on the Great White Trail* (Criterion Pictures, 1938).

939

Renfrew: You're an amazing man, Doctor. You save lives and take them with equal composure.

Sergeant Renfrew played by James Newill and Doc Howe played by Richard Alexander: Al Herman's *Renfrew on the Great White Trail* (Criterion Pictures, 1938).

940

Judge: The Doc here don't like me on account of I never send him no patients. Let's have that jug, will ya, Marshal?

Doc: All his trade goes to Jetson, the undertaker. And I happen to know he pays you $10 a head.

Judge: Only if the deceased can afford it.

Judge Kyle played by Walter Matthau and the Doc was uncredited: Jesse Hibbs' *Ride a Crooked Trail* (Universal, 1958).

941

Gil: Old Doc. You know what happened to him?

Steve: I heard he died.

Gil: That's right. Old Doc. Gave thirty years of his life to make the west safe for decent people. You'd have wept to see the way they turned out to pay tribute to him …all three of them! The mortician, the grave digger, and me.

Steve: Well, when I'm buried, I won't much care who comes to the funeral.

Gil Westrum played by Randolph Scott and Steve Judd played by Joel McCrea: Sam Peckinpah's *Ride the High Country* (MGM, 1962).

942

Doctor: It will kill ya or cure ya.

Dr. Wilkins played by Chill Wills: John Ford's *Rio Grande* (Republic, 1950).

943

Corporal: It'll be all right, miss. He lost some blood. Once the doc gets that hunk of arrow out of his arm, all he'll need is a lot of red beef and good strong tea. There's nothing like beef and tea for growing new blood.

Corporal Martin played by Milburn Stone: George Marshall's *The Savage* (Paramount, 1952).

944

Clarence: He's alive!

Annie: Did I forget to mention it?

Clarence: Yes, you forgot to mention it!

Annie: I pulled out eighteen slugs and not one of them hit his heart.

Ed: Clarence!

Clarence: How are you feeling, Ed?

Ed: Cooler. When a breeze hits me, I whistle. Ha, ha, ha! Oh, oh!

Clarence: Try not to laugh, Ed.

Ed: Do you have a bit of whiskey? It helps the pain.

Clarence: You took a lot of lead.

Ed: It doubled my body weight! Ha, ha ha! Oh, oh!

Clarence: Ed, Ed, try not and laugh. Can I get you something? Water?

Ed: Water? I only got one set of dry sheets! Ha, ha, ha, ha! Oh, oh!

Clarence: Ed, I better leave you alone for awhile.

Ed: No, no. Stay with me, Clarence! Just keep your mouth shut!

Clarence Gentry played by Fred Willard, Annie Simms played by Lela Ivey, and Ed "Shorty" Simms played by Lou Wagner: Eugene Levy's *Sodbusters* (Atlantis Releasing, 1994).

945

Doc: The bullet is lodged near the heart. It's a bad wound.

Clint: You're a doc. You know how to get it out, don't you?

Doc: Academically, yes. In practice, no. This man needs a surgeon, an M.D., a regular doctor.

Clint: A regular doctor! What are you?

Doc: D.V.M. Doctor of Veterinary Medicine.

Clint: A vet! Why you crazy drunkard fool! Why didn't you …

Lilly: Please stop it! Even a horse doctor is better than none. Do what you can.

Doc Stanton played by Morris Ankrum, Clint McDonald played by John Ireland, and Lilly played by Joanne Dru: Ray Nazarro's *Southwest Passage* (United Artists, 1954).

946

Doc: Good luck, Doctor. And remember: when in doubt about symptoms, do nothing at all. That is the secret of a successful medical practice.

Doc Stanton played by Morris Ankrum: Ray Nazarro's *Southwest Passage* (United Artists, 1954).

947

Tod: I'd never let him do that [tooth pulling] to me without laughing gas.

Spikes: Why, he's the same doctor that took out my appendix with only a quart and a half of tequila.

Tod Hayhew played by Charles Martin Smith and Harry Spikes played by Lee Marvin: Richard Fleischer's *The Spikes Gang* (United Artists, 1974).

948

Leah: Too many times, you'll find the medicine that will ease the pain …but it won't really cure you.

Leah Parker played by Marilyn Maxwell: William F. Claxton's *Stage to Thunder Rock* (Paramount, 1964).

949

Ringo: You did a good job, Doc, even if you was drunk.

Doc: Thank you, son. Professional compliments are always pleasing.

The Ringo Kid played by John Wayne and Dr. Josiah Boone played by Thomas Mitchell: John Ford's *Stagecoach* (United Artists, 1939).

950

Marshal: Hey, Doc? Do you know anything about babies?

Doc: About what?

Marshal: Babies. You know, little …babies.

Buck: They're the kind that women have.

Doc: Well, I know how they're made, and I've heard rumors about where they come from, and I believe they grow up and become people.

Marshal: That's all you know?

Doc: Well, they're messy and they make a lot of noise.

Buck: What else?

Doc: Well, I wouldn't play poker with one, and I wouldn't have one in the house.

Marshal Curley Wilcox played by Johnny Cash, Doc Holliday played by Willie Nelson, and Buck played by John Schneider: Ted Post's *Stagecoach* (TVW, 1986).

951

Doc: I've never really done this before.

Mallory: You've never delivered a baby?

Doc: No, ma'am, not even one.

Mallory: But everybody calls you Doc.

Doc: Yes, ma'am. There's something else I should tell you too. And I realize that this is not the best time to do it. But I'm not a doctor. I'm a dentist.

Mallory: A dentist?

Doc: Yes, ma'am. It's all right. Just relax. It's okay, Mrs. Mallory. It's okay. Just lay down. Just relax. You're going to be all right.

Mallory: A dentist?

Doc: Yes, ma'am.

Mallory: Do you know anything at all about what is going to happen here tonight?

Doc: Oh yes, ma'am. A lot of good things is going to happen here tonight. Great things. You can count on that. You know, one time I delivered a foal for my mare. The prettiest little filly you ever saw.

Mallory: A filly?

Doc Holliday played by Willie Nelson and Lucy Mallory played by Mary Crosby in Ted Post's *Stagecoach* (TVW, 1986).

952

Charlie: What good is a lawyer if he never gets into court?

Haven: Oh, like a doctor in a graveyard.

Charlie played by Jane Greer and Haven played by Dick Powell: Sidney Lanfield's *Station West* (RKO, 1948).

953

Latigo: This is your office?

Doc: I doctor pack mules too. If you got a pain in the ass, you come see Doc Shultz.

Latigo Smith played by James Garner and Doc Shultz played by Dub Taylor: Burt Kennedy's *Support Your Local Gunfighter* (United Artists, 1971).

954

Doc: Son, I'm the best dentist in this town. And there's only two ways to be the best dentist in the town. One of 'em is to do the finest work.

Dan: What's the other?

Doc: Be the only dentist.

Doc Thorpe played by Edgar Buchanan and Dan Thomas played by William Holden: George Marshall's *Texas* (Columbia, 1941).

955

Hefty: You see, there's been some pretty bad cases of lead poisoning around here …a regular epidemic.

Texas: You haven't been able to find a doctor that could cure the trouble?

Hefty: You can't cure dead men that's been shot in the back by unknown killers.

Hefty played by Vernon Dent and Texas Grant/ Jim Rawlins played by Tim McCoy: D. Ross Lederman's *Texas Cyclone* (Columbia, 1932).

956

Beckworth: If a doctor's brains was put in a jaybird, he'd fly backwards!

Beckworth played by Jack Oakie: George Sherman's *Tomahawk* (Universal, 1951).

957

Doc: My hypocrisy goes only so far.

[*but later*]

Doc: It appears my hypocrisy knows no bounds.

Doc Holliday played by Val Kilmer: George P. Cosmatos' *Tombstone* (Buena Vista, 1993).

958

Harkrider: This is the best liniment you can buy. Sold it myself on the midway. Chief O'Wampah's Indian Remedy, folks, made from nature's healing herbs and roots from the age old secret formula of the Chippewas. I used it a thousand times myself …that is, on my horses, I mean.

Colonel Harkrider played by George Cleveland: William Witney's *Trigger, Jr.* (Republic, 1950).

959

Fiesta: But one day she [my wife] gets bit by a rattlesnake.

Mollie: She did?

Fiesta: Yeah.

Mollie: Did the doctor get there in time?

Fiesta: No, she's already dead.

Mollie: Your wife?

Fiesta: My wife? No, no, the snake. My wife? My wife the next day, she's so angry she bites her brother. Sure, and his whole family is poisoned!

Fiesta played by Akim Tamiroff and Mollie Monahan played by Barbara Stanwyck: Cecil B. DeMille's *Union Pacific* (Paramount, 1939).

960

[*conversation among two saloon patrons*]

Patron: Doctor! Somebody get that doctor!

Patron: When Jeff shoots them, they don't need a doctor. They need an undertaker.

The two saloon patrons were uncredited. Jeff Butler played by Joel McCrea: Cecil B. DeMille's *Union Pacific* (Paramount, 1939).

961

Doctor: It's been my observation that man's appetite grows by what it feeds on. And there's no hunger like the hunger for land. It swallows everything and everybody.

Dr. Henry Crowell played by Raymond Green-

Bad guy Joe Maybe (Audie Murphy) rides into town and is mistaken for a marshal. Joe assumes the role of the marshal and becomes a good guy in the process in *Ride a Crooked Trail* (Universal, 1958).

leaf: Rudolph Mate's *The Violent Men* (Columbia, 1955).

962

Parrish: All that grass and sand ever meant to me the past three years has been a place to retain my health. And now that I've got it, there's nothing to hold me here any longer.

Doctor: Except what you owe the land …and your neighbors.

Parrish: I don't owe anybody anything.

Doctor: You came out here to die, Mr. Parrish. This country gave you back your life. And you still owe it nothing?

John Parrish played by Glenn Ford and Dr. Henry Crowell played by Raymond Greenleaf: Rudolph Mate's *The Violent Men* (Columbia, 1955).

963

Doctor: Next time you get a bullet wound, better not try to cauterize it with gunpowder.

Murrell: It worked pretty good for a snake bite.

Doctor: Then it should have worked for you!

Dr. Cameron played by Moroni Olsen and John Murrell played by Humphrey Bogart: Michael Curtiz's *Virginia City* (Warner Bros., 1940).

964

Phil: About that leg, Clay. You know, these flesh wounds can be a little tricky. You know, things happen …there are complications.

Clay: You had to amputate?

Phil: No, no, no, no, no, no! The leg is, ah, fine …a little stiff.

Clay: Well now, that's to be expected.

Phil: Well, you know, actually, Clay, ah, the leg is not the only part that's, ah, stiff. Actually, his whole body is kind of, ah, well, he's, ah, he's, ah, he's dead!

Phil Taylor played by Richard Lewis and Clayton Ferguson played by Thomas F. Duffy: Peter Markle's *Wagons East!* (Tristar, 1994).

965

Red: She's out like your last match on a windy night. I got to get the doc!

Red played by Dick Wessel: Joseph Kane's *West of the Badlands* (a.k.a. *The Border Legion*; Republic, 1940).

966

Doc: Feels like you got a slug there, pardner. A .44?

Charlie: Injun arrowhead. It don't bother me none.

Doc: You know, some members of the medical profession like to cut them things out. But I say, let 'em stay if it's that comfortable.

Doc Murdock played by John Carradine and Charlie played by Victor Kilian: Fritz Lang's *Western Union* (20th Century–Fox, 1941).

967

Doctor: Shot, hell! He's damn near froze to death! And he smells like a still! What did you do, stop off on the way to celebrate?

Dr. Fraker played by William Schallert: Tom Gries' *Will Penny* (Paramount, 1968).

968

Irish: I'll make a deal with you. I'll take out the bullet and you turn me loose.

Carlos: Can you save her?

Irish: I can try.

Arturo: If you don't, we'll bury you the same day.

Edward Creighton (Dean Jagger) is engineer for the telegraph company that is stringing wire west. They've just been attacked by white men dressed as Indians. Employee Vance Shaw (Randolph Scott), who scouts for the company but a former outlaw, is being questioned in the epic *Western Union* (20th Century–Fox, 1941).

Irish Gallager played by Van Heflin, Carlos played by Paul Fierro, and Arturo played by Rodolfo Acosta: Budd Boetticher's *Wings of the Hawk* (Universal, 1953).

969

Doc: Your leg isn't broken half as bad as you smell. How long have you been riding to work up a smell like this?

Brady: Twenty-six days.

Doc: I figured longer.

Doc Stovall played by Charles McGraw and Martin Brady played by Robert Mitchum: Robert Parrish's *The Wonderful Country* (United Artists, 1959).

970

Doc: Forget about your gun! Do you speak English?

Brady: Yes.

Doc: I'm Doc Stovall. Drink a lot of this in English. You're going to need it!

Doc Stovall played by Charles McGraw and Martin Brady played by Robert Mitchum: Robert Parrish's *The Wonderful Country* (United Artists, 1959).

971

Brady: Doc, look, how am I going to pay you?

Doc: My other patients aren't worrying. Why should you be a pioneer?

Martin Brady played by Robert Mitchum and Doc Stovall played by Charles McGraw: Robert Parrish's *The Wonderful Country* (United Artists, 1959).

972

Charlie: What brings you down this way anyway?

Ben: My doctor told me I better find a climate with a little less lead in the air.

Charlie played by Paul Fix and Ben Kane played by Robert Mitchum: Burt Kennedy's *Young Billy Young* (United Artists, 1969).

973

Regas: What happened?

Gabby: Hit by an injun arrow. Might be poisonous.

Regas: Take him to his quarters. I'll send for a doctor.

Gabby: We can't wait for no sawbones. I'll take care of him. I've done it before. Get me some hot water. Lots of it!

[*and a little later*]

Elena: You know how to do this? [*doctoring*]

Gabby: Sure I do. I've been in a hundred injun fights. Doctored five men at the same time.

Elena: How?

Gabby: Why, simplest thing you've ever seen. You just use hot water.

Elena: And what will you do with it?

Gabby: Oh, any fool knows that. You just pour the hot water in the air hole and let it drain out the other side.

Don Regas played by Hugh Sothern, Gabby Whittaker played by George "Gabby" Hayes, and Elena played by Anna Demetrio: Joseph Kane's *Young Buffalo Bill* (Republic, 1940).

Drinking

See also Saloons; Whiskey

974

Zach: A good Christian does not flinch with difficulty.

Holly: He doesn't court them by drinking either.

Zachariah Coop played by Robert Logan and Holly Smith played by Heather Rattray: Stewart Raffill's *Across the Great Divide* (Pacific International, 1976).

975

General: Where's Jim Bowie?

Captain: He's indisposed, sir.

General: Indisposed? By God if you mean drunk, you say drunk, sir!

Captain: He's drunk, sir!

General Sam Houston played by Richard Boone, Colonel Jim Bowie played by Richard Widmark, and Captain James Butler Bonham played by Patrick Wayne: John Wayne's *The Alamo* (United Artists, 1960).

976

Doc: It's amazing ...the varied uses to which men put alcohol. To each different individual, it's either a stimulant, a depressant, or antidine. Just now I'm using it as an antidine.

Doctor Mangrum played by Tom Powers: James Edward Grant's *Angel and the Badman* (Republic, 1947).

977

Lt. Glidden: Do you realize that men have been given as much as twenty years in federal prison for giving liquor to an Indian?

Lt. Glidden played by James Griffith: Hugo Fregonese's *Apache Drums* (Universal, 1951).

978

Lt. Glidden: You see, they [Indians] don't drink to get drunk. Their drinking is like praying. And then they kill.

Lt. Glidden played by James Griffith: Hugo Fregonese's *Apache Drums* (Universal, 1951).

979

Tracks: Water? Water? Why, there ain't no such thing as a good drink of water!

Tracks Williams played by Raymond Hatton: James Hogan's *The Arizona Raiders* (a.k.a. *Bad Men of Arizona*; Paramount, 1936).

980

Nita: We drink.

Bannon: It's against the law for an Indian to drink.

Nita: I drink in Spanish.

Nita played by Katy Jurado and Ed Bannon played by Charlton Heston: Charles Marquis Warren's *Arrowhead* (Paramount, 1953).

981

Henry: Sheriff, I'm so thirsty I could drink my Saturday bath ...if I had one.

Garth: One drop would kill the whole posse.

Henry Cliff played by Andy Clyde, Sheriff Bill Cummings played by Robert Barrat, and Charlie Garth played by Francis Ford: Lew Landers' *Bad Lands* (RKO, 1939).

982

Martha: If the pain gets too great, I'll ask Hallie to bring you some [wine].

McBurney: Well, this does seem like a good occasion, and I would love some wine.

Martha: It was offered for your pain, not for your pleasure!

McBurney: To be sure, ma'am. It's just that sometimes the two do go together.

Martha played by Geraldine Page, John McBurney played by Clint Eastwood, and Hallie played by Mae Mercer: Don Siegel's *The Beguiled* (Universal, 1971).

983

Morgan: Don't you want a drink?

Jagger: Water? What am I, a trout?

Chad Morgan played by Alan Ladd and Joe Jagger played by Edmond O'Brien: Gordon Douglas' *The Big Land* (Warner Bros., 1957).

984

Jim: On the level, Billy. You ought to get off the bottle.

Billy: Bottle? I was never drunk in my life.

Jim: I don't mean liquor. I mean another kind of bottle: excitement …phony adventure. It's no good, Billy.

Jim Sherwood played by Brian Donlevy and Billy the Kid played by Robert Taylor: David Miller's *Billy the Kid* (MGM, 1941).

985

Mister: I've never saw a man yet who could hold his liquor like a bottle.

Mister played by Ben Johnson: Richard Brooks' *Bite the Bullet* (Columbia, 1975).

986

Mendez: I hoped I had seen the last of you.

Frye: Maybe you're hallucinating.

Mendez: If you ain't corn liquor, son, you're just a bad nightmare.

Frye: How can you tell the difference.

Mendez: Because I can get over a hangover.

Harold Mendez played by Danny Nelson and Kirby Frye played by Cody Glenn: C.T. McIntyre's *Border Shootout* (Turner Home Entertainment, 1990).

987

Leffingwell: We don't need Tattoo. No sense dragging a lot of dead weight … especially when it is all drunken mouth.

Leffingwell played by Robert Keith and Tattoo played by John Berkes: Rudolph Mate's *Branded* (Paramount, 1951).

988

Miss Lilly: Good morning!

Lefty: What's so good about it?

Miss Lilly: Smell that fresh morning air! Look at the blue sky above!

Lefty: Have you been drinkin' some of Doc's Snakebite?

Antoinette Lilly played by Sondra Locke and Lefty LeBow played by Bill McKinney: Clint Eastwood's *Bronco Billy* (Warner Bros., 1980).

989

Blue: I'm just too old to start drinking whiskey at ten in the morning.

Calamity: Yeah, well, I'm too old to stop.

Teddy Blue played by Gabriel Byrne and Calamity Jane played by Anjelica Huston: Rod Hardy's *Buffalo Girls* (Cabin Fever Entertainment, 1995).

990

Cahill: Charlie, what are you doing in here [jail]? It ain't Thursday.

Charlie: A man has got a right to change his mind. Besides, it's going to rain on Thursday. And drinking in the rain, it's bad for your health.

Marshal J.D. Cahill played by John Wayne and Charlie Smith played by Jackie Coogan: Andrew

McLaglen's *Cahill: United States Marshal* (Warner Bros., 1973).

991

Chip: If I see one more hand touch one more jug, there may not be a jug …and there may not be a hand.

Chip Donohue played by John Dehner: Thomas Carr's *Cast a Long Shadow* (United Artists, 1959).

992

Jackson: Kid, Kid! What a time for you to fall off the wagon. Just look at your eyes!

Kid: What's wrong with my eyes?

Jackson: Well, they're red …bloodshot.

Kid: You ought to see 'em from my side!

Jackson Two Bears played by Tom Nardini and Kid Sheleen played by Lee Marvin: Elliot Silverstein's *Cat Ballou* (Columbia, 1965).

993

Clay: I've never seen a man get through a day so fast.

Clay Boone played by Michael Callan: Elliot Silverstein's *Cat Ballou* (Columbia, 1965).

994

Kid: Why don't we have a drink for old time sake?

Butch: Old time sake? That means you got no cash.

Kid Sheleen played by Lee Marvin: Butch Cassidy played by Arthur Hunnicutt: Elliot Silverstein's *Cat Ballou* (Columbia, 1965).

995

Jones: Give me about fifty cents worth of wet.

Jones played by John Ireland: Leon Klimovsky's *Challenge of the Mackennas* (Filmar Compagnia Cinematografica — Atlantida/Hemlock Enterprises, 1969).

996

Smiley: When a man is forced by bitter circumstances to drink water, you might have the common decency to turn the other way.

Smiley played by Henry Kulky: Gordon Douglas' *The Charge at Feather River* (Warner Bros., 1953).

997

Cullen: Well, sir, when I get drunk I forget what I do and I steal.

Miles: Huh, huh.

Cullen: And when I steal, I want to forget what I did so I get drunk.

Smiley: I just get drunk.

Cullen played by Dick Wesson, Miles Archer played by Guy Madison and Smiley played by Henry Kulky: Gordon Douglas' *The Charge at Feather River* (Warner Bros., 1953).

998

Cherokee Kid: Now I know you don't want to go to heaven sober …so here's one for the road.

The Cherokee Kid/Isaiah Turner played by Sinbad: Paris Barclay's *The Cherokee Kid* (HBO Pictures, 1996).

999

Bates: Who says I'm too drunk to fight? Stand up and I'll show ya!

Cisco: But, señor, I'm already standing.

Tommy Bates played by George Montgomery and the Cisco Kid played by Cesar Romero: Herbert I. Leeds' *The Cisco Kid and the Lady* (20th Century–Fox, 1939).

1000

Andy: [*Toasting*] Here's to an easy saddle and good riding, friend. May your boots never get dusty and your guns never get rusty.

Andy West played by Wallace Ford: Ray Enright's *Coroner Creek* (Columbia, 1948).

1001

Reece: How's the arm, Charlie?

Charlie: All right, boss. It's my drinking arm, not my loving arm.

Tom Reece played by Glenn Ford and Charlie played by Dick York: Delmer Daves' *Cowboy* (Columbia, 1958).

1002

Barnes: One of them has got bottle fever …threw away the cork.

Mathew Barnes played by William Fawcett: Lewis R. Foster's *Dakota Incident* (Republic, 1956).

1003

Call: Did you hit him?

Johnny: Hit who?

Call: Did you hit the Indian you shot at?

Johnny: Who shot?

Call: You shot! Are you so drunk you can't remember shooting your own gun?

Johnny: I shot? I shot?

Woodrow F. Call played by Jonny Lee Miller and Johnny was uncredited: Yves Simoneau's *Dead Man's Walk* (Cabin Fever Entertainment, 1996).

1004

Willie: [*Toasting*] Here's to green pastures and no fences.

Uncle Willie MacLeod played by Edgar Buchanan: Charles Vidor's *The Desperadoes* (Columbia, 1943).

1005

Bull: He's back there …sleeping. And being how you've known him longer than I have, you know enough to be careful how you wake him up. Because he's a bad one when he's drinking. He ain't put that stopper back in that bottle in a coon's age.

Bull Harris played by Arthur Hunnicutt: Howard Hawks' *El Dorado* (Paramount, 1967).

1006

Preacher: There will be no drinking during services!

Billy Bonney (Robert Taylor) in *Billy the Kid* (MGM, 1941).

Earl: Well, you don't mind us, Preacher, and we won't mind you.

Preacher Broyles played by Ed Begley and Earl played by Gary Lockwood: Vincent McEveety's *Firecreek* (Warner Bros.–Seven Arts, 1968).

1007

Mime: I saw this bottle. I thought it would give me my nerve back. But it took more of it away.

Uncle Mime played by James Stone: Roger Corman's *Five Guns West* (American Releasing Corp., 1955).

1008

Quale: Don't put any ice in mine. It takes up too much room.

S. Quentin Quale played by Groucho Marx: Edward Buzzell's *Go West* (MGM, 1940).

1009

Jackson: Gentlemen, I ask you to join me in a toast to a great victory by the longest winded man alive. If his words were bullets, he could win a war single-handed. To Sam Houston!

President Andrew Jackson played by G.D. Spradlin and Sam Houston played by Sam Elliott: Peter Levin's *Gone to Texas* (a.k.a. *Houston: The Legend of Texas*; TVW, 1986).

1010

Snort: [*Toasting*] Here's to the vinegarroon who jumped on the centipede's back and hollered with a laugh and a glee: "You poisonous son-of-a-bitch, I'll kill you yet if you don't kill me!"

Snort Yarnell played by Sam Shepard: Tommy Lee Jones' *The Good Old Boys* (Turner Pictures, 1995).

1011

Tom: Have another, Ahab.

Ahab: I don't know that I rightly should, Tom. In proverbs it says: "Look not upon the wine when it is red for at the last it biteth like the serpent and stingeth like the adder." On the other hand, in 1st Timothy it says: "Drink no longer water, but use a little wine for thy stomach sake." I reckon I can't refuse to help an old friend like my stomach after all it's done for me.

Tom was uncredited and Ahab Jones played by Peter Whitney: Lloyd Bacon's *The Great Sioux Uprising* (Universal, 1953).

1012

Ringo: Give me a drink.

Mac: Are you up early or out late?

Ringo: Either way you want it, partner, just so I get a drink.

Jimmy Ringo played by Gregory Peck and Mac played by Karl Malden: Henry King's *The Gunfighter* (20th Century–Fox, 1950).

1013

Townsman: I beg your pardon, both of you gentlemen, for interrupting. But this is a kind of a serious situation for me, Marshal.

Marshal: What is it?

Townsman: Well, the truth of the matter, sir, is that Les Fuller is burning my house down.

Marshal: What's he doing that for?

Townsman: Well, he just felt like it, Marshal. That's the only excuse in the world he's got. Just felt like it.

Marshal: Drunk?

Townsman: He certainly don't act like he was altogether cold sober.

The Townsman was uncredited and Marshal Mark Strett played by Millard Mitchell: Henry King's *The Gunfighter* (20th Century–Fox, 1950).

1014

Lee: Well, it's beginning to look like I neglected that boy's education. I thought I taught him to carry his liquor better than that.

Lee Hackett played by Van Heflin: Phil Karlson's *Gunman's Walk* (Columbia, 1958).

1015

Bartender: I've seen a man take two drinks of that stuff and go out and hunt bear with a willow switch.

Reb: What did he want the switch for?

The Bartender played by Bill Radovich and Reb Kittredge played by Audie Murphy: Nathan Juran's *Gunsmoke* (Universal, 1953).

1016

Cora: Say when.

Reb: Pour until your fingers get wet.

Cora DuFrayne played by Mary Castle and Reb Kittredge played by Audie Murphy: Nathan Juran's *Gunsmoke* (Universal, 1953).

1017

John: Well, if the truth be known, I haven't had a toot of the jug in a little of five, no, two days.

Matt: Well, your secret is safe with me.

John: It must be that puritan strength of yours rubbing off onto me.

Matt: Well, you better be careful there. Too little temptation might lead to …virtue.

John Parsley played by James Brolin and Matt Dillon played by James Arness: Jerry Jameson's *Gunsmoke: The Long Ride* (TVW, 1993).

1018

Louise: If you would only try to understand Mrs. Massingale, a woman who has lost two husbands to alcohol. They literally drank themselves into an early grave.

Colonel: I can only wonder why.

Louise Gearhart played by Pamela Tiffin and Colonel Thadeus Gearhart played by Burt Lancaster: John Sturges' *The Hallelujah Trail* (MGM, 1965).

1019

Averill: Billy, you're the only son-of-a-bitch I ever knew worth getting seriously drunk with.

James Averill played by Kris Kristofferson and Billy Irvine played by John Hurt: Michael Cimino's *Heaven's Gate* (United Artists, 1980).

1020

Mayor: No man should have to face morning or old man Bloodshy sober.

Mayor Ragsdale played by Darren McGavin and

Col. Thadeus Gearhart (Burt Lancaster) returns to the fort where a full-scale temperance march is in progress, led by Cora Templeton Massingale (Lee Remick), in John Sturges' *The Hallelujah Trail* (MGM, 1965).

Bloodshy played by Jim Dale: Robert Butler's *Hot Lead and Cold Feet* (Buena Vista, 1978).

1021

Barston: My throat's dryer than a woodpecker's lunch.

Barston played by Bruce Dern: Sam Pillsbury's *Into the Badlands* (TVW, 1991).

1022

Oliver: He's a hard drinker. The harder he drinks, the more he preaches about death and damnation.

Oliver Hale played by John Russell: Joseph Kane's *Jubilee Trail* (Republic, 1954).

1023

Ace: Into the mouth and over the gums, look out stomach, here she comes!

Ace Bonner played by Robert Preston: Sam Peckinpah's *Junior Bonner* (CIN, 1972).

1024

Maria: Take good care of your brother. And take good care of Billy, too. If he gets drunk and falls asleep outside, cover him up so he wouldn't freeze.

Maria Garza played by Sonia Braga and Billy Williams played by George Carlin: Joseph Sargent's *Larry McMurtry's Streets of Laredo* (Cabin Fever Entertainment, 1995).

1025

Jimmy: How did you lose it?

Woodfoot: What, the leg? Oh, I got stinkin' drunk in a blizzard and fell asleep and it froze up fast. Sandy carried me fifteen miles on his back to save my hide. But I lost my leg.

Jimmy: And you didn't give up drinking?

Woodfoot: I still got one good leg left, ain't I, son?

Jimmy played by Russ Tamblyn, Woodfoot played by Lloyd Nolan, and Sandy McKenzie played by Stewart Granger: Richard Brooks' *The Last Hunt* (MGM, 1956).

1026

Lefty: Won't you join us?

Fuzzy: Well, don't mind if I do. It sure is nice weather for drinking.

Lefty played by Lee Roberts and Fuzzy played by Al "Fuzzy" St. John: Ray Taylor's *Law of the Lash* (PRC, 1947).

1027

Roy Bean: Here you are, Whorehouse.

Whorehouse: Well, thank you, Judge.

Roy Bean: That'll be $25.

Whorehouse: $25?

Roy Bean: Yeah, when I ain't winning [poker], the beer is $25.

Whorehouse: Well, that ain't sportin'. What is a man supposed to do?

Roy Bean: Start losing or quit drinking.

Judge Roy Bean played by Paul Newman and Whorehouse Lucky Jim played by Steve Kanaly:

John Huston's *The Life and Times of Judge Roy Bean* (NGP, 1972).

1028

Majesty: Other men have quit …men who have fallen lower …men who are weaker. I have faith in you, Gene Stewart.

Stewart: If I could believe that.

Majesty: Without faith we are only dust.

Madeline "Majesty" Hammond played by Jo Ann Sayers and Gene Stewart played by Victor Jory: Lesley Selander's *The Light of the Western Stars* (Paramount, 1940).

1029

Jerri: Jack, what are you going to do?

Jack: Well, about every six months I figure I owe myself a good drunk. It rinses your insides out, sweetens your breath, and tones up your skin.

Jerri Bondi played by Gena Rowlands and Jack Burns played by Kirk Douglas: David Miller's *Lonely Are the Brave* (Universal, 1962).

1030

Jacob: Can I buy you a drink?

Riley: Oh, anybody can buy me a drink. Well, who are you?

Jacob: I'm your father.

Jacob Wade played by Jack Palance and Riley Wade played by Anthony Perkins: Henry Levin's *The Lonely Man* (Paramount, 1957).

1031

Gus: [*Toasting*] Well, here's to the sunny slopes of long ago.

Gus McCrae played by Robert Duvall: Simon Wincer's *Lonesome Dove* (TVW, 1989).

1032

Josiah: I'm a spiritual man. Sometimes I turn to the wrong kinds of spirits.

Josiah played by Ron Perlman: Geoff Murphy's *The Magnificent Seven: The Series* (TVW, Series Premiere, 1998).

1033

Twillie: I think I'll write a book …the art of rising the morning after.

Cuthbert J. Twillie played by W.C. Fields: Edward F. Cline's *My Little Chickadee* (Universal, 1940).

1034

Twillie: During one of my treks through Afghanistan, we lost our corkscrew …compelled to live on food and water for several days.

Cuthbert J. Twillie played by W.C. Fields: Edward F. Cline's *My Little Chickadee* (Universal, 1940).

1035

Bierce: Are you staring at me for any particular reason?

Arroyo: I have never seen an old man drink so much.

Bierce: The revolutionaries should study some history. In every war, the drunken nations have conquered the sober ones.

Arroyo: Drunks always talk better than they shoot.

Ambrose Bierce played by Gregory Peck and General Tomas Arroyo played by Jimmy Smits: Luis Puenzo's *Old Gringo* (Columbia, 1989).

1036

Elizabeth: Did you know that the Fentys had an apple farm back in Pennsylvania?

Rumson: Applejack, huh?

Mr. Fenty: No sir, we did not make applejack.

Rumson: Then what did you grow the apples for?

Mr. Fenty: Mr. Rumson, do you think everything that comes out of the earth should be used to make liquor?

Rumson: Whenever possible, yes.

Mrs. Fenty: You should read the Bible, Mr. Rumson.

Rumson: I have read the Bible, Mrs. Fenty.

Mrs. Fenty: Didn't that discourage you about drinking?

Rumson: No, but it sure killed my appetite for reading.

Elizabeth Woodling played by Jean Seberg, Ben Rumson played by Lee Marvin, Mr. Fenty played by Alan Baxter, and Mrs. Fenty played by Paula Trueman: Joseph Logan's *Paint Your Wagon* (Paramount, 1969).

1037

Carver: Hey Jesse, you …you ain't here for that revenge shit, are you?

Jesse Lee: I'll tell you what. Let's be two old friends having a drink. No past, no future. Just this drink: right here, right now.

Carver: Here's to here and now.

Carver played by Blair Underwood and Jesse Lee played by Mario Van Peebles who also directed *Posse* (Gramercy Pictures, 1993).

1038

Tucson: Happy, I reckon you better set up the drinks. There's no use of us mourning until we get a corpse.

Tucson Smith played by Harry Carey and Happy Hopkins played by William Desmond: Wallace Fox's *Powdersmoke Range* (RKO, 1935).

1039

Ogden: Sit down. Have a drink.

Sundown: Gunplay and liquor don't mix.

Mayor "Big Steve" Ogden played by Sam Hardy and Sundown Saunders played by Tom Tyler: Wallace Fox's *Powdersmoke Range* (RKO, 1935).

1040

Rick: Cheer up, Ben. The next best thing to finding a gal is a loyal buddy to drown your sorrows with.

Rick Harper played by Arthur Kennedy and Ben Mathews, alias Ben Martin, played by Tony

Curtis: Rudolph Mate's *The Rawhide Years* (Universal, 1956).

1041

Lamartine: Ah, I see you like a good glass! So do I. I don't cotton to a man who cries "when." If he's got to worry about drinking too much, he's not to be trusted when he does.

Lamartine played by Alan Reed: Leslie Fenton's *The Redhead and the Cowboy* (Paramount, 1951).

1042

John: Say, you look like you've seen a ghost!

Muley: I did, John! Greenish ghost you've ever seen! I seen it, I tell ya! I seen it with my own eyes ...sweeping out the saloon at Braxton!

John: A ghost sweeping out a saloon? You got to quit drinking, Muley!

Muley: I did ...when I seen that ghost!

John Pettit played by George "Gabby" Hayes and Muley Wilson played by Walter Baldwin: Ray Enright's *Return of the Badmen* (RKO, 1948).

1043

Gideon: [*Toasting*] To Captain Augusta McCrea!

Call: [*Toasting*] To the sunny slopes of long ago!

Gideon Walker played by William Peterson and Captain Woodrow F. Call played by Jon Voight: Mike Robe's *Return to Lonesome Dove* (TVW, 1993).

1044

Maybe: Why doesn't he fall down?

Deputy: I've seen him shot six times, and he never does ...unless he's drunk.

Joe Maybe played by Audie Murphy and Ben the Deputy played by Frank Chase: Jesse Hibbs' *Ride a Crooked Trail* (Universal, 1958).

1045

Chance: Don't set yourself up as being so special. You'd think you invented the hangover.

Dude: I could sure take out a patent for this one.

John T. Chance played by John Wayne and Dude played by Dean Martin: Howard Hawks' *Rio Bravo* (Warner Bros., 1959).

1046

Kathleen: [*Toasting*] To my only rival, the United States Cavalry.

Mrs. Kathleen Yorke played by Maureen O'Hara: John Ford's *Rio Grande* (Republic, 1950).

1047

McNally: Remind me to ask Tuscarora a question.

Phillips: About what?

McNally: He said you were a saintly old man that didn't hold with all the vices.

Phillips: I don't. I don't hold with them at all. But that don't stop me from taking a saintly pleasure in them whenever I get a chance.

Cord McNally played by John Wayne, Phillips played by Jack Elam, and Tuscarora played by Chris Mitchum: Howard Hawks' *Rio Lobo* (NGP, 1970).

1048

Brigham: Nothing is worth drinking yourself to hell over.

Brigham Young played by Michael Ruud: Richard Lloyd Dewey's *Rockwell* (Imperial Entertainment, 1994).

1049

Rex: I shoot better when I've had a shot. What do you say we have a drink all around?

Rex played by Hal Taliaferro: Joseph Kane's *Saga of Death Valley* (Republic, 1939).

1050

Murphy: Who's he?

Jed: A drunken liar and a lying drunk!

Murphy played by Theodore Newton and Jed Givens played by John Larch: Richard Carlson's *The Sage of Hemp Brown* (Universal, 1958).

1051

Heywood: Nobody ever loved me. Did you know I had to take my own cousin to the graduation dance? I threw up on her dress.

Saloon Girl: You're really my kind of guy!

Jesse W. Heywood played by Don Knotts and the Saloon Girl was uncredited: Alan Rafkin's *The Shakiest Gun in the West* (Universal, 1968).

1052

Gunther: Somebody peed on a bag of flour! Who was it? It's not funny! It's lazy! Even a dog knows to pee in the street. I can't sell this now!

Butch: You can sell it to a sodbuster. He won't know the difference.

Gunther: What kind of men are you? All you do is drink and pee, and drink and pee, and then kill somebody ...and then drink some more.

Gunther Schteuppin played by Steve Landesberg and Butch played by Earl Pastko: Eugene Levy's *Sodbusters* (Atlantis Releasing, 1994).

1053

Colonel: Now, Sergeant, that's for you. You drink it in good health. And may you be in heaven a half hour before the devil knows you're there!

Colonel Morgan played by Brian Keith and Sergeant Fitzsimmons played by Merlin Olsen: Andrew V. McLaglen's *something big* (NGP, 1971). *See also entry 1066.*

1054

Junior: That's the first mirror I've seen with a hangover.

Junior played by Bob Hope: Frank Tashlin's *Son of Paleface* (Paramount, 1952).

1055

Leah: [*Toasting*] To wherever we're going, Mr. Swope: heaven, hell, all the stops in between.

Leah Parker played by Marilyn Maxwell and Sam Swope played by Scott Brady: William F. Claxton's *Stage to Thunder Rock* (Paramount, 1964).

1056

Charlie: Didn't you know it's no fun to drink alone.

Haven: Not until after the first one.

Charlie played by Jane Greer and Haven played by Dick Powell: Sidney Lanfield's *Station West* (RKO, 1948).

1057

Stewart: We need a drink! I don't believe in bottle bravery, but this will tune us all up.

John Stewart played by Randolph Scott: Bruce Humberstone's *Ten Wanted Men* (Columbia, 1955).

1058

Custer: Well, he who drinks and runs away lives to drink another day.

George Armstrong Custer played by Errol Flynn: Raoul Walsh's *They Died with Their Boots On* (Warner Bros., 1941).

1059

Guthrie: I was drunk before I started drinking tonight.

Jim Guthrie played by Dana Andrews: Alfred Werker's *Three Hours to Kill* (Columbia, 1954).

1060

Marshal: Alex, have you been drinking this morning or not?

Alex: Marshal, you know I never touch a drop until the stroke of noon.

The Marshal played by Ford Rainey and Alex Potter played by Henry Jones: Delmer Daves' *3:10 to Yuma* (Columbia, 1957).

1061

Clanton: He's so drunk he can't hit nothing. In fact, you're probably seeing double.

Doc: I have two guns ...one for each of you.

Billy Clanton played by Thomas Hayden Church and Doc Holliday played by Val Kilmer: George P. Cosmatos' *Tombstone* (Buena Vista, 1993).

1062

La Boeuf: You're lucky to be where water is so handy. I've seen the time I drank out of a filthy hoofprint. And I was glad to get it!

La Boeuf played by Glen Campbell: Henry Hathaway's *True Grit* (Paramount, 1969).

Candace Bronson (Rhonda Fleming) is a Confederate spy who rides into trouble and into the arms of Gil Kyle (Glenn Ford) in *The Redhead and the Cowboy* (Paramount, 1951).

1063

Mattie: What is your opinion of the federal marshal called Rooster Cogburn?

Mrs. Floyd: Look, I've heard some terrible things about him. He loves to pull a cork, I know that.

Mattie Ross played by Kim Darby, Mrs. Floyd played by Edith Atwater, and Marshal Reuben J. "Rooster" Cogburn played by John Wayne: Henry Hathaway's *True Grit* (Paramount, 1969).

1064

General: [*Toasting*] To your virtues …and especially your vices, Sara!

General LeClaire played by Alberto Morin and Sister Sara played by Shirley MacLaine: Don Siegel's *Two Mules for Sister Sara* (Universal, 1970).

1065

McCabe: I thought I told you to take those drunks over to the courthouse.

Ward: Well, yes sir, Mr. McCabe, that's what you told me and that's what I done …didn't I, fellas? But it wasn't no use, no use at all …was it, fellas?

McCabe: Huh huh. Well now, Ward, why wasn't it any use? Or am I supposed to guess?

Ward: No sir, Mr. McCabe, not that it calls for much guessing. That's a true fact. Well, what it comes down to is that the judge himself was drunk last night …and never even showed up in court today. And so as I see it, there ain't but one thing to do. And that is to march these fellas right back to jail until the judge sobers up enough to fine 'em legal and proper.

Marshal Guthrie "Gus" McCabe played by James Stewart and Ward Corbey played by Chet Douglas: John Ford's *Two Rode Together* (Columbia, 1961).

1066

John Henry: [*Toasting*] May you be in heaven a half an hour before the devil knows you're dead.

Colonel John Henry Thomas played by John Wayne: Andrew McLaglen's *The Undefeated* (20th Century–Fox, 1969). *See also entry 1053.*

1067

Will: Ned, you remember that drover I shot through the mouth …his teeth came out the back of his head?

Ned: Yeah.

Will: I think about him now and again. He didn't do anything to deserve to get shot …at least nothing I could remember when I sobered up.

William Bill Munny played by Clint Eastwood and Ned Logan played by Morgan Freeman: Clint Eastwood's *Unforgiven* (Warner Bros., 1992).

1068

Allen: Never take another man's drink. It's bad luck.

Dick Allen played by Robert Preston: Cecil B. De-Mille's *Union Pacific* (Paramount, 1939).

1069

Honey: Say fella, if you wasn't drinking, you might wake up in the morning and find yourself seriously dead!

Honey Wiggin played by Eugene Pallette: Victor Fleming's *The Virginian* (Paramount, 1929).

1070

Mexican: Señor, you want to hear a Mexican song?

Clum: Sorry, I'm in a hurry.

Mexican: Oh, I play for one drink, and sing at the same time for two.

Clum: Later, maybe.

Mexican: But I'm thirsty now!

Clum: I'll tell you what. You start playing and I'll go look for some water.

Mexican: Water?

The Mexican was uncredited. John P. Clum played by Audie Murphy: Jesse Hibbs' *Walk the Proud Land* (Universal, 1956).

1071

Shep: The guy was dead. Self-defense, huh? Only with a hole in it …because there wasn't any gun under the guy's coat …only a bottle …busted. It went right through his heart. A joke, see? I killed a guy for reachin' for a drink!

Shep played by William Bishop: John Sturges' *The Walking Hills* (Columbia, 1949).

1072

Arizona: Oh, I sure hope they got plenty of cold beer in Silver City. My innards feel like the Big Dry set in!

Arizona played by James Parnell: Reginald LeBorg's *War Drums* (United Artists, 1957).

1073

Judge Bean: [*Toasting*] Here's to the greatest woman in the world. The fairest flower that ever bloomed …Lillie Langtry! Hold it boys! You hear that toast, stranger?

Stranger: Lillie Langtry? I thought you meant your friends. I didn't know that included me.

Judge Bean: That includes every man that drinks at my bar!

Stranger: Glad to join you. Have you ever met Miss Langtry?

Judge Bean: No, I never met her. I never met the sun. I never shook hands with the moon, and I've never been introduced to no clouds.

Stranger: That's all right! Too bad Lillie Langtry couldn't have heard that.

Judge Bean: Did you ever see her?

Stranger: No. I was in England once but didn't get around to it.

Judge Bean: Oh …you was in England once …and you could have seen her …but you never got around to it?

Stranger: Yeah.

Posse members ready for a necktie party: Stanley Andrews (uncredited), Honey Wiggen (William Frawley), the Virginian (Joel McCrea), Baldy (Vince Barnett), and Nebraska (Tom Tully). Rustlers: Shorty (Paul Guilfoyle), Steve (Sonny Tufts), and Spanish Ed (Martin Garralaga) in *The Virginian* (Paramount, 1946).

Judge Bean: Get out of my bar.

Stranger: Huh?

Judge Bean: Get out of my bar!

Judge Roy Bean played by Walter Brennan and the Stranger played by Lucien Littlefield: William Wyler's *The Westerner* (United Artists, 1940).

1074

Cole [*toasting to picture*]: To the unfortunate lady with a bullet in the face.

Judge Bean: The man that fired that bullet was hauled out of here feet first!

Cole: And he ought to be. Any man that would shoot at a picture of Lillie Langtry ought to be killed. It's just retribution!

Judge Bean: It's justifiable homicide! That was my ruling.

Cole Hardin played by Gary Cooper and Judge Roy Bean played by Walter Brennan: William Wyler's *The Westerner* (United Artists, 1940).

1075

Judge Bean: Now in honor of this great occasion, I'm dishing out free beer to one and all. And anybody found sober after sundown is liable to be arrested for disorderly conduct. And that's my ruling.

Judge Roy Bean played by Walter Brennan: William Wyler's *The Westerner* (United Artists, 1940).

1076

Yancey: Music is wine for a thirsty soul.

Yancey played by Audie Murphy: Jack Sher's *The Wild and the Innocent* (Universal, 1959).

1077

Grandpa: It's a mighty hot sun …almost tempts a man to drink water.

Grandpa played by James Barton: William A. Wellman's *Yellow Sky* (20th Century–Fox, 1948).

Dying

See also Burying; Killing

1078

Hutch: Even if you're an idiot, I don't see why you want to die so young.

Hutch played by Bud Spencer: Giuseppe Colizzi's *Ace High* (Paramount, 1967).

1079

Smitty: So many times every day you stop and give thanks. But mostly I can't catch on what you're thanking the Lord for. I mean, there's nothing special.

Parsons: I give thanks for the time and for the place.

Smitty: The time and place, Parsons?

Parsons: The time to live and the place to die. That's all any man gets. No more, no less.

Smitty played by Frankie Avalon and the Parsons played by Hank Worden: John Wayne's *The Alamo* (United Artists, 1960).

1080

George: Get your dumb thumb out of my eye!

Melody: I was just trying to see if you was dead.

George: Well, I ain't! And I don't like someone trying to gouge my eye out!

George Fury played by William Demarest and Melody Jones played by Gary Cooper: Stuart Heisler's *Along Came Jones* (RKO, 1945).

1081

Ward: Did you ever figure that maybe I won't get back?

Linus: You'll make it. People only die when they have something to live for.

Ward: I know. That's why I'm a little worried …for the first time.

Ward Kinsman played by Robert Taylor and Lt. Linus Delaney played by Don Taylor: Sam Wood's *Ambush* (MGM, 1950).

1082

Nalinle: Why did you come back, Massai?

Massai: This is where I belong.

Nalinle: Is it? Is this where you want to die?

Massai: Only a warrior chooses his place to die. I am no longer a warrior.

Nalinle played by Jean Peters and Massai played by Burt Lancaster: Robert Aldrich's *Apache* (United Artists, 1954).

1083

Sam: No bullets, no protection …not even anything worth taking a last look at.

Rev: It is God's earth, man. You wouldn't reject it in the hour of your death.

Sam Leeds played by Stephen McNally and the Reverend Griffin played by Arthur Shields: Hugo Fregonese's *Apache Drums* (Universal, 1951).

1084

Tracks: Well, now that you're dead, why don't you lay down?

Tracks Williams played by Raymond Hatton: James Hogan's *The Arizona Raiders* (a.k.a. *Bad Men of Arizona*; Paramount, 1936).

1085

Lonesome: There's a dead man in there!

Tracks: What?

Lonesome: And I think he's still alive!

Lonesome Alonzo Mulhall played by Johnny Downs and Tracks Williams played by Raymond Hatton: James Hogan's *The Arizona Raiders* (a.k.a. *Bad Men of Arizona*; Paramount, 1936).

1086

Slater: Sometimes living is not that important. I ought to take you with me. You're no good.

Jim Slater played by Richard Widmark: John Sturges' *Backlash* (Universal, 1956).

1087

Gaunt: I bring unfortunate tidings. Your father has met an untimely alleviation of existence.

Zack: What?

Gaunt: He's dead!

Undertaker Gaunt played by Carel Struycken and Zack Stone played by Richard Joseph Paul: Sam Irvin's *Backlash: Oblivion 2* (Full Moon Entertainment, 1996).

1088

Rayburn: Why, you're just a little choosy how you kick the bucket, ain't ya? You're just a figuring and a worrying in that head of yours, thinking there will be a miracle …and you won't have to die at all. Well, I used to josh myself that way once too. I sleep better now.

Rayburn played by Addison Richards: Lew Landers' *Bad Lands* (RKO, 1939).

1089

…a brave man dies only once.

Spoken by Alicia who was played by Gina Lollobrigida: Gene Martin's *Bad Man's River* (Scotia International, 1971).

1090

Cable: Josh, it's about time you earned your keep. Preach me a funeral sermon.

Hildy: Oh, for heaven's sake!

Cable: A good one. Don't make me out no saint, but don't put me down too deep.

Joshua: You mean now?

Cable: Yeah. It's not so much the dying that you hate. It's not knowing what they're going to say about you, that's all. Now all my life I've been scared of this living. Now …got to do the other. Now come on now! I can't wait all day! I ain't got any time!

Cable Hogue played by Jason Robards, Jr., Hildy played by Stella Stevens, and the Reverend Joshua Sloan played by David Warner: Sam Peckinpah's *The Ballad of Cable Hogue* (Warner Bros., 1970).

1091

Frank: Do you think he's going to make it?
Ruth: Well, he's got one foot on the other side.

Frank Badger played by Bo Hopkins and Ruth Badger played by Carrie Snodgress: Maggie Greenwald's *The Ballad of Little Jo* (Fine Line Features, 1993).

1092

Cookie: I knew I was too young and pretty to die.

Cookie played by Andy Devine: William Witney's *Bells of San Angelo* (Republic, 1947).

1093

Doc: Step back, gents, and reflect on the joys of living.

Doc Butcher played by Walter Brennan: William D. Russell's *Best of the Badmen* (RKO, 1951).

1094

Britt: A man can't live worrying about dyin', brother.

Britt Johnson played by Tony Todd: Steven H. Stern's *Blood Horse* (TV miniseries, Cabin Fever Entertainment, 1995).

1095

Sandine: My people have a saying which sums it up rather nicely. Hawk-a-hey.
Maverick: Hawk-a-hey?
Sandine: It's a good day to die. Adios, pilgrim.

Philo Sandine played by Stuart Margolin and Bret Maverick played by James Garner: Stuart Margolin's *Bret Maverick: The Lazy Ace* (TVW, 1981).

1096

Bledsoe: There's something out there that scares you, huh? But it's too late. Now you should have let yourself get killed a long time ago while you had the chance. So you may be the biggest thing that ever hit this area, but you're still two bit outlaws. I never met a soul more affable than you, Butch, or faster than the Kid. But you're still nothing but two bit outlaws on the dodge. It's over! Don't you get that? Your times is over! And you're going to die bloody. And all you can do is choose where.

Sheriff Bledsoe played by Jeff Corey: George Roy Hill's *Butch Cassidy and the Sundance Kid* (20th Century–Fox, 1969).

1097

Etta: I'm twenty-six and I'm single and a schoolteacher …and that's the bottom of the pit. And the only excitement I've known is here with me now. So I'll go with you, and I won't whine, and I'll sew your socks, and I'll stitch you when you're wounded. I'll do anything you ask of me … except one thing: I won't watch you die. I'll miss that scene if you don't mind.

Etta played by Katharine Ross: George Roy Hill's *Butch Cassidy and the Sundance Kid* (20th Century–Fox, 1969).

Butch Cassidy (Paul Newman) and the Sundance Kid (Robert Redford) on their way to the outlaw hideout, Hole in the Wall, in George Roy Hill's ***Butch Cassidy and the Sundance Kid*** (20th Century–Fox, 1969).

1098

Pee Wee: Oh no you ain't! You ain't going to get me today, you dirty beady-eyed little sons. Because old Pee Wee ain't going to die today. You filthy scavengers!

Cahill: Oh shut up, Simser! If a buzzard bites you, he'd never eat meat again.

Pee Wee Simser played by Rayford Barnes and Marshal J.D. Cahill played by John Wayne: Andrew McLaglen's *Cahill: United States Marshal* (Warner Bros., 1973).

1099

Cahill: Well, there's no use prodding around. I'm willing to die trying to keep 'em [prisoners]. The question is, are you willing to die trying to take 'em? Now I'm cold and hungry and wet and tired and short-tempered, so get on with it!

Marshal J.D. Cahill played by John Wayne: Andrew McLaglen's *Cahill: United States Marshal* (Warner Bros., 1973).

1100

Gang Leader: Tucker! Tucker! How's Coley?

Tucker: He's still alive, but his guts look mighty sick!

The Gang Leader played by Robert Dix and Tucker was uncredited: Kent Osborne's *Cain's Cutthroats* (a.k.a. *Cain's Way*; M.D.A. Associates/Fanfare, 1969).

1101

Cordoba: Remember, hombre, it's better to die on your feet than live on your knees.

General Cordoba played by Raf Vallone: Paul Wendkos' *Cannon for Cordoba* (United Artists, 1970).

1102

Martin: It's a hell of a place to die in.

Nye: There ain't no good places.

Martin Hall played by Victor French and Nye Buell played by Richard Basehart: Michael Winner's *Chato's Land* (United Artists, 1972).

1103

Nat Love: If a man can't go out in a blaze of glory, he can at least go with dignity.

Cherokee Kid: Well, I don't feel like going!

Nat Love played by Ernie Hudson and the Cherokee Kid/Isaiah Turner played by Sinbad: Paris Barclay's *The Cherokee Kid* (HBO Pictures, 1996).

1104

Deborah: Dull Knife, the old chief is much too sick. He'll never make such a trip. Listen …

Dull Knife: If he lives to ride even a mile closer to home, he will die as a man should. There will be no more dying in this place.

Deborah Wright played by Carroll Baker and Dull

Knife played by Gilbert Roland: John Ford's *Cheyenne Autumn* (Warner Bros., 1964).

1105

Spanish Woman: They will not go back. Life there is not life. They will die here.

Spanish Woman played by Dolores Del Rio: John Ford's *Cheyenne Autumn* (Warner Bros., 1964).

1106

Trent: Wake me up when it's time to die.

Chuka: Are you scared of dyin', Lou?

Trent: Not particularly. It just comes at an inconvenient time.

Lou Trent played by James Whitmore and Chuka played by Rod Taylor: Gordon Douglas' *Chuka* (Paramount, 1967).

1107

Cisco Kid: I can't believe this! I think they are really going to kill us.

Pancho: Are you afraid to die?

Cisco Kid: I'd rather live.

Pancho: Me too!

The Cisco Kid played by Jimmy Smits and Pancho played by Cheech Marin: Luis Valdez's *The Cisco Kid* (Turner Pictures, 1994).

1108

Cisco Kid: Well, come on!

Pancho: I can't [jump].

Cisco Kid: What are you afraid of, dying?

Pancho: No, I'm afraid of breaking my leg and then living!

The Cisco Kid played by Jimmy Smits and Pancho played by Cheech Marin: Luis Valdez's *The Cisco Kid* (Turner Pictures, 1994).

1109

Duke: Did Curly die happy?

Mitch: Does anybody?

Duke/Curly Washburn played by Jack Palance and Mitch Robbins played by Billy Crystal: Paul Weiland's *City Slickers II: The Legend of Curly's Gold* (Columbia, 1994).

1110

Beth: I died a hundred times while you were in there.

Steve: I nearly died …once.

Beth Donovan played by Ruth Roman and Steve Farrell played by Randolph Scott: Edwin L. Marin's *Colt .45* (Warner Bros., 1950).

1111

Soldier: Relax. Dying ain't so bad. You've been doing it since the day you was born.

An unidentified soldier's comment to a fellow comrade prior to an Indian attack: Frederick de Cordova's *Column South* (Universal, 1953).

1112

Captain: My troop has extra mounts, sir. I thought perhaps you would like to use one.

Colonel: I'm an infantryman, MacClaw. If I'm going to die, I'm not going to do it sitting down.

Captain Robert MacClaw played by Guy Madison and Colonel Janeway played by Carl Benton Reid: David Butler's *The Command* (Warner Bros., 1953).

1113

Stew: Did you ever get hit with a bullet? It's like a hunk of iron ripping and tearing into you. It sets you on fire inside. Sometimes you don't die right away. You just bleed and hurt for a long time.

Stew Shallis played by Douglas V. Fowley: Ray Enright's *Coroner Creek* (Columbia, 1948).

1114

Mrs. Cantrell: You're at the end of the road …and the devil is beside ya …waiting.

Mrs. Cantrell played by Marjorie Main. She was talking to her son, William Cantrell, played by Walter Pidgeon: Raoul Walsh's *The Dark Command* (Republic, 1940).

1115

Doc: You're dying, Richie. Don't fight it, boy. Just let it come nice and easy.

Dr. Eli Prather played by Royal Dano: Jerry Thorpe's *Day of the Evil Gun* (MGM, 1968).

1116

Nobody: I prepared your canoe with cedar boughs. It's time for you to leave now, William Blake. Time for you to go back to where you came from.

Blake: You mean, Cleveland?

Nobody: Back to the place where all the spirits came from …and where all the spirits return. This world will no longer concern you.

Nobody played by Gary Farmer and William Blake played by Johnny Depp: Jim Jarmusch's *Dead Man* (Miramax Films, 1996).

1117

Cobb: If you are determined to die, I will oblige you myself.

Colonel Caleb Cobb played by F. Murray Abraham: Yves Simoneau's *Dead Man's Walk* (Cabin Fever Entertainment, 1996).

1118

Johnny: Oh God, Bill, I hope it don't get cold again tonight. I don't mind dying …if I could just do it warm.

Johnny and Bill were uncredited: Yves Simoneau's *Dead Man's Walk* (Cabin Fever Entertainment, 1996).

1119

Bill: Did he freeze?

Bigfoot: Well, he's frozen now.

Bill was uncredited and Bigfoot Wallace played by Keith Carradine: Yves Simoneau's *Dead Man's Walk* (Cabin Fever Entertainment, 1996).

Capt. Kaleb (Bekim Fehmiu), deserter from the Army, preparing to take out some Apaches in Burt Kennedy's *The Deserter* (a.k.a. *Ride to Glory*; Paramount, 1971).

1120

Bigfoot: [*declining a blindfold*] I've seen many a man die with his eyes wide open, Major. I expect I can do the same.

Bigfoot Wallace played by Keith Carradine: Yves Simoneau's *Dead Man's Walk* (Cabin Fever Entertainment, 1996).

1121

Johnny: I can't understand why the hell you want to die. Maybe I'm nobody, but I like being alive!

Johnny Ears played by Franco Nero: Paolo Cavara's *Deaf Smith & Johnny Ears* (MGM, 1972).

1122

[*learning one's family history*]

Dying Boy: Why did my father kill himself, Marshal?
Marshal: I don't know, son.
Dying Boy: Tell me! Tell me!
Marshal: A long time ago, a man was killed …shot in the back.
Dying Boy: My father did it?
Marshal: Nobody knew for sure who did it.
Dying Boy: You knew. Why didn't you hang him?
Marshal: There was nothing to be gained by hanging. The dead man had a child, a son. Your father agreed to raise him as his own.

Will Oxley, the Dying Boy, played by Mercer Harris and Marshal Frank Patch played by Richard

Widmark: Allen Smithee's *Death of a Gunfighter* (Universal, 1969).

1123

Kaleb: O'Toole made two mistakes. He didn't test his skills …
Crawford: And he yelled when he was falling.
Kaleb: An Apache wouldn't.
Crawford: Damn it! If a man is dying, he has a right to be a little disturbed about it!
Kaleb: Not if he cares anything about the men he's with.

Captain Viktor Kaleb played by Bekim Fehmiu, Crawford played by Ian Bannen, and O'Toole played by John Alderson: Burt Kennedy's *The Deserter* (a.k.a. *Ride to Glory*; Paramount, 1971).

1124

Sikes: Are you afraid of dying?
McCall: I don't give it much thought.
Sikes: I don't know why you're here. But you ain't going to get what you're after …as long as you got something to lose. My death don't bother me. I ain't got nothing to lose.

John Sikes played by James Remar and Duell McCall played by Alex McArthur: E.W. Swackhamer's *Desperado: The Outlaw Wars* (TVW, 1989).

1125

Sikes: Are you still afraid of dying, McCall? Huh? I want you to feel the bullet because that's going to be me inside you. Take a deep breath, McCall, because here I come!

John Sikes played by James Remar and Duell McCall played by Alex McArthur: E.W. Swackhamer's *Desperado: The Outlaw Wars* (TVW, 1989).

1126

Zeke: I was always one of them fellas that wanted to die with my boots off, in bed, with people standing around and crying over me.

Zeke Carmody played by Edgar Buchanan: Anthony Mann's *Devil's Doorway* (MGM, 1950).

1127

Ellen: They all think that any decent woman would prefer to die than live as an Apache squaw. Maybe they're right.
Jess: Death comes soon enough. Anyone that hurries it is a damn fool.

Ellen Grange played by Bibi Anderson and Jess Remsberg played by James Garner: Ralph Nelson's *Duel at Diablo* (United Artists, 1966).

1128

Chata: You white eyes want us all dead. But when I die, it will not be as a tamed reservation Indian. I will die Apache …killing my enemies.

Chata played by John Hoyt: Ralph Nelson's *Duel at Diablo* (United Artists, 1966).

1129

Mace: You've been so clever, I thought I might learn a little something talking to you. They say a dyin' man's words are interesting.

Mace Ballard played by Kenneth MacDonald: Lambert Hillyer's *The Durango Kid* (Columbia, 1940).

1130

Larkin: How long ago did he die?
Evelyn: Ten years.
Larkin: And you've buried yourself in this town ever since!
Evelyn: I object to the word "buried."
Larkin: Object away! You're living further in the past than I am!

Bob Larkin played by Henry Fonda and Evelyn played by Inger Stevens: Vincent McEveety's *Firecreek* (Warner Bros.–Seven Arts, 1968).

1131

Matanza: There's nothing much surer than being dead, amigo.

Matanza was uncredited: Aldo Florio's *Five Giants from Texas* (Miro Cinematografica/P.C. Balcazar, 1966).

1132

Billy: You're going to die looking like a brave man!

Billy Candy played by Jonathan Haze: Roger Corman's *Five Guns West* (American Releasing Corp., 1955).

1133

Pacer: Don't try to help me, Clint. I've been killed already. I'm just stubborn about dying.

Pacer Burton played by Elvis Presley and Clint Burton played by Steve Forrest: Don Siegel's *Flaming Star* (20th Century–Fox, 1960).

1134

Arch: Maybe our luck has run out on us.
Jesse: I make my own damn luck!
Cole: Yeah, but do we have to die to prove that?
Jesse: It's not our fate to die on the trail.

Arch Clements played by Nick Sadler, Jesse James played by Rob Lowe, and Cole Younger played by Randy Travis: Robert Boris' *Frank & Jesse* (Vidmark Entertainment, 1995).

1135

Sarah: John, do you remember in the hospital when I read aloud to you from *Julius Caesar*?
Doc: Yeah.
Sarah: Well, there was a line in the first act that went something like this: "Cowards die many times before their death, but brave but once."
Doc: I'm a coward?

Sarah: You've become one, John. You're afraid of living and you're afraid of dying.
Doc: No, not afraid of dying.
Sarah: Yes, afraid of dying. Oh, all this going around killing and hoping to be killed isn't courage. Well, that's just a cover for fear.

Sarah Allen played by Nancy Kelly and John "Doc" Holliday played by Cesar Romero: Allan Dwan's *Frontier Marshal* (20th Century–Fox, 1939).

1136

Billy: You know, Brady, it's not the dying that bothers me. It's the suffering.

Billy Montana played by Bruce Boxleitner and Brady played by Kenny Rogers: Dick Lowry's *The Gambler, Part III — The Legend Continues* (TVW, 1987).

1137

Luke: How many times do you have to die to get it done once?

Luke Daly played by Cameron Mitchell: Henry Hathaway's *Garden of Evil* (20th Century–Fox, 1954).

1138

Fiske: There it [sunset] goes, Hooker. Everyday it goes. And somebody always goes with it. Today it's me.

Fiske played by Richard Widmark and Hooker played by Gary Cooper: Henry Hathaway's *Garden of Evil* (20th Century–Fox, 1954).

1139

Sieber: Goddamn, I never thought I'd get killed trying to help save an Apache.
Davis: We got 'em, Mr. Sieber. We got 'em all.
Sieber: I've been gunshot and arrow shot seventeen times …twenty years chasing old Geronimo! There's nothing I know better than being hurt. Finis.
Gatewood: You don't have to account for yourself to me, Al. You're a brave man.
Sieber: [*dying*] I never did have no kind of luck. Never did. So …I'm going to catch me a little sleep here for …a minute or two. Rotten sons-a-bitches!

Al Sieber played by Robert Duvall, Lt. Britton Davis played by Matt Damon, and Lt. Charles Gatewood played by Jason Patric: Walter Hill's *Geronimo: An American Legend* (Columbia, 1993).

1140

General: Some things never die, do they Harrod?
Harrod: Only men die, General.

General Frederick McCabe played by Andrew Duggan and Captain Demas Harrod played by Tom Tryon: Arnold Laven's *The Glory Guys* (United Artists, 1965).

1141

Harrod: And now I'm back for one last fight. Only this time he's put me in

charge of the expendables. Why, these recruits can't ride, can't shoot, can't fight …can't even button their pants twice the same way. But for General "Glory" McCabe, we can all do one thing superbly …we can die.

Captain Demas Harrod played by Tom Tryon: Arnold Laven's *The Glory Guys* (United Artists, 1965).

1142

Sol: If you aim to die, you're going at it the wrong way. Drink deep, ride hard, take a hold of everything that comes your way. Only double. Don't look over the horizon. That's the Lord's business.

Sol Rogers played by Harve Presnell: Arnold Laven's *The Glory Guys* (United Artists, 1965).

1143

Houston: It's time the other fellas did the dying.

Sam Houston played by Sam Elliott: Peter Levin's *Gone to Texas* (a.k.a. *Houston: The Legend of Texas*; TVW, 1986).

1144

Molly: Is it …is it Hiram who's hurt?
Ben: It's Hiram, Molly. He won't hurt anymore.

Molly Cain played by Kathryn Card, Marshal Hiram Cain played by Emile Meyer, and Ben Cutler played by Fred MacMurray: Nathan Juran's *Good Day for a Hanging* (Columbia, 1958).

1145

Sheriff: He's dead.
Johnson: Aren't you gonna take him out of here [jail cell]?
Sheriff: What for? He ain't in any hurry to go anywhere.

Sheriff William Morgan played by Graham McPherson and Alan Johnson played by Christopher Reeve: Steven H. Stern's *Good Men and Bad* (TV miniseries, Cabin Fever Entertainment, 1995).

1146

Blinky: I don't want to die rich.

Blinky played by Lee Marvin: Raoul Walsh's *Gun Fury* (Columbia, 1953).

1147

Jess: You look very much alive for a dead man.

Jess Burgess played by Leo Gordon: Raoul Walsh's *Gun Fury* (Columbia, 1953).

1148

Doc: Listen, Wyatt, the only thing I'm really scared of is dying in bed. I don't want to go little by little. Someday someone has got to outshoot me and it will be over real quick.

John H. "Doc" Holliday played by Kirk Douglas and Wyatt Earp played by Burt Lancaster: John Sturges' *Gunfight at the O.K. Corral* (Paramount, 1957).

1149

Kate: You're going to die for sure if you go out there.

Doc: If I'm going to die, at least let me die with the only friend I ever had.

Kate Fisher played by Jo Van Fleet and John H. "Doc" Holliday played by Kirk Douglas: John Sturges' *Gunfight at the O.K. Corral* (Paramount, 1957).

1150

Linda: I pity you. You're a dead man already. I can see it in your eyes. They used to be so full of life. But not anymore. You have one thing to look forward to: lying face down in the street. And there will be no one there to cry for you.

Linda Yarnell played by Kay Lenz: Larry Ferguson's *Gunfighter's Moon* (Rysher Entertainment/ Cabin Fever Entertainment, 1995).

1151

Sheriff: What do you want to do? Wind up using the gunman's sidewalk? Huh? That's the middle of the street. That's where they all die sooner or later.

Sheriff Harry Brill played by Robert F. Simon: Phil Karlson's *Gunman's Walk* (Columbia, 1958).

1152

McCasslin: When you're liable to be sleeping for a long while, you try to crowd in as much living as you can with the time that's left.

Hazel McCasslin played by Madge Meredith: George Marshall's *The Guns of Fort Petticoat* (Columbia, 1957).

1153

Emiliano: Chris, how old do you have to be to die?

The little boy, Emiliano Zapata, played by Tony Davis and Chris played by George Kennedy: Paul Wendkos' *Guns of the Magnificent Seven* (United Artists, 1969).

1154

Emiliano: Max, what did Chris say?

Max: He said the cowards die many deaths …the brave only one.

Emiliano Zapata played by Tony Davis, Max played by Reni Santoni, and Chris played by George Kennedy: Paul Wendkos' *Guns of the Magnificent Seven* (United Artists, 1969).

1155

John: I guess I'm going to find out for sure now.

Matt: What's that, John?

John: When you're passing over, they say that you can see into the next world as you're going …see the fields of ambrosia.

John Parsley played by James Brolin and Matt Dillon played by James Arness: Jerry Jameson's *Gunsmoke: The Long Ride* (TVW, 1993).

1156

Devlin: Forget me.

Soledad: Oh no, no! Never!

Devlin: Oh, I know you. You'll mourn me until the day after tomorrow, then swap my horse for a ticket to Abilene.

Soledad: Not Abilene. New Orleans.

Davlin: You'll sell my guns, too, for that new bonnet that I never got around to buying you.

James Devlin played by Steve Forrest and Soledad Villegas played by Barbara Luna: Michael Caffey's *The Hanged Man* (TVW, 1974).

1157

Frank: My leg is killing me!

Rufus: Well, I sure hope bleeding is good for it, Frank, because you really struck blood there!

Rufus Clemens played by Strother Martin and Frank Clemens played by Jack Elam: Burt Kennedy's *Hannie Caulder* (Paramount, 1971).

1158

Sheriff: Look, Steve, no man gets to be my age. Well, it ain't that he minds dying. It's just that he likes to feel that it was all worthwhile.

Sheriff Sim Hacker played by Robert Burton and Steve Burden played by Guy Madison: George Sherman's *The Hard Man* (Columbia, 1957).

1159

Moxon: How does it feel knowing you only have a few seconds left to live?

Moxon played by Mirko Ellis: Domenico Paolella's *Hate for Hate* (MGM, 1967).

1160

Beck: I figured we taught you not to stray, Andrews.

Andrews: We come here for a purpose, Beck.

Beck: Well, if your purpose is to end up dead in the street, I reckon you come to the right place.

Asa Beck played by John Anderson and Scotty Andrews played by Ed Bakey: Lee H. Katzin's *Heaven with a Gun* (MGM, 1969).

1161

Grimes: Well now, what do you suppose hell is going to look like?

Russell: We all die. It's just a question of when.

Grimes played by Richard Boone and John Russell played by Paul Newman: Martin Ritt's *Hombre* (20th Century–Fox, 1967).

1162

Hondo: Indians place great value on male children.

Angie: They also place a great value on dying well. Did Ed die well?

Hondo: He died well.

Hondo Lane played by John Wayne, Angie played by Geraldine Page, and Ed Lowe played by Leo Gordon: John Farrow's *Hondo* (Warner Bros., 1953).

1163

Hondo: Everybody gets dead. It was his turn.

Hondo Lane played by John Wayne: John Farrow's *Hondo* (Warner Bros., 1953).

1164

Aaron: Shoot him in the belly. I want him to die hard.

Aaron played by John Russell: R.G. Springsteen's *Hostile Guns* (Paramount, 1967).

1165

Doc: What did he [Wyatt's dying brother] say?

Wyatt: When we were kids, we used to argue about whether when you were dying your whole life flashed in front of you or not. He said, it ain't so, Wyatt.

Doc Holliday played by Jason Robards, Jr. and Wyatt Earp played by James Garner: John Sturges' *The Hour of the Gun* (United Artists, 1967).

1166

Jules: You know, it's a funny thing. A man crazy to live takes a chance and dies. A man who doesn't care takes the same chance and gets away with it.

Jules Gaspard D'Estaing played by Yul Brynner: Richard Wilson's *Invitation to a Gunfighter* (United Artists, 1964).

1167

Old Tom: Look, everybody is looking at me. It's the first time I ever felt important.

Dying words of Old Tom, played by John Carradine, in Nicholas Ray's *Johnny Guitar* (Republic, 1954).

1168

Roy: Did he go fast?

Jory: He was dead before he hit the floor.

Roy played by John Marley and Jory Walden played by Robby Benson: Jorge Fons' *Jory* (Avco Embassy, 1972).

1169

O'Fallon: It's no use, kid. A man always knows when he gets the one with his number on it. That, that was it.

O'Fallon played by Will Geer: Kurt Neumann's *The Kid from Texas* (Universal, 1950).

1170

Hardin: Don't sit there, go outside and die. Nobody wants you dyin' in here. This is a proper saloon.

Blacksmith: Boy, it hurts!

Hardin: Well, I expect so. That's what a .44 slug is meant to do.

John Wesley Hardin played by Randy Quaid: Joseph Sargent's *Larry McMurtry's Streets of Laredo* (Cabin Fever Entertainment, 1995).

One of the most famous showdowns ever: Johnny Ringo (John Ireland), Ike Clanton (Lyle Bettger), and Tom McLowery (Jack Elam) await Wyatt Earp (Burt Lancaster), John "Doc" Holliday (Kirk Douglas), Virgil Earp (John Hudson), and Morgan Earp (DeForest Kelley) in John Sturges' *Gunfight at the O.K. Corral* (Paramount, 1957).

1171

Mox Mox: Build a fire, Jimmy. It's chilly.

Jimmy: No more fires for you, Mox.

Mox Mox: Why not? What's wrong with you?

Jimmy: Not near as much as is wrong with you. I ain't shot in the lung and I ain't dying …and you're both. Building you a fire would be a waste of time. And I ain't got the time to waste on a man that's dying.

Mox Mox: I ain't dying! I'm just shot up a little. I'll live if I can get warm.

Jimmy: Hellfire will warm you, Mox. You'll be plenty warm there.

Mox Mox played by Kevin Conway and Quick Jimmy played by Fredrick Lopez: Joseph Sargent's *Larry McMurtry's Streets of Laredo* (Cabin Fever Entertainment, 1995).

1172

Major: Frank, no! A coward dies a thousand times, Frank. Let this one die a few thousand more.

Major Edwards played by Ed Bruce and Frank James played by Johnny Cash: William A. Graham's *The Last Days of Frank and Jesse James* (TVW, 1986).

1173

Henrietta: One thing about facing death: I'm not afraid to let anything into my heart anymore.

Alfred: I won't stand for that attitude, you're not facing death!

Henrietta: Yes, I am. It's just that you won't see it. And that makes me terribly lonely. Do you know what I worry about? That when I die, you'll hold it against me.

Mrs. Henrietta Kroeber played by Anne Archer and Professor Alfred Kroeber played by Jon Voight: Harry Hook's *The Last of His Tribe* (HBO Pictures, 1994).

1174

Ellison: No one knows who killed him or where he's buried.

Padre: Do you always think in violence? Cannot a man die in peace?

Brad Ellison played by Jock Mahoney and Padre Jose played by Eduard Franz: George Sherman's *The Last of the Fast Guns* (Universal, 1958).

1175

Munro: Death and honor are thought to be the same. But today I have learned that sometimes they are not.

Colonel Munro played by Maurice Roeves: Michael Mann's *The Last of the Mohicans* (20th Century–Fox, 1992).

1176

Drune: What's he trying to do? Die with his boots on?

Emerson: Can you think of a better way for him to go?

Sampson Drune played by Charles Bickford and Robert Emerson played by Warner Anderson: Alfred Werker's *The Last Posse* (Columbia, 1953).

1177

Linda: I'm not like you. I don't want to die for law and order.

Linda played by Carolyn Jones: John Sturges' *Last Train from Gun Hill* (Paramount, 1959).

1178

Todd: Well, death is a path we're all on, son. The Indians say a warrior dies well if he gives his life for his loved ones.

"Comanche" Todd played by Richard Widmark: Delmer Daves' *The Last Wagon* (20th Century–Fox, 1956).

1179

Brandt: Pull off my boots! I sweared to my ma I wouldn't die with 'em on.

Frame: You ain't a gonna die, Brandt!

Brandt: No use our playing poker, Frame. I ain't a gonna grow much older.

Ed Brandt played by Harry Carey and Frame Johnson played by Walter Huston: Edward L. Cahn's *Law and Order* (Universal, 1932).

1180

Horses Ghost: It's a good day for dying!

Horses Ghost played by Nick Mancuso: Mel Damski's *The Legend of Walks Far Woman* (TVW, 1982).

1181

Bean: What are you doing in Vinegarroon?

Adams: All my life I've been cold. I've come south to die where it's warm.

Bean: Well, it's warm here, but there will be no illegal dying. The only people that die in my town are those I shoot or hang. Get along with ya!

Adams: Can't die here, can't die there! A man can't even die where he sees fit to. I don't want no part of what this world is coming to, and glad my days are at an end.

Judge Roy Bean played by Paul Newman and Grizzly Adams played by John Huston: John Huston's *The Life and Times of Judge Roy Bean* (NGP, 1972).

1182

Hayworth: Only the good die young.

Nat Hayworth played by Morris Ankrum: Lesley Selander's *The Light of the Western Stars* (Paramount, 1940).

1183

Old Lodge Skins: I won't eat with you because I'm going to die soon.

Little Big Man: Die, grandfather?

Old Lodge Skins: Yes, my son. I want to die in my own land where human beings are buried in the sky.

Little Big Man: But why do you want to die, grandfather?

Old Lodge Skins: Because there's no other way to deal with the white man, my son. Whatever else you can say about them, it must be admitted: you cannot get rid of 'em.

Little Big Man: No, I suppose not, grandfather.

Old Lodge Skins: There is an endless supply of white men, but there has always been a limited number of human beings. We won today …we won't win tomorrow.

Old Lodge Skins played by Chief Dan George and Little Big Man/Jack Crabb played by Dustin Hoffman: Arthur Penn's *Little Big Man* (NGP, 1971).

1184

Old Lodge Skins: It is a good day to die.

Old Lodge Skins played by Chief Dan George: Arthur Penn's *Little Big Man* (NGP, 1971).

1185

[*a classroom discussion*]

Nancy: Miss Plum?

Teacher: Yes, Nancy?

Nancy: Could I ask Albert a question?

Teacher: Certainly.

Nancy: What's it like, knowing you're going to die?

Teacher: Nancy, I don't think that's any of your business!

Albert: That's all right, Miss Plum. I don't mind talking about it. [*pause*] Well, at first I was scared …and angry. But, you know, once I started to think about my life, I found that I had made myself some really wonderful memories. You know, things I've done, all the good times, all the good friends. And you know, the best thing about it all is that they all took place right here [Walnut Grove]. And that's why I came back. Because there's no better place on God's earth. Just don't waste the time you have on it. All of you: go out, you have a good time, make yourself lots of good friends. You see, that way … you see, that way when it's your time to look back and find your memories, you'll see that you won't be scared or angry either.

Nancy Olsen played by Allison Balson, Teacher Etta Plum played by Leslie Landon, and Albert Ingalls played by Matthew Laborteaux: Victor French's *Little House on the Prairie: Look Back to Yesterday* (TVW, 1983).

1186

Dog Face: I hurt bad. Go ahead, shoot me.

Blue Duck: You won't catch me wasting a bullet on you. Monkey can cut your damn throat if he wants to!

Monkey: Nah, he'll die soon enough.

Dog Face played by David Ode, Blue Duck played by Frederic Forrest, and Monkey John played by Matthew Cowles: Simon Wincer's *Lonesome Dove* (TVW, 1989).

1187

Old Man: Well, should you die before our journey is through, happy days! All is well.

The Old Man played by John Marley: Vic Morrow's *A Man Called Sledge* (Columbia, 1971).

1188

McCabe: Well, I just didn't want to get killed.

Lawyer: Until people stop dying for freedom, they ain't going to be free.

John McCabe played by Warren Beatty and Lawyer Clement Samuels played by William Devane: Robert Altman's *McCabe & Mrs. Miller* (Warner Bros., 1971).

1189

Watson: Why did you come back?

Benjie: Because I live here.

Watson: You could die here too, Benjie.

Benjie: A man could die any place. I've been learning that for four years [Civil War]. It just depends on what he's dying for.

Watson played by R.G. Armstrong and Benjie played by Brock Peters: Alf Kjellin's *The McMasters* (Jayjen/Chevron, 1970).

1190

Tom Horn: One shot …no pain. He never knew what hit him.

Ernestina: That's good …isn't it?

Tom Horn played by David Carradine and Ernestina Crawford played by Karen Black: Jack Starrett's *Mr. Horn* (TVW, 1979).

1191

Dan: Your grandfather was a good man. You were lucky to have him as long as you did.

Nika: Why does everyone have to die?

Dan: Death ain't the end of everything.

Dan played by Joel McCrea and Nika played by Nika Mina: John Champion's *Mustang Country* (Universal, 1976).

1192

Jack: Well, now that you got me in the history books, how do I quit?

Nobody: There's only one way.

Jack: How's that?

Nobody: You got to die.

Jack Beauregard played by Henry Fonda and Nobody played by Terence Hill: Tonino Valerii's *My Name Is Nobody* (Universal, 1973).

1193

Santiago: Drink!

Vicente: I'm frightened.

Santiago: Ah, you know how to die. You watched plenty others.

Vicente: I'm going to hell.

Santiago: This will give you courage.

Santiago played by Arthur Kennedy and Vicente played by Tony Martinez: Edgar G. Ulmer's *The Naked Dawn* (Universal, 1955).

1194

Howie: And it's your choice, Ben. A bullet right here on the trail or a rope in Abilene.

Ben: Choosing a way to die, what's the difference? Choosing a way to live, that's the hard part.

Howard "Howie" Kemp played by James Stewart and Ben Vandergroat played by Robert Ryan: Anthony Mann's *The Naked Spur* (MGM, 1953).

1195

Jesse: I got it coming. Do business with the Devil and you get it every time.

Jesse Tate played by Millard Mitchell: Anthony Mann's *The Naked Spur* (MGM, 1953).

1196

Kit: You always said I would die with my boots on. Do me a favor, will ya? Take 'em off.

Kit played by Alan Bridge: Carl Pierson's *The New Frontier* (Republic, 1935).

1197

Harriet: Why did you tell him he was dying?

Bierce: A man deserves the truth at least once before he dies.

Harriet: He didn't need the truth, he needed comfort. It must be horrible to die, frightened and alone.

Bierce: Very few have the foresight and opportunity of planning any other kind of death.

Harriet: You're so eloquent when you say such appalling things.

Bierce: Well, that's the story of my life, my dear. Everybody appreciates the form and is frightened of the content.

Harriet Winslow played by Jane Fonda and Ambrose Bierce played by Gregory Peck: Luis Puenzo's *Old Gringo* (Columbia, 1989).

1198

Bierce: The poor captain. He was only trying to impress us with

His courthouse and saloon were called "The Jersey Lilly." He was the "law west of the Pecos." It was located in the County of Vinegarroon. And this was *The Life and Times of Judge Roy Bean* (NGP, 1972).

his bravery in the face of death ...proving he could die admirably.

Ambrose Bierce played by Gregory Peck and Captain Ovando played by Pedro Damian: Luis Puenzo's *Old Gringo* (Columbia, 1989).

1199

Hayes: Go out in a blaze of glory. Is that it?

John Henry: Why not? It ain't every day a man gets to die doing what he does.

Oren Hayes played by Richard Widmark and John Henry Lee played by Willie Nelson: Burt Kennedy's *Once Upon a Texas Train* (TVW, 1988).

1200

Cheyenne: Hey, Harmonica. When they do you in, pray it's somebody who knows where to shoot.

Cheyenne played by Jason Robards, Jr. and Harmonica Man played by Charles Bronson: Sergio Leone's *Once Upon a Time in the West* (Paramount, 1969).

1201

Verdugo: Well, I hope you know how to die. I admire a man who dies well.

General Verdugo played by Fernando Lamas: Tom Gries' *100 Rifles* (20th Century–Fox, 1969).

1202

Bounty Hunter: I'm looking for Josey Wales.

Josey Wales: That'll be me.

Bounty Hunter: You're wanted, Wales.

Josey Wales: I reckon I'm right popular. You a bounty hunter?

Bounty Hunter: A man's got to do something for a living these days.

Josey Wales: Dyin' ain't much of a livin', boy. You know this isn't necessary. You can just ride on.

The Bounty Hunter played by John Chandler and Josey Wales played by Clint Eastwood who also directed *The Outlaw Josey Wales* (Warner Bros., 1976).

1203

Jamie: Josey, I got to tell you something. I'm scared of dyin', Josey!

Jamie played by Sam Bottoms and Josey Wales played by Clint Eastwood who also directed *The Outlaw Josey Wales* (Warner Bros., 1976).

1204

Jamie: If I don't make it, Josey, I want you to know ...I'm prouder than a game rooster to have rid with ya.

Josey: You are a game rooster, boy. Now shut up!

Jamie played by Sam Bottoms and Josey Wales played by Clint Eastwood who also directed *The Outlaw Josey Wales* (Warner Bros., 1976).

1205

Clint: Me? I kind of relish getting old. It takes the bother out of living.

Clint Priest played by James Whitmore: Roy Rowland's *The Outriders* (MGM, 1950).

Old friends meet ...but the times are changing. Pat Garrett (James Coburn) is now working for the establishment and tells Billy the Kid (Kris Kristofferson) they want him out of the country: "I'm asking ya ...but in five days I'm making ya," in Sam Peckinpah's *Pat Garrett & Billy the Kid* (MGM, 1973).

1206

Will: You got to let the dead stay dead.

Will Owen played by Joel McCrea: Roy Rowland's *The Outriders* (MGM, 1950).

1207

Jessie: What an awful way to die!

Granger: Do you know of a good one?

Jessie Lorraine played by Adele Jergens and Ross Granger played by Jock Mahoney: Fred F. Sears' *Overland Pacific* (United Artists, 1954).

1208

Bowdre: They killed me! I'm gunshot for sure!

Bowdre played by Charles Martin Smith: Sam Peckinpah's *Pat Garrett and Billy the Kid* (MGM, 1973).

1209

Queen Tika: Attend to him, Rab. He must not die.

Rab: He's dead!

Queen Tika: No one is dead in Murania unless we do not wish to revive them.

Queen Tika played by Dorothy Christie and Head Surgeon Rab played by Warner Richmond: Otto Brower and B. Reeves (Breezy) Eason's *The Phantom Empire* (Mascot serial, Chapter 7 in "From Death to Life," 1935).

1210

First Sgt.: You did not take his life. He gave it to you.

First Sergeant Emmett Bell played by Jeff Chandler: George Marshall's *Pillars of the Sky* (Universal, 1956).

1211

Baker: There's a first time for everything except dyin'. And that ain't a first time …it's an only time.

Gilmore: You sure are a deep thinker, J.D.!

J.D. Baker played by Paul Drake and Gilmore played by Gary Bisig: Arthur Allan Seidelman's *Poker Alice* (TVW, 1987).

1212

Glascow: Am I going to die?

Tucson: We all got to go sometime, Glascow. You wouldn't want to go without making a clean breast of things, would ya?

Glascow: It's all Ogden's fault. He got me into this and I'm going to see that he gets his. He rustled over 3,000 head of Tress Bar cattle. A lot of them with his Box 8 brand.

Tucson: How about the deed and the record book?

Glascow: He's got 'em in his safe.

Doctor: Is he hurt bad?

Tucson: No. He'll live to serve a jail sentence.

Glascow: You said I was going to die!

Brose Glascow played by Adrian Morris, Tucson Smith played by Harry Carey, Mayor "Big Steve" Ogden played by Sam Hardy, and the Doctor played by Henry Roquemore: Wallace Fox's *Powdersmoke Range* (RKO, 1935).

1213

Raza: You know, of course, one of us must die.

Dolworth: Maybe both of us.

Raza: To die for money is foolish.

Dolworth: To die for a woman is more foolish.

Bill Dolworth played by Burt Lancaster and Captain Jesus Raza played by Jack Palance: Richard Brooks' *The Professionals* (Columbia, 1966).

1214

Dolworth: Nothing is for always …except death.

Bill Dolworth played by Burt Lancaster: Richard Brooks' *The Professionals* (Columbia, 1966).

1215

Fierro: It is not proper to laugh at a man who is about to die.

Fierro played by Rafael Bertrand: Richard Brooks' *The Professionals* (Columbia, 1966).

1216

Fierro: It is a sacrilege to die with a lie lodged in your teeth.

Fierro played by Rafael Bertrand: Richard Brooks' *The Professionals* (Columbia, 1966).

1217

Gentry: Learning can be slow. But there ain't very many rules to worry about if dying comes fast.

Gentry/John Coventry played by Fred MacMurray: Harry Keller's *Quantez* (Universal, 1957).

1218

Spangler: I don't like to kill friends, Clint.

Clint: That makes us even, Spang. I'm kind of against dying.

Spangler played by Ted De Corsia and Clint Cooper played by Audie Murphy: Sidney Salkow's *The Quick Gun* (Columbia, 1964).

1219

Nathan: What happens to an old crazy man like that?

Julian: Somebody will kill him. That's what he wants.

Nathan: How come?

Julian: Because that's all he's got left …his own dying.

Nathan played by Bryan Fowler and the Reverend Julian Shay played by Willie Nelson: William Wittliff's *Red Headed Stranger* (Alive Films/Charter Entertainment, 1987).

1220

Morgan: Elk Woman, to give up hope is to die.

John Morgan/Shunkawakan played by Richard Harris and Elk Woman played by Gale Sonder-gaard: Irving Kershner's *The Return of a Man Called Horse* (United Artists, 1976).

1221

Marshal: You must be awfully tired of life.

Wyatt: No, not tired of life. Tired of death. It keeps on following me.

Marshal: Maybe it finally caught up with you.

Marshal Will Parker played by Mort Mills and Ben Wyatt played by Robert Taylor: James Neilson's *Return of the Gunfighter* (TVW, 1966).

1222

Boone: The way I look at it, it ain't near as hard for a man if he knows why he's going to die.

Sam Boone played by Pernell Roberts: Budd Boetticher's *Ride Lonesome* (Columbia, 1959).

1223

Steve: When I became a lawman, the world lost a first-class bookkeeper. So, just to pass the time one day, I sort of calculated what it was worth getting shot at. I figured it about $100 a shot.

Gil: You'd have earned quite a sum by now.

Steve: Getting hit, I figured that's worth anywhere from a thousand on up.

[*and later on*]

Steve: How did we figure? A thousand dollars a shot?

Gil: Yeah.

Steve: Those boys sure made me a lot of money. They put 'em all in one spot.

Steve Judd played by Joel McCrea and Gil Westrum played by Randolph Scott: Sam Peckinpah's *Ride the High Country* (MGM, 1962).

1224

Rio: It's strange, Padre, how the most valuable thing in the world is always the cheapest …life.

Father: That is only when there is no love in it. It is the way to life and to God. And there is no other way.

Rio: Well, then it's a good night for life, Padre. It keeps you …and loses me. Adios.

Rio played by Robert Taylor and Father Antonio played by Kurt Kasznar: John Farrow's *Ride, Vaquero!* (MGM, 1953).

1225

Hays: I'm not trying to horn my way in with the Almighty. I just want an edge when I line up for the last showdown.

Hank Hays played by Richard Boone: Sidney Salkow's *Robbers' Roost* (United Artists, 1955).

1226

Gabby: And then I said, Rain-in-the-Face …that was the chief's name …you're a dead injun.

Belle: And what did he say?

Gabby: Well, with rigor mortis having set in, he remained incommunicado.

Gabby Hornaday played by George "Gabby" Hayes and Belle Starr played by Sally Payne: Joseph Kane's *Robin Hood of the Pecos* (Republic, 1941).

1227

Pap: Do you reckon them buzzards have lost something around here?

Plank: It looks a little like they don't believe we're leaving.

Pap: I never did like them things studying on me. It ain't because the buzzards know what they're doing. But it brings the question to mind: do I know what I'm doing?

Pap Dennison played by Guinn "Big Boy" Williams and Plank played by Slim Pickens: William Keighley's *Rocky Mountain* (Warner Bros., 1950).

1228

Deneen: He died before he knew very much about living.

Mr. Deneen played by Donald Crisp: Robert Parrish's *Saddle the Wind* (MGM, 1958).

1229

Bryant: I'm afraid this man is done for, Sheriff.

Jones: Yeah, I'm cheating the rope.

John Bryant played by John Wayne and Joseph Conlon, alias Bob Jones, played by Lane Chandler: Armand Schaefer's *Sagebrush Trail* (Lone Star/Monogram, 1933).

1230

Ptewaquin: Do not be sad, little one. It is a good journey. I go on now. There is nothing to fear. No pain …no hate.

Ptewaquin played by Irene Tedrow: William Witney's *Santa Fe Passage* (Republic, 1955).

1231

Deaks: Did she have any last words?

Jody: No, not that I heard. She died pretty hard.

Deaks: Yeah, you live hard and die hard. That's what most of us come to.

Deaks played by Robert Wilke and Jody played by Michael Burns: Gary Nelson's *Santee* (Crown International Pictures, 1973).

1232

Sergeant: You're already dead but you don't know it.

The Sergeant was uncredited: Werner Knox/Bruno Mattei's *Scalps* (Imperial Entertainment, 1987).

1233

Caldwell: So you think I'm a traitor. I told you I'd be better off dead.

Osceola: No man is better off dead, my friend.

Lieutenant Lance Caldwell played by Rock Hudson and Chief Osceola/John Powell played by Anthony Quinn: Budd Boetticher's *Seminole* (Universal, 1953).

1234

Lomax: Your friends! They took turns gunning old Trooper in his wheelchair. Shot him in the belly so he died real slow. Do you know what happens when you're shot in the belly? Well, you can't move. You can't breathe. You feel yourself filling up with blood …with pain! And you can't die!

Clay Lomax played by Gregory Peck and Trooper played by Jeff Corey: Henry Hathaway's *Shoot Out* (Universal, 1971).

1235

Books: Well, my being here, maybe that's news. But dying is my own business. Keep it under your hat, will ya?

Marshal: All right. Just don't take too long to die. Be a gent and convenience everybody and do it soon.

John Bernard Books played by John Wayne and Marshal Thibido played by Harry Morgan: Don Siegel's *The Shootist* (Paramount, 1976).

1236

Stranger: There are two sure things: death and taxes.

The Stranger played by Tony Anthony: Vance Lewis' (Luigi Vanzi) *The Silent Stranger* (a.k.a. *Stranger in Japan*; MGM, 1969).

1237

Mal: I got there just short of too late.

Mal played by Danny Glover: Lawrence Kasdan's *Silverado* (Columbia, 1985).

1238

Ma Mondier: Life goes on in spite of trouble, Laurie. Life goes on.

Ma Mondier played by Lorna Thayer and Laurie Cullen played by Susan Houston: Joseph Kane's *Smoke in the Wind* (Frontier Productions/Gamalex, 1975).

1239

Laura: Why do you care whether any of us live or die?

Brett: I don't see any reason for people to throw their lives away.

Laura Evans played by Piper Laurie and Brett Halliday played by Dana Andrews: Jerry Hopper's *Smoke Signal* (Universal, 1955).

1240

Spikes: I don't know when I liked a boy so much. He was never noisy …never rude. A born gentleman by nature. Well, let's hope the ground that covers his grave will always be green.

Will: He's not dead yet!

Spikes: He's a goner. Say goodbye and let's go.

Will: He's still alive!

Spikes: Put a hat over his face. He ain't gonna make it.

Will: He's still breathing! Now, we're gonna take him to a doctor.

Spikes: Just loading him on a horse will be his end.

Will: We ain't leaving Tod behind!

Spikes: That posse will be back. We're already short a horse. We won't make it unless we leave him.

Les: Then we won't make it!

Spikes: I'd stay by his side if I thought it would do him any good and me no harm. But that ain't the way it lies.

Will: Don't you care nothing about him? You just said you did.

Spikes: I've left men dead behind me. I've left men dying behind me. And I've left 'em calling my name. What you do is shut your ears and close your eyes and run like hell. If you boys were older and been in it longer, you'd know that's the only way to stay alive.

Harry Spikes played by Lee Marvin, Will Young played by Gary Grimes, Les Richter played by Ron Howard, and Tod Hayhew played by Charles Martin Smith: Richard Fleischer's *The Spikes Gang* (United Artists, 1974).

1241

Les: Well, one thing is for sure. I can't die any poorer than I started.

Les Richter played by Ron Howard: Richard Fleischer's *The Spikes Gang* (United Artists, 1974).

1242

Marshal: Buck, just because a man doesn't want to die doesn't mean he's yellow.

Marshal Curley Wilcox played by Johnny Cash and Buck played by John Schneider: Ted Post's *Stagecoach* (TVW, 1986).

1243

Peacock: Marshal, you understand I'm not concerned for myself. But I would hate to see good whiskey wasted on Geronimo. I must insist that we return to Tonto.

Marshal: Sorry, mister. But in this court, majority rules.

Billy: That means if there are three people, and two of them vote to die, then the third one has to die with 'em.

Trevor Peacock played by Anthony Newley, Marshal Curley Wilcox played by Johnny Cash, and Billy "Ringo" Williams played by Kris Kristofferson: Ted Post's *Stagecoach* (TVW, 1986).

1244

Buck: Does the sight of blood bother you much?

Marshal: Only if it's mine.

Buck played by John Schneider and Marshal Curley Wilcox played by Johnny Cash: Ted Post's *Stagecoach* (TVW, 1986).

1245

Sarah: I didn't have the courage to die. I knew what I had to do to stay alive.

Sarah Carter played by Eva Marie Saint: Robert Mulligan's *The Stalking Moon* (NGP, 1968).

1246

Valerie: Oh, Mrs. Kenyon, what about that wounded man?

Ann: You get used to everything around here, especially the wounded and the dying. You just get used to it.

Valerie Kendrick played by Julia Adams and Ann Kenyon played by Jaclynne Greene: Lee Sholem's *The Stand at Apache River* (Universal, 1953).

1247

Pike: Dying is a way of life for some people, Tyree. Make sure you don't have that problem.

Pike played by Jim Brown and Tyree played by Fred Williamson: Anthony M. Dawson's *Take a Hard Ride* (20th Century–Fox, 1975).

1248

Corinne: If I'm to die, I want it all at once, and with you. I'm not going anyplace else to die in little pieces.

Corinne Michaels played by Jocelyn Brando: Bruce Humberstone's *Ten Wanted Men* (Columbia, 1955).

1249

Andrew: It would be better to die by the hand of someone who loves you.

Andrew Hall played by David Strollery: William Beaudine's *Ten Who Dared* (Buena Vista, 1960).

1250

Lonetta: Have you no wish to live?

Don Andrea: I wish to live. But what is life without honor?

Lonetta: What is honor without life?

Lonetta played by Tina Marquand and Don Andrea Baldasar played by Alain Delon: Michael Gordon's *Texas Across the River* (Universal, 1966).

1251

El Guapo: You want to die like dogs?

Dusty: Well, if there's anyway of avoiding that part of it …

El Guapo played by Humberto Arau and Dusty Bottoms played by Chevy Chase: John Landis' *Three Amigos!* (Orion, 1986).

1252

Phillips: We're all dying on our feet and haven't got sense enough to know it.

John Phillips played by John Wayne: Bernard Vorhaus' *Three Faces West* (Republic, 1940).

1253

Polly: Oh, Marty, is there anything you believe in?

Marty: Yes. Living.

Polly: Then you better get out of town.

Polly played by Carolyn Jones and Marty Lasswell played by Laurence Hugo: Alfred Werker's *Three Hours to Kill* (Columbia, 1954).

1254

Marshal: Safe? Who knows what's safe. I knew a man who dropped dead looking at his wife. My own grandmother fought the Indians for sixty years, then choked to death on lemon pie. Do I have two volunteers?

The Marshal played by Ford Rainey: Delmer Daves' *3:10 to Yuma* (Columbia, 1957).

1255

Innocencio: Sometimes a soldier does not live well. But they always die well.

Innocencio played by Gilbert Roland: Rudolph Mate's *Three Violent People* (Paramount, 1956).

1256

Cinch: You know, the fact that men die heroes doesn't change the fact that they're dead before their time.

Cinch Saunders played by Tom Tryon: Rudolph Mate's *Three Violent People* (Paramount, 1956).

1257

Capt.: Do you read Shakespeare?

Lt.: Do I what?

Capt.: A posture of victory always. But we are all born with a debt to death. Pay it today and we don't owe it tomorrow.

Captain Stephen Maddocks played by Richard Boone and Lieutenant Curtis McQuade played by George Hamilton: Joseph Newman's *A Thunder of Drums* (MGM, 1961).

1258

Tulsa: A funny thing about living, Captain. You never can count on it.

Tulsa played by Raymond Burr and Captain David Storm played by Dane Clark: Frank McDonald's *Thunder Pass* (Republic, 1954).

1259

Wolcott: I can see men dying for their country. That's my duty. But I can't see men dying for your honor …or mine.

Major Wolcott played by Glenn Ford: Phil Karlson's *A Time for Killing* (Columbia, 1967).

1260

McCord: Oh, that reminds me. Coroner's certificate …my formal affidavit that Jamerson died suddenly but thoroughly. One gunshot.

Dr. McCord played by John McIntire: Anthony Mann's *The Tin Star* (Paramount, 1957).

1261

Morgan: Wyatt, do you believe in God? Now come on, really, do you?

Wyatt: Yeah. Maybe. Hell, I don't know.

Morgan: Well, what do you think happens when you die?

Wyatt: Something. Nothing. Hell, I don't know.

Morgan: Well, I read this book …a book on spiritualism.

Virgil: Oh God, here he goes again!

Morgan: It said that a lot of people when they die, they see this light …like in a tunnel. They say it's the light leading you to heaven.

Wyatt: Really? Well, what about hell? They got a sign there or what?

Morgan Earp played by Bill Paxton, Wyatt Earp played by Kurt Russell, and Virgil Earp played by Sam Elliott: George P. Cosmatos' *Tombstone* (Buena Vista, 1993).

1262

Morgan: Remember what I said about seeing a light when you're dying?

Wyatt: Yeah, yeah.

Morgan: It ain't true. I can't see a damn thing!

Morgan Earp played by Bill Paxton and Wyatt Earp played by Kurt Russell: George P. Cosmatos' *Tombstone* (Buena Vista, 1993).

1263

Wyatt: How are we feeling today, Doc?

Doc: I'm dyin'. How are you?

Wyatt Earp played by Kurt Russell and Doc Holliday played by Val Kilmer: George P. Cosmatos' *Tombstone* (Buena Vista, 1993).

1264

Priest: Let the living die, he said, so the dead can live.

The Town Priest played by Fernando Rey: Robert Parrish's *A Town Called Hell* (a.k.a. *A Town Called Bastard*; Scotia International, 1971).

1265

Noble: The blood's dark. The bullet's in my liver. I'll be dead in an hour.

Noble Adams played by Kris Kristofferson: John Guillermin's *The Tracker* (HBO Pictures, 1988).

1266

Grady: Yeah, when a man can't hold his liquor, that's the first sign [of getting old].

Jesse: What about your women?

Grady: What about 'em?

Jesse: Well, don't tell me you don't run 'em as much as you used to.

Grady: Jesse, now I wouldn't want this to get around …but the last time I was over to Kate's in Tucson, I spent the whole night listening to a fella play the piano.

Jesse: Could he play good?

Grady: Worst I've ever heard!

Jesse: Oh, you just wasn't in the mood.

Grady: I'm not getting any younger! That's what I'm trying to tell ya, Jesse. And neither are you.

Jesse: What the hell do you want me to do? Just roll over and die?

It's showdown time at the O.K. Corral with Doc Holliday (Val Kilmer), Virgil Earp (Sam Elliott), Wyatt Earp (Kurt Russell), and Morgan Earp (Bill Paxton) in *Tombstone* (Buena Vista, 1993).

Grady: All I'm saying is …don't get old. You'll live to regret it.

Grady played by Rod Taylor and Wil Jesse played by Ben Johnson: Burt Kennedy's *The Train Robbers* (Warner Bros., 1973).

1267

Lon: Easy, Hoby, don't move. I'll get a doctor.

Hoby: No! A man that can do what I've done shouldn't live.

Lon Cordeen played by Gordon Scott and Hoby Cordeen played by James Mitchum: Albert Band's *The Tramplers* (Embassy Picture Release, 1965).

1268

Ruth: When you think you're going to die, you grow up fast.

Ruth Harris played by Shelley Winters: George Sherman's *The Treasure of Pancho Villa* (RKO, 1955).

1269

Rudock: I ain't ready to die yet. I got too many good times left in me.

Jeremy Rudock played by James Cagney: Robert Wise's *Tribute to a Bad Man* (MGM, 1956).

1270

Miller: I was a boy when I entered Mr. Rodock's valley. But when I left, I wasn't a boy anymore. I picked up a few pointers on how men die quickly, and how they keep from dying quickly.

Steve Miller played by Don Dubbins and Jeremy Rudock played by James Cagney: Robert Wise's *Tribute to a Bad Man* (MGM, 1956).

1271

Marshal: I can't do a thing for you, son. Your partner has killed you and I've done for him.

Moon: Don't leave me lying here! Don't let those wolves get me!

Marshal: I'll see that you get buried.

Marshal Reuben J. "Rooster" Cogburn played by John Wayne and Moon played by Dennis Hopper: Henry Hathaway's *True Grit* (Paramount, 1969).

1272

Euphemia: Why does Baby Jesus need so much company?

Young Euphemia Ashby played by Tina Majorino: Karen Arthur's *True Women* (TVW, 1997).

1273

Bill: What are you up to anyway?

Pete: Nothin', Bill. Just dyin'.

Skinner Bill Bragg played by Wallace Beery and Piute Pete played by Leo Carrillo: Richard Thorpe's *20 Mule Team* (MGM, 1940).

1274

Leach: There's only one thing wrong about dying in the snow, Jefferson. A fellow is liable to catch cold.

Leach Overmile played by Lynne Overman and Jeff Butler played by Joel McCrea: Cecil B. De-Mille's *Union Pacific* (Paramount, 1939).

1275

Fierro: Go outside and die. Where are your manners?

Fierro played by Charles Bronson: Buzz Kulik's *Villa Rides!* (Paramount, 1968).

1276

Steve: Yeah, what's life anyway? A few winters waiting for spring. A few summers wishing they'd last. A few bottles of whiskey and a half a dozen girls you can remember. And then you're a little six by three feet under the ground …and that's all. It might as well be now as later.

Steve played by Richard Arlen: Victor Fleming's *The Virginian* (Paramount, 1929). *See also entry 1277.*

1277

Spanish Ed: Don't get nervous, Shorty. You can die only once.

Steve: And what's life anyway? A few winters waiting for spring. A few summers wishing they'd last. A few bottles of whiskey and maybe a half dozen girls you can remember. And then you're a little three by six under ground, and that's all. It might as well by now as later.

Spanish Ed played by Martin Garralaga and Steve played by Sonny Tufts: Stuart Gilmore's *The Virginian* (Paramount, 1946). *See also entry 1276.*

1278

Siringo: He had to die sooner or later, Etta.
Etta: Later would have been better.

Charlie Siringo played by Steve Forrest and Etta Place played by Katharine Ross: Lee Philips' *Wanted: The Sundance Woman* (TVW, 1976).

1279

Vickers: He died too easy.

John Vickers played by Edmond O'Brien: Byron Haskin's *Warpath* (Paramount, 1951).

1280

Adam: A man shouldn't lie, Holderness, when he's so close to death.

Adam Naab played by J. Farrell MacDonald and Judson Holderness played by David Landau: Henry Hathaway's *When the West Was Young* (a.k.a. *Heritage of the Desert*; Paramount, 1932).

1281

Germany: We're not afraid of a good fight.
Cross: There's no such thing as a good fight if you could end up dead.

Germany played by Delta Burke and Cross played by Willie Nelson: Burt Kennedy's *Where the Hell's That Gold?!!!* (a.k.a. *Dynamite & Gold*; TVW, 1988).

1282

Little Dog: Words have too many shadows. I want no more words.
Tanner: As your friend, Little Dog, I am here to ask you not to die.
Little Dog: I will not go with the soldiers. I will die here. But I will not die alone.

Little Dog played by Jeffrey Hunter and Josh Tanner played by Robert Wagner: Robert Webb's *White Feather* (20th Century–Fox, 1955).

1283

Catherine: You have to get to a doctor immediately.
Dutchy: Too late for a doctor. No, I'm just a dying cowboy.
Catherine: Well, there must be something I could do.
Dutchy: Maybe you could hold my hand?

Catherine Allen played by Joan Hackett and Dutchy played by Anthony Zerbe: Tom Gries' *Will Penny* (Paramount, 1968).

1284

Dutchy: Hey, Will? What he said about that shrine …is he right, do you think? Am I going to die?
Will: Oh, it happens to all of us, Dutchy.
Dutchy: Oh no, Will, you know what I mean. Is now my time?

Will: Oh, we'll get you to that doctor right now.
Dutchy: Will?
Will: I don't know, Dutchy! How the hell do I know?
Dutchy: There's a whole lot I ain't done yet …cowboyin' around.

Dutchy played by Anthony Zerbe and Will Penny played by Charlton Heston: Tom Gries' *Will Penny* (Paramount, 1968).

1285

Blue: He's a good old boy. And this ain't no good way for him to go, Will.
Will: I'll tell ya, Blue. There ain't no good way to go.

Blue played by Lee Majors and Will Penny played by Charlton Heston: Tom Gries' *Will Penny* (Paramount, 1968).

1286

Raquel: Time runs out for all of us. There's nothing we can do to change it.

Raquel played by Julia Adams: Budd Boetticher's *Wings of the Hawk* (Universal, 1953).

1287

Nicholas: Do you think you're the first man to lose someone? That's what life is all about …loss. But we don't use it as an excuse to destroy ourselves. You go on …all of us.

Nicholas Earp played by Gene Hackman: Lawrence Kasdan's *Wyatt Earp* (Warner Bros., 1994).

Forts

See also Indians

1288

Colonel: General, I assume you're ordering me to …
General: Damn it! I am ordering you to command! How and what you do is your problem!

Colonel William Travis played by Laurence Harvey and General Sam Houston played by Richard Boone: John Wayne's *The Alamo* (United Artists, 1960).

1289

Crockett: Step down off your high horse, Mister. You don't get lard unless you boil the hog!

Colonel David "Davy" Crockett played by John Wayne: John Wayne's *The Alamo* (United Artists, 1960).

1290

General: Travis, I've never been able to like you. But you are another one of the very few men I would trust with the life of Texas.

General Sam Houston played by Richard Boone and Colonel William Travis played by Laurence Harvey: John Wayne's *The Alamo* (United Artists, 1960).

1291

Crockett: Well, what do you think, Jim?
Bowie: I hate to say anything good about that long-winded jackanapes, but he does know the short way to start a war.

Colonel David "Davy" Crockett played by John Wayne and Colonel Jim Bowie played by Richard Widmark: John Wayne's *The Alamo* (United Artists, 1960).

1292

Crockett: Travis says that [Colonel] Fannin's coming.

Bowie: Travis says! I wouldn't take Travis' word that night's dark and day's light!

Colonel David "Davy" Crockett played by John Wayne, Colonel Jim Bowie played by Richard Widmark, and Colonel William Travis played by Laurence Harvey: John Wayne's *The Alamo* (United Artists, 1960).

1293

Ward: You sure must need those ten big dollars a day the Army paid you to come up here.
Holly: I got a sick wife.
Ward: It beats a sick widow!

Ward Kinsman played by Robert Taylor and Frank Holly played by John McIntire: Sam Wood's *Ambush* (MGM, 1950).

1294

Linus: Well, I never thought I'd live to see the day.

Ward: That's the point, isn't it? To live to see the day.

Lt. Linus Delaney played by Don Taylor and Ward Kinsman played by Robert Taylor: Sam Wood's *Ambush* (MGM, 1950).

1295

Bill: It seems like the Army is always nearby but never there.

Bill Gibson played by Arthur Hunnicutt: R.G. Springsteen's *Apache Uprising* (Paramount, 1966).

1296

Major: We are presently reduced to a skeletal force that couldn't defend against a stiff breeze!

Major Gaskill played by Harry Morgan: Vincent McEveety's *The Apple Dumpling Gang Rides Again* (Buena Vista, 1979).

1297

Andy: Gambler, gunfighter, and now a deserter?

Bart: Yeah.

Andy: It looks like you added color to the list.

Major Andrew Pepperis played by Carleton Young and Bart Laish played by Sterling Hayden: Lesley Selander's *Arrow in the Dust* (Allied Artists, 1954).

1298

Christella: We're not moving?

Major: Yes.

Christella: Tonight?

Major: Tonight.

Christella: But we can't, Major.

Major: Why not?

Christella: The trip will be too hard on the wounded soldiers.

Major: Miss Burke, back where I came from, there happened to be dead soldiers.

Christella Burke played by Coleen Gray and Bart Laish, assuming the identity of Major Andrew Pepperis, played by Sterling Hayden: Lesley Selander's *Arrow in the Dust* (Allied Artists, 1954).

1299

Bannon: Pick another way back to the post anyway, Colonel.

Colonel: We're at peace.

Bannon: It's a good way to stay alive while you're at peace.

Ed Bannon played by Charlton Heston and Colonel Waybright played by Lewis Martin: Charles Marquis Warren's *Arrowhead* (Paramount, 1953).

1300

Sandy: Captain, you're a smart man. You have lots of brains. You're real intelligent. You're just kind of stupid.

Sandy MacKinnon played by Milburn Stone and Captain Bill North played by Brian Keith: Charles Marquis Warren's *Arrowhead* (Paramount, 1953).

1301

Bannon: You're as blind as the Colonel if that's possible …and it's possible.

Ed Bannon played by Charlton Heston and Colonel Waybright played by Lewis Martin: Charles Marquis Warren's *Arrowhead* (Paramount, 1953).

1302

Lake: I figured you for a good soldier. I should have known better. Good soldiers never volunteer.

Sergeant George Lake played by Barton MacLane: John Sturges' *Backlash* (Universal, 1956).

1303

Captain: I thought the worst of it was over. Now I think this is the worst of it …coming back.

Stacey: You did what you could, Captain.

Captain: Did I?

Stacey: It's no crime to lose a battle.

Captain: Isn't it?

Captain Richard Hillman played by John Crawford and Stacey Wyatt played by Richard Denning: William Castle's *Battle of Rogue River* (Columbia, 1954).

1304

Major: Sometimes a big bark is more effective than a little bite, Lieutenant.

Major Frank Archer played by George Montgomery: William Castle's *Battle of Rogue River* (Columbia, 1954).

1305

Brett: Tell me, Major, is this peace with the Indians going to last?

Major: Well, it's lasted this long.

Brett: But you don't believe in it, do you?

Major: As a soldier, I believe peace is something you have to fight for, Miss McClain.

Brett McClain played by Martha Hyer and Major Frank Archer played by George Montgomery: William Castle's *Battle of Rogue River* (Columbia, 1954).

1306

Brett: Then you should know that a fighting man needs time to live between battles.

Major: He also needs to learn how to stay alive during battles. It's better for a man to come back to a woman than kiss her goodbye and never come back.

Brett: You surprise me, Major. I had thought women had no place in your plans at all.

Major: It may also surprise you to know, Miss McClain, that my own mother was a woman.

Brett McClain played by Martha Hyer and Major Frank Archer played by George Montgomery: William Castle's *Battle of Rogue River* (Columbia, 1954).

1307

Major: My troops are under orders to open fire ten minutes from when I started up here. I haven't looked at my watch lately, but time isn't running backwards.

Major Jeff Clanton played by Robert Ryan: William D. Russell's *Best of the Badmen* (RKO, 1951).

1308

Colonel: Soldiers don't make wars, Mr. Johnson. We just fight them.

Colonel McKenzie played by Lawrence Dane and Alan Johnson played by Christopher Reeve: Steven H. Stern's *Black Fox* (TV miniseries, Cabin Fever Entertainment, 1995).

1309

Johnson: Well, I hope when the war's over, I can buy you a drink.

Colonel: After the war, I hope I got no holes in me so I can hold a drink.

Colonel McKenzie played by Lawrence Dane and Alan Johnson played by Christopher Reeve: Steven H. Stern's *Black Fox* (TV miniseries, Cabin Fever Entertainment, 1995).

1310

Sergeant: My men are soldiers in the United States Cavalry! And they are prepared to die for their country!

Beauchamp: With all due respect, sir, you're out of your fuckin' mind!

Sergeant Hastings played by Adam Baldwin and Beauchamp played by James Oscar Lee in Richard Spence's *Blind Justice* (HBO Home Video, 1994).

1311

Pike: Keep your troops back, Captain Calhoun. Parade regulations …colored companies fifteen yards behind whites.

General Pike played by Tom Bower: Charles Haid's *Buffalo Soldiers* (Turner Pictures/Trilogy Group, 1997).

1312

Archer: Mr. Scott! I told you to cover that flank!

Scott: I'm sorry, sir.

Archer: From now on, you don't scratch until I itch! Is that clear?

Captain Thomas Archer played by Richard Widmark and Second Lieutenant Scott played by Patrick Wayne: John Ford's *Cheyenne Autumn* (Warner Bros., 1964).

1313

Archer: Scott, tell me something.

Scott: Sir?

Archer: What put the blood in your eyes?

Scott: It's just a private matter, sir.

Archer: Nothing that affects an officer's conduct is private.

Captain Thomas Archer played by Richard Widmark and Second Lieutenant Scott played by Patrick Wayne: John Ford's *Cheyenne Autumn* (Warner Bros., 1964).

1314

Doc: Listen to me, Miss Wright. You're a Quaker and you're dedicated to

Chief of Scouts Ed Bannon (Charlton Heston) and Apache Chief Toriano (Jack Palance) agree to meet at daybreak, and come empty-handed, to settle a long-standing dispute. Although blood brothers, there is bad blood between them as depicted in this daybreak scene where Toriano appears to be no longer empty-handed. *Arrowhead* (Paramount, 1953).

self-sacrifice. Well, I'm dedicated to self-preservation. You know, you want me to go out there, don't you? Yeah, and take me future, me career, and me pension …and throw it down the drain. Is that what you want, huh? Yeah, well …that's exactly what I'm going to do.

Dr. O'Carberry played by Sean McClory and Deborah Wright played by Carroll Baker: John Ford's *Cheyenne Autumn* (Warner Bros., 1964).

1315

Colonel: It will be wonderful to dine instead of to feed. It seems to be the routine when men in a country like this are isolated. I miss the conversation …the eloquence of dining in mixed company.

Colonel Stuart Valois played by John Mills: Gordon Douglas' *Chuka* (Paramount, 1967).

1316

Capt. Whitlock: What is it, honey? What's wrong?

Ms. Whitlock: Oh, everything. I can't stand this place, Lee.

Capt. Whitlock: Well, I'll admit it's nothing like home. But after we get it fixed up, it will be …

Ms. Whitlock: No. No, it's not just the house. It's that and everything else: the dirt, the cold, Indians sneaking around at night, and rude officers. I just hate it, that's all.

Captain Lee Whitlock played by Robert Sterling and Marcy Whitlock, the Captain's sister, played by Joan Evans: Frederick de Cordova's *Column South* (Universal, 1953).

1317

Capt. Whitlock: The time may come, Lieutenant, when the North and

the South are at each other's throat. But as of right now, there's no war being fought. We are all in the same army.

Lt. Sayre: I'm glad you feel that way, sir.

Capt. Whitlock: That's the way I expect every officer and man in this post to feel. And if they don't feel it, they can act it.

Capt. Lee Whitlock played by Robert Sterling and Lt. Jed Sayre played by Audie Murphy: Frederick de Cordova's *Column South* (Universal, 1953).

1318

Lt. Chalmers: You know, if you two put off hating each other so much, you might find you'd like each other a lot.

Lt. Chalmers played by Palmer Lee/Greg Palmer. He was talking to Lt. Jed Sayre played by Audie Murphy: Frederick de Cordova's *Column South* (Universal, 1953).

1319

Captain: Sir, may I suggest that my troop act as a rear guard?

Colonel: Where did you learn cavalry tactics, Captain?

Captain: Well, infantry isn't mobile …

Colonel: Neither is dead cavalry! Ask Custer!

Captain Robert MacClaw played by Guy Madison and Colonel Janeway played by Carl Benton Reid: David Butler's *The Command* (Warner Bros., 1953).

1320

Captain: The riflemen are going to fight from the wagons.

Major: Fight from wagons?

Captain: Well, why not?

Major: It's never been done! Wagons are supposed to be used as a defense.

Captain: So the book says. Let's keep a closed book and an open mind, Major.

Captain Robert MacClaw played by Guy Madison and Major Gibbs played by Don Shelton: David Butler's *The Command* (Warner Bros., 1953).

1321

Sergeant: Well, injuns fight two ways, Captain. When they're running against a little outfit, they go ring around right away, and close it quick for the kill. But if they're running against a big outfit, like we're tied up with now, they'll keep hacking and chopping away at your weak spots until they wear you down. Then make a ring around. And once they get you in a circle, they know you're finished.

Sergeant Elliott played by James Whitmore and Captain Robert MacClaw played by Guy Madison: David Butler's *The Command* (Warner Bros., 1953).

1322

Colonel: Mr. O'Hirons. Mr. O'Hirons! Regulations stipulate $10 a month additional for command functions. When we reach the Paradise, notify he paymaster that Captain MacClaw has commanded with distinction. The government owes him $3.30.

Colonel Janeway played by Carl Benton Reid, Mr. O'Hirons played by Bob Nichols, and Captain Robert MacClaw played by Guy Madison: David Butler's *The Command* (Warner Bros., 1953).

1323

Martha: You hate being a soldier, and you hate killing. Yet you do it.

Captain: I got a uniform and a conscience. Right now, the uniform covers the conscience.

Martha played by Joan Weldon and Captain Robert MacClaw played by Guy Madison: David Butler's *The Command* (Warner Bros., 1953).

1324

Custer: As professional soldiers, we best leave the question of morality to those whose job it is. Our job is to fight.

Lieutenant Colonel George Armstrong Custer played by Wayne Maunder: Norman Foster's *Crazy Horse and Custer: The Untold Story* (TVW, 1967).

1325

Sheridan: You know, Custer, you could become a living legend …or get yourself killed. Dead men make better legends.

General Sheridan played by Lawrence Tierney and George Armstrong Custer played by Robert Shaw: Robert Siodmak and Irving Lerner's *Custer of the West* (Security Pictures/Cinerama, 1968).

1326

Sheridan: If there's any doubt about the policy of my command, I'll give it to you in one sentence: The only good Indian is a dead Indian. Clear enough?

General Sheridan played by Lawrence Tierney: Robert Siodmak and Irving Lerner's *Custer of the West* (Security Pictures/Cinerama, 1968).

1327

Bitteroot: One thing is for sure: If the Army's around, trouble can't be far off.

Bitteroot played by Dub Taylor: David Lowell Rich's *The Daughters of Joshua Cabe Return* (TVW, 1975).

1328

Forbes: They're deserters!

Warfield: Well, is that a fact?

Captain: Renegades is a better word. It implies a spirit of adventure. Desertion is cowardly. We're not that.

Owen Forbes played by Arthur Kennedy, Lorn Warfield played by Glenn Ford, and Captain Jefferson Addis played by John Anderson: Jerry Thorpe's *Day of the Evil Gun* (MGM, 1968).

1329

Colonel: Would you like to inspect the fort, General?

General: Hell, no! How do you get a drink around here?

Colonel Brown played by Richard Crenna and General Miles played by John Huston: Burt Kennedy's *The Deserter* (a.k.a. *Ride to Glory*; Paramount, 1971).

1330

Kaleb: There's a good chance he won't come back, General.

General: That's the price of glory.

Captain Viktor Kaleb played by Bekim Fehmiu and General Miles played by John Huston: Burt Kennedy's *The Deserter* (a.k.a. *Ride to Glory*; Paramount, 1971).

1331

Cranshaw: I wish that there was some way that you could cut regulations and bring her out here. It sure would make things

more tolerable. She could even sleep with me. Just like at home.

Lieutenant: You can't bring your wife out here until you are a three striper!

Cranshaw: Wife, sir? I ain't got none.

Lieutenant: Well, you can't take your girlfriend into the barracks either!

Cranshaw: She ain't no human girl. She's the best old blue-tick coonhound in Kentuck[y].

Cranshaw played by Bobby Bare and Lieutenant Matthew Hazard played by Troy Donahue: Raoul Walsh's *A Distant Trumpet* (Warner Bros., 1964).

1332

Lieutenant: There's nothing the matter with the recruits, sir. The matter is with the training and the discipline.

Lieutenant Matthew Hazard played by Troy Donahue: Raoul Walsh's *A Distant Trumpet* (Warner Bros., 1964).

1333

Kitty: You're a hard man. A duty man. It's your only love really.

Lieutenant: Is there a better kind?

Kitty: Well, speaking as a normal woman, yes; as an Army woman, no.

Kitty played by Suzanne Pleshette and Lieutenant Matthew Hazard played by Troy Donahue: Raoul Walsh's *A Distant Trumpet* (Warner Bros., 1964).

1334

Lieutenant: He once said at the Academy, the Army is a jealous mistress.

Laura: And he loves her. That's why he's an old bachelor.

Lieutenant Matthew Hazard played by Troy Donahue and Laura played by Diane McBain: Raoul Walsh's *A Distant Trumpet* (Warner Bros., 1964).

1335

General Canby: Sometimes it is as necessary to take risks to win peace as it is in war to win victories.

General Canby played by Warner Anderson: Delmer Dave's *Drum Beat* (Warner Bros., 1954).

1336

Toller: You used to be a pretty good sergeant yourself, McAllister. But now you're just a …a rank officer.

Toller played by Sidney Poitier and Lieutenant Scotty McAllister played by Bill Travers: Ralph Nelson's *Duel at Diablo* (United Artists, 1966).

1337

Colonel: It's hard to know what to do, Roper. Am I losing my nerve or am I getting old? Go ahead and say it.

Roper: This is hard country to stay alive in, Colonel, much less stay young.

Colonel Owens played by Carl Benton Reid and Captain Roper played by William Holden: John Sturges' *Escape from Fort Bravo* (MGM, 1953).

1338

Cabot: When do we go [escape]? Why does it have to be such a big secret? Because I'm not supposed to have any brains?

Campbell: That's a good question ...but an even better answer.

Cabot Young played by William Campbell and Campbell played by William Demarest: John Sturges' *Escape from Fort Bravo* (MGM, 1953).

1339

Lt. Col.: Mr. Meacham, you're a blackguard, a liar, a hypocrite, and a stench in the nostrils of honest men. If it were up to me, I would hang you from the nearest tree and leave your carcass for the buzzards. But as you are a representative of the United States Government, I pledge you the protection and cooperation of my command.

Lt. Col. Owen Thursday played by Henry Fonda and Silas Meacham played by Grant Withers: John Ford's *Fort Apache* (RKO, 1948).

1340

Lt. Col.: This Lt. O'Rourke. Are you by chance related?

Sgt. Major: Not by chance, sir, by blood. He's my son.

Lt. Col.: I see. How did he happen to get into West Point?

Sgt. Major: It happened by presidential appointment, sir.

Lt. Col.: Are you a former officer, O'Rourke?

Sgt. Major: During the war, I was major in the 69th New York Regiment ...the Irish Brigade, sir.

Lt. Col.: Still, it's been my impression that presidential appointments were restricted to sons of holders of the Medal of Honor.

Sgt. Major: That is my impression too, sir. Will that be all, sir?

Lt. Col.: Yes, Sergeant, it will.

Lt. Col. Owen Thursday played by Henry Fonda and Sgt. Major Michael O'Rourke played by Ward Bond: John Ford's *Fort Apache* (RKO, 1948).

1341

Captain: Colonel, if you send out the regiment, Cochise will think I tricked him.

Lt. Col.: Exactly! We have tricked him! Tricked him into returning to American soil. And I intend to see that he stays here.

Captain: Colonel Thursday, I gave my word to Cochise. No man is gonna make a liar out of me, sir.

Lt. Col.: Your word to a breach-clouted savage? An illiterate, uncivilized

George Armstrong Custer (Robert Shaw) rides into glory (and into the whole Sioux Indian Nation!) at the Little Bighorn in *Custer of the West* (Security Pictures/Cinerama, 1968).

murderer and treaty-breaker? There's no question of honor, sir, between an American officer and Cochise.

Captain: There is to me, sir.

Captain Kirby York played by John Wayne and Lt. Col. Owen Thursday played by Henry Fonda: John Ford's *Fort Apache* (RKO, 1948).

1342

Lt. Col.: I'll trouble you for your saber, Captain.

Captain: My saber?

Lt. Col.: I must rejoin my command.

Captain: The command is wiped out, sir. There's nothing we can do about it.

Lt. Col.: I'm not asking your opinion, Captain York. When you command this regiment, and you probably will, command it! Your saber, sir! Any questions, Captain?

Lt. Col. Owen Thursday played by Henry Fonda and Captain Kirby York played by John Wayne: John Ford's *Fort Apache* (RKO, 1948).

1343

Reporter 1: He's become almost a legend already. He's the hero of every school boy in America.

Reporter 2: But what of the men who died with him? What of Collinworth and …

Lt. Col.: Collinwood.

Reporter 2: Oh, of course, Collinwood.

Reporter 3: That's the irony part of it. We always remember the [Colonel] Thursbys, but the others are forgotten.

Lt. Col.: You're wrong there. They aren't forgotten because they aren't dead. They're living …right out there. Collinwood and the rest. And they'll keep on living as long as the regiment lives. Pay is thirteen dollars a month, and their diet is beans and hay …maybe horse meat before this campaign is over. They'll fight over cards or rot-gut whiskey, but share the last drop in their canteen. The faces may change, and the names, but they're there. They're the regiment, the regular army …now and fifty years from now.

The Reporters were played by Frank Ferguson, William Forrest, and Archie Twitchell. Lt. Col. Kirby York played by John Wayne: John Ford's *Fort Apache* (RKO, 1948).

1344

Pendleton: You shouldn't have sent out such a green man.

Vinson: I didn't hear you volunteer.

Pendleton: Well, why should I have? I was wounded.

Vinson: That bullet only creased you, Pendleton. It didn't even hurt your feelings.

Pvt. Pendleton played by George Neise and Sgt. Vinson played by Joel McCrea: Joseph Newman's *Fort Massacre* (United Artists, 1958).

1345

Vinson: Look, you want these stripes? You can have them! They weigh a ton!

Sgt. Vinson played by Joel McCrea: Joseph Newman's *Fort Massacre* (United Artists, 1958).

1346

Vinson: I don't think! I'm a sergeant! I do what I'm taught like a trained dog.

Sgt. Vinson played by Joel McCrea: Joseph Newman's *Fort Massacre* (United Artists, 1958).

1347

McGurney: I should have more respect for government property. Even when a thing is useless, you pin a medal on it and toot a horn and bury it in a deep hole. And, of course, you got to have proper orders. Yes. Orders, the date, the regimental seal …signed by three colonels, two generals, maybe even the pope himself. Isn't that right, sir? You can't even spit without that.

McGurney played by Forrest Tucker: Joseph Newman's *Fort Massacre* (United Artists, 1958).

1348

McGurney: There's no such thing as cowards. There's only degrees of fright.

McGurney played by Forrest Tucker: Joseph Newman's *Fort Massacre* (United Artists, 1958).

1349

Travis: Not that it's any of my business, but why did you kill that last Apache? He was ready to surrender.

Vinson: You said it yourself, Travis. You don't know brass buttons from hot rocks. Those Apaches hate us. Do you understand! They hate us so much they quit being human. Hate can do that. It swells up inside you until it pushes out every other feeling: pain, love, even fear. And when a man gets like that, bursting with it, the only way for that hate to come out is through a neat round bullet hole.

Travis played by John Russell and Sgt. Vinson played by Joel McCrea: Joseph Newman's *Fort Massacre* (United Artists, 1958).

1350

Colonel: Captain, there are two ways to get men through a door: kick 'em through or you can lead 'em through.

Captain: That's right, sir. They wind up the same place anyway.

Colonel Reed played by Byron Morrow and Captain Bruce Coburn played by Audie Murphy: William Witney's *40 Guns to Apache Pass* (Columbia, 1967).

1351

Narrator: One month before my twenty-second birthday, I reported for duty in the Arizona territory. It was my first posting to garrison life. And looking back, it is now clear to me that I was as much a stranger to myself as I was to the great western desert.

Narration by Lt. Britton Davis, played by Matt Damon: Walter Hill's *Geronimo: An American Legend* (Columbia, 1993).

1352

Sieber: I know you don't like me much, Lieutenant, and I don't really care. I know I'm rough in some of my ways …I guess. I ain't the gentleman type. But, ah, I think, ah, compared to you, I am somewhat honest. No offense intended, Lieutenant, I'm just speaking off the record, sir. I just, ah, figure you're a real sad case. You don't know who you're fighting for, and you don't hate who you're fighting against.

Gatewood: Perhaps I could learn to hate with a proper vigor from you, Al?

Sieber: Well, maybe you could, Lieutenant.

Al Sieber played by Robert Duvall and Lt. Charles Gatewood played by Jason Patric in Walter Hill's *Geronimo: An American Legend* (Columbia, 1993).

1353

Miles: I hate an idealist. There's always something messy about them.

Brigadier General Nelson Miles played by Kevin Tighe: Walter Hill's *Geronimo: An American Legend* (Columbia, 1993).

1354

Harrod: It is my opinion that in a very short time, he will have you engaged in a major battle against the Sioux. In other words, it is likely that in a month from now some of you …maybe all of you …including myself will be dead.

Captain Demas Harrod played by Tom Tryon: Arnold Laven's *The Glory Guys* (United Artists, 1965).

1355

Dakota: What you can't get through your head, Captain, is that a man can live on hate as well as love.

Captain: You'll live to find it's a bitter substitute.

Dakota played by John Matthews and Captain Benton played by Darren McGavin: Sidney Salkow's *The Great Sioux Massacre* (Columbia, 1965).

1356

Ben: Bat, you got to light out of here right now. This is a soldier's town. Whenever one of 'em gets it, no matter how hated he was, the whole platoon suddenly falls in love with him.

Ben Thompson played by Walter Coy and Bat Masterson played by Joel McCrea: Joseph M. Newman's *The Gunfight at Dodge City* (United Artists, 1959).

Cochise (Miguel Inclan) and warriors await battle with the soldiers from *Fort Apache* (RKO, 1948). This was the first of John Ford's cavalry trilogy, the other two being *She Wore a Yellow Ribbon* (1949) and *Rio Grande* (1950).

1357

Sergeant: We got a morale problem, sir.
Colonel: Take care of it, Buell.
Sergeant: I think the Colonel will have to root it out, sir. It's right at the core. The ladies are taking baths …in the nude.

Master Sergeant Buell played by John Anderson and Colonel Thadeus Gearhart played by Burt Lancaster: John Sturges' *The Hallelujah Trail* (MGM, 1965).

1358

Colonel: Duty is a cruel master.

Colonel Thadeus Gearhart played by Burt Lancaster: John Sturges' *The Hallelujah Trail* (MGM, 1965).

1359

Hondo: How is he?
Buffalo: He'll make out. He don't know much. He led us into an ambush, but I ain't ashamed of him no how. The bullet holes are in the front of him.

Hondo: All those youngsters from the [West] Point are like that.
Buffalo: Well, they got to learn.
Hondo: Partly they learn and partly they die. But I've got to float my stick same as you. I've never saw one of 'em I had to be ashamed of.

Hondo Lane played by John Wayne and Buffalo played by Ward Bond: John Farrow's *Hondo* (Warner Bros., 1953).

1360

Kendall: As usual, I'm trying to present the grim facts of life. Colonel Secord doesn't seem to understand that the coffee tastes better if the latrines are dug downstream instead of upstream. How do you like your coffee, Colonel?

Major Henry Kendall played by William Holden and Colonel Phil Secord played by Willis Bouchey: John Ford's *The Horse Soldiers* (United Artists, 1959).

1361

Hunter: I suppose when the time comes to testify against you, I'd be handicapped with a broken jaw, wouldn't I?
Colonel: I'd say so.

Hannah Hunter played by Constance Towers and Colonel John Marlowe played by John Wayne: John Ford's *The Horse Soldiers* (United Artists, 1959).

1362

Sgt. Major: I could be a sweet time happier where I was going, sir.
Colonel: Well, you got me there.
Sgt. Major: No sir, you got me here!

Sergeant Major Kirby played by Judson Pratt and Colonel John Marlowe played by John Wayne: John Ford's *The Horse Soldiers* (United Artists, 1959).

1363

Carson: I'm sure now. The only difference between a donkey and a soldier is a uniform.

Kit Carson played by Jon Hall: George B. Seitz's *Kit Carson* (United Artists, 1940).

1364

Fremont: You boys don't sound as if you think much of soldiers.

Carson: We don't. Where you find soldiers, you find trouble. But when you find trouble, you can't find the soldiers.

Captain John C. Fremont played by Dana Andrews and Kit Carson played by Jon Hall: George B. Seitz's *Kit Carson* (United Artists, 1940).

1365

Zeb: Now look, I told the Colonel you're the man for the job while I'm gone. You let me down and you'll be looking for your praying bones. Meantime, don't you forget what I taught you: You shoot 'em where they look the biggest. And don't go as far as hell for no woman.

Zeb Macahan played by James Arness: Bernard McEveety's *The Macahans* (TVW, 1976).

1366

Dundee: Lieutenant Graham.

Graham: Yes, sir.

Dundee: When I left I gave you a specific order. You failed to carry it out.

Graham: No, sir. You gave me a command. From then on, I gave the orders.

Dundee: You surely did. Have a cigar.

Major Amos Charles Dundee played by Charlton Heston and Lieutenant Graham played by Jim Hutton: Sam Peckinpah's *Major Dundee* (Columbia, 1965).

1367

Waller: You'll be shot for this, Amos.

Dundee: My executioners will have to stand in line.

Captain Frank Waller played by Karl Swenson and Major Amos Charles Dundee played by Charlton

Heston: Sam Peckinpah's *Major Dundee* (Columbia, 1965).

1368

Crawford: In case you've been wondering, I had the audacity to dispute a general over tactics. But that wasn't my mistake, you see. And it also wasn't because the dispute happened in front of a group of my fellow officers. No, my error was simply this: I turned out to be right.

Captain Emmet Crawford played by Jeremy Slate: Jack Starrett's *Mr. Horn* (TVW, 1979).

1369

Sieber: There's three kinds of people in this world: There is colored peoples, there is white peoples, and there is jackasses. All soldiers is jackasses.

Kit Carson (Jon Hall) advises Capt. John C. Fremont (Dana Andrews) to skirt the mountains, that the hills are swarming with Shoshoni. The Captain ignores the advice and moves out, and Carson laments, "I'm sure now. The only difference between a donkey and a soldier is the uniform," in *Kit Carson* (United Artists, 1940).

Al Sieber played by Richard Widmark: Jack Starrett's *Mr. Horn* (TVW, 1979).

1370

Horn: How bad is Miles?

Sieber: There is four kinds of peoples in this world. There is colored peoples, there is white peoples, there is jackasses …and there is General Miles.

Al Sieber played by Richard Widmark, Tom Horn played by David Carradine and General Nelson Miles played by Stafford Morgan: Jack Starrett's *Mr. Horn* (TVW, 1979).

1371

Sieber: General, I said some insulting things to you when you fired me. I was mad and my pride was hurt. But I just want you to know one thing. I meant every damn word I said!

Al Sieber played by Richard Widmark: Jack Starrett's *Mr. Horn* (TVW, 1979).

1372

Unger: I don't care a bubble in a dirty river what you think of me. The big point is I don't like the way you let your schoolboy ideas stand in the way of doing a man's job.

Lt. Colonel Unger played by Forrest Tucker: Joseph Kane's *Oh! Susanna* (Republic, 1951).

1373

Sergeant: Yes sir, Mr. Cutter, I figured maybe you could set me straight.

Lieutenant: On what, Sergeant?

Sergeant: Why is it, sir, meaning no disrespect, sir, nobody wants to be a second lieutenant?

Lieutenant: All right, I guess every shave-tail that's been out on a day's patrol with you has had to listen to this one. Let's have it, Sergeant.

Sergeant: Well, sir, and I'll give up a day's pay if I'm wrong. A private wants to be a corporal, and a corporal wants to be a sergeant. But does a sergeant want to be a second lieutenant? Captains are right glad to be captains; majors and colonels are glad to be majors and colonels. But even a second lieutenant don't want to be a second lieutenant. Looking for something, sir?

Lieutenant: Yes, a good answer, Sergeant.

Sergeant Barhydt played by Chill Wills and Lieutenant Cutter played by John Compton: Joseph Kane's *Oh! Susanna* (Republic, 1951).

1374

Captain: Corporal, you seem to feel that each man has a right to consult his conscience and decide which orders he will obey and which he will disobey.

Captain Stewart played by Pat Hingle and Corporal Clint Keys played by James Garner: Bernard McEveety's *One Little Indian* (Buena Vista, 1973).

1375

Captain: The Army doesn't shoot prisoners, Joe!

Scout: I'm a civilian!

Captain Richard Lance played by Gregory Peck and Army Scout Joe Harmony played by Jeff Corey: Gordon Douglas' *Only the Valiant* (Warner Bros., 1951).

1376

Captain: You're lying, aren't you?

Trooper: That's an enlisted man's privilege, Captain.

Captain Richard Lance played by Gregory Peck and Trooper Rutledge played by Warner Anderson: Gordon Douglas' *Only the Valiant* (Warner Bros., 1951).

1377

Major: What countermeasures have you ordered this time?

Lieutenant: None, sir. These Indians are back in the woods shooting long range. It would be luck if they even bounced a shot into the fort.

Major: It's an old Sioux trick …to keep us awake and nervous. It works, too, when troops are under canvas.

Major Roland Dane played by Edward Platt and Lt. Niles Ord played by John Ericson: Paul Landres' *Oregon Passage* (Warner Bros., 1958).

1378

Colonel: Tell this man who makes war with women that my orders are to build a fort. And rightfully so and in accordance with the treaty he and these chiefs have signed.

Holden: He can understand you, Colonel, if you will speak with him.

Colonel: I do not threaten, nor do I speak with men who threaten.

Colonel Edson Stedlow played by Willis Bouchey and Dr. Joseph Holden played by Ward Bond: George Marshall's *Pillars of the Sky* (Universal, 1956).

1379

First Sgt.: Learn to tie your moccasins before you try to become a scout.

First Sergeant Emmett Bell played by Jeff Chandler in George Marshall's *Pillars of the Sky* (Universal, 1956).

1380

Major: Well, that's Sergeant Bell, Colonel. Away from his scouts, he's half drunk all the time, all drunk half the time. And rebelliously insubordinate, drunk or sober. He's a shame and a disgrace to his uniform. But if you had a hundred more like him, you could ride into hell and put out the fires.

Major Donahue played by Walter Coy, First Sergeant Emmett Bell played by Jeff Chandler, and Colonel Edson Stedlow played by Willis Bouchey: George Marshall's *Pillars of the Sky* (Universal, 1956).

1381

Stiles: I'm saying that as long as the Cheyenne see men like you wearing the uniform of the U.S. Army, we'll continue to have trouble.

Hickok: Did you do any fighting during the war?

Stiles: That isn't the point.

Hickok: I guess it isn't, at that. Like you said, the only thing wrong with these uniforms is what grows inside 'em.

Lt. Stiles played by Bradford Dillman and Wild Bill Hickok played by Don Murray: David Lowell Rich's *The Plainsman* (Universal, 1966).

1382

Lassiter: Friend, the only other thing you have to know is that the further we get from the fort, the further you are from a rope.

James Lassiter played by Richard Boone: Gordon Douglas' *Rio Conchos* (20th Century–Fox, 1964).

1383

Lassiter: You are stupid enough to become a general!

James Lassiter played by Richard Boone: Gordon Douglas' *Rio Conchos* (20th Century–Fox, 1964).

1384

Yorke: I don't want you men to be fooled about what's coming up for you. Torture, at least that. The war department promised me 180 men. They sent me 18 all told. You are the eighteen. So each one of you will have to do the work of 10 men. If you fail, I'll have you spread-eagled on a wagon wheel. If you desert, you'll be found, tracked down, and broken into bits. That is all.

Lt. Col. Kirby Yorke played by John Wayne: John Ford's *Rio Grande* (Republic, 1950).

1385

Yorke: But put out of your mind any romantic ideas that it's a way of glory. It's a life of suffering and hardship, an uncompromising devotion to your oath and your duty.

Lt. Col. Kirby Yorke played by John Wayne: John Ford's *Rio Grande* (Republic, 1950).

1386

Yorke: But he must learn that a man's word to anything, even his own destruction, is his honor.

Lt. Col. Kirby Yorke played by John Wayne: John Ford's *Rio Grande* (Republic, 1950).

1387

Sheridan: I'm going to issue you an order and give it to you personally. I want you to cross the Rio Grande, hit the Apache and burn him out. I'm tired of hit-and-run. I'm sick of diplomatic hide-and-seek.

General Philip Sheridan played by J. Carrol Naish: John Ford's *Rio Grande* (Republic, 1950).

1388

Batoche: You could always ask Benton for a transfer.
O'Rourke: I know where he'd tell me where to go.

Batoche played by J. Carrol Naish and Sergeant Thomas O'Rourke played by Alan Ladd: Raoul Walsh's *Saskatchewan* (Universal, 1954).

1389

Benton: It takes some men longer to become good soldiers than it does others. I happen to be one of the some ones.

Inspector Benton played by Robert Douglas: Raoul Walsh's *Saskatchewan* (Universal, 1954).

1390

Martin: Even this kind of a campaign don't make good sense.

Ahern: You mean the Army's wrong?
Martin: Well, about half and half, my way of figuring. We ain't got the right to push them Indians on the reservation. But they ain't got the right to claim all this land either. They got to move over and give the next fella a little more room.
Ahern: They won't move over.
Martin: That's the general trouble with people. They won't give elbow room. We won't budge and they won't either. So the Army has got to do some pushing with bullets and bayonets.
[*and later*]
Martin: Hey, don't tell me them Sioux are running away?
Ahern: No, not running away. Just moving over to give the other fella a little elbow room.

Corporal Martin played by Milburn Stone and Jim Ahern/Warbonnet played by Charlton Heston: George Marshall's *The Savage* (Paramount, 1952).

1391

Beecher: Who is Captain Buffalo?
Cantrell: Oh, he's ah, well, when the Plains Indians first saw the troopers of the 9th Cavalry, it was in the dead of winter and they were all wearing buffalo coats to keep them warm … and buffalo caps on …they looked like buffaloes. Well, consequently, the Indians started calling them buffalo soldiers. And Captain Buffalo is, ah, well, he's the ideal soldier. You know …giant size …kind of like Paul Bunyan.

Mary Beecher played by Constance Towers and Lieutenant Thomas Cantrell played by Jeffrey Hunter: John Ford's *Sergeant Rutledge* (Warner Bros., 1960).

Movie poster to *She Wore a Yellow Ribbon* (RKO, 1949) with John Wayne as Capt. Nathan Brittles. This was the second of John Ford's cavalry triology, the other two being *Fort Apache* (1948) and *Rio Grande* (1950).

1392

Lieutenant: Well, you're a good man. And in another nine or ten years, you're going to make corporal.

Lieutenant Thomas Cantrell played by Jeffrey Hunter: John Ford's *Sergeant Rutledge* (Warner Bros., 1960).

1393

Rutledge: Because the 9th Cavalry was my home, my real freedom, and my self-respect. The way I was deserting it, I was nothin' but a swamp-running nigger, and I ain't that. Do you hear me? I'm a man!

First Sergeant Braxton Rutledge played by Woody Strode: John Ford's *Sergeant Rutledge* (Warner Bros., 1960).

1394

Corporal: I guess I've played taps over one thousand times since I've been in the Army, sir. But tonight, somehow it was different.

Captain: Yes, tonight I think I really heard it and understood it for the first time.

Corporal: It's a sad call, sir. Sort of like saying goodbye to old friends.

Captain: Requiem for the regiment.

Corporal Morrison played by Harry Carey, Jr. and Captain Tom Benson played by Randolph Scott: Joseph H. Lewis' *7th Cavalry* (Columbia, 1956).

1395

Brittles: Never apologize, mister. It's a sign of weakness.

Captain Nathan Brittles played by John Wayne: John Ford's *She Wore a Yellow Ribbon* (RKO, 1949).

1396

Captain: Six more days. Six more days and I retire.

Sergeant: The Army will never be the same when we retire, sir.

Captain: The Army is always the same. The sun and the moon change, but the Army knows no seasons.

Sergeant: Here we are in our prime, and they are turning us out to pasture. It's an abuse of the taxpayers' money.

Captain: The only tax you ever paid was a whiskey tax.

Captain Nathan Brittles played by John Wayne and Sergeant Quincannon played by Victor McLaglen: John Ford's *She Wore a Yellow Ribbon* (RKO, 1949).

1397

Narrator: So here they are: the dog-faced soldiers, the regulars, the fifty-cents-a-day professionals ...riding the outposts of the nation. From Fort Reno to Fort Apache, from Sheridan to Stark, they were all the same. Men in dirty-shirt blue, and only a gold page in the history books to mark their passage. But wher-ever they rode, and whatever they fought for, that place became the United States.

The narrator was Irving Pichel: John Ford's *She Wore a Yellow Ribbon* (RKO, 1949).

1398

Custer: An order seems to be something of a little stumbling block for you. Major, you've been a burr under my saddle ever since you came west. You were an aide to General Grant when I first knew you. A colonel! Now you seem to be traveling downwards in rank.

Parris: Well, we seem to be traveling the same direction, Colonel Custer. You used to be a general.

Colonel George A. Custer played by Douglas Kennedy and Major Robert Parris played by Dale Robertson: Sidney Salkow's *Sitting Bull* (United Artists, 1954).

1399

Sergeant: Why, I remember when I was with the 7th Cavalry back in Kansas. We were fighting the Cheyenne. It was the Battle of the Chickasaw. I don't know how it happened but all of a sudden there I was, all alone, all by myself. So I whipped my horse around and started back to the regiment. There, right in front of me, were 50 Indians! So I turned around and started to retreat. There, blocking my path, was 100 Indians! So quick, I turned to the left and, coming right at me, 200 Indians! So I turned around to take to the right ...300 Indians bearing down on me! All around me, Indians! Indians in front of me, Indians in back of me, Indians to the left of me, and Indians to the right of me!

Hardsaddle: What happened?

Sergeant: What happened? I got killed!

Hardsaddle: If you were killed, how come you're still living?

Sergeant: You call this living?

Sergeant McIntosh played by Andy Devine and Hardsaddle played by Lew Bedell: Irving Allen's *Slaughter Trail* (RKO, 1951).

1400

Sergeant: I thought you said you was the hottest Indian fighter east of the Rio Grande?

Hardsaddle: That was east of the Rio Grande. West of the Rio Grande I ain't so hot.

Sergeant McIntosh played by Andy Devine and Hardsaddle played by Lew Bedell: Irving Allen's *Slaughter Trail* (RKO, 1951).

1401

Narrator: The Arikara called him Creeping Panther who comes in the night. The Crow called him Son of the Morning Star who attacks at dawn.

In describing George Armstrong Custer, the voice of Kate Bighead played by Buffy Sainte-Marie: Mike Robe's *Son of the Morning Star* (TVW, 1991).

1402

Beale: There's what's left of the Army surveyors. Kit Carson said we wouldn't get this far.

Lt. Owens: Apaches ...or they ran out of water?

Tall Tale: It don't make no never mind which. Either way you get powerful dead.

Edward Beale played by Rod Cameron, Lt. Owens played by Stuart Randall, and Tall Tale played by Guinn "Big Boy" Williams: Ray Nazarro's *Southwest Passage* (United Artists, 1954).

1403

Hudson: Erin, you know what I would do if I were you? I think you ought to go home to your son. This is a man's world out here, and you don't belong. But just remember this: People don't always act the way you expect them to. It doesn't mean that they aren't fond of you, or they don't love you. It simply means they may have a star to follow that's stronger than any personal tie.

Lt. Colonel John Hudson played by Paul Kelly and Erin Kearney played by Phyllis Thaxter: Andre De Toth's *Springfield Rifle* (Warner Bros., 1952).

1404

McCool: Kind of used of giving orders, aren't you?

Kearney: What's worse, I'm used to being obeyed.

Austin McCool played by David Brian and Major Lex Kearney played by Gary Cooper: Andre De Toth's *Springfield Rifle* (Warner Bros., 1952).

1405

Marshal: Lieutenant, it seems to me that there could come a time when common sense would overrule Army orders.

Lieutenant: Common sense has never overwritten Army orders!

Marshal Curley Wilcox played by Johnny Cash and Lt. Blanchard played by Merritt Butrick: Ted Post's *Stagecoach* (TVW, 1986).

1406

Sergeant: You sure picked a hell of a way to end fifteen years with the Army!

Sam: I don't mind getting out alive.

Sergeant Rudabaugh played by Henry Beckman and Sam Varner played by Gregory Peck: Robert Mulligan's *The Stalking Moon* (NGP, 1968).

1407

Major: One more year! That's all I ask!

Sam: That's all you asked last year!

Major: That's all I'll ask next year!

The Major played by Frank Silvera and Sam

Varner played by Gregory Peck: Robert Mulligan's *The Stalking Moon* (NGP, 1968).

1408

Stallman: If I weren't in uniform, I might teach you a few manners.

Haven: If you could teach me anything, you wouldn't be in a uniform!

Lieutenant Stallman played by Steve Brodie and Haven played by Dick Powell: Sidney Lanfield's *Station West* (RKO, 1948).

1409

Lieutenant: I would like a word with you, sir. I've been deliberating since last night on the total effect of the Medal of Honor upon my career. And I'm very grateful to you, sir, but I've decided to stand on my privilege as an officer by requesting that my case be removed from consideration.

Major: Why?

Lieutenant: Well, there's an old service maxim, sir, that I'm sure you're well aware of. Career officers should make themselves as inconspicuous as possible …particularly junior officers.

Major: I wasn't aware of it.

Lieutenant: Well, it's true, sir. Too outstanding an exploit too early in one's career would make one a marked man, a sure victim of the jealousy of one's superiors.

Lieutenant William Fowler played by Tab Hunter and Major Thomas Thorn played by Gary Cooper: Robert Rossen's *They Came to Cordura* (Columbia, 1959).

1410

Sharp: What made you one of the Army by choosing it as a career?

Custer: Glory, Mr. Sharp, glory. I want to leave a name behind me that the nation will honor. There's a great many more statues for soldiers than there are for civilians, I noticed.

Sharp: I am sure you'll fit right in with the statues, Mr. Custer …just like part of the horse.

Ned Sharp, Jr. played by Arthur Kennedy and George Armstrong Custer played by Errol Flynn:

Raoul Walsh's *They Died with Their Boots On* (Warner Bros., 1941).

1411

Sheridan: We don't concern ourselves with the making of wars here, Senator …only the fighting of them.

Colonel Phil Sheridan played by John Litel and Senator Sharp played by Walter Hampden: Raoul Walsh's *They Died with Their Boots On* (Warner Bros., 1941).

1412

Taipe: And as for his record, George Armstrong Custer has the lowest marks and the highest demerits of any cadet who ever attended this [West Point] academy …including Ulysses S. Grant.

Sheridan: Huh. I wondered what happened to Grant?

Major Romulus Taipe played by Stanley Ridges and Colonel Phil Sheridan played by John Litel: Raoul Walsh's *They Died with Their Boots On* (Warner Bros., 1941).

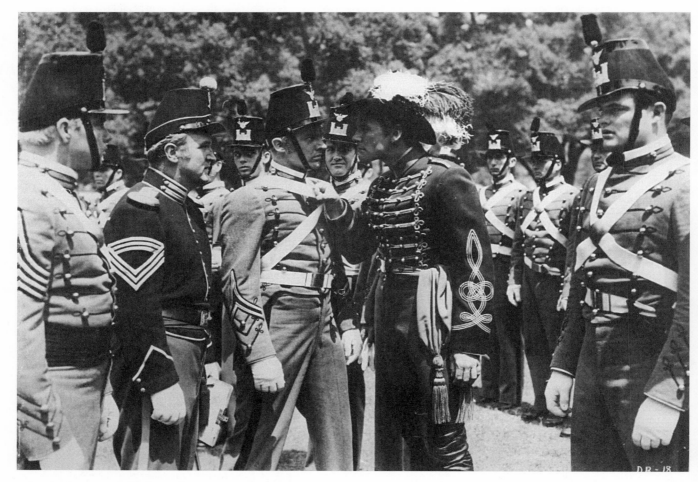

When Cadet George Armstrong Custer (Errol Flynn) shows up at West Point in his tailor-made uniform, Sgt. Doolittle (Joseph Sawyer) salutes him mistaking him for a general. Cadet Ned Sharp, Jr. (Arthur Kennedy), then plays a trick on Custer which nearly gets him canned in Raoul Walsh's *They Died with Their Boots On* (Warner Bros., 1941).

1413

Custer: I needn't tell most of you that a regiment is something more than just 600 disciplined fighting men. Men die …but a regiment lives on. Because a regiment has an immortal soul of its own. Well, the way to begin is to find it; to find something that belongs to us alone. Something to give us that pride in ourselves that will make men endure and, if necessary, die with their boots on.

George Armstrong Custer played by Errol Flynn: Raoul Walsh's *They Died with Their Boots On* (Warner Bros., 1941).

1414

And so was born the immortal 7TH U.S. CAVALRY which cleared the plains for a ruthlessly advancing civilization that spelled doom to the red man.

Caption: Raoul Walsh's *They Died with Their Boots On* (Warner Bros., 1941).

1415

Custer: You may be right about money, Sharp. Quite right. But there's one thing to be said for glory.
Sharp: Yeah, what's that?
Custer: You can take glory with you when it's your time to go.

George Armstrong Custer played by Errol Flynn and Ned Sharp, Jr. played by Arthur Kennedy: Raoul Walsh's *They Died with Their Boots On* (Warner Bros., 1941).

1416

Custer: The regiment rides in about an hour. You can ride with it if you want.
Sharp: Where is the regiment riding?
Custer: To hell, Sharp …or to glory. It depends on one's point of view.

George Armstrong Custer played by Errol Flynn and Ned Sharp, Jr. played by Arthur Kennedy: Raoul Walsh's *They Died with Their Boots On* (Warner Bros., 1941).

1417

Captain: Where are your sidearms, mister?
Doctor: I didn't think surgeons were supposed to carry arms, Captain, according to regulations.
Captain: Redskins don't observe the rules of war, mister. In fact, they never heard of them.

Captain Peter Blake played by Phil Carey and Doctor Allen Seward played by Robert Francis: Phil Karlson's *They Rode West* (Columbia, 1954).

1418

Doctor: Captain, these men can't fight off another attack.

Captain: I know it and they know it. And maybe somehow we can bluff 'em. You see, Doctor, men have got to hope for something. Even when within their hearts they know they're going to die.

Doctor Allen Seward played by Robert Francis and Captain Peter Blake played by Phil Carey: Phil Karlson's *They Rode West* (Columbia, 1954).

1419

Captain: I'm aware of your name, mister. Your orders preceded you. I endorsed them unfavorably.
Lieutenant: Unfavorably, sir?
Captain: That's correct. And you're reporting in here a week ahead of time. Out here, don't ever jump the gun, mister. Don't be early, and don't be late!

Captain Stephen Maddocks played by Richard Boone and Lieutenant Curtis McQuade played by George Hamilton: Joseph Newman's *A Thunder of Drums* (MGM, 1961).

1420

Captain: Now you get that lovely brothel stench of glory out of your nostrils! On this post a green officer leads nothing, and commands nothing, until I have hand-tooled and troop-schooled him myself!

Captain Stephen Maddocks played by Richard Boone: Joseph Newman's *A Thunder of Drums* (MGM, 1961).

1421

Captain: Now …there are three things a man can do to relieve the boredom of these lonely one-troop posts. He can drink himself into a straitjacket. He can get his throat cut chasing squaws. Or he can dedicate himself to the bleak monastic life of a soldier and become a good officer. I hope you choose the latter. That's all, mister.

Captain Stephen Maddocks played by Richard Boone: Joseph Newman's *A Thunder of Drums* (MGM, 1961).

1422

Sergeant: I don't like officers much. And I don't have to. But I got to trust them. I don't know what a gentleman is …but a real one ain't a back-fighter.

Sergeant Rodermill played by Arthur O'Connell: Joseph Newman's *A Thunder of Drums* (MGM, 1961).

1423

Captain: I'm a long way from a Bible thumper, but one thing I do believe: The sum total of man's experience

with morality is the Ten Commandments. If we don't try to live by them, we throw away the God-given chance for decency.

Captain Stephen Maddocks played by Richard Boone: Joseph Newman's *A Thunder of Drums* (MGM, 1961).

1424

Captain: It's not in the book, mister, but it's one of the hard lessons we learn out here.
Lieutenant: What's that?
Captain: Bachelors make the best soldiers. All they have to lose is their loneliness.

Captain Stephen Maddocks played by Richard Boone and Lieutenant Curtis McQuade played by George Hamilton: Joseph Newman's *A Thunder of Drums* (MGM, 1961).

1425

Colonel: If you bungle this job, I'll have you transferred to the Indian territory for the rest of your life …which won't be for very long!

Lt. Colonel Chandler played by Henry Hull: Andre De Toth's *Thunder Over the Plains* (Warner Bros., 1953).

1426

Dancy: It's the oldest rule in the Army, Captain. Don't disobey orders when you can't win.

Lieutenant Rob Dancy played by Alex Nicol and Captain Fetterman played by Arthur Randall: George Sherman's *Tomahawk* (Universal, 1951).

1427

Taglito: Your cavalrymen move with the silence of buffalo.

Taglito played by Tommy Rall: Jesse Hibbs' *Walk the Proud Land* (Universal, 1956).

1428

Colonel: Ah, still a sergeant, hey Schermerhorn?
Sergeant: Yes, sir. I guess soldiers are like water: They find their own level.

Colonel Jackson Meade played by John McIntire and Sergeant Luke Schermerhorn played by Charles Drake: George Sherman's *War Arrow* (Universal, 1954).

1429

Clarke: I'll tell you something, Tolson. One way to judge an officer is how many fights you've been in and whether you're still alive. You're still living.

Sergeant Clarke played by Charles McGraw and

Tolson played by Peter Graves: Lesley Selander's *War Paint* (United Artists, 1953).

1430

Tolson: You know, Martin, all we live for is the big moment. The moment when we finally take what we want.

Martin: Where are you going to find it in the Army?

Tolson played by Peter Graves and Martin played

by James Parnell: Lesley Selander's *War Paint* (United Artists, 1953).

1431

Captain: Anything you wish to add, Mr. Killian?

Killian: Well, Captain, what you didn't say ain't worth saying. Of course, there ain't much you didn't say.

Captain Charring played by Richard Kelton and Killian played by Hugh O'Brian: Don Taylor's *Wild Women* (TVW, 1970).

1432

Major: Harmon, I'd go easy if I were you. You haven't got much evidence to arrest a man on.

Marshal: If he's innocent, he's got nothing to worry about.

Major: If he's guilty, he'll face a court martial.

Marshal: If he's guilty, he'll face me!

Major Lucas played by Peter Mark Richman and Marshal Dave Harmon played by Clint Walker: Ted Post's *Yuma* (TVW, 1971).

Gambling

See also Drinking; Saloons; Whiskey

1433

Jason: Are you really a trickster?

Zach: Oh, I think most people are at a certain level. But remember this: You can't trick a man unless he's aiming to trick you.

Jason: How come?

Zach: Well, because people in general like the idea of getting something for nothing. And the trickster affords him that opportunity.

Jason Smith played by Mark Edward Hall and Zachariah Coop played by Robert Logan: Stewart Raffill's *Across the Great Divide* (Pacific International, 1976).

1434

Zach: I'm going to give up gambling until I get you there. And that's a promise.

Holly: I don't believe it.

Zach: Well, I'd be willing to bet ya.

Zachariah Coop played by Robert Logan and Holly Smith played by Heather Rattray: Stewart Raffill's *Across the Great Divide* (Pacific International, 1976).

1435

Sam: I guess the winning hand always comes up after the game has been played. That's the way it always is.

Sam Leeds played by Stephen McNally: Hugo Fregonese's *Apache Drums* (Universal, 1951).

1436

Billie: Carlos, how can I take you seriously? All those escapades ...and not forgetting that weakness for gambling either. I don't like it.

Carlos: Billie, I've given that up. Honest!

Billie: Wanna make a bet?

Carlos: Why, sure, anything!

Billie Colby played by Dale Evans and Carlos Vega played by Russ Vincent: William Witney's *Apache Rose* (Republic, 1947).

1437

Homer: Welcome to Quaker City, Donovan. Looks like luck is against you.

Donovan: Well, there's one good thing about luck. It always changes. And I got a feeling mine is just around the corner.

Homer McCoy played by Harry Morgan and Russell Donovan played by Bill Bixby: Norman Tokar's *The Apple Dumpling Gang* (Buena Vista, 1975).

1438

Amos: How much money do you figure that dude's got in front of him?

Theodore: About five hundred.

Amos: Five hundred? Wow! You know, that'll be, huh, that's two hundred apiece!

Amos Tucker played by Tim Conway and Theodore Ogilvie played by Don Knotts: Norman Tokar's *The Apple Dumpling Gang* (Buena Vista, 1975).

1439

Laramie: Say, that's cheatin'!

Tracks: Yeah, I've been cheatin' myself all my life.

Laramie: Ever catch yourself?

Tracks: No, I'm too smart for that!

Laramie Nelson played by Larry "Buster" Crabbe and Tracks Williams played by Raymond Hatton: James Hogan's *The Arizona Raiders* (a.k.a. *Bad Men of Arizona*; Paramount, 1936).

1440

Sheriff: You look like a man who wants to cash his chips. Keep on talking that way and somebody might accommodate you.

Sheriff Bill Cummings played by Robert Barrat: Lew Landers' *Bad Lands* (RKO, 1939).

1441

Ringo: Never enter into a deal for less than thirty percent.

Ringo played by Giuliano Gemma: Duccio Tessari's *Ballad of Death Valley* (a.k.a. *The Return of Ringo*; Mediterranee-Balcazar/Rizzoli Film, 1966).

1442

Cole: Never mix marriage with gambling. Percentage is all against it.

Emerson Cole Garret played by Arthur Kennedy: Anthony Mann's *Bend of the River* (Universal, 1952).

1443

Drummond: My daughter, Celie, was getting married.

Buford: Celie?

Drummond: That's right! When Tropp come for me, she was in the middle of getting married. And they're holding up the "love, honor, and obey" part until I get back.

Wilcox: You mean you walked out in the middle of the wedding?

Drummond: I did! I ain't been late for this [poker] game in sixteen years and I ain't about to start now ...wedding or no wedding.

Henry Drummond played by Jason Robards, Jr., Jesse Buford played by John Qualen, Dennis Wilcox played by Robert Middleton, Celie Drummond played by Louise Glenn, and Benson Tropp played by Charles Bickford: Fielder Cook's *A Big Hand for the Little Lady* (Warner Bros., 1966).

1444

Wilcox: Now look, mister, the first rule of the game of poker, whether you're playing eastern or western rules, or the kind they play at the North Pole, is put up or shut up!

Dennis Wilcox played by Robert Middleton: Fielder Cook's *A Big Hand for the Little Lady* (Warner Bros., 1966).

1445

Mary: Gentlemen are all such gallant gentlemen.

Drummond: We're gallant on Sunday. This is Friday, and we're playing poker.

Mary played by Joanne Woodward and Henry Drummond played by Jason Robards, Jr.: Fielder Cook's *A Big Hand for the Little Lady* (Warner Bros., 1966).

1446

[banker's response upon being offered a poker hand as collateral]

Ballinger: Forty-six years ago, I started lending money in Larry Bingham's back room. My first customer was a drover named Penny. He wanted $2 on a Brindle cow at 6 percent interest. He said she gave six quarts of milk a day. You know what I made him do? I made him move that cow into my back yard for a whole week. And I watched him milk her every day. Sure enough, she gave an average of 6½ quarts a day. So I gave him the money at 6½ percent interest. Not only that, I kept the 60 pounds of manure she left behind. When you show me collateral, madam, you better make sure it's good collateral. For forty-six years I've been lending money on good old-fashioned principles. I stand here now to tell you one and all that I've never been offered a better piece of collateral than I hold in my hand right now!

C.P. Ballinger played by Paul Ford: Fielder Cook's *A Big Hand for the Little Lady* (Warner Bros., 1966).

1447

Billy: Yeah, I'll play along, Hickey. You just keep four aces in the deck.

Billy the Kid played by Robert Taylor and Dan Hickey played by Gene Lockhart: David Miller's *Billy the Kid* (MGM, 1941).

1448

Johnny: Now, no offense, but …ah …fighting with your hands is a losing game.

Johnny Liam played by Rod Cameron: Spencer G. Bennet's *The Bounty Killer* (Embassy/Premiere, 1965).

1449

Bass: I was worried you wouldn't make it, Maverick.

Maverick: Well, Bass, now you can start worrying that I did.

Ramsey Bass played by Bill McKinney and Bret Maverick played by James Garner: Stuart Margolin's *Bret Maverick: The Lazy Ace* (TVW, 1981).

1450

Mike: He'll cool down. And when he does, he'll take the deal. He's too smart not to. Ain't that right, Ben?

Ben: I don't know. But anybody that throws $10,000 in a spittoon makes me nervous.

Mike Devereaux played by Hugh O'Brian and Ben Devereaux played by Richard Widmark: Edward Dmytryk's *Broken Lance* (20th Century–Fox, 1954).

1451

Lottie: Oh, I bet you know how to spend money, Sam.

Sam: Well now, I tell you. I've never been able to save any.

Lottie played by Ruta Lee and Sam Ward played by Darren McGavin: R.G. Springsteen's *Bullet for a Badman* (Universal, 1964).

1452

Etta: Why is there never any money, Butch?

Butch: Well, I swear now, I don't know. I've been working like a dog all my life and I can't get a penny ahead.

Etta: Sundance says it's because you are a soft touch, and always taking expensive vacations, and buying drinks for everyone, and you're a rotten gambler.

Butch: Well, that might have something to do with it.

Etta Place played by Katharine Ross, Butch Cassidy played by Paul Newman, and the Sundance Kid played by Robert Redford: George Roy Hill's *Butch Cassidy and the Sundance Kid* (20th Century–Fox, 1969).

1453

Pennock: You know, Trumbo, if ever you grow up you'll learn that a woman is like a poker game: What you take in one hand you drop in the next.

Booth Pennock played by Galvin Muir and Jonathan Trumbo played by Ray Milland: John Farrow's *California* (Paramount, 1946).

1454

Lily: He was a gambler. He played the Mississippi boats. He always used to say: "It's your cheat who's most afraid of being cheated." You better stay on your horse after this, Trumbo. It makes you look a lot more important than you really are. Another thing my father told me: "Always leave a man burying money."

Lily Bishop played by Barbara Stanwyck and Jonathan Trumbo played by Ray Milland: John Farrow's *California* (Paramount, 1946).

1455

Logan: This is Jacksonville, Clench. U.S.A. We sail with the tide.

Clench: All Americans think that. They think the tide flows forever for them. But mark me, Logan. Gold veins run out, crops fail, men starve, wars come.

Logan: And businesses fail …until we get a new deck and deal again.

Logan Stuart played by Dana Andrews and Clenchfield played by Halliwell Hobbes: Jacques Tourneur's *Canyon Passage* (Universal, 1946).

1456

Matt: Do you know what it's like not having a name? It's like being an extra joker in a deck of cards. You're nothing. You don't belong in the game.

Matt Brown played by Audie Murphy: Thomas Carr's *Cast a Long Shadow* (United Artists, 1959).

1457

Guinevere: You thought this was the prettiest dress you ever saw. Why, you couldn't take your eyes off it.

Wyatt: Well now, that was when I was ten high. Now I'm ace high.

Miss Guinevere Plantagenet played by Elizabeth Allen and Marshal Wyatt Earp played by James Stewart: John Ford's *Cheyenne Autumn* (Warner Bros., 1964).

1458

Pluthner: Was there any trouble?

Wes: A little. The marshal picked up Reno and Duke.

Pluthner: What? Ah, that was a tough break. They was good boys. But that's the game for ya …all part of the game. You and me, Wes …just you and me left out of that fine parcel of men. Of course, we end up with the money, you and me. But, that's how the cards fall.

Wes: Look, Pluthner! This deck has had so much bottom-dealing that it's dog-eared. Too many jokers turned up.

Pluthner played by Harry Woods and Wes McQueen played by Joel McCrea: Raoul Walsh's *Colorado Territory* (Warner Bros., 1949).

1459

Cutter: It's time we both quit, Crow. You don't like losing to me, and I don't like winning from you.

Jake Cutter played by John Wayne and Crow played by Lee Marvin: Michael Curtiz's *The Comancheros* (20th Century–Fox, 1961).

1460

Silver: There's one cartridge in this gun and five empty chambers. This slug with your name on it may be in first or the last …or somewhere in between.

Denver: Chief, that's one for the book.

Silver: I thought you'd like that. I'm going to give you a gambling chance. If you give me an honest answer to my question, you walk out that door a free man.

Strap: You expect me to believe that?

Silver: That's another gamble you'll have to take. At the moment, the odds are five to one that this is an empty chamber.

Silver Kirby played by William Bishop, Denver Jones played by Don Porter, and Strap Galland played by Richard Egan: Ray Nazarro's *Cripple Creek* (Columbia, 1952).

1461

Rose: Oh honey, don't think about him. They tell me he plays women just like he plays poker. Riffle, shuffle, fast cut, big deal, the sky's the limit; and then all of a sudden you're lying there in the discard.

Rose Dalton played by Lisa Davis: Reginald LeBorg's *The Dalton Girls* (United Artists, 1957).

1462

Illinois: The name's Illinois Grey …gambler. Not very moral, not very brave.

But I don't welsh and I don't squeal. I'm my own law and my own man. I don't hold myself above you, or you me.

W.T. "Illinois" Grey played by John Russell: Reginald LeBorg's *The Dalton Girls* (United Artists, 1957).

1463

Mason: You must be the joker in the deck.
Ben: Well, one thing's for certain. I ain't the queen.
Mason: Well, I'm not so sure. You're acting like an old woman.

John Mason played by John Wayne and Ben played by Reed Howes: R.N. Bradbury's *The Dawn Rider* (Lone Star/Monogram, 1935).

1464

Datry: A kingsnake eats nothing but other snakes …preferably rattlesnakes. That is its sole diet. You see, it would go against my nature to cheat an honest man. I couldn't sleep nights. But the other kind? I sleep like a baby!

Norbert Datry played by Matt Frewer: Brad Turner's "Fool's Gold" episode to the series premiere *Dead Man's Gun* (Showtime, 1997).

1465

McCall: Are you still after the bounty on my head?
Cates: No, I gave up that line of work. It's too dangerous.
McCall: Well, cheating at cards ain't a whole hell of a lot safer.
Cates: I wasn't cheating. Cards aren't my main occupation anyhow.
McCall: What is?
Cates: Damn if I know.

Duell McCall played by Alex McArthur and Charlie Cates played by Whip Hubley: E.W. Swackhamer's *Desperado: The Outlaw Wars* (TVW, 1989).

1466

Boris: Frenchy, have I got you beat?
Frenchy: Why don't you call me and find out?
Boris: I'll call. I'll bet my pants!
Frenchy: Two aces.
Boris: I was right! Why didn't I listen to myself?
Frenchy: Hand over those pants!
Boris: Oh, but now Frenchy, I can't! It's undignified! Think of my position! I've met every king in Europe!
Frenchy: Now you've met two aces in Bottleneck. Off with those pants!

Boris Callahan played by Mischa Auer and Frenchy played by Marlene Dietrich: George Marshall's *Destry Rides Again* (Universal, 1939).

1467

Lem: Why, the game was as crooked as a hog's tail.

Lem Claggett played by Tom Fadden: George Marshall's *Destry Rides Again* (Universal, 1939).

1468

Marshal: Just a minute! I'm probably wasting my breath, but I'm going to give you some advice. Get out of town pronto. Get yourself a job and quit poker. Poker is a man's game.
The Kid: I can take care of myself.
Marshal: Oh sure, I know you're fast with your guns. But sooner or later you'll meet a man that's faster, or that doesn't fight square. And then you'll move to Boot Hill. No, you're bucking a sucker's game, kid. You can't beat it.
The Kid: I guess that's good advice, Marshal. But I ain't taking it. Besides, how to handle a six gun and poker is all I know.

The Marshal/Lightning played by Stephen McNally and the Silver Kid played by Audie Murphy: Don Siegel's *The Duel at Silver Creek* (Universal, 1952).

1469

Sam: I smell a stinkin' cheater!
Ebenezer: On the contrary, Mr. Benson. It is the distinct odor of a loser!

Sam Benson played by Rick Schroder and Ebenezer Scrooge played by Jack Palance: Ken Jubenvill's *Ebenezer* (TVW, 1997).

1470

Maudie: Well, there I was …stranded. A gambler's widow and not a chip to my name.

Maudie played by Charlene Holt: Howard Hawks' *El Dorado* (Paramount, 1967).

1471

Morgan: You know, when a gambler lets his game wind up in a killing, pretty soon he don't have a game.

Van Morgan played by Dean Martin: Henry Hathaway's *Five Card Stud* (Paramount, 1968).

1472

Haggard: You got a lot to learn about patience.
Hale: I'm patient enough when the chips are on the table. I just want the game to get started.

J.C. Haggard played by Paul Birch and Hale Clinton played by Michael "Touch" Connors: Roger Corman's *Five Guns West* (American Releasing Corp., 1955).

1473

Wylie: Now the first thing to learn about a deck of cards is how to handle them. They're a whole lot like women. Usually, when you pick one up, you wished you hadn't.

Wolf Wylie played by William Frawley: Joseph Kane's *Flame of Barbary Coast* (Republic, 1945).

1474

Wylie: Did I ever tell you that women and cards don't mix?
Duke: I don't intend mixing them.
Wylie: Well, which comes first?
Duke: Cards.
Wylie: I may have to remind you of that occasionally.

Wolf Wylie played by William Frawley and Duke Fergus played by John Wayne: Joseph Kane's *Flame of Barbary Coast* (Republic, 1945).

1475

Johnny: And on top of that, it's colder than a tinhorn gambler's heart.

Johnny Tallon played by Dane Clark: John Rawlins' *Fort Defiance* (United Artists, 1951).

1476

Lunsford: It seems like my luck is running out. The higher I stack the chips, the worse it goes.
Britt: You even stacked your life on it!
Lunsford: If a man wants to hit the jackpot, Ned, he's got to take chances. Oh, if I got killed, of course I would regret it.

Blair Lunsford played by David Brian and Ned Britt played by Randolph Scott: Edwin Marin's *Fort Worth* (Warner Bros., 1951).

1477

Vance: You think you're top man on God's green earth, don't you?
Darrow: I'm a gambler. When I'm losing, I cut my bets to the minimum. When I'm winning, I let it ride.

Vance Jeffords played by Barbara Stanwyck and Rip Darrow played by Wendell Corey: Anthony Mann's *The Furies* (Paramount, 1950).

1478

Hawkes: Gambling can take hold of a man. He's got to be able to walk away from it.

Brady Hawkes played by Kenny Rogers: Dick Lowry's *The Gambler* (TVW, 1980).

1479

Hawkes: Poker is a trade, son. An honest one. It's fellows like you that give gambling a bad name …like drunks give drinking.

Brady Hawkes played by Kenny Rogers: Dick Lowry's *The Gambler* (TVW, 1980).

1480

Hawkes: Kid, I tell you what. If you don't make it as a gambler, you'll do real good at spreading fertilizer.

Brady Hawkes played by Kenny Rogers: Dick Lowry's *The Gambler* (TVW, 1980).

1481

Billy: How'd you know?
Doc: You just paid to see the cards, boy. Lessons come extra.

Billy Montana played by Bruce Boxleitner and Doc Palmer played by Lance LeGault: Dick Lowry's *The Gambler* (TVW, 1980).

1482

General: Gentlemen, I have a full house …threes over jacks.
Hawkes: Eights over fours. I guess my house was fuller than yours.

General Nelson Miles played by George Kennedy and Brady Hawkes played by Kenny Rogers: Dick Lowry's *The Gambler, Part III — The Legend Continues* (TVW, 1987).

1483

Poker Player 1: Four kings.

Poker Player 2: I got four kings!

Poker Player 3: Wait a minute! I got four kings!

Billy: Four aces! You lose! Yes, siree, gentlemen, there wouldn't be no winners if we didn't have any losers.

The three poker players were uncredited. Billy Montana played by Bruce Boxleitner: Dick Lowry's *The Gambler, Part III — The Legend Continues* (TVW, 1987).

1484

Hawkes: Gambling is really not about money. It's just our way of keeping score.

Brady Hawkes played by Kenny Rogers: Dick Lowry's *The Gambler Returns: The Luck of the Draw* (TVW, 1991).

1485

Bat: You know, Brady, it isn't how much luck you have. It's when you have it. And right now, my luck seems to be running out on me.

Bat Masterson played by Gene Barry and Brady Hawkes played by Kenny Rogers: Dick Lowry's *The Gambler Returns: The Luck of the Draw* (TVW, 1991).

1486

O'Malley: Mr. Hawkes, it's good that you believe in the cards. But it's better that you believe in yourself.

Butterfingers O'Malley played by Zelda Rubinstein and Brady Hawkes played by Kenny Rogers: Dick Lowry's *The Gambler Returns: The Luck of the Draw* (TVW, 1991).

1487

Burgundy: All women are gamblers whether they know it or not.

Burgundy Jones played by Reba McEntire: Dick Lowry's *The Gambler Returns: The Luck of the Draw* (TVW, 1991).

1488

Fiske: You never trust me.

Hooker: They always told me, cut the deck. You can't win but you can last longer.

Fiske played by Richard Widmark and Hooker played by Gary Cooper: Henry Hathaway's *Garden of Evil* (20th Century–Fox, 1954).

1489

Joe Grant: Hey, kid!

Three soldiers of fortune, Luke Daly (Cameron Mitchell), Fiske (Richard Widmark), and Hooker (Gary Cooper), are hired by Leah Fuller (Susan Hayward) to rescue her husband who is trapped in a mine. It turns out to be a gold mine ...and a *Garden of Evil* (20th Century–Fox, 1954), directed by Henry Hathaway.

Sioux girl Nah-Lin (Judy Walsh) tends to wounded brave while tribe members look on in *The Half-Breed* (RKO, 1952).

Billy: Yes, sir.
Joe Grant: I'll make you a bet.
Billy: Well, I like gambling. What's the bet?
Joe Grant: That I will kill a man tonight before you do.

Joe Grant played by Red West and Billy the Kid played by Val Kilmer: William A. Graham's *Gore Vidal's Billy the Kid* (Turner Pictures, 1989).

1490

Steely: You know, gentlemen, it's a peculiar thing. The more I tell people that the game is crooked and they can't win, the more they seem to enjoy losing.

Steely Edwards played by Brian Donlevy: William A. Wellman's *The Great Man's Lady* (Paramount, 1942).

1491

Jess: There's only one kind of a deal he understands. The kind that comes out of a gun.

Jess Burgess played by Leo Gordon: Raoul Walsh's *Gun Fury* (Columbia, 1953).

1492

Doc: You may not know it, but there's rumors about you all over town.
Bat: About me?
Doc: They say you deal black jack with three fingers: thumb, index, and trigger.

Doc played by John McIntire and Bat Masterson played by Joel McCrea: Joseph M. Newman's *Gunfight at Dodge City* (United Artists, 1959).

1493

John: Doc, you're walking into a stacked deck. If Bailey don't get you, the marshal will. You'd be smart to get out while you can. You act as if you want to get killed!
Doc: Maybe I do.

John Shanssey played by George Mathews, Ed Bailey played by Lee Van Cleef, and John H. "Doc" Holliday played by Kirk Douglas: John Sturges' *Gunfight at the O.K. Corral* (Paramount, 1957).

1494

Wyatt: Of course, you'll guarantee you won't lose.
Doc: I never lose. You see, poker is played by desperate men who cherish money. I don't lose because I have nothing to lose …including my life.

Wyatt Earp played by Burt Lancaster and John H. "Doc" Holliday played by Kirk Douglas: John Sturges' *Gunfight at the O.K. Corral* (Paramount, 1957).

1495

Wyatt: I've done some foolish things in my life. I'm about to do another. I'm going to let you stay in town.
Doc: Why so generous?
Wyatt: Let's say I like your cut. You can stay and you can play on one condition: no knives, no guns, and no killings.

Wyatt Earp played by Burt Lancaster and John H.

"Doc" Holliday played by Kirk Douglas: John Sturges' *Gunfight at the O.K. Corral* (Paramount, 1957).

1496

Nate: You know, I used to think I was a high-rolling gambler. But then, all I was ever willing to risk was money. I got a lot more at stake now …and all bets right on you.

Nate Harlan played by Warren Stevens: Earl Bellamy's *Gunpoint* (Universal, 1966).

1497

Nate: It never pays to even the odds.

Nate Harlan played by Warren Stevens: Earl Bellamy's *Gunpoint* (Universal, 1966).

1498

Craig: When you gamble and lose, you're a fool. When you gamble and win …you're a crook.

Dan Craig played by Robert Young: Stuart Gilmore's *The Half-Breed* (RKO, 1952).

1499

Craig: Rule number one in gambling, Marshal: Never bet on the losing side.

Dan Craig played by Robert Young: Stuart Gilmore's *The Half-Breed* (RKO, 1952).

1500

Ben: Can I play?
Claire: Can you lose?
Ben: Half of what I win.

Ben played by Julian Mateos and Claire played by Norma Bengell: Sergio Corbucci's *The Hellbenders* (Embassy Pictures, 1967).

1501

Reb: Jubal, there ain't no law that says you have to play every hand that's dealt you …or play hands you can't afford to have. You can always pass.
Jubal: Suppose the time comes when you don't want to pass?

Reb Haislipp played by Charles Bronson and Jubal Troop played by Glenn Ford: Delmer Daves' *Jubal* (Columbia, 1956).

1502

Randall: It looks like he ain't so smart after all, Mr. Slack. He played right into your hands.
Slack: Maybe he's not so smart and, then again, maybe he is.
Randall: What do you mean?
Slack: I was just wandering: Is he playing into my hands, or is he trying to get me to play into his?

Randall played by Robert Mitchum and Dan Slack played by Victor Jory: Joseph E. Henabery's *Leather Burners* (United Artists, 1943).

1503

Judge: Do you know there's a city ordinance against disturbing a man who's

deciding whether to raise or call? It's a misdemeanor. You could be shot for it!

Judge Roy Bean played by Paul Newman: John Huston's *The Life and Times of Judge Roy Bean* (NGP, 1972).

1504

Jacob: You've stacked your last deck!

Jacob Wade played by Jack Palance: Henry Levin's *The Lonely Man* (Paramount, 1957).

1505

Gus: I'll tell you what. Let's cut cards. Now if you're high, you win the $50.00 and forget the poke. Now if I'm high, I'll still give you the $50.00, but I get the poke. All right?
Lorena: What about Jake? I thought he was your good friend?
Gus: I ain't trying to cut Jake out. I just want a poke.
(after Gus wins the cut)
Lorena: You cheated, didn't ya?
Gus: Well, I wouldn't say I did and I wouldn't say I didn't. But I will say this: A man who wouldn't cheat for a poke don't want one bad enough. Come on, darling!

Gus McCrae played by Robert Duvall, Lorena Wood played by Diane Lane, and Jake Spoon played by Robert Urich: Simon Wincer's *Lonesome Dove* (TVW, 1989).

1506

Hooker: The odds are getting shorter.
Old Man: And our shares are getting bigger.

Hooker played by Claude Akins and the Old Man played by John Marley: Vic Morrow's *A Man Called Sledge* (Columbia, 1971).

1507

Mitch: Ain't you superstitious?
Doc: Only when I'm winning. I don't like to break my luck by killing a man. But when I'm losing …

Mitch played by Gregg Barton and Doc Holliday played by James Griffith: William Castle's *Masterson of Kansas* (Columbia, 1954).

1508

Bret: You know, my old pappy always used to say: There is no more deeply moving religious experience than cheatin' on a cheater.

Bret Maverick played by Mel Gibson: Richard Donner's *Maverick* (Warner Bros., 1994).

1509

Bret: Now ever since I was a kid, I believed I had a gift: that if I thought hard enough about a card, I'd be able to cut straight to it. Of course, my old pappy always said I was a damn fool. But I knew if I really believed and made it happen, well then, that would be nothing short of magic. Of course, it didn't always work. As a matter of fact, it had never worked.

Bret Maverick played by Mel Gibson: Richard Donner's *Maverick* (Warner Bros., 1994).

1510

Laurinda: Kraut strung him up three days ago. He said he was cheating at cards. They'll pull him down tomorrow, I guess.

Laurinda played by Nicoletta Machiavelli and Kraut played by Mario Brega: Franco Giraldi's *A Minute to Pray, a Second to Die* (Selmur/Cinerama, 1967).

1511

Laurent: A gambling loss is a debt of honor.

Laurent Dureau played by John Baer: Rudolph Mate's *The Mississippi Gambler* (Universal, 1953).

1512

Zeb: Is this a game of chance?
Twillie: Not the way I play it, no.

Cousin Zeb played by Fuzzy Knight and Cuthbert J. Twillie played by W.C. Fields: Edward F. Cline's *My Little Chickadee* (Universal, 1940).

1513

Roy: It's just like I told you, Trigger. Sometimes it's fun and sometimes it's tough. You got to take the breaks the way they come. Life is sort of like gambling. You can't always win.

Dialogue between Roy Rogers and his horse, Trigger: Frank McDonald's *My Pal Trigger* (Republic, 1946).

1514

Scoville: Well, what do you think of it?
Gabby: I think that horse was running backwards.
Scoville: Would you like to make a bet?
Gabby: I ain't making no bets! I quit gambling!
Scoville: Ha! Ha! Ha! That's a laugh!
Gabby: Well, you want to bet on it!

Brett Scoville played by Jack Holt and Gabby Kendrick played by George "Gabby" Hayes: Frank McDonald's *My Pal Trigger* (Republic, 1946).

1515

Narrator: Hunted, hiding …The Kid continued to play his cards the way he saw them …and by his own rules.

Narration: Lloyd Bacon's *The Oklahoma Kid* (Warner Bros., 1939).

1516

Jason: I ain't ready to cash in my chips. Come to think about it, I ain't even got any!

Jason Pitch played by Jack Elam: Burt Kennedy's *Once Upon a Texas Train* (TVW, 1988).

1517

George: Now, I don't want to hold up a good poker game over some picky little squabble over the rules. But seven aces in one deck! That's a lot of aces!

Gentleman George played by Chill Wills: Jean Yarbrough's *The Over-the-Hill Gang* (TVW, 1969).

1518

Rumson: He calls himself Rotten Luck Willie. But that's just to get the suckers. You couldn't beat him with five aces, so don't go play with him.
Pardner: Oh, I don't gamble, Mr. Rumson.
Rumson: Neither does he.

Ben Rumson played by Lee Marvin, Pardner played by Clint Eastwood, and Rotten Luck Willie played by Harve Presnell: Joseph Logan's *Paint Your Wagon* (Paramount, 1969).

1519

Billy: Don't press your luck.
Garrett: I ain't worried about my luck.

Billy the Kid played by Kris Kristofferson and Pat Garrett played by James Coburn: Sam Peckinpah's *Pat Garrett and Billy the Kid* (MGM, 1973).

1520

Alice: This book [the Bible] and a royal flush are the only two things in my life that have never changed.

Poker Alice Moffit played by Elizabeth Taylor: Arthur Allan Seidelman's *Poker Alice* (TVW, 1987).

1521

Alice: Only a loser smiles at a poker table.

Poker Alice Moffit played by Elizabeth Taylor: Arthur Allan Seidelman's *Poker Alice* (TVW, 1987).

1522

Alice: I've never shaved a deck. I've never marked an ace. I don't deal from the bottom, and I have never double-discarded. When I sit in on a poker game, I don't cast shadows!

Poker Alice Moffit played by Elizabeth Taylor: Arthur Allan Seidelman's *Poker Alice* (TVW, 1987).

1523

McCarthy: Are you familiar with a card game called stud poker?
Alice: Well, I have played it.
McCarthy: I assure you that anything you lose will be returned to you after the game. My friends and I would never think of taking money from a lady. It is your company that we prize.
Alice: What if I by some strange happenchance, I should win?
McCarthy: Naturally, you would keep your winnings, Miss Moffit. Our loss to you would be our pleasure.
Alice: Oh, how fortunate for the weaker sex!

McCarthy played by Pat Corley and Poker Alice Moffit played by Elizabeth Taylor: Arthur Allan Seidelman's *Poker Alice* (TVW, 1987).

1524

McCarthy: Jake, lend me a few thousand. I can't let her get away with a bluff like that.
Jake: What makes you think she's bluffin', McCarthy?
McCarthy: Oh, she's gotta be bluffin'. No woman can have a run of luck like that!
Jake: The cards don't know she's a woman!

McCarthy played by Pat Corley and Jake Sears played by Richard Mulligan: Arthur Allan Seidelman's *Poker Alice* (TVW, 1987).

1525

Little J: You see, I ain't much on people, Time. Money is great, and booze is all right. But for me, most of all, it's the thrill. You know, that thrill of knowing you can win it all …or lose it all in a blink of an eye.

Little J played by Stephen Baldwin and Father Time played by Big Daddy Kane: Mario Van Peebles' *Posse* (Gramercy Pictures, 1993).

1526

Sundown: I guess it just wasn't in the cards for me to stay on.

Sundown Saunders played by Tom Tyler: Wallace Fox's *Powdersmoke Range* (RKO, 1935).

1527

Farlan: I can understand you getting into a crap game and losing $700.00 you didn't have. But how did you lose your pants?
Dolworth: In a lady's bedroom trying to raise the cash.

Henry Rico Fardan played by Lee Marvin and Bill Dolworth played by Burt Lancaster: Richard Brooks' *The Professionals* (Columbia, 1966).

1528

Ace: Do you want to play poker with me, young lady?
Ellen: It looks like you're having a pretty good time playing with yourself.

Ace Hanlon played by Lance Henriksen and Ellen played by Sharon Stone: Sam Raimi's *The Quick and the Dead* (Tristar, 1995).

1529

Kirby: What's your angle?
Randolph: Like my aces, I prefer to keep that up my sleeve. Let's just say that I'd like very much to see Mr. Montgomery put to bed …with a pick and shovel.

Tex Kirby played by Rory Calhoun and John Randolph played by Rex Reason: John Sherwood's *Raw Edge* (Universal, 1956).

1530

Ben: I think you owe me an apology, sir.
Marshal: Don't push your luck, boy. If you were cheating, and I have no doubt you were, you'll slip up one of these days.

Opposite: **Movie poster from *A Minute to Pray, a Second to Die* (Selmur/Cinerama Releasing, 1967), a good spaghetti western with gunman Clay McCord (Alex Cord) who comes down with paralytic seizures at the worst of times.**

And when you do, the law will be on the side of the man that kills you. Now move along!

Ben Mathews played by Tony Curtis and Marshal Sommers played by William Gargan: Rudolph Mate's *The Rawhide Years* (Universal, 1956).

1531

Carrico: Isn't it customary to give a man a chance to get even?

Matt: Why, I wouldn't know. I'm not familiar with the niceties of the game.

Carrico: I figured you for a man of high ideals. It seems that I was wrong.

Matt: You did. I figured you for a bad loser. I was right.

Carrico played by Donald Randolph and Matt Comfort played by Minor Watson: Rudolph Mate's *The Rawhide Years* (Universal, 1956).

1532

Groot [Old Timer on cattle drive trying to get store-bought teeth back from Indian that he lost in poker game]: If you was half human, you'd give 'em back to me. You can see I could use 'em. Besides, it'd help keep the dust out of my mouth.

Quo: Keep mouth shut. Dust not get in.

Groot: I bet I ate ten pounds in the last 16 days. Before this shenanigan is over, I'll probably eat enough land to incorporate me into the Union.

Groot Nadine played by Walter Brennan and Quo played by Chief Yowlachie: Howard Hawks' *Red River* (United Artists, 1948).

1533

Drury: There's one point you fooled me on, Simms. I didn't figure you for a coward. You haven't got the nerve to give me a break in a fair fight.

Simms: You asked to play a lone hand, didn't ya? Well, you're gonna play it …all by yourself!

John Drury played by John Wayne and Henry Simms, alias The Hawk, played by Frank Hagney: Fred Allen's *Ride Him, Cowboy* (Warner Bros., 1932).

1534

Rio: Now amigo, I'll bet you something. I'll bet you all this money that I can shoot a cigarette out of your mouth at ten paces …without killing you.

Vaquero: How can I win?

Rio: If I win, you won't have any money to worry about. If I miss, you won't have

Above: Tom Dunson (John Wayne) and adopted son Matthew Garth (Montgomery Clift) have a confrontation on their trail drive to the *Red River. Opposite:* Movie poster from Howard Hawks' masterpiece, *Red River* (United Artists, 1948).

any further need of money, or worry of any kind. What could be better than that?

Rio played by Robert Taylor and Vaquero played by Charles Stevens: John Farrow's *Ride, Vaquero!* (MGM, 1953).

1535

Smokey: You must have cut your teeth on a poker deck.

Smokey played by Warren Stevens: Sidney Salkow's *Robbers' Roost* (United Artists, 1955).

1536

Dolan: 49 percent of something is better than 100 percent of nothing.

Dolan played by George Peppard: Arnold Laven's *Rough Night in Jericho* (Universal, 1967).

1537

Tell: Mister, we're just 40 dollar-a-month hard-rock miners. There's no need to use no Mississippi riverboat card trick on us.

Tell Sackett played by Sam Elliott: Robert Totten's *The Sacketts* (TVW, 1979).

1538

Ryker: Be reasonable. After all, there are just so many hands in a deck of cards.

Ryker played by Emile Meyer: George Stevens' *Shane* (Paramount, 1953).

1539

Quince: Jason, there are good losers and there are bad losers. And you know how I hate bad losers …especially when they haven't lost yet.

Quince Drew played by Larry Hagman and Jason O'Rourke played by Lou Gossett: Burt Kennedy's *Sidekicks* (TVW, 1974).

1540

Eamon: A desperate man should never lay all his cards on the table when doing business, Mr. Roe.

Eamon McCree played by Alan Bates and Prescott Roe played by Richard Harris: Sam Shepard's *Silent Tongue* (Trimark Pictures, 1994).

1541

Clint: From now on, honey, we'll be playing with a whole new deck of cards.
Lilly: What good is a new deck …if you go on dealing them off the bottom.

Clint McDonald played by John Ireland and Lilly played by Joanne Dru: Ray Nazarro's *Southwest Passage* (United Artists, 1954).

1542

Roy: Come on! Like they say in poker, let's draw to a busted pair.
Cherry: I think you better toss in all your cards, mister. Like they say in poker, there's a new deal coming up.

Roy Glennister played by Jeff Chandler and Cherry Malotte played by Anne Baxter: Jesse Hibbs' *The Spoilers* (Universal, 1955).

1543

Mallory: Are you saying you win by dishonest means?
Hatfield: No, ma'am. I win by any means.

Lucy Mallory played by Mary Crosby and Hatfield played by Waylon Jennings: Ted Post's *Stagecoach* (TVW, 1986).

1544

Mallory: But why were they going to hang you?
Hatfield: I lost the payroll.
Mallory: You misplaced it?
Hatfield: You know, they used a lot of words, but I don't think misplaced was one of them.
Mallory: I'm sorry, I don't understand.
Hatfield: You see, I lost the payroll in a game of seven card stud. The more I lost, the more certain I was that I was going to win until finally there wasn't nothing left.
Mallory: You gambled away the regimental payroll?
Hatfield: Don't make it sound so easy. It took me 17 hours. You know, I believe that's the hardest work I ever did, the coldest deck I ever saw, and the biggest mistake I ever made.

Lucy Mallory played by Mary Crosby and Hatfield played by Waylon Jennings: Ted Post's *Stagecoach* (TVW, 1986).

1545

Charlie: He taught me one thing: As long as men think they can beat the table, all you have to do is get a table.

Charlie played by Jane Greer: Sidney Lanfield's *Station West* (RKO, 1948).

1546

Jeff: I've found that in playing for big stakes, Mr. Mourret, you better make sure you hold the right cards.

Jeff Travis played by Randolph Scott and Jules Mourret played by George Macready: Andre De Toth's *The Stranger Wore a Gun* (Columbia, 1953).

1547

Hap: He's trying to play an honest game with a crooked deck.

Hap Sutton played by Lane Chandler: Lesley Selander's *Tall Man Riding* (Warner Bros., 1955).

1548

Powell: And so, the die was cast. There was no turning back.

Major John Wesley Powell played by John Beal: William Beaudine's *Ten Who Dared* (Buena Vista, 1960).

1549

Reynolds: Did you ever think about killing him yourself?

Turner: Why should I when I can hire someone like you to do it for me? Here's your stack [of money]. We'll split 50-50 on anything you win [at poker].

Reynolds: What's my take if I win and kill him too?

Turner: 75 percent.

Reynolds: And if I lose?

Turner: A free funeral.

Reynolds played by Myron Healey and Turner played by Anthony Caruso: Allan Dwan's *Tennessee's Partner* (RKO, 1955).

1550

Luke: You know we all got out weaknesses. Mine is I'm a bad loser.

Jess: You might have to get used to it.

Luke: I got a better way. I fix it so I always win.

Luke Starr played by Broderick Crawford and Jess

Carlin played by Audie Murphy: Lesley Selander's *The Texican* (Columbia, 1966).

1551

Custer: I'll gamble! I'll gamble with anything! My money, my sword, my life if necessary. But there's one thing I won't gamble with …and that's my good name.

George Armstrong Custer played by Errol Flynn: Raoul Walsh's *They Died with Their Boots On* (Warner Bros., 1941).

1552

Morgan: We're going into business for ourselves, Doc. Wyatt just got us a faro game.

Doc: Oh, since when is faro a business?

Wyatt: Didn't you always say that gambling is an honest trade?

Doc: No, I said poker is an honest trade.

Morgan Earp played by Bill Paxton, Doc Holliday played by Val Kilmer, and Wyatt Earp played by Kurt Russell: George P. Cosmatos' *Tombstone* (Buena Vista, 1993).

1553

Rosser: Any deal from you would be from a crooked deck.

Tom Rosser played by Dana Andrews: Lesley Selander's *Town Tamer* (Paramount, 1965).

1554

McNulty: When the dice have left your hand, you've got to ride all the way with the number.

McNulty played by Stephen McNally: Robert Wise's *Tribute to a Bad Man* (MGM, 1956).

1555

Dusty: You know, a man ought to think real hard before he gambles with stakes he can't afford to lose.

Dusty Fog played by Christopher Atkins: David Lister's *Trigger Fast* (Vidmark, 1994).

1556

Trampas: Always play percentages. Never try to be a hog. Percentages, Steve. I learned that dealing faro. Remember that!

Trampas played by Walter Huston: Victor Fleming's *The Virginian* (Paramount, 1929).

1557

Beaudray: The bet's $50.00, pal.

Card Hustler: You gotta honor my marker.

Beaudray: I wouldn't honor your mama!

The Card Hustler played by Larry Golden and Beaudray Demerille played by Peter Fonda who also directed *Wanda Nevada* (MGM/UA, 1979).

1558

Vance: The first thing we got to find out is what sort of game we're sitting in on.

Vance Shaw played by Randolph Scott: Fritz Lang's *Western Union* (20th Century–Fox, 1941).

1559

Red: George, you can cheat me out of most anything: booze, happiness, women. But when it comes to money, my honor is at stake.

Red Dillon played by Richard Widmark and George played by Evans Stevens: Stuart Millar's *When the Legends Die* (20th Century–Fox, 1972).

1560

Jones: Do you know why it is that a man can always beat a dog at poker?

Fargo Man: No, sir.

Jones: A dog gets a good hand, he always wags his tail.

Jones played by Gerald McRaney and the Young Wells Fargo Man played by John David Garfield: Burt Kennedy's *Where the Hell's That Gold?!!!* (a.k.a. *Dynamite & Gold*; TVW, 1988).

1561

Luke: Murray, if there had been any other way, I'd had played it differently. You know that, don't you? The only cards I had were the ones you dealt me.

Luke "Whispering" Smith played by Alan Ladd and Murray Sinclair played by Robert Preston: Leslie Fenton's *Whispering Smith* (Paramount, 1948).

1562

Jane: A man that cheats at cards ain't got no religion.

Calamity Jane played by Ellen Barkin: Walter Hill's *Wild Bill* (MGM/United Artists, 1995).

1563

Will: It's too late for me. I ain't a good gamble for you. I wish luck to you though. I surely do that.

Will Penny played by Charlton Heston: Tom Gries' *Will Penny* (Paramount, 1968).

Gold

See also Lawlessness; People; Rough and Tough; West

1564

Colonel: The worst kind of informer. For gold he would have betrayed his own mother …or us.

Colonel Skimmel played by Gerald Haerter: Frank Kramer's *Adios, Sabata* (United Artists, 1971).

1565

Van Hock: You know, there's not a rich man that doesn't want to be richer.

Peter Van Hock played by Alan Ladd: Delmer Daves' *The Badlanders* (MGM, 1958).

1566

Bob: We're going to California. We hear there's gold out there.

Doc: There's gold in the mint at Denver, too, and it's a lot closer.

Bob Younger played by Jack Buetel and Doc

Shorty Hoolihan (Jack Oakie) discovers gold in the wild Yukon with Claire Blake (Loretta Young) and Jack Thornton (Clark Gable) looking on in William Wellman's *The Call of the Wild* (20th Century–Fox, 1935).

Butcher played by Walter Brennan: William D. Russell's *Best of the Badmen* (RKO, 1951).

1567

Mister: Ever prospected? Ever hit pay dirt? I've dug for gold, silver, lead, mercury. I've dug more holes than a whole regiment of gophers. I ain't never dug out a decent day's wages yet.
Mister played by Ben Johnson: Richard Brooks' *Bite the Bullet* (Columbia, 1975).

1568

Jonathan: Gold. You know, next to the Lord and maybe the land, I reckon it's the most powerful thing there is.
Jonathan Kent played by Tyrone Power: Henry Hathaway's *Brigham Young* (20th Century–Fox, 1940).

1569

Jonathan: I'm sorry, Gramps, it looks like I'll be holding you back.

Michael: I'm in no hurry. The earth and the sun and the sky will still be there when we get there, Johnny.
Jonathan: Yeah, but not the gold, Grandpa. Not the gold.
Jonathan Trumbo played by Ray Milland and Michael Fabian played by Barry Fitzgerald: John Farrow's *California* (Paramount, 1946).

1570

Shorty: Gee, I wonder what it's going to be like having things instead of wishing for 'em?
Claire: It's not nearly as much fun.
Jack: You're wrong, Claire. Wishing never got anybody anyplace. It's owning something that counts. And taking it when you can't get it any other way. That's all right too. It's the law up here …the law of the Klondike. If there is something you need, grab it! Take it away from the other guy. It's a good law. It works.

Claire: No, it only works when you deserve to have what you take. Otherwise, it's stealing. Perhaps that particular commandment isn't respected up here.
Jack: They all get broken. That one gets splintered.
Shorty Hoolihan played by Jack Oakie, Claire Blake played by Loretta Young, and Jack Thornton played by Clark Gable: William Wellman's *The Call of the Wild* (20th Century–Fox, 1935).

1571

Catlow: Now you keep those mules moving or we'll have those asses full of lead instead of gold.
Jed Catlow played by Yul Brynner: Sam Wanamaker's *Catlow* (MGM, 1971).

1572

Catlow: Ben, it's maverick gold. It belongs to anyone who can round it up.

Cowan: It don't belong to you. You can't steal from a man just because you don't know his name.

Jed Catlow played by Yul Brynner and Ben Cowan played by Richard Crenna: Sam Wanamaker's *Catlow* (MGM, 1971).

1573

Billie: Hey, Cisco, wait a minute! What about the gold mine?

Cisco: The gold of the rising sun is much more beautiful, señorita. And it is ours for as long as we live.

Billie Graham played by Virginia Field and the Cisco Kid played by Cesar Romero: Herbert I. Leeds' *The Cisco Kid and the Lady* (20th Century–Fox, 1939).

1574

Mendoza: He says the medals belong to him …that he stole them himself.

Brett: Well, tell him the next time to steal something with some gold in it.

Mendoza played by Rodolfo Acosta and Brett Stanton played by Dale Robertson: Harmon Jones' *City of Bad Men* (20th Century–Fox, 1953).

1575

Anderson: A fool comes to town with a fistful of gold dust, and every jackass from 50 miles around lights out after him.

Wil Anderson played by John Wayne: Mark Rydell's *The Cowboys* (Warner Bros., 1972).

1576

Gold is where you find it.

Prologue: Ray Nazarro's *Cripple Creek* (Columbia, 1952).

1577

Deacon: Now we made a bargain. I'm gonna build you a church, and you're

gonna lead me to some gold. Remember? But Lord, you're not helping at all!

The Deacon played by Jack Starrett who also directed *Cry Blood, Apache* (Golden Eagle/Goldstone, 1970).

1578

Jack: Did you ever go fishing, Norbert?

Norbert: Sure, lots of times. I'm good at fishing.

Jack: All right. If you want to catch a fish, you have to think like one. You have to think, where would I be hiding? Gold mining is like that. You have to think like what you want to find. And ask yourself: If I was gold, where would I'd be hiding …and look there!

Jack Fleetwood played by John Glover and Norbert Datry played by Matt Frewer: Brad Turner's "Fool's Gold" episode to the series premiere *Dead Man's Gun* (Showtime, 1997).

Jeff (James Stewart) outbids Ronda (Ruth Roman) for Yukon Sam's (Eddy C. Waller) claim in Anthony Mann's ***The Far Country*** (Universal, 1955).

1579

Jack: Try to understand, Norbert, finding gold isn't the hard part.

Norbert: It's not?

Jack: No, the hard part is keeping it.

Jack Fleetwood played by John Glover and Norbert Datry played by Matt Frewer: Brad Turner's "Fool's Gold" episode to the series premiere, *Dead Man's Gun* (Showtime, 1997).

1580

Luke: Well, I knew it was coming. I warned you I did. Where there's gold, there's stealing. Where there's stealing, there's killing. I knew it was coming. I just did know it.

Luke played by Royal Dano: Anthony Mann's *The Far Country* (Universal, 1955).

1581

Stranger: Now what do you suppose they're carrying in that coach?

Silvanito: It would be easy to find out. You get up close to it and take a little look what's in it. If they fire at you, you know it's gold.

The Stranger (Joe) played by Clint Eastwood and Silvanito played by Pepe Calvo: Sergio Leone's *A Fistful of Dollars* (United Artists, 1964; U.S. 1967).

1582

Morgan: It's a funny thing about gold. It don't look like gold until it gets to be money.

Van Morgan played by Dean Martin: Henry Hathaway's *Five Card Stud* (Paramount, 1968).

1583

Hale: You sure got one idea in your mind, Govern. You can't get your mind off that gold, can you?

Govern: You get your mind on too many things, you wind up with nothin'.

Hale Clinton played by Michael "Touch" Connors and Govern Sturges played by John Lund: Roger Corman's *Five Guns West* (American Releasing Corp., 1955).

1584

Fiske: Say, Hooker, before you became an idiot looking for gold, what were you?

Hooker: An idiot without any.

Fiske played by Richard Widmark and Hooker played by Gary Cooper: Henry Hathaway's *Garden of Evil* (20th Century–Fox, 1954).

1585

John: That's all I ever meant to you …a pick and shovel …to get you gold.

John Fuller played by Hugh Marlowe: Henry Hathaway's *Garden of Evil* (20th Century–Fox, 1954).

1586

Hooker: The Garden of Evil. If the earth was made of gold, I guess men would die for a handful of dirt.

Hooker played by Gary Cooper: Henry Hathaway's *Garden of Evil* (20th Century–Fox, 1954).

1587

Hannah: Why don't you go, too …like all the others …over the next hill?

Steely: Because I've already come over that hill, Hannah. This is all I want.

Hannah Sempler played by Barbara Stanwyck and Steely Edwards played by Brian Donlevy: William A. Wellman's *The Great Man's Lady* (Paramount, 1942).

1588

Nielson: You know, if you could find gold the way you find women, you'd be the richest man in the world.

Nielson played by Jan Merlin: Frank McDonald's *Gunfight at Comanche Creek* (Allied Artists, 1964).

1589

Jamie: Ain't it funny, father. Here we are going to California to find gold, and we already found it.

McPheeters: Better not count your nuggets before they're hatched, Jamie.

Jamie McPheeters played by Kurt Russell and Doctor McPheeters played by Russ Conway: Boris Sagal's *Guns of Diablo* (MGM, 1964).

1590

Dillon: You had your own church, John?

John: Yes, sir. Missouri. Yeah, in Pike County I had myself over 250 God-fearing, hymn-singing, straight-back, brother-loving damn Christians. And sir, my word was gospel.

Dillon: What happened?

John: Gold, that's what happened! There I was, preaching the inner wealth of the soul and suddenly they started walking out the door two-by-two for the mother lode. Then word come back that two of them had struck pay-dirt beyond their wildest dreams. And there went the rest of them.

Dillon: And then you went to preach in the gold camp?

John: No, hell, I come on out after 'em to pick up that vile yellow lucre myself. Damn if I didn't have the fever …groveling in the gravel stream beds with the rest of 'em.

Matt Dillon played by James Arness and John Parsley played by James Brolin: Jerry Jameson's *Gunsmoke: The Long Ride* (TVW, 1993).

1591

Matt: That's what won the war. Not courage or being in the right. Just gold.

Matt Stewart played by Randolph Scott: Roy Huggins' *Hangman's Knot* (Columbia, 1952).

1592

Ryan: Carter, you're gonna lead us to where that gold is or none of ya are gonna see daylight again.

Joe Ryan played by Harry Woods: Mack Wright's *Haunted Gold* (Warner Bros., 1932).

1593

Hawks: Looks like gold. Feels like it. Tastes like gold. Where does it live?

Red Cloud: I hope you never learn.

Hawks: Why?

Red Cloud: It would make me unhappy to see your hair growing on a stick. Anyone of my people who tells the white man …dies.

Hawks: But you're rich! Gold will buy horses, blankets. You're very rich!

Red Cloud: Will it bring back the buffalo your people will kill? Will it clean the streams your people will fill with filth as they search for the yellow iron? Will it bring back the beauty of the land? I'm already rich, and the only wealth I want is that which you see above us.

Johnny Hawks played by Kirk Douglas and Red Cloud played by Eduard Franz: Andrew De Toth's *The Indian Fighter* (United Artists, 1955).

1594

Narrator: Many men had sought it, few had found it, and more than a few there were who had never returned from the quest.

Narration by Richard Dreyfuss: Peter Svatek's *Jack London's The Call of the Wild: Dog of the Yukon* (Hallmark Entertainment, 1997).

1595

Kehoe: Buried gold doesn't draw much interest.

Bartender: It draws an awful lot of interest around here!

Dan Kehoe played by Clark Gable and the Bartender played by Jay C. Flippen: Raoul Walsh's *The King and Four Queens* (United Artists, 1956).

1596

Barker: Gold mines, horses, and women. Gee, I wish I could hang on to 'em.

Bonanza Bill Barker played by Harry Carey: Glenn Tryon's *The Law West of Tombstone* (RKO, 1938).

1597

McTavish: If I let them escape, they'll return. And not alone! Not alone, but with a hundred men. And they will massacre my people for the gold. Is that what you want?

Bel-Air: It was never our intention to harm your people.

McTavish: I don't live my life on the best intentions of others!

McTavish played by Serge Houde and Charles Bel-Air played by Georges Corraface: Rene Manzor's *Legends of the North* (Cinevideo Plus, 1995).

1598

Banker: How's the claim coming?

Jake: Oh, still coughing up a few color.

The Banker, Mr. Williams, played by Earl Dwine and Jake Benson played by George "Gabby" Hayes: Robert Bradbury's *The Lucky Texan* (Lone Star/Monogram, 1934).

1599

Narrator (Storm): When you're sick with gold fever, you have no patience with caution.

Narration by Barry Storm played by William Prince: Sylvan Simon's *Lust for Gold* (Columbia, 1949).

1600

Narrator (Storm): I'd just gone in to look for gold. I didn't want to find lead from the business end of a killer's gun.

Narration by Barry Storm played by William Prince: Sylvan Simon's *Lust for Gold* (Columbia, 1949).

1601

Storm: I'm on my way back to Superstition [Mountain] right now.

Walter: You better be careful. There's still a killer up there.

Storm: I got nothing to lose …except my life.

Barry Storm played by William Prince and Walter played by Jay Silverheels: Sylvan Simon's *Lust for Gold* (Columbia, 1949).

1602

Martin: Are you sure it's all right to do this [drugs]?

Morgan: I find …when you're in the gold fields, it's the best cure for not finding gold.

Martin played by Gerry Duggan and Daniel Morgan played by Dennis Hopper: Philippe Mora's *Mad Dog Morgan* (Motion Picture Company/BEF, 1976).

1603

Sledge: How much gold did you say they carry in that wagon?

Old Man: Enough for a man to die on …more than that maybe.

Luther Sledge played by James Garner and the Old Man played by John Marley: Vic Morrow's *A Man Called Sledge* (Columbia, 1971).

1604

Spur: Let this be a lesson to ya, Jim: I find a little bit of gold and suddenly, after all these years, the relatives turn up.

Spur played by Kirk Douglas and Jim Craig played by Tom Burlinson: George Miller's *The Man from Snowy River* (20th Century–Fox, 1982).

1605

Ramos: Don't be discouraged, my friends. Gold is where you find it. What you got to worry about is …how you're gonna spend it. Come on, keep digging!

Ramos played by Peter Mamakos: Gerald Mayer's *The Marauders* (MGM, 1955).

1606

Nugget: Prospectin' is my trade …stayin' single is my hobby.

Nugget Clark played by Eddy Waller: Philip Ford's *Marshal of Amarillo* (Republic, 1948).

1607

Gimp: A man would be a fool to tell anybody if he did strike it rich.

Magruder: Probably a dead fool.

Gimp played by Jack Elam and Lloyd Magruder played by Trevor Bardette: Ray Nazarro's *Montana Territory* (Columbia, 1952).

1608

Jason: Why don't you deputize more men, Sheriff?

Sheriff: The job's open. Do you want it?

Jason: Talk sense, I'm a busy man. Who would run my store and my gold mine?

Sheriff: There's your answer. Most folks are too busy making money to spend any time protecting it.

Jason Waterman played by Hugh Sanders and Sheriff Henry Plummer played by Preston Foster: Ray Nazarro's *Montana Territory* (Columbia, 1952).

1609

Monica: Imagine what it would have been like if your father had struck it rich and mine hadn't?

Cain: I can't.

Monica Alton played by Anne Francis and Cain played by Clint Walker: Robert Sparr's *More Dead Than Alive* (United Artists, 1968).

1610

Scape: Two things go straight to a man's heart: bullets and gold.

Scape played by Geoffrey Lewis: Tonino Valerii's *My Name Is Nobody* (Universal, 1973).

1611

Jesse: I've seen fellas too drunk to walk fall on their face and find gold. But never me.

Jesse Tate played by Millard Mitchell: Anthony Mann's *The Naked Spur* (MGM, 1953).

1612

Tanner: Dyke, you like gold?

Dyke: You can make pretty teeth out of it.

Tanner: You get me out of here [jail], and I'll give you enough gold to make everybody in Nevada a set of teeth.

Dyke: If everybody had 'em, nobody would want 'em.

Tanner: Well, there's lots of other things you could do with gold.

Dyke: Yeah, I know. I've had all kind of fever: typhoid, yellow, scarlet. I've never yet got the gold fever. If you're rich, someone wants it. If they can't steal it, they'll kill ya for it. Either way, you're better off if you had stayed poor.

Tom Tanner played by Forrest Tucker and Sheriff/

Dentist Dyke Merrick played by Charles Kemper in Gordon Douglas' *The Nevadan* (Columbia, 1950).

1613

Mitch: You know, I read something a long time ago: Follow the rainbow …but don't wait for the gold to be in it.

Dan: Look for the silver in-between. Yeah, I know. I went to school once, too. Say, what are you? Are you some kind of do-gooder or something? You want to save my soul, mister?

Mitch: No, I want a few men with anger and guts enough to follow that rainbow and grab a pot full of gold …not petty silver in-between.

Mitch Barrett played by Alan Ladd and Dan Keats played by Don Murray: James B. Clark's *One Foot in Hell* (20th Century–Fox, 1960).

1614

Mad Jack: If you so much as open your mouth about this tunnel, I'll put a stick of dynamite in it. You tell no one, you hear?

Horton: I swear before God!

Mad Jack: I said, no one!

Mad Jack Duncan played by Ray Walston and Horton Fenty played by Tom Ligon: Joseph Logan's *Paint Your Wagon* (Paramount, 1969).

1615

Holbrook: All those in favor of bringing prostitutes to this camp, say Aye!

Haywood Holbrook played by Benny Baker: Joseph Logan's *Paint Your Wagon* (Paramount, 1969).

1616

If You Drink, Don't Talk. If You Talk, Don't Drink.

Sign on miner's cart in secret gold mine: Joseph Logan's *Paint Your Wagon* (Paramount, 1969).

1617

Spider: One nugget! I'd like to find me one big nugget. I'd shove it so far up La-Hood's ass he'd wink at it when he washes his teeth.

Spider Conway played by Doug McGrath: Clint Eastwood's *Pale Rider* (Warner Bros., 1985).

1618

Kirby: Listen, Wagner, no one ever double-crossed me and lived to tell about it! I'm giving you just 24 hours to get that gold back!

Lee Kirby played by John Calvert and Thomas J. Wagner played by Hal Price: Derwin Abrahams' *The Return of the Durango Kid* (Columbia, 1945).

1619

Gil: What's this about mercenary desires?

Knudsen: You're on your way to Coarse Gold, ain't you?

Gil: Yes.

Knudsen: Well, them that travel there do so for one reason only: to traffic in gold. Which to possess is to live in fear; to traffic is to live in sorrow.

Steve: But we're not trafficking, sir …merely transporting.

Gil Westrum played by Randolph Scott, Joshua Knudsen played by R.G. Armstrong, and Steve Judd played by Joel McCrea: Sam Peckinpah's *Ride the High Country* (MGM, 1962).

1620

Gil: Like the fella said, gold is where you find it.

Steve: And if it's not yours, don't covet it.

Gil: Don't worry, boy. The Lord's bounty may not be for sale, but the Devil's is …if you can pay the price.

Gil Westrum played by Randolph Scott and Steve Judd played by Joel McCrea: Sam Peckinpah's *Ride the High Country* (MGM, 1962).

1621

Sam: You know, finding the gold, that's only part of it. You still got to dig it out and bring it back. And you can't do that alone. You got to have somebody to help ya. You know, somebody you can trust. And that's the hell of it. You can't trust nobody.

Sam Cooper played by Van Heflin: Giorgio Capitani's *The Ruthless Four* (PCM-Eichberg/Goldstone, 1968).

1622

Tell: My pa used to say that gold and trouble usually come in pairs.

Tell Sackett played by Sam Elliott: Robert Totten's *The Sacketts* (TVW, 1979).

1623

Orrin: Do you recall what pa used to say? Gold is risky business at best.

Orrin Sackett played by Tom Selleck: Robert Totten's *The Sacketts* (TVW, 1979).

1624

Brown: But in the new world, men are equal. And it is gold that makes them so.

John George "Kootenai" Brown played by Tom Burlinson: Allan Kroeker's *Showdown at Williams Creek* (Republic Pictures Home Video, 1991).

1625

Brown: Jim had good luck finding gold, but bad luck keeping it.

Nobody trusts nobody in *Lust for Gold* (Columbia, 1949). In this scene, Jacob Walz/the Dutchman (Glenn Ford) and Wiser (Edgar Buchanan) plot to follow two prospectors, who "seem to know where they're going," in pursuit of lost Spanish gold.

John George "Kootenai" Brown played by Tom Burlinson and Jim Blessing played by Brent Stait: Allan Kroeker's *Showdown at Williams Creek* (Republic Pictures Home Video, 1991).

1626

Tall Tale: That's California ahead.

Clint: How can you tell?

Tall Tale: Just raise your fingers into the air and rub them together. That pretty feeling between them is gold dust.

Tall Tale played by Guinn "Big Boy" Williams and Clint McDonald played by John Ireland: Ray Nazarro's *Southwest Passage* (United Artists, 1954).

1627

Flapjack: They went and hopped my claim, and I ain't gonna take it sitting down!

Cherry: Oh, you're gonna do some shooting, hey Flapjack?

Flapjack: You bet I am! And some hitting at what I shoot at!

Cherry: Now, now, now! Don't be in a rush. Maybe we better think this over. I don't want to have to walk out one morning and find you standing under that old sycamore with your feet just off the ground.

Flapjack Simms played by Russell Simpson and Cherry Malotte played by Marlene Dietrich: Ray Enright's *The Spoilers* (Universal, 1942).

1628

Roy: Where did he get you [shoot you], old timer?

Flapjack: If you get my claim back, Roy, turn it over to Banty and kind of bury me at sea on account of I always hankered to be a sailor.

Roy: I hate to disappoint you, Flapjack, but I never heard of anyone dying from a scratch like that.

Flapjack: You mean to say I ain't dying?

Roy: I'm afraid not.

Flapjack: Oh, dangnabbit! Just when a fella thinks he's got shed of his troubles, something has to happen!

Banty: That's the nearest I ever come to owning a mine in my whole life!

Roy Glennister played by John Wayne, Flapjack Simms played by Russell Simpson, and Banty played by George Cleveland: Ray Enright's *The Spoilers* (Universal, 1942).

1629

Haven: Who steals the gold?

Charlie: Who doesn't? All they have to do is put on a mask and they all look like Black Bart.

Haven played by Dick Powell and Charlie played by Jane Greer: Sidney Lanfield's *Station West* (RKO, 1948).

1630

Sheriff: Well, do you see anything?

Jake: No. What are we looking for?

Sheriff: What are we looking for? We're looking for nuggets, veins, the mother lode!

Jake: What's the mother lode?

Sheriff: I'm beginning to get the horrible feeling you know even less about gold mining than I do, Jake.

Jake: Of course I don't know anything about gold mining!

Sheriff: Well, why do you think I brought you along for? I thought everyone around here knew about mining.

Jake: Well, I don't! I might be able to give you a few tips about shoveling horse …working around the stable, but I don't know nothing about hunting gold.

Sheriff Jason McCullough played by James Garner and Jake played by Jack Elam: Burt Kennedy's *Support Your Local Sheriff!* (United Artists, 1969).

1631

Sheriff: I thought you might want to know. Some prospectors just tried to beat up Duchess and the girls.

Tennessee: Why?

Sheriff: They're all set for a gold rush but they don't know where to rush …and it's driving them crazy.

The Sheriff played by Leo Gordon, Elizabeth "Duchess" Farnham played by Rhonda Fleming, and Tennessee played by John Payne: Allan Dwan's *Tennessee's Partner* (RKO, 1955).

1632

Lane: Gold has a way of bringing out the larceny in all of us, Mrs. Lowe.

Lane played by John Wayne and Mrs. Lowe played by Ann-Margret: Burt Kennedy's *The Train Robbers* (Warner Bros., 1973).

1633

Homer: Why, in the old days a man could take a hat and wheelbarrow, go out and gather up a fortune before breakfast. But it's the seeking that's best …not the finding. I struck gold, my brother Ben and I. And I count that the unluckiest day of my life.

David: Why?

Homer: Because money is filthy stuff. I despise it. It corrupts. It eats out the heart. It separates brother from brother.

Doc Homer Brown played by William Powell and David played by Tommy Ivo: Ted Tetzlaff's *The Treasure of Lost Canyon* (Universal, 1952).

1634

Juan: You know I wouldn't cut your throat for a woman, no more than you would mine. But for the gold …maybe.

Juan Castro played by Gilbert Roland: George Sherman's *The Treasure of Pancho Villa* (RKO, 1955).

1635

Tom: We'll all die if we don't get some water pretty soon.

Juan: You're a funny man. First you want gold, now you want water. Why don't you want one thing at a time?

Tom: My trouble is you can't drink gold.

Tom Bryan played by Rory Calhoun and Juan Castro played by Gilbert Roland: George Sherman's *The Treasure of Pancho Villa* (RKO, 1955).

It's a standoff! Sheriff Jason McCullough (James Garner) and his dimwit deputy Jake (Jack Elam) have prisoner Joe Danby (Bruce Dern) tied to a cannon. Pa Danby (Walter Brennan), sons Tom Danby (Gene Evans) and Luke Danby (Dick Peabody) and company aren't sure it's a bluff in Burt Kennedy's *Support Your Local Sheriff!* (United Artists, 1968).

1636

Juan: They are going to trade a lot of lead for this gold. Lots of it.
Tom: Our rate of exchange will be high, amigo.

Juan Castro played by Gilbert Roland and Tom Bryan played by Rory Calhoun: George Sherman's *The Treasure of Pancho Villa* (RKO, 1955).

1637

Howard: As long as there's no find, the noble brotherhood will last. But when the piles of gold begin to grow, that's when the trouble starts.

Howard played by Walter Huston: John Huston's *The Treasure of the Sierra Madre* (Warner Bros., 1948).

1638

Howard: I never knew a prospector yet that died rich.

Howard played by Walter Huston: John Huston's *The Treasure of the Sierra Madre* (Warner Bros., 1948).

1639

Howard: I know what gold does to men's souls.

Howard played by Walter Huston: John Huston's *The Treasure of the Sierra Madre* (Warner Bros., 1948).

1640

Corporal: That's, ah, a lot of gold for one inside man to guard.

Captain: That's a lot of soldier, Corporal.
Corporal: Well, I still say that's a lot of gold, sir.

Corporal Blyth played by Jim Boles and Captain Shipley played by James Whitmore: William A. Graham's *Waterhole No. 3* (Paramount, 1967).

1641

Ramsey: How are you panning out, Hank?
Hank: I ain't. I'm only holding on to this claim until I find somebody I hate bad enough to give it to.

Ramsey MacKay played by Joel McCrea and Hank York played by Bob Burns: Frank Lloyd's *Wells Fargo* (Paramount, 1937).

1642

In 1864 the War Between the States was at a stalemate. Gold, the lifeblood of both armies was running dangerously low — gold to buy guns, ammunition and equipment. For the North it meant increasing the flow of bullion from California, across three thousand miles of hazardous country …For the South it meant stopping those gold shipments at all costs. Victory hung in the balance.

Prologue to Budd Boetticher's *Westbound* (Warner Bros., 1959).

1643

Bixby: Mr. Otis, a tenderfoot like you ain't thinking of staking a claim in the Black Hills?

Otis: It says there [newspaper], a new land of promise.
Bixby: It don't promise nothing but a quick grave in a Sioux boneyard.

Amos Bixby played by John Carradine and Wild Bill Hickok/James Otis played by Charles Bronson: J. Lee Thompson's *The White Buffalo* (United Artists, 1977).

1644

Walrus: We're sure going to be mighty rich corpses.

Walrus played by Charles Kemper: William A. Wellman's *Yellow Sky* (20th Century–Fox, 1948).

1645

Montez: You must tell me the location of the hidden mine which is the secret of our tribe.
Akuna: Our secrets are which only the chiefs may know.
Montez: We were born of the same mother.
Akuna: But different fathers. Yours was a white man and Americano. So the secret of the gold mine is only for me.

Montez played by Trevor Bardette and Akuna played by Chief Thundercloud: Joseph Kane's *Young Buffalo Bill* (Republic, 1940).

1646

Baxter: It ain't so easy to stop a gold rush.

Baxter played by Hal Taliaferro/Wally Wales: Spencer Bennet's and Wallace Grissell's *Zorro's Black Whip* (Republic serial, Chapter 7: "Wolf Pack," 1944).

Good Guys

See also Cowboys; Men; People; Women

1647

Ballantine: You saved my life just now. They say if you save a man's life, it makes you responsible for him …for the rest of his days. It makes me feel quite secure.

Ballantine played by Dean Reed: Frank Kramer's *Adios, Sabata* (United Artists, 1971).

1648

Wylie: Just remember, Fievel: One man's sunset is another man's dawn. I don't know what's out there beyond those hills. But if you ride yonder …head up, eyes steady, heart open …I think one day you'll find that you're the hero you've been looking for.

The voice of the cartoon character, Wylie Burp, was that of James Stewart: Phil Nibbelink and Simon Wells' *An American Tail: Fievel Goes West* (Universal, 1991).

1649

Bradley: So that's Quirt Evans. He's quite a man with the gals. He's closed the eyes of many men …and opened the eyes of many women.

Bradley played by Olin Howlin and Quirt Evans played by John Wayne: James Edward Grant's *Angel and the Badman* (Republic, 1947).

1650

Major: It doesn't matter what you've been or what you've done. There must still be some good left in you. Or have you changed so much, Bart?

Major Andrew Pepperis played by Carleton Young and Bart Laish played by Sterling Hayden: Lesley Selander's *Arrow in the Dust* (Allied Artists, 1954).

1651

Karyl: Why don't you leave him alone and let him get out of here?

Jim: Get out? Why would he want to do that?
Karyl: Because he has a chance to lead a decent life. He's a good man. Doesn't that mean anything to you?
Jim: You could be wrong about him. True, I haven't seen him since he was born. But it's my blood that flows in his veins …and it's a little thicker than water.

Karyl Orton played by Donna Reed and Jim Bonniwell played by John McIntire: John Sturges' *Backlash* (Universal, 1956).

1652

Warden: I've never been able to figure you out. This place is for murderers, scum, riffraff, badlanders. Not for a man of your education and talents.

The Warden played by Ford Rainey: Delmer Daves' *The Badlanders* (MGM, 1958).

1653

Eric: You know, things are going to happen in this county. Guns and shooting are going out. Law and order is on the march. You better look out or they'll run you over. The good people want to live together as good, peaceful citizens. And when they get together, there isn't a man fast enough on the draw or tough enough to stand against them. Not even Hannibal, Napoleon, or Billy the Kid.

Eric Keating played by Ian Hunter: David Miller's *Billy the Kid* (MGM, 1941).

1654

Choya: All my life I've been a snake. I've lived by my wits. I've gotten what I've wanted anyway I wanted it. Just lately I've been wondering just for once if I couldn't do something straight …do something a little decent.

Choya played by Alan Ladd: Rudolph Mate's *Branded* (Paramount, 1951).

1655

Sheriff: Ladies and gentlemen. There's no need for me to tell you. The emergency arose and the man appeared. Mr. Douglas, it's not often a man gets to do so much for his neighbors, and do it like you did. We want you to know we'll be forever grateful …and you'll be in our hearts always.

Douglas: Thank you …and in your prayers …please.

Sheriff Elroy Sanchez played by Herbert Rudley and Jim Douglas played by Gregory Peck: Henry King's *The Bravados* (20th Century–Fox, 1958).

1656

Bronco Billy: Now look! I don't take kindly to kids playin' hooky from school. I think every kid in America ought to go to school …at least up to the eighth grade.

Young Kid: We don't go to school today, Bronco Billy. It's Saturday!

The Young Kid was uncredited and Bronco Billy played by Clint Eastwood who also directed *Bronco Billy* (Warner Bros., 1980).

1657

Cody: Mr. President. Ladies and gentlemen. I was afraid I was going to make a fool of myself in front of you tonight. But that would have been all right. Because a man can make a fool of himself when he's off his own stamping grounds. But when a man makes a fool of himself on his own stamping grounds, there's no excuse for him. I don't hold with General Sherman that a good Indian is a dead Indian. From what I've seen, the Indian is a free-born American who'll fight for his folks, for his land, and for his living …just like any other American.

Buffalo Bill Cody played by Joel McCrea: William Wellman's *Buffalo Bill* (20th Century–Fox, 1944).

1658

President: Where will you sleep, Buffalo Bill?

Ed: You can sleep with me, Uncle Will.

Buffalo Bill: No, Ed, I will sleep out on the prairie underneath the moon and listen to the lullaby of the coyotes. You see, I ain't always been a comfortable man.

President: You know, it's a man like that that made this country what it is today!

President Grover Cleveland played by Pat McCormick, Ed played by Harvey Keitel, and Buffalo Bill played by Paul Newman: Robert Altman's *Buffalo Bill and the Indians, or Sitting Bull's History Lesson* (United Artists, 1976).

1659

John: You hit that dog one more time, I'm gonna kill ya.

Hal: Go to hell! He's mine and I'll do what I like with him.

John: I shot four varmits already this morning. One more don't matter none to me.

John Thornton played by Charlton Heston and Hal played by Horst Heuck: Ken Annakin's *The Call of the Wild* (MGM-UA, 1972).

1660

Douglas: The trouble being a hero is the morning after.

Captain Rod Douglas played by George Peppard: Paul Wendkos' *Cannon for Cordoba* (United Artists, 1970).

1661

Kate: You really do care. You like helping people, don't you?

Adams: Well, when you come to think about it, all that a person has is other folks. And I reckon there's a lot of folks in these parts that could use a helping hand.

Kate Brady played by Kim Darby and Grizzly Adams played by Dan Haggerty: Don Keeslar's *The Capture of Grizzly Adams* (TVW, 1982).

1662

Harley: I thought you know me better than that, John, after all the years we rode together.

John: Well, I guess it just goes to prove that you never really know a man until the chips are down and you need him most.

Harley Sullivan played by Henry Fonda and John O'Hanlan played by James Stewart: Gene Kelly's *The Cheyenne Social Club* (NGP, 1970).

1663

Pepper: You know, there's an old saying, Miss Sally. There's no law west of Dodge, and no God west of the Pecos. Right, Mr. Chisum?

Chisum: Wrong, Mr. Pepper. Because no matter where people go, sooner or later there's the law. And sooner or later they find that God's already been there.

James Pepper played by Ben Johnson, Miss Sally Chisum played by Pamela McMyler, and John Chisum played by John Wayne: Andrew McLaglen's *Chisum* (Warner Bros., 1970).

1664

Sally: You know, Pat, there's been a lot of stories about John Chisum …about how wild he was.

Pat: Those were wild times.

Sally: I think in some ways the two of them are a lot alike.

Pat: Who?

Sally: Uncle John and Billy Bonney. Don't you think they are? Don't you?

Pat: Not in the important things.

Sally: Like what?

Pat: Oh, Mr. Chisum has changed with the times. He doesn't like to let on, but he cares …about the people here, and in town …about the Indians and the territory. Well, he's independent and he likes to do things his own way, but he cares.

Sally: And Billy doesn't?

Pat: I guess he can't help it. But you heard him. All he cares about is getting those men.

Sally: In a way, doesn't it amount to the same thing?

Pat: No. Billy wants revenge. Mr. Chisum wants justice. There's a big difference.

Miss Sally Chisum played by Pamela McMyler, Pat Garrett played by Glenn Corbett, John Chisum played by John Wayne, and Billy the Kid played by Geoffrey Deuel: Andrew McLaglen's *Chisum* (Warner Bros., 1970).

1665

Sol: They will always talk about Yancy. He's gonna be part of the history of the great Southwest. It's men like him that build the world. The rest of them, like me …why …we just come along and live in it.

Sol Levy played by George E. Stone and Yancy Cravat played by Richard Dix: Wesley Ruggles' *Cimarron* (RKO, 1931).

1666

Lylah: You've just proven that you can still do the right thing.

Don: It'll probably be the last time I'll ever be fool enough to do it.

Lylah Sanford played by Pauline Moore and Don Burke played by Milburn Stone: Joseph Kane's *Colorado* (Republic, 1940).

1667

Mrs. Lowe: If, if you had a woman, taken by the Comanche and, and you got her back …how would you feel knowing?

Cody: Dobie, when we get to Lawrenceburg, you can ride along with me for a ways. A man gets tired being all the time alone.

Dobie played by Richard Rust, Frank played by Skip Homeier, and Jefferson Cody played by Randolph Scott: Budd Boetticher's *Comanche Station* (Columbia, 1960).

1669

Cutter: Let him make a run for it, I'd say to myself.
Regret: And then what would you say?
Cutter: And then I'd say back to myself, you can't let him run. You swore an oath when they put that badge on you.
Regret: And that's important to you?
Cutter: I said I swore an oath.
Regret: Words!
Cutter: Monsieur, words are what men live by ...words they say and mean.

Jake Cutter played by John Wayne and Paul Regret played by Stuart Whitman: Michael Curtiz's *The Comancheros* (20th Century–Fox, 1961).

1670

Bender: What about this fella, Reece?
Curtis: He's all right if you're all right.
Bender: When does he pay off? At the end of the run?
Curtis: You ask him for what's coming in the middle of a river crossing, and he'll pay you off. He'll pay you off in dry bills.

Doc Bender played by Brian Donlevy and Paul Curtis played by Richard Jaeckel: Delmer Daves' *Cowboy* (Columbia, 1958).

1671

Mary: I thought they bred men of flesh and blood in Texas. I was wrong. You're made of granite!
Bob: No, Mary, just common clay. It bakes kind of hard in Texas.

Mary McCloud played by Claire Trevor and Bob Seton played by John Wayne: Raoul Walsh's *The Dark Command* (Republic, 1940).

1672

Nora: We have a chance to get away. Let's take it.
Duell: I can't do that.
Nora: Then where does it end? Either you'll be killed or somebody else is going to die if you go back there.

Buffalo Bill (Joel McCrea) waving to his fans in his wild west show in William Wellman's *Buffalo Bill* (20th Century–Fox, 1944).

Cody: If I loved her, it wouldn't matter.
Mrs. Lowe: Wouldn't it?
Cody: No ma'am, it wouldn't matter at all.

Mrs. Nancy Lowe played by Nancy Gates and Jefferson Cody played by Randolph Scott: Budd Boetticher's *Comanche Station* (Columbia, 1960).

1668

Dobie: Me and Frank were riding together up Val Verde way. Frank was alone, same as me. And we heard about this fella who was looking for some young guns. We've been with him ever since.
Cody: You'll end up on a rope, Dobie. You know that.
Dobie: Yes, sir.
Cody: You could break with him?
Dobie: I've thought about that. I've thought about that a lot. Frank says: A man gets used to a thing.

Duell: I know, I know that.

Nora: Why do you have to take on everybody else's troubles?

Duell: Nora, I've been living on borrowed time. There could be a bullet waiting around the next bend for me. But until then, I've got to do what I feel is right.

Nora: There's a town called Opportunity about a hundred miles south. I'll wait there for you.

Nora played by Lise Cutter and Duell McCall played by Alex McArthur: Richard Compton's *Desperado: Avalanche at Devil's Ridge* (TVW, 1988).

1673

Destry: You know, I don't hold too much for first impressions. The way I figure it, the last impression is important.

Destry played by Audie Murphy: George Marshall's *Destry* (Universal, 1954).

1674

Tex: You know, you got to run steel through a little fire before it's any good.

Tex Martin played by Tex Ritter: Lambert Hillyer's *The Devil's Trail* (Columbia, 1942).

1675

Cowboy: You overestimate me, Padre.

Padre: Oh no, you underestimate your self.

The Cowboy played by Emilio Estevez and the Padre was uncredited: Gene Quintano's *Dollar for the Dead* (TVW, 1998).

1676

Doolin: Somebody once said: No man's bad enough to be shot in the back.

Bill Doolin played by Randolph Scott: Gordon Douglas' *The Doolins of Oklahoma* (Columbia, 1949).

1677

Senator: So that's where you stand!

Jesse: I think I'd rather be on the side of the victims than of the murderers.

The father, Senator McCanles, played by Lionel Barrymore and the son, Jesse McCanles, played by Joseph Cotten: King Vidor's *Duel in the Sun* (Selznick Releasing Organization, 1946).

1678

Ebenezer: My father said, the world is not an easy place. But that doesn't mean I can't try to make it better.

Ebenezer Scrooge played by Jack Palance: Ken Jubenvill's *Ebenezer* (TVW, 1997).

Two sons battle over the beautiful and passionate Pearl Chavez (Jennifer Jones). Bad son Lewt McCanles (Gregory Peck) is less than a second away from receiving the back of good son Jesse McCanles' (Joseph Cotten) hand in King Vidor's classic, ***Duel in the Sun*** (Selznick Releasing Organization, 1946).

1679

Sheriff: That's the way it is, Cole. I guess you're supposed to take care of [kill] me.

Cole: Well, not that I couldn't do it, Harrah, but I don't think I'd like that.

Sheriff: I'm glad to hear you say that …not that I couldn't handle you. But, ah, I don't think I'd like that either.

Sheriff J.P. Harrah played by Robert Mitchum and Cole Thornton played by John Wayne: Howard Hawks' *El Dorado* (Paramount, 1967).

1680

Maudie: Have you known him a long time?

Sheriff: Yeah, I've known him a long time. Since before the war. We've traveled some together.

Maudie: Sure, I know what that means. It means either you saved his life or he saved yours, or both. And neither of you will talk about it. Men!

Maudie played by Charlene Holt and Sheriff J.P. Harrah played by Robert Mitchum: Howard Hawks' *El Dorado* (Paramount, 1967).

1681

Mississippi: Are you sure your friend is worth helping?

Cole: You just spent two years chasing some fellas that killed a friend of yours. Do you think your friend was worth two years?

Mississippi: I guess I asked a fool question.

Cole: You did.

Alan Bourdillon Traherne ("Mississippi") played by James Caan and Cole Thornton played by John Wayne: Howard Hawks' *El Dorado* (Paramount, 1967).

1682

Blake: You see, Mr. Breen, you're a hero. And in the heroic tradition, you must wait for me to make the first move. Personally, I think that's rather foolish. In your position, I wouldn't hesitate. It's strange, isn't it? The very thing that makes you a hero is the very thing that makes you vulnerable to a man like me.

Blake Randolph played by John Howard and John Breen played by John Wayne: George Waggner's *The Fighting Kentuckian* (Republic, 1949).

1683

Faro: A red-headed cowboy with an injun kid? Was this cowboy wearin' batwing chaps with an 'R' on 'em?

Windy: Come to think of it, he was. Why, do you know him?

Faro: Know him? Sure I know him! His name is Red Ryder!

Faro played by John Hart and Windy played by Lane Bradford: Lewis D. Collins' *The Fighting Redhead* (Equity Pictures/Eagle-Lion, 1950).

1684

Johnny: Unless people take a stand, there won't be any place in this world for the Larkins to hide. Henrietta said we settled for a lot less here. And, well, maybe we did …maybe we did. But I'm fighting for my home. And I'm fighting for my boys taking over someday …and making the name Firecreek heard …and making this valley a place we got some pride in!

Johnny Cobb played by James Stewart: Vincent McEveety's *Firecreek* (Warner Bros.–Seven Arts, 1968).

1685

Jackson: Sam, some people have destiny sitting right on the backs of their necks. You're one of 'em. You're a born leader. When you talk, people listen because you love 'em. You'll fight for 'em and you'll die for 'em if you have to …and they know it.

Andrew Jackson played by Carl Benton Reid and Sam Houston played by Joel McCrea: Byron Haskin's *The First Texan* (Allied Artists, 1956).

1686

Marisol: Why do you do this for us?

Stranger: Why? Because I knew someone like you once and there was no one there to help.

Marisol played by Marianne Koch and the Stranger (Joe) played by Clint Eastwood: Sergio Leone's *A Fistful of Dollars* (United Artists, 1964; U.S. 1967).

1687

Danver: Duke, there's a certain something inside a man that makes him do things. Unpleasant things. Things for which there's no reward. But you can't always do the things you'd like to, and you can't always get the things you want. But you got to be able to live with yourself. You got to be able to look at yourself in the mirror when you shave.

Cyrus Danver played by Russell Hicks and Duke Fergus played by John Wayne: Joseph Kane's *Flame of Barbary Coast* (Republic, 1945).

1688

Angel: Come on, you heard him. You and I are going to fight together now, Chad.

Chad: Against who?

Angel: Against what? Against them! That's who! Come on!

Chad: That don't seem right, Angel, us fighting together. Why?

Angel: Why? Because they are the bad guys, that's why!

Chad: Ain't we the bad guys?

Angel: No, we're the good guys!

Angel played by Nick Dennis and Chad played by Mike Mazurki: Robert Aldrich's *Four for Texas* (Warner Bros., 1964).

1689

Blue: This country ain't got enough good people in it where it can afford to lose a family like the Calloways.

Blue Hannigan played by Larry Mahan: Tommy Lee Jones' *The Good Old Boys* (Turner Pictures, 1995).

1690

Spring: If wealth was measured in friends, you'd be the wealthiest man that ever lived.

Spring Renfro played by Sissy Spacek: Tommy Lee Jones' *The Good Old Boys* (Turner Pictures, 1995).

1691

Kristen: Jordan, who's Frank Morgan?

Jordan: He's some kind of gunfighter.

Old Harry: Oh, no, he ain't! Calling Frank Morgan a gunfighter is like calling a desert dry. He's a hell of a lot more than a gunfighter, Jordan. He's an honest-to-God walking-around legend. That's what Frank Morgan is!

Kristen Yarnell played by Nikki DeLoach, Jordan Yarnell played by David McIlwraith, Old Harry played by Walter Marsh, and Frank Morgan played by Lance Henriksen: Larry Ferguson's *Gunfighter's Moon* (Rysher Entertainment/Cabin Fever Entertainment, 1995).

1692

Father Joseph: God must see some good in you …though I grant He has very sharp eyes to see it.

Father Joseph played by Sam Jaffe: Henri Verneuil's *Guns for San Sebastian* (MGM, 1967).

1693

Leon: He saw God in people and not in the stones of the church.

Leon Alastray played by Anthony Quinn: Henri Verneuil's *Guns for San Sebastian* (MGM, 1967).

1694

Reb: I guess that squares us, Johnny.

Johnny: I'm glad to hear it, Reb. I never did like to shoot my friends.

Reb Kittredge played by Audie Murphy and Johnny Lake played by Charles Drake: Nathan Juran's *Gunsmoke* (Universal, 1953).

1695

Uncle Ben: Here, let me help you!

Cassidy: Oh, I can hop along by myself. Ole Hopalong Cassidy, that's me!

Red: You're a better man with one leg than the whole outfit put together!

Uncle Ben played by George "Gabby" Hayes, Hopalong Cassidy played by William Boyd, and Red Connors played by Frank McGlynn, Jr.: Howard Bretherton's *Hopalong Cassidy* (a.k.a. *Hopalong Cassidy Enters*; Paramount, 1935).

1696

Wood: I always thought we measured human progress by something more than our inventions ...by the way men treat each other ...with justice and compassion.

Captain Wood played by Sam Elliott: Richard T. Heffron's *I Will Fight No More Forever* (TVW, 1975).

1697

Tom: Well, it looks like I'll have to go.
Ellen: Why? Why should you risk your life for a lot of riffraff?
Tom: Well, they're people. They need help.
Ellen: Oh, you and your high ideals! Where did they ever get you? Why, they're the very same people that turned against you. They even tried to hang you!
Tom: Oh, that doesn't enter into it.
Ellen: Well if it doesn't it should!

Tom Craig played by John Wayne and Ellen Sanford played by Helen Parrish: William McGann's *In Old California* (Republic, 1942).

1698

Narrator: As he [Sam Houston] crossed the river, the new times he brought would be called history.

Narration by Charlton Heston: Richard Lang's *James A. Michener's Texas* (TVW, 1995).

1699

Gamecock: Maybe that's what the Almighty intended. Maybe He wanted you to do one wrong so that, to right it, you'd do a lot of good.

Gamecock played by Morris Ankrum: Lesley Selander's *Knights of the Range* (Paramount, 1940).

1700

Father: Well, I know how hard it is when people start ...I mean especially your friends ...when they start saying things that hurt.
Son: I told Rollie Adams that I would punch him in the nose if ...
Father: Hey now, none of that! You can't go around hitting people because they say things you don't want to hear. And you can't run because they say 'em.
Son: Then what can I do?
Father: Well, when a horse starts to bucking, you got to take a good hold of the reins and just try to hang on.
Son: You mean I should do nothing?
Father: It takes more sand to do that than it does to hit somebody ...or run away. And someday, I hope you'll see the sense of it.

The father, Will Spence, played by Richard Widmark; the son, Adam, played by Sparky Marcus: Vincent McEveety's *The Last Day* (Paramount, 1975).

1701

Jed: I like him. His face don't lie to me.

Jed Cooper played by Victor Mature: Anthony Mann's *The Last Frontier* (Columbia, 1955).

1702

Calem: You know what happens when you put a lid on a boiling pot? It either boils over or explodes.
Asaph: Unless you put the fire out under it.
Calem: I guess we should pray for rain, huh?
Asaph: You're storm enough, Calem. You're putting out the fire and I'm grateful.

Marshal Calem Ware played by Randolph Scott and Asaph Dean played by James Bell: Joseph H. Lewis' *A Lawless Street* (Columbia, 1955).

1703

Maddox: I never drew first on a man in my life. That's the only way to stay clean. You play it by the rules. Without the rules, you're nothing.

Marshal Jared Maddox played by Burt Lancaster: Michael Winner's *Lawman* (United Artists, 1971).

1704

Book: They say he rides into trouble like an angel from heaven. And that white suit of his ...gleaming in the sunlight. No one's tougher, no one's faster. He's the best shot alive. Hammer has killed men all right, but it's always been for the good ...for true justice.

Joshua "Book" Brown played by Carl Franklin: Alan J. Levi's *The Legend of the Golden Gun* (TVW, 1979).

1705

John: Hammer is a good man. Every gunfight he's fought has been on the side of true justice.

John Golden played by Jeff Osterhage and Jim Hammer played by Hal Holbrook: Alan J. Levi's *The Legend of the Golden Gun* (TVW, 1979).

1706

Hammer: Evil has its way of tipping the odds in its favor sometimes. It's best to make your own. That seventh bullet is for evil.
Johnny: For Quantrill?
Hammer: No! You didn't stumble on me by accident, Johnny. It was fate ...destiny. Quantrill is only a small part of what you've got ahead of you. I didn't train you to go out there bent on revenge and kill him. I trained you to carry out a quest ...to fight against evil and injustice. To go out there and ride as a saviour, not some cheap kind of killer. Do you understand?
Johnny: I reckon I do.
Hammer: Then go out there and do it.

Jim Hammer played by Hal Holbrook and John Golden played by Jeff Osterhage: Alan J. Levi's *The Legend of the Golden Gun* (TVW, 1979).

1707

Narrator: With his friend, Tonto, the daring and resourceful Masked Rider of the Plains led the fight for law and order in the early western United States. Nowhere in the pages of history can one find a greater champion of justice. The Lone Ranger rides again!

Narration: William A. Fraker's *The Legend of the Lone Ranger* (Universal, 1981).

1708

Crecencio: Ned took on that old man not because he's brave, but because he don't know what fear is. But you, mi amigo, you got a whole belly full of fear.
Sticks: Yes, sir, I do.
Crecencio: But you jumped over that fear and came back. That's what brave is ...jumping over your own fear to do what your heart tells you is the right thing to do. The bigger the fear, the braver the man who jumps over it.

Crecencio played by Luis Avalos and Sticks Packwood played by Tim Scott: Jack Bender's *Lone Justice II* (Triboro Entertainment Group, 1995).

1709

In this forge, upon this anvil, was hammered out a man who became a legend. A man who hated thievery and oppression. His face masked, his true name unknown, he thundered across the West upon a silver white stallion. Appearing out of nowhere to strike down injustice or outlawry, and then vanishing as mysteriously as he came. His sign was a silver bullet. His name was ...the Lone Ranger!

Prologue: Stuart Heisler's *The Lone Ranger* (Warner Bros., 1956).

1710

Governor: Kemo Sabe?
Tonto: Ah, that my friend. Indian word mean trusted scout.

The Governor played by Charles Meredith and Tonto played by Jay Silverheels: Stuart Heisler's *The Lone Ranger* (Warner Bros., 1956).

1711

Tonto: Me call you, Kemo Sabe. It mean, trusty scout.

Tonto played by Jay Silverheels: George B. Seitz's *The Lone Ranger* (Television Series, earliest episodes, Sept. 1949).

1712

But every once in awhile, a man comes along who is as big as his dream ...who fights for law and order and tries to make the world a better and safer place to be. Of course, it helps that he's the fastest gun in the West ...faster than his own shadow. That man is Lucky Luke. I should know, I'm his trusty, white horse, Jolly Jumper. And he's my cowboy.

Roger Miller was the voice of the horse, Jolly Jumper: Terence Hill's *Lucky Luke* (Silvio Berlusconi Communications, 1991).

1713

Sheriff: How about you, Douglas?

Douglas: Douglas! Just plain Douglas, hey? And you call him Mr. McLintock. Why?

Sheriff: Well, Douglas, I guess it's because he earned it.

Sheriff Lord played by Chuck Roberson, Matt Douglas played by Gordon Jones, and George Washington McLintock played by John Wayne: Andrew V. McLaglen's *McLintock!* (United Artists, 1963).

1714

McLintock: Now, we'll all calm down!

Drago: Boss, he's just a little excited.

McLintock: I know, I know. I'm going to use good judgment. I haven't lost my temper in 40 years. But, pilgrim, you've caused a lot of trouble this morning that might have got someone killed. And somebody ought to belt you in the mouth. But I won't! I won't! The hell I won't!

George Washington McLintock played by John Wayne, Drago played by Chill Wills, and the pilgrim, Jones, played by Leo Gordon: Andrew V. McLaglen's *McLintock!* (United Artists, 1963).

1715

Village Boy: We're ashamed to live here. Our fathers are cowards.

O'Reilly: Don't you ever say that again about your fathers, because they are not cowards. You think I am brave because I carry a gun. Well, your fathers are much braver because they carry responsibility …for you, your brothers, your sisters, and your mothers. And this responsibility is like a big rock that weighs a ton. It bends and it twists them until finally it buries them under the ground. And there's nobody says they have to do this. They do it because they love you and because they want to. I have never had this kind of courage. Running a farm, working like a mule every day with no guarantee anything will ever come of it …this is bravery.

O'Reilly played by Charles Bronson: John Sturges' *The Magnificent Seven* (United Artists, 1960).

1716

Pard: There are two kinds of people in this life, my friend. Those who seek battle and seem not to fear death …like them [gunfighters]. And those who avoid battle but will stand and fight to the death if their loved ones are threatened …like them [villagers]. That is true courage.

Pard played by Anthony Starke: Geoff Murphy's

Movie poster for *The Lone Ranger* (Warner Bros., 1956) with the Lone Ranger (Clayton Moore), his white horse Silver, and his faithful Indian companion, Tonto (Jay Silverheels).

In a silent classic, Douglas Fairbanks, Sr., is Zorro, the masked rider who protects the oppressed and leaves his mark upon the oppressor ... *The Mark of Zorro* (United Artists, 1920).

The Magnificent Seven: The Series (TVW, Series Premiere, 1998).

1717

Lockhart: Why are you sticking your neck out for me, Charlie?

Charlie: I'm a lonely man, Mr. Lockhart. So are you. I don't suppose we spoke ten words coming down here. But I feel that I know you. And I like what I know.

Will Lockhart played by James Stewart and Charlie O'Leary played by Wallace Ford: Anthony Mann's *The Man from Laramie* (Columbia, 1955).

1718

Oppression — by its very nature — creates the power that crushes it. A champion arises — a champion of the oppressed — whether it be Cromwell or someone unrecorded, he will be there. He is born.

Caption: Fred Niblo's silent film, *The Mark of Zorro* (United Artists, 1920).

1719

Fra: Are you trying to make me the receiver of stolen goods?

Don Diego: No, Padre ...the dispenser.

Fra Felipe played by Eugene Pallette and Don Diego Vega/Zorro played by Tyrone Power: Rouben Mamoulian's *The Mark of Zorro* (20th Century–Fox, 1940).

1720

Soldier: He's got a Z on his chest!

The Soldier was uncredited: Rouben Mamoulian's *The Mark of Zorro* (20th Century–Fox, 1940).

1721

Ernestina: You rescued him.

Tom Horn: I didn't rescue him. He died.

Ernestina: Emmet was nothing to you.

Tom Horn: Are you going to be around Bowie for long?

Ernestina: Don't you try to change the subject on me. You didn't have to do anything. Why did you go out after him at all?

Tom Horn: Well, I couldn't think of a good reason not to.

Ernestina Crawford played by Karen Black and Tom Horn played by David Carradine: Jack Starrett's *Mr. Horn* (TVW, 1979).

1722

H.D. [discussing aging father with sister]: Just don't give up on him. He never quit on us.

Cheryl: H.D., he cannot take care of himself. He needs a babysitter.

H.D.: He ain't an old pair of boots going to Goodwill! He's a hero! He's my hero! You don't put away your heroes!

Cheryl: Oh really? Well tell me, what do you do with them when they are old and sick and tired and worn out and unable to function anymore?

H.D.: You honor 'em, Cheryl! You honor 'em! They ain't plastic! You don't throw 'em away!

H.D. Dalton played by Scott Glenn and Cheryl Hornby played by Tess Harper: Stuart Rosenberg's *My Heroes Have Always Been Cowboys* (Samuel Goldwyn Company, 1991).

1723

Nobody: But a hero can't run away from his destiny.

Jack: My destiny is to get the hell out of here!

Nobody played by Terence Hill, Jack Beauregard played by Henry Fonda: Tonino Valerii's *My Name Is Nobody* (Universal, 1973).

1724

Kit: And you called him yellow! You better pick another color!

Kit played by Alan Bridge: Carl Pierson's *The New Frontier* (Republic, 1935).

1725

Kit: There goes the squarest man I've ever met. He's a great friend and I'd hate to have him for an enemy. No man ever double-crossed him. They liked him too well. They're afraid of him maybe. I can't figure it out. But whatever it is, there ain't two like him. He found me once with a bullet in my back and a price on my head. And packed me forty miles into town.

Cowboy: To the law?

Kit: No …to the doctors. He took care of me until I was well and then fetched me back to where he found me. He said there was no harm done to the law for what he'd done for me. You can't cross a fella like that.

Kit played by Alan Bridge: Carl Pierson's *The New Frontier* (Republic, 1935).

1726

Niles: I can't dry-gulch a man that's saying his prayers.

Lt. Niles Ord played by John Ericson: Paul Landres' *Oregon Passage* (Warner Bros., 1958).

1727

Ben: I can't think of one commandment I ain't shattered regular. I never did fancy my mother and father let alone respect them when around them. And I've coveted my neighbor's wife …whenever I had a neighbor …and whenever he had a wife. And I gamble and I cheat at cards. But there is one thing I do not do. I ain't never galled a pardner.

Ben Rumson played by Lee Marvin: Joseph Logan's *Paint Your Wagon* (Paramount, 1969).

1728

Preacher: The vote you took the other night showed courage. You voted to stick together. That's just what you should do. Spider made a mistake. He went into town alone. A man alone is easy prey. Only by standing together are you going to be able to beat the La-Hoods of the world. No matter what happens tomorrow, don't you forget that.

The Preacher played by Clint Eastwood, Spider Conway played by Doug McGrath, and Coy La-Hood played by Richard Dysart: Clint Eastwood's *Pale Rider* (Warner Bros., 1985).

1729

Frankie: All right, all raise your right hand and repeat after me! I, as a member of the Junior Thunder Riding Club …promise to follow the creed of our organization and help Gene Autry who's in trouble.

Frankie Baxter played by Frankie Darro: Otto Brower and B. Reeves (Breezy) Eason's *The Phantom Empire* (Mascot serial, Chapter 4: "Phantom Broadcast," 1935).

1730

Benson: By going out and doing what he did, he made a coward out of every man who stayed behind. None of you can forgive him for that.

Welles: Yeah, and you scared ones, who hate him the most right now, will be the ones who will want him to stay on as a lawman the most. You'll want a man like him standing between you and the next bad man who comes along.

Benson: I know how you feel, Banner, and I don't blame you. But if you've known one or two men in your life who were willing to go out and chance dying with you, then you've known more than most. But there are some who don't reach that high point of being a man, and who are still worthwhile. Think on it. Maybe you will come up with some reasons of your own that will make you choose to stay.

Benson played by James Bell, Dr. Welles played by Forrest Lewis, and Banner Cole played by Audie Murphy: Herbert Coleman's *Posse from Hell* (Universal, 1961).

1731

Colonel: We are neighbors, señor. We do not close our doors to one another because there is a mad dog in the streets.

The Colonel was uncredited: Douglas Heyes' *Powderkeg* (TVW, 1971).

1732

Dolworth: Maybe there's only one revolution: the good guys against the bad guys. The question is, who are the good guys?

Bill Dolworth played by Burt Lancaster: Richard Brooks' *The Professionals* (Columbia, 1966).

1733

Jake: Mr. D., whatever got a lovely man like you in the dynamite business?

Dolworth: Well now, I'll tell ya. I was born with a powerful passion to create. I can't write, I can't paint, I can't make up a song.

Ehrengard: So you explode things?

Dolworth: Well, that's how the world was born. The biggest damn explosion you ever saw.

Jacob "Jake" Sharp played by Woody Strode, Bill Dolworth played by Burt Lancaster, and Hans Ehrengard played by Robert Ryan: Richard Brooks' *The Professionals* (Columbia, 1966).

1734

Autry: Thanks a lot, folks. Speeches are not exactly my strong point so …maybe I better sing. I'm dedicating this number to a man we should all be mighty grateful to. You old timers remember about 30 years ago this town was plenty wild. Gunfights took place in this very street that claimed the lives of my folks and some of yours. Then a young fella named Doniphon was elected sheriff. He didn't have much equipment …just his guns and his nerves. He still carries the scars of those battles. But he made this a place where decent folks could live and raise their families. And that's why I'd like to dedicate "Old Buckaroo" to Matt Doniphon.

Gene Autry played by himself and Sheriff Matt Doniphon played by William Farnum: Joseph Kane's *Public Cowboy No. 1* (Republic, 1937).

1735

Duncan: There's something you should know before you leave. You've angered me, you've embarrassed me, you've shamed me, and you certainly worried the hell out of me. But through it all, there's something I've always responded to: There's a kindness in you, Vallian. That's what I'll miss.

Duncan McKaskel played by Tom Conti and Con Vallian played by Sam Elliott: Richard Day's *The Quick and the Dead* (HBO Pictures, 1987).

1736

Ben: Say, you try pretty hard to be fair, don't you mister?

Matt: Well, I just find it's the easiest way. You've been doing things the hard way, son.

Ben Mathews played by Tony Curtis and Matt Comfort played by Minor Watson: Rudolph Mate's *The Rawhide Years* (Universal, 1956).

1737

Larry: He'd charge hell with a bucket of water.

Larry played by Larry Melton: Michael Parks' *The Return of Josey Wales* (Multi-Tacar/Reel Movies International, 1987).

1738

During the pioneering days of the West, some unscrupulous men, greedy for money and power, flouted the law and trampled the rights of the early settlers. But there were other men willing to risk their lives in defense of people unable to protect themselves. Such was the Durango Kid, a mysterious masked rider whose name became a byword in Texas — 1875.

Prologue: Derwin Abrahams' *The Return of the Durango Kid* (Columbia, 1945).

1739

Chris: I'll be damned.

Vin: I doubt that. I doubt that very much.

Vin played by Robert Fuller and Chris played by Yul Brynner: Burt Kennedy's *Return of the Seven* (United Artists, 1966).

1740

Gideon: It's your heart that amazes me.

Clara: Mine?

Gideon: It's a rare thing for someone to lose everything they own and still show more concern for others than for their own loss. It's the tender-loving heart you have, Clara. It fills me up just to watch it.

Gideon Walker played by William Peterson and Clara Allen played by Barbara Hershey: Mike Robe's *Return to Lonesome Dove* (TVW, 1993).

1741

Quiberon: Well, if you think my word is worth something, yes, I give you my word.

Benedict: It's worth what you make it worth.

Quiberon played by Roger Hanin and John Benedict played by William Holden: Daniel Mann's *The Revengers* (NGP, 1972).

1742

Gil: Partner, you know what's on the back of a poor man when he dies? The clothes of pride. And they're not a bit warmer to him dead than they were when he was alive. Is that all you want, Steve?

Steve: All I want is to enter my house justified.

Gil Westrum played by Randolph Scott and Steve Judd played by Joel McCrea: Sam Peckinpah's *Ride the High Country* (MGM, 1962).

1743

Elsa: My father says there's only right and wrong, good and evil ...nothing in-between. It isn't that simple, is it?

Steve: No, it isn't. It should be, but it isn't.

Elsa Knudsen played by Mariette Hartley and Steve Judd played by Joel McCrea: Sam Peckinpah's *Ride the High Country* (MGM, 1962).

1744

Eula: Ruben, I have to say it. Living with you has been an adventure any woman would relish for the rest of time. And look at ya! With your burned-out face, and your big belly, and your bear-like paws ...and your shining eye! But I have to say: You're a credit to the whole male sex, and I'm proud to have you for my friend!

Rooster: I'll be damned if she didn't get the last word in again! Well!

Eula Goodnight played by Katharine Hepburn and Rooster Cogburn played by John Wayne: Stuart Millar's *Rooster Cogburn* (Universal, 1975).

1745

Bob: Ever face another good guy before?

Rex: No.

Bob: Me neither.

Rex: Kind of makes you wonder what will happen.

Bob: I guess the good guy will win, just like always.

Rex: Yeah, except we're both good guys.

Bob: Then I reckon the most good, good guy will win.

Rex: That's the way I figure too.

Bob Barber played by Patrick Wayne and Rex O'Herlihan played by Tom Berenger: Hugh Wilson's *Rustlers' Rhapsody* (Paramount, 1985).

1746

Ann: They [ranchers] need a leader. Someone with strength and courage.

Roy: But why me? I'm a newcomer here and ...

Ann: But you are the only one ...our only hope!

Ann Meredith played by Doris Day and Roy Reynolds played by Roy Rogers: Joseph Kane's *Saga of Death Valley* (Republic, 1939).

1747

Caldwell: He was a great man. He loved his people.

Muldoon: He loved all people, Lance. That's what made him great.

Lieutenant Lance Caldwell played by Rock Hudson and Revere Muldoon played by Barbara Hale: Budd Boetticher's *Seminole* (Universal, 1953).

1748

Narrator (Gillom): His name was J.B. Books. And he had a matched pair of 45's with antique ivory grips which were something to behold. He wasn't an outlaw. The fact is, for awhile he was a lawman. Long before I met Mr. Books, he was a famous man. I guess his fame was why somebody or other

was always after him. The wild country had taught him to survive. He lived his life and herded by himself. He had a credo that went: "I won't be wronged, I won't be insulted, and I won't be laid a hand on. I don't do these things to other people, and I require the same from them."

Narration by Gillom played by Ron Howard and John Bernard Books played by John Wayne: Don Siegel's *The Shootist* (Paramount, 1976).

1749

Quince: It's no time to stop trusting me.

Jason: Oh, I've never trusted you, Quince. I've always liked you, but I've never trusted you.

Quince Drew played by Larry Hagman and Jason O'Rourke played by Lou Gossett: Burt Kennedy's *Sidekicks* (TVW, 1974).

1750

Howard: A western actor can't afford a weakness. The public will forgive a dramatic actor. But a western star belongs to the kids ...the kids and the P.T.A.

Richard L. Howard played by Walter Reed: Richard H. Bartlett's *Slim Carter* (Universal, 1957).

1751

Destiny: I'm no hero, Joe Jr. Your pa is the real hero.

Joe Jr.: Am I missing something?

Destiny: You ever see a shootin' star, Joe Jr.? They look real impressive like they're showing off for all the other stars. The fact is, they got no place to go. They just burn themselves out. But it's all the other stars, the little ones you can hardly see, but you can depend on being there night after night ...like your pa. Does that make any sense?

Destiny played by Kris Kristofferson and Joe Gentry Jr. played by Cody Jones: Eugene Levy's *Sodbusters* (Atlantis Releasing, 1994).

1752

Destiny: It's a tough thing for a boy when his hero turns out to be a fake. I don't blame you for feeling bad. You see, Joe Jr., a hero ain't a hero at all unless it's in the eyes of someone else. And I guess I wanted to be a hero in your eyes today. Even risked my life for it.

Destiny played by Kris Kristofferson and Joe Gentry Jr. played by Cody Jones: Eugene Levy's *Sodbusters* (Atlantis Releasing, 1994).

1753

Marshal: Pick up all the men you can and let every rider wear a white cloth around his head so we can distinguish ourselves from the outlaws!

U.S. Marshal John Travers played by John Wayne:

Robert Bradbury's *The Star Packer* (Lone Star/Monogram, 1934).

1754

Gabby: That ain't your fight, Roy!

Roy: Why isn't it? Four against one doesn't look fair to me!

Gabby Whittaker played by George "Gabby" Hayes and Roy Rogers played by himself: Joseph Kane's *Sunset on the Desert* (Republic, 1942).

1755

Stark: There goes the only man I ever respected. He's what every boy thinks he's going to be when he grows up ...and wishes he had been when he's an old man.

Nathan Stark played by Robert Ryan: Raoul Walsh's *The Tall Men* (20th Century–Fox, 1955).

1756

Daniel: Pa, Pecos Bill ain't real.

Jonas: He's out there ...where there's still enough elbow room for a man to wander. He's out there ...where the land is still young and wild. You don't believe me? I swear to you by the code of the West, Pecos Bill is as real as you and me. Now, you know the code of the West, don't ya?

Daniel: Yeah, Pa. I know.

Jonas: Respect the land, defend the defenseless, and don't ya never spit in front of women or children.

Daniel Hackett played by Nick Stahl and Jonas Hackett played by Stephen Lang: Jeremiah S. Chechik's *Tall Tale: The Incredible Adventure* (Buena Vista, 1995).

1757

Pecos Bill: I ought to plug you two right now. But I make it a rule never to kill a man on Sunday.

Pecos Bill played by Patrick Swayze: Jeremiah S. Chechik's *Tall Tale: The Incredible Adventure* (Buena Vista, 1995).

1758

Julie: You don't have to live wild like you do. You could be a big man.

Bridger: I have my own idea of bigness.

Julie Madden played by Yvonne De Carlo and Jim Bridger played by Van Heflin: George Sherman's *Tomahawk* (Universal, 1951).

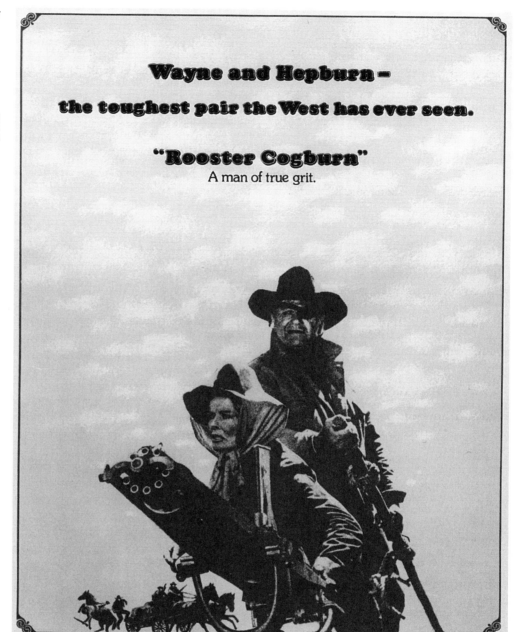

When you put Rooster Cogburn (John Wayne) and Eula Goodnight (Katharine Hepburn) on a raft loaded with nitroglycerin and a Gatling gun, you can expect plenty of rough riding in this action western. *Rooster Cogburn* (Universal, 1975).

1759

Reynolds: It's been a long fight, Major, but we've won.

Major: Yes, and we owe our thanks to those three gallant men [the Three Mesquiteers] whose brave efforts made it possible!

Reynolds played by Rex Lease and Major R.C. Kelton played by Tom Chatterton: George Sherman's *The Trail Blazers* (Republic, 1940).

1760

Lane: I hate to have to tell you this, Ben, but whether you like it or not you're a man ...and you're stuck with it. You're going to find yourself standing your ground and fighting when you ought to run; speaking out when you ought to keep your mouth shut; and doing things that, well, seem wrong to a lot of people …but you'll do them all the same.

Lane played by John Wayne and Ben Young played by Bobby Vinton: Burt Kennedy's *The Train Robbers* (Warner Bros., 1973).

1761

Mattie: They tell me you are a man with true grit.

Mattie Ross played by Kim Darby and Marshal Reuben J. "Rooster" Cogburn played by John Wayne: Henry Hathaway's *True Grit* (Paramount, 1969).

1762

Rooster: That Texican …saved my life twice. Once after he was dead.

Marshal Reuben J. "Rooster" Cogburn played by John Wayne and the Texican, La Boeuf, played by Glen Campbell: Henry Hathaway's *True Grit* (Paramount, 1969).

1763

Leach: I declare, he seems like a right nice young fella. I hope he lives long enough so we can get acquainted.

Leach Overmile played by Lynne Overman: Cecil B. DeMille's *Union Pacific* (Paramount, 1939).

1764

Hewie: You always stand up for him, don't you, Owen?

Owen: When you're loyal to a man, Hewie, you're loyal to everything about him …even his faults.

Hewie played by Charlton Carpenter and Owen Daybright played by Burt Lancaster: Richard Thorpe's *Vengeance Valley* (MGM, 1951).

1765

Don Luis: Señor Arnold, do not worry. You may not be at home, but tonight you will be in your own house.

Don Luis Gonzalez played by Robert Carricart and Lee Arnold played by Robert Mitchum: Buzz Kulik's *Villa Rides!* (Paramount, 1968).

1766

Virginian: If folks came to think me a coward, I couldn't look 'em square in the eye ever again …or you either.

Molly: But that's just pride!

Virginian: I don't know what you call it. But it's something in the feelings of a man …down deep inside. Something a man can't go back on. If anybody would happen to say I was a thief, I couldn't let 'em go on saying it. It wouldn't matter what other people thought …but I would have to know inside of me that I

thought enough of my own honesty to fight for it.

Molly: Then it will be like this always. When will it ever end?

Virginian: There'll always be killing to do until this country ain't a meeting place for men like Trampas.

Molly: Then think of us …you and me …our life together!

Virginian: That's what I am thinking of.

The Virginian played by Gary Cooper and Miss Molly Stark Wood played by Mary Brian: Victor Fleming's *The Virginian* (Paramount, 1929).

1767

Pancho Villa: Those who have friends are rich.

Pancho Villa played by Hector Elizondo: Lee Philips' *Wanted: The Sundance Woman* (TVW, 1976).

1768

Dusty: You know, it was right around here that I picked you up 12 years ago. You was more dead than alive.

Hayden: I'll never forget that night, Dusty. A flash of guns …a shot from murdering men …and the courage of my Dad …sheltering me and fighting a helpless fight. Riddled with bullets, he fell across me, whispering: "Lay still, Ted boy, they'll think you're dead."

Dusty Rhodes played by George "Gabby" Hayes and Ted Hayden played by John Wayne: Robert N. Bradbury's *West of the Divide* (Lone Star/Monogram, 1934).

1769

John: And the answer men is: We must band together. You, Carter! And you, Russell! And every man here who has suffered from the injustices of these gangs. And it's up to us to clean them out. Now, my plan is this: Every man here will ride a white horse, wear a black shirt and white scarf. In this way, we will know each other in battle. I'm asking for single men only. And men who'll stick!

John Wyatt played by John Wayne and Carter played by Glenn Strange: Robert Bradbury's *Westward Ho* (Republic, 1935).

1770

Boone: A lot of thanks I get, working to keeping you alive!

Cross: Having you work for me is like losing two good men!

Boone played by Jack Elam and Cross played by Willie Nelson: Burt Kennedy's *Where the Hell's That Gold?!!!* (a.k.a. *Dynamite & Gold*; TVW, 1988). *See also entry 638.*

1771

Wyatt Earp: It's not a question of who's right …it's a question of what's right.

Wyatt Earp played by Joel McCrea: Jacques Tourneur's *Wichita* (Allied Artists/Warner Bros., 1955).

1772

Charlie: I don't know why this matters to me …except I'd miss Bill's company …but every time there is a death of a hero, we are all the less. It drags down the morale, people get anxious and depressed, they drink more, they fight more, causing more killings …until the general uncertainty destroys whatever useful or good remains.

Charlie Prince played by John Hurt and Wild Bill Hickok played by Jeff Bridges: Walter Hill's *Wild Bill* (MGM/United Artists, 1995).

1773

Tector: He's going to get us all killed. I'm going to get rid of him.

Pike: You're not going to get rid of anybody. We're gonna stick together just like it used to be. When you side with a man, you stay with him. And if you can't do that, you're like some animal …you're finished! We're finished! All of us!

Tector Gorch played by Ben Johnson and Pike Bishop played by William Holden: Sam Peckinpah's *The Wild Bunch* (Warner Bros.–Seven Arts, 1969).

1774

Lin: You've been real fine people, High Spade, riding along with me.

High Spade: That's what friends are for, isn't it? At least ways, that's the way your dad always said it.

Lin: Yeah, he did, didn't he? He said if a man had one friend, he was rich. I'm rich.

Lin McAdam played by James Stewart and Johnny "High Spade" Williams played by Millard Mitchell: Anthony Mann's *Winchester '73* (Universal, 1950).

1775

Steve: Damn good riding with you, Chavez.

Chavez: Many nights, my friend, many nights I've put a blade to your throat while you were sleeping. I'm glad I never killed you, Steve. You're all right.

Dirty Steve Stephens played by Dermot Mulroney and Chavez Y. Chavez played by Lou Diamond Phillips: Christopher Cain's *Young Guns* (20th Century–Fox, 1988).

1776

Gonzales: Gentlemen, this is becoming ridiculous! The next thing we know, someone will be accusing you of being Zorro.

Don Diego: Why, I believe I'd be flattered!

Gonzales played by Edmund Cobb and Don Diego Vega/Zorro played by Reed Hadley: William Witney's and John English's *Zorro's Fighting Legion* (Republic serial, Chapter 9: "The Golden Arrow," 1939).

1777

Don Diego: What Diego can't do, Zorro can!

Don Diego Vega/Zorro played by Reed Hadley: William Witney's and John English's *Zorro's Fighting Legion* (Republic serial, Chapter 10: "Mystery Wagon," 1939).

1778

Don Alejandro: Let me tell you one thing. Things will never get better anywhere if people try to run from their problems.

Don Alejandro de la Vega played by George J. Lewis: Charles Barton's *Zorro, the Avenger* (TVW, 1959).

Gunfighters

See also Bad Guys; Good Guys; Guns; Showdown

1779

George: Look Melody, you couldn't hit the hind end of your horse with a handful of buckshot ...and you know it. And you ain't a gunfighter, that's all. You ain't even a good shot. You're just a plain no good bronc stomper that's been hit in the seat of the pants so many times ...

George Fury played by William Demarest and Melody Jones played by Gary Cooper: Stuart Heisler's *Along Came Jones* (RKO, 1945).

1780

George: You always want to shoot 'em in their right eye. It spoils their aim.

George Fury played by William Demarest: Stuart Heisler's *Along Came Jones* (RKO, 1945).

1781

Stranger: I got a rule: when there's a man to shoot, shoot to kill.

The Stranger played by George Hilton: Enzo G. Castellari's *Any Gun Can Play* (Golden Eagle/RAF, 1968).

1782

Bill: Kind of close back there. That little sidewinder was about to draw down on you.

Jim: Oh, he was just looking to carve another notch in his gun.

Bill Gibson played by Arthur Hunnicutt and Jim Walker played by Rory Calhoun: R.G. Springsteen's *Apache Uprising* (Paramount, 1966).

1783

Grandpa: Never wait too long between shots or your finger may change its mind.

Grandpa played by Russell Simpson: Preston Sturges' *The Beautiful Blonde From Bashful Bend* (20th Century–Fox, 1949).

1784

Dawson: Say, you don't look too good. The sight of blood bother you?

McCandles: Only my own.

Pop Dawson played by Harry Carey, Jr., and Jacob McCandles played by John Wayne: George Sherman's *Big Jake* (NGP, 1971).

1785

Zeb: Keep your eyes open. If you see anything, shoot. Don't bother to aim because you probably couldn't hit nothing no how.

Zeb Calloway played by Arthur Hunnicutt: Howard Hawks' *The Big Sky* (Winchester/RKO, 1952).

1786

Brady: There ain't no permanence in this business. You just begin to like somebody and he turns up dead.

Lance: You can lose a lot of people you don't like that way too.

Jersey Brady played by Percy Kilbride and Lance Hardeen played by Jeffrey Lynn: George Sherman's *Black Bart* (Universal, 1948).

1787

Early: Maybe that's the difference between an amateur and a professional. The professional knows he can make only one mistake.

Bob Early played by David Orrick: Earl Bellamy's *Blackjack Ketchum, Desperado* (Columbia, 1956).

1788

Dee: Yeah, I didn't know how good I was myself until I heard you telling the boys at the inquest how many men I had killed. It's a fine reputation you give me. Eleven men. That's quite a record. Hard to top it. But I'd like to make it an even dozen the next time I meet up with you.

Dee Havalik played by William Tannen: Earl Bellamy's *Blackjack Ketchum, Desperado* (Columbia, 1956).

1789

Sheriff: You are the Kid!

Jim: Was. Yeah, I was the Kid.

Sheriff: Well, what happened?

Jim: Oh well, it got so that every kid prairie punk who thought he could shoot a gun would ride into town to try out the Waco Kid. I must have killed more men than Cecil B. De Mille. Got pretty gritty. I started to hear the word "draw" in my sleep. Then one day, I was just walking down the street and I heard a voice behind me say, "Reach for it, mister!" And I spun around ...and there I was, face-to-face with a six year old kid. Well, I just threw my guns down and walked away. The little punk shot me in the ass! So I limped to the nearest saloon, crawled inside a whiskey bottle, and I've been there ever since.

Sheriff Bart played by Cleavon Little and Jim played by Gene Wilder: Mel Brooks' *Blazing Saddles* (Warner Bros., 1974).

1790

Jim: No, no, don't do that! Don't do that! If you shoot him [Mongo], you'll just make him mad.

Jim played by Gene Wilder and Mongo played by Alex Karras: Mel Brooks' *Blazing Saddles* (Warner Bros., 1974).

1791

Jim: I've been mixed up in a lot of things, Tate. But up to now, I've never been hired for my guns.

Tate: Can you afford to be particular?

Jim Garry played by Robert Mitchum and Tate Riling played by Robert Preston: Robert Wise's *Blood on the Moon* (RKO, 1948).

1792

Sundeen: I thought you hired out to anybody with a price?

Jordan: So did I. But sometimes you get to thinking about things you thought you already knew.

Good guy Johnny Carter (Ray Milland) being chased by gang of outlaws in John Farrow's *Copper Canyon* **(Paramount, 1950).**

Phil Sundeen played by Jeff Kaake and Clay Jordan played by Russell Todd: C.T. McIntyre's *Border Shootout* (Turner Home Entertainment, 1990).

1793

Rubriz: So what do they call you?
Choya: Choya.
Rubriz: Choya. It is a name I have heard. Not too often. Not with the biggest reputation. Small things with a gun.
Choya: Big enough that the rangers want to do a little hanging.
Rubriz: Me they wish to hang a thousand times.

Rubriz played by Joseph Calleia and Choya played by Alan Ladd: Rudolph Mate's *Branded* (Paramount, 1951).

1794

Rubriz: You young ones have not heard enough bullets to know the song of them. When I rode with Juarez, I heard them by the hundreds. Enough bullets to know their music.

Rubriz played by Joseph Calleia: Rudolph Mate's *Branded* (Paramount, 1951).

1795

Goldie: He's the best gunhand in Griffin so I hired him. It doesn't mean I like him.
Logan: Who's the pushy kid with him?
Goldie: Jeff? When Pink's cold, Jeff sneezes. He'll learn better if he lives long enough.

Goldie played by CeCe Whitney, Logan Keliher played by Audie Murphy, and Pink played by Skip Homeier: R.G. Springsteen's *Bullet for a Badman* (Universal, 1964).

1796

Nat Love: Every time you shoot at someone, plan on dying.

Nat Love played by Ernie Hudson: Paris Barclay's *The Cherokee Kid* (HBO Pictures, 1996).

1797

Harley: I've never known it before, John, but a good gunfight sure makes a man hungry.

Harley Sullivan played by Henry Fonda and John

O'Hanlan played by James Stewart: Gene Kelly's *The Cheyenne Social Club* (NGP, 1970).

1798

Matthew: You ain't gonna last long, son. There ain't no soft-hearted gunfighters.

Matthew Sebanek played by Warren Oates: Monte Hellman's *China 9, Liberty 37* (a.k.a. *Gunfire*; Titanus, 1978).

1799

Sheriff: You're smarter than the rest of them. A lot of you all rode into this town. But you are the only one that saw anything. You noticed the change. The others don't look past the end of their guns. You saw the handwriting on the wall. They don't even see the wall because their backs are against it. Their days are over. They don't know it. You know it.

Sheriff Gifford played by Hugh Sanders: Harmon Jones' *City of Bad Men* (20th Century–Fox, 1953).

1800

Travis: Remember when I told you once about never having to dodge bullets from a dead man? Well, that still goes.

Deputy Sheriff Lane Travis played by Macdonald Carey: John Farrow's *Copper Canyon* (Paramount, 1950).

1801

Silver: Now I wonder what Cabeau saw in those two to worry about?
Denver: Maybe it's the way they sling the artillery ...Texas style: low and handy.

Silver Kirby played by William Bishop, Emil Cabeau played by John Dehner, and Denver Jones played by Don Porter: Ray Nazarro's *Cripple Creek* (Columbia, 1952).

1802

Largo: You shot nothing but holes in the sky!

Rick Largo played by John Doucette: Lewis R. Foster's *Dakota Incident* (Republic, 1956).

1803

Talby: Third lesson: never get between a gun and its target.

Frank Talby played by Lee Van Cleef: Tonino Valerii's *Day of Anger* (a.k.a. *Days of Wrath*; Sancrosiap/Corona Film/KG Divina Film/National General, 1967).

1804

Talby: Fourth lesson: punches are like bullets. If you don't make the first ones count, Scotty, you might just be finished.

Frank Talby played by Lee Van Cleef and Scott Mary played by Giuliano Gemma: Tonino Valerii's *Day of Anger* (a.k.a. *Days of Wrath*; Sancrosiap/Corona Film/KG Divina Film/National General, 1967).

1805

Talby: Scott, remember: a man on horseback has to divide his attention between his horse and his gun. So you cannot let them dismount.

Frank Talby played by Lee Van Cleef and Scott

Mary played by Giuliano Gemma: Tonino Valerii's *Day of Anger* (a.k.a. *Days of Wrath*; Sancrosiap/Corona Film/KG Divina Film/National General, 1967).

1806

Scott: Doc Holliday was the best shot in all the west. Him …not his pistol!

Murph: Him …and his pistol! There can be an experience of a lifetime in a gun. But it's not enough to be able to draw faster than the other guy if the other guy knows a trick that you don't know. In my day, we had to either learn the tricks …or we gave work to the grave-diggers.

Scott Mary played by Giuliano Gemma and Murphallan played by Walter Rilla: Tonino Valerii's *Day of Anger* (a.k.a. *Days of Wrath*; Sancrosiap/Corona Film/KG Divina Film/National General, 1967).

1807

Harry: You don't know it, but you're about to witness a legend being made.

Brittany: You look the same to me.

Harry McDonacle played by John Ritter and Brittany played by April Telek: Joseph L. Scanlan's "The Great McDonacle" episode to the series premiere, *Dead Man's Gun* (Showtime, 1997).

1808

Cole: Maybe I am different. But I beat those men. It's not the gun …it's me.

Cole played by Frank Whaley: Neill Fearnley's "My Brother's Keeper" episode to the series premiere, *Dead Man's Gun* (Showtime, 1997).

1809

Beesly: Don't take a bullet in the head. It'll ruin a good picture.

Beesly played by John M. Jackson: Alan J. Levi's *Dead Man's Revenge* (MCA/Universal Home Video, 1994).

1810

Sam: Do you think you can shoot with those as well as you can handle them?

Tom: Well enough.

Sam: Now that's something that no man does: shoot well enough. Sooner or later, if you keep looking, you'll find somebody that can slap leather faster.

Tom: Do you figure that will happen to you?

Sam: Oh, I don't plan to live forever.

Sam Garrett played by Wayne Morris and Tom Cameron played by James J. Lydon: Thomas Carr's *The Desperado* (Allied Artists, 1954).

1811

Slaten: I want to tell you something, young man. Your heroics will be forgotten in a month, so don't be so full of yourself. A smart man, he saves his glory days for the latter part of his life.

Silas Slaten played by Rod Steiger: Richard Compton's *Desperado: Avalanche at Devil's Ridge* (TVW, 1988).

1812

Willie: I'm a lot older than you, Jack. In my time, I've seen a lot of men with itchy trigger fingers like you. And they're all in Boot Hill with dirt in their face. Somebody cured them of that itch.

Uncle Willie MacLeod played by Edgar Buchanan and Jack Lester played by Bernard Nedell: Charles Vidor's *The Desperadoes* (Columbia, 1943).

1813

Sheriff: Are you sure you can't remember anything about him, Allison?

Allison: Yes, Steve. The way I remember him, he wouldn't come out last in a gunfight. He seems awful quick, Steve.

Sheriff: Did you ever see how fast I can duck?

Sheriff Steve Upton played by Randolph Scott and Allison MacLeod played by Evelyn Keyes: Charles Vidor's *The Desperadoes* (Columbia, 1943).

1814

Kid: I've got to learn [to shoot], Mr. Holliday.

Doc: Why did you come after me, and not somebody else?

Kid: Because they say you're the best there is. Because I've read all about you in them dime novels, Mr. Holliday. Because …because you're a legend.

The Kid played by Denver John Collins and John "Doc" Holliday played by Stacy Keach: Frank Perry's *Doc* (United Artists, 1971).

1815

Doc: How old are you?

Kid: I'm eighteen.

Doc: What are you going to do with your life? Don't you have any ambition?

Kid: Yes, Mr. Holliday. I want to be like you.

John "Doc" Holliday played by Stacy Keach and the Kid played by Denver John Collins: Frank Perry's *Doc* (United Artists, 1971).

1816

Friend: There's always someone faster.

Gambler: He's the one.

Friend: What one?

Gambler: The one who's always faster.

Reager's Friend played by Bill Pickel and the Gambler was uncredited: Gene Quintano's *Dollar for the Dead* (TVW, 1998).

1817

Dooley: You're a hell of a shot, Cowboy. But in the human being department, you barely meet basic requirements.

Dooley played by William Forsythe and Cowboy played by Emilio Estevez: Gene Quintano's *Dollar for the Dead* (TVW, 1998).

1818

Dooley: Patience isn't exactly his strong suit.

Colby: What is?

Cowboy: Shooting people who make me impatient.

Dooley played by William Forsythe, Jacob Colby played by Ed Lauter, and Cowboy played by Emilio

Estevez: Gene Quintano's *Dollar for the Dead* (TVW, 1998).

1819

Mayor: What was that shooting?

Editor: Just his way of putting periods to his sentences.

Mayor Ephraim played by Len Birman and the Newspaper Editor, Eugene Lippert, played by Graham McPherson: Steven H. Stern's *Draw!* (TVW, 1984).

1820

Billy Ray: Maybe you can tell me where I could find a man named Kid Durango?

Van Leek: Why do you want him for?

Billy Ray: They say he's the fastest gun in the west.

Van Leek: Oh yeah?

Billy Ray: I want to hire him for a job.

Van Leek: You got any money?

Billy Ray: Maybe.

Van Leek: Well …hire me. I ain't as fast as I used to be …but I cheat real good. Fast don't mean a whole lot these days. Us professional folks are tired of fighting fair …and dying for it.

Billy Ray Smith played by Anthony Edwards and Thomas Van Leek played by Louis Gossett, Jr.: Peter Markle's *El Diablo* (HBO Pictures, 1990).

1821

Van Leek: What are you looking at?

Billy Ray: You just shot him in the back!

Van Leek: His back was to me!

Van Leek (later): Damn, boy! You shot him in the back!

Billy Ray: Well his back was to me!

Thomas Van Leek played by Louis Gossett, Jr. and Billy Ray Smith played by Anthony Edwards: Peter Markle's *El Diablo* (HBO Pictures, 1990).

1822

Bart: Well, perhaps the law doesn't quite see it my way. But since when did hired guns get choosy? You're paid to …

Cole: I'm paid to risk my neck! And I'll decide where and when I'll do it. This isn't it!

Bart Jason played by Edward Asner and Cole Thornton played by John Wayne: Howard Hawks' *El Dorado* (Paramount, 1967).

1823

MacDonald: Well, I'm waiting to hear what happened.

Cole: Well, I'll tell you what happened. You left a boy out there to do a man's job.

Kevin MacDonald played by R.G. Armstrong and Cole Thornton played by John Wayne: Howard Hawks' *El Dorado* (Paramount, 1967).

1824

Benny: I didn't expect the word to travel so far.

Talion: Oh, the word about bounty hunters …that travels pretty far pretty fast. It'll always beat you home, boy.

Benny Wallace played by Patrick Wayne and Talion played by Robert Lansing: Michael Moore's *An Eye for an Eye* (Columbia, 1966).

1825

Temple: Well, before you know it, top guns from all over will be coming to Cross Creek to find out just how fast I am.

Reverend: How do you know that?

Temple: Because trouble collects around a fast gun. You know, there's a certain, certain kind of scum that will go a hundred miles out of their way for a good fight. This is a nice town. This is a good town. And you don't want them here.

Reverend: These men that you say will come. How would they hear about it?

Temple: The story of a fast gun gets around. The faster the gun, the faster the story travels.

George Kelby, Jr., alias George Temple, played by Glenn Ford and the Reverend played by Joseph Sweeney: Russell Rouse's *The Fastest Gun Alive* (MGM, 1956).

1826

Temple: That's right. I'm George Kelby's son. My father's business was guns. He was very good at it, and he was very proud about it. And he taught me everything he knew about guns. He taught me until I was faster than he was. But there's certain things that one man can't teach another man. I've never drawn against a man. That's right. And all the time he was teaching me, I hated guns. I hated them. Then the day comes when somebody shows up who thinks he's faster than you are. He thinks he can outdraw you, and he wants a showdown. And you realize why you hate guns. It's because you're scared. You're scared right here! You're afraid. He told me, my father said, he said you can run if you want to …and you can go ahead. You can run but the Kelby's name will always have to stay, and will always have to fight. So he did stay, and he fought, and he was killed. I couldn't, I couldn't even fight the killer of my own father.

George Kelby, Jr., alias George Temple, played by Glenn Ford: Russell Rouse's *The Fastest Gun Alive* (MGM, 1956).

1827

Vinnie: My name is Harold. Vinnie Harold. The money is to get him a headstone …to say he was killed by the fastest gun there is.

Blind Man: That's not so.

Vinnie: What?

Blind Man: There's a faster gun than yours.

Vinnie: Who carries it?

Blind Man: You'll find out.

Vinnie: Who carries it?

Blind Man: You'll find out when you least expect it …in a place where you'd never expect it.

Vinnie: You couldn't see me draw. How could you say anyone's faster? How could you say anyone's faster?

Blind Man: Because there always is. No matter how fast you are, there's always somebody faster.

Vinnie Harold played by Broderick Crawford and the Blind Man was uncredited: Russell Rouse's *The Fastest Gun Alive* (MGM, 1956).

1828

Tex: Who was the hombre that got himself shot?

Doc: A gent named Ed Poke. He fancied himself with a six gun …and tried to make a fast reputation by ventilating Tombstone Jack.

Tex McCloud played by Sterling Hayden, Doc Fallon played by George Cleveland, and Ed Poke played by Ethan Laidlaw: Ray Enright's *Flaming Feather* (Paramount, 1952).

1829

Chico: Can you see me as a farm dog? Me? I cut my teeth on a gun.

Wes: They're still milk teeth. Remember what Pa says: they who labor in the earth are the chosen people of God.

Chico: But I don't want to be a chosen people. I want to be Griff's third gun!

Chico Bonnell played by Robert Dix, Wes Bonnell played by Gene Barry, and Griff Bonnell played by Barry Sullivan: Samuel Fuller's *Forty Guns* (20th Century–Fox, 1957).

1830

Albright: I'd like to thank you for what you did today. Or rather, didn't do.

Earp: What the hell are you talking about?

Albright: Your shooting and surrounding me [with bullets] the way you did.

Earp: Around you? Bull plop! I tried to get you, jackass! I did my best.

Albright: I don't understand.

Earp: Well, you wouldn't. Every one of those damn bullets was meant for ya.

Albright: To hit me?

Earp: To kill ya!

Albright: Why am I still here?

Earp: How do you hit someone that I keep splitting in two?

Albright: Wait a minute! Are you saying you missed me unintentionally? Six times in a row?

Earp: Six lousy, stinking times!

Albright: Fast on the draw and blind as a bat!

Earp: Why do you think I stayed in the saloon all day drinking myself sick?

Albright: You should have asked me to stand closer.

Earp: Guess what?

Albright: You almost did!

Ernest Albright played by Judge Reinhold and Wyatt Earp played by Fred Ward: Piers Haggard's *Four Eyes and Six-Guns* (Turner Pictures, 1992).

1831

Gypsy: I ain't nothing but a gunslinger. I can't teach you nothing but how to kill people. You got a chance to learn books. That's where the power is. It's better than guns.

Gypsy Smith played by Sidney Poitier: David Greene's *A Good Day to Die* (a.k.a. *Children of the Dust*; Vidmark Entertainment, 1995).

1832

Tuco: When you have to shoot, shoot! Don't talk!

Tuco played by Eli Wallach: Sergio Leone's *The Good, the Bad, and the Ugly* (United Artists, 1966; U.S. 1968).

1833

Old Timer: Any damn fool can get himself shot full of holes.

Cole: It ain't hard getting shot. It's the getting back up.

The Old Timer played by William Challee and Cole Younger played by Cliff Robertson: Philip Kaufman's *The Great Northfield, Minnesota Raid* (Universal, 1972).

1834

Boy: Come on, Cole. Take off your shirt so we can see your bullet wounds.

Cole: Oh hell, ain't no difference from any other man's bullet holes.

The Boy was uncredited and Cole Younger was played by Cliff Robertson: Philip Kaufman's *The Great Northfield, Minnesota Raid* (Universal, 1972).

1835

Abe: Jenny, there is nobody faster with a gun than me. I've known it ever since I was a kid, ever since the first time I picked up a gun. There's nothing good or bad about it, and certainly nothing brave or noble. But that's just the way it is. It's something I can do, and something I can do better than anybody in the whole world.

Abe Cross played by Johnny Cash and Jenny Simms played by Karen Black: Lamont Johnson's *A Gunfight* (Paramount, 1971).

1836

John: You know, I've yet to see the guy pick a fight. Trouble just naturally seems to find him. It's gotten so every would-be gunmen on the frontier wants the honor of putting him in Boot Hill. You know how it is when a man gets a reputation.

John Shanssey played by George Mathews: John Sturges' *Gunfight at the O.K. Corral* (Paramount, 1957).

1837

Doc: Want a gun hand?

Wyatt: You? No thanks.

Doc: I do handle one pretty well. The only trouble is, those best able to testify to my aim aren't around for comment.

Cole Younger (Cliff Robertson) and Jesse James (Robert Duvall) in *The Great Northfield, Minnesota Raid* (Universal, 1971).

John H. "Doc" Holliday played by Kirk Douglas and Wyatt Earp played by Burt Lancaster: John Sturges' *Gunfight at the O.K. Corral* (Paramount, 1957).

1838

Billy: It's not that I want to be a gunfighter exactly. It's just …I don't know, sometimes I get lonely.

Wyatt: All gunfighters are lonely. They live in fear. They die without a dime or a woman or a friend.

Billy: You know, I never thought about it like that.

Wyatt: Well, think about it. Think about it!

Billy Clanton played by Dennis Hopper and Wyatt Earp played by Burt Lancaster: John Sturges' *Gunfight at the O.K. Corral* (Paramount, 1957).

1839

Wyatt: You think you're pretty tough, don't you son? I never saw a gunslinger yet so tough he lived to celebrate his 35th birthday. I learned one rule about gunslingers: there's always a man faster on the draw that you are. And the more you use a gun, the sooner you're gonna run into that man.

Wyatt Earp played by Burt Lancaster: John Sturges' *Gunfight at the O.K. Corral* (Paramount, 1957).

1840

Ringo: I heard you made your reputation against a bunch of drunks.

Johnny Ringo played by John Ireland: John Sturges' *Gunfight at the O.K. Corral* (Paramount, 1957).

1841

In the Southwest of the 1880s the difference between death and glory was often but a fraction of a second.

Prologue: Henry King's *The Gunfighter* (20th Century–Fox, 1950).

1842

Eddie: He don't look so tough to me.

Cowboy: Well, if he ain't so tough there's been an awful lot of sudden natural deaths in his vicinity.

Eddie played by Richard Jaeckel and Cowboy was uncredited: Henry King's *The Gunfighter* (20th Century–Fox, 1950).

1843

Hunt: What does he look like?

Johnny: He's a kind of natural man. He don't look much different from a lot of other fellas.

Pablo: He looks mighty average to be such a big man.

Barber: About as big as they come, I guess.

Hunt: How many hands does he got?

Barber: Well, I never counted them to tell you the truth.

Hunt: Well, he's got two hands just like anybody else. And some of these days, somebody is going to make a big name for himself by proving that's all he got.

Johnny: A big name …right on his tombstone.

Hunt: Well, it's got to come sooner or later, ain't it? You don't expect him to go on forever do you?

Swede: As far as I'm concerned he can.

Hunt Bromley played by Skip Homeier, Johnny played by Michael Branden, Pablo played by Alberto Morin, the Barber played by Eddie Parkes, and Swede played by Kenneth Tobey: Henry King's *The Gunfighter* (20th Century–Fox, 1950).

1844

Hunt: You're asking for trouble, Mr. Ringo.

Ringo: You already got it, partner, because I got a gun on you under this table. And it's pointed smack at your belly. Now, are you going to get out of here or not?

Hunt: I'm kind of disappointed in you, Mr. Ringo. We heard a lot about you around here. But I guess they forgot to tell us about the gun under the table.

Ringo: The older you grow the more you learn, son.

Hunt Bromley played by Skip Homeier and Jimmy Ringo played by Gregory Peck: Henry King's *The Gunfighter* (20th Century–Fox, 1950).

1845

Barber: Now wait a minute, Hunt. You're good but maybe you ain't that good.

Hunt: How do you know I ain't?

Johnny: If you ain't, can I have your saddle?

The Barber played by Eddie Parkes, Hunt Bromley played by Skip Homeier, and Johnny played by Michael Branden: Henry King's *The Gunfighter* (20th Century–Fox, 1950).

1846

Marshal: Now listen to me, yellow belly! Ringo fixed you good. You're going to get it exactly like you give it to him. Because there are a thousand cheap, dirty, crooked, little squirts like you waiting right now for the chance to kill the man that killed Jimmy Ringo. But it ain't going to be here, sonny. Not in my territory. So get going now. Get killed somewhere else!

Marshal Mark Strett played by Millard Mitchell and Jimmy Ringo played by Gregory Peck: Henry King's *The Gunfighter* (20th Century–Fox, 1950).

1847

Hunt: It looks like everybody is drawing behind your back these days.

Deputy: All the smart ones.

Hunt Bromley played by Skip Homeier and Deputy Charlie played by Anthony Ross: Henry King's *The Gunfighter* (20th Century–Fox, 1950).

1848

Doc: You sound as though you liked him.

Dan: Why not?

Doc: Well, if someone was out to shoot me, I think I could work up a reasonable dislike for him.

Dan: Ah, he's just doing his job. You can't hate a man for that.

Doc: Well, under the circumstances, I could try real hard!

The frightened people of Lago hire the Stranger (Clint Eastwood) to protect them from a trio of bad guys. The gunslinger is given carte blanche over town affairs whereupon he appoints the dwarf Mordecai (Billy Curtis) as the new mayor in *High Plains Drifter* (Universal, 1972).

Doc Farrell played by Chubby Johnson and Dan Saxon played by Paul Kelly: Nathan Juran's *Gunsmoke* (Universal, 1953).

1849

Colonel: It's a miracle!

Captain: I beg your pardon, sir?

Colonel: A miracle …of the highest order …that so many bullets could have missed so many people in so small of an area in such a short space of time!

Colonel Thadeus Gearhart played by Burt Lancaster and Captain Paul Slater played by Jim Hutton: John Sturges' *The Hallelujah Trail* (MGM, 1965).

1850

Thomas: Judging distance is not the most important thing, but damn near it. At sunset a man will cast a long shadow and give you the idea that there is a great distance between ya …and there may not be. At noon there's no shadow, the sun is directly overhead. You'll feel you can reach out and touch him. If you'll too close to a man, you see too much of him. You can watch him sweat, wet his mouth, blink. And while your eyes are taking all that in, he can kill ya. Back off. See everything …and nothing. And hit him right here [pointing to middle of chest]. Right there! And after you fire, move!

Thomas Luther Price played by Robert Culp: Burt Kennedy's *Hannie Caulder* (Paramount, 1971).

1851

Burden: It's my turn now. I'm telling you to get out of town. You and me, Rodman, we're killers. That's what we draw pay for. We know it's not a man's speed that counts. It's his nerve. We know that, don't we, Rodman? Don't we, Rodman? You make a man sweat and you got him beat. And you're sweating now, Rodman. Your nerve is gone. You're going to keep on breathing, but you're dead. You know it and I know it.

Steve Burden played by Guy Madison and John Rodman played by Rudy Bond: George Sherman's *The Hard Man* (Columbia, 1957).

1852

Billy: Sheep and range bums don't usually stop in Lago. Life here is a little too quick for 'em. Maybe you think you're fast enough to keep up with us, huh?

Stranger: I'm faster than you'll ever live to be.

Billy Borders played by Scott Walker and The Stranger played by Clint Eastwood: Clint Eastwood's *High Plains Drifter* (Universal, 1973).

1853

Preacher: Well, nevertheless, my conscience will not allow me to be a party to the hiring of professional gunfighters.

Morgan: Well, maybe you would like to go out there and stand them off yourself, Preacher.

Preacher: I'm just a simple man of God.

Drake: Well, it's time we unsimplified you, Reverend.

The Preacher played by Robert Donner, Morgan Allen played by Jack Ging, and Dave Drake played by Mitchell Ryan: Clint Eastwood's *High Plains Drifter* (Universal, 1973).

1854

Drake: Well now, maybe a little bonus will make you a little more appreciative.

Stranger: How little?

Drake: $500.00 a head.

Stranger: $500.00 a ear!

Drake: Done …done.

Dave Drake played by Mithell Ryan and The Stranger played by Clint Eastwood: Clint Eastwood's *High Plains Drifter* (Universal, 1973).

1855

Sheriff: If you had your gun in your hand and he had his in his holster, he'd still win. The only possible way of beating him …shooting him in the back.

Sheriff Foster played by Klaus Kinski: Don Reynolds' *His Name Was King* (New Pacific, 1971).

1856

Pecos Jack: Shoot first and argue afterwards! That's my advice.

Pecos Jack Anthony played by Kenneth Thomson: Howard Bretherton's *Hopalong Cassidy* (a.k.a. *Hopalong Cassidy Enters*; Paramount, 1935).

1857

Townsman: I've got a half dollar that says he's a skinny runt tied to a big gun. You know, them skinny ones is the ones that get handy with a gun. They got to, you know.

The Townsman was uncredited: Richard Wilson's *Invitation to a Gunfighter* (United Artists, 1964).

1858

Sam: I sent Crane Adams to Amarillo to hire a lawman …who's able to flush that Reb out of these hills and end this war we thought was over.

Ruth: A lawman, Mr. Brewster? Crane went to find a gunfighter. A gunfighter kills the man he goes after. No trial, no jury. Guilty or innocent, he kills him. Are you asking us to …?

Sam: I'm asking you nothing, Mrs. Adams. Woman don't vote here!

Sam Brewster played by Pat Hingle, Ruth Adams played by Janice Rule, and Crane Adams played by Clifford David: Richard Wilson's *Invitation to a Gunfighter* (United Artists, 1964).

1859

Sam: You got him in the arm.

Crane: I aimed for his Reb heart.

Sam: Your performance is never up to your intentions.

Sam Brewster played by Pat Hingle and Crane Adams played by Clifford David: Richard Wilson's *Invitation to a Gunfighter* (United Artists, 1964).

1860

Vienna: Thanks, Mr. Andrews, but I'm not trusting to luck. A good gunfighter doesn't depend on four leaf clovers.

Vienna played by Joan Crawford and Mr. Andrews played by Rhys Williams: Nicholas Ray's *Johnny Guitar* (Republic, 1954).

1861

Dancin' Kid: I've always wanted to shoot me a guitar man.

Vienna: That's a worthy ambition.

The Dancin' Kid played by Scott Brady and Vienna played by Joan Crawford: Nicholas Ray's *Johnny Guitar* (Republic, 1954).

1862

Blaine: You know something, Lot? It appears to me you got too much conscience for all this gunfighting. Because one of these days, you're going to feel that you are in the wrong. And then you're going to lose. You ever think of that? A good pistolero has to be sure of himself.

Lot: From what I hear, you've killed enough men to know.

Marshal Dan Blaine played by Glenn Ford and Lot McGuire played by Chad Everett: Richard Thorpe's *The Last Challenge* (MGM, 1967).

1863

Lot: I'm nothing to him. I'm just another fellow come to town with his gun tied to his leg with a piece of rawhide.

Lot McGuire played by Chad Everett: Richard Thorpe's *The Last Challenge* (MGM, 1967).

1864

Spence: I had a hand in wiping out the Dalton's. That's all folks around here are going to remember. Now word will spread that Will Spence is in Coffeyville. There'll be men coming off the plains to try me.

Betty: That would hold true no matter where we went. People who have to bear the past bury it! They do it!

Spence: Do you think we can?

Betty: We have to!

Will Spence played by Richard Widmark and Betty Spence played by Barbara Rush: Vincent McEveety's *The Last Day* (Paramount, 1975).

1865

Frank: One of these days, you'll shoot yourself into a female.

Frank James played by Johnny Cash: William A. Graham's *The Last Days of Frank and Jesse James* (TVW, 1986).

1866

Potter: Too bad you're not vaccinated against lead poisoning.

Trooper Rusty Potter played by Mickey Shaughnessy: Andre De Toth's *Last of the Comanches* (Columbia, 1952).

1867

Ellison: You wanted to see me?

Forbes: I wanted to see the winner.

Ellison: Nobody wins in a gunfight.

Forbes: You seem to be quite careful.

Ellison: They give you a choice. Get careful or get dead.

Forbes: I understand the man you killed had quite a reputation.

Ellison: He rode tall enough.

Forbes: And how do you ride?

Ellison: They'll dig me the same six feet.

Brad Ellison played by Jock Mahoney and John Forbes played by Carl Benton Reid: George Sherman's *The Last of the Fast Guns* (Universal, 1958).

1868

Ellison: I ride gun for another man to protect his property and his cattle. Sometimes I have to kill to do it. The money you make with a gun, you got to spend fast before it starts to stare back at you.

Brad Ellison played by Jock Mahoney: George Sherman's *The Last of the Fast Guns* (Universal, 1958).

1869

Reporter: Wounded 16 times! That's unbelievable!

Bitter Creek: Well, I wouldn't play that up too much if I were you. Bullet holes in a man weren't all that uncommon back then. Even today, they ain't exactly a certificate of smart.

The Reporter was uncredited and Bitter Creek played by Matt Clark: Dan Curtis' *Last Ride of the Dalton Gang* (TVW, 1979).

1870

Deadwood: With the life we're following, we're going to get a belly full of lead for breakfast sooner or later!

Deadwood played by Raymond Hatton: Edward L. Cahn's *Law and Order* (Universal, 1932).

1871

Lucas: You and I sit at the same table, Jared. The virtuous need us but they don't like the smell.

Lucas played by Joseph Wiseman and Marshal Jared Maddox played by Burt Lancaster: Michael Winner's *Lawman* (United Artists, 1971).

1872

Bronson: And Marc Corman is dead?

Ryan: He's dead.

Bronson: How did it happen?

Ryan: He came up against the wrong man. I don't know the details.

Harvey: Marc was a good man with a gun.

Ryan: He was a big mouth who thought he was a good man with a gun. There's a cold hole in the ground between the two.

Vincent Bronson played by Lee J. Cobb, Marshal Cotton Ryan played by Robert Ryan, and Harvey Stenbaugh played by Albert Salmi: Michael Winner's *Lawman* (United Artists, 1971).

1873

Tom: Hey Charlie! You notice the way he straps his gun?

Charlie: So?

Tom: Yeah, ties her down too.

Charlie: That don't mean he's a bandit.

Tom: Well, it don't mean he's a preacher neither!

Tom Folliard played by James Best and Charlie Boudre played by James Congdon: Arthur Penn's *The Left Handed Gun* (Warner Bros., 1958).

1874

Hammer: You got to have patience to be a good [gun] fighter ...to know when the time is right. You waited five days to lose your temper. That's good. Any less than four, I'd had figured you a hothead. More than six, a coward.

Jim Hammer, alias J.R., played by Hal Holbrook: Alan J. Levi's *The Legend of the Golden Gun* (TVW, 1979).

1875

Majesty: I can't trust you out of my sight! Liquor, women, gunfighting ...that's all you ever think about!

Madeline "Majesty" Hammond played by Jo Ann Sayers: Lesley Selander's *The Light of the Western Stars* (Paramount, 1940).

1876

Caroline: You sold your gunfighter outfit? Turning in your gun?

Jack Crabb: Well, I'm sorry Caroline.

Caroline: There ain't nothing in this world more useless than a gunfighter who can't shoot people.

Caroline played by Carole Androsky and Jack Crabb played by Dustin Hoffman: Arthur Penn's *Little Big Man* (NGP, 1971).

1877

Gunfights came easy in the west. A fella seemed to get shot faster than they had time to die from typhoid or even a snake bite. You know, in the Old West gun control meant hittin' what you aimed at.

Roger Miller was the voice of the horse, Jolly Jumper: Terence Hill's *Lucky Luke* (Silvio Berlusconi Communications, 1991).

1878

Chico: How can you talk like this? Your gun has got you everything you have. Is that not true? Huh? But isn't it true?

Vin: Yeah, sure, everything. After awhile you can call bartenders and faro dealers by their first names ...maybe two hundred of 'em. Rented rooms you live in ...five hundred. Meals you eat in hash houses ...a thousand. Home? None. Wife? None. Kids? None. Prospects? Zero. Suppose I left anything out?

Chico played by Horst Buchholz and Vin played by Steve McQueen: John Sturges' *The Magnificent Seven* (United Artists, 1960).

1879

Vin: We deal in lead, friend.

Calvera: So do I. We are in the same business, huh?

Vin: Only as competitors.

Vin played by Steve McQueen and Calvera played by Eli Wallach: John Sturges' *The Magnificent Seven* (United Artists, 1960).

1880

Buck: Now you don't fan your guns! That spoils your aim. One good shot is better than six bad ones!

Buck played by Dale Midkiff: Geoff Murphy's *The Magnificent Seven: The Series* (TVW, Series Premiere, 1998).

1881

Nadine: How does a man like you become a gunman?

Wes: Well, it's pretty easy once it starts. You learn how to handle a gun and maybe learn to handle it better than anybody else.

Nadine: It must be quite an art.

Wes: It's one that some people never master.

Nadine Corrigan played by Mary Murphy and Wes Steele played by Ray Milland: Ray Milland's *A Man Alone* (Republic, 1955).

1882

Bret: What's your occupation?

Johnny: I'm a gunfighter.

Bret: Well, I have to assume since you're still alive and playing cards with us here that you're good at it.

Johnny: Care to find out?

Bret Maverick played by Mel Gibson and Johnny Hardin played by Max Perlich: Richard Donner's *Maverick* (Warner Bros., 1994).

1883

Horn: Is it true you've been shot 28 times?

Sieber: Who told you that?

Horn: That's what you hear.

Sieber: Damn people will say anything. Who can be shot 28 times and live? I've been wounded 28 times. Some with knives, some with arrows, at least a couple of clubs. Twenty-eight times shot? Ridiculous!

Tom Horn played by David Carradine and Al Sieber played by Richard Widmark: Jack Starrett's *Mr. Horn* (TVW, 1979).

1884

Billy: Cain, how come no one went for your back? It's a big enough target.

Cain: Well, a fella did once but his aim was low. I got a scar on my ass to prove it.

Billy Eager played by Paul Hampton and Cain

Marshal Jared Maddox (Burt Lancaster) says, "I'm just a lawman." In this scene, the corpus delicti decided to call the marshal out rather than give himself up in *Lawman* (United Artists, 1970).

played by Clint Walker: Robert Sparr's *More Dead Than Alive* (United Artists, 1968).

1885

Cain: You see, when you're a little bit afraid and not quite sure of yourself, even the fastest gun can be beat. Things are different when the target can shoot back. You remember that.

Cain played by Clint Walker: Robert Sparr's *More Dead Than Alive* (United Artists, 1968).

1886

Jack: How come you know so much about me?

Nobody: Everyone knows about Jack Beauregard …the only hope for law and order in the west.

Jack: Son, let me give you a little advice. Instead of admiring someone, pretty soon you're envious so you start showing off …taking chances. And before you know it, you're dead.

Nobody: Well, it ain't good for some folks to live too long.

Jack Beauregard played by Henry Fonda and Nobody played by Terence Hill: Tonino Valerii's *My Name Is Nobody* (Universal, 1973).

1887

Jonas: You know, handling one of these things [gun] is only half of it. The other part is learning human nature. That's gonna take ya the rest of your life so you damn well better not trust anybody till you do. Now you want to plan your

moves, pick your place to fight, don't make any threats, and don't you ever walk away from one. You here?

Jonas Cord played by Brian Keith: Henry Hathaway's *Nevada Smith* (Paramount, 1966).

1888

Sheriff: He's a hired assassin. He was sent here to kill somebody. That's his job.

Asa: You sound mighty positive.

Sheriff: Well, you know the man's reputation, Asa.

Asa: Sure, but that's all I know. I don't know the man.

Sheriff: Well, in this case the reputation is the man.

Sheriff Buck Hastings played by Willis Bouchey and Asa Canfield played by R.G. Armstrong: Jack Arnold's *No Name on the Bullet* (Universal, 1959).

1889

Sheriff: Gant is like a disease that they haven't found a cure for. Except for this [pistol]. He's supposed to be better with this kind of medicine than anyone.

Sheriff Buck Hastings played by Willis Bouchey and John Gant played by Audie Murphy: Jack Arnold's *No Name on the Bullet* (Universal, 1959).

1890

Della: You made your reputation as a fast gun, Case. But there were fast guns before you, and there will be fast guns after you. It's just that someday a faster one will live …and you won't.

Della Haines played by Lyn Thomas and Case Britton played by Jim Davis: Edward L. Cahn's *Noose for a Gunman* (United Artists, 1960).

1891

Jason: Who goes there?
Herald: It's me, Jason.
Jason: Advance and be recognized! Halt!
Herald: Jason, it's me. Herald!
Jason: Herald who?
Herald: Your brother!
Jason: Oh, I thought I recognized your voice there, Herald. What can I do for you?
Herald: Well, for one thing, you can point that shotgun in another direction.
Jason: Oh, it ain't loaded. See!
Herald: It's loaded, Jason.
Jason: It is? Oh, I could have sworn I …
Herald: It could have killed me, too!
Jason: Oh, I wouldn't do that. You're my brother.

Jason Pitch played by Jack Elam and Herald Pitch played by Harry Carey, Jr.: Burt Kennedy's *Once Upon a Texas Train* (TVW, 1988).

1892

Charlie: You couldn't hit a bull in the butt with a banjo!

Charlie Lee played by Dub Taylor: Burt Kennedy's *Once Upon a Texas Train* (TVW, 1988). *See also entry 1939.*

1893

Lone Watie: You know, every man that I ever knew who was good with a gun, and lived, always had an edge. And some of them would like to have the sun behind their back.
Josey Wales: That's always a good idea. Yeah, sure pays to have an edge.

Lone Watie played by Chief Dan George and Josey Wales played by Clint Eastwood: Clint Eastwood's *The Outlaw Josey Wales* (Warner Bros., 1976).

1894

Josey Wales: I kind of liked her. But then, it's always like that.
Lone Watie: Like what?
Josey Wales: Whenever I get to liking someone, they ain't around long.
Lone Watie: I notice when you get to disliking someone, they ain't around for long neither.

Josey Wales played by Clint Eastwood and Lone Watie played by Chief Dan George: Clint Eastwood's *The Outlaw Josey Wales* (Warner Bros., 1976).

1895

Lone Watie: How did you know which one was going to shoot first?
Josey Wales: Well, the one in the center, he had a flap holster and he was in no itchin' hurry. And the one second from the left, he had scared eyes. He wasn't going to do nothing. But the one on the far left, he had crazy eyes. I figured him to make the first move.
Lone Watie: How about the one on the right?
Josey Wales: I never paid him no mind. You were there!

Lone Watie played by Chief Dan George and Josey Wales played by Clint Eastwood who also directed *The Outlaw Josey Wales* (Warner Bros., 1976).

1896

Torrance: That kid couldn't hit water if he fell out of a boat.

Jesse Ray Torrance played by Kris Kristofferson: Bill Corcoran's *Outlaw Justice* (TVW, 1999).

1897

Torrance: If you could shoot like you kiss, you'd be one dangerous hombre.

Jesse Ray Torrance played by Kris Kristofferson: Bill Corcoran's *Outlaw Justice* (TVW, 1999).

1898

Torrance: It's just possible you're the worst shot I ever saw. It's a toss-up between you and Judge Crammer. Crammer had the advantage though …he was blind!

Jesse Ray Torrance played by Kris Kristofferson: Bill Corcoran's *Outlaw Justice* (TVW, 1999).

1899

John: I meant to shoot over his head. Was it my fault he stood up at the same time I pulled the trigger?

John played by George Hamilton: Arthur Allan Seidelman's *Poker Alice* (TVW, 1987).

1900

Strawhorn: Every day above ground is a good day.

Jack Strawhorn played by Bruce Dern: Kirk Douglas' *Posse* (Paramount, 1975).

1901

Davenport: What's their customary fee?
Buckner: A blank check, Mr. Davenport. You see, they feel like this: if you can put a price on it, you don't need 'em bad enough.

Cyrus Davenport played by John McIntire and Major Bill Buckner played by William Bryant: Douglas Heyes' *Powderkeg* (TVW, 1971).

1902

Sundown: How did you know I wasn't accurate at over fifty yards?
Tucson: Well, I …I figured you always planned your fights when the sun was

gone down, when the light was weak so you could draw your victims up close. And that's why they called you Sundown.
Sundown: Outsmarted me, huh?

Sundown Saunders played by Tom Tyler and Tucson Smith played by Harry Carey: Wallace Fox's *Powdersmoke Range* (RKO, 1935).

1903

Ogden: I understand you're the fastest draw in the southwest.
Sundown: Nobody has ever proved different.

Mayor "Big Steve" Ogden played by Sam Hardy and Sundown Saunders played by Tom Tyler: Wallace Fox's *Powdersmoke Range* (RKO, 1935).

1904

Tucson: That trick of getting a man accidently shot is so old it's got a beard.

Tucson Smith played by Harry Carey: Wallace Fox's *Powdersmoke Range* (RKO, 1935).

1905

Will: Well, when you ride far enough and long enough, you kind of get used to the smell of gunpowder.

Will Hansen played by Chuck Connors: Ferde Grofé Jr.'s *The Proud and the Damned* (Media Trend-Prestige/Columbia, 1972).

1906

Teach: I may be a stranger to this country, but I'm no stranger to a gun.

Teach played by John Gavin: Harry Keller's *Quantez* (Universal, 1957).

1907

Kid: I'm so damn fast I can wake up at the crack of dawn and rob two banks, a train and a stagecoach, shoot the tail feathers off of a duck's ass at 300 feet, and still be back in bed before you wake up next to me.

The Kid played by Leonardo DiCaprio: Sam Raimi's *The Quick and the Dead* (Tristar, 1995).

1908

Herod: I always wanted to fight you, Cort. Ever since the first time I saw you. You're just this itch that I had to scratch.

John Herod played by Gene Hackman and Cort played by Russell Crowe: Sam Raimi's *The Quick and the Dead* (Tristar, 1995).

1909

Herod: You know, your mouth gets faster every day. It's a pity your hands are so slow.

John Herod played by Gene Hackman: Sam Raimi's *The Quick and the Dead* (Tristar, 1995).

1910

Grant: Your guns have gotten too fast and too sudden. And from what I hear about your reputation, they have gotten a lot faster and a lot suddener in the last two years.

Scotty Grant played by James Best: Sidney Salkow's *The Quick Gun* (Columbia, 1964).

1911

Cagle: Well, he sure wasn't bluffing about them barricades, or them gunhands he's got behind them.

Spangler: Gunhands? There ain't ten men in the whole town that knows which end of the gun does the shooting.

Donovan: Yeah, well, I'd sure hate to find out by having them practicing on me!

Spangler: Listen to me! I'll tell you just when you get shot and when not! You understand that? Don't forget it!

Cagle played by Mort Mills, Spangler played by Ted De Corsia, and Donovan played by Gregg Palmer: Sidney Salkow's *The Quick Gun* (Columbia, 1964).

1912

Wyatt: Ah, one last word which you'll probably pay no attention to. Stop trying to prove how good you are. There's always somebody in the next town just a little bit faster.

Ben Wyatt played by Robert Taylor: James Neilson's *Return of the Gunfighter* (TVW, 1966).

1913

Chris: He's fast!

Frank: As fast as you are?

Chris: I'd hate to have to live on the difference.

Chris played by Yul Brynner and Frank played by Claude Akins: Burt Kennedy's *Return of the Seven* (United Artists, 1966).

1914

Benedict: Just a minute! You missed my heart by one inch! Now, any son of mine can learn to shoot better than that!

John Benedict played by William Holden: Daniel Mann's *The Revengers* (NGP, 1972).

1915

Elizabeth: I was looking at your handgun. The trigger is tied back and the holster smells of hog grease. Are you a gunfighter?

Elizabeth Riley played by Susan Hayward: Daniel Mann's *The Revengers* (NGP, 1972).

1916

Judge: I never give a trigger-happy gunman an even break.

Judge Kyle played by Walter Matthau: Jesse Hibbs' *Ride a Crooked Trail* (Universal, 1958).

1917

Jane: He's a gunman, isn't he?

Bern: Well, I know this. Between Tull and death, there was not the breath of the littlest hair.

Jane Withersteen played by Amy Madigan, Bern Venters played by Henry Thomas, and Deacon Tull played by Norbert Weisser: Charles Haid's *Riders of the Purple Sage* (Turner Home Entertainment, 1996).

1918

Kid Ringo: Consider yourself lucky I don't plug ya!

Poster for *The Riders of the Purple Sage* (20th Century–Fox, 1941) featuring the legendary figure Lassiter (George Montgomery).

Kid Ringo played by Tom Tyler: Lesley Selander's *Riders of the Range* (RKO, 1950).

1919

Dude: Is he as good as I used to be?

Chance: It would be pretty close. I'd hate to have to live on the difference.

Dude played by Dean Martin and John T. Chance played by John Wayne: Howard Hawks' *Rio Bravo* (Warner Bros., 1959).

1920

Chance: It's nice to see a smart kid for a change.

Stumpy: Yeah, he ain't like the usual kid with a gun.

Dude: I wonder if he's as good as Wheeler said.

Chance: I'd say he is. I'd say he's so good he doesn't feel he has to prove it.

John T. Chance played by John Wayne, Stumpy played by Walter Brennan, Dude played by Dean Martin, and Pat Wheeler played by Ward Bond: Howard Hawks' *Rio Bravo* (Warner Bros., 1959).

1921

Fowler: How would you like to earn this, Vance?

Vance: For a double job, I ain't cheap!

Fowler: Well, how much?

Vance: Twice that much.

Fowler: Suppose you miss?

Vance: You only lose money …I lose my life. But I never miss.

Fowler played by John Holland and Vance played by Tom Tyler: Lesley Selander's *Rio Grande Patrol* (RKO, 1950).

1922

Sam: Listen, you're been having the time of your life wet-nursing me all these years. You like to tell people what to do.

You and your settling down …you and your future!

Bill: All right, you take that bull head of yours west and I'll take my future east. One last sermon: if you intend to live by that thing [gun], you'll always find a man who can outdraw ya. An empty head and a loaded gun are bad partners.

Sam: I'm still the fastest draw you ever saw!

Bill: I taught you, remember? And I've known a fair number of real fast draws. They all got one thing in common: they're all dead!

Sam Mayhew played by Skip Homeier and Bill Mayhew played by John Payne: Joseph Kane's *The Road to Denver* (Republic, 1955).

1923

Hickman: The difference between an amateur and a professional: a professional

Above: Stumpy (Walter Brennan) decides to use dynamite to blast out the bad guys. *Opposite:* Colorado Ryan (Ricky Nelson) and John T. Chance (John Wayne) decide to exchange lead rather than prisoners with the baddies in Howard Hawks' action western, *Rio Bravo* (Warner Bros., 1959).

figures out a way to cut down the odds before he makes his move.

Ben Hickman played by John McIntire: Arnold Laven's *Rough Night in Jericho* (Universal, 1967).

1924

Mat: Sometimes it don't matter so much how fast you are. It's where you put the first bullet that counts.

Mat Dow played by James Cagney: Nicholas Ray's *Run for Cover* (Paramount, 1955).

1925

Steve: I'm only asking you to remember one thing. In every gunfight, there's one who walks up to the bar and buys the drinks. And there's the other who gets his name carved into a stone.

Steve Sinclair played by Robert Taylor: Robert Parrish's *Saddle The Wind* (MGM, 1958).

1926

Joan: What will become of him, Steve?

Steve: If he keeps on the way he's going, some day he'll meet somebody faster with a gun than he is because that's the way it happens. They'll bury him. If he's lucky, he'll have a marker. And if he isn't, it won't make too much difference because there won't be anybody to mourn him ...except me.

Joan Blake played by Julie London and Steve Sinclair played by Robert Taylor: Robert Parrish's *Saddle the Wind* (MGM, 1958).

1927

Mona: You don't talk like a gunman.

Brown: Do you think I am one?

Mona: You get beaten up. You worry about heading south. You feel empty without a gun. That sounds like a gunman.

Mona Langley played by Beverly Garland and Hemp Brown played by Rory Calhoun: Richard Carlson's *The Sage of Hemp Brown* (Universal, 1958).

1928

Bad Penny: You couldn't hit a bleeding elephant in the snow!

Penelope "Bad Penny" Cushings played by Barbara Rhoades: Alan Rafkin's *The Shakiest Gun in the West* (Universal, 1968).

1929

Shane: You've lived too long. Your kind of days are over.

Ryker: My days? What about your days, gunfighter?

Shane: The difference is I know it.

Shane played by Alan Ladd and Ryker played by Emile Meyer: George Stevens' *Shane* (Paramount, 1953).

1930

Shane: I got to be going on.

Joey: Why, Shane?

Shane: A man has to be what he is, Joey. He can't break the mold. I tried it and it didn't work for me.

Joey: We want you, Shane.

Shane: Joey, there's no living with ...with a killing. There's no going back for me. Right and wrong ...it's a brand. A brand sticks. There's no going back. Now you run home to your mother and tell her ...tell her everything is all right.

And that there ain't any more guns in the valley.

Shane played by Alan Ladd and Joey Starrett played by Brandon de Wilde: George Stevens' *Shane* (Paramount, 1953).

1931

Books: It isn't always being fast or even accurate that counts. It's being willing. I found out early that most men, regardless of cause or need, aren't willing. They blink an eye or draw a breath before they pull a trigger. I won't.

John Bernard Books played by John Wayne: Don Siegel's *The Shootist* (Paramount, 1976).

1932

Gillom: [Bat Masterson] says that a man has to have …ah …guts, deliberation, and a proficiency with firearms.
Books: Did he mention that third eye you better have?
Gillom: Third eye?
Books: For that dumb-ass amateur. It's usually some six-fingered buster that couldn't hit a cow in the tit with a tin can that does you in. But then Bat Masterson always was full of sheep dip.

Gillom Rogers played by Ron Howard and John Bernard Books played by John Wayne: Don Siegel's *The Shootist* (Paramount, 1976).

1933

Books: In my profession, if you trust too much, you don't celebrate many birthdays. I kind of like it around here.

John Bernard Books played by John Wayne: Don Siegel's *The Shootist* (Paramount, 1976).

1934

Jesse: You said that you'd been with men for money. Can you remember what any of them looked like? It's the same with the ones I go up against. I can't remember one by his face. That's how we are able to make our way, you and me, doing the things we do. You see, Kelly, you ain't no better than I am. No better at all.

Frank Jesse played by Dan Duryea and Kelly played by Joan O'Brien: Harry Keller's *Six Black Horses* (Universal, 1962).

1935

Spikes: What's your name?
Kid White: Oh, I got a lot of names. Billy Blanco, Kid White. Take your pick.
Spikes: Why, I've heard of you. You've put a few in Boot Hill, haven't you?
Kid White: Two or three rows.
Spikes: Took some from behind I heard.
Kid White: That's right, brother. If that was the way they was facing.

Harry Spikes played by Lee Marvin and Kid White played by Arthur Hunnicutt: Richard Fleischer's *The Spikes Gang* (United Artists, 1974).

1936

Jud: I'm supposed to pretend I'm Swifty Morgan? Goodbye!
Latigo: They're willing to pay.
Jud: How much?
Latigo: One thousand dollars. We'll split it fifty-fifty. That means four hundred for you.
Jud: That seems fair. But I think that …
Latigo: No, no you don't! That's part of the deal. I do the thinking. You stand around and look tough.

Jud May played by Jack Elam and Latigo Smith played by James Garner: Burt Kennedy's *Support Your Local Gunfighter* (United Artists, 1971).

1937

Barton: If I'd known you were going to send this pip-squeak against a man like Swifty Morgan …
Colorado: Now look, Mr. Barton, I can't help it …
Barton: Don't take offense, lad. But after all, you've never killed anybody outside of this county. You're just local stuff.

Taylor Barton played by Harry Morgan and Colorado played by Ben Cooper: Burt Kennedy's *Support Your Local Gunfighter* (United Artists, 1971).

1938

Jud: You know, I may not have too much of a chance with Swifty Morgan. But suppose I down him?
Latigo: Well, suppose you don't? And the odds are about a thousand to one that you won't. Well, you'll just end up an unknown character under a wooden cross on Boot Hill.

Jesse W. Haywood (Don Knotts), the eastern correspondence-school dentist gone west, is, hands-down, *The Shakiest Gun in the West* (Universal, 1968).

Jud: Well, everybody winds up dead sooner or later.

Latigo: Well, the smart ones try to postpone it as long as possible.

Jud May played by Jack Elam and Latigo Smith played by James Garner: Burt Kennedy's *Support Your Local Gunfighter* (United Artists, 1971).

1939

Orville: You couldn't hit a bull in the ass with a banjo!

Orville Bud Barton played by Dick Curtis: Burt Kennedy's *Support Your Local Gunfighter* (United Artists, 1971). *See also entry 1892.*

1940

Jason: You beat that poor man to the draw. He's dead and you're alive. That's the idea of this game, isn't it?

Jason McCullough played by James Garner: Burt Kennedy's *Support Your Local Sheriff!* (United Artists, 1969).

1941

Cibo: Tell the Peso Kid I want to see him.

Reva: You play with a loaded gun and you're going to get into trouble. The Peso Kid is a loaded gun.

Cibo: I think you should remember, Reva, that the one thing I don't want from you is advice.

Cibo Pearlo played by John Baragrey, Reva the Saloon Singer played by Peggie Castle, and the Peso Kid played by Paul Richards: Lesley Selander's *Tall Man Riding* (Warner Bros., 1955).

1942

Bailey: If word gets around that someone is pretty fast with a gun, there's always some man who wants to prove he's faster. That's a good thing to remember.

Wes Tancred, alias John Bailey, played by Richard Egan: Charles Marquis Warren's *Tension at Table Rock* (RKO, 1956).

1943

Cinch: I remember my first sight of Mr. Cable at Bar S with his gun slung real low. Funny thing …all the show-offs who want you to think they're gunslingers carry their guns like that.

Cinch Saunders played by Tom Tryon: Rudolph Mate's *Three Violent People* (Paramount, 1956).

1944

Lane: Grady, where did you find these two peckerwoods?

Grady: Well, they're standing up to you. That ought to prove something.

Lane: I don't need two of 'em standing up to me! I need 'em standing along side of me!

Turner: All we want to know is what did we ride here for?

Lane: What a gun rides anywhere for …money. The more there is of it, the more chances you take.

Lane played by John Wayne, Grady played by Rod Taylor, and Sam Turner played by Jerry Gatlin: Burt Kennedy's *The Train Robbers* (Warner Bros., 1973).

1945

Jesse: Calhoun and Sam, them I only just met. But from what I've heard, they haven't made up their minds what side of the law they're on. That's the trouble with young guns. It's mighty tempting to cross over to the wild side.

Wil Jesse played by Ben Johnson, Calhoun played by Christopher George, and Sam Turner played by Jerry Gatlin: Burt Kennedy's *The Train Robbers* (Warner Bros., 1973).

1946

Jesse: We just run from a fight. That's a bad habit for a man to get into that makes his way with a gun.

Lane: There's twenty of 'em back there, Jesse!

Jesse: I'd say they were a little shorthanded …and so would you …if it wasn't for the woman being along.

Wil Jesse played by Ben Johnson and Lane played by John Wayne: Burt Kennedy's *The Train Robbers* (Warner Bros., 1973).

1947

Ruth: What you believe in isn't changed by being paid when you fight for it.

Tom: What I believe in is taking care of number one. I'm here because the dough is good, and better than I could get doing something else.

Ruth: You're being very explicit, but you'll excuse me if I don't go along with that story. No man would fight the way you did just for money.

Tom: In my business, if you're a bum you don't live long. Sure, I know about George Washington, but I don't need George Washington. All I need is his little hatchet.

Ruth: You're telling me you're a mercenary.

Tom: That's a $3.00 word. You mean I'm a hired gun? Yeah, that's me.

Ruth Harris played by Shelley Winters and Tom Bryan played by Rory Calhoun: George Sherman's *The Treasure of Pancho Villa* (RKO, 1955).

1948

Rudock: You oughtn't move in on a gunfight until you've figured out which side is which.

Jeremy Rudock played by James Cagney: Robert Wise's *Tribute to a Bad Man* (MGM, 1956).

1949

Trace: I hope you're as fast with that gun of yours as you are with your mouth.

Trace was uncredited: David Lister's *Trigger Fast* (Vidmark, 1994).

1950

Mallick: You just cost me three good men.

Mark: Well, I guess they weren't that good.

Brent Mallick played by Corbin Bernsen and Mark played by James Van Helsen: David Lister's *Trigger Fast* (Vidmark, 1994).

1951

…A man of notoriously vicious and intemperate disposition.

Part of the prologue and epilogue: Clint Eastwood's *Unforgiven* (Warner Bros., 1992).

1952

Little Bill: Look, Son, being a good shot means quick with a pistol. That don't do no harm, but it don't mean much next to being cool headed. A man who will keep his head, not get rattled under fire, likely as not will kill ya.

Beauchamp: But if the other fella is quicker and fires first …

Little Bill: Then he'll be hurrying and miss.

Little Bill Daggett played by Gene Hackman and W.W. Beauchamp played by Saul Rubinek: Clint Eastwood's *Unforgiven* (Warner Bros., 1992).

1953

Taw: Are you going to shoot me in the back?

Lomax: You deserve it. You caused me a lot of embarrassment.

Taw: How?

Lomax: You're the only man I ever shot that I didn't kill.

Taw: Well, if it makes you feel any better, that slug you put in me kept me in the hospital for six months.

Taw Jackson played by John Wayne and Lomax played by Kirk Douglas: Burt Kennedy's *The War Wagon* (Universal, 1967).

1954

Lomax: Mine hit the ground first!

Taw: Mine was taller!

Lomax played by Kirk Douglas and Taw Jackson played by John Wayne: Burt Kennedy's *The War Wagon* (Universal, 1967).

1955

Blaisdell: People generally begin to resent me. I don't mind when it happens. It's part of the job.

Richardson: Marshal, let me assure you …

Blaisdell: But it will happen. I come here as your salvation at a very high wage. I establish order and ride roughshod over offenders. At first, you're pleased because there's a good deal less trouble. And then a very strange thing happens. You begin to feel I'm too powerful. You begin to fear me. Not me, but what I am. And when that happens, we shall have had full satisfaction from one another. And it will be time for me to leave.

When the town hired Clay Blaisdell (Henry Fonda) to clean up their town, they also got his partner, Tom Morgan (Anthony Quinn). "I've never known him to commit an evil act," says Clay. Pictured here is Tom committing an evil act in *Warlock* (20th Century–Fox, 1959).

Jessie: You speak of this from great experience, Marshal. Has this happened in many towns?
Blaisdell: Yes ma'am, in a lot of towns.
Clay Blaisdell played by Henry Fonda, Richardson played by Vaughn Taylor, and Jessie Marlow played by Dolores Michaels: Edward Dmytryk's *Warlock* (20th Century–Fox, 1959).

1956
Skinner: Three hits. One through the throat …two not a finger apart …through the heart.
Morgan: Well, I must be losing my touch. All three were chest aimed.
Skinner played by Regis Toomey and Tom Mor-

gan played by Anthony Quinn: Edward Dmytryk's *Warlock* (20th Century–Fox, 1959).

1957
Hickok: Charlie, you know what I hate more than anything else in the world?
Charlie: More than Injuns?
Hickok: Even more than dying.
Charlie: What?
Hickok: Being afraid.
Wild Bill Hickok/James Otis played by Charles Bronson and Charlie Zane played by Jack Warden: J. Lee Thompson's *The White Buffalo* (United Artists, 1977).

1958
Mayor: I explained to our border friend here there's a great difference between gunmen and gunfighters.
Wyatt: How did you know which one I am, Mr. Mayor?
Mayor: Well, I judge a man by what I see him do. A gunfighter is a man on the side of the law. That's what you were today.
The Mayor played by Carl Benton Reid and Wyatt Earp played by Joel McCrea: Jacques Tourneur's *Wichita* (Allied Artists/Warner Bros., 1955).

1959
Charlie: He fashioned himself [Wild Bill Hickok] as just an ordinary man and no way special. But of course that was a deception. By luck or design, it had fallen to him to play the hero's part …and to the very end he embraced his fate.
Charlie Prince played by John Hurt: Walter Hill's *Wild Bill* (MGM/United Artists, 1995).

1960
Charlie: The theatre of Bill's [Wild Bill Hickok] life had come to demand that he walk up the center of a muddy street rather than use the boardwalk. He had discovered that being Wild Bill was a profession in its own right.
Charlie Prince played by John Hurt: Walter Hill's *Wild Bill* (MGM/United Artists, 1995).

1961
Tector: That damn railroad [holdup] you're talking about sure as hell ain't getting no easier.
Sykes: And you boys ain't getting any younger either.
Pike: We gotta start thinking beyond our guns. Those days are closin' fast.
Tector Gorch played by Ben Johnson, Old Sykes played by Edmond O'Brien, and Pike Bishop played by William Holden: Sam Peckinpah's *The Wild Bunch* (Warner Bros.-Seven Arts, 1969).

1962
Doc: Wyatt, did you ever wonder why we have been a part of so many unfortunate incidents here and we're still walking around? I have figured it out. It's nothing

much …just luck. And you know why it's nothing much, Wyatt? Because it doesn't matter much whether we're here today or not. I wake up every morning looking into the face of Death. And you know what? He ain't half bad. I think the secret old Mr. Death is holding is that it's better for some of us over on the other side. I know it can't be any worse for me.

Doc Holliday played by Dennis Quaid and Wyatt Earp played by Kevin Costner: Lawrence Kasdan's *Wyatt Earp* (Warner Bros., 1994).

1963

Bat: You got yourself a bit of a reputation, Wyatt.

Wyatt: It's a tricky thing, a reputation business, Bat.

Ed: I got to tell ya, Wyatt, not all a man hears is good. We heard about you all the way over in Abilene.

Morgan: What are they saying?

Ed: They say people in Dodge are complaining that you're too quick to bash a man just because you don't like the way he looks.

Morgan: Well, you just tell me what son of a bitch is complaining, and I'll go bash him! Look, there's plenty of people around here who like Wyatt. There's me, there's Virgil …there's me …

Bat Masterson played by Tom Sizemore, Wyatt Earp played by Kevin Costner, Ed Masterson played by Bill Pullman, and Morgan Earp played by Linden Ashby: Lawrence Kasdan's *Wyatt Earp* (Warner Bros., 1994).

1964

Billy: Is he any good?

Charley: He's killed more people than smallpox.

William H. "Billy" Bonney played by Emilio Estevez and Charley Bowdre played by Casey Siemaszko:

Christopher Cain's *Young Guns* (20th Century–Fox, 1988).

1965

Hendry: I guess what I'm trying to say is …you're called Kid; and Rudabaugh is called Arkansas Dave; and I dare say Doc's Christian name is Doc.

Bonney: You want a name?

Hendry: Yes, sir, I would like that, I would like that very much indeed.

Bonney: You have to earn it, Hendry. And until then, you're stuck with plain ole Hendry. I'm sorry.

Hendry French played by Alan Ruck, William H. Bonney, alias Billy the Kid, played by Emilio Estevez, Arkansas Dave Rudabaugh played by Christian Slater, and Doc Scurlock played by Kiefer Sutherland: Geoff Murphy's *Young Guns II* (20th Century–Fox, 1990).

Guns

See also Dying; Gunfighters; Killing.

1966

Escudo: Do you think he's trying to trick us?

Sabata: Just don't let him get out of your rifle range.

Escudo played by Pedro Sanchez and Sabata played by Yul Brynner: Frank Kramer's *Adios, Sabata* (United Artists, 1971).

1967

Kansas: Pete, put the gun down.

Pete: They say I'm the fastest draw west of the Colorado. You care to try me, Kansas?

Kansas: I don't know. I'm not that good at geography.

Brisco County, Jr., alias "Kansas," played by Bruce Campbell and Pete Hutter played by John Pyper-Ferguson: Bryan Spicer's *Adventures of Brisco County, Jr.* (TVW, Series Premiere, 1993).

1968

[*Kansas takes gun from Pete*]

Scratchy: My God! He touched Pete's piece!

Outlaw: Nobody touches Pete's piece!

Pete: You're touching my piece, Kansas!

Kansas: Then I apologize. Forget about it.

[*Kansas returns gun to Pete*]

Pete: Forget about it? You mean, rip it from my memory like a picture from a book? A picture of a small boy …kind

of shy …with big ears who only wanted to be liked. And the laughing faces of his classmates, mocking him because he forgot to wear his pants to school. Is that what you mean?

Kansas: You lost me, Pete.

Pete: I'm calling you out, Kansas!

Kansas: You don't want to do that.

Scratchy: You touched Pete's piece. That's something you don't want to do with Pete!

Scratchy played by Charles Noland, Pete Hutter played by John Pyper-Ferguson, and Brisco County, Jr., alias "Kansas," played by Bruce Campbell: Bryan Spicer's *Adventures of Brisco County, Jr.* (TVW, Series Premiere, 1993).

1969

Penny: Surely you can walk to the barn without that!

Quirt: What?

Penny: The gun!

Quirt: Oh, well, it balances me. One leg is longer than the other. You know, the weight.

Prudence "Penny" Worth played by Gail Russell and Quirt Evans played by John Wayne: James Edward Grant's *Angel and the Badman* (Republic, 1947).

1970

Marshal: Only a man that carries a gun ever needs one.

Marshal Wistful McClintock played by Harry Carey: James Edward Grant's *Angel and the Badman* (Republic, 1947).

1971

Massai: I must hunt with the bow again. I may not be back tonight.

Nalinle: You will come back?

Massai: You know I would not leave my rifle.

Massai played by Burt Lancaster and Nalinle played by Jean Peters: Robert Aldrich's *Apache* (United Artists, 1954).

1972

Tom: All right, Peso, you can stay.

Peso: Thanks, Tom.

Tom: But I'll take your guns.

Peso: Oh, there's no reason for that, boy. My guns? Why, I'd be chilly without 'em. I might even catch cold.

Tom Herrera played by Robert Horton and Peso played by Gilbert Roland: Harold Kress' *Apache War Smoke* (MGM, 1952).

1973

Matt: The next time you point a gun at me, you better pull the trigger. Because I'm going to blow you into so many pieces your friends will get tired looking for you.

Matt played by Marlon Brando: Sidney J. Furie's *The Appaloosa* (Universal, 1966).

1974

Frank: A bullet hole can be explained in various ways.

Frank Hudson played by Hugh O'Brian: Joseph Pevney's *Back to God's Country* (Universal, 1953).

1975

Paul: Don't go away, Frank. I might need your help.

Frank: Well, you better get your gun. It will help you more than I will.

Paul Blake played by Steve Cochran and Frank Hudson played by Hugh O'Brian: Joseph Pevney's *Back to God's Country* (Universal, 1953).

1976

Clara: I don't dance very well when my partner has a gun in his hand.

Clara Clayton played by Mary Steenburgen: Robert Zemeckis' *Back to the Future, Part III* (Universal, 1990).

1977

Salesman: Young man, young man! I'd like you to have this new Colt Peacemaker and gunbelt. Free of charge.

Marty: Free?

Salesman: I want everybody to know that the gun that shot Buford Tannen was a Colt Peacemaker!

Marty: Hey, no problem. Thanks a lot!

Salesman: Of course, you understand, that if you lose I'm taking it back.

Marty: Thanks again.

The Colt Gun Salesman played by Burton Gilliam, Marty McFly played by Michael J. Fox, and Buford "Mad Dog" Tannen played by Thomas F. Wilson: Robert Zemeckis' *Back to the Future, Part III* (Universal, 1990).

1978

Johnny: I notice you use a tie down. Does that mean you're fast? Everybody west of the Pecos thinks that they're fast.

Johnny Cool played by William Campbell: John Sturges' *Backlash* (Universal, 1956).

1979

Bonniwell: You know, I've never seen it fail. When you take a trigger-happy bunch sitting it out like this, somebody's bound to start fooling with his gun.

Jim Bonniwell played by John McIntire: John Sturges' *Backlash* (Universal, 1956).

1980

Doc: Men that put away their guns can't argue with the men that still carry them.

Doc Grant played by Andrew Tombes: Tim Whelan's *Badman's Territory* (RKO, 1946).

1981

Stranger: Give me that rifle!

Cable: I'll give you what's in it!

The Stranger played by Darwin W. Lamb and Cable Hogue played by Jason Robards, Jr.: Sam Peckinpah's *The Ballad of Cable Hogue* (Warner Bros., 1970).

1982

Ringo: You know, we got an old sayin' in Texas: God created men equal …but the six gun made 'em different.

Ringo played by Giuliano Gemma: Duccio Tessari's *Ballad of Death Valley* (a.k.a. *The Return of Ringo*; Mediterranee-Balcazar/Rizzoli Film, 1966).

1983

Karl: Well, do you ever have any partners on this kind of stuff?

Barbarosa: No thank you.

Karl: Well, I've killed a man.

Barbarosa: Well, that ain't no high recommendation.

Karl: Well, he was a great big one. He was twice as big as me.

Barbarosa: Old Sam Colt makes everyone just about the same size.

Karl played by Gary Busey and Barbarosa played by Willie Nelson: Fred Schepisi's *Barbarosa* (Universal, 1982).

1984

Mello: You're a little naked to go calling on Hendricks. You ain't wearin' a gun.

Captain Mello played by Chubby Johnson and Tom Hendricks played by Howard Petrie: Anthony Mann's *Bend of the River* (Universal, 1952).

1985

Hickey: Left handed, hey?

Billy: I'm saving my right to shake hands with friends.

Dan Hickey played by Gene Lockhart and Billy the Kid played by Robert Taylor: David Miller's *Billy the Kid* (MGM, 1941).

1986

Stevens: Make yourself comfortable and keep your hand away from your gun. You'd be filled with lead before you knew where it's coming from.

Cat Stevens played by Terence Hill: Giuseppe Colizzi's *Boot Hill* (Film Ventures, 1969).

1987

Johnny: And while you're at it, you learn how to use this [gun] and hang onto it. You can get by without a dime in your pocket out in this country. But without this iron, you're nothing.

Willie: Oh, it can't be as bad as you say.

Johnny: Now maybe where you come from the law comes in books. But in this country, a man carries it on his hip.

Johnny Liam played by Rod Cameron and Willie Duggan played by Dan Duryea: Spencer G. Bennet's *The Bounty Killer* (Embassy/Premiere, 1965).

1988

Ruth: You don't have to wear them [guns] around here.

Choya: I wouldn't feel dressed without them.

Ruth Lavery played by Mona Freeman and Choya played by Alan Ladd: Rudolph Mate's *Branded* (Paramount, 1951).

1989

Billy: Well, I guess if I am going to be a wanted man, I might as well wear this [a gun].

The Kid: Every well-dressed bad man does, Billy.

Billy and the Kid were uncredited: John Bushelman's *The Broken Land* (20th Century–Fox, 1962).

1990

Chito: Drop that pistol or this one will start leaking lead!

Chito Rafferty played by Richard Martin: Lesley Selander's *Brothers in the Saddle* (RKO, 1949).

1991

Diggs: Nobody's gun is ever on anybody's side out of plain kindness of heart. A man's nature is too pure cussed for that.

Diggs played by George Tobias: R.G. Springsteen's *Bullet for a Badman* (Universal, 1964).

1992

Sundance: Now let me tell you something. I could drop you right here. So don't be telling me how stupid I am. I'm as smart as you are. Now, you got that?

Butch: Now with that [gun] in your hand, you're a damn genius!

The Sundance Kid played by William Karr and Butch Cassidy played by Tom Berenger: Richard Lester's *Butch and Sundance: The Early Days* (20th Century–Fox, 1979).

1993

Joel: I've never saw anybody take to anything the way you have to a gun. A man would think you've been shooting all your life.

Bass: It's just like anything else. Decide where you want to go, then get there the best way you can.

Joel Collins played by Lloyd Bridges and Sam Bass played by Howard Duff: George Sherman's *Calamity Jane and Sam Bass* (Universal, 1949).

1994

Tom: No notches?

Farrell: New job …new gun.

Tom McCord played by Gene Evans and Farrell played by Ronald Reagan: Allan Dwan's *Cattle Queen of Montana* (RKO, 1954).

1995

Connors: Say, is this really a repeater?

Sergeant: A repeater? Son, you can load this on Sunday and shoot it all week.

Connors played by James Brown and the Supply

Sergeant was uncredited: Gordon Douglas' *The Charge at Feather River* (Warner Bros., 1953).

1996

A gun, like any other source of power, is a force for either good or evil, being neither in itself, but dependent upon those who possess it.

Prologue: Edwin L. Marin's *Colt .45* (Warner Bros., 1950).

1997

Steve: The first Colt repeating pistols in this territory, Sheriff. The finest guns ever made. Here's law and order in six-finger doses. Yes, sir, easy to load and as durable as your mother-in-law.

Steve Farrell played by Randolph Scott and the Sheriff of Redrock played by Charles Evans: Edwin L. Marin's *Colt .45* (Warner Bros., 1950).

1998

Sheriff: A pistol don't make a man. It's the gent before the gun that counts.

The Sheriff of Redrock played by Charles Evans: Edwin L. Marin's *Colt .45* (Warner Bros., 1950).

1999

Luke: Don't turn your back on me, mister!

Frank: Don't let your mouth overload your hardware, cowboy.

Luke played by Luke Askew and Frank Culpepper played by Billy Green Bush: Dick Richards' *The Culpepper Cattle Company* (20th Century–Fox, 1972).

2000

Banner: I know it's not very sociable, but I've got a gun aimed right at your belly.

John Banner played by Dale Robertson: Lewis R. Foster's *Dakota Incident* (Republic, 1956).

2001

Joshua: The word is respect. You don't like guns or hate 'em. You start respecting a gun in what it is, what it can do, why you might use it. You learn all that and more, and then you learn to shoot one.

Joshua Cabe played by Dan Daily: David Lowell Rich's *The Daughters of Joshua Cabe Return* (TVW, 1975).

2002

Willford: Think of the violence. It's what I call an evil gun. I'll never know how one man can kill another.

Willford played by Parley Baer: Jerry Thorpe's *Day of the Evil Gun* (MGM, 1968).

2003

Nobody: William Blake, do you know how to use this weapon?

Blake: Not really.

Nobody: That weapon will replace your tongue. You will learn to speak through it. And your poetry will now be written with blood.

Nobody played by Gary Farmer and William Blake played by Johnny Depp: Jim Jarmusch's *Dead Man* (Miramax Films, 1996).

Advertisement for Anthony Mann's *Bend of the River* (Universal, 1952). Glyn McLynrock (James Stewart) leads wagon trains to Oregon with plenty of action along the way.

2004

Narrator: In the American West, a gun touched by evil passed from hand to hand, changing the lives of all who possessed it. As its legend grew, it became to be known as ... "the dead man's gun."

Narration by Kris Kristofferson to the series premiere, *Dead Man's Gun* (Showtime, 1997).

2005

Willy: Like I said before, Cole, ain't no good can come from a dead man's gun. Get rid of it! It's bad luck!

Cole: For him, not me!

Willy played by Sebastian Spence and Cole played by Frank Whaley: Neill Fearnley's "My Brother's Keeper" episode to the series premiere, *Dead Man's Gun* (Showtime, 1997).

2006

Sam: Bad guns are like bad friends. They'll let you down when you need them the most. Here, take them [guns]. I got them off a fella at the border. He was in no condition to object.

Sam Garrett played by Wayne Morris: Thomas Carr's *The Desperado* (Allied Artists, 1954).

2007

Sam: They put sights on a gun for a reason. Try using them. The drawing can come later.

Sam Garrett played by Wayne Morris: Thomas Carr's *The Desperado* (Allied Artists, 1954).

2008

Sam: Some folks will tell you that a good shot only needs one gun. That's a lot of foolishness. Two of anything is better than one. Now loosen your belt and let your guns hang so that your palms brush the gun butts. Boot Hill is full of guys who had to reach for that extra inch.

Sam Garrett played by Wayne Morris: Thomas Carr's *The Desperado* (Allied Artists, 1954).

2009

Wild Bill: If you don't want to die with your boots on, let that gun lie!

Wild Bill Hickok played by Bill Elliott: Lambert Hillyer's *The Devil's Trail* (Columbia, 1942).

2010

Clum: You're not going to solve anything with a gun.

Wyatt: Now you'd be surprised the things you can solve with a gun.

Editor Clum played by Dan Greenburg and Wyatt Earp played by Harris Yulin: Frank Perry's *Doc* (United Artists, 1971).

2011

Colby: What's the gun for?

Cowboy: It helps to cut out the small talk.

Jacob Colby played by Ed Lauter and the Cowboy played by Emilio Estevez: Gene Quintano's *Dollar for the Dead* (TVW, 1998).

2012

Cole: Well, if you're going to stay around here, I got two pieces of advice for you: get rid of that hat and learn how to use a gun.

Cole Thornton played by John Wayne: Howard Hawks' *El Dorado* (Paramount, 1967).

2013

Swede: I think I got just the gun you're looking for.

Cole: Well, good. Wow! How wide will that shot spread? I mean, how big a pattern?

Swede: I don't know. The fella who used it before, he couldn't see too good. He just shoot where he hear somebody talk.

Mississippi: What happened to him?

Swede: Oh, he had a fight in a saloon. The piano player, he made so much noise, he couldn't hear the other man. So he just shoot the piano player, and they hanged him!

The Swedish Gunsmith played by Olaf Wieghorst, Cole Thornton played by John Wayne, and Alan Bourdillon Traherne ("Mississippi") played by James Caan: Howard Hawks' *El Dorado* (Paramount, 1967).

2014

Bull: What are you looking at?

Mississippi: Somebody is out there with a gun.

Bull: Everybody in town has got a gun.

Mississippi: Yeah, but not pointing at us though!

Bull Harris played by Arthur Hunnicutt and Alan Bourdillon Traherne ("Mississippi") played by James Caan: Howard Hawks' *El Dorado* (Paramount, 1967).

2015

Ellen: You look different ...bigger.

Kincaid: Well, maybe it's the gun. It would make anyone look bigger.

Ellen Bailey played by Dorothy Green and Jim Larsen, alias Ray Kincaid, played by Fred MacMurray: Paul Wendkos' *Face of a Fugitive* (Columbia, 1959).

2016

Johnny: Don't move, fella! In case you're interested, I can kill ya with this [shooting guitar], and play your funeral march at the same time. So just drop the gun!

Johnny played by Roy Orbison: Michael Moore's *The Fastest Guitar Alive* (MGM, 1967).

2017

Dora: That gun means more to you than me or your child or anything else. And the terrible part of it is ...you'll never be free of it until you put another notch on it.

Dora Temple played by Jeanne Crain: Russell Rouse's *The Fastest Gun Alive* (MGM, 1956).

2018

Ramon: When you want to kill a man, you must shoot for his heart. And the Winchester is the best weapon.

Stranger: That's very nice but I'll stick with my .45.

Ramon: When a man with a .45 meets a man with a rifle, the man with the pistols will be a dead man. That's an old Mexican proverb, and it's true.

Ramon Rojo played by Gian Maria Volonte and the Stranger (Joe) played by Clint Eastwood: Sergio Leone's *A Fistful of Dollars* (United Artists, 1964; U.S. 1967).

2019

Nick: Do you figure to be the conscience for this town, Mr. Rudd?

Rudd: Oh, it could use one.

Nick: Did somebody elect you?

Rudd: God ...and Mr. Colt ...first name Samuel. Sort of biblical, isn't it?

Nick: Mr. Colt votes a lot of people in. He also votes a lot of them out.

Nick Evers played by Roddy McDowall and Reverend Jonathan Rudd played by Robert Mitchum: Henry Hathaway's *Five Card Stud* (Paramount, 1968).

2020

Nick: From here on, I'll wear my gun tied down. And if I have to, I'm gonna use it.

Morgan: A man would be a fool not to wear a gun. He would be a bigger fool if he used it too fast.

Nick Evers played by Roddy McDowall and Van Morgan played by Dean Martin: Henry Hathaway's *Five Card Stud* (Paramount, 1968).

2021

Shanks: Fast on the draw?

Cameron: Fast enough.

Shanks: Draw, Mr. Cameron!

Cameron: It's kind of risky business, Mr. Shanks.

Shanks: Just a friendly test of speed.

Cameron: When I bring my gun out, Mr. Shanks, I bring it out shooting. It's just an old habit of mine. However, if you don't mind, I don't.

Al Shanks played by Roy Roberts and Cash Blackwell, alias Tex Cameron, played by Victor Mature: Bruce Humberstone's *Fury at Furnace Creek* (20th Century–Fox, 1948).

2022

Billy: And that derringer is not going to do it. You pull that trigger twice, that little old gun is gonna be emptier than a banker's heart.

Billy Montana played by Bruce Boxleitner: Dick Lowry's *The Gambler* (TVW, 1980).

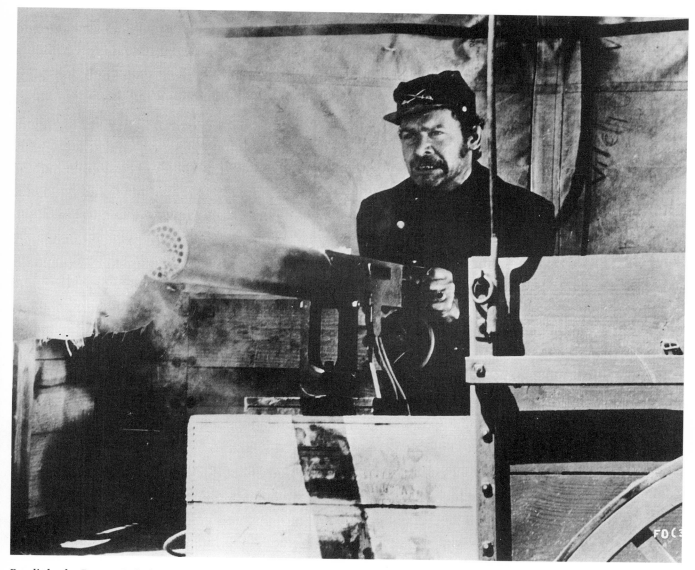

Bandit leader Ramon Rojo (Gian Maria Volonte) says "There's plenty of space for everybody in this town." That's because earlier in the day, Ramon created some space by reducing the population of the San Miguel area by about fifty soldiers with the aid of a Gatling gun in Sergio Leone's *A Fistful of Dollars* (United Artists, 1964).

2023
Sarah: It's Good Friday, men. Let's not talk about guns today.
Sarah Johnson played by Nancy Sorel: Steven H. Stern's *Good Men and Bad* (TV miniseries, Cabin Fever Entertainment, 1995).

2024
Blondie: Put your drawers on and take your gun off!
Blondie played by Clint Eastwood: Sergio Leone's *The Good, the Bad, and the Ugly* (United Artists, 1966; U.S. 1968).

2025
Blondie: You see, in this world there's two kinds of people, my friend. Those with loaded guns and those who dig. You dig!
Blondie played by Clint Eastwood: Sergio Leone's *The Good, the Bad, and the Ugly* (United Artists, 1966; U.S. 1968).

2026
Blondie: Every gun makes its own tune.
Blondie played by Clint Eastwood: Sergio Leone's *The Good, the Bad, and the Ugly* (United Artists, 1966; U.S. 1968).

2027
Adam: Men are all different, but guns are all the same.
Adam Saxon played by Horst Frank: Giancarlo Santi's *The Grand Duel* (Ital./Fr., 1972).

2028
Cal: Let me tell you something. A man wears a gun …it means he's ready to use it.
Cal Wayne played by Bobby Darin: William Hale's *Gunfight in Abilene* (Universal, 1967).

2029
Lee: Look, habit is a strong thing in a man, Ed. You got to learn to respect a gun. Knowing when to shoot it is just as important as knowing how.
Lee Hackett played by Van Heflin and Ed Hackett played by Tab Hunter: Phil Karlson's *Gunman's Walk* (Columbia, 1958).

2030

Davy: Last time I was in Jackson City, there wasn't one man I saw, barring the Sheriff, who was wearing a gun. I could see folks staring at us.

Lee: Sure they stare! Don't you think I know that? I want 'em to. A bunch of Johnny-come-lately's …sodbusters. Let 'em get a good look!

Davy: Why?

Lee: I'll tell you why. I want them to know that this ain't their country. After all, they're trying to take it over. I just want to remind them that some of us got here first. And we're the ones that had to fight for it. And with this [gun]!

Davy Hackett played by James Darren and Lee Hackett played by Van Heflin: Phil Karlson's *Gunman's Walk* (Columbia, 1958).

2031

Town Woman 1: He's wearing a pistol!

Town Woman 2: And I know that's against the law!

Town Man: Yeah, but you see, the Hacketts got here before the law did.

The three townfolks were uncredited: Phil Karlson's *Gunman's Walk* (Columbia, 1958).

2032

Ed: From now on, I'm going on my own. Me! Ed Hackett! And before I'm through, Ed Hackett is going to be a bigger name in this territory than Lee Hackett ever was.

Lee: What? As a gunman? A killer? Is that all my name ever meant to you? Do you think a gun is all that I had to be proud of?

Ed: Tell me what else? What else do you wear it for? What else have I heard about you until I'm sick of hearing it? How many men you've killed and how many Indians. Do you want me to run through the whole list for you?

Ed Hackett played by Tab Hunter and Lee Hackett played by Van Heflin: Phil Karlson's *Gunman's Walk* (Columbia, 1958).

2033

Craig: You better hand it over. Hand it over or you won't have a hand to hand it with!

Dan Craig played by Robert Young: Stuart Gilmore's *The Half-Breed* (RKO, 1952).

2034

Rufus: Always two against one! You'd lay off me fast enough if Pop was still alive.

Emmett: He still would be if you hadn't shot him!

Rufus: How many times do I have to tell you! I was cleaning my gun! There ain't a night that goes by that I don't think of Pop's face.

Town representative Sam Brewster (Pat Hingle) hires gunfighter Jules Gaspard D'Estaing (Yul Brynner) to rid the town of a menace. The so-called menace turns out to be the good guy, the town representative turns out to be the bad guy, and the gunfighter turns out to be the menace in *Invitation to a Gunfighter* (United Artists, 1964).

Frank: You mean what was left of it.

Rufus Clemens played by Strother Martin, Emmett Clemens played by Ernest Borgnine, and Frank Clemens played by Jack Elam: Burt Kennedy's *Hannie Caulder* (Paramount, 1971).

2035

Ramirez: Does the sound of guns frighten you that much?

Amy Kane: No, Mrs. Ramirez, I've heard guns. My father and my brother were killed by guns. They were on the right side, but that didn't help 'em when the shooting started.

Helen Ramirez played by Katy Jurado and Amy Kane played by Grace Kelly: Fred Zinnemann's *High Noon* (United Artists, 1952).

2036

Bang, bang! You're dead, Kane!

Kids shouting as Kane (Gary Cooper) walks alone through the streets of Hadleyville: Fred Zinnemann's *High Noon* (United Artists, 1952).

2037

Ruth: I heard shots. They woke me.

Jules: Just a little gunplay at the saloon. Nobody hurt.

Ruth: Gunplay? Guns is a play thing to you?

Jules: Play and work, Mrs. Adams. Work and play.

Ruth Adams played by Janice Rule and Jules Gaspard D'Estaing played by Yul Brynner: Richard Wilson's *Invitation to a Gunfighter* (United Artists, 1964).

2038

Darcy: A cold-fingered gun. An instrument of death for those we neither love nor hate.

Luke Darcy played by Jeff Chandler: Melvin Frank's *The Jayhawkers* (Paramount, 1959).

2039

Priest: Today is the feast of St. James the Apostle, one of the first martyrs. I will tell the people to pray to him for his strength and courage. St. James was beheaded rather than deny his faith.

Kidd: You wouldn't have a gun around here would you, padre?

The Priest played by Pepe Hern and Joe Kidd played by Clint Eastwood: John Sturges' *Joe Kidd* (Universal, 1972).

2040

Roy: What do you think you're trying to prove with Jocko's guns?

Jory: A real man can't live without guns.

Roy: Guns don't make a man …it just gives him something else to hide behind.

Roy played by John Marley and Jory Walden played by Robby Benson: Jorge Fons' *Jory* (Avco Embassy, 1972).

2041

Jameson: It's a queer thing about wearing guns. A gun draws trouble to you.

Jameson played by Shepperd Strudwick: Kurt Neumann's *The Kid from Texas* (Universal, 1950).

2042

Cannonball: He's got so many notches carved on his gun now, he ain't got hardly any handle left!

Cannonball played by Dub Taylor: Lambert Hillyer's *King of Dodge City* (Columbia, 1941).

2043

Deputy: Say, you oughtn't to have that pistol cocked, you know. You might have a bad dream and jerk and shoot your knee off.

Judge: It might rain whores out of the sky, too …but I doubt it.

Deputy Ted Plunkert played by Tristan Tait and Judge Roy Bean played by Ned Beatty: Joseph Sargent's *Larry McMurtry's Streets of Laredo* (Cabin Fever Entertainment, 1995).

2044

Hawkins: I got a prisoner here. I'm bringing him back from New Mexico. I'd like to lock him up for the night.

Jailer: Do you got extradition papers on him?

Hawkins: Well, ah, I figured I wouldn't need 'em. I, ah, extradited him with a gun.

Hawkins played by Douglas Kennedy and the Jailer was uncredited: Paul Landres' *Last of the Badmen* (Allied Artists, 1957).

2045

Ellison: Pick it up! Pick it up or die looking at it!

Brad Ellison played by Jock Mahoney: George Sherman's *The Last of the Fast Guns* (Universal, 1958).

2046

Frame: There don't seem to be no shortage of six-guns around here.

Frame Johnson played by Walter Huston: Edward L. Cahn's *Law and Order* (Universal, 1932).

2047

Brandt: Ah come on, let's get going. This country is too peaceful for me.

Deadwood: What do you mean, Brandt? No Injun country is peaceful.

Luther: Them Apaches are bad medicine.

Frame: No, no, it ain't Injuns that has caused all the trouble in the West. It's the six-gun. They made a mistake when they passed that out. It even made skunks brave.

Ed Brandt played by Harry Carey, Deadwood played by Raymond Hatton, Luther Johnson played by Russell Hopton, and Frame Johnson played by Walter Huston: Edward L. Cahn's *Law and Order* (Universal, 1932).

2048

Fin: What happened, Kurt?

Kurt: I dropped my gun and it went off and the bullet hit him!

Fin Elder played by Alphonse Ethier and Kurt Northrup played by Richard Alexander: Edward L. Cahn's *Law and Order* (Universal, 1932).

2049

Bronson: It took guns to get the land …guns to keep it …guns to make things grow. The guns that pride called out. And each time we buried the cost.

Vincent Bronson played by Lee J. Cobb: Michael Winner's *Lawman* (United Artists, 1971).

2050

Tonto: Try this.

Lone Ranger: A silver bullet.

Tonto: It's more accurate. Travel chiefs first used silver on their arrows. It makes them fly longer and straighter. Silver is pure. It has been a symbol of justice and purity since the year of the sun.

Tonto played by Michael Horse and the Lone Ranger played by Klinton Spilsbury: William A. Fraker's *The Legend of the Lone Ranger* (Universal, 1981).

2051

Dempsey: Look, know this: twirling a gun never saved a man's life. There's only one thing you got to learn: get it out fast, and then …put it away slow.

Dempsey Rae played by Kirk Douglas: King Vidor's *Man Without a Star* (Universal, 1955).

2052

Billy: Hell, I just wish …I just wish I'd been living in those days. The way I handle a gun, boy, I'll tell ya …

Cain: The way you handle a gun, you would be a dead man. Somebody would have shot you in the back because they were afraid to face up to you. That's the way it was, and don't you think different.

Billy Eager played by Paul Hampton and Cain played by Clint Walker: Robert Sparr's *More Dead Than Alive* (United Artists, 1968).

2053

Utica Kid: That's a pretty good rig.

Howdy: Too good for the guy that owned it. Remember that draw you taught me? It worked. He went down with his gun in the leather.

Utica Kid: And now you're an in-case man.

Howdy: In-case?

Utica Kid: Yeah, in case you miss six times with one, you draw the other …if you have time.

The Utica Kid played by Audie Murphy and Howdy Sladen played by Tommy Cook: James Neilson's *Night Passage* (Universal, 1957).

2054

Jim: This [gun] is the only law that I know is worth a hoot in this part of the country. The only law.

Jim Kincaid/Oklahoma Kid played by James Cagney: Lloyd Bacon's *The Oklahoma Kid* (Warner Bros., 1939).

2055

Morton: How does it feel setting behind that desk, Frank?

Frank: It's almost like holding a gun …only much more powerful.

Morton played by Gabriele Ferzetti and Frank played by Henry Fonda: Sergio Leone's *Once Upon a Time in the West* (Paramount, 1969).

2056

Frank: My weapons might look simple to you, Mr. Morton. But they can still shoot holes big enough for our little problems.

Frank played by Henry Fonda and Morton played by Gabriele Ferzetti: Sergio Leone's *Once Upon a Time in the West* (Paramount, 1969).

2057

Pat: I thought you might want to have Doc's guns as a keepsake.

Billy: Say, I sure would. Thanks, Pat. Thanks a lot. I've never had an extra pair. And black holsters too! They'd go nice with Sunday clothes if I ever get any.

Billy the Kid played by Jack Buetel, Doc Holliday played by Walter Huston, and Pat Garrett played by Thomas Mitchell: Howard Hughes' *The Outlaw* (United Artists, 1943).

2058

Torrance: Best you move your self-righteous butt or this heathen rifle is gonna blow out your candle!

Jesse Torrance played by Kris Kristofferson: Bill Cocoran's *Outlaw Justice* (TVW, 1999).

2059

Torrance: A nice thing about a knife is …it's hard to shoot your foot off with it.

Jesse Torrance played by Kris Kristofferson: Bill Cocoran's *Outlaw Justice* (TVW, 1999).

2060

George: Well, you almost outdrew him, Nash.

Nash: Almost gets a man a quick funeral!

Gentleman George played by Chill Wills and Nash Crawford played by Walter Brennan: Jean Yarbrough's *The Over-the-Hill Gang* (TVW, 1969).

2061

Sheriff: He couldn't find his gun in the daylight.

Sheriff Clyde Barnes played by Jack Elam: Jean Yarbrough's *The Over-the-Hill Gang* (TVW, 1969).

2062

George: Now, you see that light in Cassie's Saloon over there? I'm going to shoot

A gun battle nearly erupts when Wes Handley (Ward Bond) interrupts Jim Kincaid/Oklahoma Kid (James Cagney) singing "I Don't Want to Play in Your Yard." Indian Jack Pasco (Trevor Bardette), Piano Player/the Professor (Ray Mayer), and outlaw leader Whip McCord (Humphrey Bogart) look on in *The Oklahoma Kid* (Warner Bros., 1939).

through the door and shoot that light out. That bullet is going to bounce against that pot belly stove, ricochet across the street, hit that anvil in front of the blacksmith's shop, ricochet across the street again, hit that cowbell over that store, come back towards me …and I'm going to catch that lead slug with my teeth!

Deputy: There ain't a man alive that good!

Gentleman George played by Chill Wills and the Deputy played by Myron Healey: Jean Yarbrough's *The Over-the-Hill Gang* (TVW, 1969).

2063

Jason: We just wear 'em for balance. I took mine off once and toppled over.

Jason Fitch played by Edgar Buchanan: George McCowan's *The Over-the-Hill Gang Rides Again* (TVW, 1970).

2064

Pepper: I told you my garter would bring you good luck.

Potter: Ah, thanks! Lucky thing I had a gun too.

Pepper played by Iris Adrian and Painless Peter Potter played by Bob Hope: Norman Z. McLeod's *The Paleface* (Paramount, 1948).

2065

Storyteller: A Colt .45 …single shot. You had to cock it every time you shot. It's called the Peacemaker …but I haven't seen much peace that it brought.

The Storyteller played by Woody Strode: Mario Van Peebles' *Posse* (Gramercy Pictures, 1993).

2066

Gentry: A gun has got a way of killin' a man who wears 'em.

Gentry/John Coventry played by Fred MacMurray: Harry Keller's *Quantez* (Universal, 1957).

2067

Marston: Are you familiar with the Army revolver, Mr. Quigley?

Quigley: Well sir, I never had much use for one.

Marston: A recent invention of your countryman, Colonel Colt.

Quigley: God created all men, and they say Sam Colt made them equal …more or less.

Elliott Marston played by Alan Rickman and Matthew Quigley played by Tom Selleck: Simon Wincer's *Quigley Down Under* (MGM-United Artists, 1990).

2068

Chris: How would you like to use that gunbelt for something more than just holding up your pants?

Chris played by Yul Brynner: Burt Kennedy's *Return of the Seven* (United Artists, 1966).

2069

Frank: So what do we do now?

Brigade: Sit there and watch your brother hang!

Frank: You don't mean that.

Brigade: Don't I?

Frank: He's only a boy!

Brigade: He's as old as his gun!

Frank played by Lee Van Cleef and Ben Brigade played by Randolph Scott: Budd Boetticher's *Ride Lonesome* (Columbia, 1959).

2070

Sheriff: What would you be in this town without your gun?

Rio: Just another funeral nobody went to.

Sheriff Parker played by Ted De Corsia and Rio played by Robert Taylor: John Farrow's *Ride, Vaquero!* (MGM, 1953).

2071

Burdette: If he says it wasn't murder, why do you say it was?

Chance: A man gets shot that has a gun, well, there's room for reasonable doubt. A man gets shot that hasn't got a gun, what would you call it?

Nathan Burdette played by John Russell and John T. Chance played by John Wayne: Howard Hawks' *Rio Bravo* (Warner Bros., 1959).

2072

McNally: That scatter gun is useless!

Phillips: You don't mind if I shoot, do you? It makes me feel better!

Cord McNally played by John Wayne and Phillips played by Jack Elam: Howard Hawks' *Rio Lobo* (NGP, 1970).

2073

Jim: You're pretty handy with a gun too. Fast. It could get you in trouble someday.

Sam: It could get me out too.

Jim: What's your line?

Sam: Anything. Most anything at all.

Jim Donovan played by Lee J. Cobb and Sam Mayhew played by Skip Homeier: Joseph Kane's *The Road to Denver* (Republic, 1955).

2074

Fenton: No gunplay, you understand! Unless you have to.

Odie Fenton played by Gordon/Bill Elliott: Gus Meins' *Roll Along, Cowboy* (20th Century–Fox, 1937).

2075

Roy: If you can find anything that will shoot, grab it!

Roy played by Roy Rogers: Joseph Kane's *Rough Riders' Round-Up* (Republic, 1939).

2076

Helga: Do you think putting a gun in his hand will cure what is in his heart?

Helga Swenson played by Viveca Lindfors: Nicholas Ray's *Run for Cover* (Paramount, 1955).

2077

Joan: I'm no slut, Mr. Sinclair! He didn't buy me like he bought that gun!

Joan Blake played by Julie London: Robert Parrish's *Saddle the Wind* (MGM, 1958).

2078

Steve: The use of it [gun], you may have got from me. But what about the love for it? Where did you get the love of it, Tony?

Steve Sinclair played by Robert Taylor and Tony Sinclair played by John Cassavetes: Robert Parrish's *Saddle the Wind* (MGM, 1958).

2079

Brown: You'll be traveling light. You won't need that heavy gun. So unbuckle it and let it drop!

Hemp Brown played by Rory Calhoun: Richard Carlson's *The Sage of Hemp Brown* (Universal, 1958).

2080

Franchea: Because he is not an enemy, that does not make him a friend. We'll keep the gun until we know.

Franchea played by Paquita Rico: Michael Carreras' *The Savage Guns* (MGM, 1961).

2081

Fallon: Don't let the fact that you're a woman make you think they won't kill you, ma'am. They shoot at the hand that holds the gun.

Steve Fallon played by Richard Basehart: Michael Carreras' *The Savage Guns* (MGM, 1961).

2082

Luke: It's the code of the West: you never mess with another man's guns.

Luke Morgan played by Corey Carrier: Dean Hamilton's *Savage Land* (Herndale Communications/Savage Land Productions, 1994).

2083

Miles: Sharps [rifles]. Take 'em. They'll knock the stripes off of a skunk from 500 yards.

Sheriff Miles Gillette played by R.G. Armstrong: Andrew V. McLaglen's *The Shadow Riders* (TVW, 1982).

2084

Shane: A gun is a tool, Marion. No better or no worse than any other tool: an axe, a shovel or anything. A gun is as good or as bad as the man using it. Remember that.

Shane played by Alan Ladd and Marion Starrett played by Jean Arthur: George Stevens' *Shane* (Paramount, 1953).

2085

Sheriff: Any man that carries a gun is advertising that he is ready and willing to use it.

Sheriff Jim Trask played by Jock Mahoney: Charles Haas' *Showdown at Abilene* (Universal, 1956).

2086

Quince: I don't think it's healthy for a man with your position in life to be that good with a gun.

Jason: A man with my position in life, with you as a friend, better be good at something!

Quince Drew played by Larry Hagman and Jason O'Rourke played by Lou Gossett: Burt Kennedy's *Sidekicks* (TVW, 1974).

2087

Jesse: I don't suppose you ever give much thought to hiring out your gun.

Lane: My gun?

Jesse: There, on your hip.

Frank Jesse played by Dan Duryea and Ben Lane played by Audie Murphy: Harry Keller's *Six Black Horses* (Universal, 1962).

2088

Destiny: It's a Colt Paterson. I took it off an hombre in Amarillo a long time ago. It's the first time I touched it in twenty years.

Joe Jr.: It sure is a beauty!

Destiny: They don't make them like this anymore. A perfect balance, fast action, deadly sights, and a grip as reassuring as an old friend's handshake.

Destiny played by Kris Kristofferson and Joe Gentry Jr. played by Cody Jones: Eugene Levy's *Sodbusters* (Atlantis Releasing, 1994).

2089

Joe Jr.: How's that, Destiny?

Destiny: Not bad …not bad. It could have been better.

Joe Jr.: What am I doing wrong?

Destiny: What were you looking at when you pulled the trigger?

Joe Jr.: The can.

Destiny: It couldn't have been the can. Because if you were looking at the can, your eyes would have been opened.

Joe Jr.: Then how did I see the can?

Destiny: You didn't see the can! You couldn't have seen the can. Because you got to have your eyes open to see something!

Joe Jr.: Maybe it's this gun. Maybe it ain't as good as you think it is.

Joe Gentry Jr. played by Cody Jones and Destiny played by Kris Kristofferson: Eugene Levy's *Sodbusters* (Atlantis Releasing, 1994).

2090

Slade: When a man don't wear a gun, I suppose the only thing he can shoot off is his mouth.

Slade Cantrell played by John Vernon: Eugene Levy's *Sodbusters* (Atlantis Releasing, 1994).

2091

Doc: I'll take that shotgun, Luke.

Luke: You'll take it in the belly if you don't get out of my way!

Dr. Josiah Boone played by Thomas Mitchell and Luke Plummer played by Tom Tyler: John Ford's *Stagecoach* (United Artists, 1939).

2092

Dallas: Going bye bye, Doc?

Doc: I got business in another town, Dallas.

Dallas: Oh, it must be serious …with you wearing your irons.

Doc: Well, a friend of mine in Tombstone said I should travel light and come well-balanced.

Dallas played by Elizabeth Ashley and Doc Holliday played by Willie Nelson: Ted Post's *Stagecoach* (TVW, 1986).

2093

Tobias: Our faith is in the hands of the Lord.

Trinity: Yeah, but He doesn't carry a gun either. You can't get much help there. Look, I don't think the Lord would take it wrong if you defended yourself.

Tobias: We cannot kill our fella man.

Trinity: But they ain't your fella man! They're lower than rattlesnakes! You can't go on turning the other cheek forever.

Tobias: We shall see what God wills.

Trinity: I hope he wills a couple guns!

Tobias played by Dan Sturkie and Trinity played by Terence Hill (Mario Girotti): E.B. Clucher's (Enzo Barboni) *They Call Me Trinity* (West Film/Avco Embassy, 1970).

2094

Tobias: Have you seen what faith can do?

Bambino: It'll work …if you put it in a rifle barrel.

Tobias played by Dan Sturkie and Bambino played by Bud Spencer (Carlo Pedersoli): E.B. Clucher's (Enzo Barboni) *They Call Me Trinity* (West Film/Avco Embassy, 1970).

2095

Carter: Carrying a gun! Go ahead, use it! That's your answer to everything!

Guthrie: No, it's my answer to another gun!

Carter Mastin played by Richard Webb and Jim Guthrie played by Dana Andrews: Alfred Werker's *Three Hours to Kill* (Columbia, 1954).

2096

Hickman: Try and hold 'em …with a shotgun. It talks louder to a crowd.

Morg Hickman played by Henry Fonda: Anthony Mann's *The Tin Star* (Paramount, 1957).

2097

Ruth: Tom, how did you ever get so good with guns?

Tom: Ah, it's a job.

Ruth: I can think of safer and pleasanter ones.

Tom: When you grow up in a border town, a gun is the pleasantest thing there is. Every time one goes off, somebody makes money. Once I found that out, I knew I had it made.

Ruth Harris played by Shelley Winters and Tom Bryan played by Rory Calhoun: George Sherman's *The Treasure of Pancho Villa* (RKO, 1955).

2098

Tom: Any man who has a gun in his hand after the count of three will be in bad health.

Tom Bryan played by Rory Calhoun: George Sherman's *The Treasure of Pancho Villa* (RKO, 1955).

2099

Sarah: I swear, the guns in this house are cleaner than the pots and pans!

Sarah McClure played by Dana Delany: Karen Arthur's *True Women* (TVW, 1997).

2100

Fatty: Jesus, Clyde, you got three pistols and you only got one arm, for Christ sake!

Clyde: I just don't want to get killed for lack of shooting back.

Fatty Rossiter played by Jefferson Mappin and Clyde Ledbetter played by Ron White: Clint Eastwood's *Unforgiven* (Warner Bros., 1992).

2101

Mollie: Why do you keep on loading when there's shooting to be done?

Jeff: Because you wasted a shot on that cigar store Indian out there!

Mollie Monahan played by Barbara Stanwyck and Jeff Butler played by Joel McCrea: Cecil B. De-Mille's *Union Pacific* (Paramount, 1939).

2102

Handsome: This is a seven shot six-shooter.

Handsome Stranger played by Arnold Schwarzenegger: Hal Needham's *The Villain* (a.k.a. *Cactus Jack*; Columbia, 1979).

2103

Trampas: And who's talking to you?

Virginian: I'm talking to you, Trampas.

Trampas: If I want to know anything from you, I'll tell you …you long legged son-of-a …

Virginian: If you want to call me that …smile!

Trampas: With a gun against my belly, I …I always smile.

Trampas played by Walter Huston and the Virginian

Jason O'Rourke (Lou Gossett, Jr.) and Quince Drew (Larry Hagman) unintentionally end up in an outlaw camp led by Boss (Jack Elam). They quickly contrive a story that they are bank robbers and that Jason is an explosives expert in Burt Kennedy's *Sidekicks* (TVW, 1974).

played by Gary Cooper: Victor Fleming's *The Virginian* (Paramount, 1929).

2104

Virginian: When you call me that, smile.
Trampas: With a gun against my belly, I always smile.

The Virginian played by Joel McCrea and Trampas played by Brian Donlevy: Stuart Gilmore's *The Virginian* (Paramount, 1946).

2105

Murdock: Colonel Colt's Navy revolver …you just load it up on Sunday and shoot it the rest of the week.

Abner Murdock played by James Read: Craig Clyde's *Walking Thunder* (Majestic Entertainment/Sunset Hill Partners, 1997).

2106

Peter: I'm just curious, how much do they weigh?
John: Three or four pounds.
Peter: That heavy? Do they have much of a kick?

John: A Colt .45?
Peter: Well, I never fired one before. Hey, what about that thing where you go like this over the gun?
John: Fanning?
Peter: Yeah.
John: What about it?
Peter: Is that hard to do? Now, when they give you the gunbelt, does it have those strings to tie around your leg?
John: If that's the kind you want.
Peter: That's the kind I want. I think it's probably better for quick draw, you know.
John: It all depends.
Peter: What kind of gunbelt did you have the last time?
John: I had the one without the strings.
Peter: And you could draw fast?
John: Ah huh.
Peter: Well, maybe it doesn't matter after all. The guns they give you …are real guns?
John: Ah huh. Real guns.

Peter: That's incredible!

Peter Martin played by Richard Benjamin and John Blane played by James Brolin: Michael Crichton's *Westworld* (MGM, 1973).

2107

Judson: What's the matter, Lefty? You ain't afraid of them psalm-singin' angels?
Lefty: Well, they're maybe angels, boss, but them things hangin' from their belts ain't harps!

Judson Holderness played by David Landau and Lefty played by Guinn "Big Boy" Williams: Henry Hathaway's *When the West Was Young* (a.k.a. *Heritage of the Desert*; Paramount, 1932).

2108

Chip: You broke it! You broke it!
Yancey: Now you know it's a hand … not just something on the end of a gun!

Chip Miller played by Peter Breck and Yancey played by Audie Murphy: Jack Sher's *The Wild and the Innocent* (Universal, 1959).

2109

Angel: Would you give guns to someone to kill your father or your mother or your brother?

Pike: Ten thousand [dollars] cuts an awful lot of family ties.

Angel played by Jaime Sanchez and Pike Bishop played by William Holden: Sam Peckinpah's *The Wild Bunch* (Warner Bros.–Seven Arts, 1969).

2110

Hugh: What's one of those [gun] worth?

Rusty: Your life …when you need to use it.

Hugh: I mean, money?

Rusty: Why do you need a six-gun?

Hugh: Two men need killing.

Rusty: Take a six-shooter like this. It's worth about seven steers. On this trip it could be worth the whole herd.

Hugh Breslin played by Gary Gray and Rusty played by Casey Tibbs: Charles Haas' *Wild Heritage* (Universal, 1958).

2111

Hugh: How about a fast draw on a gun?

Brazos: That's the last thing you learn, boy. You got to learn your gun, learn yourself, before you fool with any gun-slick tricks.

Hugh Breslin played by Gary Gray and Brazos played by Christopher Dark: Charles Haas' *Wild Heritage* (Universal, 1958).

2112

Hugh: How long does it take to get that fast?

Rusty: You drew faster than I did …but I hit it [tree branch]. The point is, there's no use trying to draw fast until you can hit a target. And the hardest target to hit are the ones that move …and shoot back at you.

Hugh Breslin played by Gary Gray and Rusty played by Casey Tibbs: Charles Haas' *Wild Heritage* (Universal, 1958).

2113

Dutch: What happened at Little Big Horn?

Joe: Haven't you heard? Sioux jumped Custer. Wiped out the whole command.

Yes sir, it's getting to be mighty tough country to travel …without a gun.

Dutch Henry Brown played by Stephen McNally and Joe Lamont played by John McIntire: Anthony Mann's *Winchester '73* (Universal, 1950).

2114

Stretch: I wish you wouldn't keep pointing that thing at me. Women got no business carrying guns. They'll have to shoot somebody they don't mean to.

Mike: Not me.

Stretch played by Gregory Peck and Mike played by Anne Baxter: William A. Wellman's *Yellow Sky* (20th Century–Fox, 1948).

2115

Gabby: Get his gun, Calamity.

Calamity: He ain't got none.

Gabby: Well then, give him one and take it away from him!

Gabby Whittaker played by George "Gabby" Hayes and Calamity Jane played by Sally Payne: Joseph Kane's *Young Bill Hickok* (Republic, 1940).

Hanging

See also Burying; Dying; Justice; Killing

2116

Janie: If you're going to hang, I'll hang with you. That's the least you can let me do.

Janie played by Claire Trevor: William A. Seiter's *Allegheny Uprising* (RKO, 1939).

2117

George: Who is it?

Melody: That used to be Packard, the Express Company fella.

George: Well that cinched the duck! Now they got a corpus delicti!

Melody: A what?

George: A dead body! That's the way the law says it. Corpus delicti. Means that if they got a corpse, you're delicti! Before this, even if they hung ya, we could have proved it was a mistake.

George Fury played by William Demarest and Melody Jones played by Gary Cooper: Stuart Heisler's *Along Came Jones* (RKO, 1945).

2118

Marshal: You know, Quirt, I always figured on using a new rope in hanging you …because I kind of respected ya. You never took the best of things, and all your men went down looking at ya.

Marshal Wistful McClintock played by Harry Carey and Quirt Evans played by John Wayne:

James Edward Grant's *Angel and the Badman* (Republic, 1947).

2119

Marshal: When are you and Laredo Stevens going to get around to killing one another?

Quirt: Laredo? Well, we water our horses out of the same trough.

Marshal: Well, I'm sure looking forward to hanging the survivor.

Marshal Wistful McClintock played by Harry Carey, Laredo Stevens played by Bruce Cabot, and Quirt Evans played by John Wayne: James Edward Grant's *Angel and the Badman* (Republic, 1947).

2120

Sheriff: When they hear about this, they're going to come looking for you.

Slater: Seems logical.

Sheriff: If it's your idea to shoot it out with them, you're going to lose.

Slater: Could be.

Sheriff: And even if you beat 'em, you're going to lose …because I'm going to hang the man that wins.

Sheriff J.C. Marson played by Edward Platt and Jim Slater played by Richard Widmark: John Sturges' *Backlash* (Universal, 1956).

2121

Bishop: You know, I've always been sort of curious about your job.

Hangman: Well, there's a lot more to it than most folks think. There's nothing worse than a sloppy hanging. Now back in Oklahoma, I once watched 'em hang a fella five times before it took.

Bishop: Five times? Five? Well now, just exactly what do you have to know, Mr. Grimes, in order to make a good clean professional job of it?

Hangman: Just about everything. You have to know how tall your subject is …how much he weighs …his neck size …and how he feels about it all. Then you have to be certain …

Bishop: Well now, excuse me. You mean to say that you have to know how the fella you're going to hang feels about it?

Hangman: Oh, yes sir. A scared man is a crying and praying and shaking and moving all around. He's a lot harder to send to his Maker than one who's decided to just stand there and take it.

Bishop: Huh huh.

Hangman: Well, I had a subject last year, took me the most part of an hour just to get him up off his knees.

Bishop: Is that a fact?

Sidekick George Fury (William Demarest) with saddlemate Melody Jones (Gary Cooper) in *Along Came Jones* (RKO, 1945).

Hangman: That's a fact! Now, you can't hang a subject when he's on his knees. It just don't look right.

Mace Bishop played by James Stewart and Ossie Grimes, The Hangman, played by Guy Raymond: Andrew McLaglen's *Bandolero!* (20th Century–Fox, 1968).

2122

Hangman: Ossie Grimes is the name, Sheriff. I'm down from Oklahoma to prove once more than the sins of the father are a visit on the son. And that's true in Texas just like anyplace else. The southwest will be a better place to live once our work is finished.

The Hangman disguised as Ossie Grimes played by Mace Bishop: Andrew McLaglen's *Bandolero!* (20th Century–Fox, 1968).

2123

Hangman: You're expecting a big crowd, I imagine?

Sheriff: Well, it's a free country. If folks want to watch a hanging, they got a right to.

Hangman: Huh, huh. Well then, I'd like to advise you about two things, Sheriff. I found out from bitter experience that when folks come into town for a hanging, all guns should be confiscated until after the proceedings …and all saloons should be closed.

Sheriff: Well, I'll see what I can do.

Hangman: Good, good. These men deserve to hang. But they don't deserve to hang cold sober while a bunch of drunks stand around and watch 'em.

The Hangman disguised as Ossie Grimes played by Mace Bishop, and Sheriff July Johnson played by George Kennedy: Andrew McLaglen's *Bandolero!* (20th Century–Fox, 1968).

2124

Bobbie: Have you no plan, laddie?

Babe: My plan is to stay away from a rope.

Bobbie O'Hara played by Sean McClory and Babe

Jenkins played by Clint Richie: Andrew McLaglen's *Bandolero!* (20th Century–Fox, 1968).

2125

Major: I'll hang him from the highest tree …and his friends with him.

Belle: Wouldn't that require a great deal of rope?

Major: Fortunately, we have an ample supply.

Major Thomas Crail played by Dana Andrews and Belle Shirley Starr played by Gene Tierney: Irving Cummings' *Belle Starr* (20th Century–Fox, 1941).

2126

Marshal: Thorpe, why don't you get back on the Penzy Belle [riverboat] and make yourself scarce? If you're here when the boat pulls out, the boys will certainly lead your pony out from under ya.

The Marshal played by Alphonse Ethier and Bill Thorpe played by Ian Keith: Raoul Walsh's *The Big Trail* (Fox, 1930).

2127

Flack: Well, if it ain't Bill Thorpe, hey? I always thought you was hung and planted, I'd expect.

Thorpe: No, my time ain't arrive yet, Flack. But it looks as though it might be drawing close.

Flack: How come?

Thorpe: Well, I've been promised a hanging bee if I don't get out on the Penzy Belle [riverboat]. And the Captain promised me a necktie party if I set foot on the boat. It's a case of nowhere to go.

Flack: It appears to me you do your shooting by daylight, with too many people looking on, hey?

Red Flack played by Tyrone Power, Sr. and Bill Thorpe played by Ian Keith: Raoul Walsh's *The Big Trail* (Fox, 1930).

2128

Zeke: When a man begins to do a lot of talking about hanging, he better make pretty sure as to who is going to decorate the end of the rope.

Zeke played by Tully Marshall: Raoul Walsh's *The Big Trail* (Fox, 1930).

2129

Boles: I'd still like to know why you blew up that tree. You might have killed somebody.

Brady: I figured it all out. No tree, no hanging.

Charles E. Boles played by Dan Duryea and Jersey Brady played by Percy Kilbride: George Sherman's *Black Bart* (Universal, 1948).

2130

Douglas: You're wasting a lot of good lumber. A tree does just as well.

Sheriff: They were sentenced to be hanged …not lynched!

Jim Douglas played by Gregory Peck and Sheriff Elroy Sanchez played by Herbert Rudley: Henry King's *The Bravados* (20th Century–Fox, 1958).

2131

Cleve: I now ask you, sir, do you remember the names Charlie Monger, Red Dog Johnson, or Carlos Rameriez?

Devereaux: No.

Cleve: The incident may be too trivial to recall. But isn't it true that you summarily hanged all three of these men on the afternoon of June 4th …

Devereaux: They were stealing my cattle!

Cleve: I thought you didn't remember them.

Devereaux: I didn't ask them their names!

Cleve: You just hanged 'em?

Devereaux: By the neck until they were dead! They were thieves!

Van Cleve played by Philip Ober and Matthew Devereaux played by Spencer Tracy: Edward Dmytryk's *Broken Lance* (20th Century–Fox, 1954).

2132

Sheriff: Let's take him over to the jailhouse and wait for him to come to. When I hang a man, I like him to know what's going on.

Sheriff Lou Agry played by Barry Kelley: Budd Boetticher's *Buchanan Rides Alone* (Columbia, 1958).

2133

Cahill: Oh, MacDonald! This is Cahill. How are you?

MacDonald: Fine. Leastwise no one has tried to hang me lately.

Marshal J.D. Cahill played by John Wayne and MacDonald played by Royal Dano: Andrew McLaglen's *Cahill: United States Marshal* (Warner Bros., 1973).

2134

Hanson: I ain't gonna swing alone!

Hanson played by Tom London: Lesley Selander's *Call of the Rockies* (Republic, 1944).

2135

Bragg: What do you have against me?

Logan: You ought to know.

Bragg: You're talking in riddles, Logan. What's in your mind?

Logan: A picture of a tree …with you swingin' from it.

Honey Bragg played by Ward Bond and Logan Stuart played by Dana Andrews: Jacques Tourneur's *Canyon Passage* (Universal, 1946).

2136

Logan: There was a lot of good in George.

Johnny: He sure panned out no color.

Logan: There's a thin margin, Johnny, between what could be and what is.

Johnny: Yeah. It was thin for you last night. We were a mind to hang ya.

Logan: You see how thin the margin is.

Logan Stuart played by Dana Andrews and Johnny Steele played by Lloyd Bridges: Jacques Tourneur's *Canyon Passage* (Universal, 1946).

2137

Gabby: You ain't gonna hang nobody without a fair trial!

Lee: Trial? What for?

Gabby: This place ain't gonna get no Hangtown reputation.

Gabby Whittaker played by George "Gabby" Hayes and Lee Jessup played by Bob Steele: Joseph Kane's *The Carson City Kid* (Republic, 1940).

2138

Miller: Now, how good are you on a horse?

Catlow: As good as the next man.

Miller: You ain't heard the conditions. You ride this bronc with your hands tied behind your back. And your neck in that noose!

Miller played by Leonard Nimoy and Jed Catlow played by Yul Brynner: Sam Wanamaker's *Catlow* (MGM, 1971).

2139

Morton: You're going to shoot us, ain't you Chisum.

Chisum: I thought about it. Then I thought about something Henry Tunstall once said. He watched a man walk to the gallow …saw him hang. He said it was ghastly. Well, I've seen men hang. And that's the word: ghastly. You two are going to hang.

Morton played by Robert Donner, John Chisum played by John Wayne, and Henry Tunstall played by Patrick Knowles: Andrew McLaglen's *Chisum* (Warner Bros., 1970).

2140

Marshal: That's a nice sight [hanging] for anybody with a train-robbing itch.

The U.S. Marshal played by Morris Ankrum: Raoul Walsh's *Colorado Territory* (Warner Bros., 1949).

2141

Mrs. Quary: You got to hang that killer! I want to see it! I want to hear that neck of his crack with my own two ears!

Mrs. Quary played by Peggy Converse: Harry Keller's *Day of the Bad Man* (Universal, 1958).

2142

Sheriff: Maybe we can try him this afternoon and hang him right away and save the county the expense of feeding him.

The Sheriff of Rattlesnake Gulch played by Frank Brownlee: Cullen Lewis's (Lew Collins) *The Desert Trail* (Monogram/Lone Star, 1935).

2143

Blackie: Only about twelve hours now until you boys get some exercise …walking on air!

The Deputy, Blackie, played by Edward Pawley: Charles Vidor's *The Desperadoes* (Columbia, 1943).

2144

Judge: Why, I aim to give Red Valley a couple hangings that they'll be proud of in days to come.

Judge Cameron played by Raymond Walburn: Charles Vidor's *The Desperadoes* (Columbia, 1943).

2145

Marshal: Yes ma'am, we're going to wrap a necklace of good Kentucky hemp around that little neck of yours. Have you ever heard the sound a broke neck bone makes? It's like a carrot.

Marshal Bill Speaks played by Sam Elliott: P.J. Pesce's *The Desperate Trail* (Turner Home Entertainment, 1995).

2146

Hatton: I'm going to have you indicted for murder as an accessory after the fact.

Taylor: I had nothing to do with it!

Opposite: **Advertisement for *Black Bart* (Universal, 1948), the story of the infamous highwayman who has it in for the Wells Fargo Company.**

HIS <u>RECKLESS DARING</u> BLAZED
A TRAIL OF GUNSMOKE!
HER <u>FLAMING DANCES</u>
SET THE WEST AFIRE!

A stirring saga
of thrilling
love and wild
adventure
in a land
beyond
the *LAW!*

Universal-International presents
Yvonne **De CARLO**
Dan **DURYEA**
Jeffrey **LYNN**

BLACK BART

COLOR BY
TECHNICOLOR!

with PERCY KILBRIDE

THEATRE
MAT NO. 204

Screenplay by LUCI WARD, JACK NATTEFORD and WILLIAM BOWERS · Directed by GEORGE SHERMAN
Original Story by Luci Ward and Jack Natteford · Produced by LEONARD GOLDSTEIN

Hatton: You're going to be dancing in thin air just the same as Yancey. Now, do you want to swing or do you want to tell me and save your neck?

Wade Hatton played by Errol Flynn, Bud Taylor played by Ward Bond, and Yancey played by Victor Jory: Michael Curtiz's *Dodge City* (Warner Bros., 1939).

2147

Little Bill: Old Ben Franklin said, "we shall hang together, or assuredly, we shall all hang separately." Now that fits us, just like it fit them.

Little Bill played by Noah Beery, Jr.: Gordon Douglas' *The Doolins of Oklahoma* (Columbia, 1949).

2148

Malloy: Hold it! Hold it! Hold it! Now let's not get carried away with blood lust. Where is our cup of human kindness? Where's it runneth to?

Cowboy: It runneth right up your ass! That's where it runneth to! Somebody get the rope!

Charlie Malloy played by George Segal and the Cowboy was uncredited: Melvin Frank's *The Duchess and the Dirtwater Fox* (20th Century–Fox, 1976).

2149

Gannon: Now it becomes my duty to carry out the sentence which I have imposed on these men for killing and stealing within the territory under my jurisdiction. However, I want it strictly understood that there will be no undo shooting or cheering or drunken talk when I pull that lever …on account it would offend the dignity of the occasion.

Gannon played by John McIntire: Anthony Mann's *The Far Country* (Universal, 1955).

2150

Gannon: Have a nice trip! I'll hang ya when you come back!

Gannon played by John McIntire: Anthony Mann's *The Far Country* (Universal, 1955).

2151

Benson: The man is wanted for a murder in Seattle.
Gannon: Well, Seattle will have to wait. He's wanted here for busting up a hanging.

Captain Benson played by Stuart Randall and Gannon played by John McIntire: Anthony Mann's *The Far Country* (Universal, 1955).

2152

Morgan: Anything new on the hanging?
Marshal: Oh, nothing to hang anybody else with. The fella was new in town. We haven't even turned up his name.
Morgan: What do you do in a case like that?

Bad guys Jeff Surrett (Bruce Cabot) and Yancy (Victor Jory) get reacquainted with good guy Wade Hatton (Errol Flynn) in Michael Curtiz's classic western, *Dodge City* (Warner Bros., 1939).

Marshal: Oh, you bury the man but keep him in mind.

Van Morgan played by Dean Martin and Marshal Dana played by John Anderson: Henry Hathaway's *Five Card Stud* (Paramount, 1968).

2153

Avram: And what if I give back the money?
Tommy: You mean your half!
Avram: Yes, I mean my half!
Tommy: Well, first, they'll string you up by your balls until you tell them where the other half is. Then they'll hang ya!

Avram Belinsky played by Gene Wilder and Tommy played by Harrison Ford: Robert Aldrich's *The Frisco Kid* (Warner Bros., 1979).

2154

Bird: You're new around here, Cameron. When a man shoots somebody in the back, he don't get a trial. He just gets hung.

Bird played by Fred Clark and Cash Blackwell, alias Tex Cameron, played by Victor Mature: Bruce Humberstone's *Fury at Furnace Creek* (20th Century–Fox, 1948).

2155

Grinder [*Sgt. ordering troopers to cut down two hung Indians*]: All right, cut 'em down.
Grinder [*upon seeing how the order was about to be executed*]: Hey! Don't cut that! That's a good rope! Untie 'em!

Sergeant Calvin Grinder played by Matt Clark: Dick Lowry's *The Gambler, Part III — The Legend Continues* (TVW, 1987).

2156

Sheriff: Mr. Moon? It's about that time.
Moon: What about my last meal?
Sheriff: You're smoking it.

Sheriff Kyle played by Richard Bradford and Henry Moon played by Jack Nicholson: Jack Nicholson's *Goin' South* (Paramount, 1978).

2157

Tallant: I came to talk to you about the execution.
Ben: We don't have to talk about that, do we?
Tallant: Oh, but we do. There hasn't been a hanging in Nebraska in a long time. There's been some new ordinances passed.
Ben: Oh, like what?
Tallant: Like you can't take a man out to a tall tree or stand him on a barrel anymore.

Tallant Joslin played by Wendell Holmes and Ben Cutler played by Fred MacMurray: Nathan Juran's *Good Day for a Hanging* (Columbia, 1958).

2158

Beeson: I'm going to hang you like they hung Bob. I might even let Nez here cut your balls off first.

Boss Beeson played by Eric Keenlyside and Nez played by Charles Andre: David Greene's *A Good Day to Die* (a.k.a. *Children of the Dust*; Vidmark Entertainment, 1995).

2159

Shelby: I've been haunted by my mother's death for so many years now.
Rachel: I'm haunted too. I found my mother hanging from the ceiling when I was just a kid.
Shelby: It's a cruel message for a mother to leave her daughter.
Rachel: Yes, it was. She seemed to be saying that life is too difficult, too painful, too empty to keep on struggling; that it was better to die than go through it. I don't want to be like her. I want to have a life filled with love and joy and family.

Shelby Hornbeck played by Hart Bochner and Rachel played by Joanna Going: David Greene's *A Good Day to Die* (a.k.a. *Children of the Dust*; Vidmark Entertainment, 1995).

2160

Tuco: There are two kinds of people in the world, my friend. Those with a rope around their neck, and the people who have the job of doing the cutting. Listen, the neck at the end of the rope is mine. I run the risks. So the next time, I want more than half [of the reward].
Blondie: You may run the risks, my friend, but I do the cutting. If we cut down my percentage, it's liable to …cigar? …interfere with my aim.

Tuco played by Eli Wallach and Blondie played by Clint Eastwood: Sergio Leone's *The Good, the Bad, and the Ugly* (United Artists, 1966; U.S. 1968).

2161

Tuco: You've never had a rope around your neck! Well, I'm going to tell you something. When that rope starts to pull tight, you can feel the devil bite your ass.

Tuco played by Eli Wallach: Sergio Leone's *The Good, the Bad, and the Ugly* (United Artists, 1966; U.S. 1968).

2162

Angel Eyes: People with ropes around their necks don't always hang.

Angel Eyes played by Lee Van Cleef: Sergio Leone's *The Good, the Bad, and the Ugly* (United Artists, 1966; U.S. 1968).

2163

Jake: Sentencing a man to a rope death is one thing; getting it done is another.

Jake Marant played by Howard Kruschke: Clay Borris' *The Gunfighters* (TVW, 1989).

2164

Keno: Do you want to know my name before you hang me?

Judge: Not particularly. Just your last words.

Keno played by Monte Markham and the Judge was uncredited: Paul Wendkos' *Guns of the Magnificent Seven* (United Artists, 1969).

2165

Bliss: Save your breath. I don't know who hung you or why. But if you're innocent, the Judge will set you free. And if you ain't, we'll have to take the trouble of hanging you again.

Sheriff Dave Bliss played by Ben Johnson: Ted Post's *Hang 'em High* (United Artists, 1968).

2166

Prisoner: Always uses top grade hemp, Schmidt does. He oils it so it slides real good. Snaps your neck like a dried out twig.

The Prisoner played by James Westerfield and Schmidt the Hangman played by Bert Freed: Ted Post's *Hang 'em High* (United Artists, 1968).

2167

Eubie: And when you feel that rope around your neck, oh, you're going to give us a dandy show. Crying, begging for mercy …but too late. They'll put that gunnysack on your head and drop you through that trapdoor to hell.

Eubie Turpin played by John Mitchum: Michael Caffey's *The Hanged Man* (TVW, 1974).

2168

Donnie: What do you suppose it is that makes people want to watch another man hang?

Donnie played by Kelly Lebrock: Jim Wynorski's *Hard Bounty* (Triboro Entertainment, 1995).

2169

Sheriff: I wish you'd do me a favor and try to get away. I'd like to save the state all that rope.

The Sheriff played by Jack Rockwell: David Howard's *In Old Santa Fe* (Mascot, 1934).

2170

Darcy: A man must die with dignity.
Blecker: What's the difference? The man's dead!
Darcy: No. There's a thousand ways to die and each man finds his own. But to strangle at the end of a rope with your eyes bulging, your feet kicking, your tongue hanging out. That's for a clown or an animal. Not men.
Blecker: You're really scared of hanging, aren't you?

Luke Darcy played by Jeff Chandler and Cam Blecker played by Fess Parker: Melvin Frank's *The Jayhawkers* (Paramount, 1959).

2171

Governor: Blecker, you might take a notion to cross me. If you do, remember this: I'll get him and I'll get you. And I'll string you both up one at a time on the same day I string up the rest of those Jayhawkers.

Blecker: Governor, you sound like somebody who just come into an awful lot of rope.

Governor William Clayton played by Herbert Rudley and Cam Blecker played by Fess Parker: Melvin Frank's *The Jayhawkers* (Paramount, 1959).

2172

Stribling: I'm gonna see that you hang, O'Malley.

O'Malley: Oh, hanging is a long time proposition.

Dana Stribling played by Rock Hudson and Brendan O'Malley played by Kirk Douglas: Robert Aldrich's *The Last Sunset* (Universal, 1961).

2173

Belden: It don't take no guts to kill a man when he's cuffed.

Morgan: It takes guts not to. It would be too easy on you. You'd die too quick. I know an old man who would like to kill you, Belden. The Indian way …slow. That's how I'm going to do it …slow …but the white man's way. First, you'll stand trial. That takes a fair amount of time and you'll do a lot of sweating. Then they'll sentence ya. I've never seen a man who didn't get sick to his stomach when he heard the kind of sentence you'll draw. And then after that, you'll sit in a cell and wait, maybe for months, thinking how that rope will feel around your neck. Then they'll come around some cold morning, just before sunup. They'll tie your arms behind you. You'll start blubbering, kicking, yelling for help. But it won't do you any good. They'll drag you out in the yard and heave ya up on that platform, fix that rope around your neck, and leave you out there all alone with a big black hood over your eyes. You know the last sound you hear? Kind of a thump when they kick the trapdoor catch and down you go. And you'll hit the end of that rope like a sack of potatoes …all dead weight. You'll be white hot around your neck and your Adam's Apple will turn to mush. You'll fight for your breath, but you haven't got any breath. Your brain will begin to boil, you'll scream and holler. But nobody will hear you. You'll hear it! But nobody else. Finally, you'll just be swinging there …all alone and dead.

Rick Belden played by Earl Holliman and U.S. Marshal Matt Morgan played by Kirk Douglas: John Sturges' *Last Train from Gun Hill* (Paramount, 1959).

2174

Sheriff: I heard of a hanging up by Cheyenne. It took nearly half an hour for the fella to die …just choking to death. You're going to break that record.

Sheriff Bull Harper played by George Mathews: Delmer Daves' *The Last Wagon* (20th Century–Fox, 1956).

2175

Frame: Johnny, do you realize that you're the first fellow to be hung legal in Tombstone?

Johnny: Am I, Mr. Johnson?

Frame: Yes sir, you're the first man to be hung in this county according to Hoyle.

Johnny: You don't say, Mr. Johnson.

Frame: Yep, that's right. Everybody will be watching.

Johnny: Will you hang me, Mr. Johnson?

Frame Johnson played by Walter Huston and Johnny Kinsman played by Andy Devine: Edward L. Cahn's *Law and Order* (Universal, 1932).

2176

McNelly: Don't get too fond of him, Duncan. If you want to sing his praises, maybe you'll get the chance to recite a eulogy over his grave …after we hang him.

Captain W. H. McNelly of the Texas Rangers played by Tom Jackson: Raoul Walsh's *The Lawless Breed* (Universal, 1952).

2177

Deputy: The Judge said Friday. Monday, Tuesday, Wednesday …Thursday, Friday. That's your day. That's the day we're going to hang you.

Deputy Ollinger played by Denver Pyle: Arthur Penn's *The Left Handed Gun* (Warner Bros., 1958).

2178

Roy Bean: Hanging is the outlaws' path to glory …and much too good for the likes of you.

Judge Roy Bean played by Paul Newman: John Huston's *The Life and Times of Judge Roy Bean* (NGP, 1972).

2179

Bart: Have you got a minute, Judge?

Judge: What's on your mind, Bart?

Bart: We would like to talk to you about something.

Judge: Go right ahead.

Bart: The railroad is a comin'.

Whorehouse: But we don't think the train is even going to stop here. What with a man hanging right out in clear view.

Bart: Don't get us wrong, Judge. We ain't against hanging. We just feel that it should be done private like.

Fermel: Yeah, in Dallas they do it in a barn and outside of town.

Judge: In a barn? Like they was ashamed of it? Why, I'd rather give up hanging. No sir, the law says the guilty shall be punished. And I say it shall be done in broad daylight, in the open …not sneaking around like you was the one that was guilty, not them.

Frank Gass: But what about the ladies, Judge, and their delicate sensibilities? And the children?

Judge: Children? It's exactly what children need! It sets an example. It shows them what will happen if they don't walk the straight and narrow.

Bart Jackson played by Jim Burk, Judge Roy Bean played by Paul Newman, Whorehouse Lucky Jim played by Steve Kanaly, Fermel Parlee played by Bill McKinney, and Frank Gass played by Roddy McDowall: John Huston's *The Life and Times of Judge Roy Bean* (NGP, 1972).

2180

Sheriff: Now maybe you better slow down too, Mr. Kilgore. You're burning with rope fever.

Kilgore: You're a fool, Kimberley.

Sheriff: We ain't arging that. I'm a peace officer and this badge says nobody, white or Indian, gets strung up unless the proper Judge and jury says to.

Sheriff Kimberley played by John Pickard and Reece Kilgore played by Lyle Bettger: Stuart Heisler's *The Lone Ranger* (Warner Bros., 1956).

2181

Burke: Sid, did you bring your rope?

Sid: Yeah, if I'm going to hang I want to be comfortable.

Devereaux Burke played by Clark Gable and Sid Yoakum played by Trevor Bardette: Vincent Sherman's *Lone Star* (MGM, 1952).

2182

Roy: Where is he going?

Gus: To pick out a tree to hang you from, son.

Jake: Gus …

Gus: You know how it works, Jake. You ride with an outlaw, you die with an outlaw. I'm sorry you crossed the line.

Roy Suggs played by Jerry Biggs, Gus McCrae played by Robert Duvall, and Jake Spoon played by Robert Urich: Simon Wincer's *Lonesome Dove* (TVW, 1989).

2183

Gus: I'm sorry. It's just that I got to do this, Jake. I wish it had fallen to somebody else.

Jake: Well, hell boys, I damn sight rather be hung by my friends than by a bunch of strangers.

Gus McCrae played by Robert Duvall and Jake Spoon played by Robert Urich: Simon Wincer's *Lonesome Dove* (TVW, 1989).

2184

Gus: I'll say this for you, son. You're the kind of man that's a pleasure to hang!

Gus McCrae played by Robert Duvall: Simon Wincer's *Lonesome Dove* (TVW, 1989).

2185

Rosie: What's all the noise out there?

Big Ed: Is this Saturday? Lynch night! Lynch night!

Rosie Velez played by Divine and Big Ed played by Nedra Volz: Paul Bartel's *Lust in the Dust* (Fox Run/New World, 1985).

2186

Chris: Judge Parker said to me once: the men I hanged never killed again …but plenty that I didn't hang, did.

Chris played by Lee Van Cleef: George McGowan's *The Magnificent Seven Ride* (United Artists, 1972).

2187

Wade: Where did you come from?

Stoud: Town.

Wade: Why did you leave?

Stoud: I had a little throat trouble.

Dawes: They were going to hang him!

Jess Wade played by Victor Jory, John Stoud played by Glenn Ford, and Dawes played by Neville Brand: Budd Boetticher's *The Man from the Alamo* (Universal, 1953).

2188

Jeff: Well, I guess I got to thank you again.

Dempsey: For what?

Jeff: Well, you kept me from getting hung.

Dempsey: You can get hung any day you want.

Jeff Jimson played by William Campbell and Dempsey Rae played by Kirk Douglas: King Vidor's *Man Without a Star* (Universal, 1955).

2189

Jane: We had a famous painter out here last year …did natural scenes. That man must have painted ten square miles of canvas …and not one human face! And I wish he could have been here to paint that boy, Sandy, hanging up there so decoratively against the mountains. Because his pink tongue and his white face would have just set off the green of Montana splendidly. I mean, it would have made the damnedest bank calendar you ever saw!

Jane Braxton played by Kathleen Lloyd:

Advertisement for King Vidor's *Man Without a Star* (Universal, 1955). Drifter Dempsey Rae (Kirk Douglas) tells a saddle pal that "everybody has got a star to follow" but "I never got around to picking one for myself."

Arthur Penn's *The Missouri Breaks* (United Artists, 1976).

2190

Logan: I understand you had to hang someone here.
Braxton: I did that.
Logan: Ah, that's tough. What was this, some kind of a desperado?
Braxton: No, he was a thief …with probably a million good reasons for being on hard times. The main thing is that we put him out of his misery.

Tom Logan played by Jack Nicholson and David Braxton played by John McLiam: Arthur Penn's *The Missouri Breaks* (United Artists, 1976).

2191

Padre: Did you ever see Him [crucifix] before?
Max: Yeah, once. It was on the end of a little silver chain.
Padre: He's the Son of God. He came to earth to teach men love by example.
Max: Well, He must have missed somebody. That looks worse than hanging!

Father Zaccardi played by Raf Vallone and Max Sand/Nevada Smith played by Steve McQueen: Henry Hathaway's *Nevada Smith* (Paramount, 1966).

2192

John Henry: If a man don't know the ropes in this business, he's liable to wind up with one around his neck.

John Henry Lee played by Willie Nelson: Burt Kennedy's *Once Upon a Texas Train* (TVW, 1988).

2193

Rio: You're dying to get me hung, aren't you?
Sheriff: No, kid. You've been trying to get yourself hung for the past ten years, and this time I think you're going to make it.

Rio played by Marlon Brando and Sheriff Dad Longsworth played by Karl Malden: Marlon Brando's *One-Eyed Jacks* (Paramount, 1961).

2194

Rio: You're forgetting one thing, Lon.
Lon: Yeah, what's that?
Rio: I ain't hung yet.
Lon: Yeah, but you will be, brother. You ain't getting no older than tomorrow.

Rio played by Marlon Brando and Lon, the Deputy, played by Slim Pickens: Marlon Brando's *One-Eyed Jacks* (Paramount, 1961).

2195

Jessie: You're sick. And the only cure for that is hanging.

Jessie Lorraine played by Adele Jergens: Fred F. Sears' *Overland Pacific* (United Artists, 1954).

2196

Martin: Well, we must be pretty important or else awfully dangerous.
Greer: It ain't that you're so dangerous. It's just that most of the men ain't never seen a real triple hanging.

Donald Martin played by Dana Andrews and Ma

(Jenny) Grier played by Jane Darwell: William Wellman's *The Ox-Bow Incident* (20th Century–Fox, 1943).

2197

Ollinger: I'm going to tell you one last thing personal, Kid. It's going to be a loose rope and a long drop.

Deputy Bob Ollinger played by R.G. Armstrong and Billy the Kid played by Kris Kristofferson: Sam Peckinpah's *Pat Garrett and Billy the Kid* (MGM, 1973).

2198

Calico: I wish I was in Sonora with a swell gal I know.
Whit: Why? You scared of hanging?
Calico: No, but it'll sure keep me from seeing that gal in Sonora!

Calico played by Paul Fix and Whit Lacey played by Forrest Tucker: Jospeh Kane's *The Plunderers* (Republic, 1948).

2199

Strawhorn: You know what I regret the most is killing that sheriff out there in the street. Because, mister, that should have been you.
Marshal: I don't usually attend hangings. They make me sick to my stomach. But in your case, I might make an exception.

Jack Strawhorn played by Bruce Dern and Marshal Howard Nightingale played by Kirk Douglas: Kirk Douglas' *Posse* (Paramount, 1975).

2200

Blacksmith: Hey, you're in luck! You can look right out your window there and see that fella being hanged. The righteous shall rejoice when he seest a vengeance! Psalms 58, verse 10.
Bracket: Yeah, well, maybe we're not gonna be all that righteous.

The Blacksmith was uncredited and Hank Bracket played by Rod Taylor: Douglas Heyes' *Powderkeg* (TVW, 1971).

2201

Quentin: This isn't right, Tank. It just isn't right, damn it! You just can't let this happen.
Tank: The hell I can't. They got a dozen deputies standing around here saying it can happen. Well, maybe I didn't bushwhack that fellow. But, then, maybe I did. It don't make no difference. I've done enough in life to hang …at least once. Shad, let's get on with the proceedings. Don't I get to say some last words.
Shad: Heck, Tank, I didn't know you wanted any.
Tank: Oh, I've changed, Shad. When I had to give up women and guns, I turned to drink and I've become sort of a man of letters. Now this might seem a little flowery to you, but I wrote it myself and I want it to be my epitaph. All right?

Now that my soul seeks rains and rest
Beyond that Great Divide

They planted me here in this lonely stretch
That's sunny, free, and wide.
Let the cattle rub my tombstone down
And coyotes mourn my kin.
Let the horses paw and tromp this mound
But pard …don't fence me in!

Quentin Baudine played by Tim Matheson, Tank Logan played by Brian Keith, and Shadrack Peltzer played by Cameron Mitchell: Lee H. Katzin's *The Quest* (TVW, 1976).

2202

Teeler: Now you can get your Bible and read over us after you shoot us.
Dunson: I'm going to hang you!

Teeler Yacy played by Paul Fix and Tom Dunson played by John Wayne: Howard Hawks' *Red River* (United Artists, 1948).

2203

Dryden: A tough man's neck doesn't take any longer to break than a coward's.

Marcus Dryden played by Robert Foxsworth: E.W. Swackhamer's *The Return of Desperado* (TVW, 1988).

2204

Josey: They're going to hang Tenspot in the morning.
Paco: Why in the morning?
Josey: Well, I've seen a few hangings. And they always hang 'em in the morning. I think they got it figured out. I've been doing some thinking on it. You see, in the morning time, every thing is fresh, kind of being born, and everything comes to life. It just hurts more getting hanged in the morning. It's lonesome. You hang some poor boy in the evening time, now, and the day is dying, and everything goes to sleep. And it becomes a comfort to him.

Paco played by Paco Vela and Josey Wales played by Michael Parks who also directed *The Return of Josey Wales* (Multi-Tacar/Reel Movies International, 1987).

2205

Whitey: I can't sleep …too much on my mind.
Deputy: That figures. They can only hang you once.
Whitey: But once can be awful permanent.

Whitey Kincade played by Dan Duryea and Deputy Clay O'Mara played by Audie Murphy: Jesse Hibbs' *Ride Clear of Diablo* (Universal, 1954).

2206

Sheriff: We're sorry about this, ma'am.
Catherine: I hope you hang them!
Sheriff: Don't worry. They've seen their last sunrise.

Sheriff Quint Mapes played by Brandon Carroll and Catherine played by Katherine Squire: Monte Hellman's *Ride in the Whirlwind* (Jack H. Harris/Proteus Films, 1966).

2207

Lassiter: Well now, I didn't know they could hang you for trading with Apaches.
Rodriguez: Oh, no, no! They say it was for fighting. And that is unjust. This soldier

had a gun and I had only a knife. That's all.

Lassiter: And the soldier had a wife?

Rodriguez: Oh, amigo, such a wife! But I have always been unlucky: locked up here, I cannot even console the poor widow.

James Lassiter played by Richard Boone and Juan Rodriguez played by Tony Franciosa: Gordon Douglas' *Rio Conchos* (20th Century–Fox, 1964).

2208

Leech: They'll be using a brand new rope for your big send-off …a big knot behind your neck. If they do it right, you won't feel a thing. If they do it wrong, you can squirm awhile.

Roscoe: Leech, there ain't a dime worth of difference between you and me.

Leech: There's a big difference, Roscoe. You're in there [jail] …and I'm out here!

Quinton Leech played by Kenny Rogers and Roscoe was uncredited: Rod Hardy's *Rio Diablo* (TVW, 1993).

2209

Stokes: It looks like they're going to have a necktie party in town.

Banning: No?

Stokes: Yeah, the people around here are getting the lynchin' fever mighty bad.

Stokes played by Glenn Strange and Banning played by Edward Pauley: Joseph Kane's *Romance on the Range* (Republic, 1942).

2210

Flood: There's still time to buy you a last drink.

Dolan: Only minutes ahead of a rope makes swallowing too tough.

Alex Flood played by Dean Martin and Dolan played by George Peppard: Arnold Laven's *Rough Night in Jericho* (Universal, 1967).

2211

Morgan: My partner out there, did he get it quick? I seen a fellow dangle once for twenty minutes. He flopped around like a fish out of water.

Morgan played by Ernest Borgnine: Nicholas Ray's *Run for Cover* (Paramount, 1955).

2212

Mrs. O'Meara: There's no hiding place for what ails you, Son. We're all under one flag now.

O'Meara: I want to tell you something, Mother. I'll hang. I'll hang before I'll recognize that flag.

Mrs. O'Meara: Maybe a broken neck is the best answer for what ails ya?

O'Meara: Maybe, Mama. Maybe.

Mrs. O'Meara played by Olive Carey and O'Meara played by Rod Steiger: Samuel Fuller's *Run of the Arrow* (RKO, 1957).

2213

Bryant: You know, we ought to give up this racket though. It's going to lead us both to a rope necktie one of these days.

John Bryant played by John Wayne: Armand Schaefer's *Sagebrush Trail* (Lone Star/Monogram, 1933).

2214

Brown: I am now quite certain that I am worth inconceivably more to hang than for any other purpose.

John Brown played by Raymond Massey: Charles Marquis Warren's *Seven Angry Men* (Allied Artists, 1955).

Abolitionist John Brown (Raymond Massey) and his six sons: Frederick (John Smith), Jason (James Best), Oliver (Larry Pennell), Owen (Jeffrey Hunter), John Jr. (Dennis Weaver), and Salmon (Guy Williams). Also present: Green (James Edwards), Thompson (James Anderson), and Wilson (John Pickard) in *Seven Angry Men* (Allied Artists, 1955).

2215

Flood: You know, if I had to face life without cigars, whiskey, women, steak and cards, I'd much rather they take me out and string me up.

Jim Flood played by Barry Sullivan: Harry Keller's *Seven Ways from Sundown* (Universal, 1960).

2216

Quince: You really wouldn't want to see two innocent men hung would you, Miss?

Prudy: Better than not seeing anybody hung at all!

Quince Drew played by Larry Hagman and Prudy Jenkins played by Blythe Danner: Burt Kennedy's *Sidekicks* (TVW, 1974).

2217

Sheriff: While you two are waiting to be hung, I'll expect you to conduct yourself like gentlemen!

The Sheriff played by Harry Morgan: Burt Kennedy's *Sidekicks* (TVW, 1974).

2218

Coulter: I've come so close to hanging so many times, you'd think I get used to it.

Sam Coulter played by Houseley Stevenson: Alfred E. Green's *Sierra* (Universal, 1950).

2219

Paden: I hate to see any man swing. It's bad luck.

Paden played by Kevin Kline: Lawrence Kasdan's *Silverado* (Columbia, 1985).

2220

Huckaby: I never thought you all would want to see old Smoky the way he is now, ma'am. He looks pretty bad …him being hung and all.

Stapp Hunkaby played by Bill Foster and Smoky Harjo played by Henry Kingi: Joseph Kane's *Smoke in the Wind* (Frontier Productions, 1975).

2221

Trinity: Would you like the cork?

Bambino: Cork?

Sheriff: What cork?

Bambino: Yeah, what cork?

Trinity: Well, sometimes fear gets the better of a man. I mean, he soils himself. But I maintain that all men who are about to meet their Maker have a right to self-respect. That's why I heartily suggest the cork.

Sheriff: I'm all for the cork! The undertaker will be grateful.

Trinity, pretending to be the Hangman, played by Heath Kizzier, Bambino played by Keith Neubert, and the Sheriff played by Ronald Nitschke: E.B. Clucher's *Sons of Trinity* (Triboro Entertainment, 1996).

2222

Townsman: Orval, if you ask me, this is just a waste of time and money. In the old days, we didn't build no scaffold for no hanging.

Orval: These ain't the old days. Since Bill Jorden has been sheriff, everything has got to be done legal …even hanging.

Townsman: Well, a good tree was good enough for my pappy, and I reckon it's good enough for me.

The Townsman was uncredited, Orval Jones played by James Gleason, and Sheriff Bill Jorden played by John Agar: Charles Haas' *Star in the Dust* (Universal, 1956).

2223

Sheriff: I never saw the like. Every time I want to hang a fellow, there ain't no tree.

Deputy: There's a big oak about a mile back, sheriff.

Ramsey: Hey, you can't do that without a trial!

Sheriff: As sheriff and justice of the peace, I hereby find you guilty and sentence you to be hanged. Get on your horse!

The Sheriff played by Don Beddoe, the Deputy played by Ralph Peters, and Tod Ramsey played by Glenn Ford: George Marshall's *Texas* (Columbia, 1941).

2224

Sheriff: Do you think that Wickett fella was the first one to be hanged in El Crossing? Or that he'll be the last one? Runaway slaves, squatters, Yankee carpetbaggers …Cordeen is waiting for them all. And he's not running out of rope!

The Sheriff played by Dino Desmond, Fred Wickett played by Claudio Gora, and Temple Cordeen played by Joseph Cotten: Albert Band's *The Tramplers* (Embassy Picture Release, 1965).

2225

Miller: What's hanging fever, Mr. McNulty?

McNulty: It's hanging men, even if they are thieves, without trial and jury. And it's a sickness. A fella could die of it.

Steve Miller played by Don Dubbins and McNulty played by Stephen McNally: Robert Wise's *Tribute to a Bad Man* (MGM, 1956).

2226

Jo: You've become sick. You got hanging fever.

Rudock: Where did you hear about hanging fever?

Jo: I was here my first week, not so long ago, when you caught the thief and hanged him.

Rudock: He stole my horse!

Jo: And what did the hanging steal from you? He died, and you died a little too. You're not the law!

Rudock: I'm the only law I got!

Jocasta "Jo" Constantine played by Irene Papas and Jeremy Rudock played by James Cagney: Robert Wise's *Tribute to a Bad Man* (MGM, 1956).

2227

Mother: I declare, I've never seen such unloving kin brothers the likes of you two. The only family tie you ever felt was the hangman's noose.

The Mother played by Jessica Dublin: E.B. Clucher's (Enzo Barboni) *Trinity Is Still My Name* (West Film/Avco Embassy, 1971).

2228

Photographer: Hi! Remember me? I know this isn't a real good time for you right now, but I was just wondering …if you could look toward the camera when the noose tightens. It'll make a fitting back cover to my book …which you already have the front. Ah, you see if you look into the lens …or into the eyes of the reader if you will …well, then I can catch the last moment of your miserable and useless life.

The Photographer played by John David Caffield: Terence Hill's *The Troublemakers* (Rialto Film, 1994).

2229

Marshal: Now wait a minute! Wait a minute! I'm here to tell you you're getting amnesty.

Bragg: Amnesty? I stand on my constitutional right for a straight hanging!

The Marshal played by Minor Watson and Skinner Bill Bragg played by Wallace Beery: Richard Thorpe's *20 Mule Team* (MGM, 1940).

2230

Mrs. Taylor: He did what he had to do because it was his duty.

Molly: His duty? To lynch a man?

Mrs. Taylor: There's no likeness between this and lynching. When you lynch a man, you take him out of jail, out of the rightful hands of the law. Here, we have no policemen, no courts, and no jails. So we have to do things in our own way.

Mrs. Taylor played by Fay Bainter and Molly Wood played by Barbara Britton: Stuart Gilmore's *The Virginian* (Paramount, 1946).

2231

Marshal: I'm afraid we're going to have to hang you, son.

Dusty: What are you afraid about? I'm the one who's going to be hung!

The Marshal played by Donald Barry and Dusty played by Bob Denver: Jack Arnold, Oscar Rudolph, Bruce Bilson, and Earl Bellamy's *The Wackiest Wagon Train in the West* (Topar Films, 1976).

2232

[Two cowboys in the saloon]

1st Cowboy: How was the hanging?

2nd Cowboy: Well, his neck didn't hardly stretch a foot!

The two cowboys were uncredited: William Wyler's *The Westerner* (United Artists, 1940).

2233

Judge Bean: Now you men get some rope and string him up.

Chickenfoot: String him up? Well …he's dead already!

Judge Bean: We hang horse thieves, don't we? String him up!

Judge Roy Bean played by Walter Brennan and Chickenfoot played by Paul Hurst: William Wyler's *The Westerner* (United Artists, 1940).

2234

Deputy: The young kid stole a horse. Somebody said the Chinaman looked the wrong way at a white woman. And the Injun was in town trading when we got the word about Custer. We're going to hang 'em all Saturday!

The Deputy was uncredited: Walter Hill's *Wild Bill* (MGM/United Artists, 1995).

2235

Tower: Where have you been?

Morrell: Did you ever have a bad dose of lead poisoning? No, of course not! Well, it takes a lot of curing.

Tower: Well, you've taken enough time to recover from a severe case of hanging.

Nicholas Tower played by John Miljan and Morrell played by Hal Taliaferro/Wally Wales: Joseph Kane's *Young Bill Hickok* (Republic, 1940).

2236

Charley: Goddamnit, Billy! Have you ever seen a man hanged? His face turns flat purple and his eyes come upon him.

Billy: Yeah, I seen Red Smitty hang. I seen his head come clean off. It was a hell of a sight.

Doc: Billy, I don't think Charley wants to hear about Red Smitty. I think what he would like to hear is that we're not gonna hang.

Charley: You mess your trousers, they say. Gals watching and everything.

Billy: Well, if we get caught, Charley, we're going to hang. But there's many a slip betwixt the cup and the lip.

Charley Bowdre played by Casey Siemaszko, William H. "Billy" Bonney played by Emilio Estevez, and Josiah "Doc" Scurlock played by Kiefer Sutherland: Christopher Cain's *Young Guns* (20th Century–Fox, 1988).

2237

Jeff: There's nothing like being hung to reform a man.

Jeff Shelby played by Jody McCrea: Maury Dexter's *Young Guns of Texas* (20th Century–Fox, 1963).

2238

Chavez: When the neck is broken, there is only a sharp pain …fast. And then if the other place accepts you, the Spirit Horse comes and takes you to the other side. So don't worry too much. When you die you're going to see the Spirit Horse. She'll come for you, my friend.

Doc: Great! Let me tell you something, Chavez. I don't really want to catch the Spirit Horse. I don't even want to see the other side. And I sure as hell don't want to have my neck broke to a sharp quick pain. The only thing I really want to do is get the hell out of here!

Chavez Y. Chavez played by Lou Diamond Phillips and Doc Scurlock played by Kiefer Sutherland: Geoff Murphy's *Young Guns II* (20th Century–Fox, 1990).

Holdups

See also Bad Guys; Chase; Outlaws, Cattle Rustlers and Horse Thieves

2239

Jet: You've been out looking for the man who stuck up the train?

Bravo: I figure I got more trail dust than he did dollars.

Jet Younger played by Jack Lambert and Sheriff Bravo Trimble played by Edgar Buchanan: Edwin Marin's *Abilene Town* (United Artists, 1946).

2240

Cacopoulos: So don't worry. I just need a small amount. Just enough for the bare necessities.

[*looks at the money*]

Well, no. Money corrupts men, it softens him. So to keep you young and pure, I think I'll take everything.

Cacopoulos played by Eli Wallach: Giuseppe Colizzi's *Ace High* (Paramount, 1967).

2241

Holly: Now drop your pants and put your hands on your head!

Holly Smith played by Heather Rattray: Stewart Raffill's *Across the Great Divide* (Pacific International, 1976).

2242

Sam: I is the robber and you is the robbee!

Sam Spade played by Richard Pryor: Fred Williamson's *Adios Amigo* (Atlas, 1975).

2243

Bandit: I think I kill both of ya!

Sam: Now wait a minute! I said I didn't have the money here. I didn't say I didn't know where it was.

Bandit: Good! Now we go somewhere!

Sam: Yeah, we go somewhere! I get on my horse, I go get the money and come back!

Bandit: You go? Come back? Kill him!

Sam: Hold it! No, no! Look, I think you misunderstand my plan! See, I go …I leave my amigo here. If I don't come back, you kill him!

Ben: Hey, now wait a minute!

Bandit: You keep quiet!

Ben: I don't like that idea. I go get the money …you kill him!

The Bandit was uncredited, Sam Spade played by Richard Pryor, and Ben played by Fred Williamson who also directed *Adios Amigo* (Atlas, 1975).

2244

Lon: You fellas bound for Woodward?

Al: Yeah. We thought maybe you could tell us something about the town.

Lon: You sure stopped the right party, son. I know all about Woodward. It's a riproaring town if there ever was one. Growing like a weed and wide open. Oh, but the prices there. Costs you a fortune for anything you buy. So I hope you boys brought plenty of money along with ya.

Frank: Oh, we brought enough.

Lon: Well in that case just step right down off them horses and hit the ground with your hands in the air!

Lon Tuttle played by Guinn "Big Boy" Williams, Al Jennings played by Dan Duryea, and Frank Jennings played by Dick Foran: Ray Nazarro's *Al Jennings of Oklahoma* (Columbia, 1951).

2245

Stagecoach Guard: If this is a holdup, you're dead.

Slater: If I did it this way, I'd deserve to be.

The Stagecoach Guard was uncredited and Jim Slater played by Richard Widmark: John Sturges's *Backlash* (Universal, 1956).

2246

Hobbs: You go ahead and eat your beans, Joe. Me and the boys can take 'em easy. There's only two.

Big Joe: My boy, if it was a blind woman in a wheelchair, I'd still give her the odds.

Hobbs played by Geoffrey Lewis and Big Joe played by David Huddleston: Robert Benton's *Bad Company* (Paramount, 1972).

2247

Alicia: What business are you in, Mr. King?

King: Ah …banking. I transfer funds from, ah, one place to another.

Alicia played by Gina Lollobrigida and King played by Lee Van Cleef: Gene Martin's *Bad Man's River* (Scotia International, 1971).

2248

Orozco: I would like to make you a deal, Mr. King.

King: I already got a deal.

Orozco: Look, I am a bandit, and you rob banks. Right?

King: Get to the point.

Orozco: So we both want the same thing: other people's money. Right? So you and I are on the same side. We are amigos!

Orozco played by Luis Rivera and King played by Lee Van Cleef: Gene Martin's *Bad Man's River* (Scotia International, 1971).

2249

Van Hock: How about being an outside partner?

McBain: No, I wouldn't make a partnership with God.

Peter Van Hock played by Alan Ladd and John McBain played by Ernest Borgnine: Delmer Daves' *The Badlanders* (MGM, 1958).

2250

Coyote: Where are you headed for next, Bob?

Bob: Two banks.

Coyote: Double-header, huh?

Jim Badger (alias The Coyote Kid), played by George "Gabby" Hayes and Bob Dalton played by Steve Brodie: Tim Whelan's *Badman's Territory* (RKO, 1946).

2251

Dee: You robbed a bank? You, Mace?

Mace: Well, Dee, the bank was there …and I was there …and there wasn't much of anybody else there. And it just seemed like the thing to do.

Dee Bishop played by Dean Martin and Mace Bishop played by James Stewart: Andrew McLaglen's *Bandolero!* (20th Century–Fox, 1968).

2252

Marquette: You know, the only thing that kept all our men together was a need for violence and money. This morning they got their share of the violence. Now all they want is their share of the money …and to split up.

Marquette played by Kerwin Mathews: Gordon Douglas' *Barquero* (United Artists, 1970).

2253

Jasper: Stealin' what's yours ain't stealin'.

Jasper Trench played by Olin Howlin: Irving Cummings' *Belle Starr* (20th Century–Fox, 1941).

2254

Stage Driver: You're Jeff Clanton. I've seen your picture!

Doc: Now, what could you do with $5,000 in a cemetery?

Jeff Clanton played by Robert Ryan and Doc Butcher played by Walter Brennan: William D. Russell's *Best of the Badmen* (RKO, 1951).

2255

Marshal: Watching out for the old man, huh, breed? Well, he's not out there. He's down in Mexico leaning up against some cantina bar, puking up all that money you and him and your dead partner stole. Yeah, all that money. $420.00. You had to kill somebody at that. I don't like no kind of law breaker, breed. But the kind I hate worse is the cheap one. And cheaper than you and your friend, they just don't come!

Marshal Henry Gifford played by Jack Warden and the breed, Billy, played by Desi Arnaz, Jr.: Ted Kotcheff's *Billy Two Hats* (United Artists, 1973).

2256

Boles: Lola, I've been working on something for two years. Something that will make me the biggest man in this part of the country. I'm within an inch of doing it now. You wouldn't want me to quit at this point.

Lola: The biggest man in the cemetery is still pretty small.

Charles E. Boles, alias Black Bart, played by Dan Duryea and Lola Montez played by Yvonne De Carlo: George Sherman's *Black Bart* (Universal, 1948).

2257

Clark: I've got an idea that's bigger than anything you've ever heard. It'll take time …and it'll take brains.

Boles: I got plenty of time.

Clark played by John McIntire and Charles E. Boles, alias Black Bart, played by Dan Duryea: George Sherman's *Black Bart* (Universal, 1948).

2258

Brady: Are we splitting up?

Boles: That's the general idea.

Lance: Why?

Boles: You're bad news, Lance. You're not interested enough in growing old.

Lance: You have to take a few chances in this line of work.

Boles: Not as many as I've been taking with you.

Jersey Brady played by Percy Kilbride, Charles E. Boles, alias Black Bart, played by Dan Duryea, and Lance Hardeen played by Jeffrey Lynn: George Sherman's *Black Bart* (Universal, 1948).

2259

Bass: You make your deposit, Maverick, and I'll make my withdrawal.

Ramsey Bass played by Bill McKinney and Bret Maverick played by James Garner: Stuart Margolin's *Bret Maverick: The Lazy Ace* (TVW, 1981).

2260

Sundance: You know, I've been thinking…

Butch: That could be dangerous!

The Sundance Kid played by William Karr and Butch Cassidy played by Tom Berenger: Richard Lester's *Butch and Sundance: The Early Days* (20th Century–Fox, 1979).

2261

Butch: If he'd just pay me what he's spending to make me stop robbing him, I'd stop robbing him!

Butch Cassidy played by Paul Newman: George Roy Hill's *Butch Cassidy and the Sundance Kid* (20th Century–Fox, 1969).

2262

Garris: Will you two beginners cut it out!

Butch: Well, we're just trying to spot an ambush, Mr. Garris.

Garris: Morons! I've got morons on my team! Nobody is going to rob us going down the mountain! We have got no money going down the mountain! When we have got the money, on the way back up, then you can sweat!

Percy Garris played by Strother Martin and Butch Cassidy played by Paul Newman: George Roy Hill's *Butch Cassidy and the Sundance Kid* (20th Century–Fox, 1969).

2263

Joel: Well, we could've had our ranch out of that [strong] box.

Bass: No, we couldn't, Joel. The way we did it, even if this thing comes out, people will know that we took back only what he stole from us. They'll be on our side.

Dakota: Sure, we wouldn't want 'em to think we robbed this stage dishonestly.

Joel Collins played by Lloyd Bridges, Sam Bass played by Howard Duff, and Dakota played by Houseley Stevenson: George Sherman's *Calamity Jane and Sam Bass* (Universal, 1949).

2264

Captain: I don't suppose you remember the combination.

Griffin: I never had a head for figures.

Captain Apache played by Lee Van Cleef and Griffin played by Stuart Whitman: Alexander Singer's *Captain Apache* (Scotia International, 1971).

2265

Holly: You just got a new lease on life, gents, so don't break it by moving!

Holly Dalton played by Merry Anders: Reginald LeBorg's *The Dalton Girls* (United Artists, 1957).

2266

Gabby: Let me tell you something, young fella. Never have nothing to do with no banks. If you got any money to protect, get yourself a good dog …like Whiskers here. It'd be a whole lot safer with him.

Gabby Whittaker played by George "Gabby" Hayes: Joseph Kane's *Days of Jesse James* (Republic, 1939).

2267

Lewis: I cannot in good conscience allow myself to be party to this deception.

Jack: How much?

Lewis: I beg your pardon?

Jack: How much is your conscience going to cost me?

Palmer Lewis played by Malcolm Stewart and Jack Fleetwood played by John Glover: Brad Turner's "Fool's Gold" episode to the series premiere, *Dead Man's Gun* (Showtime, 1997).

2268

Nitro: Come on, let's go!

Cheyenne: Well, why? What's the hurry? We're not in any hurry.

Nitro: Oh yes we are. I just robbed a bank!

Nitro Rankin played by Guinn "Big Boy" Williams and Cheyenne Rogers played by Glenn Ford: Charles Vidor's *The Desperadoes* (Columbia, 1943).

2269

Sarah: So what do you need money so bad for? I thought you said you was a farmer?

Jack: Well, I am. Or I'm going to be.

Sarah: In the meantime, you just rob people, right?

Jack: Sometimes you got to do some wrong to do some good. You know what I mean?

Sarah O'Rourke played by Linda Fiorentino and Jack Cooper played by Craig Sheffer: P.J. Pesce's *The Desperate Trail* (Turner Home Entertainment, 1995).

2270

Dingus: Now we go to Mexico.

Anna: Mexico?

Dingus: When you steal money, that's where you go. That's the code of the west.

Dingus Magee played by Frank Sinatra and Anna played by Michele Carey: Burt Kennedy's *Dirty Dingus Magee* (MGM, 1970).

2271

Hardin: Empty your pockets!

Dingus: Yes sir, Mr. Hardin.

Hardin: You know my name, huh?

Dingus: Yes sir. There ain't a fence post or tree stump anywhere in these parts that don't have a John Wesley Hardin picture on it.

Hardin: Is that a fact?

Dingus: Yes, sir.

Hardin: Ain't I seen a poster on you somewhere?

Dingus: Yes, sir. The name's Magee. Dingus Magee.

Hardin: Oh, that ten dollar outlaw.

Dingus: None but.

Hardin: Ha! Ha! Ha! Hell, if I had known that, I never would have held you up. But I got to steal something from you. Never stop a man for robbing unless you at least take something. That's the code of the west.

John Wesley Hardin played by Jack Elam and Dingus Magee played by Frank Sinatra: Burt Kennedy's *Dirty Dingus Magee* (MGM, 1970).

2272

Belle: Get that filthy thing off my carpet!

Hoke: I got good news for you, Belle. This here is the chest from the stagecoach robbery. And Dingus Magee estimates there may be as much as a million dollars in gold and silver pieces inside.

Belle: Well, the money ain't rightly ours, is it?

Hoke: Finders keepers. That's the code of the west, ain't it?

Belle: Give me that crowbar!

Belle played by Anna Jackson and Hoke played by George Kennedy: Burt Kennedy's *Dirty Dingus Magee* (MGM, 1970).

2273

Arkansas: Come on, come on. Let's go!

Doolin: What's the hurry? We're taking a rest, remember?

Arkansas: I'm telling you we got to get out of here.

Doolin: What's all the rush?

Arkansas: I just robbed a bank!

Little Bill: Alone?

Arkansas: Well, there was only one bank!

Arkansas played by Charles Kemper, Bill Doolin played by Randolph Scott, and Little Bill played by Noah Beery, Jr.: Gordon Douglas' *The Doolins of Oklahoma* (Columbia, 1949).

2274

Lippert: He wants a horse and an empty street.

Eugene Lippert played by Graham McPherson: Steven H. Stern's *Draw!* (TVW, 1984).

2275

Malloy: I think we're safe.

Duchess: You thought taking the money was gonna be a cinch too.

Malloy: Taking the money was a cinch. It's keeping it that's getting to be a pain in the ass!

Charlie Malloy played by George Segal and Amanda Quaid, alias "Duchess" played by Goldie Hawn: Melvin Frank's *The Duchess and the Dirtwater Fox* (20th Century–Fox, 1976).

2276

Malloy: You know something? A man has got to know what he wants in life. Ain't that right, Duchess?

Duchess: Sure, Charlie.

Malloy: And a man has to fight for what he wants. Ain't that right?

Duchess: Sure, Charlie.

Malloy: That why I'm going back and get my money.

Duchess: What!

Malloy: I stole it fair and square and nobody is going to take it away from me!

Charlie Malloy played by George Segal and Amanda Quaid, alias "Duchess," played by Goldie Hawn: Melvin Frank's *The Duchess and the Dirtwater Fox* (20th Century–Fox, 1976).

2277

Sam: But I ain't got nothing left!

Ebenezer: That's a double negative, Mr. Benson. Shame on you.

Sam: Huh?

Sam Benson played by Rick Schroder and Ebenezer Scrooge played by Jack Palance: Ken Jubenvill's *Ebenezer* (TVW, 1997).

2278

Luke: You can get killed and just as dead going after a hundred as a million [dollars].

Luke played by Jim Brown: John Guillermin's *El Condor* (NGP, 1970).

2279

Teacher: It was pretty clear why they were there. They had an appointment with the bank, and it wasn't to make a deposit.

Teacher Billy Ray Smith played by Anthony Edwards: Peter Markle's *El Diablo* (HBO Pictures, 1990).

2280

Shorty: Don't move, gents! Stand where you are! Drop that rifle, Waller. I got a bead on your back. And you, Lunsford, I got a lead pill all labeled for you!

Shorty played by Bob Steele: Edwin Marin's *Fort Worth* (Warner Bros., 1951).

2281

Cully: We may be taking the Cholla Bank tomorrow.

Bronco: It's been tried three times in the past five years. They got a big graveyard in Cholla. About the biggest this side of Gallop.

Yaqui: We're all gonna land in one sooner or later. Why you worry?

Bronco: I just don't want to get shoved!

Ray Cully played by Rory Calhoun, Bronco played by George Nader, and Yaqui played by Jay Silverheels: Richard Carlson's *Four Guns to the Border* (Universal, 1954).

2282

Tommy: All right now, you all put your hands on top of your heads. Good! That's real good! Now, we're all gonna play like we're in church. You got something for the collection, sir?

Tommy played by Harrison Ford: Robert Aldrich's *The Frisco Kid* (Warner Bros., 1979).

2283

Burgundy: I wouldn't give you the sweat off my horse's butt!

Burgundy Jones played by Reba McEntire: Dick Lowry's *The Gambler Returns: The Luck of the Draw* (TVW, 1991).

2284

Mayor: Wait, wait, wait! Wait a minute, Jim Boy! Now calm down! Holdup?

Posse? We haven't used those words in …in years!

Flagg: Well, in case you're forgotten, Mayor, they mean trouble. Which is exactly what we're going to have if we don't stop jawing and start moving!

Mayor Randolph Wilker played by Martin Balsam and Marshal Jim Flagg played by Robert Mitchum: Burt Kennedy's *The Good Guys and the Bad Guys* (Warner Bros., 1969).

2285

Mayor: Wait a minute now, Jim Boy! Maybe Mr. McKay here has something constructive to contribute.

McKay: There's only one plan and it's as plain as the nose on your face. You can't stop them from getting the money once the train gets into town. And since they are coming to the telegraph, you can't stop the train from coming into town. What you got to do is stop the train from stopping in town.

Mayor: Stop the train from …

Flagg: The train just steams right on through.

McKay: The fellas down at the depot would be looking mighty foolish.

Mayor: But the train will stop. It always does!

Flagg: Not if someone boards it and tells them not to.

Mayor: Oh, a tremendous idea! That is bold, that is inventive! It is audacious! It is worthy of your reputation, Mr. McKay. I am impressed! Well, that's the plan, Jim Boy. We ride out of town, board the train, and just roar right on through.

Flagg: What do you mean, we?

Mayor: Well, of course I'm coming. You don't think I'd let an opportunity like this slip by, do you? I mean, have you any idea what this could do for my career? Oh, I can see it now. Criss-crossing the country, delivering lectures on law and order. The need for positive action, civic responsibility. Yes, I could write a book. I could write a weekly column, syndicated all over the country …the world! You know, I could be Governor. Maybe even President! President Randolph Wilker. Oh boy, there would be no stopping me!

McKay: Oh, Mr. President.

Mayor: Yes!

McKay: I should mention something kind of important.

Mayor: Please, go ahead.

McKay: If you're going to pull this off, you're going to have to board a train at a dead run. And if you ain't careful …

Mayor: Dead run? That means while it's moving?

Flagg: While it's moving.

McKay: And if you ain't careful, you could wind up like Dusty Boggs.

Mayor: Dusty Boggs?

Flagg: He boarded a train once.

Mayor: Well, what happened to him?

McKay: I don't know. All we found was a grease slick along the cinder bed.

Mayor: You make an excellent point, Mr. McKay. Yes, I should be more prudent, I have a whole town to worry about. If this was for my own safety, there would be no hesitation. But I do have a public trust.

McKay: The country has just lost a President!

Mayor Randolph Wilker played by Martin Balsam, Big John McKay played by George Kennedy, and Jim Flagg played by Robert Kennedy's *The Good Guys and the Bad Guys* (Warner Bros., 1969).

2286

Bill: How do you plan to rob these banks?

Danny: Simple. All I need is four or five guys with guns and guts.

Bill: Well, that sounds simple enough.

Bill Miner played by Richard Farnsworth and Danny Young played by Stephan E. Miller: Phillip Borsos' *The Grey Fox* (United Artists, 1982).

2287

Miner: The identity of Miner's accomplice remains unknown. The train crew describes this man as short, dirty, nervous, and unintelligent.

Shorty: I've never been nervous in my life!

Bill Miner, played by Richard Farnsworth, reading a newspaper article to his sidekick. Shorty played by Wayne Robson: Phillip Borsos' *The Grey Fox* (United Artists, 1982).

2288

Danny: I figured we would do some holdups. That's your line, right?

Miner: No, I just rob stagecoaches.

Danny: Well, have you tried to find one nowadays? Besides, stagecoaches, banks, stores …it's all the same.

Miner: No, it's not the same. The professional always specializes.

Danny: Well, yours is gone …just like a buffalo.

Danny Young played by Stephan E. Miller and Bill Miner played by Richard Farnsworth: Phillip Borsos' *The Grey Fox* (United Artists, 1982).

2289

Chad: But that's blood money!

Jubal: It's payable in gold coin, Chad. They say blood washes off gold, but I know better.

Chad Santee played by Buster Crabbe and Jubal played by Neville Brand: Sidney Salkow's *Gun Brothers* (United Artists, 1956).

2290

Wailer: Well, you don't expect a man to go on a bank raid with an empty gun. We may have to shoot our way out.

Troop: When you keep a rattlesnake around, you always pull its fangs.

Wailer was uncredited and Amos Troop played by De Forest Kelley: Frank McDonald's *Gunfight at Comanche Creek* (Allied Artists, 1964).

2291

Tortilla: Now tell me, how much money you got?

Kettle: None! I told you …none!

Tortilla: Oh amigo, I must shoot you for lying.

Kettle: I'm not lying …I'm not! My pockets are empty. Search!

Salt Pork: Then I'm going to have to shoot you for lying with no money.

Kettle: Will you tell your boys to stop this joke and cut me down out of here?

Kipper: I wish I could, my friend. But we're in somewhat of a dilemma. If you're lying, he has to shoot you. And if you have no money, he has to [shoot you].

Salt Pork: Now what's it going to be?

Tortilla played by Nestor Paiva, Kettle played by Sean McClory, Salt Pork played by Ray Teal, and Kipper played by James Griffith: George Marshall's *The Guns of Fort Petticoat* (Columbia, 1957).

2292

Emmett: You blew up the money, you dummy! You dummy!

Emmett Clemens played by Ernest Borgnine: Burt Kennedy's *Hannie Caulder* (Paramount, 1971).

2293

Rufus: Are you calling me a liar? Emmett, he's calling me a liar!

Emmett: Well, you are!

Rufus: You name one time when I didn't tell the truth!

Emmett: When you said there was no shotgun guard on that stagecoach that we tried to rob. That's when!

Frank: Damn near got us all shot!

Emmett: Yeah!

Rufus: Well, that was a mistake, not a lie! Anyway, I never said that I was perfect. All I have said …

Emmett: Oh, shut the hell up, Rufus! I'm trying to think.

Rufus: With what?

Rufus Clemens played by Strother Martin, Emmett Clemens played by Ernest Borgnine, and Frank Clemens played by Jack Elam: Burt Kennedy's *Hannie Caulder* (Paramount, 1971).

2294

Kitty: Can I help count the money, please?

Jonas: The only thing I'm counting …is miles between here and home and a new beginning.

Kitty played by Maria Martin and Jonas played by Joseph Cotten: Sergio Corbucci's *The Hellbenders* (Embassy Pictures, 1967).

2295

Jonas: You're too greedy, friend, you can't carry all that!

Beggar: You got a point there, señor. What about your coffin? The stuff would fit real snug in there.

Jonas: That sacrilege! You got to respect the dead!

Beggar: I don't even respect the living, friend!

Jonas played by Joseph Cotten and the Beggar played by Al Mulock: Sergio Corbucci's *The Hellbenders* (Embassy Pictures, 1967).

2296

Stacey: Give me that combination, Morg.

Morgan: I wouldn't give you the combination to the gates of hell!

Stacey Bridges played by Geoffrey Lewis and Morgan Allen played by Jack Ging: Clint Eastwood's *High Plains Drifter* (Universal, 1973).

2297

Jessie: What are you doing here?

Braden: Going bad, honey.

Jessie played by Diane Cilento and Frank Braden played by Cameron Mitchell: Martin Ritt's *Hombre* (20th Century–Fox, 1967).

2298

Charlie: Sheriff, Sheriff! Gone, all gone, Sheriff!

Sheriff: What's all gone?

Charlie: Money …money all gone …stolen!

Sheriff: You kept your money in here [box]?

Charlie: Yes!

Sheriff: How much was there?

Charlie: All.

Sheriff: All? All your savings?

Charlie: Sure. When it's safe to go back to China, Sheriff. In back of ironing board …nobody bother. Broke in washing room last night. Just find empty box. Was going to put money in …Sheriff, no money left now. Money for many years.

Sheriff: Well, that's what we got banks for, Charlie.

Charlie: What we got sheriff for?

The Chinese laundry man, Charlie, was uncredited and Sheriff Sam Galt played by Sterling Hayden: Sidney Salkow's *The Iron Sheriff* (United Artists, 1957).

2299

Jesse: Everybody sit quiet and nobody will get hurt!

Jesse James played by Tyrone Power: Henry King's *Jesse James* (20th Century–Fox, 1939).

2300

Bick: Listen to me! We can get that money. It would be just like the old days. We could get it!

A scene from *Jesse James* (20th Century–Fox, 1939) with Frank James (Henry Fonda), Zee (Nancy Kelly), newspaperman Major Rufus Cobb (Henry Hull), and Jesse James (Tyrone Power). Etched on Jesse's tombstone at the end is "Murdered By A Traitor And Coward Whose Name Is Not Worthy To Appear Here."

Mendoza: No, they would catch our ass.

Bick: We can get that money if you would listen to me. I mean it! We can get it! We can get that payroll. Look, I don't know nothing about Jesus, but I know He …He'd would want us to have it. Are you with me on this?

Mendoza & Old Coyote: Amen …amen …amen!

Bick: All we need is guns and horses.

Mendoza & Old Coyote: Amen …amen …amen!

Bickford Wanner, alias Kid Blue, played by Dennis Hopper, Mendoza played by Jay Varela, and Old Coyote played by Jose Torvay: James Frawley's *Kid Blue* (20th Century–Fox, 1973).

2301

Provo: Are you in or out?

Gant: Man, for four thousand in gold, I'd cut my old man in a town square …and let the vultures feed on his carcass!

Zach Provo played by James Coburn and Will Gant played by John Quade: Andrew V. McLaglen's *The Last Hard Men* (20th Century–Fox, 1976).

2302

Bruce: Every time I show my face, that reward takes another jump.

Hawkins: We can't all ride in wearing masks, Bruce. People get suspicious. Somebody has got to go in first and throw 'em off guard.

Bruce: Why does it always have to be me?

Hawkins: What do you got to lose? In another few months, you'll be so famous you can run for President.

Taylor: The only difference is your platform will have a trapdoor in it.

Dan Barton, alias Jack Bruce, played by George Montgomery, Hawkins played by Douglas Kennedy, and Taylor played by Robert Foulk: Paul Landres' *Last of the Badmen* (Allied Artists, 1957).

2303

Bitter Creek: We ain't never robbed a bank before!

Bob Dalton: That's right, Bitter Creek. That's why we ain't going to rob one now. We're going to rob two! In the same town and on the same day!

Emmett Dalton: Great day, that's bigger than Northfield.

Bill Doolin: Yes, and if I remember right, ole Jesse and Cole got shot up pretty good back there.

Emmett Dalton: Don't pay any attention to him, Bob. He's just jealous that he didn't come up with the idea. Where are we going to hit them?

Bob Dalton: Coffeyville.

Bitter Creek played by Matt Clark, Bob Dalton

played by Cliff Potts, Emmett Dalton played by Larry Wilcox, and Bill Doolin played by Bo Hopkins: Dan Curtis' *Last Ride of the Dalton Gang* (TVW, 1979).

2304

Barker: Say, you know I ain't had so much fun since me and Jesse James held up …I mean, ah, since me and General Grant upheld the glory of old Stars & Stripes at Vicksburg.

Bonanza Bill Barker played by Harry Carey: Glenn Tryon's *The Law West of Tombstone* (RKO, 1938).

2305

Kane: I mean, Australia is a colony. You see, so if you rob a bank back there, you're wanted all over the country. But in America, you can rob banks in five different states. You still got another thirty. Cross the border and you run free. No worries. Yeah, democracy is a wonderful thing.

Lightning Jack Kane played by Paul Hogan: Simon Wincer's *Lightning Jack* (Savoy Pictures, 1994).

2306

Younger: Shoot, what's there to know about robbing a bank? You ride into town like thunder and cannonballs, guns blazing, scaring just about every person in sight until they're frozen. Then you ride right into the bank without getting off your horse. You dynamite the safe and ride off with the loot …hooting and hollering the same damn way as you came in.

John Younger played by Kevin Brophy: Walter Hill's *The Long Riders* (United Artists, 1980).

2307

Frank: Don't worry, ladies and gentlemen. We're just taking a permanent loan from the Rock Island payroll.

Frank James played by Stacy Keach: Walter Hill's *The Long Riders* (United Artists, 1980).

2308

Colorado: Say, you have been most kind and we are grateful. We ask no more of your hospitality than the loan of a few horses and mules which we need. And some food for our journey. Also, we will take your wife. Because if we run into trouble with the cavalry, she may come in useful. If we pass this way again, God-willing, I will sell her back to you. That is a true promise.

Colorado played by Omar Sharif: J. Lee Thompson's *MacKenna's Gold* (Columbia, 1969).

2309

Dock: All it takes to make this work is guts. Who's got 'em?

Dock Tobin played by Lee J. Cobb: Anthony Mann's *Man of the West* (United Artists, 1958).

2310

Zorro: And now, señora, that little trinket.

Señora: You'd rob a woman?

Zorro: I can't afford gallantries.

Don Diego Vega/Zorro played by Tyrone Power and Señora Inez Quintero played by Gale Sondergaard: Rouben Mamoulian's *The Mark of Zorro* (20th Century–Fox, 1940).

2311

Zorro: It is not theft to steal from a thief. It's merely irony.

Zorro/Don Diego played by Frank Langella: Don McDougall's *The Mark of Zorro* (TVW, 1974).

2312

Bret: Blowing my head off is not going to make you any richer.

Cowboy: It's sure gonna make me feel better!

Bret Maverick played by Mel Gibson and the Cowboy was uncredited: Richard Donner's *Maverick* (Warner Bros., 1994).

2313

Badger: And as for that tenderfoot Sheriff? Why, he couldn't keep his nose out of a bottle long enough to holdup a dog's tail …much less a stagecoach!

Jeff Badger/The Masked Bandit played by Joseph Calleia: Edward F. Cline's *My Little Chickadee* (Universal, 1940).

2314

Fitch: Nobody takes another drink from now until we're finished! I don't want any jumpy riders and nervous triggers. This isn't going to be any cowhand Saturday night spree a hollerin' and shootin' up the town. We're going to move in fast, hit hard, and run! Every man for himself!

Henchman: We shoot to kill?

Fitch: Is there any other way?

Tom Fitch played by Karl Malden: Henry Hathaway's *Nevada Smith* (Paramount, 1966).

2315

Fitch: A few of us is liable to get knocked off. Scare ya?

Smith: No. I ain't planning on being one of 'em. And there will be more [loot] for the rest of us.

Tom Fitch played by Karl Malden and Max

Sand/Nevada Smith played by Steve McQueen: Henry Hathaway's *Nevada Smith* (Paramount, 1966).

2316

Jim: Listen, I learned this about human nature when I was but so high. And that is: that the strong take away from the weak, and the smart take it away from the strong.

Jim Kincaid/Oklahoma Kid played by James Cagney: Lloyd Bacon's *The Oklahoma Kid* (Warner Bros., 1939).

2317

Gene: We're going out to arrest the O'Keefes for highway robbery.

Frog: Oh, don't kid me! They couldn't even find a highway!

Gene Autry played himself, and Frog Millhouse was played by Smiley Burnette: Joseph Kane's *The Old Corral* (Republic, 1936).

2318

Harmonica: The reward for this man is $5,000, is that right?

Cheyenne: Judas was content for $4,970 less.

Harmonica: There were no dollars in them days.

Cheyenne: But sons-of-bitches …yeah!

Harmonica played by Charles Bronson and Cheyenne played by Jason Robards, Jr.: Sergio Leone's *Once Upon a Time in the West* (Paramount, 1969).

2319

Lee: If you're gonna rob me, at least stand downwind.

Lee Walker played by Willie Nelson: Bill Cocoran's *Outlaw Justice* (TVW, 1999).

2320

Doc: Dobbs was wondering how we were gonna split up the goods. Anybody want his boots?

Doc Shabitt played by Matt Clark and Johnny Dobbs played by R.L. Tolbert: Richard Day's *The Quick and the Dead* (HBO Pictures, 1987).

2321

Black: Where's the $30,000? Well, where's the money?

Spike: We didn't get it. It wasn't in the safe.

Black: What do you mean you didn't get it?

Spike: I'm telling you we couldn't find it.

Black: And you call yourself bad men! Huh! I should have left you where I found you …branding calves!

Marvin Black played by George "Gabby" Hayes and Spike played by Yakima Canutt: Harry

Fraser's *Randy Rides Alone* (Lone Star/Monogram, 1934)

2322

Link: Folks, me and my friends are going to put on a little wild west show for you. Some of you may have heard about it. It's called a holdup. Now, don't get scared or do anything stupid and you'll be all right. Just relax …and enjoy yourself.

Link played by Charles Bronson: Terence Young's *Red Sun* (NGP, 1971).

2323

Gauche: Quite a hold for you, Alec: one third.

Link: Yeah. Not bad for Sabbath work, huh?

Gauche played by Alain Delon and Alec Link played by Charles Bronson: Terence Young's *Red Sun* (NGP, 1971).

2324

Heesman: Let's clean 'em out now!

Hays: We'll do it my way, Heesman. A bite at a time.

Heesman played by Peter Graves and Hank Hays played by Richard Boone: Sidney Salkow's *Robbers' Roost* (United Artists, 1955).

2325

Chavez: There is old saying: a fair exchange is no robbery.

Chavez played by Anthony Caruso: William Witney's *Santa Fe Passage* (Republic, 1955).

2326

Billy: Art, I got to hand it to you. The whole thing went off as slick as spit on a round door knob.

Billy Massey played by Dean Martin and Art Williams played by Donald Moffat: George Seaton's *Showdown* (Universal, 1973).

2327

Jason: Anybody got a match?

Boss: That is the best powder man in the business?

Quince: Oh, with powder he's great. But with matches, he leaves a little to be desired.

Jason O'Rourke played by Lou Gossett, the Boss (of the gang) played by Jack Elam, and Quince Drew played by Larry Hagman: Burt Kennedy's *Sidekicks* (TVW, 1974).

2328

Jason: I got to hand it to you, Quince. You really came up with a plan this time. A good plan! It is a good plan, isn't it Quince?

Jason O'Rourke played by Lou Gossett and Quince Drew played by Larry Hagman: Burt Kennedy's *Sidekicks* (TVW, 1974).

2329

Ginger: You're so careless with your money, you always leave it lying around in your wallet.

Ginger played by Susan Clark: Paul Bogart's *Skin Game* (Warner Bros., 1971).

2330

Pablo: What you got there?

Frog: Now you look here! You can't have that watch! That's a heirloom. I swiped, ah, my grandfather gave me that!

Pablo played by Dick Botiller and Frog Millhouse played by Smiley Burnette: George Sherman's *South of the Border* (Republic, 1939).

2331

Will: Mr. Spikes is never broke. He's never hungry either.

Tod: What made you think of him all of a sudden?

Will: Looking at that bank. You know what he would do if he was in our shoes? He'd walk in that bank, pull out his gun, and say: it's all baloney, so slice me some.

Will Young played by Gary Grimes, Tod Hayhew played by Charles Martin Smith, and Harry Spikes played by Lee Marvin: Richard Fleischer's *The Spikes Gang* (United Artists, 1974).

2332

Rawlins: The first one that makes a move gets lead between the eyes!

Jess Rawlins played by Bill Kennedy: Lesley Selander's *Storm Over Wyoming* (RKO, 1950).

2333

Doc: I guess it did look kind of bad to the sheriff, finding your partner with that money after the stage was held up.

Dan: Yeah, I guess it did.

Doc: How did you get it [money]?

Dan: Well, me and my partner held up the bandits. Then, when I was out running down some beef, the Sheriff held up my partner. So I held up the Sheriff.

Doc Thorpe played by Edgar Buchanan and Dan Thomas played by William Holden: George Marshall's *Texas* (Columbia, 1941).

2334

Floyd: I've had my share of the big ones all right.

Pitman: Big jobs, big outfits, is that right?

Floyd: That's right. They had to be. You're only as good as your worst man.

Floyd Moon played by Warren Oates and Paris Pitman, Jr., played by Kirk Douglas: Joseph L. Mankiewicz's *There Was a Crooked Man* (Warner Bros., 1970).

2335

Will: Wanna help me count this stuff, Kid?

Kid: I trust you, Will.

Will: Don't go trusting me too much.

William "Bill" Munny played by Clint Eastwood and

When lawman Chuck Jarvis (Rock Hudson) and outlaw Billy Massey (Dean Martin) get together, and neither has a hankerin' for a career change, it can only lead to a *Showdown* (Universal, 1973).

the Schofield Kid played by Jaimz Woolvett: Clint Eastwood's *Unforgiven* (Warner Bros., 1992).

2336
Cactus Jack: Take another step and I'll ventilate you!
Cactus Jack Slade played by Kirk Douglas: Hal Needham's *The Villain* (a.k.a. *Cactus Jack*; Columbia, 1979).

2337
Pancho Villa: Fierro, now you give him one more chance to contribute the money. If he refuses, shoot him …but not in church.
Pancho Villa played by Hector Elizondo and Fierro played by Hector Elias: Lee Philips' *Wanted: The Sundance Woman* (TVW, 1976).

2338
Jack: I've been robbed!
Old Timer: Welcome to the Yukon.
Jack Conroy played by Ethan Hawke and the Old Timer played by Clifford Fossman: Randal Kleiser's *White Fang* (Buena Vista, 1991).

2339
Pike: I'd like to make one good score and back off.
Dutch: Back off to what?
Pike Bishop played by William Holden and Dutch Engstrom played by Ernest Borgnine: Sam Peckinpah's *The Wild Bunch* (Warner Bros.–Seven Arts, 1969).

2340
Sutton: That's U.S. Government property! That's just plain stealin'!
Sergeant Tobe Sutton played by Leroy "Satchel" Paige: Robert Parrish's *The Wonderful Country* (United Artists, 1959).

2341
Stretch: Whether you like it or not, we're giving them their full share. If that don't suit you, you got a fight on your hands, and you better get at it quick!
Lengthy: It's a free country ain't it? Majority rules. I say we take a vote on it.
Stretch: I told you once before I don't like votes.
Stretch played by Gregory Peck and Lengthy played by John Russell: William A. Wellman's *Yellow Sky* (20th Century–Fox, 1948).

Horses

See also Cattle; Cowboys; Ranch and Range

2342

Holly: Has a horse ever been down through there before?

Ward: A horse has got too much sense to try.

Frank Holly played by John McIntire and Ward Kinsman played by Robert Taylor: Sam Wood's *Ambush* (MGM, 1950).

2343

Mr. Keon: The kid can ride!

Madden: How do you know?

Mr. Keon: I ought to know, I'm his Pa.

Madden: There might be a big war party out there.

Kid: Let me ride my own horse, and there's not an Indian pony that will even smell his dust.

Mr. Keon played by Ray Bennett, Joe Madden played by Willard Parker, and the Kid (Bert Keon) played by James Best: Hugo Fregonese's *Apache Drums* (Universal, 1951).

2344

Leonard: Donovan! I haven't seen you since, ah …

Donovan: Santa Fe.

Leonard: Right!

Donovan: When you sold me the Marshal's horse.

Leonard: Right. I was just funnin', Donovan.

Donovan: The Marshal wasn't amused.

Leonard Sharpe played by John McGiver and Russell Donovan played by Bill Bixby: Norman Tokar's *The Apple Dumpling Gang* (Buena Vista, 1975).

2345

Harriet: Please, be careful! As of my father's death, that horse developed a bad reputation.

Laramie: A lot of us that have that don't deserve it. Maybe he's one of them.

Harriet Lindsay played by Marsha Hunt and Laramie Nelson played by Larry "Buster" Crabbe: James Hogan's *The Arizona Raiders* (a.k.a. *Bad Men of Arizona*; Paramount, 1936).

2346

Tracks: I saved him from committing a downright dishonest act.

Laramie: I don't doubt it. Go on with your story.

Tracks: Over in Colorado, Arledge took a right-size herd of horses from a fella without the fella knowing it at that time.

Laramie: And I suppose you talked him into giving them back?

Tracks: Well, I done even better than that. In order to make sure that the owner got them back, I took them horses myself. I started looking for that fella. But, you know, I looked and I looked and I looked, and I never, I never could locate him. Finally, I had to sell them horses myself.

Tracks Williams played by Raymond Hatton, Laramie Nelson played by Larry "Buster" Crabbe, and Luke Arledge played by Don Rowan: James Hogan's *The Arizona Raiders* (a.k.a. *Bad Men of Arizona*; Paramount, 1936).

2347

Bannon: Apaches don't like horses, Sergeant. They ride 'em until they drop …kill 'em and eat 'em …and then steal some more.

Ed Bannon played by Charlton Heston and Sergeant Stone played by Robert J. Wilke: Charles Marquis Warren's *Arrowhead* (Paramount, 1953). *See also entry 2386.*

2348

Marshal: Oh, that suite is taken. So is every room in the hotel. And every other hotel in town. You might try the stable across the bridge.

Van Hock: I like horses, Marshal, but not as roommates.

The Marshal played by Karl Swenson and Peter Van Hock played by Alan Ladd: Delmer Daves' *The Badlanders* (MGM, 1958).

2349

Marty: You talk about an empire. This whole country is my empire. I don't have my brand on anything or anybody. I don't need it. I don't have a brand on my horse. But you let some man try to ride him!

Marty played by himself, Marty Robbins: Bill Ward's *Ballad of a Gunfighter* (Bill Ward Production, 1964).

2350

Major: Horse thief! You'll get life!

Doc: Major, I collect bridles for souvenirs. And on the end of one, I was plumb surprised to find a horse!

Major Jeff Clanton played by Robert Ryan and Doc Butcher played by Walter Brennan: William D. Russell's *Best of the Badmen* (RKO, 1951).

2351

Doc: Hey, wait a minute! I've always liked bridles with rosettes on 'em. I ought to take this along as a souvenir.

And what do you know? It's got a horse on the end of it!

Doc Butcher played by Walter Brennan: William D. Russell's *Best of the Badmen* (RKO, 1951).

2352

Jacob: Throw a blanket over 'im [horse].

James: I can ride without a blanket!

Jacob: I'm not worrying about your butt! It's his back!

Jacob McCandles played by John Wayne and James McCandles played by Patrick Wayne: George Sherman's *Big Jake* (NGP, 1971).

2353

Billy: I've got a horse and the west is wide.

Billy the Kid played by Robert Taylor: David Miller's *Billy the Kid* (MGM, 1941).

2354

Lance: What about that $3,000 we have buried at Sage Fork?

Boles: We split it.

Lance: How?

Boles: We can't all go together. The first one there takes his share and leaves the rest.

Lance: You must trust me a lot, Charlie.

Boles: I do. Besides, I've got a faster horse.

Lance Hardeen played by Jeffrey Lynn and Charles E. Boles, alias Black Bart, played by Dan Duryea: George Sherman's *Black Bart* (Universal, 1948).

2355

Sgt.: Do these dead men belong to you?

Canaan: They just came with those horses.

Sergeant Hastings played by Adam Baldwin and Canaan played by Armand Assante: Richard Spence's *Blind Justice* (HBO Home Video, 1994).

2356

Maverick: Boy, it's getting bad when you have to con your own horse for a ride.

Bret Maverick played by James Garner: Stuart Margolin's *Bret Maverick: The Lazy Ace* (TVW, 1981).

2357

Cowan: Well, you see, all I own is a couple of guns and a tin star. And of course a beautiful new horse and saddle.

Christina: Is that how you judge the worth of a man? By how much he owns?

Ben Cowan played by Richard Crenna and Christina played by Jo Ann Pflug: Sam Wanamaker's *Catlow* (MGM, 1971).

2358

Bartender: Headin' somewhere special?

Jones: No, just following my horse. When he gets tired, I get tired.

Matthew the Bartender was uncredited and Jones played by John Ireland: Leon Klimovsky's *Challenge of the Mackennas* (Filmar Compagnia Cinematografica — Atlantida/Hemlock Enterprises, 1969).

2359

Miles: We'll go from here on foot. Dismount!

Cullen: Dismount? You'd think if we're all gonna get killed by a bunch of blood-thirsty savages, they'd at least let us ride.

Ryan: Cullen, it's about time you learn that the cavalry loves horses …and hates men.

Miles Archer played by Guy Madison, Cullen played by Dick Wesson, and Ryan played by Steve Brodie: Gordon Douglas' *The Charge at Feather River* (Warner Bros., 1953).

2360

John: Well, how much money does she need to get her liver fixed?

Jenny: $500.00.

John: $500.00 for a liver?

Jenny: That's what the big doctor in Chicago charges. And he's got all kinds of fancy letters in back of his name.

John: I don't care what he has in back of his name! $500.00! That's more than you have to pay for a good horse!

John O'Hanlan played by James Stewart and Jenny played by Shirley Jones: Gene Kelly's *The Cheyenne Social Club* (NGP, 1970).

2361

Chino: Now, what the hell is that?

Louise: That's a side saddle.

Chino: A side saddle? You mean to tell me you're gonna put that on the side of a horse?

Chino Valdez played by Charles Bronson and Louise played by Jill Ireland: John Sturges' *Chino* (Coral Film/Intercontinental Releasing Corporation, 1973).

2362

Jamie: Are you going to bust him?

Chino: Do you know what it means …bustin' a horse?

Jamie: Showing it you can't be thrown.

Chino: No, that ain't all of it. Bustin' a horse means just exactly that: you bust him. And that takes all the spunk out a horse …it breaks him. And I'm not gonna bust a Valdez horse.

Jamie Wagner played by Vincent Van Patten and Chino Valdez played by Charles Bronson: John Sturges' *Chino* (Coral Film/Intercontinental Releasing Corporation, 1973).

2363

Neemo: So if you want these horses, I sell them to you. Did you bring some gold with you?

Chisum: No.

Neemo: Silver?

Chisum: Just lead!

Neemo played by Lloyd Batista and John Chisum played by John Wayne: Andrew McLaglen's *Chisum* (Warner Bros., 1970).

Pat Garrett (Glenn Corbett), John Chisum (John Wayne), and James Pepper (Ben Johnson) watch as Billy the Kid rides out of town to avenge the killing of Alex McSween (Andrew Prine), who was shot dead (foreground), in *Chisum* (Warner Bros., 1970).

2364

Station Agent: Mister, the way I figure it, you got quite a reward coming from Wells Fargo. Just leave me your name and address and our superintendent will get in touch with you.

Mr. Rogers: Thanks, but I'll settle for a good horse and saddle.

The Station Agent played by Oliver Blake and Wes McQueen, alias Mr. Chet Rogers, played by Joel McCrea: Raoul Walsh's *Colorado Territory* (Warner Bros., 1949).

2365

Cowboy: It beats me how women can go for you cowboys.

Charlie: Oh, yeah. Women like the smell of a horse on a man. That makes them giggle.

Cowboy: Well, the smell of a horse on me never did me no good. Just makes them get up and move away.

Charlie: Maybe you've been associating with the wrong horses.

The Cowboy played by Strother Martin and Charlie played by Dick York: Delmer Daves' *Cowboy* (Columbia, 1958).

2366

Reece: And all that hogwash about horses! The loyalty of the horse! The intelligence of the horse! The intelligence? You know a horse has a brain just about the size of a walnut. They're mean, they're treacherous, and they're stupid. There isn't a horse born that had enough sense to move away from a hot fire. No sensible man loves a horse. He tolerates the filthy animal only because riding is better than walking.

Tom Reece played by Glenn Ford: Delmer Daves' *Cowboy* (Columbia, 1958).

2367

Sergeant: All right, let's start from the beginning! This is a horse. It's got four legs. Two more than you got. It is something you ride. And in order to ride it, you got to get on top of it.

Sergeant James Bustard played by Peter Palmer: Norman Foster's *Crazy Horse and Custer: The Untold Story* (TVW, 1967).

2368

Ben: Sure is a nice horse. What's his name?

Luke: You don't have to put a name on something you might have to eat.

Ben Mockridge played by Gary Grimes and Luke played by Luke Askew: Dick Richards' *The Culpepper Cattle Company* (20th Century–Fox, 1972).

2369

Sheridan: I didn't recognize you without your horse.

General Sheridan (addressing George Custer) played by Lawrence Tierney: Robert Siodmak and

Irving Lerner's *Custer of the West* (Security Pictures/Cinerama, 1968).

2370

Jagade: I'm looking for the blacksmith.

Blacksmith: What do you want?

Jagade: My horse could use a shoe.

Blacksmith: Not on Sunday.

Jagade: Now he don't know it's Sunday. He thinks it's Saturday. I've got twenty dollars that says he right.

Jagade played by Dale Robertson and the Blacksmith was uncredited: Harmon Jones' *A Day of Fury* (Universal, 1956).

2371

Coolan: That's a big horse you're riding there. It's a long fall off of it.

Poole: Like you said, he's a big horse.

Verne Coolan played by Louis Calhern and Lance Poole played by Robert Taylor: Anthony Mann's *Devil's Doorway* (MGM, 1950).

2372

Tex: Hickok, I don't like to tie a man on a horse if he has to travel. But I don't mind shootin' him off of one if he tries to get away.

Tex Martin played by Tex Ritter and Wild Bill Hickok played by Bill Elliott: Lambert Hillyer's *The Devil's Trail* (Columbia, 1942).

2373

Willard: My horse is dead and you're back. It should have been the other way around.

Willard Grange played by Dennis Weaver: Ralph Nelson's *Duel at Diablo* (United Artists, 1966).

2374

Narrator: Long before the myths began, it was primitive …unforgiving. But in that vast limitless space man had one ally …the horse.

Narration by Pike, played by Martin Sheen: Anthony Harvey's *Eagle's Wing* (Eagle's Wing Productions/Rank, 1979).

2375

Sonny: Do me a favor, will ya, Alice? Don't go trying to think like a horse.

Sonny Steele played by Jane Fonda: Sydney Pollack's *The Electric Horseman* (Columbia/Universal, 1979).

2376

Beecher: Just one question, Roper. Why did you run off the horses?

Roper: If you've ever been pinned down in the desert with a dead horse, you'd know.

Lieutenant Beecher played by Richard Anderson and Captain Roper played by William Holden: John Sturges' *Escape from Fort Bravo* (MGM, 1953).

2377

Vinson: You never stick your neck out, do you Travis?

Travis: I'm just something that comes with the horse.

Sgt. Vinson played by Joel McCrea and Travis played by John Russell: Joseph Newman's *Fort Massacre* (United Artists, 1958).

2378

Zack: I'm gonna take the horses. All of them.

Joe: What about me?

Zack: Did you hear what the Injun said when they asked him how come he was riding and the squaw was walking? He said, she got no horse!

Zack Thomas played by Frank Sinatra and Joe Jarrett played by Dean Martin: Robert Aldrich's *Four for Texas* (Warner Bros., 1964).

2379

Joe: And .. ah .. then there are the kids.

Zack: Kids?

Joe: Huh, huh. All twenty-five of 'em.

Zack: Twenty-five? You must have the fastest horse in Texas!

Zack Thomas played by Frank Sinatra and Joe Jarrett played by Dean Martin: Robert Aldrich's *Four for Texas* (Warner Bros., 1964).

2380

Major: But we got the right on our side! We're bound to win!

Rusty: Oh, it's not in the cards, Major. A handful of men against a great big city.

Major: Is that so? Well, the Greeks did it. Why, they took the city of Troy with less men than we got.

Rusty: No! How did they work it?

Major: With a wooden horse.

Rusty: A wooden horse?

Major Stephen Braddock played by Eddy Waller and Rusty Joslin played by Raymond Hatton: George Sherman's *Frontier Horizon* (a.k.a. *New Frontier*; Republic, 1939).

2381

Sieber: Well, sir, your Apache rides a horse to death and eats him …and steals another. I mean, the horse is just mobile food.

Al Sieber played by Robert Duvall: Walter Hill's *Geronimo: An American Legend* (Columbia, 1993).

2382

Gus: A horse ain't never dead until he's dead, boss.

Gus played by Burl Ives: Louis King's *Green Grass of Wyoming* (20th Century–Fox, 1948).

2383

Amos: I'm sorry, mister. These horses are already hired.

Hadley: You rented them pretty fast.

Amos: Look, mister, I ain't got nothing against you personally. It's just that my horses are pretty particular who they work for.

Amos Stearnes played by George Selk and Jim

Hadley played by Alan Ladd: Robert D. Webb's *Guns of the Timberland* (Warner Bros., 1960).

2384

Emmett: Come on, get on your horse!

Rufus: Well, I can't find it!

Emmett: What do you mean, you can't find it? How can you lose anything as big as a horse?

Rufus: Because you're sitting on it!

Emmett Clemens played by Ernest Borgnine and Rufus Clemens played by Strother Martin: Burt Kennedy's *Hannie Caulder* (Paramount, 1971).

2385

Narrator: Sometimes it's worse than killing a man to steal his horses.

Narration by Noel Hickman (played by Chuck Pierce, Jr., as boy and Charles B. Pierce as old man): Charles B. Pierce's *Hawken's Breed* (Vidmark Entertainment, 1987).

2386

Hondo: And the Apache is the best rider in the world. His ponies can outrun any of ours.

Johnny: How come?

Hondo: Well, that pony knows that if he stops on him, that Apache will eat him.

Hondo Lane played by Ralph Taeger and Johnny Dow played by Buddy Foster: Lee H. Katzin's *Hondo and the Apaches* (TVW, 1967). *See also entry 2347.*

2387

Hopalong: I don't like to see human beings getting trampled by a horse. It upsets my peace of mind.

Hopalong Cassidy played by William Boyd: Howard Bretherton's *Hopalong Cassidy* (a.k.a. *Hopalong Cassidy Enters*; Paramount, 1935).

2388

Billy: The fact of the matter is …if you ain't the lead horse, the scenery never changes.

Billy Kelton played by Jeff Kober: Andy Tennant's *Keep the Change* (Turner Home Entertainment, 1992).

2389

Carson: I feel like a wild mustang turned loose in a corral with a string of thoroughbreds!

Kit Carson played by Jon Hall: George B. Seitz's *Kit Carson* (United Artists, 1940).

2390

Call: What are you doing in jail?

Billy: Oh, some years back the Sheriff caught that old Kickapoo [Indian] eating a dead horse. He decided it was stolen. The Sheriff ain't forgot.

Call: Why was Pea arrested?

Billy: Consorting with a horse-eater, I guess.

Captain Woodrow F. Call played by James Garner, Billy Williams played by George Carlin, and Pea

Eye Parker played by Sam Shepard: Joseph Sargent's *Larry McMurtry's Streets of Laredo* (Cabin Fever Entertainment, 1995).

2391

O'Reilly: Do you think you can ride that horse?

Ellison: I don't think anyone should. Some things just aren't meant to be broken.

Michael O'Reilly played by Lorne Greene and Brad Ellison played by Jock Mahoney: George Sherman's *The Last of the Fast Guns* (Universal, 1958).

2392

Hammer: I've been trying to get that buckskin for a couple months now. He won't have anything to do with me. A horse is keen to people …for what they're worth. If that horse just picked you as his master, I'm inclined to trust his judgment. I'd like you to count me as a friend.

Jim Hammer played by Hal Holbrook: Alan J. Levi's *The Legend of the Golden Gun* (TVW, 1979).

2393

Tonto: Him a beauty. Like mountain with snow. Silver white.

Lone Ranger: Silver! That would be a name for him. Here, Silver!

Tonto played by Jay Silverheels and the Lone Ranger played by Clayton Moore: George B. Seitz's *The Lone Ranger* (Television Series, earliest episodes, Sept. 1949).

2394

Narrator: Here is no conflict between animal and master. Here, instead, is a partnership between horse and rider. The Lone Ranger and Silver accept each other as equal.

The Lone Ranger played by Clayton Moore. Narration: George B. Seitz's *The Lone Ranger* (Television Series, earliest episodes, Sept. 1949).

2395

Jacob: I'm through triggering. You know that, don't you?

Ben: Sure, Jacob. You quit outlawing to settle down and break wild horses. I could do with a few myself. You could break a real strong wild one, and you could run away from any posse horse in the county.

Jacob Wade played by Jack Palance and Ben Ryerson was played by Robert Middleton: Henry Levin's *The Lonely Man* (Paramount, 1957).

2396

Jolly Jumper: The Dalton horses have conditioned reflexes. Whatever town they're in, they'll stop either at the bank or at the saloon. Of course, they don't always get their priorities right.

Roger Miller was the voice of the horse, Jolly Jumper: Terence Hill's *Lucky Luke* (Silvio Berlusconi Communications, 1991).

2397

California: Son, I remember once back in '86. It rained so hard I had to tie a log on each side of my horse to keep him floating down the trail.

California Carlson played by Andy Clyde: Georg Archainbaud's *The Marauders* (United Artists, 1947).

2398

Avery: Any questions?

Ramos: That's a difficult climb. A man could break his leg.

Avery: Likewise, a horse. And I'm sure you're aware what happens to a horse with a broken leg. Keep that in mind …all of you!

Avery played by Dan Duryea and Ramos played by Peter Mamakos: Gerald Mayer's *The Marauders* (MGM, 1955).

2399

Henry: I traded a good pinto for her [squaw]. Of course, I stole them [horses] from her pappy first.

Tyler (later): What happened to your squaw?

Henry: I traded her back to her pappy for the pinto.

Tyler: You ain't riding her.

Henry: The old fart stole him [pinto] back again!

Henry Frapp played by Brian Keith and Bill Tyler played by Charlton Heston: Richard Lang's *The Mountain Men* (Columbia, 1980).

2400

Griff: I know what your trouble is. You still got bronc fever. You don't want to go back home until you get a loop on that stallion.

Griff played by Robert Fuller: John Champion's *Mustang Country* (Universal, 1976).

2401

Dan: Those wild horses never gave up easy. They were fearless and fast as greased lightning. That's why the Spanish called them mestengo …meaning running wild. In our lingo, that came up mustang.

Dan played by Joel McCrea: John Champion's *Mustang Country* (Universal, 1976).

2402

Dan: There's a heap to know about broncbusting, and nobody ever learns it all. Like they say, there ain't no horse that can't be rode, and there ain't no rider that can't be thrown.

Dan played by Joel McCrea: John Champion's *Mustang Country* (Universal, 1976). *See also entry 2447.*

A scene in a cantina with Granger (Robert Taylor), Buffalo Baker (Noah Beery, Jr.) and Hondo Lane (Ralph Taeger) in *Hondo and the Apaches* (TVW, 1967).

2403
Rob: Mares are funny about death. They won't hang around a dead foal. But after they get away from it, they remember it …and start to whinny and hunt for it.
Rob McLaughlin played by Preston Foster: Harold Schuster's *My Friend Flicka* (20th Century–Fox, 1943).

2404
Gus: A rather pretty little flicka she is.
Ken: Flicka, what does that mean?
Gus: Swedish, for little girl.
Ken: Flicka, that's what I'll call her!
Gus played by James Bell and Ken McLaughlin played by Roddy McDowall: Harold Schuster's *My Friend Flicka* (20th Century–Fox, 1943).

2405
Ken: She tried to jump that fence when she knew she shouldn't.

2406
Rob: She's given us a lot of trouble, son. But she's taught us a few things too. You …responsibility. Me …that there is such a thing as hope beyond hope. That sometimes when things are at their lowest ebb, all we need to do is have a little more love, a little more patience, a little more faith.
Rob McLaughlin played by Preston Foster: Harold Schuster's *My Friend Flicka* (20th Century–Fox, 1943).

Rob: Anyone can try the impossible once. You know the old saying: it couldn't be done, but the old darn fool didn't know it, and went ahead and did it anyway.
Ken McLaughlin played by Roddy McDowall and Rob McLaughlin played by Preston Foster: Harold Schuster's *My Friend Flicka* (20th Century–Fox, 1943).

2407
Honest John: Hey, make him pay first [for the horse]!
Nobody: Why?
Honest John: Because you don't look like you're going to live long enough to get credit.
Honest John played by R.G. Armstrong and Nobody played by Terence Hill: Tonino Valerii's *My Name Is Nobody* (Universal, 1973).

2408
Roy: Time to be here and here he is. You're kind of quick on the trigger, son.
Walling: What are you going to name him, Roy?
Roy: I just did. It's Trigger!
Roy Rogers played himself and Mr. Walling played by Paul E. Burns: Frank McDonald's *My Pal Trigger* (Republic, 1946).

2409

Seton: Haven't you ever rode a horse before?

Harris: Oh yes, yes. It was quite a while ago though. I remember that the horse had rockers under it.

Seton played by Henry Hull and Neal Harris played by Fred MacMurray: Gene Fowler Jr.'s *The Oregon Trail* (20th Century–Fox, 1959).

2410

Josey Wales: I didn't know there were others that hadn't surrendered.

Lone Watie: I didn't surrender neither. But they took my horse and made him surrender.

Josey Wales played by Clint Eastwood and Lone Watie played by Chief Dan George: Clint Eastwood's *The Outlaw Josey Wales* (Warner Bros., 1976).

2411

Crawford: Well, there you are, Henry. That's every cent I got to my name. I've been saving it to pay for my burying.

Henry: Well, that critter [horse] is just liable to toss you off, stomp you in the dirt, and bury you free.

Nash Crawford played by Walter Brennan and Henry the Liveryman played by Guy Wilkerson: Jean Yarbrough's *The Over-the-Hill Gang* (TVW, 1969).

2412

Megan: And I looked, and behold a pale horse; and his name that sat on him was Death …and hell followed with him.

Megan Wheeler played by Sydney Penny: Clint Eastwood's *Pale Rider* (Warner Bros., 1985).

2413

Lullaby: I'll take the horse over to the stable. I'll probably feel more at home there myself.

Stony: Yeah, if the horses don't mind.

Lullaby Joslin played by Max Terhune and Stony Brooke played by John Wayne: George Sherman's *Pals of the Saddle* (Republic, 1938).

2414

Kern: When this is all over with, I hope I never see another horse the rest of my life!

Seymour Kern played by John Saxon: Herbert Coleman's *Posse from Hell* (Universal, 1961).

2415

Laurie: Is your horse worth the life of this man?

Julian: I couldn't say. I didn't know him.

Laurie played by Katharine Ross and Reverend Julian Shay played by Willie Nelson: William Wittliff's *Red Headed Stranger* (Alive Films/Charter Entertainment, 1987).

2416

Grover: Now, can you raise a posse or can't you?

Deputy: I think I can take care of it.

Grover: Who are you taking with you?

Deputy: Nobody.

Grover: You mean you're going alone? Just one man?

Deputy: They only stole one horse, didn't they?

Matt Grover was uncredited and Deputy Clay O'Mara was played by Audie Murphy: Jesse Hibbs' *Ride Clear of Diablo* (Universal, 1954).

2417

Judge: This court is now in session! Folks, this trial is unusual in my experience …but there ain't no reason I can see why a horse shouldn't have a fair trial same as a man. So if ain't anybody got no objections, we'll proceed.

Judge Barlett played by Charles Sellon: Fred Allen's *Ride Him, Cowboy* (Warner Bros., 1932).

2418

Jane: You'll never be able to ride him. He's an outlaw [horse].

Lassiter: That's what some people call me. Maybe Wrangle and I will understand each other.

Jane Withersteen played by Mary Howard and Jim Lassiter played by George Montgomery: James Tinling's *Riders of the Purple Sage* (20th Century–Fox, 1941).

2419

Yorke: Is it dark enough for you to get in there?

Tyree: With two men I pick, sir.

Yorke: Two men you pick? I know that you are an excellent judge of horse flesh, Trooper Tyree. You proved that when you stole my horse. But how are you as a judge of men for a dangerous mission?

Tyree: I consider myself a good judge of the men I trust, sir.

Lt. Col. Kirby Yorke played by John Wayne and Trooper Tyree played by Ben Johnson: John Ford's *Rio Grande* (Republic, 1950).

2420

Mark: Are you going to kill him?

Matt: Mark, look! There's a law: you can't steal a man's horse. In this land that's like stealing his life.

Mark Calder played by Tommy Rettig and Matt Calder played by Robert Mitchum: Otto Preminger's *The River of No Return* (20th Century–

2421

Sutton: You got a room?

Mayhew: No, but my horse has. I'll tell him to move over.

John Sutton played by Ray Middleton and Bill Mayhew played by John Payne: Joseph Kane's *The Road to Denver* (Republic, 1955).

2422

Ben: Now I hate to do this to you, horse, but you have thrown, you've kicked, and you have dragged me for the last time. Howdy, start the truck.

Howdy: What are you going to do?

Ben: I'm going to run over this knot-head.

Howdy: Run over him?

Ben: Yeah. He tried to kill me, I'm gonna kill him!

Howdy: You can't do that!

Ben: Oh, can't I? You just watch and see! What I'm gonna do is, I'm gonna go way back there and get a good run at him. He'll never know what hit him. There's more than one way to break a horse!

Ben Jones played by Glenn Ford and Howdy Lewis played by Henry Fonda: Burt Kennedy's *The Rounders* (MGM, 1965).

2423

Ben: Come spring, I'm gonna buy this no-good animal from Jim Ed Love.

Howdy: Buy him?

Ben: Yeah, then I'm gonna load him in that truck over there. And I'm gonna take him to town. And I'm gonna see him to a soap factory. And then I'm gonna buy the first cake of soap made out of him. And I'm gonna find myself a great big manure pile and I'm going to wallow around in it for about a week. And then I'm gonna take a bath with him. And from then on, every time I wash my hands, I'm gonna laugh like hell. That's what I'm going to do!

Ben Jones played by Glenn Ford and Howdy Lewis played by Henry Fonda: Burt Kennedy's *The Rounders* (MGM, 1965).

2424

Cap: You know something, son. It's one thing to shoot a man's legs out from under him. But when they take your horse away from ya, that's down right hellacious!

Cap Roundtree played by Ben Johnson: Robert Totten's *The Sacketts* (TVW, 1979).

2425

Witcher: See, the Paiutes, when the horse goes lame, they take a thorn off a snowberry bush and they shove it in one of his veins. It dies quicker than a crow can fly across this river.

Lum Witcher played by Jack Elam: Charles B. Pierce's *Sacred Ground* (Pacific International Enterprises/Wilderness Family, 1983).

2426

Magpie: I don't want anybody grabbing for the reins until the horses are hitched!

Magpie Harper played by John Elliott: S. Roy Luby's *Saddle Mountain Roundup* (Monogram, 1941).

2427

Gabe: That horse will kick you right into a funeral procession!

Gabe McBride played by Robert Conrad: Michael

Keusch's *Samurai Cowboy* (Den Pictures/Entertainment Securities/Saban Entertainment, 1993).

2428

Ethan: A human rides a horse until it dies, and then he goes on foot. A Comanche comes along, gets that horse up, rides him twenty more miles ...and then eats him.

Ethan Edwards played by John Wayne: John Ford's *The Searchers* (Warner Bros., 1956).

2429

Lomax: A little scrub like that. I figure he'd might be worth, ah, a couple dollars.

Page: He's got a sentimental value; belonged to my late wife.

Lomax: Why don't you put a sentimental price on him?

Page: Oh, ah, $20.00?

Lomax: Got a saddle that goes with it?

Page: My late wife's!

Clay Lomax played by Gregory Peck and Homer Page played by Arthur Hunnicutt: Henry Hathaway's *Shoot Out* (Universal, 1971).

2430

Sergeant: How do I know this is your horse?

Paden: Can't you see this horse loves me?

Sergeant: I had a gal do that to me. It didn't make her my wife!

The Cavalry Sergeant played by Sheb Wooley and Paden (who was kissing his horse) played by Kevin Kline: Lawrence Kasdan's *Silverado* (Columbia, 1985).

2431

Parris: Sam, there's no sense riding a dead horse.

Captain Robert Parris played by Dale Robertson and Sam played by Joel Fluellen: Sidney Salkow's *Sitting Bull* (United Artists, 1954).

2432

Quincy: The first time I met him, I conned him. I sold him a horse.

Ginger: What's wrong with that?

Quincy: It was the sheriff's horse.

Quincy Drew played by James Garner and Ginger played by Susan Clark: Paul Bogart's *Skin Game* (Warner Bros., 1971).

2433

Roy: When Trigger sees the spot we're in, he'll get us out. He's got horse sense.

Junior: If he had any sense, he wouldn't be a horse!

Roy Rogers played himself and Junior was played by Bob Hope: Frank Tashlin's *Son of Paleface* (Paramount, 1952).

2434

Beale: Lt. Owens tells me you saved three of our horses.

Clint: One of them was mine.

Beale: It must have been a pretty good horse. You risked your life for him.

Ethan Edwards (John Wayne) is in search of his niece kidnapped by the Comanches. He is torn between rescuing her and killing her for becoming a squaw in John Ford's classic and masterpiece, *The Searchers* (Warner Bros., 1956).

Clint: All that I own was on him.

Edward Beale played by Rod Cameron, Lt. Owens played by Stuart Randall, and Clint McDonald played by John Ireland: Ray Nazarro's *Southwest Passage* (United Artists, 1954).

2435

Curley: You can find another wife.

Chris: Sure, I can find another wife. But she take my rifle and horse. Oh, I'll never sell her. I love her so much. I beat her with a whip and she never get's tired.

Doc: Your wife?

Chris: No, my horse. I can find another wife easy, yes. But not a horse like that!

Sheriff Curley Wilcox played by George Bancroft, Chris played by Chris-Pin Martin, and Dr. Josiah Boone played by Thomas Mitchell: John Ford's *Stagecoach* (United Artists, 1939).

2436

Marshal: Luke Plummer cleared you, and as far as I'm concerned you're on the right side of the law ...except for those horses you're stealing.

Billy: These horses have been stolen so many times they can't give their own right names anymore.

Marshal Curley Wilcox played by Johnny Cash and Billy "Ringo" Williams played by Kris Kristofferson: Ted Post's *Stagecoach* (TVW, 1986).

2437

Red Ryder: I guess folks and horses are a lot alike. It all depends on how they're saddle-broke whether the good or bad crops out. And the thing that counts most ought to be how they finish the race.

Red Ryder played by Allan "Rocky" Lane: R.G. Springsteen's *Stagecoach to Denver* (Republic, 1946).

2438

Walt: Listen, son, if he starts running the rails, empty that saddle like it was hot.

Autry: Yeah, no glory riding. It's better to pull up than to reach your shadow on the ground.

Walt Bailey played by Jack Holt and Gene Autry played himself: John English's *The Strawberry Roan* (Columbia, 1948).

2439

Autry: You know, Joe, I had a horse once that piled into a fence. He healed all right but he never was any use to anybody. The boys said it broke his spirit and might as well shoot him.

Joe: Why didn't you?

Autry: Well, that would have been a waste. I know he had good stuff and anybody might have thought he just got scared and quit. I've seen horses busted up ten times worse and still come out of it. All he needed was a little time and patience to give him confidence. He turned out to be the best cow pony I've ever had. Well, I've got to go to work. You know, Joe, I was just thinking: horses are a lot like people.

Gene Autry played himself and Joe Bailey played by Dick Jones: John English's *The Strawberry Roan* (Columbia, 1948).

2440

Tom Horn: That's a mother-in-law horse. Do you know what that is?

Stable Hand: No.

Tom Horn: A mother-in-law horse is a horse you put your mother-in-law on. You send 'em both up in the hills and hope they don't ever come back!

Tom Horn played by Steve McQueen and the Stable Hand played by Elisha Cook, Jr.: William Wiard's *Tom Horn* (Warner Bros., 1980).

2441

Curly Bill: Hey, Johnny? What did that Mexican mean, a sick horse is going to get us, huh?

Johnny Ringo: He's was quoting the Bible ...Revelations: Behold a pale horse; the man who sat on him was Death ...and hell followed with him.

Curly Bill played by Powers Boothe and Johnny Ringo played by Michael Biehn: George P. Cosmatos' *Tombstone* (Buena Vista, 1993).

2442

Billy: Larkin, you make one move and there will be an empty horse walking down the street!

Billy Burns played by George "Gabby" Hayes and Lance Larkin played by Harry Woods: Ray Enright's *Trail Street* (RKO, 1947).

2443

Rudock: One thing you got to learn though. Horses are a man's slave. But treat 'em like a slave, and you ain't a man.

Jeremy Rudock played by James Cagney: Robert Wise's *Tribute to a Bad Man* (MGM, 1956).

2444

Rooster: Well, La Boeuf, you're quite a horse shooter!

La Boeuf: I was trying for Ned Pepper.

Rooster: Well, next time try for the horse and maybe you'll hit Pepper!

Marshal Reuben J. "Rooster" Cogburn played by John Wayne, La Boeuf played by Glen Campbell, and Ned Pepper played by Robert Duvall: Henry Hathaway's *True Grit* (Paramount, 1969).

2445

McIntosh: Lieutenant, a horse will run so far, so fast, for so long. And then he'll lie down on ya. When a horse lies down on an Apache, he puts a fire under his belly and gets him back up on his feet. When the horse dies, he gets off, eats a bit of it, and steals another.

McIntosh played by Burt Lancaster and Lieutenant Garnett DeBuin played by Bruce Davison: Robert Aldrich's *Ulzana's Raid* (Universal, 1972).

2446

Giles: Just a minute! You're selling horses to Maximilian in preference to your own country's army?

John Henry: No, I'm selling horses for $35.00 in preference to $25.00!

D.J. Giles, a government horse buyer, played by Guy Raymond and Colonel John Henry Thomas played by John Wayne: Andrew McLaglen's *The Undefeated* (20th Century–Fox, 1969).

2447

Johnny: There ain't a man that can't be thrown ...and there ain't a horse that can't be rode.

Johnny Portugal played by John Saxon: John Huston's *The Unforgiven* (United Artists, 1960). *See also entry 2402.*

2448

Urbina: I swear, ever since we've been fighting, my horse gets more [loving] than I do.

Fierro: Your horse has more to offer than you do.

Urbina played by Robert Viharo and Fierro played by Charles Bronson: Buzz Kulik's *Villa Rides!* (Paramount, 1968).

2449

Steve: Why, she's got you roped, hog-tied, and branded. The only difference between you and that horse is ...he's got sense enough to buck.

Steve played by Sonny Tufts: Stuart Gilmore's *The Virginian* (Paramount, 1946).

2450

Virginian: Oh, but now that you have a horse, maybe you'd go riding with me?

Molly: I'm afraid I'll be busy at school.

Virginian: Oh, there's always afternoons and Sundays.

Molly: Besides, I've never riden western style.

Virginian: Oh, I can learn you easy.

Molly: Teach me, not learn me.

Virginian: Huh?

Molly: You teach, I learn.

Virginian: Well, that's what I said.

Molly: I'm talking about grammar. Teach is a transitive verb taking an object. Learn is an intransitive verb.

Virginian: Well, what does it take?

The Virginian played by Joel McCrea and Molly Wood played by Barbara Britton: Stuart Gilmore's *The Virginian* (Paramount, 1946).

2451

Dusty: She's really a beauty, isn't she? A genuine Appalachian.

Callahan: It's not an Appalachian, it's Appaloosa. And it's not a she, it's a he.

Dusty: I don't care if it's a boy Appaloosa or a girl Appalachian! It's a beauty!

Dusty played by Bob Denver and Callahan played by Forrest Tucker: Jack Arnold, Oscar Rudolph, Bruce Bilson, and Earl Bellamy's *The Wackiest Wagon Train in the West* (Topar Films, 1976).

2452

Gardner: If you really want to live, you mustn't be afraid to take a chance. You got to learn to leap first and look afterwards.

Somers: That's what happened to my horse. He broke his neck!

Jim "Hunk" Gardner played by Albert Dekker and Dan Somers played by John Wayne: Albert S. Rogell's *War of the Wildcats* (Republic, 1943).

2453

[Conversation following sheriff's daughter being assaulted and horse stolen]

Sheriff: He took my Big Blue [horse] out in that desert!

Billee: Oh, Daddy, is that all you care about?

Sheriff: No. I'll make it up to you, Billee. You got to remember: a man picks his pleasure from the nearest tree. Why, if you weren't my daughter, I ...I mean, there's worse things. He could have killed you! Now, that would have been worse, wouldn't it? I think.

Billee: You bring him back!

Sheriff: Yeah, well, I'll bring him back. My election to a third term of sheriff depends on it. And my honor!

Billee: Your honor?

Sheriff: Oh darling, I can only keep my mind on one offense at a time.

Sheriff John Copperud played by Carroll O'Connor and Billee Copperud played by Margaret Blye: William Graham's *Waterhole No. 3* (Paramount, 1967).

2454

Sergeant: As we say in the cavalry: without a horse, a man is afoot.

Sergeant Henry Foggers played by Claude Akins: William Graham's *Waterhole No. 3* (Paramount, 1967).

2455

Judge Bean: People of Vinegarroon are against ya. You can use any name you like.

Cole: Cole Harden.

Judge Bean: What are ya doing in Vinegarroon?

Cole: Well, just passing through.

Judge Bean: Homesteader?

Cole: No.

Judge Bean: Where do you hail from?

Cole: No place in particular.

Judge Bean: Where ya heading for?

Cole: No place special.

Judge Bean: Oh, saddle bum, huh? Well, it's all right to live on a horse if it's your horse.

Judge Roy Bean played by Walter Brennan and Cole Hardin played by Gary Cooper: William Wyler's *The Westerner* (United Artists, 1940).

2456

Judge Bean: You're charged with stealing a horse. Guilty or not guilty?

Cole: Not guilty.

Judge Bean: Where's exhibit A?

Chickenfoot: Huh?

With the conflict-resolution talks concluded, Marshal Rooster Cogburn (John Wayne) yells across a glade to outlaw Ned Pepper and gang, "Fill your hand, you son-of-a-bitch!" in Henry Hathaway's *True Grit* (Paramount, 1969).

Judge Bean: Where's the horse? Bring in the horse, Chickenfoot!

Judge Roy Bean played by Walter Brennan, Cole Hardin played by Gary Cooper, and Chickenfoot played by Paul Hurst: William Wyler's *The Westerner* (United Artists, 1940).

2457

Yancey: Do you know how to get a job?

Rosalie: Well, I guess I'll just ask folks like Pa does.

Yancey: I never figured him asking for work.

Rosalie: Once he did, but then he got caught stealing somebody's horse. And if we hadn't cried and hollered some-thing terrible, they would have strung him up.

Yancey: That must have been awful.

Rosalie: It was. We sure needed that horse!

Yancey played by Audie Murphy and Rosalie Stocker played by Sandra Dee: Jack Sher's *The Wild and the Innocent* (Universal, 1959).

2458

Sketter: You know, I found a rope one time ...with a horse on the end of it. I liked to get into a lot of trouble!

Sketter Burke played by Sketter Bill Robins: Richard Thorpe's and Sidney Algier's *Wild Horse* (Allied-Astor, 1931).

2459

Cowboy 1: Being a tenderfoot, you might not know that hanging around other man's horses ain't considered genteel.

Cowboy 2: A fella looked at a horse a couple weeks ago. He looked at him so long he must have got confused. He thought it was his. Last mistake that poor fella would ever make.

Cowboy 1: Yeah, died with a broken neck right there after. Ah, the rope done it!

The Cowboys were uncredited: Reginald LeBorg's *Wyoming Mail* (Universal, 1950).

2460

Stretch: A horse is a useful animal. There's no use letting him suffer just because he belongs to a jackass.

Stretch played by Gregory Peck: William A. Wellman's *Yellow Sky* (20th Century–Fox, 1948).

2461

Colonel: Why, I never could teach a horse anything. What's the secret?

Gene: The secret in teachin' a horse, Colonel, is that you have to know more than the horse!

Colonel Frog Millhouse played by Smiley Burnette and Gene Autry played himself: Joseph Kane's *Yodelin' Kid from Pine Ridge* (Republic, 1937).

2462

Colonel: We've been hearing about you …buffalo hunter …Chief Scout of General Sheridan. And it seems to me you broke a lot of records riding pony express.

Buffalo Bill: Well, I'm afraid I had to ride fast, Colonel. I generally had some Indians chasing me.

Colonel Calhoun played by Wade Boteler and Buffalo Bill played by Roy Rogers: Joseph Kane's *Young Buffalo Bill* (Republic, 1940).

2463

Bonney: Now you remember something, Pat. I never stole a horse from someone I didn't like. If I didn't like him, I just wouldn't even bother with 'em.

Rudabaugh: Yeah, he'd just kill 'em!

William H. Bonney, alias Billy the Kid, played by Emilio Estevez and Arkansas Dave Rudabaugh played by Christian Slater: Geoff Murphy's *Young Guns II* (20th Century–Fox, 1990).

Indians

See also Forts

2464

Jason: How come you can speak Indian?

Zach: Well, my mother was the daughter of a Cheyenne chief.

Jason: Really?

Zach: Yeah.

Jason: What was she like?

Zach: I don't really remember because she died two years before I was born.

Jason Smith played by Mark Edward Hall and Zachariah Coop played by Robert Logan: Stewart Raffill's *Across the Great Divide* (Pacific International, 1976).

2465

Narrator: My father told me that for the first time, he saw these Indians as he had never seen them before: As people with homes and traditions and ways of their own. Suddenly, they were no longer savages. They were people who laughed and loved and dreamed.

Narration by Howard Keel: William Wellman's *Across the Wide Missouri* (MGM, 1951).

2466

Callendar: They're real friendly like, the injuns.

MacDougall: The only friendly Indians are dead Indians, I say.

Callendar played by Brian Donlevy and MacDougall played by Wilfrid Lawson: William A. Seiter's *Allegheny Uprising* (RKO, 1939).

2467

Capt: What do you think of the entire plan of action? You didn't say.

Ward: I wasn't asked.

Capt: You are now.

Ward: The plan is based upon what Diablito should do. You better be ready for what he can't possibly do, but probably will.

Captain Ben Lorrison played by John Hodiak and Ward Kinsman played by Robert Taylor: Sam Wood's *Ambush* (MGM, 1950).

2468

Holly: I say we ain't much time before they [Indians] pick up our trail.

Ward: Time is what gives a man gray hair.

Frank Holly played by John McIntire and Ward Kinsman played by Robert Taylor: Sam Wood's *Ambush* (MGM, 1950).

2469

Massai: You call that life? If an Apache cannot live in his home mountains like his fathers before him, he is already dead!

Massai played by Burt Lancaster: Robert Aldrich's *Apache* (United Artist, 1954).

2470

Massai: You have a woman and …yet you carry the water?

Glagg: Some of the white man's ways are hard.

Massai, an Apache, played by Burt Lancaster and Glagg, a Cherokee, played by Ian MacDonald: Robert Aldrich's *Apache* (United Artists, 1954).

2471

Santos: Even a hawk is an eagle among crows.

Santos played by Paul Guilfoyle: Robert Aldrich's *Apache* (United Artists, 1954).

2472

Massai: If the Cherokee is like the white man, then he is Massai's enemy.

Glagg: I am the enemy of no man.

Massai: Then the Cherokee is a woman!

Glagg: I am no woman! My people have fought the white men many times but have always been driven west. First from a place called Carolina, then to the land of Tennessee, and then at last to Oklahoma. But there our chiefs grew wise. They did not fight and they did not run.

Massai: Neither does the turtle.

Glagg: Are you afraid of the turtle? Then put your knife away.

Massai played by Burt Lancaster and Glagg played by Ian MacDonald: Robert Aldrich's *Apache* (United Artists, 1954).

2473

Massai: Apaches are warriors, not farmers.

Glagg: You have seen the world of the white man …their numbers like leaves of the trees. That taught you nothing? The warriors' day is over. Once we Cherokees were like the Apaches. We feasted when the hunting was good. We starved when it was bad. But the white man ate the whole year around …because he raised his own food. We found we could live with the white man …only if we lived like him.

Massai played by Burt Lancaster and Glagg played

by Ian MacDonald: Robert Aldrich's *Apache* (United Artists, 1954).

2474

Nalinle: But will they not say that growing corn is woman's work?

Massai: I am a warrior. What I do can never be woman's work.

Nalinle played by Jean Peters and Massai played by Burt Lancaster: Robert Aldrich's *Apache* (United Artists, 1954).

2475

Nalinle: My father wronged you. Many men have wronged you. But now you make yourself worse than they are. Now there is nothing in you but hate. You fight only for yourself. You kill only for yourself. You are like a dying wolf biting at its own wounds.

Nalinle played by Jean Peters: Robert Aldrich's *Apache* (United Artists, 1954).

2476

Sieber: You want us to kill you, don't you Massai? Right out here in front of all your blood-thirsty brothers …so they could sing your praises around the campfire and start another war in your honor. That would be a sweet death, wouldn't it Massai? A warrior's death! But you're not a warrior anymore. You're just a whooped injun!

Al Sieber played by John McIntire and Massai played by Burt Lancaster: Robert Aldrich's *Apache* (United Artists, 1954).

2477

Sieber: I knew Geronimo and Cochise when they were that buck's age. That's another one of the same breed. A real bronco Apache.

Al Sieber played by John McIntire: Robert Aldrich's *Apache* (United Artists, 1954).

2478

Massai: I cannot stop fighting. I am the last real Apache in all the world …except for the little one to be.

Massai played by Burt Lancaster: Robert Aldrich's *Apache* (United Artists, 1954).

2479

Sieber: It looks like he called the war off.

Lt. Col.: Then why are you looking so glum about?

Sieber: I'm getting old, I guess. This is the only war we had. And we ain't likely to find another.

Al Sieber played by John McIntire and Lt. Colonel Beck played by Walter Sande: Robert Aldrich's *Apache* (United Artists, 1954).

2480

Sam: I like your notion, Reverend, that Apaches are just evils the Lord created to try honest men. I'm saved! I'm not an honest man.

Sam Leeds played by Stephen McNally and the Reverend Griffin played by Arthur Shields: Hugo Fregonese's *Apache Drums* (Universal, 1951).

2481

Walker: Do you know what the word "Apache" means? It means enemy. A twenty-four hour a day enemy. An enemy that's anything that walks on two legs.

Jim Walker played by Rory Calhoun: R.G. Springsteen's *Apache Uprising* (Paramount, 1966).

2482

Walker: Well, the time to start worrying is when you don't see 'em.

Captain: We'll be ready for 'em when they come.

Walker: Well, nobody is ever ready for the Apache. They'll fight you on their own terms. If you and your men are tired enough, and thirsty enough, and far enough away from the fort, that's when you'll find them. They'll isolate the town, and they'll lead you into an ambush. Now, that's something you didn't learn at West Point.

Captain: And what do you know of that?

Walker: Enough to know they've never written a book that's worth a tinkers-darn on how to fight Apaches.

Captain: That's a matter of opinion.

Walker: You could change yours, Gannon. The Apaches can't read …but he can sure kill ya!

Jim Walker played by Rory Calhoun and Captain Gannon played by Richard Arlen: R.G. Springsteen's *Apache Uprising* (Paramount, 1966).

2483

Bill: Tonto's …the worst kind!

Jim: As mean as they come.

Bill: Yeah. I've seen them take a man and cut his feet and make him walk on cactus. And that is merely before they begin to torture him.

Bill Gibson played by Arthur Hunnicutt and Jim Walker played by Rory Calhoun: R.G. Springsteen's *Apache Uprising* (Paramount, 1966).

2484

Walker: I had a partner once who got caught by some of Victorio's Mescaleros. They staked him out on an ant hill, slit his eye lids, and then let nature take its course.

Jim Walker played by Rory Calhoun: R.G. Springsteen's *Apache Uprising* (Paramount, 1966).

2485

Peter: A wagon train come in headin' for California and I'm joinin' up with it.

Phoebe: When?

Peter: Sundown.

Phoebe: Well, sundown is a good time to leave. Indians don't hanker much for night fightin'.

Peter Muncie played by William Holden and Phoebe Titus played by Jean Arthur: Wesley Ruggles' *Arizona* (Columbia, 1940).

2486

Phoebe: Mr. Oury, am I hearing you right? Are you talking about giving Arizona back to the Indians?

Oury: That's one way of saying it, Phoebe.

Judge: Like Oury says, it's better to leave what we built here than get our bones picked clean by the buzzards.

Phoebe: What did you ever build?

Phoebe Titus played by Jean Arthur, Grant Oury played by Regis Toomey, and Judge Bogardus played by Edgar Buchanan: Wesley Ruggles' *Arizona* (Columbia, 1940).

2487

Major: It's clearly common knowledge out here that most Indians do not like to fight at night. An Indian killed at night, they believe, wanders forever in darkness.

Bart Laish, assuming the identity of Major Andrew Pepperis, played by Sterling Hayden: Lesley Selander's *Arrow in the Dust* (Allied Artists, 1954).

2488

Bannon: Chattez, you were always the wise one. There is a new thinking in the beat of your drums …a new dance. I want to be told what they mean.

Chattez: So that we may more easily be killed?

Ed Bannon played by Charlton Heston and Chief Chattez played by Frank de Kova: Charles Marquis Warren's *Arrowhead* (Paramount, 1953).

2489

Sandy: Which way are you going back to the post?

Colonel: The way every detail goes back.

Bannon: Pick another way, Colonel.

Colonel: These Apaches were here for peace. Do you see any paint on their faces?

Bannon: They don't have to have it on their faces. But they can't fight without paint. They got to have it on them somewhere.

Sandy MacKinnon played by Milburn Stone, Colonel Waybright played by Lewis Martin, and Ed Bannon played by Charlton Heston: Charles Marquis Warren's *Arrowhead* (Paramount, 1953).

2490

Johnny: Toriano is more than my friend. We played together when we were young. Look at this [scar on wrist]. We made ourselves blood brothers.

Bannon: There's just one way an Apache can put an end to that relationship. He kills ya!

Johnny Gunther played by John M. Pickard, Toriano played by Jack Palance, and Ed Bannon played by Charlton Heston: Charles Marquis Warren's *Arrowhead* (Paramount, 1953).

2491

Sandy: I think they're swinging too wide for a circle, Ed. Maybe they're not using a pattern at all.

Bannon: Apaches always use a pattern for their campaigns. I've seen 'em fight in a circle covering hundreds of miles or in an x as big as the whole territory. Even a zigzag pattern. We got to be sure which one they're using now.

Sandy MacKinnon played by Milburn Stone and Ed Bannon played by Charlton Heston: Charles Marquis Warren's *Arrowhead* (Paramount, 1953).

2492

Toriano: In my thoughts there have been visions. The Great One put us here on earth first. He is displeased with those who have come second. To please Him, we must rid the earth of these second-comers. The Ghosts of our Fathers demand it, and they have shown us a way. To please the Great One, we must dance before we kill. We must dance so that the Ghost of our Fathers know that we obey their wishes. We must dance the Ghost Dance! And I will show you how it is done as it was given to me in my vision.

Toriano played by Jack Palance: Charles Marquis Warren's *Arrowhead* (Paramount, 1953).

2493

Captain: What is it?

Bannon: Prophecy.

Captain: Prophecy?

Bannon: They never talk it. It was always written: carved in a tree, painted on a rock. The Invisible One would appear and lead them to victory over the white eyes. It would be one of their people. He'd come out of the east.

Captain: That fits Toriano

Bannon: That's why he went back East to school ...so he could make it fit.

Captain Bill North played by Brian Keith and Ed Bannon played by Charlton Heston: Charles Marquis Warren's *Arrowhead* (Paramount, 1953).

2494

Bannon: The Apaches have a saying: think what you want to think. You have to live with your thoughts.

Ed Bannon played by Charlton Heston: Charles Marquis Warren's *Arrowhead* (Paramount, 1953).

2495

Captain: Give me your attention. This command is going after Toriano. Now, on my responsibility, we'll take our orders from Mr. Bannon.

Bannon: I'll make it short. There's only one way to beat the Apache: fight the way he fights ...hit and run until he can't run anymore.

Captain Bill North played by Brian Keith, Toriano played by Jack Palance, and Ed Bannon played by Charlton Heston: Charles Marquis Warren's *Arrowhead* (Paramount, 1953).

2496

Tom: Those savages are crazy! They come running in here, jabbin' at us with those sticks, and then runnin' off hollerin'. One of 'em got me right here in the shoulder ...just light as a feather!

July: Countin' coup.

Tom: What?

July: I'm saying that's just like the Indian ...for the glory of it, that's all. They ain't much on killin'.

Tom Jefferd played by Ty Hardin and July played by Richard Roundtree: Clyde Ware's *Bad Jim* (RCA/Columbia Home Video, 1990).

2497

Garth: They sure say a lot with a little smoke.

Charlie Garth played by Francis Ford: Lew Landers' *Bad Lands* (RKO, 1939).

2498

Garth: Apaches don't do night work. It's against the rules of their God. They prefer the rosy dawn for murder.

Sheriff: Of course, Apache Jack's influence will be pretty ungodly.

Charlie Garth played by Francis Ford and Sheriff Bill Cummings played by Robert Barrat: Lew Landers' *Bad Lands* (RKO, 1939).

2499

Chief: The river runs red with the blood of your people and mine. Why should our voices speak when theirs are silent?

Chief Mike played by Michael Granger: William Castle's *Battle of Rogue River* (Columbia, 1954).

2500

Chief: Among my people, when the word of a chief is challenged, he must kill the challenger in combat or admit that he is no chief.

Chief Mike played by Michael Granger: William Castle's *Battle of Rogue River* (Columbia, 1954).

2501

Major: Well, there's one thing in our favor. The Indian gods don't permit them to attack before dawn.

Major Frank Archer played by George Montgomery: William Castle's *Battle of Rogue River* (Columbia, 1954).

2502

Chief: Let the talk begin ...not from your tongue but from your heart. Many times we have talked with the white chiefs and

no two of them talk alike. With my people there is but one chief. And so we wish to speak with the true chief. Are you, then, the true chief?

Capt: Among my people, the people themselves are chief. I speak for them.

Chief Mike played by Michael Granger and Major Frank Archer played by George Montgomery: William Castle's *Battle of Rogue River* (Columbia, 1954).

2503

Chief: We will test this peace of yours for thirty days. But if war shall come, let me say this to you now. You are a true chief and a worthy enemy. I will kill you with regret.

Chief Mike played by Michael Granger: William Castle's *Battle of Rogue River* (Columbia, 1954).

2504

Brave: Your voice rings louder than those who came before you. But in death, your voice will be as silent as theirs. I take your words to my chief. He will answer them with guns.

Major: And if I should meet him with two guns for each one of his, what will he do?

Brave: Why, then, each one of his guns will fire twice.

The Brave played by Steve Ritch and Major Frank Archer played by George Montgomery: William Castle's *Battle of Rogue River* (Columbia, 1954).

2505

Glyn: I thought we were out of Cheyenne country. What do you make of that?

Cole: Shoshoni. Real mean when they want to be. Lately, they want to be.

Glyn McLyntock played by James Stewart and Emerson Cole Garret played by Arthur Kennedy: Anthony Mann's *Bend of the River* (Universal, 1952).

2506

Jacob: Give us a room.

Hotel Clerk: The dog is all right, but, ah, we do not allow Indians.

Jacob McCandles played by John Wayne and the Hotel Clerk was uncredited: George Sherman's *Big Jake* (NGP, 1971).

2507

Zeb: Blackfeet ...proud injuns. They ain't gonna let no white men spy on their country. The only thing they are feared of is a white man's sickness.

Boone: What's that?

Zeb: Grabs. White men don't see nothing pretty unless they want to grab it. The more they grab, the more they want to grab. It's like a fever and they can't get cured. The only thing for them to do is to keep on grabbin' until everything belongs to white men, and then start grabbin' from each other. I reckon injuns got no reason to love nothing white.

Zeb Calloway played by Arthur Hunnicutt and Boone played by Dewey Martin: Howard Hawks' *The Big Sky* (Winchester/RKO, 1952).

2508

Jourdonnais: Calloway, what do you think? Do you think they gone went, huh?

Calloway: They gone went. But the question is, will they stay gone went?

Jourdonnais played by Steven Geray and Zeb Calloway played by Arthur Hunnicutt: Howard Hawks' *The Big Sky* (Winchester/RKO, 1952).

2509

Zeb: Boone, this is Teal's father, Chief Red Horse. Chief Red Horse wants to see you on account he wants to know how much you're gonna pay for his daughter.

Boone: Pay for Teal?

Zeb: You married her, didn't ya? He gets paid.

Boone: Well, I reckon that's the custom.

Zeb: Well, yes and no. In this here particular case, it's yes.

Zeb Calloway played by Arthur Hunnicutt and Boone played by Dewey Martin: Howard Hawks' *The Big Sky* (Winchester/RKO, 1952).

2510

Boone: Why did she want to grab this?

Zeb: That's a Blackfoot scalp you got, and she knows it. Ain't you ever thought of why an injun takes a scalp?

Deakins: Why?

Zeb: To shame an enemy. The way she figures it, there's a Blackfoot brave somewhere that can't show his face in the hereafter until that thing is buried under the ground.

Boone played by Dewey Martin, Zeb Calloway played by Arthur Hunnicutt, and Jim Deakins played by Kirk Douglas: Howard Hawks' *The Big Sky* (Winchester/RKO, 1952).

2511

Ruth: Look how queer his horse is acting!

Zeke: Yeah, he's riding zigzag. That's Indian sign that he wants to palavra. There's the chief riding out to meet him now for a powwow.

Ruth Cameron played by Marguerite Churchill and Zeke played by Tully Marshall: Raoul Walsh's *The Big Trail* (Fox, 1930).

2512

Billy Jack: It's funny, isn't it? Only the white man wants everything put in writing. And only then so he can use it against you in court. You know, among the Indians a promise is good enough.

Billy Jack played by Tom Laughlin: T.G. Frank's (Tom Laughlin) *Billy Jack* (Warner Bros.–National Student Film Corp., 1971).

2513

Billy Jack: Being an Indian is not a matter of blood …it's a way of life.

Billy Jack played by Tom Laughlin: T.G. Frank's (Tom Laughlin) *Billy Jack* (Warner Bros.–National Student Film Corp., 1971).

2514

Barbara: What is the snake ceremony?

Jean: A ceremony where Billy becomes a brother to the snake.

Barbara: How does he do that?

Jean: By going on the mountain and being bitten by the snake over and over. Then he passes into unconsciousness for the last time. And if he lives, he has a vision. And in this vision, he finds out what his life's mission will be and who the spirit will be to guide him on this mission.

Barbara played by Julie Webb, Jean Roberts played by Delores Taylor, and Billy Jack played by Tom Laughlin: T.G. Frank's (Tom Laughlin) *Billy Jack* (Warner Bros.–National Student Film Corp., 1971).

2515

Spencer: Well, Indians don't fight in the dark. It's against their religion.

Deans: Did they seem all that religious to you?

Spencer played by John Pearce and Arch Deans played by Gregory Peck: Ted Kotcheff's *Billy Two Hats* (United Artists, 1973).

2516

Spencer: How many [Indians] do you think there are?

Deans: Four, I think.

Spencer: How do you know there's four?

Deans: I counted their feet and divided by two.

Spencer played by John Pearce and Arch Deans played by Gregory Peck: Ted Kotcheff's *Billy Two Hats* (United Artists, 1973).

2517

Johnson: From everything I've heard about these Indians, they get along about as well as in-laws.

Alan Johnson played by Christopher Reeve: Steven H. Stern's *Black Fox* (TV miniseries, Cabin Fever Entertainment, 1995).

2518

Chomina: Tomorrow, do not cry out.

The crazed Indian, Poordevil (Hank Worden), in Howard Hawks' *The Big Sky* (Winchester/RKO, 1952).

Daniel: If we do cry out, will they stop [torturing us]?

Chomina: No, they will not stop. But if you cry out when you die, they will have your spirit.

Chomina played by August Schellenberg and Daniel played by Aden Young: Bruce Beresford's *Black Robe* (Samuel Goldwyn, 1991).

2519

Daniel: They have an afterworld of their own.

Laforgue: They have no concept of one.

Daniel: Annuka has told me, they believe that in the forest at night the dead can see. The souls of men hunt the souls of animals.

Laforgue: Is that what she told you? It is childish, Daniel.

Daniel: Is it harder to believe in than Paradise where we all sit on clouds and look at God?

Daniel played by Aden Young and Father Laforgue played by Lothaire Bluteau: Bruce Beresford's *Black Robe* (Samuel Goldwyn, 1991).

2520

Running Dog: A Kiowa and a Texan will never be friends. I walk the path of peace now, but I'll keep my war horse and arrows handy.

Running Dog played by Raoul Trujillo: Steven H. Stern's *Blood Horse* (TV miniseries, Cabin Fever Entertainment, 1995).

2521

Chuluka: You move too quiet for a white man.

Danaher: Well, maybe you make too much noise for an Indian.

Chuluka played by Michael Ansara and Sheriff John Danaher played by Glenn Ford: C.T. McIntyre's *Border Shootout* (Turner Home Entertainment, 1990).

2522

O'Brien: What the hell are they shooting?

Pearce: When you tell an Indian things will be a certain way and then they're not, he's inclined to think maybe you crossed him.

Frank O'Brien played by Charles Durning and Nathan Pearce played by Ben Johnson: Tom Gries' *Breakheart Pass* (United Artists, 1976).

2523

Pearce: There's more ways to pacify Indians than shootin' holes in them!

Nathan Pearce played by Ben Johnson: Tom Gries' *Breakheart Pass* (United Artists, 1976).

2524

Sandine: My people have a custom: when you save a life, you own that life. I am your servant. I am your brother.

Maverick: I already have a brother and I don't want a servant ...particularly some bogus Indian who thinks he's Sitting Bull!

Sandine: Standing Bear! And my life belongs to you.

Maverick: I don't want it!

Sandine: You got it, pilgrim!

Philo Sandine played by Stuart Margolin and Bret Maverick played by James Garner: Stuart Margolin's *Bret Maverick: The Lazy Ace* (TVW, 1981).

2525

Brigham: Indians can't be any worse than some Christians I know. But just the same, until we find out a little bit more about them, we mean to trust in you, Lord, and to keep our powder dry.

Brigham Young played by Dean Jagger: Henry Hathaway's *Brigham Young* (20th Century–Fox, 1940).

2526

Porter: Zigzag. That means he wants to talk in peace. You zigzag out to meet him.

Porter Rockwell played by John Carradine: Henry Hathaway's *Brigham Young* (20th Century–Fox, 1940).

2527

Tom: Cochise can't even read a map. But he and his men know every gully, every foot of mountain, every waterhole in Arizona. His horses can go twice as far as yours in a day, and his men can run on foot as far as a horse can run. He can't write his name, but his intelligence service knows when you got to Fort Grant and how many men you got. He stopped the Butterfield Stage from running. He stopped the U.S. Mail from going through. And for the first time in Indian history, he has all the Apaches from all the tribes fighting under one command.

Tom Jeffords played by James Stewart and Cochise played by Jeff Chandler: Delmer Daves' *Broken Arrow* (20th Century–Fox, 1950).

Cochise (Jeff Chandler) and cavalry scout Tom Jeffords (James Stewart) trying to find peace in Delmer Daves' *Broken Arrow* (20th Century–Fox, 1950).

2528

Cochise: You should always wipe your hands on your arm after eating, tall one. The grease is good for them.

Tom: Ah, among white men we wash it off.

Cochise: What a waste!

Cochise played by Jeff Chandler and Tom Jeffords played by James Stewart: Delmer Daves' *Broken Arrow* (20th Century–Fox, 1950).

2529

Cochise: To talk of peace is not hard. To live it is very hard.

Cochise played by Jeff Chandler: Delmer Daves' *Broken Arrow* (20th Century–Fox, 1950).

2530

Cochise: I break the arrow. I will try the way of peace.

Cochise played by Jeff Chandler: Delmer Daves' *Broken Arrow* (20th Century–Fox, 1950).

2531

Cochise: Now I say this: the Americans keep cattle but they are not soft or weak. Why should not the Apache be able to learn new ways? It is not easy to change but sometimes it is required. The Americans are growing stronger while we are growing weaker. If a big wind comes, a tree must bend …or be lifted out of its roots.

Cochise played by Jeff Chandler: Delmer Daves' *Broken Arrow* (20th Century–Fox, 1950).

2532

Juan: Remember this: if you see him, do not lie to him. Not in the smallest thing. His eyes will see into your heart. He is greater than other men.

Juan played by Bill Wilkerson: Delmer Daves' *Broken Arrow* (20th Century–Fox, 1950).

2533

Tom: They found a pouch on one of the wounded men. And in the pouch there were three Apache scalps. So they dug a pit in the ground and they rubbed his face with the juice of a mescal plant. And they made me watch the ants come.

Tom Jeffords played by James Stewart: Delmer Daves' *Broken Arrow* (20th Century–Fox, 1950).

2534

Seth's wife: But you must be careful not to become so fond of their [white] ways that you ever forget who and what you are.

Seth's wife played by Buffy Sainte-Marie: Lamont Johnson's *The Broken Chain* (Turner Pictures, 1993).

2535

Brant: With my people, our mothers have taught us to bring into our home those we capture. Bring them into our lives, have them come as one with our nations, share our home fires.

Joseph Brant played by Eric Schweig: Lamont Johnson's *The Broken Chain* (Turner Pictures, 1993).

2536

Brant: As we turned our face to Canada, we left behind a new nation …the United States of America. A nation that was created in our image and that was paid for with the blood of the Iroquois people. But the people of the Long House will survive as long as we keep the Tree of Peace growing and the spirit of the council fire bright. For it is a spirit and a fire that must never be allowed to die. And as long as the people believe in it, they shall live on through all the ages. And they shall have the sanction of the Holder of the Heavens forever.

Joseph Brant played by Eric Schweig: Lamont Johnson's *The Broken Chain* (Turner Pictures, 1993).

2537

Franklin: What does it take to break a single arrow? Nothing! But bound together …unbreakable!

Ben Franklin played by John Hagadorn: Lamont Johnson's *The Broken Chain* (Turner Pictures, 1993).

2538

Yellow Hand: Men of the Nation. There's a black cloud coming from the east to cover us all. We, the Cheyenne, have called our brothers of the Sioux so we can hear the words about this thing. Yesterday, the buffalo was many as the blades of grass upon the prairie. Today, the buffalo is few as the leaves on an oak tree in winter. The white man has done this thing so the red man will starve. When the buffalo is done, we starve. We'll have no meat to eat, no hide to make tepees, no robes to make beds. Brothers, it's not good for man to hear his woman and children crying. It's a bad thing for a man to starve. There are better ways to die.

Yellow Hand played by Anthony Quinn: William Wellman's *Buffalo Bill* (20th Century–Fox, 1944).

2539

Ned: You know the Indian, Cody, don't you?

Cody: Nobody knows the Indian. I've had to fight them since I was fourteen. Pony Express, stage driver, scouting. Indians never do what you'd expect.

Ned Buntline played by Thomas Mitchell and Buffalo Bill Cody played by Joel McCrea: William Wellman's *Buffalo Bill* (20th Century–Fox, 1944).

2540

Cody: When you do an Indian a favor, he never forgets it. But if you do him bad, he never forgets that either.

Buffalo Bill Cody played by Joel McCrea: William Wellman's *Buffalo Bill* (20th Century–Fox, 1944).

2541

Louisa: What is she doing here all alone?

Cody: She's just old. When Indians get too old to travel, why they're left behind with a little food and fuel.

Louisa: To die?

Cody: Yeah.

Louisa: That's terrible! Can't we do something for her?

Cody: It's the way of the people. There's nothing we can do.

Louisa: Here am I, going to bring a new life into the world, and leaving an old woman behind to die.

Cody: That's nature way, Louisa. When anything becomes too old to be useful, it's just pushed aside.

Louisa: But it shouldn't be! That's why we have civilization!

Louisa Cody played by Maureen O'Hara and Buffalo Bill Cody played by Joel McCrea: William Wellman's *Buffalo Bill* (20th Century–Fox, 1944).

2542

Yellow Hand: Now there is no debt and no friendship between us. If we meet in battle, as a brave of the Cheyenne, I will take the scalp of Pahashka and hang it on his lodge pole.

Buffalo Bill: It may be easier to hang it than to take it, Yellow Hand.

Yellow Hand played by Anthony Quinn and Buffalo Bill Cody played by Joel McCrea: William Wellman's *Buffalo Bill* (20th Century–Fox, 1944).

2543

Burke: Don't worry about how you feel about where you ought to be …just come on over here where you should be.

Major Burke played by Kevin McCarthy: Robert Altman's *Buffalo Bill and the Indians, or Sitting Bull's History Lesson* (United Artists, 1976).

2544

Halsey: Great Father, Sitting Bull has waited to ask you a very simple thing for his people.

President: Mr. Halsey, I remind you that in government …nothing is simple.

William Halsey played by Will Sampson, President Grover Cleveland (the Great Father) played by Pat McCormick, and Sitting Bull played by Frank Kaquitts in Robert Altman's *Buffalo Bill and the Indians, or Sitting Bull's History Lesson* (United Artists, 1976).

2545

[*Ned Buntline explaining why Sitting Bull should be in a wild west show*]

Buntline: A rock ain't a rock once it becomes gravel.

Ned Buntline played by Burt Lancaster: Robert Altman's *Buffalo Bill and the Indians, or Sitting Bull's History Lesson* (United Artists, 1976).

2546

Buffalo Bill: The difference between a white man and an injun in all situations is that an injun is red. And an injun is red for a very good reason. So we can tell us apart!

Buffalo Bill played by Paul Newman: Robert Altman's *Buffalo Bill and the Indians, or Sitting Bull's History Lesson* (United Artists, 1976).

2547

Crutch: Come here, Mr. Buntline! Come over here and look at Sitting Bull! The son-of-a-bitch must be seven feet tall!

Buntline: He's getting smaller every year.

Crutch played by Bert Remsen, Ned Buntline played by Burt Lancaster, and Sitting Bull played by Frank Kaquitts: Robert Altman's *Buffalo Bill and the Indians, or Sitting Bull's History Lesson* (United Artists, 1976).

2548

Buntline: I bring up this dream business because, well, because things are beginning to take on an unreal shape. Now I was thinking of Sitting Bull. Just put yourself in that Injun's place. You sit in your tepee and you dream. And then you go to wherever the dream may take place …it might come true. And you wait for real life to catch up.

Ned Buntline played by Burt Lancaster and Sitting Bull played by Frank Kaquitts: Robert Altman's *Buffalo Bill and the Indians, or Sitting Bull's History Lesson* (United Artists, 1976).

2549

Buntline: Injuns gear their lives to dreams. And what an injun dreams, no matter how farfetched, will wait until he dies for it to come true. The white men, they're different. The only time they dream is when things are going their way. I'm no expert on the subject, but it seems to me that what Sitting Bull does is a hell of a lot cheaper than mounting a wild west show …which is just dreaming out loud.

Ned Buntline played by Burt Lancaster and Sitting Bull played by Frank Kaquitts: Robert Altman's *Buffalo Bill and the Indians, or Sitting Bull's History Lesson* (United Artists, 1976).

2550

[*talking to the ghost of Sitting Bull*]

Buffalo Bill: My God, look at ya! Look at ya! You want to stay the same! Well, that's going backwards!

Buffalo Bill played by Paul Newman and Sitting Bull played by Frank Kaquitts: Robert Altman's *Buffalo Bill and the Indians, or Sitting Bull's History Lesson* (United Artists, 1976).

2551

Halsey: Sitting Bull says that history is nothing more than disrespect for the dead.

William Halsey played by Will Sampson and Sitting Bull played by Frank Kaquitts: Robert Altman's *Buffalo Bill and the Indians, or Sitting Bull's History Lesson* (United Artists, 1976).

2552

No Ears: All massacres are alike: the smell of death, the big birds to pick the bones clean.

No Ears played by Floyd Red Crow Westerman: Rod Hardy's *Buffalo Girls* (Cabin Fever Entertainment, 1995).

2553

Wyatt: When an enemy praises an enemy, the smart man listens.

First Sergeant Washington Wyatt played by Danny Glover: Charles Haid's *Buffalo Soldiers* (Turner Pictures/Trilogy Group, 1997).

2554

[*Indian Chief speaking to Buffalo Soldier*]

Victorio: Why do you murder my people for those who made you less than cattle?

Victorio played by Harrison Lowe: Charles Haid's *Buffalo Soldiers* (Turner Pictures/Trilogy Group, 1997).

2555

Cahill: I thought an Indian didn't show pain. Especially a bona fide Comanche war chief.

Lightfoot: Who in the hell ever told you that? A damn white man?

Marshal J.D. Cahill played by John Wayne and Lightfoot played by Neville Brand: Andrew McLaglen's *Cahill: United States Marshal* (Warner Bros., 1973).

2556

Danny: One thing I hate more than a Comanche is half of one.

Cahill: His name is Lightfoot. And I wouldn't call him breed to his face if I were you. Not if you want to reach maturity.

Danny Cahill played by Gary Grimes and J.D. Cahill played by John Wayne: Andrew McLaglen's *Cahill: United States Marshal* (Warner Bros., 1973).

2557

Captain: It's the spirit that dances, not the man. Indian proverb.

Captain Apache played by Lee Van Cleef: Alexander Singer's *Captain Apache* (Scotia International, 1971).

2558

Cat: Jackson, what's happening?

Jackson: It's ghost sickness.

Cat: What?

Jackson: In this Indian religion, see, we believe what the gods did when they made

a man crazy was they made him fall in love.

Cat Ballou played by Jane Fonda and Jackson Two Bears played by Tom Nardini: Elliot Silverstein's *Cat Ballou* (Columbia, 1965).

2559

Merridew: You trust that injun?

Catlow: Well, they trust you.

Merridew: In that desert, I wouldn't trust no one. Especially me!

Merridew played by Jeff Corey and Jed Catlow played by Yul Brynner: Sam Wanamaker's *Catlow* (MGM, 1971).

2560

Colorados: And you go back to your settlement. Tell them that there are Indians who do not wish death to all whites …but peace.

Sierra Nevada: You're going to help us?

Colorados: Is it so hard to believe that I am a human being too?

Colorados played by Lance Fuller and Sierra Nevada Jones played by Barbara Stanwyck: Allan Dwan's *Cattle Queen of Montana* (RKO, 1954).

2561

Red Lance: My son, the time is not far when you must wear this buffalo helmet which is now mine. Your worries will be great, your problems many. But the greatest is not how to deal with the whites …but how to keep your own tribe together.

The Indian Chief Red Lance was uncredited: Allan Dwan's *Cattle Queen of Montana* (RKO, 1954).

2562

Colorados: The first thing you must learn from a white man is never ask reason.

Colorados played by Lance Fuller: Allan Dwan's *Cattle Queen of Montana* (RKO, 1954).

2563

Miles: I don't get it. Indians don't like to fight at night.

Grover: Why?

Miles: Because if they get killed in the dark, it'll always be dark in their happy hunting grounds.

Miles Archer played by Guy Madison and Grover Johnson played by Onslow Stevens: Gordon Douglas' *The Charge at Feather River* (Warner Bros., 1953).

2564

Grover: Well, if they had squaws with them, they would hardly be on the warpath, would they?

Miles: Anybody who tells you he can figure Indians …he's lyin'!

Grover Johnson played by Onslow Stevens and Miles Archer played by Guy Madison: Gordon Douglas' *The Charge at Feather River* (Warner Bros., 1953).

Chief Sitting Bull, played by William Halsey (Will Sampson), challanges Buffalo Bill (Paul Newman) to a duel to the death in the Wild West Show. *Buffalo Bill and the Indians or Sitting Bull's History Lesson* (United Artists, 1976).

2565

Archer: They'll charge again as soon as they pick a new chief.

Miles Archer played by Guy Madison: Gordon Douglas' *The Charge at Feather River* (Warner Bros., 1953).

2566

Quincey: Apaches don't leave tracks unless they got a reason.

Quincey Whitmore played by Jack Palance: Michael Winner's *Chato's Land* (United Artists, 1972).

2567

Joshua: I've seen Comanches in Texas. And, boy, I'll never want to see one again …I can tell you that.

Quincey: Well, you don't see Apaches. You don't hear 'em and you don't see 'em. It's like an act of God.

Joshua Everette played by James Whitmore and Quincey Whitmore played by Jack Palance: Michael Winner's *Chato's Land* (United Artists, 1972).

2568

Archer: Dull Knife! Little Wolf! What happened today changes nothing. The In-

dian Bureau is still pledged to provide you with adequate clothing and rations. And you're still pledged to abide by the law. Remember that!

Little Wolf: We are asked to remember much. The white man remembers nothing.

Captain Thomas Archer played by Richard Widmark and Little Wolf played by Ricardo Montalban: John Ford's *Cheyenne Autumn* (Warner Bros., 1964).

2569

Narrator: But this wasn't just another day to the Cheyenne. Far from their homeland, as out of place in this desert as eagles in a cage, their three great chiefs prayed over the Sacred Bundles …that at last the promises made to them when the white man sent them more than a year ago would today be honored. The promises that had led them to give up their own way of life in their own green and fertile country …1,500 miles to the north.

Narration by Richard Widmark: John Ford's *Cheyenne Autumn* (Warner Bros., 1964).

2570

Spanish Woman: They are angry …because my son fired the first shot.

Deborah: Does it ever matter who fires the first shot?

Spanish Woman played by Dolores Del Rio and Deborah Wright played by Carroll Baker: John Ford's *Cheyenne Autumn* (Warner Bros., 1964).

2571

Archer: Have you ever seen a Cheyenne?

Deborah: Of course I have.

Archer: No you haven't! All you've ever seen is reservation Indians looking pitiful as fish out of water. But give them a chance, and they're the greatest fighters in the world. Will you listen to me? It takes a blue coat to make a white man a soldier. But a Cheyenne is a soldier from the first slap on his butt. War is his life. He's fierce, he's smart …and he's meaner than sin!

Captain Thomas Archer played by Richard Widmark and Deborah Wright played by Carroll Baker: John Ford's *Cheyenne Autumn* (Warner Bros., 1964).

2572

Narrator: And so when the Nation was safe, the Sacred Bundle, symbol of the Chief of Chiefs, was passed on. For no one could carry it who had shed the blood of another Cheyenne.

Narration by Richard Widmark: John Ford's *Cheyenne Autumn* (Warner Bros., 1964).

2573

Little Wolf: I pray the young one will give me sons. But I want them to be born where I, and all my people before me, were born.

Dull Knife: Even a dog can go where he likes …but not a Cheyenne.

Little Wolf played by Ricardo Montalban and Dull Knife played by Gilbert Roland: John Ford's *Cheyenne Autumn* (Warner Bros., 1964).

2574

Little Wolf: You spoke the truth for us. This we will not forget. But there will be no more school.

Deborah: Oh, no! Oh, no, please don't do that to the children!

Little Wolf: The white man's words are lies. It is better that our children not learn them.

Deborah: It is not the words …but who speaks them. Has speaking white men's words made you a liar?

Dull Knife: Our words were learned long ago when some white men still spoke truth.

Little Wolf played by Ricardo Montalban, Deborah Wright played by Carroll Baker, and Dull Knife played by Gilbert Roland: John Ford's *Cheyenne Autumn* (Warner Bros., 1964).

2575

Little Wolf: This I say: we have always thought as one. Never has the thickness of a straw come between us.

Dull Knife: We still think as one.

Little Wolf: As war chief, I may raise my hand only against my enemy.

Dull Knife: We still think as one.

Little Wolf: That is why I must sleep with no wife …saving all my strength for a fight against the soldiers. But your son tries to steal my youngest wife.

Dull Knife: This can not be! He is my blood. And my blood has never been bad.

Little Wolf: He is of your blood …but he is not you.

Little Wolf played by Ricardo Montalban and Dull Knife played by Gilbert Roland: John Ford's *Cheyenne Autumn* (Warner Bros., 1964).

2576

Barkley: It's them Pawnee you got to watch out for. They'll kill ya just as soon as look at ya. They'll scalp ya with the right hand and …snatch your balls off with the left.

Barkley played by Dan Haggerty: Mark Griffiths' *Cheyenne Warrior* (Concorde — New Horizons Corp., 1994).

2577

Crazy Horse: How many times must the white man break his word? How short are your memories that you can again accept their promises? Has Old Man Afraid forgotten the peace talks on the Shell River? Has Sitting Bull forgotten the peace talks at Blue Water? Has Dull Knife forgotten the peace talks at Sand Creek? And Red Cloud? Has he forgotten our people who came to this fort before us, who has grown sick and old before their time? No, our nation will not be divided as it was at Shell River, at Blue Water, and at Sand Creek. I would like to ask my friend, Twist, a question. Why is today's promises any different from those of yesterday?

Twist: All I know is the Commissioner wants this fighting stopped.

Crazy Horse: He's put his name to the paper too many times before.

Twist: Always as a friend of the Lakotas.

Crazy Horse: Then the Lakotas prefer its enemies! I set my face against this treaty. This is our country …the sacred land of our fathers. I will fight for it …and I will die for it!

Crazy Horse played by Victor Mature and Major Twist played by John Lund: George Sherman's *Chief Crazy Horse* (Universal, 1955).

2578

Crazy Horse: My father looks at his son with eyes blinded by the lodge smoke.

Crazy Horse played by Victor Mature: George Sherman's *Chief Crazy Horse* (Universal, 1955).

2579

General: Why hunt buffalo? We're giving your people what they need.

Crazy Horse: But with my people, the buffalo hunt isn't the same as that with the whites. We don't hang the buffalo's head on a pole in the lodge and boast of our hunting skill. By eating his flesh, our flesh becomes strong. His skin makes our clothing, his bones our arrows, his hair makes the ropes for our horses. Even the covering on our feet comes from him. The buffalo is truly our friend …sent to us to give us life. Take this hunt from us and we are no longer Lakotas. We're no longer men. We're nameless and dead.

General Crook played by James Millican and Crazy Horse played by Victor Mature: George Sherman's *Chief Crazy Horse* (Universal, 1955).

2580

Mantz: It isn't often we get such fine pelts as you brought us …or such pretty yellow stones. Where did you get them?

Little Big Man: From the Lakota burial grounds. They ward off evil spirits. They are big medicine.

Jeff Mantz played by Robert F. Simon and Little Big Man played by Ray Danton: George Sherman's *Chief Crazy Horse* (Universal, 1955).

2581

Conquering Bear: Hear my words. Life melts from me. My eyes see into the midst. Someday a great warrior leader will arise among us. His medicine will be very strong against the whites. He will unite all the tribes of the Lakotas …and lead us to victory. But drive envy and jealousy from your hearts. For when this great warrior dies, it will be at the hand of a Lakota.

Conquering Bear played by Morris Ankrum: George Sherman's *Chief Crazy Horse* (Universal, 1955).

2582

Crazy Horse: I'm not speaking of visions. I'm speaking of a way to silence their guns without death. Time after time we've gone into battle like a herd of buffalo made crazy by fear. Knowing this, their soldiers have cut us down. I have watched their soldiers many, many times …and how their young men are held back by the commands of their leaders …until the time for the killing. Our young warriors must learn this. They must be obedient! They must be like the lance …that is obedient to the hand until it is thrown.

Crazy Horse played by Victor Mature: George Sherman's *Chief Crazy Horse* (Universal, 1955).

2583

Mantz: Take a good look, Little Big Man! Make up your mind. You'll see plenty more blood spilled and for a long time to come …until this country becomes civilized.

Jeff Mantz played by Robert F. Simon: George Sherman's *Chief Crazy Horse* (Universal, 1955).

2584

Chino: Anyway, a bunch of Indians stole my horses once. I went along and stole them back. And while they was chasing me, I came off my horse and got run over.

Jamie: Why didn't they kill you?

Chino: Hell, boy, they was my friends!

Chino Valdez played by Charles Bronson and Jamie Wagner played by Vincent Van Patten: John Sturges' *Chino* (Coral Film/Intercontinental Releasing Corporation, 1973).

2585

Chino: That's the way Indians bury their dead. They'd rather be close to the sun than have dirt thrown in their faces.

Chino Valdez played by Charles Bronson: John Sturges' *Chino* (Coral Film/Intercontinental Releasing Corporation, 1973).

2586

Colonel: I've discovered, Mr. Chuka, that to a savage kindness means weakness. He'll despise you for it. The moment you turn your back, he'll put a knife in it. I offer you that piece of intelligence, sir. It might save your life one day.

Chuka: Colonel, they're awful hungry out there. I think they're mean. And unless you give them food or the rifles to hunt their own, they're gonna come in here and take it. That's a little piece of intelligence that might save your life sometime.

Colonel Stuart Valois played by John Mills and Chuka played by Rod Taylor: Gordon Douglas' *Chuka* (Paramount, 1967).

2587

Steve: Chief, if you break the peace now, you'll make enemies of a lot of innocent people.

Chief: Dead enemies best way to peace.

Steve Farrell played by Randolph Scott and Chief Walking Bear played by Chief Thundercloud: Edwin L. Marin's *Colt .45* (Warner Bros., 1950).

2588

Lt. Sayre: My orders are to move you out.

Menquito: You speak of a place where vultures grow fat from the bodies of those who die without food in winter and without water in summer. This is our home. We will not move!

Lt. Sayre: Hear me well, Menquito. If you haven't given the word to your people by the time that cloud passes the sun, I'll open fire!

Lt. Jed Sayre played by Audie Murphy and Menquito played by Dennis Weaver: Frederick de Cordova's *Column South* (Universal, 1953).

2589

Ms. Whitlock: Listen carefully. I don't care if your [Indian] friend is the most important chief in the entire West. To me, he's just a redskin savage, and I can't

stand the stench long enough to stay in the same room with him.

Lt. Sayre: It wasn't him. You just got a good whiff of your own soul. And lady, all the perfume in the world wouldn't cover that up!

Ms. Marcy Whitlock played by Joan Evans and Lt.

Advertisement for *Colt .45* (Warner Bros., 1950). A gun salesman (Randolph Scott) has his Colt pistols stolen, and he sets out to get them back and apprehend the thief.

Jed Sayre played by Audie Murphy: Frederick de Cordova's *Column South* (Universal, 1953).

2590

Lt. Sayre: The point is, I don't think Barney was murdered by a Navajo or any other Indian.

Capt. Whitlock: Well, how can you say that? Half the man's head was gone!

Lt. Sayre: You didn't see an arrow sticking in him, did you?

Capt. Whitlock: Proving what?

Lt. Sayre: Proving this: an Indian may scalp a man, but he'll always stick an arrow in the body. It's superstition. It's supposed to pin the spirit to the corpse so it won't go rising up and haunting the guilty Indian or his friends.

Lt. Jed Sayre played by Audie Murphy and Captain Lee Whitlock played by Robert Sterling: Frederick de Cordova's *Column South* (Universal, 1953).

2591

Lt. Sayre: Then the peace is strong, Menquito?

Menquito: It will always be strong so long as there are men with strong minds to guard it well.

Lt. Jed Sayre played by Audie Murphy and Menquito played by Dennis Weaver: Frederick de Cordova's *Column South* (Universal, 1953).

2592

Read: So that's the way it is. Comanches kill Mexicans …to get even with the Spanish. And the Mexicans kill Comanche in revenge for that. It's become a way of life.

Ward: I can see how it began. But the Comanche must throw away their war paint, or we will have to make them.

Jim Read played by Dana Andrews and the Indian Bureau Chief John Ward played by Lowell Gilmore: George Sherman's *Comanche* (United Artists, 1956).

2593

Read: Oh, that young Mexican girl. No harm will come to her?

Chief: Tawalka and Morning Star will care for her. She's a captive. She belongs to the tribe.

Jim Read played by Dana Andrews and Chief Quanah Parker played by Kent Smith: George Sherman's *Comanche* (United Artists, 1956).

2594

Black Cloud: It is Comanche that no man leads unless others follow.

Black Cloud played by Henry Brandon: George Sherman's *Comanche* (United Artists, 1956).

2595

Flat Mouth: Medicine Mound. Sacred. Comanche only go there to meet Great Spirit.

Flat Mouth played by Mike Mazurki: George Sherman's *Comanche* (United Artists, 1956).

2596

Read: Let's head for Medicine Mound. You can see for miles. The Comanche don't go there except to die.

Jim Read played by Dana Andrews: George Sherman's *Comanche* (United Artists, 1956).

2597

General: You got here fast.

Read: You said it was urgent, General, so we cut across the Stake Plains.

General: With Comanches loose?

Read: We traveled at night mostly. Comanches hold up at night. It's bad medicine for them.

General Miles played by John Litel and Jim Read played by Dana Andrews: George Sherman's *Comanche* (United Artists, 1956).

2598

Chief: The Mexicans still collect gold from the government for Comanche scalps. Would you have me treat them as brothers?

Read: They will no longer buy Comanche scalps. I ask you to call the Americans and the Mexicans …brothers.

Chief: You ask me to be better than my enemies.

Read: I ask you to be greater. A great man can grant great favors.

Chief Quanah Parker played by Kent Smith and Jim Read played by Dana Andrews: George Sherman's *Comanche* (United Artists, 1956).

2599

Chief: But our numbers do not increase. And the Americans are without number …they are like weeds …like drops of rain .. no end to them.

Read: The time has come to walk the path of the Americans.

Chief: This has long been on my mind. The Americans are brave. They know many things. We must learn from them …or the sun will set on us forever.

Chief Quanah Parker played by Kent Smith and Jim Read played by Dana Andrews: George Sherman's *Comanche* (United Artists, 1956).

2600

Chief: I do not think of Americans. I think only of Comanches …and the children of Comanches …and the children that will come from those children. The Americans are here. They will stay. We cannot drive them out. They will grow strong while we will not. We must learn from them so that our children will not hunger …so they will be warm in winter …so they will grow strong as the Americans are strong.

Chief Quanah Parker played by Kent Smith: George Sherman's *Comanche* (United Artists, 1956).

2601

Chief: If my brother dies, the white man's death will not be as swift as his. We will see your tongue torn out by the root.

Chief Quanah Parker played by Kent Smith:

George Sherman's *Comanche* (United Artists, 1956).

2602

Chief: There are two white faces. Later, we will find out how long their spirits can stay in their bodies under endless torment.

Chief Quanah Parker played by Kent Smith: George Sherman's *Comanche* (United Artists, 1956).

2603

Bowie: So this is the mighty Quisima who sat on the council of the white man in Washington. This is Quisima who gave one hand in friendship to his white brothers while the other hand held a knife. This is Quisima whose words is shifting as the wind, whose tongue twists like a river of many branches. This is Quisima, breaker of treaties. Today, the Comanche is held in honor and respect like the mountain that never yields, or the sun that never changes. Tomorrow he will be driven off like a dog that wanders close to a campfire to take his place among men.

James Bowie played by Macdonald Carey and Quisima played by Pedro de Cordoba: George Sherman's *Comanche Territory* (Universal, 1950).

2604

Stacey: You all know what we're here for. I had you men picked because I think you all feel the way I do. We didn't come out here for the good of the glorious West …but for our own good. And that being so, we're moving in on Comanche territory tonight.

Stacey Howard played by Charles Drake: George Sherman's *Comanche Territory* (Universal, 1950).

2605

Quisima: If Comanches must die, they will die like men …but never give up sacred soil of their fathers.

Quisima played by Pedro de Cordoba: George Sherman's *Comanche Territory* (Universal, 1950).

2606

Seeger: You'll find this mighty interesting, Jim. Them bucks out there come galloping by and see how close they can come to us with their arrows. And then they try again ten paces further on …and so on.

Bowie: It's that "so on" that bothers me.

Dan'l Seeger played by Will Geer and James Bowie played by Macdonald Carey: George Sherman's *Comanche Territory* (Universal, 1950).

2607

Cutter: You see those dark markings? A cross patch over light. It makes him look like a rattler. But you can see a thousand like that one. But when you see your first rattlesnake, you'll know the difference.

Regret: You still haven't told me how you tell a Comanche from a tame Indian.

Cutter: Just like your first rattler. One look and you'll know.

Jake Cutter played by John Wayne and Paul Regret played by Stuart Whitman: Michael Curtiz's *The Comancheros* (20th Century–Fox, 1961).

2608

Martha: You sympathize with them. Why?

Captain: Perhaps because we destroyed the Indian's ability to make a distinction between the good and the bad. He has a child's logic: the white man hurt him …therefore, all white men are bad.

Martha played by Joan Weldon and Captain Robert MacClaw played by Guy Madison: David Butler's *The Command* (Warner Bros., 1953).

2609

Sergeant: Never say an injun is dumb. He just waits for the chance to use his one good cavalry tactic: ring around and close in.

Sergeant Elliott played by James Whitmore: David Butler's *The Command* (Warner Bros., 1953).

2610

McCloud: You keep a close lookout for Indians, ma'am. They ain't been troublesome lately, but you never can tell when they might start up again. Never give 'em anything. They take that as a sign of fear. Make 'em trade. They cotton to that.

Charlie McCloud played by Barry Corbin: Reynaldo Villalobos' *Conagher* (Turner Pictures, 1991).

2611

Major: It is a custom of our people, the handshake. It means we each give our word to what has been said.

Major Thomas Burke played by Robert Stack: William Castle's *Conquest of Cochise* (Columbia, 1953).

2612

Consuelo: Cochise, I'm sorry.

Cochise: You know about Terua?

Consuelo: Yes.

Cochise: You must never be sorry. People who are no longer with us have gone to another life …one that is much richer than ours …where there is no sickness, pain, death, or sorrow. We wish them well, and then never think about it again. I will start from the beginning …now, as if Terua never existed.

Consuelo de Cordova played by Joy Page, Terua played by Carol Thurston, and Cochise played by John Hodiak: William Castle's *Conquest of Cochise* (Columbia, 1953).

2613

Consuelo: Why does he turn his back on her? Doesn't he like her?

Cochise: This is the mother of his bride. Our custom forbids the husband to talk to his mother-in-law …forever.

Consuelo: How strange.

Cochise: In some ways, the custom of the Apache is superior to that of the white.

Consuelo de Cordova played by Joy Page and Cochise played by John Hodiak: William Castle's *Conquest of Cochise* (Columbia, 1953).

2614

Cochise: These young ones are being taught discipline and endurance. They all start off running, not full speed, but trotting. Somewhere along the road, a brave with water in a little container gives it to the runner and says, "take a mouthful, but do not swallow it." They run four miles with the water in their mouths. At the end of the course, each is inspected to see if he still has the water. If one has swallowed, the trainers see to it that he does not do it a second time.

Cochise played by John Hodiak: William Castle's *Conquest of Cochise* (Columbia, 1953).

2615

Major: Will Cochise, for the sake of a few raids on Mexican haciendas, force upon his people a war with the Americans? Or will he be for peace?

Cochise: I will be for peace …but my people may be for war.

Major: What will happen then?

Cochise: They will choose another chief …and make war.

Major Thomas Burke played by Robert Stack and Cochise played by John Hodiak: William Castle's *Conquest of Cochise* (Columbia, 1953).

2616

Terua: You do not want war with the white man?

Cochise: No.

Terua: Then do not do it. You are chief of the Apaches.

Cochise: Sometimes the will of his people is stronger than the will of their chief.

Terua played by Carol Thurston and Cochise played by John Hodiak: William Castle's *Conquest of Cochise* (Columbia, 1953).

2617

Cochise: Sometimes it is easier for the heart to do the talking.

Consuelo: But it is not always easy for the heart to make itself understood.

Cochise played by John Hodiak and Consuelo de Cordova played by Joy Page: William Castle's *Conquest of Cochise* (Columbia, 1953).

2618

Reporter: What about the Indians, General? And aren't the Black Hills officially Sioux land from the Treaty of 1868?

Custer: Whatever the right or wrong isn't the question. The Indians must be dispossessed. The practical question is how the inevitable can be accomplished with the least inhumanity to the Indians.

Reporter: Didn't General Polk say that?

Custer: I believe in destiny, you see. For individuals as well as nations. Nothing can stop the movement of history.

The Reporter played by James Hatzell and General George Custer played by Peter Horton: John Irvin's *Crazy Horse* (Turner Pictures, 1996).

2619

Conquering Bear: In 1865, the Civil War ended. As the flow of settlers heading westward increased, so did the disputes between the government, the settlers, and the Indians. Conflict was inevitable …

Voice of Conquering Bear played by Jimmy Herman in the prologue: John Irvin's *Crazy Horse* (Turner Pictures, 1996).

2620

Red Cloud: Our way of life is finished. There is only the white man's way, and we will learn it …or we will all die.

Crazy Horse: I speak only for myself. I'll live the way of my fathers …as a warrior.

Red Cloud played by Wes Studi and Crazy Horse played by Michael Greyeyes: John Irvin's *Crazy Horse* (Turner Pictures, 1996).

2621

Custer: They are a brave people. Their time has passed. History moves on.

General George Custer played by Peter Horton: John Irvin's *Crazy Horse* (Turner Pictures, 1996).

2622

To be a leader among men. That's what it was to be made a shirt wearer among the Lakota. Shirt wearers led the people and protected them at all times. Shirt wearing was the honor that usually went to the sons of chiefs and tribal leaders.

Voice of Conquering Bear played by Jimmy Herman: John Irvin's *Crazy Horse* (Turner Pictures, 1996).

2623

Crazy Horse: My first time in battle, I went against my vision. That's why I was wounded.

Worm: There will be plenty more battles, my son. Remember what your vision promised: you'll be a strong shield for the people.

Crazy Horse played by Michael Greyeyes and Worm was uncredited: John Irvin's *Crazy Horse* (Turner Pictures, 1996).

2624

You looked at me and saw what happens to a man of peace in times of war. Now I see what happens to man of war in times of peace. Come with me now, Crazy Horse.

Voice of Conquering Bear played by Jimmy Herman: John Irvin's *Crazy Horse* (Turner Pictures, 1996).

2625

Anyone can kill a man. Anyone can take a scalp. But only the bravest warrior can count coup and fight with no weapon at all.

Voice of Conquering Bear played by Jimmy Herman: John Irvin's *Crazy Horse* (Turner Pictures, 1996).

2626

Crazy Horse: White man eat raw oysters …cook frogs …but grow pale about eating worms. You have strange ways, Yellow Hair.

Crazy Horse played by Michael Dante and Lieutenant Colonel George Armstrong Custer ("Yellow Hair") played by Wayne Maunder: Norman Foster's *Crazy Horse and Custer: The Untold Story* (TVW, 1967).

2627

Pitcalin: I figure I'll meet the Apaches sooner or later. I guess I'd rather it be later.

Pitcalin played by Jody McCrea: Jack Starrett's *Cry Blood, Apache* (Golden Eagle, Goldstone, 1970).

2628

Custer: I'll make it very simple for you. The fact that we seem to be pushing you clear off the earth is not my responsibility. The problem is precisely the same as when you Cheyenne decided to take another tribe's hunting ground. You didn't ask them about their rights. You didn't care if they had been there a thousand years. You just had more men and more horses. You destroyed them in battle. You took what you wanted. And right or wrong, for better or worse, that is the way things seem to get done. That's history. I'm talking about history. You are a militarily defeated people. You are paying the price for being backward.

George Armstrong Custer played by Robert Shaw: Robert Siodmak and Irving Lerner's *Custer of the West* (Security Pictures/Cinerama, 1968).

2629

[*Senator attempting to reason with hidden Indians*]

Indian brothers, hear me! I extend my hand to you in friendship. Soon I go to the tents of your many chiefs to speak of peace and smoke the pipe in everlasting brotherhood. The promises I make you will be honored. If you allow us to go in peace and safety, then my mission can be fulfilled. And once again, you can lay aside your war drums and return to your families, raise your corn, and hunt your buffalo. Tell me that my words are not blown away with the wind. Tell me that I am heard. Tell me that you will leave here now in peace and go to your villages. Speak to me, Indian brothers, so that I may know. So that …

[*whiff of an arrow into Senator's gut*]

You were right, Miss Clarke. Words aren't enough. But perhaps they just didn't understand.

Senator Blakely played by Ward Bond and Amy Clarke played by Linda Darnell: Lewis R. Foster's *Dakota Incident* (Republic, 1956).

2630

Chester: Maybe we oughtn't have a fire if there's Indians around.

Minstrel: With the moon as high, it won't make no difference. Anyhow, injuns don't need to see. They got an uncanny ear for hearing. They can hear a shadow moving over peach fuzz …a goose bump rising on a white man.

Mark Chester played by Whit Bissell and Minstrel played by Regis Toomey: Lewis R. Foster's *Dakota Incident* (Republic, 1956).

2631

Indian: I make you present [Indian's horse].

Banner: White man thanks Indian.

Clarke: But, your people! They went away, they left you!

Indian: I walk back to my home over the mountains.

Banner: But why?

Indian: It is the custom of my people. The walk is part of the gift.

The Indian played by Charles Horvath, John Banner played by Dale Robertson, and Amy Clarke played by Linda Darnell: Lewis R. Foster's *Dakota Incident* (Republic, 1956).

2632

Chester: What do them savages know about God? What kind of religion does an Indian got?

Blakely: Well, among other things, the religion of taking only from the land that which is necessary for his survival. The Indian takes his food from the small end of the Horn of Plenty. The white man spills his from the large end, and leaves it to rot upon the ground.

Minstrel: Just like a politician spilling words out of the big end. Senator, your Horn of Plenty is the same at both ends …no small end, none at all!

Mark Chester played by Whit Bissell, Senator Blakely played by Ward Bond, and Minstrel played by Regis Tooney: Lewis R. Foster's *Dakota Incident* (Republic, 1956).

2633

Blakely: These things are bound to happen. Until we can find a common ground, a common language …

Clarke: You can't kill an Indian with words.

Blakely: Never underestimate the power of words, Miss Clarke. It only takes one word to start a war: charge. There's also a single word to end one: armistice.

Clarke: Have you found the words to end this one?

Senator Blakely played by Ward Bond and Amy Clarke played by Linda Darnell: Lewis R. Foster's *Dakota Incident* (Republic, 1956).

2634

Blakely: In my small way, I'm trying to unite our people: the Indians and the white.

Clarke: I hope your scalp is glued on tight. Have you ever met an Indian face-to-face?

Blakely: Only in the literary sense. You see, I happen to be a student of anthropology.

Clarke: So was General Custer. It didn't help him very much.

Senator Blakely played by Ward Bond and Amy Clarke played by Linda Darnell: Lewis R. Foster's *Dakota Incident* (Republic, 1956).

2635

Wind In His Hair: We will shoot some arrows into the white man. If he truly has medicine, he will not be hurt. If he has no medicine, he will be dead.

Wind In His Hair played by Rodney A. Greene: Kevin Costner's *Dances with Wolves* (TIG/Orion, 1990).

2636

Warfield: What happened to my family? Where are they?

Jimmy: All I know is that the Apaches delivered them up for death.

Warfield: What does that mean?

Jimmy: I don't know.

Lorn Warfield played by Glenn Ford and Jimmy Noble played by Dean Jagger: Jerry Thorpe's *Day of the Evil Gun* (MGM, 1968).

2637

Blake: What is your name?

Nobody: My name is Nobody.

Blake: Excuse me?

Nobody: My name is Xamichee, "he who talks loud says nothing."

Blake: "He who talks"? I thought you said your name was Nobody.

Nobody: Well, I prefer to be called Nobody.

William Blake played by Johnny Depp and Nobody played by Gary Farmer: Jim Jarmusch's *Dead Man* (Miramax Films, 1996).

2638

Nobody: The eagle never lost so much time as when he submitted to learn from the crow.

Nobody played by Gary Farmer: Jim Jarmusch's *Dead Man* (Miramax Films, 1996).

2639

Colonel: Tell him he is welcome. And throw in some guff about what a great chief he is, how he is stronger than the buffalo and wiser then the bear. Tell him his name is enough to freeze Mexican blood. We need some wind here. They expect it.

Colonel Caleb Cobb played by F. Murray Abraham: Yves Simoneau's *Dead Man's Walk* (Cabin Fever Entertainment, 1996).

2640

McCrae: I wonder why he pointed that lance at us?

Bes Das: He said that both of you belong to him. He says he will take you when he is ready, but not today. He is coming to eat supper with the Colonel and will bring his wives.

McCrae: Now how does he figure that we belong to him?

Bes Das: You cheated his lance. His lance is hungry for your liver.

McCrae: Well, it can just stay hungry!

Augustus McCrae played by David Arquette and Bes Das played by Jimmie F. Skaggs: Yves Simoneau's *Dead Man's Walk* (Cabin Fever Entertainment, 1996).

2641

Shadrach: That Mexican didn't have no way to kill hisself …didn't have no gun.

Bigfoot: No, but he had a knife. A knife is adequate if you know where to cut.

Woodrow: Where would you cut?

Bigfoot: You cut at the jugular …right here [pointing]. Now you could do it with a broken bottle or even poke a big mesquite thorn in there …if that's all you got available. You want to cut two or three times though. That way you bleed to death before they get a chance to do much torture.

Bill: Me, I'll shoot myself in the head if I got time.

Bigfoot: Well, that could go wrong, too. Don't be sticking no gun in your mouth unless it's a shotgun.

Augustus: Why not? It's hard to miss your head with a gun in your mouth.

Bigfoot: No, it ain't. That bullet could ricochet off a tooth …come out your ear. You'd still be healthy enough for them to torture for a week. You shove the butt of a gun up against an eyeball …and pull. Now, that's sure. Then if some squaw comes along and chews off your privates, you won't know the difference.

Augustus: Mercy!

Major: My, this is a cheery conversation!

Bigfoot: Some of these boys are inexperienced, Major. If they don't know the proper way to finish themselves, they could wind up prisoners of the Comanche some day. They would be real bad. A Comanche can keep a captive alive three or four days while they have their fun with them.

Major: Back in the Tidewater, Mr. Wallace, we usually refrain from discussing suicide methods over breakfast.

Augustus: They got no call chewing on people like that!

Bigfoot: Oh, there's worse than that happens.

Bill: What's worse than having your privates chewed off?

Bigfoot: Oh, having 'em pull out the end of your gut and tie it to a dog. And then chase the dog around the camp for awhile until there's about 50 foot of your gut strung out for the brats to eat.

Augustus: Oh, God!

Bill: To eat? To eat?

Shadrach: Comanche brats eat guts like white brats eat candy.

Major: [departing] Well, I'm certainly glad I wasn't hungry this morning! Talk like this might unsettle it …delicate stomach. Gentlemen.

Bigfoot: Or they might run a stick up the fundament and set it on fire. That way your guts will done be cooked when they pull them out.

Woodrow: What's a fundament?

Shadrach: It's a hole in your body. It ain't your nose or your mouth or either of your ears. Figure it out.

Shadrach played by Harry Dean Stanton, Bigfoot Wallace played by Keith Carradine, Woodrow F. Call played by Jonny Lee Miller, Bill was uncredited, Augustus McCrae played by David Arquette, and Major Chevallie played by Brian Dennehy: Yves Simoneau's *Dead Man's Walk* (Cabin Fever Entertainment, 1996).

2642

Hetty: Then you're not sure then that the Hurons will give him up.

Deerslayer: Well, that depends upon what they want the most: Old Tom or the scalps of their dead.

Harry: What makes you think they want them scalps at all?

Deerslayer: Well, all Indians are superstitious. Hurons more than most. They believe that the spirit of the scalped warrior can never rest …until the scalp is reclaimed.

Harry: And then you can't go the Happy Hunting Grounds without his hair on, huh?

Hetty played by Rita Moreno, Deerslayer played by Lex Barker, Harry Marsh played by Forrest Tucker, and Old Tom Hutter played by Jay C.

Flippen: Kurt Neumann's *The Deerslayer* (20th Century–Fox, 1957).

2643

Old Tom: Thank ye, oh Lord, for delivering my enemies into my hands. When them blood-lustin' heathen Hurons come loping this way, I'm going to give 'em hellfire, and damnation right out of the mouth of my cannon. I'm going to smite 'em hip and thigh like the Good Book says …and teach 'em the error of their sinful ways. Amen, Lord.

Old Tom Hutter played by Jay C. Flippen: Kurt Neumann's *The Deerslayer* (20th Century–Fox, 1957).

2644

Natachai: Before the beginning of time, a great warrior God battled the father of all eagles in the mountain higher than the sky. And when he defeated that giant eagle, he sat alone on the mountain. He sat, and he soon found that the sorrow called death must come not only to the father of all eagles, but to all men as well. And in his love for all things alive, and for his sorrow for all things dead, he became born again. And when this happened, the eagle came magically to life and soared high within his heart. As long as men have love for all things living, and sorrow for all things dead, then will warriors have two lives …but die only once.

Narachai played by Ricardo Montalban: Burt Kennedy's *The Deserter* (a.k.a. *Ride to Glory*; Paramount, 1971).

2645

Crawford: I thought Apaches were supposed to be so damn quiet?

Kaleb: They yell like that to scare you.

Crawford: They sure as hell did!

Crawford played by Ian Bannen and Captain Viktor Kaleb played by Bekim Fehmiu: Burt Kennedy's *The Deserter* (a.k.a. *Ride to Glory*; Paramount, 1971).

2646

Lance: The whites outnumber us, Father. The war is over. All the wars …even yours. The country is growing up. They gave me these stripes without testing my blood. I led a squad of white men. I slept in the same blankets with them, ate out of the same pan. I held their heads when they died. Why should it be any different now?

Mr. Poole: You are home. You are again an Indian.

Lance Poole played by Robert Taylor and Mr. Poole played by Fritz Leiber: Anthony Mann's *Devil's Doorway* (MGM, 1950).

2647

Lance: It's hard to explain how an Indian feels about the earth. It's the pumping of our blood …the love we got to have. My father said the earth is our mother. I was raised in the valley, and now I'm part of it. Like the mountains and the hills, the deer, the pine trees and the wind. Deep in my heart I know I belong. If we lose it now, we might as well all be dead.

Lance Poole played by Robert Taylor: Anthony Mann's *Devil's Doorway* (MGM, 1950).

2648

Lance: Every Shoshoni boy has to go through that. It's a test. Before a boy turns into a man, the tribe wants to know if he measures up.

Mrs. Masters: Well, what does he have to do?

Lance: He's given a knife, nothing else. No food, no water. He has to go up into the mountains above the snow line …and bring back the talons of an eagle. He has three days to do it in. He has to be back on the third day before the sun goes down.

Orrie: Isn't it rather cruel?

Lance: It depends upon your point of view. You see, Shoshoni are a small tribe. Every man counts. Suppose one day that boy had to fight for his people. Wouldn't it be a good idea if they knew they could depend upon him?

Lance Poole played by Robert Taylor, Mrs. Masters played by Spring Byington, and Orrie Masters played by Paula Raymond: Anthony Mann's *Devil's Doorway* (MGM, 1950).

2649

Mr. Poole: Drop my body in a deep shaft. Then you must keep this earth always, for I am part of it. An Indian without land loses his soul …and his heart with it. Sweet Meadows is our mother …the earth.

Mr. Poole played by Fritz Leiber: Anthony Mann's *Devil's Doorway* (MGM, 1950).

2650

Sergeant: Indians, sir!

General: My God, we're in luck. We will make our stand here. Sergeant!

Sergeant: Yes sir!

General: Circle the wagons!

Sergeant: We ain't got enough, sir.

General: Well, make a half moon!

The Sergeant played by Terry Wilson and the General played by John Dehner: Burt Kennedy's *Dirty Dingus Magee* (MGM, 1970).

2651

Monk: These injuns smell a little gamely, Captain. They rub skunk oil on themselves to keep off the bugs and flies.

Monk played by Arthur Hunnicutt amd Captain Quincy Wyatt played by Gary Cooper: Raoul Walsh's *Distant Drums* (Warner Bros., 1951).

2652

Wyatt: An interesting thing about the way the Seminoles bury their warriors. They sit 'em up and put war paint on 'em, set a bowl of fresh food along side of 'em and then stick their favorite weapon in their hands. And then they cover 'em up. With a great chief like that over yonder, they throw in the first new born child to be born after he died.

Tufts: Why do they do a thing like that for?

Wyatt: Well, they believe when a man dies, his spirit leaves the body and enters that of the first new born. And in regarding a chief high like that, they don't want the spirit to be passed on down to somebody that ain't fit to carry it.

Captain Quincy Wyatt played by Gary Cooper and Richard Tufts played by Richard Webb: Raoul Walsh's *Distant Drums* (Warner Bros., 1951).

2653

Wyatt: They still don't like fighting at night. But they'll come a hootin' and a hollerin' at dawn!

Monk: It makes me fonder than ever of moonshine!

Captain Quincy Wyatt played by Gary Cooper and Monk played by Arthur Hunnicutt: Raoul Walsh's *Distant Drums* (Warner Bros., 1951).

2654

Lieutenant: All right, now take a good look at them. It's going to make killing Apaches a lot easier. They were buried alive. Those ants are eating their brains out!

Lieutenant Matthew Hazard played by Troy Donahue: Raoul Walsh's *A Distant Trumpet* (Warner Bros., 1964).

2655

MacKay: Peace is going to be awfully hard to get.

Bill: That's your business …not mine!

MacKay: Bill, I need your help. Don't go running off half wild killin' Modocs. Only one got Lily.

Bill: You think she was worth only one of them devils? You dish out your peace, Johnny. I'll dish out my end!

Peace Commissioner Johnny MacKay played by Alan Ladd and Bill Satterwhite played by Robert Keith: Delmer Daves' *Drum Beat* (Warner Bros., 1954).

2656

Mr. Dyar: You see, Doc, out this way the Bible and brotherly love get all mixed up with injun hate.

Mr. Dyar played by Frank Ferguson and Dr.

Thomas played by Richard Gaines: Delmer Daves' *Drum Beat* (Warner Bros., 1954).

2657

Gen. Canby: We want to stop this purposeless killing. Any war that doesn't bring about a peace with honor is futile.

Mr. Dyar: Well, peace with honor and peace with Captain Jack are apt to be jackasses of two mighty different colors.

General Canby played by Warner Anderson and Mr. Dyar played by Frank Ferguson: Delmer Daves' *Drum Beat* (Warner Bros., 1954).

2658

MacKay: Have you met Captain Jack yet?

Dr. Thomas: I look forward to the pleasure.

MacKay: That's one thing it won't be.

Mr. Dyar: You can say that in spades!

Peace Commissioner Johnny MacKay played by Alan Ladd, Dr. Thomas played by Richard Gaines, and Mr. Dyar played by Frank Ferguson: Delmer Daves' *Drum Beat* (Warner Bros., 1954).

2659

Nellie: Have you actually seen Indians bite the dust?

MacKay: They don't really bite it, Miss. They hit it.

Nellie was the daughter of President Ulysses Grant. Johnny MacKay played by Alan Ladd: Delmer Daves' *Drum Beat* (Warner Bros., 1954).

2660

President: What kind of a man is he [Captain Jack]?

MacKay: Well, some people say he's got a little white blood in him …because of his white eye. But I think it's mostly bad blood.

President Ulysses Grant played by Hayden Rorke, Johnny MacKay played by Alan Ladd, and Captain Jack played by Charles Bronson: Delmer Daves' *Drum Beat* (Warner Bros., 1954).

2661

MacKay: And thus ended the killing in the Modoc country. And the peace began among our people that lives to this day. A peace that wasn't won by just wanting it, but costs plenty …but left scars. But it showed the country something we had to learn and remember: that among the Indians, as amongst our people, the good in heart outnumber the bad, and they will offer their lives to prove it.

Johnny MacKay played by Alan Ladd: Delmer Daves' *Drum Beat* (Warner Bros., 1954).

2662

Preacher: You'll never want for anything in heaven, Jack. When you go through those

Indian girl Toby (Marisa Pavan) tells peace men that they would be ill-advised to meet with Captain Jack, leader of the Modoc tribe. *Sitting:* Dr. Thomas (Richard Gaines), Gen. Canby (Warner Anderson), Johnny MacKay (Alan Ladd), and Mr. Dyar (Frank Ferguson). Manok (Anthony Caruso) is Toby's brother in *Drum Beat* (Warner Bros., 1954).

Pearly Gates, you'll find everything there …even without you asking for it.

Capt. Jack: You say this heaven nice place, huh? You like this place you call heaven?

Preacher: Yes. it's a beautiful place!

Capt. Jack: Then I tell you what, Preacher. You like it so much, you take my place out there [gallows]. You go to heaven instead of me. What do you say?

Preacher: Well now, I'll be ready when the great day comes.

Capt. Jack: You not ready now …me not ready neither!

The Preacher was uncredited and Captain Jack played by Charles Bronson: Delmer Daves' *Drum Beat* (Warner Bros., 1954).

2663

Capt. Jack: Red man think he go to good place when he die. Good hunting …good shooting …no white man. None! You're not like preacher who talk about Pearly Gates. You got sense. You

tell me, Johnny, you believe there is place like this?

MacKay: Yes, I believe that, Jack. Except I think it's open for all of us when we die. I think they, ah, even let white men in.

Capt. Jack: If I see that it's for red man only up there, maybe someday I tell them: you let Johnny MacKay in, he good fighter!

MacKay: Thanks, Jack. Maybe I'll see you up there. Goodbye …and good luck …and good hunting!

Captain Jack played by Charles Bronson and Johnny MacKay played by Alan Ladd: Delmer Daves' *Drum Beat* (Warner Bros., 1954).

2664

MacKay: More killing means war, Jack.

Capt. Jack: Then there will be war.

MacKay: War is no good. In war, only one side wins. In peace, both sides win.

Peace Commissioner Johnny MacKay played by Alan Ladd and Captain Jack played by Charles Bronson: Delmer Daves' *Drum Beat* (Warner Bros., 1954).

2665

Chief Ouray: I fought the enemies of peace, no matter who, while I lived. I will fight them after my death.

Chief Ouray played by Morris Ankrum: Nathan Juran's *Drums Across the River* (Universal, 1954).

2666

Willard: You mean you like living with a bunch of savages?

Ellen: You don't understand.

Willard: Well, no, I don't understand. Lots of white women have been grabbed off by the Indian. And many a decent one of them would have killed herself before she let them turn her into an Indian squaw.

Ellen: I'm not that decent, I guess!

Willard: Oh, don't shout. They'll hear ya.

Ellen: You don't care what happens to me …but only what people think about you!

Willard: I do business with them people.

Ellen: The same people who treat your wife like dirt. I was better off with the Indians!

Willard Grange played by Dennis Weaver and Ellen Grange played by Bibi Anderson: Ralph Nelson's *Duel at Diablo* (United Artists, 1966).

2667

Lem: There's a funny glow in the sky tonight, ain't there? I remember once hearing one of them injun legends about how their ancestors lit bonfires in the sky when the chief's son was a dying.

Lem Smoot played by Harry Carey: King Vidor's *Duel in the Sun* (Selznick Releasing Organization, 1946).

2668

Pike: I thought you traded regular with the Comanche?

Henry: Yeah, and I walk in rattlesnake country too. I'm just careful how I do it.

Pike played by Martin Sheen and Henry played by Harvey Keitel: Anthony Harvey's *Eagle's Wing* (Eagle's Wing Productions/Rank, 1979).

2669

Pesky: I sure hope them Indians aren't the scalping variety!

Pesky played by George "Gabby" Hayes: Lewis Foster's *El Paso* (Paramount, 1949).

2670

Govern: Don't string out. Indians like to pick off the last man.

Govern Sturges played by John Lund: Roger Corman's *Five Guns West* (American Releasing Corp., 1955).

2671

Indian: Are you my brother beyond the wall?

Half-Breed: Yeah.

Indian: Then why light go out when friend come in peace?

Half-Breed: Why does a friend who come in peace wait until the sun is gone?

Indian: Warrior ride when stars are alive.

Half-Breed: Only a guest has enemies.

Indian: In the world of white men, there are men who are not enemies nor friends.

Buffalo Horn played by Rodolfo Acosta and Pacer Burton, the half-breed, played by Elvis Presley: Don Siegel's *Flaming Star* (20th Century–Fox, 1960).

2672

Captain: I have some experience with the Shawnee. While they have great respect for courage, they have no patience for the sick or the wounded.

The Captain (British officer) was uncredited: Martin Davidson's *Follow the River* (Hallmark Home Entertainment, 1995).

2673

Snake Stick: You must know that they adopt captives to replace Shawnee people killed by white men.

Snake Stick played by Jimmie F. Skaggs: Martin Davidson's *Follow the River* (Hallmark Home Entertainment, 1995).

2674

Kirby: Well, if you saw them, sir, they weren't Apache.

Captain Kirby York played by John Wayne: John Ford's *Fort Apache* (RKO, 1948).

2675

Vinson: Now don't get the idea that Charlie and Adele are Indian lovers. They're just business people …dealing flour, sugar, rifles, dead soldiers.

Charlie: Look, Sergeant, I know you don't like us. But look at it from our standpoint.

Vinson: If I had my way, your standpoint would be up against a wall.

Sgt. Vinson played by Joel McCrea and Charlie played by Irving Bacon: Joseph Newman's *Fort Massacre* (United Artists, 1958).

2676

Pawnee: Indians believe it is wrong to kill. Paint face …fool God.

Pawnee, an Army Scout, played by Anthony Caruso: Joseph Newman's *Fort Massacre* (United Artists, 1958).

2677

Pawnee: There is much talk of heaven. Very fine place. But who is anxious to go there?

Pawnee, an Army Scout, played by Anthony Caruso: Joseph Newman's *Fort Massacre* (United Artists, 1958).

2678

Piute Girl: Piutes say that all journeys are without reason. You move from the place where you were born to where you will die.

The Piute Girl played by Susan Cabot: Joseph Newman's *Fort Massacre* (United Artists, 1958).

2679

Pawnee: You will learn: what is in man's heart is more dangerous than what is in his hand.

Pawnee, the Army Scout, played by Anthony Caruso: Joseph Newman's *Fort Massacre* (United Artists, 1958).

2680

Dick: They look like Sioux. I wonder what they are doing here?

Carey: I don't know, but they look like trouble to me.

Dick: No, if they were in a killing mood, we would have been full of arrows long ago.

Dick Ross played by James Craig and Carey played by Keith Larsen: Lesley Selander's *Fort Vengeance* (Allied Artists, 1953).

2681

Sitting Bull: It is forbidden to speak of the dead unless it concerns vengeance.

Sitting Bull played by Michael Granger: Lesley Selander's *Fort Vengeance* (Allied Artists, 1953).

2682

Sitting Bull: Can a wolf be told he is now a rabbit easier than a Sioux warrior can be told he must forget his heritage?

Crowfoot: I am an old man, and I have seen many animals. My favorite among them is the fox …who is not helpless like the rabbit, nor hated like the wolf.

Sitting Bull played by Michael Granger and Chief Crowfoot played by Morris Ankrum: Lesley Selander's *Fort Vengeance* (Allied Artists, 1953).

2683

Cochise: A man who turns on his friends cannot be trusted by his enemies.

Cochise played by Michael Keep: William Witney's *40 Guns to Apache Pass* (Columbia, 1967).

2684

Lolly: They say Indians don't talk much. But give them some smoke and they chatter like women at the church social.

Lolly Bhumer played by Colleen Miller: Richard Carlson's *Four Guns to the Border* (Universal, 1954).

2685

Dutch: I don't like this dang weather. It's injun weather.

Dutch played by John McIntire: Richard Carlson's *Four Guns to the Border* (Universal, 1954).

2686

Chief: Your heart is big …not as big as your mouth …but you have good feelings inside.

Chief Gary Cloud played by Val Bisoglio: Robert Aldrich's *The Frisco Kid* (Warner Bros., 1979).

2687

Avram: What did they want?

Tommy: They wanted our horses, our guns, our scalps! Jesus, I don't know …they wanted our asses, that's what they wanted!

Avram: But why? What did we do?

Tommy: They've been shit on by white men so long they don't ask questions no more.

Avram Belinsky played by Gene Wilder and Tommy played by Harrison Ford: Robert Aldrich's *The Frisco Kid* (Warner Bros., 1979).

2688

Charles Afraid of Bear: If I steal what belongs to me, how can I be stealing?

Charles Afraid of Bear played by Jimmie F. Skaggs: Dick Lowry's *The Gambler, Part III — The Legend Continues* (TVW, 1987).

2689

Buffalo Bill: If the other chiefs do sign [treaty] and you do not, what will happen to you and your people?

Sitting Bull: There will be no real Indians left but me.

Buffalo Bill played by Jeffrey Jones and Chief Sitting Bull played by George American Horse: Dick Lowry's *The Gambler, Part III — The Legend Continues* (TVW, 1987).

2690

Mary: Some Sioux believe that the Ghost Dance is the last chance they have to regain their land, bring back the buffalo, and live in peace.

Mary Collins played by Linda Gray: Dick Lowry's *The Gambler, Part III — The Legend Continues* (TVW, 1987).

2691

Iron Dog: It is easy to be fair and honest while pointing a rifle at another's man heart.

Iron Dog played by Richard Chaves: Dick Lowry's *The Gambler, Part III — The Legend Continues* (TVW, 1987).

2692

Billy: What are they saying?

Buffalo Bill: The little one wants to kill us right now. The big one says he has to take us to Sitting Bull and let him decide.

Brady: I like the big one!

Billy Montana played by Bruce Boxleitner, Buffalo Bill played by Jeffrey Jones, Brady Hawkes played by Kenny Rogers, and Chief Sitting Bull played by George American Horse: Dick Lowry's *The Gambler, Part III — The Legend Continues* (TVW, 1987).

2693

Leah: After the volcano, it became sacred to the Indians …a place of evil spirits.

Hooker: Only you don't believe in them.

Leah: Do you?

Hooker: I believe in Indians!

Leah Fuller played by Susan Hayward and Hooker played by Gary Cooper: Henry Hathaway's *Garden of Evil* (20th Century–Fox, 1954).

2694

Luke: Hey, what's this all about?

Hooker: There's Indians here somewhere and they left a message.

Luke: What did it say?

Hooker: It's Apache.

Luke: Well, what else?

Hooker: Well, that's enough!

Luke Daly played by Cameron Mitchell and Hooker played by Gary Cooper: Henry Hathaway's *Garden of Evil* (20th Century–Fox, 1954).

2695

Geronimo: You have your own horse now, Giantah. You're a man. From now on you act like a man.

Giantah: Yes, Geronimo.

Geronimo: You ride with your shoulders back and your head held proud. And when anyone asks you who you are, you say: "I am an Apache," and they won't ask you again.

Geronimo played by Chuck Connors and Giantah played by Mario Navarro: Arnold Laven's *Geronimo* (United Artists, 1962).

2696

Geronimo: This time we don't fight just to stay alive like before. This time we declare war.

Mangus: Fifty men declare war against the whole United States? What kind of war is that?

Geronimo: Don't laugh at me!

Mangus: I'm not laughing, I'm crying. Because you're crazy, you know. Geronimo, we have no chance. We can't win, and we'll probably all die. Even I know that!

Geronimo: No Mangus, we can win. We can win because we have no chance, and yet we fight. But we got to fight long enough. Long enough for the people of the United States to begin to wonder why such a small handful of men go on fighting a war against such a big country as theirs. Long enough until they ask themselves, why do the Apaches starve and die instead of surrender? That's when they will begin to understand. And when they do, maybe their leader, Mr. Washington himself, will come right here. And he'll have a new treaty. A treaty that says how important it is for all men to be proud and strong …and believe in what they are.

Mangus: I love you. Of course, you have no sense. You have a soul, but no sense.

Geronimo played by Chuck Connors and Mangus played by Ross Martin: Arnold Laven's *Geronimo* (United Artists, 1962).

2697

Captain: Have you ever seen an Apache before, Lieutenant?

Lieutenant: No, sir.

Captain: Well, take a good long look and keep facing front. You might keep your hair.

Captain William Maynard played by Pat Conway and Lieutenant John Delahay played by Adam West: Arnold Laven's *Geronimo* (United Artists, 1962).

2698

[*Geronimo talking to young Apache boy on reservation*]

Geronimo: They take away. First they take the land. Then they take your people one at a time. Then your food …your music …your dance. And then even your words …and your thoughts.

Boy: So what?

Geronimo played by Joseph Runningfox: Roger Young's *Geronimo* (Turner Pictures, 1993).

2699

[*Young Geronimo asking father for hand of daughter*]

Nosopo: Your family is poor. You have no horses, only a half dead mule. You have no standing in the tribe.

Geronimo: There is nothing I would not do for your daughter. You must believe me.

Nosopo: Eight horses! That is what you must do. Bring me eight horses and I will know you are serious.

Geronimo: Is that all you want? I can't believe you'd give her away so cheaply.

Nosopo: Make it twelve then.

Geronimo: Make it sixteen! One for each of her years.

[*and later — Geronimo's sister talks with brother*]

Sister: Idiot! You idiot! Sixteen horses! I spoke with her cousin this morning. She says she's been crying non-stop. She had to cut her hair off, and her mother had to hold her down. Are you listening? She says she hates you now. She says you threw her away. You just threw her away with your stinking pride. And she's right.

Geronimo: [*grabbing his sister*] I'm going to get the horses!

Sister: Brother, you are hurting me!

Geronimo: I didn't throw her away. I just thought eight horses was a high price, and it is. But there are a few that can raise that many. But none could raise sixteen. And he can't take less for her now. She won't stand for it. So you see, I have her!

Sister: Except for sixteen horses!

Nosopo played by Jonothon Gill, Geronimo as a Youth played by Ryan Black, and Ketsu (Sister) played by Jessica Cruz: Roger Young's *Geronimo* (Turner Pictures, 1993).

2700

Geronimo: You know I went to the mountains. I stayed long. I didn't care whether I lived or died. I did not care. But then a voice spoke. It called my name four times.

Friend: A spirit?

Geronimo: It said that no gun could kill me. He said that he would take the bullets from the Mexican guns. He said that he would guide me in battle.

Friend: A spirit always wants something in return.

Geronimo: Revenge is close now. This is the only thing I live for.

Geronimo played by Joseph Runningfox: Roger Young's *Geronimo* (Turner Pictures, 1993).

2701

Daklugle: I only wished I had been old enough to fight, to die like my father …fighting for his people.

Geronimo: The fighting is over, but the struggle is not. And for this you must learn about the whites. I fought with your father, and I know your work is harder than his. Because it is easier to die in a world you understand than to live on in one that makes no sense. But you must live on. The Apache people must live on.

Cadet Daklugle played by Brian Frejo and Geronimo as an Old Man played by Jimmy Herman: Roger Young's *Geronimo* (Turner Pictures, 1993).

2702

Geronimo: No one knows why the One God let the white eye take our land. Why did there have to be so many of them? Why did they have so many guns, so many horses? For many years, the One God made me a warrior. No gun, no bullets, could ever kill me. That was my power. Now my time is over. Now, maybe, the time of our people is over.

Geronimo played by Wes Studi: Walter Hill's *Geronimo: An American Legend* (Columbia, 1995).

2703

Davis: Over the years, the events surrounding Geronimo's campaign have continued to haunt me. I carry the memory of those days …days of bravery and cruelty, of heroism and deceit. And I'm still faced with an undeniable truth: a way of life that endured a thousand years was gone. This desert, this land that we look out on …would never be the same.

Lt. Britton Davis played by Matt Damon: Walter Hill's *Geronimo: An American Legend* (Columbia, 1993).

2704

Geronimo: It was told by a medicine man that many more Apaches will die fighting white eye. And in the end, we will win because we will die free of them.

Gatewood: The only way for an Apache to be free is to die?

Geronimo played by Wes Studi and Lt. Charles Gatewood played by Jason Patric: Walter Hill's *Geronimo: An American Legend* (Columbia, 1993).

2705

Sieber: If you ever get in a fight with an Apache and things go bad, you save the last bullet for yourself. You don't want to be taken alive. No, sir. They have lots of ways to kill you. Now one of their favorites is to strip you, tie you upside down to a wagon wheel, they pour pitch on you, and light you on fire.

Al Sieber played by Robert Duvall: Walter Hill's *Geronimo: An American Legend* (Columbia, 1993).

2706

Crook: The problem was Geronimo. I knew Cochise. He was a king. He was a wise ruler of his people. I knew Victorio. He was a proud leader. And I know Geronimo …who doesn't want to lead, or rule, or be wise. He just wants to fight!

Brigadier General George Crook played by Gene Hackman: Walter Hill's *Geronimo: An American Legend* (Columbia, 1993).

2707

Joe: See, you got the chief mad. Let me talk to him.

Quale: Can you talk Indian?

Joe: I was born in Indianapolis.

Joe Panello played by Chico Marx and S. Quentin Quale played by Groucho Marx: Edward Buzzell's *Go West* (MGM, 1940).

2708

Loftus: When an injun, like a Comanche or an Apache, gets himself into a scrape, he rides his horse until that horse dies. Then he draws the blood from that horse, and he keeps on. He uses that horse's blood for water.

Loftus played by Jesse Vint: John Badham's *The Godchild* (TVW, 1974).

2709

Corby: I'm not gonna let them hang me. Indians say that if man dies from strangling, his spirit can't get out of his body and travel to the Spirit Land. He has to wander forever.

Corby/White Wolf played by Billy Wirth: David Greene's *A Good Day to Die* (a.k.a. *Children of the Dust*; Vidmark Entertainment, 1995).

2710

Running Wolf: The ground on which I stand is sacred ground. It is the blood and dust of my ancestors. Oh, Great Spirit, you have made the forest and the animals in the forest which we hunt. But they are all leaving. In a few more summers they will be here no more. Great Spirit, I am afraid for my people. For the white man is coming. He will cause us to turn to dust and bone. And we shall blow across the prairie like the great winds of summer.

Running Wolf played by Paul Fix: Charles B. Pierce's *Grayeagle* (American International, 1977).

2711

Willis: Well, Indian, what we got here is a simple case of mistaken identity.

Trapper Willis played by Jack Elam: Charles B. Pierce's *Grayeagle* (American International, 1977).

2712

Running Wolf: It is the way of the Cheyenne that when a child is born to a chief that his eyes must look upon that child before his death …or his spirit will wander in the skies forever.

Running Wolf played by Paul Fix: Charles B. Pierce's *Grayeagle* (American International, 1977).

2713

Benton: How can the Indians respect our rights if we disregard theirs? Trespassing on their lands, herding them into filthy reservations, starving them to death while corrupt Indian agents steal the food out of their mouth?

Captain Benton played by Darren McGavin: Sidney Salkow's *The Great Sioux Massacre* (Columbia, 1965).

2714

Senator: Just remember: Indians can't vote.

Senator Blaine played by Don Haggerty: Sidney Salkow's *The Great Sioux Massaure* (Columbia, 1965).

2715

Dakota: Colonel, when I pay for a haircut, I like to get my money's worth. That's why I don't want to get scalped.

Major: I can think of several other good reasons.

Dakota played by John Matthews, Major Reno played by Joseph Cotten, and Colonel Custer played by Philip Carey: Sidney Salkow's *The Great Sioux Massacre* (Columbia, 1965).

2716

Crazy Horse: They march in column of three.

Sitting Bull: That is good. The branches will break more easily than the trunk.

Crazy Horse played by Iron Eyes Cody and Sitting Bull played by Michael Pate: Sidney Salkow's *The Great Sioux Massacre* (Columbia, 1965).

2717

Captain: You're the ranking officer here. You give the order to die.

Major: Charge!

Captain Benton played by Darren McGavin and Major Reno played by Joseph Cotten: Sidney Salkow's *The Great Sioux Massacre* (Columbia, 1965).

2718

Westgate: I do not say that all the people on my side are good. I do not pretend that we have always treated you justly.

And I do not promise that if you help us now, there will be eternal brotherhood between all of you and all of us. I was taught by a wise man, by Chief Red Cloud, not to promise that which is not in my power to keep. He who makes promises for other men and other times lies ...and he knows it.

Jonathan Westgate played by Jeff Chandler and Chief Red Cloud played by John War Eagle: Lloyd Bacon's *The Great Sioux Uprising* (Universal, 1953).

2719

Major: Let there always be peace between us.
Red Cloud: When there is justice, there will always be peace.

Major McKay played by Stephen Chase and Red Cloud played by John War Eagle: Lloyd Bacon's *The Great Sioux Uprising* (Universal, 1953).

2720

Shawnee: You better stop spoiling her [Indian]. The first thing you know, she'll be following you around like a shadow.
Chad: Yeah, if we had done a little Indian spoiling in the past, it would have saved a heap of fighting ...and a heap of dying!

Shawnee Jack played by Michael Ansara and Chad Santee played by Buster Crabbe: Sidney Salkow's *Gun Brothers* (United Artists, 1956).

2721

Loving: They [Indians] always looked at my hair lovingly. They never seen much red hair, I reckon. Now that it's turning gray, I sure feel safer around them, I'll tell you that.

Loving played by Chill Wills: Abner Biberman's *Gun for a Coward* (Universal, 1957).

2722

Nate: I must have made 'em mad. I was afraid I'd make a few enemies when I killed those four scouts.
Chad: A few? It looks like you brought the whole Apache nation down our necks!

Nate Harlan played by Warren Stevens and Sheriff Chad Lucas played by Audie Murphy: Earl Bellamy's *Gunpoint* (Universal, 1966).

2723

Chad: Is this your first taste of Indians?
Mark: Yeah. They look different in town.
Chad: They act different too. Now, when they charge, don't try to shoot them all at once. Pick out one at a time.

Sheriff Chad Lucas played by Audie Murphy and Mark Emerson played by David Macklin: Earl Bellamy's *Gunpoint* (Universal, 1966).

2724

Charlie Wolf: We come to speak with our tongues, not our guns.

Kraemer: Apaches are as full of tricks as a dog is of fleas.

Charlie Wolf played by Jack Buetel and Kraemer played by Porter Hall: Stuart Gilmore's *The Half-Breed* (RKO, 1952).

2725

Craig: Just remember this: he was raised an Apache. Scratch him and he'll bleed Apache.

Dan Craig played by Robert Young: Stuart Gilmore's *The Half-Breed* (RKO, 1952).

2726

Narrator: The Indian was back on the reservation where the Peace Commission of 1867 had met with various warlike tribes and secured certain promises from them. In return, papers were given to Indians, certifying them to be good citizens who would obey the laws of the land.

Narration by John Dehner: John Sturges' *The Hallelujah Trail* (MGM, 1965).

2727

Hawken: How did you come by her [squaw] anyway?
Jeb: She was a gift.
Hawken: Gift?
Jeb: Yeah, plain out gift from an old Shawnee chief. He gave her to me for healing him.
Hawken: Healing him?
Jeb: Yeah, healing him of the hiccups.
Hawken: Hiccups?
Jeb: Yeah! He had 'em for over a year. He couldn't get shut of 'em. He asked me if I could cure 'em.
Hawken: And?
Jeb: Simple as hell! I cured him! You know, the best way to cure hiccups is to scare 'em away.
Hawken: Maybe, but I reckon it'd be most difficult to scare anything away from an old Shawnee chief.
Jeb: I took him out behind the cabin, bent him over a fallen tree, and tied his ankles to his hands, pulled his britches down, shoved a candle up his ass, and lit it! I told him, you better be thinking more about that fire than you are the hiccups. He never hiccuped again!

Hawken played by Peter Fonda and Jeb played by Bill Thurman: Charles B. Pierce's *Hawken's Breed* (Vidmark Entertainment, 1987).

2728

Lowe: They [Indians] won't bother me ...us, I mean. We've always got along very well.
Hondo: People I know, a man and his wife, got along real well for twenty years. And then one day she up and blew a hole in him big enough to drive a stagecoach through. She got mad. Apaches are mad.

Angie Lowe played by Geraldine Page and Hondo Lane played by John Wayne: John Farrow's *Hondo* (Warner Bros., 1953).

2729

Hondo: The whites are learning to live with each other. The red man and white man must do the same thing.
Vittoro: This is our land! Apache land!
Hondo: That's right, it is, for two hundred years. But before that, it was Pima land. Apaches took it away from the Pimas because they were stronger. Now the soldiers are stronger.

Hondo Lane played by Ralph Taeger and Vittoro played by Michael Pate: Lee H. Katzin's *Hondo and the Apaches* (TVW, 1967).

2730

Angie: You lived with the Apaches?
Hondo: When you're married to one, it's better to live with her than have her live with you.

Angie Dow played by Kathie Browne and Hondo Lane played by Ralph Taeger: Lee H. Katzin's *Hondo and the Apaches* (TVW, 1967).

2731

Hondo: Apaches teach their children while they're young. A boy your age has to take in a mouthful of water and run two miles through the desert and then spit out the whole mouthful of water.

Hondo Lane played by Ralph Taeger: Lee H. Katzin's *Hondo and the Apaches* (TVW, 1967).

2732

Angie: I'm still not sure we shouldn't have moved on tonight.
Hondo: I am.
Angie: But I thought Indians didn't attack at night.
Hondo: If dead men talked, some might tell you different.

Angie Dow played by Kathie Browne and Hondo Lane played by Ralph Taeger: Lee H. Katzin's *Hondo and the Apaches* (TVW, 1967).

2733

Vittoro: Sometimes it is harder to keep the peace than to make war.

Vittoro played by Michael Pate: Lee H. Katzin's *Hondo and the Apaches* (TVW, 1967).

2734

Colonel: When you find Vittoro, tell him ...tell him if he'll live in peace, I'll be the best friend he ever had. But if wants war, I'll be his worst enemy.

Colonel Crook played by William Bryant: Lee H. Katzin's *Hondo and the Apaches* (TVW, 1967).

2735

Silva: We will keep our land! Even if we have to be buried in it!

Silva played by Victor Lundin: Lee H. Katzin's *Hondo and the Apaches* (TVW, 1967).

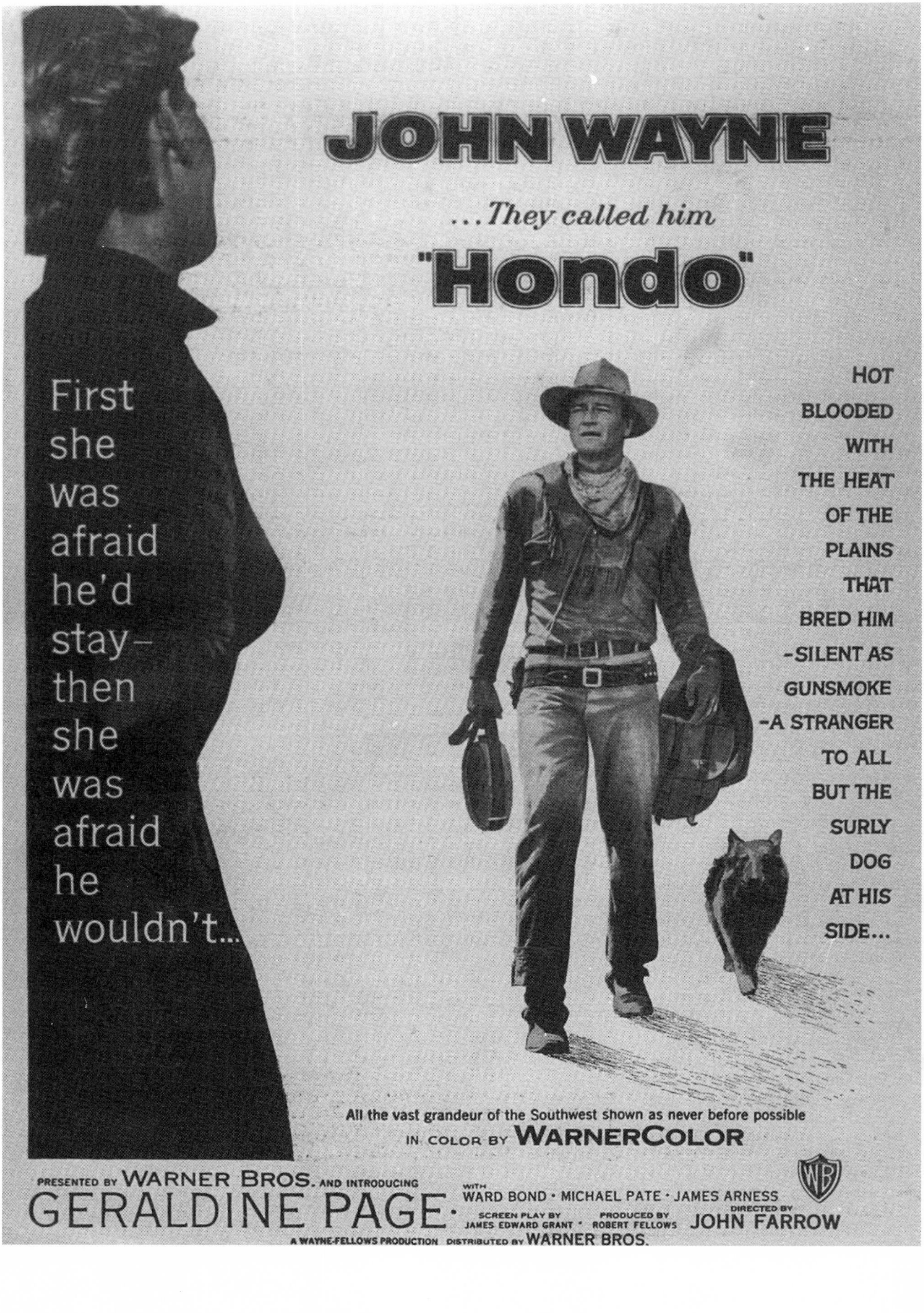
JOHN WAYNE
...They called him
"Hondo"
First she was afraid he'd stay– then she was afraid he wouldn't...
HOT BLOODED WITH THE HEAT OF THE PLAINS THAT BRED HIM –SILENT AS GUNSMOKE –A STRANGER TO ALL BUT THE SURLY DOG AT HIS SIDE...
All the vast grandeur of the Southwest shown as never before possible
IN COLOR BY WARNERCOLOR
PRESENTED BY WARNER BROS. AND INTRODUCING
GERALDINE PAGE
WITH WARD BOND · MICHAEL PATE · JAMES ARNESS
SCREEN PLAY BY JAMES EDWARD GRANT · PRODUCED BY ROBERT FELLOWS
DIRECTED BY JOHN FARROW
A WAYNE-FELLOWS PRODUCTION DISTRIBUTED BY WARNER BROS.

2736

King: Did you get any word about those two men that were killed today?

Rawlings: I tracked the Arapahos and talked to the chief. Those men were a mile off the right-of-way where they had no business …drunk …and chasing squaws. It was as much their fault as it was the Indians.

King: Is that a fact? Well, soldier boy, your job is to fight Indians, not to agree with them?

Rawlings: Mr. King, there were two hundred Arapahos and I had twenty men. Now to me, agreeing seemed wiser than fighting.

Mike King played by Richard Widmark and Zeb Rawlings played by George Peppard: John Ford's, George Marshall's, and Henry Hathaway's *How the West Was Won* (MGM, 1962).

2737

Chief Joseph: It is easy to raise the rifle. It is hard to put it down.

Chief Joseph played by Ned Romero: Richard T. Heffron's *I Will Fight No More Forever* (TVW, 1975).

2738

Chief Joseph: We are all men …chiefs. Do we fight the rain? Do we make war against the wind? As the melted snow floods the rivers, as fires sweep the dry land, the white man is here. He is strong. We must live with his force …or he will destroy us forever.

Chief Joseph played by Ned Romero: Richard T. Heffron's *I Will Fight No More Forever* (TVW, 1975).

2739

Rainbow: Joseph, you are wise. Where do we go?

Chief Joseph: We can look back over many snows and see it all. But at tomorrow's sun we know nothing. Even the wise are blind. We have only hope to lead us …and our warriors.

Rainbow played by Nick Ramus and Chief Joseph played by Ned Romero: Richard T. Heffron's *I Will Fight No More Forever* (TVW, 1975).

2740

Chief Joseph: Our weapons have won battles …but not victories. It is finished.

Chief Joseph played by Ned Romero: Richard T. Heffron's *I Will Fight No More Forever* (TVW, 1975).

2741

Hawks: I'm here to see your brother. Red Cloud and I happen to be friends.

Grey Wolf: There can be no friendship between red man and white. The fight is to the end. Ride back to your people. There is no room for you here!

Hawks: You've grown a big mouth since I saw you last, Grey Wolf. But I didn't come here to talk to a big mouth. I've come here to talk to a big man.

Johnny Hawks played by Kirk Douglas and Grey Wolf played by Harry Landers: Andrew De Toth's *The Indian Fighter* (United Artists, 1955).

2742

Preacher Bob: Now I say, come down here, son. It ain't that cold and it ain't deep enough to scare ya.

Father of Boy: Preacher Bob, I just can't see letting my little boy being baptized in the water with them injuns. I don't think that God would have wanted it that way.

Preacher Bob: Well, I'm the one who knows what God wants. Who the devil are you to tell a preacher about God? Now I say to you again, send that boy down here right now! All right! All right then! It's no skin off my butt if your child burns in hell!

Preacher Bob played by Peter Boyle: James Frawley's *Kid Blue* (20th Century–Fox, 1973).

2743

Old Coyote: You say when we get pushed under the water, our spirits will be safe forever. We're children of God.

Preacher Bob: Well, that's the teachin'.

Mendoza: Yeah, and the children of God, do they get their land back?

Preacher Bob: Well, I didn't exactly say that.

Mendoza: You said that this man God …

Preacher Bob: Wait a minute, Mendoza! God ain't a man!

Mendoza: Well, Jesus is His son.

Preacher Bob: Well, it's a tricky situation.

Mendoza: You put Old Coyote under the water real soon. And then he'll get our land back. And we'll have a place to live.

Preacher Bob: It's more complicated than that!

Mendoza: Wait, now have you been lying about God?

Preacher Bob: You hold on, boy! I never lied about no God.

Old Coyote: Then, push me under the water!

Preacher Bob: All right then! The next time we go out, you go in!

Old Coyote played by Jose Torvay, Preacher Bob played by Peter Boyle, and Mendoza played by Jay Varela: James Frawley's *Kid Blue* (20th Century–Fox, 1973).

2744

Carson: Lucky for us Indians are superstitious about attacking at night. Our only chance is to get out of here before daylight.

Kit Carson played by Jon Hall: George B. Seitz's *Kit Carson* (United Artists, 1940).

2745

Lopez: Scalps, señorita, is a very good thing to have. When the Indians know that his enemy collects scalps, he not jump so quick.

Ape: You see, Miss, a brave can't get into injun heaven without his scalp on. That's why he's so scared to lose it.

Lopez played by Harold Huber and Ape played by Ward Bond: George B. Seitz's *Kit Carson* (United Artists, 1940).

2746

Vince: Well, Major, you know as far as I'm concerned there is no problem. There's only Apaches.

Vince Carden played by Telly Savalas and Major Tanner played by Guy Rolfe: Nathan Juran's *Land Raiders* (Columbia, 1969).

2747

Vince: Remember what he [Colonel Chivington] told his men at Sand Creek: kill them all, big and little …nits make lice.

Vince Carden played by Telly Savalas: Nathan Juran's *Land Raiders* (Columbia, 1969).

2748

Pea-Eye: How about you? How are your children?

Famous Shoes: They were great children. Comanche killed all of them. I came back to the Brazos to be near their spirits and the spirit of their grandfather …but I didn't find his spirit.

Pea-Eye: What about your children? Did you find their spirit?

Famous Shoes: No, they were too young. Their spirits were too light. They had blown away to another part of the world.

Pea-Eye Parker played by Sam Shepard and Famous Shoes played by Wes Studi: Joseph Sargent's *Larry McMurtry's Streets of Laredo* (Cabin Fever Entertainment, 1995).

2749

Blaine: What were you selling those Indians? Watered-down whiskey or worn-out weapons?

Scarned: Just peaceable dealings, that's all.

Marshal Dan Blaine played by Glenn Ford and Ernest Scarned played by Jack Elam: Richard Thorpe's *The Last Challenge* (MGM, 1967).

Opposite: Advertisement for a first-rate western with John Wayne as Hondo Lane in John Farrow's *Hondo* (Warner Bros., 1953). Have your 3-D glasses ready for this one!

2750

Indian Girl: White Buffalo! You take away our food. And now you kill our religion.

The Indian Girl played by Debra Paget: Richard Brooks' *The Last Hunt* (MGM, 1956).

2751

Kroeber: Mr. Witney is from the Department of the Interior.

Witney: The Bureau of Indian Affairs to be precise …Wild Indian Division.

Waterman: There's a Wild Indian Division? There are no more wild Indians.

Witney: That's why it's being phased out. So …what's to be done with him [Indian]?

Kroeber: He'll stay here with us of course.

Witney: Well, my job is to make him happy.

Waterman: If you'll pardon me, Mr. Witney, but that sounds just like our government. We do everything we can to eliminate these people from the face of the earth. And then when one manages to survive, we send someone around to make sure he's happy.

Professor Alfred Kroeber played by Jon Voight, Mr. Witney played by Daniel Benzali, and Tom Waterman played by Jack Blessing: Harry Hook's *The Last of His Tribe* (HBO Pictures, 1994).

2752

Henrietta: What do you mean, the trail of the dead?

Alfred: That's their view of the after life. The trail of the dead leads to the land of the ancestors. When you die, you walk along the trail for a long way until at last you come to your own lodge where your family is gathering around the firepit waiting for you.

Henrietta: Do you believe in that?

Alfred: The trail of the dead?

Henrietta: Well, if not …something? Heaven, I suppose.

Alfred: Well, I don't think our view of the after life is any more valid than theirs.

Mrs. Henrietta Kroeber played by Anne Archer and Professor Alfred Kroeber played by Jon Voight: Harry Hook's *The Last of His Tribe* (HBO Pictures, 1994).

2753

Lillian: The Indian shaped the character of our entire nation.

Gates: We picked a hell of a way to say thank you, didn't we?

Lillian: Well, what happened was inevitable. The way it happened was unconscionable!

Professor Lillian Sloan played by Barbara Hershey and Lewis Gates played by Tom Berenger: Tab Murphy's *Last of the Dogmen* (Savory Pictures, 1995).

2754

Chingachgook: Great Spirit. A warrior goes to you …swift, straight, and unseen like arrow shot into sun. Let him sit at council fire of my tribe. For he is Uncas, my son. My fire is ashes; your fire is bright. Now all my tribe is there

Buffalo hunter Sandy McKenzie (Stewart Granger) takes aim on a herd of bison, then pauses and realizes that he is no longer going to participate in this senseless slaughter, in *The Last Hunt* (MGM, 1956).

but one. I, Chingachgook, last of Mohicans.

Chingachgook played by Robert Barrat: George B. Seitz's *The Last of the Mohicans* (United Artists, 1936).

2755

Major: What on earth are you doing?

Chingachgook (with ear to ground): Listen to beaver downstream. Indian sentry. When canoe come, beaver flap tail.

Major Duncan played by Henry Wilcoxon and Chingachgook played by Robert Barrat: George B. Seitz's *The Last of the Mohicans* (United Artists, 1936).

2756

Hawkeye: You can do what you want with your own scalp, Major. But don't start telling us what to do with ours!

Hawkeye played by Randolph Scott and Major Duncan played by Henry Wilcoxon: George B. Seitz's *The Last of the Mohicans* (United Artists, 1936).

2757

Hawkeye: Ms. Munro, I've seen more savages in lace collars and velvet pants than in war paint.

Hawkeye played by Steve Forrest and Cora Munro played by Michele Marsh: James L. Conway's *Last of the Mohicans* (TVW, 1977).

2758

Heyward: These are savages!

Hawkeye: By whose reckoning? The British who chopped off a red man's hand for stealing? Or the French who taught him the finer points of torture? The meaning of the word "savage" depends on who's speaking it.

Major Heyward played by Andrew Prine and Hawkeye played by Steve Forrest: James L. Conway's *Last of the Mohicans* (TVW, 1977).

2759

Gamut: Why did those heathens spare my life?

Uncas: They believe you are the son of a spirit …that you are crazy. Such people cannot be harmed. It is law.

Gamut: That's a good law.

David Gamut played by Robert Easton and Uncas played by Don Shanks: James L. Conway's *Last of the Mohicans* (TVW, 1977).

2760

Hawkeye: When a Mohican lad is on the brink of becoming a brave, he sets out alone into the forest looking for signs. Things that will tell him who he is or who he's gonna be. Sacred things. And he puts those in his pouch of life. He believes they'll protect him against evil spirits. So you see, that leather bag means more to him than his own scalp.

Hawkeye played by Steve Forrest: James L. Conway's *Last of the Mohicans* (TVW, 1977).

2761

Hawkeye: There's something big in the wind.

Hawkeye played by Steve Forrest: James L. Conway's *Last of the Mohicans* (TVW, 1977).

2762

Sachen: The white man came and night entered our future with him.

Sachen played by Mike Phillips: Michael Mann's *The Last of the Mohicans* (20th Century–Fox, 1992).

2763

Hawkeye: My father's people say that at the birth of the sun and its brother, the moon, their mother died. So the sun gave to the earth her body from which was to spring all life. And he drew forth from her breasts the stars …stars he threw into the night sky to remind him of her soul.

Nathaniel Poe/Hawkeye played by Daniel Day-Lewis: Michael Mann's *The Last of the Mohicans* (20th Century–Fox, 1992).

2764

Chingachgook: Great Spirit, and the Maker of our life, a warrior goes to You swift and straight as an arrow shot into the sun. Welcome him and let him take his place at the council fire of my people. Uncas, my son, tell them to be patient and ask death for speed …for they are all there but one …I, Chingachgook, last of the Mohicans.

Chingachgook played by Russell Means and Uncas played by Eric Schweig: Michael Mann's *The Last of the Mohicans* (20th Century–Fox, 1992).

2765

Magua: When the Grey Hair is dead, Magua will eat his heart. Before he dies, Magua will put his children under the knife so the Grey Hair will know his seed is wiped out forever.

Magua played by Wes Studi: Michael Mann's *Last of the Mohicans* (20th Century–Fox, 1992).

2766

Britten: Why did you kill the trader, Mc-Quade?

Geronimo: He sold my men bad whiskey and bad guns. The whiskey poisoned them, and the guns blew the heads off many Indians. He deserved to die. I do not understand why we are put in jail for killing him.

Britten: When I think of a good reason, I'll let you know.

Vance Britten, alias Major Thomas Riordan, played by Ronald Reagan, Geronimo played by John War Eagle, and Sam McQuade played by

John Ridgely: Lewis R. Foster's *The Last Outpost* (Paramount, 1951).

2767

Delacourt: Well, haven't you people ever seen smoke before?

Lt. Crosby: In this country, where there's smoke, there's apt to be Indians under it.

Mr. Delacourt played by Lloyd Corrigan and Lieutenant Crosby played by Peter Hanson: Lewis R. Foster's *The Last Outpost* (Paramount, 1951).

2768

Delacourt: Colonel, you really don't expect them to attack, do you? They wouldn't be so fool-hearted.

Colonel: We killed their chief. They outnumber us 50 to 1. What do you think?

Delacourt: They might be fool-hearted.

Mr. Delacourt played by Lloyd Corrigan and Colonel Jeb Britten played by Bruce Bennett: Lewis R. Foster's *The Last Outpost* (Paramount, 1951).

2769

Todd: I know it sounds kind of foolish to most whites, but Indians don't suffer when somebody gets killed. Not like you. You see, Indians believe the brave dead go to the high ground and that's a good place. Game is never short and winter is never too hard …and plenty of water and plenty of grass.

"Comanche" Todd played by Richard Widmark: Delmer Daves' *The Last Wagon* (20th Century–Fox, 1956).

2770

Todd: Well, when we started out on this trip, I promised nothing. Now it looks like even promising that was too much. We can't neither turn back nor go ahead. And we got three bullets against three hundred Apaches. It ain't hardly enough!

"Comanche" Todd played by Richard Widmark: Delmer Daves' *The Last Wagon* (20th Century–Fox, 1956).

2771

Jake: We probably got more Indians surrounding us right now than Custer had to fight at Big Horn.

Wexler: So what? We don't have to worry until it's light, and we'll probably be out of here by then.

Jake: Who says you don't have to worry until it gets light?

Burke: Indians don't attack at night! Everybody knows that!

Jake: Apaches don't attack at night. But they're the only ones that don't. These are Comanches!

Jake Wade played by Robert Taylor, Wexler played by DeForest Kelley, and Burke played by Eddie

Firestone: John Sturges' *The Law and Jake Wade* (MGM, 1958).

2772

Rennie: They're Comanches, and what are we doing about it? We're sitting around here like customers in a barber shop …waiting our turn to get a nice close hair cut.

Rennie played by Henry Silva: John Sturges' *The Law and Jake Wade* (MGM, 1958).

2773

Chief: White man promise much …but give little.

Chief Barking Fox played by Chief Many Treaties: Alan James' *The Law Rides Again* (Monogram, 1943).

2774

Jimmy Black Legs: Little Dog, no talk. Him only think.
Bill Barker: How do you know he thinks?
Jimmy Black Legs: Cause him never talk.

Jimmy Black Legs was uncredited, Chief Little Dog played by Kermit Maynard, and Bonanza Bill Barker played by Harry Carey: Glenn Tryon's *The Law West of Tombstone* (RKO, 1938).

2775

We will put fresh earth to the roots of the tree of peace so that it may live and flourish while the sun shines and the rivers run.

Del Hardy, played by Fess Parker, interpreting the words of Chief Cuyloga, played by Joseph Calleia: Herschel Daugherty's *The Light in the Forest* (Buena Vista, 1958).

2776

Hardy: When a captive isn't killed, he's usually adopted …mostly for a dead relative. They baptize you in the river to wash away your white meanness and put brave Indian thoughts into your head. And when that's done, your flesh are their flesh, and blood of their blood. And they're not going to let you go …not ever!

Del Hardy played by Fess Parker: Herschel Daugherty's *The Light in the Forest* (Buena Vista, 1958).

2777

Niskitoon: I do not fight children. But on the warpath, it is easier to carry a scalp than a prisoner.

Niskitoon played by Norman Frederic: Herschel Daugherty's *The Light in the Forest* (Buena Vista, 1958).

2778

Kane: Why didn't we shoot them? They're Comanche. We don't know their names. You don't know nothing about injuns, do you? You kill a Comanche, and you don't know his name, his spirit goes into an owl. And every night that owl will come around calling out: Hoot! Hoot! If you can't sing out the right name, he'll follow you forever. Bad medicine.

Lightning Jack Kane played by Paul Hogan: Simon Wincer's *Lightning Jack* (Savoy Pictures, 1994).

2779

Lana: Jack, folks in town said this trail leads through hostile Apache country.
Jack: Good. See this, it's a spirit bag. I bought it off an Apache medicine man. That makes me a full blood brother to the Apache. I'm practically family. And for only $50.00.
Lana: Well, even if it works for you, what about me and Ben?
Jack: No problem! You see, this covers my whole family.

Lana played by Beverly D'Angelo, Lightning Jack Kane played by Paul Hogan, and Ben Doyle played by Cuba Gooding, Jr.: Simon Wincer's *Lightning Jack* (Savoy Pictures, 1994).

2780

Old Lodge Skins: This boy is no longer a boy. He's a brave. He's little in body but his heart is big. His name shall be Little Big Man.

Old Lodge Skins played by Chief Dan George and Little Big Man/Jack Crabb played by Dustin Hoffman: Arthur Penn's *Little Big Man* (NGP, 1971).

2781

Little Big Man: Well, grandfather, all the whites aren't crazy.
Old Lodge Skins: I'm glad to hear that, my son. I thought they were.
Little Big Man: Oh no. I know of one who is as brave as any human being.
Old Lodge Skins: I'd like to meet this man and smoke with him. What is he called?
Little Big Man: He's called General Custer.
Old Lodge Skins: General Custer? What does the name mean, my son?
Little Big Man: Well, it means, ah, long hair.
Old Lodge Skins: Good name. How did he win it?
Little Big Man: He won it in the war of the whites to free the black man.
Old Lodge Skins: Oh yes, the black white men. I know of them. It is said that a black white man once became a human being. But most maybe are strange creatures. Not as ugly as the white, true, but they're just as crazy.

Little Big Man/Jack Crabb played by Dustin Hoffman and Old Lodge Skins played by Chief Dan George: Arthur Penn's *Little Big Man* (NGP, 1971).

2782

Narrator: The next morning I found myself in that Indian camp all alone. But the Cheyenne who call themselves the human beings had no idea to hurt me. I was an honored guest and they gave me a real treat for breakfast …broiled dog. Dog ain't bad neither. Now, dog is greasy, I'll admit, but you'd be surprised how down-right delicate the flavor is …especially when you're starving!

Narration by Jack Crabb/Little Big Man played by Dustin Hoffman: Arthur Penn's *Little Big Man* (NGP, 1971).

2783

Younger Bear: I'm a very important man. More important than you. I have a wife and four horses.
Little Big Man: I have a horse and four wives!

Younger Bear played by Cal Bellini and Little Big Man/Jack Crabb played by Dustin Hoffman: Arthur Penn's *Little Big Man* (NGP, 1971).

2784

Little Big Man: Grandfather! What happened to your neck, grandfather?
Old Lodge Skins: It's a wound that cut the tunnel through which light travels through the heart.
Little Big Man: You …you mean you're blind?
Old Lodge Skins: Oh, no. My eyes still see, but my heart no longer receives it.
Little Big Man: How did it happen?
Old Lodge Skins: White man.

Little Big Man/Jack Crabb played by Dustin Hoffman and Old Lodge Skins played by Chief Dan George: Arthur Penn's *Little Big Man* (NGP, 1971).

2785

Custer: Well, what's your answer, mule skinner?
Jack Crabb: General, you go down there.
General: You're advising me to go into the coolie?
Jack Crabb: Yes, sir.
Custer: There are no Indians there, I suppose?
Jack Crabb: I didn't say that. There are thousands of Indians down there. And when they get done with you, there won't be nothing left but a greasy spot. This ain't the Washita River, General. And them ain't helpless women and children waiting for ya. They're Cheyenne braves and Sioux! You go down there if you got the nerve!
Custer: Still trying to outsmart me, aren't you, mule skinner? You want me to think that you don't want me to go down there. But the subtle truth is, you really don't want me to go down there!

General George A. Custer played by Richard Mulligan and Jack Crabb/Little Big Man played by Dustin Hoffman: Arthur Penn's *Little Big Man* (NGP, 1971).

2786

Narrator: The time had come to look the devil in the eye and send him to hell where he belonged. The only question was: how to get him there.

Narration by Jack Crabb/Little Big Man played by Dustin Hoffman: Arthur Penn's *Little Big Man* (NGP, 1971).

2787

Old Lodge Skins: When they looked back, they saw the body of Little Man …lied down among his friends. Little Man was small, but his bravery was big.

Old Lodge Skins played by Chief Dan George: Arthur Penn's *Little Big Man* (NGP, 1971).

2788

Angry Horse: Red Hawk no more tell what do. Red Hawk old …no more fight. Angry Horse not old. Better Angry Horse be chief.

Lone Ranger: Always the young buffalo wishes to kill the old buffalo and take his place. And he does kill the old buffalo because he has youth …and strength. But has he the wisdom to lead the herd …to keep it out of danger? I say Angry Horse has not the wisdom and cannot be the chief of a tribe that wishes to live in peace.

Angry Horse played by Michael Ansara, Red Hawk played by Frank De Kova, and the Lone Ranger played by Clayton Moore: Stuart Heisler's *The Lone Ranger* (Warner Bros., 1956).

2789

Tonto: You have the tongue and the courage of the coyote. You speak much, but you say nothing.

Tonto played by Jay Silverheels: Lesley Selander's *The Lone Ranger and the Lost City of Gold* (United Artists, 1958).

2790

Pea-Eye: What Indians is it we're fighting anyhow?

Gus: They didn't introduce themselves!

Pea-Eye Parker played by Tim Scott and Gus McCrae played by Robert Duvall: Simon Wincer's *Lonesome Dove* (TVW, 1989).

2791

Call: Do you want me to do anything about them Indians that shot you?

Gus: We got no call to be vengeful. They didn't invite us here.

Captain Woodrow F. Call played by Tommy Lee Jones and Gus McCrae played by Robert Duvall: Simon Wincer's *Lonesome Dove* (TVW, 1989).

2792

Blue Duck: I got a treatment for women that try to run away. I cut a little hole in their stomachs, pull out a gut, and wrap it around a limb. And then I drag them thirty or forty feet and tie 'em down.

That way they can watch what the coyotes are having for supper.

Blue Duck played by Frederic Forrest: Simon Wincer's *Lonesome Dove* (TVW, 1989).

2793

Luke: Indians believe that a warrior killed at night will spend eternity in darkness. Indians don't attack at night.

Lucky Luke played by Terence Hill: Terence Hill's *Lucky Luke* (Silvio Berlusconi Communications, 1991).

2794

Narrator: A thousand years ago in the southwest, there was an Apache legend. It told about a hidden canyon guarded by the Apache gods, and rich with gold. As long as the Apaches kept the canyon a secret and never touched the gold, they would be strong and powerful. That was the legend.

Narration by Victor Jory: J. Lee Thompson's *MacKenna's Gold* (Columbia, 1969).

2795

Yellow Hawk: When lies are loud, the truth may not be heard.

Yellow Hawk played by Jay Silverheels: William Castle's *Masterson of Kansas* (Columbia, 1954).

2796

Bret: Well, he says we can go if one of us passes the Indian bravery test. But one of us has to go with him.

Annabelle: Well, what's the Indian bravery test?

Bret: You see that? He cuts off both of your hands. If you don't make a sound, you pass.

[*a moment later*]

Bret: Well …now when they cut my hands off, my lucky shirt will fit.

Bret Maverick played by Mel Gibson and Annabelle Bransford played by Jodie Foster: Richard Donner's *Maverick* (Warner Bros., 1994).

2797

McLintock: The Comanche say: we are an old people and a proud people. When the white man first came among us, we were as many as the grass is of the prairie. Now we are few. But we are still proud. For if a man loses pride in manhood, he is nothing. You tell us now that if we will let you send us away to this place called Fort Sill, you will feed us and care for us. Let us tell you this: it is the Comanche law that no chief ever eats unless first he sees that the pots are full of meat at the lodges of the widows and orphans. It is the Comanche way of life. This that the white man calls charity is a fine thing for widows and orphans. But no warrior can accept it. For if he does, he is no longer a man.

And when he is no longer a man, he is nothing …and better off dead. You say to the Comanche: you are widows and orphans. You are not men. And we the Comanche say we would rather be dead. It will not be a remembered fight when you kill us because we are few now and have few weapons. But we will fight. And we will die Comanche.

George Washington McLintock played by John Wayne: Andrew V. McLaglen's *McLintock!* (United Artists, 1963).

2798

Katherine: Now, Mr. McLintick, we have an awful lot to talk over.

McLintock: The first thing I learned about Indian fighting was to wait for daylight.

Katherine: And what does our conversation got to do with Indian fighting?

McLintock: Indian fighting is good experience for our kind of conversations. It'll wait.

Katherine McLintock played by Maureen O'Hara and George Washington McLintock played by John Wayne: Andrew V. McLaglen's *McLintock!* (United Artists, 1963).

2799

Fauntleroy: Doggone it, folks! Let's don't let a little old Indian raid break up a good barbecue and a rodeo!

Fauntleroy played by Big John Hamilton: Andrew V. McLaglen's *McLintock!* (United Artists, 1963).

2800

Benjie: They're gonna take my land!

White Feather: Well, that's just it. That land don't belong to you. It don't belong to nobody. We say, we belong to the land.

Benjie played by Brock Peters and White Feather played by David Carradine: Alf Kjellin's *The McMasters* (Jayjen/Chevron, 1970).

2801

Sam: You know, they say these mountains are the closest thing there is to heaven. The trouble is, word spreads, and now you got your missionaries and preachers trekking up here all around with the mighty word and holy water. Hey, Chief, don't let 'em go baptizing you now, you here?

Sam Webster played by John Dennis Johnston and Chief Washakie played by Rino Thunder: Kevin James Dobson's *Miracle in the Wilderness* (TVW, 1991).

2802

Morgan: My brothers, when the heart is full, the tongue speaks idle words.

Tom Morgan played by Tom Mix: Armand Schaefer and B. Reeves Eason's *The Miracle Rider* (Mascot serial, Chapter 8: "Guerrilla Warfare," 1935).

2803

Sieber: Everybody hates everybody. Mickey is Apache, but he hates Geronimo because Mickey is Tonto Apache and Geronimo is Chiricahua Apache. Hate is a lot of crap.

Al Sieber played by Richard Widmark, Mickey Free played by Lewis James Oliver, and Geronimo played by Enrique Lucero: Jack Starrett's *Mr. Horn* (TVW, 1979).

2804

Sieber: He [Geronimo] didn't get where he got by being dumb.

Al Sieber played by Richard Widmark and Geronimo played by Enrique Lucero: Jack Starrett's *Mr. Horn* (TVW, 1979).

2805

Geronimo: When we attack, it is a massacre. When you attack, it is a battle.

Geronimo played by Enrique Lucero: Jack Starrett's *Mr. Horn* (TVW, 1979).

2806

Heavy Eagle: But you and I are the same. A few passing suns will see us no more. Our bones will bleach in the sun with the bones of the buffalo. But we shall be remembered. Tomorrow, you will see your last sunrise.

Heavy Eagle played by Stephen Macht: Richard Lang's *The Mountain Men* (Columbia, 1980).

2807

Iron Belly: In the mountains of the River of Wind …there is a valley.
Bill Tyler: The Wind River Range?
Iron Belly: It's the land of our enemy, the Blackfeet. Their hearts are bad …their eyes red with blood.

Iron Belly played by Victor Jory and Bill Tyler played by Charlton Heston: Richard Lang's *The Mountain Men* (Columbia, 1980).

2808

Running Moon: I came from another village. My father sold me to Heavy Eagle: one horse and one gun.
Bill Tyler: Slave?
Running Moon: Wife …the same.

Running Moon played by Victoria Racimo and Bill Tyler played by Charlton Heston: Richard Lang's *The Mountain Men* (Columbia, 1980).

2809

Bill Tyler: You got any ideas?
Henry: No. Maybe if we could hold them off until dark. That would get us out of here and up to that village before sunup. Because you know that Heavy Eagle ain't going to try to butcher us until daybreak. By then, we would be halfway to Yellowstone.
Bill Tyler: What makes you think he won't butcher us at night?

Henry: Well, Blackfeet don't fight at night, you know that.
Bill Tyler: Henry, you ain't got the brains God gave geese.

Bill Tyler played by Charlton Heston and Henry Frapp played by Brian Keith: Richard Lang's *The Mountain Men* (Columbia, 1980).

2810

Henry: Did I ever tell you about the time the Arapaho chased me up a canyon over in the Big Loss?
Tyler: No, but I reckon you're going to tell me.
Henry: Well, I was over on the Horse Prairie. This band of Arapahos had been chasing me three days. So I seen this canyon and I figured I'll whip in there and then I'll slip out. The trouble was that there was a way in but no way out at all. Nothing but cliffs, a half mile high, all the way around. A whole tribe of Blackfoot down there just madder than turpentine and wildcats. So I holed up behind some rocks, but that didn't do no good because they just keep on a coming. The entire Sioux nation! Me out of powder …out of lead.
Tyler: Well, what happend?
Henry: Well, I got killed, of course!

Henry Frapp played by Brian Keith and Bill Tyler played by Charlton Heston: Richard Lang's *The Mountain Men* (Columbia, 1980).

2811

Gideon: Was that chap dragging you across the prairie a full-blooded Indian?
Twillie: Quite the antithesis. He's very anemic!

Mrs. Gideon played by Margaret Hamilton and Cuthbert J. Twillie played by W.C. Fields: Edward F. Cline's *My Little Chickadee* (Universal, 1940).

2812

Pierre: Paul, she's a half-breed. You know what that means? The whites despise her and the Indians don't trust her. She's got no real people.

Pierre played by Jacques Weber and Paul played by Jeff Fahey: Arnaud Selignac's *Northern Passage* (Trimark, 1994).

2813

Ledbetter: We didn't move out yesterday when some whipper-snapper Lieutenant told us to, and we're not moving out today! The yellow stuff in that creek back there tells us we're going to stay right here for quite a spell.
Trooper: Answer me this. How do they better themselves with the top of their heads gone?

Jake Ledbetter played by Alan Bridge and Trooper Muro played by Wally Cassell: Joseph Kane's *Oh! Susanna* (Republic, 1951).

2814

Cpt: Open the gate, Sergeant. Muro, give me your saber.
Sgt: Sir, you're not going to let 'em in!
Cpt: That's the sign for a palaver. I'm going out.
Sgt: But they're Sioux! That don't mean nothing but a trap. I'm going with you!
Cpt: You'll stay here …just in case. Open the gate!
Sgt: Just in case he don't come back.
Muro: If he don't come back, there won't be any case.

Captain Webb Calhoun played by Rod Cameron, Sergeant Barhydt played by Chill Wills, and Trooper Muro played by Wally Cassell: Joseph Kane's *Oh! Susanna* (Republic, 1951).

2815

Barhydt: You notice he's still got his hair? That's so when he walks around in the hereafter, everybody will know he wasn't even worth scalping.

Sergeant Barhydt played by Chill Wills: Joseph Kane's *Oh! Susanna* (Republic, 1951).

2816

Mark: Clint, we got nothing to eat. Cheyenne quiet. I steal.
Clint: Now look! You got to get over the idea that anytime you want anything, you can just go steal it. We'll wait until they quiet down …then I'll steal the bacon.

Mark played by Clay O'Brien and Clint Keys played by James Garner: Bernard McEveety's *One Little Indian* (Buena Vista, 1973).

2817

Lt.: Who is she?
Nato: Little Deer. She not belong to this tribe. She come from north.
Lt.: Yes, I can see that. Her skin is much too light. What's she doing here?
Nato: Virgin bride for Black Eagle. Make purified for two weeks. Big steam every day. Like white man do lobster.

Lt. Niles Ord played by John Ericson, Nato played by Paul Fierro, Little Deer played by Toni Gerry, and Black Eagle played by H.M. Wynant: Paul Landres' *Oregon Passage* (Warner Bros., 1958).

2818

Little Deer: Do you know what the old Indians say? The devil is in the heart of a light-haired woman.
Lt.: You keep those Indian fairy tales to yourself. And don't keep pulling that one about my owning you just because I rescued you! That's Chinese anyway.

Little Deer played by Toni Gerry and Lt. Niles Ord played by John Ericson: Paul Landres' *Oregon Passage* (Warner Bros., 1958).

2819

Dobson: Niles says the Indians are too superstitious to come through a graveyard.

A lot of their own people are buried here too.

Lt. Baird Dobson played by Jon Shepodd and Lt. Niles Ord played by John Ericson: Paul Landres' *Oregon Passage* (Warner Bros., 1958).

2820

Lone Watie: We wore this frock coat to Washington before the war. We wore them because we belonged to the Five Civilized Tribes. We dressed ourselves up like Abraham Lincoln. You know, we got to see the Secretary of the Interior. And he said: Boy, you boys sure look civilized. He congratulated us and he gave us medals for looking so civilized. We told him about how our land had been stolen and our people were dying. When we finished, he shook our hands and said: endeavor to persevere!

Lone Watie played by Chief Dan George: Clint Eastwood's *The Outlaw Josey Wales* (Warner Bros., 1976).

2821

Lone Watie: I thought you might be someone who would sneak up behind me with a gun.

Josey Wales: Where did you ever get an idea like that? And besides, it ain't supposed to be easy to sneak up behind an Indian.

Lone Watie: I'm an Indian all right. But here in the Nation they call us the civilized tribe. They call us civilized because we're easy to sneak up on. White men has been sneaking up on us for years.

Lone Watie played by Chief Dan George and Josey Wales played by Clint Eastwood: Clint Eastwood's *The Outlaw Josey Wales* (Warner Bros., 1976).

2822

Lone Watie: I'm going to take up tepee living if it's like this! You know, she thinks I'm some kind of a Cherokee chief.

Josey Wales: Now, I wonder where she ever got that idea?

Lone Watie played by Chief Dan George and Josey Wales played by Clint Eastwood: Clint Eastwood's *The Outlaw Josey Wales* (Warner Bros., 1976).

2823

Josey Wales: You be Ten Bears?

Ten Bears: I am Ten Bears.

Josey Wales: I'm Josey Wales.

Ten Bears: I have heard. You are the gray rider. You would not make peace with the blue coats. You may go in peace.

Josey Wales: I reckon not. I got nowhere to go.

Ten Bears: Then you will die.

Josey Wales: I came here to die with you …or live with you. Dying ain't so hard for men like you and me. It's living that's hard when all you have ever cared

about has been butchered and raped. Governments don't live together, people live together. With governments, you don't always get a fair word or fair fight. Well, I've come here to give you either one …or get either one from you. I came here like this so that you'll know my word of death is true. And then my word of life is then true. The bear lives here. The wolf, the antelope, the Comanche. And so will we. Now we'll only hunt what we need to live on, same as the Comanche does. And every spring, when the grass turns green and the Comanche moves north, he can rest here in peace, butcher some of our cattle, and jerk beef for the journey. The sign of the Comanche, that will be on our lodge. That's my word of life.

Ten Bears: And your word of death?

Josey Wales: It's here in my pistols and there in your rifles. I'm here for either one.

Ten Bears: These things you say we will have. We already have.

Josey Wales: That's true. I ain't promising ya nothing extra. I'm just giving you life and you're giving me life. And I'm saying that men can live together without butchering one another.

Ten Bears: It's sad that governments are cheapened by the Devil's tongue. And there is iron in your words of death for all Comanche to see. And so there is iron in your words of life. No signed paper can hold the iron. It must come from men. The words of Ten Bears carries the same iron of life and death. It is good that warriors such as we meet in the struggle of life …or death. It shall be life.

Josey Wales played by Clint Eastwood and Ten Bears played by Will Sampson: Clint Eastwood's *The Outlaw Josey Wales* (Warner Bros., 1976).

2824

Jane: You're not afraid of a few Indians are you?

Potter: Oh, it's not the Indians I'm afraid of. It's their attitude. They're hatchet happy!

Calamity Jane played by Jane Russell and Painless Peter Potter played by Bob Hope: Norman Z. McLeod's *The Paleface* (Paramount, 1948).

2825

Sgt. Timothy: He said the treaty is broken. The talk was of stock.

Colonel: Stock? Is that their word for war?

Sgt. Bell: Not just war, Colonel. Extermination. Bloody and total.

Indian Scout Sergeant Timothy played by Sydney Chaplin, Colonel Edson Stedlow played by Willis Bouchey, and First Sergeant Emmett Bell played by Jeff Chandler: George Marshall's *Pillars of the Sky* (Universal, 1956).

2826

Kamiakin: These mountains mark our land. Our fathers know not even these boundaries. But we have promised to live here between the pillars of the sky though our people are crowded one upon the other. There's not game enough to feed a single tribe. Now these soldiers say even this is too much. There's no talk left! There is only stock!

The Indian Chief Kamiakin played by Michael Ansara: George Marshall's *Pillars of the Sky* (Universal, 1956).

2827

Holden: Three eagle feathers. Kamiakin sends a truce.

Doctor Joseph Holden played by Ward Bond and Kamiakin played by Michael Ansara: George Marshall's *Pillars of the Sky* (Universal, 1956).

2828

1st Sgt.: Sometime tonight, Kamiakin will hit us with everything he's got. And then you'll have your answer.

Lt. Winston: But I heard that Indians wouldn't fight at night. Something about their ghosts not being able to find their heaven in the dark.

1st Sgt.: These Indians don't believe in ghosts, Lieutenant. Thanks to Doctor Holden, they're Christians!

First Sergeant Emmett Bell played by Jeff Chandler, Chief Kamiakin played by Michael Ansara, Lieutenant Winston played by Glen Kramer, and Dr. Joseph Holden played by Ward Bond: George Marshall's *Pillars of the Sky* (Universal, 1956).

2829

1st Sgt.: The pillars of the sky, Doc. They were sacred to the tribes long before you came with the word of God.

First Sergeant Emmett Bell played by Jeff Chandler in George Marshall's *Pillars of the Sky* (Universal, 1956).

2830

Sgt. Timothy: You speak of our Fathers. My father's bow would have torn the arm from my shoulder before it broke. We have lost the skills of our father's Chief of the Palute. We lost them a thousand suns ago when we first took an iron knife from the white man. And now we have this [white man's rifle]. You cannot fight or hunt without one. Can you make one? The food in your bellies, the iron pot you cook it with, the tobacco in your pipes. These belong to the white man. The medicines when you are sick, the whiskey that turns you mad, both are his. And so it is. The good in your lives, and the bad, are bound up with the white man.

Kamiakin: So you say, let them brush us to one side as though we were dead leaves. I say we will fight.

Sgt. Timothy: Then you will fight. But even should you drive him away, you will have lost. For if the white man goes, then we must follow. For we no longer know how to live without him.
Isaiah: And what is the end?
Sgt. Timothy: The end is this: the white man and the red will live together. Though it will not come in our time, Cordalie. And until it does, it will be hard. But from the white man, too, there comes a faith that will help us wait.
Kamiakin: Then take their faith! But for me, there is this: I will stay on his land. And if there is no game, then my belly will be lean. And if there are no hides, then I will run naked. And if I have no gun and my bow breaks, I will fight with a club or stone. I will heal myself or I will die and put my faith in the ghost of my fathers. But I will live as my own man as I have been taught. And if my tribe be lost, let it be lost in battle …not swallowed up in the belly of a different people.
Indian Scout Sergeant Timothy played by Sydney Chaplin, Chief Kamiakin played by Michael Ansara, and Chief Isaiah played by Richard Hale: George Marshall's *Pillars of the Sky* (Universal, 1956).

2831
1st Sgt: There will be no genuine Sioux scalps for sale! The last time we met up with recruits, there wasn't a horse left in the troop with a whole tail!
First Sergeant Emmett Bell played by Jeff Chandler: George Marshall's *Pillars of the Sky* (Universal, 1956).

2832
Sgt: There is an old saying amongst those Indian fighters. I just made it up: first you lose your nerve and then you lose your scalp. And the Colonel is a nervous man.
Sergeant Lloyd Carracart played by Lee Marvin: George Marshall's *Pillars of the Sky* (Universal, 1956).

2833
Hickok: What started you on the warpath, Yellow Hand?
Yellow Hand: Where sun rise, white man's land. Where sun set, Indian land. White man come, take our land, kill buffalo, our food. White man promise us food. White man lie. Now Cheyenne buy white man thunder stick. Soon war drum sound in all Indian land. All tribes ride with Yellowhand. We drive white man, like buffalo, away back to rising sun. Yellow Hand has spoken.
Wild Bill Hickok played by Gary Cooper and Chief Yellow Hand played by Paul Harvey: Cecil B. DeMille's *The Plainsman* (Paramount, 1936).

2834
Tony: Hey, why don't you want to get a haircut?
Hickok: Short hair makes the Indians mad, and they're mad enough already.
Tony the Barber played by Charles Judels and Wild Bill Hickok played by Gary Cooper: Cecil B. DeMille's *The Plainsman* (Paramount, 1936).

2835
Black Kettle: Who speaks the truth, Hickok or Crazy Knife?
Hickok: I never lied to you.
Black Kettle: Crazy Knife is my blood.
Hickok: Truth is stronger than blood.
Chief Black Kettle played by Simon Oakland, Wild Bill Hickok played by Don Murray, and Crazy Knife played by Henry Silva: David Lowell Rich's *The Plainsman* (Universal, 1966).

2836
Crazy Knife: I hear the voice of the Ghost Dancer. He will come soon. Then all the Cheyenne who are dead will rise. And on that day all the guns of our enemy will bend and no bullets will enter our skin. We will dance the Ghost Dance and win every battle. Peace is our enemy.
Crazy Knife played by Henry Silva: David Lowell Rich's *The Plainsman* (Universal, 1966).

2837
Black Kettle: Hickok, listen! In here [*pointing to head*] is peace. But in here [*pointing to stomach*] is war.
Chief Black Kettle played by Simon Oakland and Wild Bill Hickok played by Don Murray: David Lowell Rich's *The Plainsman* (Universal, 1966).

2838
Pioneer Girl: Well, I hope you don't find your hair drying in a Sioux tepee!
The Pioneer Girl played by Mary Ruth Wade: Joseph Kane's *The Plunderers* (Republic, 1948).

2839
Chief: This new world is not ours anymore.
Chief Powhatan played by Gordon Tootoosis: Daniele J. Suissa's *Pocahontas: The Legend* (Goodtimes Entertainment — Alliance Releasing, 1995).

2840
Pocahontas: When a woman loses family in battle, she can adopt a captive from another tribe to take his place.
Pocahontas played by Sandrine Holt: Daniele J. Suissa's *Pocahontas: The Legend* (Goodtimes Entertainment — Alliance Releasing, 1995).

2841
Smith: Kocoum has much anger in his soul.
Mochiqus: A brave needs anger. A brave does not have to hide behind a woman.
Smith: A man does not need anger when he can share in the wisdom of a woman.
John Smith played by Miles O'Keeffe, Kocoum played by Billy Merasty, and Mochiqus played by Billy Two Rivers: Daniele J. Suissa's *Pocahontas: The Legend* (Goodtimes Entertainment — Alliance Releasing, 1995).

2842
Pemberton: I'm taking the stage back to California tonight.
Cooper: The stage doesn't travel at night anymore. Indians.
Pemberton: I was told Indians wouldn't fight at night.
Cooper: I was told that, too, but I guess nobody told the Indians.
Pemberton played by Stuart Randall and Cooper played by Henry Brandon: Jerry Hopper's *Pony Express* (Paramount, 1953).

2843
Jimmy: He caught an arrow in the back.
Jimmy D. Richardson played by Stewart Petersen: Robert Totten's *Pony Express Rider* (Doty-Dayton, 1976).

2844
Standing Bear: When a man gives his word, duties go with it.
Standing Bear played by Stuart Randall: Joseph M. Newman's *Pony Soldier* (20th Century–Fox, 1952).

2845
Calhoun: Talk with an Indian? Well, take it from me, from Jess Calhoun, the only talk an Indian understands is hot lead in its belly.
Duncan: The Indian figures that's the only language the white man understands.
Jess Calhoun played by Robert Horton and Constable Duncan MacDonald played by Tyrone Power: Joseph M. Newman's *Pony Soldier* (20th Century–Fox, 1952).

2846
Tank: Well, I dropped him. I bored that Apache clean through with a .44. And that was one buck that departed for the trail of permanent sleep.
Tank Logan played by Brian Keith: Lee H. Katzin's *The Quest* (TVW, 1976).

2847
Vallian: Mrs. McKaskel, hand me your Bible.
Duncan: A Bible! You want me to throw it at them?
Villain: I'm going to watch you preach.
Duncan: What are you talking about? I'm not a preacher!
Villain: You preach to the earth, to the sky, to the grass, and to the Sioux!
Duncan: I'll look like a fool!
Villain: The crazier they think you are, the safer you're gonna be. Indians don't see

any point in killing crazy people …even white ones.

Con Vallian played by Sam Elliott, Duncan McKaskel played by Tom Conti, and Susanna McKaskel played by Kate Capshaw: Richard Day's *The Quick and the Dead* (HBO Pictures, 1987).

2848

Quantrill: Why did you deceive me? Do we not walk the same trail? Are we not brothers?

Little Crow: We are not brothers, white man. The deer travels with the coyote for fear of the snake. The coyote is not brother to the deer.

Quantrill played by John Ireland and Little Crow played by Jay Silverheels: William Dieterle's *Red Mountain* (Paramount, 1951).

2849

Groot: Why do Indians always want to be burning up good wagons?

Groot Nadine played by Walter Brennan: Howard Hawks' *Red River* (United Artists, 1948).

2850

Morgan: There is no evil spirits …only evil men.

John Morgan/Shunkawakan played by Richard Harris: Irving Kershner's *The Return of a Man Called Horse* (United Artists, 1976).

2851

Morgan: The smoke from this Sacred Pipe, mixed with my breath, will rise and spread throughout the universe and become one with the breath of the Great Spirit who has now shown me the way.

John Morgan/Shunkawakan played by Richard Harris: Irving Kershner's *The Return of a Man Called Horse* (United Artists, 1976).

2852

Elk Woman: If Yellow Hands all die, that is the way it will be.

Morgan: You're not afraid of death?

Elk Woman: Are you afraid to die? You have forgot much.

Morgan: Elk Woman, help me! Help me!

Elk Woman: You must forget yourself. Fast for four days and four nights to purify your body and seek your vision. You must suffer for the people. Then you will be reborn.

Elk Woman played by Gale Sondergaard and John Morgan/Shunkawakan played by Richard Harris: Irving Kershner's *The Return of a Man Called Horse* (United Artists, 1976).

2853

Call: You done right by me. I owe you. Of course, it don't change who I am.

Chief: You fight my people?

Call: All my life. Comanche, Kiowa, Mescalero, Apache. I ain't never been a friend of your people.

Jean Arthur is Calamity Jane in Cecil D. DeMille's epic western, *The Plainsman* (Paramount, 1936).

Chief: I take many scalps like yours. But always with honor. Do you not fight with honor?

Call: I do.

Chief: Then our hearts have same scar.

Captain Woodrow F. Call played by Jon Voight and the Indian Chief was uncredited: Mike Robe's *Return to Lonesome Dove* (TVW, 1993).

2854

Jack: I grew up with Indians. One thing about them, they always play games. Even when they become men …always play games. But they got plans for you. It's called honeypop. What they do is …they bury a man …all but his head …beside an ant hill …slide over with honey …on your mouth …your nose …and your ears. They slit your [eye] lids so you don't miss nothing. But you won't have to worry about that. I says to them, it's too easy for a man like you …Ranger …famous Indian fighter. I say to them they should show you some respect …let you run arrows.

Cherokee Jack Jackson played by Dennis Haysbert: Mike Robe's *Return to Lonesome Dove* (TVW, 1993).

2855

Hoop: That's an awful lot of Comanches, Greaser. I'm going to get on my horse and haul ass!

William P. "Bill" Hoop played by Ernest Borgnine and Cholo, referred to as "Greaser," played by

Jorge Martinez De Hoyos: Daniel Mann's *The Revengers* (NGP, 1972).

2856

Wid: Well, we got a treaty with the Mescaleros, ain't we?

Sam: It's just words on paper, Wid.

Wid: Yeah, we've been getting along.

Sam: I knew a man once who got along with his wife. One day she up and head shot him.

Wid: Dead? But why?

Sam: Got mad. Mescaleros, they're mad.

Wid: We ain't done nothing to them.

Sam: We're white. That's good enough.

Wid played by James Coburn and Sam Boone played by Pernell Roberts: Budd Boetticher's *Ride Lonesome* (Columbia, 1959).

2857

Bloodshirt: Lassiter. Lassiter. They tell me there is such a man. Great killer of my people. Often I think, what kind of man is this Lassiter that hunts the Apache like the Apache hunts the white eye. Now I look. I see. Same as me. Same hate here [heart].

Bloodshirt played by Rodolfo Acosta and James Lassiter played by Richard Boone: Gordon Douglas' *Rio Conchos* (20th Century–Fox, 1964).

2858

Franklyn: Doing like they do don't make it right.

Sergeant Ben Franklyn played by James Brown: Gordon Douglas' *Rio Conchos* (20th Century–Fox, 1964).

2859

Yorke: Any liquor in this village?

Tyree: Mucha tequila. They were slugging it down copious like when I left.

Yorke: Drums? Singing?

Tyree: Yes, sir.

Yorke: Vengeance dance. They'll dance until dawn.

Lt. Col. Kirby Yorke played by John Wayne and Trooper Tyree played by Ben Johnson: John Ford's *Rio Grande* (Republic, 1950).

2860

Mark: What will we do if they come with paint on?

Matt: We'll fight 'em. We cleared this land, son. It's ours. We'll stay on it …or under it.

Mark Calder played by Tommy Rettig and Matt Calder played by Robert Mitchum: Otto Preminger's *The River of No Return* (20th Century–Fox, 1954).

2861

Pap: I don't mind the sniping. They can't hit nothing from down there. But I could sure use a lot less of them drums.

Plank: The louder they bang them, the better I like it. It's when they stop that I'm gonna start to sweat.

Pap Dennison played by Guinn "Big Boy" Williams and Plank played by Slim Pickens:

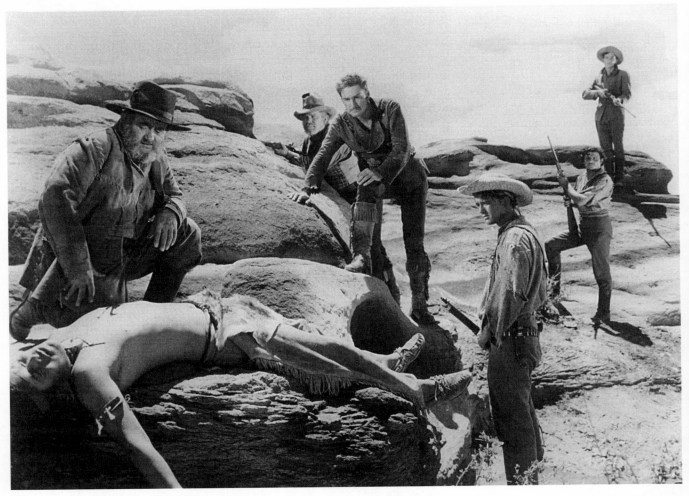

A detachment of Confederate cavalry on secret mision out west. Gil Craigie (Chubby Johnson), Pap Dennison (Guinn "Big Boy" Williams), Lafe Barstow (Errol Flynn), Jim Wheat (Dick Jones), Pierre Duchesne (Peter Coe), Kip Waterson (Buzz Henry), and a dead Indian on Ghost Mountain, also known as *Rocky Mountain* (Warner Bros., 1950).

William Keighley's *Rocky Mountain* (Warner Bros., 1950).

2862

Pap: It looks like the end of the line.

Lafe: They've seen our backs. Let's show them our faces!

Pap Dennison played by Guinn "Big Boy" Williams and Lafe Barston played by Errol Flynn: William Keighley's *Rocky Mountain* (Warner Bros., 1950).

2863

Walking Coyote: The game is called "Run of the Arrow." When we get to the spot where his arrow fell, we start running. They run after us.

O'Meara: On feet?

Walking Coyote: Yeah, except they're not barefooted like we are.

O'Meara: He fired the arrow quite a ways. Maybe we got a chance.

Walking Coyote: That's the idea. They torture us with a chance to make an escape.

O'Meara: You cannot outrun them. You're too old.

Walking Coyote: You ain't. There's one thing I got to tell you, son. Nobody ever made the run and lived to tell about it.

Walking Coyote played by Jay C. Flippen and O'Meara played by Rod Steiger: Samuel Fuller's *Run of the Arrow* (RKO, 1957).

2864

O'Meara: Wait a minute! You said awhile back that you could have been a Sioux chief.

Walking Coyote: That's true.

O'Meara: Well, why didn't you?

Walking Coyote: Ah, I can't stomach politics!

O'Meara played by Rod Steiger and Walking Coyote played by Jay C. Flippen: Samuel Fuller's *Run of the Arrow* (RKO, 1957).

2865

Yellow Moccasin: A Sioux can watch an American skinned alive. An American cannot watch.

Yellow Moccasin played by Sarita Montiel: Samuel Fuller's *Run of the Arrow* (RKO, 1957).

2866

Prairie Fox: The white man's law is the thunder sticks that kills us.

Prairie Fox played by Eloy Phil Casados: Charles B. Pierce's *Sacred Ground* (Pacific International Enterprises/Wilderness Family, 1983).

2867

Witcher: The Paiutes only send one warrior after a lone enemy. It's sort of like a code of honor or something or another.

Lum Witcher played by Jack Elam: Charles B. Pierce's *Sacred Ground* (Pacific International Enterprises/Wilderness Family, 1983).

2868

Witcher: You know what you've done? You made 'em mad! You made their spirits mad! And the way they look at it, when their dead is restless, they just roam around up there in heaven and they never get to their happy hunting grounds.

Lum Witcher played by Jack Elam: Charles B. Pierce's *Sacred Ground* (Pacific International Enterprises/Wilderness Family, 1983).

2869

Yutaka: I don't belong here. I'm not a cowboy. And I never will be.

Eagle Eye: You know, my grandfather said that each person comes into this world from one of the great four directions. The bear from the west, the buffalo from the north, the eagle from the east, and the mouse from the south.

Yutaka: I know. I am the mouse. I feel like a mouse.

Eagle Eye: There is nothing wrong with the mouse. He comes from a place of innocence and trust. But he is a small creature. He only sees what's at the end of his nose. The mouse went to find the Great River. The river was a powerful experience. But most powerful was the sight of the Sacred Mountains. Once he saw them, he knew he had to go. The journal across the prairie would have been impossible, but two animals helped him: the dying buffalo and the wolf who lost his memory. And to each he made a sacrifice to return them to health. To each he gave an eye.

Yutaka: But then he was blind!

Eagle Eye: He gave up the mouse's way of seeing. And there he stood at the bottom of the mountain waiting to die. But something swooped down and carried him away. He was terrified. But suddenly, he began to see colors. And the voice called out to him: hold on to the wind and trust. Higher and higher he went. And the higher he went, the clearer he could see. And the mouse flew over the Great River and saw his friend the buffalo. And the buffalo said: Okay! Hello! You have a new name …peta …eagle.

Yutaka: So the mouse became the eagle!

Eagle Eye: Yes. He left his beginning and experienced a new direction. It takes great courage.

Yutaka Sato played by Hiromi Go and Eagle Eye played by Byron Chief Moon: Michael Keusch's *Samurai Cowboy* (Den Pictures/Entertainment Securities/Saban Entertainment, 1993).

2870

Sam: If they're gonna lift your scalp, I want to peek under it and see what you've been using for brains.

Sam Beckman played by Slim Pickens: William Witney's *Santa Fe Passage* (Republic, 1955).

2871

White Thunder: White men are our friends. Have they not told us so? In our treaty, they said our people could live forever in peace and friendship in the Black Hills. They said we could hunt in peace and friendship as far south as the Great River. They said their soldiers would protect us against other white men who might seek to steal our land, spoil our hunting. Those are the things they promised. This is the treaty I, White Thunder, signed in blood. But the white men found yellow iron in the Black Hills. They built an iron road across our land, and brought the iron horse. Some of our people tried to stop these white men. The soldiers came as they had promised. But they were not the soldiers who made the treaty. Their chiefs were not the chiefs who signed the treaty. They punished our people who tried to stop these invaders. They drove our people from our hills. But do not be angry at the white men. Remember, they are our friends. Soon they will be coming to protect you, to take you to the reservations. They will give you cow, beef and white flour to eat. You will hunt no more. They will take away your weapons and ponies. In peace and friendship, you who were once great warriors will sit by the fire and mumble stories to your grandchildren. And they will laugh behind your bent backs.

White Thunder played by John Miljan: George Marshall's *The Savage* (Paramount, 1952).

2872

Colonel: You'd like some action with us, is that it? I'm sorry, I can't promise you that. You see, we have a treaty with the hostiles.

Ahern: Hostiles?

Colonel: Indians. We're waiting to hear from Washington whether the hostiles are willing to let civilization move further west.

Colonel Ellis played by Howard Negley and Jim Ahern/Warbonnet played by Charlton Heston: George Marshall's *The Savage* (Paramount, 1952).

2873

Colonel: I want the area outside well lighted at every interval just in case they forgot their superstition and make a night attack.

Colonel Ellis played by Howard Negley: George Marshall's *The Savage* (Paramount, 1952).

2874

Iron Beast: White Thunder himself will speak tomorrow.

Yellow Eagle: I've heard words from greater chiefs.

Iron Beast: They say even the white men fear him.

Pehangi: They say. Small men easily give the name of greatness to feel less small themselves.

Iron Beast played by Ted De Corsia, White Thunder played by John Miljan, Yellow Eagle played by Ian MacDonald, and Pehangi played by Angela Clarke: George Marshall's *The Savage* (Paramount, 1952).

2875

Colonel: A lot of white trappers take scalps, Vaugant. Out there with the Indians they learn to keep their own scalp and take the other fella's. It's not different than our own souvenir hunting soldiers.

Colonel Ellis played by Howard Negley and Captain Arnold Vaugant played by Richard Rober: George Marshall's *The Savage* (Paramount, 1952).

2876

Skyano: And always remember: first there's family ...and then there's all else.

Luke: Did someone very wise once say that?

Skyano: Yeah ...I did.

Skyano played by Graham Greene and Luke Morgan played by Corey Carrier: Dean Hamilton's *Savage Land* (Herndale Communications/Savage Land Productions, 1994).

2877

Simon: We do a rain dance because we want rain ...to make things grow ...because we're hungry. I mean, if you want to get some Indians to dance, I'm sure you can get some. But not me. To me, it's something special. I mean, it's very old. And, well, I think you do it out of need. It's like a religion.

Simon played by Burt Reynolds: George McCowan's *Savage Run* (TVW, 1970).

2878

Indian Girl: My father say, everyone has guiding spirit. And even the white man has guiding spirit in his body. I not die, you see, as long as the spirit of my father shows the way and stays within me ...as the spirit of your wife guides you. The souls we love dearly stay in us. Love is like hate. It never dies.

The Indian Girl, daughter of Chief Black Eagle, played by Mapy Galan: Werner Knox/Bruno Mattei's *Scalps* (Imperial Entertainment, 1987).

2879

Nesby: I don't like it.

Clayton: What don't you like?

Nesby: Indians on the raid generally hide their dead. And if they don't care anything about us knowing, it only spells one thing: they ain't afraid of us following ...or of us catching up with 'em either.

Nesby played by Bill Steele and Captain Reverend Samuel Clayton played by Ward Bond: John Ford's *The Searchers* (Warner Bros., 1956).

2880

Ethan: ...But what that Comanche believes: if he ain't got no eyes, he can't enter the Spirit Land. He has to wander forever between the wind.

Ethan Edwards played by John Wayne: John Ford's *The Searchers* (Warner Bros., 1956).

2881

Kajeck: It was I who killed your sentry. I wished to do away with Osceola. He was blinded and made weak by your promises and treachery. A chief must be strong. Strong enough to face the enemy in his own camp without fear or faith of any false white flags that flutter within the wind.

Kajeck played by Hugh O'Brian and Chief Osceola/John Powell played by Anthony Quinn: Budd Boetticher's *Seminole* (Universal, 1953).

2882

Kulak: You will stay, my son. To look for peace is unwise when hate blinds the eyes. The rashness of the young is not needed.

Kulak played by Ralph Moody: Budd Boetticher's *Seminole* (Universal, 1953).

2883

Seven: I thought Indians always did a lot of hollering?

Flood: Well, they do that mainly when they're trying to build up their nerve. They don't think they got any particular problem here.

Seven Jones played by Audie Murphy and Jim Flood played by Barry Sullivan: Harry Keller's *Seven Ways from Sundown* (Universal, 1960).

2884

Flood: Look at them run! I guess they decided to do something easy, like attack an Army fort, rather than tackle with you and me.

Jim Flood played by Barry Sullivan: Harry Keller's *Seven Ways from Sundown* (Universal, 1960).

2885

Bates: They left us a warning. Sitting Bull don't want no white men in the valley of the Big Horn.

Benson: For once you're right, Bates. He's made the battlefield his personal big medicine ground.

Kruger: And when we take out those bodies, we disturb his medicine.

Benson: Little Big Horn is now a Sioux holy place ...part of their religious belief.

Kruger: Well, for us coming in here is like bustin' into a church and shootin' it up.

Sergeant Bates played by Jay C. Flippen, Captain Tom Benson played by Randolph Scott, and Sergeant Kruger played by Frank Faylen: Joseph H. Lewis' *7th Cavalry* (Columbia, 1956).

2886

Kroomak: I will find many words to say nothing.

Kroomak played by Toshiro Mifune: Jacques Dorfmann's *Shadow of the Wolf* (Triumph Releasing, 1993).

2887

Shalako: Chato, we've fought too much in the past.

Chato: Yes, we fight. We both live. My spirit live forever ...if I kill you before I die.

Shalako played by Sean Connery and Chato played by Woody Strode: Edward Dmytryk's *Shalako* (CIN, 1968).

2888

Brittles: Pony That Walks, my heart is sad at what I see. Your young men painted for war. Their scalp knives red, the medicine drums talking. It is a bad thing.

Captain Nathan Brittles played by John Wayne and Pony That Walks played by Chief John Big Tree: John Ford's *She Wore a Yellow Ribbon* (RKO, 1949).

2889

Reeves: It's just a hunting party.

Eamon: Just a hunting party! And what do you suppose they might be hunting? I'm telling ya now, if we don't turn back, their dogs will be eating our testicles by nightfall.

Reeves McCree played by Dermot Mulroney and Eamon McCree played by Alan Bates: Sam Shepard's *Silent Tongue* (Trimark Pictures, 1994).

2890

Marshal: Indians train themselves to endure thirst by running long distances with a mouthful of water. The idea is not to swallow any of it.

Marshal John Llewellyn played by Barry Corbin: Kevin G. Cremin's *Siringo* (TVW, 1994).

2891

Parris: What is your plan, Sitting Bull?

Sitting Bull: My braves will hold their arrows. But your chief must come here.

He will meet me between the two armies in the open country.

Parris: You mean bring the President here?

Sitting Bull: If this meeting fails, then both armies will come together. The chiefs in the middle will die first. This is the Indian way.

Captain Robert Parris played by Dale Robertson and Chief Sitting Bull played by J. Carrol Naish: Sidney Salkow's *Sitting Bull* (United Artists, 1954).

2892

Sitting Bull: Great Spirit, Father of my Fathers, here lies the body of my son. Killed without reason. Listen to the death chant of the women. Listen to the war cries of the chiefs. Give me your counsel, Mighty One. Must there be war? Is this land not big enough for all people? Guide me now, oh God of my people. War or peace? War or peace?

Chief Sitting Bull played by J. Carrol Naish: Sidney Salkow's *Sitting Bull* (United Artists, 1954).

2893

Sitting Bull: There have been battles. But when the white soldiers win a battle, they call it victory. When the Indians win, they call it massacre.

Chief Sitting Bull played by J. Carrol Naish: Sidney Salkow's *Sitting Bull* (United Artists, 1954).

2894

Bighead: The women, they punctured his [Custer's] ears with their sewing awl. They did this so that he would hear better. He had promised never again to make war on the Cheyenne. And we had promised his death if he did. He forgot his promise. He did not remember our words. In the next life, he should hear us better.

The voice of Kate Bighead played by Buffy Sainte-Marie: Mike Robe's *Son of the Morning Star* (TVW, 1991).

2895

Bighead: They called it Custer's last stand. But it was not his. It would be our last stand.

The voice of Kate Bighead played by Buffy Sainte-Marie: Mike Robe's *Son of the Morning Star* (TVW, 1991).

2896

Tall Tale: I didn't like what I seen, boss.

Beale: Oh, what was it?

Tall Tale: Nothing.

Beale: No Apaches?

Tall Tale: Nothing but scenery. Where they was they ain't. And that's the time to start worrying about 'em!

Tall Tale played by Guinn "Big Boy" Williams and Edward Beale played by Rod Cameron: Ray Nazarro's *Southwest Passage* (United Artists, 1954).

2897

Tall Tale: Apaches won't jump until daybreak.

Lt. Owens: That's what they said about the Cheyenne. It didn't turn out that way. I was there.

Tall Tale: But these Apaches are different. You see, they got a special War God who sleeps all night. They believe that if he sees a warrior die while fighting, he'll take him straight up into heaven. So they wait until it's light enough so Old Sleepy can see what's going on.

Beale: We'll keep a strong guard anyway …in case Old Sleepy wakes up early.

Tale Tale played by Guinn "Big Boy" Williams, Lt. Owens played by Stuart Randall, and Edward Beale played by Rod Cameron: Ray Nazarro's *Southwest Passage* (United Artists, 1954).

2898

Tall Tale: Nobody sees Apaches before they attack …only when.

Tall Tale played by Guinn "Big Boy" Williams: Ray Nazarro's *Southwest Passage* (United Artists, 1954).

2899

Lt. Owens: We haven't got enough ammunition left to stop another charge if they make it.

Tall Tale: They'll make it all right. I reckon we're all in for a short haircut.

Lt. Owens played by Stuart Randall and Tall Tale played by Guinn "Big Boy" Williams: Ray Nazarro's *Southwest Passage* (United Artists, 1954).

2900

Sir George: There is a divine order to life. It starts with God, followed by the angels, then the king. Then the rest of us according to our positions in the world. Your position, Indian, is lower than the animal. You're not a human being. You're livestock.

Sir George played by Michael Gambon: Xavier Koller's *Squanto: A Warrior's Tale* (Buena Vista, 1994).

2901

Squanto: I will wear their ashes and carry their spirits with me.

Squanto played by Adam Beach: Xavier Koller's *Squanto: A Warrior's Tale* (Buena Vista, 1994).

2902

Squanto: Like him [my father], I would be a leader and a warrior one day. But you will become a different kind of leader, he said. Your eyes will see far beyond our horizons. I did not yet understand his words of wisdom.

Squanto played by Adam Beach: Xavier Koller's *Squanto: A Warrior's Tale* (Buena Vista, 1994).

2903

Doc: They say Geronimo has two virtues: he can kill without being killed, and steal without getting caught.

Hatfield: Those don't seem like virtues to me.

Doc: Well, you would if you were an Apache with a white man coming out from under every rock.

Hatfield: You know, you actually sound like you admire him.

Doc: I really do. I'd admire anybody who would fight for their survival against odds that they know is going to overwhelm them in the end.

Doc Holliday played by Willie Nelson and Hatfield played by Waylon Jennings: Ted Post's *Stagecoach* (TVW, 1986).

2904

Lane Dakota: The government as big as ours doesn't always know the mistakes that are made by its helpers.

Cara Blanca: Is it too much to ask that the White Chief know when its promises are made into lies?

Sheriff Lane Dakota played by Stephen McNally and Cara Blanca played by Edgar Barrie: Lee Sholem's *The Stand at Apache River* (Universal, 1953).

2905

Sheriff: Wouldn't the reservation be safer for you and the women?

Cara Blanca: Now there is no choice …because you have always won the wars against us. But you have never won our trust. Can you ever win it by punishment?

Sheriff Lane Dakota played by Stephen McNally and Cara Blanca played by Edgar Barrie: Lee Sholem's *The Stand at Apache River* (Universal, 1953).

2906

Sheriff: When Indians attack, no one is a hero.

Sheriff Lane Dakota played by Stephen McNally: Lee Sholem's *The Stand at Apache River* (Universal, 1953).

2907

Allison: There's more Sioux out there than there are fleas on a dog!

Ben Allison played by Clark Gable: Raoul Walsh's *The Tall Men* (20th Century–Fox, 1955).

2908

Cochise: One last wish. Let no white eyes find the ground where Cochise makes the Big Sleep.

Cochise played by Jeff Chandler: Douglas Sirk's *Taza, Son of Cochise* (Universal, 1954).

2909

Captain: What's it all about?

Taza: The drums say: all the Apache warriors must be ready to fight or die because the soldiers will come soon to kill them.

Captain: That's crazy!

Sergeant: They don't go in for idle talk, Captain.

Captain Burnett played by Gregg Palmer, Taza played by Rock Hudson, and Sergeant Hamma played by Joseph Sawyer: Douglas Sirk's *Taza, Son of Cochise* (Universal, 1954).

2910

Tecumseh: White promises! I hope you live to see them.

Black Hoof: Not a good way to think, my son. You'd be happier if you lived in peace.

Tecumseh: Aren't you happy that we are still free? Isn't it better to die under the white man's gun than under his boot?

Black Hoof: In the end, the leader cannot bear the crying mothers and wives, the loss of sons and brothers. At last he says: no more tears, no more blood. Give me your treaty. Let me sign it.

Tecumseh played by Jesse Burrego and Black Hoof played by August Schellenberg: Larry Elikann's *Tecumseh: The Last Warrior* (Turner Pictures, 1995).

2911

Tecumseh: They have stolen everything from us: our homes, our religion, our children. All they have left us with is hate. From now on, it will be a war of vengeance. I'll fight the long knives to my death. I swear it to the Master of Life!

Tecumseh played by Jesse Burrego: Larry Elikann's *Tecumseh: The Last Warrior* (Turner Pictures, 1995).

2912

Harrison: What we ask now is simple: that you cease your efforts to organize the tribes against us. And that you join us in making one last agreement, giving us title to the land …

Tecumseh: One last agreement? Every treaty you have ever made with the red man since coming upon this land you promised was to be the last. And each time you invaded us again! You asked us to have confidence in your promises. When Jesus Christ came upon the earth, you killed him. The son of your own God! And only after he was dead did you worship him, and start killing those who would not. Who could trust the word of such people?

William Henry Harrison played by David Morse and Tecumseh played by Jesse Burrego: Larry Elikann's *Tecumseh: The Last Warrior* (Turner Pictures, 1995).

2913

Tecumseh: I will speak plainly. We have learned your ways. And we know that your treaties are for us to keep and you to break.

Tecumseh played by Jesse Burrego: Larry Elikann's *Tecumseh: The Last Warrior* (Turner Pictures, 1995).

2914

Loud Noise: Whites are evil. But our misery is not their fault. It's our own. We are corrupt. Sick in spirit. We have lost our own spiritual ways.

Loud Noise played by Lorne Cardinal: Larry Elikann's *Tecumseh: The Last Warrior* (Turner Pictures, 1995).

2915

A great war chief is honored by being buried close to where he died. They painted his face black and put him in the ground with bark around him. He lies with his head toward the setting sun. There is no stone or metal in the grave. And at the end, there is a hole in the bark so his spirit can pass through.

Voice of Turtle Mother: Larry Elikann's *Tecumseh: The Last Warrior* (Turner Pictures, 1995).

2916

His American enemies, to whom he had never yielded in life, could not capture my son in death.

Voice of Turtle Mother: Larry Elikann's *Tecumseh: The Last Warrior* (Turner Pictures, 1995).

2917

Blue Jacket: It's a book.

Tecumseh: A book?

Blue Jacket: Whites put their talk in 'em.

Blue Jacket played by Holt McCallany and Tecumseh played by Jesse Burrego: Larry Elikann's *Tecumseh: The Last Warrior* (Turner Pictures, 1995).

2918

Hardstriker: You're destined to be a great warrior, Tecumseh. And a warrior must always remember that he belongs to the people. Once he learns that, he has nothing to fear.

Hardstriker played by Jimmie F. Skaggs and Tecumseh played by Jesse Burrego: Larry Elikann's *Tecumseh: The Last Warrior* (Turner Pictures, 1995).

2919

Black Hoof: No one is without fear. But one can stay above this fear. That is what a warrior must do.

Tecumseh: How do I do that?

Black Hoof: What did your father, Hardstriker, teach you?

Tecumseh: That I, that I have nothing to fear. That I belong to the people.

Black Hoof: You forgot that in battle. You forgot the needs of your people. You thought only of yourself.

Tecumseh: Yes.

Black Hoof: That's your answer. Remember that!

Black Hoof played by August Schellenberg, Tecumseh played by Jesse Burrego, and Hardstriker played by Jimmie F. Skaggs: Larry Elikann's *Tecumseh: The Last Warrior* (Turner Pictures, 1995).

2920

Harrison: Contrary to his legend, gentleman, he [Tecumseh] is not all that big. Although when he springs up before you with his tomahawk, he does seem rather, rather imposing. Take it from one who knows. But then, as the maxim goes: the greater the enemy, the greater the victory.

William Henry Harrison played by David Morse and Tecumseh played by Jesse Burrego: Larry Elikann's *Tecumseh: The Last Warrior* (Turner Pictures, 1995).

2921

Chiksika: Promise when I fall, you will not lose heart.

Tecumseh: I promise. If you fall, I will revenge your death.

Chiksika: Revenge is spit in the wind. It comes back in your face.

Chiksika played by Gregory Norman Cruz and Tecumseh played by Jesse Burrego: Larry Elikann's *Tecumseh: The Last Warrior* (Turner Pictures, 1995).

2922

Tecumseh: Yes, my friend, tomorrow we will be in the smoke of the long-knife guns again. It seems the gun is the only talk the Americans understand.

Tecumseh played by Jesse Burrego: Larry Elikann's *Tecumseh: The Last Warrior* (Turner Pictures, 1995).

2923

Don Andrea: This is night. Are you going to sleep?

Sam Hollis: Well, it ain't healthy to travel through that Comanche territory in the daytime. So we'll travel at night.

Don Andrea: Oh, when we ride, the savage sleeps. Yes?

Sam Hollis: Yep. Them Comanches believe the moon is an evil spirit.

Don Andrea Baldasar played by Alain Delon and Sam Hollis played by Dean Martin: Michael Gordon's *Texas Across the River* (Universal, 1966).

2924

Sam Hollis: Why you dumb, fool tenderfoot! Are you trying to take on that whole tribe single-handed?

Don Andrea: When one is alone, one must become an army.

Sam Hollis played by Dean Martin and Don Andrea Baldasar played by Alain Delon: Michael Gordon's *Texas Across the River* (Universal, 1966).

2925

Capt: As for the Apache, well, you know he is a path master at making his pony tell lies about where he was yesterday and the day before.

Captain Stephen Maddocks played by Richard Boone: Joseph Newman's *A Thunder of Drums* (MGM, 1961).

2926

Lt.: They found the homesteader's wife and daughter violated …and freshly murdered yesterday.

Capt: Mr. Gresham, Comanches rape their own. That's their idea of courtship. But they don't generally fancy white women.

Lieutenant Gresham played by James Douglas and Captain Stephen Maddocks played by Richard Boone: Joseph Newman's *A Thunder of Drums* (MGM, 1961).

2927

Ancient: You know, somehow, I got a feeling that tomorrow is going to be a little too late for the lot of us.

Ancient played by Raymond Hatton: Frank McDonald's *Thunder Pass* (Republic, 1954).

2928

Captain: I got you all together here so I could give it to you real straight. We may not be able to make it out of this valley. But if everybody obeys orders, we stand a chance. A lot of good blood has been donated to these plains by settlers who didn't obey orders.

Captain Dave Storm played by Dane Clark: Frank McDonald's *Thunder Pass* (Republic, 1954).

2929

Tulsa: But Captain, we can't leave this here place. Ancient and me got our whole future tied up in this mine.

Scout: If you don't get out of here, mister, your whole future is liable to be tied up in your past.

Tulsa played by Raymond Burr, Captain Dave Storm played by Dane Clark, and Ancient played

by Raymond Hatton: Frank McDonald's *Thunder Pass* (Republic, 1954).

2930

Wolcott: Do you boys know what happens to stragglers? Indians get 'em. And when they do, they pull their innards out and make 'em walk around a tree. Now if that doesn't scare you, maybe this will. A man's intestines is 30 feet long, and that's more walking than you two have ever done put together!

Major Wolcott played by Glenn Ford: Phil Karlson's *A Time for Killing* (Columbia, 1967).

2931

Nona: They say the only good Indian is a dead Indian. And when they find one with a man's pride and courage to stand up as an equal …they kill him. And it isn't called murder. They just made him a good Indian.

Nona Mayfield played by Betsy Palmer: Anthony Mann's *The Tin Star* (Paramount, 1957).

2932

Horn: Geronimo is a man so great that Corbett there would have to stand on his mother's shoulders to kiss his ass.

Tom Horn played by Steve McQueen and "Gentleman" Jim Corbett played by Steve Oliver: William Wiard's *Tom Horn* (Warner Bros., 1980).

2933

Civilian: What did he say, Mr. Bridger?

Bridger: Well, he said that the white man's promises are written in water. In other words, gentlemen, he said that you all are a pack of liars and that this peace conference is a fake.

The Civilian was uncredited and Jim Bridger played by Van Heflin: George Sherman's *Tomahawk* (Universal, 1951).

2934

Sergeant: What are they singing?

Beckworth: It's a death chant. They always sing that before they start a ruckus.

Sergeant Newell played by Stuart Randall and Sol Beckworth played by Jack Oakie: George Sherman's *Tomahawk* (Universal, 1951).

The Tall Men (20th Century–Fox, 1955) is a story of men riding away from past memories and toward a new beginning …tall men with long shadows. Upon seeing a man hanging in a tree, Ben Allison (Clark Gable) remarks to his brother, "looks like we're getting close to civilization" in Raoul Walsh's classic western.

2935

Johnny: Apaches have a saying: death comes anyway …why go to meet him?

Johnny Dogwood played by Eddie Little Sky: Robert Parry/Lesley Selander's *Tomahawk Trail* (United Artists, 1957).

2936

McCoy: At least we'll be able to send a few of them back to join their ancestors.

Reynolds: That's what the Apache wants, isn't it, Sergeant? To die in battle? They can't lose, can they?

McCoy: Nope.

Sergeant Wade McCoy played by Chuck Connors and Private Tim Reynolds played by John Smith: Robert Parry/Lesley Selander's *Tomahawk Trail* (United Artists, 1957).

2937

McCoy: But if the Apaches weren't actually at war for the moment, I knew they weren't ever at peace.

Sergeant Wade McCoy played by Chuck Connors: Robert Parry/Lesley Selander's *Tomahawk Trail* (United Artists, 1957).

2938
Nanchez: You are more Indian than you know.
Hook: I've taught myself to think like my enemy.
Nanchez: I am familiar with your mind. You will not let the blood of my son make you soft.
Hook: You leave me no choice.
Nanchez: And you think you have left me with no choice.
Hook: Maybe you're more white than you know. You love your son too much to see him killed.
Chief Nanchez played by Rodolfo Acosta and Sergeant Hook played by Joel McCrea: Charles Marquis Warren's *Trooper Hook* (United Artists, 1957).

2939
Consuela: Why haven't they attacked before, Sergeant?
Sergeant: They'll do that when it's convenient for them. If they don't jump us before dark, we got the rest of the night to get as close to Tucson as we can. They're superstitious about fighting after the sun goes down. So hold tight. We'll start worrying hard when it counts.
Consuela played by Susan Kohner and Sergeant Hook played by Joel McCrea: Charles Marquis Warren's *Trooper Hook* (United Artists, 1957).

2940
Jim: I better be pushing on. I got to catch up with Aguila.
Prospector: With one six-gun? Mister, it seems to me that water ain't the only thing you're low on!
Jim Harvey played by Audie Murphy and the Prospector played by Harry Harvey: Nathan Juran's *Tumbleweed* (Universal, 1953).

2941
Seth: Well, anyway, Indians won't fight after dark.
Jim: Aguila ain't just an Indian!
Seth played by Ross Elliott and Jim Harvey played by Audie Murphy: Nathan Juran's *Tumbleweed* (Universal, 1953).

2942
Aguila: You have heard of the death without sleep? At dawn we will cut your eyelids so you can watch the sun.
Aguila played by Ralph Moody: Nathan Juran's *Tumbleweed* (Universal, 1953).

2943
Bill: Well, I ain't running from no Indian, dead or alive!
Pete: Please, Bill, I run away for both of us!

Skinner Bill Bragg played by Wallace Beery and Piute Pete played by Leo Carrillo: Richard Thorpe's *20 Mule Team* (MGM, 1940).

2944
Son: I ain't eatin' with no savage! I don't want nothing to do with 'em!
Hugh: Listen, there ain't nothing more savage than a white man!
Son Holland played by Scott Bairstow and Hugh Allison played by Kris Kristofferson: Rod Hardy's *Two for Texas* (Turner Pictures, 1998).

2945
Major: I don't know how the word got out but somehow it did. And they have been expecting a Messiah, a Moses …come to deliver their children from bondage. And I've got to send them you!
Major Frazer played by John McIntire: John Ford's *Two Rode Together* (Columbia, 1961).

2946
Indian Agent: What are you trying to tell me to do? Give them extra rations?
McIntosh: Just don't water the beef before you weigh 'em. You'd be surprised how many steaks there are in two gallons of river water.
Indian Agent Steegmeyer played by Otto Reichow and McIntosh played by Burt Lancaster: Robert Aldrich's *Ulzana's Raid* (Universal, 1972).

2947
Lieutenant: Do you hate Apaches, Mr. McIntosh?
McIntosh: No.
Lieutenant: Well, I do.
McIntosh: Well, it might not make you happy, Lieutenant, but it sure won't make you lonesome. Most white folks hereabouts feel the same as you do.
Lieutenant: Why don't you feel that way?
McIntosh: It would be like hating the desert because there ain't no water on it. For now, I can get by being pretty scared of 'em.
Lieutenant Garnett DeBuin played by Bruce Davison and McIntosh played by Burt Lancaster: Robert Aldrich's *Ulzana's Raid* (Universal, 1972).

2948
McIntosh: Half of what they say is lies. The other half ain't true.
McIntosh played by Burt Lancaster: Robert Aldrich's *Ulzana's Raid* (Universal, 1972).

2949
Lieutenant: Why are your people like that? Why are they so cruel? What is the reason?
Ke-Ni-Tay: This how they are.
Lieutenant: But why?
Ke-Ni-Tay: This how they are. They have always been like that.
Lieutenant: Are you like that? Would you kill a man like that?

Ke-Ni-Tay: Yes.
Lieutenant: Why?
Ke-Ni-Tay: To take the power. Each man that die, the man who kill him, takes his power. Man give up his power when he die. Like fire with heat. Fire that burn long time. Many can have heat.
Lieutenant: You mean you'd torture a man for hours? And you can get power from watching some poor creature suffering? What kind of power is that?
Ke-Ni-Tay: Here in this land man must have power.
Lieutenant Garnett DeBuin played by Bruce Davison and Ke-Ni-Tay played by Jorge Luke: Robert Aldrich's *Ulzana's Raid* (Universal, 1972).

2950
Lieutenant: Why didn't they kill the boy?
Ke-Ni-Tay: Man cannot take power from boy …only from man.
Lieutenant Garnett DeBuin played by Bruce Davison and Ke-Ni-Tay played by Jorge Luke: Robert Aldrich's *Ulzana's Raid* (Universal, 1972).

2951
Major: What we have to determine, Mr. McIntosh, is how many of them there are and whether they are hostile.
McIntosh: Well, the first is open to question; the second you can bet on!
Major Cartwright played by Douglas Watson and McIntosh played by Burt Lancaster: Robert Aldrich's *Ulzana's Raid* (Universal, 1972).

2952
McIntosh: Apache war parties come in all sizes. There's the kind with 100 braves …and the kind with one.
McIntosh played by Burt Lancaster: Robert Aldrich's *Ulzana's Raid* (Universal, 1972).

2953
Lieutenant: Well, killing, I expect, Mr. McIntosh. But mutilation and torture? I cannot accept that as readily as you seem to be able to.
McIntosh: What bothers you, Lieutenant, is you don't like to think of white men behaving like Indians. It kind of confuses the issue, don't it?
Lieutenant Garnett DeBuin played by Bruce Davison and McIntosh played by Burt Lancaster: Robert Aldrich's *Ulzana's Raid* (Universal, 1972).

2954
Bone: Hey! Hear them war drums? They'll stop in a minute. Then hang on to your hair!
Dave Bone played by Mike Mazurki: Cecil B. De-Mille's *Unconquered* (Paramount, 1947).

2955
Holden: In case of an Indian war, which side would you be on?
Garth: I've killed men for [saying] less than that!

Holden: Much less!

Captain Christopher Holden played by Gary Cooper and Martin Garth played by Howard da Silva: Cecil B. DeMille's *Unconquered* (Paramount, 1947).

2956

Ben: I'm going to parley. Don't shoot unless you have to.

Cash: When is that?

Ben: When they break the peace and kill me.

Ben Zachary played by Burt Lancaster and Cash Zachary played by Audie Murphy: John Huston's *The Unforgiven* (United Artists, 1960).

2957

Sid: What's a dead Indian more or less?

Sid Campeua played by Brian Donlevy: Cecil B. DeMille's *Union Pacific* (Paramount, 1939).

2958

Cactus Jack: I come to speak with straight tongue.

Nervous Elk: Tongue may be straight, but mouth hide many sharp teeth.

Cactus Jack Slade played by Kirk Douglas and Nervous Elk played by Paul Lynde: Hal Needham's *The Villain* (a.k.a. *Cactus Jack*; Columbia, 1979).

2959

Dusty: Put the wagons in a circle! Put the wagons in a circle!

Callahan: We only got two wagons!

Dusty played by Bob Denver and Callahan played by Forrest Tucker: Jack Arnold, Oscar Rudolph, Bruce Bilson, and Earl Bellamy's *The Wackiest Wagon Train in the West* (Topar Films, 1976).

2960

Hetty: Get down here and grab one these guns!

Abby: I won't do it!

Hetty: Well, at least you can help me reload.

Abby: I won't be part of the killing of any human.

Hetty: You'll change your mind when one of 'em starts lifting your hair with a scalping knife.

Hetty Masters played by Leila Bennett and Abby Masters played by Jan Duggan: Charles Barton's *Wagon Wheels* (Paramount, 1934).

2961

Eskiminzin: We beaten people. No more need for Apache chief.

John Clum: Yes there is. Much has been taken away from your people ...more than your land. Much has been taken from your hearts too, and your pride ...and your whole way of living. And now I'm here to see that some of these things are given back. I'm not here to rule the reservation, but to help you rule.

Eskiminzin played by Robert Warwick and John P. Clum played by Audie Murphy: Jesse Hibbs' *Walk the Proud Land* (Universal, 1956).

2962

Clum: Why do you Apaches use that word "maybe" so much?

Taglito: It is because we are never sure of anything ...maybe.

John P. Clum played by Audie Murphy and Taglito played by Tommy Rall: Jesse Hibbs' *Walk the Proud Land* (Universal, 1956).

2963

Clum: What happened to her?

Sweeney: Oh, she's in mourning for her husband. They make a big thing out it, these Apache women. They chop off their hair, they dirty up their clothes with soil. It shows they're not interested in other men.

John P. Clum played by Audie Murphy and Tom Sweeney played by Charles Drake: Jesse Hibbs' *Walk the Proud Land* (Universal, 1956).

2964

Tianay: It is proper for me to choose because I am a widow. In the Apache way, it is wrong for a woman to belong to a man before she is married. But for a widow who has no man, it is all right.

Tianay played by Anne Bancroft: Jesse Hibbs' *Walk the Proud Land* (Universal, 1956).

2965

Eskiminzin: A man's heart must lead him. May yours be a wise one.

Eskiminzin played by Robert Warwick: Jesse Hibbs' *Walk the Proud Land* (Universal, 1956).

2966

Sweeney: But they still outnumber us three to one!

Clum: That's why we have to take them by surprise. Now if we split up and send only our police group to the trading post, the rest could go through the mountains and cover us from above.

Taglito: Now you are thinking like an Apache.

Cash Zachary (Audie Murphy) and Ben Zachary (Burt Lancaster) are brothers. Cash is a bigot and a racist. When the truth is learned that their "adopted sister" is actually an Indian by birth, Cash and their neighbors turn against the family in John Huston's *The Unforgiven* (United Artists, 1960).

Clum: No …Gideon.

Sweeney: Who?

Clum: Gideon. He conquered his enemies with the help of the Lord. It's in the Bible [Judges: 7,8].

Sweeney: The Bible?

Clum: Gideon was outnumbered by the Midianites. The Lord told him to divide his men into three companies and surround the camp. At a signal, they blew on their trumpets. The noise frightened the Midianites and made them think he had thousands of men. As the Bible puts it: they stood every men in his place, 'round about camp, and all the hosts ran, cried, and fled.

Sweeney: Yeah, but this Gideon fellow, he never fought any Apaches!

Tom Sweeney played by Charles Drake, John P. Clum played by Audie Murphy, and Taglito played by Tommy Rall: Jesse Hibbs' *Walk the Proud Land* (Universal, 1956).

2967

Narrator: The Sioux have a saying …what is life? It's the flash of the firefly in the night. It's the breath of the buffalo in the wintertime. It's the little shadow which runs across the tall grass and loses itself. Life is not long or short. It just is.

Narration by Brian Keith: Craig Clyde's *Walking Thunder* (Majestic Entertainment/Sunset Hill Partners, 1997).

2968

Walking Thunder, hear me! The voice I send is weak …it's my heart that speaks. Give them the strength to walk the soft earth, that they may face the wind and walk the good road until the day of quiet. Hear me, because the time has accomplished as you have shown.

A prayer of Dark Wind played by Chief Ted Thin Elk and narrated by Brian Keith: Craig Clyde's *Walking Thunder* (Majestic Entertainment/Sunset Hill Partners, 1997).

2969

Murdock: He's leaving a few things to bless your lodge with: Salt from the deer lick so you'll have savor into your life; jerked elk meat so you won't know hunger; and a dream catcher to hang above your door.

Jacob: What's a dream catcher?

Murdock: The Sioux believe that dreams fill the lodge and then come true. A dream catcher catches the bad dreams while you sleep …so only good dreams come true.

Abner Murdock played by James Read and Jacob McKay played by David Tom: Craig Clyde's *Walking Thunder* (Majestic Entertainment/Sunset Hill Partners, 1997).

2970

Pino: A house is good because of how you live in it …not how it is made.

Pino played by Dennis Weaver: George Sherman's *War Arrow* (Universal, 1954).

In pursuit of a peace treaty, Commissioner Kirby (Richard Cutting) manages to get himself killed and scalped by Taslik (Keith Larsen) before the opening credits can be shown in Lesley Selander's *War Paint* (United Artists, 1953).

2971

Corwin: The talk is that you'll never train the Seminoles to fight.

Major: The only thing that talk ever trained, Mrs. Corwin, is the parrot.

Mrs. Elaine Corwin played by Maureen O'Hara and Major Howell Brady played by Jeff Chandler: George Sherman's *War Arrow* (Universal, 1954).

2972

Mangas: Hear me, warriors of the Apaches! I've tried hard to keep the peace with the Americanos, but this is no longer possible. Today they have broken the peace treaty. I take the knife …I take the arrow …I take the lance …I shall not lay these weapons down until the Americanos have been driven from the land of the Apache!

Mangas Coloradas played by Lex Barker: Reginald LeBorg's *War Drums* (United Artists, 1957).

2973

Mangas: The peace words of your people are written on the wind. They are not to be trusted. I close my ears to them!

Mangas Coloradas played by Lex Barker: Reginald LeBorg's *War Drums* (United Artists, 1957).

2974

Fargo: But right now, Washington has ordered me to kill all Apache warriors and bring the women and children to Fort Stanton …unless the Apaches throw down their weapons and move onto government reservations.

Mangus: Our reservation and Apache warrior will be as an eagle with broken wings.

Fargo: But he would be given food, blankets, sheep to raise, corn to grow. He will live in peace.

Mangus: It is not for Washington to tell the Apache where they may live. Here is our home, the spirit land of our fathers. We will fight or die to keep it!

Luke Fargo played by Ben Johnson and Mangas Coloradas played by Lex Barker: Reginald LeBorg's *War Drums* (United Artists, 1957).

2975

Judge: A fine friend he is! He eats your food and rides off without a word!

Fargo: An Apache never says goodbye. He just goes away.

Judge Bolton played by Richard Cutting and Luke Fargo played by Ben Johnson: Reginald LeBorg's *War Drums* (United Artists, 1957).

2976

Arizona: Hey, Luke! Take a look at them smoke signals. And there's another one over there! They don't look like no regular Apache palaver.

Luke: It ain't! It's war talk! Some blasted lunatic must have tossed bear grease in the fire.

Arizona played by James Parnell and Luke Fargo played by Ben Johnson: Reginald LeBorg's *War Drums* (United Artists, 1957).

2977

Fargo: Those smoke signals are Apache telegraphs. Right now they're ordering all their tribes to go on the warpath. And in a little while, it will be a blood bath.

Luke Fargo played by Ben Johnson: Reginald LeBorg's *War Drums* (United Artists, 1957).

2978

Gardner: Arrange a powwow with Big Tree for tomorrow.

Desprit: Just a plain introduction?

Gardner: Oh, just how plain?

Desprit: Oh, a howdy …a couple ok's.

Gardner: How much [money] to tell him what a great guy I am?

Desprit: That'll cost you money. If I'm going to stretch the truth, I got to get paid for it. You know, I got a very delicate conscience.

Jim "Hunk" Gardner played by Albert Dekker and Desprit Dan played by George "Gabby" Hayes: Albert S. Rogell's *War of the Wildcats* (Republic, 1943).

2979

Taslik: My father believes in the honor of the white man. But I know when you do not need him, you will break the treaty. And when we cry for food, you will tell us to eat grass.

Taslik played by Keith Larsen: Lesley Selander's *War Paint* (United Artists, 1953).

2980

Solider: Why do you paint up for war now? There's no fighting.

Indian: Do you not wear war clothes?

The soldier, Clancy, played by Douglas Kennedy and the Indian, Taslik, played by Keith Larsen: Lesley Selander's *War Paint* (United Artists, 1953).

2981

Vickers: Well, make your circle. Your fight has come to you.

John Vickers played by Edmond O'Brien: Byron Haskin's *Warpath* (Paramount, 1951).

2982

Mekoki: You must purify your mind for the hunt …or the animals will refuse to die for you.

Rod: What do you mean?

Mekoki: They will not offer themselves …they will hide from your gun.

Rod: How can I purify my mind?

Mekoki: Look around you. The rivers speak …the trees speak. Listen to their advice.

Mekoki played by Jimmy Herman and Rod Elliot played by Lukas Haas: Rene Manzor's *Warrior Spirit* (Cinevideo Plus, 1994).

2983

Mekoki: Hunting is not a sport. It is a prayer.

Mekoki played by Jimmy Herman: Rene Manzor's *Warrior Spirit* (Cinevideo Plus, 1994).

2984

Summers: [The Chief] doesn't like what you're giving him.

Tadlock: What does he want?

Summers: Whiskey.

Tadlock: Whiskey?

Lije: Get 'em liquored up …and maybe we could sneak off.

Summers: You got a choice. You could give it to 'em or they'll take it. I agree that the first one might be a little dangerous. But the second one could prove fatal.

Dick Summers played by Robert Mitchum, Senator William J. Tadlock played by Kirk Douglas, and Lije Evans played by Richard Widmark: Andrew V. McLaglen's *The Way West* (United Artists, 1967).

2985

Lije: I guess we'll have to fight, Dick.

Dick: Well, all right, but some of us are gonna have to settle for a piece of ground a little short of Oregon.

Lije Evans played by Richard Widmark and Dick Summers played by Robert Mitchum: Andrew V. McLaglen's *The Way West* (United Artists, 1967).

2986

Hank: You know that tap you got in the shoulder? That means your scalp belongs to him now anytime he wants to claim it.

Hank Breckenridge played by Jeff York: William Beaudine's *Westward Ho the Wagons* (Buena Vista, 1956).

2987

Wyatt: The chief says their arrows are not strong against our bullets. I think we are all right for awhile. He says there will be another time. There will be!

Buck Wyatt played by Robert Taylor: William Wellman's *Westward the Women* (MGM, 1952).

2988

Ito: Big boss, what's that?

Wyatt: Indian burial ground. They bury them high [in trees]. It gives them a start up to the Happy Hunting Grounds.

Ito played by Henry Nakamura and Buck Wyatt played by Robert Taylor: William Wellman's *Westward the Women* (MGM, 1952).

2989

Lt.: What does it mean?

Cross: Apache.

Boone: Is that all?

It's Happening At Paramount—"Will Penny"

—MONTANA, SEPT. 1967 There was "High Noon." Then there was "Shane." Now it's "Will Penny," starring Charlton Heston, that will have people talking about the great American Western. His realistic portrayal of a rugged cowboy who suddenly begins to question his life is sure to be one of Heston's most memorable performances. Add a unique villain played by English star Donald Pleasence, and you have a motion picture of true award-caliber. The film is scheduled for release early next year.

CREDITS
PARAMOUNT PICTURES PRESENTS CHARLTON HESTON, JOAN HACKETT AND DONALD PLEASENCE IN "WILL PENNY." INTRODUCING LEE MAJORS. PRODUCED BY FRED ENGEL AND WALTER SELTZER. WRITTEN AND DIRECTED BY TOM GRIES. AN ENGEL-GRIES-SELTZER PRODUCTION. TECHNICOLOR.

Advertisement for *Will Penny* (Paramount, 1968). He's a loner, he's a drifter, he's a cowboy. He can't read and he takes a bath maybe eight or nine times a year. He's aging and his future doesn't look much different. He's Will Penny (Charlton Heston) and he's about to meet Catherine Allen (Joan Hackett) in Tom Gries's superb western.

Cross: That's enough! Let's get out of here!

The Lieutenant played by Michael Wren, Cross played by Willie Nelson, and Boone played by Jack Elam: Burt Kennedy's *Where the Hell's That Gold?!!!* (a.k.a. *Dynamite & Gold*; TVW, 1988).

2990

Settler: That's a bald eagle. The Apaches, I hear, believe it to be a witness of time.

They think it's eternal …writing men's destiny in the sky.

The Settler was uncredited: Vincent Dawn/Bruno Mattei's *White Apache* (Imperial Entertainment, 1984).

2991

Chief: A wolf becomes a dog only when it is forced to live outside the forest.

The Chief was uncredited: Vincent Dawn/Bruno

Mattei's *White Apache* (Imperial Entertainment, 1984).

2992

Crazy Bull: The pain of death is evil. It brings bad luck. And what's more, it makes you unhappy.

Crazy Bull was uncredited: Vincent Dawn/Bruno Mattei's *White Apache* (Imperial Entertainment, 1984).

2993

Worm: Long hair, why are you whites in my country? I did not ask the whites to come here. The Great Spirits gave us these hills as a home. You say, why do we not become civilized? We do not want your civilization.

Hickok: You've spoken red truth.

Worm: Tell me then white truth, long hair.

Hickok: In the first place, the Great Spirit did not give you these hills. You took this land by force. You took it from the Cheyenne, the Shoshoni, and the Arapaho. You took it with lance and tomahawk. And now the white man makes war on you. What's the difference?

Worm: The whites have no honor.

Crazy Horse/Worm played by Will Sampson and Wild Bill Hickok played by Charles Bronson: J. Lee Thompson's *The White Buffalo* (United Artists, 1977).

2994

Worm: But long hair, though you and I are brothers, we must never meet again. Hear me, my friend. These are my words: we must never cross paths in the tomorrow. For if we do, I will see only a white enemy …and you will see only an Indian.

Crazy Horse/Worm played by Will Sampson: J. Lee Thompson's *The White Buffalo* (United Artists, 1977).

2995

Charlie: You really got no guts for injuns, do you?

Hickok: Like Phil Sheridan said, I ain't never seen a good Indian that wasn't dead.

Charlie Zane played by Jack Warden and Wild Bill Hickok/James Otis played by Charles Bronson: J. Lee Thompson's *The White Buffalo* (United Artists, 1977).

2996

Old Worm: Crazy Horse, my son, it is not fitting that the war chief of the Oglalas weep like a young woman. Therefore, I take away your true name. You shall be called Worm.

Old Worm played by Chief Tug Smith and Crazy Horse/Worm played by Will Sampson: J. Lee Thompson's *The White Buffalo* (United Artists, 1977).

2997

Sheriff: For someone who's trying to live like a white man, you're sure turning out to be one hell of a Comanche!

Sheriff Logan played by Joseph Cotten: Gilbert Lee Kay's *White Comanche* (International Producers Corp., 1967).

2998

Notah: Does Kah-To have something to say?
Kah-To: I will make a place to put him.
Notah: No time. The dead will find their own place.
Kah-To: If he is not put to the fire, his spirit will go forever in darkness.

Notah played by William Shatner and Kah-To played by Luis Rivera: Gilbert Lee Kay's *White Comanche* (International Producers Corp., 1967).

2999

Moses: For three days you will fast and drink only this. To hunt is a sacred act. You must purify your body to be worthy of the kill. Your mind must be clear of all else …no distractions.

Moses Joseph played by Al Harrington: Ken Olin's *White Fang II: Myth of the White Wolf* (Buena Vista, 1994).

3000

Tanner: I was hoping to see someone practicing the signing of a peace treaty.
Little Dog: Peace treaty? We are Cheyenne. The treaty pen does not fit our hand as well as the arrow.

Josh Tanner played by Robert Wagner and Little Dog played by Jeffrey Hunter: Robert Webb's *White Feather* (20th Century–Fox, 1955).

3001

Tanner: A Cheyenne is a warrior. He's too proud to attack us with our backs turned.

Josh Tanner played by Robert Wagner: Robert Webb's *White Feather* (20th Century–Fox, 1955).

3002

Little Dog: I will go into the hills by myself. The spirits will tell me what to do. They will not lie to me.

Little Dog played by Jeffrey Hunter: Robert Webb's *White Feather* (20th Century–Fox, 1955).

3003

Chief: A white feather. It is a challenge. My son and American Horse are not bound by your paper. They have chosen to fight and they wait for you in the hills.
Colonel: Just the two of them?

Chief: This is their challenge. They expect you to honor it.
Colonel: You mean, American Horse and Little Dog want to meet the troops in battle? Two men?
Chief: Yes, this is true. They are waiting.

Chief Broken Hand played by Eduard Franz, Colonel Lindsay played by John Lund, American Horse played by Hugh O'Brian, and Little Dog played by Jeffrey Hunter: Robert Webb's *White Feather* (20th Century–Fox, 1955).

3004

Joe: Don't kill him, Bill!
Wild Bill: The man knows what he wants.
Joe: It's bad luck to kill an injun in a religious frame of mind!

California Joe played by James Gammon and Wild Bill Hickok played by Jeff Bridges: Walter Hill's *Wild Bill* (MGM/United Artists, 1995).

3005

Mit-O-Ne: To seek a truce, use words. But when a battle approaches, no words are needed.

Mit-O-Ne played by Cynthis Hull: Don Taylor's *Wild Women* (TVW, 1970).

3006

Boy: How come Indians are all red and sunburned like that?
Will: That ain't sunburn. They come that way. Injuns don't get sunburned much.
Boy: But how come?
Will: Well, they're smart. You've seen them sunflowers that grows in the spring.
Boy: Yeah.
Will: Well, injuns take the seeds and grind them up in a kind of butter-like. And then they spread it all over their selves …to keep the sun out.
Boy: Ah, no!
Will: Yeah, that's the straight up truth! Injuns make do with what nature gives.
Boy: How do you know all these things?
Will: Even a blind hog will root up an acorn now and then.

The Boy, Horace Greeley Allen, played by Jon Francis and Will Penny played by Charlton Heston: Tom Gries' *Will Penny* (Paramount, 1968).

3007

Young Bull: All white men are thieves. In peace, they steal our land. In war, they kill our women. And you are a white man!

Young Bull played by Rock Hudson: Anthony Mann's *Winchester '73* (Universal, 1950).

3008

Joe: Indian smoke always means the same …trouble.

Joe Lamont played by John McIntire: Anthony Mann's *Winchester '73* (Universal, 1950).

3009

Lin: Say, ah, about these Indians. It seems like they hardly ever attack at night.
Sergeant: Why?
Lin: Well, they figure if they are killed in the dark, the Great Spirit can't find their souls and whip 'em up to heaven …or something like that.

Lin McAdam played by James Stewart and Sergeant Wilkes played by Jay C. Flippen: Anthony Mann's *Winchester '73* (Universal, 1950).

3010

Lin: Yeah, I hear 'em.
Johnny: I told you night riding wasn't smart.
Lin: I guess you did.
Johnny: Now, we're smack in the middle of 'em.
Lin: I guess you're right again.
Johnny: Being right ain't gonna do us any good. What will we do now?
Lin: Well, keep riding.
Johnny: With injuns all around us?
Lin: Maybe you'd feel better if we stopped?
Johnny: Ah …no.
Lin: Well, then maybe we better just keep on riding.

Lin McAdam played by James Stewart and Johnny "High Spade" Williams played by Millard Mitchell: Anthony Mann's *Winchester '73* (Universal, 1950).

3011

Johnny: It was such pretty hair. I've had it ever since I was a kid. A little thin on top …but I sure would like to keep it.

Johnny "High Spade" Williams played by Millard Mitchell: Anthony Mann's *Winchester '73* (Universal, 1950).

3012

Windwalker: Do not fear death. As spring begins with the winter …so death begins with birth. It is only a step …in the great circle of life.

Windwalker played by Trevor Howard: Keith Merrill's *Windwalker* (Windwalker/Pacific International, 1980).

3013

Carter: They won't dare attack me. War Eagle is my friend.
Raven: War Eagle may be your friend but to those cutthroat bucks of his, you're just another white man with hair worth liftin'!

King Carter played by Harry Woods and Raven played by Trevor Bardette: Ford Beebe's and Ray

Taylor's *Winners of the West* (Universal serial, Chapter 2: "The Wreck At Red River Gorge," 1940).

3014

Fireknife: Wait, Adam. My father gave me this [bow]. He said when I wish a strong friendship to find the man that can string the bow. I give it to you, Adam.

Fireknife played by Lee Van Cleef and Adam played by Rory Calhoun: Lesley Selander's *The Yellow Tomahawk* (United Artists, 1954).

3015

Katherine: You say yourself that the Indians are in the hills. They'll kill us one by one. Adam, you can't fight an enemy you can't see.

Adam: You can't run away from one either.

Katherine played by Peggie Castle and Adam played by Rory Calhoun: Lesley Selander's *The Yellow Tomahawk* (United Artists, 1954).

3016

Adam: You got your massacre! Go on out and look at it! Touch it! Smell it!

Adam played by Rory Calhoun: Lesley Selander's *The Yellow Tomahawk* (United Artists, 1954).

3017

Adam: Will another blood bath make your dreams easy?

Katherine: You're not defending them!

Adam: No, but if massacre breeds massacre, where's the end of it?

Adam played by Rory Calhoun and Katherine played by Peggie Castle: Lesley Selander's *The Yellow Tomahawk* (United Artists, 1954).

3018

Kelly: That's the trouble with Indians. You never know what they'll do next. They don't either.

Kelly played by Clint Walker: Gordon Douglas' *Yellowstone Kelly* (Warner Bros., 1959).

3019

Kelly: When you were a boy, did you ever go out in the woods and catch something wild …a rabbit or bird …take it home with you to keep?

Harper: Yes, sir.

Kelly: Well, what happened?

Harper: Well …

Kelly: I'll tell you what happened. It either got sick, ran away, or died. It's the same way with an Indian. You go trying to tame them, make them live white …it just won't work.

Kelly played by Clint Walker and Anse Harper played by Edward Byrnes: Gordon Douglas' *Yellowstone Kelly* (Warner Bros., 1959).

3020

Harper: I wish he would take that grin off his face.

Kelly: He's proud …counting coup on us.

Harper: Coup?

Kelly: That stick he clubbed us with? A coup stick. Horseback Indians figure anybody can stand safe off and kill a man. But if you can get in close enough to touch him and then ride away alive, that's something to tell your squaw about.

Anse Harper played by Edward Byrnes and Kelly played by Clint Walker: Gordon Douglas' *Yellowstone Kelly* (Warner Bros., 1959).

3021

Kelly: Planning on crossing the river, are you?

Major: I told you I was going to drive the Sioux back to the Dakotas. That's what I intend to do.

Kelly: I knew a man once …he intended to kill a bear with a stick. I buried him.

[*and a little later*]

Kelly: I'll tell you once more, Major, on this side [of the river] you're in trouble; over there you're dead!

Kelly played by Clint Walker and Major Towns played by Rhodes Reason: Gordon Douglas' *Yellowstone Kelly* (Warner Bros., 1959).

3022

Kelly: I'd rather lose some sleep than my hair.

Kelly played by Clint Walker: Gordon Douglas' *Yellowstone Kelly* (Warner Bros., 1959).

3023

Jerry: I haven't seen any Indians.

Buffalo Bill: That's the kind to be careful of …the kind you can't see.

Jerry played by Gaylord Pendleton and Buffalo Bill played by Roy Rogers: Joseph Kane's *Young Buffalo Bill* (Republic, 1940).

3024

Gabby: You know, that reminds me of the time I captured fifty Indians all by myself …singlehanded.

Pancho: You did?

Gabby: Yeah.

Pancho: How did you do this?

Gabby: Simple enough. I surrounded them!

Gabby Whittaker played by George "Gabby" Hayes and Pancho played by Julian Rivero: Joseph Kane's *Young Buffalo Bill* (Republic, 1940)

3025

Chavez: We have come to a place where we are lost, no? When an Indian is lost, he must reach into the spirit world to find a way. On the spirit road, he'll be shown a sign. This is the way to the spirit road. We're lost right now, but I'll find us the way.

Chavez Y. Chavez played by Lou Diamond Phillips: Christopher Cain's *Young Guns* (20th Century–Fox, 1988).

3026

Charley: Hey Chavez, how come they ain't killin' us?

Steve: Because we're in the spirit world, asshole! They can't see us!

Charley Bowdre played by Casey Siemaszko, Dirty Steve Stephens played by Dermot Mulroney, and Chavez Y. Chavez played by Lou Diamond Phillips: Christopher Cain's *Young Guns* (20th Century–Fox, 1988).

Justice

See also Good Guys; Lawlessness; Lawmen; West

3027

Major: I would not have given you the honor of being executed by a firing squad.

The Major played by Antonio Gradoli: Frank Kramer's Adios, *Sabata* (United Artists, 1971).

3028

Al: There's an old saying about juries: the longer they're out, the better your chances.

Al Jennings played by Dan Duryea: Ray Nazarro's *Al Jennings of Oklahoma* (Columbia, 1951).

3029

Melody: But you don't want to forget: when a posse makes a mistake, it's a mighty hard thing to unmake.

Melody Jones played by Gary Cooper: Stuart Heisler's *Along Came Jones* (RKO, 1945).

Six regulators hired for their guns to "take care of business": Dick Brewer (Charlie Sheen), Dirty Steve Stephens (Dermot Mulroney), Josiah "Doc" Scurlock (Kiefer Sutherland), William H. Bonney (Emilio Estevez), Charley Bowdre (Casey Siemaszko), and Chavez Y. Chavez (Lou Diamond Phillips) in *Young Guns* (20th Century–Fox, 1988).

3030

Ann: Justice! That's what you promised, ain't it? I told you what he'd get. Cattlemen's justice! A trial in the dead of night so you could hang him quicker. Are you satisfied now?

Judge: Young woman, I can understand your anxiety for your father. But justice does not vary with the time of day. Your father can receive as fair a trial in darkness as in daylight.

Ann Keith played by Virginia Mayo and the Judge played by Charles Meredith: Raoul Walsh's *Along the Great Divide* (Warner Bros., 1951).

3031

Judge: This court is now in session. The Honorable Homer McCoy presiding. Theodore Ogilvie. Amos Tucker. You're charged with attempted bank robbery. How do you plead? Guilty or not guilty?

Theodore: Not guilty?

Judge: Guilty!

Amos: That was the wrong one.

Judge: This court sentences you to be hung by the neck until dead. And I'm fining you an extra ten bucks for perjury. Let 'em out [of custody], Leonard. Be down at the oak tree near Boot Hill at twelve o'clock sharp for your hanging.

Justice of the Peace Homer McCoy played by Harry Morgan. Theodore Ogilvie played by Don Knotts, Amos Tucker played by Tim Conway, and

Leonard Sharpe played by John McGiver: Norman Tokar's *The Apple Dumpling Gang* (Buena Vista, 1975).

3032

Judge: Hey, Joe Briggs. I've got some time on my hands, Joe, and there's a charge against you. I might as well hold court out here where it don't smell so bad. Are you ready to stand trial?

Joe: Well, I don't have much time. Can you hurry it up?

Judge: Sure enough. Just step in a little more where it's shady. Now, the prisoner at the bar, the charge against you is that you up and blowed the head plumb off of Gus Modesko. In consequence of which said shooting said Gus is deader than blazes. Are you guilty or not guilty?

Joe: Well, Judge, I don't reckon I could say not guilty when everybody seen me do it.

Judge: Now what in tunket made you act like that, Joe?

Joe: Drinking. Just drinking.

Judge: Well, the verdict of this here tribunal is that Joe Briggs is fined $5.00 for disturbing the peace. The court is hereby adjourned to Lazarus Ward's Bar where said fine will duly be disposed of.

Judge Bogardus played by Edgar Buchanan and Joe Briggs played by Earl Crawford: Wesley Ruggles' *Arizona* (Columbia, 1940).

3033

B.D.: Well, as you said, it was them or us.

John: Well, it should have been us. They was the ones in the right!

B.D. played by James Brolin and John T. Coleman played by John Clark Gable: Clyde Ware's *Bad Jim* (RCA/Columbia Home Video, 1990).

3034

Reverend: Vengeance is mine sayeth the Lord.

Cable: Well, that's fair enough with me …just as long as he don't take too long and I can watch.

The Reverend Joshua Sloan played by David Warner and Cable Hogue played by Jason Robards, Jr.: Sam Peckinpah's *The Ballad of Cable Hogue* (Warner Bros., 1970).

3035

Abernathy: Had he stayed, a posse would have come …not thirsting for justice …but thirsting for his blood.

Lawyer Abernathy played by Barry Corbin: Robert M. Young's *The Ballad of Gregorio Cortez* (Embassy Pictures, 1983).

3036

Ruth: They say you're going to hunt down Flack and Lopez.

Breck: That's what I aim to do.

Ruth: But you can't do this awful thing …take two lives.

Breck: Frontier justice.

Ruth Cameron played by Marguerite Churchill and Breck Coleman played by John Wayne: Raoul Walsh's *The Big Trail* (Fox, 1930).

3037

Bascom: What did they do, Coleman?

Breck: Killed my best friend. And I've been on their trail ever since.

Bascom: That's a serious charge. If you're sure, we'll call a settler's meeting in the morning to try 'em.

Breck: You can call a settlers' meeting to bury 'em!

Bascom: What do you mean?

Breck: That I kill my own rats!

Pa Bascom played by Frederick Burton and Breck Coleman played by John Wayne: Raoul Walsh's *The Big Trail* (Fox, 1930).

3038

Posse Member: This is your last chance to say anything.

Lance: You're hanging two innocent men!

Posse Member: Innocent? You were caught leaving town with the mayor's wife, riding stolen horses, and carrying the money from two bank holdups!

Boles: You call that evidence?

Lance Hardeen played by Jeffrey Lynn and Charles E. Boles, alias Black Bart, played by Dan Duryea: George Sherman's *Black Bart* (Universal, 1948).

3039

Jared: I want Dee Havalik freed by that coroner's jury …fair and square.

Grat: Well, how fair …and how square?

Jared: Well, I don't mean a packed jury or a bought jury. What I mean is …a jury of towners.

Grat: Not no cattlemen on it, nor ranchers?

Jared: That's the idea. The local cowmen have become prejudiced against the Four T and should be kept off the jury in the best interest of justice.

Grat: You mean you're going to give them a free rein?

Jared: The Four T brand represents progress …and power. Ordinary people are afraid of power, and these townspeople are just ordinary. I want them scared. Not shot, no guns …but scared. I suggest you give the town an example of Four T power just in case their idea of justice is misguided.

Grat: Sure boss! The biggest outfit is entitled to the biggest justice.

Grat Barbey played by Wes Hudman and Jared Tetlow played by Victor Jory: Earl Bellamy's *Blackjack Ketchum, Desperado* (Columbia, 1956).

3040

Waldo: All right! Quiet, quiet, everybody! Your trial is about to start. Now Jim here is going to pass among you with a tray and the Judge wants me to have you put all your glasses in that tray …empty! The Judge don't want no more liquored-up opinion like he had in that last trial.

Waldo Peek played by Robert Anderson: Budd Boetticher's *Buchanan Rides Alone* (Columbia, 1958).

3041

Ed: It's a question of law and order, Annie. Uncle Will keeps the law …and Sitting Bull is out of order.

Ed played by Harvey Keitel, Annie Oakley played by Geraldine Chaplin, Buffalo Bill (Uncle Will) played by Paul Newman, and Sitting Bull played by Frank Kaquitts: Robert Altman's *Buffalo Bill and the Indians, or Sitting Bull's History Lesson* (United Artists, 1976).

3042

Cassidy: It's the greatest country in the world. Guilty as hell! Free as a bird!

Mike Cassidy played by Michael C. Gwynne: Richard Lester's *Butch and Sundance: The Early Days* (20th Century–Fox, 1979).

3043

Kincaid: We'll give him a fair trial, won't we boys?

Dobbie: Sure, we'll hang him legal …after we're through with him!

Silent Jeff Kincaid played by Randolph Scott and Dobbie was uncredited: Andre De Toth's *Carson City* (Warner Bros., 1952).

3044

Sheriff: Well, how do you expect one to keep law and order in this town if everytime I bring 'em in, you keep turning 'em loose?

Judge: You keep the order and I'll look after the law!

Sheriff Ben Anderson played by Carl Raff and Judge George Perkins played by Louis Prendes: Sidney W. Pink's *The Christmas Kid* (Producers Releasing Organization, 1966).

3045

Don: You know, in Mexico they have a way of sparing prisoners of all that [*waiting to be hung*]. When a fella is gonna be executed, they give him a chance to run for it …and shoot him when he's trying to escape. Ley de Fuga they call it, I think.

Jerry: I know …the law of flight.

Don Burke played by Milburn Stone and Jerry Burke played by Roy Rogers: Joseph Kane's *Colorado* (Republic, 1940).

3046

Judge: Major here has told me what your troubles are. I've been thinking it over and in light of my forty years experience in legal jurisprudence, I have come to the positive conclusion that there ain't no way to do this legal and honest. But, being good sensible Texans, we'll do it illegal and dishonest! Now all the boys here in the room have agreed to sign a paper I have prepared. They all are going to commit perjury. That's legal language for just a plain dumb blasted lie.

Judge Bean played by Edgar Buchanan: Michael Curtiz's *The Comancheros* (20th Century–Fox, 1961)

3047

Judge Bean: Most say, except for them who are unfair minded, that I have the finest legal mind in the entire southwest. So you can have faith in your lawyer, son. How much money do you got?

Regret: I don't have any.

Judge Bean: Well, I'm beginning to doubt your chances against the law.

Judge Bean played by Edgar Buchanan and Paul Regret played by Stuart Whitman: Michael Curtiz's *The Comancheros* (20th Century–Fox, 1961)

3048

Kate: Chris, there is something or someone bigger than all of us that takes care of our injuries, and squares things for us.

Chris: I'll do my own squaring, Kate.

Kate: Vengeance is mine, I will repay. Remember?

Chris: I also remember, an eye for an eye.

Kate Hardison played by Marguerite Chapman and Chris Danning played by Randolph Scott: Ray Enright's *Coroner Creek* (Columbia, 1948).

3049

Teddy Bear: Mr. Ferguson has a statement to make, folks. Haven't you, buster?

Ferguson: Well, I did have, but I'm kind of forgetful.

Roy: Where are you taking him [Ferguson]?

Teddy Bear: To the memory room.

Ferguson: Wait a minute! It's coming back to me! I'm beginning to remember!

Teddy Bear played by Guinn "Big Boy" Williams, Ferguson played by Hal Taliaferro/Wally Wales, and Roy played by Roy Rogers: Joseph Kane's *Cowboy and the Señorita* (Republic, 1944).

3050

Judge: What happened out there?

Marshal: The law got itself done.

Judge John J. McLean played by Carl Benton Reid and Marshal Allan Burnett played by Jock Mahoney: Harmon Jones' *A Day of Fury* (Universal, 1956).

3051

Jagade: I don't trust your ways, Judge. You sniff a gun and decide it's been fired …then string a man up. Then pat yourself on the back for getting rid of another gunslinger.

Jagade played by Dale Robertson and Judge John

J. McLean played by Carl Benton Reid: Harmon Jones' *A Day of Fury* (Universal, 1956).

3052

Charlie: What's the sentence going to be?

Judge: The court convenes at eleven at the church. Get there early if you want a seat.

Howard: I want to know now.

Judge: Well, what you want and what you get are not one and the same.

Charlie Hayes played by Robert Middleton, Judge Jim Scott played by Fred MacMurray, and Howard Hayes played by Skip Homeier: Harry Keller's *Day of the Bad Man* (Universal, 1958).

3053

Major: In the jar there are white beans and black beans. You will each draw a bean. The man who draws white beans will live; the man who draws black beans will die. We have a priest as you can see …and we have a firing squad. So, gentleman, who will be the first to draw a bean?

The Major was uncredited: Yves Simoneau's *Dead Man's Walk* (Cabin Fever Entertainment, 1996).

3054

Ballard: There'll be a trial when the circuit judge comes to town. Do you know him? We go hunting quail together when he's here. He's a damn fine shot and a very fair man …completely impartial. He'll hear the case, weigh the evidence …and Duell McCall will hang!

Gentleman Johnny Ballard played by David Warner: Virgil W. Vogel's *Desperado* (TVW, 1987).

3055

Judge: …Four, five, six, seven, eight, nine, ten, eleven, twelve. Well, gents, there's twelve of you, and it takes twelve to make a jury. Now we got two men here to hang. But we are going to do it by the law. Hank, you be foreman.

Hank: Huh? Oh, all right judge.

Judge: Lift your right hand. Do you solemnly swear to put the law on them bank robbers, so help ya?

Hank: I do.

Judge: That's the stuff, Hank! Now wait a minute, we got to have a little evidence …but very little!

Judge Cameron played Raymond Walburn and Hank played by Francis Ford: Charles Vidor's *The Desperadoes* (Columbia, 1943).

3056

Tom: Now the next time you fellas start any of this here promiscuous shooting around the streets, you're going to land in jail! You understand?

Tom Destry, Jr., played by James Stewart: George Marshall's *Destry Rides Again* (Universal, 1939).

3057

Tom: Reminds me of a kid I used to know. He done in both his pa and ma with a crowbar.

Wash: No!

Tom: Yes, he did. Now the judge said to him, he said: "Do you got anything to say for yourself?" And the kid said, "Well, I just hope that your honor has some regard for the feelings of a poor orphan."

Tom Destry, Jr., played by James Stewart and Sheriff Washington Dimsdale played by Charles Winninger: George Marshall's *Destry Rides Again* (Universal, 1939).

3058

Slade: According to the provisions of the statutes of our territorial commonwealth, you gentlemen of the jury have been selected as representative citizens of our fair community. We want to see that the public's faith is justified. So when you boys retire to consider a verdict, stay out for awhile. Mr. Kent will see that you are plentifully provided with liquid refreshments. And after you have deliberated sufficiently, weighed all the evidence fair and square, and brought in a verdict of not guilty, you will be amply rewarded. You understand?

Judge Hiram Slade played by Samuel Hinds: George Marshall's *Destry Rides Again* (Universal, 1939).

3059

Sheriff: I think it was them easterners on that jury. They don't care what the custom was before. They just want the gunfight to stop now.

Billy: So they turned a page of their calendar over on me, huh?

Sheriff: Well, it's progress I guess you'd call it.

The Sheriff played by Morris Ankrum and Billy Reynolds played by Dale Robertson: Alfred Werker's *Devil's Canyon* (RKO, 1953).

3060

Lance: I envy you, ma'am, you being a lawyer.

Orrie: Well, I …

Lance: You got a faith, something to go by …like a religion. With you it's the law.

Orrie: My father wanted me to study law. It means a great deal to me.

Lance: Yes, it must. I've always wanted something like that. Something to tell me what's right or wrong.

Orrie: I'm glad you feel the way you do.

Lance: Because then you don't have to bother about your conscience. It's written out for you to follow …no matter what it does to people. It's the law. And changing the law is something you don't have to worry about.

Lance Poole played by Robert Taylor and Orrie Masters played by Paula Raymond: Anthony Mann's *Devil's Doorway* (MGM, 1950).

3061

Hatton: About ten days [in jail] for this customer, Tex. Five to cool off and five to think it over.

Wade Hatton played by Errol Flynn and Tex Baird played by Guinn "Big Boy" Williams: Michael Curtiz's *Dodge City* (Warner Bros., 1939).

3062

Clayton: Now if the judge is drunk, we haven't got a chance. He's got to be sober for that trial!

Clayton Fletcher played by John Payne: Lewis Foster's *El Paso* (Paramount, 1949).

3063

[*Poster placed on tree*]

NOTICE
In order to save time
the trial of John Elkins
will he held under this tree
next Tuesday morning. The public
is welcome to witness
this trial [*crossed out with the words* "this hanging"]

From *El Paso*, directed by Lewis Foster (Paramount, 1949).

3064

Tex: Be sure that somebody don't talk you into paroling that gang. Especially that Chinaman! He made a lot of threats against me if I had only understood 'em.

Tex Murdock played by Charles "Chic" Sale: Charles Barton's *The Fighting Westerner* (a.k.a. *Rocky Mountain Mystery*; Paramount, 1935).

3065

Britt: Money sure polluted you. You used to believe in a fair draw.

Ned Britt played by Randolph Scott: Edwin Marin's *Fort Worth* (Warner Bros., 1951).

3066

Judge: Is there something you want me to do, Mr. Leverett?

Leverett: Yes, come in here. Shut the door. A fine figure of judicial authority! Now listen to me and get this straight! Do you still remember how to run a court?

Judge: Why, yes, I guess so. Why?

Leverett: Be at Miner's Hall tomorrow morning at ten o'clock …shaved and sober. You're going to preside at a murder trial.

Judge: Me?

Leverett: Yes, you! I'll see you before the trial and tell you just what to say and when. Now get him out of here and clean him up!

The drunken Judge played by George Cleveland and Edward Leverett played by Albert Dekker: Bruce Humberstone's *Fury at Furnace Creek* (20th Century–Fox, 1948).

Stranger/lawyer Clayton Fletcher (John Payne) enters a saloon where drunken Judge Jeffers (Henry Hull) is conducting court and quickly finds himself in contempt of court. Defending the court are corrupt townsmen Burt Donner (Sterling Hayden) and Sheriff LaFarge (Dick Foran) in *El Paso* (Paramount. 1949).

3067

Deputy: You got extradition papers on you?

Troop: No, I extradited him with a gun.

The Deputy was uncredited and Amos Troop played by DeForest Kelley: Frank McDonald's *Gunfight at Comanche Creek* (Allied Artists, 1964).

3068

[*Dying Ringo giving advice to his killer*]

Marshal: We got him, Son. He ain't getting away with it.

Ringo: No, I drew first. I was ahead of him.

Marshal: I seen it, Jimmy. You don't have to say anything like that. I seen who drew first.

Ringo: You heard what I said, Mark! I drew first! Now don't argue with me! I know what I'm doing.

Hunt: You don't have to do me no favors, Pappy.

Deputy: Keep your mouth shut!

Ringo: If I was doing you a favor, I'd let 'em hang you right now and get it over with. But I don't want you to get off that light. I want you to go on …being a big tough gunnie. I want you to see what it means to have to live like a big tough gunnie. So don't thank me yet, partner. You'll see what I mean. Just wait!

Marshal Mark Strett played by Millard Mitchell, Jimmy Ringo played by Gregory Peck, Hunt Bromley played by Skip Homeier, and Deputy Charlie played by Anthony Ross: Henry King's *The Gunfighter* (20th Century–Fox, 1950).

3069

Cole: I haven't heard anything about a fair trial.

Sheriff: He'll get a trial. We do believe in justice.

Cole: Justice? Around here justice is blind, deaf, and dumb!

Cole Everett played by Art Hindle and Sheriff Burrows played by Wendell Smith: Clay Borris' *The Gunfighters* (TVW, 1989).

3070

Matt: I never shot no one before, Cole. It was self-defense. He came at me with his gun in his hand.

Cole: In this town that doesn't count. Kate's father is the sheriff. You're an Everett. He's going to do everything he can to stick your neck in a noose.

Dutch: You're going to have to get out of here.

Matt: What do you mean?

Cole: He means out of Kansas.

Matt: That's the same as saying I'm guilty. I ain't never run from nothin' in my life.

Cole: You know the lay of the land as well as we do. Deke Turner runs everything, including the law. That makes you guilty as sin.

Matt Everett played by Tony Addabbo, Cole Everett played by Art Hindle, and Dutch played by Reiner Schoene: Clay Borris' *The Gunfighters* (TVW, 1989).

3071

Clee: Mr. Hackett, I don't want your son's life in exchange for my brother's. But I do want him to admit that what he did was wrong …and that he be ashamed …and that a man's life, even if he is part stinkin' Sioux, as I am, is worth more than a mare and one hundred dollars.

Clee Chouard played by Kathryn Grant: Phil Karlson's *Gunman's Walk* (Columbia, 1958).

3072

Lee: Now there's another way to look at it: that this shooting was just a little misunderstanding. And for the harm done, well, let's just say, ah: $5, that string of horses, and the same story that you told in court. Now are you strong enough to nob your head …or are you fool enough to shake it?

Lee Hackett played by Van Heflin: Phil Karlson's *Gunman's Walk* (Columbia, 1958).

3073

Hadley: If you're not going to uphold the law, we will.

Sheriff: No matter who gets hurt?

Hadley: No matter.

Sheriff: Mr. Hadley, I don't condone law breaking of any kind. But there are laws and laws …some big and some small. Occasionally, it's better to break a small law to keep a big one.

Jim Hadley played by Alan Ladd and Sheriff Taylor played by Regis Toomey: Robert D. Webb's *Guns of the Timberland* (Warner Bros., 1960).

3074

Cooper: There'll be no hanging here.

Cowboy: These men killed my father and brother. They're gonna get what's coming to 'em.

Cooper: They're gonna get what the law says is coming to 'em.

Jed Cooper played by Clint Eastwood and the Cowboy was uncredited: Ted Post's *Hang 'Em High* (United Artists, 1968).

3075

Judge: You think I judged him too harshly? Used him like a piece of kindling for my fire of justice?

Judge Adam Fenton played by Pat Hingle: Ted Post's *Hang 'Em High* (United Artists, 1968).

3076

Cooper: You're lynching those boys. Why?

Judge: Why? Because of you, Cooper. Because of that beautiful, that magnificent journey you took to bring three killers to justice. Because if the law didn't hang them, the next posse that goes out will

say: hang 'em and hang 'em high, there's no justice in Fort Grant. And if there's no justice in Fort Grant, Cooper, there will be no statehood for this territory.

Cooper: Well, I don't care how you slice it. Whether there's nine men out in the plains with a dirty rope or a judge with his robe on in front of the American flag, those boys are going to be just as dead as if they'd been lynched.

Judge: That's right, Cooper, just as dead. But they wouldn't have been lynched. They would have been judged. And if you can't see the difference, you better take off that star, and right now!

Jed Cooper played by Clint Eastwood and Judge Adam Fenton played by Pat Hingle: Ted Post's *Hang 'Em High* (United Artists, 1968).

3077

Thomas: Vengeance is mine, saith the Lord.

Hannie: He said it, I didn't.

Thomas Luther Price played by Robert Culp and Hannie Caulder played by Raquel Welch: Burt Kennedy's *Hannie Caulder* (Paramount, 1971).

3078

Hopalong: That's what it says in the book: whatever measure you give out, that same measure shall be given out to you.

Hopalong Cassidy played by William Boyd: Howard Bretherton's *Hopalong Cassidy* (a.k.a. *Hopalong Cassidy Enters*; Paramount, 1935).

3079

Judge: Now this is going to be a fair trial …conducted legally. A boy's life hangs in the balance.

Spectator: That's about the only place he'll hang!

The Judge played by Will Wright: Sidney Salkow's *The Iron Sheriff* (United Artists, 1957).

3080

Annie: Mrs. McGuinness, that's what we need! We'll have a women's jury! That ought to be very simple. And none of this men's business about being open-minded and not prejudice as they say. We want a good prejudiced jury!

Annie played by Loretta Young and Mrs. McGuinness played by Jessie Ralph: Frank Lloyds' *Lady from Cheyenne* (Universal, 1941).

3081

Hardin: I'll give you a little free advice, killer. You said it yourself: stealin' is a more dangerous habit in these parts than killin'. But if you have a tendency to steal, you best stay clear of Judge Roy Bean. He can't abide a thief. If he catches his money in your pockets, he'll hang you promptly and keep the money.

John Wesley Hardin played by Randy Quaid and Judge Roy Bean played by Ned Beatty: Joseph Sargent's *Larry McMurtry's Streets of Laredo* (Cabin Fever Entertainment, 1995).

3082

Bob: What do you mean, Judge? Are you going to let us go?

Judge: If those bureaucratic nincompoops in Washington found out that three of the men I hired as deputies had to be hung as horse thieves, armed robbers, and consorting with women of low repute …so I'm going to let you go.

Grat: Well, I just want to tell you, Judge, that I think that's mighty nice of you.

Judge: Shut up, you unpardonable imbecile! I'm gonna repeat it. I'm gonna let you go. All of you …but with a warning. You get out of this territory by sundown tonight. And if I ever catch you, or any one of your worthless friends in my jurisdiction again, then I personally am gonna select the tallest cottonwood tree in the state of Arkansas. And on it, I'm going to hang you from the first light of dawn until the next full moon. Do you understand that?

Bob Dalton played by Cliff Potts, Judge Isaac Parker played by Dale Robertson, and Grat Dalton played by Randy Quaid: Dan Curtis' *Last Ride of the Dalton Gang* (TVW, 1979).

3083

Frank: The Judge has got him measured for a pine box.

Frank Dalton played by Don Collier: Dan Curtis' *Last Ride of the Dalton Gang* (TVW, 1979).

3084

Durango Kid: Why didn't you shoot me when you had the chance?

Marshal: I'm hired to keep the peace, not to kill people.

Durango Kid: It seems like the two of them sort of go hand in hand.

Marshal: Well, at least you got the satisfaction of knowing you'll get hung legal.

Durango Kid: That may be some satisfaction to you, but I can't help thinking you'll wind up dead either way.

The Durango Kid played by Wally Cassell and Marshal Frame Johnson played by Ronald Reagan: Nathan Juran's *Law and Order* (Universal, 1953).

3085

Quirt: The law don't want proof. The law wants justice.

Quirt played by Don Johnson: Virgil W. Vogel's *Law of the Land* (TVW, 1976).

3086

Judge: Does the prisoner have anything to say?

Hardin: Yes I have, your honor. If you and the jury weren't afraid of public opinion, I never would have been convicted. Because I shot Charlie Webb in self-defense and you all know it. Maybe I did wrong. Maybe I deserve to be punished.

But I'm not a murderer. I never killed a man who didn't try to kill me first.

The Judge played by Stephen Chase and John Wesley Hardin played by Rock Hudson: Raoul Walsh's *The Lawless Breed* (Universal, 1952),

3087

Lieutenant: Did you see the shooting?

Old Timer: I've seen nothing. Ain't seen my wife in a week. What time is it?

Lieutenant: Everybody has gone blind and dumb around here at the same time!

The Lieutenant was uncredited and the Old Timer played by Francis Ford: Raoul Walsh's *The Lawless Breed* (Universal, 1952).

3088

Maddox: He'll go back to Bannock and stand trial.

Laura: Will they hang him?

Maddox: The circuit judge is no hanging judge. In fact, a man like Bronson could buy him cheap.

Laura: I don't mean just the judge. I mean the town, the good people with the rope.

Maddox: It's my town, Laura. Nobody gets a mob rope in my town. You know that. I give you my word. If he comes in peaceful, there will be no hurt come to him.

Laura: You never did give much away.

Marshal Jared Maddox played by Burt Lancaster and Laura Shelby played by Sheree North: Michael Winner's *Lawman* (United Artists, 1971).

3089

Tom: Amnesty. Nobody gets hung. Nobody goes to jail. We're all forgiven for our sins, man!

Tom Folliard played by James Best: Arthur Penn's *The Left Handed Gun* (Warner Bros., 1958).

3090

Roy Bean: I'm the new judge. There's going to be law. There's going to be order, progress, civilization, and peace. Above all, peace. And I don't care who I have to kill to get it.

Judge Roy Bean played by Paul Newman: John Huston's *The Life and Times of Judge Roy Bean* (NGP, 1972).

3091

Bean: Ordinarily, I'd take you into my court and try ya and hang ya. But if you got money for whiskey, I guess we can dispense with those proceedings.

Judge Roy Bean played by Paul Newman: John Huston's *The Life and Times of Judge Roy Bean* (NGP, 1972).

3092

Bart: Do you get much judging around here?

Bean: What do you mean?

Bart: Ah, I mean, what's the use being a judge if you ain't got no one to law?

Bean: I got a whole graveyard of previous cases!

Bart Jackson played by Jim Burk and Judge Roy Bean played by Paul Newman: John Huston's *The Life and Times of Judge Roy Bean* (NGP, 1972).

3093

Tector: Hear ye, hear ye! The Court of Vinegarroon is in session. There'll be no drinking! Judge Roy Bean presiding.

Judge: Do you have anything to say before we find you guilty?

Sam: I'm not guilty of nothing! There's no crime that I've done wrong.

Judge: Do you deny the killing?

Sam: I do not deny it. But there's no place in that book where it says nothing about killing a Chinese. And no one I know ever heard of a law on greasers, niggers, or injuns.

Judge: All men stand equal before the law. And I'll hang a man for killing anyone …including chinks, greasers, or niggers. I'm very advanced in my views …and outspoken.

Sam: There's no place in that book that …

Judge: Trust in my judgment of The Book. Besides, you're going to hang no matter what it says in there because I'm the law. And the law is the handmaiden of justice. Get a rope!

Tector Crites played by Ned Beatty, Judge Roy Bean played by Paul Newman, and Sam Dodd played by Tab Hunter: John Huston's *The Life and Times of Judge Roy Bean* (NGP, 1972).

3094

Judge: I ain't gonna sentence ya, boy, but I am gonna warn ya. If you ain't out of town here in five minutes, I'm gonna open court and earn it.

Pimp: I ain't even got a horse!

Judge: Steal one! A fast one! Remember, we hang horse thieves around here!

Judge Roy Bean played by Paul Newman and the Pimp played by Jack Colvin: John Huston's *The Life and Times of Judge Roy Bean* (NGP, 1972).

3095

Tector: We don't stand a chance. The law is on his side!

Rose: The law!

Tector: Yes, law. I didn't say anything about justice.

Tector Crites played by Ned Beatty and Rose Bean played by Jacqueline Bisset: John Huston's *The Life and Times of Judge Roy Bean* (NGP, 1972).

3096

Blessing: Someday I'm gonna make him pay for what he did to my father. I swear it!

Crecencio: Yes, he will pay with or without you. That is the way of the world. When one pees into the wind, he's gonna get his own feet wet. But remember this too, Mi Hijo: just as evil brings evil back on the doer, so does kindness bring kindness. That is the place to put your heart, Mi Hijo ...not on revenge.

Blessing: Can you teach me to use a gun?

Young Ned Blessing played by Sean Baca and Crecencio played by Luis Avalos: Peter Werner's *Lone Justice* (Academy Entertainment, 1994).

3097

Governor: But why the mask?

Lone Ranger: Governor, outlaws live in a lonesome world. A world of fear. Fear of the mysterious. I made this mask from my dead brothers clothing. I've worked from behind it ever since. I'll wear this mask until justice has been dealt to the last murderer and outlaw. I hope that answers your questions.

The Governor played by Charles Meredith and the Lone Ranger played by Clayton Moore: Stuart Heisler's *The Lone Ranger* (Warner Bros., 1956).

3098

Lone Ranger: All I want out of this place is enough silver for some immediate needs. Other than that, all you can dig is yours.

Jim Blane: Oh now, I couldn't!

Lone Ranger: You're entitled to it, Jim. You'll have to do all the work.

Jim Blane: You know, I could refine a little ore right here.

Lone Ranger: That's just what I want you to do, Jim. Then in the future, whenever Tonto and I come back here, we can get the pure metal for money and bullets.

Jim Blane: Bullets?

Lone Ranger: Yes. I want some of the ore cast into silver bullets.

Jim Blane: Thunderation, what's the matter with lead bullets? They'll kill just as well as ...

Lone Ranger: You forget, I told you I vowed never shoot to kill. Silver bullets will serve as sort of a symbol. Tonto suggested the idea.

Jim Blane: Symbol? Of what?

Lone Ranger: A symbol which means justice by law. I want to become known to all who see the silver bullets that I live and fight only to see the eventual defeat and the proper punishment by law of any criminal in the west.

Jim Blane: There will be an awful lot of silver shot up before you're through!

The Lone Ranger played by Clayton Moore, Jim Blane played by Ralph Littlefield, and Tonto played by Jay Silverheels: George B. Seitz's *The Lone Ranger* (Television Series, earliest episodes, Sept. 1949).

3099

Cobham: I've been meaning to tell you, Judge, how much I admire the severity of your sentences.

Judge: My goodness, Cobham, I didn't take you to be a simpleton! I give long sentences because we got roads to build.

Superintendent Cobham played by Frank Thring and Judge Barry played by Peter Collingwood: Philippe Mora's *Mad Dog Morgan* (Motion Picture Company/BEF, 1976).

3100

Johnny: Maybe you don't believe it, Judge, but there's two kinds of justice: yours and other peoples. Just don't forget that!

Johnny Howard played by Jerome Courtland and Judge Owen Devereaux played by Glenn Ford: Henry Levin's *The Man from Colorado* (Columbia, 1948).

3101

Valance: Lawyer, huh? Well, I'll teach you law. Western law!

Liberty Valance played by Lee Marvin: John Ford's *The Man Who Shot Liberty Valance* (Paramount, 1962).

3102

Soldier: He's got a Z on his chest!

The Soldier was uncredited: Rouben Mamoulian's *The Mark of Zorro* (20th Century–Fox, 1940).

3103

Calvin: A 44.40 and a brain pan would be my sentence for him. Now I don't know why you don't want to go along with that, Tom!

Calvin played by Harry Dean Stanton and Tom Logan played by Jack Nicholson: Arthur Penn's *The Missouri Breaks* (United Artists, 1976).

3104

Jason: We'll be at the relay station in a few minutes ...where you'll get a quick trial and a quicker hanging.

Jason Waterman played by Hugh Sanders: Ray Nazarro's *Montana Territory* (Columbia, 1952).

3105

Judge: Young lady, are you trying to show contempt for this court?

Flower Belle: No, I'm doing my best to hide it.

The Judge played by Addison Richards and Flower Belle Lee played by Mae West: Edward F. Cline's *My Little Chickadee* (Universal, 1940).

3106

Nell: What do you suppose will happen to Vinnie and Judge Crupper?

Brett: Oh, Judge Crupper will get a fine. And they'll give him a reprimand and suspended sentence. Vinnie is going to be doing time in a federal penitentiary.

Nell: Why? They both of them are guilty of the same crime.

Ben: Well, as my old grandpappy used to say, one man's political disgrace is another man's prison sentence.

Nell McGarahan played by Susan Blanchard, Brett

Maverick played by James Garner, Ben Maverick played by Charles Frank, and Judge Austin Crupper played by Eugene Roche: Hy Averback's *The New Maverick* (TVW, 1978).

3107

Tucson: And with Don Luis exposed as a fraud, charges against us will be dropped.

Lullaby: And if they ain't, we'll be dropped by firing squad.

Tucson Smith played by Ray Corrigan and Lullaby Joslin played by Max Terhune: George Sherman's *The Night Riders* (Republic, 1939).

3108

John: In the end, I'll see that the law gets you. And it won't be just to run you out of town. It'll be at the end of a rope.

John Kincaid played by Hugh Sothern: Lloyd Bacon's *The Oklahoma Kid* (Warner Bros., 1939).

3109

Captain: General! It is a crime to murder an officer without proper trial.

General: No one is going to murder you, Captain. We're just going to kill you!

Captain Ovando played by Pedro Damian and General Tomas Arroyo played by Jimmy Smits: Luis Puenzo's *Old Gringo* (Columbia, 1989).

3110

Sheriff: Now I'm letting you go. But if you ever come back here again, I'll shoot you down like a dog in the street.

Sheriff Dad Longsworth played by Karl Malden: Marlon Brando's *One-Eyed Jacks* (Paramount, 1961).

3111

Rio: I am going to get a trial, ain't I Dad?

Sheriff: Oh sure, kid, sure. You'll get a fair trial. And then I'm going to hang you ...personally!

Rio played by Marlon Brando and Sheriff Dad Longsworth played by Karl Malden: Marlon Brando's *One-Eyed Jacks* (Paramount, 1961).

3112

Curly: You didn't have to shoot him in the back!

Duke: Shoot him in the back? What are you talking about? The fellow went for a gun! I've got eight witnesses to prove it. Or maybe I've only got seven. How about it, Curley?"

Curly: Oh no, Dukey, you have eight!

Curly played by Nacho Galindo and Duke Rankin played by Bob Steele: William Whitney's *The Outcast* (Republic, 1954).

3113

Fletcher: You promised me those men would be decently treated!

Senator: They were decently treated! They were decently fed, and then they were decently shot!

Fletcher played by John Vernon and Senator Lane played by Frank Schofield: Clint Eastwood's *The Outlaw Josey Wales* (Warner Bros., 1976).

3114

Jason: Well, it ain't often a man gets the honor and privilege of drinking with a famous judge ...appointed by the Governor himself.

Judge: Now, I got a secret for you, Jason. I wasn't appointed by the Governor. I paid $10.00 for my office, two buffalo skins, and a case of whiskey.

Jason: No? Say, that's a good one! Why didn't you buy the mayor's job? Why did you want to be judge for?

Judge: Well, I wanted to be where I could do people the most good. And, by golly, I was too! Because I wasn't in there two days and I let ten of my best friends out of jail. That's doing good!

Jason Fitch played by Edgar Buchanan and Judge Amos Polk played by Andy Devine: Jean Yarbrough's *The Over-the-Hill Gang* (TVW, 1969).

3115

Martin: Why do you keep asking me all these questions? You don't believe anything I tell you.

Tetley: There's truth in lies, too, if you can get enough of 'em.

Donald Martin played by Dana Andrews and Major Tetley played by Frank Conroy: William Wellman's *The Ox-Bow Incident* (20th Century–Fox, 1943).

3116

Martin: Even in this God-forsaken country, I've got a right to a trial!

Tetley: You're getting a trial with 28 of the only kind of judges [that] murderers and rustlers get in what you call this God-forsaken country!

Donald Martin played by Dana Andrews and Major Tetley played by Frank Conroy: William Wellman's *The Ox-Bow Incident* (20th Century–ox, 1943).

3117

Martin: Justice? What do you care about justice? You don't even care whether you got the right men or not! All you know is you lost something and somebody has got to be punished!

Donald Martin played by Dana Andrews: William Wellman's *The Ox-Bow Incident* (20th Century–Fox, 1943).

3118

Martin: Man just naturally can't take the law into his own hands and hang people without hurting everybody in the world. Because then he's just not breaking one law, but all laws. Laws are a lot more than words you put into a book ...or judges or lawyers or sheriffs you hire to

Bob Ford shot Jesse James in the back and Frank James (Henry Fonda) is out for revenge in Fritz Lang's *The Return of Frank James* (20th Century–Fox, 1940).

carry it out. It's everything people ever have found out about justice, and what's right and wrong. It's the very conscience of humanity. There can't be any such thing as civilization unless people have a conscience. Because if people touch God anywhere, where is it except through their conscience. And what is anybody's conscience except a little piece of the conscience of all men that ever lived.

Excerpts of a letter written by Donald Martin played by Dana Andrews and read by Gil Carter played by Henry Fonda: William Wellman's *The Ox-Bow Incident* (20th Century–Fox, 1943).

3119

Queen: The Captain of the Thunder Guards failed again. What shall I do with him?

Argo: According to the law of Murania, there is no third chance.

Queen Tika played by Dorothy Christie and Lord Argo played by Wheeler Oakman: Otto Brower and B. Reeves (Breezy) Eason's *The Phantom Empire* (Mascot serial, Chapter 3: "The Lightning Chamber," 1935).

3120

Chief: Justice must not only be carried out …it must be seen to be carried out.

Chief Powhatan played by Gordon Tootoosis: Daniele J. Suissa's *Pocahontas: The Legend* (Goodtimes Entertainment — Alliance Releasing, 1995).

3121

Mayor: You boys are going to get a fair trial as God is my witness.

Papa Joe: Your witness, Mayor? Is that the same God that witnessed you all puttin' black folks into slavery and stealin' the Indians' land?

Mayor Bigwood played by Paul Bartel and Papa Joe played by Melvin Van Peebles: Mario Van Peebles' *Posse* (Gramercy Pictures, 1993).

3122

Mayor: Papa Joe, you ought to be working on saving your black soul.

Papa Joe: Shit, I'm working on saving my black ass!

Mayor Bigwood played by Paul Bartel and Papa Joe played by Melvin Van Peebles: Mario Van Peebles' *Posse* (Gramercy Pictures, 1993).

3123

Judge: Now we'll go on to the next charge. That's, ah, assault. Now, did Jeb Burleigh strike the first blow or did you?

Chandler: Well, that's hard to say.

Judge: I don't see what's so hard about it. It seems simple enough to me. Either Jeb Burleigh struck the first blow or you did.

Chandler: It's not so simple. A lot of wars begin before the shooting starts.

Judge Morley played by Henry Hull, John Chandler played by Alan Ladd, and Jeb Burleigh played by Harry Dean Stanton: Michael Curtiz's *The Proud Rebel* (MGM, 1958).

3124

Tank: What do you think the verdict is gonna be?

Shad: You're gonna swing.

Tank Logan played by Brian Keith and Shadrack Peltzer played by Cameron Mitchell: Lee H. Katzin's *The Quest* (TVW, 1976).

3125

Averell: I believe in law and order myself, Sheriff. But there's also a thing called justice.

Jessup: And I'm dealing some out!

Jim Averell played by William Bishop and Matt Jessup played by Dennis Weaver: Lee Sholem's *The Redhead from Wyoming* (Universal, 1953).

3126

Clem: It's just like my papaw always said: there ain't no law for poor folks except at the end of a gun.

Clem played by Jackie Cooper: Fritz Lang's *The Return of Frank James* (20th Century–Fox, 1940).

3127

Prosecutor: Tell me, just where was the watchman Wilson when he was hit?

Frank: Well, let me see. I think …

Prosecutor: Never mind what you think! Where was he?

Frank: I'm sorry, I can't talk without thinking …not being a lawyer.

The prosecutor played by Russell Hicks and Frank James played by Henry Fonda: Fritz Lang's *The Return of Frank James* (20th Century–Fox, 1940).

3128

Sheriff: Wait a minute now. This is a court of law. And don't ever let it be said that I didn't give everyone a fair hearing. You got anything to say for yourself, prisoner?

Prisoner: You bet I got something to say for myself. You stole those cattle from me in the first place, and I got …

Sheriff: Shut up! I find the prisoner guilty of first degree robbery. Does the jury second that?

Sheriff McNally played by Robert Barrat and the Prisoner/Tough played by Ward Bond: Herbert I. Leeds' *The Return of the Cisco Kid* (20th Century–Fox, 1939).

3129

Reverend: What do you plan on doing now?

Clay: What would you do if you were in my position?

Reverend: That's a pretty difficult question. Many people would be inclined to seek some sort of retribution. I'd have to advise against it.

Clay: Vengeance is mine, sayeth the Lord?

Reverend: It's more or less what I had in mind.

Clay: Yeah, but I'm not a minister.

Reverend: I know that. That's what disturbs me.

Reverend Moorehead played by Denver Pyle and Clay O'Mara played by Audie Murphy: Jesse Hibbs' *Ride Clear of Diablo* (Universal, 1954).

3130

Sheriff: Shut up and listen! You're appearing as a defense witness for Whitey Kincade.

Ringer: Why should I defend him? I hope they hang him.

Sheriff: You'll hang right along side him if they do. He knows enough to ruin us all. And he won't mind talking if he doesn't like the verdict.

Ringer: I'm not going to get up there and lie for nothing.

Sheriff: You've been lying for nothing all your life!

Sheriff Fred Kenyon played by Paul Birch and Jed Ringer played by Russell Johnson: Jesse Hibbs' *Ride Clear of Diablo* (Universal, 1954).

3131

Judge: Well, you've brought him to the proper spot. We'll hold court right here in the old Tequila Bar …surrounded by tender memories of the past.

Judge E. Clarence Jones played by Otis Harlan: Fred Allen's *Ride Him, Cowboy* (Warner Bros., 1932).

3132

Judge: Hey there! No rough stuff with the prisoner until after the trial! We'll hang this prisoner in accordance with the law made and provided in all such cases to the contrary notwithstanding.

Cowboy: Hey, Judge!

Judge: Well?

Cowboy: Can we hang the critter first and then try him afterwards?

Judge: No sir. This here will be a regular trial by due process of the law. And the prisoner will get every consideration. Prisoner, don't you forget to stand up after the jury pronounces you guilty so I can pass sentence on ya!

Judge E. Clarence Jones played by Otis Harlan: Fred Allen's *Ride Him, Cowboy* (Warner Bros., 1932).

3133

Judge: Order in this court! Being that we ain't got any Bible, and no one here has ever seen one anyway, the jury will not be sworn in.

Judge E. Clarence Jones played by Otis Harlan: Fred Allen's *Ride Him, Cowboy* (Warner Bros., 1932).

3134

Judge: Well, seeing as how the prosecution has rested, I am now ready to hear arguments for the defense. What have you got to say for yourself?

Drury: I want to say again that Henry Simms is …

Judge: Out of order! Your testimony is incompetent, irrelevant, immaterial, unnecessary, and extraneous! Have you got anything further to say for yourself?

Judge E. Clarence Jones played by Otis Harlan and John Drury played by John Wayne: Fred Allen's *Ride Him, Cowboy* (Warner Bros., 1932).

3135

Judge: Seeing that the defense rests, now if there isn't any arguments on either side, I will …Holy Smoke! I forgot! Does the prisoner plead guilty or not guilty?

Drury: Not guilty.

Judge: Not that it makes a darn bit of difference, but, ah, the trial's got to be regular.

Judge E. Clarence Jones played by Otis Harlan and John Drury played by John Wayne: Fred Allen's *Ride Him, Cowboy* (Warner Bros., 1932).

3136

Judge: Gentlemen, you have heard the evidence. The last and final step before the hanging will be to let the jury retire to deliberate. The jury will rise. The case is in your hands, gents. And don't spend too much time arguing!

Judge E. Clarence Jones played by Otis Harlan: Fred Allen's *Ride Him, Cowboy* (Warner Bros., 1932).

3137

Judge: Now as soon as the prisoner arrives, the court will come to order. We'll give him a fair trial, and then we'll hang him.

Judge Dyer played by Robert Barrat: James Tinling's *Riders of the Purple Sage* (20th Century–Fox, 1941).

3138

Gabby: You folks just sit back and give me a chance. I've got a little witnessing to do for myself.

Judge: You're the prisoner!

Gabby: I am.

Judge: Who's your witness?

Gabby: I am.

Judge: Who's your attorney?

Gabby: I am.

Judge: Who's your …

Gabby: Now, everything that is, I am!

Gabby Hornaday played by George "Gabby" Hayes and Judge Cravens played by Robert Strange: Joseph Kane's *Robin Hood of the Pecos* (Republic, 1941).

3139

Eula: You have ridden the Hoot Owl Trail and tasted the fruits of evil. But justice will catch up with you to demand payment.

Eula Goodnight played by Katharine Hepburn: Stuart Millar's *Rooster Cogburn* (Universal, 1975).

3140

Mayor: You think I let 'em off pretty easy, don't you?

Sheriff: Well, I wouldn't exactly say you made an example out of 'em.

Mayor: Law and order is an awful lot like hard liquor. Too big a dose the first time is liable to pull a man off of it for life. You got to get used to it gradual. Maybe that isn't what is said in Blackstone, but he didn't live out west.

Mayor Walsh played by John Miljan and Sheriff Mat Dow played by James Cagney: Nicholas Ray's *Run for Cover* (Paramount, 1955).

3141

Yutaka: If you want to fight, fight fair and square.

Flint: Well, it's more fun this way.

Yutaka Sato played by Hiromi Go and Flint played by Mark Acheson: Michael Keusch's *Samurai Cowboy* (Den Pictures/Entertainment Securities/Saban Entertainment, 1993).

3142

Judge: One more word from you and I'll fine you for contempt of this court!

Stony: Words fail to express my contempt for this court!

Judge Henry J. Hixon played by Ferris Taylor and Stony Brooke played by John Wayne: George Sherman's *Santa Fe Stampede* (Republic, 1938).

3143

Marshal: Judge Hixon, the prisoner seems to want an early trial. Do you think you can accommodate him?

Judge: Why yes, Marshal, I think I can arrange it. I've done it before.

Marshal: Oh no, Judge! This is going to be a fair trial!

Marshal Wood played by Tom London and Judge Henry J. Hixon played by Ferris Taylor: George Sherman's *Santa Fe Stampede* (Republic, 1938).

3144

Long Mane: He who has lived without honor must die without honor.

Iron Beast: It is the law. It is just.

Long Mane played by Michael Tolan and Iron Beast played by Ted De Corsia: George Marshall's *The Savage* (Paramount, 1952).

3145

Judge: Dan, there isn't much that I can say. But I think I can speak for all of us. We're sorry.

Dan: You're sorry? A moment ago, you wanted to kill me. You forced me to kill …to defend myself, to save my own life. You wouldn't believe me, you wouldn't believe what I said. A man's life can hang in the balance …on a piece of paper. And you're sorry!

Judge Cranston played by Robert Warwick and Dan Ballard played by John Payne: Allan Dwan's *Silver Lode* (RKO, 1954).

3146

Cobb: And we're going to give you a fair trial …followed by a first-class hanging!

Sheriff Cobb played by Brian Dennehy: Lawrence Kasdan's *Silverado* (Columbia, 1985).

3147

Valerie: Well, how can you say they're guilty of something until it's proven?

Colonel: Law is an unusual interest for a woman.

Valerie: I'm not talking about law! I'm referring to justice, Colonel!

Colonel: Then justice is an unusual interest for women.

Valerie Kendrick played by Julia Adams and Colonel Morsby played by Hugh Marlowe: Lee Sholem's *The Stand at Apache River* (Universal, 1953).

3148

Gabby: Justice ain't only blind in this town, it's deaf too!

Gabby Whittaker played by George "Gabby" Hayes: Joseph Kane's *Sunset on the Desert* (Republic, 1942).

3149

Windy: Here's the fine for both of 'em.

Judge: Well, that's a little bit irregular, Mr. Miller.

Windy: Everything is irregular in this two by four court, including your remark about [General] Lee and [General] Beauregard.

Judge: What?

Windy: And there's twenty dollars for the fine for Thatch Delaney. Come on, Thatch!

Judge: Why, he ain't entered his plea!

Windy: He pleads guilty!

Judge: Why, that's a twenty, and the fine is only ten!

Windy: Take the change and get some of the stink out of this place!

Windy Miller played by George Bancroft and the Judge played by Raymond Hatton: George Marshall's *Texas* (Columbia, 1941).

3150

Hollis: Baldy's grave is down by the corral. The jury dug it before the trial started.

Sam Hollis played by Dean Martin and Don Andrea Baldasar played by Alain Delon: Michael Gordon's *Texas Across the River* (Universal, 1966).

3151

Posse Member: The jury is coming in, Buck.

Buck: How do they look?

Posse Member: Well, they look like of posse of pallbearers.

The Posse Member played by Ben Johnson and

You always felt safe just knowing the Three Mesquiteers were within a day's ride. Saddled and ready for another adventure are Lullaby Joslin (Max Terhune), Stony Brooke (John Wayne), and Tuscon Smith (Ray Corrigan) in George Sherman's *Santa Fe Stampede* (Republic, 1938).

Marshal Perley "Buck" Sweet played by Ward Bond: John Ford's *The 3 Godfathers* (MGM, 1948).

3152
Judge: I hereby give you the minimum sentence under the law: one year and one day. Court's closed …bar's open …double bourbon, bartender!
The Judge played by Guy Kibbee: John Ford's *The 3 Godfathers* (MGM, 1948).

3153
Sheriff: You're a wanted man, Jim. Anyone in this town can put a bullet through your back and they wouldn't have to answer for it.
Sheriff Ben East played by Stephen Elliott and Jim Guthrie played by Dana Andrews: Alfred Werker's *Three Hours to Kill* (Columbia, 1954).

3154
Hickman: Fair fight. You won't find any bullet holes in his back.

Morg Hickman played by Henry Fonda: Anthony Mann's *The Tin Star* (Paramount, 1957).

3155
Granny: It ain't honorable to take a family feud to court. It won't spill no blood for you.
Mark: I want no blood spilled for me.
Granny: Then you're puttin' yourself above the Prophets! An eye for an eye and a tooth for a tooth. It's in The Book!
Granny Hayden played by Eugenie Besserer and Mark Hayden played by Egon Brecherin: Henry Hathaway's *To the Last Man* (Paramount, 1933).

3156
Judge: Jed Colby, you have been found guilty. But on account of peculiar circumstances and feelings in the community, the court has decided not to have a hanging. But you'll have to go to the State Penitentiary for fifteen years for the murder of Judd Spelvin.

Jed: Murder? Why, it was feudin', pure and simple!
The Judge played by Erville Alderson and Jed Colby played by Noah Beery, Sr.: Henry Hathaway's *To the Last Man* (Paramount, 1933).

3157
Burke: Tom, they're gonna have you come to court very quickly. Have you ever been tried for anything before?
Horn: Yeah, once. It was a military trial a long time ago. A couple scouts and myself.
Burke: What were you charged with?
Horn: Invasion of Mexico.
Defense Counsel Thomas Burke played by Harry Northrup and Tom Horn played by Steve McQueen: William Wiard's *Tom Horn* (Warner Bros., 1980).

3158
Judge: I think what the prosecutor is trying to say to you, Mr. Horn, is that we would keenly like to have you reply

specifically to the accusation that you killed this boy.

Horn: You want me to say whether I did or I didn't do it?

Judge: Well, in effect, yes. Although a plea of innocence has been entered.

Horn: Well, I'm not going to give you the satisfaction. Now whether you, or Stoll, or that sold-out son-of-a-bitchin' Marshal Joe Belle want to see me guilty, well, you go right ahead. But I'm not going to give you any more satisfaction than I have to. Now whether you shoot me, hang me, or take my rifle or my horse …one reason is as good as another. And I believe that, I do. That's my last word on this matter!

Judge Scott played by Bert Williams, Tom Horn played by Steve McQueen, Prosecutor Walter Stoll played by Geoffrey Lewis, and U.S. Marshal Joe Belle played by Billy Green Bush: William Wiard's *Tom Horn* (Warner Bros., 1980).

3159

Stillwell: Are you going to hang me?

Noble: No.

Stillwell: Are they going to send me back to Yuma?

Noble: No, they won't.

Stillwell: They won't?

Noble: Because I'm sending you to hell!

John "Red Jack" Stillwell played by Scott Wilson and Noble Adams played by Kris Kristofferson: John Guillermin's *The Tracker* (HBO Pictures, 1988).

3160

Billy: Larkin, you're going to get thirty days for that killin'. Then we're going to hang you!

Billy Burns played by George "Gabby" Hayes and Lance Larkin played by Harry Woods: Ray Enright's *Trail Street* (RKO, 1947).

3161

Cody: You know, you got to hand it to the Mexicans when it comes to swift justice. Once the federales get their mitts on a criminal, they know just what to do with him. They hand him a shovel, tell him where to dig. When he's dug deep enough, they tell him to put the shovel down, smoke a cigarette, and say his prayers. In another five minutes, he's being covered over with the earth he dug out.

James Cody played by Bruce Bennett: John Huston's *The Treasure of the Sierra Madre* (Warner Bros., 1948).

3162

Miller: It was always Mr. Rudock's valley …just as the horses of the country were always known as Rudock horses. And when they hung a horse thief, they called it Mr. Rudock's justice.

Steve Miller played by Don Dubbins and Jeremy Rudock played by James Cagney: Robert Wise's *Tribute to a Bad Man* (MGM, 1956).

3163

Defense: I believe you testified that you backed away from old man Worden.

Marshal: Yes, sir.

Defense: Which direction were you going?

Marshal: Backward. I always go backward when I'm backing away.

The Defense Lawyer Goudy played by Alfred Ryder and Marshal Reuben J. "Rooster" Cogburn played by John Wayne: Henry Hathaway's *True Grit* (Paramount, 1969).

3164

Mattie: This man wants to take Chaney back to Texas. That's not what I want.

Rooster: He wants him caught and punished. So do you.

Mattie: I want Tom Chaney to hang for killing my father! It's little to me how many dogs and senators he killed in Texas!

Mattie Ross played by Kim Darby, Tom Chaney played by Jeff Corey, and Marshal Reuben J. "Rooster" Cogburn played by John Wayne: Henry Hathaway's *True Grit* (Paramount, 1969).

3165

Stonehill: I'll take it up with my attorney!

Mattie: And I'll take it up with mine …Lord Daggett. And he will make money, and I will make money, and your lawyer will make money. And you, Mr. Licensed Auctioneer, you will foot the bill!

Stonehill: You are a damn nuisance! Lawyer Daggert, lawyer Daggert! Who is this famous pleader whose name I was happily ignorant of ten minutes ago?

Mattie: Have you ever heard of the Great Arkansas River, Vicksbury, Gulf & Steamship Company?

Stonehill: I had done business with the G.A.V.& G., yes.

Mattie: Well, he was the one that forced them into receivership. They tried to mess with him.

Stonehill: All right, come inside.

Colonel G. Stonehill played by Strother Martin and Mattie Ross played by Kim Darby: Henry Hathaway's *True Grit* (Paramount, 1969).

3166

Little Bill: I guess you know, Bob, that …ah …if I see you again, I'm just going to start shooting and figure it self-defense.

Little Bill Daggett played by Gene Hackman and English Bob played by Richard Harris: Clint Eastwood's *Unforgiven* (Warner Bros., 1992).

3167

Vance: See you at the trial tomorrow, Glenn.

Glenn: I'll be there, Vance. But don't sit up tonight writing my obituary.

Clayton Vance played by Douglas Spencer and Glenn Denbow played by Scott Brady: Hugo Fregonese's *Untamed Frontier* (Universal, 1952).

3168

Vickers: Ever since then, all I've ever known is what you called vengeance. I call it retribution. It's the one thing that kept me going all these years.

John Vickers played by Edmond O'Brien: Byron Haskin's *Warpath* (Paramount, 1951).

3169

Cole: I didn't break any law, Sheriff.

Sheriff: No? Well, what about stealing my horse, huh?

Cole: I needed that horse to recover the gold.

Sheriff: Locking me in my own jail?

Cole: I wanted you behind me.

Sheriff: Murder?

Cole: Self-defense.

Sheriff: Raping!

Cole: Assault with a friendly weapon?

Lewton Cole played by James Coburn and Sheriff John Copperud played by Carroll O'Connor: William Graham's *Waterhole No. 3* (Paramount, 1967).

3170

Cole: A man can dream, can't he?

Sheriff: Oh well, a man can dream. But there ain't no use …cause even if they don't stretch your neck, why, you'll probably be wearing a number into the 20th century.

Lewton Cole played by James Coburn and Sheriff John Copperud played by Carroll O'Connor: William Graham's *Waterhole No. 3* (Paramount, 1967).

3171

Cole: Well, your Honor, I was just trying to get the lay of the land.

Southeast: You will, too, at the end of a rope!

Judge Bean: Southeast, no anticipating!

Cole Hardin played by Gary Cooper, Southeast played by Chill Wills, and Judge Roy Bean played by Walter Brennan: William Wyler's *The Westerner* (United Artists, 1940).

3172

Judge Bean: What's the verdict?

Chickenfoot: You know what the verdict is …guilty!

Judge Bean: There's only one thing I can do. You're sentenced to hang. That's my ruling. Turn loose of the prisoner's hands.

Southeast: Judge, you just ruled …

Judge Bean: I didn't finish my ruling. The court sentenced the prisoner to hang.

The court didn't say when, so long as there is a reasonable doubt.

Chickenfoot: What reasonable doubt, Judge?

Stranger: We just caught him on Chickenfoot's horse!

Southeast: There ain't any room for doubt!

Judge Bean: Order! I've been talking to the prisoner. He's a friend of Lillie Langtry. It stands to reason no friend of Lillie Langtry goes around stealing horses. Least ways there's a reasonable doubt.

Chickenfoot: You mean you're setting aside your own ruling?

Judge Bean: That ain't what I said! When I make a ruling, it stands!

Southeast: But Judge, you just sentenced a man!

Judge Bean: The sentence is suspended for …for a couple weeks until I can look into the matter further. That's my ruling!

Judge Roy Bean played by Walter Brennan, Chickenfoot played by Paul Hurst, and Southeast played by Chill Wills: William Wyler's *The Westerner* (United Artists, 1940).

3173

Judge Bean: Mr. Hardin, it's my duty to inform you that the larceny of an equine is a capital offense punishable by death. But you can rest assure that in this court a horse thief always gets a fair trial before he's hung.

Judge Roy Bean played by Walter Brennan and Cole Hardin played by Gary Cooper: William Wyler's *The Westerner* (United Artists, 1940).

3174

Cole: Now look, those people don't take up much room with their little shirt-size pieces of land. Why don't you be a real judge …for all the people. Why don't you try to see their side of it, and try to help 'em instead of fight 'em. Make peace around here instead of war. There's plenty of room for everybody. And then everybody would look up to you. And then someday maybe they would put up a statue out there in the street. A statue with carvings on it: To Roy Bean, A Real Judge.

Cole Hardin played by Gary Cooper and Judge Roy Bean played by Walter Brennan: William Wyler's *The Westerner* (United Artists, 1940).

3175

Cross: He said that firing squad couldn't hit a bull in the ass with a banjo!

Cross played by Willie Nelson: Burt Kennedy's *Where the Hell's That Gold?!!!* (a.k.a. *Dynamite & Gold*; TVW, 1988).

3176

Ibran: So, Cardiff! You, too, suffer from white man's justice.

Cardiff: Yeah, there's a short rope and a long drop waiting for me.

Ibran played by Geno Silva and Hugh Cardiff played by Sam Elliott: Richard Compton's *Wild Times* (TVW, 1980).

3177

Charlie: There's two kinds of justice: one you deserve and one you don't.

Charlie Veer played by Douglas Kennedy: Fred Sears' *Wyoming Renegades* (Columbia, 1955).

3178

Judge: It is therefore considered by the court here that said defendant, William H. Bonney, alias Kid, alias William Antrim, alias Henry McCathy, be confined in prison in said Lincoln County by the Sheriff of said county until on the day aforesaid he be taken from such prison to a suitable and convenient place of execution within said county and there be hanged by the neck until he be dead, dead, dead! Now do you have anything to say, young man?

Bonney: Yes, your honor, I do. You can go to hell, hell, hell!

Judge Bristol played by Tony Frank and William H. Bonney, alias Billy the Kid, played by Emilio Estevez: Geoff Murphy's *Young Guns II* (20th Century–Fox, 1990).

3179

Bonney: I should have dusted his excellency's regal ass when I had the chance!

William H. Bonney, alias Billy the Kid, played by Emilio Estevez: Geoff Murphy's *Young Guns II* (20th Century–Fox, 1990).

3180

Felipe: I propose that Kala be hanged in the public square tomorrow morning.

Gonzales: Excellent …make an example of him!

Pablo: I also agree. Show the Yaquis they cannot break our laws and live, and we'll have little to fear from that quarter.

Don Diego: Except bloodshed and death.

Felipe played by Leander de Cordova, Kala played by Paul Marion, Gonzales played by Edmund Cobb, Pablo/Don del Oro played by C. Montague Shaw, and Don Diego Vega/Zorro played by Reed Hadley: William Witney's and John English's *Zorro's Fighting Legion* (Republic serial, Chapter 11: "Face To Face," 1939).

Killing

See also Burying; Dying; Showdown

3181

Big Smith: Nice work, Kansas. You just killed my four best men: Pete and Scratchy, and …those other two.

Kansas: Oh, I'm sorry, Big. I guess I was just thinking of myself.

Big Smith played by M.C. Gainey and Brisco County, Jr., alias "Kansas," played by Bruce Campbell: Bryan Spicer's *Adventures of Brisco County, Jr.* (TVW, Series Premiere, 1993).

3182

Tennessean: We sure killed many of brave men today.

Gambler: Funny, I was proud of 'em. Even while I was killing 'em, I was proud of 'em. It speaks well for men that so many ain't afraid to die when they think right is on their side. It speaks well.

The Tennessean played by Chuck Roberson and the Gambler played by Denver Pyle: John Wayne's *The Alamo* (United Artists, 1960).

3183

Cherry: Why did you shoot that old man?

Monte: Because he came asking for it. Anytime somebody comes asking for it, they're gonna get it.

Cherry de Longpre played by Loretta Young and Monte Jarrad played by Dan Duryea: Stuart Heisler's *Along Came Jones* (RKO, 1945).

3184

McCall: Ah, you know, Quirt, I hate to shoot people. Remember I shot a wattie once in Montana. I dreamed about it all the next night. And then, of course, there's always witnesses. And then you got to shoot the witnesses.

Randy McCall played by Lee Dixon and Quirt Evans played by John Wayne: James Edward Grant's *Angel and the Badman* (Republic, 1947).

3185

Massai: Every white man, every Indian, is my enemy. I cannot kill them all. And someday they will kill me.

Nalinle: And then we will live until some-day.

Massai played by Burt Lancaster and Nalinle played by Jean Peters: Robert Aldrich's *Apache* (United Artists, 1954).

3186

Matt: I'm having a little trouble getting started, Father.

Priest: You are in the House of God now, my son. Speak from your heart.

Matt: Well, I've done a lot of killin'. I've killed a lot of men and sinned a lot of women. But the men I killed needed killin', and the women wanted sinnin', and well, I never was one much to argue.

Matt played by Marlon Brando and the Priest played by Larry D. Mann: Sidney J. Furie's *The Appaloosa* (Universal, 1966).

3187

Hickman: Blood atonement. That made it easy. Save a wicked man's soul by spilling his blood. And raise your own self up in the process. Salvation for the victim …exaltation for the slayer. A good deal for both parties.

Bill Hickman played by Tom Bower: Craig R. Baxley's *The Avenging Angel* (Turner Home Entertainment, 1995).

3188

Long: It's easy enough to assassinate a powerful man. The real trick, the art of it, is finding someone else to put the blame on.

Milton Long played by Jeffrey Jones: Craig R. Baxley's *The Avenging Angel* (Turner Home Entertainment, 1995).

3189

Miles: You bastard! I'm sending you to hell!

Eliza: No, Miles, don't! I'm all right. Don't kill him, please! Don't kill him!

Miles: After all he's done! After all the death and deceit, you're trying to save his soul?

Eliza: No, I'm trying to save your soul!

Miles played by Tom Berenger and Eliza Rigby played by Leslie Hope: Craig R. Baxley's *The Avenging Angel* (Turner Home Entertainment, 1995).

3190

Bonniwell: What's on your mind?

Slater: I've spent six months looking for a killer. What do you do when he turns out to be your father?

Bonniwell: Killer? Aren't you a little careless with your words, son? Yes, I kill when I have to. But I've never killed a man who wasn't trying to kill me. And that goes for the Sheriff in spite of his badge.

Jim Bonniwell (Father) played by Jim McIntire

and Jim Slater (Son) played by Richard Widmark: John Sturges' *Backlash* (Universal, 1956).

3191

Doc: They're going to kill you with no hard feelings.

Doc Velie played by Walter Brennan: John Sturges' *Bad Day at Black Rock* (MGM, 1955).

3192

Josh: You're dead! I just ain't killed ya yet.

Josh McCoy played by Dermot Mulroney: Jonathan Kaplan's *Bad Girls* (20th Century–Fox, 1994).

3193

Hampton: You know, I could kill you for what you just done.

Coyote: Yea, you've killed a lot for a lot less.

Bill Hampton played by Morgan Conway and Jim Badger (alias The Coyote Kid) played by George "Gabby" Hayes: Tim Whelan's *Badman's Territory* (RKO, 1946).

3194

Esteban: But I warn you: if you kill me while I'm lying here, I'll slit your throat!

Esteban played by Fernando Sancho: Duccio Tessari's *Ballad of Death Valley* (a.k.a. *The Return of Ringo*; Mediterranee-Balcazar/Rizzoli Film, 1966).

3195

Ringo: Dead, huh? Well they say: early to bed, early to rise, gets ya shot between the eyes.

Ringo played by Giuliano Gemma: Duccio Tessari's *Ballad of Death Valley* (a.k.a. *The Return of Ringo*; Mediterranee-Balcazar/Rizzoli Film, 1966).

3196

California: I'm worried.

Bradley: What are you worried about?

California: What chance have we got when the shooting starts?

Hopalong: We'll have as good a chance as Quirt had.

California: Sure, and look what happened to him! A man that would get himself killed to prove a point has got a mule beat for stubbornness.

California Carlson played by Andy Clyde, Lin Bradley played by George Reeves, and Hopalong Cassidy played by William Boyd: Lesley Selander's *Bar 20* (United Artists, 1943).

3197

Capt: May I ask you a question, Corbett? When you are about to kill a man, what do you look at? I've asked this question of other men and do you know what they always say? They look at his hands. I don't. I look at his eyes. Because a moment before he moves his hands, his eyes betray him. And you can always read death in them. Yours …or his.

Captain Von Schulenberg played by Gerald

Herter, and Jonathan Corbett played by Lee Van Cleef: Sergio Sollima's *The Big Gundown* (Columbia, 1968).

3198

Corbett: If you don't kill me right now, it will be the last mistake you'll ever make.

Cuchilo: No, but to kill you is a big mistake. If I kill you, they will just send another man after me who is much smarter …much! Anyway, now you'll owe me something. I could have killed you, I didn't. Now, we have an account to settle, you and I.

Jonathan Corbett played by Lee Van Cleef and Cuchilo played by Tomas Milian: Sergio Sollima's *The Big Gundown* (Columbia, 1968).

3199

Jacob: Well, if you can shoot that far, a quarter of a mile straight along the edge of my nose is a mountain buck. Shoot it.

Michael: I don't kill to make a point, Father.

Jacob: Michael, there's two reasons to kill: survival and meat. We need meat!

Jacob McCandles played by John Wayne and Michael McCandles played by Chris Mitchum: George Sherman's *Big Jake* (NGP, 1971).

3200

Jagger: Well, you know my problem. What's yours?

Morgan: I should have killed a man the other day.

Jagger: Killed a man? What for?

Morgan: He needed it.

Joe Jagger played by Edmond O'Brien and Chad Morgan played by Alan Ladd: Gordon Douglas' *The Big Land* (Warner Bros., 1957)

3201

Billy: I'm awful sorry to hear about your daughter. How did it happen?

Eva: My Lisa is dead. The marks of a vampire are on her throat.

Billy: Vampire?

Billy the Kid played by Chuck Courtney and Eva Oster played by Hannie Landman: William Beaudine's *Billy the Kid vs. Dracula* (Circle/Embassy Pictures, 1966).

3202

Carbo: All this hardware. I ain't never been in a gunfight.

Jones: Killing a man don't prove you're a man.

Carbo played by Jan-Michael Vincent and Miss Jones played by Candice Bergen: Richard Brooks' *Bite the Bullet* (Columbia, 1975).

3203

Johnny: Something bothering you?

Willie: One minute he was alive and then

he was dead. I've never seen a man killed before.

Johnny: Everybody dies.

Willie: Don't you feel anything? He was a human being.

Johnny: His kind don't deserve the name. I'd feel worse about killing a helpless animal.

Johnny Liam played by Rod Cameron and Willie Duggan played by Dan Duryea: Spencer G. Bennet's *The Bounty Killer* (Embassy/Premiere, 1965).

3204

Youth: Well, you can say what you want. But he's done more to clean up the territory in six months than any ten men wearing stars.

Townsman: I'm not arguing that. What I'm saying is that he's done more killing than most of the men he's gunning down.

The Youth played by Peter Duryea and the Townsman played by Edmund Cobb: Spencer G. Bennet's *The Bounty Killer* (Embassy/Premiere, 1965).

3205

Cochise: You know what I am thinking? Maybe someday you will kill me or I will kill you. But we will not spit on each other.

Cochise played by Jeff Chandler: Delmer Daves' *Broken Arrow* (20th Century–Fox, 1950).

3206

Bronco Billy: Killin's too good for you!

Bronco Billy played by Clint Eastwood: Clint Eastwood's *Bronco Billy* (Warner Bros., 1980).

3207

Logan: We were friends once, Sam. It's not easy to shoot an old friend.

Sam: Friend? That's a long way back, Logan. And I got one big advantage over you. You won't kill me unless you have to. I won't hesitate one second about killing you.

Logan Keliher played by Audie Murphy and Sam Ward played by Darren McGavin: R.G. Springsteen's *Bullet for a Badman* (Universal, 1964).

3208

Sundance Kid: I didn't want to kill him! I just wanted to put a bullet …just wanted to put a hole in him!

The Sundance Kid played by William Karr: Richard Lester's *Butch and Sundance: The Early Days* (20th Century–Fox, 1979).

3209

Sundance: What was this guy like?

Butch: Who?

Sundance: Hanks.

Butch: Okay, really.

Sundance: Thanks a lot.

Bad guy Quirt Rankin (Francis McDonald), bushwhacked by his own gang, lies dying in the company of good guy Hopalong Cassidy (William Boyd) and saddlepals California (Andy Clyde) and Lin Bradley (George Reeves). *Bar 20* (United Artists, 1943).

Butch: What for?

Sundance: Oh, I wanted you to tell me he was a lousy bastard that didn't deserve to live. Did he have any family?

Butch: Just the five kids.

Sundance: Did he?

Butch: No! And will you quit torturing yourself! He didn't have any kids. He didn't even have a wife …just some old hag he lived with. Sundance, when you go get yourself in gunfights, you can't just pick orphans to do it with.

The Sundance Kid played by William Karr and Butch Cassidy played by Tom Berenger: Richard Lester's *Butch and Sundance: The Early Days* (20th Century–Fox, 1979).

3210

Sundance: You say they are hired permanent?

Etta: No, just until they kill you.

The Sundance Kid played by Robert Redford and Etta Place played by Katharine Ross: George Roy Hill's *Butch Cassidy and the Sundance Kid* (20th Century–Fox, 1969).

3211

Cain: So help me God, I'll kill 'em! I'll kill every last one of 'em!

Preacher: Vengeance is mine sayeth the Lord! He will seek out your enemies and smite them down.

Cain: Then the Lord will have to get there before I do.

Captain Justice Cain played by Scott Brady and Preacher Sims played by John Carradine: Kent Osborne's *Cain's Cutthroats* (a.k.a. *Cain's Way*; M.D.A. Associates/Fanfare, 1969).

3212

Preacher: The point of your revenge has passed. Now it's lust …lust for killing!

Preacher Sims played by John Carradine: Kent Osborne's *Cain's Cutthroats* (a.k.a. *Cain's Way*; M.D.A. Associates/Fanfare, 1969).

3213

Lynch: I'm going to keep getting up so you better get your gun. You're going to have to kill me to keep me down.

Steve: I don't want to kill you, I want to hire you!

Lynch played by Alan Hale, Jr. and Steve Patrick played by George Montgomery: Harmon Jones' *Canyon River* (Allied Artists, 1956).

3214

Jubal: I ought to woop you.

Elias: But you won't, Jubal, because you know I'd put a hole in your gut.

Jubal Hooker played by Simon Oakland and Elias Hooker played by Ralph Waite: Michael Winner's *Chato's Land* (United Artists, 1972).

3215

Gavin: Maybe he isn't a killing man.

Jubal: He's half Apache, isn't he? You mix dog and wolf, you wind up with a killing animal.

Gavin Malechie played by Roddy McMillan and Jubal Hooker played by Simon Oakland: Michael Winner's *Chato's Land* (United Artists, 1972).

3216

Matthew: I think he's come to kill me, Catherine. Hired by the railroad, I imagine.

Catherine: Why are you letting him stay [with us]?

Matthew: Because …when he's ready, it ain't gonna do no good to hide.

Matthew Sebanek played by Warren Oates and Catherine played by Jenny Agutter: Monte Hellman's *China 9, Liberty 37* (a.k.a. *Gunfire*; Titanus, 1978).

3217

Claytun: Who will they send to get me? You?

Matthew: No. Probably just some ordinary man whose morals wouldn't keep him from shooting you in the back.

Claytun Drumm played by Fabio Testi and Matthew Sebanek played by Warren Oates: Monte Hellman's *China 9, Liberty 37* (a.k.a. *Gunfire*; Titanus, 1978).

3218

Catherine: I killed my husband. He found out [about us] and started beating me. He was gonna come after you. I didn't mean to kill him.

Claytun: A man's life for a moment's weakness. It doesn't seem like a fair exchange.

Catherine played by Jenny Agutter and Claytun Drumm played by Fabio Testi: Monte Hellman's *China 9, Liberty 37* (a.k.a. *Gunfire*; Titanus, 1978).

3219

Sheriff: He's deader than a can of corn beef. You just had to kill him, huh?

Nodeen: A whole lot less trouble that way.

Sheriff Brady played by Bruce Cabot and Dan Nodeen played by Christopher George: Andrew McLaglen's *Chisum* (Warner Bros., 1970).

3220

Colonel: How many men have you killed?

Chuka: I stopped counting at sixteen.

Colonel: Were they fair fights? Mr. Chuka! I said, were they fair fights?

Chuka: Fifteen were fair.

Colonel: And what is fair to you, Mr. Chuka?

Chuka: They were facing me, they had a chance at me.

Colonel: And the sixteenth?

Chuka: I shot him in the back of the head. But like the doctor here, I can't prove that he stuck a knife in me and was stealing my horse.

Colonel Stuart Valois played by John Mills and

Chuka played by Rod Taylor: Gordon Douglas' *Chuka* (Paramount, 1967).

3221

Sabra: Did you have to kill him?

Yancy: No, I could have let him kill me.

Sabra Cravat played by Irene Dunne and Yancy Cravat played by Richard Dix: Wesley Ruggles' *Cimarron* (RKO, 1931).

3222

Doolin: I've got a rule of my own that might do you good to remember: there will be no killing unless it's forced on us.

Bill Doolin, alias The Cimarron Kid, played by Audie Murphy: Budd Boetticher's *The Cimarron Kid* (Universal, 1951).

3223

1st Townsman: Why, those men were trying to kill each other!

2nd Townsman: Yep.

1st Townsman: What's it all about? Do you know them?

2nd Townsman: Yep. Barney, that's the fella that just went off. He don't like Flint. That's the one he was shooting at. And Flint, he ain't got no use for Barney.

1st Townsman: Well, I figured they weren't exactly friends.

The Townsmen were played by Frank Ferguson and Percy Helton, and Flint played by Alan Dexter: Harmon Jones' *City of Bad Men* (20th Century–Fox, 1953).

3224

Stewpot: I got a feeling that the real fight is going to be outside of the ring.

Brett: Well, if the killing starts, you can forget about your fistfight. This town will empty like a cyclone hit it.

Stewpot: Will you be staying or leaving?

Brett: That depends upon which way the winds blowing.

Stewpot played by Harry Hines and Brett Stanton played by Dale Robertson: Harmon Jones' *City of Bad Men* (20th Century–Fox, 1953).

3225

Mitch: Hi, Curly. Kill anyone today?

Curly: The day ain't over yet.

Mitch Robbins played by Billy Crystal and Curly played by Jack Palance: Ron Underwood's *City Slickers* (Columbia, 1991).

3226

Beth: He's an animal. You should have seen him behind those guns today. I think he kills just to see men die.

Beth Donovan played by Ruth Roman: Edwin L. Marin's *Colt .45* (Warner Bros., 1950).

3227

Regret: How do you know you killed him?

Cutter: There wasn't time not to!

Paul Regret played by Stuart Whitman and Jake Cutter played by John Wayne: Michael Curtiz's *The Comancheros* (20th Century–Fox, 1961).

3228

Cutter: It would break my heart if I had to put a bullet in your back.

Regret: It would make me sad also.

Jake Cutter played by John Wayne and Paul Regret played by Stuart Whitman: Michael Curtiz's *The Comancheros* (20th Century–Fox, 1961).

3229

Johnny: Why didn't you draw on Kiowa?

Conagher: You mean, was I afraid? Staples didn't need killing. He needed to be taught a lesson.

Johnny: He'd had killed you if he had the chance.

Conagher: He might have. But I'll tell you something, kid. Any man who kills when he could do otherwise is crazy. Just plumb crazy. Some men take to a side of killing, Johnny. Just make sure when the killing time comes, you're standing on the right side.

Johnny McGivern played by Daniel Quinn, Kiowa Staples played by Paul Koslo, and Conn Conagher played by Sam Elliott: Reynaldo Villalobos' *Conagher* (Turner Pictures, 1991).

3230

Parnell: Hell, you're so weak you can hardly stand.

Conagher: If you want to see how weak I am, try for your gun.

Parnell: No, you've got just enough sand left in ya to kill me.

Smoke Parnell played by James Gammon and Conn Conagher played by Sam Elliott: Reynaldo Villalobos' *Conagher* (Turner Pictures, 1991).

3231

Carter: When you kill a man, he dies just as bad or just as stupid as the moment when you put the bullet in him. If you let him live, he's still got a chance to learn things.

Travis: Well, that's smart …provided he learns the right things.

Johnny Carter played by Ray Milland and Deputy Sheriff Lane Travis played by Macdonald Carey: John Farrow's *Copper Canyon* (Paramount, 1950).

3232

Custer: War isn't just killing you know. It's a contest. It's a man against a man. That's [Gatling gun] a machine! Personal courage wouldn't count. Honor, duty, loyalty …everything a soldier lives by would be wiped out. All you would have left is statistics. How many men would the machine murder today? One hundred? A thousand? Ten thousand? If this is the future, I don't want any part of it.

George Armstrong Custer played by Robert Shaw: Robert Siodmak and Irving Lerner's *Custer of the West* (Security Pictures/Cinerama, 1968).

3233

Sandy: That's papa! He's shooting at us!

Devlin: All I want to know is: do you take after papa or mama?

Sandy: Papa always wants to shoot things out. He has no more sense than you have. I do hope he doesn't kill us. He'd never get over it.

Devlin: Well, I'd feel kind of regretful about it myself.

Sandy played by Vera Ralston and John Devlin played by John Wayne: Joseph Kane's *Dakota* (Republic, 1945).

3234

Clarke: You once killed a man over a bottle of whiskey …winner take all. How many Indians would you kill for a canteen of water?

Banner: That's not the way I look at it. The point is, I don't want 'em to kill the only real friend I got …me!

Amy Clarke played by Linda Darnell and John Banner played by Dale Robertson: Lewis R. Foster's *Dakota Incident* (Republic, 1956).

3235

Blakely: How could you hate a man so much?

Banner: I didn't hate him. He was my brother!

Senator Blakely played by Ward Bond and John Banner played by Dale Robertson: Lewis R. Foster's *Dakota Incident* (Republic, 1956).

3236

Red Stick: Why you no kill me?

Crockett: Maybe because of another law. We have trouble living up to it. But it ain't bad for red man or white man alike: thou shall not kill.

Chief Red Stick played by Pat Hogan and Davy Crockett played by Fess Parker: Norman Foster's *Davy Crockett, King of the Wild Frontier* (Buena Vista, 1955).

3237

Talby: Fifth lesson: if you wound a man, you better kill him. Because sooner or later he's gonna kill you.

Frank Talby played by Lee Van Cleef: Tonino Valerii's *Day of Anger* (a.k.a. *Days of Wrath*; Sancrosiap/Corona Film/KG Divina Film/National General, 1967).

3238

Turner: I hope he's dead, the bastard!

Talby: You're going to hell, Turner. Find out down there!

Turner played by Ennio Balbo and Frank Talby played by Lee Van Cleef: Tonino Valerii's *Day of Anger* (a.k.a. *Days of Wrath*; Sancrosiap/Corona Film/KG Divina Film/National General, 1967).

3239

Warfield: You ever kill a man?

Forbes: Why?

Warfield: Well now, suppose before this thing is over you have to kill a few Indians?

Forbes: I'll manage. It's not the same thing as men gunning each other down in the middle of the street.

Lorn Warfield played by Glenn Ford and Owen Forbes played by Arthur Kennedy: Jerry Thorpe's *Day of the Evil Gun* (MGM, 1968).

3240

Vic: I don't hold for killin'.

Starrett: You don't have to …as long as you got somebody to do it for you.

Vic played by Donald Elson and Blaise Starrett played by Robert Ryan: Andre De Toth's *Day of the Outlaw* (United Artists, 1959).

3241

Big George: Good God, I'm hit! Lord have mercy! Burns like hellfire! You son-of-a-bitch! I'm gonna have to kill somebody now!

Big George Drakoulious played by Billy Bob Thornton: Jim Jarmusch's *Dead Man* (Miramax Films, 1996).

3242

Beesly: Sir, you look like a man of means. Maybe you'd like to purchase one of these rare prints. The name's Beesly …professional photographer and visual historian …specializing in the dead.

Bodeen: Dead what?

Beesly: Whatever chooses to be, sir …made eternal by the science of photochemistry. I particularly favor the criminal element as there appears to be a cultural victory in their death and a social interest in their lives. Sir, you appear to be somewhat of that caliber yourself. And if you think you might be getting killed soon, I'd sure be obliged to know.

Bodeen: Who's the latest?

Beesly: Oh, a man named Luck who appears just plumb out of it.

Beesly played by John M. Jackson, Bodeen/Tom Hatcher played by Keith Coulouris, and Luck Hatcher played by Michael Ironside: Alan J. Levi's *Dead Man's Revenge* (MCA/Universal Home Video, 1994).

3243

Bigfoot: Life's a peculiar business, Captain. Old Shad had been shot at by some of the best marksmen in the west. Now there he lays …killed by a blind man.

Bigfoot Wallace played by Keith Carradine, Captain Salazar played by Edward James Olmos, and Shadrach played by Harry Dean Stanton: Yves Simoneau's *Dead Man's Walk* (Cabin Fever Entertainment, 1996).

3244

Yellowleg: You don't know me well enough to hate me that much. Hating is a subject I know a little something about. You got to be careful it don't bite you back. I know somebody who spent five years looking for a man he hated. Hating and wanting revenge was all that kept him alive. He spent all those years tracking that other man down. And when he caught up with him, it was the worst day in his life. He'd get his revenge all right, but then he'd lose the one thing he had to live for.

Yellowleg played by Brian Keith: Sam Peckinpah's *The Deadly Companions* (Paramount, 1961).

3245

Johnny: I'm not getting myself killed for nothing!

Johnny Ears played by Franco Nero: Paolo Cavara's *Deaf Smith & Johnny Ears* (MGM, 1972).

3246

Dan: It's awful seeing a man kill himself. One minute he's there …alive …then he's dead. Blood and the smell of powdersmoke. And it's all over and done with. It's awful!

Dan Joslin played by Michael McGreevey: Allen Smithee's *Death of a Gunfighter* (Universal, 1969).

3247

Bill: Before anybody kills me, they got to get my okay. And I don't think I'll give it to 'em.

Bill played by John Phillip Law: Giulio Petroni's *Death Rides a Horse* (United Artists, 1967).

3248

Sam: Bart, I think you done a fool thing. After all that searching around, it seems like you would have been satisfied to just kill him on sight.

Bart: Even a rattler gives a warning.

Sam played by Noah Beery, Jr., and Bart Allison played by Randolph Scott: Budd Boetticher's *Decision at Sundown* (Columbia, 1957).

3249

Ferguson: He seemed to come straight out of the glare of the sun. We never knew what hit us.

General: Did he say anything?

Ferguson: He said it was a lot easier to kill men than it was to capture them. Next time, he'll stop us the easy way.

Lieutenant Ferguson played by Brandon De Wilde and General Miles played by John Huston: Burt Kennedy's *The Deserter* (a.k.a. *Ride to Glory*; Paramount, 1971).

3250

Sam: I should have killed him. A man like me has no business with silly scruples.

Sam Garrett played by Wayne Morris: Thomas Carr's *The Desperado* (Allied Artists, 1954).

3251

McCall: Jim, did you ever kill anybody?

Buckner: I've been with posses that shot at men. Some of 'em fell. I figure my bullets was in there somewhere.

Duell McCall played by Alex McArthur and Jim Buckner played by Dwier Brown: Richard Compton's *Desperado: Avalanche at Devil's Ridge* (TVW, 1988).

3252

Lester: Killin' me don't make sense.

Nitro: It never does to the fella that's getting killed.

Jack Lester played by Bernard Nedell and Nitro Rankin played by Guinn "Big Boy" Williams: Charles Vidor's *The Desperadoes* (Columbia, 1943).

3253

Tex: Harris tried to murder me, but he got the bullet with the period on it.

Tex Martin played by Tex Ritter and Harris played by Bub Osborne: Lambert Hillyer's *The Devil's Trail* (Columbia, 1942).

3254

Dooley: You sure are pretty good at killing.

Cowboy: It's not a talent I wished for.

Dooley played by William Forsythe and the Cowboy played by Emilio Estevez: Gene Quintano's *Dollar for the Dead* (TVW, 1998).

3255

Dooley: Why are them regulators trying to kill ya?

Cowboy: Religious differences.

Dooley played by William Forsythe and the Cowboy played by Emilio Estevez: Gene Quintano's *Dollar for the Dead* (TVW, 1998).

3256

Friend: Well, dead is dead.

Reager: I don't want him dead. I want to kill him!

Reager's Friend played by Bill Pickel and Reager played by Howie Long: Gene Quintano's *Dollar for the Dead* (TVW, 1998).

3257

Duchess: You just shot a man, Malloy!

Malloy: No shit!

Duchess: How many men have you shot dead in your life?

Malloy: Including that one?

Duchess: Yea.

Malloy: One.

Amanda Quaid, alias "Duchess," played by Goldie Hawn and Charlie Malloy played by George Segal: Melvin Frank's *The Duchess and the Dirtwater Fox* (20th Century–Fox, 1976).

3258

Billy Ray: I don't condone killin', but this paztosso probably deserved it. If he traveled with El Diablo, he had some severe character flaws I was sure.

Billy Ray Smith played by Anthony Edwards: Peter Markle's *El Diablo* (HBO Pictures, 1990).

3259

Milt: You killed Charlie because he killed your friend, right?

Mississippi: That's right.

Milt: Well, it happens that Charlie was a good friend of mine.

Milt played by Robert Donner and Alan Bourdillon Traherne ("Mississippi") played by James Caan: Howard Hawks' *El Dorado* (Paramount, 1967).

3260

Doctor: Roper, there's two big businesses in the world. One of them is to keep people alive. The other one seems to be yours.

Roper: It's not a world I made.

Doctor Miller played by Forrest Lewis and Captain Roper played by William Holden: John Sturges' *Escape from Fort Bravo* (MGM, 1953).

3261

Cabot: You must have missed.

Campbell: No, we just killed the same one twice!

Cabot Young played by William Campbell and Campbell played by William Demarest: John Sturges' *Escape from Fort Bravo* (MGM, 1953).

3262

Roper: Everything nice and peaceful?

Chavez: Beautiful, Captain. Beautiful!

Roper: It's crazy, Chavez, all this beautiful country and in one canyon a lot of men trying to kill each other.

Chavez: Very crazy.

Roper: It'll make sense someday.

Chavez: Only to the living, Captain.

Captain Roper played by William Holden and Chavez played by Alex Montoya: John Sturges' *Escape from Fort Bravo* (MGM, 1953).

3263

Reed: Riley, if I have to kill you, I don't much care whether it's tomorrow or now. You can save us both time by starting the trouble now.

Reed Williams played by Alan Baxter and Sheriff Mark Riley played by Lin McCarthy: Paul Wendkos' *Face of a Fugitive* (Columbia, 1959).

3264

Larkin: A lesson I learned a long time ago: a man worth shootin' is a man worth killin'.

Bob Larkin played by Henry Fonda: Vincent McEveety's *Firecreek* (Warner Bros.-Seven Arts, 1968).

3265

Baxter: I saw the whole thing! You killed all four of them! You'll pay all right! You'll be strung up!

Stranger: Who are you?

Volunteers at the Alamo survey Santa Anna's Mexican forces. From right to left: George Russell (Buddy Ebsen), Davy Crockett (Fess Parker), Bustedluck (Nick Cravat), and Thimblerig (Hans Conried) in *Davy Crockett, King of the Wild Frontier* (Buena Vista, 1955).

Baxter: Don't fire a shot. I'm John Baxter …Sheriff.

Stranger: Yea, well, if you're the sheriff you better get these men under ground.

John Baxter played by Wolfgang Lukschy and the Stranger (Joe) played by Clint Eastwood: Sergio Leone's *A Fistful of Dollars* (United Artists, 1964; U.S. 1967).

3266

Nick: Just what were you doing in that street this afternoon? You're not here to stop killing, you're here to do some!

Rudd: Let's just say I'm particular about who gets killed.

Nick Evers played by Roddy McDowall and Reverend Jonathan Rudd played by Robert Mitchum: Henry Hathaway's *Five Card Stud* (Paramount, 1968).

3267

Johnny: Don't be in such a rush to get killed. It might come to you soon enough.

Johnny Tallon played by Dane Clark: John Rawlins' *Fort Defiance* (United Artists, 1951).

3268

Charlie: There never was much law here before the war. Even less now. Men kept coming through, don't know where they're going or no notion of what they're going to do. They got so used to killin' that killin' is the only thing they're sure of.

Uncle Charlie Tallon played by George Cleveland: John Rawlins' *Fort Defiance* (United Artists, 1951).

3269

Johnny: A man that gets killed doing his duty ain't any more alive that a man who just gets plain killed.

Johnny Tallon played by Dane Clark: John Rawlins' *Fort Defiance* (United Artists, 1951).

3270

Griff: In my heart I've always asked forgiveness before I killed. Just like an Indian asking forgiveness from an animal before the slaughter. You can't ask after you kill. It's too late then.

Griff Bonnell played by Barry Sullivan: Samuel Fuller's *Forty Guns* (20th Century–Fox, 1957).

3271

Jesse: He needs to die, Frank.

Frank: I can't argue that.

Jesse James played by Rob Lowe and Frank James played by Bill Paxton: Robert Boris' *Frank & Jesse* (Vidmark Entertainment, 1995).

3272

Cole: I know I can kill you. I'm just not convinced you'd stay dead.

Cole Younger played by Randy Travis: Robert Boris' *Frank & Jesse* (Vidmark Entertainment, 1995).

3273

Frank: Goddamn it, Jesse, I said no bloodshed! You gave me your word!

Jesse: He was provoking me.

Frank James played by Bill Paxton and Jesse James

played by Rob Lowe ian Robert Boris' *Frank & Jesse* (Vidmark Entertainment, 1995).

3274

Cole: Do it, Jesse. Give him lead poisoning!

Cole Younger played by Randy Travis and Jesse James played by Rob Lowe: Robert Boris' *Frank & Jesse* (Vidmark Entertainment, 1995).

3275

Sarah: John?
Doc: Yes, Sarah?
Sarah: Isn't it more thrilling to give life than to take it?

Sarah Allen played by Nancy Kelly and John "Doc" Holliday played by Cesar Romero: Allan Dwan's *Frontier Marshal* (20th Century–Fox, 1939).

3276

Luke: Dead men don't recognize anybody.

The outlaw, Luke Johnson, was uncredited: Joseph Kane's *Frontier Pony Express* (Republic, 1939).

3277

General: I think it's rotten luck the way he got himself killed.
Brady: Oh, it was rotten luck all right.

General Nelson Miles played by George Kennedy and Brady Hawkes played by Kenny Rogers: Dick Lowry's *The Gambler, Part III — The Legend Continues* (TVW, 1987).

3278

Kirby: Senator, I have found out about [your dog] Bonaparte.
Sernator: Bonaparte? Where is he?
Kirby: He's dead.
Senator: Dead?
Kirby: He was killed by some of your railroad construction workers …foreigners.
Senator: Why? Why? Did he do something? Did he bite someone?
Kirby: They ate him.
Senator: Ate my dog?
Kirby: You see, Senator, he's a delicacy …ah, where they're from. I'm sure he was well received.

The Senator's aide, Kirby, was uncredited. Senator Henry Colton played by Charles Dunning: Dick Lowry's *The Gambler, Part III — The Legend Continues* (TVW, 1987).

3279

Uncle Bawley: Bick, you should have shot that fellow a long time ago. Now he's too rich to kill!

Uncle Bawley Benedict played by Chill Wills and Jordan "Bick" Benedict played by Rock Hudson: George Stevens *Giant* (Warner Bros., 1956).

3280

Grundy: If you go getting killed, don't come running back here.

Grundy played by Douglas V. Fowley: Burt Kennedy's *The Good Guys and the Bad Guys* (Warner Bros., 1969).

3281

Johnson: Son, I got one rule in life. I only shoot people that need killin'. If you challenge me one more time, you're gonna fall right into that category.

Alan Johnson played by Christopher Reeve: Steven H. Stern's *Good Men and Bad* (TV miniseries, Cabin Fever Entertainment, 1995).

3282

Tommy: You'll be back, won't you Uncle Hewey? You won't let some old bronc kill ya?
Hewey: Tommy, I ain't never been killed in my life.

Tommy Calloway played by Blayne Weaver and Hewey Calloway played by Tommy Lee Jones: Tommy Lee Jones' *The Good Old Boys* (Turner Pictures, 1995).

3283

Billy: I killed people who needed killin'.

Billy the Kid played by Val Kilmer: William A. Graham's *Gore Vidal's Billy the Kid* (Turner Pictures, 1989).

3284

Bill: You're not worth killin'. But if you come at me again, I'll put a window through your head, so help me!

Bill Miner played by Richard Farnsworth: Phillip Borsos' *The Grey Fox* (United Artists, 1982).

3285

Warren: I've seen enough and I've had enough of killing. I'm sick of violence and force. I learned one thing: bullets are very democratic. They kill good men as well as bad.

Ben Warren played by Rock Hudson: Raoul Walsh's *Gun Fury* (Columbia, 1953).

3286

Estella: Sooner or later I'll kill you!
Slayton: Let's make it later!

Estella Morales played by Roberta Haynes and Frank Slayton played by Phil Carey: Raoul Walsh's *Gun Fury* (Columbia, 1953).

3287

Warren: Will killin' him make any difference? Will you feel any better when he's dead?
Estella: Yes.

Ben Warren played by Rock Hudson and Estella Morales played by Roberta Haynes: Raoul Walsh's *Gun Fury* (Columbia, 1953).

3288

Gifford: You know, it's a funny thing about nerve. It takes a special kind to kill a man.

Bob Gifford played by Audie Murphy: Frank McDonald's *Gunfight at Comanche Creek* (Allied Artists, 1964).

3289

Billy: What's it like to kill a man?

Masterson: Well, Billy, I'll tell ya. It's not so good. First, you're standing there facing him. And you're scared. And you want to run and hide, hide anywhere. But you don't because you can't. And you can't because you know if you make even the slightest move, he's bound to draw. So you watch his eyes, praying to God Almighty he'll back down or say something, anything, to give you a chance to get out of it. Then you try and make yourself say something. But before you can, it's too late. He's not there anymore. He's on the floor. The cuspidor spills and it's running all over him. People are screaming and they run in and want to buy you a drink and tell ya he drew first. And then you break away and run outside somewhere where no one will see you, and vomit.

Billy played by Wright King and Bat Masterson played by Joel McCrea: Joseph M. Newman's *The Gunfight at Dodge City* (United Artists, 1959).

3290

Bat: If you had come in here five minutes ago, Regan, I would have killed you! Now, I'm only going to half kill you!

Bat Masterson played by Joel McCrea and Jim Regan played by Don Haggerty: Joseph M. Newman's *The Gunfight at Dodge City* (United Artists, 1959).

3291

Ringo: That's a fine life, ain't it? Just trying to stay alive. Not really living, not enjoying anything, not going anywhere. Just trying to keep from getting killed.

Jimmy Ringo played by Gregory Peck: Henry King's *The Gunfighter* (20th Century–Fox, 1950).

3292

Molly: He was found in the alley shot through the back of the head.
Ringo: Well, didn't he leave you anything?
Molly: Yea. A horse and a saddle, two guns, and $15.00.

Molly played by Jean Parker and Jimmy Ringo played by Gregory Peck: Henry King's *The Gunfighter* (20th Century–Fox, 1950).

3293

Deke: Everett, you should have killed me. You're a fool with a soft heart and it's gonna cost ya. I'll live to see the three of you hang.

Deke Turner played by George Kennedy and Cole Everett played by Art Hindle: Clay Borris' *The Gunfighters* (TVW, 1989).

3294

Ab: Come on, Bull, let's kill 'em.
Bull: Nah, let's enjoy 'em for awhile longer. We ain't had no visitors since those settlers showed up.

Ab played by Kelly Thordsen and Bull played by

Edgar Buchanan: Earl Bellamy's *Gunpoint* (Universal, 1966).

3295

Linc: Let's don't get ourselves killed before we're ready.

Linc Murdock played by Charles Bronson: Boris Sagal's *Guns of Diablo* (MGM, 1964).

3296

Wyatt: You're gonna murder me!
Morgan: No, merely eliminate ya.

Matt Wyatt played by Tony Barrett and Morgan played by Steve Brodie: Lesley Selander's *Guns of Hate* (RKO, 1948).

3297

Sheriff: Mr. Hadley, I want to talk to you.
Hadley: It's a little late for that.
Sheriff: It's never too late to stop people from killin' each other.

Sheriff Taylor played by Regis Toomey and Jim Hadley played by Alan Ladd: Robert D. Webb's *Guns of the Timberland* (Warner Bros., 1960).

3298

John: Eighteen buckshot in each two [chambers], fellas. It makes for an ugly and oozy cadaver.

John Parsley played by James Brolin: Jerry Jameson's *Gunsmoke: The Long Ride* (TVW, 1993).

3299

Charlie Wolf: You understand Apache?
Craig: You don't have to know the whole language to know when a man wants to kill you.

Charlie Wolf played by Jack Buetel and Dan Craig played by Robert Young: Stuart Gilmore's *The Half-Breed* (RKO, 1952).

3300

Carrie: You know how I feel about executions. There's some good in every man. And killing him kills that too.

Carrie Gault played by Sharon Acker: Michael Caffey's *The Hanged Man* (TVW, 1974).

3301

Matt: What's happened to you? Is it that easy to kill a man?
Rolph: Well, isn't it? What else have we been doing for the last five years?

Matt Stewart played by Randolph Scott and Rolph Bainter played by Lee Marvin: Roy Huggins' *Hangman's Knot* (Columbia, 1952).

3302

Sheriff: There you are. One hundred dollars even [bounty money]. Damn it, woman, you didn't have to cut him in half, did you?
Hannie: Both halves match, don't they?

The Sheriff was uncredited and Hannie Caulder played by Raquel Welch: Burt Kennedy's *Hannie Caulder* (Paramount, 1971).

3303

Hannie: You're a bounty hunter?
Thomas: I am.
Hannie: You kill men for money?
Thomas: You know a better reason?

Hannie Caulder played by Raquel Welch and Thomas Luther Price played by Robert Culp: Burt Kennedy's *Hannie Caulder* (Paramount, 1971).

3304

Rufus: Did I get him?
Emmett: There ain't no part of 'em you didn't!

Rufus Clemens played by Strother Martin and Emmett Clemens played by Ernest Borgnine: Burt Kennedy's *Hannie Caulder* (Paramount, 1971).

3305

Kanning: I don't like to shoot anybody I don't have to …especially so early in the morning.

Kanning played by Matt McCoy: Jim Wynorski's *Hard Bounty* (Triboro Entertainment, 1995).

3306

Cooper: I thought I told you, no killin'.
Moxon: You told me, no shootin'.

Cooper played by John Ireland and Moxon played by Mirko Ellis: Domenico Paolella's *Hate for Hate* (MGM, 1967).

3307

Killian: And the rest of ya! There'll be no killin' around this church …unless I do the killin'! Amen.

Jim Killian played by Glenn Ford: Lee H. Katzin's *Heaven with a Gun* (MGM, 1969).

3308

Beck: Mr. Killian, I hired good boys. They're not afraid to fight, nor am I. I'd sure hate to lose two, maybe three, trying to cut you down. Considering that, I'd rather pay ya than kill ya.
Killian: Why, Mr. Beck, I consider that the act of a generous man.

Asa Beck played by John Anderson and Jim Killian played by Glenn Ford: Lee H. Katzin's *Heaven with a Gun* (MGM, 1969).

3309

Sheriff: Well, what's it about is …Billy Borders.
Stranger: Don't know the man.
Sheriff: Well, you missed your chance cause you shot him yesterday. Him and Ike Sharp and Fred Morris. And, and you know, those are just the names in case you're interested.
Stranger: Well, I'm not really interested, Sheriff.
Sheriff: Well, I can't say I blame ya. You know, Billy, he wasn't a loved man, you know. And he didn't have much personality. What he did have was all bad …just bad.

Stranger: What you're trying to say is there's no charge [for killing them], right?
Sheriff: Well, forgive and forget, you know. That's our motto.

Sheriff Sam Shaw played by Walter Barnes and The Stranger played by Clint Eastwood: Clint Eastwood's *High Plains Drifter* (Universal, 1973).

3310

Russell: If he tries to leave with nothing, shoot him once. If he takes the money, shoot him twice. And if he picks up the water, you empty your gun!

John Russell played by Paul Newman: Martin Ritt's *Hombre* (20th Century–Fox, 1967).

3311

Grimes: Mister, you got a lot of hard bark on you …walking down here like this. Now I owe you. You put two holes in me.
Russell: It's usually enough for most of 'em.

Grimes played by Richard Boone and John Russell played by Paul Newman: Martin Ritt's *Hombre* (20th Century–Fox, 1967).

3312

Homer: It don't take long to kill things. Not like it does to grow.

Homer Bannon played by Melvyn Douglas: Martin Ritt's *Hud* (Paramount, 1963).

3313

Dawson: Thunderation, I've killed men before.
Lacey: Yea, but shooting out in the open has something square and fair about it. Killing with poison is sneaky and low down.

Britt Dawson played by Albert Dekker and Lacey Miller played by Binnie Barnes: William McGann's *In Old California* (Republic, 1942).

3314

Darcy: You humiliated him. Someday he'll have to kill you, but not until I say so.
Blecker: Then I still have a little time?
Darcy: That's all any of us have, friend …a little time. Most of it lonely. It goes so fast. A man sings, loves, fights …and then he's nothing. Dust. A leaf that falls and is gone.

Luke Darcy played by Jeff Chandler and Cam Blecker played by Fess Parker: Melvin Frank's *The Jayhawkers* (Paramount, 1959).

3315

Vienna: I'm offering you an opportunity to get rich.
Andrews: An opportunity to get killed would be more accurate.

Vienna played by Joan Crawford and Mr. Andrews played by Rhys Williams: Nicholas Ray's *Johnny Guitar* (Republic, 1954).

3316

Vienna: I hired you for protection. I won't have any killing.

Johnny: What do you think they're coming to do to you? Make up your mind. To stay is to fight.

Vienna: I'm going to stay. I'm going to fight. But I won't kill.

Johnny: To fight you got to kill. I don't know any other way.

Vienna played by Joan Crawford and Johnny Guitar played by Sterling Hayden: Nicholas Ray's *Johnny Guitar* (Republic, 1954).

3317

Kate: Kill 'em and bury 'em …all in a day's work, huh?

Kate Clarke played by Marguerite Chapman: Ray Enright's *Kansas Raiders* (Universal, 1950).

3318

Tex: I'm superstitious. I hate to see anybody shot in the back.

Tex Rawlings played by Tex Ritter: Lambert Hillyer's *King of Dodge City* (Columbia, 1941).

3319

Frog: Roy, you're dead. And as long as you stay dead, you ain't gonna get killed.

Frog Millhouse played by Smiley Burnette and Roy Rogers played himself: Joseph Kane's *King of the Cowboys* (Republic, 1943).

3320

Lorena: If killin' is the only reason you can think of to live, then you might as well die.

Lorena Parker played by Sissy Spacek: Joseph Sargent's *Larry McMurtry's Streets of Laredo* (Cabin Fever Entertainment, 1995).

3321

Brookshire: He's just playing with us now. He can kill us any time he wants to, and he knows it. I have spent nothing but cold nights since I got to Texas. And I'll be damned if I'm going to spend another cold night squatting on my heels just to get shot in the morning. He can just shoot me now and spare me the shivering!

Ned Brookshire played by Charles Martin Smith: Joseph Sargent's *Larry McMurtry's Streets of Laredo* (Cabin Fever Entertainment, 1995).

3322

Hardin: Call is economical. He don't kill just anybody who needs killin'.

John Wesley Hardin played by Randy Quaid and Captain Woodrow F. Call played by James Garner: Joseph Sargent's *Larry McMurtry's Streets of Laredo* (Cabin Fever Entertainment, 1995).

3323

Frank: Revenge has lost its taste. And there's no bottom to it.

Frank James played by Johnny Cash: William A.

Graham's *The Last Days of Frank and Jesse James* (TVW, 1986).

3324

Jed: You know, Colonel, there's something eating you. I've seen it before, mostly in Indians, when they get so full of hate they can't wait to kill. I've done some killin' myself, but I never went out looking for it.

Jed Cooper played by Victor Mature and Colonel Frank Marston played by Robert Preston: Anthony Mann's *The Last Frontier* (Columbia, 1955).

3325

Sandy: I've changed my mind, mister. You want to go slaughtering buffalo, you go ahead. Me? I want to get the stink off of my insides. I'm fed up on killin'. Seems like all I've ever known since I was a kid is killin' one way or another.

Gilson: Well, there ain't nothing wrong with that. Killin' is natural.

Sandy: Not to me it ain't.

Gilson: Sure it is, the war taught me that. The more you kill, the better man you was. Killin', fightin', war, that's the natural state of things. Peace time is only the resting time in between, so you can go on fightin'.

Sandy McKenzie played by Stewart Granger and Charles Gilson played by Robert Taylor: Richard Brooks' *The Last Hunt* (MGM, 1956).

3326

Gilson: Killin' is like the only real proof you're alive.

Charles Gilson played by Robert Taylor: Richard Brooks' *The Last Hunt* (MGM, 1956).

3327

Ellison: Did you see the draw?

Sheriff: From my office.

Ellison: Fair fight?

Sheriff: Some call it murder. The law calls it a killing. Says there is a difference.

Brad Ellison played by Jock Mahoney and the Sheriff played by Richard Cutting: George Sherman's *The Last of the Fast Guns* (Universal, 1958).

3328

Hawkeye: Scalps to the Indians, Major, are like your medals. They're gotten by the same means …killing.

Hawkeye played by Randolph Scott and Major Duncan played by Henry Wilcoxon: George B. Seitz's *The Last of the Mohicans* (United Artists, 1936).

3329

Morgan: I ought to kill ya for that!

Belden: Why don't ya? Why don't ya kill me?

Morgan: You saved my life. I've paid you back. But from here on in, they're all free shots.

U.S. Marshal Matt Morgan played by Kirk Dou-

glas and Craig Belden played by Anthony Quinn: John Sturges' *Last Train from Gun Hill* (Paramount, 1959).

3330

Todd: How many men have you killed?

General: You mean on the battlefield?

Todd: Any place. How many?

General: Why do you ask?

Todd: If a man hangs me, I want to know if he knows the meaning of hanging.

General: There's a difference between war and murder, a great difference.

Todd: Tell me the difference.

General: In war, you kill the enemies of your people.

Todd: Why, that's what I did. Wasn't them people you killed in the Civil War your people?

General: My people? The Confederates?

Todd: They was American, wasn't they? And they're Americans now. And they're your friends now that it's over, ain't they?

General: Well, of course.

Todd: Then you killed your friends. You see, with my people it's different. We only kill our enemies.

General: Your people?

Todd: The Comanches.

General: But you're a white man!

Todd: I was.

"Comanche" Todd played by Richard Widmark and General Howard played by Carl Benton Reid: Delmer Daves' *The Last Wagon* (20th Century–Fox, 1956).

3331

Clint: Wexler, you go ahead and kill anybody you want to. It's a free country. But if you do it with hate in your heart, you'll end up with nothing but an upset stomach.

Clint Hollister played by Richard Widmark and Wexler played by DeForest Kelley: John Sturges' *The Law and Jake Wade* (MGM, 1958).

3332

Marv: I tell you, it was murder! Murder in the first degree! Habeas corpus. That means he's real dead!

Marv the Bartender played by Richard Wessel: Raoul Walsh's *The Lawless Breed* (Universal, 1952),

3333

Bronson: What do you want to do? Ride into Sabbath and gun him down? Those days have passed. Times have changed. There are other ways. You buy him. And if he doesn't sell, you buy the man above him. Those killing days were for younger men.

Vincent Bronson played by Lee J. Cobb: Michael Winner's *Lawman* (United Artists, 1971).

A very unusual but superior western with gambling saloon owner Vienna (Joan Crawford) and Johnny Guitar (Sterling Hayden): Nicholas Ray's *Johnny Guitar* (Republic, 1954).

3334

Maddox: It's always the same. If you post a man, he has to come into town to prove he's a man. Or you kill a man, and he's got a friend or kin, and he just has to come against you. And for no reason. No reason that makes any sense. And it don't make a damn to the man already in the ground. Nobody wins.

Marshal Jared Maddox played by Burt Lancaster: Michael Winner's *Lawman* (United Artists, 1971).

3335

Crowe: You killed Harvey Stenbaugh!
Maddox: You got a bad memory, son. Stenbaugh had it in mind to kill me.
Crowe: He didn't have a chance. You don't even care, do you, Maddox?
Maddox: No. No, I don't care. You say he didn't have a chance. He went for his gun first. When he does that, he uses up all his chances.

Crowe Wheelwright played by Richard Jordan and Marshal Jared Maddox played by Burt Lancaster: Michael Winner's *Lawman* (United Artists, 1971).

3336

Crowe: Ryan thinks you're pretty good. He says you could kill me anytime you wanted to. I see it different. I think I'm faster.
Maddox: Are you asking me who's faster or whether I could kill you if I chose to? Because if it's the second, the answer is yes.
Crowe: You're pretty damn sure.
Maddox: I'm pretty damn sure. You think it's a game, don't you? A contest between gentlemen. You ever kill a man, Crowe? You're a cowman. You carry a side gun for protection …snakes. You learn to use it sometimes fairly well. Sometimes you become really good. But you're still a cowman. I'm lawman. You know what a lawman is, Crowe? He's a killer of men. That's what the job calls for. There are nicer ways to put it, but it reads the same. That's the difference between us. And it's all the difference I need.

Crowe Wheelwright played by Richard Jordan and Marshal Jared Maddox played by Burt Lancaster: Michael Winner's *Lawman* (United Artists, 1971).

3337

Maddox: You can't break the rules, Laura.
Laura: Oh, the rules! I forgot about the rules. You think they change the killing? Because you never draw on a man first, you think that really matters? Do you know what they call you, Jared? The widow-maker!

Marshal Jared Maddox played by Burt Lancaster and Laura Shelby played by Sheree North: Michael Winner's *Lawman* (United Artists, 1971).

3338

Rev: The first time I saw Roy Bean, he was set on killing me. He thought I was the devil come to take him. It was an understandable thought considering all the carnage that he had so recently brought forth.

Narration by the Reverend LaSalle who played by Anthony Perkins: John Huston's *The Life and Times of Judge Roy Bean* (NGP, 1972).

3339

Little Big Man: I don't understand it, Grandfather. Why would they [white men] kill women and children?
Old Lodge Skins: Because they are strange. They do not seem to know where the center of the earth is.

Little Big Man/Jack Crabb played by Dustin Hoffman and Old Lodge Skins played by Chief Dan George: Arthur Penn's *Little Big Man* (NGP, 1971).

3340

Frances: Why did they kill him?
Padre: Same as before …no apparent reason.

Frances Henderson played by Noreen Nash and Padre Vincente Esteban played by Ralph Moody: Leslie Selander's *The Lone Ranger and the Lost City of Gold* (United Artists, 1958).

3341

Ada: Why did Jacob leave Red Bluff?
Ben: He killed a sheriff. You kill a badge man in this country, they hang you quick.

Ada Marshall played by Elaine Aiken, Ben Ryerson played by Robert Middleton, and Jacob Wade played by Jack Palance: Henry Levin's *The Lonely Man* (Paramount, 1957).

3342

Rosie: Don't kill me, please! You promised on your mother's grave.
Hard Case: So I did. But you'll be sorry to hear that the old bitch is still alive and kicking!

Rosie Velez played by Divine and Hard Case Williams played by Geoffrey Lewis: Paul Bartel's *Lust in the Dust* (Fox Run/New World, 1985).

3343

Forbes: There sure has been a lot of killing since I met you.

Noah Forbes played by Michael Callan: George McGowan's *The Magnificent Seven Ride* (United Artists, 1972).

3344

Dundee: Don't get youself killed. That would inconvenience me.

Major Amos Charles Dundee played by Charlton Heston: Sam Peckinpah's *Major Dundee* (Columbia, 1965).

3345

Lockhart: I came a thousand miles to kill you.
Hansbro: You're crazy! I never did anything to you!

3345 (continued)

Lockhart: I'm not going to rush it. I've waited a long time for this.
Hansbro: What are you talking about? I've never laid eyes on you until that day at the salt flats. You got no cause to shoot me.
Lockhart: Shooting is too good for you.
Hansbro: What did I do to you? Tell me, what did I do? I've got a right to know!
Lockhart: Yea, I guess a man's got the right to know what he's going to die for.

Will Lockhart played by James Stewart and Vic Hansbro played by Arthur Kennedy: Anthony Mann's *The Man from Laramie* (Columbia, 1955).

3346

Grobart: I told you I didn't want anybody killed back there!
Dawes: Yea, well, I forgot.

Jay Grobart played by Burt Reynolds and Dawes played by Jack Warden: Richard C. Sarafian's *The Man Who Loved Cat Dancing* (MGM, 1973).

3347

Stoddard: What's the matter? Is everybody in this country kill crazy?

Ransom Stoddard played by James Stewart: John Ford's *The Man Who Shot Liberty Valance* (Paramount, 1962).

3348

Stoddard: Isn't it enough to kill a man without trying to build a life on it?

Ransom Stoddard played by James Stewart: John Ford's *The Man Who Shot Liberty Valance* (Paramount, 1962).

3349

Miles: If you were a man, I'd kill you.
Reed: Strange, I thought you only shot at boys.

Steve Miles played by Richard Boone and Reed Bowman played by Jeanne Crain: King Vidor's *Man Without a Star* (Universal, 1955).

3350

Nugget: I still don't get it. Why did they want to kill a U.S. Marshal?
Marshal: It's an old outlaw trick, Nugget. And a good one when it works. If you want to kill a law officer, kill him and his prisoner. It'll look like they killed each other.

Nugget Clark played by Eddy Waller and Marshal Rocky Lane played by Allan "Rocky" Lane: Philip Ford's *Marshal of Amarillo* (Republic, 1948).

3351

Doc: No bet, gentlemen. I don't kill for profit. But on the other hand, I'd just as soon kill Masterson for nothing. So that disposes of the ethics.
Fry: Then what's stopping you?
Doc: Call it a superstition. Every gambler has one. To me, killing is a jinx. It never fails to break a winning streak. And I'm having one. But win or lose, if I kill a

man, it's for personal reasons. And, personally, I don't like any of you any more than I like Masterson.

Doc Holliday played by James Griffith and Charlie Fry played by William A. Henry: William Castle's *Masterson of Kansas* (Columbia, 1954).

3352

White Feather: You go back, they kill you now for sure.

Benjie: I ain't dead yet.

White Feather: How dead you wanna get?

White Feather played by David Carradine and Benjie played by Brock Peters: Alf Kjellin's *The McMasters* (Jayjen/Chevron, 1970).

3353

Ernestina: Have you really killed a hundred men?

Tom Horn: A thousand.

Ernestina: I was serious.

Tom Horn: How did you know I wasn't?

Ernestina: Now why do you talk like that?

Tom Horn: The more they think I've done, the less I'll have to do. The more afraid, the better.

Ernestina Crawford played by Karen Black and Tom Horn played by David Carradine: Jack Starrett's *Mr. Horn* (TVW, 1979).

3354

Marshal: How many men have you really killed, huh?

Tom Horn: I never killed anybody that didn't need it.

Marshal Joe LeFlors played by John Durren and Tom Horn played by David Carradine: Jack Starrett's *Mr. Horn* (TVW, 1979).

3355

Yeager: I could kill ya for this, Plummer.

Plummer: There isn't whiskey enough to give you the nerve, Yeager. There's not country enough for you to hide in if you ever try it.

Yeager played by Robert Griffin and Sheriff Henry Plummer played by Preston Foster: Ray Nazarro's *Montana Territory* (Columbia, 1952).

3356

Billy: How did you do it? How did you kill 'em, I mean?

Cain: Different men, different ways.

Billy: Different men, different ways? But you always let 'em draw first, right?

Cain: No, not if there was a chance I might get beat. The code I had was to let 'em know I was coming.

Billy: Yea, yea... but, but you never bush-whacked anyone, did ya?

Cain: Well, like I said, they knew I was coming, so they all had guns. And none of 'em got it in the back.

Billy: Yea, well, see I thought...

Cain: You thought that I marched down the street, called 'em out, and waited for 'em to draw. Huh?

Billy: Yea.

Cain: No, Billy, I was hired to use my gun and I did.

Billy: Ah huh. Well, I... I'd let anyone draw first because I can out-draw anyone. It's hard for me to believe that you never were as good as I am.

Cain: Good at what, Billy? Hitting branches or killing men? There's a difference!

Billy Eager played by Paul Hampton and Cain played by Clint Walker: Robert Sparr's *More Dead Than Alive* (United Artists, 1968).

3357

Billy: Say, Ruff, who did he come gunning for?

Ruffalo: Oh, some cattleman.

Billy: Yea, but did he get him?

Ruffalo: Does an outhouse stink?

Billy Eager played by Paul Hampton and Dan Ruffalo played by Vincent Price: Robert Sparr's *More Dead Than Alive* (United Artists, 1968).

3358

Ben: If you're going to murder me, Howie, don't make it look like something else.

Ben Vandergroat played by Robert Ryan and Howard "Howie" Kemp played by James Stewart: Anthony Mann's *The Naked Spur* (MGM, 1953).

3359

Navajo Kid: Dead men can't talk.

Tom Kirk/Navajo Kid played by Bob Steele: Harry Fraser's *Navajo Kid* (Producer's Releasing Corp., 1945).

3360

Jonas: You an old hand at killin'?

Max: I killed my share of deer and rabbits.

Jonas: You ever hold a gun on a man?

Max: No.

Jonas: You're setting out to kill three of 'em, huh? Bang, bang, bang. You figure you're going to make it because you got right on your side?

Max: It helps.

Jonas: They bury a sheriff about once a week out here.

Jonas Cord played by Brian Keith and Max Sand/Nevada Smith played by Steve McQueen: Henry Hathaway's *Nevada Smith* (Paramount, 1966).

3361

Jonas: Look, just to find 'em, you're gonna have to comb out every saloon, gambling hall, hog farm, and whorehouse between here and Mexico. What do you think you're after, three preachers? Are you gonna gun 'em down at 80 yards when they're coming out of a church social? You're hunting three men that steal because they're too damn lazy to work, and they kill because they love to. And

then they hide out like rats in the garbage. So if you're gonna get 'em, you're gonna have to eat, drink, and wallow in the garbage right with 'em until you get so you think like 'em and smell like 'em.

Max: I'll do what I have to do.

Jonas: It ain't that easy, kid. Finding 'em is one thing... killing 'em is another.

Jonas Cord played by Brian Keith and Max Sand/Nevada Smith played by Steve McQueen: Henry Hathaway's *Nevada Smith* (Paramount, 1966).

3362

Fitch: Come on, come on, get it over with. Get it over with! For God's sake, get it over with! You're waited years for this, so get it over with! Come on... oh... finish me... finish me. Finish me! You haven't got the guts! You're yellow! Finish me!

Max: You're just not worth killing.

Tom Fitch played by Karl Malden and Max Sand/Nevada Smith played by Steve McQueen: Henry Hathaway's *Nevada Smith* (Paramount, 1966).

3363

John: What is it?

Tom: He was killed.

John: What?

Tom: Yes. Shot in the back... at the First Chance Saloon. He went there for us... to make peace.

John Dawson played by John Wayne and Tom Lewis played by Murdock McQuarrie: Carl Pierson's *The New Frontier* (Republic, 1935).

3364

Marshal: All right, go on about your business... all of ya. You've seen dead men before.

Marshal Tom Evans played by Walter Sande: Edward L. Cahn's *Noose for a Gunman* (United Artists, 1960).

3365

Nitro: I ain't never killed anybody young before.

Fargo: You ain't never killed anybody before.

Nitro: I wounded that deputy in Sweetwater.

Kelly: Oh, you hit him in the head with a stick of dynamite.

Nitro: It got the job done.

Nitro Jones played by Royal Dano, Fargo Parker played by Gene Evans, and Kelly Sutton played by Ken Curtis: Burt Kennedy's *Once Upon a Texas Train* (TVW, 1988).

3366

Morton: Tell me, was it necessary that you killed all of them? I only told you to scare them.

Frank: People scare better when they're dying.

Morton played by Gabriele Ferzetti and Frank played by Henry Fonda: Sergio Leone's *Once Upon a Time in the West* (Paramount, 1969).

3367

Cheyenne: I'll kill anything... but never a kid. It'd be like killing a priest... a Catholic priest, that is.

Cheyenne played by Jason Robards, Jr.: Sergio Leone's *Once Upon a Time in the West* (Paramount, 1969).

3368

Cheyenne: You know, ma'am, when you kill four it's easy to make it five.

Cheyenne played by Jason Robards, Jr.: Sergio Leone's *Once Upon a Time in the West* (Paramount, 1969).

3369

Cheyenne: I don't have to kill you now. You leave a slime behind you like a snail.

Cheyenne played by Jason Robards, Jr.: Sergio Leone's *Once Upon a Time in the West* (Paramount, 1969).

3370

McBain: But, but they were his men! And they tried to kill him!

Harmonica: They must have found somebody who pays better.

McBain: And you! You saved his life!

Harmonica: I didn't let them kill him, and that's not the same thing.

Jill McBain played by Claudia Cardinale and the Harmonica Man played by Charles Bronson: Sergio Leone's *Once Upon a Time in the West* (Paramount, 1969).

3371

Billy: Pat, I want you to know I'm sorry. I honestly am. Last night I was ready to kill you. But in the daylight I can see things much better.

Billy the Kid played by Jack Buetel and Pat Garrett played by Thomas Mitchell: Howard Hughes' *The Outlaw* (United Artists, 1943).

3372

Fletcher: I don't want to hear Wales dead. I want to see Wales dead!

Fletcher played by John Vernon and Josey Wales played by Clint Eastwood: Clint Eastwood's *The Outlaw Josey Wales* (Warner Bros., 1976).

3373

Bryce: Hey, Lee, did my father shoot anybody when he rode with you?

Lee: Nobody that didn't have it coming... and never in the back.

Bryce played by Chad Willett and Lee Walker played by Willie Nelson: Bill Corcoran's *Outlaw Justice* (TVW, 1999).

3374

Stewart: Why did you do that [shoot him]?

Jason: I thought it was the 4th of July.

Stewart: He had seen the light.

Jason: Well, just in case he didn't, I let a little [light] through him.

Del Stewart played by William Bishop and Jason played by Chris Alcaide: Fred F. Sears' *Overland Pacific* (United Artists, 1954).

3375

Louisa: Will, does he kill like that?

Cody: Ain't a corpse-maker like him, honey!

Louisa Cody played by Helen Burgess and Buffalo Bill Cody played by James Ellison: Cecil B. DeMille's *The Plainsman* (Paramount, 1936).

3376

Evelyn: All I know is that no good can come from men who murder to get what they want.

Evelyn Hastings played by Rhonda Fleming: Jerry Hopper's *Pony Express* (Paramount, 1953).

3377

King David: Well, better to wait forever than to fight. Because when you start killin' for a dream, you usually end up killin' the dream too. And that's what hell is... watching your dreams die.

King David played by Robert Hooks: Mario Van Peebles' *Posse* (Gramercy Pictures, 1993).

3378

Fierro: Put down your gun.

Fardan: Well now, if I did that, how do I know that you would still be friendly?

Fierro: Do I got to kill you to prove I like ya?

Fierro played by Rafael Bertrand and Henry Rico Fardan played by Lee Marvin: Richard Brooks' *The Professionals* (Columbia, 1966).

3379

Hank: Will, did you have to shoot him? Couldn't you've pistol-whipped him instead or something?

Will: I'm sorry, I couldn't help it. But he didn't need a lesson... he needed killin'.

Hank played by Henry Capps and Will Hansen played by Chuck Connors: Ferde Grofe Jr.'s *The Proud and Damned* (Media Trend-Prestige/Columbia, 1972).

3380

Chico: You know, pride can kill a man faster than a bullet.

Silver: So can over-confidence, Chico.

Chico played by Rodolfo Acosta and Marshal Cass Silver played by Robert Ryan: Robert D. Webb's *The Proud Ones* (20th Century–Fox, 1956).

3381

Gentry: It's not a good thing to watch a man die. But it will grow faint in remembering. It will pass... except for the person who pulls the trigger.

Gentry/John Coventry played by Fred MacMurray: Harry Keller's *Quantez* (Universal, 1957).

3382

Quentin: It must be a great way to make a living: running cattle to the railhead.

Tank: Ah yea, but it's nothing compared to what I used to do.

Quentin: What was that?

Tank: I used to kill people.

Quentin Baudine played by Tim Matheson and Tank Logan played by Brian Keith: Lee H. Katzin's *The Quest* (TVW, 1976).

3383

Morgan: You murdered him!

Tank: No, he died of sheer stupidity.

Morgan Baudine, also known as Two Persons, played by Kurt Russell and Tank Logan played by Brian Keith: Lee H. Katzin's *The Quest* (TVW, 1976).

3384

Morgan: So you shot at people for the invested interest.

Tank: Oh, I didn't shoot at 'em, son. I shot into 'em. Of course, I never murdered anybody. I always had due cause... because they were trying to kill me, or else they were intending to.

Morgan: But you killed them whatever.

Tank: Sober I'd admit to it and drunk I'd swear to it. I tell ya, I bragged about so many killings, I can't remember which ones were mine and which ones was the Lord's. For that matter, neither can anybody else. So it don't make no difference. In fact, if I had to go in a court of law, that would be my defense.

Morgan Baudine, also known as Two Persons, played by Kurt Russell and Tank Logan played by Brian Keith: Lee H. Katzin's *The Quest* (TVW, 1976).

3385

Vallian: I wonder why it is that men who plead for mercy never get it.

Con Vallian played by Sam Elliott: Richard Day's *The Quick and the Dead* (HBO Pictures, 1987).

3386

Vallian: If you have to shoot, shoot to kill. Wounds won't impress 'em. They've all been shot before.

Con Vallian played by Sam Elliott: Richard Day's *The Quick and the Dead* (HBO Pictures, 1987).

3387

Ellen: I'm going to kill you if I have to ride all the way to hell to do it!

Herod: Do you have some particular problem with me?

Ellen played by Sharon Stone and John Herod played by Gene Hackman: Sam Raimi's *The Quick and the Dead* (Tristar, 1995).

Jacob Sharp (Woody Strode), Henry Rico Farden (Lee Marvin), Hans Ehrengard (Robert Ryan), and Bill Dolworth (Burt Lancaster) are *The Professionals* (Columbia, 1966) who rescue a kidnapped girl from a notorious Mexican bandit.

3388

Ellen: Don't you even want to fight back?

Cort: Of course I do. I'd like to kill them all for what they've done. But I won't. Killing people is wrong.

Ellen: Some people deserve to die.

Ellen played by Sharon Stone and Cort played by Russell Crowe: Sam Raimi's *The Quick and the Dead* (Tristar, 1995).

3389

Clint: So it finally happened. A Reno brother got killed.

Sim: Clint, we don't want no preaching.

Frank: Take it easy, Sim.

Clint: The baby of the family dying in the streets, and his brave brothers running away. Not even animals would do a thing like that!

John: Dead in the streets… not dying.

Clint: As if that made any difference!

Clint Reno played by Denver Pyle, Simeon Reno played by J. Carrol Naish, Frank Reno played by Forrest Tucker, and John Reno played by Myron Healey: Tim Whelan's *Rage at Dawn* (RKO, 1955).

3390

McElroy: We don't approve of killing ordinarily, but we might have to force ourselves.

John G. McElroy played by Brian Keith: Herschel Daugherty's *The Raiders* (Universal, 1964).

3391

Vern: I'm going to kill you, Kinch, but I'm not going to murder you. I'll give you an even chance.

Vern Haskell played by Arthur Kennedy and Kinch played by Lloyd Gough: Fritz Lang's *Rancho Notorious* (RKO, 1952).

3392

Dunson: You should have let them kill me because I'm going to kill you. I'll catch up with you. I don't know when, but I'll catch up. And every time you turn around, expect to see me. Because one time you'll turn around and I'll be there. And I'll kill you.

Tom Dunson played by John Wayne: Howard Hawks' *Red River* (United Artists, 1948).

3393

Lamartine: Shots fired in the air rarely kill men on the ground.

Lamartine played by Alan Reed: Leslie Fenton's *The Redhead and the Cowboy* (Paramount, 1951).

3394

Gil: War makes everybody a little quick on the trigger.

Gil Kyle played by Glenn Ford: Leslie Fenton's *The Redhead and the Cowboy* (Paramount, 1951).

3395

Eleanor: Tell me, is it more important for you to kill a man than to save the life of an innocent one?

Eleanor Stone played by Gene Tierney. She was talking to Frank James who played by Henry Fonda: Fritz Lang's *The Return of Frank James* (20th Century–Fox, 1940).

3396

Lopez: How do you feel to be killed?

Cisco: Ah, it did not hurt one bit.

Lopez played by Cesar Romero and the Cisco Kid played by Warner Baxter: Herbert I. Leeds' *The Return of the Cisco Kid* (20th Century–Fox, 1939).

3397

Vin: I wish the hell I knew for sure.

Chris: Knew what?

Vin: Whether I'm here because Chico is a friend of mine, or if I'm just on the prod for a fight like Frank. Killing can get inside you.

Chris: And you think that's happened to you?

Vin: Why else would I be here? Sure, Chico is a friend of mine. But, hell, I don't even know his last name.

Chris: Neither do I.

Vin: Don't it make you wonder?

Chris: No.

Vin: How the hell come, Chris?

Chris: Because in all the years I made my way with a gun, I never once shot a man just to see him fall. If that time ever comes, I'll throw my guns in a water bucket and ride out. So will you.

Vin played by Robert Fuller, Chris played by Yul Brynner, Frank played by Claude Akins, and Chico played by Julian Mateos: Burt Kennedy's *Return of the Seven* (United Artists, 1966).

3398

Newt: Did you have to kill him?

Gideon: He would have killed you.

Newt: He wouldn't have killed me. I can take care of myself.

Gideon: I couldn't be sure of that. A man that won't kill to protect his own is either a coward or a fool. And I don't take myself as either.

Newt Dobbs played by Rick Schroder and Gideon Walker played by William Peterson: Mike Robe's *Return to Lonesome Dove* (TVW, 1993).

3399

Elizabeth: My father had this notion to kill a man who done him some injustice. And my grandfather said to him: Shaun, he said, you best learn that you live your life in your heart. And you got to be most careful what you put in your heart. If you fill it with vengeance and hate, he said, there'll be no room left for love or laughter or tears. And your heart will rot.

Elizabeth Riley played by Susan Hayward: Daniel Mann's *The Revengers* (NGP, 1972).

3400

Jimmy: Are you going to enjoy this killing?

Judge: Not exactly. There ain't nobody in his right mind enjoys a killing. It's worse when it's someone you like.

Jimmy played by Eddie Little Sky and Judge Kyle played by Walter Matthau: Jesse Hibbs' *Ride a Crooked Trail* (Universal, 1958).

3401

Rio: Dead men don't talk.

Rio played by Robert Taylor: John Farrow's *Ride, Vaquero!* (MGM, 1953).

3402

Lassiter: I can't kill a man just for hate. Hate ain't the same with me since I loved you.

Jim Lassiter played by Ed Harris: Charles Haid's *Riders of the Purple Sage* (Turner Home Entertainment, 1996).

3403

Lassiter: These people are slow to kill. That's the only good I ever seen in their religion.

Jim Lassiter played by Ed Harris: Charles Haid's *Riders of the Purple Sage* (Turner Home Entertainment, 1996).

3404

Lassiter: We had a slight disagreement and I dissolved the partnership.

James Lassiter played by Richard Boone: Gordon Douglas' *Rio Conchos* (20th Century–Fox, 1964).

3405

Tabor: You know, killing don't mean spit to you, does it?

Leech: One thing you learn quick in my business, boy: there ain't no such thing as an innocent man… just some less guilty. I gave him his choices. He just took the wrong one. He wouldn't leave it alone.

Benjamin Tabor played by Travis Tritt and Quinton Leech played by Kenny Rogers: Rod Hardy's *Rio Diablo* (TVW, 1993).

3406

Leech: Did you ever kill a man? Killing ain't hard… unless, of course, he's of mind to kill you. Revenge is a mighty cold supper, Benny. You never get enough to satisfy that pain you're feeling.

Quinton Leech played by Kenny Rogers and Benjamin Tabor played by Travis Tritt: Rod Hardy's *Rio Diablo* (TVW, 1993).

3407

Amelita: Turn around, Sheriff. I want you to see who's going to kill ya.

Amelita played by Sherry Lansing: Howard Hawks' *Rio Lobo* (NGP, 1970).

3408

Mark: You shot him in the back?

Matt: That's right! I shot him in the back, or in the front. What does it matter how you kill a snake? What does it matter which way he's facing?

Mark Calder played by Tommy Rettig and Matt Calder played by Robert Mitchum: Otto Preminger's *The River of No Return* (20th Century–Fox, 1954).

3409

Hays: Why didn't you drop him? You had us with ya.

Tex: I never shot a man just because I had a chance to.

Hays: Now, me, I work on the opposite principle. And I'll live longer than you.

Hank Hays played by Richard Boone and Tex played by George Montgomery: Sidney Salkow's *Robbers' Roost* (United Artists, 1955).

3410

Dolan: The way I look at it, a man starts choking a woman is looking to go to hell in a hurry. All I did was oblige him.

Dolan played by George Peppard: Arnold Laven's *Rough Night in Jericho* (Universal, 1967).

3411

Ben: Yes, well now, because of what we've been through, you know, I'm gonna do something for you, Bull. Yes, sir, I'm gonna give you the greatest gift that one man could give another.

Bull: You're going to kill yourself for me?

Ben Jones played by Glenn Ford and Bull played by Denver Pyle: Burt Kennedy's *The Rounders* (MGM, 1965).

3412

Blue Buffalo: You are a Christian. Will you kill Christians in battle?

O'Meara: Well, my nation fought for liberty against the United States. And Christianity is always the brother of liberty in all wars.

Blue Buffalo played by Charles Bronson and O'Meara played by Rod Steiger: Samuel Fuller's *Run of the Arrow* (RKO, 1957).

3413

Sam: Well, it was him or me.

Mason: Dead men tell no tales.

Sam Cooper played by Van Heflin and Mason played by Gilbert Roland: Giorgio Capitani's *The Ruthless Four* (PCM-Eichberg/Goldstone, 1968).

3414

Sabata: Now Father Brown will have it in for you, too. He already spends most of his time saying masses for the dead, and nobody pays.

Sabata played by Lee Van Cleef and Father Brown played by R. Lodi: Frank Kramer's *Sabata* (United Artists, 1969).

3415

Tom: Are you afraid of me, Tye?
Tyrel: I seen you kill too many men not to be.

Tom Sunday played by Glenn Ford and Tyrel Sackett played by Jeff Osterhage: Robert Totten's *The Sacketts* (TVW, 1979).

3416

Deneen: How does your brother feel after having killed his first human being?
Steve: Healthier than if he turned his back.

Mr. Deneen played by Donald Crisp and Steve Sinclair played by Robert Taylor: Robert Parrish's *Saddle the Wind* (MGM, 1958).

3417

Hardin: I wouldn't be alive except for Charlie. And he wouldn't be dead except for me.

Clay Hardin played by Errol Flynn and Charlie Bell played by John Litel: David Butler's *San Antonio* (Warner Bros., 1945).

3418

Santee: You're right in part. Your father didn't have a chance. But, you know, he had a choice. You see, I bring them in alive whenever I can. It's up to them. But even a coward would rather die with his boots on than be dragged up before a hangman. And your father was no coward.

Santee played by Glenn Ford: Gary Nelson's *Santee* (Crown International Pictures, 1973).

3419

Summers: That was a cold-blooded killing!
Fallon: What other kind is there?

Mike Summers played by Don Taylor and Steve Fallon played by Richard Basehart: Michael Carreras' *The Savage Guns* (MGM, 1961).

3420

Henderson: You are thinking about killing me?
Tulugak: We are thinking about it.

Henderson played by Donald Sutherland and Tulugak played by Qalingo Tookalak: Jacques Dorfmann's *Shadow of the Wolf* (Triumph Releasing, 1993).

3421

Ryker: I'll kill him if I have to.
Wilson: You mean I'll kill him if you have to.

Ryker played by Emile Meyer and Jack Wilson played by Jack Palance: George Stevens' *Shane* (Paramount, 1953).

3422

Books: I don't believe I ever killed a man that didn't deserve it.

J.B. Books played by John Wayne: Don Siegel's *The Shootist* (Paramount, 1976).

3423

Brown: I said I was a soldier. I was not a killer.
McTooth: Subtle distinction.

John George "Kootenai" Brown played by Tom Burlinson and McTooth/Eben Campbell played by Donnelly Rhodes: Allan Kroeker's *Showdown at Williams Creek* (Republic Pictures Home Video, 1991).

3424

Drunk: Say, you're the fastest thing I ever did see. I didn't even see your hand move. I, ah, I want to thank you for not killing me… although I would have understood perfectly well if you had. I, ah, I need a drink!

The Drunk played by Denver Pyle: Burt Kennedy's *Sidekicks* (TVW, 1974).

3425

Ed: Well, the Boss would rather not have too much killing on this job. Oh, he don't mind, but sometimes it just complicates things.
Quince: I'll hold him down to a decent limit.

Ed played by Dick Peabody, Quince Drew played by Larry Hagman, and the Boss (of the gang) played by Jack Elam: Burt Kennedy's *Sidekicks* (TVW, 1974).

3426

Jason: I think the Boss really intends to kill us.
Quince: You just leave that little detail to me.
Jason: Death is a little detail?

Jason O'Rourke played by Lou Gossett, Quince Drew played by Larry Hagman, and The Boss (of the gang) played by Jack Elam: Burt Kennedy's *Sidekicks* (TVW, 1974).

3427

Ballard: If you kill one man, it's not so hard to kill the second. The third one is easy.

Dan Ballard played by John Payne: Allan Dwan's *Silver Lode* (RKO, 1954).

3428

Colonel: Well, how many people would you say he's killed during his life?
Junior: Well, none that didn't deserve it.
Colonel: How many have you killed, Junior?
Junior: None that didn't deserve it. Me and Bill was very particular about that. We never killed church folks neither. Of course, there was a Baptist that got in the way once… but very seldom!

Colonel Morgan played by Brian Keith and Junior Frisbee played by Denver Pyle: Andrew V. McLaglen's *something big* (NGP, 1971).

3429

Sheriff: Nobody has got a natural need to kill. That grows in a man. It's put there after he's born.

Sheriff Lane Dakota played by Stephen McNally: Lee Sholem's *The Stand at Apache River* (Universal, 1953).

3430

Turner: You did hear what the man said.
Tennessee: If I heard him, I might have to kill him.

Turner played by Anthony Caruso and Tennessee played by John Payne: Allan Dwan's *Tennessee's Partner* (RKO, 1955).

3431

Luke: If you want somebody to kill ya, kid, you better find someone else to do it.

Luke Starr played by Broderick Crawford: Lesley Selander's *The Texican* (Columbia, 1966).

3432

Ruby: They're like that. Always willing to get killed or kill if they think they're right. And they always think they're right.

Ruby LaSalle played by Elaine Stritch: Rudolph Mate's *Three Violent People* (Paramount, 1956).

3433

Hickman: As long as you're wearing that badge, you got to walk up, tell 'em to throw 'em up, then watch which way his hands move. They go up, you got yourself a prisoner. They go down, he's dead… or you are. A decent man doesn't want to kill. But if you're going to shoot, you shoot to kill.

Morg Hickman played by Henry Fonda: Anthony Mann's *The Tin Star* (Paramount, 1957).

3434

Horn: Listen, I figured folks would have to do something about me sooner or later… the frontier clothes and all. Hell, I never knew anybody that knew anything but just killing and getting killed. After awhile, that's all you know.

Tom Horn played by Steve McQueen: William Wiard's *Tom Horn* (Warner Bros., 1980).

3435

McCoy: Ellen, sometimes life gives you no choice. Sometimes you got to either kill or be killed. It's as simple as that.

Sergeant Wade McCoy played by Chuck Connors and Ellen Carter played by Susan Cummings: Robert Parry/Lesley Selander's *Tomahawk Trail* (United Artists, 1957).

3436

Doc: Don't try it alone! They'll kill ya!

Armed with a Spencer rifle and an intemperate disposition, Bill Munny (Clint Eastwood) is about to blast Little Bill Daggett (Gene Hackman) into the past tense in *Unforgiven* (Warner Bros., 1992).

Rosser: It's my job, Doc. Killing... and getting killed.

Doctor Kent played by Richard Arlen and Tom Rosser played by Dana Andrews: Lesley Selander's *Town Tamer* (Paramount, 1965).

3437

Noble: If anything goes wrong, don't stop to argue about it. Shoot to kill!

Noble Adams played by Kris Kristofferson: John Guillermin's *The Tracker* (HBO Pictures, 1988).

3438

Stillwell: He just came out of nowhere. But I was too quick for him. I filled him so full of holes he wouldn't float in brine.

John "Red Jack" Stillwell played by Scott Wilson in John Guillermin's *The Tracker* (HBO Pictures, 1988).

3439

Jesse: You should have let me kill him.
Frank: You really like killing, don't you?
Jesse: It comes easy in our business.
Frank: Is that why you chose the business? So you could go on killing?
Jesse: You've done your share.
Frank: Yea, well, I'm not proud of it.
Jesse: Well I am! Jesse James... that name means something!

Jesse James played by Robert Wagner and Frank James played by Jeffrey Hunter: Nicholas Ray's *The True Story of Jesse James* (20th Century–Fox, 1957).

3440

Russell: He won't be in a position to say anything when the time comes.
Deputy: What do you mean?

Russell: Dead men can't talk!

Bob Russell played by Wheeler Oakman and Deputy Sheriff Bendix played by Walter Brennan: Ross Lederman's *Two Fisted Law* (Columbia, 1932).

3441

Colonel: This is better than killing each other, no?
Hogan: I only figured there was going to be one funeral... Catholic.
Colonel: Oh? I didn't know that you were Catholic.

Colonel Beltran played by Manolo Fabregas and Hogan played by Clint Eastwood: Don Siegel's *Two Mules for Sister Sara* (Universal, 1970).

3442

Lieutenant: Where will he fight us?
McIntosh: He don't mean to fight you no place, Lieutenant. He only means to kill ya.

Lieutenant Garnett DeBuin played by Bruce Davison and McIntosh played by Burt Lancaster: Robert Aldrich's *Ulzana's Raid* (Universal, 1972).

3443

Abby: You're not a man. You're a walking loaded rifle with the one blood-thirsty purpose to kill Garth. You haven't blood in your veins. You've gunpowder!

Abigail Martha "Abby" Hale played by Paulette Goddard and Martin Garth played by Howard da Silva: Cecil B. DeMille's *Unconquered* (Paramount, 1947).

3444

Mrs. Langdon: You went out there to talk! Why did you have to shoot the man?
John Henry: The conversation kind of dried up, ma'am!

Mrs. Ann Langdon played by Marian McCargo and Colonel John Henry Thomas played by John Wayne: Andrew McLaglen's *The Undefeated* (20th Century–Fox, 1969).

3445

Kid: That was the first one.
Will: First one what?
Kid: First one I've ever killed.
Will: Yea.
Kid: You know how I said I shot five men. It wasn't true. That Mexican that come after me with a knife? I just busted his leg with a shovel. I didn't kill him or nothing neither.
Will: Well, you sure killed the hell out of that fella today.

The Schofield Kid played by Jaimz Woolvett and William "Bill" Munny played by Clint Eastwood: Clint Eastwood's *Unforgiven* (Warner Bros., 1992).

3446

Will: Just 'cause we're going on this killin', that don't mean I'm going back to the way I was.

William "Bill" Munny played by Clint Eastwood:

Clint Eastwood's *Unforgiven* (Warner Bros., 1992).

3447

Will: It's a hell of a thing... killin' a man. You take away all he's got... and all he's ever gonna have.
Kid: Yea, well, I guess they had it comin'.
Will: We all have it comin', kid.

William "Bill" Munny played by Clint Eastwood and the Schofield Kid played by Jaimz Woolvett: Clint Eastwood's *Unforgiven* (Warner Bros., 1992).

3448

Rachel: I've never killed anybody before.
Ben: The gun does the killing.

Rachel Zachary played by Audrey Hepburn and Ben Zachary played by Burt Lancaster: John Huston's *The Unforgiven* (United Artists, 1960).

3449

Priest: You should announce youself. I could have shot you.
Jackson: Killed by a priest. I'd be the laughing stock of hell!

The Priest played by Ted Haler and Jackson played by Christopher Boyer: Michael Bohusz's *Uninvited* (Imperial Entertainment, 1993).

3450

Pancho: You know you amaze me, gringo. You run guns and you don't care who gets killed... so long as you get paid and you don't have to watch. It must be a terrible thing: to kill a man without hating him.

Pancho Villa played by Yul Brynner: Buzz Kulik's *Villa Rides!* (Paramount, 1968).

3451

Judith: That's right, find an excuse to stay here and fight. Men can always find a reason to murder each other. I know you think you're doing right, but there's no right to killing. I'd like to know what good it's ever done. It has only brought on more killing.

Judith Wilkison played by Dianne Foster: Rudolph Mate's *The Violent Men* (Columbia, 1955).

3452

Clay: I remember when I first killed a man. It was clear and had to be done... though I went home afterwards and puked my insides out.

Clay Blaisdell played by Henry Fonda: Edward Dmytryk's *Warlock* (20th Century–Fox, 1959).

3453

Mekoki: You kill every time you buy meat... only you use money instead of a gun.

Mekoki played by Jimmy Herman: Rene Manzor's *Warrior Spirit* (Cinevideo Plus, 1994).

3454

Gentry: Dead men tell no tales.

Gentry played by Lloyd Whitlock: Robert N. Bradbury's *West of the Divide* (Lone Star/Monogram, 1934).

3455

Charlie: You want me to foreclose on his mortgage?

Charlie Zane played by Jack Warden: J. Lee Thompson's *The White Buffalo* (United Artists, 1977).

3456

Bartell: It's not your fault, boy. Killin' is the fault of the time we live in.

Sheriff Paul Bartell played by Gilbert Roland: Jack Sher's *The Wild and the Innocent* (Universal, 1959).

3457

Wild Bill: I'm gonna give you a chance in life, Jack. I don't want to kill nobody so young and confused about things. Joe, give him a horse, would you? Put him on it and point him east.
Joe: Yep, east is where fellas like him ought to live. But my recommendation is still to kill him.

Wild Bill Hickok played by Jeff Bridges, Jack McCall played by David Arquette, and California Joe played by James Gammon: Walter Hill's *Wild Bill* (MGM/United Artists, 1995).

3458

Boy: How many people have you shot?
Will: I don't think that's anything to brag on to a nice boy like you. Come on, sit down and rest.
Boy: Oh, I ain't so nice. You can tell me.
Will: Well, I guess there was a few times.
Boy: How did it feel?
Will: Bad. Bad scared before and bad sorry after.

The Boy, Horace Greeley Allen, played by Jon Francis and Will Penny played by Charlton Heston: Tom Gries' *Will Penny* (Paramount, 1968).

3459

Ike: I ain't gonna fight you tonight, Doc. But your fight's coming soon enough.
Doc: My mama always told me never put off til tomorrow people you can kill today.

Ike Clanton played by Jeff Fahey and Doc Holliday played by Dennis Quaid: Lawrence Kasdan's *Wyatt Earp* (Warner Bros., 1994).

3460

Lengthy: It sure was mighty inconsiderate of old Jeb to get himself killed like that. He owed me six bits.

Lengthy played by John Russell and Jeb played by Robert Alder: William A. Wellman's *Yellow Sky* (20th Century–Fox, 1948).

3461

Ben: Don't get jumpy. It's not much of a posse.
Billy: It was a fair fight!
Ben: Well, the law is kind of like a fence line. It puts the grass into two pastures. On the one side the grass is thick and green... registered stock, branded, and grazing peacefully. And on the other side the grass gets kind of thin and mean.
Billy: Killin' that Sheriff puts me some across that line, don't it?
Ben: Some.

Ben Kane played by Robert Mitchum and Billy Young played by Robert Walker, Jr.: Burt Kennedy's *Young Billy Young* (United Artists, 1969).

3462

Dick: Rumor has it you killed a man, Billy. You don't seem like the killing sort.
Steve: Yea, Billy, what did you kill him for?
Billy: He was hackin' on me.

Dick Brewer played by Charlie Sheen, Dirty Steve Stephens played by Dermot Mulroney, and William H. "Billy" Bonney played by Emilio Estevez: Christopher Cain's *Young Guns* (20th Century–Fox, 1988).

3463

Billy: Are you really going to kill Billy the Kid?
Joe Grant: Does a horse piss where she pleases?

William H. "Billy" Bonney played by Emilio Estevez and Texas Joe Grant played by Tom Callaway: Christopher Cain's *Young Guns* (20th Century–Fox, 1988).

3464

Billy: Alex, if you stay they're gonna kill ya. And then I'm gonna have to go around and kill all the guys that killed you. That's a lot of killin'!

William H. "Billy" Bonney played by Emilio Estevez and Alex McSween played by Terrance O'Quinn: Christopher Cain's *Young Guns* (20th Century–Fox, 1988).

3465

Chisum: You just killed yourself, Bonney. You are a fool. You call yourself the scourge of New Mexico. Well, by God, I am New Mexico! And you are dead!
Bonney: Let me tell you something, Mr. New Mexico. I wouldn't give a bucket of piss for your future.

John Chisum played by James Coburn and William H. Bonney, alias Billy the Kid, played by Emilio Estevez: Geoff Murphy's *Young Guns II* (20th Century–Fox, 1990).

Lawlessness

See also Bad Guys; Dying; Gunfighters; Killing; Outlaws, Cattle Rustlers and Horse Thieves

3466
Frank: Any of the old bunch still around?
Lon: Not many. Fred Salter is in jail for cattle rustling. Sammy Page and Doc Wrightmire got themselves hung for horse stealing. And the last I heard of Pete Kincaid, he was down in Indian country for his health. He got a sudden attack of lead poisoning running away from a posse. That leaves me and Buck and Slim Harris.
Frank: Things must be pretty quiet around here.
Frank Jennings played by Dick Foren, Lon Tuttle played by Guinn "Big Boy" Williams, Fred Salter played by Harry Shannon, Sammy Page played George J. Lewis, Doc Wrightmire played by Edwin Parker, and Pete Kincaid played by Robert Bice: Ray Nazarro's *Al Jennings of Oklahoma* (Columbia, 1951).

3467
The turbulent Pecos River, west of which there existed no law of God or man.
Caption: Thomas Carr's *Alias Billy the Kid* (Republic, 1946).

3468
Crown: If your laws don't include me, well then, they just don't apply to me either.
Anita Crown played by Mary Stuart Masterson: Jonathan Kaplan's *Bad Girls* (20th Century–Fox, 1994).

3469
But an unusual mistake was made in this race for statehood. A strip of land was completely overlooked... forgotten. It was left without law or sheriff. This strip had no legal basis for government of any kind. And in the closing decade of the 19th century, it became a hideout for the outlaws who infested the west. No United States Marshal dared venture there. It was called... Badman's Territory.
Prologue: Tim Whelan's *Badman's Territory* (RKO, 1946).

3470
Dan: Billy, if a mob can pass judgment on one man, then they can do it to anybody they want to, and anytime they want. That's why we have laws, son. Not just to protect us from the bad men, but a mob's righteous men can get out of hand.

Dan Baker played by Clint Walker and Billy Baker played by Lee Montgomery: Lyman Dayton's *Baker's Hawk* (Doty/Dayton, 1976).

3471
Boone: I'm about sick of this senseless killin'! What are we gonna do about it?
Boone Choate played by Tom Bower: Robert M. Young's *The Ballad Of Gregorio Cortez* (Embassy Pictures, 1983).

3472
Shorty: The law won't let you get away with this.
Glyn: What law?
Shorty played by Harry Morgan and Glyn McLyntock played by James Stewart: Anthony Mann's *Bend of the River* (Universal, 1952).

3473
Hannassey: I'm a law-abiding man. That is, if there's any law to abide by.
Rufus Hannassey played by Burl Ives: William Wyler's *The Big Country* (United Artists, 1958).

3474
Posner: We got the law here, Billy Jack.
Billy Jack: When policeman break the law, then there isn't any law... just the fight for survival.
Posner played by Bert Freed and Billy Jack played by Tom Laughlin: T.G. Frank's (Tom Laughlin) *Billy Jack* (Warner Bros.–National Student Film Corp., 1971).

3475
Mac: The only time there's any law and order is when there's more of it than anything else. And this time there was more of Jared Tetlow.
Mac Gill played by Don C. Harvey and Jared Tetlow was played by Victor Jory: Earl Bellamy's *Blackjack Ketchum, Desperado* (Columbia, 1956).

3476
Reverend: Well, I don't have to tell you good folks what has been happening here in our beloved little town. Sheriff murdered, crops burned, stores looted, people stampeded, and cattle raped. Now the time has come to act... and act fast. I've leaving!
Reverend Johnson played by Liam Dunn: Mel Brooks' *Blazing Saddles* (Warner Bros., 1974).

3477
Lamarr: Be ready to attack Rock Ridge tomorrow. Here's your badge.

Bandit: Badges? We don't need no stinking badges!
The Mexican Bandit was uncredited and Hedley Lamarr played by Harvey Korman: Mel Brooks' *Blazing Saddles* (Warner Bros., 1974).

3478
Canaan: You the law?
Sgt.: The closest thing they got to it in this shit hole, yes.
Canaan played by Armand Assante and Sergeant Hastings played by Adam Baldwin: Richard Spence's *Blind Justice* (HBO Home Video, 1994).

3479
Alacran: The whole world is turning to shit!
Alacran played by Robert Davi: Richard Spence's *Blind Justice* (HBO Home Video, 1994).

3480
Major: I've come over here to warn you. You better get your people out of here just as fast as you can.
Young: Why?
Major: Because I've held off those mobs as long as I'm able. From now on, I can't be responsible.
Young: You mean you want us to leave everything we fought all our lives for?
Major: I mean if you don't go, and go quickly, blood is going to run like water in the streets. And there's nothing I can do to stop it.
Young: We're not budging one inch!
Major: Well, I'm sorry that's your answer. But I'm afraid the law can't help you much.
Young: The law? What law? The law that let's a pack of scoundrels come in here and hunt us down like wild animals... burn our homes, ruin our crops, arrest our leader on trumped-up charges, and then look the other way when a mob breaks in and mur-ders him? If they call that law, let 'em keep it! We don't want any more of it!
The Major played by Russell Simpson and Brigham Young played by Dean Jagger: Henry Hathaway's *Brigham Young* (20th Century–Fox, 1940).

3481
Murphy: There's a fundamental difference between Mr. Chisum and me.
Sheriff: Yeah, what's that?

Murphy: Mr. Chisum is a man who respects the law. And around here, I'm the one who owns it.

Lawrence Murphy played by Forrest Tucker and Sheriff Brady played by Bruce Cabot: Andrew McLaglen's *Chisum* (Warner Bros., 1970).

3482

Sabra: Do you feel nervous about your sermon, dear?

Yancy: I'd rather plead to a Texas jury than preach to this gang!

Sabra Cravat played by Irene Dunne and Yancy Cravat played by Richard Dix: Wesley Ruggles' *Cimarron* (RKO, 1931).

3483

Sheriff: Take a look outside, gentlemen. Take a good look. They look harmless enough, just lounging around. When you came in just now, you probably took them for cowhands if you noticed them at all. But every one of them have had his share of killin'. They are waiting for me to make up my mind too. And the longer it takes me, the more of them there will be.

Brady: But they're only a handful. You can't let them influence you.

Sheriff: That's an awful tough handful.

Brady: If you turn that man loose, you're letting them run this town.

Sheriff: Mr. Brady, they can start running this town anytime they want to. But they're too shiftless, lazy. They need something to start them off. Like Flint [prisoner]. If they have to break him out, they won't stop there. Before they're through, they will go for each other's throats like a pack of mad dogs, and we'll be caught in the middle.

Brady: But, but this isn't the wild west anymore. Jesse James is dead. You haven't got the pony express, you got the railroads now. You even got an automobile here in town. You're talking in the past. Civilization is here.

Sheriff: So are they! And they are not interested in civilization!

Sheriff Gifford played by Hugh Sanders and William Brady played by Douglas Evans: Harmon Jones' *City of Bad Men* (20th Century–Fox, 1953).

3484

Preacher: The wrath of the Lord must move through his servants. Evil has come to us and it must be driven out.

Marshal: Crowds get can unruly, Preacher. Our common problem is a matter for the law.

Preacher: You're the law! And since you do nothing, I must!

Marshal: If you don't respect the cloth you're wearing, I won't either. You're inciting a lynch mob and I've got to stop you.

Preacher: If you're accusing me of hiding behind the cloth, I'm out front now. This morning, Marshal, I was all fired up about performing a wedding over you. Now if you make one move to stop us, I'm going to have to perform something else.

Preacher Jason played by John Dehner and Marshal Allan Burnett played by Jock Mahoney: Harmon Jones' *A Day of Fury* (Universal, 1956).

3485

Charlie: Now listen, Sheriff. I've got something to say so pay attention because I don't like to repeat. Us Hayes are in town on a matter of importance. We get real annoyed if some sly sheriff like yourself took to interfering. So you just keep your nose in your own pocket and maybe you'll get to see the sun go down.

Charlie Hayes played by Robert Middleton and Sheriff Barney Wiley played by John Ericson: Harry Keller's *Day of the Bad Man* (Universal, 1958).

3486

Big George: That's terrible.

Sally: It's horrible!

Big George: Terrible is what it is.

Big George Drakoulious played by Billy Bob Thornton and Salvatore "Sally" Jenko played by Iggy Pop: Jim Jarmusch's *Dead Man* (Miramax Films, 1996).

3487

Lou: Civilization is a wonderful thing, ain't it Doc?

Doc: If they ever got it started it might work.

Lou Trinidad played by John Saxon and Doc Adams played by Dub Taylor: Allen Smithee's *Death of a Gunfighter* (Universal, 1969)

3488

McCall: You're not the law!

Bede: You see how stupid you are! The Company is the law in this town... and I'm the Company!

Duell McCall played by Alex McArthur and Bede was played by Yaphet Kotto: Virgil W. Vogel's *Desperado* (TVW, 1987).

3489

Decker: The only law I believe in is the law of self-preservation.

Decker played by Lyle Bettger: George Marshall's *Destry* (Universal, 1954).

3490

Tom: Nobody is going to set themselves up above the law around here. Do you understand? I got something to say to you. I think maybe I could illustrate it a little better if I could tell you a story. I used to have a friend that was an opera singer. And he went into the cement business. And one day he fell into the cement. And now he's the cornerstone of the post office in St. Louis, Missouri. He should have stuck to his own trade. You better stick to yours!

Tom Destry, Jr., played by James Stewart: George Marshall's *Destry Rides Again* (Universal, 1939).

3491

Janice: Please don't mind my brother, Mr. Destry. He's always threatening to blow people's heads off.

Tom: I had, I had a friend once. His name was Stubbs. He was always going around threatening to blow people's heads off. One day a fella came along and took him up on it.

Jack: Well?

Tom: Well, folks say that now Stubbs' forehead is holding up the prettiest tombstone in Greenlawn Cemetery.

Janice Tyndall played by Irene Hervey, Jack Tyndall played by Jack Carson, and Tom Destry, Jr,. played by James Stewart: George Marshall's *Destry Rides Again* (Universal, 1939).

3492

Joe: It's kind of sad to see the country grow up, ain't it? People like you and me just ain't gonna know how to live in a place where killin' is illegal.

Joe played by Tom Powers: Alfred Werker's *Devil's Canyon* (RKO, 1953).

3493

Henchman: McQuade's all right. He's just been law here so long sometimes you have to remind him the government is moving west.

The Henchman played by Tris Coffin and Bull McQuade played by Noah Beery, Sr.: Lambert Hillyer's *The Devil's Trail* (Columbia, 1942).

3494

Doolin: I see you still have the habit of sleeping outside.

Arkansas: Yeah, you live longer that way. See, when the shooting starts, I don't have to stop to open no door.

Bill Doolin played by Randolph Scott and Arkansas played by Charles Kemper: Gordon Douglas' *The Doolins Of Oklahoma* (Columbia, 1949).

3495

Clayton: Law? What good is law without enforcement? What good is justice if you are afraid to accept it? You saw what happened when a court of law was held up to scorn and ridicule. You saw a judge killed for daring to render an honest decision. You saw a man and woman brutally murdered for obeying the mandates of that court. The scales of justice are tipped too far out of balance here in El Paso. There's only one way to even them up... with a gun and a rope!

The newly appointed black sheriff of Rock Ridge, Bart (Cleavon Little), is about to be greeted by its all-white town citizens in Mel Brooks' outrageous *Blazing Saddles* (Warner Bros., 1974).

The time has come to take the law into your own hands! Will you follow me?

Clayton Fletcher played by John Payne: Lewis Foster's *El Paso* (Paramount, 1949).

3496

Clayton: These men had to take the law into their own hands in order to defend the rights of their people.

Judge: The rights of the people? That has been the rallying cry of hoodlums since the beginning of time. Is that your justification for the heinous crimes you and these men have committed?

Clayton Fletcher played by John Payne and Judge Fletcher played by H.B. Warner: Lewis Foster's *El Paso* (Paramount, 1949).

3497

Clayton: Mob rule is no good no matter how we try to justify it. We've broken the law too. Did you ever stop to think who and what could be trying us someday?

Clayton Fletcher played by John Payne: Lewis Foster's *El Paso* (Paramount, 1949).

3498

Larkin: Where you find no law, you set your own. We tried him... found him guilty.

Bob Larkin played by Henry Fonda: Vincent McEveety's *Firecreek* (Warner Bros.–Seven Arts, 1968).

3499

Ramon: You mean you don't admire peace?

Stranger: It's not really easy to like something you don't know nothing about.

Ramon Rojo played by Gian Maria Volonte and the Stranger (Joe) played by Clint Eastwood: Sergio Leone's *A Fistful of Dollars* (United Artists, 1964; U.S. 1967).

3500

Matanza: It ain't no good sittin' here getting shot at.

Matanza was uncredited: Aldo Florio's *Five Giants from Texas* (Miro Cinematografica/P.C. Balcazar, 1966).

3501

Where life had no value, death, sometimes, had it's price. That is why the bounty killers appeared.

Prologue: Sergio Leone's *For a Few Dollars More* (United Artists, 1965; U.S. 1967).

3502

Quale: There's only one law in the west: the law of blood and bullets. It's either shoot or get shot. What are we gonna do?

Joe: Sue 'em!

S. Quentin Quale played by Groucho Marx and Joe Panello played by Chico Marx: Edward Buzzell's *Go West* (MGM, 1940).

3503

Drusilla: Sometimes it's so hard to under-stand that when there's so much beauty in the world how there can be such hate… such cruelty.

Drusilla played by Regina Taylor: David Greene's *A Good Day to Die* (a.k.a. *Children of the Dust*; Vidmark Entertainment, 1995).

3504

Teresa: You came back and talked of a new life. Instead, you brought the old one with you… death and violence.

Teresa played by Malila St. Duval: Paul Hunt's *The Great Gundown* (Sun Productions, 1977).

3505

Ballard: There must be some sense of honor left in you.

Slayton: There isn't much of that left any-where in the world.

Ballard: Ordinary men live by ordinary laws. I'm not an ordinary man. The laws I need, I make at my own convenience.

Jennifer Ballard played by Donna Reed and Frank Slayton played by Phil Carey: Raoul Walsh's *Gun Fury* (Columbia, 1953).

3506

Bat: It's not enough just to say no to any-one who's threatening you. You have to make it very clear to them that every street runs both ways.

Bat Masterson played by Joel McCrea: Joseph M. Newman's *The Gunfight at Dodge City* (United Artists, 1959).

3507

Max: It is hard to respect the law when you feel the heel of its boot on your back.

Max played by Reni Santoni: Paul Wendkos' *Guns of the Magnificent Seven* (United Artists, 1969).

3508

Charlie Wolf: It seems that white man not have peace even among each other.

Charlie Wolf played by Jack Buetel: Stuart Gilmore's *The Half-Breed* (RKO, 1952).

3509

Sheriff: You know, you'd be doing me a big favor, Miss Caulder, if you would just get yourself right the hell out of my town before some innocent people get caught in your crossfire.

Hannie: I wonder if you didn't say the same thing to the Clemens.

Sheriff: They weren't bothering nobody. They were just riding around being wanted. You're shooting the hell out of the place!

The Sheriff was uncredited and Hannie Caulder played by Raquel Welch: Burt Kennedy's *Hannie Caulder* (Paramount, 1971).

3510

Averill: The whole damn country will be nothing but widows and orphans soon.

James Averill played by Kris Kristofferson: Michael Cimino's *Heaven's Gate* (United Artists, 1980).

3511

Clanton: Get this through your heads! If this were back east, I could make law the way they do. But the best thing I can do out here is buy it!

Ike Clanton played by Robert Ryan: John Sturges' *The Hour of the Gun* (United Artists, 1967).

3512

Narrator: The law was in the hands of whoever could shoot fast and straight.

Narration by Spencer Tracy: John Ford's, George Marshall's, and Henry Hathaway's *How the West Was Won* (MGM, 1962).

3513

Hud: Well, I always say the law was meant to be interpreted in a lenient manner. And that's what I try to do. Sometimes I lean to one side of it, sometimes I lean to the other.

Hud Bannon played by Paul Newman: Martin Ritt's *Hud* (Paramount, 1963).

3514

Ann: What's the reason for all this vio-lence and terrorism?

Sam: Well, honey, if we had the answers to those questions, we wouldn't have to be cleaning these firearms now.

Ann Bolton played by Linda Sterling and Sam Bolton played by Tom London: Fred C. Brannon and Thomas Carr's *Jesse James Rides Again* (Re-public serial, Chapter 1: "The Black Raiders," 1947).

3515

Harlan: If the sheriff here can't stop him, I will, mister. I got claim to 935 sections. That's nearly 600,000 acres. And I'm not going to permit some sheep herder by the name of Luis Chama to get away with cutting fences and stirring up the Mexican population with talk about land reform. Nor am I going to waste time arguing in court.

Frank Harlan played by Robert Duvall and Luis Chama played John Saxon: John Sturges' *Joe Kidd* (Universal, 1972).

3516

Harlan: I came here to hunt Chama, not kill people in cold blood. I told you once before, I don't have time for court hear-ings. Now if these people want to fight me, then I'll blow 'em straight to hell!

Frank Harlan played by Robert Duvall and Luis Chama played John Saxon: John Sturges' *Joe Kidd* (Universal, 1972).

3517

Jory: Roy? Well, now that we're in Texas, I've been thinking.

Roy: Texas sure makes you think.

Jory: Yeah. Is there any place in Texas where a fella can become a lawyer?

Roy: Ha! Ha! Ha! A lawyer in Texas?

Jory Walden played by Robby Benson and Roy played by John Marley: Jorge Fons' *Jory* (Avco Embassy, 1972).

3518

Brookshire: Nothing that happens out here makes any sense. It's all just killing.

Ned Brookshire played by Charles Martin Smith: Joseph Sargent's *Larry McMurtry's Streets Of Laredo* (Cabin Fever Entertainment, 1995).

3519

Austin: Something's wrong with this val-ley. The war's over but the killin' don't stop.

Austin Dodd played by Patrick Kilpatrick: Dick Lowry's *Last Stand at Saber River* (Turner Net-work Television, 1997).

3520

In the wake of the pioneer came a back-wash of lawlessness which gave birth to the gun-man. Weak men were made strong by the aid of leaden death.

Prologue: Edward L. Cahn's *Law and Order* (Uni-versal, 1932).

3521

Janet: I don't wish to appear ungrateful, but was it quite necessary to shoot that man?

Tipton: No, ma'am. I could have let him shoot me.

Major: Why, I've been of the opinion that most arguments can be settled peace-ably.

Tipton: Well, out here they still rely on the guns, sir.

Janet Carter played by Ann Rutherford, John Tip-ton played by John Wayne, and Major Carter played by George "Gabby" Hayes: Joseph Kane's *The Lawless Nineties* (Republic, 1936).

3522

Near the turn of the last century, the Pecos River marked the boundaries of civilization in western Texas. West of the Pecos there was no law, no order, and only bad men and rattlesnakes lived there.

Prologue to John Huston's *The Life and Times of Judge Roy Bean* (NGP, 1972).

3523

Roy Bean: [*reading book cover*] "Revised Laws & Statutes of the State of Texas." What's that doing here?

Mexican Leader: For the whores to piss on!

Roy Bean played by Paul Newman and the Mexi-can Leader played by Frank Soto: John Huston's *The Life and Times of Judge Roy Bean* (NGP, 1972).

3524

Rev: Blessed is the Lord thy strength which teaches thy hand to war and thy fingers to fight. I shall pray for you, Bean. This land abounds in ruffians and varlets. Their numbers are legion, their evil skills commensurate.

Bean: Piss on 'em!

The Reverend LaSalle played by Anthony Perkins and Judge Roy Bean played by Paul Newman: John Huston's *The Life and Times of Judge Roy Bean* (NGP, 1972).

3525

Majesty: This is the 20th century! There's supposed to be no more frontiers where men can shoot their fellow creatures without being punished!

Madeline "Majesty" Hammond played by Jo Ann Sayers: Lesley Selander's *The Light of the Western Stars* (Paramount, 1940).

3526

Ned: I should have run them out of the country the first day they showed up.

Judge: Well, we tried. Then one morning we woke up to find a pickle jar sitting on top of the bar down at the saloon… and Sheriff Larssen's head was floating inside. Well, the town got the message then.

Ned Blessing played by Brad Johnson and Judge Longley played by Richard Riehle: Jack Bender's *Lone Justice II* (Triboro Entertainment Group, 1995).

3527

Commodore: Coop, your security isn't worth a damn! Everybody's got a gun!

Commodore Duvall played by James Coburn and Marshal Zane Cooper played by James Garner: Richard Donner's *Maverick* (Warner Bros., 1994).

3528

Landers: What would the Judge think, John, about vigilantes taking the law into their own hands?

John: Well, my father had said many times that the three worst disasters that could happen to mankind were pestilence, famine, and mob rule.

Bill Landers played by Myron Healey and John Malvin played by Lon McCallister: Ray Nazarro's *Montana Territory* (Columbia, 1952).

3529

Sheriff: But I have no sympathy, and never will have, with you men who want to substitute mob rule for the law. Do the people of a diseased-ridden community throw out their doctor just because there are too many sick people for him to cure?

Jason: Maybe not. But if they got any sense, they would pitch in and do some doctoring themselves.

Sheriff: Yeah and kill more people than they'll cure. And that's what will happen to the people if you take the law into your own hands.

Jason Waterman played by Hugh Sanders and Sheriff Henry Plummer played by Preston Foster: Ray Nazarro's *Montana Territory* (Columbia, 1952).

3530

Tom: How long can we go on living under this constant roar of guns… not knowing which one of us will be next? Mike Sawyer was a fine man… the fourth to be killed since we've been here. We've got to have law in this new frontier before these men tear down completely the thing we are trying to build.

Tom Lewis played by Murdock McQuarrie: Carl Pierson's *The New Frontier* (Republic, 1935).

3531

Judge: Luke, I haven't sat on the bench in ten years. The laws on the books may have changed, but the law itself hasn't. Law is the manifest will of the people, the conscious rule of the community. And when the mechanics of law enforcement break down, they must be re-established.

Judge Benson played by Edgar Stehli and Dr. Luke Canfield played by Charles Drake: Jack Arnold's *No Name on the Bullet* (Universal, 1959).

3532

Ferguson: There's only one law left in this town now… and that's every man for himself!

Jim Ferguson played by Harry Carey, Jr.: Edward L. Cahn's *Noose for a Gunman* (United Artists, 1960).

3533

Ned: Pop is counting on you bringing law in this territory, Judge.

Judge: That's going to be some job, judging from the scum of the west I've seen drifting in here.

Ned Kincaid played by Harvey Stephens and Judge Hardwick played by Donald Crisp: Lloyd Bacon's *The Oklahoma Kid* (Warner Bros., 1939).

3534

Davies: Wait a minute, men. Don't let's go off half-cocked and do something we'll be sorry for. We want to act in a reasoned and legitimate manner, not like a lawless mob.

Smith: The trouble with you, Davies, is you have been store-keeping too long. You don't see any profit in this. Now if any of you fellas would offer to buy the rope from him…

Arthur Davies played by Harry Davenport and Monty Smith played by Paul Hurst: William Wellman's *The Ox-Bow Incident* (20th Century–Fox, 1943).

3535

Priest: Murderers! Thieves! Destroyers! Blasphemy, murdering, and more than this… destroying my furniture!

The Priest played by Alberto Fernandez in Eugenio Martin's *Pancho Villa* (Granda/Scotia International, 1975).

3536

John Druin: I'm an officer in the United States Cavalry! I order you all to disperse!

Mob Member: Let's lynch him too!

John Druin played by Rod Cameron: Jospeh Kane's *The Plunderers* (Republic, 1948).

3537

Rhondo: I have seen violence many times, amigo… in many places. It is easier when one learns to live with it.

Rhondo played by John Saxon: Joseph Pevney's *The Plunderers* (Allied Artists, 1960).

3538

Parkinson: Where are your police? Have you no laws in this God-forsaken country?

Ricardo: Si, señorita, we have laws… and men to break them.

Beth Parkinson played by Tisha Sterling and Ricardo Sandoval played by Reni Santoni: Douglas Heyes' *Powderkeg* (TVW, 1971).

3539

Montgomery: Maybe I'm not the law you like, but I'm the only law there is.

Gerald Montgomery played by Herbert Rudley: John Sherwood's *Raw Edge* (Universal, 1956).

3540

Rick: I wish you'd settle down to a life of crime and forget these distractions. The world is ours! Another town, another poker game, a handy bank to be cracked. What do you say?

Ben: I'll tell you in a few moments. But just to be on the safe side, buy us a couple horses.

Rick Harper played by Arthur Kennedy and Ben Mathews, alias Ben Martin, played by Tony Curtis: Rudolph Mate's *The Rawhide Years* (Universal, 1956).

3541

Marshal: I wish you were as handy with common sense as you were with a gun and a rope.

Marshal Roberts played by Francis McDonald: William Dieterle's *Red Mountain* (Paramount, 1951).

3542

Gil: He was shot in the back.

Lamartine: These are difficult times.

Gil Kyle played by Glenn Ford and Lamartine played by Alan Reed: Leslie Fenton's *The Redhead and the Cowboy* (Paramount, 1951).

3543

Cherokee Jack: It's a nice world of yours, Captain. But we ain't part of it.

Cherokee Jack Jackson played by Dennis Haysbert and Captain Woodrow F. Call played by Jon Voight: Mike Robe's *Return to Lonesome Dove* (TVW, 1993).

3544

Dub: And that council of Durham's is going to slap on some taxes and hire us some law. Well, there's a lot of us around here that ain't geared to taxes.

Dub Stokes played by Gary Merrill and Brooks Durham played by Michael Rennie: Bernard McEveety's *Ride Beyond Vengeance* (Columbia, 1966).

3545

Esqueda: In the name of the law, Sheriff, I'm taking this town!

Sheriff: What law?

Esqueda: The law of the bullet. You think that does not make the law?

Sheriff: No, never!

Esqueda: Then we disagree?

Sheriff: We do.

Esqueda: Then you force me to prove my argument.

Jose Esqueda played by Anthony Quinn and Sheriff Parker played by Ted De Corsia: John Farrow's *Ride, Vaquero!* (MGM, 1953).

3546

Ballard: It's very difficult to deal moderately with people of lawless character.

Davis: Have you tangible evidence of this lawlessness?

Ballard: A jail full!

Ambrose Ballard played by Cy Kendall and Colonel Davis played by Henry Hall: Joseph Kane's *Robin Hood of the Pecos* (Republic, 1941).

3547

Molly: Hired killers.

Dolan: The badge gives them a license.

Dolan played by George Peppard and Molly Lang played by Jean Simmons: Arnold Laven's *Rough Night in Jericho* (Universal, 1967).

3548

Jed: Which of your two legs do you want broke first?

Jed Hooker played by Ossie Davis: Arnold Laven's *Sam Whiskey* (United Artists, 1969).

3549

Dell: Mr. Sweet, be careful!

Sweet: I guess that's just about the most unnecessary advice anybody ever got.

Dell Payton played by Shirley MacLaine and Jason Sweet played by Glenn Ford: George Marshall's *The Sheepman* (MGM, 1958).

Cordelia Cameron (Ava Gardner) takes exception to the Mexican bandit's comment that the meek shall inherit only six feet of the earth. The bandit is Jose Esqueda (Anthony Quinn) and his half-brother is Rio (Robert Taylor) who can't decide which side he's on in John Farrow's *Ride, Vanquero!* (MGM, 1953).

3550

Marshal: Listen to me, folks. Ballard can't get away. The roads are blocked and I'm deputizing every man in this town. Go home and get your guns!

Judge: Marshal! Men! Listen to me! Mob violence is the death to any town.

Ned McCarthy, pretending to be a Marshal from another jurisdiction, played by Dan Duryea. Judge Cranston played by Robert Warwick: Allan Dwan's *Silver Lode* (RKO, 1954).

3551

Mal: What about the law?

Ezra: Whose law? The law here runs a man down just like he's cattle.

Mal: That ain't right! I've had enough of what ain't right!

Mal played by Danny Glover and Ezra played by Joe Seneca: Lawrence Kasdan's *Silverado* (Columbia, 1985).

3552

John: Why can't we get some straight answers? Why didn't you tell us that Bass was shot in the back?

Sheriff: When a man is killed, does it make a whole lot of difference which direction the bullet came from?

John: It makes all the difference if you're trying to find out whether he was murdered or not!

John Elder played by John Wayne and Sheriff Billy Wilson played by Paul Fix: Henry Hathaway's *The Sons of Katie Elder* (Paramount, 1965)

3553

During the Alaskan gold rush, claim-jumping and mine stealing became an everyday occurrence — lawlessness was rampant.

Prologue to Ray Enright's *The Spoilers* (Universal, 1942).

3554

Cherry: Glad to see you out of jail again, Mr. Skinner!

Skinner: It's a temporary arrangement only. I'll be back in again by nightfall, I dare say.

Cherry Malotte played by Marlene Dietrich and Mr. Skinner played by Jack Norton: Ray Enright's *The Spoilers* (Universal, 1942).

3555

Alex: It's not only against the law to rob a bank, Glennister, but there's a local ordinance against killin' marshals!

Alex McNamara waa played by Rory Calhoun and Roy Glennister played by Jeff Chandler: Jesse Hibbs' *The Spoilers* (Universal, 1955).

3556

Rawlins: The only law we have: Sundown Valley is the law of the gun and the rope.

Jess Rawlins played by Bill Kennedy: Lesley Selander's *Storm Over Wyoming* (RKO, 1950).

3557

Rocklin: What's wrong with law and order?

Dave: Well, it depends on who's dishing it out. Now I never was much for orders. And as far as the law, you'll find out what that means around these parts.

Rocklin played by John Wayne and Dave played by George "Gabby" Hayes: Edwin L. Marin's *Tall in the Saddle* (RKO, 1944).

3558

Deputy: Did you have a ruckus with some of the boys in town yesterday?

Willard: To be more exact about it, they had a ruckus with me.

Deputy: One of them is dead.

Willard: That's why I'm alive.

Deputy Jeff Barkley played by Mickey Simpson and Rex Willard played by William Ching: Lesley Selander's *Tall Man Riding* (Warner Bros., 1955).

3559

Stewart: Campbell has grown as big as he can within the law. Now he's using violence to take him to the top. I'm standing in his way.

Corinne: You'll be killed. The last to fight and the first to die.

John Stewart played by Randolph Scott, Corinne Michaels played by Jocelyn Brando, and Wick Campbell played by Richard Boone: Bruce Humberstone's *Ten Wanted Men* (Columbia, 1955).

3560

Governor: This territory has laws for men to live by. And that's the real point of everything. When you haven't got laws, you got lawlessness… and that leads to crime.

The Governor played by J. Edward McKinley: Joseph L. Mankiewicz's *There Was a Crooked Man* (Warner Bros., 1970).

3561

Ben: What do I do now?

Morg: Wait. They got to get wound up first. It takes time and plenty of liquor. A mob is only as tough as its leader. You only got one man to lick.

Sheriff Ben Owens played by Anthony Perkins and Morg Hickman played by Henry Fonda: Anthony Mann's *The Tin Star* (Paramount, 1957).

3562

Belle: Handling rustlers after your experience with the Apache warriors should be like shootin' fish in a barrel.

Horn: Well now, you're talking about the high side of shootin' and the low side of the law.

Belle: Bring 'em to trial if you like. I feel in what I know about you, you're going to want to go ahead and shoot. But from the standpoint of the Association, that's going to be entirely up to you.

Horn: Whether I bring them in… or shoot?

Belle: That is your problem.

Horn: Listen, you're a U.S. Marshal. You tell me, what's the difference between a U.S. Marshal and… and an assassin?

Belle: The Marshal's checks come in on time.

U.S. Marshal Joe Belle played by Billy Green Bush and Tom Horn played by Steve McQueen: William Wiard's *Tom Horn* (Warner Bros., 1980).

3563

Rosser: Vigilantes don't solve any problem. They only create new ones.

Tom Rosser played by Dana Andrews: Lesley Selander's *Town Tamer* (Paramount, 1965).

3564

Condor: You see, the vigilantes are a mob. These badges make us legal. We're the law. And the law has the right to shoot up a mob.

Riley Condor played by Bruce Cabot: Lesley Selander's *Town Tamer* (Paramount, 1965).

3565

Masterson: Listen, friends. Logan Maury's men are drunk with liquor. You're drunk with anger. That's worse and it's more dangerous. Mob rule is a poor substitute for law and order and can only bring wholesale murder. Why, this kind of wild talk makes lawbreakers out of decent citizens like yourself.

Bat Masterson played by Randolph Scott and Logan Maury played by Steve Bodie: Ray Enright's *Trail Street* (RKO, 1947).

3566

Mayor: A murderous crew tried to run Dodge City once. And then Bat Masterson stepped in. After a wholesale funeral on Boot Hill, the town went suddenly peaceful again.

The Mayor played by Harry Harvey: Ray Enright's *Trail Street* (RKO, 1947).

3567

Carmody: We take care of our own troubles here in Liberal.

Masterson: You don't do a very good job of it. If I hadn't happened along, you'd have had to hang this man for murder.

Carmody: You talk like a peace officer.

Masterson: Every citizen is a peace officer where the peace is violated. This is a free country by statutes.

Carmody: The statutes haven't reached this part of Kansas yet. You have plenty to learn, my friend. Among other things, I'll inform you that no cowboy will ever hang in Liberal.

Masterson: Liberal is the county seat. According to law, it's where killers hang when convicted.

Carmody: Let's put it this way… if they're convicted, they hang. I'll advise you to get acquainted with our town.

Carmody played by Billy House and Bat Masterson played by Randolph Scott: Ray Enright's *Trail Street* (RKO, 1947).

3568

Gold Hat: We are federales. You know, the mounted police.

Dobbs: If you are the police, where are your badges?

Gold Hat: Badges? We ain't got no badges! We don't need no badges! I don't have to show you no stinkin' badges!

Gold Hat played by Alfonso Bedoya and Fred C. Dobbs played by Humphrey Bogart: John Huston's *The Treasure of the Sierra Madre* (Warner Bros., 1948).

3569

Magruder: Out here we don't take kindly to strangers who come among us and try to use our law to settle their private grudges.

Magruder played by James Westerfield: Rudolph Maté's *The Violent Men* (Columbia, 1955).

3570

Molly: Don't you realize that was down right murder?

Taylor: Now there ain't no use talking about it, dearie. Crime is ranked differently in different countries. And out here, stealing is about the meanest, the lowest thing a man can do.

Molly: But that doesn't justify killing. And Steve, his friend?

Taylor: It ain't a question of friends or enemies. It's a question of right and wrong. Why, if we didn't hold a rope and a six-shooter over them outlaws, you couldn't teach your school at all. Why, our lives wouldn't be worth living.

Molly: You think I'll teach my children to believe in that? You think I'll praise the new generation to approve of murder?

Taylor: Where you come from they have policemen and courts and jails to enforce the law. Here, we got nothing. So when we have to, we do things our own

way. Do you think it was easy for him to have to hang a friend? It was a darn sight harder for him to do it than us to bear it.

Miss Molly Stark Wood played by Mary Brian and Mrs. Taylor played by Helen Ware: Victor Fleming's *The Virginian* (Paramount, 1929).

3571

Creighton: Well then, I guess I better see the law about this.

Slade: You'll have to go back to Omaha if you do. It don't run beyond there.

Creighton: I'll make some of my own!

Edward Creighton played by Dean Jagger and Jack Slade played by Barton MacLane: Fritz Lang's *Western Union* (20th Century–Fox, 1941).

3572

Mayor: I heard he was treed in Ellsworth a couple years ago.

Masterson: Treed?

Whiteside: A western expression… meaning terrified.

The Mayor played by Carl Benton Reid, Bat Masterson played by Keith Larsen, and Whiteside played by Wallace Ford: Jacques Tourneur's *Wichita* (Allied Artists/Warner Bros., 1955).

3573

Ramsey: Carter, do you remember the time I told you that civilization was gonna catch up to you whether you liked it or not? Well, it has. And it's passed ya.

Jeff Ramsay played by Dick Foran and King Carter played by Harry Woods: Ford Beebe's and Ray Taylor's *Winners of the West* (Universal serial, Chapter 13: "Barricades Blasted," 1940).

3574

Nicholas: I've got to tell you something, Wyatt. I told your brothers when they went off to fight, and I suppose the time has come for you. You know, I am a man that believes in the law. After your family, it's about the only thing you got to believe in. But there are plenty of men who don't care about the law. Men who will take part in all kind of vicious-

ness, and don't care who gets hurt. In fact, the more they get hurt, the better. When you find yourself in a fight with such viciousness, hit first if you can. And when you do hit, hit to kill. You'll know. Don't worry. You'll know when it comes to that. The Earps always know!

Nicholas Earp played by Gene Hackman and Wyatt Earp played by Kevin Costner: Lawrence Kasdan's *Wyatt Earp* (Warner Bros., 1994).

3575

Warren: Wyatt, you're still a marshal around here, ain't ya?

Doc: Sure, but now he's going to be a marshal and an outlaw… the best of both worlds, son.

Warren Earp played by James Caviezel, Doc Holliday played by Dennis Quaid, and Wyatt Earp played by Kevin Costner: Lawrence Kasdan's *Wyatt Earp* (Warner Bros., 1994).

3576

Earp: My name is Wyatt Earp! It all ends now!

Wyatt Earp played by Kevin Costner: Lawrence Kasdan's *Wyatt Earp* (Warner Bros., 1994).

3577

Alex: What the hell happened, Doc?

Doc: There's a whirlwind out there. When you're in it, you can't get out.

Alex McSween played by Terrance O'Quinn and Josiah "Doc" Scurlock played by Kiefer Sutherland: Christopher Cain's *Young Guns* (20th Century–Fox, 1988).

3578

Bonney: If there was one thing an outlaw feared in the New Mexico territory it was lynch mob justice. With no patience for courts and trials, they did it their own way. And there was no stopping 'em. Mainly because the so-called law had no damn intentions of stopping 'em.

William H. Bonney, alias Billy the Kid, played by Emilio Estevez: Geoff Murphy's *Young Guns II* (20th Century–Fox, 1990).

Lawmen

See also Chase; Good Guys; Gunfighters; Justice

3579

Marshal: Now, Bravo, I thought we were old friends.

Sheriff: We are, Dan, we are. But you got the idea that you ought to kick up a fuss about things that are bound to happen

anyway. I don't figure that way. A man's got to live. Cows get lost, sometimes accidents happen, and fellas get killed. Why get hot under the collar about it? And why go hunting for fellas that don't want to be found?

Marshal Dan Mitchell played by Randolph Scott and Sheriff Bravo Trimble played by Edgar Buchanan: Edwin Marin's *Abilene Town* (United Artists, 1946).

Deputy Jeff Barkley (Mickey Simpson) knows more about a killing than he's willing to share with Larry Madden (Randolph Scott) in Lesley Selander's *Tall Man Riding* (Warner Bros., 1955).

3580

Marshal: I understand you filed for reelection next fall, Bravo.

Sheriff: Yeah, they talked me into it. I figured on opening up a saloon or maybe going back to practicing dentistry. But somebody has got to keep law and order in the county.

Marshal Dan Mitchell played by Randolph Scott and Sheriff Bravo Trimble played by Edgar Buchanan: Edwin Marin's *Abilene Town* (United Artists, 1946).

3581

Jonah: So, Marshal Brisco County, now that you have rounded up the thirteen most notorious outlaws in all the west, including John Bly, what do you do for an encore?

Marshal: I believe I'll smoke this pipe.

Jonah Collier played by Dan Gerrity and Marshal Brisco County played by R. Lee Ermey: Bryan Spicer's *Adventures of Brisco County, Jr.* (TVW, Series Premiere, 1993).

3582

Carson: The Governor gave me orders to start pushing law west of the Pecos. And here's where I start pushing!

Sunset Carson played himself: Thomas Carr's *Alias Billy the Kid* (Republic, 1946).

3583

Ed: Who are you?

Marshal: My name is Merrick. I'm a United States Marshal here.

Dan: You're new in the territory.

Marshal: The law isn't.

Ed Roden played by Morris Ankrum, Marshal Len Merrick played by Kirk Douglas, and Dan Roden played by James Anderson: Raoul Walsh's *Along the Great Divide* (Warner Bros., 1951).

3584

Stillwell: Anytime you got one of them down-home sheriffs, you always got a town full of vigilantes.

Frank Stillwell played by Slim Pickens: Norman Tokar's *The Apple Dumpling Gang* (Buena Vista, 1975).

3585

Sheriff: I didn't know you had any dealings with Indians.

Rile: You still don't know. That's what I pay you for: not to know anything.

Sheriff: What is it, Tom? Are you selling the Apaches whiskey or guns?

Rile: You better put that blindfold back on.

Sheriff: It's no wonder you got so many gunslingers working for you.

Rile: You know, you'd look a lot healthier with that usual dumb look on your face.

Sheriff: Tom, I can only go so far with that dumb look and then something gets stuck in my craw, and I can't get it out.

Rile: Yeah, what? Your conscience?

Sheriff Grover played by Barton MacLane and Tom Rile played by Scott Brady: Lesley Selander's *Arizona Bushwhackers* (Paramount, 1968).

3586

Sweeney: You're straight-foward, Marshal. I like a man after my own heart. Well, actually, not always. Once there was a man after my own heart, and I had to strangle him with his own intestines.

Sweeney played by Maxwell Caulfield and Marshal Zack Stone played by Richard Joseph Paul: Sam Irvin's *Backlash: Oblivion 2* (Full Moon Entertainment, 1996).

3587

Sheriff: Don't you understand? You know, when you wear this badge, you're the law. And when somebody

does something against the law, then you're supposed to do something about it. I did nothing. And that's what's eating me. What kind of prescription do you got for that?
Doc: I don't know. I haven't found one for myself.

Sheriff Tim Horn played by Dean Jagger and Doc Velie played by Walter Brennan: John Sturges' *Bad Day at Black Rock* (MGM, 1955).

3588
Smith: Tim, you're just a lost ball in the high weeds. I told you a long time ago nothing happened for you to worry about.
Tim: The thing is, I do worry. Maybe I ain't much else, but I sure am a worrier. And I still am the law.

Reno Smith played by Robert Ryan and Sheriff Tim Horn played by Dean Jagger: John Sturges' *Bad Day at Black Rock* (MGM, 1955).

3589
Clayborne: If you were anything more than a pile of manure with a badge on it, my Colonel might still be alive.

The Widow Clayborne played by Zoaunne LeRoy: Jonathan Kaplan's *Bad Girls* (20th Century–Fox, 1994).

3590
B.D.: Now, that town marshal, he don't look like much neither. But I don't believe they give him that badge just to keep his vest from a flappin'.

B.D. played by James Brolin: Clyde Ware's *Bad Jim* (RCA/Columbia Home Video, 1990).

3591
Coyote: Daggone it, Sheriff, you should have been an outlaw!

Jim Badger, alias The Coyote Kid, played by George "Gabby" Hayes: Tim Whelan's *Badman's Territory* (RKO, 1946).

3592
Henryette: I'd advise you to remove that star.
Sheriff: Well, thanks, but I think maybe I can take care of myself.
Henryette: The life expectancy of a sheriff can be very short in Quinto.

Henryette Alcott played by Ann Richards and Sheriff Mark Rowley played by Randolph Scott: Tim Whelan's *Badman's Territory* (RKO, 1946).

3593
Mark: Johnny, if you were an outlaw camped down there on the creek and saw a posse coming up behind you, what would you do?
Johnny: I'd head up this cut to open country where a man could use a fresh horse.
Mark: Right! Now, as a deputy sheriff who's figured out the outlaw's next move?

Johnny: I'd sneak up behind those trees.
Mark: Right!
Johnny: And pump lead into 'em as they come up.
Mark: Wrong! A good officer don't kill except in self-defense. The law says every man has a right to a fair trial.
Johnny: Outlaws? Train robbers?
Mark: And even murderers. No one's guilty until he's convicted. So try to take your man alive.
Johnny: But what if he shows fight?
Mark: That's different! Shoot and don't miss!

Sheriff Mark Rowley played by Randolph Scott and Deputy Sheriff Johnny Rowley played by James Warren: Tim Whelan's *Badman's Territory* (RKO, 1946).

3594
Billy: Well, how many bad men are you supposed to chase if you're a deputy?
Jeremy: I guess five a week or so.
Billy: It seems like you'd run out of people in town to chase.
Jeremy: Nah, there's always new ones to chase. My pa says decent people live on farms. Anybody who lives in town is a thief or makes their living off what they steal.

Billy Baker played by Lee Montgomery and Jeremy played by Brian Williams: Lyman Dayton's *Baker's Hawk* (Doty/Dayton, 1976).

3595
Boone: Well, you know how it is in this business. One slipup... adios!

Boone Choate played by Tom Bower: Robert M. Young's *The Ballad of Gregorio Cortez* (Embassy Pictures, 1983).

3596
Billy: Don't he get a badge or something?
Eric: Well, they didn't give me a badge for him. But... wait... there's a United States eagle on this dollar. That's all you need!

Billy The Kid played by Robert Taylor and Eric Keating played by Ian Hunter: David Miller's *Billy the Kid* (MGM, 1941).

3597
Copeland: Ain't you forgot something?
Marshal: What?
Copeland: Swear me in as your deputy.
Marshal: All right, raise your hand.
Copeland: Which one?
Marshal: Hell, I don't care... all right, you're sworn.
Copeland: Is that all there is to it?
Marshal: That's all.
Copeland: Well, hell, that ain't much.
Marshal: Well, it ain't much of a job.

Copeland played by David Huddleston and Marshal Henry Gifford played by Jack Warden: Ted Kotcheff's *Billy Two Hats* (United Artists, 1973).

3598
Sheriff: Tetlow, if you're so legal you ought to know I can't clear your man, Havalik. Only a coroner's jury can do that... at an official inquest.
Tetlow: Well, under the circumstances, that seems like an unnecessary formality.
Havalik: Yeah, and I ain't wasting my time listening to some jury tell me a lot of stuff I already know. Besides, Carson got no more lead than he asked for.
Sheriff: Did I hear you refuse to appear before the coroner's jury?
Havalik: Well, you ain't deaf are you?

Sheriff Mach played by Ken Christy, Jared Tetlow played by Victor Jory, and Dee Havalik played by William Tannen: Earl Bellamy's *Blackjack Ketchum, Desperado* (Columbia, 1956).

3599
Tindal: Why, you've been a deputy here for 20 years and look at ya! You're insolent, you're illiterate, you haven't taken a bath in a month... and you dress like a buffalo hunter!

R.D. Tindal played by Sam Smiley: C.T. McIntyre's *Border Shootout* (Turner Home Entertainment, 1990).

3600
Frye: I don't think you understood who I am, mister.
Davis: Oh, we understand who you are. You're a horse's ass lawman who has lost his badge. So I guess that just makes you a plain old horse's ass, don't it?

Kirby Frye played by Cody Glenn and Lieutenant Davis played by Josef Ranier: C.T. McIntyre's *Border Shootout* (Turner Home Entertainment, 1990).

3601
Edith: Frye must have done something really stupid.
Haig: Oh, he did! He tried to uphold the law in this piss-ant town.

Edith Hanasain played by Charlene Tilton, Haig Hanasain played by Don Starr, and Kirby Frye played by Cody Glenn: C.T. McIntyre's *Border Shootout* (Turner Home Entertainment, 1990).

3602
Crow: Pay no attention to Sheriff Guthrie. He's just a little bit bitter because he's about to become a footnote in Sweetwater's past.

Crow played by Ramon Bieri and Sheriff Tom Guthrie played by Ed Bruce: Stuart Margolin's *Bret Maverick: The Lazy Ace* (TVW, 1981).

3603
Guthrie: Well, there's no law against buying votes. Some of the folks around here need the money more than they need the choice. That's just the way it's done now. Now if you'll excuse me.

Rodney: Well, M.L. says you should give longer speeches.

Guthrie: So she has told me more than once. Speech-making and hand-shaking don't have anything to do with being a good sheriff. When I came to this town, they didn't even have elections. I ran off the Bannavich Gang and they hired me. It was as simple as that. Now, a man has got to kiss babies… among other things.

Sheriff Tom Guthrie played by Ed Bruce and Rodney played by David Knell: Stuart Margolin's *Bret Maverick: The Lazy Ace* (TVW, 1981).

3604

Marshal: You see, no man really knows right from wrong. That's why laws are invented. I've lived by them all my life. It's the only way I can be sure of myself.

The Marshal played by Kent Taylor: John Bushelman's *The Broken Land* (20th Century–Fox, 1962).

3605

Waitress: How long will he hold you?

The Kid: It's hard to tell. He's got a real bad case… like none I've ever seen.

Waitress: A case of what?

The Kid: I call it blood hunger. It eats away at a man's guts and it don't matter which side of the law he's on.

The Waitress played by Diana Darrin and The Kid was played by Jack Nicholson: John Bushelman's *The Broken Land* (20th Century–Fox, 1962).

3606

Cahill: Any of you want to surrender?

Ben: Now what did you say?

Cahill: I said, any of you want to surrender?

Ben: Five of us and one of you! I'll say one thing for you, J.D., you got style! Yes sir, you got style!

Marshal J.D. Cahill played by John Wayne and Ben Tildy played by Scott Walter: Andrew McLaglen's *Cahill: United States Marshal* (Warner Bros., 1973).

3607

Constable: Oh, we don't have gunfighters up here [Canada].

Ben: No?

Billy: How come?

Constable: There's no need. That's the difference.

Ben: Between what?

Constable: This side of the line and yours.

Ben: Are you claiming there is something wrong with the States of America?

Constable: Oh, I guess I am in a way.

Billy: That ain't very friendly.

Constable: Well, doesn't it ever make you think though?

Ben: About what?

Constable: That you have to tie a gun to your leg wherever you go.

Ben: You mean you don't here?

Constable: No.

Billy: Why?

Constable: The force. You see, we arrived in this territory long before any whites moved in. The law got here first you might say. It's the other way around in your country. The settlers come, crime gets out of hand. They pin a star on a man. Like it or not, he gets the job done. But it sure makes for a lot of dead men in the street.

Constable Springer played by Burt Metcalfe, Ben played by Scott Peters, and Billy played by Richard Alden: Burt Kennedy's *The Canadians* (20th Century–Fox, 1961).

3608

Kate: Do you really believe it's the sheriff's duty to hang a man we all know is innocent?

Kate Brady played by Kim Darby: Don Keeslar's *The Capture of Grizzly Adams* (TVW, 1982).

3609

Frankie: Well now, there's a game for a sheriff: liar's poker. We got our unemployed off the street and made Wolf City safe all in one brilliant stroke.

Frankie Ballou played by John Marley: Elliot Silverstein's *Cat Ballou* (Columbia, 1965).

3610

Murphy: The Sheriff here has formed his posse. Oh, have you got anything you want to add to that, Sheriff?

Sheriff: Just this: now you people can either help me or stay the hell out of my way!

Lawrence Murphy played by Forrest Tucker and Sheriff Dan Nodeen played by Christopher George: Andrew McLaglen's *Chisum* (Warner Bros., 1970).

3611

Sheriff: Hi everybody! I'm serving notice on all of you evil-doers to make yourself scarce because the majesty of the law has just arrived.

Sheriff O'Hea played by Edgar Buchanan: Ray Enright's *Coroner Creek* (Columbia, 1948).

3612

Reece: You know being a town marshal, I always figured that was a pretty good job. What made you give it up?

Bender: Same old story. You know, a man gets a reputation with a gun, he's just got to do too much killin'.

Tom Reece played by Glenn Ford and Doc Bender played by Brian Donlevy: Delmer Daves' *Cowboy* (Columbia, 1958).

3613

Weatherby: Now these are orders, Mr. Hickok. Your patriotic duty demands that…

Wild Bill: Sonny, there are duty scars all over my hide. From now on, folks are going to buy tickets just to look at 'em on a stage of a theater.

Weatherby: You mean you're going to be an actor?

Wild Bill: Why not? You're what marshaling has petered down to!

Martin Weatherby played by Leif Erickson and Wild Bill Hickok played by Reed Hadley: Stuart Heisler's *Dallas* (Warner Bros., 1950).

3614

Wild Bill: Marshal, I'm glad I met you while you were still with us. You're going to be the shortest lived marshal on record.

Wild Bill Hickok played by Reed Hadley: Stuart Heisler's *Dallas* (Warner Bros., 1950).

3615

Doc: You know, you could make something out of yourself if you tried.

Bob: Yeah?

Doc: Yeah. You could run for marshal.

Bob: Me being a marshal? Are you loco?

Doc: Well, you could try. It's better for a young fella like you to be working for Uncle Sam rather than against him.

Bob: I can't read or write. You know that!

Doc: Listen, you don't read or write a man into jail.

Doc Grunch played by George "Gabby" Hayes and Bob Seton played by John Wayne: Raoul Walsh's *The Dark Command* (Republic, 1940).

3616

Seton: Folks, it's true. I don't know much about the law. Ain't had much book learning. But the good Lord gave me a nose for smelling a horse thief a mile off. And what you need in these parts is a marshal that's better at smelling than spelling.

Bob Seton played by John Wayne: Raoul Walsh's *The Dark Command* (Republic, 1940).

3617

Cantrell: Learning, studying, working like a dog… and what does it get me? The first chance I have to be somebody [Marshal], I'm beaten out of it by an ignorant cowhand who can't even write his own name! Well, I can write mine… and I'm going to write it across the territory in letters of fire and blood if I have to! I'm going to be somebody in this country! Somebody big!

William Cantrell played by Walter Pidgeon: Raoul Walsh's *The Dark Command* (Republic, 1940).

3618

Sheriff: If you're in town by sundown tomorrow, I'm going to throw you in jail.

Rapp: On what charge?

Sheriff: Disturbing my peace of mind!

Sheriff Cauthen played by Edgar Buchanan and Jimmy Rapp played by Alex Nicol: George Sherman's *Dawn at Socorro* (Universal, 1954).

3619

Sheriff: Hey, take it easy. They ain't going to run out of that stuff [whiskey].

Rapp: When I stop drinking, you start worrying.

Sherirf: It's too late. I've already started worrying. Let's have your gun.

Rapp: I'm naked without it.

Sheriff: That's all right. I won't arrest you for being naked.

Sheriff Cauthen played by Edgar Buchanan and Jimmy Rapp played by Alex Nicol: George Sherman's *Dawn at Socorro* (Universal, 1954).

3620

Brett: I was just listing my friends.

Sheriff: What about your enemies?

Brett: All my friends are my enemies. I hate 'em because I have to leave 'em.

Sheriff: Yeah, that's the part I like best... you leaving.

Brett Wade played by Rory Calhoun and Sheriff Cauthen played by Edgar Buchanan: George Sherman's *Dawn at Socorro* (Universal, 1954).

3621

Marshal: You don't belong. There's no place for your...

Jagade: You can save the rest of that speech. I've heard it. There's no place for your kind. Civilization has come to the west. The good people! They made all the rules. You either live by 'em or you're driven out. And what they can't do with the fear of God, they do with a hired gun. Only they call him a marshal.

Marshal Allan Burnett played by Jock Mahoney and Jagade played by Dale Robertson: Harmon Jones' *A Day of Fury* (Universal, 1956).

3622

Judge: Wiley, just what did you expect to do when you came on as Sheriff here?

Sheriff: I didn't say I wouldn't do the job. I'm just not interested in committing suicide, that's all. Are you?

Judge Jim Scott played by Fred MacMurray and Sheriff Barney Wiley played by John Ericson: Harry Keller's *Day of the Bad Man* (Universal, 1958).

3623

Conway: I'll tell you one thing: if that there Blake fella keeps on shootin' marshals, I might end up liking the bastard!

Conway Twill played by Michael Wincott and William Blake played by Johnny Depp: Jim Jarmusch's *Dead Man* (Miramax Films, 1996).

3624

Sheriff: Captain Vesser, you got to be taught a lesson. You got to learn that to fight in a war at peace time is the business of peace officers, not private citizens. We have law in this country. And if a man breaks the law against you, you're just as guilty as him if you break the law trying to get back at him.

Sheriff Ed Johnson played by James Burke and Captain Jim Vesser played by Edmond O'Brien: Byron Haskin's *Denver and Rio Grande* (Paramount, 1952).

3625

Ballard: Marshal Dancey! I had no idea it's our time of the month to have you here!

Marshal: You make it sound like a physical affliction.

Gentleman Johnny Ballard played by David Warner and Marshal Dancey played by Pernell Roberts: Virgil W. Vogel's *Desperado* (TVW, 1987).

3626

McCall: You're not the law. There is no law! You're just another man with a gun. Only you're paid by a better class of people.

Duell McCall played by Alex McArthur and Bede was played by Yaphet Kotto: Virgil W. Vogel's *Desperado* (TVW, 1987).

3627

Marshal: Oh, these posters on Duell McCall... they're not legal. That's bounty hunting.

Ballard: He's an enemy of the Company.

Marshal: The Company is not the law.

Ballard: The Company pays more than the law. How much does the law pay you, Marshal?

Marshal: Are you trying to bribe me, Mr. Ballard?

Ballard: If I have to try to bribe a man, Marshal, he's probably unbribable.

Marshal Dancey played by Pernell Roberts and Gentleman Johnny Ballard played by David Warner: Virgil W. Vogel's *Desperado* (TVW, 1987).

3628

Cates: You know, I tried most ways of making a living. But they're all too much like hard work. Hell, I wouldn't even mind being sheriff... if I could find a town soft enough.

Charlie Cates played by Whip Hubley: E.W. Swackhamer's *Desperado: The Outlaw Wars* (TVW, 1989).

3629

Destry: Oh listen, Mayor. I've got a little problem I'd like to take up with you. It's sort of official.

Mayor: Well, I'm always glad to talk over any problems concerning the welfare of the community.

Destry: Yeah, I know. That's why I came to see ya. You see, Rags and I don't seem to be getting much cooperation.

Mayor: That so?

Destry: Yeah. Every time I start asking questions, the people kind of look vague and sort of drift away.

Mayor: What kind of questions do you ask?

Destry: Oh, just ordinary things. Like, what really happened to Sheriff Bailey?

Mayor: I knew a fella once who made himself real unpopular asking questions. It got so nobody talked to him. He died lonely. You might keep that in mind.

Destry: I will. Sounds like a pretty awful way to die.

Destry played by Audie Murphy, Mayor Hiram Sellers played by Edgar Buchanan, and Rags Barnaby played by Thomas Mitchell: George Marshall's *Destry* (Universal, 1954).

3630

Destry: Boys, hold the music, will ya? Folks, I hate to interrupt your fun, but I got something important to say to you. I just found out how Sheriff Bailey died.

Decker: I understood Bailey died of a heart attack.

Destry: That seems to be the rumor around town. If he did die of a heart attack, that's because he heard a bullet coming at him.

Destry played by Audie Murphy and Decker played by Lyle Bettger: George Marshall's *Destry* (Universal, 1954).

3631

Bartender: Are you going to take over the whole job now?

Destry: What job?

Bartender: Well, Rags was just in here and traded this [badge] for a jug. I guess he figured it was better to be a first-rate drunk than a second-rate sheriff.

The Bartender played by Ralph Peters, Destry played by Audie Murphy, and Sheriff Rags Barnaby played by Thomas Mitchell: George Marshall's *Destry* (Universal, 1954).

3632

Mayor: Friends... fellow citizens. As the poet says: life is real... life is earnest... and the goal is but the grave. Or words to that affect. It is my sorrowful duty to inform you that one of our fellow townsmen has just made the goal. Our esteemed sheriff, Joseph Bailey, is no longer with us. In the absence of other officials, and in the interest of law and order, and in accordance with ordinance number eight thousand and, ah, six-five-four, I must appoint a temporary successor. I have considered this matter seriously, and sought the advice of prominent citizens. I have decided to appoint a sheriff, a man who is not without experience as a peace officer. A man you all love and respect. Mr.... ah, er, what's his name again?

Mayor Hiram Sellers played by Edgar Buchanan: George Marshall's *Destry* (Universal, 1954).

3633

Wash: Frenchy, am I really the sheriff?

Frenchy: Sure you are.

Wash: Then I'm off the liquor! A man has got to choose between the bottle and the badge.

Sheriff Washington Dimsdale played by Charles Winninger and Frenchy played by Marlene Dietrich: George Marshall's *Destry Rides Again* (Universal, 1939).

3634
Wash: Here's your badge. Don't let anyone see it… without guns.

Sheriff Washington Dimsdale played by Charles Winninger: George Marshall's *Destry Rides Again* (Universal, 1939).

3635
Abby: Do you still feel the weight of that tin star on your shirt?

Abby Nixon played by Virginia Mayo: Alfred Werker's *Devil's Canyon* (RKO, 1953).

3636
Tex: Hey wait! You ain't going to keep me in here [jail], are you?
Hatton: I'm sorry, Tex, but you read that notice the same as anyone else. Three days in there won't do you a bit of harm.
Tex: Ah, but you can't do this to me after all we have been through together. We fought a war together, built a railroad together. We ate, drank, slept, lived and died together.
Hatton: And now we are going to be in jail together. You in there and me out here.

Tex Baird played by Guinn "Big Boy" Williams and Wade Hatton played by Errol Flynn in Michael Curtiz's *Dodge City* (Warner Bros., 1939).

3637
Surrett: You see, I make $100,000 a year one way or another. Frankly, I don't need that much money. So naturally I'd be willing to make a deal with anyone that would, ah, well, sort of see things my way. It would make a mighty good deal for both of us.
Hatton: You mean a little friendly bribery, huh?
Surrett: Well, you can catch more flies with molasses than you can with vinegar.

Jeff Surrett played by Bruce Cabot and Wade Hatton played by Errol Flynn: Michael Curtiz's *Dodge City* (Warner Bros., 1939).

3638
Sheriff: Remember, we, the law, will beat them. Because the right is on our side. And that makes a big difference.

Sheriff Sam Hughes played by George Macready: Gordon Douglas' *The Doolins of Oklahoma* (Columbia, 1949).

3639
Holland: It won't be the first time a lawman holed me in the back, Sheriff. But I always did get one or two shots off… in acknowledgement you might say.

Handsome Harry H. Holland played by Kirk Douglas: Steven H. Stern's *Draw!* (TVW, 1984).

3640
Johnny: I'm reformed, but my friend here isn't. His name is Blake from Tombstone. And he don't like marshals.
Marshal: Maybe there's a good reason why you don't like marshals.
Blake: None of 'em live long enough for us to get acquainted.
Marshal: You've been meeting the wrong kind of marshals.

Johnny Sombrero played by Eugene Iglesias, Rat Face Blake played by Kyle James/James Anderson, and Marshal/Lightning played by Stephen McNally: Don Siegel's *The Duel at Silver Creek* (Universal, 1952).

3641
Dusty: Lightning, Johnny has been talking big since word got around that you were wounded. He figured it's bound to have slowed you down.
Lightning: I never had much respect for Johnny's figuring.

Dusty Fargo played by Susan Cabot, Marshal/Lightning played by Stephen McNally, and Johnny Sombrero played by Eugene Iglesias: Don Siegel's *The Duel at Silver Creek* (Universal, 1952).

3642
Joey: Good morning, Sheriff.
Sheriff: Joey, I'm taking a bath!
Joey: Oh, don't mind me, Sheriff. I was raised with four brothers.
Sheriff: Well, I'm not your brother!

Joey MacDonald played by Michele Carey and Sheriff J.P. Harrah played by Robert Mitchum: Howard Hawks' *El Dorado* (Paramount, 1967).

3643
Cole: I'm looking at a tin star with a drunk pinned on it!

Cole Thornton played by John Wayne: Howard Hawks' *El Dorado* (Paramount, 1967).

3644
Sheriff: Look, Cole, I may be a drunk. I may not be able to load my own gun. But I don't need you to tell me how to do my job.

Sheriff J.P. Harrah played by Robert Mitchum and Cole Thornton played by John Wayne: Howard Hawks' *El Dorado* (Paramount, 1967).

3645
Bull: Here's a couple badges. Now raise your right hand. I forgot the words but you better say, I do.
Cole & Mississippi: I do.
Bull: Now you're deputies.
Mississippi: Do you suppose these [badges] will do us any good if someone takes a shot at us?

Bull: It will give them a good mark to shoot at.

Bull Harris played by Arthur Hunnicutt, Cole Thornton played by John Wayne, and Alan Bourdillon Traherne ("Mississippi") played by James Caan: Howard Hawks' *El Dorado* (Paramount, 1967).

3646
Clayton: I was under the impression that an officer of the law was hired to keep the peace, not break it.

Clayton Fletcher played by John Payne: Lewis Foster's *El Paso* (Paramount, 1949).

3647
Larkin: Two dollars a month! The homemade badge! You got no business laying your life on the line!

Bob Larkin played by Henry Fonda: Vincent McEveety's *Firecreek* (Warner Bros.–Seven Arts, 1968).

3648
[*Two posses unknowingly end up in a shootout*]
Pierce: Now hold it! You fellas haven't a tinker's chance. Throw down your guns. You'll get a fair trial. I'll give you my word on that.
Lord: What? Fair trial? What kind of shit is that? We're the law! You're all under arrest!
Pierce: Arrest? What the hell? What did you say?
Lord: We're the law! We're the law! You're all under arrest!
Pierce: What?

Sheriff Allan Pierce played by John Anderson and Sheriff Martin Lord played by William Bryant: Ron Joy's *Five Savage Men* (X.Y.Z. Productions, 1971).

3649
Clevenger: But I don't like to go to court!
Sheriff: I don't reckon you do, Gabe. I don't reckon anybody does. But, but this here warrant says you're sure going to court.
Clevenger: What warrant?
Sheriff: Mr. Britt signed murder charges against ya. Well now, don't get mad at me, Gabe. I ain't setting in judgment.
Clevenger: You're just arresting me, huh?
Sheriff: That's all!

Gabe Clevenger played by Ray Teal and the Sheriff played by Chubby Johnson: Edwin Marin's *Fort Worth* (Warner Bros., 1951).

3650
Ruth: You could take that badge off and throw it in the dirt and walk away from it, and no one would blame you.
Ben: No one but me.
Ruth: Is your pride worth more to you than your daughter?

Ben: It's not just pride, Ruth. It's a lot
of other things all mixed together.
It's the oath I took on the Bible, the
land I live in and love. But mostly,
it's... well, it's a matter of justice
and the law. I happen to believe in
them.

Ruth Granger played by Maggie Hayes and Ben
Cutler played by Fred MacMurray: Nathan Juran's
Good Day for a Hanging (Columbia, 1958).

3651

Howard: Hey look, Jim, I don't pretend to
be half the man you are. I doubt if I
ever will be. I'd appreciate it if you
would take the badge back.
Jim: No, you keep the badge, Howard. I'm
a retired man.
Howard: Yeah, but the town needs
you.
Jim: Not anymore. No, you'll do just
fine, Howard. Just one thing.
Howard: What's that?
Jim: You have to learn to tell the good
guys from the bad guys.

Howard Boyle played by Dick Peabody and Jim
Flagg played by Robert Mitchum: Burt Kennedy's
The Good Guys and the Bad Guys (Warner Bros.,
1969).

3652

Sheriff: Jubal was hit right over there by
the woods. I gunned him down myself.
He can't have got far.
Deputy: We combed the woods. He's either lit out, holed up, or dead.
Sheriff: Well, if he's still around, he'll
need some grub and blankets and bandages.

Sheriff Jorgen played by Roy Barcroft and the
Deputy was uncredited: Sidney Salkow's *Gun
Brothers* (United Artists, 1956).

3653

Bat: It never hurt a sheriff to have a reputation with a gun.

Bat Masterson played by Joel McCrea: Joseph M.
Newman's *The Gunfight at Dodge City* (United
Artists, 1959).

3654

Lily: He's a very clever man, our sheriff.
He's got two hats he keeps taking off
and putting on. The white one is for
making speeches, kissing babies, and
attending rodeos. The black one is
for funerals and for collecting his
percentage of every business in
town.

Lily played by Nancy Gates: Joseph M. Newman's
The Gunfight at Dodge City (United Artists, 1959).

3655

Cowboy 1: It looks like you folks went and
elected yourself a crazy sheriff. Figure
he'll last a week?

Kid Shelleen (Lee Marvin), the drunken gunfighter and dime novel hero, in *Cat Ballou*
(Columbia, 1965).

Cowboy 2: I don't know. We'll find out
tonight, I reckon. Ain't nobody ever
tried to stop the guns around here on a
Saturday night.
Cowboy 1: Well, if he does, he's just asking
to be shot up.
Cowboy 2: Yeah, and it would be a shame,
too. He seems like a right nice fella,
doesn't he?

The two cowboys were uncredited: Joseph M.
Newman's *The Gunfight at Dodge City* (United
Artists, 1959).

3656

Doc: I give you our new sheriff, Bat Masterson!
Bat: Thank you very much everyone. I
never made a speech in my life and I'm
not going to try to make one now. I'd
just like to tell you what I have in mind
concerning law enforcement. There'll be
law... and there'll be enforcement.
Thank you!

Doc played by John McIntire and Bat Masterson

played by Joel McCrea in Joseph M. Newman's *The Gunfight at Dodge City* (United Artists, 1959).

3657

John: Funny, I never figured you for a lawman. You was always pretty reckless and
wild.

Wyatt: I never figured myself for a lawman
either.

John Shanssey played by George Mathews and
Wyatt Earp played by Burt Lancaster: John
Sturges' *Gunfight at the O.K. Corral* (Paramount,
1957).

3658

Wilson: I've been a lawman for twenty-
five years. Worked every hell hole in
the territory. You know what I got to
show for it? A twelve dollar a month
room in the back of a cruddy boarding
house and a tin star. You think I like
winding up in a place like this? It's the
end of the line for me, Wyatt. It will
happen to you someday. Just like it happens to all of us.

Sheriff Cotton Wilson played by Frank Faylen:
John Sturges' *Gunfight at the O.K. Corral* (Paramount, 1957).

3659

Wilson: There's $20,000 in it for you…
cash.

Wyatt: $20,000? The ways of sin are rising.

Wilson: Twenty thousand against a six
foot hole in Boot Hill, or a $20.00 a
month pension if you live long enough
to collect it.

Sheriff Cotton Wilson played by Frank Faylen and
Wyatt Earp played by Burt Lancaster: John
Sturges' *Gunfight at the O.K. Corral* (Paramount,
1957).

3660

Wyatt: Look, Holliday, as long as I'm the
law here, not one of those cowfolks is
going to cross that Deadline with a gun.
I don't care if his name is Shanghai
Pierce.

Doc: Well spoken. I'll repeat those words
at your funeral.

Wyatt Earp played by Burt Lancaster, Abel Head
(alias Shanghai Pierce) played by Ted De Corsia,
and John H. "Doc" Holliday played by Kirk Douglas: John Sturges' *Gunfight at the O.K. Corral*
(Paramount, 1957).

3661

Wyatt: Hold up your right hand. Do you
solemnly swear to uphold… oh, this is
ridiculous! You're deputized! Grab some
gear. I'll get the horses.

Doc: Wait a minute! Don't I get to wear a
tin star? Wyatt: Not on your life!

Wyatt Earp played by Burt Lancaster and John H.
"Doc" Holliday played by Kirk Douglas: John
Sturges' *Gunfight at the O.K. Corral* (Paramount,
1957).

3662

Wilson: Why don't you get off that pulpit,
Wyatt? Ellsworth, Wichita, Dodge
City… and what have they got you but a
life full of misery and a woman who
walked out on you… and the friendship
of a killer [Doc Holliday]!

Cotton Wilson played by Frank Faylen, Wyatt
Earp played by Burt Lancaster and John H. "Doc"
Holliday was played by Kirk Douglas: John Sturges'
Gunfight at the O.K. Corral (Paramount, 1957).

3663

Wyatt: Ike's called a play. We'll do it his
way now.

Doc: Don't do that, Wyatt. That's what
they want. Don't let them push you into
a personal fight.

Wyatt: That's mighty funny comin' from
you.

Doc: You're a lawman, Wyatt. Don't throw
away a lifetime's work. Where's your
logic?

Wyatt: To hell with logic! That's my
brother lyin' there!

Wyatt Earp played by Burt Lancaster and John H.
"Doc" Holliday played by Kirk Douglas: John
Sturges' *Gunfight at the O.K. Corral* (Paramount,
1957).

3664

Sheriff: If I think he might be coming back
to hide out at your place, you can be
sure I'll come looking.

Cole: You step foot on our land and I'll
shoot you down like a horse thief.

Sheriff: I'm the law!

Cole: Burrows, you stand for everything
the law is against!

Sheriff Burrows played by Wendell Smith and
Cole Everett played by Art Hindle: Clay Borris'
The Gunfighters (TVW, 1989).

3665

Governor: This territory is hell on wheels.
Renegades, cattle rustlers, guns for hire.
I need men to do battle with that breed.
Not just a few soldiers. I need real men,
like you. Gunfighters… but… legal.

Matt: You mean you're asking us to be
lawmen?

Governor: Let me put it to you this way.
Either you work for me as marshals or
you go back to Kansas and hang.

Dutch: What if we leave Wyoming?

Governor: You'll be hunted down and shot!

Dutch: Just asking!

Governor: Outside of this territory you're
still outlaws. If you stray, the Pinkertons
will be waiting for you.

Cole: You don't give us many choices.

Governor: No… none! Well?

Cole: [picking up badge] We'd be honored!

Governor Hornback played by Michael Kane,
Matt Everett played by Tony Addabbo, Dutch
played by Reiner Schoene, and Cole Everett

played by Art Hindle: Clay Borris' *The Gunfighters*
(TVW, 1989).

3666

Sheriff: Take that bottle out of your mouth
when I'm talking to you!

Ed: Sheriff, I don't use my mouth to listen
with. I use my ears.

Sheriff Harry Brill played by Robert F. Simon and
Ed Hackett played by Tab Hunter: Phil Karlson's
Gunman's Walk (Columbia, 1958).

3667

Avery: Don't you realize the importance of
questioning Sieverts before he dies?

Sheriff: You sure wouldn't get anywhere
questioning him afterwards, would you?

Purcell Avery played by Edward Platt, Jensen
Sieverts played by Ray Teal, and Sheriff Harry
Brill played by Robert F. Simon: Phil Karlson's
Gunman's Walk (Columbia, 1958).

3668

Lee: Harry, you ain't going after that boy
with any shotgun.

Sheriff: I'm not but the law is.

Lee: It seems to me you've been overwork-
ing that law of yours against Ed ever
since we got to town. A man can take
just so much pushing.

Sheriff: That goes for the law too, Lee.

Lee Hackett played by Van Heflin and Sheriff
Harry Brill played by Robert F. Simon: Phil Karlson's *Gunman's Walk* (Columbia, 1958).

3669

Nate: Those Apaches don't have much
respect for law and order, Sheriff.
You might as well get rid of that tin
star.

Sheriff: I think I'll just keep it for awhile
longer. I may want to pin that big
mouth of yours with it.

Nate Harlan played by Warren Stevens and Sheriff
Chad Lucas played by Audie Murphy: Earl Bellamy's *Gunpoint* (Universal, 1966).

3670

Nate: You know, down here in New Mexico we both have equal authority. So
we'll go together and make a citizen's arrest.

Sheriff: It'd be about like teaming a sheep
dog with a wolf.

Nate Harlan played by Warren Stevens and Sheriff
Chad Lucas played by Audie Murphy: Earl Bellamy's *Gunpoint* (Universal, 1966).

3671

Bull: [*reading badge*] So you're a sheriff?
"Sheriff …Lodgepole, Colorado."

Ode: I didn't know you could read.

Bull: I can read badges! That's what I
learned to read on in jail.

Bull played by Edgar Buchanan and Ode played by

Royal Dano: Earl Bellamy's *Gunpoint* (Universal, 1966).

3672

Sheriff: I like everybody… until they start breaking the law. That's when people don't like me.

Sheriff Taylor played by Regis Toomey: Robert D. Webb's *Guns of the Timberland* (Warner Bros., 1960).

3673

Dillon: You know where I come from, Sheriff, the badge means one thing. You either do what needs to be done… or take it off.

Matt Dillon played by James Arness: Jerry Jameson's *Gunsmoke: The Long Ride* (TVW, 1993).

3674

Monaghan: How many bullet holes you got in you, Dillon?

Dillon: I've had my share.

Monaghan played by Patrick Dollaghan and Matt Dillon played by James Arness: Jerry Jameson's *Gunsmoke: The Long Ride* (TVW, 1993).

3675

Judge: Nineteen marshals and one court to commandeer 70,000 square miles. A happy hunting ground filled with bushwhackers, horse thieves, whiskey peddlers, counterfeiters, hide peelers, mauraders. They'd kill ya for a hat band. Now that's why there's a badge in my desk, Cooper, itching to sit on somebody's chest… and no takers!

Judge Adam Fenton played by Pat Hingle: Ted Post's *Hang 'Em High* (United Artists, 1968).

3676

Judge: Pick up that badge or leave justice to me and my men!

Judge Adam Fenton played by Pat Hingle: Ted Post's *Hang 'Em High* (United Artists, 1968).

3677

Bovard: I seem to be a minority of one in this town.

Weston: You ain't popular.

Deputy U.S. Marshal MacKenzie Bovard played by Robert Taylor and Sheriff Buck Weston played by Fess Parker: Michael Curtis' *The Hangman* (Paramount, 1959).

3678

Bovard: Well, a long time ago by a fluke I had to put on a badge… and then I found out I couldn't take it off. Always more rats to run down. The human race is full of 'em. You finally get so you don't trust anybody.

Deputy U.S. Marshal MacKenzie Bovard played by Robert Taylor: Michael Curtis' *The Hangman* (Paramount, 1959).

3679

Howe: It's a great life. You risk your skin catching killers, and the juries turn 'em loose so they can come back and shoot at you again. If you're honest, you're poor your whole life. And in the end, you wind up dying all alone on some dirty street. For what? For nothing. For a tin star.

Martin Howe played by Lon Chaney, Jr.: Fred Zinnemann's *High Noon* (United Artists, 1952).

3680

Sheriff: And look, friend. We sure would like it if you would help us with our problem.

Stranger: The only problem you got, Sheriff, is a short supply of guts.

Sheriff Sam Shaw played by Walter Barnes and The Stranger played by Clint Eastwood who also directed *High Plains Drifter* (Universal, 1973).

3681

Braden: I've been working since I was ten years old, Jessie. Cleaning spittoons at a dime a day. Now, thirty years later, all I see out the window is a dirt road going nowhere. The only thing that changes the view is a spotted dog lifting his leg against a wall over there. On Saturday nights, I haul in the town drunks. I get their twenty-five cent dinners and their rot-gut liquor heaved up over the front of my one good shirt. I wear three pounds of iron strapped to my leg. That makes me fair game for any punk cowboy that's had one too many. No, Jess, I don't need a wife. I need out!

Frank Braden played by Cameron Mitchell and Jessie played by Diane Cilento: Martin Ritt's *Hombre* (20th Century–Fox, 1967).

3682

Sheriff: Hold it! He's here!

Mayor: Who?

Sheriff: He is! Rattlesnake. But don't worry. It's gonna be all right. I got the edge on him.

Mayor: You do? Why?

Sheriff: Because he's here and I know he's here. And he knows I know he's here. But he doesn't know I know he knows I know he's here. But I know. I got the edge.

Mayor: Let's leave this up to the Sheriff, son.

The Sheriff/Denver Kid played by Don Knotts, Mayor Ragsdale played by Darren McGavin, and Rattlesnake played by Jack Elam: Robert Butler's *Hot Lead and Cold Feet* (Buena Vista, 1978).

3683

Wyatt: I don't care about the rules anymore. I'm not that much of a hypocrite.

Doc: The whole thing is hypocrisy. The rules they tack on today that unless you're wearing that badge or a soldier's uniform, you can't kill. But they're the only rules there are. They are more important to you than you think. Play it that way, Wyatt, or you'll destroy yourself.

Wyatt Earp played by James Garner and Doc Holliday played by Jason Robards, Jr.: John Sturges' *The Hour of the Gun* (United Artists, 1967).

3684

Frog: Say, wasn't that [Ranger] Stevens that just left here? Ha! Ha! He couldn't catch a cold!

Frog Millhouse played by Smiley Burnette and Chief Ranger Bob Stevens played by Onslow Stevens: Joseph Kane's *Idaho* (Republic, 1943).

3685

Benjie: Dad, you can't believe what he said. You can't!

Sheriff: No, I believe you, Benjie. But I got to prove it. Somehow I got to prove it.

Benjie: To the people here… or to yourself?

Benjie Galt played by Darryl Hickman and Sheriff Sam Galt played by Sterling Hayden: Sidney Salkow's *The Iron Sheriff* (United Artists, 1957).

3686

Judge: Do you know it's against the law to hunt on reservation land?

Kidd: Well, the deer didn't know where he was and I wasn't sure either.

The Judge played by John Carter and Joe Kidd played by Clint Eastwood: John Sturges' *Joe Kidd* (Universal, 1972).

3687

Sheriff: I'm Sheriff Mean John Simpson, ma'am.

Conforto: Why would anyone call you mean?

Sheriff: To them folks that I like, I can be a real nice person. To them that I don't like, they would rather fall in a cactus patch than to see me get stirred up.

Sheriff "Mean John" Simpson played by Ben Johnson and Janet Conforto played by Janice Rule: James Frawley's *Kid Blue* (20th Century–Fox, 1973).

3688

Judge: This town don't need a sheriff anymore.

Cannonball: I thought you gave me this badge?

Judge: Yeah, that's why I gave it to you.

Judge Lynch played by Rick Anderson and Cannonball played by Dub Taylor: Lambert Hillyer's *King of Dodge City* (Columbia, 1941).

3689

Judge: You ought to retire, Willie. You're losing your eyesight.

Billy: Just in the left eye.

Marshal Jed Cooper (Clint Eastwood) gets the drop on murderer and cattle rustler Miller (Bruce Dern) in Ted Post's *Hang 'Em High* (United Artists, 1967). Inasmuch as the marshal reports directly to a "hangin' judge," the disposition of the case was never in doubt.

Judge: A man that's as blind as you oughtn't be riding that river. You're liable to fall in a hole and get swallowed up.

Billy: You're blind drunk nine days out of ten. What's to keep you from stumbling off into a hole and getting swallowed up?

Judge: The fact is, I hold court nine days out of ten. And I'm too busy to wander out there and find myself a hole big enough. I particularly hate thieves. A man who would steal 50 cents off of ya would steal a million dollars.

Billy: Ain't too many folks around here got 50 cents much less a million dollars.

Judge: I've got 50 cents and I aim to keep it too.

Billy: If I stole your 50 cents, would you hang me?

Judge: I'd hang you as soon as I could find my rope. Now, I may not be able to put my hand on my hanging rope right off, so if you was quick, you might escape.

Billy: Who says you could be a judge anyway? I'd want to see some papers before I'd let you hang me.

Judge: If you could see, you'd see that we're west of the Pecos. And out here, if you want to be a judge bad enough, you can be. And I want to be one bad enough.

Billy: What if it was a dime I stole? Would you still hang me?

Judge: I cannot tolerate the loss of any sum… officially. You want to put this whiskey you've been drinking on your bill, is that correct?

Billy: Put it anywhere you want to put it!

Judge Roy Bean played by Ned Beatty and Billy Williams (referred to as Willie) played by George Carlin: Joseph Sargent's *Larry McMurtry's Streets of Laredo* (Cabin Fever Entertainment, 1995).

3690

Marshal: You know something, Harry? I swear, you'd just sit there and suffocate before you'd do anything about it!

Marshal Dan Blaine played by Glenn Ford and Deputy Harry Bell played by Robert Sorrells: Richard Thorpe's *The Last Challenge* (MGM, 1967).

3691

Lot: Why don't you just hang it up, Marshal? Put your guns away and turn to preachin'.

Blaine: Oh, that's my excuse for living. See, you don't have one. That's why you're looking to get yourself killed.

Lot McGuire played by Chad Everett and Marshal Dan Blaine played by Glenn Ford: Richard Thorpe's *The Last Challenge* (MGM, 1967).

3692

Judge: Now raise your right hands! Do you swear to uphold the laws of this territory and the constitution of the United States, so help you God? Well, for better or worse, you're now Parker men which means that you'll receive $25.00 a month salary minus whatever field expense you have for whatever men you might kill in the line of duty. That is to discourage the indiscriminate shooting of citizens. But the wearing of that badge means a great deal more than just a generous wage. It means that you're now a part of the cutting edge of the awesome sword of the law. Stand up tall, hold your head proud, keep your weapons primed, and watch your back trail. Good day!

Judge Isaac Parker played by Dale Robertson: Dan Curtis' *Last Ride of the Dalton Gang* (TVW, 1979).

3693

Stribling: I got a warrant for your arrest. I'm taking you back to Frio County, Texas, to stand trial. Will you come voluntarily, or will I have to take you?

O'Malley: Say, it just happens that I'm headed for Texas right now… to Crazy Horse. Of course it isn't Frio County, but you'd die a lot closer to home than if I had to kill you here.

Dana Stribling played by Rock Hudson and Brendan O'Malley played by Kirk Douglas: Robert Aldrich's *The Last Sunset* (Universal, 1961).

3694

Marshal: Tell Lute to start packing our gear. We're pulling out.

Jimmy: Well, what about your job?

Marshal: I'm all through.

Jimmy: Because I was in that lynch mob?

Marshal: That's part of it. I've been at it too long. I'm tired of trying to give people something that they don't seem to want anymore.

Marshal Frame Johnson played by Ronald Reagan, Lute Johnson played by Alex Nicol, and Jimmy Johnson played by Russell Johnson: Nathan Juran's *Law and Order* (Universal, 1953).

3695

Deputy: Pat, what are you doing out here? It's cold!

Sheriff: Oh, I was just hoping some clean air might stir up some clear thoughts.

Deputy Brad Jensen played by Nicholas Hammond and Sheriff Pat Lambrose: Virgil W. Vogel's *Law of the Land* (TVW, 1976).

3696

Jane: You never gave me an answer as to why a deputy.

Tom: Well, I thought about being a lawyer. But there is no way the whites could trust the Indian half, and no way the Indians could afford the white half.

Jane Adams played by Barbara Parkins and Tom Condor played by Cal Bellini: Virgil W. Vogel's *Law of the Land* (TVW, 1976).

3697

Sheriff: How would you like to make yourself $12.00 a week?

Quirt: Wearing a star?

Sheriff: You could do a lot worse and stand as tall as the man who wore it last. Mind ya, I'm not saying you're up to that.

Quirt: Sounds a little like a dare to me, Sheriff.

Sheriff: No, son, it's a challenge. There's a difference.

Sheriff Pat Lambrose played by Jim Davis and Quirt played by Don Johnson: Virgil W. Vogel's *Law of the Land* (TVW, 1976).

3698

Sheriff: I ain't never lost a prisoner yet.

Dusty: You never had one to lose.

The Sheriff played by Jack Rockwell and Dusty played by George "Gabby" Hayes: Robert Bradbury's *The Lawless Frontier* (Lone Star/Monogram, 1934).

3699

Tobin: Nice, agreeable, and appreciative Sheriff you got here.

Dusty: Yeah. He started off all right, but he's sure gone to seed.

John Tobin played by John Wayne and Dusty played by George "Gabby" Hayes: Robert Bradbury's *The Lawless Frontier* (Lone Star/Monogram, 1934).

3700

Marshal: Do you want the job?

John: Well, I've made a lot of quick changes in my life, but this is the first time from a jail bird to a star packer.

The Marshal played by Jack Curtis and John Middleton played by John Wayne: Robert N. Bradbury's *Lawless Range* (Republic, 1935).

3701

Marshal: No, I've got just once chance, only one… to outlast the times. And I'm gambling I'll live to see it.

Doc: Ah, you're fooling yourself, Calem. Duty is one thing, self-preservation is another. You walk the streets a legend, yet all the time you're afraid men will know you're human.

Marshal Calem Ware played by Randolph Scott and Dr. Amos Wynn played by Wallace Ford: Joseph H. Lewis' *A Lawless Street* (Columbia, 1955).

3702

Calem: When we met, you knew I was a peace officer, that I was going to be the marshal at Apache Wells.

Tally: Yes, you told me that. But I didn't know what it was like for a man to make his living by his guns, walking the streets a living target. I died a little more each day, and I died more at night.

Marshal Calem Ware played by Randolph Scott and Tally Dickinson played by Angela Lansbury: Joseph H. Lewis' *A Lawless Street* (Columbia, 1955).

3703

Maddox: I remember you at Fort Bliss.

Ryan: That's my trouble. Everybody remembers me at Fort Bliss. That's all I got, Maddox, a bunch of yesterdays. It's a long ride down from the high country… with stops all the way down.

Marshal Jared Maddox played by Burt Lancaster and Marshal Cotton Ryan played by Robert Ryan: Michael Winner's *Lawman* (United Artists, 1971).

3704

Ryan: It's a great life. If you were some cheap gunsel with a big name running out in front of you, they'd all be buying you drinks… rubbing up against you… fixing up what they're going to tell their kids and the ones who weren't there. But if you're a lawman, you're a disease. They need you, but they hate you.

Maddox: It comes with the job.

Marshal Cotton Ryan played by Robert Ryan and Marshal Jared Maddox played by Burt Lancaster: Michael Winner's *Lawman* (United Artists, 1971).

3705

Roy Bean: Raise your right hands! Do you solemnly swear to uphold the letter of the law as enforced in the Revised Statutes of Texas of 1855? And furthermore, do you swear solemn allegiance and vow to uphold the honor of Lillie Langtry?

Marshals: I do!

Tector: Ah, Judge! Ah, Judge! Can I be the bartender? I've had my fill at being shot at for money.

Roy Bean: What about that part about Miss Langtry?

Tector: That's the most beautiful woman I've ever seen in all my born days!

Roy Bean: By the power invested in me through God and the great and honorable State of Texas, I hereby proclaim you to be Marshals of the Court for the County of Greater Vinegarroon. For Texas and Miss Lillie!

Marshals: For Texas and Miss Lillie!

Judge Roy Bean played by Paul Newman. The Marshals were Tector Crites played by Ned Beatty, Bart Jackson played by Jim Burk, Nick the Brub played by Matt Clark, Whorehouse Lucky Jim played by Steve Kanaly, and Fermel Parlee played by Bill McKinney: John Huston's *The Life and Times of Judge Roy Bean* (NGP, 1972).

3706

Crecencio: Well, if you're going to be sheriff, hijo, we're going to have to stop stealing for awhile.

Crecencio played by Luis Avalos: Jack Bender's *Lone Justice II* (Triboro Entertainment Group, 1995).

3707

Here beyond the reach of law and order, might was right. The best shot was the best man. Born of necessity in this chaotic period of westward expansion, an organization was developed to combat the evil forces of the times. An organization called… The Texas Rangers.

Prologue: George B. Seitz's *The Lone Ranger* (Television series first episode, "Enter the Lone Ranger," 9/15/49).

3708

Lone Ranger: Tonto, from this moment on, I'm going to devote my life to establishing law and order in this new frontier… to make the west a decent place to live.

Tonto: That good! But when Cavendish Gang know you escape ambush, you marked man. They hunt you down… many against one.

Lone Ranger: No one is going to know that I'm alive. I'm supposed to be dead and I'm going to stay that way. I'll hide my identity somehow. I'll wear a disguise of some sort.

Tonto: You mean like mask?

Lone Ranger: That's it, Tonto! From now on, I'll wear a mask!

The Lone Ranger played by Clayton Moore and Tonto played by Jay Silverheels: George B. Seitz's *The Lone Ranger* (Television series, earliest episodes, Sept. 1949).

3709

Buck: As your new sheriff, I pledge to uphold one basic law: we must learn to live together as brothers or we shall die together as fools.

Buck played by Paul Lazar: Jean-Marc Vallee's *Los Locos* (PolyGram Filmed Entertainment/Gramercy Pictures, 1997).

3710

Virgil: You mean I can be your deputy? But I want Saturdays off… and I always take my mother fishing every Friday afternoon.

Luke: I said all right!

Virgil played by Neil Summers and Lucky Luke played by Terence Hill who also directed *Lucky Luke* (Silvio Berlusconi Communications, 1991).

3711

Sledge: Don't believe all that crap about your tin star. You bleed just like we do.

Luther Sledge played by James Garner: Vic Morrow's *A Man Called Sledge* (Columbia, 1971).

3712

Marshal: It seems mighty funny to me that every time this gang organizes a rodeo, their own men win all the first prizes. When it begins to look like an outsider is going to win, he gets sick. Two or three has even died from it.

Weston: Well, you can't arrest them for that, Marshal.

Marshal: No, maybe not. But it's might peculiar that when these outsiders fall off them top broncs they're suffering from snake bite. I tell ya, it just ain't natural.

Weston: What do you want me to do? Get snake bit?

Marshal George Higgins played by George "Gabby" Hayes and John Weston played by John Wayne: Robert Bradbury's *The Man from Utah* (Lone Star/Monogram, 1934).

3713

Amy: Bat, is that really a name… Bat?

Bat: William Barclay Masterson, it says in the family Bible. When I was a kid, we lived by a big cave that was full of bats. We used to go target practicing there. Folks used to say nobody could never hit a crazy zig-zagging bat on the wing. So I… I had to try… kept trying. Kept trying until I could. And they called me the boy who shot the bats. Finally, it shook down to just Bat.

Amy Merrick played by Nancy Gates and Sheriff Bat Masterson played by George Montgomery: William Castle's *Masterson of Kansas* (Columbia, 1954).

3714

Bat: Wyatt Earp is as fine a man as ever that wore a badge. But he's got a blind spot… Doc Holliday.

Sheriff Bat Masterson played by George Montgomery, Wyatt Earp played by Bruce Cowling, and Doc Holliday played by James Griffith: William Castle's *Masterson of Kansas* (Columbia, 1954).

3715

Clay: Smoking is bad for your health.

Colby: So is holding a gun on a marshal!

Clay McCord played by Alex Cord and Marshal Roy Colby played by Arthur Kennedy: Franco Giraldi's *A Minute to Pray, a Second to Die* (Selmur/Cinerama, 1967).

3716

Clay: Hey boys, they tried to surrender. Why did you kill them?

Deputy: We don't go for any of that old white flag stuff around these parts.

Clay McCord played by Alex Cord and the Deputy was uncredited: Franco Giraldi's *A Minute to Pray, a Second to Die* (Selmur/Cinerama, 1967).

3717

Marshal: I'm getting old.

Tom: That's quite an accomplishment for a man to grow old in this country… especially with the Daltons around.

Marshal Ripple played by Gene Roth and Tom

Bradfield played by George Brent: Allan Dwan's *Montana Belle* (RKO, 1952).

3718

Jason: The law is for protection. If you haven't got protection, you haven't gotten any law. What are you asking us to do, Plummer? Keep on getting robbed and murdered just so you can wear a fancy badge?

Jason Waterman played by Hugh Sanders and Sheriff Henry Plummer played by Preston Foster: Ray Nazarro's *Montana Territory* (Columbia, 1952).

3719

Sheriff: Raise your right hand. Do you solemnly swear to uphold the law and carry out the orders of this office, and conduct yourselves as peace officers at all times?

Deputies: Uh huh… I do.

Sheriff: Here, wear these [badges] and take plenty of ammunition with you!

Sheriff Henry Plummer played by Preston Foster: Ray Nazarro's *Montana Territory* (Columbia, 1952).

3720

Sheriff: Goodbye, Rogers. I hope I won't see you again under these circumstances.

Roy: You won't… under any circumstances!

The Sheriff played by Sam Flint and Roy Rogers played himself: Frank McDonald's *My Pal Trigger* (Republic, 1946).

3721

Sheriff: What do you want?

Navajo Joe: That [*pointing to sheriff's badge*].

Sheriff: What?

Hannah: You want us to appoint you as Sheriff, is that it?

Navajo Joe: That's right.

Sheriff: But you can't. An Indian Sheriff? The only ones elected in this country are Americans.

Navajo Joe: My father was born here… in the mountains. His father before him, and his father before him, and his father before him. Where was your father born?

Sheriff: What has that to do with it?

Navajo Joe: I said, where was he born?

Sheriff: Ah, in Scotland.

Navajo Joe: My father was born here in America. His father before him, and his father before him, and his father before him. Now which of us is American?

Sheriff Elmo Reagan played by Gianni Di Stolfo, Navajo Joe played by Burt Reynolds, and Hannah Blackwood Lynne played by Valeria Sabel: Sergio Corbucci's *Navajo Joe* (United Artists, 1966).

3722

Deputy: I'm taking these leg irons off so you can stretch. But I'm warning you, don't try to stretch your legs too far!

Deputy Morgan played by Stanley Andrews: Gordon Douglas' *The Nevadan* (Columbia, 1950).

3723

Sheriff: I'm going to have to ask you to leave town.
Gant: Why should I leave?
Sheriff: We've just put a law in the books against a public nuisance. Mr. Gant, you're a public nuisance.
Sheriff Buck Hastings played by Willis Bouchey and John Gant played by Audie Murphy: Jack Arnold's *No Name on the Bullet* (Universal, 1959).

3724

Marshal: Case will only be in town a few hours. And while he's here, I don't want any trouble from you… and that's an order!
Link: Is your gun fast enough to give me orders, Marshal?
Marshal Tom Evans played by Walter Sande and Link Roy played by Leo Gordon: Edward L. Cahn's *Noose for a Gunman* (United Artists, 1960).

3725

Folsey: And you better have a good excuse for not showing Case Britton to jail!
Marshal: When I have to start giving excuses for what I do, I'll turn in my badge.
Ed Folsey played by Lane Chandler and Marshal Tom Evans played by Walter Sande: Edward L. Cahn's *Noose for a Gunman* (United Artists, 1960).

3726

Vaqui Joe: How come they only gave you a badge in the first place?
Lyedecker: Well, I guess I took a job that nobody else wanted. And even at that, it took me a whole year to get it.
Vaqui Joe: How much are they going to give you for taking me back?
Lyedecker: Two hundred dollars and a job permanent like.
Vaqui Joe: Shoot, they ain't even hardly worth bothering about.
Lyedecker: Well, Joe, that depends on what you got in the first place.
Vaqui Joe: Yeah. I ain't ever been worth a damn in my whole damn life. I've never been worth nothing to talk about. I've never even had a job permanent like. Now I finally done something for somebody. Me! I finally amounted to something.
Lyedecker: Yeah, you robbed a bank!
Vaqui Joe Herrera played by Burt Reynolds and Lyedecker played by Jim Brown: Tom Gries' *100 Rifles* (20th Century–Fox, 1969).

3727

Sheriff: It ain't safe here no more! All my deputies are either dead or they left town. I ain't got no backup!
Mayor: You shot one of them yourself!
Sheriff Clyde Barnes played by Jack Elam and Mayor Nard Lundy played by Edward Andrews:

Jean Yarbrough's *The Over-the-Hill Gang* (TVW, 1969).

3728

Nash: No ranger retires perpendicular.
Nash Crawford played by Walter Brennan: Jean Yarbrough's *The Over-the-Hill Gang* (TVW, 1969).

3729

Captain: First of all, I want to tell you that I'm grateful for the way you responded to my call… quickly and loyally, no questions asked. I appreciate that. But I want to apologize for doing it. You see, I'd forgotten that you retired honorably from the Rangers to set up new lives for yourselves because you were, well, you were tired of guns and fighting.
Nash: Well, that ain't so, Captain. We just used up all the bad injuns and outlaws in town.
George: We just cleaned ourselves out of business.
Jason: We didn't retire. We just ran out of something to do.
Captain: No. No, there was a time when we could have set this town on its ears. But, we got to face it, we're over-the-hill now.
Captain Oren Hayes played by Pat O'Brien, Nash Crawford played by Walter Brennan, Gentleman George played by Chill Wills, and Jason Fitch played by Edgar Buchanan: Jean Yarbrough's *The Over-the-Hill Gang* (TVW, 1969).

3730

Mayor: You know, we can't go out and just hire any man for Marshal. No sir! We got to have a name that those drifters and gunmen respect. Why, half of the success of this job is respect.
Nash: Don't the one you got have respect?
Mayor: Oh, lots of respect… for a dead man.
The Mayor played by Parley Baer and Nash Crawford played by Walter Brennan: George McCowan's *The Over-the-Hill Gang Rides Again* (TVW, 1970).

3731

George: Of course, we're all rangers. But we're so far over that hill, I can't even remember seeing the hump.
George Agnew played by Chill Wills: George McCowan's *The Over-the-Hill Gang Rides Again* (TVW, 1969).

3732

Nash: You said it before, Kid. You got too much pride. And I agree. What you got to do is find a decent height. You try to stand too tall, you'll want everyone looking up at you. If they don't, then you fall down in the gutter and let them look down on you. Now there is a middle ground there, Kid, and it's just about eye level… where you can look at

the world straight in the face, and without shame.
Nash Crawford played by Walter Brennan and the Baltimore Kid played by Fred Astaire: George McCowan's *The Over-the-Hill Gang Rides Again* (TVW, 1969).

3733

Sheriff: It's like this, Granger. I'm an old man. Peace officers get scared. And they get hungry. They pick them up off the ground dead every day. The only thing that comes out of their pockets is pennies. You know what I mean?
Granger: Overtures bore me. If this is going to be an opera, sing!
Sheriff Blaney played by Chubby Johnson and Ross Granger played by Jock Mahoney: Fred F. Sears' *Overland Pacific* (United Artists, 1954).

3734

Preacher: This is no ordinary kind of marshal. His name is Stockburn. He travels with six deputies. And they uphold whatever law pays them the most. Killin' is a way of life with them.
The Preacher played by Clint Eastwood and Stockburn played by John Russell: Clint Eastwood's *Pale Rider* (Warner Bros., 1985).

3735

Dr. Carter: Sheriff, what you need is a bottle of Dr. Carter's Indian Remedy. It will put venom and vigor in that body of yours, and make you more fit for your job, Sheriff. I'll be glad to take your order anytime you want, Sheriff. Good for a man or beast. Better buy your horse a bottle.
Sheriff: Never mind that! You'll need more than Indian Remedy if you ever come back in this county again!
Dr. Carter played by Earle Hodgins and the Sheriff played by Henry Hall: Carl Pierson's *Paradise Canyon* (Monogram, 1935).

3736

Rodriguez: I cannot arrest voices in the dark.
Captain Rodriguez played by Raymond Burr: Allan Dawn's *Passion* (RKO, 1954).

3737

Billy: It wasn't long ago when I was the law, riding with Chisum. And ole Pat [Garrett] was an outlaw. The law's a funny thing, ain't it?
Billy the Kid played by Kris Kristofferson and Pat Garrett played by James Coburn: Sam Peckinpah's *Pat Garrett and Billy the Kid* (MGM, 1973).

3738

Marshal: How about me deputizing you, Hickok? Right now.
Hickok: Well, no thanks, Marshal. That badge would make me do a lot of things I don't want to do, and keep me from

doing a lot of things I got a hankering to do.

The Marshal was uncredited and Wild Bill Hickok played by Don Murray: David Lowell Rich's *The Plainsman* (Universal, 1966).

3739

Sheriff: Give a fool a gun and he's still a fool... only a louder one.

Sheriff Sam Borden played by George Cleveland: Jospeh Kane's *The Plunderers* (Republic, 1948).

3740

Deputy: You sure let him jingle his spurs out loud.

Sheriff: Still waters run deep.

Sheriff Tap Lawrence played by Grant Withers: Jospeh Kane's *The Plunderers* (Republic, 1948).

3741

Inspector: You get paid 75 cents a day to carry the law where there is none. This is your first patrol, Constable, and you haven't earned your pay.

Inspector Frazer played by Howard Petrie: Joseph M. Newman's *Pony Soldier* (20th Century–Fox, 1952).

3742

Thad: I can take care of myself.

Marshal: Taking care of yourself is one thing. Taking care of a town is another.

Thad played by Jeffrey Hunter and Marshal Cass Silver played by Robert Ryan: Robert D. Webb's *The Proud Ones* (20th Century–Fox, 1956).

3743

[*City councilman asking marshal to resign*]

Bolton: I hope you don't take this as a personal reflection on you.

Marshal: No, Sam, I don't. I take it as a personal reflection on you. All of you!

Sam Bolton played by Whit Bissell and Marshal Cass Silver played by Robert Ryan: Robert D. Webb's *The Proud Ones* (20th Century–Fox, 1956).

3744

Marshal: Your first lesson comes right now. At night, always walk in the shadows. You can see better. In the daytime, walk away from the sun. You'll live longer.

Marshal Cass Silver played by Robert Ryan: Robert D. Webb's *The Proud Ones* (20th Century–Fox, 1956).

3745

Brooks: Look, the last man we would want handling this thing is [Deputy] Glen. Why, he'd shoot the eyes out of a dove for singing too early in the day.

Brooks played by John David Souther and Deputy Glen played by Donnie Wahlberg: Uli Edel's *Purgatory* (TVW, 1999).

3746

Randy: I'm afraid you got me wrong, Sheriff. I didn't do anything...

Sheriff: It looks like we got you right.

Randy Bowers played by John Wayne and the Sheriff played by Earl Dwire: Harry Fraser's *Randy Rides Alone* (Lone Star/Monogram, 1934).

3747

Judge: People are going to be proud to see this badge, Marshal. And I think you'd be proud to show it. [*Judge reads names inscribed on inside of badge*] Two good men, both of them dead. How come your name ain't on it?

Marshal: I'm not dead!

Judge Kyle played by Walter Matthau and Joe Maybe, alias Marshal Joe Newland, played by Audie Murphy: Jesse Hibbs' *Ride a Crooked Trail* (Universal, 1958).

3748

Judge: You're a lucky man, Marshal. I've seen Dan kill bigger men than you. Well, they were taller!

Judge Kyle played by Walter Matthau: Jesse Hibbs' *Ride a Crooked Trail* (Universal, 1958).

3749

Judge: We'll give you $10.00 a day, cartridges, and a brand new hat. Is that fair enough?

Judge Kyle played by Walter Matthau: Jesse Hibbs' *Ride a Crooked Trail* (Universal, 1958).

3750

Wheeler: Would you mind telling me what this is all about?

Chance: We got Joe Burdette in here.

Wheeler: Joe Burdette in jail? Nathan's brother?

Chance: That's right.

Wheeler: What are you holding him for?

Chance: We were about to bury the reason when you were coming in.

Wheeler: Murder?

Chance: There's no other word for it.

Pat Wheeler played by Ward Bond and John T. Chance played by John Wayne: Howard Hawks' *Rio Bravo* (Warner Bros., 1959).

3751

Colorado: If I'm going to get shot at, I might as well get paid for it. How do I get a badge?

Colorado Ryan played by Ricky Nelson: Howard Hawks' *Rio Bravo* (Warner Bros., 1959).

3752

Feathers: How does a man get to be a sheriff?

Chance: He gets lazy and tired of selling his gun all over... decides to sell it in one place.

Feathers played by Angie Dickinson and John T. Chance played by John Wayne: Howard Hawks' *Rio Bravo* (Warner Bros., 1959).

3753

Leech: This is none of your business.

Tabor: They killed my wife! What business is that of yours?

Leech: That's exactly what it is... it's a business.

Quinton Leech played by Kenny Rogers and Benjamin Tabor played by Travis Tritt: Rod Hardy's *Rio Diablo* (TVW, 1993).

3754

McNally: Tell me, what's going on around here?

Dr. Jones: Well, the man really running things and putting up all the money is a man named Ketcham. He came in here right after the war. Hendricks killed the sheriff we had, and Ketcham made Hendricks the new sheriff.

Cord McNally played by John Wayne and Dr. Ivor Jones played by David Huddleston: Howard Hawks' *Rio Lobo* (NGP, 1970).

3755

Judge: Rooster, any deputy who shoots and kills sixty-four suspects in eight years is breaking the law, not aiding and abetting it!

Rooster: Now let's get this straight, Judge. Only sixty of 'em died! None was shot but in the line of duty or in defense of my person, or fleeing justice.

Judge: You have been in the service of this court for almost two lustrums. You're a strong man and you're a brave man, Rooster. And you have at times executed your duties faithfully and well. But all too often you have acted with excessive zeal and with...

Rooster: What is a lustrum, Judge?

Judge: Five years. Don't interrupt me while I'm talking!

Rooster: Yes, sir.

Judge: Pay attention to me!

Rooster: Yes, sir.

Judge: This is not just another formal reprimand!

Rooster: Yes, sir.

Judge: People with money to invest go where they're protected by the law, not shot by it!

Rooster: Is that the kind of law my deputy got yesterday? I was proud to tell his wife I shot his killers!

Judge: It seems you cannot serve the papers of this court and effect arrest without breaking heads and spraying bullets about. The west is changing and you haven't changed with it. I want your badge!

Rooster: Well, Judge, out there in the territory, they don't know about all these new fangle laws. We know it but they don't. They're still shooting in the same direction. At me!

Judge: Your badge, Cogburn! You've let yourself go, Rooster. Look at your belly!

Retired Texas Rangers saddle up to rescue the Baltimore Kid (Fred Astaire in white hat); Nash Crawford (Walter Brennan), George Agnew (Chill Wills), Amos Polk (Andy Devine), and Jason Fitch (Edgar Buchanan) in *The Over-the-Hill Gang Rides Again* (TVW, 1970).

You can't even close your coat over it! You drink too much!

Rooster: I ain't had a drink since breakfast! And I only wear this coat in your court. It was always good enough when you needed what was in it!

Judge: You've gone to seed, Rooster... gone to seed. Next case!

Judge Parker played by John McIntire and Rooster Cogburn played by John Wayne: Stuart Millar's *Rooster Cogburn* (Universal, 1975).

3756

Davey: What's that for? [*putting folded money in gun cylinder*].

Sheriff: A decent burial. Where I come from, all the peace officers carry around their own burial money. A custom of the country.

Davey: Suppose you need that chamber?

Sheriff: I'm not that fast. If I haven't hit what I'm aiming at by the time I squeeze off the first five, I'll be needing a pine box instead of another bullet.

Davey Bishop played by John Derek and Mat Dow played by James Cagney: Nicholas Ray's *Run for Cover* (Paramount, 1955).

3757

Mayor: We've had enough gunslingers wearing badges. We figure it's about time we had a man with some character in the job.

Mayor Walsh played by John Miljan: Nicholas Ray's *Run for Cover* (Paramount, 1955).

3758

Ma: Remember what Mr. Sackett said: you always ride with the law, you never ride against it. Ya hear?

Ma Sackett played by Mercedes McCambridge: Robert Totten's *The Sacketts* (TVW, 1979).

3759

Sheriff: You haven't any notion who his enemies was, have ya?

Nancy: I didn't know he had any.

Sheriff: Well, he must have had one anyway.

The Sheriff played by Jack Holmes and Nancy Henderson played by Lita Conway: S. Roy Luby's *Saddle Mountain Roundup* (Monogram, 1941).

3760

Clayton: This is a job for a whole company of Rangers, or it's a job for one or two men. Right now, we're too many and not enough.

Captain Reverend Samuel Clayton played by Ward Bond: John Ford's *The Searchers* (Warner Bros., 1956).

3761

Clayton: …You'll faithfully discharge your duties as such without recompense or monetary consideration. Amen. That means no pay!

Captain Reverend Samuel Clayton played by Ward Bond: John Ford's *The Searchers* (Warner Bros., 1956).

3762

Flood: Well, that's just like the Rangers. They're always short of something: men, money, or brains!

Jim Flood played by Barry Sullivan: Harry Keller's *Seven Ways from Sundown* (Universal, 1960).

3763

Billy: Stop worrying! The Sheriff in Cumbres is so fat he uses a barrel hoop for a belt. And he couldn't catch a milk cow if it had a bell on it.

Billy Massey played by Dean Martin: George Seaton's *Showdown* (Universal, 1973).

3764

Sheriff: You stick to practicing law… I'll enforce it!

Sheriff Chuck Jarvis played by Rock Hudson: George Seaton's *Showdown* (Universal, 1973).

3765

Sheriff: Well, maybe you better get down to Wilson's office. He's waiting for you.

Jack: Oh, no hurry. He'll take ten minutes talking about how the President appointed him to bring law and order to this lawless community.

Sheriff: Yeah. You'd think he'd save some of that breath for breathing.

Sheriff Chuck Jarvis played by Rock Hudson, P.J. Wilson played by John McLaim, and Jack Bonney was played by Philip L. Mead: George Seaton's *Showdown* (Universal, 1973).

3766

Bonney: You figuring on getting yourself killed, Sheriff?

Sheriff: I got a good chance at it.

Jack Bonney played by Philip L. Mead and Sheriff Chuck Jarvis played by Rock Hudson: George Seaton's *Showdown* (Universal, 1973).

3767

Deputy: You know, the trouble with this business is that it makes a man old before his time. You know, I never did hear of a sheriff living to be a ripe old age. Did you?

Sheriff: Sure! Ed Murdock. They didn't shoot him until he was thirty-eight.

Deputy Verne Ward played by David Janssen and Sheriff Jim Trask played by Jock Mahoney: Charles Haas' *Showdown at Abilene* (Universal, 1956).

3768

Sheriff: Now I am going to have to arrest you two.

Jason: What for?

Sheriff: Gunfighting in the streets. We can't have a gunfight without someone being arrested.

Quince: Well, I didn't start it, Sheriff. The other guy did.

Sheriff: I know, but he got away.

Quince: Well, he's right there in the saloon!

Sheriff: I know, but he also happens to be one of our most prominent ranchers, while you ain't nothing but two itinerant vagrant bums!

Jason: Who says so?

Sheriff: You got any money?

Quince: What does money have to do with it, Sheriff?

Sheriff: If you ain't got any, you ain't nothing but two itinerant vagrant bums! I'll take that derringer. I ain't never seen anyone hit anything with one of these before. I'll take that gun too. Let's go to jail.

Quince: What are the formal charges against us, Sheriff?

Sheriff: Shooting a concealed weapon from an exposed position at a prominent drunk.

Jason: I was pretty sure it would be something like that.

The Sheriff played by Harry Morgan, Jason O'Rourke was played by Lou Gossett, and Quince Drew played by Larry Hagman: Burt Kennedy's *Sidekicks* (TVW, 1974).

3769

Sheriff: The law works kind of slow sometimes, Jess. It's like fishing. There's nothing we can do except keep the hooks out and keep them baited.

Sheriff Tom Davisson played by Rory Calhoun and Jess Harker played by Robert Wagner: Harmon Jones' *The Silver Whip* (20th Century–Fox, 1953).

3770

Jess: I've been wondering, Tom. What if Race really tried to take the prisoner? You wouldn't have shot him, would you? Plug a man like Race to save an outlaw?

Tom: Race is the best friend I've ever had. But he still figures he has the law in his holster. He's got to learn different.

Jess Harker played by Robert Wagner, Sheriff Tom Davisson played by Rory Calhoun and Race Crim played by Dale Robertson: Harmon Jones' *The Silver Whip* (20th Century–Fox, 1953).

3771

Paden: What is it you want from me?

Sheriff: Nothing. Do nothing. Don't get between us.

Paden: I'm a great believer in doin' nothing.

Paden played by Kevin Kline and Sheriff Cobb played by Brian Dennehy: Lawrence Kasdan's *Silverado* (Columbia, 1985).

3772

Sheriff: Ben, the trouble with you is… you're like an owl. The more light you shine on him, the less he sees.

Sheriff Billy Wilson played by Paul Fix and Deputy Sheriff Ben Latta played by Jeremy Slate: Henry Hathaway's *The Sons of Katie Elder* (Paramount, 1965).

3773

Lt.: Do I have to ask what's going on here?

Marshal: Yeah. I just told this man to hand over his rifle and he's still got it. I guess he never saw what double-aught buck can do to a two-dollar shirt.

Lt.: Are you placing this man under arrest?

Marshal: I certainly hope so… because it's a bad place for a funeral. There's not a choir or flower within three hundred miles. Now what's it going to be, Ringo?

Lieutenant Blanchard played by Merritt Butrick and Marshal Curley Wilcox played by Johnny Cash: Ted Post's *Stagecoach* (TVW, 1986).

3774

Billy: And you're going into Lordsburg all by yourself to take on all the Plummers?

Marshal: It's what you were going to do, ain't it?

Billy: Well, you're going to need some help.

Marshal: If I deputized an escaped convict, I'd be run out of the territory!

Billy: It's better than being carried out!

Billy "Ringo" Williams played by Kris Kristofferson and Marshal Curley Wilcox played by Johnny Cash: Ted Post's *Stagecoach* (TVW, 1986).

3775

Billy: Did the marshal tell you you're under arrest?

Luke: He might have mentioned it.

Billy: You're not sure though?

Luke: Well now, I never really paid much attention to what the law had to say. I did hear tell, though, that you're his deputy.

Billy: Yeah, well, good help is hard to find.

Billy "Ringo" Williams played by Kris Kristofferson and Luke Plummer played by David Allan Coe: Ted Post's *Stagecoach* (TVW, 1986).

3776

Matt: It was our votes that elected him. We believed in him the same as you did. But he has sold out to Braydon! And if he forces us to a showdown, he'll find out that we got just as many guns as votes.

Matt Disher played by Forrest Taylor and Braydon played by Wheaton Chambers: R.G. Springsteen's *Stagecoach to Denver* (Republic, 1946).

3777

Orval: Do I get my deputy's badge?

Deputy: When they start pinning stars on a courthouse janitor, that's when I throw mine in.

Sheriff: Easy, Mac. Keep your eyes open. I'm going to take another look around.

Orval: If I had a deputy's badge, I could help out better when the shooting started.

Deputy: Why Orval, you wouldn't know which end of this [rifle] to shoot through!

Orval Jones played by James Gleason, Deputy Mike MacNamera played by Paul Fix, and Sheriff Bill Jorden played by John Agar: Charles Haas' *Star in the Dust* (Universal, 1956).

3778

Travers: Men, I was sent here from Washington. I'm swearing you all in as deputy marshals. Today, you're riding for the United States Government!

U.S. Marshal John Travers played by John Wayne: Robert Bradbury's *The Star Packer* (Lone Star/Monogram, 1934).

3779

This is a tribute to men of courage and perseverance… men who were steadfast in danger and hardship… and whose history is the pride and heritage of the Lone Star State… they had no uniforms… they lived hard… they fought hard… they died hard… carrying out a record of glory in which every American shares… To the Texas Rangers.

Prologue: Leslie Fenton's *Streets of Laredo* (Paramount, 1949).

3780

Major: One of the first responsibilities of a Ranger is to know the meaning of the word "responsibility."

Major Bailey played by Stanley Ridges: Leslie Fenton's *Streets of Laredo* (Paramount, 1949).

3781

Sheriff: Well, everything seems to be in order.

Mayor: Our last sheriff was a good organizer. Yellow clean through… but a good organizer.

Sheriff Jason McCullough played by James Garner and Mayor Olly Perkins played by Harry Morgan: Burt Kennedy's *Support Your Local Sheriff!* (United Artists, 1969).

3782

Danby: I believe you got one of my children in the jail here.

Sheriff: How dare you walk into my office and pull a gun on me!

Danby: Get your finger out of the end of my gun!

Sheriff: How dare you pull a gun on me!

Danby: I said, take your finger out of the end of my gun!

Sheriff: Well, until I do, you better take your finger off that trigger… and let the hammer down real slow.

Danby: If that gun had gone off, it would have blown up right in my face!

Sheriff: Well, it wouldn't have done my finger a hell of a lot of good either, would it?

Pa Danby played by Walter Brennan and Sheriff Jason McCullough played by James Garner: Burt Kennedy's *Support Your Local Sheriff!* (United Artists, 1969).

3783

Sheriff: Say, Jake, what did you do before you became my deputy?

Jake: Well, I did odd jobs.

Sheriff: Well, like what?

Jake: Well, for one thing I was a whore holder at Madame Horses …ah …horse holder at Madame Orr's House.

Sheriff: You were a what?

Jake: Horse holder. You see, on Saturday night that hitch rack out front would get full. And I'd hold the extra horses, sometimes all night.

Sheriff: It seems to me like you spent a lot time with horses.

Jake: One end or the other. Of course, I come about it natural. My daddy stole horses for a living. They hung him.

Sheriff Jason McCullough played by James Garner and Deputy Jake played by Jack Elam: Burt Kennedy's *Support Your Local Sheriff!* (United Artists, 1969).

3784

Preacher: Now just because we've lost three sheriffs don't mean we're going to lose four.

Fred: Our luck is bound to change.

Mayor: What about his luck?

Preacher Henry Jackson played by Henry Jones, Fred Johnson played by Walter Burke, and Mayor Olly Perkins played by Harry Morgan: Burt Kennedy's *Support Your Local Sheriff!* (United Artists, 1969).

3785

Sheriff: You got a name?

Jake: Jake.

Sheriff: Well, Jake, I want you to go in the Mint Saloon. There's a fella in there by the name of Joe Danby. You tell him I remember his name, he's under arrest for murder, and I'll be in to pick him up in about twenty minutes.

Jake: Are you talking to me?

Sheriff: Are you hard of hearing?

Jake: You want me to tell Joe Danby that he's under arrest for murder? What are you going to do after he kills me?

Sheriff: Then I'll arrest him for both murders.

Sheriff Jason McCullough played by James Garner, Jake played by Jack Elam, and Joe Danby played by Bruce Dern: Burt Kennedy's *Support Your Local Sheriff!* (United Artists, 1969).

3786

Pa Danby: Now I'm going to take a little trip tomorrow. And I want you two to behave yourselves while I'm gone. I don't want nobody to make no martyr out of this here sheriff.

Tom Danby: What's a martyr?

Pa Dandy: Oh, I'm sorry. They didn't use words like that in the third grade, did they?

Tom Dandy: Well, how would I know? I didn't get that far!

Pa Danby played by Walter Brennan and Tom Danby played by Gene Evans: Burt Kennedy's *Wes Tour Local Sheriff!* (United Artists, 1969).

3787

Mayor: You interested in the job of sheriff?

Jason: Oh, maybe. How much does it pay?

Townsman: Well, none of our sheriffs ever lived long enough to find out!

Mayor Olly Perkins played by Harry Morgan and Sheriff Jason McCullough played by James Garner: Burt Kennedy's *Support Your Local Sheriff!* (United Artists, 1969).

3788

Jason: Is there some kind of badge that goes with this job?

Mayor: Oh, you bet there is. I'm afraid it's a little bent up.

Jason: Well, it must have saved the life of whoever was wearing it.

Mayor: Well, it sure would have if it hadn't been for all them other bullets flying in from everywhere!

Jason McCullough played by James Garner and Mayor Olly Perkins played by Harry Morgan: Burt Kennedy's *Support Your Local Sheriff!* (United Artists, 1969).

3789

Jason: Gentlemen, do we have a jail here?

Mayor: Do we have a jail? A brand new one with two cells that the whole community pitched in and built last month!

Fred: Just like a barn raising.

Preacher: Even the dancehall girls showed up. They made sandwiches and carried on like crazy.

Mayor: It was designed to be practically escape proof.

Jason: Well, good, because I think I'm going to have to throw a couple in it.

Mayor: There's only one thing. This new jail is sure got everything.

Fred: Even a new stove with a coffee pot already on it.

Mayor: The only thing it hasn't got is iron bars for the cells.

Jason: You're kidding?

Mayor: Which we had to send away for 'em and they ain't arrived yet.

Fred: But it's got everything else! It's got glass windows, and brooms, and kerosene lamps, and you name it.

Jason: Just no bars for the cells.

Mayor: That's right!

Jason: Well, all right, I'll think of something.

Mayor: You ain't wanted for anything anywhere, are you Mr. McCullough? Not that it matters! Because we understand how them little things can happen.

Jason McCullough played by James Garner, Mayor Olly Perkins played by Harry Morgan, Fred Johnson played by Walter Burke, and Preacher Henry Jackson played by Henry Jones: Burt Kennedy's *Support Your Local Sheriff!* (United Artists, 1969).

3790

Sheriff: Jake, how would you like the job as my deputy?

Jake: I'd hate it! Even if I lived through it, I'd hate it!

Sheriff Jason McCullough played by James Garner and Jake played by Jack Elam: Burt Kennedy's *Support Your Local Sheriff!* (United Artists, 1969).

3791

Mayor: That must have been some show you put on at the saloon this afternoon. It kind of sobered up the whole town.

Sheriff: Well, that's good.

Mayor: Maybe… maybe not. It has been a lot of fun around here up to now. I mean, everything all kind of wide-open and relaxed. Nobody looking down their noses at anybody who happened to shoot somebody else. Nobody poking their noses into nobody else's business without them getting their big noses blasted off in the process. Ah, I guess now that we got law and order, churches will start moving in.

Sheriff: Yeah, that's usually the next thing that happens.

Mayor: And then the women will start forming committees and having bazaars. And then they'll chase Madame Orr's girls out of town, or make them get married, or something even worse. But, what the hell, like you said, the law's the law, and we all got to face up to it sometime.

Sheriff: When did I say that?

Mayor Olly Perkins played by Harry Morgan and Sheriff Jason McCullough played by James Garner: Burt Kennedy's *Support Your Local Sheriff!* (United Artists, 1969).

3792

Mayor: Some people think you could have waited a couple days before you stuck your nose in the biggest hornet's nest we got.

Sheriff: Well, when you set out to clean up a mess, you don't just sit around and watch that mess get bigger and bigger.

Mayor: Well, I guess you know what you're doing, Sheriff.

Sheriff: I don't know what I could have said to give you that idea, Mayor.

Mayor Olly Perkins played by Harry Morgan and Sheriff Jason McCullough played by James Garner: Burt Kennedy's *Support Your Local Sheriff!* (United Artists, 1969).

3793

Conroy: Sorry to make you boys so much trouble.

Tim: When you're wearin' a badge, trouble is your business.

Conroy played by Walter Reed and Tim played by Tim Holt: Stuart Gilmore's *Target* (RKO, 1952).

3794

Moran: An honest marshal never gets rich.

Marshal Terry Moran played by Linda Douglas: Stuart Gilmore's *Target* (RKO, 1952).

3795

Tim: Marshal is not the job we're after. The man that wears the badge is a target for every two-bit gunslinger that comes to town. And you know something?

Chito: What?

Tim: Bullets don't bounce!

Tim played by Tim Holt and Chito Rafferty played

by Richard Martin: Stuart Gilmore's *Target* (RKO, 1952).

3796

Sheriff: I could use a deputy, though, for the next few days.

Bailey: No thanks, that's out of my line.

Sheriff: Oh, anything against it?

Bailey: Yeah. A man's liable to get shot!

Sheriff Fred Miller played by Cameron Mitchell and Wes Tancred, alias John Bailey, played by Richard Egan: Charles Marquis Warren's *Tension at Table Rock* (RKO, 1956).

3797

Higgins: I've killed my best friend.

Dickson: You were only doing your duty, Higgins. Why take it so to heart?

Higgins: When duty makes it necessary to take the life of a man like old Dan Matthews, well then I'm through with duty.

John Higgins played by John Wayne and Joe Dickson played by LeRoy Mason: Robert N. Bradbury's *Texas Terror* (Lone Star/Monogram, 1935).

3798

Sheriff: Where are you going?

Deputy: Out to take a look around.

Sheriff: It's a quiet day today. See that it ends up the way it started.

Sheriff Bambino played by Bud Spencer and Deputy Trinity played by Terence Hill: E.B. Clucher's *They Call Me Trinity* (West Film/Avco Embassy, 1970).

3799

Marshal: Now, the way I figured it, the faster we get him out of here, the safer.

Alex: That's right! We'll outsmart 'em every step! We'll outsmart 'em!

Marshal: We only got two, three hours' head start. They'll probably figure we're going to take him over to Fort Huachuca and turn him in there.

Alex: Sure they will!

Marshal: And if they don't figure that, they'll figure we've taken him to Benson.

Alex: That's a fact!

Marshal: And if they don't figure that, then they'll figure we've taken him over to Contention City and put him on the 3:10 to Yuma.

Alex: Sure they will… bound to!

Marshal: Alex, will you let me finish! Then you can agree!

Alex: Sure, Will!

The Marshal (Will) played by Ford Rainey and Alex Potter played by Henry Jones: Delmer Daves' *3:10 to Yuma* (Columbia, 1957).

3800

Ben: You think I'm a fool?

Morg: Any man that wears that badge is. I know why you like it. Everybody slaps you on the back, tells you how important you are. Decent people look up to

Mistake one was messin' with Katie Elder. Mistake two was messin' with *The Sons of Katie Elder* (Paramount, 1965) in a good shoot-'em-up western by Henry Hathaway. Pictured here are sons John Elder (John Wayne) and Tom Elder (Dean Martin).

you. They are all your friends. I've seen it before.

Sheriff Ben Owens played by Anthony Perkins and Morg Hickman played by Henry Fonda: Anthony Mann's *The Tin Star* (Paramount, 1957).

3801

Sheriff: I only want to be good enough to keep this badge.

Hickman: Study men. Paste this in your head: a gun is only a tool. You can master a gun if you got the knack. It's harder to learn men.

Sheriff Ben Owens played by Anthony Perkins and Morg Hickman played by Henry Fonda: Anthony Mann's *The Tin Star* (Paramount, 1957).

3802

Hickman: She knows what's wrong with that badge. A man pins it on, he can't take it off. They'll give ya a nice funeral.

Morg Hickman played by Henry Fonda: Anthony Mann's *The Tin Star* (Paramount, 1957).

3803

Sheriff: What did I do that was wrong?

Hickman: Everything! You let him stop you. You let him talk. You listened to what he was saying instead of watching what he was doing. You pulled your gun when you didn't have to.

Sheriff: Oh no, he'd have pulled his first.

Hickman: When you walk right up to a man, chances are he won't gunfight. Because at three feet he knows he'd get hurt… maybe killed even if he draws first. Pulling your gun, you just gored him into trying to get you. You better take off that tin star and stay alive.

Sheriff Ben Owens played by Anthony Perkins and Morg Hickman played by Henry Fonda: Anthony Mann's *The Tin Star* (Paramount, 1957).

3804

Hickman: How come they picked you?

Sheriff: I'm only temporary.

Hickman: You're more temporary than you think.

Morg Hickman played by Henry Fonda and Sheriff Ben Owens played by Anthony Perkins: Anthony Mann's *The Tin Star* (Paramount, 1957).

3805

Behan: All right, all of you are under arrest!

Wyatt: I don't think I'll let you arrest us today, Behan.

Sheriff John Behan played by Jon Tenney and Wyatt Earp played by Kurt Russell: George P. Cosmatos' *Tombstone* (Buena Vista, 1993).

3806

Wyatt: Forget it. I'm retired.

Marshal: Excuse me?

Wyatt: I said forget it. I don't want the job and that's final.

Marshal: I don't think you understand!

Wyatt: No, you don't understand, Marshal. I did my duty, and now I'd like to get on with my life. I'm going to Tombstone.

Marshal: Oh, I see. To strike it rich. Well, all right, that's fine. I'll tell you one thing though. I never saw a rich man that didn't wind up with a guilty conscience.

Wyatt: I already got a guilty conscience. I might as well have the money too.

Wyatt Earp played by Kurt Russell and U.S. Marshal Crawley Dake played by Gary Clark: George P. Cosmatos' *Tombstone* (Buena Vista, 1993).

3807

Virgil: There's six of 'em. Damn, this is like a bad dream!

Wyatt: Stay calm and use your head. It'll be all right. Just the same, though, I guess maybe you better swear me in.

Virgil Earp played by Sam Elliott and Wyatt Earp played by Kurt Russell: George P. Cosmatos' *Tombstone* (Buena Vista, 1993).

3808

Billy: Before Bat Masterson gets through with this town, this jail will be more populous than a hound dog with the fleas.

Billy Burns played by George "Gabby" Hayes: Ray Enright's *Trail Street* (RKO, 1947).

3809

Carmody: Now listen. While you're doing it, if a stray bullet should happen to catch Masterson accidentally, I got an idea there will be a big reward for a man who would shoot so bad.

Carmody played by Billy House: Ray Enright's *Trail Street* (RKO, 1947).

3810

Billy: You're the Mayor of Liberal. How much longer do we got to put up with such goings on?

Mayor: Until we get a new marshal, I reckon. But it will have to be somebody who ain't particular about livin' long.

Billy Burns played by George "Gabby" Hayes and the Mayor played by Harry Harvey: Ray Enright's *Trail Street* (RKO, 1947).

3811

Masterson: It will only be a part-time job.

Billy: What you mean is a short-time job!

Bat Masterson played by Randolph Scott and Billy Burns played by George "Gabby" Hayes: Ray Enright's *Trail Street* (RKO, 1947).

3812

Dusty: Are you acting Marshal?

Trace: No, I ain't the Marshal. But around here, I am the law.

Dusty Fog played by Christopher Atkins and Trace was uncredited: David Lister's *Trigger Fast* (Vidmark, 1994).

3813

Dusty: My pa always said, you don't not do something that's right just because it's unwise. That's what makes a lawman.

Dusty Fog played by Christopher Atkins: David Lister's *Trigger Fast* (Vidmark, 1994).

3814

Tex: You men can drop your guns! It'll make it easier to get your hands over your heads!

Tex Masters played by Tex Ritter: Robert Bradbury's *Trouble in Texas* (Grand National, 1937).

3815

Sheriff: Well, I suppose you'll be wanting your reward?

Moses: Uh huh.

Sheriff: Well, let's see… two hundred each man times five, that makes six hundred. I'll get the…

Moses: None of your hanky panky with me now, huh! Five men, at two hundred each, that makes seven hundred… plus fifty!

Sheriff Fox played by Ron Carey and Moses played by Bud Spencer: Terence Hill's *The Troublemakers* (Rialto Film, 1994).

3816

Defense: How many men have you shot since you became a marshal, Mr. Cogburn?

Marshal: I never shot nobody I didn't have to.

Defense: That was not the question. How many?

Marshal: Ah, shot or killed?

Defense: Oh, let's restrict it to kill so we may have a manageable figure.

Marshal: Well, twelve to fifteen… stopping men in flight and defending myself.

Defense: Twelve to fifteen? So many that you cannot keep a specific count. I have examined the records, Mr. Cogburn. A much more accurate figure is available. Come now, how many?

Marshal: Well, counting those two Wordens… twenty-three.

Defense: I felt you would come to it with a little effort. Twenty-three dead men in four years! That makes about six men a year!

Marshal: It's a dangerous business!

Defense: Oh, and how much more dangerous for those arrested by you!

The Defense Lawyer Goudy played by Alfred Ryder and Marshal Reuben J. "Rooster" Cogburn played by John Wayne: Henry Hathaway's *True Grit* (Paramount, 1969).

3817

Mattie: Do you know a Marshal Rooster Cogburn?

Stonehill: Most people around here have heard of Rooster Cogburn, and some people live to regret it.

Mattie Ross played by Kim Darby and Colonel G. Stonehill played by Strother Martin: Henry Hathaway's *True Grit* (Paramount, 1969).

3818

Tanner: I don't know how you horse shit them people into givin' a greaser a tin star, but you don't horseshit Frank Tanner!

Frank Tanner played by Jon Cypher: Edwin Sherin's *Valdez Is Coming* (United Artists, 1971).

3819

Sheriff: I have even gotten married.

Siringo: That can be hard on a lawman.

Sheriff: You mean, a woman being afraid of you getting killed?

Siringo: No, them making you afraid.

The Sheriff played by Warren Berlinger and Charlie Siringo played by Steve Forrest: Lee Philips' *Wanted: The Sundance Woman* (TVW, 1976).

3820

Sheriff: Well, do you want the job, Buck?

Buck: For what? Forty dollars a month and a free pine box?

Sheriff Keller played by Hugh Sanders and Buck Slavin played by Bartlett Robinson: Edward Dmytryk's *Warlock* (20th Century–Fox, 1959).

3821

Sheriff: I just wish there was some bank robbers up around here for us to chase after.

Deputy: Well, you done scared them all away by bringing them back dead!

Sheriff: Well, that's the way they wanted them: dead or alive.

Deputy: On that last job, though, you only brought back half the loot.

Sheriff: Half is better than none, ain't it? You know something, Turpin? You probably wouldn't believe this, but I once had a gold robbery in the works. I mean, me! I was really going to do it.

Deputy: What happened?

Sheriff: Oh well, I had to give it up when I was elected sheriff. I started to believe my own slogan. But I'm going to tell you: if this job wasn't so sweet and soft, why I, ah, I might just elect to follow the criminal profession.

Deputy: You'd be real good, too, John.

Sheriff John Copperud played by Carroll O'Connor and Deputy Tippen played by Bruce Dern: William Graham's *Waterhole No. 3* (Paramount, 1967).

3822

Cole: You show me an honest sheriff and I'll show you a man without money.

Lewton Cole played by James Coburn: William Graham's *Waterhole No. 3* (Paramount, 1967).

3823

Willets: Of all the lug-headed sheriffs I've ever saw, you western ones are the dumbest!

Officer Willets played by Robert Emmett Keane: Joseph Kane's *West of the Badlands* (a.k.a. *The Border Legion*; Republic, 1940).

3824

Mayor: Serving God and serving the law are two different things.

Whiteside: I disagree. To do either one takes a dedicated man.

The Mayor played by Carl Benton Reid and Whiteside played by Wallace Ford: Jacques Tourneur's *Wichita* (Allied Artists/Warner Bros., 1955).

3825

Mayor: Wait a minute, Wyatt! Raise your right hand. Do you solemnly swear to uphold the laws of the United States of America and this community?

Wyatt: I do.

Mayor: I hereby appoint you Marshal of Wichita.

Lawman: He's as good as dead right now!

The Lawman was uncredited. The Mayor played by Carl Benton Reid and Wyatt Earp played by Joel McCrea: Jacques Tourneur's *Wichita* (Allied Artists/Warner Bros., 1955).

3826

Virgil: Now Wyatt, you are going to get this office so cluttered up with six-guns, a man won't have a place to spit. You've got half the guns in Kansas hanging on the wall right now.

Lin: It's an awful lot of law for a little cowtown.

Wyatt: This is the kind of cowtown that needs a lot of law.

Virgil played by Guy Wilkerson, Lin McAdam played by James Stewart, and Wyatt Earp played by Will Geer: Anthony Mann's *Winchester '73* (Universal, 1950).

3827

Behan: Wyatt, I'm going to have to arrest you.

Wyatt: I'm not going to be arrested today, Johnny. Not by you and not by anybody else.

Johnny Behan played by Mark Harmon and Wyatt Earp played by Kevin Costner: Lawrence Kasdan's *Wyatt Earp* (Warner Bros., 1994).

3828

Clem: You couldn't have been trying to arrest him, Wyatt. Not with close to twenty bullet holes in his body.

Wyatt: No, I wasn't trying to arrest him.

John Clem played by Randle Mell and Wyatt Earp played by Kevin Costner: Lawrence Kasdan's *Wyatt Earp* (Warner Bros., 1994).

3829

Cushman: Look, Mr. Kane, I don't like your kind any more than you like mine.

Kane: What kind am I, Miss Cushman?

Cushman: A hired killer.

Kane: Let me tell you something, Miss Cushman. Something for you and all the other gentle hearts in Lordsburg to think about. I've been indicted for murder in every town I've ever worn a badge. Not by the ones I hunted, but by the people I was paid to protect. Like you, Miss Cushman. You're all alike. You hire a man and then you grab his gun arm and tell him to hold off …let the bad ones shoot first so you can make damn good and sure they're bad. Even if it means getting a hole blown in that tin star they pin on you.

Cushman: But you don't work that way?

Kane: I'm alive!

Evvie Cushman played by Deana Martin and Ben Kane was played by Robert Mitchum: Burt Kennedy's *Young Billy Young* (United Artists, 1969).

3830

Kane: I never knew a lawman yet that died from old age.

Ben Kane played by Robert Mitchum: Burt Kennedy's *Young Billy Young* (United Artists, 1969).

3831

Deputy: It looks like it's getting pretty near to supper time. You boys hungry? I got two lots of news for ya …good and bad. I'll give ya the bad news first. All we got for supper is horseshit.

Prisoner: What the hell's the good news?

Doc: There's tons of it!

Deputy Bob Ollinger played by Leon Rippy and Doc Scurlock played by Kiefer Sutherland: Geoff Murphy's *Young Guns II* (20th Century–Fox, 1990).

Lone Rider

See also Cowboys; Good Guys; Gunfighters; Men

3832

Rita: You know, I think what I like least about you is that you're so sure of yourself.

Marshal: When a man rides down the middle of Texas Street, confidence is all he's got.

Rita played by Ann Dvorak and Marshal Dan Mitchell played by Randolph Scott: Edwin Marin's *Abilene Town* (United Artists, 1946).

3833

Williams: I guess if you're gonna spend your life with yourself, you might as well learn to be good company.

David Williams played by James Caan: Claude Lelouch's *Another Man, Another Chance* (United Artists, 1977).

3834

Slater: There's things a man has to know and has to do, and it's best that he does them alone.

Jim Slater played by Richard Widmark: John Sturges' *Backlash* (Universal, 1956).

3835

Dan: Billy, you got to learn to control your own life. Folks can help you along and kind of point out the general direction sometimes. But nobody can really show you the way as such. Any man who says he can is either after votes, money, or he just plain don't know what he's talking about.

Dan Baker played by Clint Walker and Billy Baker played by Lee Montgomery: Lyman Dayton's *Baker's Hawk* (Doty/Dayton, 1976).

3836

Terrill: Here in the west, Jim, a man is still expected to defend himself. If he allows people to think he won't, he's in trouble. Bad trouble.

Major Henry Terrill played by Charles Bickford and Jim McKay played by Gregory Peck: William Wyler's *The Big Country* (United Artists, 1958).

3837

Travis: You got any friends?

Choya: My guns.

Travis: Kinfolk?

Choya: My horse.

Dad Travis played by Edward Clark and Choya played by Alan Ladd: Rudolph Mate's *Branded* (Paramount, 1951).

3838

Waitress: First it was the Army uniform. Now it's a badge. Someday you'll make a mistake and stand all alone.

The Waitress played by Diana Darrin: John Bushelman's *The Broken Land* (20th Century–Fox, 1962).

3839

Preacher: May the Lord be with you, Brother Cain. Because if He isn't, you'll ride alone.

Preacher Sims played by John Carradine: Kent Osborne's *Cain's Cutthroats* (a.k.a. *Cain's Way*; M.D.A. Associates/Fanfare, 1969).

3840

Sgt.: Where are you from?

Chuka: Anywhere I happen to be.

Sergeant Otto Hansback played by Ernest Borgnine and Chuka played by Rod Taylor: Gordon Douglas' *Chuka* (Paramount, 1967).

3841

Seaborn: I don't know you, cowboy, and you don't know me. But if you got any ideas about bucking trouble, I'm afraid you're going to have to go it alone.

Conagher: You want to help me?

Seaborn: Well, I'm up into my 70s, boy. And I got a bum kicker to boot. I was kind of hoping to just live out my days and not die out on some sandy slope with lead in my guts. If they get me out on that range, they'll kill me for sure. And then just take my cattle as they please …with nobody to stop 'em.

Conagher: What if they come after you?

Seaborn: If they come after me, I damn sure will fight.

Conagher: You better keep a rifle handy.

Seaborn Tay played by Ken Curtis and Conagher played by Sam Elliott: Reynaldo Villalobos' *Conagher* (Turner Pictures, 1991).

3842

Reece: You're getting old, Doc.

Doc: No, it ain't that. A man has to have something besides a gun and a saddle. You just can't make it all by yourself.

Tom Reece played by Glenn Ford and Doc Bender played by Brian Donlevy: Delmer Daves' *Cowboy* (Columbia, 1958).

3843

Kit: It's strange. I feel I know you better than any man I've ever known. Yet I hardly know you at all.

Kit played by Maureen O'Hara: Sam Peckinpah's *The Deadly Companions* (Paramount, 1961).

3844

Ryan: We both got an old account to settle with the same people. Only I want to take first crack at 'em.

Bill: We could go on together.

Ryan: No, son, you got too much hate in you. Sooner or later that's gonna get you in trouble.

Bill: Hate is hate. There's no two ways.

Ryan: Somebody once wrote that revenge is a dish that has to be eaten cold. As hot as you are, you're liable to end with indigestion. No, I'm going it alone.

Ryan played by Lee Van Cleef and Bill played by John Phillip Law: Giulio Petroni's *Death Rides a Horse* (United Artists, 1967).

3845

Dooley: Where are you from?

Cowboy: No place in particular.

Dooley: Where are you headed?

Cowboy: Same place.

Dooley played by William Forsythe and the Cowboy played by Emilio Estevez: Gene Quintano's *Dollar for the Dead* (TVW, 1998).

3846

Rose: Well, they say a man's the best company when he's alone.

Rose of Cimarron played by Louise Allbritton: Gordon Douglas' *The Doolins of Oklahoma* (Columbia, 1949).

3847

Ned: Sometimes I get the feeling that you don't want to know us, and you don't want us to know you.

Ben: No, it ain't that.

Ned: Well, it's something. Just because I can't see with my eyes don't mean I can't see.

Ned Tallon played by Peter Graves and Ben Shelby played by Ben Johnson: John Rawlins' *Fort Defiance* (United Artists, 1951).

3848

Luther: Whoever that be?

Britt: Somebody with a taste for solitude. The Texas Trail makes for lonely riding for a man alone.

Luther Wick played by Dick Jones and Ned Britt played by Randolph Scott: Edwin Marin's *Fort Worth* (Warner Bros., 1951).

3849

Will: Where are you going that's better than where you've been?

Will Tenneray played by Kirk Douglas: Lamont Johnson's *A Gunfight* (Paramount, 1971).

3850

Rita: How are you getting along with Kittredge?

Curly: I can take him or leave him alone. If given a choice, I'd leave him alone.

Rita Saxon played by Susan Cabot, Reb Kittredge played by Audie Murphy, and Curly Mather played by Jack Kelly: Nathan Juran's *Gunsmoke* (Universal, 1953).

3851

Kanning: Some things are better left in the past.

Sheriff: Unless that past has come back to haunt you.

Kanning played by Matt McCoy and the Sheriff played by Ross Hagen: Jim Wynorski's *Hard Bounty* (Triboro Entertainment, 1995).

3852

Sarah: Be careful. You're a man who makes people afraid. And that's dangerous.

Stranger: Well, it's what people know about themselves inside that makes them afraid.

Sarah Belding played by Verna Bloom and The Stranger played by Clint Eastwood: Clint Eastwood's *High Plains Drifter* (Universal, 1973).

3853

Sarah: Have you ever heard the name Jim Duncan?

Stranger: I've heard a lot of things. Why?

Sarah: He was town marshal here. He's lying out there in an unmarked grave. They say the dead don't rest without a marker of some kind. Do you believe that?

Stranger: What makes you think I care?

Sarah: I don't know. He's the reason this town is afraid of strangers.

Sarah Belding played by Verna Bloom and The Stranger played by Clint Eastwood who also directed *High Plains Drifter* (Universal, 1973).

3854

Hondo: If you don't mind, ma'am, I'd rather you didn't feed him [dog].

Lowe: Oh, I see, you don't want him to get in the habit of taking food from anyone else. Well, you can hand it to him.

Hondo: No, ma'am, I don't feed him either. Sam's independent. He doesn't need anybody. I want him to stay that way. It's a good way.

Lowe: Well, everyone needs someone.

Hondo: Yes, ma'am, most everyone. Too bad, isn't it?

Hondo Lane played by John Wayne and Angie Lowe played by Geraldine Page: John Farrow's *Hondo* (Warner Bros., 1953).

3855

Amy: Don't go, Jory.

Jory: I got to go, Amy. Everything here has your father's brand …even you. I've got to do what Roy said …got to find a place with my own name on it. I've got to find my Promised Land.

Amy played by Linda Purl, Jory Walden played by Robby Benson, and Roy played by John Marley: Jorge Fons' *Jory* (Avco Embassy, 1972).

3856

Gernet: John, don't you ever get tired of the trail?

John: I guess I was meant to keep moving. It's all right for some folks to stay in one place, I guess.

Gernet Hale played by Joan Leslie and John Ives played by Forrest Tucker: Joseph Kane's *Jubilee Trail* (Republic, 1954).

3857

Junior: I got to go down my own road.

Junior Bonner played by Steve McQueen: Sam Peckinpah's *Junior Bonner* (CIN, 1972).

3858

Maria: You are a long way from home.

Ellison: A man always is until he has one of his own.

Uncas (Phillip Reed) defending Cora Munro (Heather Angel) against the menacing Magua (Bruce Cabot) on the edge of a cliff in *The Last of the Mohicans* (United Artists, 1936).

Maria O'Reilly played by Linda Cristal and Brad Ellison played by Jock Mahoney: George Sherman's *The Last of the Fast Guns* (Universal, 1958).

3859

Alice: I came to ask you to stay.

Hawkeye: You know I don't belong here. There's a fence between your world and mine.

Alice: And you have a trail to follow?

Hawkeye: Huh uh.

Alice: You know, it's a very sad trail that leads back to no one.

Hawkeye: There's an old Indian saying: a trap awaits the otter who follows the same trail twice.

Alice Munro played by Binnie Barnes and Hawkeye played by Randolph Scott: George B. Seitz's *The Last of the Mohicans* (United Artists, 1936).

3860

O'Malley: Look, Belle, I know this hasn't been a good trip for you. But, well,
we're gonna have smooth sailing from here on out.

Belle: You don't really want smooth sailing, Brendan. You carry your own storm wherever you go.

O'Malley: Only when I travel alone.

Brendan O'Malley played by Kirk Douglas and Belle Breckenridge played by Dorothy Malone: Robert Aldrich's *The Last Sunset* (Universal, 1961).

3861

Ryan: Some men just go to things in a straight line, Mr. Bronson. They don't bend and they don't trade.

Bronson: Are you telling me Maddox is like that?

Ryan: He's got the mark.

Harvey: That's too bad. Then he's going to buy himself a lot of pain.

Marshal Cotton Ryan played by Robert Ryan, Vincent Bronson played by Lee J. Cobb, and Harvey Stenbaugh played by Albert Salmi: Michael Winner's *Lawman* (United Artists, 1971).

3862

Jack: Do you know what a loner is? He's a low cripple. He's crippled because the only person he can live with is himself. His life is the way he wants to live it. It's all for him. A guy like that, he'd kill to have a woman like you. But he couldn't love you ...not the way you are loved.

Jack Burns played by Kirk Douglas: David Miller's *Lonely Are the Brave* (Universal, 1962).

3863

Henry: He learned young to live alone and be his own man. And all the years we was together, he never let me become close enough to ask: What's on your mind, Zack, what's bothering ya? He drew a circle-like around himself. Nobody dared enter it.

Captain Filmore Henry played by John Huston and Zachary Bass played by Richard Harris: Richard C. Sarafian's *Man in the Wilderness* (Warner Bros., 1971).

3864

Cheyenne: People like that have something inside ...something to do with death.

Cheyenne played by Jason Robards, Jr.: Sergio Leone's *Once Upon a Time in the West* (Paramount, 1969).

3865

Josey Wales: Sometimes trouble just follows a man.

Josey Wales played by Clint Eastwood: Clint Eastwood's *The Outlaw Josey Wales* (Warner Bros., 1976).

3866

1st Sgt.: It's mean hard for a man to be alone.
Holden: A man is never alone, Emmett.

First Sergeant Emmett Bell played by Jeff Chandler and Doctor Joseph Holden played by Ward Bond: George Marshall's *Pillars of the Sky* (Universal, 1956).

3867

Susanna: Pardon me, but we don't even know your name.
Vallian: Names don't count for much out here, ma'am.
Duncan: He's called the dark stranger of the prairie.

Susanna McKaskel played by Kate Capshaw, Con Vallian played by Sam Elliott, and Duncan McKaskel played by Tom Conti: Richard Day's *The Quick and the Dead* (HBO Pictures, 1987).

3868

Susanna: You're not going to stay here with us?
Vallian: I try never to be around where I'm thought to be, ma'am.

Susanna McKaskel played by Kate Capshaw and Con Vallian played by Sam Elliott: Richard Day's *The Quick and the Dead* (HBO Pictures, 1987).

3869

McCall: I ain't got nothing against you, Pickett. It's just the less people I know, the less people get killed.

Duell McCall played by Alex McArthur and Nathaniel Pickett played by Victor Love: E.W. Swackhamer's *The Return of Desperado* (TVW, 1988).

3870

Jesse: Jonas, there's no need to leave.
Jonas: There's none to stay.

Jesse played by Kathryn Hays and Jonas Trapp played by Chuck Connors: Bernard McEveety's *Ride Beyond Vengeance* (Columbia, 1966).

3871

Rex: Look, Peter, I don't have a sidekick. I ride alone, and that's my style.
Peter: But you could use a sidekick, couldn't you?
Rex: No, no, sorry, but even my theme song says I ride alone: yo lady, yo lady, I ride alone.
Peter: Change it!
Rex: What do you mean, change it? It took me four years to get that right!
Peter: It did?
Rex: Now look, there is no sidekick openings. So if you'll excuse me!

Rex O'Herlihan played by Tom Berenger and Peter, the Town Drunk, played by G.W. Bailey: Hugh Wilson's *Rustlers' Rhapsody* (Paramount, 1985).

3872

Joe: I wouldn't ask you where you're bound.
Shane: One place or another. Some place I've never been.

Joe Starrett played by Van Heflin and Shane played by Alan Ladd: George Stevens' *Shane* (Paramount, 1953).

3873

Swiss: Don't go through life dragging a stone. He travels fastest who travels alone.

Blanc De Blanc/"Swiss" played by Giuliano Gemma: Sergio Corbucci's *Shoot First ...Ask Questions Later!* (a.k.a. *The White, the Yellow, and the Black*; Mntex Entertainment, It/Sp/Fr).

3874

Lomax: I ain't getting into any trouble until I find the trouble I want.

Clay Lomax played by Gregory Peck: Henry Hathaway's *Shoot Out* (Universal, 1971).

3875

Slade: You ever see him before?
Butch: Maybe ...maybe not ...hard to tell. They all look the same.
Slade: Who?
Butch: Strangers.
Slade: What the hell are you talking about?
Butch: I don't know. I'm just making conversation.
Slade: Get inside and order me a whiskey, you dumb jackass!

Slade Cantrell played by John Vernon and Butch played by Earl Pastko: Eugene Levy's *Sodbusters* (Atlantis Releasing, 1994).

3876

Cole: Go tell Cantrell a stranger is coming.
Butch: Are your boots on a holiday? Tell him yourself!

Cole played by John Hemphill and Butch played by Earl Pastko: Eugene Levy's *Sodbusters* (Atlantis Releasing, 1994).

3877

Slade: I expected you to be long gone by now, stranger.
Destiny: Then I reckon you better lower your expectations.

Slade Cantrell played by John Vernon and Destiny played by Kris Kristofferson: Eugene Levy's *Sodbusters* (Atlantis Releasing, 1994).

3878

Tyree: Have you always been a loner, Pike? You kind of got that look in your eye that tells people to stay away.
Pike: It depends on the people.

Tyree played by Fred Williamson and Pike played by Jim Brown: Anthony M. Dawson's *Take a Hard Ride* (20th Century–Fox, 1975).

3879

Bailey: That leaves it right up to you. One of us is lying. You can back him or you can back me. But remember, once a lie gets a hold of you, there's only one way you can go. And no matter how far you go, you don't get anywhere. Because you're running from yourself. If you don't mind being alone the rest of your life, you got an easy choice. But I don't figure you for that kind of a man. Make up your mind. It's got to be one way or the other. There's no middle.

Wes Tancred, alias John Bailey, played by Richard Egan: Charles Marquis Warren's *Tension at Table Rock* (RKO, 1956).

3880

Pat: I never could stay in one place long enough to be happy.

Pat Westall played by Dean Stockwell: Albert Band's *Texas in Flames* (a.k.a. *She Came to the Valley*; Raja Films, 1977).

3881

Lester: You stand still too long in one spot, Mrs. Westall, you start blowing yourself.

Bill Lester played by Scott Glenn and Willy Westall played by Ronee Blakley: Albert Band's *Texas in Flames* (a.k.a. *She Came to the Valley*; Raja Films, 1977).

3882

Pat: I never could figure out a drifter.

Pat Westall played by Dean Stockwell: Albert Band's *Texas in Flames* (a.k.a. *She Came to the Valley*; Raja Films, 1977).

3883

Nona: You're so generous!
Morg: Don't fool yourself. A man lives alone like me gets kind of selfish. If he gives you anything, you can be sure he's getting his money's worth.

Nona Mayfield played by Betsy Palmer and Morg Hickman played by Henry Fonda: Anthony Mann's *The Tin Star* (Paramount, 1957).

3884

Vance: I like being alone.
Creighton: The best place to be alone sometimes is in a crowd.
Vance: That's the way I figured it ...until I ran into you.

Vance Shaw played by Randolph Scott and Edward Creighton played by Dean Jagger: Fritz Lang's *Western Union* (20th Century–Fox, 1941).

3885

Wyatt: I guess I was born under a troublesome star. Things like that are always happening to me.

Wyatt Earp played by Joel McCrea: Jacques Tourneur's *Wichita* (Allied Artists/Warner Bros., 1955).

Marriage and Romance

See also Men; People; Wild Women; Woman

3886

Sherry: Oh, Dan, if you care anything about me at all, take me away.

Marshal: Sherry, I …I wouldn't be any good to you running away. Being afraid would take half the fun out of life for me.

Sherry Balder played by Rhonda Fleming and Marshal Dan Mitchell played by Randolph Scott: Edwin Marin's *Abilene Town* (United Artists, 1946).

3887

Smith: Put that gun down!

Janie: I won't! I'm not going to be a widow before I'm even a wife.

Jim Smith played by John Wayne and Janie played by Claire Trevor: William A. Seiter's *Allegheny Uprising* (RKO, 1939).

3888

Melody: Pa gave me a piece of advice that ain't never failed me yet. Son, he says, if you ever fool around with a woman, always hide a dollar in the toe of the boot and you'll come out a dollar to the good. That is, pa says, if you keep your boots on.

Melody Jones played by Gary Cooper: Stuart Heisler's *Along Came Jones* (RKO, 1945).

3889

George: Who is she?

Melody: I've never seen her before.

George: That time in Cheyenne when you was kicked in the head and you was missing four days. Are you sure you didn't marry somebody while you was out of your head?

Melody: I wasn't that far out of my head!

George Fury played by William Demarest and Melody Jones played by Gary Cooper: Stuart Heisler's *Along Came Jones* (RKO, 1945).

3890

Massai: And there is no place in Massai's life for love. Love is for men who can walk without looking behind. For men who can live summer and winter in the same place.

Massai played by Burt Lancaster: Robert Aldrich's *Apache* (United Artists, 1954).

3891

Homer: I've never teamed two more unlikely prospects. You go together like ice cream and whiskey. But I guess you'd be man and wife same as regular people, and nobody could say different.

Justice of the Peace Homer McCoy played by Harry Morgan: Norman Tokar's *The Apple Dumpling Gang* (Buena Vista, 1975).

3892

Phoebe: Are you asking me to marry you?

Peter: Around about. Is there still something you don't like about me?

Phoebe: No, it's not that. If there wasn't something I didn't like about a man, I couldn't stand the sight of him.

Phoebe Titus played by Jean Arthur and Peter Muncie played by William Holden: Wesley Ruggles' *Arizona* (Columbia, 1940).

3893

Tracks: The trouble with you is, you don't know what romance is.

Laramie: Sure I do. Romance is when a man runs after a woman until she catches him.

Tracks Williams played by Raymond Hatton and Laramie Nelson played by Larry "Buster" Crabbe: James Hogan's *The Arizona Raiders* (a.k.a. *Bad Men of Arizona*; Paramount, 1936).

3894

Laramie: Lonesome, are you sure you love this girl?

Lonesome: I'm sure I do. I'd die for her.

Tracks: It's a pretty bad case, Laramie. He's half dead already.

Laramie Nelson played by Larry "Buster" Crabbe, Lonesome Alonzo Mulhall played by Johnny Downs, and Tracks Williams played by Raymond Hatton: James Hogan's *The Arizona Raiders* (a.k.a. *Bad Men of Arizona*; Paramount, 1936).

3895

Abernathy: Well, this here is a huntin' license. But according to Hoyle, I need only to change a word or two to make it a bona fide marriage license.

Boswell Abernathy played by Richard Carle: James Hogan's *The Arizona Raiders* (a.k.a. *Bad Men of Arizona*; Paramount, 1936).

3896

Abernathy: It becomes legal the moment I get my fee. The marriage become legal directly after I receive my fee!

Boswell Abernathy played by Richard Carle: James Hogan's *The Arizona Raiders* (a.k.a. *Bad Men of Arizona*; Paramount, 1936).

3897

Frank: What did you try to do? Make love to her while telling her she just became a widow?

Frank Hudson played Hugh O'Brian: Joseph Pevney's *Back to God's Country* (Universal, 1953).

3898

Mace: How did you come to marry your husband, Mrs. Stoner?

Maria: He bought me, Mr. Bishop. He found me in the back room of a cantina. He liked me, and he bought me. He gave my father five cows and a gun. He made my father the richest man in all the village.

Mace Bishop played by James Stewart and Maria Stoner played by Raquel Welch: Andrew McLaglen's *Bandolero!* (20th Century–Fox, 1968).

3899

Dee: I was just thinking. We make a perfect pair …you and me. I'm broke without a woman, and you're rich and without a man.

Dee Bishop played by Dean Martin: Andrew McLaglen's *Bandolero!* (20th Century–Fox, 1968).

3900

Mace: You two have gotten pretty close, haven't you?

Dee: Oh, nothing has been said.

Mace: Well, nothing has to be said.

Dee: It's just a feeling, Mace. You know, just a feeling, but ….

Mace: But what?

Dee: I don't know if she has the same feeling.

Mace: Have you thought about asking her?

Dee: Asking?

Mace: Dee, I know you don't believe in talking. And you've said that talking never got you anywhere. But how in the world are you ever going to find out anything from anybody if you don't talk?

Mace Bishop played by James Stewart and Dee Bishop played by Dean Martin: Andrew McLaglen's *Bandolero!* (20th Century–Fox, 1968).

3901

Patricia: But if he loved me, why would he let me think he was a coward?

Julie: If you love him, why would you think it? How many times does a man have to win you?

Patricia Terrill played by Carroll Baker and Julie

Maragon played by Jean Simmons: William Wyler's *The Big Country* (United Artists, 1958).

3902

Patricia: Well, even when you rode Old Thunder, everybody knew it. Ramon knew it, Julie knew it. But me? Not a word! Why? You know how much it meant to me …with everybody laughing at me. And don't tell me they weren't. But you wouldn't do it for me. Why not? Why not for me?

McKay: There's some things a man has to prove to himself alone …not to anyone else.

Patricia: Not even to the woman he loves?

McKay: Least of all to her …if she loves him.

Patricia Terrill played by Carroll Baker and Jim McKay played by Gregory Peck: William Wyler's *The Big Country* (United Artists, 1958).

3903

Hannassey: Treat her right. Take a bath sometime.

Rufus Hannassey played by Burl Ives: William Wyler's *The Big Country* (United Artists, 1958).

3904

Tropp: Any man who gets himself married is automatically stupid.

Benson Tropp played by Charles Bickford: Fielder Cook's *A Big Hand for the Little Lady* (Warner Bros., 1966).

3905

Boone: What's all the noise about?

Zeb: They're [Indians] celebrating your wedding.

Boone: Wedding?

Zeb: You maybe don't know it, but you're a married man now.

Boone: Married? And I don't got nothing to say about it?

Zeb: Wouldn't do you no good to say it.

Boone played by Dewey Martin and Zeb Calloway played by Arthur Hunnicutt: Howard Hawks' *The Big Sky* (Winchester/RKO, 1952).

3906

Mother-in-Law: I was with your wife, Sarah, and she gave birth to twins.

Gussie: Twins? Are they both mine?

Gussie's mother-in-Law played by Louise Carver and Gussie played by El Brendel: Raoul Walsh's *The Big Trail* (Fox, 1930).

3907

Jones: Rosie, how many times have you been married?

Rosie: Eleven. Ten without a preacher or license.

Jones: Well, did you love any of 'em?

Rosie: Oh, all of 'em! Every one of 'em! The good and the bad. It's a shame to waste all that prime beef on a guy serv-ing three to five in a prison. Do you keep in touch?

Jones: Oh, he's kind of a lousy letter writer.

Rosie: A lousy bank robber too!

Miss Jones played by Candice Bergen and Rosie played by Jean Willes: Richard Brooks' *Bite The Bullet* (Columbia, 1975).

3908

Lola: There's enough uncertainty about marriage without sitting home wondering what tree your husband is hanging from that night.

Lola Montez played by Yvonne DeCarlo: George Sherman's *Black Bart* (Universal, 1948).

3909

Lola: Wouldn't it be a little crowded on the honeymoon? You and me and the hanging party?

Boles: I'll leave them at home.

Lola: Mr. and Mrs. Black Bart. Somehow it doesn't sound very permanent.

Boles: You'll have to admit, it doesn't sound dull.

Lola Montez played by Yvonne DeCarlo and Charles E. Boles, alias Black Bart, played by Dan Duryea: George Sherman's *Black Bart* (Universal, 1948).

3910

Wanda Mae: If you was to kiss me, I'd be mighty obliged.

Johnny: [*following the kiss*] My mouth's burning!

Wanda Mae: Shucks, I'm sorry, Johnny. It's my chaw.

Wanda Mae was uncredited and Johnny Geyser played by John Hammond: Andrew V. McLaglen's *The Blue and the Gray* (TV miniseries, 1982).

3911

Ridgeway: No daughter of mine is going to be an outlaw bride.

Matthew Ridgeway played by Richard Arlen: Spencer G. Bennet's *The Bounty Killer* (Embassy/Premiere, 1965).

3912

Miss Lilly: But why do I hate him so?

Running Water: The Apaches have a word for that …it's called love.

Antoinette Lilly played by Sondra Locke and Lorraine Running Water played by Sierra Pecheur: Clint Eastwood's *Bronco Billy* (Warner Bros., 1980).

3913

Miss Lilly: Have you ever been married?

Bronco Billy: Sure. A long time ago.

Miss Lilly: Did you love her?

Bronco Billy: With all my heart. Sometimes that just isn't enough.

Miss Lilly: What happened?

Bronco Billy: I caught her in bed with my best friend.

Miss Lilly: What did you do to him?

Bronco Billy: I shot her.

Miss Lilly: What! What about him?

Bronco Billy: He was my best friend!

Antoinette Lilly played by Sondra Locke and Bronco Billy played by Clint Eastwood: Clint Eastwood's *Bronco Billy* (Warner Bros., 1980).

3914

Indian Girl: I believe what my grandfather used to tell me: that eyes that meet the way ours did, and hold tightly, are meant to meet again …many times.

The Delaware Indian girl played by Carmen Moore: Mark Sobel's *Brothers of the Frontier* (TVW, 1996).

3915

Jude: Ah, well, being in love ain't going to hurt him. Ain't no harm in that. It's getting hitched is where the trouble begins.

Jude Pilchuck played by Raymond Hatton: Henry Hathaway's *Buffalo Stampede* (a.k.a. *The Thundering Herd*; Paramount, 1934).

3916

Cahill: Lightfoot, Amy and me tried for a lot of years to have children …but maybe they came along too late in my life.

Lightfoot: J.D.?

Cahill: Yeah.

Lightfoot: There ain't nothing too late …if you love it.

Marshal J.D. Cahill played by John Wayne and Lightfoot played by Neville Brand: Andrew McLaglen's *Cahill: United States Marshal* (Warner Bros., 1973).

3917

White Squaw: Mr. Gannon?

Gannon: Yes.

White Squaw: If you met a woman, a woman like me, that had been taken by the Sioux, how would you feel knowing that?

Gannon: If I loved her, it wouldn't matter.

White Squaw: It wouldn't?

Gannon: No, ma'am, it wouldn't matter at all.

White Squaw played by Teresa Stratas and Inspector Gannon played by Robert Ryan: Burt Kennedy's *The Canadians* (20th Century–Fox, 1961).

3918

Logan: George, when is this girl going to marry you?

George: I doubt if she knows herself, Logan. When are you taking me, Lucy?

Lucy: George, do you like poetry?

George: Must I like poetry to be your husband?

Lucy: We'll be married when the leaves fall.

George: You see, Logan, she strings me up and lets me swing. You mean the maple leaves that fall early, or the pine needles that never fall at all?

Logan Stuart played by Dana Andrews, George Camrose played by Brian Donlevy, and Lucy Overmire played by Susan Hayward: Jacques Tourneur's *Canyon Passage* (Universal, 1946).

3919

Ben: If you want to catch a man, you got to work at it.
Caroline: I want no man I have to catch.
Ben: Why sure, you catch him and he catches you. A man always figures that he does the catching. The truth is, it's the woman that brings him up on the rope ...and him not quite knowing it.

Ben Dance played by Andy Devine and Caroline Marsh played by Patricia Roc: Jacques Tourneur's *Canyon Passage* (Universal, 1946).

3920

Sam: You know what I just decided love is? Having someone to talk to ...someone you don't have to choose your words with.

Sam Brassfield played by Robert Taylor: Tay Garnett's *Cattle King* (MGM, 1963).

3921

Maggie: Falling in love is like being hit with a bullet. You don't know it's happened until you're dead.

Maggie played by Annabella Incontrera: Leon Klimovsky's *Challenge of the Mackennas* (Filmar Compagnia Cinematografica — Atlantida/Hemlock Enterprises, 1969).

3922

Maggie: Love is the only form of death you recover from.

Maggie played by Annabella Incontrera: Leon Klimovsky's *Challenge of the Mackennas* (Filmar Compagnia Cinematografica — Atlantida/Hemlock Enterprises, 1969).

3923

Cullen: All the women west of the Mississippi, and we got to wind up with a war chief's bride!

Cullen played by Dick Wesson: Gordon Douglas' *The Charge at Feather River* (Warner Bros., 1953).

3924

Ryan: I was shot at by the whole Confederate Army. You think I'm scared of one husband?

Ryan played by Steve Brodie: Gordon Douglas' *The Charge at Feather River* (Warner Bros., 1953).

3925

Jenny: Three days. So much can happen to the human heart in three days. It beats 239,000 times in three days. It can break, it can be torn apart. But it just keeps on beating ...and beating.

Jenny played by Sally Kirkland: Rod McCall's *Cheatin' Hearts* (Trimark Pictures, 1993).

3926

Harley: Then there was my cousin, Jim. He sure was a fine figure of a man. But he fell to pieces when he got married. He got fat, his hair started fallin' out, his teeth went bad. The worse lookin' he got, the better lookin' she got. I mean, she weren't no vampire ...nothing like that, at least ways nobody could prove it ...but, Lord of Mercy, the worse lookin' he got the better lookin' she got ...until there wasn't nothing much left of him ...and she went off back east somewhere and took up with a stone mason.

Harley Sullivan played by Henry Fonda: Gene Kelly's *The Cheyenne Social Club* (NGP, 1970).

3927

John: I never knew you were married?
Harley: Well John, it ain't something I like to talk about, but I was married once. And once is enough for any man. You can't smoke, chew, dip, drink, scratch in the parlor, or cuss. When you leave the house, they ask you where'd you go. And when you come home, they ask you where have you been. And right now with you, it is just like when I was married.
John: Why, how is that, Harley?
Harley: Well John, when a woman's talking to you, you can be pretty sure that she thinks she's in control. And when she's not talking to you, you can be pretty certain you're in control.

John O'Hanlan played by James Stewart and Harley Sullivan played by Henry Fonda: Gene Kelly's *The Cheyenne Social Club* (NGP, 1970).

3928

Jenny: Did you ever love a woman, Johnny? I mean, really love her?
John: Yeah. Thought I did once. Come to find out it was indigestion.

Jenny played by Shirley Jones and John O'Hanlan played by James Stewart: Gene Kelly's *The Cheyenne Social Club* (NGP, 1970).

3929

Billy: Did you ever think on getting married?
Pat: I've been three years a buffalo hunter.
Billy: What's that got to do with getting married?
Pat: Smell.
Billy: What smell?
Pat: Death. Buffalo hunters smell like old guts all the time.
Billy: Well, I'm downwind from you and I don't smell it.
Pat: I'm upwind and I smell it on you, Billy.
Billy: What? Old guts?
Pat: Death.

Billy The Kid played by Geoffrey Deuel and Pat

Garrett played by Glenn Corbett: Andrew McLaglen's *Chisum* (Warner Bros., 1970).

3930

Yancy: Wife and mother ...stainless woman ...hide me, hide me in your love.

Yancy Cravat played by Richard Dix: Wesley Ruggles' *Cimarron* (RKO, 1931).

3931

Wife: Look at you! You're a priest now!
Pancho: I did it for you so no woman would want me no more!

The wife, Rosa, played by Yareli Arizmendi and Pancho played by Cheech Marin: Luis Valdez's *The Cisco Kid* (Turner Pictures, 1994).

3932

Cisco: Amigo, if the young lady refuses to say, "I do," shoot the gentleman in the leg.
Gordito: Oh, si.
Cisco: And if the gentleman refuses to say, "I do," shoot him in the other leg. It only comes twice in the ceremony, no?
Saunders: Ah ...yes!
Cisco: Good! He's got enough legs.

The Cisco Kid played by Cesar Romero, Gordito played by Chris-Pin Martin, and Justice of the Peace Pop Saunders played by James Burke: Herbert I. Leeds' *The Cisco Kid and the Lady* (20th Century–Fox, 1939).

3933

Mitch: Women need a reason to have sex; men just need a place.

Mitch Robbins played by Billy Crystal: Ron Underwood's *City Slickers* (Columbia, 1991).

3934

Mitch: Ed, have you noticed: the older you get, the younger your girlfriends get. Soon you'll be dating sperm.

Mitch Robbins played by Billy Crystal and Ed Furillo played by Bruno Kirby: Ron Underwood's *City Slickers* (Columbia, 1991).

3935

Gabby: Doggone it! There's another good man gone and got himself roped and hog-tied in spite of all my warnings!

Gabby Whittaker played by George "Gabby" Hayes: Joseph Kane's *Colorado* (Republic, 1940).

3936

Ben: Oh, I admit I've never had much luck when it comes to women. Oh, I've run with a few, but nothing you could call serious. Except maybe that little gal down in Sonora. She said right out she loved me. Wanted to marry me. She told everybody. Everybody but her husband. Oh, he came within that of doing me with a scatter gun. That taught me a lesson though: always check the brand to make sure you ain't driving another man's stock.

Ben Lane played by Claude Akins: Budd Boetticher's *Comanche Station* (Columbia, 1960).

3937

Black Buffalo Woman: Don't forget me.
Crazy Horse: I could sooner forget to breathe.

Black Buffalo Woman played by Irene Bedard and Crazy Horse played by Michael Greyeyes: John Irvin's *Crazy Horse* (Turner Pictures, 1996).

3938

Lt. Dunbar: We are trying for a baby.
Kicking Bird: No waiting?
Lt. Dunbar: No waiting.
Kicking Bird: I was just thinking that of all the trails in this life …there is one that matters most. It is the trail of a true human being. I think you are on this trail, and it is good to see.

Lt. John J. Dunbar played by Kevin Costner and Kicking Bird played by Graham Greene: Kevin Costner's *Dances with Wolves* (TIG/Orion, 1990).

3939

Mary: Now, will you please get to the point and tell me what you want?
Bob: I want to marry you.
Mary: You what?
Bob: Well, I ain't got no job right now, but I figure to get one. And outside of a snort of hooch now and then, I got no bad habits.
Mary: I'd say asking a perfect stranger to marry you is a very bad habit!

Mary McCloud played by Claire Trevor and Bob Seton played by John Wayne: Raoul Walsh's *The Dark Command* (Republic, 1940).

3940

Brett: What's your destination, Miss Hayes?
Hayes: Socorro.
Brett: What's your destiny? Marriage?
Hayes: Yes.
Brett: It's not the answer I was hoping for.
Hayes: Don't you believe in marriage?
Brett: I once had many beliefs. One of them was marriage.

Brett Wade played by Rory Calhoun and Rannah Hayes played by Piper Laurie: George Sherman's *Dawn at Socorro* (Universal, 1954).

3941

Brittany: Aren't you supposed to be married?
Harry: Forbidden fruit always taste the sweetest.

Brittany played by April Telek and Harry McDonacle played by John Ritter: Joseph L. Scanlan's "The Great McDonacle" episode to the series premiere, *Dead Man's Gun* (Showtime, 1997).

3942

Brittany: What about your wife?

Harry: What about her? She stuck with me when I was nobody. She has faith in me. She's kind …loyal.
Brittany: If that's all you want, Harry, why not get a dog?

Brittany played by April Telek and Harry McDonacle played by John Ritter: Joseph L. Scanlan's "The Great McDonacle" episode to the series premiere, *Dead Man's Gun* (Showtime, 1997).

3943

Claire: You did mean it, didn't you?
Frank: Mean what?
Claire: About marrying me?
Frank: Yeah.
Claire: When, Frank?
Frank: Right now.
Claire: Can a bride have an hour to get ready?
Frank: It'll take you that long?
Claire: Ah huh.
Frank: Well, all right, but hurry up.
Claire: Frank?
Frank: Yeah.
Claire: What about the preacher? He might want to be in on this.

Claire Quintana played by Lena Horne and Marshal Frank Patch played by Richard Widmark: Allen Smithee's *Death of a Gunfighter* (Universal, 1969).

3944

Chief: You like daughter?
Dingus: Ah, yeah.
Chief: Me like gun. We make trade. I take gun. You take daughter. Marry.
Dingus: Oh well, ah, sir, she's a mighty nice girl and I like her a lot. But that's a fine looking rifle there.
Chief: Me keep rifle! You take daughter! Go honeymoon. Crazy Blanket has spoken!

Chief Crazy Blanket played by Paul Fix and Dingus Magee played by Frank Sinatra: Burt Kennedy's *Dirty Dingus Magee* (MGM, 1970).

3945

Don Cesar: I shall see you again.
Dolores: You presume.
Don Cesar: I assume.

Don Cesar de Vega played by Douglas Fairbanks and Dolores de Muro played by Mary Astor: Donald Crisp's silent film, *Don Q, Son of Zorro* (United Artists, 1925).

3946

Arkansas: Oh, come on Melissa! Marry me, please?
Melissa: Ask me sometime when you're sober, Arkansas.
Arkansas: It's a funny thing. She won't marry me when I'm drunk, and I won't marry her when I'm sober.

Arkansas played by Charles Kemper and Melissa Price played by Lee Patrick: Gordon Douglas' *The Doolins of Oklahoma* (Columbia, 1949).

3947

Arkansas: Bill Doolin …married to a woman!
Little Bill: Yeah, they make the best wives.

Arkansas played by Charles Kemper and Little Bill played by Noah Beery, Jr.: Gordon Douglas' *The Doolins of Oklahoma* (Columbia, 1949).

3948

Elaine: You know, this is my first opportunity to show off my new husband.
Doolin: New husband! Was there an old one?

Elaine Burton played by Virginia Huston and Bill Doolin played by Randolph Scott: Gordon Douglas' *The Doolins of Oklahoma* (Columbia, 1949).

3949

Deacon: You're dead, Bill. And I don't want my daughter married to a dead man.

Deacon Burton played by Griff Barnett and Bill Doolin played by Randolph Scott: Gordon Douglas' *The Doolins of Oklahoma* (Columbia, 1949).

3950

Lana: Do you like me as much as you do your old farm?

Lana Borst Martin played by Claudette Colbert: John Ford's *Drums Along the Mohawk* (20th Century–Fox, 1939).

3951

Malloy: Duchess, how many times have you been in love?
Duchess: Including this time?
Malloy: Ah huh.
Duchess: Once.

Charlie Malloy played by George Segal and Amanda Quaid, alias "Duchess,' played by Goldie Hawn: Melvin Frank's *The Duchess and the Dirtwater Fox* (20th Century–Fox, 1976).

3952

Wife: It's as if I'm not even here, isn't it?
Husband: Huh? What?

Rebecca played by Jocelyn Loewen and Young Ebenezer played by Aaron Pearl: Ken Jubenvill's *Ebenezer* (TVW, 1997).

3953

Erica: I want to marry a man who's breathing, not one who's six feet under.

Erica played by Amy Locane and Sam Benson played by Rick Schroder: Ken Jubenvill's *Ebenezer* (TVW, 1997).

3954

Kellie: I love you. You don't have to be perfect for me.
Lane: You mean that? You may have to prove it.
Kellie: I will.
Lane: Right now …I'm covered in horseshit!

Kellie Frost played by Cynthia Geary and Lane Frost played by Luke Perry: John G. Avildsen's *8 Seconds* (New Line Cinema, 1994).

3955

Carla: Women always look beautiful when they get married …and the men always look scared.

Roper: They both get over it.

Carla Forester played by Eleanor Parker and Captain Roper played by William Holden: John Sturges' *Escape from Fort Bravo* (MGM, 1953).

3956

Campbell: Don't it occur to you that the girl and Roper are getting kind of thick?

Marsh: Yes, it does.

Campbell: You trust her pretty good, huh?

Marsh: Ah huh, pretty good.

Campbell: Only it still cuts you a little, huh?

Marsh: Well, not enough to bleed.

Campbell played by William Demarest and Captain John Marsh played by John Forsythe: John Sturges' *Escape from Fort Bravo* (MGM, 1953).

3957

Mark: Are you trying to tell me I should ask her to marry me now? Tonight?

Ray: That's what I'm trying to tell you.

Mark: Don't you realize that I might be killed in the morning?

Ray: Anybody can be killed …any day.

Mark: Anybody is me! Any day is tomorrow!

Sheriff Mark Riley played by Lin McCarthy and Jim Larson, alias Ray Kincaid, played by Fred MacMurray: Paul Wendkos' *Face of a Fugitive* (Columbia, 1959).

3958

Sue: I've decided you love me.

Johnny: I'm glad you told me!

Sue: And you know how I know? It's, well, it's like eating peanuts.

Johnny: What's like eating peanuts?

Sue: Ever since that kiss on the stage in San Francisco …I've wanted more.

Johnny: Well, for your information, peanuts give me heartburn!

Sue played by Joan Freeman and Johnny played by Roy Orbison: Michael Moore's *The Fastest Guitar Alive* (MGM, 1967).

3959

Flora: Well, don't let her pull the wool over your eyes.

Larry: Maybe I like wool pulled over my eyes.

Flora Ballard played by Kathleen Burke and Larry Sutton played by Randolph Scott: Charles Barton's *The Fighting Westerner* (a.k.a. *Rocky Mountain Mystery*; Paramount, 1935).

3960

Jessica: What's happened to us is like a war. Easy to start …hard to stop.

Jessica Drummond played by Barbara Stanwyck: Samuel Fuller's *Forty Guns* (20th Century–Fox, 1957).

3961

Joe: Marriage? Marriage is for …ah …married people!

Joe Jarrett played by Dean Martin: Robert Aldrich's *Four for Texas* (Warner Bros., 1964).

3962

Bronco: Are you going to marry her off to a plow pusher?

Simon: Well, she sure ain't going to marry no gunslinger!

Bronco played by George Nader and Simon Bhumer

Indians display some displeasure with having settlers moving in next door in John Ford's *Drums Along the Mohawk* (20th Century–Fox, 1939).

played by Walter Brennan: Richard Carlson's *Four Guns to the Border* (Universal, 1954).

3963

Vance: I don't think I like being in love. It puts a bit in my mouth.

Vance Jeffords played by Barbara Stanwyck: Anthony Mann's *The Furies* (Paramount, 1950).

3964

Ruby Roy: Marryin' him is better than hangin' him.

Ruby Roy Bean played by Julie Donald: Dick Lowry's *The Gambler Returns: The Luck of the Draw* (TVW, 1991).

3965

Ruby Roy: Well, [my daddy] always says: when you find your man, corral him, put a saddle on him, he's all yours. Ethan slipped his bridle and I need to round him up.

Ruby Roy Bean played by Julie Donald and Ethan Cassidy played by Rick Rossovich: Dick Lowry's *The Gambler Returns: The Luck of the Draw* (TVW, 1991).

3966

Leslie: The best part about quarreling is the making up.

Leslie Lynnton Benedict played by Elizabeth Taylor: George Stevens' *Giant* (Warner Bros., 1956).

3967

Sgt.: What's the matter, boy? The law ain't after you, is it?

Hale: Oh, no sir. I run away from getting married.

Sgt.: Shotgun wedding?

Hale: Yeah, my cousin. She moved in with us last fall. Inside of a month, half the fellows in town have been to the barn with her. You know how jolly some girls are?

Sgt.: Yeah, I know.

Hale: Well, about five months later, my father says to put on my Sunday suit. Seems she is gonna have a baby, and I'm elected. I said all I ever did was kiss her. And he says, yeah, she sure looks that way! Anyway, he said it was time I quit schooling and settle down. Marriage was just what I needed. So when he went downstairs to meet the preacher, I went out the back window. When I got here, I enlisted. I'm just wondering what happens if he finds me here?

Sgt.: You're government property now, son. Ain't nobody got any claim on you except Uncle Sam. So stop worrying.

Sergeant James Gregory played by Slim Pickens and Martin Hale played by Michael Anderson, Jr.: Arnold Laven's *The Glory Guys* (United Artists, 1965).

3968

Sol: All right, I'm asking you now. Will you marry me?

Lou: You're already married, Sol, to yourself, to your freedom …taking off whenever the mood comes over you.

Sol Rogers played by Harve Presnell and Lou Woodward played by Senta Berger: Arnold Laven's *The Glory Guys* (United Artists, 1965).

3969

Quale: I'm not in business for love, you know. I was in love once, and I got the business.

S. Quentin Quale played by Groucho Marx: Edward Buzzell's *Go West* (MGM, 1940).

3970

Henry: Well, you know what they say: a lady loves an outlaw like a little boy loves a stray dog.

Henry Moon played by Jack Nicholson who also directed *Goin' South* (Paramount, 1978).

3971

Henry: Of course, a good husband is hard to find.

Julia: You weren't hard to find. You were standing in front of the whole town with a rope around your neck.

Henry Moon played by Jack Nicholson and Julia Tate played by Mary Steenburgen: Jack Nicholson's *Goin' South* (Paramount, 1978).

3972

Henry: I'll never forget you, Hermine. You're the first woman I didn't have to pay for.

Henry Moon played by Jack Nicholson and Hermine played by Veronica Cartwright: Jack Nicholson's *Goin' South* (Paramount, 1978).

3973

Laurie: You couldn't love anybody. There's too much hate in you.

Laurie Cutler played by Joan Blackman: Nathan Juran's *Good Day for a Hanging* (Columbia, 1958).

3974

Drusilla: I'm sorry but I'm not having any bastards, thank you. There's too many in the world as it is.

Gypsy: I kind of hate to hear you talking about bastards. I happen to be one.

Drusilla: So am I. That's why I'm not having any.

Gypsy: I'm not the marrying kind.

Drusilla: Well, I am!

Drusilla played by Regina Taylor and Gypsy Smith played by Sidney Poitier: David Greene's *A Good Day to Die* (a.k.a. *Children of the Dust*; Vidmark Entertainment, 1995).

3975

Undertaker: You can have everything, everything I own, my dear. Do you know what that means? A secure future,

a family. What, what does it take to have you say …yes?

Whore: Easy. Pay me the usual price. Just $10.00, like everybody else has to.

Two uncredited characters: Giancarlo Santi's *The Grand Duel* (Ital./Fr., 1972).

3976

Saxon: Brothers are the worst bosses …after wives.

Adam Saxon played by Horst Frank: Giancarlo Santi's *The Grand Duel* (Ital./Fr., 1972).

3977

Weatherby: I almost got married once myself. It was all set until her family came west in a covered wagon. If you could have seen her family, you'd know why the wagon was covered.

Weatherby played by Forrest Lewis: Raoul Walsh's *Gun Fury* (Columbia, 1953).

3978

Wyatt: We'd like you to come to the wedding, Doc, if it doesn't interfere with your poker.

Doc: I'm not good at weddings …only funerals. Deal me out.

Wyatt Earp played by Burt Lancaster and John H. "Doc" Holliday played by Kirk Douglas: John Sturges' *Gunfight at the O.K. Corral* (Paramount, 1957).

3979

Laura: Wyatt, when I first met you, I told you I wouldn't follow you from town to town, sitting in the darkness, waiting for someone to bring the news you've been killed. I won't live that way. We're not going to start a life together with a gun in your hand.

Laura Denbow played by Rhonda Fleming and Wyatt Earp played by Burt Lancaster: John Sturges' *Gunfight at the O.K. Corral* (Paramount, 1957).

3980

Reb: Are you in love with Curly?

Rita: He wants to marry me.

Reb: That's not what I asked you.

Rita: I don't know why that should interest you.

Reb: I don't want to stake my claim on range that's already taken up.

Reb Kittredge played by Audie Murphy and Rita Saxon played by Susan Cabot: Nathan Juran's *Gunsmoke* (Universal, 1953).

3981

Pastor: You may kiss the bride and close the deal, son.

Pastor Zach played by Victor Izay: Jerry Jameson's *Gunsmoke: The Long Ride* (TVW, 1993).

3982

Bovard: You're too young to understand a man like me. And maybe I'm too old to understand a girl like you. Time is like a barb wire fence; when too many years pile up, we can't get across to each other.

Deputy U.S. Marshal MacKenzie Bovard played by Robert Taylor: Michael Curtiz' *The Hangman* (Paramount, 1959).

3983

Clyde: You got what you wanted. Now you got to take what comes with it.

Clyde Stewart played by Rip Torn: Richard Pearce's *Heartland* (Wilderness Women/Filmhaus, 1980).

3984

Jack: Well, I never did care much for weddings.
Elinore: Well, I never did care much for 'em myself. But they're a sight better than funerals.

Jack played by Barry Primus and Elinore Randall Stewart played by Conchata Ferrell: Richard Pearce's *Heartland* (Wilderness Women/Filmaus, 1980).

3985

Tom: Why don't you get married and settle down? Why, you're running around like a maverick without a brand on.
Dare: Well, I don't like branding. It hurts in the wrong place.

Tom Fillmore played by Johnny Mack Brown and Dare Rudd played by John Wayne: Charles Barton's *Hell Town* (a.k.a. *Born to the West*; Paramount, 1937).

3986

Arch: I wonder what your wife is gonna say to you when she lays eyes on you, Harry? What I mean, what kind of nature does she have?
Harry: Oh, I don't rightly recall. I only lived with her for about a year and nine months.
Arch: Well, if I had a horse for a year and nine months, I'd sure know how many teeth he had.
Harry: Well, she had three teeth. I remember that.

Arch Harris played by Warren Oates and Harry Collings played by Peter Fonda: Peter Fonda's *The Hired Hand* (Universal, 1971).

3987

Billy Lee: You try living with a 24-hour belly-achin' and see how you like it!
Jessie: Well, that's the price you pay if you want it where you can nudge it in the night.

Billy Lee Blake played by Peter Lazer and Jessie played by Diane Cilento: Martin Ritt's *Hombre* (20th Century–Fox, 1967).

3988

Rattlesnake: My sister says you insulted her. No man insults my sister and stays alive.

Denver Kid: Insulted her? I asked her to marry me!
Rattlesnake: So she was right! Get ready to slap leather!

Rattlesnake played by Jack Elam and the Denver Kid played by Don Knotts: Robert Butler's *Hot Lead and Cold Feet* (Buena Vista, 1978).

3989

Prescott: Mr. Morgan, all my life I've wanted to marry a rich husband. Can I blame Cleve for wanting to marry a rich wife? Most of us may have been born for the poor house, but we're not the kind to like it.

Lilith Prescott played by Debbie Reynolds, Roger Morgan played by Robert Preston, and Cleve Van Valen played by Gregory Peck: John Ford's, George Marshall's, and Henry Hathaway's *How the West Was Won* (MGM, 1962).

3990

Morgan: Wet or dry, you're the handsomest woman I ever did see. A spirit and a fine sturdy body. It's a noble combination, Ms. Prescott. Why, for you, child-bearing would come as easy as rolling off a log.
Prescott: Well, I think I'd rather roll off a log, Mr. Morgan.

Roger Morgan played by Robert Preston and Lilith Prescott played by Debbie Reynolds: John Ford's, George Marshall's, and Henry Hathaway's *How the West Was Won* (MGM, 1962).

3991

Gabby: You two ought to get along just like that span of mules over there. They've been wearing the same harness for eleven years.

Gabby Whittaker played by George "Gabby" Hayes: Joseph Kane's *In Old Caliente* (Republic, 1939).

3992

Kentucky: Gee, it's kind of warm in here, isn't it?
Lila: I like the moonlight too.
Kentucky: Why, I didn't say anything about the moonlight!
Lila: I did.

Kentucky played by Ken Maynard and Lila Miller played by Evalyn Knapp: David Howard's *In Old Santa Fe* (Mascot, 1934).

3993

Benito: The land is good, Mattie, but the love of a man for a woman is better.
Mattie: Well, sometimes the love for a dream is the greatest of all.
Benito: Like Texas.
Mattie: Yes.
Benito: But you cannot make love to Texas.

Benito Garza played by Benjamin Bratt and Mattie Quimper played by Chelsea Field: Richard Lang's *James A. Michener's Texas* (TVW, 1995).

3994

Benito: You once told me that sometimes the greatest love is for a dream. I wish we had the same dream.

Benito Garza played by Benjamin Bratt: Richard Lang's *James A. Michener's Texas* (TVW, 1995).

3995

Johnny: It looks like the girl did a smart thing in getting rid of him.
Vienna: She was smart all right. She learned not to love anybody again.
Johnny: Five years is a long time. There must have been quite a few men in between.
Vienna: Enough.
Johnny: What do you suppose would happen if this man was to come back?
Vienna: When a fire burns itself out, all you have left is ashes.

Johnny Guitar played by Sterling Hayden and Vienna played by Joan Crawford: Nicholas Ray's *Johnny Guitar* (Republic, 1954).

3996

Johnny: How many men have you forgotten?
Vienna: As many women as you've remembered.

Johnny Guitar played by Sterling Hayden and Vienna played by Joan Crawford: Nicholas Ray's *Johnny Guitar* (Republic, 1954).

3997

Ellie: I just don't give a damn anymore. As far as I'm concerned, you can go to hell or Australia …but not with me!
Ace: Well, they're both down under.
Ellie: Dreams and sweet talk. That's all you are.

Elvira "Ellie" Bonner played by Ida Lupino and Ace Bonner played by Robert Preston: Sam Peckinpah's *Junior Bonner* (CIN, 1972).

3998

Quantrill: My dear Kate, I'm too old a man to have any illusions about the constancy of women, or to be seriously disturbed by the lack of it.

Colonel Quantrill played by Brian Donlevy and Kate Clarke played by Marguerite Chapman: Ray Enright's *Kansas Raiders* (Universal, 1950).

3999

Susie: Sometimes people can ruin what they love.

Susie played by Diane Lynn: Burt Lancaster's *The Kentuckian* (United Artists, 1955).

4000

Brookshire: What's wrong with your man? Is he sick?
Call: No, he ain't sick. He's married!

Ned Brookshire played by Charles Martin Smith and Captain Woodrow F. Call played by James Garner: Joseph Sargent's *Larry McMurtry's Streets of Laredo* (Cabin Fever Entertainment, 1995).

4001

Mother: Go ahead and marry him if you want to. But if you do, you'll sip sour with a spoon, I'll promise ya.

Kate's Mother played by Virginia Brissac: Joseph Kane's *The Last Bandit* (Republic, 1949).

4002

Emmett: Now honey, I tried honest work. The best I could do was a ranch hand ...at twelve dollars a month. Twelve dollars! You want to get married, don't you?

Julia: Yes.

Emmett: Well, twelve dollars don't buy nothing except maybe beans and misery.

Emmett Dalton played by Tim Matheson and Julia Johnson played by Kathleen Cody: Vincent McEveety's *The Last Day* (Paramount, 1975).

4003

Old Timer: My cousin walked into them mountains twenty years ago. He never come out.

Gates: Any message in case I come across him?

Old Timer: Yeah. Tell him I run off with his wife!

The Old Timer played by Robert Donley and Lewis Gates played by Tom Berenger: Tab Murphy's *Last of the Dogmen* (Savory Pictures, 1995).

4004

Jenny: Your wife? Was she a Comanche girl?

Todd: Huh huh.

Jenny: Young?

Todd: Fifteen when she come to me.

Jenny: That seems awfully young.

Todd: Well, girls and ponies both, the younger you break 'em in the better. They're apt to get wild otherwise.

Jenny played by Felicia Farr and "Comanche" Todd played by Richard Widmark: Delmer Daves' *The Last Wagon* (20th Century–Fox, 1956).

4005

Jeannie: You're big and you're ugly and you're stupid, and I happen to be in love with you.

Jeannie Bristow played by Dorothy Malone: Nathan Juran's *Law and Order* (Universal, 1953).

4006

Mandy Lou: You a baptist?

Mose: No, ma'am. Ain't never been to church but once in my whole life. And then something terrible happened to me.

Mandy Lou: No! What?

Mose: I got married!

Mandy Lou played by Etta McDaniel and Mose played by Fred "Snowflake" Toones: Joseph Kane's *The Lawless Nineties* (Republic, 1936).

4007

Whip: So you really want to get married, huh?

Laura: I don't want to get married ...you want to get married.

Whip: I didn't say I want to get married. I said the next time I got married, I wanted to get married and then get drunk ...and see if that works.

Laura: If anybody needs a drink, it's me, because I ain't gonna marry you sober.

Whip played by Randy Quaid and Laura Flemming played by Macha Grenon: Rene Manzor's *Legends of the North* (Cinevideo Plus, 1995).

4008

Leola: Wren has got a tongue on her, don't she papa?

Verlon: Yeah, just like your mama did.

Leola: Yeah, but mama wasn't a whore.

Verlon: Well, I reckon she was a whore. Married to me and run off with another man. What's that if it ain't no whore?

Leola: Run off? I thought you said mama died.

Verlon: She did die ...and him, too. They both died!

Leola Borgers played by Gregory Scott Cummins, Verlon Borgers played by Bill McKinney, and Wren played by Brenda Bakke: Jack Bender's *Lone Justice II* (Triboro Entertainment Group, 1995).

4009

Martha: But now that you mentioned it, why don't you have a wife?

Burke: No woman ever said yes.

Martha: How many have you asked?

Burke: None.

Martha Ronda played by Ava Gardner and Devereaux Burke played by Clark Gable: Vincent Sherman's *Lone Star* (MGM, 1952).

4010

John: Is there someone who is going to miss you too, Jed? A wife? A sweetheart?

Jed: You darn tootin'! They'll both miss me. That's why I didn't go back to Missouri.

John Ashley played by John Wayne and Jed played by Jim Toney: Joseph Kane's *The Lonely Trail* (Republic, 1936).

4011

Clara: He wanted what I wouldn't give, and I wanted what he didn't have.

Clara played by Anjelica Huston: Simon Wincer's *Lonesome Dove* (TVW, 1989).

4012

Cole: First getting shot, then getting married. Bad habits.

Cole Younger played by David Carradine: Walter Hill's *The Long Riders* (United Artists, 1980).

4013

Frank: I got a question for you.

Clell: Fire away, Frank. Fire away and fall back.

Frank: Have you ever been in love?

Clell: Oh God, yeah. It's terrible ...an affliction ...really miserable ...nothing but trouble. It drove me crazy.

Frank: It was that bad, really?

Clell: Yeah. She was wonderful!

Frank James played by Stacy Keach and Clell Miller played by Randy Quaid: Walter Hill's *The Long Riders* (United Artists, 1980).

4014

Cathy: We don't want you to go, Vance. This is your home. We all love you.

Vance: A home can be full of too much love, Cathy. Then one night it burns up ...and everybody in it.

Cathy played by Debra Paget and Vance Reno played by Richard Egan: Robert D. Webb's *Love Me Tender* (20th Century–Fox, 1956).

4015

Mrs. Hill: When a man gets married, it halves his territory. But a woman doubles hers.

Mrs. Hill played by Fionnula Flanagan: Martin Donovan's *Mad at the Moon* (1992).

4016

Daughter: I can't help the way I feel when I look at James Miller. I feel nothing. I don't feel anything. When I look at him, I don't see anybody. I don't see the man I'm going to marry.

Mother: But that's romance, my darling. This is life!

Jenny Hill (daughter) played by Mary Stuart Masterson, Mrs. Hill (mother) played by Fionnula Flanagan, and James Miller played by Stephen Blake: Martin Donovan's *Mad at the Moon* (1992).

4017

Marietta: There's one thing I've learned in cowtowns from Abilene to the Dakotas: never run after a married man. You might catch him. And if you do, his good wife runs you right out of town.

Marietta played by Barbara Luna: Burt Kennedy's *Mail Order Bride* (MGM, 1964).

4018

Preacher: If there be any present here who can show just cause why these two should not be joined in holy wedlock, let him speak now or forever hold his peace?

Bridegroom: Me!

Preacher: You don't count!

Preacher Pope played by Denver Pyle and Lee Carey, the Bridegroom, played by Keir Dullea: Burt Kennedy's *Mail Order Bride* (MGM, 1964).

4019

Barbara: I want to be your wife, Vic. But if I can't get you to leave with me, I'm not going to stay around to become your widow.

Vic: I don't die so quick.

Barbara Waggoman played by Cathy O'Donnell

and Vic Hansbro played by Arthur Kennedy: Anthony Mann's *The Man from Laramie* (Columbia, 1955).

4020

Alec: You know, Davey, you're just like your mother. She always listened. She never understood.

Alec Waggoman played by Donald Crisp and Dave Waggoman played by Alex Nicol: Anthony Mann's *The Man from Laramie* (Columbia, 1955).

4021

Will: Suppose you had known before our marriage that I meant to go after Merritt. Would you have married me?

Laure: What a brutal question!

Will: Thank you for the compliment.

Will Isham played by Alexander Knox, Laure Bidwell played by Joan Leslie, and Owen Merritt played by Randolph Scott: Andre De Toth's *Man in the Saddle* (Columbia, 1951).

4022

Brett: We better get an understanding. I don't like women, never have liked women, and never will!

Alice: I'm not at all interested in your problems.

Brett Dale played by Randolph Scott and Alice Gaynor played by Verna Hillie: Henry Hathaway's *Man of the Forest* (Paramount, 1933).

4023

Alice: I don't know what to say to you.

Brett: I do, but we'll have to wait until we'll get more time.

Alice Gaynor played by Verna Hillie and Brett Dale played by Randolph Scott: Henry Hathaway's *Man of the Forest* (Paramount, 1933).

4024

Alice: I'll kill you the next time!

Brett: If you do, I'll spank you again!

Alice Gaynor played by Verna Hillie and Brett Dale played by Randolph Scott: Henry Hathaway's *Man of the Forest* (Paramount, 1933).

4025

California: A marriage is worse than a funeral. In a marriage, your troubles just begin. In a funeral …they're over.

California Carlson played by Andy Clyde: George Archainbaud's *The Marauders* (United Artists, 1947).

4026

Maria: If you take the challenge out of the sport, you ruin the hunt.

Teresa: He's coming to dine, not to hunt.

Maria: You are young, inexperienced. To a man, there is only the hunt …the challenge. The sport is important whether it be a blood sport or a love sport. Remember that!

Maria played by Inez Perez and Teresa played by Anne Archer: Don McDougall's *The Mark of Zorro* (TVW, 1974).

Big Eli (Burt Lancaster) and son, Little Eli, set off for Texas and find plenty of adventure along the way in *The Kentuckian* (United Artists, 1955).

4027

Don Diego: I have a servant — a wonder at the guitar. Tonight I shall order him to come out and play beneath your window.

Lolita: I have a servant passionately fond of music.

Don Diego/Zorro played by Douglas Fairbanks, Sr. and Lolita played by Marguerite de la Motte: Fred Niblo's silent film, *The Mark of Zorro* (United Artists, 1920).

4028

McLintock: There's something I ought to tell you. I guess now is as good a time as any. You're gonna have every young buck west of the Missouri around here trying to marry you. Mostly because you're a handsome filly. But partly because I own everything in this country from here to there, and they'll think you're going to inherit it. Well, you're not! I'm going to leave most of it to, well, to the nation really …for a park where no lumbermen will cut down all the trees for houses with leaky roofs …and nobody will kill all the beaver for hats or dudes …or murder the buffalo for ropes. What I'm gonna give you is a 500 cow spread on the upper Green River. Now that may not seem like much, but it's more than we had …your mother and I. Some folks are gonna say I'm doing all this so I can sit up there in the hereafter and look down on a park named after me. Or that I was disappointed in you and didn't want you to get all that money. But the real reason, Becky, is because I love you. And I want you and some young man to have what I had. Because all the gold in the United States Treasury, and all the harp music in heaven, can't equal what happens between a man and a woman with all that growing together!

George Washington McLintock played by John

Wayne and Becky McLintock played by Stefanie Powers: Andrew V. McLaglen's *McLintock!* (United Artists, 1963).

4029
Sam: Hell, Jericho, you used to tell jokes so dirty they'd mortify a tent preacher two canyons away. Now look at ya! Family …married to a church-going woman!
Jericho: There ain't a church within a hundred miles of here!
Sam: Hell, they bring 'em with 'em! They always do! First, it's the whiskers. The next thing you know, you'll be plantin' things in rows!
Sam Webster played by John Dennis Johnston and Jericho Adams played by Kris Kristofferson: Kevin James Dobson's *Miracle in the Wilderness* (TVW, 1991).

4030
Bess: You know, Hoyce, there's one thing to be said for a fence post.
Hoyce: Yeah, which is?
Bess: They're predictable.
Bess Guthrie played by Gena Rowlands and Hoyce Guthrie played by Richard Crenna: William A. Graham's *Montana* (TVW, 1990).

4031
Bess: You go to hell!
Hoyce: I'd go and pay rent if I knew they wouldn't let you in!
Bess Guthrie played by Gena Rowlands and Hoyce Guthrie played by Richard Crenna: William A. Graham's *Montana* (TVW, 1990).

4032
Dalton: I'm not asking you to be grateful, Belle. I'm asking you to love me.
Belle: No thanks. I was married to an outlaw. And the last payoff is always the same …Boot Hill.
Bob Dalton played by Scott Brady and Belle Starr played by Jane Russell: Allan Dwan's *Montana Belle* (RKO, 1952).

4033
Monica: Who would have thought back in Boston …that I'd be saying "yes" in a cheap hotel room in Arizona …to a tall gunslinger in black!
Monica Alton played by Anne Francis: Robert Sparr's *More Dead Than Alive* (United Artists, 1968).

4034
Twillie: It is not good for a man to be alone.
Flower Belle: It's no fun for a woman either.
Twillie: Is it possible for us to be lonesome together?
Cuthbert J. Twillie played by W.C. Fields and Flower Belle Lee played by Mae West: Edward F. Cline's *My Little Chickadee* (Universal, 1940).

4035
Carter: Aren't you forgetting that you're married?
Flower Belle: I'm doing my best!
Wayne Carter played by Dick Foran and Flower Belle Lee played by Mae West: Edward F. Cline's *My Little Chickadee* (Universal, 1940).

4036
Sam: My only politics …anti-wife. Any woman who devotes herself to making one man miserable instead of a lot of men happy, don't get my vote.
Sam McCord played by John Wayne: Henry Hathaway's *North to Alaska* (20th Century–Fox, 1960).

4037
Sam: George, a wonderful thing about Alaska is that matrimony hasn't hit up here yet. Let's keep it a free country.
Sam McCord played by John Wayne and George Pratt played by Stewart Granger: Henry Hathaway's *North to Alaska* (20th Century–Fox, 1960).

4038
Angel: A bullet through the brain is always the best cure for love.
Michelle "Angel" played by Capucine: Henry Hathaway's *North to Alaska* (20th Century–Fox, 1960).

4039
April: Aren't you married?
Dusty: I've always held that a bachelor is a fella who never makes the same mistake once.
April Logan played by Madeleine Carroll and Dusty Rivers played by Gary Cooper: Cecil B. DeMille's *North West Mounted Police* (Paramount, 1940).

4040
April: Is there anything in the regulations about the mounted police always getting their woman?
Brett: No, but there should be!
April Logan played by Madeleine Carroll and Sgt. Jim Brett played by Preston Foster: Cecil B. DeMille's *North West Mounted Police* (Paramount, 1940).

4041
Logan: You're the sweetest poison that ever got into a man's blood.
Constable Ronnie Logan played by Robert Preston: Cecil B. DeMille's *North West Mounted Police* (Paramount, 1940).

4042
Ado Annie: Ali, Laurey and me have been having an argument.
Ali: About what, baby?
Ado Annie: About what you meant when you said that about driving with me to the end of the world.

Ali: Well, I didn't really mean to the end of the world.
Ado Annie: Well then, how far did you want to go?
Ali: About as far as, say, Claremore.
Ado Annie: What's at Claremore?
Ali: The hotel. In front of the veranda, inside is the lobby …and upstairs, baby, might be paradise.
Ado Annie: I thought they was just bedrooms?
Ado Annie played by Gloria Grahame and Ali Hakim played by Eddie Albert: Fred Zinnemann's *Oklahoma!* (Magna, 1955).

4043
Maria: I love you. You must know that.
John: It's easy to mistake gratitude for love.
Maria: I'm old enough to know the difference!
Maria Smith played by Gloria Talbott and Dr. John Brighton played by Joel McCrea: Francis D. Lyon's *The Oklahoman* (Warner Bros., 1957).

4044
Babb: Love is so insidious. It's constantly interfering with the pursuit of true happiness.
Miss Amity Babb played by Martha Hyer: Hal Kanter's *Once Upon a Horse* (Universal, 1958).

4045
Bert: That lady from Virginia sure changed the Major.
Cal: Wait until after the marriage and he'll get his same old even disposition back …always mad.
Bert played by Harry Carey, Jr., Cal Prince played by James Millican, and Major Cosgrave played by Jim Davis: William Whitney's *The Outcast* (Republic, 1954).

4046
Judy: I don't suppose I'm the first girl you've kissed. But I don't care …as long as I'm the last.
Judy Polsen played by Joan Evans: William Whitney's *The Outcast* (Republic, 1954).

4047
Jet: But after the wedding, don't throw the flowers away. You may need them for a funeral.
Jet Cosgrave played by John Derek: William Whitney's *The Outcast* (Republic, 1954).

4048
Doc: The crazier a man is about a woman, the crazier he thinks and the crazier he does.
Doc Holliday played by Walter Huston: Howard Hughes' *The Outlaw* (United Artists, 1943).

4049
Louise: Now do you understand, Reverend, why I insisted on a rehearsal?

Parson: I certainly do!

Jason: Well, that's what has got me so nervous, all this rehearsing.

Louise: Now, Jason.

Jason: But it's true. If you're going to tie a horse up to a rail, you don't lead him in first to see if the wood is strong enough to hold him. Why don't we just do it and get it over with?

Louise Murphy played by Lillian Bronson, the Parson played by Jonathan Hole, and Jason Fitch played by Edgar Buchanan: George McCowan's *The Over-the-Hill Gang Rides Again* (TVW, 1970).

4050

Stewart: Look, Jessie, we've been through for a long time. The fire is out. There's nothing left but ashes.

Del Stewart played by William Bishop and Jessie Lorraine played by Adele Jergens: Fred F. Sears' *Overland Pacific* (United Artists, 1954).

4051

Pardner: A woman can't have two husbands!

Elizabeth: Well, I was married to a man [Mormon] who had two wives. Why can't a woman have two husbands?

Pardner played by Clint Eastwood and Elizabeth Woodling played by Jean Seberg: Joseph Logan's *Paint Your Wagon* (Paramount, 1969).

4052

Megan: I think I love you.

Preacher: There's nothing wrong with that. If there was more love in the world, there probably would be a lot less dyin'.

Megan: So there can't be anything wrong with making love either.

Preacher: I think it's best just to practice loving for awhile before you think about the other.

Megan: If I practiced this loving for awhile, will you teach me the other?

Preacher: Megan, most folks around kind of associate that with marriage.

Megan: I'll be fifteen next month!

Megan Wheeler played by Sydney Penny and the Preacher played by Clint Eastwood: Clint Eastwood's *Pale Rider* (Warner Bros., 1985).

4053

Megan: Were Grandma and Grandpa happy when you got married, Ma?

Sarah: I'm afraid they didn't have a thimble full of choice in the matter.

Megan: Were they surprised?

Sarah: Your grandpa took the measles and your grandma got drunk.

Megan Wheeler played by Sydney Penny and Sarah Wheeler played by Carrie Snodgress: Clint Eastwood's *Pale Rider* (Warner Bros., 1985).

4054

Jane: Now remember, Painless. You promised to love, honor, and protect me.

Painless: Yeah, but let's do it in the order named.

Calamity Jane played by Jane Russell and Painless Peter Potter played by Bob Hope: Norman Z. McLeod's *The Paleface* (Paramount, 1948).

4055

1st Sgt: As for me, I still drink, I'm still broke, and I still draw a sergeant's pay.

Calla: Is that what you've been telling yourself?

1st Sgt: Any other reason why you didn't marry me?

First Sergeant Emmett Bell played by Jeff Chandler and Calla Gaxton played by Dorothy Malone: George Marshall's *Pillars of the Sky* (Universal, 1956).

4056

Hickok: I got a restless toe. I can't tie up with anybody.

Wild Bill Hickok played by Don Murray: David Lowell Rich's *The Plainsman* (Universal, 1966).

4057

Whit: Running into you gave me an idea.

Druin: Where do I fit in?

Whit: You're getting married.

Druin: Me?

Whit: Yes, Johnny, you.

Druin: Oh, no. I always figured on passing up getting married.

Whit: Well, I don't generally go around endorsing it. But any sensible man would figure that's better than having his wind cut off with a six-strand rawhide rope.

Druin: Since you put it that way, who's the bride?

Whit Lacey played by Forrest Tucker and John Druin played by Rod Cameron: Joseph Kane's *The Plunderers* (Republic, 1948).

4058

Martin: Almost all relationships are compromises, Lin. And marriages, too. Now look what I got to offer: a way out of this life, money, security. Lin, marriages aren't made in heaven.

Lin: Maybe not. But wouldn't it be wonderful if they were?

Eben Martin played by Taylor Holmes and Lin Conner played by Ilona Massey: Joseph Kane's *The Plunderers* (Republic, 1948).

4059

Druin: I always figured a man a fool to get married. It weights him down. He never walks as wide or as tall from the minute he's got a woman hanging on his arm. But I want to marry you. It doesn't matter from then on if I walk an inch narrow and only a foot tall.

John Druin played by Rod Cameron: Joseph Kane's *The Plunderers* (Republic, 1948).

4060

Lana: Do you know how to cheat Mr. Death? By making love. Because, you know, every time you make love you can make another life. And that makes Mr. Death mad as hell.

Lana played by Salli Richardson: Mario Van Peebles' *Posse* (Gramercy Pictures, 1993).

4061

Dolworth: Rico, buddy, this will come as a shock for both of us: I'm a born sucker for love.

Rico: That bullet must have knocked some of your brains out.

Dolworth: Or let some in.

Bill Dolworth played by Burt Lancaster and Henry Rico Fardan played by Lee Marvin: Richard Brooks' *The Professionals* (Columbia, 1966).

4062

Walton: No whelp of the Turner litter can marry my daughter …unless it's over my dead body!

Clint: That would be one way of doing it!

John Walton played by Ed LeSaint and Clint Turner played by John Wayne: Ross Lederman's *The Range Feud* (Columbia, 1931).

4063

Cheyenne: It may not be lady-like to talk like this but, well, thank goodness I'm not a lady. If I loved a man and he wanted me, I wouldn't wait for orange blossoms and a honeymoon in California. Why, I'd marry him in a blizzard in the middle of the desert.

Cheyenne played by Anne Jeffreys: Ray Enright's *Return of the Badmen* (RKO, 1948).

4064

Billy: You know, Elder, I hate to get married with one of my brothers smelling bad enough to gag a dog off a gut wagon.

Billy Hammond played by James Drury and Elder Hammond played by John Anderson: Sam Peckinpah's *Ride the High Country* (MGM, 1962).

4065

Billy: Here she is, folks! My bride to be! Elsa, this here is Judge Tolliver.

Judge: Pleased to meet your acquaintance, my dear.

Billy: And that there is Kate. She's your bridesmaid.

Kate: Welcome to Kate's Place, honey!

Billy Hammond played by James Drury, Judge Tolliver played by Edgar Buchanan, Kate played by Jenie Jackson, and Elsa Knudsen played by Mariette Hartley: Sam Peckinpah's *Ride the High Country* (MGM, 1962).

4066

Judge: A good marriage is like a rare animal. It's hard to find; it's almost impossible to keep.

"No man takes a woman I want away from me and lives," say Bob Dalton (Scott Brady) to outlaw Mac (Forrest Tucker) in Allan Dwan's *Montana Belle* (RKO, 1952).

Judge Tolliver played by Edgar Buchanan: Sam Peckinpah's *Ride the High Country* (MGM, 1962).

4067
Elder: You can't take a wife away from her husband!
Judge: It's a pure case of breaking and entering!
Elder Hammond played by John Anderson and Judge Tolliver played by Edgar Buchanan: Sam Peckinpah's *Ride the High Country* (MGM, 1962).

4068
Cordelia: Cam, is there anything I can do to make you forgive me?
Cameron: I can forgive anything that you can forget.
Cordelia Cameron played by Ava Gardner and King Cameron played by Howard Keel: John Farrow's *Ride, Vaquero!* (MGM, 1953).

4069
Feathers: I thought you were never going to say it.

Chance: Say what?
Feathers: That you loved me.
Chance: I said I would arrest you!
Feathers: It means the same thing, you know that. You just won't say it. Oh, we're different. I'll have to get used to you.
Feathers played by Angie Dickinson and John T. Chance played by John Wayne: Howard Hawks' *Rio Bravo* (Warner Bros., 1959).

4070
Chito: She's the kind of girl that makes you promise her something. She kept saying that her finger is cold because it has no ring on it.
Chito Rafferty played by Richard Martin: Lesley Selander's *Rio Grande Patrol* (RKO, 1950).

4071
Dan: You know, there's only one thing wrong with getting married. It's the people you're apt to get married to.

Dan Corrigan played by Rod Cameron: George Sherman's *River Lady* (Universal, 1948).

4072
Clay: When you get older, you'll understand things a lot better. Like men and women. Just because a man kisses a girl doesn't mean he …well, he can kiss her and not want to have her around all the time.
Clay played by Robert Sterling: Mark Robson's *Roughshod* (RKO, 1949).

4073
Ben: How's the wife and kids?
Bull: Fine.
Howdy: How many do you got now?
Bull: Wives?
Howdy: Kids.
Bull: Ten …but I ain't been home in a week. Which reminds me, I better be getting on.
Ben Jones played by Glenn Ford, Bull played by Denver Pyle, and Howdy Lewis played by Henry

Fonda: Burt Kennedy's *The Rounders* (MGM, 1965).

4074

Joan: You kissed me like you paid for the privilege. I don't like that kind of kiss!

Joan Blake played by Julie London: Robert Parrish's *Saddle the Wind* (MGM, 1958).

4075

Grace: Mr. Batoche, that's quite a family you got there.

Batoche: Well, my wife, Crowshank, she always wanted to be married to a chief. So I figured the only way I could become a chief was to raise a tribe of my own.

Grace: That's quite a project!

Batoche: Oh, I suppose it could be faster to adopt some …but there's no fun in that.

Grace Markey played by Shelley Winters and Batoche played by J. Carrol Naish: Raoul Walsh's *Saskatchewan* (Universal, 1954).

4076

Warbonnet: I know sometimes there is a great separation between father and son …like the empty space between two mountain tops. But I also know there is love between us. And while this love lives, the empty space grows very small.

Jim Ahern/Warbonnet played by Charlton Heston: George Marshall's *The Savage* (Paramount, 1952).

4077

Marty: You know, Laurie, I was just thinking that maybe it's about time you and me started going steady, huh?

Laurie: Well, Marty Pauley! You and me have been going steady since we was three years old!

Marty: We have?

Laurie: It's about time you find out about it!

Marty Pauley played by Jeffrey Hunter and Laurie Jorgensen played by Vera Miles: John Ford's *The Searchers* (Warner Bros., 1956).

4078

Jesse: Those two got to be loco.

Mac: I think they call that love, little brother.

Jesse: It amounts to the same thing, don't it?

Jesse Traven played by Jeffrey Osterhage and Mac Traven played by Tom Selleck: Andrew V. McLaglen's *The Shadow Riders* (TVW, 1982).

4079

Penelope: Now look, Mr. Welsh, I have got to get on this wagon train.

Welsh: No single women. Company rules.

Penelope: Well, I got to find some way.

Welsh: Well, the only thing I can recommend is you find yourself a husband by five o'clock tomorrow morning.

Penelope: A husband?

Welsh: All you need is something wearing pants.

Penelope "Bad Penny" Cushings played by Barbara Rhoades and Wagonmaster Welsh played by Terry Wilson: Alan Rafkin's *The Shakiest Gun in the West* (Universal, 1968).

4080

Countess: Julia, it is one thing to try to arrange a marriage. It's another to insist on it.

Countess Irini Lazaar played by Brigitte Bardot and Lady Julia Daggett played by Honor Blackman: Edward Dmytryk's *Shalako* (CIN, 1968).

4081

Sam: Well, I'll come straight to the point of the matter, sir. I want to ask for your daughter's hand.

Charlie: You mean you want to marry her, Sam?

Sam: Yes, sir.

Charlie: Why?

Sam: Sir?

Charlie: Why do you want to marry her?

Sam: Well, I …well, I love her, Mr. Anderson.

Charlie: Well, that's not good enough, Sam.

Sam: I beg your pardon?

Charlie: Do you like her?

Sam: I just said I …

Charlie: No, no. You said you loved her. There's some difference between loving and liking. When I married Jennie's mother, I didn't love her. I liked her. I liked her a whole lot. I liked Martha for at least three years after we were married …and then one day it just dawned on me I loved her. I still do. You see, Sam, when you love a woman without liking her, the night can be long and cold …and contempt comes up with the sun.

Sam played by Doug McClure and Charlie Anderson played by James Stewart: Andrew V. McLaglen's *Shenandoah* (Universal, 1965).

4082

Ann: Here's something else you must remember: husbands like to be alone once in awhile.

Jennie: Why?

Ann: You never know why, but I can always tell when James wants to be alone. A mood comes over him. I can always see it in his eyes before it gets there. I don't know where the mood comes from or why. But that's when I leave him alone. It seems sometimes things get so fickle in a man that he comes to feel that everything is closing in on him. And that's when he wants to be left alone. You understand, don't you?

Jennie: No!

Ann Anderson played by Katharine Ross and Jennie played by Rosemary Forsyth: Andrew V. McLaglen's *Shenandoah* (Universal, 1965).

4083

Billy: I often wondered why you and me never hooked up, Kate.

Kate: Hook up to the tail of a kite with no string on it? Uh, uh.

Billy: It might have been a fun ride.

Billy Massey played by Dean Martin and Kate Jarvis played by Susan Clark: George Seaton's *Showdown* (Universal, 1973).

4084

Bartender: Ain't you joining the party, Dolly?

Dolly: Yeah, what's the celebration for?

Bartender: It started out for Dan Ballard's wedding. Now, it's his funeral.

Dolly: Don't tell me he's dead.

Herbert: Not yet, but soon.

Joe the Bartender played by Ralph Sanford, Dolly played by Dolores Moran, and Paul Herbert played by Frank Sully: Allan Dwan's *Silver Lode* (RKO, 1954).

4085

Quincy: Well I never said it was over, did I?

Ginger: Men never do. They just start acting rotten until the lady kind of figures it out for herself.

Quincy Drew played by James Garner and Ginger played by Susan Clark: Paul Bogart's *Skin Game* (Warner Bros., 1971).

4086

Ginger: I always found the best way to hold a man is to get a firm grip on his bank book.

Ginger played by Susan Clark: Paul Bogart's *Skin Game* (Warner Bros., 1971).

4087

Lilac: Do you find me attractive, Destiny?

Destiny: A man would be a fool if he didn't.

Lilac: Then what do I have to do to get you to notice me?

Destiny: Lilac, you're married to my employer!

Lilac: Oh, don't hold that against me!

Lilac Gentry played by Wendle Meldrum and Destiny played by Kris Kristofferson: Eugene Levy's *Sodbusters* (Atlantis Releasing, 1994).

4088

Junior: Oh boy! This is going to be a happy marriage because, well, you're a woman and I'm a man and, well, those are the people that usually get married!

Junior played by Bob Hope: Frank Tashlin's *Son of Paleface* (Paramount, 1952).

4089

Leah: I loved you for what you seemed to be, and hated you for what you were.

Leah Parker played by Marilyn Maxwell: William F. Claxton's *Stage to Thunder Rock* (Paramount, 1964).

4090

Marshal: How pregnant?

Buck: You ever thump a watermelon and get an echo back?

Marshal Curley Wilcox played by Johnny Cash

and Buck played by John Schneider: Ted Post's *Stagecoach* (TVW, 1986).

4091

Dave: Look, let's get it straight right here and now! I'm the kind of a guy who will never have much money. And you're very rich.

Jessie: But I can change that.

Dave: You would get awful tired of being poor once the novelty wore off.

Dave played by Tim Holt and Jessie played by Jeff Donnell: Lew Landers' *Stagecoach Kid* (RKO, 1949).

4092

Arnold: Young man, are you able to support my daughter in the manner in which she is accustomed?

Dave: No.

Arnold: Splendid! Then you have my blessing …and my sympathy!

Arnold played by Thurston Hall and Dave played by Tim Holt: Lew Landers' *Stagecoach Kid* (RKO, 1949).

4093

Ann: I won't die waiting for a man I don't even love.

Valerie: Did you ever tell him?

Ann: If you didn't love the man you were going to marry, could you tell him?

Ann Kenyon played by Jaclynne Greene and Valerie Kendrick played by Julia Adams: Lee Sholem's *The Stand at Apache River* (Universal, 1953).

4094

Valerie: Being loved isn't enough, is it? Being loved and not loving back the same way is like …it's like being alone.

Valerie Kendrick played by Julia Adams in Lee Sholem's *The Stand at Apache River* (Universal, 1953).

4095

Valerie: To marry a man just because you're miserable if you don't just makes life a misery for both.

Valerie Kendrick played by Julia Adams: Lee Sholem's *The Stand at Apache River* (Universal, 1953).

4096

Charlie: Did you ever tell a woman you loved her?

Haven: All of them.

Charlie: How did you get away?

Haven: I was always in the doorway when I said it.

Charlie: You never said it to me.

Haven: Let's get over to the doorway.

Charlie played by Jane Greer and Haven played by Dick Powell: Sidney Lanfield's *Station West* (RKO, 1948).

4097

Doc: Patience, you got to stop shooting at people. You know something? If you wasn't such a miserable shot, there wouldn't be a young man alive in all of Purgatory. I heard you shot at Elmer Price in the lobby of the hotel yesterday evening.

Patience: Well, he asked me to marry him!

Doc: You think that's reason enough to shoot at a man?

Doc Shultz played by Dub Taylor and Patience Barton played by Suzanne Pleshette: Burt Kennedy's *Support Your Local Gunfighter* (United Artists, 1971).

4098

Patience: I hope I didn't hurt you too much when I hit you with the chair.

Latigo: I'm all right. The Doc just said so.

Patience: I just couldn't help feeling the way I did, you know.

Latigo: I understand.

Patience: I mean, what if we kept going together and we got married, and you'd been killed in an accident, and I'd been brought in to identify the body? I mean, wouldn't I look the fool. I mean, there you'd be laid out with some other woman's name on your chest: "I Love Goldie." Now wouldn't that be awful?

Latigo: I told you I understood. Now just let it go!

Patience: What if we went to a picnic and you got some ants in your shirt, and you had to rip it off and everybody would see it on your chest. Oh, I wish you would have had T.B. instead of that damn rotten tattoo!

Patience Barton played by Suzanne Pleshette and Latigo Smith played by James Garner: Burt Kennedy's *Support Your Local Gunfighter* (United Artists, 1971).

4099

Mayor: I want you to meet my daughter, Sheriff. She's a good cook, a mighty fine looking girl. Takes after her dear departed mother.

Sheriff: Mother died, huh?

Mayor: No, she just departed.

Mayor Olly Perkins played by Harry Morgan and Sheriff Jason McCullough played by James Garner: Burt Kennedy's *Support Your Local Sheriff!* (United Artists, 1969).

4100

Mayor: She's a rich little old gal in her own name, Sheriff. The sole owner of the Miller Trymore Memorial Mining Company.

Sheriff: You meanin' whoever marries her gets the mine.

Mayor: Shaft and all!

Mayor Olly Perkins played by Harry Morgan and Sheriff Jason McCullough played by James Garner: Burt Kennedy's *Support Your Local Sheriff!* (United Artists, 1969).

4101

Phoebe: I don't want to be a widow before I am a bride.

Phoebe Ann Taylor played by Rosemary Forsyth: Michael Gordon's *Texas Across the River* (Universal, 1966).

4102

Lonetta: A man looks at many things. But sometimes he does not see what is under his eyes.

Don Andrea: That is true, Lonetta. I myself have known such men.

Lonetta: A campfire gives flame, smoke. This you see.

Don Andrea: Of course.

Lonetta: A fire inside gives no flame, no smoke. But it burns as hot.

Don Andrea: A fire inside?

Lonetta: In me there is such a fire. You do not see it, but it burns for you.

Lonetta played by Tina Marquand and Don Andrea Baldasar played by Alain Delon: Michael Gordon's *Texas Across the River* (Universal, 1966).

4103

Aunt Martha: Now listen, honey, all men are like jackasses when they are in love.

Aunt Martha Hubbard played by Fern Emmett: Robert N. Bradbury's *Texas Terror* (Lone Star/Monogram, 1935).

4104

Lalu: There is a river between us.

Jim: But the magpies have built a bridge for us to cross over. We are together now.

Lalu Nathoy/Polly Bemis played by Rosalind Chao and Jim/Li Po played by Dennis Dun: Nancy Kelly's *Thousand Pieces of Gold* (Greycat Films, 1991).

4105

Rosita: Would you like to kiss me?

Dusty: Yeah!

Rosita: Well?

Dusty: What? Now? Here?

Rosita: Well, we could take a walk and you could kiss me on the veranda.

Dusty: The lips would be fine.

Rosita played by Benita and Dusty Bottoms played by Chevy Chase: John Landis' *Three Amigos!* (Orion, 1986).

4106

Conchita: Carmen, today is El Guapo's birthday. And tonight, you are to be El Guapo's woman.

Carmen: I would sooner die.

Conchita: Let me prepare you for the way El Guapo makes love. Tell me, Carmen, do you know what foreplay is?

Carmen: No.

Conchita: Good! Neither does El Guapo!

Conchita played by Loyda Ramos and Carmen played by Patrice Martinez: John Landis' *Three Amigos!* (Orion, 1986).

4107

Jefe: Why don't you take her? When you want cattle, you take the cattle. When you want food, you take the food. When you want a woman, you just take the woman. Why don't you just take her?

El Guapo: Jefe, you do not understand women. You cannot force open the petals of the flowers. When the flower is ready, it opens itself up to you.

Jefe: When do you think Carmen will open up her flower to you?

El Guapo: Tonight ...or I will kill her!

Jefe played by Tony Plana and El Guapo played by Humberto Arau: John Landis' *Three Amigos!* (Orion, 1986).

4108

Phillips: I guess I'm gonna find out what happens to a fella when he's kissed a girl right under her father's nose.

Father: Better find out what happens when you kiss the girl under her own nose!

John Phillips played by John Wayne and the Father, Dr. Karl Braun, played by Charles Coburn: Bernard Vorhaus' *Three Faces West* (Republic, 1940).

4109

Dr. Braun: It's not easy to know where loyalty ends and love begins.

Dr. Karl Braun played by Charles Coburn: Bernard Vorhaus' *Three Faces West* (Republic, 1940).

4110

Luis: If you think you're in love, it's the same thing as to be in love, huh papa?

Innocencio: No, it's not the same. If you were really in love, this would be to the other as ...as gold is to lead ...as fine wine is to muddy water ...as mountain air is to the stench of stables. When true love comes, a man has more strength. His eyes are clear and he can see farther away. And instead of time passing fast, it stands still. That, muchachos, is a moment of ecstasy. That is true love.

Luis played by Leo Castillo and Innocencio played by Gilbert Roland: Rudolph Mate's *Three Violent People* (Paramount, 1956).

4111

Innocencio: Señora, we have a saying in Spanish: that a glad heart is all that one should ask of God. For that is real happiness. My heart is glad. You, too, have a glad heart. It shines in your eyes.

Innocencio played by Gilbert Roland: Rudolph Mate's *Three Violent People* (Paramount, 1956).

4112

Capt.: It's not my advice, mister, it's the rule of the game. Bachelors make the best soldiers. All they have to lose is their loneliness.

Captain Stephen Maddocks played by Richard Boone: Joseph Newman's *A Thunder of Drums* (MGM, 1961).

4113

Wyatt: I have nothing left, nothing to give you. I have no pride, no dignity, no money. I don't even know how we'll make a living, but I promise I'll love you the rest of your life.

Josephine: Don't worry, Wyatt ...my family is rich.

Wyatt Earp played by Kurt Russell and Josephine played by Dana Delany: George P. Cosmatos' *Tombstone* (Buena Vista, 1993).

4114

Lane: I got a saddle that's older than you are, Mrs. Lowe.

Lane played by John Wayne and Mrs. Lowe played by Ann-Margret: Burt Kennedy's *The Train Robbers* (Warner Bros., 1973).

4115

Rudock: A fella doesn't die of a broken heart from his first love ...only from his last.

Jeremy Rudock played by James Cagney: Robert Wise's *Tribute to a Bad Man* (MGM, 1956).

4116

Father: But you could get married though. Say, there's a couple beauties down at the saloon that would like nothing better than a husband to light down with.

Mother: Yes sir, they make the best wives!

Father: That's right, they make the best wives! Say, you should have seen your mother the day we got married. Of course, you were too young to remember. You were just knee high. And you [another son] were still crawling. But we had a wing-ding in that saloon!

The Father played by Harry Carey, Jr., and the Mother played by Jessica Dublin: E.B. Clucher's (Enzo Barboni) *Trinity Is Still My Name* (West Film/Avco Embassy, 1971).

4117

Mitch: Hey, hold on now! Here, take it easy! Why, a lady ain't supposed to throw spittoons at a gent until after she's married to him!

Mitch played by Noah Beery, Jr.: Richard Thorpe's *20 Mule Team* (MGM, 1940).

4118

Sara: Don't you want a woman of your own?

Hogan: What for?

Sara: To share your name, bear your children, be a companion.

Hogan: To ask me to quit drinking, quit gambling, and save money? And to bitch about her aches and pains all day? No thanks!

Sister Sara played by Shirley MacLaine and Hogan played by Clint Eastwood: Don Siegel's *Two Mules for Sister Sara* (Universal, 1970).

4119

Margaret: You know, I've been thinking an awful lot about home.

James: I have too, Maggie. And my home is you.

Margaret Langdon played by Lee Meriwether and Colonel James Langdon played by Rock Hudson: Andrew McLaglen's *The Undefeated* (20th Century-Fox, 1969).

4120

Emma: Don't you believe in love?

Cecilia: Yeah, as long as it lasts five minutes and pays for the full hour!

Emma played by Bari Buckner and Cecilia played by Erin Noble: Michael Bohusz's *Uninvited* (Imperial Entertainment, 1993).

4121

Glenn: Well, just don't stand there! Think of something, Max!

Max: There's only one way out. In the State of Texas, a wife may not testify against her husband.

Glenn: Wife? Do you mean I have to marry that ...

Max: It's that ...or your life. And you got to do it before the trial.

Glenn Denbow played by Scott Brady and Max Wickersham played by John Alexander: Hugo Fregonese's *Untamed Frontier* (Universal, 1952).

4122

Matt: So you're going to marry my son, hey? Do you love him?

Jane: Very much, Mr. Denbow. And I'll do my best to make him a very good wife.

Matt: We'll see. It's been my experience, Miss Stevens, that you can never tell about cattle ...or women ...until they've been on your range for awhile.

Matt Denbow played by Minor Watson and Jane Stevens played by Shelley Winters: Hugo Fregonese's *Untamed Frontier* (Universal, 1952).

4123

Pancho: You see, gringo, all women want to get married no matter what they say. Right? Now you know and I know that these marriages don't mean a thing.

Arnold: I didn't know that.

Pancho: But it makes them happy. It's the eleventh time for me, I think.

Pancho Villa played by Yul Brynner and Lee Arnold played by Robert Mitchum: Buzz Kulik's *Villa Rides!* (Paramount, 1968).

4124

Julia: No matter how much a man is in love, he really wonders whether the woman is quite good enough for him or not. But when a woman is in love, well, she's just in love and that's the end of it.

Julia Hayne played by Miriam Hopkins: Michael Curtiz's *Virginia City* (Warner Bros., 1940).

4125

Julia: I've often wondered what brought you together.

Kerry: Oh, just luck ...like you and I. The interesting part is what keeps people together, don't you think?

Julia Hayne played by Miriam Hopkins and Kerry Bradford played by Errol Flynn: Michael Curtiz's *Virginia City* (Warner Bros., 1940).

4126

Honey: Yeah, the bishop is making a trip special ...just to marry them.

Slim: You don't say! I ain't never seen a bishop. What's a bishop look like?

Honey: Oh, just like an ordinary shoe drummer ...except he wears half his clothes backwards.

Honey Wiggin played by Eugene Pallette and Slim played by Jack Pennick: Victor Fleming's *The Virginian* (Paramount, 1929).

4127

Abby: I'm willing to marry you, Jim Burch. But you got to write to my father in Indiana and ask for my hand.

Jim: But it takes a letter a year to get there and back.

Abby: I can't help that. It's proper. Here! [*handing him a quill pen*].

Jim: But, Abby, I can't write!

Abby Masters played by Jan Duggan and Jim Burch played by Raymond Hatton: Charles Barton's *Wagon Wheels* (Paramount, 1934).

4128

Fleurety: You like him, don't you?

Denver: I don't want to see him full of bullet holes if that's what you mean!

Fleuretty Phyffe played by Ruth Clifford and Denver played by Joanne Dru: John Ford's *Wagonmaster* (RKO, 1950).

4129

Belle: Bastard!

Slade: Could be. I don't know if my ma and pa were married. I killed my pa before I could ask.

Belle played by Ellen Greene and John Slade played by Ed Lauter: Peter Markle's *Wagons East!* (TriStar, 1994).

4130

Clancy: Hamilton, let me straighten you out on something. You know, there's only two mistakes a man can make with a woman. Asking her too soon and having her say yes; or asking her too late, and having her say no. Now it's the smart laddie who knows how to pick his

spot and slide right in between. So take your time, huh?

Clancy played by Douglas Kennedy and Corporal Hamilton played by Charles Nolte: Lesley Selander's *War Paint* (United Artists, 1953).

4131

Sheriff: How come at your age, a fella like you ain't tied down yet?

Cole: Well, I was ...once.

Sheriff: What did you do to her?

Cole: Well, I don't know. Just ...got on separate trains, I guess.

Sheriff John Copperud played by Carroll O'Connor and Lewton Cole played by James Coburn: William Graham's *Waterhole No. 3* (Paramount, 1967).

4132

Tadlock: You know, it's no easy matter to share a vision ...particularly for a man and a woman.

Senator William J. Tadlock played by Kirk Douglas in Andrew V. McLaglen's *The Way West* (Untied Artists, 1967).

4133

Roy: The men want wives and they've put up the money to get 'em. They're as sick at this as I am ...saloons, gambling. Well, you know.

Buck: Yeah, I know ...and I like it!

Roy: Okay, Buck, but you and I are going to Chicago. I'll recruit the women and you guide them across the country. Two thousand miles of trail and you know every inch of it. You brought wagon trains to Oregon, Sacramento, Santa Fe. You're the man to bring the women here to my valley.

Buck: There is only two things in this world that scares me. And a good woman is both!

Roy Whitman played by John McIntire and Buck Wyatt played by Robert Taylor: William Wellman's *Westward the Women* (MGM, 1952).

4134

Roy: You see, you overlooked one thing.

Buck: What was that?

Roy: The will of a woman when there's a wedding ring in sight.

Roy Whitman played by John McIntire and Buck Wyatt played by Robert Taylor: William Wellman's *Westward the Women* (MGM, 1952).

4135

Buck: How many good women are you figuring on bringing?

Roy: Well, there are a hundred men signed up for wives.

Buck: Better recruit 150 of them then. If we're lucky, we'll only lose one out of three.

Buck Wyatt played by Robert Taylor and Roy Whitman played by John McIntire: William Wellman's *Westward the Women* (MGM, 1952).

4136

Lije: It takes money to get married. If you'd ever been out of these mountains and down to a town, you'd know. Females like pretty things. Why, some of 'em won't even live in a house unless it's got a window.

Uncle Lije Hawkes played by George Mitchell: Jack Sher's *The Wild and the Innocent* (Universal, 1959).

4137

Brady: Look, what we did, maybe that was wrong ...but not what we feel.

Ellen: What a pity then that life is what we do ...and not just what we feel.

Martin Brady played by Robert Mitchum and Ellen Colton played by Julie London: Robert Parrish's *The Wonderful Country* (United Artists, 1959).

4138

Wahleeah: No man can take my love. It must be given as the sun gives warmth to the gray of dawn.

Wahleeah played by Andra Martin: Gordon Douglas' *Yellowstone Kelly* (Warner Bros., 1959).

Men

See also Bad Guys; Good Guys; Gunfighters; People

4139

Ethan: I like that man.

Granville: You never were a very good judge of character, Ethan.

Ethan Emerson played by James Drury and Granville Thorogood played by Stuart Whitman: Bryan Spicer's *Adventures of Brisco County, Jr.* (TVW, Series Premiere, 1993).

4140

Sam: Some men are makers. They got to

sweat for what they want. I'm a taker. I got to be one.

Sally: You could be good and honest.

Sam: I saw my father work his heart out on a lathe in Bridgeport. He died young and he died broke. He was an honest man. I never want to be one.

Sam Leeds played by Stephen McNally and Sally played by Coleen Gray: Hugo Fregonese's *Apache Drums* (Universal, 1951).

4141

Shelby: Mr. Grover, hadn't you better take at least some of this [money]?

Grover: What for?

Shelby: A man can't live without money.

Grover: I'll tell you something, son. When it's that kind of money, a man can't live with it.

Dan Shelby played by John Ireland and Sheriff Grover played by Barton MacLane: Lesley

Union soldiers Olaf "Moose" Swenson (Alan Hale), Kerry Bradford (Errol Flynn), and Marblehead (Guinn "Big Boy" Williams) watch as Mexican bandits (led by Humphrey Bogart) attack a wagon train (led by Randolph Scott) which is loaded with gold and destined for the Confederacy in Michael Curtiz's *Virginia City* (Warner Bros., 1940).

Selander's *Arizona Bushwhackers* (Paramount, 1968).

4142

Hector: I believe a man is nothing unless he stands up for what's rightfully his. What do you think?

Hector David played by Lee Marvin: John Sturges' *Bad Day at Black Rock* (MGM, 1955).

4143

Smith: I believe a man is as big as what will make him mad. Nobody around here seems big enough to get you mad.

Reno Smith played by Robert Ryan: John Sturges' *Bad Day at Black Rock* (MGM, 1955).

4144

Doc: There comes a time, Tim, when a man has just got to do something.

Doc Velie played by Walter Brennan and Sheriff Tim Horn played by Dean Jagger: John Sturges' *Bad Day at Black Rock* (MGM, 1955).

4145

Zeb: A man leaves when he ain't got nothin' to stay for.

Zeb Calloway played by Arthur Hunnicutt: Howard Hawks' *The Big Sky* (Winchester/RKO, 1952).

4146

Fallon: Stop thinking so hard, Frenchie. You're liable to get yourself a bad headache.

Jim Fallon played by Kirk Douglas and French LeCrois played by John Archer: Felix Feist's *The Big Trees* (Warner Bros., 1952).

4147

Alicia: Men have been known to change.
Burns: Oh, lady, even I have been given up by women reformers! The biggest mistake a woman can make is to pick the wrong man and try to make him right.

Alicia Chadwick played by Eve Miller and Walter

"Yukon" Burns played by Edgar Buchanan: Felix Feist's *The Big Trees* (Warner Bros., 1952).

4148

Mary: If he's a follower of Jesus, I'm a horse's behind!

Mary Johnson played by Janet Bailey: Steven H. Stern's *Blood Horse* (TV miniseries, Cabin Fever Entertainment, 1995).

4149

Lincoln: It's well known that the more a man speaks, the less he's understood.

Abraham Lincoln played by Gregory Peck: Andrew V. McLaglen's *The Blue and the Gray* (TV miniseries, 1982).

4150

Tex: Tim, my boy, I'm afraid you're in this up to your neck.
Tim: Worse than that, I'm in over my head!

Tex Weaver played by Ralph Byrd and Tim Ross

played by Tim McCoy: Sam Newfield's *Border Caballero* (Puritan Pictures, 1936).

4151

Running Water: He's like all men …a big kid in a man's body.

Lorraine Running Water played by Sierra Pecheur: Clint Eastwood's *Bronco Billy* (Warner Bros., 1980).

4152

Buntline: Bill, any youngster like yourself who figures to set the world on fire best not forget where he got the matches.

Ned Buntline played by Burt Lancaster and Buffalo Bill played by Paul Newman: Robert Altman's *Buffalo Bill and the Indians, or Sitting Bull's History Lesson* (United Artists, 1976).

4153

Buffalo Bill: Remember, son, the last thing that a man wants to do is the last thing he does.

Buffalo Bill played by Paul Newman: Robert Altman's *Buffalo Bill and the Indians, or Sitting Bull's History Lesson* (United Artists, 1976).

4154

Nate: I'm the only partner Bill Cody ever had who tells him the truth. And in the end, we always agree.

Ned: I was taught that when two partners always agree, one of them ain't necessary.

Nate Salsbury played by Joel Grey and Ned Buntline played by Burt Lancaster: Robert Altman's *Buffalo Bill and the Indians, or Sitting Bull's History Lesson* (United Artists, 1976).

4155

Coffin: I've heard such talk from pulpits: the meek shall inherit the earth. No, Mr. Trumbo, the earth belongs to the men who make the law. And the law belongs to the men who can lay it down.

Pharoah Coffin played by George Coulouris and Jonathan Trumbo played by Ray Milland: John Farrow's *California* (Paramount, 1946).

4156

Jackson: He's young, but he'll settle down.

Douglas: How far? Six feet?

Sergeant Jackson Harkness played by Don Gordon and Captain Rod Douglas played by George Peppard: Paul Wendkos' *Cannon for Cordoba* (United Artists, 1970).

4157

George: You have strange friends, Jack.

Jack: I didn't say that I liked him or that I trust him.

George: What's your idea of a friend?

Jack: Any man, I suppose, who believes as I do that the human race is a horrible mistake.

George Camrose played by Brian Donlevy and Jack Lestrade played by Onslow Stevens: Jacques Tourneur's *Canyon Passage* (Universal, 1946).

4158

Janet: You talk about how you grow and how a big shadow you're going to cast. Matt, you're getting smaller.

Janet Calvert played by Terry Moore and Matt Brown played by Audie Murphy: Thomas Carr's *Cast a Long Shadow* (United Artists, 1959).

4159

Chip: If you're just half as big a man as you want us to think you are, you'll admit you're wrong before there is any damage done.

Chip Donohue played by John Dehner: Thomas Carr's *Cast a Long Shadow* (United Artists, 1959).

4160

Hortensia: You say there is nothing here to keep you. I think when you go, you leave behind more than you take with you.

Hortensia played by Rita Lynn: Thomas Carr's *Cast a Long Shadow* (United Artists, 1959).

4161

Catlow: You know, for a smart boy like you, Rio, you're just plain dumb.

Jed Catlow played by Yul Brynner and Rio played by Michael Delano: Sam Wanamaker's *Catlow* (MGM, 1971).

4162

President: I, too, have discovered that when a man tries to stand up to his responsibilities, there's a good chance that he'll make many enemies. And sadly, he may even lose some of his old friends.

President Chester A. Arthur played by Larry Gates: Tay Garnett's *Cattle King* (MGM, 1963).

4163

Harry: I've never been sure of anything my whole life long, you know that. I guess that is hard for you to understand, isn't it Sam? You know where you're going, every move you're gonna make. Well, I don't! I wake up every morning …scared. And if I don't start something, at least I know I won't fail finishing it.

Harry Travers played by William Windom and Sam Brassfield played by Robert Taylor: Tay Garnett's *Cattle King* (MGM, 1963).

4164

Jenny: Some famous male writer once wrote: you can't sleep with all the women in the world, but you must try! That pretty much sums up the attitude of every man I've known …except my daddy.

Jenny played by Sally Kirkland: Rod McCall's *Cheatin' Hearts* (Trimark Pictures, 1993).

4165

John: I don't like to say this about my own brother, but he just never was what you'd call an outstanding citizen. The truth is, he, well, he wasn't worth the sweat on a waterbag!

John O'Hanlan played by James Stewart: Gene Kelly's *The Cheyenne Social Club* (NGP, 1970).

4166

Jamie: I ain't never going to get mixed up with women folk.

Chino: Well, what a man says and what a man does, doesn't always end up to be the same thing.

Jamie Wagner played by Vincent Van Patten and Chino Valdez played by Charles Bronson: John Sturges' *Chino* (Coral Film/Intercontinental Releasing Corporation, 1973).

4167

Colonel: Please don't allow the actions and therefore the discipline of one man to disturb you.

Veronica: In a lifetime, Colonel Valois, I have learned that one man is the image of all men.

Colonel Stuart Valois played by John Mills and Veronica Kleitz played by Luciana Paluzzi: Gordon Douglas' *Chuka* (Paramount, 1967).

4168

Curly: I crap bigger than you!

Curly played by Jack Palance: Ron Underwood's *City Slickers* (Columbia, 1991).

4169

Etta Mae: Men are all alike. They can't be trusted. None of 'em!

Etta Mae played by Maude Eburne: Joseph Kane's *Colorado* (Republic, 1940).

4170

Ben: A lot of money has a way of making a man go all greed inside.

Cody: Such as?

Ben: It can get him to thinking of doing things that he might not otherwise do. You know, it's a long way to Lawrenceburg. It wouldn't surprise me if somebody didn't try to take that woman away from you.

Cody: Like you, for instance?

Ben: Like me, in particular.

Ben Lane played by Claude Akins and Jefferson Cody played by Randolph Scott: Budd Boetticher's *Comanche Station* (Columbia, 1960).

4171

Cimarron: Why don't you put me in charge?

Anderson: A big mouth don't make a big man.

Cimarron played by A Martinez and Wil Anderson played by John Wayne: Mark Rydell's *The Cowboys* (Warner Bros., 1972).

4172

Banner: Hamilton, you're the only man I ever knew that didn't put his thoughts right out on his face where everybody could read them.

John Banner played by Dale Robertson and Carter Hamilton played by John Lund: Lewis R. Foster's *Dakota Incident* (Republic, 1956).

4173

Hamilton: I'm no hero, friend. I'd be a fool to let chivalry carry me off in a box.

Banner: It's only a real scared man who stands up and shouts how brave he is.

Carter Hamilton played by John Lund and John Banner played by Dale Robertson: Lewis R. Foster's *Dakota Incident* (Republic, 1956).

4174

Mary: I thought they bred men of flesh and blood in Texas. I was wrong. You're made of granite!

Bob: No, Mary, just common clay. It bakes kind of hard in Texas.

Mary McCloud played by Claire Trevor and Bob Seton played by John Wayne: Raoul Walsh's *The Dark Command* (Republic, 1940).

4175

Big George: I don't give a shit who said what, and who did what, or who did who!

Big George Drakoulious played by Billy Bob Thornton: Jim Jarmusch's *Dead Man* (Miramax Films, 1996).

4176

Flagg: None of us knows the future, Willy. A man has to grasp his opportunities as they come.

Flagg played by Michael Hogan and Willy played by Sebastian Spence: Neill Fearnley's "My Brother's Keeper" episode to the series premiere, *Dead Man's Gun* (Showtime, 1997).

4177

Bodeen: Drop your pants!

Jessup: What?

Bodeen: I find it takes the threat out of a man looking that ridiculous.

Bodeen/Tom Hatcher played by Keith Coulouris and Jessup Bush played by Vondie Curtis-Hall: Alan J. Levi's *Dead Man's Revenge* (MCA/Universal Home Video, 1994).

4178

Luck: Son, as your father, nothing on earth means more to me than knowing you're alive. But you've picked the worst damn time to announce it!

Luck Hatcher played by Michael Ironside: Alan J. Levi's *Dead Man's Revenge* (MCA/Universal Home Video, 1994).

4179

Bart: I'm glad to hear he's doing so well. When a man's riding high, the ground comes up and hits him a lot harder when he falls.

Bart Allison played by Randolph Scott: Budd

Boetticher's *Decision at Sundown* (Columbia, 1957).

4180

Pike: I just want to be my own man in my own way. You can't be your own man when you're polishing someone else's boots.

Pike played by Martin Sheen: Anthony Harvey's *Eagle's Wing* (Eagle's Wing Productions/Rank, 1979).

4181

Ebenezer: When a man has everything to lose, Mr. Benson, he has everything to gain. It is at that very point when you must summon up the last vestige of true courage or walk away a coward.

Ebenezer Scrooge played by Jack Palance and Sam Benson played by Rick Schroder: Ken Jubenvill's *Ebenezer* (TVW, 1997).

4182

Carolyn: Honey, I'd judge a man more by the size of his heart than his rear. It's likely to do you more good.

Carolyn Kyle played by Ronnie Claire Edwards: John G. Avildsen's *8 Seconds* (New Line Cinema, 1994).

4183

Hallie; You know, you're gonna screw up your whole life!

Sonny: Ha! Ha! Ha! I'm trying' to unscrew it, lady !

Hallie Martin played by Jane Fonda and Sonny Steele played by Robert Redford: Sydney Pollack's *The Electric Horseman* (Columbia/Universal, 1979).

4184

Cabot: You act like he was your kid brother.

Marsh: All men are brothers, Cabot …and most of 'em are kids.

Cabot Young played by William Campbell and Captain John Marsh played by John Forsythe: John Sturges' *Escape from Fort Bravo* (MGM, 1953).

4185

Mark: Now, no man is as important enough to walk wherever he wants. He's bound to run into something that will stop him.

Sheriff Mark Riley played by Lin McCarthy: Paul Wendkos' *Face of a Fugitive* (Columbia, 1959).

4186

Flo: Men are so stupid. When a woman wants something from a man, she makes love to him. When a man wants something from a man, he goes to war for it.

Sue: Gee, Sis, I wish I could think of things to say like that!

Flo played by Maggie Pierce and Sue played by

Joan Freeman: Michael Moore's *The Fastest Guitar Alive* (MGM, 1967).

4187

Earl: Now, we've been your men, Bob. But maybe we'll start voting on what gets done around here and what doesn't.

Larkin: When did you ever show enough brains to vote on what gets done?

Earl played by Gary Lockwood and Bob Larkin played by Henry Fonda: Vincent McEveety's *Firecreek* (Warner Bros.–Seven Arts, 1968).

4188

George: Well, I guess a man has got to be a damn fool once in a while. It proves he's still alive, huh?

Little George played by Yaphet Kotto: Henry Hathaway's *Five Card Stud* (Paramount, 1968).

4189

Vinson: More men find themselves in the wilderness than lose themselves in it.

Sgt. Vinson played by Joel McCrea: Joseph Newman's *Fort Massacre* (United Artists, 1958).

4190

Jessica: I need a strong man to carry out my orders.

Griff: And a weak man to take them.

Jessica Drummond played by Barbara Stanwyck and Griff Bonnell played by Barry Sullivan: Samuel Fuller's *Forty Guns* (20th Century–Fox, 1957).

4191

Jess: I'm just his father, Eliza, not his conscience. A man's life isn't worth a hill of beans except he lives up to his own conscience.

Jess Birdwell played by Gary Cooper and Eliza Birdwell played by Dorothy McGuire: William Wyler's *Friendly Persuasion* (Allied Artists, 1956).

4192

Wyatt: You talk too much for a fighting man, Pringle.

Wyatt Earp played by Randolph Scott and Pringle played by Lon Chaney, Jr.: Allan Dwan's *Frontier Marshal* (20th Century–Fox, 1939).

4193

Vance: If he's smiling, be smart. If he's not smiling, be smarter.

Vance Jeffords played by Barbara Stanwyck: Anthony Mann's *The Furies* (Paramount, 1950).

4194

Cash: You got to believe me and trust me.

Molly: My pa used to say that when a man ask you to trust him, it's time to get out of his firing range.

Cash Blackwell played by Victor Mature and Molly Baxter played by Coleen Gray: Bruce Humberstone's *Fury at Furnace Creek* (20th Century–Fox, 1948).

4195

Leverett: One of the penalties for success is that you make enemies. A man at the top is like the bull's-eye on a target. Everybody is after him.

Edward Leverett played by Albert Dekker: Bruce Humberstone's *Fury at Furnace Creek* (20th Century–Fox, 1948).

4196

Geronimo: He's a fine looking boy. Through him your husband lives.

Geronimo played by Chuck Connors: Arnold Laven's *Geronimo* (United Artists, 1962).

4197

Flagg: I expected you to keep your word.
McKay: I promised. I never gave you my word.
Flagg: Well, what the hell is the difference?
McKay: One is a promise, the other is my word! That's the difference! Oh no, it'll never be said on a day that Big John broke his word to a friend or an enemy!

Jim Flagg played by Robert Mitchum and Big John McKay played by George Kennedy: Burt Kennedy's *The Good Guys and the Bad Guys* (Warner Bros., 1969).

4198

Eve: A man with a woman to help and encourage him can make a garden out of a desert.
Hewey: If he's like me, he'll make a desert out of a garden.

Eve Calloway played by Frances McDormand and Hewey Calloway played by Tommy Lee Jones who also directed *The Good Old Boys* (Turner Pictures, 1995).

4199

Tuco: I like big fat men like you. When they fall, they make more noise. And sometimes they never get up.

Tuco played by Eli Wallach: Sergio Leone's *The Good, the Bad, and the Ugly* (United Artists, 1966; U.S. 1968).

4200

Joan: When will a gentleman learn that there are some ladies who do not have to be helped off horses.
Cook: I don't know. It's fun to be stupid.

Joan Britton played by Faith Domergue and Stephen Cook played by Lyle Bettger: Lloyd Bacon's *The Great Sioux Uprising* (Universal, 1953).

4201

Jake: It ain't what a man thinks, son. It's what he knows.

Jake played by Will Wright: Louis King's *Green Grass of Wyoming* (20th Century–Fox, 1948)

4202

Will: A man's got to learn to live in this land. You've nursed Bless so long he's

between a mountain and a river. He'll get lost for sure.
Mother: Then I'll take the boy's hand and he won't get lost.
Will: Then you'll lose the man.

Will Keough played by Fred MacMurray, Bless Keough played by Jeffrey Hunter, and Mrs. Keough played by Josephine Hutchinson: Abner Biberman's *Gun for a Coward* (Universal, 1957).

4203

Hade: You're standing in front of him again, Will.
Will: I stand in front of you too, Hade.
Hade: But you don't cover me with your shadow.

Hade Keough played by Dean Stockwell and Will Keough played by Fred MacMurray: Abner Biberman's *Gun for a Coward* (Universal, 1957).

4204

Loving: Leave him alone, Stringer. Can't you see the boy's got grief enough.
Stringer: Grieving is for women. Fighting is for men.

Loving played by Chill Wills and Stringer played by John Larch: Abner Biberman's *Gun for a Coward* (Universal, 1957).

4205

Aud: Pa, Bless maybe needs help.
Andy: It's time he helped himself.
Aud: You don't understand him because he won't fight for a small purpose.
Andy: A man fights for his name.

Aud Niven played by Janice Rule and Andy Niven played by Paul Birch: Abner Biberman's *Gun for a Coward* (Universal, 1957).

4206

Warren: Well, I learned one thing, Jess. A man's got to do his own growing …no matter how tall his father was.

Ben Warren played by Rock Hudson and Jess Burgess played by Leo Gordon: Raoul Walsh's *Gun Fury* (Columbia, 1953).

4207

Will: A man goes on pretending long enough, he, well, he starts forgetting what he's become.

Will Tenneray played by Kirk Douglas: Lamont Johnson's *A Gunfight* (Paramount, 1971).

4208

Lily: You're sure you know what you're doing?
Bat: I'm sure.
Lily: Men usually don't, you know.

Lily played by Nancy Gates and Bat Masterson played by Joel McCrea: Joseph M. Newman's *The Gunfight at Dodge City* (United Artists, 1959).

4209

Lee: Listen, son, you let a man do things for you, things you should be doing yourself, and sooner or later he's going

to get the idea that he's a better man than you are. Now you remember that.

Lee Hackett played by Van Heflin: Phil Karlson's *Gunman's Walk* (Columbia, 1958).

4210

Lee: You know, I think it's high time I shook a rope at that boy. Teach him to have a little more respect for his father.
Bob: Are you his father, Lee? Now where did I get the notion that you just wanted to be one of the boys? Whose idea was it to have him call you Lee instead of Dad or Pa, huh?

Lee Hackett played by Van Heflin and Bob Selkirk played by Paul Birch: Phil Karlson's *Gunman's Walk* (Columbia, 1958).

4211

Lee: Son, I raised you the best way I knew how.
Ed: You raised me like a shadow. Only you didn't want it to grow any bigger than you were. Because if it did, how would people know which was the man and which was the shadow?

Lee Hackett played by Van Heflin and Ed Hackett played by Tab Hunter: Phil Karlson's *Gunman's Walk* (Columbia, 1958).

4212

Linc: Who's the flunky that's getting me a horse?
Maria: That's my father.
Linc: Well, there's no fool like a man who puts his foot in his own mouth.

Linc Murdock played by Charles Bronson and Maria Macklin played by Susan Oliver: Boris Sagal's *Guns of Diablo* (MGM, 1964).

4213

Peterson: Oh come now, no hard feelings! It's a big man who knows how to lose, Hadley.
Hadley: It's a bigger man who knows how to win.

The Store Owner, Sam Peterson, was uncredited and Jim Hadley played by Alan Ladd: Robert D. Webb's *Guns of the Timberland* (Warner Bros., 1960).

4214

Haney: Ben Bodine? Why, he has only the span of his own lifetime, Mr. Coburn. But men who live by faith live an eternity.

Clem Haney played by Kevin Hagen, Ben Bodine played by Vaughn Taylor, and Chip Coburn played by Mark Stevens: Thomas Carr's *Gunsmoke in Tucson* (Allied Artists, 1958).

4215

Ma: Treat an Indian like a white man and he'll start acting like one.
Helen: Is that an improvement?

Ma Higgins played by Connie Gilchrist and Helen

played by Janis Carter: Stuart Gilmore's *The Half-Breed* (RKO, 1952).

4216

Craig: The boy in him ran away, but the man in him will think it over and come back.

Dan Craig played by Robert Young: Stuart Gilmore's *The Half-Breed* (RKO, 1952).

4217

Thomas: Not a bad life, I guess …a home and kids. A man ought to leave something else behind him …besides a headstone. So should a woman.

Thomas Luther Price played by Robert Culp: Burt Kennedy's *Hannie Caulder* (Paramount, 1971).

4218

Clint: Well, I ain't a man to look for trouble. But I don't run from it.

Tom: I usually run from it.

Clint Mabry played by Steve Forrest and Tom Healy played by Anthony Quinn: George Cukor's *Heller in Pink Tights* (Paramount, 1960).

4219

Helen: You're a good-looking boy. You have big, broad shoulders. But he's a man. It takes more than big, broad shoulders to make a man, Harv, and you have a long way to go!

Helen Ramirez played by Katy Jurado and Harvey Pell played by Lloyd Bridges: Fred Zinnemann's *High Noon* (United Artists, 1952).

4220

Hannah: A man that's in a woman's bed thinks he's her boss.

Hannah Collings played by Verna Bloom: Peter Fonda's *The Hired Hand* (Universal, 1971).

4221

Hannah: A man don't ask the things of another man like a woman does. He's easy to please and he don't get bitter about the same things.

Hannah Collings played by Verna Bloom: Peter Fonda's *The Hired Hand* (Universal, 1971).

4222

Lon: What do you sleep in?

Alma: In my own room with the door locked.

Lon: Do you ever wear any of those little shorty things?

Alma: What kind of question is that?

Lon: I just wondered.

Alma: Does your mind usually run in that direction?

Lon: Yea, it seems to.

Alma: Boys with impure thoughts come out in acne, do you know that?

Lon Bannon played by Brandon De Wilde and Alma played by Patricia Neal: Martin Ritt's *Hud* (Paramount, 1963).

4223

Hud: A man like that sounds no better than a heel.

Alma: Aren't ya all?

Hud: Honey, don't go shootin' all the dogs because one of 'em got fleas.

Hud played by Paul Newman and Alma played by Patricia Neal: Martin Ritt's *Hud* (Paramount, 1963).

4224

Hud: This world is so full of crap, a man is going to get into it sooner or later whether he's careful or not.

Hud played by Paul Newman: Martin Ritt's *Hud* (Paramount, 1963).

4225

Homer: He ain't such a bad fellow. He's just got a cruddy job.

Homer Bannon played by Melvyn Douglas: Martin Ritt's *Hud* (Paramount, 1963).

4226

Johnny: You know some men got the craving for gold and silver. Others need lots of land with herds of cattle. And there's those that got the weakness for whiskey and for women. When you boil it all down, what does a man really need? Just a smoke and a cup of coffee.

Johnny Guitar played by Sterling Hayden: Nicholas Ray's *Johnny Guitar* (Republic, 1954).

4227

Turkey: You talk like I was a boy. I'm a man!

Vienna: Every man is entitled to be a boy for a little while.

Turkey Ralston played by Ben Cooper and Vienna played by Joan Crawford: Nicholas Ray's *Johnny Guitar* (Republic, 1954).

4228

Dancin' Kid: Bart, you don't drink! You don't smoke! You're mean to horses! What do you like?

The Dancin' Kid played by Scott Brady and Bart Lonergan played by Ernest Borgnine: Nicholas Ray's *Johnny Guitar* (Republic, 1954).

4229

Old Tom: What are you going to do with him?

Vienna: I can't keep him here.

Old Tom: He can't travel.

Vienna: Then I'll have to turn him over to the posse.

Old Tom: But they'll hang him. He's just a boy!

Vienna: Boys who play with guns have to be ready to die like men.

Old Tom played by John Carradine and Vienna played by Joan Crawford: Nicholas Ray's *Johnny Guitar* (Republic, 1954).

4230

Jory: What's so different about Texas? It looks the same to me.

Roy: It's the men in it that's different, boy, not the dirt.

Jory Walden played by Robby Benson and Roy played by John Marley: Jorge Fons' *Jory* (Avco Embassy, 1972).

4231

Florinda: Men don't come in to drink and be merry with me because they think there is something fine in me, dear. They think just the opposite. That's why they gather around.

Florinda Grove/Julie Latour played by Vera Ralston: Joseph Kane's *Jubilee Trail* (Republic, 1954).

4232

Big Eli: I'm trying to be a right father to you. I'm trying to think what kind of man you'll grow up to be.

Little Eli: What kind of man are you coming to be? That's the worst of all!

Little Eli played by Donald MacDonald and Big Eli Wakefield played by Burt Lancaster who also directed *The Kentuckian* (United Artists, 1955).

4233

Fremont: It takes courage to tell a man the truth …when the truth hurts.

Captain John C. Fremont played by Dana Andrews: George B. Seitz's *Kit Carson* (United Artists, 1940).

4234

Myra: All men are alike in the springtime. There's only room in their heads for two things: fighting and kissing.

Myra Ripple played by Ethel Wales: Lesley Selander's *Knights of the Range* (Paramount, 1940).

4235

Hamilton: Let me tell you something, Bruce. You just stop thinking. You're gonna live a lot longer.

Ted Hamilton played by James Best and Dan Barton, alias Jack Bruce, played by George Montgomery: Paul Landres' *Last of the Badmen* (Allied Pictures, 1957).

4236

Sheriff: A man works hard enough …he'll make his mark.

Sheriff Pat Lambrose played by Jim Davis: Virgil W. Vogel's *Law of the Land* (TVW, 1976).

4237

Calem: A man's tongue works like a shovel sometimes, Cody. It can dig him his own grave.

Marshal Calem Ware played by Randolph Scott and Cody Clark played by John Emery: Joseph H. Lewis' *A Lawless Street* (Columbia, 1955).

4238

Maddox: A man gets caught in his own doing. You can't change what you are. And if you try, something always calls you back.

Marshal Jared Maddox played by Burt Lancaster: Michael Winner's *Lawman* (United Artists, 1971).

4239

Old Grandfather: It's harder to find a good man than a good horse. Believe me, no horse ever chased a woman.

Old Grandfather played by George Clutesi: Mel Damski's *The Legend of Walks Far Woman* (TVW, 1982).

4240

Bud: Mr. Burke, I thought you said a smart man knows when he's whipped.
Burke: Who says I'm smart?

Bud Yoakum played by Ralph Reed and Devereaux Burke played by Clark Gable: Vincent Sherman's *Lone Star* (MGM, 1952).

4241

Cobham: I will tell you one thing, Doctor.

The more I see of man, the more I admire dogs.

Superintendent Cobham played by Frank Thring and Dr. Dobbyn played by Kurt Beimel: Philippe Mora's *Mad Dog Morgan* (Motion Picture Company/BEF, 1976).

4242

Harry: Right now, he's like an itch I can't scratch.

Harry Luck played by Brad Dexter: John Sturges' *The Magnificent Seven* (United Artists, 1960).

4243

Dundee: Men can understand fighting. I guess maybe they need it sometimes. The truth is, it's easy. You forget about your problems, responsibilities …just let someone feed ya, tell ya what to do.

Major Amos Charles Dundee played by Charlton Heston: Sam Peckinpah's *Major Dundee* (Columbia, 1965).

4244

Lockhart: Well, nobody likes being whipped. But most men get over it.

Will Lockhart played by James Stewart: Anthony Mann's *The Man from Laramie* (Columbia, 1955).

4245

Dawes: Women tend to themselves, huh? Men just take a piss.

Dawes played by Jack Warden: Richard C. Sarafian's *The Man Who Loved Cat Dancing* (MGM, 1973).

4246

Grobart: Never try and bribe a man with something he can take anyway.

Jay Grobart played by Burt Reynolds: Richard C. Sarafian's *The Man Who Loved Cat Dancing* (MGM, 1973).

4247

Bret: You couldn't sneak up on a corpse, Coop! Not any more. You're just another decrepit old has-been!

Bret Maverick played by Mel Gibson and Marshal Zane Cooper played by James Garner: Richard Donner's *Maverick* (Warner Bros., 1994).

Seven gunmen unite to defend a Mexican village …and become *The Magnificent Seven* in the process (United Artists, 1960). Chris (Yul Brynner), Vin (Steve McQueen), Chico (Horst Buchholz), O'Reilly (Charles Bronson), Lee (Robert Vaughn), Harry Luck (Brad Dexter), and Britt (James Coburn). And a magnificent musical score by Elmer Bernstein.

4248
McCabe: Well, I'll tell you something. I got poetry in me. I do. I got poetry in me. But I ain't gonna put it down on paper. I ain't no educated man. I've got sense enough not to try.
John McCabe played by Warren Beatty: Robert Altman's *McCabe & Mrs. Miller* (Warner Bros., 1971).

4249
McLintock: I saw your picture in the paper at the Governor's Ball. You were dancing with the Governor.
Katherine: At least he's a gentleman!
McLintock: I doubt that. You have to be a man first before you're a gentleman. He misses on both counts.
George Washington McLintock played by John Wayne and Katherine McLintock played by Maureen O'Hara: Andrew V. McLaglen's *McLintock!* (United Artists, 1963).

4250
Ernestina: All I want from a man is that he outlives me.
Ernestina Crawford played by Karen Black: Jack Starrett's *Mr. Horn* (TVW, 1979).

4251
Hogan: What's so funny?
Mary: Men. My husband used to sit on that keg all the time. I couldn't get him used to a chair.
Hogan: Sometimes men just aren't comfortable when they're comfortable.
"Silver" Ward Hogan played by Jock Mahoney and Mary Kingman played by Kim Hunter: Richard Bartlett's *Money, Women and Guns* (Universal, 1958).

4252
Emmett: Why don't you take a bath?
Pete: What's the use? A man just gets dirty all over again.
Emmett Dalton played by Ray Teal and Pete Bivins played by Andy Devine: Allan Dwan's *Montana Belle* (RKO, 1952).

4253
H.D.: I never did know what to say to a woman until after midnight.
H.D. Dalton played by Scott Glenn: Stuart Rosenberg's *My Heroes Have Always Been Cowboys* (Samuel Goldwyn Company, 1991).

4254
Ben: Now ain't that the way. A man gets set for trouble head-on, and it sneaks up behind him every time.
Ben Vandergroat played by Robert Ryan: Anthony Mann's *The Naked Spur* (MGM, 1953).

4255
Nell: A man gets to thinking how he'd look sitting on a cement horse out in front of the courthouse.

Nell McGarahan played by Susan Blanchard: Hy Averback's *The New Maverick* (TVW, 1978).

4256
Ben: Brett, you'll never be happy running with the herd. You got what most men spend a whole life fighting for.
Brett: Yea?
Ben: Freedom.
Brett: Oh well, as my old pappy used to say: freedom has got a lot to do with what you're carrying in your hip pocket. And I'm carrying about 85 cents.
Ben Maverick played by Charles Frank and Brett Maverick played by James Garner: Hy Averback's *The New Maverick* (TVW, 1978).

4257
Jim: There ain't a man alive that hasn't got trouble. It's how he handles that trouble is what counts.
Angela: How he goes looking for that trouble is what makes him a fool.
Jim Cole played by Clint Walker and Angela Cole played by Martha Hyer: Joseph Pevney's *The Night of the Grizzly* (Paramount, 1966).

4258
Anne: What are you talking about? You can't tell me that everybody there thinks something is going on between John and Maria. That's ridiculous!
Waynebrook: What's ridiculous about it? Did you take a look at Maria?
Anne: I did.
Waynebrook: Of course you did. Everybody did. She's the prettiest little thing I've ever saw in my life.
Anne: I still know John well enough to know he wouldn't …he isn't that kind of a man.
Waynebrook: The kind of man John is has nothing to do with it. He's a man!
Anne Barnes played by Barbara Hale, Mrs. Waynebrook played by Verna Felton, and Maria Smith played by Gloria Talbott: Francis D. Lyon's *The Oklahoman* (Warner Bros., 1957).

4259
Bierce: Man, as you know, is one of the most pathetic creatures on earth. Condemned to a desire that contradicts all the laws of nature …to close the gap between two human beings.
Ambrose Bierce played by Gregory Peck: Luis Puenzo's *Old Gringo* (Columbia, 1989).

4260
Dan: It's time you learned, Doc, the only thing in this life a man can earn is friendship. Everything else you can steal.
Dan Casey played by Dan Rowan: Hal Kanter's *Once Upon a Horse* (Universal, 1958).

4261
Wobbles: You've known me for a long time, Frank. You know you can trust me.

Frank: Wobbles, how can you trust a man that wears both a belt and suspenders? The man can't even trust his own pants!
Wobbles played by Marco Zuanelli and Frank played by Henry Fonda: Sergio Leone's *Once Upon a Time in the West* (Paramount, 1969).

4262
Hayes: My boy, a man never really sees himself until he looks at the friends he once knew.
Captain Oren Hayes played by Pat O'Brien: Jean Yarbrough's *The Over-the-Hill Gang* (TVW, 1969).

4263
Nash: A man ain't through until he's dead.
George: Sometimes a man's dead when he ain't no use anymore.
Nash Crawford played by Walter Brennan and Gentleman George played by Chill Wills: Jean Yarbrough's *The Over-the-Hill Gang* (TVW, 1969).

4264
George: That's always the way it is: when a man starts handing out good advice, he ain't up to set no more bad examples.
Gentleman George played by Chill Wills: Jean Yarbrough's *The Over-the-Hill Gang* (TVW, 1969).

4265
Granger: Dead men can't hurt ya. It's the live ones you have to watch.
Ross Granger played by Jock Mahoney: Fred F. Sears' *Overland Pacific* (United Artists, 1954).

4266
Ben: Now you ain't gonna tell me that you ain't never had a woman either!
Horton: Well, no sir, I haven't.
Ben: That's, that's, well, that's terrible! Do you know you could go blind?
Ben Rumson played by Lee Marvin and Horton Fenty played by Tom Ligon: Joseph Logan's *Paint Your Wagon* (Paramount, 1969).

4267
[*Introducing boy to prostitute*]
Ben: I give you the boy. Give me back the man.
Ben Rumson played by Lee Marvin: Joseph Logan's *Paint Your Wagon* (Paramount, 1969).

4268
Mr. Fenty: Horton, how did that bottle get into your pocket? Horton, how long have you been drinking hard liquor?
Horton: Well, since this afternoon. I know you don't approve, Pa. But believe me, until you've had a good cigar and a shot of whiskey, you're missing the second and third best things in life.
Ben: Horton!
Pardner: Where did you take him, Ben?
Elizabeth: Damn you, Ben Rumson! What are you going to teach this boy next? How to cheat at cards? Or just physical education with one of Willie's floozies?

Horton: That's the best one, Pa!

Mr. Fenty played by Alan Baxter, Horton Fenty played by Tom Ligon, Ben Rumson played by Lee Marvin, Pardner played by Clint Eastwood, and Elizabeth Woodling played by Jean Seberg: Joseph Logan's *Paint Your Wagon* (Paramount, 1969).

4269

Potter: Brave men run in my family.

Painless Peter Potter played by Bob Hope: Norman Z. McLeod's *The Paleface* (Paramount, 1948).

4270

Pershing: Every great man was once a bandit.

General Pershing played by Walter Coy: Eugenio Martín's *Pancho Villa* (Granada/Scotia International, 1975).

4271

Reverend: God places men together in a special relationship so that in the rubbing together they polish each other.

Reverend Jacob Karns played by Dennis O'Keefe: Lewis R. Foster's *Passage West* (Paramount, 1951).

4272

Ricardo: You were once a man of the people. Your name was spoken with admiration ...like that of Zapata. You stood side by side with him. How do you wish to be remembered? As you were then ...or for what you do now?

Morales: And how do you wish to be remembered, huh? With a bullet hole between your eyes?

Ricardo: I'm just asking you to be the man you could be and have been.

Ricardo Sandoval played by Reni Santoni and Chucho Morales played by Fernando Lamas: Douglas Heyes' *Powderkeg* (TVW, 1971).

4273

Grant: You bastard!

Fardan: Yes sir. In my case, an accident of birth. But you sir? You're a self-made man!

J.W. Grant played by Ralph Bellamy and Henry Rico Fardan played by Lee Marvin: Richard Brooks' *The Professionals* (Columbia, 1966).

4274

Teach: I haven't asked for any help. I don't want any.

Gentry: We can all use help. When a man reaches a crossroad, it's no shame to ask which way to point his feet.

Teach played by John Gavin and Gentry/John Coventry played by Fred MacMurray: Harry Keller's *Quantez* (Universal, 1957).

4275

Sam: Well, I didn't break anything. I just chipped my pride, I guess.

Jeff: That seems to hurt worse than anything, don't it Sam?

Sam Burnett played by James Stewart and Jeff

Harter played by Ben Johnson: Andrew V. McLaglen's *The Rare Breed* (Universal, 1966).

4276

Tom: She's doing what you ought to do once in awhile ...take a bath.

Sam: Keep dry outside and wet inside. That's what a man does in this country.

Tom Owens played by Tyrone Power and Sam Todd played by Edgar Buchanan: Henry Hathaway's *Rawhide* (20th Century–Fox, 1951).

4277

Lamartine: There was a time when war was the property of gentlemen ...of men on horseback who fought under a rigid, ethical code. Unfortunately, my dear, those times have passed.

Lamartine played by Alan Reed: Leslie Fenton's *The Redhead and the Cowboy* (Paramount, 1951).

4278

Kate: What brought you here?

Stan: Just passing through.

Kate: Drifting?

Stan: You don't like that?

Kate: A man knows where he's going.

Kate Maxwell played by Maureen O'Hara and Stan Blaine played by Alex Nicol: Lee Sholem's *The Redhead from Wyoming* (Universal, 1953).

4279

Kate: It seems to me that all men want to do is fight ...even when they talk about peace, like you, with a gun in their hands. It's high time women took a hand in running this world!

Kate Maxwell played by Maureen O'Hara and Stan Blaine played by Alex Nicol: Lee Sholem's *The Redhead from Wyoming* (Universal, 1953).

4280

Pickett: You know, if you save a man's life in China, the man you save has to dedicate his whole life to the one who did the saving.

McCall: It's a good thing we're in New Mexico!

Nathaniel Pickett played by Victor Love and Duell McCall played by Alex McArthur: E.W. Swackhamer's *The Return of Desperado* (TVW, 1988).

4281

Josey: The only thing I worry about now is your brain. You see, your brain runs with tequila and women ...and nothing else.

Josey Wales played by Michael Parks who also directed *The Return of Josey Wales* (Multi-Tacar/Reel Movies International, 1987).

4282

Call: Gideon Walker, you are in a different world.

Gideon: Same world, Captain ...different times. Gus used to say: a man is like a

river ...he got to keep on flowing where the force of nature takes you.

Captain Woodrow F. Call played by Jon Voight and Gideon Walker played by William Peterson: Mike Robe's *Return to Lonesome Dove* (TVW, 1993). Captain Augusta "Gus" McCrea was Call's deceased friend.

4283

Jonas: Dub says a man will wear out or rust out, and it ain't my bend to rust.

Jonas Trapp played by Chuck Connors and Dub Stokes played by Gary Merrill: Bernard McEveety's *Ride Beyond Vengeance* (Columbia, 1966).

4284

Steve: Boys nowadays ...no pride, no self-respect. Plenty of gall, but no sand.

Steve Judd played by Joel McCrea: Sam Peckinpah's *Ride the High Country* (MGM, 1962).

4285

Rio: A man should have faith only in his dog and his enemies.

Rio played by Robert Taylor: John Farrow's *Ride, Vaquero!* (MGM, 1953).

4286

Esqueda: What a man takes, he has to keep it at his own risk whether it be a country or a woman.

Jose Esqueda played by Anthony Quinn: John Farrow's *Ride, Vaquero!* (MGM, 1953).

4287

Chito: I always know what I'm doing! I think!

Chito Rafferty played by Richard Martin: Lesley Selander's *Riders of the Range* (RKO, 1950).

4288

Dan: I've seen too many men work themselves to death for an ambitious woman.

Dan Corrigan played by Rod Cameron: George Sherman's *River Lady* (Universal, 1948).

4289

Beauvais: Go ahead, make a gentleman out of him. He's just stupid enough to be good material. But after he gets to be a gentleman, he'll want a lady ...not you.

Beauvais played by Dan Duryea: George Sherman's *River Lady* (Universal, 1948).

4290

Egbert: Men are created equal to women. That's why you have no right to order me around the way you do. Abe Lincoln said so.

Effie: He also said you can fool some of the people some of the time and all of the people some of the time. But you can't fool me, Egbert Floud, any of the time!

Egbert "Sourdough" Floud played by Charles Ruggles and Effie Floud played by Mary Boland: Leo McCarey's *Ruggles of Red Gap* (Paramount, 1935).

4291

Ruggles: I feel like jumping in the river.
Judson: Well, go ahead! And jump in at
  the bend. It's deeper there!

Colonel Marmaduke "Bill" Ruggles played by
Charles Laughton and Mrs. Judson played by
ZaSu Pitts: Leo McCarey's *Ruggles of Red Gap*
(Paramount, 1935).

4292

Tom: You know, Orrin's a good man.
  Where did he inherit all that charm?
Tyrel: My pa. He could talk a pump handle
  into believing it was a windmill.

Tom Sunday played by Glenn Ford and Tyrel
Sackett played by Jeff Osterhage: Robert Totten's
The Sacketts (TVW, 1979).

4293

Jody: Well, what do I do?
Deaks: Grow! Every man has to ...on his
  own. Grow. You grow big, you hear?

Jody played by Michael Burns and Deaks played
by Robert Wilke: Gary Nelson's *Santee* (Crown
International Pictures, 1973).

4294

Valerie: Jody, I want to tell you something.
  No two men are ever alike. No two men
  ever do anything exactly the same way.
  Walk in your own footprints. Don't follow someone else.

Valerie played by Dana Wynter and Jody played by
Michael Burns: Gary Nelson's *Santee* (Crown International Pictures, 1973).

4295

Hennessey: The only thing a man can
  know about what Jim is going to do is
  that he darn sure will never know.

Sergeant Hennessey played by John McIntire and
Jim Flood played by Barry Sullivan: Harry Keller's
Seven Ways from Sundown (Universal, 1960).

4296

Seven: Flood is what every man wants to
  be, I guess ...wild and free.

Seven Jones played by Audie Murphy and Jim
Flood played by Barry Sullivan: Harry Keller's
Seven Ways from Sundown (Universal, 1960).

4297

Johnny: You didn't have to go through all
  that to pick a fight with me.
Jason: Well, you see, when I'm dealing
  with a very devious man, and I'm very
  straightforward, that puts me at a big
  disadvantage.

Johnny Bledsoe, alias Colonel Stephen Bedford,
played by Leslie Nielsen and Jason Sweet played
by Glenn Ford: George Marshall's *The Sheepman*
(MGM, 1958).

4298

Charlie: That fella, Tinkham. He's the only
  man I know that started at the bottom
  and went down in the world. He'd steal
horses for nothing and now he gets paid
for it.

Charlie Anderson played by James Stewart and
Tinkham played by Lane Bradford: Andrew V.
McLaglen's *Shenandoah* (Universal, 1965).

4299

Sammy: It's a funny thing about him. As
  far as I can remember back, he was either fighting against ya or fighting for
  ya.

Sammy Lane played by Betty Field: Henry Hathaway's *The Shepherd of the Hills* (Paramount,
1941).

4300

Swiss: You know what my grandma always
  used to say? Stay away from men who
  wear black. They're either lawmen or
  undertakers.

Blanc De Blanc/"Swiss" played by Giuliano Gemma:
Sergio Corbucci's *Shoot First ...Ask Questions
Later!* (a.k.a. *The White, the Yellow, and the Black*;
Mntex Entertainment, It/Sp/Fr).

4301

Lavalle: You and Pickett, neither one of
  you could make it alone. Maybe together you might make one good man.
  But pull you apart? You're like an oyster:
  you're a coupla shells sharing one set of
  guts.

Lavalle played by Harold J. Stone and Bert Pickett played by Charles Drake: R.G. Springsteen's
Showdown (Universal, 1963).

4302

Augie: Where are you going?
Jake: Well, I got things to do, kid. I'm a
  busy man.
Augie: I'll go with ya!
Jake: A grown man can't have a little boy
  with him everywhere he goes.
Augie: Well, who's a grown man?

Augie played by Tom Brown and Jake played by
Kevin Costner: Lawrence Kasdan's *Silverado* (Columbia, 1985).

4303

Clint: There's some things you can't
  explain to some people. And the
  few you can explain to, you don't need
  to.

Clint played by Fess Parker: George Sherman's
Smoky (20th Century–Fox, 1966).

4304

Ramon: You told me I must be a man, so I
  ...
Carlos: So you grew a mustache!

Ramon played by George J. Lewis and Carlos
played by Buck Jones: Lambert Hillyer's *South of
the Rio Grande* (Columbia, 1932).

4305

Leah: When are you men going to stop
  shooting each other?
Horne: When are you women going to
  stop being women?

Leah Parker played by Marilyn Maxwell and Sheriff
Horne played by Barry Sullivan: William F. Claxton's *Stage to Thunder Rock* (Paramount, 1964).

4306

Charlie: You see, I believe that every man
  has his price.
Haven: Some men don't believe that.
Charlie: But every woman knows it.

Charlie played by Jane Greer and Haven played by
Dick Powell: Sidney Lanfield's *Station West* (RKO,
1948).

4307

Dawkins: I figure that a man's friendship
  for another man is about as honest as
  anything that comes along.

Jim Dawkins played by William Holden: Leslie
Fenton's *Streets of Laredo* (Paramount, 1949).

4308

Stark: People build monuments to men
  who make good. Fools wind up in unmarked graves.

Nathan Stark played by Robert Ryan: Raoul
Walsh's *The Tall Men* (20th Century–Fox, 1955).

4309

Allison: There's nothing like a cold bath to
  make a boy feel like a man.

Ben Allison played by Clark Gable: Raoul Walsh's
The Tall Men (20th Century–Fox, 1955).

4310

Cowpoke: A man can take almost anything ...except being made a bigger fool
  than he already is.

Cowpoke played by Ronald Reagan: Allan Dwan's
Tennessee's Partner (RKO, 1955).

4311

Whitney: I'll tell ya, son. It ain't what you
  do that spoils your sleep. It's what you
  missed. Take it from an old man.

Whitney played by Douglas Fowley: Richard Fleischer's *These Thousand Hills* (20th Century–Fox,
1959).

4312

Adelaide: They're only men ...and damn
  poor specimens at that!

Adelaide Geary played by Rita Hayworth: Robert
Rossen's *They Came to Cordura* (Columbia, 1959).

4313

Adelaide: One act of cowardice doesn't
  make a man a coward forever. Just as
  one act of bravery doesn't make a man a
  hero forever.

Adelaide Geary played by Rita Hayworth: Robert
Rossen's *They Came to Cordura* (Columbia, 1959).

4314

Charlie: Say, you think we're all still
  demons? Well, maybe you're right.

Maybe we are. But some of us, we just need an angel like you to save us from ourselves.

Charlie played by Chris Cooper: Nancy Kelly's *Thousand Pieces of Gold* (Greycat Films, 1991).

4315

Rosita: Which one do you like best, Carmen?

Carmen: I like the one who's not too smart.

Rosita: Which one is that?

Rosita played by Benita and Carmen played by Patrice Martinez: John Landis' *Three Amigos!* (Orion, 1986).

4316

Ruby: Men who aren't afraid of guns or Indians or rattlesnakes are afraid of a little laughter behind their backs.

Ruby LaSalle played by Elaine Stritch: Rudolph Mate's *Three Violent People* (Paramount, 1956).

4317

Cinch: I wonder if it's heredity or environment. Do only stubborn men come to Texas? Or does the Texas air make all men stubborn?

Cinch Saunders played by Tom Tryon: Rudolph Mate's *Three Violent People* (Paramount, 1956).

4318

Carrington: Did you ever notice? Trouble seems to make us women forget differences. With men, it seems to turn them into snapping dogs.

Mrs. Carrington played by Ann Doran: George Sherman's *Tomahawk* (Universal, 1951).

4319

Fabian: My dear, you have such a gaze upon the quintessential frontier type. Note the lean silhouette; eyes closed by the sun, they're sharp as a hawk. He's got the look of both predator and prey.

Josephine: I want one!

Fabian: Happy hunting!

Mr. Fabian played by Billy Zane and Josephine played by Dana Delany: George P. Cosmatos' *Tombstone* (Buena Vista, 1993).

4320

Splinters: Well, what I lack in brains, I make up for in ignorance.

Splinters McGonigle played by Gordon Jones: William Whitney's *Trail of Robin Hood* (Republic, 1950).

4321

Hoby: Oh, I can't complain. We're a hard-luck family, Lon. There's nothing that's going to change that.

Lon: A man makes his own luck.

Hoby: I used to think so. Now I believe different.

Hoby Cordeen played by James Mitchum and Lon Cordeen played by Gordon Scott: Albert Band's *The Tramplers* (Embassy Picture Release, 1965).

4322

Pablo: Sometimes I have the feeling that you do not trust me.

Juan: I trust you all right …as far as I can spit.

Pablo Morales played by Joseph Calleia and Juan Castro played by Gilbert Roland: George Sherman's *The Treasure of Pancho Villa* (RKO, 1955).

4323

Rudock: A man ought to be able to have something and believe he's got it. And that it's his and he ain't gonna lose it ever.

Jeremy Rudock played by James Cagney: Robert Wise's *Tribute to a Bad Man* (MGM, 1956).

4324

Mother: Why didn't you write your ma?

Trinity: Because I don't know how to write. And you don't know how to read.

Father: Yea, you got a point there.

The Mother played by Jessica Dublin, Trinity played by Terence Hill, and the Father played by Harry Carey Jr.: E.B. Clucher's (Enzo Barboni) *Trinity Is Still My Name* (West Film/Avco Embassy, 1971).

4325

Pete: You ever have a father, Bill?

Bill: Sure I had a father! He had twelve other sons too. I was the youngest and puniest of 'em all. He was a fine fella …never raised his hand to any of us boys, only in self-defense.

Piute Pete played by Leo Carrillo and Skinner Bill Bragg played by Wallace Beery: Richard Thorpe's *20 Mule Team* (MGM, 1940).

4326

Jesus: Señor, the widow Gomez has delivered a son this morning …a boy.

McCabe: Well, a boy for the widow Gomez.

Jesus: But señor, it has been more than a year ago since Señor Antonio Gomez has been buried in the church house.

McCabe: Well, some men you just can't trust to stay where you put them.

Jesus was uncredited and Guthrie "Gus" McCabe played by James Stewart: John Ford's *Two Rode Together* (Columbia, 1961).

4327

Belle: You'd think a woman with my experience would know more about men.

Jim: Yea, well I guess ole Gus finally found something he wanted more than ten percent.

Belle Aragon played by Annelle Hayes, Lieutenant Jim Gary played by Richard Widmark, and Guthrie "Gus" McCabe played by James Stewart: John Ford's *Two Rode Together* (Columbia, 1961).

4328

Mollie: Jeff, no one has ever put any sense in a man's brain through a bullet hole in his head.

Mollie Monahan played by Barbara Stanwyck and Jeff Butler played by Joel McCrea: Cecil B. DeMille's *Union Pacific* (Paramount, 1939).

4329

Wilkison: A man makes many mistakes in his life, but most as he grows old and sees time running short. He gets in too big of a hurry to get things done. He loses sight of what's gone on around him.

Lew Wilkison played by Edward G. Robinson: Rudolph Mate's *The Violent Men* (Columbia, 1955).

4330

Lulu: Any man who wears suspenders and a belt is always prepared.

Lulu played by Jeannine Riley: Jack Arnold, Oscar Rudolph, Bruce Bilson, and Earl Bellamy's *The Wackiest Wagon Train in the West* (Topar Films, 1976).

4331

Narrator: I know I'd never be a mountain man like him, and I told him so. He told me I'd do better to be a man like my father anyway; that a real man was someone who took care of the folks who counted on him.

Narration by Brian Keith, speaking as the voice of Jacob McKay played by David Tom: Craig Clyde's *Walking Thunder* (Majestic Entertainment/Sunset Hill Partners, 1997).

4332

Siringo: Come on back to me, Lola!

Lola: Well, if you weren't such a pig-headed man about woman's suffrage, I just might think about it.

Siringo: Me?

Lola: I see you snickering in your beer every time the suffragettes have a rally.

Siringo: Oh, not me! No, I think you have a perfect right to vote …as long as it's not in any election.

Charlie Siringo played by Steve Forrest and Lola Watkins played by Stella Stevens: Lee Philips' *Wanted: The Sundance Woman* (TVW, 1976).

4333

Wilks: That fella could charm the Rocky Mountains into going south for the winter!

Sergeant Augusta Wilks played by Noah Beery, Jr.: George Sherman's *War Arrow* (Universal, 1954).

4334

Tadlock: We're mere men, but a man's nature is enormous. It contains both the great and the small. Even the meanest of us can be as large as this whole continent.

When John McCabe (Warren Beatty) refuses to sell his interest in a saloon and whorehouse, three men are sent in to "take care of business." "I don't make deals" says bad guy Dog Butler (Hugh Millais) with gunman Breed (Jace Vander Veen) standing behind him with rifle in Robert Altman's *McCabe & Mrs. Miller* (Warner Bros., 1971).

Senator William J. Tadlock played by Kirk Douglas in Andrew V. McLaglen's *The Way West* (United Artists, 1967).

4335

Lije: You know, for a smart man you ain't got a lick of sense!

Lije Evans played by Richard Widmark: Andrew V. McLaglen's *The Way West* (Untied Artists, 1967).

4336

Blue: I'll never be a man in my own eyes until I am in yours.

Will Blue played by Henry Fonda: Burt Kennedy's *Welcome to Hard Times* (MGM, 1967).

4337

Sheriff: I can't ask men to drive them wagons into certain death!

Steve: Some men, Sheriff, aren't worth asking.

The Sheriff played by Hal Taliaferro/Wally Wales and Steve Kells played by Roy Rogers: Joseph Kane's *West of the Badlands* (a.k.a. *The Border Legion*; Republic, 1940).

4338

Hank: How does it feel to be a mighty important man instead of a mighty dead one?

Hank Breckenridge played by Jeff York: William Beaudine's *Westward Ho the Wagons* (Buena Vista, 1956).

4339

Cross: A man starts telling everybody his business, pretty soon he don't have any.

Cross played by Willie Nelson: Burt Kennedy's

Where the Hell's That Gold?!!! (a.k.a. *Dynamite & Gold*; TVW, 1988).

4340

Boone: Sometimes I don't understand you, Cross. One time you're fighting for the good side; next with the bad.

Cross: A man's got to make a living, Boone.

Boone played by Jack Elam and Cross played by Willie Nelson: Burt Kennedy's *Where the Hell's That Gold?!!!* (a.k.a. *Dynamite & Gold*; TVW, 1988).

4341

Wild Bill: Go drown in crap, Charlie!

Wild Bill Hickok played by Jeff Bridges and Charlie Prince played by John Hurt: Walter Hill's *Wild Bill* (MGM/United Artists, 1995).

4342

Thompson: Your pa has got grit, I'll say that.

Virgil: Yes sir, he has.

Thompson: It'll do him as much good as a sulfur match in a wind storm.

Thompson played by Jack Elam and Virgil Tanner played by Ron Howard: Robert Totten's *The Wild Country* (Buena Vista, 1971).

4343

Arn: This is a country for men. A man carries a gun, he better be ready to use it.

Arn played by John Beradino: Charles Haas' *Wild Heritage* (Universal, 1958).

4344

Claire: Well, I don't understand how you men can take these things so lightly.

Jeff: Well, as long as you got to take 'em, that's the only way to do it.

Claire Hartford played by Anne Nagel and Jeff Ramsay played by Dick Foran: Ford Beebe's and Ray Taylor's *Winners of the West* (Universal serial, Chapter 4: "Trapped By Redskins,' 1940).

4345

Rusty: Well, this a fine way to treat a couple of friendly strangers.

Will: Friendly? How do I know you're friendly?

Tucson: You'll have to take our word for it.

Will: Don't give me that. I'll take the wind's word that it's going to rain. And I'll take the sun's word that it's going to be clear. But I've learned never to take a man's word for anything!

Rusty Joslin played by Raymond Hatton, Will Parker played by Donald "Red" Barry, and Tucson Smith played by Ray Corrigan: George Sherman's *Wyoming Outlaw* (Republic, 1939).

4346

Charlie: I'm a little old for regrets but, ah, young enough for some hope.

Charlie Veer played by Douglas Kennedy: Fred Sears' *Wyoming Renegades* (Columbia, 1955).

4347

Ben: Let me give you a little advice, friend. The next time you got a job for a boy, don't send for a man. And don't you ever send for this man!

Ben Kane played by Robert Mitchum: Burt Kennedy's *Young Billy Young* (United Artists, 1969).

4348

Cole: I wouldn't turn my back on you.

Jesse: It shows you got good sense some-times.

Cole Younger played by Willard Parker and Jesse James played by Ray Stricklyn: William F. Claxton's *Young Jesse James* (20th Century–Fox, 1960).

4349

Cole: Say, I thought you were dead.

Jesese: You always said I was too mean to die.

Cole Younger played by Willard Parker and Jesse James played by Ray Stricklyn: William F. Claxton's *Young Jesse James* (20th Century–Fox, 1960).

4350

Cole: Never send a boy on a man's errand.

Cole Younger played by Wayne Morris: Edwin L. Marin's *The Younger Brothers* (Warner Bros., 1949).

4351

Don Diego: Bernardo, no man has such a mad desire for power unless he secretly knows that he's weak.

Don Diego de la Vega/Zorro played by Guy Williams and Bernardo played by Gene Sheldon: Charles Barton's *Zorro, the Avenger* (TVW, 1959).

Newspapers, Telegraphs, and the Pony Express

See also People; Towns

4352

Doc: You know, the worse thing about a reputation is you can't outrun the thing. The press never lets up. They're on a body like stink on a dead man.

Doc Holliday played by John McLiam: Stuart Margolin's *Bret Maverick: The Lazy Ace* (TVW, 1981).

4353

Tom: When the Indian wishes to signal his brother, he does so by smoke sign. This is the white man's signal. My brothers far away can look at this and understand my meaning. We call this mail. And the men who carry the mail are like the air that carries the Apache smoke signals.

Tom Jeffords played by James Stewart: Delmer Daves' *Broken Arrow* (20th Century–Fox, 1950).

4354

Sgt: I've been waiting for you. Somebody has written you a letter.

Cody: Who, me?

Sgt: That's right, my boy. Who in the world would be writing to you?

Cody: I don't know but if you give me the letter, I'll find out.

Sgt: You'll get yours in your proper turn. The mail is delivered according to rank. And there's plenty ranker than you!

Sergeant Chips played by Edgar Buchanan and Buffalo Bill Cody played by Joel McCrea: William Wellman's *Buffalo Bill* (20th Century–Fox, 1944).

4355

Senator: Well, that's it! That's my letter telling you I was coming [out west]. I mailed it a week before I left.

Sgt: That's nothing. Private Mulligan didn't get the letter with his reprieve until days after they hung him. Come to think about it, he never did get it.

Senator Frederici played by Moroni Olsen and Sergeant Chips played by Edgar Buchanan: William Wellman's *Buffalo Bill* (20th Century–Fox, 1944).

4356

Big Jack: It looks as if your newspaper hadn't quite the influence we thought it had.

Zeke: Well, as long as I got ink to print it with, I'm going to keep on trying.

Big Jack Davis played by Raymond Massey and Zeke Mitchell played by Don Beddoe: Andre De Toth's *Carson City* (Warner Bros., 1952).

4357

Zeke: You don't agree with me, do you?

Susan: As you're so fond of saying, quote: I disapprove of what you say, but I'll defend to the death your right to say it!

Zeke Mitchell played by Don Beddoe and Susan Mitchell played by Lucille Norman: Andre De Toth's *Carson City* (Warner Bros., 1952).

4358

Olsen: I bring the west to the east. People say I write lies. But the truth is …it's dead …in a year or less.

Wilbur Olsen played by Sam Peckinpah: Monte Hellman's *China 9, Liberty 37* (a.k.a. *Gunfire*; Titanus, 1978).

4359

Claytun: What do you want?

Olsen: To buy a little legend …the touch of pulchritude for the people back east …a piece of the American west they can believe in.

Claytun: You mean lie to them?

Olsen: Of course, the lies they need, we all need.

Claytun: My life is not for sale!

Olsen: Nonsense! It's only a question of who pays and when.

Claytun Drumm played by Fabio Testi and Wilbur Olsen played by Sam Peckinpah: Monte Hellman's *China 9, Liberty 37* (a.k.a. *Gunfire*; Titanus, 1978).

4360

Yancy: I'll show them first crack that the *Oklahoma Wigwam* prints all the news all the time …knowing no law except the law of God and the government of these United States. Say, that's a pretty good slogan! Top of the page …just ahead of the editorial column!

Yancy Cravat played by Richard Dix: Wesley Ruggles' *Cimarron* (RKO, 1931).

4361

Dr. Irving: I'll tell you, Ellen, we're the public disgrace of America. You know what the New York newspapers are saying? There's no law west of Chicago …and west of Dodge City, no God.

Dr. Irving played by Henry Travers and Mrs. Ellen Irving played by Georgia Caine: Michael Curtiz's *Dodge City* (Warner Bros., 1939).

4362

Juan: Salute, Pancho.

Pancho: Don't give me the salute, give me the news!

Juan: I'm sorry, Pancho, I don't find out anything.

Pancho: Oh, you big disappointment. You don't find nothing? The next time there's nothing to be done, I do it myself.

Juan played by Duncan Renaldo and Pancho Grande played by Harold Huber: Joseph Santley's *Down Mexico Way* (Republic, 1941).

4363

Clevenger: I tell ya, boys, you just keep working on this town and it won't support no newspaper. Them that are smart enough to read get wise enough to move.

Gabe Clevenger played by Ray Teal: Edwin Marin's *Fort Worth* (Warner Bros., 1951).

4364

Happy Jack: Now don't tell me you're afraid of your own shadow …afraid to throw lead at some ink jobber.

Clevenger: He throws lead, jughead! Type. And it's got plenty scatter to it. You drill one of those newspaper fellas and what do you got? A dozen more ready to step in and blast the print at you!

Happy Jack Harvey was uncredited and Gabe Clevenger played by Ray Teal: Edwin Marin's *Fort Worth* (Warner Bros., 1951).

4365

Garvin: News comes in pieces, boys. Like a set of clothes. Don't ever sport the jacket unless you're sure you got the britches on.

Ben Garvin played by Emerson Treacy: Edwin Marin's *Fort Worth* (Warner Bros., 1951).

4366

Garvin: Did you ever wonder why I never got married? Boy, I was a foolish human once. She was pretty, just as pretty as Flora. But I printed her old man into the pen …where he belonged!

Ben Garvin played by Emerson Treacy: Edwin Marin's *Fort Worth* (Warner Bros., 1951).

4367

Britt: Thank old Ben Garvin. He made the rules for the paper. One was: never to pitchfork the dead.

Ned Britt played by Randolph Scott and Ben Garvin played by Emerson Treacy: Edwin Marin's *Fort Worth* (Warner Bros., 1951).

4368

Murphy: So you think the press created Jesse James?

Pinkerton: You created the myth. And in that, you share the responsibility.

Zack Murphy played by Sean Patrick Flanery, Allan Pinkerton played by William Atherton, and Jesse James played by Rob Lowe: Robert Boris' *Frank & Jesse* (Vidmark Entertainment, 1995).

4369

Editor: Listen to this, Andy. "Yesterday, Big Nose Jackson was buried in Boot Hill. He was shot to death by an unknown party. Joe Triplett, who officiates as coroner when not busy in the assay office, rendered the following verdict: body rich in lead …too badly punctured to hold whiskey."

The Editor played by Harlan Briggs: Allan Dwan's *Frontier Marshal* (20th Century–Fox, 1939).

4370

Press: Brady Hawkes? The Gambler? You know Brady Hawkes?

Wyatt: Son, I think the best way to write that is that he knows Wyatt Earp.

The Press Man played by Dean Cochran, Wyatt Earp played by Hugh O'Brian, and Brady Hawkes played by Kenny Rogers: Dick Lowry's *The Gambler Returns: The Luck of the Draw* (TVW, 1991).

4371

Wyatt: Son, like the man said: when legend becomes fact, print the legend.

Wyatt Earp played by Hugh O'Brian: Dick Lowry's *The Gambler Returns: The Luck of the Draw* (TVW, 1991).

4372

Narrator: Even while north and south were being torn apart, east and west had been drawn together by the Pony Express, the most daring mail route in history. Eighty riders were in the saddle at all times, night and day, and in all weather; half of 'em riding east, half riding west, between Missouri and Sacramento, carrying mail across country in days instead of months. Unarmed they rode to save weight. Five dollars a letter the mail cost, and on thin paper too. It was courage, skill, and speed against hostile Indians, bandits, hell, and occasional high water. Even as they rode, men were already building a faster message carrier across the country: the overland telegraph.

Narration by Spencer Tracy: John Ford's, George Marshall's, and Henry Hathaway's *How the West Was Won* (MGM, 1962).

4373

Editor: Everything had changed by 1882 …including Sam Hatch. He lived in a comfortable home provided by the town. Some felt he had grown soft. Others allowed that he had become a relic of the past. Only the sage frontier journalist knew that he had reverted to the avenging shootist he was when he first arrived in the town of Independence. A red-eyed man rising from hell with his hair on fire. A man possessed with meting out private justice.

Truman: It's a little strong isn't it, sir?

Editor: You had to be there, Truman. You had to be there. New paragraph!

Editor Sterling Mott played by Sandy McPeak and Truman played by Scott Jones: John Patterson's *Independence* (TVW, 1987).

4374

Editor: Roy!

Roy: Yes sir!

Editor: Take an editorial on lawyers.

Roy: Lawyers?

Editor: That'll do. We'll begin easy …paragraph. "If we are ever to have law and order in the west, first thing we got to do is take out all the lawyers and shoot 'em down like dogs." Paragraph!

[*and later on*]

Editor: Roy! Start the press! Take a new editorial on railroad presidents!

Roy: Yes sir!

Editor: Paragraph. "If we are ever to have law and order in the west, the first thing we got to do is take out all the railroad presidents and shoot 'em down like dogs." Paragraph!

[*and later on*]

Editor: Roy!

Roy: Yes sir!

Editor: Take an editorial on …dentists!

Roy: Yes sir!

Editor: Paragraph. "If we are ever to have law and order in the west, first thing we got to do is take out all the dentists and…"

Roy: …and shoot 'em down like dogs!

[*and later on*]

Editor: Roy, you got that editorial on dentists started yet?

Roy: Yes sir!

Editor: Well, change it from dentist to governors, and finish it like the one we did last week on horse thieves …except this time it's governors!

Mayor Rufus Cobb (also Editor/Publisher of the Liberty Weekly Gazette) played by Henry Hull and Roy played by John Chandler: Henry King's *Jesse James* (20th Century–Fox, 1939).

4375

Jimmy: Did you know that we are in the newspapers, Hardin? They say we are the worst to ever hit the west.

Hardin: I rarely bother with folks who read the papers.

Quick Jimmy played by Fredrick Lopez and John Wesley Hardin played by Randy Quaid: Joseph Sargent's *Larry McMurtry's Streets of Laredo* (Cabin Fever Entertainment, 1995).

4376

Major: In that type lies the power of the press. It can dethrone kings …make history.

Plummer: You know, Major, the last editor was standing right there when they shot him.

Major Carter played by George "Gabby" Hayes and Charles K. Plummer played by Harry Woods: Joseph Kane's *The Lawless Nineties* (Republic, 1936).

4377

Steele: This never was a very healthy climate for editors.

Steele played by Alan Bridge: Joseph Kane's *The Lawless Nineties* (Republic, 1936).

4378

Forbes: The name's Noah Forbes, Marshal. I've decided to do for you what Ned Buntline did for Bill Cody.

Marshal: Make a damn fool of me?

Forbes: Make you famous.

Marshal: You're a writer?

Forbes: You name a big city newspaper and I've worked on it.

Marshal: That means you're pretty good …or you can't hold a job.

Noah Forbes played by Michael Callan and the Marshal, Chris, played by Lee Van Cleef: George

McGowan's *The Magnificent Seven Ride* (United Artists, 1972).

4379

Ransom: You're not going to use the story, Mr. Scott?

Scott: No sir. This is the west, sir. When the legend becomes fact, print the legend.

Ransom Stoddard played by James Stewart and Maxwell Scott played by Carleton Young: John Ford's *The Man Who Shot Liberty Valance* (Paramount, 1962).

4380

Harris: Questions seem to bother you a lot, Mr. Wayne.

Wayne: Only the man who asks them.

Harris: Well, that's too bad because my livelihood happens to depend on questions.

Wayne: Then I suggest you go back East and ask them. Out here, questions can get you killed.

Neal Harris played by Fred MacMurray and Captain George Wayne played by William Bishop: Gene Fowler Jr.'s *The Oregon Trail* (20th Century–Fox, 1959).

4381

Mayor: You know, a smart man who is handy with words, he's a tough opponent. But when he starts to smear you with the truth, he's deadly!

Mayor Nard Lundy played by Edward Andrews: Jean Yarbrough's *The Over-the-Hill Gang* (TVW, 1969).

4382

Male Old Folk: This telegram just came for you!

Female Old Folk: Somebody's dead.

Male Old Folk: It don't have a black border.

The male Old Folks Home Resident played by Burt Mustin and the female Old Folks Home Resident played by Almira Sessions: Jean Yarbrough's *The Over-the-Hill Gang* (TVW, 1969).

4383

[*swearing in a pony express rider*]

Bob Jay: Raise your right hand. Now what did you say your name was?

Jimmy: Jimmy D. Richardson.

Bullfrog: You don't have to swear him in way the hell out here, Jay!

Bob Jay played by Slim Pickens, Jimmy D. Richardson played by Stewart Peterson, and Bullfrog Fry played by Ace Reid: Robert Totten's *Pony Express Rider* (Doty-Dayton, 1976).

4384

Wiley: Well boys, we're about to make ourselves famous. They'll be reading about us all over the territory.

Kern: Not from the obituaries, I hope.

Jack Wiley played by Paul Carr and Seymour Kern played by John Saxon: Herbert Coleman's *Posse from Hell* (Universal, 1961).

4385

Major Cobb: Now, read it back to me, Roy.

Roy: "If we are ever going to have law and order in this part of the country, we got to take vipers like those Fords and that slimy railroad detective Runyon and shoot 'em down like dogs."

Major Rufus Cobb, a newspaper publisher, played by Henry Hull. Roy played by George Chandler: Fritz Lang's *The Return of Frank James* (20th Century–Fox, 1940).

4386

Esqueda: The history of men will always be written in both blood and ink. You have written mine in ink. I will not flatter you by writing yours in blood.

Jose Esqueda played by Anthony Quinn: John Farrow's *Ride, Vaquero!* (MGM, 1953).

4387

Mona: I don't even know your name. I won't know who to look for in the obituary column.

Brown: Don't look. Just stick to the front page.

Mona Langley played by Beverly Garland and Hemp Brown played by Rory Calhoun: Richard Carlson's *The Sage of Hemp Brown* (Universal, 1958).

4388

John: Still haven't got a newspaper around here, huh?

Sheriff: No, but we do have a gossip about every twenty feet!

John Elder played by John Wayne and Sheriff Billy Wilson played by Paul Fix: Henry Hathaway's *The Sons of Katie Elder* (Paramount, 1965).

4389

Editor: Billy! Billy! Kill that story about the Republican Convention in Chicago and take this down! "The Ringo Kid was killed on Main Street in Lordsburg tonight! And among the additional dead were" …leave that blank for a spell.

Billy: I didn't hear any shootin', Ed.

Editor: You will, Billy, you will!

The Lordsburg Editor played by Robert E. Homans: John Ford's *Stagecoach* (United Artists, 1939).

4390

The early west saw crime and lawlessness triumphant. Vital information could travel no faster than a horse could run. A system capable of welding the scattered law-enforcing bodies was needed. This system was the telegraph.

Prologue: George Sherman's *The Trail Blazers* (Republic, 1940).

4391

Hank: The old Wells Fargo Company sure done its part in opening up the west. Some people goes as far as to say that it

DOWN MEXICO WAY
Gene AUTRY and SMILEY BURNETTE

A REPUBLIC PICTURE

Upon learning from Juan (Duncan Renaldo) that he has nothing to report, Pancho (Harold Huber) quips, "the next time there's nothing to be done, I do it myself." Gene Autry (himself) and sidekick Frog Millhouse (Smiley Burnette) look on in *Down Mexico Way* (Republic, 1941).

helped keep the United States united. But now we got trains running across the country, and we got the telegraph. Now, some folks seem to think that the telegraph is helping to keep country united. But I kind of hate to think that these United States was just held together by a bunch of wire.

Hank York played by Bob Burns: Frank Lloyd's *Wells Fargo* (Paramount, 1937).

4392

Vance: He says you come in peace today. But there won't be any peace if you try to take the singing wire through the Oglala nation.

Creighton: Well, tell him that the great white father who speaks with lightning over the singing wire is sorry for the wounding of his Indian son. But the

lightning talk is strong medicine and it must go through.

Vance Shaw played by Randolph Scott and Edward Creighton played by Dean Jagger: Fritz Lang's *Western Union* (20th Century–Fox, 1941).

4393

Wallace: Whiteside, you're a drunk newspaper editor! One thing I hate is a drunk newspaper editor …or a sober one!

Wallace played by Walter Sande and Whiteside played by Wallace Ford: Jacques Tourneur's *Wichita* (Allied Artists/Warner Bros., 1955).

4394

Hugh: Bob, I recall the time that me and Caleb here was carrying dispatches for an …

Doc: That was, ah, Phil Sheridan, I recall.

Hugh: Yeah, General Phil Sheridan. We was crossing through some hostile Indian country. And we got jumped on by a band of forty Cheyenne.

Caleb: And thirty Arapaho and two Ute.

Hugh: And old Caleb here, he took care of thirteen of them Cheyenne with those two pistols you see hanging there right there in that belt. And understand, Bob, he only fired twelve shots. Now one of 'em went through two of those Indians and killed 'em both.

Caleb: It had probably gone on and killed another one except there weren't any left. We had all killed them all by that time.

Hugh Cardiff played by Sam Elliott, Doc Bogardus played by Ben Johnson, Caleb Rice played by Timothy Scott, and Bob Halburton (correspondent) played by Pat Hingle: Richard Compton's *Wild Times* (TVW, 1980).

4395

Doc: From what I read in the newspaper, you're worth $2,000.00 ...alive or dead.

Hugh: Man, I always knew I'd amount to something!

Doc Holliday played by Dennis Hopper and Hugh Cardiff played by Sam Elliott: Richard Compton's *Wild Times* (TVW, 1980).

4396

(Billy the Kid dictating letter to Governor)

Dear Governor Axtell: I've heard that you will give $200 for my head. Perhaps we should meet and talk. I am at the Juarez village at the border. Send three men and instruct them not to shoot as I am unarmed. In short, sir, I surrender. Your obedient servant, William H. Bonney.

[*and then upon reflection*]

P.S. I changed my mind. Kiss my ass!

William H. "Billy" Bonney played by Emilio Estevez: Christopher Cain's *Young Guns* (20th Century–Fox, 1988).

4397

Pat: I want to hire you for a job.

Ash: You do?

Pat: I want you to document the hunt for the most famous man in New Mexico. I want a book written on it ...so the people will understand the situation. I want you to ride along with me and record the dangers of the expedition.

Ash: Ride along with ya? On a horse? No, this I can't do. I come out west to save my last lung. I'm a journalist.

Pat: You're a broke journalist. And you're a drunk!

Pat Garrett played by William Petersen and Ashmun Upson played by Jack Kehoe: Geoff Murphy's *Young Guns II* (20th Century–Fox, 1990).

Outlaws, Cattle Rustlers, and Horse Thieves

See also Bad Guys; Gunfighters; Holdups

4398

Sam: That Marshall girl and her gang jumped us again. They stampeded the herd and winged Jack.

Matt: Did you save anything?

Sam: No, you can't dodge bullets and chase cattle at the same time.

Sam played by Pierce Lyden and Matt Conroy played by Roy Barcroft: Thomas Carr's *Alias Billy the Kid* (Republic, 1946).

4399

Quirt: He swung a wide loop in his younger days, I think.

Penny: Wide loop?

Quirt: He wasn't too careful whose calf he threw his rope at.

Quirt Evans played by John Wayne and Prudence "Penny" Worth played by Gail Russell: James Edward Grant's *Angel and the Badman* (Republic, 1947).

4400

Maria: From here south is the territorial bandoleros.

Dee: Well, what's that? Territorial bandoleros?

Maria: Bandit country. They kill every gringo they can find.

Dee: You don't look too worried.

Maria: I am not a gringo.

Maria Stoner played by Raquel Welch and Dee Bishop played by Dean Martin: Andrew McLaglen's *Bandolero!* (20th Century–Fox, 1968).

4401

Adams: The bolder the outlaw, the more brazen his actions.

Richard Adams played by Robert Mitchum: Lesley Selander's *Bar 20* (United Artists, 1943).

4402

Doc: We heard tale about an outlaw that was on the loose. So we just followed the trail of shot-up saloons and worn-out posses.

Doc Butcher played by Walter Brennan: William D. Russell's *Best of the Badmen* (RKO, 1951).

4403

The history of the west was written with the blood of men both good and bad. In 1880 the last frontier was being won to the music of six-shooters on the cattle range. At this time, and into this stirring scene, there rode a young outlaw who lived his violent hour in defiance of an advancing civilization. His name has gone down in legend as "Billy the Kid."

Prologue to David Miller's *Billy the Kid* (MGM, 1941).

4404

Jim: Don't you get fed up sometimes?

Billy: Fed up with what?

Jim: Oh, rollin' around like a tumbleweed, being hunted, and never knowin' who's behind the next rock. I mean ...

Billy: I know what you mean. I like it!

Jim Sherwood played by Brian Donlevy and Billy the Kid played by Robert Taylor: David Miller's *Billy the Kid* (MGM, 1941).

4405

Dan: Nobody quits my outfit ...and stays healthy!

Billy: Which one of you guys wants to start making me unhealthy?

Dan Hickey played by Gene Lockhart and Billy the Kid played by Robert Taylor: David Miller's *Billy the Kid* (MGM, 1941).

4406

Thus, as the ways of law came to the last frontier, the last of the men of violence found his peace.

Epilogue to David Miller's *Billy the Kid* (MGM, 1941).

4407

Alacran: I should kill you for letting him get past you. But I have a feeling I'm gonna need all my men ...even a piece of shit like you. Cut off his ear!

Alacran played by Robert Davi: Richard Spence's *Blind Justice* (HBO Home Video, 1994).

4408

Luther: He and his bunch are the worst cutthroats in this territory. And you got him, Mr. Duggan! Now you can collect the bounty on him.

Duggan: Bounty?

Luther: Seddon has a $250.00 price on his head.

Duggan: $250.00? Not bad! But, ah, how do they grade men out here? Who fixes the price?

Luther: It depends on how much in demand their heads are, I reckon. The more you're wanted by the law, the higher the prices. It's like buying meat at the market, really. Except in here, it's the worst that gets the best price.

Luther played by Fuzzy Knight and Willie Duggan played by Dan Duryea: Spencer G. Bennet's *The Bounty Killer* (Embassy/Premiere, 1965).

4409

Butch: Listen, what do I call …what is your name anyway?

Sundance: Longwell. Harry Longwell.

Butch: Longwell. That's not an outlaw name. You don't have an outlaw face either. You better do something about that.

Sundance: Yeah, like what?

Butch: I don't know. Get yourself a nice scar or grow a mustache. Something.

Sundance: I am growing a mustache!

Butch: Where?

Sundance: Right here, see?

Butch: How long have you been working on that?

Sundance: Not long.

Butch: How long?

Sundance: Not long. What's the difference? It's slow starting. Come on, are we going to rob something or not?

Butch Cassidy played by Tom Berenger and The Sundance Kid played by William Karr: Richard Lester's *Butch and Sundance: The Early Days* (20th Century–Fox, 1979).

4410

Butch: You don't know who I am?

Old Robber: No, I'm sorry, sir. I don't.

Butch: Well, I'm a fairly well known outlaw.

Old Robber: Oh?

Butch: Maybe not so much around these parts here, but …ah …Utah, Wyoming.

Old Robber: I believe I have heard of you! Mr. …ah …

Butch: Cassidy.

Old Robber: Cassidy! That's right! Dutch Cassidy!

Butch Cassidy played by Tom Berenger and the Old Robber played by Peter Brocco: Richard Lester's *Butch and Sundance: The Early Days* (20th Century–Fox, 1979).

4411

Sheriff: You're out of prison for one week and you come back to Brown's Hole! Get the hell out of here! Get a job or something! And stay out of trouble!

Butch: I don't want a job, Ray. That kind of life doesn't suit me.

Sheriff: Damn it, what about your promise to the Governor?

Butch: That was Wyoming.

Sheriff: Oh, and this is Utah! Is that it?

Butch: Yeah, that's right.

Sheriff: You might have the decency to think about me! I don't want to arrest you again. It would be too damn embarrassing!

Butch: Okay, Ray, same deal. I'll stay out of your jurisdiction.

Sheriff: How many places can you promise to stay out of?

Butch: It's a big country.

Sheriff Ray Bledsoe played by Jeff Corey and Butch Cassidy played by Tom Berenger: Richard Lester's *Butch and Sundance: The Early Days* (20th Century–Fox, 1979).

4412

Butch: Boy, you know every time I see Hole-in-the-Wall again, it's like seeing it fresh for the first time. And every time that happens, I keep asking myself the same question: how could I be so damn stupid as to keep coming back here?

Butch Cassidy played by Paul Newman: George Roy Hill's *Butch Cassidy and the Sundance Kid* (20th Century–Fox, 1969).

4413

Maddox: Tell me, in your wide circle of acquaintances, would there be any rustlers?

Graycoe: Some of my best friends!

Maddox played by Walter Sande and Graycoe played by Robert Wilke: Harmon Jones' *Canyon River* (Allied Artists, 1956).

4414

Parnell: Kill him? Kid, you don't know what you're talking about. I may be an outlaw, but I've never murdered anybody in cold blood …and least of all an hombre!

Smoke Parnell played by James Gammon: Reynaldo Villalobos' *Conagher* (Turner Pictures, 1991).

4415

Weatherby: But Marshal! This …this outlaw, if you don't arrest him, I shall.

Wild Bill: Outlaw! Let me tell you something, son. This ain't Boston. We had a war down here and you'll find men in high offices who are thieves and cutthroats. You'll find others who are branded outlaws that are only fighting for what's their own. There's those known as bad men and those as are bad men. You better learn to tell the difference!

Martin Weatherby played by Leif Erickson and Wild Bill Hickok played by Reed Hadley: Stuart Heisler's *Dallas* (Warner Bros., 1950).

4416

Captain: I'll take the horse. Don't be a fool, Mr. Forbes. Turn around! Alive, you can still walk. Dead, you can only lay down.

Captain Jefferson Addis played by John Anderson and Owen Forbes played by Arthur Kennedy: Jerry Thorpe's *Day of the Evil Gun* (MGM, 1968).

4417

McCay: You know, I've always felt that horse thieves ought to be treated like treasure …buried with care and affection.

Payton McCay played by Bruce Dern: Alan J. Levi's *Dead Man's Revenge* (MCA/Universal Home Video, 1994).

4418

Ray: Didn't you hear what I said? He's Sam Garrett! He's killed twenty men! He'll kill that many more if somebody doesn't stop him. Stopping a man like that isn't just a job for the law. It's a job for every man who wants to live in peace …for every man who wants law and order to come back to Texas.

Tom: And for every man who wants to save his hide and collect $10,000 bounty! Stop making righteous speeches, Ray!

Ray Novack played by Rayford Barnes and Tom Cameron played by James J. Lydon: Thomas Carr's *The Desperado* (Allied Artists, 1954).

4419

Sam: A fella in my boots can't go liking anybody …and stay alive. You start worrying about somebody else and you forget about yourself.

Sam Garrett played by Wayne Morris: Thomas Carr's *The Desperado* (Allied Artists, 1954).

4420

McCall: Where are you headed?

Cates: Nowhere in particular. Just need to make some fast money.

McCall: I'm needing the same thing. Maybe we ought to go visit your friend, Sikes.

Cates: Well, that's not a bad idea. John is always looking for an extra gun or two.

McCall: Why is that?

Cates: Because the old ones keep getting killed.

Duell McCall played by Alex McArthur and Charlie Cates played by Whip Hubley: E.W. Swackhamer's *Desperado: The Outlaw Wars* (TVW, 1989).

4421

And so ended the Doolin Gang. The trails they rode were of their own choosing.

Part of the epilogue: Gordon Douglas' *The Doolins of Oklahoma* (Columbia, 1949).

4422

Holland: Moses, I want you to get these foolish ideas of Billy the Kid out of your head, huh? Oh, he could maybe take a life, but he could never live one.

Handsome Harry H. Holland played by Kirk Douglas and Moses played by Jason Michas: Steven H. Stern's *Draw!* (TVW, 1984).

4423

Zack: Tell me something, Mr. Jarred. How many states would you say you're wanted in?

Joe: How many states are there, Mr. Thomas?

Zack: Suppose I could get you a pardon in Texas?

Joe: For how much?

Zack: $100,000.

Joe: Oh, I give you $100,000 and you'll get me a pardon, right? You know, in most states I could buy a pardon for $5,000, and they would throw in a governor.

Zack: Of course, you must be thinking of Rhode Island. This is Texas. And here your life goes with it!

Zack Thomas played by Frank Sinatra and Joe

Jarrett played by Dean Martin: Robert Aldrich's *Four for Texas* (Warner Bros., 1964).

4424

Buchanan: The James-Younger Gang has become an itch I can't scratch. I want to see them killed!

Buchanan, the Railroad C.E.O., played by Dennis Letts: Robert Boris' *Frank & Jesse* (Vidmark Entertainment, 1995).

4425

Murphy: You know, Jesse is an outlaw …a bandit. And yet he still captures the imagination of the country. I admit it baffles me.

Frank: It baffles me too.

Annie: You mean you're surprised that America isn't ashamed of him?

Murphy: Yes, ma'am. Exactly.

Annie: Well, maybe it's because he's bold and lawless like everybody wants to be just for a little while.

Frank: You'll have to forgive my wife. She's educated.

Zack Murphy played by Sean Patrick Flanery, Frank James played by Bill Paxton, Annie played by Dana Wheeler-Nicholson, and Jesse James played by Rob Lowe: Robert Boris' *Frank & Jesse* (Vidmark Entertainment, 1995).

4426

Amanda: I never heard of the Buck Bowers Gang until today.

Graham: Well, that's because old Buck is shrewd. You know, the more famous a gang gets, the sooner they get caught. So whenever we pull a job, we blame it on the Jameses or the Daltons.

Amanda: But they'll go down in history and you'll be unremembered.

Graham: Who cares about history?

Amanda Starbuck played by Jill Ireland and Graham Dorsey played by Charles Bronson: Frank D. Gilroy's *From Noon Till Three* (United Artists, 1976).

4427

Frank: I'm tired of moving from house to house, town to town, city to city. I'm tired of running and dodging. I'm tired of being a thief. Jess, we've never enjoyed one cent of the money we've stolen. Well, I'm through. Mary and I are going to Europe. When we come back, I'm going to settle down in one place. I want to be able to look people in the eye. I want to be able to look at my wife.

Frank James played Wendell Corey, Jesse James played by Macdonald Carey, and Mary Bauer James played by Lois Chartrand: Gordon Douglas' *The Great Missouri Raid* (Paramount, 1951).

4428

Even before the wounds of the Civil War had healed in Missouri, the railroads came swarming in to steal the land. Everywhere men from the railroads were driving poor, defenseless families from their homes. And that's when a fresh wind suddenly began to blow. It was other Clay County farmers, the James and Younger boys, coming to the rescue. They tarred and feathered the railroad men, and drove them from the land. From that moment onward, they were outlaws. But the people of Missouri would never forget what the boys had done for them.

Prologue: Philip Kaufman's *The Great Northfield, Minnesota Raid* (Universal, 1972).

4429

Chief Detective: Legislators are here to make laws. We're here to make examples. They're supposed to think that fifteen years of criminal behavior can be legislated away. But in the event this amnesty does come into being, we'll already have done our duty. They'll enjoy their amnesty in the hereafter.

The Chief Detective of the Pinkerton Agency played by Herbert Nelson: Philip Kaufman's *The Great Northfield, Minnesota Raid* (Universal, 1972).

4430

Bill: Are you going to help us steal 'em [horses]? I didn't think so. You're real good at figuring out the angles but …you don't have much stomach for the risky parts, do you?

Jack: Well, that's how come I spend more time outside of prison than in it.

Bill Miner played by Richard Farnsworth and Jack Budd played by Ken Pogue: Phillip Borsos' *The Grey Fox* (United Artists, 1982).

4431

Slayton: You shouldn't judge a man by his face. Curly has been a thief and an outlaw since he was fifteen.

Frank Slayton played by Phil Carey and Curly Jordan played by Robert Herron: Raoul Walsh's *Gun Fury* (Columbia, 1953).

4432

Linda: Jesus, Frank, is there any scum in this entire country you haven't run with?

Linda Yarnell played by Kay Lenz and Frank Morgan played by Lance Henriksen: Larry Ferguson's *Gunfighter's Moon* (Rysher Entertainment/ Cabin Fever Entertainment, 1995).

4433

Judge: Stealing a man's horse in this country is worse than stealing his wife. There has been too much of that thing going on, and I'm gonna put a stop to it.

Keno: Horse stealing or wife stealing, Judge?

The Judge was uncredited and Keno played by Monte Markham: Paul Wendkos' *Guns of the Magnificent Seven* (United Artists, 1969).

4434

Cobb: There ain't no question about it. Jesse was an outlaw, a bandit, a criminal. Even those that loved him ain't got no answer to that. But we ain't ashamed of him. I don't know why, but I don't think even America is ashamed of Jesse James. Maybe it's because he was bold and lawless like we all of us like to be sometimes. Maybe it's because we understand a little that he wasn't altogether to blame …for what his times made him. Maybe it's because for ten years he licked the tar out of five states. Or maybe it's because he was so good at what he was doing. I don't know. All I do know is he was one of the dog-gonest, gal-dingest, dag-blamest buckaroos that ever rode across these United States of America!

Mayor Rufus Cobb (also Editor/Publisher of the Liberty Weekly Gazette) played by Henry Hull: Henry King's *Jesse James* (20th Century–Fox, 1939).

4435

Zee: Oh Jesse, listen. It isn't only now, although this is bad enough. It's what's going to happen to you …inside of you. Do you understand? I mean, right now you are a hero to yourself and to a lot of other people too. It's the fight you're in, and it's the railroad that started it. But that's not going to last, Jesse. The more luck you have, the worse you'll get. The shooting and robbing and …it will get in your blood, Jesse. You'll get like a wolf: just doing it because it's your nature. That'll be your appetite for shooting and robbing until something happens to you. And if anything ever happened to you, Jesse, it would be like it was happening to me too. Oh darling, there's only one way out. Come in! Give up!

Zee played by Nancy Kelly and Jesse James played by Tyrone Power: Henry King's *Jesse James* (20th Century–Fox, 1939).

4436

Reese: Molly always did think outlaws were romantic.

Bick: Can I tell you something? Of all the things that I stole, it wouldn't make the pile big enough that would stop a midget from jumping over it.

Reese Ford played by Warren Oates and Bickford Wanner, alias Kid Blue, played by Dennis Hopper: James Frawley's *Kid Blue* (20th Century–Fox, 1973).

4437

Narrator: All over New Mexico, the country was swarming with posses. From the Pecos to the Rio Grande, from Santa Fe south to the San Andreas peaks, grim men were in the saddle in one of the biggest manhunts in the history of the West. But Billy the Kid was still at large. As the weeks passed, and as his reputation spread, he even managed to attract a handful of followers. But the sands were running low.

Narration: Kurt Neumann's *The Kid from Texas* (Universal, 1950).

4438

Narrator: Historians have called him a bandit, ballad-makers a Robin Hood. But after seventy years the fairest verdict was probably that of the humble Mexicans who buried him …who called him simply el Cabrito …the Kid …and left his final judgment to God.

Narration: Kurt Neumann's *The Kid from Texas* (Universal, 1950).

4439

Tex: Which side are the horse thieves on?
Cannonball: Both of 'em, I reckon.

Tex Rawlings played by Tex Ritter and Cannonball played by Dub Taylor: Lambert Hillyer's *King of Dodge City* (Columbia, 1941).

4440

Mother: If Jim Plummer wants to be an outlaw that's all right with me, you know that. Your pa was an outlaw …until he got killed. And if I had a son, I reckon he'd follow the same trail. And welcomed. But Jim ain't got no money saved up.
Daughter: Outlaws don't generally save up money, do they Ma?
Mother: That's what I'm driving at. You wait, you just wait until the law gets a breathin' down your neck. You'll wish Jim had a pile of bank notes so you could make a getaway. Have yourself a little security.

Kate's Mother played by Virginia Brissac, Kate Foley played by Adrian Booth, and Jim Plummer played by Forrest Tucker: Joseph Kane's *The Last Bandit* (Republic, 1949).

4441

Frank: It's a tiresome weight. I can't go to the privy without these [guns]. I can't sleep a single night without hearing a twig crackling, a leaf rustling. I hear the softest footsteps.
Wood: You've been doing it nineteen years. You can't hate it all that much.
Frank: I'm strictly surviving. Nineteen years without a home. And I'm looking for a way out of it, not a way to bring more relatives into it.

Frank James played by Johnny Cash and Wood Hite played by Peter Bradshaw: William A. Graham's *The Last Days of Frank and Jesse James* (TVW, 1986).

4442

Hamilton: Look, Bruce, you did me a favor. I'm going to do you one. I'm telling you to get out. Get out quick. Or the only land you'll own will be on top of you.

Ted Hamilton played by James Best and Dan Barton, alias Jack Bruce, played by George Mont-

gomery: Paul Landres' *Last of the Badmen* (Allied Artists, 1957).

4443

Forbes: Nothing grieves a man so much as seeing a thief rewarded with the money he himself has stolen.

John Forbes played by Carl Benton Reid: George Sherman's *The Last of the Fast Guns* (Universal, 1958).

4444

Lute: Who's your friend downstairs?
Frame: A business acquaintance from Kansas.
Lute: Now what kind of business?
Frame: He dealt in cattle. Other people's cattle.
Denver: That gives a high margin of profit.
Frame: That will give a high rate of mortality, too!

Lute Johnson played by Alex Nicol, Frame Johnson played by Ronald Reagan, and Denver Cahoon played by Chubby Johnson: Nathan Juran's *Law and Order* (Universal, 1953).

4445

Dan: Grant's coming out here. He's going to hunt buffalo and make speeches. Everybody in the whole town is going to turn out there and wave little flags at him. Me? I'd like to piss on him!
John: He's the President of the United States!
Dan: He's a liar and a drunk! Piss on the President! Piss on the Cabinet! They ain't gonna help us out here, you know. In Texas, robbers are outlaws. In Washington, robbers are elected.

Dan Reid played by John Bennett Perry and John Reid played by Klinton Spilsbury: William A. Fraker's *The Legend of the Lone Ranger* (Universal, 1981).

4446

Jake: I ain't been but a day and already you boys are making a damn horse thief out of me.
Gus: Why, that's a step up for you, ain't it, Jake?

Jake Spoon played by Robert Urich and Gus McCrae played by Robert Duvall: Simon Wincer's *Lonesome Dove* (TVW, 1989).

4447

Cole: You know, Frank, when I'm older I think I'll write me a book …and make myself even more famous than I am.
Frank: If a pig had wings it would fly.

Cole Younger played by David Carradine and Frank James played by Stacy Keach: Walter Hill's *The Long Riders* (United Artists, 1980).

4448

Rixley: What do you and your brothers think about a life sentence? I mean, you're lucky they don't allow hanging in this state. Come on, Cole, tell me what you think about all this.

Cole: Ah, hell, we played a rough game …and we lost.

Mr. Rixley played by James Whitmore, Jr. and Cole Younger played by David Carradine: Walter Hill's *The Long Riders* (United Artists, 1980).

4449

Calvera: We have a saying here: a thief who steals from a thief is pardoned for 100 years.

Calvera played by Eli Wallach: John Sturges' *The Magnificent Seven* (United Artists, 1960).

4450

Calvera: You'll do much better on the other side of the border. There you can steal cattle, hold up trains. All you have to face is the sheriff or Marshal. Once I robbed a bank in Texas. Your government got after me with a whole army. A whole army! One little bank! It's clear the meaning: in Texas, only Texans can rob banks!

Calvera played by Eli Wallach: John Sturges' *The Magnificent Seven* (United Artists, 1960).

4451

Outlaw: I don't like that, Sein. It's bad luck to plug padres. They're not worth a cent.
Sein: Any priest who buddies up with an outlaw, I automatically excommunicate him …and ordain myself!

The Outlaw was uncredited and Sein played by Antonio Molino Rojo: Franco Giraldi's *A Minute to Pray, a Second to Die* (Selmur/Cinerama, 1967).

4452

Colby: So you really want to chuck this life, huh?
Clay: That's right.
Colby: You mean it?
Clay: Hand on the Bible.
Colby: You ever read it?
Clay: A little.

Marshal Roy Colby played by Arthur Kennedy and Clay McCord played by Alex Cord: Franco Giraldi's *A Minute to Pray, a Second to Die* (Selmur/Cinerama, 1967).

4453

Escondido
If You Ain't Wanted
Mister
You Ain't Wanted

A sign outside a western town: Franco Giraldi's *A Minute to Pray, a Second to Die* (Selmur/Cinerama, 1967).

4454

Logan: The first time I met Sandy, he was rustling on his own. He had a stolen cavalry pony and he kept this dog. As soon as he would kill a steer, why he'd cut the brand off and feed it to the dog. So before they could get enough evidence to convict him, they'd have to lock that dog up and pick through his shit for a week before they could find the brand.

Tom Logan played by Jack Nicholson and Sandy played by Hunter Von Leer: Arthur Penn's *The Missouri Breaks* (United Artists, 1976).

4455

Charlie: Why must you steal?

Utica Kid: Because I like to steal! Maybe I like to see what people will do when I take it away from them.

Charlie: What happens when something is taken away from you?

The Utica Kid played by Audie Murphy and Charlotte "Charlie" Drew played by Dianne Foster: James Neilson's *Night Passage* (Universal, 1957).

4456

Dan: If I told you once, I told you a hundred times: never trust a woman! See what I mean. She's nothing but a thief!

Doc: Now wait a minute! We stole that herd from her in the first place!

Dan: Well, that's different. We stole them fair and square. She cheats!

Dan Casey played by Dan Rowan and Doc Henry Logan played by Dick Martin: Hal Kanter's *Once Upon a Horse* (Universal, 1958).

4457

Hayes: They're awful young.

John Henry: And every one of 'em would shoot a man just to see him fall. Outlawing ain't what it used to be.

Hayes: It never was, John Henry.

Oren Hayes played by Richard Widmark and John Henry Lee played by Willie Nelson: Burt Kennedy's *Once Upon a Texas Train* (TVW, 1988).

4458

Governor: Aren't you a little old to go running around chasing an outlaw?

Hayes: Well, ain't he a little old to go running around robbing banks?

The Governor played by Kevin McCarthy and Oren Hayes played by Richard Widmark: Burt Kennedy's *Once Upon a Texas Train* (TVW, 1988).

4459

The Outlaw is a story of the untamed West. Frontier days when the reckless fire of guns and passions blazed an era of death, destruction, and lawlessness. Days when the fiery desert sun beat down avengingly on the many who dared defy justice and outrage decency.

Prologue: Howard Hughes' *The Outlaw* (United Artists, 1943).

4460

Doc: Sonny, that head of yours is sure screwed on tight.

Billy: If it wasn't, somebody would have knocked it off long ago.

Doc Holliday played by Walter Huston and Billy the Kid played by Jack Buetel: Howard Hughes' *The Outlaw* (United Artists, 1943).

4461

Billy: How does it feel?

Pat: It feels like times have changed.

Billy: Times maybe …but not me.

Billy the Kid played by Kris Kristofferson and Pat Garrett played by James Coburn: Sam Peckinpah's *Pat Garrett and Billy the Kid* (MGM, 1973).

4462

Druin: It's easy for a man to get on the run. A few crossed words, a fast draw. One man's dead, and the other is on the run.

John Druin played by Rod Cameron: Joseph Kane's *The Plunderers* (Republic, 1948).

4463

Tank: Bad Shad, they call him. He got his reputation killing six men in a bank holdup. Of course, as it turned out, three of 'em were innocent bystanders but that don't make no difference.

Tank Logan played by Brian Keith and Lawman Shadrack Peltzer played by Cameron Mitchell: Lee H. Katzin's *The Quest* (TVW, 1976).

4464

Tevis: And you, Yancy! You're a one-horse horse thief!

Tevis played by Jack Elam and Yancy played by Dean Jagger: Henry Hathaway's *Rawhide* (20th Century–Fox, 1951).

4465

Dalton: Why don't you get rid of him?

Doolin: He's a good man …so long as you keep him in front of ya.

Bob Dalton played by Walter Reed and Wild Bill Doolin played by Robert Armstrong: Ray Enright's *Return of the Badmen* (RKO, 1948).

4466

Vance: Look, kid, there's nothing smart about being outside the law. It just means that you haven't got the brains or the courage to keep in step with the rest of the people.

Vance played by Randolph Scott: Ray Enright's *Return of the Badmen* (RKO, 1948).

4467

Cheyenne: Well, we did all right yesterday.

Vance: Sure, you did great! You got a little quick money and a bullet hole in your arm. The next time, you'll pick up a little more gold and a little more lead. And pretty soon, if you play your cards right, you can be one of the richest outlaws buried in Boot Hill!

Cheyenne played by Anne Jeffreys and Vance played by Randolph Scott: Ray Enright's *Return of the Badmen* (RKO, 1948).

4468

Jim: I guess we fooled those outlaws by taking this trail, Curly.

Curly: Maybe, but I ain't sure of nothin' except death and taxes.

Jim (Stage Gun Guard) was uncredited and Curly (Stage Driver) played by Britt Wood: Derwin

Abrahams' *The Return of the Durango Kid* (Columbia, 1945).

4469

Rio: Here's a gift, Padre. It's money.

Father: Stolen money.

Rio: Turn it into bread. No one asks where bread comes from.

Rio played by Robert Taylor and Father Antonio played by Kurt Kasznar: John Farrow's *Ride, Vaquero!* (MGM, 1953).

4470

Herrick: There's an old proverb: set a thief to catch a thief.

Herrick played by Bruce Bennett: Sidney Salkow's *Robbers' Roost* (United Artists, 1955).

4471

Helen: Why do your songs seem to be so sad?

Happy Jack: They come to me in a sad way. From my grandfather who was buried over the matter of a horse …to my father who lost a race with a sheriff's posse. Now there is no one left but me to sing them.

Helen played by Sylvia Findley and Happy Jack played by Tony Romano: Sidney Salkow's *Robbers' Roost* (United Artists, 1955).

4472

J.C.: You know, I never rightly figured how much we're worth.

Deaks: Three thousand for you …five thousand for me.

J.C.: Kind of makes us a success, don't it?

Deaks: Not yet. We're not dead!

J.C. played by Robert Donner and Deaks played by Robert Wilke: Gary Nelson's *Santee* (Crown International Pictures, 1973).

4473

Boss: I told you that there was something funny about them two. And I ain't forgetting it was you two that busted 'em out of jail, and brought em into this gang. And vouched for em!

Ed: I didn't vouch for 'em! He did!

Sam: How could I vouch? I don't even know what it means!

The Boss played by Jack Elam, Ed played by Dick Peabody, and Sam played by Gene Evans: Burt Kennedy's *Sidekicks* (TVW, 1974).

4474

Spikes: Boys, I'm going to be your deliverance and salvation. Now, don't ask me why I'm doing it. It don't make no sense. God knows I could get a dozen better [men] out of any saloon down the street. But you got some spirit, and you got some crawl. And where I come from, you harness a mule but you give a horse a chance to run. How would you boys like to throw in with me?

Harry Spikes played by Lee Marvin: Richard Fleischer's *The Spikes Gang* (United Artists, 1974).

4475

Henry: I hear you're pretty good at robbing banks. Is that right?

Billy: I wouldn't know. I've never robbed a bank.

Henry: Oh, I see. And where do you suppose I got the idea that's what you do for a living?

Billy: Probably in one of them books you read.

Henry: Well, what do you do?

Billy: Mind my own business. You ought to try it sometime.

Henry: Why?

Billy: It's not near as dangerous as the way you're living now.

Henry Gatewood played by Tony Franciosa and Billy "Ringo" Williams played by Kris Kristofferson: Ted Post's *Stagecoach* (TVW, 1986).

4476

Jeff: A wanted man can't be choosy. He stays where they let him …and travels fast when they don't.

Jeff Travis played by Randolph Scott: Andre De Toth's *The Stranger Wore a Gun* (Columbia, 1953).

4477

Tennessee: Hopefully speaking, we're what you might call cattle separators.

Thomas: What?

Tennessee: Don't you savvy? We separate the cattle from the owners.

Tennessee played by Andrew Tombes and Dan Thomas played by William Holden: George Marshall's *Texas* (Columbia, 1941).

4478

Father: The odds are pretty good that this generous old heart of mine is gonna stop ticking mighty soon now. But before I go, I want to make sure that there is a good price on your heads. You worry me, my son. For years now you've been dragging your ass around in that litter. You still got no trade. You're a good card sharp, I hear, but I never see you with a deck of cards. I'd advise you to go on to horse rustlin'. It's a fine and difficult profession. You don't become a good horse thief overnight, you know.

The Father played by Harry Carey Jr.: E.B. Clucher's (Enzo Barboni) *Trinity Is Still My Name* (West Film/Avco Embassy, 1971).

4479

Ma: As time passes, a mother gets to wondering about her two boys. Are they married? Are they plowing their own land? Or are they still gambling and stealing horses?

Ma played by Ruth Buzzi: Terence Hill's *The Troublemakers* (Rialto Film, 1994).

4480

Janie: You're always spittin' and fightin'. Just what do you expect our young ones to grow up into?

Moses: Bounty hunters.

Moses Jr.: What about rustling horses, Pa?

Janie played by Radha Delamarter, Moses played by Bud Spencer, and Moses Jr. played by Jonathan Tucker: Terence Hill's *The Troublemakers* (Rialto Film, 1994).

4481

Remington: That's what I'm up against around here.

Lawyer: Yes …public opinion. Or better yet, public needs. Jesse James is the shooting spokesman for everyone whose life is quietly desperate. To you, he's a thief. To these people, he's already becoming a legend. One that kindles a fire in their hearts. They want him to go on.

Remington: Are you trying to tell me that nothing can be done?

Lawyer: Mr. Remington, you can't change public opinion when it suits you. When the public no longer needs Jesse James, that will be the end of him.

Remington played by Alan Baxter and Lawyer Walker played by Barry Atwater: Nicholas Ray's *The True Story of Jesse James* (20th Century–Fox, 1957).

4482

Cole: Learn a lesson, Jesse. You can't eat your cake and have it too.

Jesse: Maybe so, Cole …but bread cast upon the waters comes back before many days.

Cole Younger played by Alan Hale, Jr., and Jesse James played by Robert Wagner: Nicholas Ray's *The True Story of Jesse James* (20th Century–Fox, 1957).

4483

Charlie: We're going to miss you, Jess.

Robby: We never will get a chance to ride with you now.

Jesse: You're not missing anything.

Charlie: Why, I always thought you enjoyed it.

Jesse: I did. The excitement …and being in command. But you never get a chance to relax. Look at me. Thirty-four years old and I feel like ninety.

Charlie: Well, I didn't know the lawmen bothered you that much.

Jesse: They didn't, but as the reward goes higher your friends grow fewer. They're either killed off or turn against you. Then you worry about the old ones who might be tempted by the rewards. Or the new ones who hope to get a reputation by putting a bullet in you.

Charlie Ford played by Frank Gorshin, Robby Ford played by Carl Thayler, and Jesse James played by Robert Wagner: Nicholas Ray's *The True Story of Jesse James* (20th Century–Fox, 1957).

4484

Virginian: Don't talk that away, Steve. You and I have done a lot of loco

things together. But there's some things that are not only loco, but plumb wrong.

Steve: Ah, you take life too seriously.

Virginian: This whole country is taking things more seriously. I'm not trying to lecture you, or play Sunday on what's right or wrong. But the ranchers are getting plumb sick of having their herds trimmed out. And there'll soon be posses out with ropes on their saddles. Times are changing, Steve, and they can't get away with this sort of thing much longer.

Steve: Well, I'm carrying a nice limber rope to make it easy for them …if they catch me.

The Virginian played by Gary Cooper and Steve played by Richard Arlen: Victor Fleming's *The Virginian* (Paramount, 1929).

4485

Virginian: I passed your herd the other day, Trampas. I ought to compliment you. You have so many calves this year. It seems like your cows don't have 'em just one at a time like nature intended. They have 'em in litters like a sow.

Trampas: What do you suggest I do about it?

Virginian: If I was you, I would have a little talk with them and get 'em back closer to nature.

Trampas: You're liable to talk yourself into a lot of trouble, my friend.

Virginian: Since when was I your friend, Trampas?

The Virginian played by Joel McCrea and Trampas played by Brian Donlevy: Stuart Gilmore's *The Virginian* (Paramount, 1946).

4486

Toward the end of the 19th Century in America, civilization surged ever west. And in its wake came that inseparable pair, INJUSTICE and CRIME. In the history of the reckless violence that seized Kansas and Oklahoma, no name carried more terror than DALTON. There was more famous outlaws, but none more daring, none more desperate.

Prologue: George Marshall's *When the Daltons Rode* (Universal, 1940).

4487

Bodine: Ordinarily, it ain't my policy to look on the sorry side. But if we was to get caught, we probably would have to do about five years in the penitentiary for bank robbery. Is that right?

Post: Maybe. Maybe more.

Bodine: Yeah, but for horse stealing, no maybe. They would hang ya right now!

Ross Bodine played by William Holden and Frank Post played by Ryan O'Neal: Blake Edwards *Wild Rovers* (MGM, 1971).

Frank Post (Ryan O'Neal) is a young cowboy and Ross Bodine (William Holden) is his older cowpunching friend. Between the two of them they have but a few dollars in their poke ...so they set out to rob a bank in Blake Edwards' *Rovers* (MGM, 1971).

People

See also Bad Guys; Cowboys; Good Guys; Men; Wild Women; Women

4488

Marshal: I saw a motto on a sundial once that said: it's always later than you think.

Marshal Dan Mitchell played by Randolph Scott: Edwin Marin's *Abilene Town* (United Artists, 1946).

4489

Ben: I wish people would stop calling me amigo. That always means that something bad is about to happen.

Ben played by Fred Williamson who also directed *Adios Amigo* (Atlas, 1975).

4490

Arabella: Grandpa used to say that people are 98% water. And if you don't stir them up once in awhile, they stagnate.

Arabella Flagg played by Susanne Pleshette: James Neilson's *The Adventures of Bullwhip Griffin* (Buena Vista, 1967).

4491

Quirt: Is that Quaker stuff?
Penny: Huh, huh.
Quirt: You mean nobody can hurt you but yourself?

Penny: That's a Friend's belief.
Quirt: Well, suppose someone whacks you over the head with a branding iron? Won't that hurt?
Penny: Physically, of course. But in reality it would injure only the person doing the act or force of violence. Only the doer can be hurt by a mean or evil act.
Quirt: Are there very many of you Quakers?
Penny: Very few.
Quirt: I sort of figured that.

Quirt Evans played by John Wayne and Prudence "Penny" Worth played by Gail Russell: James

Edward Grant's *Angel and the Badman* (Republic, 1947).

4492

Molly: Everybody hopes for something.
Travis: Nobody lives without hope.

Molly played by Marilyn Maxwell and Lee Travis played by Howard Keel: Lesley Selander's *Arizona Bushwhackers* (Paramount, 1968).

4493

Jeff: You're going to talk and I'm going to listen!

Jeff Welker played by Robert J. Wilke: John Sturges' *Backlash* (Universal, 1956).

4494

Big Joe: Damn, Jackson, I wouldn't mind you being stupid if you was good company. But you ain't even that!

Big Joe played by David Huddleston and Jackson played by Raymond Guth: Robert Benton's *Bad Company* (Paramount, 1972).

4495

Smith: Tim, you got the body of a hippo but the brain of a rabbit. Now, don't overtax it!

Reno Smith played by Robert Ryan and Sheriff Tim Horn played by Dean Jagger: John Sturges' *Bad Day at Black Rock* (MGM, 1955).

4496

Doc: Well, I'd feel for ya …but I'm consumed with apathy.

Doc Velie played by Walter Brennan: John Sturges' *Bad Day at Black Rock* (MGM, 1955).

4497

Henry: Well, Adam may have been a fool, but at least they had to throw him out of Paradise.

Henry Cliff played by Andy Clyde: Lew Landers' *Bad Lands* (RKO, 1939).

4498

Billy: They ain't really going to do all those things to Mr. McGraw, are they? I mean, he ain't hurt no one.
Dan: Son, sometimes all you have to do to make people fear you and hate you is to be a little different.

Billy Baker played by Lee Montgomery and Dan Baker played by Clint Walker: Lyman Dayton's *Baker's Hawk* (Doty/Dayton, 1976).

4499

Little Jo: Why can't we just live as we are?

Little Jo Monaghan played by Suzy Amis: Maggie Greenwald's *The Ballad of Little Jo* (Fine Line Features, 1993).

4500

Lily: Do what I tell you and you'll always go wrong.

Lily Fowler played by Claire Trevor: William D. Russell's *Best of the Badmen* (RKO, 1951).

4501

Rufus: The Hannasseys know and admire a real gentleman when they see one. And they recognize the high-toned skunk when they smell one!

Rufus Hannassey played by Burl Ives: William Wyler's *The Big Country* (United Artists, 1958).

4502

Major Terrill: If there's anything I admire more than a devoted friend, it is a dedicated enemy.

Major Henry Terrill played by Charles Bickford: William Wyler's *The Big Country* (United Artists, 1958).

4503

Leech: You know, McKay, you're a bigger fool that I thought you were. And to tell you the truth, that just didn't seem possible.

Steve Leech played by Charlton Heston and Jim McKay played by Gregory Peck: William Wyler's *The Big Country* (United Artists, 1958).

4504

Buford: That's a bargain all right. But a bargain ain't a bargain unless it's something you need.

Jesse Buford played by John Qualen: Fielder Cook's *A Big Hand for the Little Lady* (Warner Bros., 1966).

4505

Jacob: You're short on ears and long on mouth!

Jacob McCandles played by John Wayne: George Sherman's *Big Jake* (NGP, 1971).

4506

Elder: Violence is not in our creed.
Yukon: Yeah, I know. And I believe in turning the other cheek …but you just about run out of cheeks. It's time you start growing some religious muscle.

Walter "Yukon" Burns played by Edgar Buchanan and Elder Bixby played by Charles Meredith: Felix Feist's *The Big Trees* (Warner Bros., 1952).

4507

Billy: You know what my name is?
Esther: It's Billy.
Billy: No. I mean my other name.
Esther: No, what?
Billy: Two Hats.
Esther: Two Hats? Billy Two Hats? How did you get a name like that?
Billy: Well, my mother was a Kiowa and I don't know who my father was except that he was white. My mother didn't know too much about him neither except she told me he was kind of important. She said that in his room he had two hats: one for special and one for ordinary. That impressed my mother a whole lot. And when I was a kid it impressed me.

Billy played by Desi Arnaz, Jr., and Esther played by Sian Barbara Allen: Ted Kotcheff's *Billy Two Hats* (United Artists, 1973).

4508

Deans: You're old enough to be half as stupid.

Arch Deans played by Gregory Peck: Ted Kotcheff's *Billy Two Hats* (United Artists, 1973).

4509

Ketchum: You can find law and order in a town, all right. It's a little harder to find it in the people.

Tom "Blackjack" Ketchum played by Howard Duff: Earl Bellamy's *Blackjack Ketchum, Desperado* (Columbia, 1956).

4510

Canaan: Are you gonna wish me luck?
Sgt: Why don't you just go to hell!
Canaan: Well, that'll do.

Canaan played by Armand Assante and Sergeant Hastings played by Adam Baldwin: Richard Spence's *Blind Justice* (HBO Home Video, 1994).

4511

Duggan: So I'm not good enough to come to meeting! Just because I'm a bounty hunter. You miserable bunch of hypocrites! Do you know why I'm a bounty hunter? Because you good people pay me to do it! That's why! You can't do your own dirty work, but you can't wait to spit on the man who does it for you!

Willie Duggan played by Dan Duryea: Spencer G. Bennet's *The Bounty Killer* (Embassy/Premiere, 1965).

4512

Springer: Some people have no shame.
Maverick: That's because others have enough for everybody.

Mary Lou Springer played by Darleen Carr and Bret Maverick played by James Garner: Stuart Margolin's *Bret Maverick: The Lazy Ace* (TVW, 1981).

4513

Brigham Young: I'm not looking for an easy religion. I'm looking for one I can bring my family up decent in.

Brigham Young played by Dean Jagger: Henry Hathaway's *Brigham Young* (20th Century–Fox, 1940).

4514

Miss Lilly: Are you for real?
Bronco Billy: I'm who I want to be.

Antoinette Lilly played by Sondra Locke and Bronco Billy played by Clint Eastwood who also directed *Bronco Billy* (Warner Bros., 1980).

4515

Calamity: Now you've been my friend for a long time, Blue. But if you feel lower than the scum at the bottom of a pond right now, you got it comin'!

Calamity Jane played by Anjelica Huston and Teddy Blue played by Gabriel Byrne: Rod Hardy's *Buffalo Girls* (Cabin Fever Entertainment, 1995).

4516

Logan: Do you make it a habit of spying on people?
Linnet: No, but I got a habit of observing people.
Logan: Is that all you have to do?
Linnet: Well, Logan, you got a big store and no time. And I got a little store and lots of time.

Logan Stuart played by Dana Andrews and Hi Linnet played by Hoagy Carmichael: Jacques Tourneur's *Canyon Passage* (Universal, 1946).

4517

Jenny: Sometimes life is like a country and western song.

Jenny played by Sally Kirkland: Rod McCall's *Cheatin' Hearts* (Trimark Pictures, 1993).

4518

Chino: Well, like they say: you can always pick your friends, but you can't pick your relatives.

Chino played by Charles Bronson: John Sturges' *Chino* (Coral Film/Intercontinental Releasing Corporation, 1973).

4519

Mrs. Wyatt: One of my ancestors was the signer of the Declaration of Independence.
Sol Levy: That's all right. A relative of mine, a fellow named Moses, wrote the Ten Commandments.

Mrs. Tracy Wyatt played by Edna May Oliver and Sol Levy played by George E. Stone: Wesley Ruggles' *Cimarron* (RKO, 1931).

4520

Warden: Hate gets under a man's skin. It spoils his whole life. It's like a bad growth, kid. You got to get rid of it.

The Warden played by Frank Ferguson: Budd Boetticher's *The Cimarron Kid* (Universal, 1951).

4521

Cisco Kid: Hombre, do you know what they call a Mexican with a good horse and money over there?
Pancho: What?
Cisco Kid: A bandit.

The Cisco Kid played by Jimmy Smits and Pancho played by Cheech Marin: Luis Valdez's *The Cisco Kid* (Turner Pictures, 1994).

4522

Phil: If hate were people, I'd be China!

Phil Berquist played by Daniel Stern: Ron Underwood's *City Slickers* (Columbia, 1991).

4523

Mitch: I'm just a little petrified of heights …which is why I am not tall.

Mitch Robbins played by Billy Crystal: Paul Weiland's *City Slickers II: The Legend of Curly's Gold* (Columbia, 1994).

4524

Duke: You know, sometimes you don't know what you have until you don't have it anymore.

Duke Washburn played by Jack Palance: Paul Weiland's *City Slickers II: The Legend of Curly's Gold* (Columbia, 1994).

4525

Colorado: You can bust out of jail, maybe, or mud holes like I was in. But you can't bust out of what you are.
Wes: You can if you're set on it.
Colorado: Can ya? Me? I was born under a chuckwagon. Never got much higher. Anything was a step up. Even getting hit by Reno was all velvet.

Colorado Carson played by Virginia Mayo and Wes McQueen played by Joel McCrea: Raoul Walsh's *Colorado Territory* (Warner Bros., 1949).

4526

Doby: A man does one thing, one thing in his life he could look back on …go proud. That's enough. Anyway, that's what my pa used to say.
Frank: He talked all the time, didn't he?
Doby: Yeah. He was a good man. Sure is a shame.
Frank: Shame?
Doby: Yeah, my pa. He never did amount to anything.

Doby played by Richard Rust and Frank played by Skip Homeier: Budd Boetticher's *Comanche Station* (Columbia, 1960).

4527

Cutter: You think I'm simple minded.
Regret: Yes, I do think you're simple minded.
Cutter: Well, don't make a point of saying that too often. And once more would be too often!

Jake Cutter played by John Wayne and Paul Regret played by Stuart Whitman: Michael Curtiz's *The Comancheros* (20th Century–Fox, 1961).

4528

Flo: You'd get your pockets picked in a graveyard!

Flo played by Barbara Payton: Stuart Heisler's *Dallas* (Warner Bros., 1950).

4529

Jackson: You've been making quite a name for yourself in local politics.
Crockett: Soft soap ain't good for nothing but washing dirty hands, General.

General Andrew Jackson played by Basil Ruysdael and Davy Crockett played by Fess Parker: Norman Foster's *Davy Crockett, King of the Wild Frontier* (Buena Vista, 1955).

4530

Crockett: I've been doing some thinking.
Russell: Me too. You know, we're pretty far down the river. Ain't it about time we decide where we're going?

Davy Crockett played by Fess Parker and George Russell played by Buddy Ebsen: Norman Foster's *Davy Crockett, King of the Wild Frontier* (Buena Vista, 1955).

4531

Jagade: That's the trouble with the world: everybody is always telling everybody else what to do.

Jagade played by Dale Robertson: Harmon Jones' *A Day of Fury* (Universal, 1956).

4532

Myra: You always expect people to do the right. Sometimes they just do the easy.

Myra Owens played by Joan Weldon: Harry Keller's *Day of the Bad Man* (Universal, 1958).

4533

Nobody: I was then taken …in a cage. I was taken to Toronto …then Philadelphia …and then to New York. And each time I arrived at another city, somehow the white men had moved all their people there ahead of me. Each new city contained the same white people as the last. And I could not understand how a whole city of people could be moved so quickly.

Nobody played by Gary Farmer: Jim Jarmusch's *Dead Man* (Miramax Films, 1996).

4534

Big George: What's a Philistine?
Sally: Well, it's just a real dirty person!

Big George Drakoulious played by Billy Bob Thornton and Salvatore "Sally" Jenko played by Iggy Pop: Jim Jarmusch's *Dead Man* (Miramax Films, 1996).

4535

Nobody: Some are born to sweet delight; some are born to endless night.

Nobody played by Gary Farmer: Jim Jarmusch's *Dead Man* (Miramax Films, 1996).

4536

Harry McDonacle is a small-time character with big-time ambition …an ego in search of a career.

Harry McDonacle played by John Ritter, and the narration was by Kris Kristofferson: Joseph L. Scanlan's "The Great McDonacle" episode to the series premiere, *Dead Man's Gun* (Showtime, 1997).

4537

Dobbs: My dear, in life it doesn't pay to examine anything too closely. You'll find that even the most perfect rose has a blemish.

Dobbs played by Jay Brazeau: Joseph L. Scanlan's "The Great McDonacle" episode to the series premiere, *Dead Man's Gun* (Showtime, 1997).

4538

Marshal: Do you want to know something, Dan?

Dan: What?

Marshal: You're a bad liar. If you want to succeed in this world, you got to learn to be a good liar.

Marshal Frank Patch played by Richard Widmark and Dan Joslin played by Michael McGreevey: Allen Smithee's *Death of a Gunfighter* (Universal, 1969).

4539

Wash: You got to listen to reason or get out of town.

Tom: Oh, I think I'll stick around. You know, I had a friend once who used to collect postage stamps. He always said the one good thing about a postage stamp is that it always sticks to one thing until it gets there. You know, I'm sort of like that too.

Sheriff Washington Dimsdale played by Charles Winninger and Tom Destry, Jr., played by James Stewart: George Marshall's *Destry Rides Again* (Universal, 1939).

4540

Wyatt: You know, you can't go through life trying to get even. You know, you can't hold a grudge forever.

Captain Quincy Wyatt played by Gary Cooper: Raoul Walsh's *Distant Drums* (Warner Bros., 1951).

4541

Dooley: What the hell would you know about a future?

Colby: Nothing, but I know enough about not having one.

Dooley played by William Forsythe and Jacob Colby played by Ed Lauter: Gene Quintano's *Dollar for the Dead* (TVW, 1998).

4542

Don Cesar: My father always said, when life plays you a trick, make it a trick for a trick.

Don Cesar de Vega played by Douglas Fairbanks: Donald Crisp's silent film, *Don Q, Son of Zorro* (United Artists, 1925).

4543

Holland: Well, there's two things in this world you got to be careful of, son. And that's where you put your trust and who you choose as your friends.

Handsome Harry H. Holland played by Kirk Douglas: Steven H. Stern's *Draw!* (TVW, 1984).

4544

Holland: Now my old man used to say: when you see a whole lot of people gathered together, lead them in song …or stay the hell away from them!

Handsome Harry H. Holland played by Kirk Douglas: Steven H. Stern's *Draw!* (TVW, 1984).

4545

McKlennar: Your thoughts are your own property, Martin, but keep 'em to yourself.

Mrs. McKlennar played by Edna May Oliver and Gilbert Martin played by Henry Fonda: John Ford's *Drums Along the Mohawk* (20th Century–Fox, 1939).

4546

Ebenezer: I'm spending tomorrow with the only person that I care about …me!

Ebenezer Scrooge played by Jack Palance: Ken Jubenvill's *Ebenezer* (TVW, 1997).

4547

Ghost: Remember this: that you are so much more than what you've become.

The Ghost of Christmas Past played by Michelle Thrush: Ken Jubenvill's *Ebenezer* (TVW, 1997).

4548

Teacher: Seven minus three equals …? Now think about this for a minute, Lon. Let's say you had seven chickens. And your neighbor came over and took away three of them. How many would you have left?

Lon: Well, I think I'd have seven 'cause my daddy would shoot him before he got out of the hen house.

Teacher: I think that's enough arithmetic for today, Lon. Why don't you sit down.

Teacher Billy Ray Smith played by Anthony Edwards and Lon played by Todd Fitzpatrick: Peter Markle's *El Diablo* (HBO Pictures, 1990).

4549

Campbell: Why don't you just take a nice nap …and I'll wake ya when you're dead.

Campbell played by William Demarest: John Sturges' *Escape from Fort Bravo* (MGM, 1953).

4550

Benny: Not long ago, you was one man I had to prove myself against. Now I'm depending upon you for my life.

Talion: There's a lot of things we think we have to prove that don't need any proving at all.

Benny Wallace played by Patrick Wayne and Talion played by Robert Lansing: Michael Moore's *An Eye for an Eye* (Columbia, 1966).

4551

Cookie: Why did you hit [your friend] Tom?

Roy: Well, I feel as bad about it as you do. But his amensia was caused by a blow on the head. And I thought maybe a shock like this would bring him back to us.

Judge Cookie Bullflacher played by Andy Devine, Roy Rogers played himself, and Tom Sharper played by Clayton Moore: William Witney's *The Far Frontier* (Republic, 1949).

4552

Rita: A nice long trip to China never hurt anybody.

Rita Dane played by Virginia Grey: Joseph Kane's *Flame of Barbary Coast* (Republic, 1945).

4553

Jess: If thee has a sword in thy heart, son, thee must pull it out and use it.

Jess Birdwell played by Gary Cooper: William Wyler's *Friendly Persuasion* (Allied Artists, 1956).

4554

Lunsford: Oh, I guess I can savvy an insult when I hear one. I don't have to have a barn fall on me.

Blair Lunsford played by David Brian: Edwin Marin's *Fort Worth* (Warner Bros., 1951).

4555

Lucy: Actually, I'm very grateful for last night. If the vail hadn't been lifted from my eyes, I might have spent the rest of my life like one of those [cattle] …blindly trailing after you in hopes that one day you'd lavish as much care and attention on me as you do on the precious lenses of yours. You may, Mr. Albright, be commended to improving the vision of others. But when it comes to opening your eyes, and most especially that locked-up heart of yours, you're as blind as a bat!

Ms. Lucy Laughton played by Patricia Clarkson and Ernest Albright played by Judge Reinhold: Piers Haggard's *Four Eyes and Six-Guns* (Turner Pictures, 1992).

4556

Darrow: I would like to make a deal with you. You stop telling lies about me, and I'll stop telling the truth about you!

Rip Darrow played by Wendell Corey: Anthony Mann's *The Furies* (Paramount, 1950).

4557

Flo: I'm bound to be lonely. Money is the only thing that makes loneliness bearable …to some slight degree.

Flo Burnette played by Judith Anderson: Anthony Mann's *The Furies* (Paramount, 1950).

4558

Vance: Aren't you getting a little old for that?

T.C.: Old? I'm just the right age. Old enough to know better, and young enough to forget what I know.

Vance Jeffords played by Barbara Stanwyck and T.C. Jeffords played by Walter Huston: Anthony Mann's *The Furies* (Paramount, 1950).

4559

Hawkes: He's not strong on brains …but he's not short on guts either. He'll learn.

Brady Hawkes played by Kenny Rogers: Dick Lowry's *The Gambler* (TVW, 1980).

4560

Leslie: Money isn't all, you know, Jett.
Jett: Not when you got it.

Leslie Lynnton Benedict played by Elizabeth Taylor and Jett Rink played by James Dean: George Stevens *Giant* (Warner Bros., 1956).

4561

Some people travel through life making friends wherever they go, while others just travel through life.

Prologue: Buster Keaton's silent film *Go West* (Metro-Goldwyn, 1925).

4562

Quale: Any resemblance between these two characters and living persons is purely accidental.

S. Quentin Quale played by Groucho Marx: Edward Buzzell's *Go West* (MGM, 1940).

4563

Quale: If you weren't smaller than me, I'd flog the daylights out of ya!

Beecher: But I'm bigger than you.
Quale: Well, that's another reason.

S. Quentin Quale played by Groucho Marx and John Beecher played by Walter Woolf King: Edward Buzzell's *Go West* (MGM, 1940).

4564

Gypsy: What good is revenge? It don't make a man feel any better. I ain't got no more stomach for it.

Gypsy Smith played by Sidney Poitier: David Greene's *A Good Day to Die* (a.k.a. *Children of the Dust*; Vidmark Entertainment, 1995).

4565

Gypsy: Ain't no shame in being ignorant …the only shame is staying ignorant.

Gypsy Smith played by Sidney Poitier: David Greene's *A Good Day to Die Die* (a.k.a. *Children of the Dust*; Vidmark Entertainment, 1995).

4566

Gypsy: We're all bits and pieces handed down to us from the ones before us; bits and pieces we pass on to the ones after. I don't know where anybody fits. I do know that your father is a great man, Little Raven. No matter where you go in this life, no matter what happens, you remember where you come from …and be proud to be his son.

Gypsy Smith played by Sidney Poitier: David Greene's *A Good Day to Die Die* (a.k.a. *Children of the Dust*; Vidmark Entertainment, 1995).

4567

Hannah: One of the meanest things about growing old …you, you forget how important everything seems to the young people.

Hannah Sempler played by Barbara Stanwyck: William A. Wellman's *The Great Man's Lady* (Paramount, 1942).

4568

Cole: There's worse things in life than having something permanent.

Wes McQueen (Joel McCrea) admonishes outlaw gang members Reno Blake (John Archer) and Duke Harris (James Mitchell) for ruffing up half-breed girl, Colorado Carson (Virginia Mayo), in Raoul Walsh's classic western *Colorado Territory* (Warner Bros.,

Cole Younger played by Cliff Robertson: Philip Kaufman's *The Great Northfield, Minnesota Raid* (Universal, 1972).

4569
Bill: You do believe me?
Kate: I believe in you.
Bill Miner played by Richard Farnsworth and Kate Flynn played by Jackie Burroughs: Phillip Borsos' *The Grey Fox* (United Artists, 1982).

4570
Bless: Why is it so hard living a life? Why does somebody always have to get hurt?
Will: Well, Bless, I guess we all just have to pay for living and being …one way or another.
Bless Keough played by Jeffrey Hunter and Will Keough played by Fred MacMurray: Abner Biberman's *Gun for a Coward* (Universal, 1957).

4571
Abe: Well, everybody's got to be somewhere doing something.
Abe Cross played by Johnny Cash: Lamont Johnson's *A Gunfight* (Paramount, 1971).

4572
Jordan: I swear to God, Harry! Sometimes talking to you is like going to the bottom of a mine without a lantern!
Jordan Yarnell played by David McIlwraith and Old Harry played by Walter Marsh: Larry Ferguson's *Gunfighter's Moon* (Rysher Entertainment/ Cabin Entertainment, 1995).

4573
Chad: No matter how you fall, you always manage to land on your feet, don't you?
Nate: I try.
Sheriff Chad Lucas played by Audie Murphy and Nate Harlan played by Warren Stevens: Earl Bellamy's *Gunpoint* (Universal, 1966).

4574
Knudson: You and me, Jamie, we're caught in the middle …too young and too old.
Knudson played by Douglas Fowley and Jamie McPheeters: Boris Sagal's *Guns of Diablo* (MGM, 1964).

4575
Keno: Why do people always have such long names?
Max: I don't know. Perhaps it's because we all have such short lives.
Keno played by Monte Markham and Max played by Reni Santoni: Paul Wendkos' *Guns of the Magnificent Seven* (United Artists, 1969).

4576
Laura: People can get mighty stubborn when you push 'em into a corner.
Hadley: That goes both ways.
Laura Riley played by Jeanne Crain and Jim Hadley played by Alan Ladd: Robert D. Webb's *Guns of the Timberland* (Warner Bros., 1960).

4577
Selah: Do you think everyone can be bought?
Bovard: Yes, I'm not a sentimentalist. I've seen too much of life.
Selah Jennison played by Tina Louise and Deputy U.S. Marshal MacKenzie Bovard played by Robert Taylor: Michael Curtiz's *The Hangman* (Paramount, 1959).

4578
Weston: You sure got a dang poor opinion of people.
Bovard: If I had taken everyone at their word, I'd have been a dead man long ago.
Weston: Seest thou a man that is hasty in his words. There is more hope of a fool than of him.
Sheriff Buck Weston played by Fess Parker and Deputy U.S. Marshal MacKenzie Bovard played by Robert Taylor: Michael Curtiz's *The Hangman* (Paramount, 1959).

4579
Martin: You worry too much.
Dennison: Maybe you don't worry enough.
Martin: Know anybody big enough to make me worry?
Rice Martin played by Lorne Greene and George Dennison played by Barry Artwater: George Sherman's *The Hard Man* (Columbia, 1957).

4580
Madge: It's your choice: gunman or preacher, heaven or hell. But don't be half and half of anything. That can really be hell.
Madge McCloud played by Carolyn Jones: Lee H. Katzin's *Heaven with a Gun* (MGM, 1969).

4581
Bridges: It's getting dangerous to be poor in this country, isn't it?
Averill: It always was.
John H. Bridges played by Jeff Bridges and James Averill played by Kris Kristofferson: Michael Cimino's *Heaven's Gate* (United Artists, 1980).

4582
Howe: People got to talk themselves into law and order before they do anything about it. Maybe because down deep they don't care. They just don't care.
Martin Howe played by Lon Chaney, Jr.: Fred Zinnemann's *High Noon* (United Artists, 1952).

4583
Jessie: Russell, if nobody ever lifted a finger until people were deserving, the whole world would go to hell. We better deal with each other out of need and forget merit …because none of us have too much of that.
Jessie played by Diane Cilento and John Russell

played by Paul Newman: Martin Ritt's *Hombre* (20th Century–Fox, 1967).

4584
Favor: I can't imagine eating a dog and not thinking anything of it.
Russell: Have you ever been hungry, lady? Not just ready for supper, but hungry enough so that your belly swells up?
Favor: I wouldn't care how hungry I got, I know I wouldn't eat one of those camp dogs.
Russell: You'd eat it. You'd fight for the bones, too!
Favor: Have you ever eaten a dog, Mr. Russell?
Russell: I've eaten 'em. I've lived like 'em.
Mrs. Audra Favor played by Barbara Rush and John Russell played by Paul Newman: Martin Ritt's *Hombre* (20th Century–Fox, 1967).

4585
Denver Kid: Well, them English names are all Greek to me.
The Denver Kid played by Don Knotts: Robert Butler's *Hot Lead and Cold Feet* (Buena Vista, 1978).

4586
Jeremiah: Do you like fighting?
Zeb: Do you remember the story Pa used to tell us about fighting that grizzly bear?
Jeremiah: Yeah.
Zeb: And I asked him. I said, well, why did you get in such a fix? Do you like fighting grizzles? He said, well, ah, not especially, ah, I just wanted to go somewhere and the bear was there first. Well, I, I guess I just want to go somewhere too.
Jeremiah Rawlings played by Claude Johnson and Zeb Rawlings played by George Peppard: John Ford's, George Marshall's, and Henry Hathaway's *How the West Was Won* (MGM, 1962).

4587
Bridie: I think the good Lord was pouring your brains in with a teaspoon and someone jiggled his arm.
Bridie played by Isabella Hofmann: John Patterson's *Independence* (TVW, 1987).

4588
Benito: I believe we were meant to be together, Mattie.
Mattie: Oh Benito, we're so different. Your people live in harmony with the land. You're easy-going, relaxed. My people? There is something in us that wants to fight it all. We feel the need to change it and tame it and conquer it.
Benito Garza played by Benjamin Bratt and Mattie Quimper played by Chelsea Field: Richard Lang's *James A. Michener's Texas* (TVW, 1995).

4589

Bowie: He's gutless. He goes whichever way the wind blows.

Houston: Well, you know the Cherokee say the willow tree is a lot stronger than the oak.

Jim Bowie played by David Keith and Sam Houston played by Stacy Keach: Richard Lang's *James A. Michener's Texas* (TVW, 1995).

4590

Ruff: It's the lawyers, dangnabbit! It's the lawyers that's messing up the whole world! What ten years ago here in Liberty we didn't have no lawyers and we got along fine. A man killed somebody, the somebody killed him, and the marshals shot 'em all and that was the end of it. But look at it today! Right here in Liberty we got hundreds of lawyers, thousands of 'em, as far as the eye can see! Nothing but lawyers!

Zee: Uncle Ruff, there are only two lawyers in Liberty.

Ruff: Huh? Two? Is that all? Well, they run around too much!

Mayor Rufus Cobb (also Editor/Publisher of the *Liberty Weekly Gazette*) played by Henry Hull and Zee played by Nancy Kelly: Henry King's *Jesse James* (20th Century–Fox, 1939).

4591

Marshal: And who are you?

Johnny: The name, sir, is Johnny Guitar.

Dancin' Kid: That's no name.

Johnny: Anybody care to change it?

Marshal Williams played by Frank Ferguson, Johnny Guitar played by Sterling Hayden, and the Dancin' Kid played by Scott Brady: Nicholas Ray's *Johnny Guitar* (Republic, 1954).

4592

Marshal: The Dancin' Kid and Vienna aren't the same.

Emma: I say they are! They both cast the same shadow.

Marshal Williams played by Frank Ferguson, the Dancin' Kid played by Scott Brady, Vienna played by Joan Crawford, and Emma Small played by Mercedes McCambridge: Nicholas Ray's *Johnny Guitar* (Republic, 1954).

4593

Sam: You know, sometimes I think it's giving the good Lord the worst of it to say He invented people.

Sam played by Noah Beery, Jr.: Delmer Daves' *Jubal* (Columbia, 1956).

4594

Barbara: What's the sense in worrying about something that probably will never happen?

Calvin: Well, if we worry enough maybe it won't happen.

Barbara Bruce played by Eve Miller and Calvin

Bruce played by Barton MacLane: Ray Nazarro's *Kansas Pacific* (Allied Artists, 1953).

4595

Astrid: You got to do something …even if it's the wrong thing.

Astrid played by Rachel Ticotin: Andy Tennant's *Keep the Change* (Turner Home Entertainment, 1992).

4596

Joe: I have a superstition about going home …of forcing the present to conform to the past.

Joe Starling played by William Petersen: Andy Tennant's *Keep the Change* (Turner Home Entertainment, 1992).

4597

Smitty: I was thinking …why did nephew Joe come home all of a sudden? Could it be because it's spring?

Joe: The same reason a dog licks his privates, Smitty. Because he can.

Uncle Smitty played by Buck Henry and Joe Starling played by William Petersen: Andy Tennant's *Keep the Change* (Turner Home Entertainment, 1992).

4598

Overstreet: You got to learn to go along to get along.

Overstreet played by Jack Palance: Andy Tennant's *Keep the Change* (Turner Home Entertainment, 1992).

4599

Fletcher: Hitting a poor scholar isn't going to cure your ignorance, my friend.

Fletcher played by John Carradine: Burt Lancaster's *The Kentuckian* (United Artists, 1955).

4600

Preacher Bob: Have you ever been baptized?

Bick: You mean dunked under water?

Preacher Bob played by Peter Boyle and Bickford Wanner, alias Kid Blue, played by Dennis Hopper: James Frawley's *Kid Blue* (20th Century–Fox, 1973).

4601

Wild Bill: You seem to be going to a lot of trouble to show me how important you are.

Morgan: I don't have to show it! It sticks out all over the state. You might say I'm sitting on a throne here.

Wild Bill: Your throne might be perched a little too high. And it doesn't seem to be resting on much of anything.

Wild Bill Hickok played by Bill Elliott and Morgan King played by Guy Usher: Lambert Hillyer's *King of Dodge City* (Columbia, 1941).

4602

Kate: You're double-crossing him, ain't ya?

Jim: That's what suckers are for, honey.

Kate Foley played by Adrian Booth and JIm Plummer played by Forrest Tucker: Joseph Kane's *The Last Bandit* (Republic, 1949).

4603

Blaine: You know, the most dangerous people in the world, Lot, are the ones that don't benefit by their own mistakes.

Marshal Dan Blaine played by Glenn Ford and Lot McGuire played by Chad Everett: Richard Thorpe's *The Last Challenge* (MGM, 1967).

4604

Dalton: Bill, you ain't got brains enough to spit downwind!

Bob Dalton played by Robert Conrad and Bill Powers played by Tom Skerritt: Vincent McEveety's *The Last Day* (Paramount, 1975).

4605

Lillian: It's just a little disconcerting to realize that the smartest member of our expedition is the dog!

Professor Lillian Sloan played by Barbara Hershey: Tab Murphy's *Last of the Dogmen* (Savory Pictures, 1995).

4606

Maria: Just how long were you standing there?

Ellison: A little while.

Maria: Exactly how long is a little while?

Ellison: Well now, ma'am, that all depends on which end of the branding iron you're holding.

Maria O'Reilly played by Linda Cristal and Brad Ellison played by Jock Mahoney: George Sherman's *The Last of the Fast Guns* (Universal, 1958).

4607

Pablo: So many of you mistake simplicity for ignorance.

Pablo played by Francisco Reyguera: George Sherman's *The Last of the Fast Guns* (Universal, 1958).

4608

Padre: You are a realist. As a dreamer, I thought I could go on forever.

O'Reilly: Nobody can escape from himself.

Padre Jose played by Eduard Franz and Michael O'Reilly played by Lorne Greene: George Sherman's *The Last of the Fast Guns* (Universal, 1958).

4609

Linda: You're just like Jimmy.

Morgan: Huh?

Linda: A fella I used to know. He was just like you. He always wanted to make everything right. He had a heart as big as a house and a brain the size of a pea.

Linda played by Carolyn Jones and U.S. Marshal Matt Morgan played by Kirk Douglas: John Sturges' *Last Train from Gun Hill* (Paramount, 1959).

4610

Sheriff: We don't all get to choose what we are in life, Tom. You should have learned that somewhere along the line.

Sheriff Pat Lambrose played by Jim Davis and Tom Condor played by Cal Bellini: Virgil W. Vogel's *Law of the Land* (TVW, 1976).

4611

Doc: They're all alike. They hire a man to fight their battle, and then call it their town.

Dr. Amos Wynn played by Wallace Ford: Joseph H. Lewis' *A Lawless Street* (Columbia, 1955).

4612

Thorne: Half of the people in this town are too yellow to fight back, and the other half look to me for a living.

Hamer Thorne played by Warner Anderson: Joseph H. Lewis' *A Lawless Street* (Columbia, 1955).

4613

Calem: The people of this town don't need a man like me any longer. It isn't just the badge that makes the law. It takes the right people to stick together, fight, and find out what it stands for.

Marshal Calem Ware played by Randolph Scott: Joseph H. Lewis' *A Lawless Street* (Columbia, 1955).

4614

Jack Crabb: After starving awhile, I took up with a swindler with the name of Allardyce T. Merriweather. After Mrs. Pendrake, his honesty was downright refreshing. Merriweather was one of the smartest men I'd ever known. But he tended to lose parts of himself. When I joined him, his left hand and his left ear were already gone. During my years with Merriweather, he lost an eye as a result of a fifth ace dropping out of his sleeve in a poker game. It didn't phase him though. Deception was his life's blood …even if it caused him to get whittled down kind of gradual like.

Jack Crabb/Little Big Man played by Dustin Hoffman, Allardyce T. Merriweather played by Martin Balsam, and Mrs. Pendrake played by Faye Dunaway: Arthur Penn's *Little Big Man* (NGP, 1971).

4615

Leola: I swear, Hugh Bell, you wake up in another world about every three minutes, don't ya?

Leola Borgers played by Gregory Scott Cummins and Hugh Bell Borgers played by Jeremy Roberts: Jack Bender's *Lone Justice II* (Triboro Entertainment Group, 1995).

4616

Craden: You don't look like a liar.

Burke: What lies have I told you?

Craden: In words, none. You merely let me believe a lie and proved me a fool.

Thomas Craden played by Broderick Crawford and Devereaux Burke played by Clark Gable: Vincent Sherman's *Lone Star* (MGM, 1952).

4617

Martha: You know they're really the best of friends although they fight all the time.

Burke: Well, that's the privilege of friendship.

Martha Ronda played by Ava Gardner and Devereaux Burke played by Clark Gable: Vincent Sherman's *Lone Star* (MGM, 1952).

4618

Gus: I guess they may have forgotten us though.

Call: Why wouldn't they forget us? We haven't been around here in years.

Gus: No, the reason is we never got killed. That's why they forgot us.

Call: That is a dang foolish thing to say.

Gus: No, it ain't. If a thousand Comanches had cornered us in a gully somewhere and wiped us out like the Sioux just done Custer, why they'd remember us sure. Hell, they'd be writing songs about us for a hundred years!

Call: Hell, there wasn't a thousand Comanches in one bunch in the whole world and you know it.

Gus: That ain't the point, Woodrow!

Call: What is it then?

Gus: In another twenty years, we'll be the Indians, that they will be trying to stick us on the reservation just to get us out of the way.

Gus McCrae played by Robert Duvall and Captain Woodrow F. Call played by Tommy Lee Jones: Simon Wincer's *Lonesome Dove* (TVW, 1989).

4619

Timothy: Nothing in this life is free. If you want something bad enough, you got to give up something to get it.

Timothy Macahan played by Richard Kiley: Bernard McEveety's *The Macahans* (TVW, 1976).

4620

1st Peasant: We know what fear is. We live with it all our lives.

2nd Peasant: Only the dead are without fear.

The two peasants were uncredited: John Sturges' *The Magnificent Seven* (United Artists, 1960).

4621

Dundee: Do you expect me to believe these Apaches will turn against their own families, and track down their own people?

Potts: Why not? Everyone else seems to be doing it.

Major Amos Charles Dundee played by Charlton

Heston and Samuel Potts played by James Coburn: Sam Peckinpah's *Major Dundee* (Columbia, 1965).

4622

Ed: Beat the drums and sound the brass …if here don't come one big horse's ass!

Ed played by James Gammon: Elliot Silverstein's *A Man Called Horse* (NGP, 1970).

4623

Spur: One of life's injustices: you never get to choose your own relatives.

Spur played by Kirt Douglas: George Miller's *The Man from Snowy River* (20th Century–Fox, 1982).

4624

Spur: Don't throw effort into foolishness.

Spur played by Kirt Douglas: George Miller's *The Man from Snowy River* (20th Century–Fox, 1982).

4625

Jim: You got to treat the mountains like a high-spirited horse. Never take them for granted.

Jessica: The same with people, too.

Jim Craig played by Tom Burlinson and Jessica Harrison played by Sigrid Thornton: George Miller's *The Man from Snowy River* (20th Century–Fox, 1982).

4626

Jeff: You didn't have to make such a fool out of me in front of her.

Dempsey: Nobody can make a fool out of you, kid. You got to do that to yourself.

Jeff Jimson played by William Campbell and Dempsey Rae played by Kirk Douglas: King Vidor's *Man Without a Star* (Universal, 1955).

4627

Lucky: You know, California, sometimes I wished we led a better life. Quiet …settle down.

California: I tried it once, Lucky.

Lucky: Yeah?

California: Yeah, I bought myself a nice little shack …and a harmonica. And I didn't go out for two whole months. But it just didn't seem to work out.

Lucky: Why not?

California: I forgot to learn how to play the harmonica.

Lucky Jenkins played by Rand Brooks and California Carlson played by Andy Clyde: George Archainbaud's *The Marauders* (United Artists, 1947).

4628

Dock Worker: People cannot sing with hatred in their hearts.

The Dock Worker played by Robert Carricart: Don McDougall's *The Mark of Zorro* (TVW, 1974).

4629

Mitch: You don't know me, Doc, but I'm your friend.

Union soldiers and Confederate prisoners join forces and cross the border into Mexico in pursuit of Apache renegades in Sam Peckinpah's *Major Dundee* (Columbia, 1965). Saddled and ready for action are Major Amos Charles Dundee (Charlton Heston) and Sgt. Gomez (Mario Adorf).

Doc: I chose my friends and I still don't know you.

Mitch played by Gregg Martell and Doc Holliday played by James Griffith: William Castle's *Masterson of Kansas* (Columbia, 1954).

4630

Dog Butler: Up in Canada right now they're blasting tunnels for under ten dollars a foot …all done by the pigtails. They got some new expensive stuff there. Fantastic stuff! They give it to a jolly Chinaman, send him in, down comes forty-five to fifty tons of rock …and one dead Chinaman. But you, sir, do you know what the fine is for killing a Chinaman? Fifty dollars …maximum! The inspector is working for the company. Four times out of five it is an accident.

Dog Butler played by Hugh Millais: Robert Altman's *McCabe & Mrs. Miller* (Warner Bros., 1971).

4631

Katherine: It's sad, these changing times.

Becky: It isn't the times that are changing, Mama.

Katherine McLintock played by Maureen O'Hara and Becky McLintock played by Stefanie Powers: Andrew V. McLaglen's *McLintock!* (United Artists, 1963).

4632

Mrs. Watson: It's a house of God. All people is welcomed there.

Mr. Watson: Since when is a nigger a person? They ain't got no soul. I told you that a million times.

Mrs. Watson played by Marion Brash and Mr. Watson played by R.G. Armstrong: Alf Kjellin's *The McMasters* (Jayjen/Chevron, 1970).

4633

Johnny: You ain't much but you're a hell of a lot better than nothin'!

Johnny Lawler played by Sam Elliott: Gary Nelson's *Molly and Lawless John* (Producers Distribution Corp., 1972).

4634

Bess: Folks ought to be careful using the word "never." You say "never" to something, it's the very thing you end up doing.

Bess Guthrie played by Gena Rowlands: William A. Graham's *Montana* (TVW, 1990).

4635

Peg: It's funny. The first resentments always end up being the last resentments.

Peg Guthrie played by Lea Thompson: William A. Graham's *Montana* (TVW, 1990).

4636

Tom: Are you sure?

Pete: I'm so sure, I'm certain!

Tom Bradfield played by George Brent and Pete Bivins played by Andy Devine: Allan Dwan's *Montana Belle* (RKO, 1952).

4637

Dally: Maybe I was wrong.

Monte: Oh no, Dally, you weren't wrong. It's just that nothing has been right these days.

Dally Johnson played by Michael Conrad and Monte Walsh played by Lee Marvin: William A. Fraker's *Monte Walsh* (NGP, 1970).

4638

Monica: It isn't what people think you are that matters. It's what you are.

Monica Alton played by Anne Francis: Robert Sparr's *More Dead Than Alive* (United Artists, 1968).

4639

Nika: I must be some kind of jinx.

Dan: There ain't no such thing. When somebody is doing their best, all there is is good luck and bad. Both of 'em are part of living.

Nika: Ok, but when do we get to the good part?

Nika played by Nika Mina and Dan played by Joel McCrea: John Champion's *Mustang Country* (Universal, 1976).

4640

Hildy: Every time I do something dumb, Mommy says I take after the old man. And every time I do something smart, Pop says I sure don't take after the old lady.

Hildy played by Diana Hale: Harold Schuster's *My Friend Flicka* (20th Century–Fox, 1943).

4641

Twillie: If a thing is worth having, it's worth cheating for.

Cuthbert J. Twillie played by W.C. Fields: Edward F. Cline's *My Little Chickadee* (Universal, 1940).

4642

Nobody: Sometimes you run smack into your destiny on the very road you take to get away from it.

Nobody played by Terence Hill: Tonino Valerii's *My Name Is Nobody* (Universal, 1973).

4643

Jack: And I also figured out the moral to your grandpa's story. The one about the cow that covered the little bird with cowpie to keep it warm, and then the coyote hauled it out and ate it. It's the moral of these new times of yours. Folks that throw dirt on you aren't always trying to hurt ya. And folks that pull you out of a jam aren't always trying to help ya. But the main point is: when you're up to your nose, keep your mouth shut!

Jack Beauregard played by Henry Fonda: Tonino Valerii's *My Name Is Nobody* (Universal, 1973).

4644

Pecos Bill: Human beings are a lot like dogs. Sometimes a kind word will bring 'em around. Others are just so bad that nothing will help 'em.

Pecos Bill/Ben Wade played by Douglas Dumbrille: Lesley Selander's *The Mysterious Rider* (a.k.a. *Mark of the Avenger*; Paramount, 1938).

4645

Frosty: Some people get all the gravy.

Frosty Kilburn played by Sidney Toler: Lesley Selander's *The Mysterious Rider* (a.k.a. *Mark of the Avenger*; Paramount, 1938).

4646

McBride: I just don't know what I ever did to deserve the misfortune of knowing you.

McBride played by Wallace Ford: Fred F. Sears' *The Nebraskan* (Columbia, 1953).

4647

Storekeeper: That's twenty-five cents for the peaches and ten cents for the book. Funny, isn't it? Ideas don't weigh much but peaches do. And the freight company charges by the weight …most people are hungrier in the stomachs than they are in the minds anyway.

The Storekeeper played by Stanley Adams: Henry Hathaway's *Nevada Smith* (Paramount, 1966).

4648

Brett: Well, as my old pappy used to say: if you're going to steal, steal from kin. They're less likely to put the law on ya.

Brett Maverick played by James Garner: Hy Averback's *The New Maverick* (TVW, 1978).

4649

Cantrell: Now, Case, you ought to trust me better than that!

Case: Sure. You trust me, I trust you. But we don't trust each other, Jack.

Jack Cantrell played by Ted de Corsia and Case Britton played by Jim Davis: Edward L. Cahn's *Noose for a Gunman* (United Artists, 1960). See also *The Quick Gun* this section.

4650

Dusty: Down where I come from, we don't jump to conclusions. It's liable to be a fella's last jump.

Dusty Rivers played by Gary Cooper: Cecil B. DeMille's *North West Mounted Police* (Paramount, 1940).

4651

Dusty: I guess I've just been having a beautiful pipe dream in the middle of a nightmare.

Dusty Rivers played by Gary Cooper: Cecil B. DeMille's *North West Mounted Police* (Paramount, 1940).

4652

Anne: Are you going to answer me or not, John?

John: Why should I? You can find out all you want by listening to rumors. Just like everyone else.

Anne: You don't care what people think of you!

John: For once, you're exactly right!

Anne Barnes played by Barbara Hale and Dr. John Brighton played by Joel McCrea: Francis D. Lyon's *The Oklahoman* (Warner Bros., 1957).

4653

Bierce: To be a gringo in Mexico, ah, that is euthanasia!

Ambrose Bierce played by Gregory Peck: Luis Puenzo's *Old Gringo* (Columbia, 1989).

4654

Arroyo: Now I know why the gringos come to Mexico: they can't stand each other!

General Tomas Arroyo played by Jimmy Smits: Luis Puenzo's *Old Gringo* (Columbia, 1989).

4655

Coates: Well, now and then for no good reason a man can figure out, life will just haul off and knock him flat …slam him against the ground so hard it seems like all his insides is busted. But it's not all like that. A lot of it is mighty fine. And you can't afford to waste the good part fretting about the bad. That makes it all bad.

Jim Coates played by Fess Parker: Robert Stevenson's *Old Yeller* (Buena Vista, 1957).

4656

Hayes: Did you ever want anything so bad you did all the wrong things to get it?

Oren Hayes played by Richard Widmark: Burt Kennedy's *Once Upon a Texas Train* (TVW, 1988).

4657

Jesse: We have been together a long time, you and me. Blanket-mates. It's been share and share alike. But you want to know something?

Will: Tell me.

Jesse: It's all over.

Will: Jesse, I'm going to flood the prairies and wash out gullies with my tears. It will rain wholesale!

Jesse Wallace played by Barry Sullivan and Will Owen played by Joel McCrea: Roy Rowland's *The Outriders* (MGM, 1950).

4658

Jason: George! Dang, you're a sight for sore eyes!

Nash: Well, your eyes must be mighty sore, Jason. I'm Nash Crawford!

Jason Fitch played by Edgar Buchanan and Nash Crawford played by Walter Brennan: Jean Yarbrough's *The Over-the-Hill Gang* (TVW, 1969).

4659

Granger: No, I don't believe in giving advice. The most interesting part of life is making mistakes.

Ross Granger played by Jock Mahoney: Fred F. Sears' *Overland Pacific* (United Artists, 1954).

4660

Jessie: Life is a long walk. If it's through a flower garden, you come out smelling sweet. If it's in the gutter, well, you keep cleaning the mud on the soles of your shoes.

Jessie Lorraine played by Adele Jergens: Fred F. Sears' *Overland Pacific* (United Artists, 1954).

4661

Pardner: I got nothin' more to say to you.

Ben: And you got nothin' I want to hear.

Pardner played by Clint Eastwood and Ben Rumson played by Lee Marvin: Joseph Logan's *Paint Your Wagon* (Paramount, 1969).

4662

Parson: Boozers, gluttons, gamblers, harlots, fornicators!

Blacksmith: What's a fornicator?

Holbrook: I don't know. I ain't a religious man.

The Parson played by Alan Dexter and Haywood Holbrook played by Benny Baker: Joseph Logan's *Paint Your Wagon* (Paramount, 1969).

4663

Holbrook: Are you moving out, Ben?

Ben: No.

Holbrook: Me neither. I guess there's two kinds in the world, Ben. People who move and people who stay. Ain't that true?

Ben: No, that ain't true.

Holbrook: Well, what's true?

Ben: Well, there's two kinds of people. Them going somewhere and them going nowhere. And that's what's true.

Holbrook: I don't agree, Ben.

Ben: That's because you don't know what the hell I'm talking about. I'm an ex-citizen of nowhere. And sometimes I get mighty homesick.

Haywood Holbrook played by Benny Baker and Ben Rumson played by Lee Marvin: Joseph Logan's *Paint Your Wagon* (Paramount, 1969).

4664

Whit: He who saves a life assumes its burden.

Whit Lacey played by Forrest Tucker: Jospeh Kane's *The Plunderers* (Republic, 1948).

4665

Whit: Oh, that's Bide and Cump. Bide is the ugliest one.

Druin: Hello, Cump.

Cump: I'm Bide, he's Cump.

Bide and Cump were uncredited. Whit Lacey played by Forrest Tucker and John Druin played by Rod Cameron: Jospeh Kane's *The Plunderers* (Republic, 1948).

4666

Collins: I'm from nowhere, trying to get somewhere, and I picked the low road to get there.

Alice: Tax collector?

Collins played by Tom Skerritt and Poker Alice Moffit played by Elizabeth Taylor: Arthur Allan Seidelman's *Poker Alice* (TVW, 1987).

4667

Trevor: For the first time in my life I feel old.

Trevor Kingman played by Henry Wilcoxon:

Robert Totten's *Pony Express Rider* (Doty-Dayton, 1976).

4668

Nightingale: Well, what has no price, even if you want it very much, sometimes costs more than one can afford.

Marshal Howard Nightingale played by Kirk Douglas who also directed *Posse* (Paramount, 1975).

4669

Cole: Maybe that's what Webb wanted me to find out: that there is always someone or something worthwhile …if we just look hard enough.

Banner Cole played by Audie Murphy and Marshal Isaac Webb played by Ward Ramsey: Herbert Coleman's *Posse from Hell* (Universal, 1961).

4670

Ramsey: I can't fly in the face of public opinion!

Bracket: Why can't ya?

Ramsey the Hotel Owner was uncredited and Hank Bracket played by Rod Taylor: Douglas Heyes' *Powderkeg* (TVW, 1971).

4671

Sharkey: Anything you don't say won't get you into trouble.

Fin Sharkey played by Ethan Laidlaw: Wallace Fox's *Powdersmoke Range* (RKO, 1935).

4672

Grant: Your hair was darker then.

Fardan: My heart was lighter then.

J.W. Grant played by Ralph Bellamy and Henry Rico Fardan played by Lee Marvin: Richard Brooks' *The Professionals* (Columbia, 1966).

4673

Dolworth: Well, I'll be damned!

Fardan: Most of us are.

Bill Dolworth played by Burt Lancaster and Henry Rico Fardan played by Lee Marvin: Richard Brooks' *The Professionals* (Columbia, 1966).

4674

Maria: Go to hell!

Dolworth: Yes, ma'am. I'm on my way.

Maria Grant played by Claudia Cardinale and Bill Dolworth played by Burt Lancaster: Richard Brooks' *The Professionals* (Columbia, 1966).

4675

Dolworth: Do you realize that people are the only animals who'll make love face-to-face?

Bill Dolworth played by Burt Lancaster: Richard Brooks' *The Professionals* (Columbia, 1966).

4676

Burleigh: Wait a minute! I'd like a little respect. I told you before I don't like people I'm talking to to walk away from me.

Look at me! You look at me when I talk to you!

Chandler: I'm looking but I don't see anything.

Jeb Burleigh played by Harry Dean Stanton and John Chandler played by Alan Ladd: Michael Curtiz's *The Proud Rebel* (MGM, 1958).

4677

Linnett: $200.00 is a lot of money, Chandler.

Chandler: $2.00 is …if you need it bad enough.

Linnett Moore played by Olivia de Havilland and John Chandler played by Alan Ladd: Michael Curtiz's *The Proud Rebel* (MGM, 1958).

4678

Gentry: It's the night you're afraid of. But look up there [at the stars]. There's always a little light.

Gentry/John Coventry played by Fred MacMurray: Harry Keller's *Quantez* (Universal, 1957).

4679

Spangler: Oh now, Clint, you ought to trust me better than that.

Clint: I trust you, Spang, and you trust me. But we just can't trust each other.

Spangler played by Ted De Corsia and Clint Cooper played by Audie Murphy: Sidney Salkow's *The Quick Gun* (Columbia, 1964). See also *Noose for a Gunman* this section.

4680

Callus: You younglings can be in hurry anywhere …even on the farside of nowhere.

Callus played by Walter Baldwin: Norman Foster's *Rachel and the Stranger* (RKO, 1948).

4681

Big Davey: The stars seem so close to you up here. It's funny how people get separated with miles in between 'em. It don't seem right.

Big Davey Harvey played William Holden: Norman Foster's *Rachel and the Stranger* (RKO, 1948).

4682

Bill: How did you ever live this long?

Mac: I'm a Presbyterian.

Bill Bell played by Sam Elliott and Mac played by Jerry O'Connell: John Kent Harrison's *The Ranger, the Cook and a Hole in the Sky* (Hallmark Home Entertainment, 1995).

4683

Martha: The trouble with appearances, Mr. Bowen, is while beauty is skin deep, meanness runs all the way through.

Martha Price played by Maureen O'Hara and Alexander Bowen played by Brian Keith: Andrew V. McLaglen's *The Rare Breed* (Universal, 1966).

4684

Tarp: You figure I could learn how to dance, Johnny?

Johnny: Well, I've seen mules trained to keep time.

Tarp Penny played by Neville Brand and Johnny Randolph played by Rex Reason: John Sherwood's *Raw Edge* (Universal, 1956).

4685

Zimmerman: Never underestimate your enemy, Mr. Fickert. It's a good way to keep alive.

Zimmerman played by Hugh Marlowe and Fickert played by Jean Heydt: Henry Hathaway's *Rawhide* (20th Century–Fox, 1951).

4686

Rick: Names don't matter, my friend. People don't remember them anyway. But faces? They never forget.

Rick Martin played by Arthur Kennedy: Rudolph Maté's *The Rawhide Years* (Universal, 1956).

4687

Rick: The next best thing to money is friendship anyhow.

Ben: Do you really mean that?

Rick: I don't know. It sounded good. But it doesn't sound like me.

Rick Martin played by Arthur Kennedy and Ben Mathews, alias Ben Martin, played by Tony Curtis: Rudolph Maté's *The Rawhide Years* (Universal, 1956).

4688

Laurie: You do hang on to your misery, don't you?

Laurie played by Katharine Ross: William Wittliff's *Red Headed Stranger* (Alive Films/Charter Entertainment, 1987).

4689

Simms: Well, I don't like to see things go good or bad. I like 'em in between.

Simms played by Hank Worden: Howard Hawks' *Red River* (United Artists, 1948).

4690

Link: Do you think you could do that again?

Kuroda: Almost certainly.

Link played by Charles Bronson and Kuroda played by Toshiro Mifune: Terence Young's *Red Sun* (NGP, 1971).

4691

Pettit: You know, Muley, there ain't much point in writing things down in books when most of the people you do business with can't write themselves.

John Pettit played by George "Gabby" Hayes and Muley Wilson played by Walter Baldwin: Ray Enright's *Return of the Badmen* (RKO, 1948).

4692

Cisco: I don't know how you can live so long and be so foolish, my friend.

The Cisco Kid played by Warner Baxter: Herbert I. Leeds' *The Return of the Cisco Kid* (20th Century–Fox, 1939).

4693

Chris: I'm not a religious man, Father, but I'll tell you this: they need you ...more now than ever before.

Priest: I've failed them.

Chris: You failed yourself. You got knocked down. Get up, Father ...at least as far as your knees!

Chris played by Yul Brynner and the Priest played by Fernando Ray: Burt Kennedy's *Return of the Seven* (United Artists, 1966).

4694

Newt: Is it people that bring him problems, Isom, or him looking to take 'em on?

Isom: Well, I can't say that it matters much, really ...as long as he handles 'em ...one problem at a time.

Newt Dobbs played by Rick Schroder and Isom Pickett played by Louis Gossett, Jr.: Mike Robe's *Return to Lonesome Dove* (TVW, 1993).

4695

Jessica: Why is accumulating things so damn important?

Jim: Because I've seen the lack of it.

Jessica Harrison played by Sigrid Thornton and Jim Craig played by Tom Burlinson: Geoff Burrowes' *Return to Snowy River* (Buena Vista, 1988).

4696

Esqueda: What an artist I might have been, Barton, had I not been thrown into the company of pigs.

Jose Esqueda played by Anthony Quinn and Barton played by Jack Elam: John Farrow's *Ride, Vaquero!* (MGM, 1953).

4697

Esqueda: When a brave man becomes a fool, he also becomes dangerous.

Jose Esqueda played by Anthony Quinn: John Farrow's *Ride, Vaquero!* (MGM, 1953).

4698

Lassiter: The longer I live, the stranger life gets.

Jim Lassiter played by Ed Harris: Charles Haid's *Riders of the Purple Sage* (Turner Home Entertainment, 1996).

4699

Burdette: Every man should have a little taste of power before he's through.

Nathan Burdette played by John Russell: Howard Hawks' *Rio Bravo* (Warner Bros., 1959).

4700

Rodriguez: How a man gets his money does not matter. It is how he spends it, amigo.

Juan Rodriguez played by Tony Franciosa: Gordon Douglas' *Rio Conchos* (20th Century–Fox, 1964).

4701

Tabor: Now just what are you trying to say?

Leech: I'm saying there's a big difference between living ...and being alive.

Benjamin Tabor played by Travis Tritt and Quinton Leech played by Kenny Rogers: Rod Hardy's *Rio Diablo* (TVW, 1993).

4702

Leech: Nobody ever said life was fair, Benny. I keep telling myself it's better than the other choice ...most of the time anyway.

Quinton Leech played by Kenny Rogers and Benjamin Tabor played by Travis Tritt: Rod Hardy's *Rio Diablo* (TVW, 1993).

4703

Cordona: You know, I like you.

Shasta: Why?

Cordona: Because you don't cry.

Shasta: Oh, but I do. You saw me.

Cordona: You cried for your friend, not for yourself. There's a lot of difference.

Pierre Cordona played by Jorge Rivero and Shasta Delaney played by Jennifer O'Neill: Howard Hawks' *Rio Lobo* (NGP, 1970).

4704

Matt: You can't just go through everything in the world, boy. Sometimes you have to back up and go around.

Matt Calder played by Robert Mitchum: Otto Preminger's *The River of No Return* (20th Century–Fox, 1954).

4705

Matt: One thing about you, though. You get somebody in trouble, you get right in it with 'em.

Kay: Only trouble should get you something. It never gets me anything.

Matt: Sure it does. It gets you more of the same.

Matt Calder played by Robert Mitchum and Kay Weston played by Marilyn Monroe: Otto Preminger's *The River of No Return* (20th Century–Fox, 1954).

4706

Bob: Here comes Gabby! He must have gotten tired of his own company.

Bob Nolan played himself and Gabby played by George "Gabby" Hayes: Joseph Kane's *Romance on the Range* (Republic, 1942).

4707

McCoy: I ain't got an ounce of goodwill in me and that's a fact! I hate everybody! I'm a cantankerous old man, and I know it. But I like myself better than anyone I've ever met. That's why I took this job, to be alone with me.

McCoy played by Strother Martin: Stuart Millar's *Rooster Cogburn* (Universal, 1975).

4708

Eula: When something unpleasant must be said, it's best to have done with it. A sharp knife cuts the quickest and hurts the least.

Eula Goodnight played by Katharine Hepburn: Stuart Millar's *Rooster Cogburn* (Universal, 1975).

4709

Mat: Why don't you stop feeling sorry for yourself. You think you are the only one in the world that ever got a raw deal?

Davey: I know, you spent six years in jail.

Mat: Yeah, and you know something else? There is a lot of people in this world who have had a tougher time than either you or me. It comes with the ticket. Nobody guarantees you a free ride. The only difference is, most people don't run for cover. They keep right on going, picking up the pieces the best way they can. But you never hear of them, but from the ones who can't take it …like you …from the ones who are looking for the free ride …who cause all the trouble everywhere.

Mat Dow played by James Cagney and Davey Bishop played by John Derek: Nicholas Ray's *Run for Cover* (Paramount, 1955).

4710

Mona: Did you ever try looking at yourself?

Brown: I don't like mirrors.

Mona Langley played by Beverly Garland and Hemp Brown played by Rory Calhoun: Richard Carlson's *The Sage of Hemp Brown* (Universal, 1958).

4711

Gabe: If anything is worth having, more than one person is gonna want it.

Gabe McBride played by Robert Conrad: Michael Keusch's *Samurai Cowboy* (Den Pictures/Entertainment Securities/Saban Entertainment, 1993).

4712

Vaugant: Civilized people don't listen in on private conversations, Mr. Ahern.

Ahern: Savages speak their insults to a man's face.

Captain Arnold Vaugant played by Richard Rober and Jim Ahern/Warbonnet played by Charlton Heston: George Marshall's *The Savage* (Paramount, 1952).

4713

Tally: Why, Jim? Why are you fighting against the Indians?

Ahern: Didn't you once tell me, primitive people have to give ground to civilization.

Tally Hathersell played by Susan Morrow and Jim Ahern/Warbonnet played by Charlton Heston: George Marshall's *The Savage* (Paramount, 1952).

4714

Flood: I'd rather do something I like and go bust than succeed at doing something dull.

Jim Flood played by Barry Sullivan: Harry Keller's *Seven Ways from Sundown* (Universal, 1960).

4715

Jason: Now say, I know I've always considered myself a pretty good judge of character. It appears to me that you're the best man for the job I got.

Milt: What kind of man do you need?

Jason: Well, mainly he's got to be a man completely without honor. A man willing to sell out anybody and everybody. There's four bits in it for him.

Milt: What?

Jason: No, huh?

Milt: No!

Jason: All right.

Milt: Just a minute. My price for that sort of thing starts at a dollar. Who do you want sold out?

Jason: Well, nobody in particular, but I thought that if you hear anything that I ought to know, you tell me. There's at least seventy-five cents in it for you.

Milt: A dollar!

Jason: A dollar.

Milt: Say, you know, you are a pretty good judge of character.

Jason Sweet played by Glenn Ford and Milt Masters played by Edgar Buchanan: George Marshall's *The Sheepman* (MGM, 1958).

4716

Granny: I wish I'd had stayed stone blind …in the good clean dark.

Granny Becky played by Majorie Main: Henry Hathaway's *The Shepherd of the Hills* (Paramount, 1941).

4717

Howitt: You know, there's a funny thing about fishing. You can let your thoughts drift downstream until they carry your troubles clean out of sight.

Daniel Howitt played by Harry Carey: Henry Hathaway's *The Shepherd of the Hills* (Paramount, 1941).

4718

Swiss: You know, Blackjack, in a gallop you could be mistaken for a horse's ass!

Blanc De Blanc/"Swiss" played by Giuliano Gemma and Blackjack played by Eli Wallach: Sergio Corbucci's *Shoot First …Ask Questions Later!* (a.k.a. *The White, the Yellow, and the Black*; Mntex Entertainment, It/Sp/Fr).

4719

Trooper: But, hell, I always liked that fella.

Lomax: So did I …until I stopped.

Trooper played by Jeff Corey and Clay Lomax played by Gregory Peck: Henry Hathaway's *Shoot Out* (Universal, 1971).

4720

Estelle: Chris, what I need now is to learn how to trust again …have faith in people …how to love. How do I start?

Chris: By taking a chance on someone again.

Estelle played by Kathleen Crowley and Chris Foster played by Audie Murphy: R.G. Springsteen's *Showdown* (Universal, 1963).

4721

Colonel: It's been over thirty years since I last heard from her. Arguments and cursed stubbornness certainly have broken up a lot of families.

Colonel White played by Wright Kramer: Howard Bretherton's *The Showdown* (Paramount, 1940).

4722

Arthur: There are good friends and there are bad. And in trust, you find treason.

Arthur Vowell played by John Pyper Ferguson: Allan Kroeker's *Showdown at Williams Creek* (Republic Pictures Home Video, 1991).

4723

Brown: How do you tell a people that they are going to disappear?

John George "Kootenai" Brown played by Tom Burlinson: Allan Kroeker's *Showdown at Williams Creek* (Republic Pictures Home Video, 1991).

4724

Boss: You know something? I can hear every word everybody is saying! I got my earsight back!

The Boss (of the gang) played by Jack Elam: Burt Kennedy's *Sidekicks* (TVW, 1974).

4725

[*During a jailbreak*]

Quince: I hope we know what we're gettin' into!

Jason: No, but we know what we're gettin' out of!

Quince Drew played by Larry Hagman and Jason O'Rourke played by Lou Gossett: Burt Kennedy's *Sidekicks* (TVW, 1974).

4726

Stranger: I never made an easy buck in my life.

The Stranger played by Tony Anthony: Vance Lewis's (Luigi Vanzi) *The Silent Stranger* (a.k.a. *Stranger in Japan*; MGM, 1969).

4727

Stella: The world is what you make it, friend. If it doesn't fit, you make alterations.

Stella played by Linda Hunt: Lawrence Kasdan's *Silverado* (Columbia, 1985).

4728

Stella: Some people think because they're stronger or meaner, they

Nobody (Terence Hill) advises Honest John (R.G. Armstrong) that "the secret to a long life is to try not to shorten it" in the comedy western *My Name Is Nobody* (Universal, 1973).

can push you around. I've seen a lot of that. But it's only true if you let it be.

Stella played by Linda Hunt: Lawrence Kasdan's *Silverado* (Columbia, 1985).

4729

Powell: My pappy always used to say ...Damn if I can remember what he used to say!

Siringo: It probably wasn't worth remembering anyway.

Powell: There you go, putting down my family!

Winton Powell played by Chad Lowe and Charlie Siringo played by Brad Johnson: Kevin G. Cremin's *Siringo* (TVW, 1994).

4730

Plunkett: I got a memory for faces, mister.

Quincy: So do I. I just hate to clutter up my mind with them.

Plunkett played by Edward Asner and Quincy Drew played James Garner: Paul Bogart's *Skin Game* (Warner Bros., 1971).

4731

Dempster: Children are usually right about people.

Captain Dempster played by Brian Donlevy: Irving Allen's *Slaughter Trail* (RKO, 1951).

4732

Slim: You got to figure on taking a punch every so often.

Boy: Sure.

Slim: You got to save up the good times to make up for the bad.

Boy: So when things go wrong, you think of something good that happened to you.

Slim: Sure, now you got the picture! That way you can roll with the punches.

Slim Carter/Hughie Mack played by Jock Mahoney and Leo Gallagher (the Boy) played by Tim Hovey: Richard H. Bartlett's *Slim Carter* (Universal, 1957).

4733

Laura: My father taught me how to think, not what to think. I've always done that by myself.

Laura Evans played by Piper Laurie: Jerry Hopper's *Smoke Signal* (Universal, 1955).

4734

Will: He was nearly as old as my grandfather. He had a safety pin holding up his pants.

Spikes: Son, where there ain't foolishness in this life, there's misery. But we got to hold ourselves together somehow ...or we would always be crying.

Will Young played by Gary Grimes and Harry

Spikes played by Lee Marvin: Richard Fleischer's *The Spikes Gang* (United Artists, 1974).

4735

McNamara: Maybe you better slip upstairs and sip a warm lemonade before you break out in a rash of righteousness.

Alexander McNamara played by Randolph Scott: Ray Enright's *The Spoilers* (Universal, 1942).

4736

Leah: Like candy, too much life can make you sick.

Leah Parker played by Marilyn Maxwell: William F. Claxton's *Stage to Thunder Rock* (Paramount, 1964).

4737

Doc: Now what are you looking at, my friend?

Henry: It's a filthy habit, smoking. Just filthy.

Doc: I have a lot of filthy habits. Most of them I find very enjoyable.

Henry: Don't you have any good ones?

Doc: You mean something that could be admired and held up to children as an example?

Henry: Yes, something like that.

Doc: No, sir. Children despise that kind of person. There's nothing that a child hates more than a good example.

Doc Holliday played by Willie Nelson and Henry Gatewood played by Tony Franciosa: Ted Post's *Stagecoach* (TVW, 1986).

4738

Arnold: Nobody around here realizes I'm an important man. I wish I were back in San Francisco.

Chito: So do we!

Arnold played by Thurston Hall and Chito Rafferty played by Richard Martin: Lew Landers' *Stagecoach Kid* (RKO, 1949).

4739

Connie: Dad said something awhile ago that seem to make sense. He said that if people are going to be neighbors, they should try to be good ones.

Connie Dawson played by Gale Storm: Lesley Selander's *Stampede* (Warner Bros., 1949).

4740

Charlie: I forgot to ask you one thing.

Haven: Well, I'm working for you now. You can ask me anything.

Charlie: How do I know if I can trust you?

Haven: You don't.

Charlie: Can I?

Haven: Only with money.

Charlie played by Jane Greer and Haven played by Dick Powell: Sidney Lanfield's *Station West* (RKO, 1948).

4741

Colonel: We share the same ancestors as far back as Adam and Eve. I desire no closer relationship to you than that.

Colonel Ames played by John Dehner: Burt Kennedy's *Support Your Local Gunfighter* (United Artists, 1971).

4742

Reva: Hate won't bring you anything but bitterness.

Reva, the Saloon Singer, played by Peggie Castle: Lesley Selander's *Tall Man Riding* (Warner Bros., 1955).

4743

Pearlo: You know when to talk and you know when to listen. The important thing is never to confuse the two.

Cibo Pearlo played by John Baragrey: Lesley Selander's *Tall Man Riding* (Warner Bros., 1955).

4744

Nella: That's important to you, isn't it? Being envied.

Stark: Frankly, very. People only envy a successful man. They envy a failure nothing.

Nella Turner played by Jane Russell and Nathan Stark played by Robert Ryan: Raoul Walsh's *The Tall Men* (20th Century–Fox, 1955).

4745

Thomas: I've never seen a person do so many things wrong in such a short time.

Dan Thomas played by William Holden: George Marshall's *Texas* (Columbia, 1941).

4746

Gil: He's a talker, you know. The kind that's all wind and no spit.

Gil played by Aldo Sambrell: Lesley Selander's *The Texican* (Columbia, 1966).

4747

Pitman: I'm putting my trust in all of you. Keep quiet!

The Kid: That's like asking a pack of coyotes to keep quiet about a dead horse!

Paris Pitman, Jr., played by Kirk Douglas and the Missouri Kid played by Burgess Meredith: Joseph L. Mankiewicz's *There Was a Crooked Man* (Warner Bros., 1970).

4748

Elizabeth: Every parting has its own fears and anxieties.

Custer: Of course. I often feel like that myself. But it has its bright side too. The more sadness in the parting, the more joy in the reunion.

Elizabeth Bacon Custer played by Olivia de Havilland and George Armstrong Custer played by Errol Flynn: Raoul Walsh's *They Died with Their Boots On* (Warner Bros., 1941).

4749

Charlie: You just got to make your peace with the devil, Polly. Why, it's the only way to get along in this world.

Charlie played by Chris Cooper and Lalu Nathoy/

Polly Bemis played by Rosalind Chao: Nancy Kelly's *Thousand Pieces of Gold* (Greycat Films, 1991).

4750

Dr. Braun: It is better not to look back. Look instead ahead.

Leni: With the eyes, yes. But with always the heart to expect.

Dr. Karl Braun played by Charles Coburn and Leni Braun played by Sigrid Gurie: Bernard Vorhaus' *Three Faces West* (Republic, 1940).

4751

Guthrie: You want to talk, Deke?

Deke: Well, it's up to the customer. I always say: when a man has a razor to his throat, he's entitled to his own thoughts.

Jim Guthrie played by Dana Andrews and the Town Barber, Deke, played by Whit Bissell: Alfred Werker's *Three Hours to Kill* (Columbia, 1954).

4752

Cinch: You know, you have very good manners. I have the sure test.

Lorna: What's that?

Cinch: Bad-mannered people just blurt it out: how did you lose your arm? Well-mannered people burn up with curiosity …but don't ask.

Lorna: I am curious. How did you lose your arm?

Cinch Saunders played by Tom Tryon and Mrs. Lorna Hunter Saunders played by Anne Baxter: Rudolph Mate's *Three Violent People* (Paramount, 1956).

4753

Lorna: Colt, listen to me. When you're raising a boy, will you try to remember something? Try to remember that people aren't perfect. They just aren't. They make mistakes. And when they do, they suffer. They pay …inside themselves. So when he makes his mistakes, and he will, try to find it in you to forgive him.

Mrs. Lorna Hunter Saunders played by Anne Baxter and Colt Saunders played by Charlton Heston: Rudolph Mate's *Three Violent People* (Paramount, 1956).

4754

Castello: I have to keep moving. I got iron in my blood. If I sit still, I rust.

Dan Castello played by Tom Tully: George Sherman's *Tomahawk* (Universal, 1951).

4755

Wyatt: I spent my whole life not knowing what I wanted out of it …just chasing my tail. Now for the first time I know exactly what I want …and who. That's the damnable misery of it.

Wyatt Earp played by Kurt Russell: George P. Cosmatos' *Tombstone* (Buena Vista, 1993).

4756

Priest: They say it's easier to repent of those sins you've already committed than those you intend to commit.

Colonel: If we have one, I intend to commit a great many.

The Town Priest played by Fernando Rey and the Colonel played by Martin Landau: Robert Parrish's *A Town Called Hell* (a.k.a. *A Town Called Bastard*; Scotia International, 1971).

4757

Alvira: The devil always wants to play God.

Priest: The devil has the largest congregation.

Alvira played by Stella Stevens and the Town Priest played by Fernando Rey: Robert Parrish's *A Town Called Hell* (a.k.a. *A Town Called Bastard*; Scotia International, 1971).

4758

Rosser: The good people in the community start the vigilante committee. But in order to make it work, you got to have more strength. So you take in more people. The first thing you know, you got a lot of people you wouldn't speak to ordinarily.

Tom Rosser played by Dana Andrews: Lesley Selander's *Town Tamer* (Paramount, 1965).

4759

Lane: You're going to spend the rest of your life getting up one more time than you're knocked down. So you better start getting used to it.

Lane played by John Wayne: Burt Kennedy's *The Train Robbers* (Warner Bros., 1973).

4760

Ruth: I read in a book somewhere, Tom, that a person must be very careful what they want in life. They're so likely to get it.

Ruth Harris played by Shelley Winters and Tom Bryan played by Rory Calhoun: George Sherman's *The Treasure of Pancho Villa* (RKO, 1955).

4761

Pablo: Courage is good, my Colonel. So is intelligence. This family needs more of the first because it lacks the second.

Pablo Morales played by Joseph Calleia: George Sherman's *The Treasure of Pancho Villa* (RKO, 1955).

4762

Howard: If you got something up your nose, blow it out! It'll do you good.

Howard played by Walter Huston: John Huston's *The Treasure of the Sierra Madre* (Warner Bros., 1948).

4763

Padre: Tell me, my son …
Bambino: What?

Padre: Well, aren't you here to confess?

Bambino: Yeah, among other things.

Padre: What other things?

Bambino: To see if you're going to absolve me too.

Padre: First you must confess. Then I'll absolve you.

Bambino: Yeah. Hey, I'm warning you, my friend! No ratting on me, huh?

Padre: No, no! Aside from myself, only He shall know [*pointing to heaven*].

Bambino: No! Either it's between you and me or nothin' doing!

The Padre played by Pupo De Luca and Bambino played by Bud Spencer: E.B. Clucher's (Enzo Barboni) *Trinity Is Still My Name* (West Film/Avco Embassy, 1971).

4764

Mattie: If I smelled as bad as you, I wouldn't live near people.

Mattie Ross played by Kim Darby: Henry Hathaway's *True Grit* (Paramount, 1969).

4765

Euphemia: Isn't there more to life than just living?

Euphemia Ashby played by Annabeth Gish: Karen Arthur's *True Women* (TVW, 1997).

4766

Woods: Life isn't just given to us, Georgia. We have to earn it.

Dr. Peter Woods played by Jeff Nordling and Georgia Lawshe played by Angelina Jolie: Karen Arthur's *True Women* (TVW, 1997).

4767

Georgia: One thing you never explained to me, Mama, is: how can the truth set you free if it's all covered over by a lie?

Georgia Lawshe played by Angelina Jolie: Karen Arthur's *True Women* (TVW, 1997).

4768

Sarah: I don't think our loved ones make our lives. But loving them does. Death cannot take that away. It stays with us …forever.

Sarah McClure played by Dana Delany: Karen Arthur's *True Women* (TVW, 1997).

4769

Frazer: In trying to spare people pain you can sometimes cause more.

Major Frazer played by John McIntire: John Ford's *Two Rode Together* (Columbia, 1961).

4770

Major: I see no reason to honor a promise to a dead man when it entails a cruel lie to the living.

Major Frazer played by John McIntire: John Ford's *Two Rode Together* (Columbia, 1961).

4771

Major: Just how much do you think human lives are worth, McCabe?

McCabe: Whatever the market will bear. No more, no less.

Major Frazer played by John McIntire and Guthrie "Gus" McCabe played by James Stewart: John Ford's *Two Rode Together* (Columbia, 1961).

4772

Ben: Hang on to these days, Rachael. And don't grow up too fast.

Ben Zachary played by Burt Lancaster and Rachel Zachary played by Audrey Hepburn: John Huston's *The Unforgiven* (United Artists, 1960).

4773

Jackson: I learned a long time ago not to rule out anything when it comes to people.

Jackson played by Christopher Boyer: Michael Bohusz's *Uninvited* (Imperial Entertainment, 1993).

4774

Jane: I like loyalty …even when it's to the wrong person.

Jane Stevens played by Shelley Winters: Hugo Fregonese's *Untamed Frontier* (Universal, 1952).

4775

Lily: I'm not afraid of living anymore.

Lily Fasken played by Sally Forrest: Richard Thorpe's *Vengeance Valley* (MGM, 1951).

4776

President: My friend, it's very much better that I die a fool trusting too much than live a tyrant trusting no one at all.

President Francisco Madero played by Alexander Knox: Buzz Kulik's *Villa Rides!* (Paramount, 1968).

4777

Arnold: Pancho Villa is a bandit, a bigamist, and a barbarian. It takes more than dumb luck to turn that into a national hero.

Lee Arnold played by Robert Mitchum and Pancho Villa played by Yul Brynner: Buzz Kulik's *Villa Rides!* (Paramount, 1968).

4778

Mary: Sometimes growing up takes a long while. And sometimes it can be done in a few days.

Mary Dennison played by Pat Crowley: Jesse Hibbs' *Walk the Proud Land* (Universal, 1956).

4779

Miller: You know something, Mr. Hayes, I don't want pity.

Hayes: Then don't look for it!

Rod Miller played by Michael Dante and John Hayes played by Randolph Scott: Budd Boetticher's *Westbound* (Warner Bros., 1959).

4780

Mace: The trouble with you, Clay, is that you're rich enough to be an honorable man. I can't afford it.

Mace played by Michael Pate and Clay Putnam played by Andrew Duggan: Budd Boetticher's *Westbound* (Warner Bros., 1959).

4781

Judge Bean: Don't you trust me, Cole?

Cole: When I was a kid, I had a pet rat-

tlesnake. I was fond of it, but I would never turn my back on it.

Judge Roy Bean played by Walter Brennan and Cole Hardin played by Gary Cooper: William Wyler's *The Westerner* (United Artists, 1940).

4782

Post: Hey, Ross? What do you think the poor folks is doing?

Bodine: Without.

Frank Post played by Ryan O'Neal and Ross Bodine played by William Holden: Blake Edwards *Wild Rovers* (MGM, 1971).

4783

Catherine: We don't all have the same choices. We just don't all have the same choice.

Catherine Allen played by Joan Hackett: Tom Gries' *Will Penny* (Paramount, 1968).

4784

Claire: Jeff, is that you?

Jeff: As near as I can tell, it is.

Claire Hartford played by Anne Nagel and Jeff Ramsay played by Dick Foran: Ford Beebe's and Ray Taylor's *Winners of the West* (Universal serial, Chapter 3: "The Bridge of Disaster," 1940).

4785

Carter: You know, Ramsay, you and I have a lot in common. It's too bad we can't work together.

Ramsay: Yes, but it's what we haven't got in common that keeps us on opposite sides of the fence.

King Carter played by Harry Woods and Jeff Ramsay played by Dick Foran: Ford Beebe's and Ray Taylor's *Winners of the West* (Universal serial, Chapter 6: "A Leap for Life," 1940).

4786

Nicholas: The closer you can keep your family, the better. They're the only ones you can rely on. Remember this, all of you: nothing counts so much as blood. The rest are just strangers.

Nicholas Earp played by Gene Hackman: Lawrence Kasdan's *Wyatt Earp* (Warner Bros., 1994).

4787

Doc: For some people, this world ain't ever gonna be right.

Doc Holliday played by Dennis Quaid: Lawrence Kasdan's *Wyatt Earp* (Warner Bros., 1994).

4788

Lily: A person's a fool when he doesn't know when to move on.

Lily Beloit played by Angie Dickinson: Burt Kennedy's *Young Billy Young* (United Artists, 1969).

4789

Billy: When you look up to somebody, you expect them to do the right thing.

Billy Young played by Robert Walker, Jr.: Burt Kennedy's *Young Billy Young* (United Artists, 1969).

Pioneers, Settlers, and Sodbusters

See also Cooks; Cowboys; Good Guys; Men; People; Women

4790
Marshal: The opinion in town is …you won't last long.
Hannaberry: The opinion here is …we will.
Marshal Dan Mitchell played by Randolph Scott and Hannaberry played by Eddy Waller: Edwin Marin's *Abilene Town* (United Artists, 1946).

4791
Peter: I figure it sounds kind of crazy to most people …going to California just to see it. But there's a gallivanted bug in my blood and that's the way I am.
Peter Muncie played by William Holden: Wesley Ruggles' *Arizona* (Columbia, 1940).

4792
Glyn: Always point this [wagon tongue] toward the North Star. Where is it? There we are. Then come morning, we'll know where we're going.
Glyn McLyntock played by James Stewart: Anthony Mann's *Bend of the River* (Universal, 1952).

4793
Doc: And Frank? Well, he was just a homesick farmer who traded his plow for a rifle, and always a mite bitter about it.
Doc Butcher played by Walter Brennan: William D. Russell's *Best of the Badmen* (RKO, 1951).

4794
Dedicated to the men and women who planted civilization in the wilderness and courage in the blood of their children.
Prairie schooners rolling west, praying for peace — but ready for battle.
The last outpost, the turning back place for the weak; the starting place for the strong.
They have not turned back, those who died; they stay, and yet they go forward. Their spirit leads.
Ten weary miles a day. There is no road, but there is a will, and history cuts the way.
Captions from Raoul Walsh's *The Big Trail* (Fox, 1930).

4795
Breck: We can't turn back! We're blazing a trail that started in England. Not even the storms of the sea could turn back those first settlers. And they carried it on further. They blazed it on through the wilderness of Kentucky. Famine, hunger, not even massacres could stop them. And now we picked up the trail again. And nothing can stop us! Not even the snows of winter, nor the peaks of the highest mountain. We're building a nation! And we got to suffer! No great trail was ever built without hardship. And you got to fight! That's right. And when you stop fighting, that's death. What are you going to do, lay down and die? Not in a thousand years! You're going on with me!
Breck Coleman played by John Wayne: Raoul Walsh's *The Big Trail* (Fox, 1930).

4796
Gussie: Zeke, did you hear that terrible crash?
Zeke: Hear it? I seen it! That was your wagon!
Gussie: Was my mother-in-law in it?
Gussie played by El Brendel and Zeke played by Tully Marshall: Raoul Walsh's *The Big Trail* (Fox, 1930).

4797
Ruth: Zack, you're not really leaving us?
Zeke: Yeah, gal, I'm pullin' out. You're all nice and settled now. And this here valley is getting altogether too civilized for me. Whenever I get more than three or four families within one hundred miles of me, I begin to feel kind of crowded.
Ruth Cameron played by Marguerite Churchill and Zeke played by Tully Marshall: Raoul Walsh's *The Big Trail* (Fox, 1930).

4798
Jim: You've got to remember that these are just simple farmers. These are people of the land …the common clay of the new west. You know …morons!
Jim played by Gene Wilder: Mel Brooks' *Blazing Saddles* (Warner Bros., 1974).

4799
Jonathan: Even though we might be the last wagon, we'd never be the first to fall out.
Jonathan Kent played by Tyrone Power: Henry Hathaway's *Brigham Young* (20th Century–Fox, 1940).

4800
Mary Ann: You're dead set against California, aren't you?

Brigham: You know human nature. Take a crowd of people to a place of milk and honey and in six months time, they won't be worth shooting.
Mary Ann Young played by Mary Astor and Brigham Young played by Dean Jagger: Henry Hathaway's *Brigham Young* (20th Century–Fox, 1940).

4801
Lucy: It's so peaceful here.
George: The illusion of peace is upon us.
Lucy: You sound rather jaded.
George: Oh, these cabin raisers jade me. People planting themselves in one rough spot for the rest of their lives. I'm more for mansions and plush furniture.
Lucy Overmire played by Susan Hayward and George Camrose played by Brian Donlevy: Jacques Tourneur's *Canyon Passage* (Universal, 1946).

4802
Matthew: Becky, we ain't going back. I'd rather die than do that, wouldn't you?
Rebecca: I don't want to die. I want to get there!
Matthew Carver played by Charles Powell and Rebecca Carver played by Kelly Preston: Mark Griffiths' *Cheyenne Warrior* (Concorde–New Horizons Corp., 1994).

4803
Barkley: You better start using your head. Dumb people just don't make it out here.
Barkley played by Dan Haggerty: Mark Griffiths' *Cheyenne Warrior* (Concorde–New Horizons Corp., 1994).

4804
In 1889, President Harrison opened the vast Indian Oklahoma Lands for white settlement …. 2,000,000 acres free for the taking, poor and rich pouring in, swarming the border, waiting for the starting gun, at noon, April 22nd ….
Caption at beginning of Wesley Ruggles' *Cimarron* (RKO, 1931).

4805
Yancy: Sugar, if we all took root and squatted, there would never be any new country.
Yancy Cravat played by Richard Dix and Sabra Cravat played by Irene Dunne: Wesley Ruggles' *Cimarron* (RKO, 1931).

4806
Cynthia: For the first time, I'm glad I came out here.

Brett: If you didn't want to come, what brought you?

Cynthia: Restlessness. I keep running after something. When I find out what it is, I'll stop. We're a lot alike.

Brett: Except I'll probably keep running.

Cynthia London played by Carole Mathews and Brett Stanton played by Dale Robertson: Harmon Jones' *City of Bad Men* (20th Century–Fox, 1953).

4807

Crane: I'll fight for what I believe, Mr. Starrett. I'll die if I have to, but I'll fight. I want you to know that.

Starrett: You got a big mouth, farmer. You got big eyes too. You came here a year ago in your broken down wagon looking for a choice spot to settle. And you think you found it. But you never stopped to think what made it such a good place. When Dan and I came here, Bitters was a nesting spot for every thief and killer in the territory. A man's life wasn't worth the price of a bullet. No woman was safe on the streets, let alone in a lonely farm house. It took more than a big mouth to get rid of the lice who infested every bend of the road you ride so safely on. I'm not saying Dan and I did it alone. But we did more than our share. We hunted them down in the freezing cold while you sat back in the east hugging your pot-belly stove. Nobody thanked us. Nobody paid us. We did it because we felt we belonged. We earned the right to belong. And all you've done is ride in here and put down your stinking roots. And now you tell us that you belong and we don't. Mr. Crane, you said you'd fight to keep what you want. Well, I've been doing that for twenty years, and I intend to keep on doing it. And no pig-belly farmer is going to stop me!

Hal Crane played by Alan Marshal and Blaise Starrett played by Robert Ryan: Andre De Toth's *Day of the Outlaw* (United Artists, 1959).

4808

Hatton: You know, out here the trail boss has sometimes even got to take the law into his own hands.

Abbie: Oh yes, pioneering, I believe you call it, don't you?

Wade Hatton played by Errol Flynn and Abbie

When a town gets infested with outlaws, citizens usually come up with ways to get rid of them. In this scene, Rancher Blaise Starrett (Robert Ryan) comes up with a novel approach: he leads them out of town! "I'm just taking some bad men out of a good town," says Blaise in Andre de Toth's *Day of the Outlaw* (United Artists, 1959).

Irving played by Olivia de Havilland: Michael Curtiz's *Dodge City* (Warner Bros., 1939).

4809

It was the custom for neighbors to come from miles around to help a newcomer clear his land.

Caption from John Ford's *Drums Along the Mohawk* (20th Century–Fox, 1939).

4810

Lewis: To those of you who want to go on, I can promise little. I can't be sure we won't dig other graves.

Meriwether Lewis played by Fred MacMurray: Rudolph Mate's *The Far Horizons* (Paramount, 1955).

4811

Mary: Mother always said: know thy enemy and never let them see that you're afraid.

Mary Ingles played by Sheryl Lee: Martin Davidson's *Follow the River* (Hallmark Home Entertainment, 1995).

4812

Impoverished by civil war, and faced with the painful labor of reconstruction, thousands of Americans cut the old ties and took the immigrant trail to the free lands of the far west ...and a new beginning.

Prologue: George Sherman's *Frontier Horizon* (a.k.a. *New Frontier*; Republic, 1939).

4813

Brady: It's a shame, Billy. You know, these people come west hoping for a new opportunity ...and they become victims of a conflict they have no say in.

Brady Hawkes played by Kenny Rogers and Billy Montana played by Bruce Boxleitner: Dick Lowry's *The Gambler, Part III — The Legend Continues* (TVW, 1987).

4814

Hooker: You think he might want to make this trip again?

Fiske: He just might want to get back from this one.

Hooker played by Gary Cooper and Fiske played

by Richard Widmark: Henry Hathaway's *Garden of Evil* (20th Century–Fox, 1954).

4815

Flaff: Nippy, huh?

Grundy: Nippy, hell! I damn near froze last night!

Flagg: Why didn't you sleep inside?

Grundy: Walls and roaches are for city folks.

Flagg: Well, then, why did you build it [cabin]?

Grundy: On account of I never built nothing like it before.

Jim Flagg played by Robert Mitchum and Grundy played by Douglas V. Fowley: Burt Kennedy's *The Good Guys and the Bad Guys* (Warner Bros., 1969).

4816

Hewey: C.C., there's a lot of people who want to own something even if it is little. They see honor in it.

Fat: The trouble with the laboring class is they're always asking more than they're worth.

Fat Gerwin played by Walter Olkewicz, C.C. Tarpley played by Wilford Brimley, and Hewey Calloway played by Tommy Lee Jones who also directed *The Good Old Boys* (Turner Pictures, 1995).

4817

Ella: Wallpaper?

Nathan: Yeah, well, it civilizes the wilderness.

Ella Watson played by Isabelle Huppert and Nathan D. Champion played by Christopher Walken: Michael Cimino's *Heaven's Gate* (United Artists, 1980).

4818

Eve: Are them injun girls pretty?

Linus: Well, now I reckon that all depends on just how long a man has gone without seeing one.

Eve: How long has it been since you've seen a white girl?

Linus: I ain't quite sure why you asked that.

Eve: How pretty do I look to you?

Linus: Ma'am, ain't you just being a little bit forward?

Eve: Well, you're headed upriver …I'm headed down. There's no time to get these questions answered.

Eve Prescott played by Carroll Baker and Linus Rawlings played by James Stewart: John Ford's, George Marshall's, and Henry Hathaway's *How the West Was Won* (MGM, 1962).

4819

Zeb: I'm just passing through.

Jethro: Through to where? Anywhere you go is like where you've been. Ain't you lost enough tail feathers back there?

Zeb: I've been plucked some. But that's what I like about this country. There's always greener grass over the next hill.

Jethro: Not no more. Not since that damn railroad come. All the green is being staked out now …with a lock on it.

Zeb: Maybe I'll just have to climb a little higher hill to find it. How about coming along?

Jethro: Are you crazy? Like the injuns say, these rocks and trees around here feel no call to move. Why should I?

Zeb: I guess I'm not an Indian, Jethro. But I'm sure not a rock nor a tree. Men belongs with his own kind …like 'em or not.

Zeb Rawlings played by George Peppard and Jethro Stuart played by Henry Fonda: John Ford, George Marshall, and Henry Hathaway's *How the West Was Won* (MGM, 1962).

4820

Craig: I got a message for you. I don't know whether to appeal to your good sense or your courage, because I don't know how much of either you have. I do know you're facing something that's going to call for both …good sense and courage.

Tom Craig played by John Wayne: William McGann's *In Old California* (Republic, 1942).

4821

Blessed By God
Bent By Toil
Busted By Bastards
Goin' Home

Sign on wagon: John Patterson's *Independence* (TVW, 1987).

4822

Harper: Have we come so far that we've forgotten what it's like to start out with nothing but a dim chance and a bright hope?

J.P. Harper played by David Ogden Stiers: Charles Haid's *Iron Will* (Buena Vista, 1994).

4823

Bowie: If it's farming you want to do, Finley MacNab, the land in Texas is so rich you can plant ten penny nails and grow yourself a crop of iron bolts.

Jim Bowie played by David Keith and Finley MacNab played by Daragh O'Malley: Richard Lang's *James A. Michener's Texas* (TVW, 1995).

4824

Sam: Colonel, only a damn small handful of men in history could lay claim to the type of pioneering you've managed to accomplish.

Austin: Ah, but bloodless pioneering, Mr. Houston. The type that scholars refer to as humble instruments that paves the way for others. The monuments and the applause are always for the military leaders …the warriors. And you, Mr. Houston, strike me as very much a warrior.

Sam Houston played by Stacy Keach and Stephen F. Austin played by Patrick Duffy: Richard Lang's *James A. Michener's Texas* (TVW, 1995).

4825

Big Eli: The way to start off new is to shuck off what's old.

Big Eli Wakefield played by Burt Lancaster who also directed *The Kentuckian* (United Artists, 1955).

4826

Steve: I was willing to go along if you played smart and let me call the moves. But when you lose your head and start plugging farmers in the back, I'm through!

Steve Lewis played by Robert Preston: Frank Lloyd's *Lady from Cheyenne* (Universal, 1941).

4827

Dalton: Your two brothers, Charlie and Henry, they're still farming …and look at them! They're already old men …scratching the dirt like chickens to make a living. Even a blind horse knows when the trough is empty.

Bob Dalton played by Robert Conrad: Vincent McEveety's *The Last Day* (Paramount, 1975).

4828

It was a hard land, a hostile land. Only the strong survived. A new American breed …the pioneer.

Prologue: Stuart Heisler's *The Lone Ranger* (Warner Bros., 1956).

4829

Brave men and women. Driven not to tame the wilderness, but to keep the wilderness from taming them.

Part of the Introduction to Simon Wincer's *Lonesome Dove* (TVW, 1989).

4830

Gus: What are you doing in my wagon?

Lippy: I jumped off a roof and here's where I landed.

Gus: Well, you better jump back up there then because this wagon is going to Montana.

Lippy: Yes sir, and I am too. Piano playing is finished around here.

Gus: Well, we got two Irishmen and a bunch of idle brain cowboys. I guess we could always use a man that wears a chamber pot on his head.

Gus McCrae played by Robert Duvall and Lippy played by William Sanderson: Simon Wincer's *Lonesome Dove* (TVW, 1989).

4831

Narrator: It's been said that the west was won with guns and gold. It was not. It was won by the courage of simple people who pushed their ponderous wagons forever west through 200,000 square miles of awesome wilderness. Some were drawn by the lure of gold. But for the most part, they were families moved by the dream of a new beginning.

Narration by William Conrad: Bernard McEveety's *The Macahans* (TVW, 1976).

4832
Timothy: Zeb, tell me something. How much would it cost to outfit a family traveling west?
Zeb: How far west are you talking about?
Timothy: California and Oregon. The places you've been writing about in your letters.
Zeb: Tim, you ain't thinking of leaving this place?
Timothy: Just, just tell me.
Zeb: Well, I reckon a family your size would be seven, eight hundred dollars. Not only that, it's, uh, well, it's too late for a wester.
Timothy: Why?
Zeb: Well, it's into April. Now if you was to leave here tomorrow, you couldn't get to Missouri until June and the last wagon train leaves St. Joe mid May.
Timothy: May? Why so early?
Zeb: Well, they leave as soon as the grass is tall enough to feed the stock, and the ground is dry enough so they won't bog down the wagons. Then at the other end, you got to get through the mountain passes before mid–October or they close with snow. If that happens, you got to winter where you're at, and start again next spring.
Timothy: We could do all that with you.
Zeb: You got the fever bad.
Timothy: Yeah, I've had it a long time.

Timothy Macahan played by Richard Kiley and Zeb Macahan played by James Arness: Bernard McEveety's *The Macahans* (TVW, 1976).

4833
Zeb: There's nobody in his right mind who'd take off across that country in a single wagon. Not unless he was drove to it. There's 200,000 square miles of nothing but wasteland out there. And every mile there's a grave of somebody that didn't make it.

Zeb Macahan played by James Arness: Bernard McEveety's *The Macahans* (TVW, 1976).

4834
Narrator: The Macahan family, like thousands of others, came and saw and endured. In a sense, they were a typical family. But they were only typical of very special breed of people. Their likes we will never see again. But they have given us a heritage and a courage that was not only unique, but has survived to become our great American tradition.

Narration by William Conrad: Bernard McEveety's *The Macahans* (TVW, 1976).

4835
Old Man: They are all farmers. Farmers talk of nothing but fertilizer and women. I've never shared their enthusiasm for fertilizer. As for women, I became indifferent when I was eighty-three.

The Old Man played by Vladimir Sokoloff: John Sturges' *The Magnificent Seven* (United Artists, 1960).

4836
Liberty: You sodbusters are a brave bunch when you're together. But don't vote any way now that you'll regret later when you're alone!

Liberty Valance played by Lee Marvin: John Ford's *The Man Who Shot Liberty Valance* (Paramount, 1962).

4837
Young Ben Sage: So the first time I find one of our hides wearing our brand hung on one them settler fences, I aim to kill me a plowboy.

Young Ben Sage played by Ed Faulkner: Andrew V. McLaglen's *McLintock!* (United Artists, 1963).

4838
Cole: Sam, is that a leanin' axe or a usin' one?

Jim Cole played by Clint Walker and Sam Potts played by Don Haggerty: Joseph Pevney's *The Night of the Grizzly* (Paramount, 1966).

4839
Doc: They wanted to start a new life. They came all the way west …here …to us. To us, my hospitable friends! That's a long way to come just to lay down and die.

Doc Seltzer played by Larry Gates: James B. Clark's *One Foot in Hell* (20th Century–Fox, 1960).

4840
Dan: My folks worked their lives out trying to make something out of a lot of worn-out dirt that nobody else would spit on.

Dan Keats played by Don Murray: James B. Clark's *One Foot in Hell* (20th Century–Fox, 1960).

4841
Sarah: Lord, thanks a lot for bringing us to this place. Pa and Daniel died at the hands of that low-down murdering trash out-of-hell that done 'em in. But they put up a good fight and died the best they could. And thanks a lot for Josey Wales who you changed from a murdering bushwhacker on the side of Satan to a better man trying to deliver us from the Philistines. And thank the Lord for getting us together in Texas.

Grandma Sarah played by Paula Trueman: Clint Eastwood's *The Outlaw Josey Wales* (Warner Bros., 1976).

4842
LaHood: Those squatters, Reverend, are standing in the way of progress.
Preacher: Theirs or yours?

Coy LaHood played by Richard Dysart and the Preacher played by Clint Eastwood: Clint Eastwood's *Pale Rider* (Warner Bros., 1985).

4843
Barret: If we sell out now, what price do we put on our dignity the next time?

Hull Barret played by Michael Moriarty: Clint Eastwood's *Pale Rider* (Warner Bros., 1985).

4844
John: A man must have land. It's his only surety.

John Sergeant played by William Shatner: Buzz Kulik's *Pioneer Woman* (TVW, 1973).

4845
Douglas: Pretty tough life for a woman without a man.
Maggie: It's a hard life, Mr. Douglas, with or without a man.

Robert Douglas played by David Janssen and Maggie Sergeant played by Joanna Pettet: Buzz Kulik's *Pioneer Woman* (TVW, 1973).

4846
Hickok: That river clipper is saying goodbye to you, ma'am. Now you're going to have three long days of this prairie clipper.
Louisa: But tomorrow is Sunday. Do we ride on Sunday?
Hickok: Well, there's no Sunday west of Junction City, no law west of Hayes City, and no God west of Carson City.

Wild Bill Hickok played by Gary Cooper and Louisa Cody played by Helen Burgess: Cecil B. DeMille's *The Plainsman* (Paramount, 1936).

4847
It shall be as it was in the past …Not with dreams, but with strength and with courage …Shall a nation be molded to last.

Epilogue to Cecil B. DeMille's *The Plainsman* (Paramount, 1936).

4848
Often intimidated or lynched if they tried to own property, and discouraged from educating themselves, most of the early black settlers were successfully kept from power.

Epilogue: Mario Van Peebles' *Posse* (Gramercy Pictures, 1993).

4849

Vallian: I'm going hunting at dawn. Do you want to come along?

Boy: I've never hunted.

Vallian: Well, I never had either until the first time.

Con Vallian played by Sam Elliott and the boy, Tom McKaskel, played by Kenny Morrison: Richard Day's *The Quick and the Dead* (HBO Pictures, 1987).

4850

Sam: Just one thing, ma'am. If you're dead set on making this trip to Texas, you're going the wrong way.

Martha: Oh, thank you, Mr. Burnett. You are a very capable guide.

Sam: Well, I can tell north from south.

Sam Burnett played by James Stewart and Martha Price played by Maureen O'Hara: Andrew V. McLaglen's *The Rare Breed* (Universal, 1966).

4851

Jane: I might be led, but I won't be driven.

Jane Withersteen played by Amy Madigan: Charles Haid's *Riders of the Purple Sage* (Turner Home Entertainment, 1996).

4852

Pa Sackett liked his horses fast, his drinks hard, and his preachers hellfire hot. And he raised his sons accordingly.

Introduction to Robert Totten's *The Sacketts* (TVW, 1979) by Louis L'Amour.

4853

Lucky: It's men like Parker that build up the west and bring progress to it …not men like you. It's the sweat and blood of the little men that makes this country the great country that it is …not the greed of the so-called big ones.

Lucky Randall played by Russell Hayden: William Berke's *Saddles and Sagebrush* (Columbia, 1943).

4854

Decky: Is it injuns?

Lomax: Worse. Worse than injuns, Decky. That there is the smell of hard times.

Decky played by Dawn Lyn and Clay Lomax played by Gregory Peck: Henry Hathaway's *Shoot Out* (Universal, 1971).

4855

Butch: It's hotter than a witch's tit.

Cole: I think you mean, colder than a witch's tit.

Butch: That ain't the way I heard it. It's hotter than a witch's tit.

Cole: Colder than a witch's tit is the proper expression.

Butch: How would you know if a witch has hot or cold tits? Have you ever felt 'em?

Cole: Jake, that expression about the witch's tit? How does it go?

Jake: Witch's tit?

Cole: Yeah …something …than a witch's tit?

Jake: Faster?

Cole: Faster? Faster than a witch's tit? Hotter or colder!

Jake: Why all of a sudden the interest in witches' tits? One of you boys seen a witch?

Butch played by Earl Pastko, Cole played by John Hemphill, and Jake played by George Buza: Eugene Levy's *Sodbusters* (Atlantis Releasing, 1994).

4856

Ed: Well, I say we got more important things to do right now. My God! Three hired hands killed in the past month! Are we just gonna lie down and let Cantrell ride roughshod over us?

Clarence: We can talk about that over brunch, Ed.

Ed: I'm through talking! Are you people blind! We got ourselves a problem here, and it's festering like a boil oozing pus!

Beth: So much for food. Come on, Roy, let's go home.

Roy: Best idea I've heard since we got here.

Ed: Go ahead, Roy! Run! Every time you smell trouble, you run and hide and stick your head in the ground like a …what do you call it? That big bird with the long neck? It can't fly! It's a bird! It sticks its head in the ground!

Annie: Why would a bird stick its head in the ground?

Ed: Well, it don't keep me up at nights thinking about it, Annie. I'm just saying that Roy reminds me of that bird.

Roy: What bird?

Ed: The bird that sticks its head in the ground! It's as big as a man! Long neck! Little wings! It sticks its head in the ground! What the hell is the name of it?

Beth: How can a bird breathe with its head in the ground, Ed?

Ed: I don't know how he can breathe with his head in the ground, Beth! That was hardly my point!

Roy: What exactly is your point?

Ed: What is my point? I'll tell you what my point is! Roy ……. I forgot my point! You all satisfied?

Ed "Shorty" Simms played by Lou Wagner, Clarence Gentry played by Fred Willard, Beth Poulet played by Maria Vacratsis, Roy Poulet played by Don Lake, and Annie Simms played by Lela Ivey: Eugene Levy's *Sodbusters* (Atlantis Releasing, 1994).

4857

Cole: Where are you from, stranger?

Destiny: Little place you probably never heard of.

Cole: Try me.

Destiny: Texas.

Cole: Texas? I heard of Texas.

Destiny: Then I reckon you are smarter than you look.

Cole: Maybe I am …maybe I'm not.

Cole played by John Hemphill and Destiny played by Kris Kristofferson: Eugene Levy's *Sodbusters* (Atlantis Releasing, 1994).

4858

Clarence: Roy, we got to stick together. It's the only way we can keep what's ours.

Roy: What's ours ain't worth keeping!

Clarence Gentry played by Fred Willard and Roy Poulet played by Don Lake: Eugene Levy's *Sodbusters* (Atlantis Releasing, 1994).

4859

Woman: What do you want?

Will: Oh, we was wondering if we could do you some chores in exchange for a dollar. Swill your pigs, clean out your barn …whatever you say.

Woman: You can scat! I don't hire saddle tramps.

Les: Ain't you heard, lady? Money is like manure. It's only good when you spread it around.

Will Young played by Gary Grimes and Les Richter played by Ron Howard: Richard Fleischer's *The Spikes Gang* (United Artists, 1974).

4860

Narrator: With the decline of the once powerful Indian nation, a new frontier began to move its way westward. Spurred on by the liberal land grant laws of 1887, men of all description fought their way across the great rivers of Missouri, the endless plains of Kansas, out into the new found territory. And a mile of land could be measured by the graves of those who died to win it. Soon the branding iron became the only law west of El Dorado. Few argued with it. Those who did were called nesters, the cattlemen's hated word for the homesteaders who spearheaded the drive across his barbed-flung empire. The war of fence and iron had begun …asking no quarter …giving none. The progress of a nation was expanding westward. But of this, the cattlemen knew little and cared less. His empire was in danger, and once again he would fight to save it.

Narration during prologue: Lesley Selander's *Stampede* (Warner Bros., 1949).

4861

Nella: You ain't thinking of butchering one of our mules?

Ben: That's no mule, grandma. That's a Missouri elk!

Nella Turner played by Jane Russell and Ben Allison played by Clark Gable: Raoul Walsh's *The Tall Men* (20th Century–Fox, 1955).

4862

Nella: Why didn't you give me a hand? You saw me out there stuck in the mud!

Ben: Mud? I thought that was quicksand!

Nella Turner played by Jane Russell and Ben Allison played by Clark Gable in Raoul Walsh's *The Tall Men* (20th Century–Fox, 1955).

4863

Blue Jacket: The American's lust for land is like a man for a woman. They can't get enough!

Blue Jacket played by Holt McCallany: Larry Elikann's *Tecumseh: The Last Warrior* (Turner Pictures, 1995).

4864

John: A little dust couldn't run her out. She could take it. She was a pioneer.

Leni: Yes, but when you are a refugee, it is different. The pioneers have everything to gain. We have lost everything.

John: The way I figure it, you stopped being a refugee when you came through Ellis Island. There's no reason you can't start being a pioneer now.

John Phillips played by John Wayne and Leni Braun played by Sigrid Gurie: Bernard Vorhaus' *Three Faces West* (Republic, 1940).

4865

Alice: What if you went into town and borrowed the money?

Dan: You know I hate to go begging other people for help.

Alice: Borrowing isn't begging. It could save us.

Alice Evans played by Leora Dana and Dan Evans played by Van Heflin: Delmer Daves' *3:10 to Yuma* (Columbia, 1957).

4866

McKeon: Bowen is like all the others around here that call themselves farmers. All they want to do is scratch the soil, throw in the seed, and then sit down and watch it grow them a fortune.

Tim McKeon played by Frank McGlynn, Jr., and Eben Bowen played by Ernie Adams: Ray Enright's *Trail Street* (RKO, 1947).

4867

Not too long ago, a lonely outpost guarded this very spot. It was called Fort Pitt. It stood at the edge of an unknown land …one of a line of forts that ran from Virginia to the Great Lakes, marking the end of the known and the beginning of the unknown. Civilization was east of the Allegheny Mountains. Conquest, opportunity, and death lay to the west.

Prologue to Cecil B. DeMille's *Unconquered* (Paramount, 1947).

4868

Yet man kept coming west. Some to build their own fortunes even at the price of Indian wars. Others to build a nation …even at the price of their own lives. These are the unconquered who pushed ever forward the frontiers of men's freedom.

Prologue to Cecil B. DeMille's *Unconquered* (Paramount, 1947).

4869

Ben: When a man sets down roots, Cash, he don't like 'em cut off.

Ben Zachary played by Burt Lancaster and Cash Zachary played by Audie Murphy: John Huston's *The Unforgiven* (United Artists, 1960).

4870

Matilda: Prairie fever.

Rachel: What's that?

Matilda: The worst thing you can get. Loneliness.

Matilda Zachary played by Lillian Gish and Rachel Zachary played by Audrey Hepburn: John Huston's *The Unforgiven* (United Artists, 1960).

4871

Ben: Well, what makes you so happy, Mama?

Matilda: Because you ain't sick or dead or scalped or something worse.

Ben: Nothing could kill me except lightning out of the sky. And then it would have to hit twice.

Ben Zachary played by Burt Lancaster and Matilda Zachary played by Lillian Gish: John Huston's *The Unforgiven* (United Artists, 1960).

4872

Julian: I'd like to recommend one of my very favorite authors to you …a woman named Jane Austen. This is a writer of just wonderfully exquisite prose. And, of course, as you can see, it's a big damn book. Oh, *Pride and Prejudice*. Harry Bob, I think you're going to get more than a run for your money out of this one.

Harry Bob: How much?

Julian: Well, I think $2.00 is a fair price.

Harry Bob: Really?

Julian: Uh huh.

Harry Bob: How much for just the "Pride"?

Julian: Well, actually, one does hate to break up the set.

Harry Bob: All right, but I got to test it first [*tearing out some pages*]. Where's the outhouse?

Julian Rodgers played by John C. McGinley and Harry Bob Ferguson played by David Dunard: Peter Markle's *Wagons East!* (TriStar, 1994).

4873

Julian: What on earth were we thinking? I mean, why in the world did we ever come out here in the first place?

Phil: Well, why don't we go back?

Ben: Back?

Phil: Yeah, back. Back east. Back home. Back! Come on!

Zeke: You're talkin' crazy, Phil.

Phil: Oh, am I?

Ben: Of course you are. You can't go east!

Phil: Why not?

Ben: Because!

Phil: Why?

Zeke: Because it is against the code!

Ben: Exactly, because it's against the code!

Phil: It's against …what code?

Ben: You know very well what code. The code of the west.

Phil: Oh, the code of the west. Isn't that the same one that says …

Ben: The only good Indian is a dead Indian.

Phil: And die with your boots on. Wait, wait a minute! I got another one. If someone steals your horse, you hang him! That's some code! Hey, this is quite a code. Let's just stay here. What a code!

Julian: It's not a very enlightened ideology.

Ben: But leaving would be like giving up.

Phil: That's exactly what it would be, Ben, giving up. So let's just give up. Let's get out of here. Let's get ourselves a wagonmaster and go home. Let's go east. What do you say?

Bartender: I say you are a bunch of gutless lily-livered yellow-belly eastern sissies. All you've done since you got here was whine and complain. Now why don't you go back and leave the west to the real men?

Julian: Well, actually, I could have the books on the wagon really quickly. And the cappucino machine, you know, is going to travel like a dream!

Julian Rodgers played by John C. McGinley, Phil Taylor played by Richard Lewis, Ben Wheeler played by Robert Picardo, Zeke played by William Sanderson, and the Bartender played by Steve Eastin: Peter Markle's *Wagons East!* (TriStar, 1994).

4874

Zeke: Howdy, Phil.

Phil: How are you doing, Zeke?

Zeke: Say, what's that wagonmaster fella's name again?

Phil: You mean Harlow?

Zeke: Harlow. Yep, that's him I reckon. He's been gnawing at me ever since I first set eyes on him. You don't forget somebody like that.

Phil: Well, what did he do?

Zeke: That's the only part I can't remember. I know it was something really good.

Phil: Yeah?

Zeke: Or really bad.

Phil: Oh well, you must remember something.

Zeke: Oh, it'll come to me. You can be sure of it …maybe not.

Zeke played by William Sanderson, Phil Taylor

played by Richard Lewis, and James Harlow played by John Candy: Peter Markle's *Wagons East!* (TriStar, 1994).

4875

Townsman: Ma'am, you people are crazy!

Belle: Crazy? What do you mean, crazy? Because we risked our lives crossing a river instead of staying on the other side? Because we have faith in ourselves? Because we believe in a wagonmaster who gave us the courage and the confidence to do things we never thought we could have done?

Townsman: No, because most people use the bridge.

The River Townsman played by Joe Bays and Belle played by Ellen Greene: Peter Markle's *Wagons East!* (TriStar, 1994).

4876

Ben: Harlow was a wagonmaster for the Donner party …before he became a vegetarian.

Ben Wheeler played by Robert Picardo and James Harlow played by John Candy: Peter Markle's *Wagons East!* (Tristar, 1994).

4877

John: We will survive, God willing.

Emma: God is not willing! That ought to be clear by now!

John McKay played by John Denver and Emma McKay played by Klara Irene Miracle: Craig Clyde's *Walking Thunder* (Majestic Entertainment/Sunset Hill Partners, 1997).

4878

Rebecca: Lije, Lije, stay home this time!

Lije: I wish I could but I can't.

Rebecca: Why?

Lije: I don't know why. It's just that I got to go where I've not been. And where I can say: this far I've come, I can't go no further. Do you understand that?

Rebecca Evans played by Lola Albright and Lije Evans played by Richard Widmark: Andrew V. McLaglen's *The Way West* (United Artists, 1967).

4879

Jenks: You ain't got the spirit of life, Isaac.

Isaac: Life? Hell, you call this life? We're buried just as sure as that frozen-like ground out there in the flats. The only difference is …we don't know it! Death is what we are.

Jenks played by Warren Oates and Isaac Maple played by John Anderson: Burt Kennedy's *Welcome to Hard Times* (MGM, 1967).

4880

Ezra: A man's a fool if he doesn't know when to move on.

Judge Roy Bean (Walter Brennan) informs Cole Hardin (Gary Cooper) that "in this court a horse thief always gets a fair trial before he's hung." Looking on is Chickenfoot (Paul Hurst), Southeast (Chill Wills), and Undertaker Mort Borrow (Charles Halton) in William Wyler's classic, *The Westerner* (United Artists, 1940).

Blue: All my life I've been moving on, Ezra. I'm going on fifty and a failure because all my life I've been moving on. I never could bring myself to stand it out in one place ... stand it out when things start going against me. I'd back up ...and move on down the road. Well, this is the end of the road, Ezra. This is as far as I go!

Will Blue played by Henry Fonda and Ezra Maple played by John Anderson: Burt Kennedy's *Welcome to Hard Times* (MGM, 1967).

4881

Cole: Do you know how to build a house?
Jane-Ellen: No, how?
Cole: Well, you ...you ...well, you have the kitchen there ...and the bedroom over there ...and the living room right in the middle.
Jane-Ellen: And it would have to have the right things in it too.
Cole: What sort of things?
Jane-Ellen: Oh, fires ...lamplight ... warm beds ...the smell of coffee in the morning ...the sound of rain on the roof.
Cole: Gee, that's a nice house, Jane-Ellen.

Cole Hardin played by Gary Cooper and Jane-Ellen Mathews played by Doris Davenport: William Wyler's *The Westerner* (United Artists, 1940).

4882

Whitman: Now you face a heartbreaking journey. To tell you of it, I'll call now on Mr. Wyatt, our guide. Mr. Wyatt!
Wyatt: We'll jump off from Independence. We'll cross the Big Blue River, the Little Blue, the Platte, the Sweetwater, the South Pass over the Rockies, down to the Big Salt Lake, and then the desert. It's a long, hard grind with no let up. Rain, hail as big as eggs, breakdowns, prairie fires, sandstorms, dust storms, alkaline water, no water, cholera, Indians, drownings, stampedes, stupid accidents. You'll pass graves everywhere ...milestones along the way. One out of every three of ya will be dead before you get to his California Valley. So if you're smart, you'll leave by that door. That's my best advice.

Roy Whitman played by John McIntire and Buck Wyatt played by Robert Taylor: William Wellman's *Westward the Women* (MGM, 1952).

4883

Wyatt: They're crazy!
Whitman: Yeah. Crazy enough to carve a home out of the wilderness. That kind of crazy I like.

Buck Wyatt played by Robert Taylor and Roy Whitman played by John McIntire: William Wellman's *Westward the Women* (MGM, 1952).

4884

Jim: It's not so much what things are, it's what they could be.

Jim Tanner played by Steve Forrest: Robert Totten's *The Wild Country* (Buena Vista, 1971).

4885

Jim: You believe in this [pioneering], don't you Kate?
Kate: I believe in you.

Jim Tanner played by Steve Forrest and Kate Tanner played by Vera Miles: Robert Totten's *The Wild Country* (Buena Vista, 1971).

4886

Jim: We can't get ahead by going back.

Jim Tanner played by Steve Forrest: Robert Totten's *The Wild Country* (Buena Vista, 1971).

4887

Virgil: If we leave now and find it hard going again, we'll move again ...and again if we have to! Mom, when do we stop starting over? When do we say, this is where we stay? When, Mom?

Virgil Tanner played by Ron Howard: Robert Totten's *The Wild Country* (Buena Vista, 1971).

4888

Rusty: Let it be a lesson for you two: you got to fight hard for everything you get. Then twice as hard to hang on to it.

Rusty played by Casey Tibbs: Charles Haas' *Wild Heritage* (Universal, 1958).

Ranch and Range
See also Cowboys; Cattle; West

4889

Pop: Put this down. "Whereas, I hereby bequeath my homestead to my daughter."
Billy: You don't need the "whereas" and the "hereby."
Pop: Well, I'll leave that up to you. But just be sure there's enough whereases in there to make any law angler set up and take notice, huh?

Timothy "Pop" Keith played by Walter Brennan and Billy Shear played by John Agar: Raoul Walsh's *Along the Great Divide* (Warner Bros., 1951).

4890

Jason: If I had thought about it, we would have stopped to eat north of the deadline.
Josie: The what?
Jason: The deadline. We passed it about ten minutes back. Sheep to the south, cattle to the north.
Josie: I don't know anything about a deadline.
Jason: Well, there's nothing complicated about it. You see, the cowmen opened up this territory and then the sheepmen tried to move in. Well, we had quite a debate. We burned up a lot of powder and a lot of lead, and we buried a few. And then finally we drew us a line across the southeast section of the state. And the sheep stay on one side and the cattle on the other.

Jason Meredith played by Peter Graves and Josie Minick played by Doris Day: Andrew V. McLaglen's *Ballad of Josie* (Universal, 1968).

4891

Maria: The ranch is not for sale.
Carter: But surely you don't expect to live out ...
Maria: I intend to keep it!
Carter: But you don't intend to run it. No woman in her right mind would attempt to operate a 150,000 acre spread!
Maria: Whether or not I succeed in operating it, Mr. Carter, is not your concern. I can take care of myself.
Carter: I think you overestimate your ability, Miss Stoner.
Maria: Perhaps I do. Good day, Mr. Carter.... Mr. Carter, I was a whore at thirteen and my family of twelve never went hungry.

Maria Stoner played by Raquel Welch and Muncie Carter played by Denver Pyle: Andrew McLaglen's *Bandolero!* (20th Century–Fox, 1968).

4892

John Fain: A ranch sure is a deserted looking place during a roundup.

John Fain played by Richard Boone: George Sherman's *Big Jake* (NGP, 1971).

4893

Sven: Oh, you boys can sleep as late as you like in the morning …so long as you get up for breakfast. Five o'clock.

Sven Johnson played by John Qualen: Gordon Douglas' *The Big Land* (Warner Bros., 1957).

4894

Estrada: And all that you see is Estrada land, the Big Sombrero.

Autry: Where's the end of it?

Estrada: Oh, it's not in sight. There's a saying of my people that when you can look far to the four corners and see only your land, then you truthfully can say: I have a rancho.

Estrellita Estrada played by Elena Verdugo and Gene Autry played himself: Frank McDonald's *The Big Sombrero* (Columbia, 1949).

4895

Clayton: No family?

Mister: Him [horse]. Oh, you know saddle tramps. They sign on, drive the beef a thousand miles, make your mark, draw your pay, and move on to the next ranch. Another roundup and another drive. Hired …fired …and move on.

Clayton: Well, it's never bothered me none.

Mister: No, me neither when I was thirty years lighter.

Sam Clayton played by Gene Hackman and Mister played by Ben Johnson: Richard Brooks' *Bite the Bullet* (Columbia, 1975).

4896

Lamarr: Unfortunately, there is one thing that stands between me and that property …the rightful owners.

Hedley Lamarr played by Harvey Korman: Mel Brooks' *Blazing Saddles* (Warner Bros., 1974).

4897

Boone: I started off with a ten dollar horse, a bucking saddle, and a rope. I went up in the hills. I caught myself a stallion and four mares. I built my herd from the ground. I fought and I clawed my way for twenty years. I wore out two wives, lost three sons, and I hung seven men for riding my brand without a bill of sale. But I built the biggest herd in Montana, and nobody is going to take a head …not one …away from me …without having me after them!

Frank Boone played by John Dehner: Burt Kennedy's *The Canadians* (20th Century–Fox, 1961).

4898

Steve: There are two things that just aren't allowed on cattle drives: women and whiskey.

Steve Patrick played by George Montgomery: Harmon Jones' *Canyon River* (Allied Artists, 1956).

4899

Matt: I gave an order. I expect any man who works for me to obey it.

Chip: No, it's not what you say that galls me. It's the way you say it.

Matt: You'll get used to it.

Chip: The question is, do I want to?

Matt: You know, when a man works the same job too long, he gets thinking no one else can do it.

Chip: I guess that makes him as big a fool as the boy who thinks if he gives enough orders, nobody will have time enough to know that most of them don't make sense.

Matt Brown played by Audie Murphy and Chip Donohue played by John Dehner: Thomas Carr's *Cast a Long Shadow* (United Artists, 1959).

4900

Winters: Seems like if a man fights for something little, he's a hero. He fights for something big and they call him a range hog or a cattle king.

Ed Winters played by Ray Teal: Tay Garnett's *Cattle King* (MGM, 1963).

4901

Johnny: I don't run this ranch. I don't think I could. Lots of times I would fight instead of wait. I talked to Ed about that once. You know what he say? He say, Johnny, the difference between Sam and you and me is that Sam knows that any fool can fight. The smart man, he fights only when he knows there's no other way.

Johnny Quatro played by Robert Loggia, Ed Winters played by Ray Teal, and Sam Brassfield played by Robert Taylor: Tay Garnett's *Cattle King* (MGM, 1963).

4902

Harley: Ain't you going to give notice you're quitting?

John: I did that when I signed on.

Harley Sullivan played by Henry Fonda and John O'Hanlan played by James Stewart: Gene Kelly's *The Cheyenne Social Club* (NGP, 1970).

4903

Harley: Did I ever tell ya how my Uncle Charlie got stowed up?

John: No, Harley.

Harley: His home set right out in the prairie. One day he went in the outhouse and got caught right in the middle of a stampede. When he went in, he said there wasn't a cow in sight. A few minutes later, 365 longhorns ran over him. Broke him up something terrible. That was nineteen years ago and he's still constipated.

Harley Sullivan played by Henry Fonda and John O'Hanlan played by James Stewart: Gene Kelly's *The Cheyenne Social Club* (NGP, 1970).

4904

Harley: I remember one winter. It was almost as cold as this down in the south of Arkansas. It got to be so cold down there that winter that just about every female in the county came up pregnant in the spring. All the following summer and fall the men and boys were praying for another cold winter.

Harley Sullivan played by Henry Fonda: Gene Kelly's *The Cheyenne Social Club* (NGP, 1970).

4905

Chisum: We may have to be neighbors, but I don't have to be neighborly.

John Chisum played by John Wayne: Andrew McLaglen's *Chisum* (Warner Bros., 1970).

4906

Charlie: I've been dreaming every night about them Mexican gals for the last week. I wouldn't take $400.00 for what I dreamed last night.

Peggy: You've been talking in your sleep too. I wish you would think of something else to dream about for a change.

Charlie: I'll tell you what you do. You think of something better to dream about …I'll dream about it.

Charlie played by Dick York and Peggy played by Guy Wilkerson: Delmer Daves' *Cowboy* (Columbia, 1958).

4907

Wil: There ain't a kid in that school over fifteen. They're between hay and grass. I need men.

Anse: How old was you when you went on your first cattle drive?

Wil: What difference does that make?

Anse: How old was you, Wil?

Wil: Well, in my day …

Anse: How old?

Wil: Thirteen! But my old man's pants fit me!

Wil Anderson played by John Wayne and Anse played by Slim Pickens: Mark Rydell's *The Cowboys* (Warner Bros., 1972).

4908

Wil: Come on, we're burning daylight!

Wil Anderson played by John Wayne: Mark Rydell's *The Cowboys* (Warner Bros., 1972).

4909

Brant: How's he gonna pay us the money he owes us if we keep topping off his herd?

Will: I don't buy mortgages to get paid back. I buy them to foreclose.

Brant Marlow played by Steve Cochran and Will Marlow played by Raymond Massey: Stuart Heisler's *Dallas* (Warner Bros., 1950).

4910

Starrett: I'm through being reasonable. I told Crane what would happen if he strung that wire.

Dan: Blaise, we've pulled over some hard hills together. And I rode behind you all the way. But a wire fence is a poor excuse to make a widow out of Crane's wife. What have you been thinking about all winter? Crane's barb wire fence or Crane's pretty wife, Helen?

Blaise Starrett played by Robert Ryan and Dan played by Nehemiah Persoff: Andre De Toth's *Day of the Outlaw* (United Artists, 1959).

4911

Lance: I got a saddlebag full of dreams I made around the campfires in the war when the nights were quiet: we'll let the valley soak in the sunlight …nurse it and pet it …until Sweet Meadows is a ranch where we can live and all the kids after us.

Lance Poole played by Robert Taylor: Anthony Mann's *Devil's Doorway* (MGM, 1950).

4912

Jessica: My father built this shack with his own hands.

Griff: You've kept it as a shrine?

Jessica: No …just as a reminder not to let go of anything.

Jessica Drummond played by Barbara Stanwyck and Griff Bonnell played by Barry Sullivan: Samuel Fuller's *Forty Guns* (20th Century–Fox, 1957).

4913

Hewey: Let him go.

Eve: I couldn't do that.

Hewey: You'll have to sooner or later. Do it now while he knows what he wants …has a real chance to go get it. One fine day he's going to pick up and follow it whether you let him or not. Let him go now …with no hard feelings.

Eve Calloway played by Frances McDormand and Hewey Calloway played by Tommy Lee Jones who also directed *The Good Old Boys* (Turner Pictures, 1995).

4914

Hade: Hey, Loving, we got us a viper in the tall grass. It like to struck at me it did.

Loving: Lucky thing for the snake. He may have died of poison.

Hade Keough played by Dean Stockwell and Loving played by Chill Wills: Abner Biberman's *Gun for a Coward* (Universal, 1957).

4915

Saxon: I built up that ranch with my own two hands. You were born there. Your mother died there. I fought Indians and snow storms, and dry years and floods to make it what it is. And I'm not going to give it up just because some two-bit gunslinger happens to come to town.

Dan Saxon played by Paul Kelly: Nathan Juran's *Gunsmoke* (Universal, 1953).

4916

Reb: Then get out of camp!

Curly: I'll leave when I'm ready.

Reb: You'll leave right now!

Curly: I reckon that's a choice I'll make for myself.

Reb: The only choice you've got is how you'll go: either riding on a horse or feet first!

Curly: You've been twirling a pretty big rope ever since you came here. Maybe it's time someone took the slack out of your rope.

Reb: Anytime you're ready.

Reb Kittredge played by Audie Murphy and Curly Mather played by Jack Kelly: Nathan Juran's *Gunsmoke* (Universal, 1953).

4917

Moore: I know we were a little rough on you, and I'm sorry for that. I'm even willing to overlook the fact that you're trespassing until we can get this thing settled.

Dakota: As I understand it, possession is nine points of the law. And as you can see, I'm in possession of this place. So until somebody changes that one way or another, it looks to me like you're trespassing!

Cal Moore played by Charles McGraw and the Stranger, Joe Dakota, played by Jock Mahoney: Richard Bartlett's *Joe Dakota* (Universal, 1957).

4918

McIvers: You better get out of here while you can, you and your men.

Vienna: We're here to stay, Mr. McIvers. You better get used to that idea.

McIvers: We don't want you here.

Vienna: This was free country when I came here. I'm not giving up a single foot of it.

Emma: You don't hear so good. We don't want you here!

Vienna: You don't own the earth, not this part of it.

McIvers: You stay and you'll keep only enough of it to bury you in!

John McIvers played by Ward Bond, Vienna played by Joan Crawford, and Emma Small played by Mercedes McCambridge: Nicholas Ray's *Johnny Guitar* (Republic, 1954).

4919

Jocko: We're going to be in Hobbs by sundown tomorrow.

Jory: Where's that?

Jocko: Hobbs, New Mexico, kid. Last stop before Texas …before the Promised Land.

Jory: Before what?

Jocko: Well, it's where each drive ends, kid. Wherever that is, that's the Promised Land. It's what you work and sweat all day for …calluses and lousy food, sun in your eyes and damn dirt in your mouth all day and all night. Why?

Jory: Oh, nothing. I just remember somebody else talking about the Promised Land, that's all. But I don't think it is the same thing.

Jocko: Well, it depends on what you want in life and what you're after.

Jocko played by B.J. Thomas and Jory Walden played by Robby Benson: Jorge Fons' *Jory* (Avco Embassy, 1972).

4920

Shep: Hey! If you fellas move any slower, you're going to be doing yesterday's work!

Shep Horgan played by Ernest Borgnine: Delmer Daves' *Jubal* (Columbia, 1956).

4921

Pinky: What are you putting on your hair? "Guaranteed to attract women and repel mosquitoes." I think they got it backwards. It should be, "guaranteed to repel women and attract bugs."

Pinky played by Rod Steiger: Delmer Daves' *Jubal* (Columbia, 1956).

4922

Mae: And everybody said he was a Wyoming cattle king. And I asked him, was he really a cattle king? He said, sure, and would I be his cattle queen and come to his castle. And then he laughed the way he does. His castle! This is where he brought me! Ten thousand acres of nothing!

Jubal: This is a fine ranch.

Mae: For men, horses, and bulls. For women, it's ten thousand acres of lonesomeness.

Mae Horgan played by Valerie French and Jubal Troop played by Glenn Ford: Delmer Daves' *Jubal* (Columbia, 1956).

4923

Pinky: Are you head man here? I'm going to tell you something, old man. You got about five minutes to hitch up and move off here and keep moving. All of you!

Shem: We're God fearing people. We don't travel on the Sabbath.

Pinky: Well now, I'm going to tell you what you're gonna do, old man. If you don't move off the land, then you better start digging holes in it …to bury yourself in …one apiece.

Pinky played by Rod Steiger and Shem Hoktor played by Basil Ruysdael: Delmer Daves' *Jubal* (Columbia, 1956).

4924

Darryl: You know, the latest joke going around is that leaving a ranch to your children constitutes child abuse.

Ranch hands cleaning up after a day's work: Sam (Noah Beery, Jr.), ruffian and bad guy Pinky (Rod Steiger), Carson (John Dierkes), and drifter Jubal Troop (Glenn Ford). Pinky wastes no time setting up confrontation with Jubal in Delmer Daves' *Jubal* (Columbia, 1956).

Darryl Burke played by Frank Collison: Andy Tennant's *Keep the Change* (Turner Home Entertainment, 1992).

4925
Belle: Now what's wrong?
Stribling: I'm just pointing the wagon tongue toward the North Star. It'll help us get our bearings in the morning.
Belle Breckenridge played by Dorothy Malone and Dana Stribling played by Rock Hudson: Robert Aldrich's *The Last Sunset* (Universal, 1961).

4926
Wes: We'll get that farm, Jane, just like I promised you. Then we'll …
Jane: Sure, I know. The place with white painted fences, green grass, and water all year around. I don't believe that anymore, Wes. And I don't think you believe it. No, you'll never have that place.

Not now. You'll never have more than six feet of ground.
John Wesley Hardin played by Rock Hudson and Jane Brown played by Mary Castle: Raoul Walsh's *The Lawless Breed* (Universal, 1952),

4927
Harvey: When it comes down to bedrock, my word don't call much, does it Vince? I'm just hired help.
Harvey Stenbaugh played by Albert Salmi and Vincent Bronson played by Lee J. Cobb: Michael Winner's *Lawman* (United Artists, 1971).

4928
Jack: Yeah, but basically, you're still an easterner.
Jerri: What are you talking about, Jack?
Jack: Oh, it's easy to understand. A westerner likes open country. That means

he's got to hate fences. And the more fences there are, the more he hates them.
Jerri: I've never heard such nonsense in my life.
Jack: It's true though. Have you ever noticed how many fences there're getting to be. And the signs they got on them: no hunting, no hiking, no admission, no trespassing, private property, closed area, start moving, go away, get lost, drop dead! Do you know what I mean?
Jack Burns played by Kirk Douglas and Jerri Bondi played by Gena Rowlands: David Miller's *Lonely Are the Brave* (Universal, 1962).

4929
Jim: Well, Gail, I guess we broke a tradition of the trail. But I don't guess anybody would mind. I sure don't.

Gail: What do you mean, Jim?
Jim: Well, on a cattle drive there are two no's: no whiskey and no women.

Jim Kirk played by Wild Bill Elliott and Gail Robinson played by Phyllis Coates: Lewis Collins' *The Longhorn* (Warner Bros., 1951).

4930
Mr. Waggoman: Who are you?
Lockhart: Oh, no one you ever heard of.
Mr. Waggoman: Well, what do you want in this town?
Lockhart: That's a big question, huh? You don't ask it very friendly.
Mr. Waggoman: I don't have to. I own this town. I own as far as you can ride in any direction for three days.
Lockhart: Yeah, so I hear. Apache land is just less than one day's ride from here. Do you own that too?
Mr. Waggoman: I have no quarrel with the Apache. It's dirt farmers and fence raisers I'm keeping out. Now which are you?

Alec Waggoman played by Donald Crisp and Will Lockhart played by James Stewart: Anthony Mann's *The Man from Laramie* (Columbia, 1955).

4931
Mr. Waggoman: Look, I want to be friends with you, Lockhart. I don't have to be, I want to be.
Lockhart: Why?
Mr. Waggoman: Well, I'd like you to work for me.
Lockhart: No, we don't speak the same language.
Mr. Waggoman: Well, maybe we could both bend a little.
Lockhart: I never owned an acre of land. I never wanted to. You couldn't live with an acre less than you got. Now just where do we bend?
Mr. Waggoman: I'm not trying to buy your friendship, Lockhart. I'm just looking for a way to reach it. Now how do I do that?

Alec Waggoman played by Donald Crisp and Will Lockhart played by James Stewart: Anthony Mann's *The Man from Laramie* (Columbia, 1955).

4932
Vic: Anybody that crosses our boundaries will grab only enough land to bury himself in!

Vic Hansbro played by Arthur Kennedy: Anthony Mann's *The Man from Laramie* (Columbia, 1955).

4933
Dempsey: Why not hire the men that bring the cattle up from Texas?
Reed: That seems like a good idea.
Strap: Well, that depends on the men. There are two kinds that drive the trail: them that knows cows, and them that knows trouble.

Dempsey: He means men that are handy with a gun.

Dempsey Rae played by Kirk Douglas, Reed Bowman played by Jeanne Crain, and Strap Davis played by Jay C. Flippen: King Vidor's *Man Without a Star* (Universal, 1955).

4934
Reed: You and your men have three days to get drunk and sober up. Then report back to the ranch ready for work.

Reed Bowman played by Jeanne Crain: King Vidor's *Man Without a Star* (Universal, 1955).

4935
McLintock: I've been punched many times in my life, but never for hiring anybody.
Devlin: Ah, I don't know what to say. I've never begged before. It turned my stomach. I suppose I should have been grateful you gave me the job.
McLintock: Gave? Boy, you got it all wrong. I don't give jobs, I hire men.
Drago: You intend to give this man a full day's work, don't you boy?
Devlin: You mean you're still hiring me, Mr. McLintock? Well, yes sir! I mean, I'll certainly deliver a fair day's work.
McLintock: For that, I'll pay you a fair day's wage. You won't give me anything and I won't give you anything. We both hold up our heads.

George Washington McLintock played by John Wayne, Devlin Warren played by Patrick Wayne, and Drago played by Chill Wills: Andrew V. McLaglen's *McLintock!* (United Artists, 1963).

4936
Jet: Did they give ya any trouble?
Duke: No. There was only one Circle C rider on the place. I sent him home tied to his saddle with some lead for balance.

Jet Cosgrave played by John Derek and Duke Rankin played by Bob Steele: William Whitney's *The Outcast* (Republic, 1954).

4937
Colonel: Now look, Dunson, you're too good a gun for me to let you leave the [wagon] train now.
Dunson: Then I'm too good a gun for you to argue with.

The Colonel played by Lane Chandler and Tom Dunson played by John Wayne: Howard Hawks' *Red River* (United Artists, 1948).

4938
Dunson: I want you all to know what you're up against. You probably already know, but I want to make sure you do. We got a thousand miles to go. Ten miles a day will be good. Fifteen will be luck. There'll be dry country and dry wells when we get to 'em. There'll be wind and rain. There's gonna be Indian territory. How bad, I don't know. And when we get to Missouri, there'll be bor-

der gangs. There's gonna be a fight all the way. But we'll get there. Now, nobody has to come along. I'll still have a job for you when we get back. But remember this: every man who signs on for this drive agrees to finish it. There'll be no quitting along the way. Not by me and not by you. There's no hard feelings if you don't want to go. But just let me know now.

Tom Dunson played by John Wayne: Howard Hawks' *Red River* (United Artists, 1948).

4939
Teeler: Well, do we go on?
Garth: Which would you rather have? What's behind or what might be ahead?

Teeler Yacy played by Paul Fix and Matthew Garth played by Montgomery Cliff: Howard Hawks' *Red River* (United Artists, 1948).

4940
Duncan: I'm warning you men, this range is taken. There is no room for squatters.
Hal: You started from scratch here yourself, Duncan.
Duncan: That was a long time past.
Matt: For you, but we're just beginning. And we aim to start with mavericks, and we aim to stay.
Duncan: You'll start just as long as you stay within the law. Which means if I find any one of you rounding up and branding cattle on my range, I'll have the right to fill ya full of lead.

Reece Duncan played by Alexander Scourby, Hal Jessup played by Palmer Lee/Gregg Palmer, and Matt Jessup played by Dennis Weaver: Lee Sholem's *The Redhead from Wyoming* (Universal, 1953).

4941
Adam: I thought my uncle ordered you to get out of this country, Venters!
Venters: Me? I like it here.
Adam: Maybe you won't like it so much when we get through with you.

Adam Dyer played by Kane Richmond and Venters played by James Gillette: James Tinling's *Riders of the Purple Sage* (20th Century–Fox, 1941).

4942
Jane: Sometimes I wish I could ride away from here.
Lassiter: Jane, you can't ride away.
Jane: What on earth do you mean? I'm an absolutely free woman.
Lassiter: You ain't anything of the kind! Years are terrible things. And for years you've been bound. Habit of years is strong as life itself.

Jane Witherston played by Amy Madigan and Jim Lassiter played by Ed Harris: Charles Haid's *Riders of the Purple Sage* (Turner Pictures, 1996).

4943
Howdy: Ben, tell me again why you hire on year after year with Jim Ed Love?

Jim Kirk (Wild Bill Elliott) and partner Andy (Myron Healey) are on their way to Oregon to get some cattle. On the way, they run into some Indians and Andy (center) ingests some lead. A rancher's daughter, Gail (Phyllis Coates), looks after Andy in *The Longhorn* (Monogram, 1951).

Ben: Because one day I'm going to save up enough money to buy myself a boat. And then I'm going to find myself a place where there ain't no grass. Because if there ain't no grass, there ain't no damn horses ...that can kick the good cowboy into being a crippled old man long before his time.

Howdy Lewis played by Henry Fonda and Ben Jones played by Glenn Ford: Burt Kennedy's *The Rounders* (MGM, 1965).

4944

Howdy: We used to have two windmills at our place back home. We had to tear one of them down. There wasn't enough wind to turn them both.

Howdy Lewis played by Henry Fonda: Burt Kennedy's *The Rounders* (MGM, 1965).

4945

Dick: Look! What do you see?

Chito: Cows, sky, grass.

Dick: It's a sight to warm a cowman's heart!

Dick played by Tim Holt and Chito Rafferty played by Richard Martin: Lesley Selander's *Rustlers* (RKO, 1949).

4946

Deneen: There are only two things I have hated all my life, Ellison. One is violence and the other is barbed wire. But I hate violence much more.

Mr. Deneen played by Donald Crisp and Clay Ellison played by Royal Dano: Robert Parrish's *Saddle the Wind* (MGM, 1958).

4947

Danny: You got too greedy, Ortega. You wanted too much.

Ortega: How much is too much? Who makes the rules? I mean to have what I want even if I have to kill ever man in Sonora to get it.

Danny: You sure got land hunger awful bad.

Ortega: Don't you want to own land, Danny?

Danny: The only land that man can be sure of is the six feet he's buried in. And I don't aim to claim that yet.

Danny Post played by Alex Nicol and Ortega played by Jose Nieto: Michael Carreras' *The Savage Guns* (MGM, 1961).

4948

Joe: Don't forget to close the gate on your way out.

Shane: Do you mind putting down your gun? Then I'll leave.

Joe: What difference does it make? You're leaving anyway.

Shane: I'd like it to be my idea.

Joe Starrett played by Van Heflin and Shane played by Alan Ladd: George Stevens' *Shane* (Paramount, 1953).

4949

Joe: God didn't make all this country just for one man like Ruker.

Lewis: He's got it though, and that's what counts!

Joe Starrett played by Van Heflin and Lewis played by Edgar Buchanan: George Stevens' *Shane* (Paramount, 1953).

4950

Dave: You tell those farmers that Chip Tomlin was trespassing on my property. And from now on, anyone else who tries it gets the same treatment.

Sheriff: You better think that over, Dave.

Dave: I've got forty men working for me. I need twenty. You think that over!

Dave Mosely played by Lyle Bettger, Chip Tomlin played by Grant Williams, and Sheriff Jim Trask played by Jock Mahoney: Charles Haas' *Showdown at Abilene* (Universal, 1956).

4951

Jeff: Where have you been working, Barkley?

Clint: Just about all over.

Jeff: Where exactly?

Clint: Texas, Arizona, Wyoming.

Jeff: No, I mean what ranch?

Clint: Most all of 'em one time or another.

Jeff: I take it then you don't light in one spot for very one?

Clint: That depends on the spot.

Jeff played by Robert Wilke and Clint played by Fess Parker: George Sherman's *Smoky* (20th Century–Fox, 1966).

4952

Dawson: This is my land. I bought it and I'm going to fence it!

Mike: Dawson, I ride this way to town. I make that ride twice a day. Habit stands up a lot longer than fences.

Dawson played by Steve Clark and Mike played by Rod Cameron: Lesley Selander's *Stampede* (Warner Bros., 1949).

4953

Ballard: We hang rustlers and horse thieves. Why shouldn't we shoot men that steal our grass?

George Ballard played by Leif Erickson: Charles Haas' *Star in the Dust* (Universal, 1956).

4954

Chito: Davy, how do you make sheep do what you tell them?

Dave: In the first place, you got to be smarter than the sheep.

Chito Rafferty played by Richard Martin and Dave played by Tim Holt: Lesley Selander's *Storm Over Wyoming* (RKO, 1950).

4955

Usher: I'm going to have me a place someday. I thought about it, I thought about it a lot. A man should have something of his own. Something to belong to …to be proud of.

Usher played by Richard Boone: Budd Boetticher's *The Tall T* (Columbia, 1957).

4956

Campbell: Mr. Stewart, this is my first job for you. You'll have to foreclose this mortgage I hold on Tom Grinnel's ranch.

Stewart: I thought Grinnel was your friend?

Campbell: That's what makes it so sad. I've known Tom for years. The first time I was ever forced to kill a man, and it had to be a friend of mine.

Wick Campbell played by Richard Boone, Adam Stewart played by Lester Matthews, and Tom Grinnel played by Clem Bevans: Bruce Humberstone's *Ten Wanted Men* (Columbia, 1955).

4957

With the ending of the Civil War, an even greater, more relentless war began …the fight for food. Famine rode the North and the South …and though countless head of cattle roamed the vast ranches of Texas, they perished. There was no transportation, no railroads. The paths to the markets were bloody trails of Indian depredations, outlaws, rustlers. It remained for a frontier adventurer of the period to find the answer. It is the year 1866, in Abilene, Kansas.

Prologue: George Marshall's *Texas* (Columbia, 1941).

4958

Tobias: There is land for all. Bring your horses to graze, sir. We will not resent their presence.

Major: No, but they would resent yours! Now, I advise you to pack up your goods, your people, your faith, and your cows, and clear out of my valley.

Tobias: But we've come two thousand miles!

Major: You can go another two thousand!

Tobias played by Dan Sturkie and Major Harriman played by Farley Granger: E.B. Clucher's (Enzo Barboni) *They Call Me Trinity* (West Film/vco Embassy, 1970).

4959

Ruby: They got a sayin' in Texas: the Rio Grande changes its course …but the Saunders don't.

Ruby LaSalle played by Elaine Stritch: Rudolph Mate's *Three Violent People* (Paramount, 1956).

4960

Billy: You call that place big? Why, back where I come from, I got a cousin by the name of Brandyhead Jones …

Mayor: Now, wait a minute, Billy! You ain't gonna tell me about Brandyhead Jones again!

Billy: Yes sir, old Brandyhead's farm is so wide that the hired man and the hired girl, following their wedding, went out to milk their cows that was grazing on the west side. When they got back, they had a child one year old!

Billy Burns and Brandyhead Jones were both played by George "Gabby" Hayes and the Mayor played by Harry Harvey: Ray Enright's *Trail Street* (RKO, 1947).

4961

Kirk: Disappointed?

Jane: Only in the Denbow men.

Kirk: Oh, we grow on people. At first, they dislike us. But later on …they get to hate us.

Kirk Denbow played by Joseph Cotten and Jane Stevens played by Shelley Winters: Hugo Fregonese's *Untamed Frontier* (Universal, 1952).

4962

McCloud: When the time comes, it will take a lot more than a Denbow fence to keep us off that range.

Denbow: If you insist on trespassing, you'll be shot. I'd hate to see you come so far just to get killed.

Ezra McCloud played by Robert Anderson and Kirk Denbow played by Joseph Cotten: Hugo Fregonese's *Untamed Frontier* (Universal, 1952).

4963

Kirk: I was a little busier than usual this morning. The west herd that you were supposed to guard last night broke through and we lost over 1200 head.

Glenn: Oh, the Denbows can afford the loss.

Kirk: Maybe, but I'm not so sure they can afford you.

Kirk Denbow played by Joseph Cotten and Glenn Denbow played by Scott Brady: Hugo Fregonese's *Untamed Frontier* (Universal, 1952).

4964

Wilkison: Here at Anchor, we don't pay much attention to this hogwash about the meek inheriting the earth.

Lew Wilkison played by Edward G. Robinson: Rudolph Mate's *The Violent Men* (Columbia, 1955).

4965

McCloud: It's a funny thing that when you work a place, you sort of become part of it. You feel for the land, everything that happens to it. When it rains or when it dries up, or when things get to die on it or grow on it ...you feel like it's happening to you.

Jim McCloud played by Warner Anderson: Rudolph Mate's *The Violent Men* (Columbia, 1955).

4966

Ranch Hand: The land is no good when there's always lead flying over it.

The Ranch Hand was uncredited: William Wyler's *The Westerner* (United Artist, 1940).

4967

Wade: This here is a big country.

Judge Bean: Yeah, but it ain't big enough for cattlemen and homesteaders and it never will be. Now clear out of here! That's my ruling!

Wade: All right, Bean, we're going. We're going back to build our fences.

Judge Bean: If you do, you'd better build coffins with 'em. Now git!

Wade Harper played by Forrest Tucker and Judge Roy Bean played by Walter Brennan: William Wyler's *The Westerner* (United Artists, 1940).

4968

Cross: Now clear off my property or get shot for trespassing!

Tanner: Mister, that advice works both ways.

Ab Cross played by Morgan Woodward and Jim Tanner played by Steve Forrest: Robert Totten's *The Wild Country* (Buena Vista, 1971).

4969

Brazos: Hey folks, ain't there no level ground anywhere in this country? I'm sea sick.

Hugh: Come over to our place. We got a big flat stretch.

Brazos: Well, I'll be over just so I can lay down straight. Every night it's the same: sleep with my feet up one hill, my back up another, and my rear end at the bottom of a gully. I'm gradually taking the shape of a horseshoe.

Brazos played by Christopher Dark and Hugh Breslin played by Gary Gray: Charles Haas' *Wild Heritage* (Universal, 1958).

4970

Dirk: What time are you leaving?

Rusty: Sunup. It comes just as early here as it does in Texas.

Dirk Breslin played by Rod McKuen and Rusty played by Casey Tibbs: Charles Haas' *Wild Heritage* (Universal, 1958).

4971

Walter: Roundup starts tomorrow morning and your boys are more interested in a two-bit whore from Kansas City!

Nell: Why is it that whenever they do something that you disapprove of they're always my boys?

Walter Buckman played by Karl Malden and Nell Buckman played by Leora Dana: Blake Edwards' *Wild Rovers* (MGM, 1971).

4972

Alex: You'll be line rider up in the ridge country. It pays $30.00 a month. Are you sure you rode line before?

Will: Sure enough to have some mighty strong feelings about it.

Alex played by Ben Johnson and Will Penny played by Charlton Heston: Tom Gries' *Will Penny* (Paramount, 1968).

4973

Shelby: Jesse, you think of everything, don't ya?

Jesse: Yeah, that's why I'm paying salaries instead of working for 'em.

Preacher Sam Shelby played by Chill Wills and Jesse Glendenning played by Robert Lowery: Maury Dexter's *Young Guns of Texas* (20th Century–Fox, 1963).

Rough and Tough

See also Cowboys; Killing; Lawlessness; West

4974

Narrator: My dad wasn't just one man named Flint Mitchell. He was a breed of men ...mountain men who lived and died in America. He used to tell me about these men he knew. Men who walked the Indian trails and blazed new ones where no man had ever been before. Men who found lakes and rivers and meadows. Men who found paths to the west and the western sea; who roamed prairies and mountains and plateaus that are now states. Men who searched for beaver and found glory. Men who died unnamed and found immortality. My father always began his story by telling me about the summer rendezvous of the mountain men. This is where they met every July after a year of trapping in the Rockies. Here they cashed in their furs, caught up on their drinking and the fighting and the gambling and the fun ...and the girls. They lived hard and they played hard.

Narrative by Howard Keel: William Wellman's *Across the Wide Missouri* (MGM, 1951).

4975

Russian: You know, I had a boy like you once. He was as ugly as dirt ...took after his ma. I ended up having to slit his throat.

Russian played by Richard Boone: Earl Bellamy's *Against a Crooked Sky* (Doty\Dayton, 1975).

4976

Hondo: Hey, why don't we just bust in?

Laredo: Because bustin' through doors with Quirt Evans on the other side isn't my idea of a healthy pastime.

Hondo was uncredited and Laredo Stevens played by Bruce Cabot: James Edward Grant's *Angel and the Badman* (Republic, 1947).

4977

Sam: Look, Reverend, you give a dog a bad name and everybody throws a stone at him. Sure, I gamble. I drink, too. I killed a man who was trying to kill me. This is a rough country and you got to take care of yourself.

Sam Leeds played by Stephen McNally and the Reverend Griffin played by Arthur Shields: Hugo Fregonese's *Apache Drums* (Universal, 1951).

4978

Deakins: Who's got it?

Boone: Got what?

Deakins: My finger! What's a man going to do without his finger?

Zeb: What do you want your finger for?

Deakins: Zeb Calloway, didn't you tell me an injun can't go to heaven unless he's whole? Didn't ya?

Zeb: That's right, I did.

Boone: You sure did.

Deakins: That's what I heard. It sounds right, too, don't it?

Zeb: Sounds right.

Boone: How can you go up there without your finger?

Deakins: That's what I'm saying! Who's got it? Who's got it? Fine thing to do to a friend!

Jim Deakins played by Kirk Douglas, Boone played by Dewey Martin, and Zeb Calloway played by Arthur Hunnicutt: Howard Hawks' *The Big Sky* (Winchester/RKO, 1952).

4979

Zeb: I remember once there being a trapper named Parker. He run smack into a big grizzly bear. The bear sure made a mess out of Parker before we killed it. Ripped one of his ears clear off. But this child just happened to have a needle and some of this here deer sinew, just like we got here. Yeah, while his ear was still hot, I picked it up and sewed it back on his head. And it growed most as good as ever.

[*and a little later*]

I said growed most as good as ever. Not hardly. It seems I sewed Parker's ear on backwards. Yeah, he hated me until the day he died. On account of every time he'd hear a rattlesnake, he'd turn the wrong direction and step smack into it!

Zeb Calloway played by Arthur Hunnicutt: Howard Hawks' *The Big Sky* (Winchester/RKO, 1952).

4980

Billy Jack: Martin, do you know what mental toughness is? Well, mental toughness is the ability to accept the fact that you're human and that you're gonna make mistakes …lots of 'em …all your life. And some of them are gonna hurt people that you love very badly. But you have the guts to accept the fact that you ain't perfect. And you don't let your mistakes crush you and keep you from doing the very best that you can.

Billy Jack played by Tom Laughlin and Martin played by Stan Rice: T.G. Frank's (Tom Laughlin) *Billy Jack* (Warner Bros.–National Student Film Corp., 1971).

4981

Ruth: What's your name?

Choya: Choya.

Ruth: That's Spanish for cactus. Why do they call you that?

Choya: Ever tried to pick one?

Ruth Lavery played by Mona Freeman and Choya played by Alan Ladd: Rudolph Maté's *Branded* (Paramount, 1951).

4982

Calamity: Them last few days of wildness was our glory days.

Calamity Jane played by Anjelica Huston: Rod Hardy's *Buffalo Girls* (Cabin Fever Entertainment, 1995).

4983

Veronica: You have become quite hard.

Chuka: Since I didn't measure up to your standards in life, madame, I had to find a way to bring people down to mine.

Veronica: With your gun, I hear, Señor Chuka.

Chuka: With my gun, Señora Kleitz.

Veronica Kleitz played by Luciana Paluzzi and Chuka played by Rod Taylor: Gordon Douglas' *Chuka* (Paramount, 1967).

4984

Dobie: A saddle and a shirt. That's all Frank had. It sure ain't much.

Cody: Sure ain't.

Dobie: It wasn't his fault though.

Cody: No?

Dobie: No, he never knew anything but the wild side.

Cody: A man can cross over anytime he has the mind.

Dobie: It ain't that easy. It ain't that easy at all.

Dobie played by Richard Rust, Frank played by Skip Homeier, and Jefferson Cody played by Randolph Scott: Budd Boetticher's *Comanche Station* (Columbia, 1960).

4985

Young Cowboy: You're a hard man, Conagher.

Conagher: It's a hard country, kid.

The Young Cowboy was uncredited and Conn Conagher played by Sam Elliott: Reynaldo Villalobos' *Conagher* (Turner Pictures, 1991).

4986

Kate: Your hatred may destroy Miles, but it can also destroy you. Hate is something that can feed on itself for only so long.

Kate Hardison played by Marguerite Chapman: Ray Enright's *Coroner Creek* (Columbia, 1948).

4987

Reece: If you had anything inside you worth saving, I'd beat you until you couldn't stand up. But it wouldn't do any good because you'll never learn. You haven't gotten tougher …you've just gotten miserable!

Tom Reece played by Glenn Ford: Delmer Daves' *Cowboy* (Columbia, 1958).

4988

Long Hair: You're a hard man, Mr. Anderson.

Anderson: Well, it's a hard life.

Long Hair played by Bruce Dern and Wil Anderson played by John Wayne: Mark Rydell's *The Cowboys* (Warner Bros., 1972).

4989

Fink: I can out-run, out-jump, out-sing, out-swim, out-dance, out-shoot, out-eat, out-drink …

Crockett: Out-talk?

Fink: Out-talk, out-cussin', out-fight anybody in the whole of Mississippi and Ohio rivers put together!

Mike Fink played by Jeff York and Davy Crockett played by Fess Parker: Norman Foster's *Davy Crockett and the River Pirates* (Buena Vista, 1956).

4990

Crockett: I'm half-horse, half-alligator, and a little attached with snapping turtle. I've got the fastest horse, the prettiest sister, the surest rifle, and the ugliest dog in Texas. My father can lick any man in Kentucky …and I can lick my father. I can hug a bear too close for comfort and eat any man alive opposed to Andy Jackson.

Davy Crockett played by Fess Parker: Norman Foster's *Davy Crockett, King of the Wild Frontier* (Buena Vista, 1955).

4991

Harriman: I've learned there's two ways to deal with a dangerous animal. One is way out of reach. And the other is right on his back.

U.S. Marshal Harriman played by Randy Travis: Alan J. Levi's *Dead Man's Revenge* (MCA/Universal Home Video, 1994).

4992

Call: Ma'am, we're back to where it's wild again.

Carey: Yes, it 'tis wild, isn't it? It's like a smell. I smelled it in Africa. And I smell it here.

Call: It means we have to be careful, ma'am.

Carey: On the contrary, Corporal Call, it means we have to be wild.

Woodrow F. Call played by Jonny Lee Miller and Lady Carey was uncredited: Yves Simoneau's *Dead Man's Walk* (Cabin Fever Entertainment, 1996).

4993

Johnny: Well, where are you heading now, Reverend?

Preacher: I'll be some visiting through the foothills. Maybe get a little marrying done among those trappers …at least the ones that don't see me coming.

Johnny: I guess they'd scatter at that. Kind of free souls up there, huh?

Johnny Cobb played by James Stewart and Preacher Broyles played by Ed Begley: Vincent McEveety's *Firecreek* (Warner Bros.–Seven Arts, 1968).

4994

Deputy: We ought to build a monument to him while he's living.

Britt: The way he's living there mightn't be much time.

Deputy Waller played by Walter Sande and Ned Britt played by Randolph Scott: Edwin Marin's *Fort Worth* (Warner Bros., 1951).

4995

Darrow: You've found a new love in your life, haven't you Van? You're in love with hate. Well, if you're patient and work hard at it, maybe it'll be all you'll need to live by. I hope it will be enough …because hate doesn't leave room enough for anything else in your life.

Rip Darrow played by Wendell Corey and Vance Jeffords played by Barbara Stanwyck: Anthony Mann's *The Furies* (Paramount, 1950).

4996

Spring: You ever come across horses that never would give up being wild?

Hewey: Oh, yes. I've seen some break their necks across fences and others just lay down and die before they would accept the saddle.

Spring: You strike me as a man who might do the same thing.

Hewey: I don't know. I've never had to face up to it.

Spring Renfro played by Sissy Spacek and Hewey Calloway played by Tommy Lee Jones who also directed *The Good Old Boys* (Turner Pictures, 1995).

4997

Cord: It's funny …a man has got to fight to live in peace.

Cord Decker played by Michael Sarrazin: William Hale's *Gunfight in Abilene* (Universal, 1967).

4998

Reb: Did you ever think of settling down in one place, Johnny?

Johnny: Yeah, I did settle down once.

Reb: What happened?

Johnny: They forgot to lock the cell one night.

Reb Kittredge played by Audie Murphy and Johnny Lake played by Charles Drake: Nathan Juran's *Gunsmoke* (Universal, 1953).

4999

Dan: I need men who can ride hard, shoot hard, and live hard.

Dan Hammond played by Robert Ryan: Budd Boetticher's *Horizons West* (Universal, 1952).

5000

Narrator: This land has a name today, and it's marked on maps. But the name and the marks and the land all had to be won. Won from nature and from primitive man. Five generations ago, a mere 125 years back, this land was known only as the west …known only to a handful of white men …lonely trappers wandering its vastness in search of beaver. They were known as mountain men …a new breed. Men like Jim Bridger, Frenchie Sublette, Linus Rawlings …more Indian than the Indians and all the blood. They held to no law but their own …drifted free as the clouds …settled nowhere …kept forever on the move …their moccasin feet and unshod horses leaving no trace on the land. Like the Indians with whom they were at peace, they wanted nothing beyond what they found …and little of that. The mountains, the forests, the harsh country were as unchanging to them as the stars …and just as unyielding.

Narration by Spencer Tracy: John Ford, George Marshall, and Henry Hathaway's *How the West Was Won* (MGM, 1962).

5001

Narrator: John Thornton asked little of man or nature. He was unafraid of the wild. With a handful of salt and rifle, he could plunge into the wilderness and fare wherever he pleased …and as long as he pleased.

Narration by Richard Dreyfuss and John Thornton played by Rutger Hauer: Peter Svatek's *Jack London's the Call of the Wild: Dog of the Yukon* (Hallmark Entertainment, 1997).

5002

Johnson: Just where is it I could find bear, beaver, and other critters worth cash money for the skins?

Robidoux: Ride due west to the sunset. Turn left at the Rocky Mountains.

Jeremiah Johnson played by Robert Redford and Robidoux played by Charles Tyner: Sydney Pollack's *Jeremiah Johnson* (Warner Bros., 1972).

5003

Johnson: Ain't that hair I see on your head?

Del Gue: It sure is. I've decided that when I depart from this life, I'd like to leave something …at least to be remembered on some man's lodge pole.

Johnson: Sound wisdom. Where are you headed?

Del Gue: Same place you are, Jeremiah. Hell in the end.

Jeremiah Johnson played by Robert Redford and Del Gue played by Stefan Gierasch: Sydney Pollack's *Jeremiah Johnson* (Warner Bros., 1972).

5004

Big Eli: We're going to Texas. We're going to live it bold.

Big Eli Wakefield played by Burt Lancaster who also directed *The Kentuckian* (United Artists, 1955).

5005

Ape: Do you figure we'll go back to the same place next year?

Lopez: We never go back nowhere.

Carson: No use going back to some place you've been when there are so many places you ain't been.

Ape: You know what's wrong with you? You got a disease …horizon fever. You always want to see what's on the other side of the hill.

Ape played by Ward Bond, Lopez played by Harold Huber, and Kit Carson played by Jon Hall: George B. Seitz's *Kit Carson* (United Artists, 1940).

5006

Woodfoot: I never knew easy money without a bad conscience.

Sandy: I already got the bad conscience. I might as well have the money.

Woodfoot played by Lloyd Nolan and Sandy McKenzie played by Stewart Granger: Richard Brooks' *The Last Hunt* (MGM, 1956).

5007

Ellison: It seems like everyone around here is bent on telling a man how to live …when the only thing important to know is how to stay alive.

Brad Ellison played by Jock Mahoney: George Sherman's *The Last of the Fast Guns* (Universal, 1958).

5008

Jed: He don't look so tough to me.

Fin: That's how he looked to a lot of people. But they're not around anymore.

Jed played by Jack Kelly and Fin Elder played by Barry Kelley: Nathan Juran's *Law and Order* (Universal, 1953).

5009

Zeb: Jeb, that's for you [knife]. It's called a Green River. It belonged to a man named Hard Luck Hayes. He killed a cougar with that.

Jeb: What happened to him? To Hard Luck, I mean?

Zeb: Well, unfortunately, the cougar killed him too.

Zeb Macahan played by James Arness and Jeb Macahan wqas played by William Kirby Cullen: Bernard McEveety's *The Macahans* (TVW, 1976).

5010

Spur: It's a hard country. It makes for hard men.

Spur played by Kirt Douglas: George Miller's *The Man from Snowy River* (20th Century–Fox, 1982).

5011

Cavish: How about Davy Crockett? Now there was a man who could charm a possum right out of a tree.

Dawes: No. When a possum saw ole Davy Crockett looking at him, he just knew that was the end. So instead of waiting to get shot, he just climbed down and dropped dead at Davy's feet.

Cavish played by John Day and Dawes played by Neville Brand: Budd Boetticher's *The Man from the Alamo* (Universal, 1953).

5012

Nan: Stay away from trouble, Owen. It comes easy to you. And it'll come still easier because you're in a frame of mind to have some.

Nan Melotte played by Ellen Drew and Owen Merritt played by Randolph Scott: Andre De Toth's *Man in the Saddle* (Columbia, 1951).

5013

Mason: I know that breed.
  They don't like to fight unless
  they have the drop on someone.

Cliff Mason played by George O'Brien:
David Howard's *The Marshal of Mesa
City* (RKO, 1939).

5014

Hank: He personified the American West in the days of its
  rowdy youth.

Hank Rate played by Sam Gilman:
Arthur Penn's *The Missouri Breaks*
(United Artists, 1976).

5015

Ernestina: You don't like talking
  about the past. Some people
  do, you know.

Tom Horn: The past has always
  been rough country for
  me, Ernestina. And I never
  meant to be here when I was
  forty.

Ernestina Crawford played by Karen
Black and Tom Horn played by David
Carradine: Jack Starrett's *Mr. Horn*
(TVW, 1979).

5016

Henry: Yeah, you got the hair of
  a bear in ya, Tyler. That's for
  sure.

Henry Frapp played by Brian Keith
and Bill Tyler played by Charlton Heston: Richard Lang's *The Mountain
Men* (Columbia, 1980).

5017

Wyeth: Haven't you ever been
  lost?

Henry: Fearsome confused for a
  month or two, but I ain't
  never been lost.

Nathan Wyeth played by John Glover
and Henry Frapp played by Brian
Keith: Richard Lang's *The Mountain
Men* (Columbia, 1980).

5018

Nobody: The secret of a long
  life is to try not to shorten
  it.

Nobody played by Terence Hill:
Tonino Valerii's *My Name Is Nobody*
(Universal, 1973).

5019

Barman: What can I do for you, ma'am?

McBain: I would like some water if it's no
  trouble.

Barman: Water? Well, you see, that word is
  poison around these parts ever since the
  day of the great flood.

McBain: You mean you never wash?

Mountain man Jeremiah Johnson (Robert Redford) and trapper Bear Claw (Will Geer) pause in
their home, the wilderness, in Sidney Pollack's *Jeremiah Johnson* (Warner Bros., 1972).

Barman: We sure do!
McBain: Well, I'd like to use the same fa-
  cilities you people do.
Barman: You sure can! I just happen to
  have a full tub in the back. And you're
  lucky. Only three people have used it
  this morning.
McBain: Used it one at a time or together?

The Barman played by Lionel Stander and Jill
McBain played by Claudia Cardinale: Sergio Leone's
Once Upon a Time in the West (Paramount, 1969).

5020

Cheyenne: Do you …are you interested in
  fashions, Harmonica?

Harmonica: I saw three of these dusters a
  short time ago. They were waitin' for a
  train. Inside the dusters there were three
  men.

Cheyenne: So?

Harmonica: Inside the men there were
  three bullets.

Cheyenne played by Jason Robards, Jr., and Harmonia Man played by Charles Bronson: Sergio Leone's *Once Upon a Time in the West* (Paramount, 1969).

5021

Ehrengard: Boiling by day, freezing at night, and alkali dust choking every hole in your body. How in the name of God does anybody live here long enough to get used to it?

Fardan: Men tempered like steel …tough breed …men who learn how to endure.

Hans Ehrengard played by Robert Ryan and Henry Rico Fardan played by Lee Marvin: Richard Brooks' *The Professionals* (Columbia, 1966).

5022

Susanna: So you're leaving?

Vallian: Well, I don't want to overstay my welcome.

Susanna: I hope you find a good life somewhere.

Vallian: Well, life ain't that bad, ma'am. For me it's the best. Always the best.

Susanna: I guess wild things don't do well in gardens.

Vallian: Wild things got to be free.

Susanna McKaskel played by Kate Capshaw and Con Vallian played by Sam Elliott: Richard Day's *The Quick and the Dead* (HBO Pictures, 1987).

5023

Vallian: Let me tell you something, McKaskel. You've been acting like the meek are gonna inherit the earth. The meek ain't gonna inherit nothing west of Chicago!

Con Vallian played by Sam Elliott and Duncan McKaskel played by Tom Conti: Richard Day's *The Quick and the Dead* (HBO Pictures, 1987).

5024

Duncan: Have you actually ever done a day's work in your life, Vallian?

Vallian: I've worked hard every day of my life, mister.

Duncan: At what?

Vallian: Stayin' alive.

Duncan McKaskel played by Tom Conti and Con Vallian played by Sam Elliott: Richard Day's *The Quick and the Dead* (HBO Pictures, 1987).

5025

Julian: You're a hard man, Scoby.

Scoby: It's a hard country, Preacher.

Reverend Julian Shay played by Willie Nelson and Scoby played by R.G. Armstrong: William Wittliff's *Red Headed Stranger* (Alive Films/Charter Entertainment, 1987).

5026

Stengel: Oswald, I like living at the peak of excitement. For life is only worthwhile when you can face death without showing any fear. In fact, I enjoy it!

Stengel played by Franco Ressel and Oswald played by Robert Hundar/Claudio Undari: Frank Kramer's *Sabata* (United Artists, 1969).

5027

Tell: Don't try riding over this man, boy. Them wrinkles are war maps. Fought Indians, grizzly, and seen a hundred struttin' peacocks like you taken down hard. Now I don't know how you got so swollen up with yourself, boy, but you are beginning to bother us.

Kid: What's the gun for?

Tell: Varmints.

Kid: What are you calling me?

Tell: A nuisance.

Kid: Stand up. I said, stand!

Tell: If I do that you're gonna force me to take hold of that pistol. Then I'll have to kill ya. And killin' don't mix well with a man's supper.

Cap: Don't crowd him, son. You wouldn't be the first one he's buried. You wouldn't even get a chance to clear leather on those hog legs. You better get some air. I said, you better get some air!

Tell Sackett played by Sam Elliott, Kid Newton played by Paul Koslo, and Cap Roundtree played by Ben Johnson: Robert Totten's *The Sacketts* (TVW, 1979).

5028

Sheriff: A six inch rattler is just as deadly as a six footer …and he sure don't like you!

Sheriff Stu Carter played by Harry Townes: Gary Nelson's *Santee* (Crown International Pictures, 1973).

5029

Mac: Now the last time you were in jail it was over a woman too. The Judge's wife, I recall. And there was shootin'.

Jack: Self-defense.

Mac: Ain't you getting a little old for that?

Jack: Well, you mean gun play?

Mac: No, I mean the other.

Jack: When I get too old for that, they'll be shovelin' dirt in my face.

Dal: About this last woman, any shootin'?

Jack: No serious shootin'.

Mac Traven played by Tom Selleck, Uncle Jack Traven played by Ben Johnson, and Dal Traven played by Sam Elliott: Andrew V. McLaglen's *The Shadow Riders* (TVW, 1982).

5030

Brown: It's a strange thing. The only way to find out what you'll do to survive …is to survive.

John George "Kootenai" Brown played by Tom Burlinson: Allan Kroeker's *Showdown at Williams Creek* (Republic Pictures Home Video, 1991).

5031

Leah: This is a hard country. A place where a woman bears a child alone, wipes him clean, slaps life into him, and then wonders if it wouldn't have been better to let him die. There is no virtue to violate, no honor to bend, no high and mighty rules to live by. There is only life and death. And it's what you want to make it that gives it the name.

Leah Parker played by Marilyn Maxwell: William F. Claxton's *Stage to Thunder Rock* (Paramount, 1964).

5032

Caslon: You're getting to be a hard man to deal with.

Iles: I'm getting to deal with some hard men.

Mrs. Mary Caslon played by Agnes Moorehead and Captain George Iles played by Tom Powers: Sidney Lanfield's *Station West* (RKO, 1948).

5033

Montana Territory 1866. They came from the South, headed for the goldfields. Ben and Clint Allison, lonely desperate men. Riding away from a heartbreak memory of Gettysburg. Looking for a new life. A story of two men — and long shadows.

Prologue: Raoul Walsh's *The Tall Men* (20th Century–Fox, 1955).

5034

Bambino: Ain't you have no ambition in life? Do something! Rustle cattle, hold up a stagecoach, or play cards or something. Once you were a good card shark. But do something!

Trinity: Whose got the time? I'm already busy doing nothing.

Bambino played by Bud Spencer (Carlo Pedersoli) and Trinity played by Terence Hill (Mario Girotti): E.B. Clucher's (Enzo Barboni) *They Call Me Trinity* (West Film/Avco Embassy, 1970).

5035

Jackass: Well, it's the first time in eight years that Skinner Bill Bragg changed his mind without being knocked unconscious.

"Jackass" Brown played by Berton Churchill and Skinner Bill Bragg played by Wallace Beery: Richard Thorpe's *20 Mule Team* (MGM, 1940).

5036

Son: I've heard stories about this knife. I didn't know if it was real or not.

Hugh: Oh, it's real all right. There's plenty of men underground who could testify to that.

Son Holland played by Scott Bairstow and Hugh Allison played by Kris Kristofferson: Rod Hardy's *Two for Texas* (Turner Pictures, 1998).

5037

[*Mountain man looking at buffalo*]

Sodbuster Torrey (Elisha Cook, Jr.) is about to be blasted into the past tense with the assistance of hired gunslinger Wilson (Jack Palance) in George Stevens' classic western *Shane* (Paramount, 1953). Bad guys Morgan (John Dierkes on bench) and Ryker (Emile Meyer in doorway) witness a scene which would redefine violence in westerns.

Murdock: We're like that, see …past our time.

Abner Murdock played by James Read: Craig Clyde's *Walking Thunder* (Majestic Entertainment/Sunset Hill Partners, 1997).

5038

Narrator: I was starting to understand about the laws of the wilderness. If you aren't the hunter, you're the prey.

Narration by Brian Keith who was the voice of Jacob McKay, played by David Tom: Craig Clyde's *Walking Thunder* (Majestic Entertainment/Sunset Hill Partners, 1997).

5039

Jacob: Mama says everyone should read at night.
Murdock: Well, I expect she's right. Not much need for it out here, though. It's more important to know how to read the signs.

Jacob: Signs?
Murdock: That's what I've been teaching you, boy. This country will speak to you if you know how to listen.

Jacob McKay played by David Tom and Abner Murdock played by James Read: Craig Clyde's *Walking Thunder* (Majestic Entertainment/Sunset Hill Partners, 1997).

5040

Constable: Survival is the thing. You said it yourself, Jules …just staying alive.
Jules: You think I couldn't throw it away?
Constable: Life? You're too full of it. Someone would have to kill it out of ya.

Constable Pedley played by Wendell Corey and Jules Vincent played by Stewart Granger: Andrew Marton's *The Wild North* (MGM, 1952).

5041

Claire: Mr. Ramsay, I called you a bully and a coward. I apologize. You're not a coward.

Claire Hartford played by Anne Nagel and Jeff Ramsay played by Dick Foran: Ford Beebe and Ray Taylor's *Winners of the West* (Universal serial, Chapter 2: "The Wreck At Red River Gorge," 1940).

5042

Carter: All's fair in love and war, you know.
Claire: We'll keep love out of this if you don't mind, and we'll talk about war.

King Carter played by Harry Woods and Claire Hartford played by Anne Nagel: Ford Beebe and Ray Taylor's *Winners of the West* (Universal serial, Chapter 7: "Thundering Terror," 1940).

5043

Tex: Never stop a good fight because you'll never know when you'll see another.

Tex Houston played by Tom Fadden: Ford Beebe and Ray Taylor's *Winners of the West* (Universal serial, Chapter 8: "The Flaming Arsenal," 1940).

Saloons

See also Drinking; Gambling; Whiskey; Wild Women

5044
Conchita: How many times must I tell you? Do not shoot the customers!

Conchita was uncredited: Enzo G. Castellari's *Any Gun Can Play* (Golden Eagle/RAF, 1968).

5045
Canaan: You're a wise man.
Ernie: Ain't so …I'm a bartender.

Canaan played by Armand Assante and Ernie Fowler played by Clayton Landey: Richard Spence's *Blind Justice* (HBO Home Video, 1994).

5046
Willie: You shouldn't be in a place like this. How long has it been?
Carole: Does it matter?
Willie: It matters to me.
Carole: I remember a preacher once said, nobody goes to hell unless they really want to. I ended up here because I wanted to.
Willie: I don't think so. We live …and learn.
Carole: That's just it. I wanted to live. Then I died …a long time ago.

Willie Duggan played by Dan Duryea and Carole Ridgeway played by Audrey Dalton: Spencer G. Bennet's *The Bounty Killer* (Embassy/Premiere, 1965).

5047
Bronco Billy: Go ahead, let the tears fall in that beer.
Miss Lilly: I'm not crying!
Bronco Billy: There's nothin' wrong with cryin'.
Miss Lilly: The smoke in here is hurting my eyes!

Antoinette Lilly played by Sondra Locke and Bronco Billy played by Clint Eastwood who also directed *Bronco Billy* (Warner Bros., 1980).

5048
Jordan: Do you know where I can find this Mr. Sutton?
Bartender: My job is making drinks, not maps.

Trace Jordan played by Tab Hunter and the Bartender played by John Doucette: Stuart Heisler's *The Burning Hills* (Warner Bros., 1956).

5049
Jones: Pretty expensive place.
Maggie: Everything is expensive here …except life.

Jones played by John Ireland and Maggie played by Annabella Incontrera: Leon Klimovsky's *Challenge of the Mackennas* (Filmar Compagnia Cinematografica — Atlantida/Hemlock Enterprises, 1969).

5050
John: Harley, this is more money than I ever dreamed! Do, do, do you know what I can do with this much money?
Harley: We passed some nice looking saloons.

John O'Hanlan played by James Stewart and Harley Sullivan played by Henry Fonda: Gene Kelly's *The Cheyenne Social Club* (NGP, 1970).

5051
Carroll: Not many men would have the guts to close down a historical monument.
John: What historical monument is that, Mr. Carroll?
Carroll: The Cheyenne Social Club, that's what historical monument!
John: The Cheyenne Social Club is a …
Carroll: It was there when there wasn't a railroad for 300 miles. It withstood prairie fires and Indian attacks. And the first ounce, O'Hanlan, the first ounce of gold discovered in this territory was spent wisely and well at the Cheyenne Social Club. And you? You come up here from Texas and close it down!
John: Well now, Mr. Carroll, I didn't figure I was doing anything all that terrible. The fact is, where I come from, it would be considered something of a public service.
Carroll: You don't say?
John: Yes sir, I do say.
Carroll: You must come from a part of Texas that I ain't heard of.

Clay Carroll played by John Dehner and John O'Hanlan played by James Stewart: Gene Kelly's *The Cheyenne Social Club* (NGP, 1970).

5052
John: Will you tell Mr. Willowby I would like to talk to him?
Harley: He's still in the Doc's office.
John: I didn't know he was sick.
Harley: He weren't until you started that fight. He was hit in the face with a piano stool, so they say. I hear that saloon looks like it was in the path of a buffalo stampede.
John: All for good cause, Harley. All for Texas.

John O'Hanlan played by James Stewart, Jedediah W. Willowby played by Dabbs Greer, and Harley Sullivan played by Henry Fonda: Gene Kelly's *The Cheyenne Social Club* (NGP, 1970).

5053
Old Cantina Lady: What do you want?
Pancho: Something to eat and a cerezas.
Cisco Kid: And I'll have a señorita.
Old Cantina Lady: I am the only señorita.
Cisco Kid: Make that two cerezas.

The Cisco Kid played by Jimmy Smits and Pancho played by Cheech Marin: Luis Valdez's *The Cisco Kid* (Turner Pictures, 1994).

5054
Bates: Excuse me, sir. Could you tell me where the school house is?
Pop: Surest thing. Up the street about two blocks …where it says Dead Eye Saloon.
Bates: Well?
Pop: That's it.
Bates: What? Dead Eye Saloon a school house?
Pop: Yep. The owner got killed so we moved the kids in there.

Tommy Bates played by George Montgomery and Pop Saunders played by James Burke: Herbert I. Leeds' *The Cisco Kid and the Lady* (20th Century–Fox, 1939).

5055
McCloud: Hey, Conagher? I'll buy the drinks.
Conagher: You buy …I'll drink.

Charlie McCloud played by Barry Corbin and Conn Conagher played by Sam Elliott: Reynaldo Villalobos' *Conagher* (Turner Pictures, 1991).

5056
Mike: One thing about operas: it sounds just as bad no matter who sings.

Mike Adams played by James Westerfield: Delmer Daves' *Cowboy* (Columbia, 1958).

5057
Brett: Look, Mr. Braden, I don't like the place you run in Socorro. Your cards are marked, dice are loaded, and your whiskey is watered.

Brett Wade played by Rory Calhoun and Dick Braden played by David Brian: George Sherman's *Dawn at Socorro* (Universal, 1954).

5058
Hayes: Well, just exactly what does my job call for?
Braden: See that my patrons spend more money at the bar and lose more money at the table than they had intended to.

You'll do this by treating every patron as if he were handsome and entertaining. And by regarding yourself as beautiful, desirable …and approachable.

Rannah Hayes played by Piper Laurie and Dick Braden played by David Brian: George Sherman's *Dawn at Socorro* (Universal, 1954).

5059

Vanryzin: Allan, you got to get back to the church at once! Preacher Jason is steaming up a crowd about Mr. Jagade. There's talk about burning him out!

Marshal: Well, isn't that just what you want?

Vanryzin: Are you crazy? They want to burn down the Silver Belle [saloon]!

Marshal: Well?

Vanryzin: I own the building!

Marshal: And that makes it illegal, doesn't it?

Vanryzin played by Howard Wendell and Marshal Allan Burnett played by Jock Mahoney: Harmon Jones' *A Day of Fury* (Universal, 1956).

5060

Preacher: I used my pulpit to teach the wrath of God: hell and damnation, the vengeance of the Lord. And I thought I had won you away from evil. But instead of conquering evil, I only made you fear God. If there's a second chance for us, perhaps I can teach you to love God and so cherish His Word that you can face evil and rise above it.

Judge: A fine sermon! You can repeat it over at the saloon. It might bring the rest of your flock back!

Preacher Jason played by John Dehner and Judge John J. McLean played by Carl Benton Reid: Harmon Jones' *A Day of Fury* (Universal, 1956).

5061

Willy: This ain't much of a town. It's only got one saloon here.

Cole: It don't matter. That's all we got money for.

Willy played by Sebastian Spence and Cole played by Frank Whaley: Neill Fearnley's "My Brother's Keeper," the premiere episode of the series *Dead Man's Gun* (Showtime, 1997).

5062

Otis: Doc, if you had been tending bars as long as I have, you wouldn't expect so much out of the human race.

Otis played by James Westerfield: Budd Boetticher's *Decision at Sundown* (Columbia, 1957).

5063

Mayor: Deliver the prisoner at 10 o'clock …Decker's Saloon. It's the only place in town big enough to hold a trial.

Mayor Hiram Sellers played by Edgar Buchanan: George Marshall's *Destry* (Universal, 1954).

5064

Nebraska: I'm going to the dance tonight. I always dance better without bullet holes.

Nebraska Kemp played by Syd Saylor: Edward F. Cline's *The Dude Ranger* (Atherton/MGM, 1934).

5065

Malone: No matter what happens over there, my place stays the same: good liquor, a few card games, and no girls.

Fred: You might lose all your customers!

Mama Malone played by Ruth Springford and Fred Carson played by Boyd "Red" Morgan: Henry Hathaway's *Five Card Stud* (Paramount, 1968).

5066

Carolina: Most men would figure walking out of here was a mistake, mister.

Tex: I like making a mistake once in a while, lady.

Carolina played by Arleen Whelan and Tex McCloud played by Sterling Hayden: Ray Enright's *Flaming Feather* (Paramount, 1952).

5067

Zack: …it's the only place in town where the women are young and the bourbon is aged.

Zack Thomas played by Frank Sinatra: Robert Aldrich's *Four for Texas* (Warner Bros., 1964).

5068

Sonora Sue: How come you don't visit my place for such a long time?

Brady: As I remember your place, the cards are too short and the nights are too long.

Sonora Sue played by Alma Martinez and Brady Hawkes played by Kenny Rogers: Dick Lowry's *The Gambler Returns: The Luck of the Draw* (TVW, 1991).

5069

Bat: The temperance movement? Well, of course, the temperance movement! I hope you close down every saloon from here to California …except, of course, the ones that I frequent.

Bat Masterson played by Gene Barry: Dick Lowry's *The Gambler Returns: The Luck of the Draw* (TVW, 1991).

5070

Kate: Where did you get this scar?

Bill: I got knifed in a saloon.

Kate: Why?

Bill: Ah, the men I worked with didn't really need a reason.

Kate Flynn played by Jackie Burroughs and Bill Miner played by Richard Farnsworth: Phillip Borsos' *The Grey Fox* (United Artists, 1982).

5071

Slayton: You left the door open. Go back and close it …from the other side.

Frank Slayton played by Phil Carey: Raoul Walsh's *Gun Fury* (Columbia, 1953).

5072

Jenny: Abe, as long as Marv is standing the drinks, why don't we sit down for a while?

Abe: Well, my dad always said: tired and broke, pack your poke.

Jenny Simms played by Karen Black, Abe Cross played by Johnny Cash, and Marv Green played by Dana Elcar: Lamont Johnson's *A Gunfight* (Paramount, 1971).

5073

Ringo: It seems like all your business is on the outside and none of it inside.

Mac: Well, that don't worry me none. Just wait until tomorrow.

Ringo: After I'm gone, huh?

Mac: This place will be famous, Jimmy. It will be like a shrine. I'll probably have to put on two more bartenders.

Jimmy Ringo played by Gregory Peck and Mac played by Karl Malden: Henry King's *The Gunfighter* (20th Century–Fox, 1950).

5074

Nate: I hate to remind you, Sheriff, but that little pointed scrap of tin you're wearing doesn't mean a thing over here.

Nate Harlan played by Warren Stevens: Earl Bellamy's *Gunpoint* (Universal, 1966).

5075

Bartender: Name your poison, gentlemen. If we haven't got it, we'll make it!

The Bartender played by Bill Radovich: Nathan Juran's *Gunsmoke* (Universal, 1953).

5076

Kanning: You're kind of young to be drinking, ain't ya son?

Benjamin: I didn't come in here for a drink.

Kanning: What can I do for you?

Benjamin: My pa gave me $2.00 for my birthday. He told me I should spend it here.

Kanning: Take your pick.

Benjamin: I like 'em both [girls].

Kanning: That may be a little dangerous, son.

Benjamin: I think I like the brunette.

Kanning: Jess will take care of ya. Go on! Scared?

Benjamin: Kind of.

Kanning: They ain't gonna bite ya. You pay extra for that.

Kanning played by Matt McCoy and Benjamin played by Jonathan Bierner: Jim Wynorski's *Hard Bounty* (Triboro Entertainment, 1995).

5077

Madge: Do you still think you're a preacher?

Killian: I tried preaching. It didn't work.

Madge: Did you really think you could
    change?
Killian: I tried.
Madge: Did you? You came here telling us
    you were a preacher. That's no bible on
    your hip. That's a .44. Don't look at me.
    Look at them [town folk]. To me,
    they've always been suckers. They pay
    for too much to drink, then they pay to
    climb the stair. But I never promised
    them heaven up there. Did you pay
    them for suckers too, Killian?

Madge McCloud played by Carolyn Jones and Jim
Killian played by Glenn Ford: Lee H. Katzin's
Heaven with a Gun (MGM, 1969).

5078
Billy: You know, James, one half of my
    drunkenness can be accounted for by
    the fact that this building is so poorly
    ventilated.

Billy Irvine played by John Hurt and James Averill played by Kris Kristofferson: Michael Cimino's
Heaven's Gate (United Artists, 1980).

5079
Harry: I'll go on over to the General Store.
    You go set up the beers.
Arch: Sounds like a reasonable division of
    labor.

Arch Harris played by Warren Oates and Harry
Collings played by Peter Fonda who also directed
The Hired Hand (Universal, 1971).

5080
Mannon: I wonder what jail is going to be
    like?
McCool: Well, it won't be much like a sa-
    loon.

Laura Mannon played by Yvonne DeCarlo and
Gid McCool played by George Montgomery: R.G.
Springsteen's *Hostile Guns* (Paramount, 1967).

5081
Jesse: Bartender, count three and duck!

Jesse James played by Tyrone Power: Henry King's
Jesse James (20th Century–Fox, 1939).

5082
Vienna: Down there [first floor of saloon]
    I sell whiskey and cards. All you can buy
    up these stairs is a bullet in the head.
    Now which do you want?

Vienna played by Joan Crawford: Nicholas Ray's
Johnny Guitar (Republic, 1954).

5083
Vienna: You haven't changed at all,
    Johnny.
Johnny: Well, what made you think I had?
Vienna: In five years a person should
    earn something.
Johnny: Five years ago, I met you in a sa-
    loon. Now I find you in one. I don't see
    much change.
Vienna: Except I own this one!

Vienna played by Joan Crawford and Johnny Gui-

tar played by Sterling Hayden: Nicholas Ray's
Johnny Guitar (Republic, 1954).

5084
Judge: The Garza boy is a competent
    marksman. He's affecting all my profits
    …shooting people who might be com-
    ing here to drink.

Judge Roy Bean played by Ned Beatty and Joey
Garza played by Alexis Cruz: Joseph Sargent's
Larry McMurtry's Streets of Laredo (Cabin Fever
Entertainment, 1995).

5085
Bartender: They came in here to get
    liquored up. Killing, blood, a good
    gunfight …it makes 'em thirsty.

The Bartender played by Val Avery: John Sturges'
Last Train from Gun Hill (Paramount, 1959).

5086
Sheriff: Take 'em into the saloon, boys!
    That's the biggest place I know to hold
    'em.

The Sheriff played by Charles King: Ray Taylor's
Law of the Lash (PRC, 1947).

5087
Barker: Again that trusty rifle cracked
    and another redskin bit the dust. But
    still those red varmints kept encircling
    that poor hopeless wagon train. Again
    and again that young man with the
    long rifle poured his lead and missiles
    of death into the ranks of those red-
    skins. And the dying screams of them
    Comanches curdled the air. The lives
    of a hundred women and children
    depended upon him. Renegade that
    he was, child of nature, foreign to the
    laws of man, he had but one thing
    on his mind: his own mother was a
    woman.
Piano Player (*crying*): My mother was a
    woman, too!

Bonanza Bill Barker played by Harry Carey and
the Piano Player was uncredited: Glenn Tryon's
The Law West of Tombstone (RKO, 1938).

5088
Paul: What happened to your face?
Jack: Oh, a bunch of guys I ran into
    down at some saloon gave it a new
    look. I guess they didn't like the old
    one.

Paul Bondi played by Michael Kane and Jack
Burns played by Kirk Douglas: David Miller's
Lonely Are the Brave (Universal, 1962).

5089
Ada: You tell him, Willie, that it's bad
    business to open a place with a killing.
    People will stay away. They will be
    afraid.

Ada Marshall played by Elaine Aiken and Willie
played by Elisha Cook, Jr.: Henry Levin's *The
Lonely Man* (Paramount, 1957).

5090
Lotta Legs: The girls have been wanting
    me to talk to you. No one goes to the sa-
    loon anymore. Everybody is afraid of
    getting arrested.
Luke: Well, if they behave themselves they
    won't.
Lotta Legs: Well, that's just the point.
    Maybe you're making Daisy Town a lit-
    tle too good.
Luke: What?
Horse: She's saying the town's boring,
    cowboy. And she's right. We haven't had
    a decent gunfight in weeks.
Lotta Legs: Well, a town that's too clean
    starts to die. You got to have a little life.
    It helps the economy.
Luke: I'm just enforcing the law!
Lotta Legs: Maybe you shouldn't enforce it
    quite so much.

Roger Miller was the voice of the horse, Jolly
Jumper. Lotta Legs played by Nancy Morgan and
Lucky Luke played by Terence Hill who also directed *Lucky Luke* (Silvio Berlusconi Communications, 1991).

5091
Don't Shoot The Piano Player. He's The
    Only One We Got.

Sign in saloon: Terence Hill's *Lucky Luke* (Silvio
Berlusconi Communications, 1991).

5092
Rosie: Who owns this dump anyway?
Red Dick: Marguerita Ventura.
Rosie: Does she need a singer?
Red Dick: Did Lincoln need John Wilkes
    Booth?

Rosie Velez played by Divine, Red Dick Barker
played by Courtney Gains, and Marguerita Ventura played by Lainie Kazan: Paul Bartel's *Lust in
the Dust* (Fox Run/New World, 1985).

5093
Callahan: I'm gonna save us both a lot of
    trouble, Sheriff. You seen him go for the
    gun?
1st Townsman: Yeah, he reached for it first
    all right.
Callahan: Is that the way you saw it?
2nd Townsman: Yeah.
Callahan: You seen it was my bottle he took?
Bartender: That's right, it was his bottle.

Diego "Macho" Callahan played by David Janssen
and the Bartender played by Steve Raines: Bernard
L. Kowalski's *Macho Callahan* (Avco Embassy
Pictures, 1970).

5094
Sheehan: You and me are going to form a
    partnership. A partnership that will keep
    away outsiders from coming in here and
    building another saloon without you
    and me saying it's all right and taking
    our cut. Huh, what do you say to that?
McCabe: Well, partners is what I come up
    here to get away from.

Sheehan: Sometimes you can't have things your own way. Sometimes you got to make a deal.
McCabe: Well, deals I don't mind. It's partners I don't like.
Sheehan played by Rene Auberjonois and John McCabe played by Warren Beatty: Robert Altman's *McCabe & Mrs. Miller* (Warner Bros., 1971).

5095
Lavetta: Ain't we done kicked you out of here already, Mr. Guthrie?
Hoyce: I sobered up. I'm starting over.
Lavetta played by Elizabeth Berridge and Hoyce Guthrie played by Richard Crenna: William A. Graham's *Montana* (TVW, 1990).

5096
Wyatt: Mac, you ever been in love?
Mac: No, I've been a bartender all my life.
Wyatt Earp played by Henry Fonda and Mac the Bartender played by J. Farrell MacDonald: John

Ford's *My Darling Clementine* (20th Century–Fox, 1946).

5097
Buck: Hard job, ain't it? Killing time.
Max: I'm working. You just can't see it. Give me a drink.
Buck: It's a hell of a way to begin a day, ain't it?
Buck Mason played by Val Avery and Max Sand/Nevada Smith played by Steve McQueen: Henry Hathaway's *Nevada Smith* (Paramount, 1966).

5098
Torrance: Excuse me. I have to go puke.
Lee: Now, it's behavior like that that gives us legends a bad name.
Jesse Ray Torrance played by Kris Kristofferson and Lee Walker played by Willie Nelson: Bill Corcoran's *Outlaw Justice* (TVW, 1999).

5099
Sheriff: Ah, George, I think it best you move on out of range. Now, why don't you go home and get some sleep?
George: I ain't got no home, Frank. I've been doing all my sleeping in Mac's saloon in yonder.
Sheriff: Oh well, if you need a bed, I could toss you in jail.
George: In jail? What for?
Sheriff: For most anything. For inciting a riot, for littering up the streets. Now come on!
George: I don't want to put you to all that bother, Frank. I'll just find myself another saloon.
Sheriff: George, you have used up every saloon in the Oklahoma Territory.
George: Well, there must be someone building a new one around here somewhere.
Sheriff Frank played by Robert Karnes and

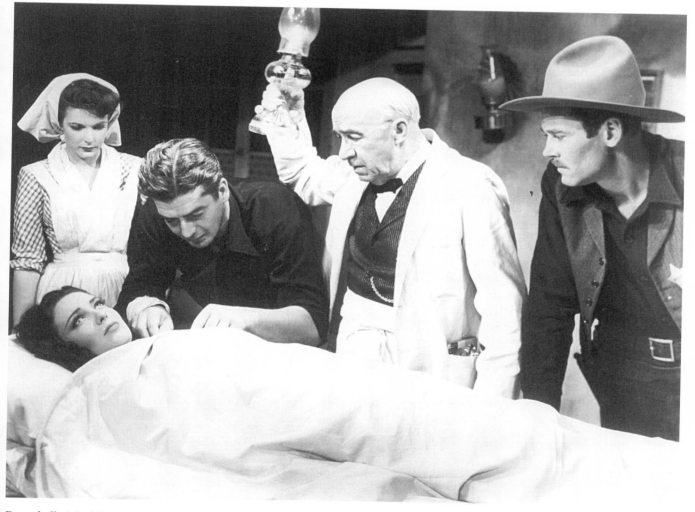
Dancehall girl Chihuahua (Linda Darnell) gets plugged and Doc Holliday (Victor Mature) is asked to operate. Clementine (Cathy Downs) pitches in as nurse while Mac, the bartender (J. Farrell MacDonald), holds the lantern. Marshal Wyatt Earp (Henry Fonda) looks on in John Ford's classic *My Darling Clementine* (20th Century–Fox, 1946).

Gentleman George played by Chill Wills: Jean Yarbrough's *The Over-the-Hill* Gang (TVW, 1969).

5100

Sheriff: She works in the Silver Dollar. It's a saloon, a gambling hall.

Granger: I've found that men that condemn such places most are usually their best customers.

Sheriff Blaney played by Chubby Johnson and Ross Granger played by Jock Mahoney: Fred F. Sears' *Overland Pacific* (United Artists, 1954).

5101

Mr. Dennison: It isn't unreasonable for a man to resent finding his daughter in a cheap gambling house.

Stewart: Now look, Mr. Dennison. That door, which incidentally you forgot to close, separates the reputable from the disreputable. The only thing that filters through the cracks is money.

Mr. Dennison played by Walter Sande and Del Stewart played by William Bishop: Fred F. Sears' *Overland Pacific* (United Artists, 1954).

5102

Jake: I don't like 53-card decks because I don't run the kind of place where you need hip boots to wade through the dead and wounded.

Jake Sears played by Richard Mulligan: Arthur Allan Seidelman's *Poker Alice* (TVW, 1987).

5103

Happy: Good evening, Sourdough. How are the bunions?

Sourdough: Plumb aggravating. Give me a beer. It all comes from wearing boots is my theory. If the human race hadn't started wearing leather on their feet, corns and bunions and such feet ailments wouldn't be, that's all.

Happy Hopkins played by William Desmond and Sourdough Jenkins played by Frank Rice: Wallace Fox's *Powdersmoke Range* (RKO, 1935).

5104

Sheriff: I'd appreciate it while you're in Refuge, that you don't curse ...except for in the saloon, of course.

Sheriff Forest played by Sam Shepard: Uli Edel's *Purgatory* (TVW, 1999).

5105

Bartender: You look like you come through the desert.

Tex: There's nothing wrong with your eyesight, mister. How good are you at guessing a man's drink?

Pop: South, I'd say ...judging by the looks of the dust on you. Texas, maybe?

Tex: Brazos.

Pop: That calls for whiskey.

Bartender: On account of we don't serve no other drink.

Bull the Bartender played by Paul Fierro, Tex Kirby played by Rory Calhoun and Pop Penny played by Emile Meyer: John Sherwood's *Raw Edge* (Universal, 1956).

5106

Ruggles: I want to make something of myself. I would like to stand on my own two feet. This is a land, sir, of great opportunity where all are created equal.

Egbert: Yeah, that's what I've been ...now you're talking! Like Lincoln said that day at Gettysburg. He hit the nail right on the nose when he said...

Ma: Well, what did he say?

Egbert: That's funny, I was going to ask you the same thing. He, uh, what did he say?

Ma: I don't know. Do you?

Judson: I don't know.

Egbert: Er, he said, er, hey Sam!

Sam: Yeah!

Egbert: What did Lincoln say that day at Gettysburg?

Sam: I don't know but I'll find out!

Colonel Marmaduke "Bill" Ruggles played by Charles Laughton, Egbert "Sourdough" Floud played by Charles Ruggles, Ma Pettingill played by Maude Eburne, Mrs. Judson played by ZaSu Pitts, and Sam played by Dell Henderson: Leo McCarey's *Ruggles of Red Gap* (Paramount, 1935).

5107

O'Herlihan: Glass of warm milk, please.

Bartender: [*no response*]

O'Herlihan: Make it a sarsaparilla.

Bartender: [*no response*]

O'Herlihan: Is this one of those really tough bars?

Bartender: [*nods affirmatively*]

O'Herlihan: Well, let me have a large glass of warm gin served with a human hair in it.

Bartender: Coming up!

Rex O'Herlihan played by Tom Berenger and the Bartender played by Alan Larson: Hugh Wilson's *Rustlers' Rhapsody* (Paramount, 1985).

5108

Pulford: You have two ways of leaving this establishment, my friend: immediately or dead!

Pulford played by Hugh O'Brian: Don Siegel's *The Shootist* (Paramount, 1976).

5109

Paden: Come on, I'll buy you a drink.

Emmett: You ain't got any money!

Paden: All right, you can buy me a drink. You know, a good smelly saloon is my favorite place in the world.

Paden played by Kevin Kline and Emmett played by Scott Glenn: Lawrence Kasdan's *Silverado* (Columbia, 1985).

5110

Doc: Jerry, I'll admit as one man to another that, economically, I haven't been

of much value to you. But do you suppose you could put one [drink] on credit?

Bartender: If talk was money, Doc, you'd be the best customer I got.

Dr. Josiah Boone played by Thomas Mitchell and Jerry the Bartender played by Jack Pennick: John Ford's *Stagecoach* (United Artists, 1939).

5111

Bartender: What I'm trying to tell you is, this is sneaking liquor you're selling. And I don't get many sneaking drinkers in here. My customers are mostly honest drunks.

[*and a little later*]

Bartender: But it's sneaking liquor! Do you want to explain it to him, Doc?

Doc: Sneaking liquor? Well, it's sort of a social comment. It's a liquor that little old ladies hide down in their petticoats and their corsets ...and in books that you won't find in a Christian store. Hypocritically, nothing like a little bracer before prayer meeting.

Salesman: My dear friend, you can't compare Kentucky bourbon with the kind of spirits old ladies hide in their knickers.

Doc: But it's prescription. It's to help their nerves and to help them sleep. It's sneaking liquor. For medicinal purposes only.

Bartender: Doc knows what he's talking about. He's a dentist!

The Bartender played by Billy Swan, Doc Holliday played by Willie Nelson, and the Whiskey Salesman, Trevor Peacock, played by Anthony Newley: Ted Post's *Stagecoach* (TVW, 1986).

5112

Haven: Doesn't he [pianist] ever stop playing?

Bartender: Sam? It don't bother him. He's deaf.

Haven played by Dick Powell and the Bartender played by John Doucette: Sidney Lanfield's *Station West* (RKO, 1948).

5113

Sheriff: Is this the kind of town you people want for yourselves? Is this the kind of life you want to lead? I mean, three killings in one saloon alone! The sun hasn't even gone down yet. Any more of this foolishness, and I'm going to close this place up tight.

Sheriff Jason McCullough played by James Garner: Burt Kennedy's *Support Your Local Sheriff!* (United Artists, 1969).

5114

Bartender: Remember what the sheriff said: no more shootin' till the sun goes down.

Townsman: Is that what he said?

Bartender: That's close enough, brother. Drinks are on the house!

The Bartender played by Dick Haynes: Burt

Kennedy's *Support Your Local Sheriff!* (United Artists, 1969).

5115

Madden: Nothing has changed much. You're even using the same cheap-smellin' toilet water.
Pearlo: You never did like that, did ya?
Madden: It'll never take the place of a bath.

Larry Madden played by Randolph Scott and Cibo Pearlo played by John Baragrey: Lesley Selander's *Tall Man Riding* (Warner Bros., 1955).

5116

King: Why don't they have saloons that women can go into?

"Mike" King played by Claire Trevor: George Marshall's *Texas* (Columbia, 1941).

5117

Pat: I ain't never seen no Main Street without a saloon.

Pat Westall played by Dean Stockwell: Albert Band's *Texas in Flames* (a.k.a. *She Came to the Valley*; Raja Films, 1977).

5118

Dusty: Well, as long as we got some time to kill, I think I'll have a beer.
Bartender: We don't have no beer …just tequila.
Ned: What's tequila?
Bartender: It's, it's like beer.

Dusty Bottoms played by Chevy Chase, the Bartender played by Fred Asparagus, and Ned Nederlander played by Martin Short: John Landis' *Three Amigos!* (Orion, 1986).

5119

Bragg: Oh come on, give me a beer. I'll pay ya! On my word of honor!
Bartender: Well, couldn't you put up something a little more valuable?

Skinner Bill Bragg played by Wallace Beery and Horsecollar the Bartender played by Eddy Waller: Richard Thorpe's *20 Mule Team* (MGM, 1940).

5120

Josie: Now listen to me, you no-good deadbeat! If I go easy on you, charging up one more [drink], it's the same as cheating my kid out of the education she's entitled to get.
Bragg: Ah, Josie, are you gonna let a hard working man die of thirst just on account of educating a kid?
Josie: That just about sums up what's wrong with the male gender, Bill Bragg. Now get out here!

Josie Johnson played by Marjorie Rambeau and Skinner Bill Bragg played by Wallace Beery: Richard Thorpe's *20 Mule Team* (MGM, 1940).

5121

Belle: Beer suit you?
Jim: You read my mind.
Belle: With most men, that's not too difficult …and not too interesting either. I can tell when a man walks through that door if he prefers blondes or brunettes, drinks whiskey or beer, plays blackjack or poker, is a cheapskate or a high roller.
Gus: Well, how do you peg old Jim here?
Belle: Beer, blonde, and solitaire.
Jim: That's me …solitaire.
Belle: And that'll be four bits, Gus, because he hasn't got a dime.
Jim: You called it, I haven't got a dime. Except I'm not so sure about blondes.
Belle: No man ever is.

Belle Aragon played by Annelle Hayes, Lieutenant Jim Gary played by Richard Widmark, and Guthrie "Gus" McCabe played by James Stewart: John Ford's *Two Rode Together* (Columbia, 1961).

5122

Little Bill: Well, sir, you are a cowardly son of a bitch! You just shot an unarmed man!
Munny: Well, he should have armed himself if he's going to decorate his saloon with my friend.

Little Bill Daggett played by Gene Hackman and William "Bill" Munny played by Clint Eastwood who also directed *Unforgiven* (Warner Bros., 1992).

5123

Owen: I always heard you were a pretty good saloon fighter, Herb. How are you without a bottle or a knife?

Owen Daybright played by Burt Lancaster and Herb Backett played by Ted De Corsia: Richard Thorpe's *Vengeance Valley* (MGM, 1951).

5124

Lomax: Sheriff, this drunk insulted the lady! Lock him up until he sleeps it off!
Saloon Lady: What did he do?
Lomax: You didn't notice?
Saloon Lady: No.
Lomax: You've been working saloons too long!

Lomax played by Kirk Douglas and Sheriff Strike played by Terry Wilson: Burt Kennedy's *The War Wagon* (Universal, 1967).

5125

Bartender: You opened your mouth to the wrong man, Lewt. He'll cut you pocket-high as soon as you start to reach.
Lewton: Yeah, well, it does look like I stepped in it a bit, doesn't it?

The Bartender played by Jay Ose and Lewton Cole played by James Coburn: William A. Graham's *Waterhole No. 3* (Paramount, 1967).

5126

Mayor: And another thing! All horses must be kept off the sidewalks. And last and most important, saloons is to be kept closed between five and six in the morning. You got to sweep 'em out sometime!

Mayor Honest John Whitaker played by George "Gabby" Hayes: Joseph Kane's *West of the Badlands* (a.k.a. *The Border Legion*; Republic, 1940).

5127

Hurricane: Stand back! I ain't gonna have no bloodshed in here! I just had this placed scrubbed!

Hurricane Hattie played by Maude Eburne: Joseph Kane's *West of the Badlands* (a.k.a. *The Border Legion*; Republic, 1940).

Showdown

See also Dying; Killing

5128

Marshal: Funny, you never know who's going to fire the first shot until the fight begins.

Marshal Dan Mitchell played by Randolph Scott: Edwin Marin's *Abilene Town* (United Artists, 1946).

5129

Bandit: Your last wish, señor?

Ben: Not to be here!

The Bandit was uncredited and Ben played by Fred Williamson who also directed *Adios Amigo* (Atlas, 1975).

5130

Pete: You ready?
Brisco: Pride comes before a fall, Pete.
Pete: So does an ounce of lead in a brain-pan.

Pete Hutter played by John Pyper-Ferguson and Brisco County, Jr., played by Bruce Campbell: Bryan Spicer's *Adventures of Brisco County, Jr.* (TVW, Series Premiere, 1993).

5131

Dakota: I'm gonna perforate his mangy carcass!

Dakota played by Tom London: Thomas Carr's *Alias Billy the Kid* (Republic, 1946).

5132

Melody: If there's anything in the world I like, it's getting saved from being shot.

Melody Jones played by Gary Cooper: Stuart Heisler's *Along Came Jones* (RKO, 1945).

5133

Pop: Just as long as you're conscious, I'm a goner. So I aim to make you unconscious.

Timothy "Pop" Keith played by Walter Brennan: Raoul Walsh's *Along the Great Divide* (Warner Bros., 1951).

5134

Doc: If I felt cynical, this would be a good opportunity to observe that we're about to see a perfect example of an eye for an eye. Unfortunately, I can't quote chapter and verse.

Doctor Mangrum played by Tom Powers: James Edward Grant's *Angel and the Badman* (Republic, 1947).

5135

Vance: You know, someday I'm going to get tired of you talking and make you pull that gun. And that will be the last thing you'll do.

Jess: Now, he didn't mean nothing, Vance. He's young. He'll learn.

Vance: He better or he won't get any older.

Vance Buckner played by John Russell and Jess Cooney played by Gene Evans: R.G. Springsteen's *Apache Uprising* (Paramount, 1966).

5136

Jim: Little man …big mouth!

Toby: Big man …big gun! Now, do you want to see how big?

Jim Walker played by Rory Calhoun and Toby Jack Saunders played by DeForest Kelley: R.G. Springsteen's *Apache Uprising* (Paramount, 1966).

5137

Theodore: You know something, Amos?

Amos: Huh?

Theodore: We got to make a decision.

Amos: What?

Theodore: Does the Hash Knife Outfit throw in its hand? Or do we go out in a blaze of glory?

Amos: Right! Huh …just what do you mean …blaze of glory?

Theodore: Fighting till the last man's killed! What's it going to be, pard?

Amos: You know, that jail in Santa Fe wasn't all that bad.

Theodore Ogilvie played by Don Knotts and Amos Tucker played by Tim Conway: Norman Tokar's *The Apple Dumpling Gang* (Buena Vista, 1975).

5138

Theodore: You know something, Amos. The Lord poured your brains in with a teaspoon and somebody juggled his

hand. I keep trying to tell you we ain't got no lead to throw, and no powder to throw it with.

Theodore Ogilvie played by Don Knotts and Amos Tucker was played by Tim Conway: Norman Tokar's *The Apple Dumpling Gang* (Buena Vista, 1975).

5139

Phoebe: Now sometime before morning, I'm going to let off both barrels of this shotgun right at you. I don't know just what time it'll happen …whenever my finger gets to itching too much. But you can depend on it. You're gonna have a double hole blown clean through you. Maybe ten minutes, maybe two hours. All you have to do is sit comfortable until I think it's the right time.

Phoebe Titus played by Jean Arthur: Wesley Ruggles' *Arizona* (Columbia, 1940).

5140

Buford: What's wrong, dude? Are you yellow? That's what I thought …a yellow belly!

Marty: Nobody calls me yellow!

Buford: Well, let's finish it! Right now!

Sidekick 1: No, not now, Buford. The marshal has got our guns.

Buford: Let's just say we'll finish this tomorrow!

Sidekick 2: Tomorrow we're robbing the Pine City Stage.

Buford: What about Monday? Are we doing anything Monday?

Sidekick 1: No, Monday would be fine. You can kill him Monday.

Buford: I'll be back this way on Monday! We'll settle this then …right there …out in the street …in front of the Palace Saloon!

Marty: Yeah, like when? High noon?

Buford: Noon? I do my killin' before breakfast! 7 o'clock!

Marty: 8 o'clock. I do my killing after breakfast!

Marty McFly played by Michael J. Fox, Buford "Mad Dog" Tannen played by Thomas F. Wilson, and Buford's sidekicks were uncredited: Robert Zemeckis' *Back to the Future, Part III* (Universal, 1990).

5141

Marty: Listen, you got a back door to this place!

Bartender: Yeah, it's in the back.

Marty McFly played by Michael J. Fox and the Bartender played by Matt Clark: Robert Zemeckis' *Back to the Future, Part III* (Universal, 1990).

5142

Marty: Listen, I'm not really feeling up to this today. So I'm gonna have to forfeit.

Buford: Forfeit. Forfeit! What's that mean?

Sidekick: Ah, it means that you win without a fight.

Buford: Without killing him? He can't do that. Hey, you can't do that!

Marty McFly played by Michael J. Fox, Buford "Mad Dog" Tannen played by Thomas F. Wilson, and Buford's sidekick was uncredited: Robert Zemeckis' *Back to the Future, Part III* (Universal, 1990).

5143

Lash: You better watch your mouth, Crowley, or I'll put a window in your head!

Lash played by Musetta Vander and Crowley played by Jeff Weston: Sam Irvin's *Backlash: Oblivion 2* (Full Moon Entertainment, 1996).

5144

Big Joe: My boy, let me give you a little piece of advice. If you're going to pull a gun on somebody, which happens from time to time in these parts, you better fire it about a half a second after you do it …because most men aren't as patient as I am.

Big Joe played by David Huddleston: Robert Benton's *Bad Company* (Paramount, 1972).

5145

Smith: Look, Mr. MacReedy, there is a law in this county against shootin' dogs. But when I see a mad dog, I don't wait for him to bite me. I swear, you're beginning to make me mad!

Reno Smith played by Robert Ryan and John J. MacReedy played by Spencer Tracy: John Sturges' *Bad Day at Black Rock* (MGM, 1955).

5146

Ringo: New game …more fun than hopscotch. The first of these gentlemen that steps forward gets a new lead bullet between his eyes.

Ringo played by Giuliano Gemma: Duccio Tessari's *Ballad of Death Valley* (a.k.a. *The Return of Ringo*; Mediterranee-Balcazar/Rizzoli Film, 1966).

5147

California: Hey! Come back here and I'll orphan your children and widow your wife!

California Carlson played by Andy Clyde: Lesley Selander's *Bar 20* (United Artists, 1943).

5148

Cole: I'll be seeing you, Glyn.

Glyn: You'll be seeing me. You'll be seeing me. Everytime you bed down for the night, you'll look back into the darkness and wonder if I'm there. And some night I will be. You'll be seeing me!

Emerson Cole Garret played by Arthur Kennedy and Glyn McLyntock played by James Stewart: Anthony Mann's *Bend of the River* (Universal, 1952).

5149

Cole: Do you know what you're doing, Doc?

Doc: Nope, I don't. But my impetuous nature got me into this …so it's going to have to get me out.

Cole Younger played by Bruce Cabot and Doc Butcher played by Walter Brennan: William D. Russell's *Best of the Badmen* (RKO, 1951).

5150

Doc: I don't know about the rest of the boys, but I'd sooner be a sensible live quitter than a stubborn dead hero.

Doc Butcher played by Walter Brennan: William D. Russell's *Best of the Badmen* (RKO, 1951).

5151

Hannassey: I'll tell you why I'm here, Major Terrill. When you come a ridin' roughshod over my land, scaring the kids and the woman folks, when you invade my home like you was the law or God Almighty, then I say to you: I've seen every kind of critter God ever made. And I ain't never see a meaner, lower, more stinking, yellow hypocrite than you. Now, you can swallow up a lot of folks and make them like it, but you ain't swallowing me. I'm stuck in your craw, Henry Terrill, and you can't spit me out. Now, hear me now! You rode into my place and beat my men for the last time. And I give you warning: you set foot in Blanco Canyon once more, and this country is going to run red with blood until there ain't one of us left!

Rufus Hannassey played by Burl Ives and Major Henry Terrill played by Charles Bickford: William Wyler's *The Big Country* (United Artists, 1958).

5152

Hannassey: He's going to be the most surprised dead man you ever saw!

Rufus Hannassey played by Burl Ives: William Wyler's *The Big Country* (United Artists, 1958).

5153

Jacob: What do you do when cockroaches get in the woodwork, Michael?
James: Smoke 'em out?
Jacob: That's right.
Michael: Why not wait until they make a move?
Jacob: Because waiting is good for them and bad for us. You get impatient, nervy, careless, and maybe dead.

Jacob McCandles played by John Wayne, James McCandles played by Patrick Wayne, and Michael McCandles played by Chris Mitchum: George Sherman's *Big Jake* (NGP, 1971).

5154

O'Brien: I hear you killed two good men in a fair fight tonight. Is that right?
James: No. Three, counting you.
O'Brien: Prove it!

O'Brien played by Glenn Corbett and James

McCandles played by Patrick Wayne: George Sherman's *Big Jake* (NGP, 1971).

5155

John: I just saw something in your eyes I don't like. I saw a foolish thought. You understand me. If anything happens, anything at all …your fault, my fault, nobody's fault …my little brother will blow that kid's head right off. It's as simple as that. No matter who else gets killed, that boy dies. If the shotgun misses him, it don't matter. You already know about the rifle on him. That won't be as messy as a shotgun at three feet, but that boy will be just as dead. You understand me?

[*and a little later when the guns are turned*]
Jacob: Now you understand. Anything goes wrong, anything at all …your fault, my fault, nobody's fault. It won't matter. I'm going to blow your head off. It's as simple as that. No matter what else happens, no matter who gets killed, I'm going to blow your head off!

John Fain played by Richard Boone and Jacob McCandles played by John Wayne: George Sherman's *Big Jake* (NGP, 1971).

5156

John Fain: You come close, mister, but no cigar!

John Fain played by Richard Boone: George Sherman's *Big Jake* (NGP, 1971).

5157

Autry: It might get a little rough.
Don Luis: You think because my bones are old, I have no stomach for danger?

Gene Autry played himself and Don Luis Alvarado played by William Edmunds: Frank McDonald's *The Big Sombrero* (Columbia, 1949).

5158

Billy Jack: I'm gonna take this right foot and I'm gonna whop you on that side of your face. And you want to know something? There's not a damn thing you're gonna be able to do about it.
Posner: Really?
Billy Jack: Really!

Billy Jack played by Tom Laughlin and Posner played by Bert Freed: T.G. Frank's (Tom Laughlin) *Billy Jack* (Warner Bros.–National Student Film Corp., 1971).

5159

Benj: Maybe it's time for a new approach.
Bronc: I only know one way …and that's head on!

Benj Cartwright played by Michael Landon, Jr. and Bronc Evans played by Ben Johnson: Jerry Jameson's *Bonanza: The Return* (TVW, 1993).

5160

Dandy Jim: You got a plan?

Kirby: Sure. We ride in and they give themselves up.
Dandy Jim: I see you've given this a lot of thought.

Dandy Jim played by Michael Horse and Kirby Frye played by Cody Glenn: C.T. McIntyre's *Border Shootout* (Turner Home Entertainment, 1990).

5161

Pearce: I reckon we come down to it, Deakin.
Deakin: You have a choice. You could throw that gun down.
Pearce: I don't think I can do that.

Nathan Pearce played by Ben Johnson and John Deakin played by Charles Bronson: Tom Gries' *Breakheart Pass* (United Artists, 1976).

5162

Maverick: Well, they got us pinned flater than a brown tick on a white dog.

Bret Maverick played by James Garner: Stuart Margolin's *Bret Maverick: The Lazy Ace* (TVW, 1981).

5163

Susan: Logan, don't take any chances. I don't want you to kill him. But if it has to be you or him, if it comes to that, I want you to come back.

Susan played by Beverley Owen and Logan Keliher played by Audie Murphy: R.G. Springsteen's *Bullet for a Badman* (Universal, 1964).

5164

Maria: My brother is not brave like our father.
Tio: Your father is dead. It is best not to be like your father.

Maria Colton played by Natalie Wood and Tio Perico played by Frank Puglia: Stuart Heisler's *The Burning Hills* (Warner Bros., 1956).

5165

Butch: Look, I don't mean to be a sore loser, but when it's done …if I'm dead …kill him!

Butch Cassidy played by Paul Newman: George Roy Hill's *Butch Cassidy and the Sundance Kid* (20th Century–Fox, 1969).

5166

Butch: We're gonna run out [of ammo] unless we can get to that mule and get some more.
Sundance: I'll go.
Butch: This is no time for bravery. I'll let ya!

Butch Cassidy played by Paul Newman and The Sundance Kid played by Robert Redford: George Roy Hill's *Butch Cassidy and the Sundance Kid* (20th Century–Fox, 1969).

5167

Old Man: If I was twenty years younger …!
Graycoe: You won't live to be twenty seconds older if you keep running off at the mouth!

The Old Man played by Francis McDonald and Graycoe played by Robert Wilke: Harmon Jones' *Canyon River* (Allied Artists, 1956).

5168

Griffin: Why do you always insult people who might kill you?

Captain: I like to see a man enjoy his work.

Griffin played by Stuart Whitman and Captain Apache played by Lee Van Cleef: Alexander Singer's *Captain Apache* (Scotia International, 1971).

5169

Briggs: Go ahead, Adams, run again!

Adams: Not this time, Briggs! A man like you has got to be stopped!

Frank Briggs played by Chuck Connors and Grizzly Adams played by Dan Haggerty: Don Keeslar's *The Capture of Grizzly Adams* (TVW, 1982).

5170

Abe: What's the matter, Brassfield? Afraid to come here alone?

Sam: What's the matter with you? Afraid to talk to me without a shotgun in your hand?

Abe Clevenger played by Malcolm Atterbury and Sam Brassfield played by Robert Taylor: Tay Garnett's *Cattle King* (MGM, 1963).

5171

Undertaker: A word of advice: don't mistake stupidity for courage.

The Undertaker/Jedediah Turner played by Gregory Hines: Paris Barclay's *The Cherokee Kid* (HBO Pictures, 1996).

5172

Pepper: What are you going to do?

Chisum: What I had done twenty-five years ago. Pat, get the men out at South Camp. Trace, you round up everybody that can ride a horse or pull a trigger. Let's break out some Winchesters!

James Pepper played by Ben Johnson and John Chisum played by John Wayne: Andrew McLaglen's *Chisum* (Warner Bros., 1970).

5173

Pepper: Would you like to listen to my opinion, Mr. John Simpson Chisum?

Chisum: Nope.

Pepper: Well, my opinion is all this speechifying, store-keeping, prayer-meeting don't amount to a spit in the river. There's only one thing that's going to make this territory know who's the bull of the woods …and sometime or sooner it's going to happen. And you know it.

Chisum: Do I?

Pepper: You do. It's just going to be you and Murphy, head-to-head and horn-to-horn …and one hell of a fight. But one of you has got to lose. So the other one walks away with the herd and the whole shebang. Now, that's my opinion.

James Pepper played by Ben Johnson and John Chisum played by John Wayne: Andrew McLaglen's *Chisum* (Warner Bros., 1970).

5174

Sgt.: Now you can pull that gun of yours and shoot me where I stand. Or you can defend yourself as best you can. Because I intend to beat you into the ground with my fists. Now, I'm waiting on ya!

Sergeant Otto Hahnsbach played by Ernest Borgnine: Gordon Douglas' *Chuka* (Paramount, 1967).

5175

John: Now don't misunderstand me, Sheriff. I don't like him any better than you do. About the most I can say for him is that he has been with me for a long time. If it was just for that, you could keep him [in jail]. But it's more than that, Sheriff. It's a matter of principle. You see, Sheriff, those men out there expect me to come out with Flint. Now, how would it look it I came out alone? You see, Sheriff, it's just a matter of principle.

John Ringo played by Richard Boone: Harmon Jones' *City of Bad Men* (20th Century–Fox, 1953).

5176

Downey: They say you're pretty good with a gun, Read. Now, just how good?

Read: I manage to stay alive.

Downey: I asked you a question, Read! How good?

Read: That's your gamble.

Art Downey played by Stacy Harris and Jim Read played by Dana Andrews: George Sherman's *Comanche* (United Artists, 1956).

5177

Regret: Gentlemen, let's remember we're gentlemen.

Cutter: Forget it! He's just spittin' out words to see where they splatter.

Paul Regret played by Stuart Whitman and Jake Cutter played by John Wayne: Michael Curtiz's *The Comancheros* (20th Century–Fox, 1961).

5178

Mahler: Damn you, Conn, you're pushing me!

Conagher: It seems to me I'm the one who's being pushed.

Mahler: You're a damn fool. They're going to clean the old man out [of his cattle] by spring. Now you can do your job and look the other way, or you can set yourself up for a target. You got a choice.

Conagher: No, you got a choice. You can throw your pack on your horse and ride out of here tonight, or you can go for that gun.

Chris Mahler played by Gavan O'Herlihy and Conn Conagher played by Sam Elliott: Reynaldo Villalobos' *Conagher* (Turner Pictures, 1991).

5179

Chris: Now, you wouldn't get an idea that my left hand is slower than your right, would you, Yordy? But if you would like to prove it …

Chris Danning played by Randolph Scott and Frank Yordy played by Joe Sawyer: Ray Enright's *Coroner Creek* (Columbia, 1948).

5180

Banner: Start walking and count to ten. And try not to deal off the bottom of the deck.

John Banner played by Dale Robertson: Lewis R. Foster's *Dakota Incident* (Republic, 1956).

5181

Station Agent: There's going to be a shooting, huh?

Wade: In two minutes.

Station Agent: Who's coming after you?

Wade: My past. Every dark, miserable day of it.

The Station Agent was uncredited and Brett Wade played by Rory Calhoun: George Sherman's *Dawn at Socorro* (Universal, 1954).

5182

Scott: Talby, now it's your turn. There's nobody out here left to be killed in your place.

Scott Mary played by Giuliano Gemma and Frank Talby played by Lee Van Cleef: Tonino Valerii's *Day of Anger* (a.k.a. *Days of Wrath*; Sancrosiap/ Corona Film/KG Divina Film/National General, 1967).

5183

Mary: What would you do, Captain, if you saw Jesse James?

Captain: There's only one thing to do: shoot first and ask questions afterwards.

Mary Whittaker played by Pauline Moore and Captain Worthington played by Harry Woods: Joseph Kane's *Days of Jesse James* (Republic, 1939).

5184

Missionary: God damn your soul to the fires of hell!

Blake: He already has!

The Trading Post Missionary played by Alfred Molina and William Blake played by Johnny Depp: Jim Jarmusch's *Dead Man* (Miramax Films, 1996).

5185

Brittany: Harry, what are you doing? He's just a boy!

Harry: Well, if he's this stupid, he's not going to grow up to be a man, now is he?

Brittany played by April Telek and Harry McDonacle played by John Ritter: Joseph L. Scanlan's "The Great McDonacle" episode of the series premiere, *Dead Man's Gun* (Showtime, 1997).

5186

Brand: You're going to hell, mister!

Willy: If I am, it won't be alone!

Brand Odom played by Jon Cuthbert and Willy played by Sebastian Spence: Neill Fearnley's "My Brother's Keeper" episode of the series premiere, *Dead Man's Gun* (Showtime, 1997).

5187

Zach: You wouldn't fire into a crowd, would you?

Bodeen: You ain't much of a crowd.

Zach was uncredited and Bodeen/Tom Hatcher played by Keith Coulouris: Alan J. Levi's *Dead Man's Revenge* (MCA/Universal Home Video, 1994).

5188

Sikes: Every man has got to know his limitations, Carl. I know mine.

Carl: Well, you ain't God Almighty either.

Sikes: Here's your chance to prove it.

John Sikes played by James Remar and Carl Turner played by Robert Knott: E.W. Swackhamer's *Desperado: The Outlaw Wars* (TVW, 1989).

5189

Jesse: If they make any noise, blast 'em!

Jesse Gorman played by Stephen McNally: Alfred Werker's *Devil's Canyon* (RKO, 1953).

5190

Stuart: Here he comes! Shall I shoot him in the back when he passes?

Hoke: No! I want this to be a fair fight. I'll shoot him in the back. It's the code of the west.

Charles Stuart played by Harry Carey, Jr., and Hoke played by George Kennedy: Burt Kennedy's *Dirty Dingus Magee* (MGM, 1970).

5191

Django: Tell Jackson that I'll be waiting at the cemetery. Understand? There's just the two of us now. I'll be waiting.

Django played by Franco Nero and Jackson played by Eduardo Fajardo: Sergio Corbucci's *Django* (B.R.C./Tecisa, 1966).

5192

MacKay: You think they're bluffin'?

Manok: We find out if they start shootin'.

Johnny MacKay played by Alan Ladd and Manok played by Anthony Caruso: Delmer Daves' *Drum Beat* (Warner Bros., 1954).

5193

Lewt: I'm riding back to that hitching post and then turning and starting to shoot.

Jesse: It's more than you did for Sam Pierce! Why all the consideration?

Lewt: I just don't want them fancy friends of yours to say you had a brother who shot you down in cold blood.

Lewt McCanles played by Gregory Peck, Jesse McCanles played by Joseph Cotten, and Sam Pierce played by Charles Bickford: King Vidor's *Duel in the Sun* (Selznick Releasing Organization, 1946).

5194

Sam: I'm calling for a showdown!

Ebenezer: Showdown?

Sam: What, are you deaf? Yes, a showdown! Tomorrow …high noon …only one bullet each. And only one man walks away alive …the cowboy way.

Sam Benson played by Rick Schroder and Ebenezer Scrooge played by Jack Palance: Ken Jubenvill's *Ebenezer* (TVW, 1997).

5195

Townsman: El Diablo is sure going to drop a load of manure in his pants when he sees you a-coming at him!

The Townsman was uncredtied: Peter Markle's *El Diablo* (HBO Pictures, 1990).

5196

Billy Ray: I had successfully shot a man in a showdown in the middle of the street at high noon. Actually, it was much later in the day, but it was still quite a thrill!

Billy Ray Smith played by Anthony Edwards: Peter Markle's *El Diablo* (HBO Pictures, 1990).

5197

Sheriff: What are you doing with that bow and arrow outfit?

Bull: Like Cole said, you got to be quiet about this.

Sheriff: Can you hit the side of a barn with that thing?

Bull: Ain't going to try to hit a barn …just a man.

Sheriff J.P. Harrah played by Robert Mitchum and Bull Harris played by Arthur Hunnicutt: Howard Hawks' *El Dorado* (Paramount, 1967).

5198

Falin: Are you the one I'm hearing about? The one that's looking all over for Falin?

Vinnie: That's right.

Falin: I'm Falin.

Vinnie: Then you're the one I'm looking for.

Falin: Have we ever met before?

Vinnie: No.

Falin: Then what's our quarrel?

Vinnie: No quarrel. They say you're faster than me.

Falin: Just that?

Vinnie: Just that.

Falin: And you aim to find out if it's true?

Vinnie: That's right.

Falin: Mister, I don't want to fight …but don't push it!

Vinnie: Mr. Falin, I'm pushin' because I got to know.

Clint Falin was uncredited and Vinnie Harold played by Broderick Crawford: Russell Rouse's *The Fastest Gun Alive* (MGM, 1956).

5199

Stranger: I don't think it's nice you laughing. You see, my mule don't like people laughing. He gets the crazy idea you're laughing at him. Now if you'll apologize like I know you're going to, I might convince him that you really didn't mean it.

The Stranger (Joe) played by Clint Eastwood: Sergio Leone's *A Fistful of Dollars* (United Artists, 1964; U.S. 1967).

5200

Stranger: When a man with a .45 meets a man with a rifle, you said the man with the pistol is a dead man. Let's see if that's true.

The Stranger (Joe) played by Clint Eastwood: Sergio Leone's *A Fistful of Dollars* (United Artists, 1964; U.S. 1967).

5201

Sean: Duck, you sucker!

Sean Mallory played by James Coburn: Sergio Leone's *A Fistful of Dynamite* (United Artists, 1971).

5202

Mortimer: I generally smoke just after I eat. Why don't you come back in about ten minutes?

Hunchback: In ten minutes you'll be smoking in hell!

Colonel Douglas Mortimer played by Lee Van Cleef and the Hunchback played by Klaus Kinski: Sergio Leone's *For a Few Dollars More* (United Artists, 1965, U.S. 1967).

5203

Deputy: If you think I won't blow your head off, try finding it in the morning.

Deputy Waller played by Walter Sande: Edwin Marin's *Fort Worth* (Warner Bros., 1951).

5204

Earp: You listen, and you listen good! Any minute a pack of cold-blooded murdering' outlaws that eat the likes of you for breakfast are going to come riding up that street. And when they do, they're not going to find Wyatt Earp waiting for 'em wearing a pair of sissy glasses.

Wyatt Earp played by Fred Ward: Piers Haggard's *Four Eyes and Six-Guns* (Turner Pictures, 1992).

5205

Earp: I may be blind, but I ain't yellow. I want to take a stand. And if that means going down with a hail of bullets, well so be it! I'll take every last one of 'em with me! All nine of those carrot-top bastards!

Wyatt Earp played by Fred Ward: Piers Haggard's *Four Eyes and Six-Guns* (Turner Pictures, 1992).

5206

Lolly: Why don't they shoot?

Simon: They will. First they got to play with us a bit …tease us like.

Lolly Bhumer played by Colleen Miller and Simon Bhumer played by Walter Brennan: Richard Carlson's *Four Guns to the Border* (Universal, 1954).

5207

Lone Rider: You better stop walking or pull iron, boy!

The Lone Rider played by Luke Askew: Robert

Boris' *Frank & Jesse* (Vidmark Entertainment, 1995).

5208

Lone Rider: Your time has come, boy. The Lord is calling you.

The Lone Rider played by Luke Askew: Robert Boris' *Frank & Jesse* (Vidmark Entertainment, 1995).

5209

Quale: I was gonna thrash 'em within an inch of their lives, but I didn't have a tape measure.

S. Quentin Quale played by Groucho Marx: Edward Buzzell's *Go West* (MGM, 1940).

5210

Colter: Bugler! Blow that bugle so they can open the gates of hell for ya …because you're comin' in!

John Colter played by Ben Johnson and Bugler played by Charles B. Pierce who also directed *Grayeagle* (American International, 1977).

5211

Tia Maria: It is you yourself you must face.

Tia Maria played by Haydee Dubarry: Paul Hunt's *The Great Gundown* (Sun Productions, 1977).

5212

Chief Detective: From here on in, men, you are farmers. Your job is to plow them under like manure!

The Chief Detective of the Pinkerton Agency played by Herbert Nelson: Philip Kaufman's *The Great Northfield, Minnesota Raid* (Universal, 1972).

5213

Chad: Trouble's broiling up inside. You can feel it. It's thick in the air.

Chad Santee played by Buster Crabbe: Sidney Salkow's *Gun Brothers* (United Artists, 1956).

5214

Gunfighter: Look, old man, why don't you step aside?
Marshal: I'm standing where I'm standing.

The Young Gunfighter played by Keith Carradine and the U.S. Deputy Marshal played by Robert J. Wilke: Lamont Johnson's *A Gunfight* (Paramount, 1971).

5215

Alverez: Ladies and gentleman. In a few minutes it will be four o'clock. And the bell in your church tower will ring four times. The last bell will be a signal for the gunfight to begin.

Francisco Alverez played by Raf Vallone: Lamont Johnson's *A Gunfight* (Paramount, 1971).

5216

Lily: Don't go out there, Bat.
Bat: I don't want to, Lily. But the difference between here and the streets is the difference between a rabbit and a man.

Lily played by Nancy Gates and Bat Masterson played by Joel McCrea: Joseph M. Newman's *The Gunfight at Dodge City* (United Artists, 1959).

5217

Clerk: Oh, Mr. Holliday!
Doc: Yes?
Clerk: Would you care to settle up your bill now? What I mean, sir, is we didn't know whether you were checking out or not.
Doc: You'll have word in fifteen minutes.

The Hotel Clerk played by Frank Carter and John H. "Doc" Holliday played by Kirk Douglas: John Sturges' *Gunfight at the O.K. Corral* (Paramount, 1957).

5218

Doc: Well, if you happen to see this, ah, gentleman …tell him I'll be waiting for him at Boot Hill. He'll have only one direction to travel from there. Down!

John H. "Doc" Holliday played by Kirk Douglas: John Sturges' *Gunfight at the O.K. Corral* (Paramount, 1957).

5219

Cap: You got a plan of action?
Chad: Yeah, we're going to fight.

Deputy Cap Hold played by Denver Pyle and Sheriff Chad Lucas played by Audie Murphy: Earl Bellamy's *Gunpoint* (Universal, 1966).

5220

Reb: How's he paying ya?
Johnny: A thousand cash …$2500.00 bonus when the job is done.
Reb: Meaning when you shoot me.
Johnny: I think your name got mentioned someplace.
Reb: Well, I've been shot at for less.

Reb Kittredge played by Audie Murphy and Johnny Lake played by Charles Drake: Nathan Juran's *Gunsmoke* (Universal, 1953).

5221

Narrator: At dawn, the morning of November 17th, the 2nd Cavalry Patrol was heading due south for Denver …with, of course, the Temperance Marchers. The Willingham Wagon Train was turning west. The 1st Cavalry Patrol was moving fast to intercept it. The Denver Citizens' Militia was making an easterly crossing of the South Platte River while the Sioux Indians were coming down from the north …picking up more braves all the time.

Narration by John Dehner: John Sturges' *The Hallelujah Trail* (MGM, 1965).

5222

Cass: You got any plans?
Matt: Uh-huh. We go out shootin' …sometime tomorrow.
Cass: I wished I hadn't asked.

Cass Browne played by Frank Faylen and Matt

Stewart played by Randolph Scott: Roy Huggins' *Hangman's Knot* (Columbia, 1952).

5223

Burden: It's coming down to you and me, Martin. Just you and me.
Martin: Only if I play it your way. All I have to do is wait. You have the weakness of every gunslinger, Burden. You can't stay away from your guns.
Burden: Like I said, Martin, just you and me.

Steve Burden played by Guy Madison and Rice Martin played by Lorne Greene: George Sherman's *The Hard Man* (Columbia, 1957).

5224

Martin: I hired me a gun, Burden. A lot of my men are in town …strangers to you. One of them is carrying a bullet …for you. You try to find which one. Because now it's your turn to sweat, to watch every shadow, to be afraid of the dark. I'm gonna wait for you to break …the way Rodman broke. And when there isn't much left of you, I'll let my man finish the job.

Rice Martin played by Lorne Greene, Steve Burden played by Guy Madison, and John Rodman played by Rudy Bond: George Sherman's *The Hard Man* (Columbia, 1957).

5225

Hawken: My fight's not with you, boys. So if you want to be leaving here alive, now's the time to walk!

Hawken played by Peter Fonda: Charles B. Pierce's *Hawken's Breed* (Vidmark Entertainment, 1987).

5226

Will: Stay at the hotel until it's over.
Amy: No, I won't be here when it's over. You're asking me to wait an hour to find out if I'm going to be a wife or a widow. I say it's too long to wait. I won't do it!

Will Kane played by Gary Cooper and Amy Kane played by Grace Kelly: Fred Zinnemann's *High Noon* (United Artists, 1952).

5227

Brewster: Can't I look you in the face, Seagull?
Seagull: Sure you can! I want to see you spit out your soul.

Jerry Brewster played by Thomas Hunter and Ken Seagull played by Nando Gazzolo: Lee W. Beaver's *The Hills Run Red* (United Artists, 1966).

5228

Russell: You better put down that gun. You got two ways to go: put it down or use it. And even if you tie me, you're going to be dead.
Favor: You persuaded me.

John Russell played by Paul Newman and Favor played by Fredric March: Martin Ritt's *Hombre* (20th Century–Fox, 1967).

5229

Bandit: Hey hombre! I compliment you on your shooting. You have put a hole in me. I never have belly ache like this since I'm a little boy. Hey, amigo! Friend! I am going to give you back this bullet.

The Mexican Bandit played by Frank Silvera: Martin Ritt's *Hombre* (20th Century–Fox, 1967).

5230

Uncle Ben: Let's go over to Meeker's and give him a little gun medicine!
Red: That'll cure him!

Uncle Ben played by George "Gabby" Hayes and Red Connors played by Frank McGlynn, Jr.: Howard Bretherton's *Hopalong Cassidy* (a.k.a. *Hopalong Cassidy Enters*; Paramount, 1935).

5231

Doc: Stilwell, if you so much as turn your head toward those men, you'll be laying in horse manure with your friends.

Doc Holliday played by Jason Robards, Jr., and Frank Stilwell played by Robert Phillips: John Sturges' *The Hour of the Gun* (United Artists, 1967).

5232

Doc: You got some kind of plan?
Wyatt: I have.
Doc: Want to tell me about it?
Wyatt: We take whoever gets in our way.
Doc: You call that a plan?
Wyatt: You got a better one?

Doc Holliday played by Jason Robards, Jr., and Wyatt Earp played by James Garner: John Sturges' *The Hour of the Gun* (United Artists, 1967).

5233

Wyatt: A man's life …for fifty dollars. I'm gonna give ya a chance to make another fifty dollars.
Warshaw: I don't want such a chance.
Wyatt: My men will stay back. I'm gonna count one, two, three. You can draw on two. I'll wait to three. If you get me, my boys won't bother you any.

Wyatt Earp played by James Garner and Andy Warshaw played by Steve Ihnat: John Sturges' *The Hour of the Gun* (United Artists, 1967).

5234

Sheriff: You're one dumb move from hell!

Sheriff Sam Hatch played by John Bennett Perry: John Patterson's *Independence* (TVW, 1987).

5235

Bridie: Can I give you a little advice?
Hatch: It appears you're about to.
Bridie: Leave while your blood is on the dark side of your skin.

Bridie played by Isabella Hofmann and Sam Hatch played by John Bennett Perry: John Patterson's *Independence* (TVW, 1987).

5236

Jack: We're going to play a game. Now, when I say shoot, we draw and shoot.

Jack played by Brad Dexter: Jorge Fons' *Jory* (Avco Embassy, 1972).

5237

Jubal: Maybe I am running from something …bad luck. I carry it with me.
Shep: Where was you aiming to take it? You know, did you ever stop to figure that maybe it takes more energy to keep running away than it does to stop and fight it out.
Jubal: Fight what out?
Shep: Whatever you're running from. You know, it comes a day, Jubal, when a man has got to decide where he's going …or he won't get nowhere.

Jubal Troop played by Glenn Ford and Shep Horgan played by Ernest Borgnine: Delmer Daves' *Jubal* (Columbia, 1956).

5238

Zack: Just you keep your powder dry. Our time to shoot will come.

Zack Wakefield played by John McIntire: Burt Lancaster's *The Kentuckian* (United Artists, 1955).

5239

Morgan: Well, if you have any idea of taking over anything from me, you'll have your hands full.
Wild Bill: That's one thing you can depend on …my hands will be full!

Morgan King played by Guy Usher and Wild Bill Hickok played by Bill Elliott: Lambert Hillyer's *King of Dodge City* (Columbia, 1941).

5240

Gamecock: You aim to get goin' or go to gunnin'?

Gamecock played by Morris Ankrum: Lesley Selander's *Knights of the Range* (Paramount, 1940).

5241

Kate: Don't get the itchy fits. You'd never have time to scratch.

Kate Foley played by Adrian Booth: Joseph Kane's *The Last Bandit* (Republic, 1949).

5242

Colonel: You don't like the man, do you?
Sergeant: I hate him.
Colonel: I don't imagine it would take much to provoke him.
Sergeant: Very little, sir.
Colonel: Provoke him.

Colonel Frank Marston played by Robert Preston and Sergeant Major Decker played by Peter Whitney: Anthony Mann's *The Last Frontier* (Columbia, 1955).

5243

Ellison: I said come here! Walk over here or die over there!

Brad Ellison played by Jock Mahoney: George Sherman's *The Last of the Fast Guns* (Universal, 1958).

5244

Kidston: Do you figure you can drop us all?
Cable: You're first, he's next. Do you care what happens after that?

Duane Kidston played by David Carradine and Cable played by Tom Selleck: Dick Lowry's *Last Stand at Saber River* (Turner Network Television, 1997).

5245

Stribling: They told me you would try to circle around to get the sun in my eyes.
O'Malley: You did a little circling yourself.
Stribling: Insurance.

Dana Stribling played by Rock Hudson and Brendan O'Malley played by Kirk Douglas: Robert Aldrich's *The Last Sunset* (Universal, 1961).

5246

Belden: You're a goner, Morgan. I know my old man. The only way you're gonna get out of here is in a box.
Morgan: Just as long as I got you with me. That's the main thing.

Rick Belden played by Earl Holliman and U.S. Marshal Matt Morgan played by Kirk Douglas: John Sturges' *Last Train from Gun Hill* (Paramount, 1959).

5247

Sheriff: As far as I'm concerned, you can go out there in the street and get yourself killed anytime you want to. But you know something? Forty years from now, the weeds will grow just as pretty on my grave as they will on yours. And nobody will even remember that I was yellow or that you died like a fool.

Sheriff Bartlett played by Walter Sande: John Sturges' *Last Train from Gun Hill* (Paramount, 1959).

5248

Poe: Now here's my proposition. I say let's you and me, right here in broad daylight, settle this man to man. Let's go out on the street, pull our guns, and go to work.

Poe Northrup played by Ralph Ince: Edward L. Cahn's *Law and Order* (Universal, 1932).

5249

Maddox: Drop that gunbelt! I'm taking you in!
Harvey: No, you're not. You got two ways to move, lawman …run, or take me!

Marshal Jared Maddox played by Burt Lancaster and Harvey Stenbaugh played by Albert Salmi: Michael Winner's *Lawman* (United Artists, 1971).

5250

Crowe: Well, Maddox called my name down in front of everybody. I ain't afraid of him, Ryan.
Ryan: You would be if you had brains enough to spit.
Crowe: Well, I figure I'm faster than him.

Ryan: Keep walking! In every town Maddox has worked, the ground is full of men who were faster.

Crowe: Yeah, well, I really am. And I aim to prove it too.

Ryan: It makes a great epitaph. You may be faster, Crowe. You may be better with a gun. But Maddox will kill you. And that's a fact. You'd be staring up at nothing before your gun even got clear. I know what I'm talking about, Crowe. You may not rate me very high, but I know men like Maddox.

Crowe Wheelwright played by Richard Jordan, Marshal Cotton Ryan played by Robert Ryan, and Marshal Jared Maddox played by Burt Lancaster: Michael Winner's *Lawman* (United Artists, 1971).

5251

Ryan: I'll tell you, Lucas, if I had somewhere to run to, I'd run. But I don't …so I'll stand.

Marshal Cotton Ryan played by Robert Ryan and Lucas played by Joseph Wiseman: Michael Winner's *Lawman* (United Artists, 1971).

5252

Bad Bob: Now listen, you tell him to prepare to go to hell. I will send him there directly. Now git!

Bad Bob played by Stacy Keach: John Huston's *The Life and Times of Judge Roy Bean* (NGP, 1972).

5253

Bad Bob: Hey, Beano! It's me, Bob. Bad Bob. Hey, Bean! I've come here to shoot your eyes out. And then I'm going to take my ivory-handled knife and cut your head off and sell it to a friend of mine in the carnival. It is my intention, Beano, to rid the ground of your shadow, and take my pleasure upon this town. I have one thing to add. Lillie Langtry is a pig-face, whore, bitch dog …and I wouldn't waste my bullet on her let alone my seed. Do you hear me, Beano? I'm ready, Beano! Come and get it, Beano! Come on, Beano! Come on, Beanie, come and get it! I'm ready for you, Beano! [*at which point Bad Bob is blasted from behind and killed …courtesy of Beano*]

Bad Bob played by Stacy Keach and Judge Roy Bean (Beano) played by Paul Newman: John Huston's *The Life and Times of Judge Roy Bean* (NGP, 1972).

5254

Caroline: All right, sit right there! Don't make no move unless you want a little daylight in your liver!

Caroline played by Carole Androsky: Arthur Penn's *Little Big Man* (NGP, 1971).

5255

Buckner: Thank whatever God you got I wasn't looking for a fight just now or else you'd be spittin' up red blood over there.

Blessing: Or you'd be lying toes up over here …with your brains leaking out of your ears.

Buckner: One or the other.

Blessing: One or the other.

Tors Buckner played by Jeff Kober and Ned Blessing played by Daniel Baldwin: Peter Werner's *Lone Justice* (Academy Entertainment, 1994).

5256

Verlon: I don't think you got enough ass in your britches to pull the trigger on me, Sticks!

Verlon Borgers played by Bill McKinney and Sticks Packwood played by Tim Scott: Jack Bender's *Lone Justice II* (Triboro Entertainment Group, 1995).

5257

Jack: Take it easy. Temper like that and one of these days you'll find yourself riding through town with your belly to the sun, your best suit on, and no place to go but hell.

Jack Burns played by Kirk Douglas: David Miller's *Lonely Are the Brave* (Universal, 1962).

5258

Ada: We could leave now and start a whole new life.

Jacob: There's no starting over for me.

Ada Marshall played by Elaine Aiken and Jacob Wade played by Jack Palance: Henry Levin's *The Lonely Man* (Paramount, 1957).

5259

Gus: They don't know it but the wrath of the Lord is about to descend on 'em.

Gus McCrae played by Robert Duvall: Simon Wincer's *Lonesome Dove* (TVW, 1989).

5260

Madron: If you want out of this …turn around. You'll live until the next time I see ya.

Madron played by Richard Boone: Jerry Hopper's *Madron* (Four Star Excelsior, 1970).

5261

Sister Mary: You turned your back on purpose!

Madron: Well, how else was I gonna get him to draw?

Sister Mary played by Leslie Caron and Madron played by Richard Boone: Jerry Hopper's *Madron* (Four Star Excelsior, 1970).

5262

Old Man: Are you ready for him? What if he comes now?

Vin: It reminds me of a fellow back home that fell off a ten story building.

Chris: Yeah, what about him?

Vin: Well, as he was falling, people on each floor kept hearing him say, "So far so good."

The Old Man played by Vladimir Sokoloff, Vin played by Steve McQueen, and Chris played by Yul Brynner: John Sturges' *The Magnificent Seven* (United Artists, 1960).

5263

Chris: We ain't headin' to a church social.

Chris played by Yul Brynner: John Sturges' *The Magnificent Seven* (United Artists, 1960).

5264

Peasant: Do your hands sweat before a fight?

Vin: Every time.

Peasant: Mine are sweating now. Funny…. hands sweat …mouth is dry. You'd think it would be the other way around.

Vin played by Steve McQueen: John Sturges' *The Magnificent Seven* (United Artists, 1960).

5265

Chris: I thought you said they were twenty [men]?

Chief: No, I ask if twenty would scare you.

Chris: Twenty, no. Forty, yes!

Chris Larabee played by Michael Biehn and the Seminole Chief played by Ned Romero: Geoff Murphy's *The Magnificent Seven: The Series* (TVW, Series Premiere, 1998).

5266

Hayes: All right, what's your plan?

Chris: Oh, I figured we'd just ride in there and shoot down anyone carrying a gun.

Andy Hayes played by James B. Sikking and Chris played by Lee Van Cleef: George McGowan's *The Magnificent Seven Ride* (United Artists, 1972).

5267

Owen: I got to thinking: a man can't run all the time. He has to fight sooner or later.

Owen Merritt played by Randolph Scott: Andre De Toth's *Man in the Saddle* (Columbia, 1951).

5268

Link: Lassu is a ghost town. And that's what you are, Dock …a ghost. You're outlived your kind, and you've outlived your time. And I'm coming to get ya!

Link Jones played by Gary Cooper and Dock Tobin played by Lee J. Cobb: Anthony Mann's *Man of the West* (United Artists, 1958).

5269

California: You mean we're just going to sit around and wait for no-good healthy trouble?

Hopalong: California, if trouble is coming, it'll find ya. You don't have to go looking for it.

Hopalong Cassidy played by William Boyd and California Carlson played by Andy Clyde: George Archainbaud's *The Marauders* (United Artists, 1947).

5270

Finley: Your friend is right. I'm not a cowpuncher, I'm a professional. And I'm not gonna draw on ya. But I'll be the one who'll be shamed. I'll ask for your forgiveness, I'll be the coward, and I'll just back away.

Abel: No, no. Whichever you move, mister, whichever muscle, I'm gonna put a bullet right between your eyes. And that includes opening up your mouth.

Finley played by Tom Laughlin and Abel played by James Andronica: Frank Laughlin's *The Master Gunfighter* (Taylor-McLaughlin/Billy Jack, 1975).

5271

Bat: Hello, Doc.

Doc: Hello, Sheriff.

Bat: That's as far as you go, Doc.

Doc: I don't think so.

Bat: There's one way to find out. Or you can turn around and go back the way you came. I'd rather not kill you, Doc.

Doc: Give me three good reasons why you shouldn't kill me if you can?

Bat: I'll give you three more steps. Each step you take is one less reason.

Sheriff Bat Masterson played by George Montgomery and Doc Holliday played by James Griffith: William Castle's *Masterson of Kansas* (Columbia, 1954).

5272

Chapman: I'm warning ya, Ranger! One more step and you'll never take another!

Chapman played by Stanley Price: Armand Schaefer and B. Reeves Eason's *The Miracle Rider* (Mascot serial, Chapter 8: "Guerrilla Warfare," 1935).

5273

Tom Horn: I challenged four men to the draw and they backed out.

Ernestina: Now why is that funny?

Tom Horn: I didn't have any bullets in my gun.

Ernestina: What if they had drawn on you, Tom?

Tom Horn: They wouldn't do that.

Tom Horn played by David Carradine and Ernestina Crawford played by Karen Black: Jack Starrett's *Mr. Horn* (TVW, 1979).

5274

Luke: Didn't anyone every tell you, boy? Never holster an empty gun.

Luke Santee played by Mike Henry: Robert Sparr's *More Dead Than Alive* (United Artists, 1968).

5275

Poker Alice: Brett, I can't let you do that …walk into an armed camp. You could get yourself killed!

Brett: Well, that's why you're going!

Poker Alice Moffit played by Susan Sullivan and Brett Maverick played by James Garner: Hy Averback's *The New Maverick* (TVW, 1978).

5276

Riel: Blood will run like water.

Corbeau: You won't notice it much. The mounted police wear red coats.

Louis Riel played by Francis McDonald and Jacques Corbeau played by George Bancroft: Cecil B. DeMille's *North West Mounted Police* (Paramount, 1940).

Trigger-happy and crazed Avery (Dan Duryea) is not very pleased with his "right-hand man," Hooks (Keenan Wynn), who just failed in an attempt to kill him. "Just don't think anymore, Mr. Hooks, you're no good at it!" in *The Marauders* (MGM, 1955).

5277

John Henry: If it's all right, we'll just wait until morning to leave your guns in the wagon. Me and the boys, we don't see too good in the dark anymore.

Cotton: Come tomorrow, you won't see at all.

John Henry: We'll see.

John Henry Lee played by Willie Nelson and Cotton played by Shaun Cassidy: Burt Kennedy's *Once Upon a Texas Train* (TVW, 1988).

5278

John Henry: Captain, I just want to tell ya that no matter how all this turns out, I'm glad to be walking down the same side of the street with ya.

Captain: I never should have let you talk me into this!

John Henry Lee played by Willie Nelson and Captain Oren Hayes played by Richard Widmark: Burt Kennedy's *Once Upon a Texas Train* (TVW, 1988).

5279

John Henry: Let me tell you something. If those boys catch us in the open out there, more than your pride is going to get hurt.

John Henry Lee played by Willie Nelson: Burt Kennedy's *Once Upon a Texas Train* (TVW, 1988).

5280

Jason: Well, I'd say it's time to put on my gunfightin' glasses.

Jason Pitch played by Jack Elam: Burt Kennedy's *Once Upon a Texas Train* (TVW, 1988).

5281

Knuckles: Frank sent us.

Harmonica Man: Did you bring a horse for me?

Knuckles: Looks like we're …looks like we're shy one horse.

Harmonica Man: You brought two too many.

Harmonica Man played by Charles Bronson and Knuckles played by Jack Elam: Sergio Leone's *Once Upon a Time in the West* (Paramount, 1969).

5282

Bob: Well, Harvey Johnson is gonna be a famous name around these parts. You're gonna get yourself killed by a fella called Rio.

Harvey: That ain't him!

Bob: It ain't, huh? I wouldn't want to lose me a handful of brains trying to find out. Now would you, Harve?

Bob Amroy played by Ben Johnson, Harvey Johnson played by Sam Gilman, and Rio played by Marlon Brando: Marlon Brando's *One-Eyed Jacks* (Paramount, 1961).

5283

Vaqui Joe: You know something?

Lyedecker: What?

Vaqui Joe: I think our string has done run out.

Lyedecker: The hell it has. We're gonna get out of this.

Vaqui Joe: Yeah?

Lyedecker: Yeah!

Vaqui Joe: How?

Lyedecker: Well, there's nothing to it. A big giant hand is gonna reach in here and pick us up and take us away and put us down someplace right in the middle of a whole bunch of women and whiskey.

Vaqui Joe Herrera played by Burt Reynolds and Lyedecker played by Jim Brown: Tom Gries' *100 Rifles* (20th Century–Fox, 1969).

5284

Doc: Well, Billy, I guess this is it. Men are pretty much like children after all. Have you ever seen two kids wrestling in the yard? They push and tussle and maybe they look like they're fighting …but they're not. They're really friends and everything is fun. Then pretty soon they play a little too rough. One of them gets mad. And in the end, somebody always gets hurt. So for you and me, this is where somebody gets hurt. But when it's over, and however it turns out, son, no hard feelings.

Doc Holliday played by Walter Huston and Billy the Kid played by Jack Buetel: Howard Hughes' *The Outlaw* (United Artists, 1943).

5285

Josey Wales: Well, are you going to pull those pistols or whistle Dixie?

Josey Wales played by Clint Eastwood who also directed *The Outlaw Josey Wales* (Warner Bros., 1976).

5286

Josey Wales: Now remember: when things look bad, and it looks like you're not gonna make it, then you got to get mean. I mean plumb mad-dog mean! Because if you lose your head and give up, then you neither live nor win. That's just the way it is. Use pistols at short range. It's more firepower and less reloading. Keep this fire going, keep an iron in it red hot. If anybody gets hit, sing out, slap iron to it. That's the fastest way to stop the blood.

Josey Wales played by Clint Eastwood who also directed *The Outlaw Josey Wales* (Warner Bros., 1976).

5287

Nash: I ain't going home! Not yet! Not until I get done what I come here to do. I ain't never crawled home with the tail between my legs in my life. And I'm too old to take on any new bad habits like that now.

Nash Crawford played by Walter Brennan: Jean Yarbrough's *The Over-the-Hill Gang* (TVW, 1969).

5288

Rumson: Pardner, there comes a time in every partnership where the party of the first part has no recourse except to knock some sense into the party of the second part.

Ben Rumson played by Lee Marvin and Pardner played by Clint Eastwood: Joseph Logan's *Paint Your Wagon* (Paramount, 1969).

5289

Ollinger: Billy, somewhere in the Good Book it says there's a time for everything. A time to live, a time to hate, a time to kill. But now it's time you got close to God.

Billy: I've heard God's fast. But I'd have to go up in front of Him myself before I'd bet on it.

Pat: You will.

Deputy Bob Ollinger played by R.G. Armstrong, Billy the Kid played by Kris Kristofferson, and Pat Garrett played by James Coburn: Sam Peckinpah's *Pat Garrett and Billy the Kid* (MGM, 1973).

5290

Billy: But if I was you all, I'd be clearing out of here. There's gonna be some hard times coming down.

Billy the Kid played by Kris Kristofferson: Sam Peckinpah's *Pat Garrett and Billy the Kid* (MGM, 1973).

5291

McKinney: Well, I hope they spell my name right in the papers.

Sheriff Kip McKinney played by Richard Jaeckel: Sam Peckinpah's *Pat Garrett and Billy the Kid* (MGM, 1973).

5292

Lemuel: You just made me have a bowel movement in my britches, Garrett! I ain't never going to forgive you for this!

Lemuel played by Chill Wills and Pat Garrett played by James Coburn: Sam Peckinpah's *Pat Garrett and Billy the Kid* (MGM, 1973).

5293

Hickok: Keep your hands off your guns or there will be more dead men here than this town can afford to bury!

Wild Bill Hickok played by Gary Cooper: Cecil B. DeMille's *The Plainsman* (Paramount, 1936).

5294

Lattimer: I'm not armed, Mr. Hickok, I'm not armed!

Hickok: I'll give you three minutes to fix that. I'll be waiting outside.

Lattimer: I'm just leaving town.

Hickok: You're not leaving town unless dead men can walk.

Wild Bill Hickok played by Gary Cooper and John Lattimer played by Charles Bickford: Cecil B. DeMille's *The Plainsman* (Paramount, 1936).

5295

Baker: This whole thing smells like an invitation to a party I don't want to go to.

J.D. Baker played by Paul Drake: Arthur Allan Seidelman's *Poker Alice* (TVW, 1987).

5296

Bates: Come on out! We all got to go to hell someday.

Jesse Lee: When you get there, tell them Jesse Lee sent ya.

Sheriff Bates played by Richard Jordan and Jesse Lee played by Mario Van Peebles who also directed *Posse* (Gramercy Pictures, 1993).

5297

Cole: When the shooting starts, try and keep a little clear. A shotgun will level anything in a ten foot square.

Kern: You mean ten square feet, not ten foot square.

Cole: I mean about the size of a wash tub, whatever that is.

Kern: Yeah, but what you said was more like the size of a wall.

Cole: You bankers sure are sticklers for detail.

Banner Cole played by Audie Murphy and Seymour Kern played by John Saxon: Herbert Coleman's *Posse from Hell* (Universal, 1961).

5298

Ogden: Am I to understand that you don't want to be friends?

Tucson: That's up to you. I'm not looking for trouble if it can be avoided. But on the other hand, me and my pals are prepared to burn plenty of powder if anyone interferes with us. Is that clear?

Ogden: Are you trying to insinuate that I …

Tucson: Take it any way you like it!

Mayor "Big Steve" Ogden played by Sam Hardy and Tucson Smith played by Harry Carey: Wallace Fox's *Powdersmoke Range* (RKO, 1935).

5299

Tucson: Now don't try to signal any of your friends. Because if you do, my first bullet will carry your address. Is that clear?

Tucson Smith played by Harry Carey: Wallace Fox's *Powdersmoke Range* (RKO, 1935).

5300

Dolworth: Now all you got to do is light this fuse. You got ten seconds to run like hell. And then, dynamite, not faith, will move that mountain into this pass. Peace, brother!

Bill Dolworth played by Burt Lancaster: Richard Brooks' *The Professionals* (Columbia, 1966).

5301

Will: If we're going to have a shootout, let's pick the place for it. This ain't the time or the place.

Will Hansen played by Chuck Connors: Ferde Grofe, Jr.'s, *The Proud and Damned* (Media Trend-Prestige/Columbia, 1972).

5302

Herod: Whatever happens, if he's still standing in the end …gun him down!

John Herod played by Gene Hackman: Sam Raimi's *The Quick and the Dead* (Tristar, 1995).

5303

Horace: Gentlemen, the street is yours!

Horace the Bartender played by Pat Hingle: Sam Raimi's *The Quick and the Dead* (Tristar, 1995).

5304

Herod: You're not fast enough for me!

Ellen: Today I am!

John Herod played by Gene Hackman and Ellen played by Sharon Stone: Sam Raimi's *The Quick and the Dead* (Tristar, 1995).

5305

Morrison: You make him draw first. You understand that? I want him dead legal.

Tom Morrison played by Walter Sande: Sidney Salkow's *The Quick Gun* (Columbia, 1964).

5306

Morrison: He won't be so big. He'll be cut down to size before this night is over. Load up!

Tom Morrison played by Walter Sande: Sidney Salkow's *The Quick Gun* (Columbia, 1964).

5307

Clint: Well, Spang, I never thought I'd see you twice in the same day.

Spangler: I don't figure it will ever happen again …seeing how you ain't got long to live.

Clint Cooper played by Audie Murphy and Spangler played by Ted De Corsia: Sidney Salkow's *The Quick Gun* (Columbia, 1964).

5308

Spangler: Any last words?

Clint: Yeah. Draw!

Spangler played by Ted De Corsia and Clint Cooper was played by Audie Murphy: Sidney Salkow's *The Quick Gun* (Columbia, 1964).

5309

Quigley: This ain't Dodge City …and you ain't Bill Hickok!

Matthew Quigley played by Tom Selleck: Simon Wincer's *Quigley Down Under* (MGM-United Artists, 1990).

5310

Powell: Men, we got to arm ourselves as best we can, and meet these desperadoes and wipe them out once and for all. And now is the time to act!

Powell played by Lloyd Ingraham: Robert N. Bradbury's *Rainbow Valley* (Lone Star/Monogram, 1935).

5311

Randolph: If I were you, I would walk around that hombre as if he were quicksand.

Tarp: You're not me.

Randolph: Your bravado talk convinces me you're not long for this world.

John Randolph played by Rex Reason and Tarp Penny played by Neville Brand: John Sherwood's *Raw Edge* (Universal, 1956).

5312

Ward: Well, Napoleon said there's a time to fight and a time to wait. So that's what we're gonna do, Sergeant. We're gonna wait!

Major Ward played by Telly Savalas: Tonino Valerii's *A Reason to Live, a Reason to Die* (a.k.a. *Massacre at Fort Holman*; Sancrosiap-Terza/Europrodis/Atlantida/Corona, 1972).

5313

Frank: Are you coming out or am I coming in?

Frank James played by Henry Fonda: Fritz Lang's *The Return of Frank James* (20th Century–Fox, 1940).

5314

Cherokee: I'm gonna get that dude and let daylight through his liver!

Cherokee played by Ray Bennett: Derwin Abrahams' *The Return of the Durango Kid* (Columbia, 1945).

5315

Bladen: Dad always told me never to wait for a showdown …go out and force it.

Bill Bladen/Durango Kid played by Charles Starrett: Derwin Abrahams' *The Return of the Durango Kid* (Columbia, 1945).

5316

Townsman: You better get off the street, stranger! Lead's gonna fly any minute!

The Townsman was uncredited: Derwin Abrahams' *The Return of the Durango Kid* (Columbia, 1945).

5317

Call: I'm gonna count to three. If you don't drop that shooter in the dirt, I'm gonna put a hole in your head.

Captain Woodrow F. Call played by Jon Voight: Mike Robe's *Return to Lonesome Dove* (TVW, 1993).

5318

Boone: There's some things a man just can't ride around.

Sam Boone played by Pernell Roberts: Budd Boetticher's *Ride Lonesome* (Columbia, 1959).

5319

Wid: We could stand off. I don't hold to ending a man with a long gun.

Wid played by James Coburn: Budd Boetticher's *Ride Lonesome* (Columbia, 1959).

5320

Esqueda: Your blessing, Father.

Father: My blessing is as good as your intention.

Jose Esqueda played by Anthony Quinn and Father Antonio played by Kurt Kasznar: John Farrow's *Ride, Vaquero!* (MGM, 1953).

5321

Saunders: Make it fast, Slippery. This is your last draw!

Singin' Sandy Saunders played by John Wayne and Slip Morgan played by Earl Dwire: Robert Bradbury's *Riders of Destiny* (Lone Star/Monogram, 1933).

5322

Tull: Mister, we're eight here. Who are you?
Lassiter: Lassiter.

Deacon Tull played by Norbert Weisser and Jim Lassiter played by Ed Harris: Charles Haid's *Riders of the Purple Sage* (Turner Home Entertainment, 1996).

5323

Lassiter: Prosateur, I reckon you better call quick on that God who reveals His Self to you on earth. Because He won't be visiting the place you're going to.

Jim Lassiter played by Ed Harris and Pastor Dyer, the Prosateur, played by G.D. Spradlin: Charles Haid's *Riders of the Purple Sage* (Turner Home Entertainment, 1996).

5324

Burrows: You're dead wrong, Ringo!
Ringo: I ain't wrong …and I ain't dead!

Burrows played by Reed Hadley and Kid Ringo played by Tom Tyler: Lesley Selander's *Riders of the Range* (RKO, 1950).

5325

Colorado: Hear that music? He told the man to play it.
Chance: What is it?
Colorado: Well, they call it the Deguello, the cutthroat song. The Mexicans played it for those Texas boys when they had them bottled up in the Alamo.
Chance: Yeah.
Colorado: They played it day and night until it was all over. Now, do you know what he means by it?
Chance: No quarter. No mercy for the loser.
Colorado: You'll be hearing a lot of it.

Colorado Ryan played by Ricky Nelson and John T. Chance played by John Wayne: Howard Hawks' *Rio Bravo* (Warner Bros., 1959).

5326

Leech: Now boys, the way I see it you got two choices. You can try me. And between the two of you, one of you will get off a shot. The question is, which one of you lives …and which one of you dies where you're standing. You can live a week or two longer if you get a good lawyer.

Quinton Leech played by Kenny Rogers: Rod Hardy's *Rio Diablo* (TVW, 1993).

5327

Hendricks: I should have taken you this morning.
McNally: You should have tried.

Sheriff Tom Hendricks played by Mike Henry and Cord McNally played by John Wayne: Howard Hawks' *Rio Lobo* (NGP, 1970).

5328

Weston: All right, Kay, I'll talk to him.
Kay: What's that [gun] for?
Weston: In case he's hard of hearing.

Harry Weston played by Rory Calhoun and Kay Weston played by Marilyn Monroe: Otto Preminger's *The River of No Return* (20th Century–Fox, 1954).

5329

Rooster: I've got a hunch we're just a little way from a lot of trouble.

Rooster Cogburn played by John Wayne: Stuart Millar's *Rooster Cogburn* (Universal, 1975).

5330

Rooster: Damn your murdering hides! Meet your Maker!

Rooster Cogburn played by John Wayne: Stuart Millar's *Rooster Cogburn* (Universal, 1975).

5331

Apache Kid: You made two fatal mistakes: knowin' too much and talkin' too much!

The Apache Kid played by Max Hoffman, Jr.: Mack V. Wright's *Rootin' Tootin' Rhythm* (Republic, 1937).

5332

Rex: This is just a warning. If you or your men draw on me, I'll shoot each man in the hand.
Blackie: In the hand?
Rex: That's right.
Blackie: Not in the face or the chest?
Rex: Nope.
Blackie: I don't like the idea of getting shot in the hand.
Rex: Then go home, Blackie.
Blackie: Go home?
Rex: That's right!
Blackie: Go home?
Rex: Yeah, and see someone about your hearing!

Rex O'Herlihan played by Tom Berenger and Blackie played by Jim Carter: Hugh Wilson's *Rustlers' Rhapsody* (Paramount, 1985).

5333

Cap: You wooled me around long enough!

Cap Roundtree played by Ben Johnson: Robert Totten's *The Sacketts* (TVW, 1979).

5334

Reed: Now we got us two sodbusters fertilizing the air. I'll sure be relieved when you boys go on back to the plow.
Tyrel: Do you play the harp, mister?
Reed: No.

Tyrel: You keep pushing, you'll end up learning.

Reed Carney played by Buck Taylor and Tyrel Sackett played by Jeff Osterhage: Robert Totten's *The Sacketts* (TVW, 1979).

5335

Tyrel: You move for that gun and you'll die …right in front of all these people …as sure as daylight. Now take a walk back to the saloon.
Reed: Huh-uh. Can't. It's gone too far.
Tyrel: Not when it comes to dyin'.

Tyrel Sackett played by Jeff Osterhage and Reed Carney played by Buck Taylor: Robert Totten's *The Sacketts* (TVW, 1979).

5336

Venables: So you want me to draw?
Tony: You got the guts?
Venables: Sonny, I got the guts and the know-how to puncture your belly six times before you could take a breath of air!

Larry Venables played by Charles McGraw and Tony Sinclair played by John Cassavetes: Robert Parrish's *Saddle the Wind* (MGM, 1958).

5337

Rex: I seen a star falling in the west today as we was riding in.
Tasker: What are you talking about?
Rex: At the same time I seen an owl fly across the new moon. Them's mighty bad signs. I've shot a lot of folks in my day, so I ain't a-kicking when it comes my time to get shot.
Tasker: You talk like a fool!
Rex: I am …always have been.

Rex played by Hal Taliaferro and Ed Tasker played by Frank Thomas: Joseph Kane's *Saga of Death Valley* (Republic, 1939).

5338

Hook: Now, mister, don't go building a whole house out of a box of matches!

Hook played by Russell Johnson: Richard Carlson's *The Saga of Hemp Brown* (Universal, 1958).

5339

Brown: I have given you fair warning. You can keep your heads or lose 'em as you wish!

Abolitionist Leader John Brown played by Raymond Massey: Michael Curtiz's *Santa Fe Trail* (Warner Bros., 1940).

5340

Oliver: Words like that won't make you live any longer.

Oliver Brown played by Larry Pennell: Charles Marquis Warren's *Seven Angry Men* (Allied Artists, 1955).

5341

Brown: I'm one hair away from sending you to hell!

Brown played by Bernard-Pierre Donnadieu: Jacques Dorfmann's *Shadow of the Wolf* (Triumph Releasing, 1993).

5342

Basch: Now wait a minute, Reverend, I ain't gonna tangle with him.
Reverend: What's the matter? Afraid he'll kill ya?
Basch: That's part of it. The main thing is: if he nicks me, why, the scar will just ruin my looks.

Matthew Basch played by Jackie Coogan and Reverend Zachary Grant played by Donald "Red" Barry: Alan Rafkin's *The Shakiest Gun in the West* (Universal, 1968).

5343

Ryker: From now on when we fight with them, the air is going to be filled with gunsmoke.

Ryker played by Emile Meyer: George Stevens' *Shane* (Paramount, 1953).

5344

Jason: Well, if it's going to take a gunfight for me to live the way I want, the sooner the better, Johnny.
Johnny: Of course, you're working at a slight disadvantage from now on.
Jason: Oh?
Johnny: Yeah, you see, I'm gonna walk over there and get on that horse and ride on right out of town. I'm not even gonna bother to look back once, because I know you wouldn't shoot me in the back. On the other hand, you can't depend on that from me at all.

Jason Sweet played by Glenn Ford and Johnny Bledsoe, alias Colonel Stephen Bedford, played by Leslie Nielsen: George Marshall's *The Sheepman* (MGM, 1958).

5345

Mal: Now I don't want to kill you and you don't want to be dead.

Mal played by Danny Glover: Lawrence Kasdan's *Silverado* (Columbia, 1985).

5346

Jesse: It's been coming down to this all along, ain't it?
Lane: There's some things a man can't ride around.

Frank Jesse played by Dan Duryea and Ben Lane played by Audie Murphy: Harry Keller's *Six Black Horses* (Universal, 1962).

5347

Ma Mondier: I never liked to hear the sound of a mourning dove this time of day.

Ma Mondier played by Lorna Thayer: Joseph Kane's *Smoke in the Wind* (Frontier Productions/Gamalex, 1975).

5348

Ed: It's about time somebody stood up to these goons!

Butch: Well, you can stand up anytime you're ready, Shorty!

Ed "Shorty" Simms played by Lou Wagner and Butch played by Earl Pastko: Eugene Levy's *Sodbusters* (Atlantis Releasing, 1994).

5349

Clarence: Ed Simms almost died for us. It seems to me there comes a time in a man's life when he has to take a stand …when he has to fight for what's rightfully his. That time is now.
Roy: Inspirational words, Clarence.
Clarence: And?
Roy: And …it's been nice knowing you!

Clarence Gentry played by Fred Willard and Roy Poulet played by Don Lake: Eugene Levy's *Sodbusters* (Atlantis Releasing, 1994).

5350

Slade: You know you're not riding out of here alive. Not this time!

Slade Cantrell played by John Vernon: Eugene Levy's *Sodbusters* (Atlantis Releasing, 1994).

5351

Andreo: Yesterday, you were my good friend. Today, you are just my friend. Tomorrow?

Andreo Mendoza played by Duncan Renaldo: George Sherman's *South of the Border* (Republic, 1939).

5352

Reese: Horne, I didn't mean it!
Horne: Open your mouth again, Reese, and I'll blow it off your face!

Reese Sawyer played by Ralph Taeger and Sheriff Horne played by Barry Sullivan: William F. Claxton's *Stage to Thunder Rock* (Paramount, 1964).

5353

Ringo Kid: Well, there are some things a man just can't run away from.

The Ringo Kid played by John Wayne: John Ford's *Stagecoach* (United Artists, 1939).

5354

Buck: If I was you, I'd let 'em shoot it out.
Curley: Let who?
Buck: Luke Plummer and the Kid. There would be a lot more peace in this territory if that Luke Plummer was so full of lead he couldn't hold his liquor.

Buck Rickabaugh, the Stagecoach Driver, played by Andy Devine and Sheriff Curley Wilcox played by George Bancroft: John Ford's *Stagecoach* (United Artists, 1939).

5355

Red Ryder: When folks start shootin' at me, I don't run. I find out who and why.

Red Ryder played by Allan "Rocky" Lane: R.G. Springsteen's *Stagecoach to Denver* (Republic, 1946).

5356

Deputy: I remember being in a cyclone once. Just before she hit, there was a

feeling of emptiness like the air had been sucked out of space. I got that same feeling.

Deputy Mike MacNamera played by Paul Fix: Charles Haas' *Star in the Dust* (Universal, 1956).

5357

Clerk: Say, I'm naturally sentimental, being sort of a poet.
Haven: Naturally.
Clerk: I keep a bunch of gem cracks: an old-time sheriff's gun, a bullet from a dead bandit, a rosary from some fellow they hung.
Haven: Well, that's nice. A hobby, huh?
Clerk: Yeah, in a way. I just wondered if there was something that you wanted to leave me?

The Hotel Clerk played by Burl Ives and Haven played by Dick Powell: Sidney Lanfield's *Station West* (RKO, 1948).

5358

Bull: I thought I heard something.
Josie: Feel how still the air is. It's just like before a cyclone or a storm …or death.

Bull Slager played by Ernest Borgnine and Josie Sullivan played by Claire Trevor: Andre De Toth's *The Stranger Wore a Gun* (Columbia, 1953).

5359

Lorn: Jim, you're crazy! I could give you the count of three with your gun already out, and you know it!
Jim: Yeah, you're fast. But that won't mean anything this time.

Lorn Reming played by Macdonald Carey and Jim Dawkins played by William Holden: Leslie Fenton's *Streets Of Laredo* (Paramount, 1949).

5360

Latigo: Patience, there are some things a man can't ride around …but then again, maybe he can.

Latigo Smith played by James Garner and Patience Barton played by Suzanne Pleshette: Burt Kennedy's *Support Your Local Gunfighter* (United Artists, 1971).

5361

Madden: I'm set to get him one way or the other.
Ames: What do you mean, one way or the other?
Madden: I want to look at Tuck Ordway through gunsmoke first.

Larry Madden played by Randolph Scott, Ames Luddington played by John Dehner, and Tucker "Tuck" Ordway played by Robert Barrat: Lesley Selander's *Tall Man Riding* (Warner Bros., 1955).

5362

Brennan: I'm going to finish this. If they come, I'm going to finish this once and for all.
Mrs. Mims: Oh, but why?
Brennan: Some things a man can't ride around.

Pat Brennan played by Randolph Scott and Mrs. Doretta Mims played by Maureen O'Sullivan: Budd Boetticher's *The Tall T* (Columbia, 1957).

5363

Wes: You're going to have to earn that two thousand the hard way, Jim. You're going to have to go through me.

Jim: You mean that?

Wes: You know I don't bluff.

Jim: You and me? I got to admit, I always wondered how I'd turn out.

Wes: So did I.

Jim: I know.

Wes: I'll be across the street if you want to find out.

Wes Tancred, alias John Bailey, played by Richard Egan and Jim Breck played by DeForest Kelley: Charles Marquis Warren's *Tension at Table Rock* (RKO, 1956).

5364

Don Andrea: Ten paces.

Sam Hollis: Ten paces?

Don Andrea: Why, that is customary. Do you wish to give the command to begin or shall I?

Sam Hollis: I don't know what you got in mind, Baldy, but I'm here for a shootout.

Don Andrea: Precisely. You take ten steps that way, I take ten steps this way. Then we turn and...

Sam Hollis: Turn? Step? I ain't here for no square dance! Now which end of town do you want to come from?

Don Andrea: End of town?

Sam Hollis: Now quit stallin'. You want to come from that end, or yonder?

Don Andrea: No! You stand so, I stand so. And then...

Sam Hollis: Back to back? Now what kind of shootout is that?

Don Andrea: Please, Sam Hollis. I have dueled many times in Spain and I'm ...

Sam Hollis: But this isn't Spain! It's Texas!

Don Andrea: Even a simple duel you cannot perform in a civilized manner!

Sam Hollis: We have had civilized killings around here for years. I come from one end of town like this, and you come from the other end. And when you get the itch, you draw.

Don Andrea: We walk all the way there, then back here, when we are already here? Foolish!

Sam Hollis: What's foolish about it? That's the way we always do it.

Don Andrea: Why?

Sam Hollis: Because that's the way it's always done in the west!

Don Andrea: There is no need to shout. Even in death one can still be a gentleman.

Sam Hollis: Which end of town do you want to come from?

Don Andrea Baldasar played by Alain Delon and

Sam Hollis played by Dean Martin: Michael Gordon's *Texas Across the River* (Universal, 1966).

5365

Utah: I didn't get out of town when the going got too hot.

Texas: Maybe it didn't get hot enough for you.

Utah: Maybe. Are you still aiming to make it hot enough?

Texas: It depends on you.

Utah: Meaning what?

Texas: Meaning I'll be slinging lead in your direction if you ever aim to jump me out!

Utah Becker played by Wheeler Oakman and Texas Grant/Jim Rawlins played by Tim McCoy: D. Ross Lederman's *Texas Cyclone* (Columbia, 1932).

5366

Luke: You see those doors? If you aren't out of town when the sun hit's 'em, you ain't gonna live to see it set!

Luke Starr played by Broderick Crawford: Lesley Selander's *The Texican* (Columbia, 1966).

5367

Pete: Let's rush 'em!

Bob: Six-shooters against Winchesters? I've seen enough!

Pedro "Pete" Roca Fuerta played by Pedro Armendariz and Robert Marmaduke Hightower played by John Wayne: John Ford's *The 3 Godfathers* (MGM, 1948).

5368

Marshal: Turn around, Texas. Turn around and draw!

Texas: Well, Perley, you old hayshaker, you got me!

Marshal Perley "Buck" Sweet played by Ward Bond and Robert Marmaduke Hightower, referred to as "Texas" by the Marshal, played by John Wayne: John Ford's *The 3 Godfathers* (MGM, 1948).

5369

Wade: Well, the street seems to be clear and everybody going inside. I guess they figure a storm is blowing up, huh Dan?

Ben Wade played by Glenn Ford and Dan Evans played by Van Heflin: Delmer Daves' *3:10 to Yuma* (Columbia, 1957).

5370

Wyatt: Go ahead! Go ahead, skin it! Skin that smoke wagon and see what happens!

Wyatt Earp played by Kurt Russell: George P. Cosmatos' *Tombstone* (Buena Vista, 1993).

5371

McMasters: If I know Ringo, he's headed straight for us. If they were my brothers, I would want revenge too.

Doc: No, make no mistake. It's not revenge he's after, it's a reckoning.

Sherman McMasters played by Michael Rooker, Johnny Ringo played by Michael Biehn, and Doc Holliday played by Val Kilmer: George P. Cosmatos' *Tombstone* (Buena Vista, 1993).

5372

Wyatt: The cowboys are finished, you understand me? I see a red sash, I kill the man wearing it. So run, you cur, run! And tell all the other curs the law is coming! You tell 'em I'm coming! And hell's coming with me, you hear! Hell's coming with me!

Wyatt Earp played by Kurt Russell: George P. Cosmatos' *Tombstone* (Buena Vista, 1993).

5373

Ike: I swear to God, lawdog, if you don't step aside we'll tear you apart!

Wyatt: All right, you die first ...get it! Your friends might get me in a rush, but not before I make your head into a canoe, you understand?

Billy: He's bluffin'. Let's rush him!

Ike: He ain't bluffin'!

Wyatt: You're not as stupid as you look, Ike.

Ike Clanton played by Stephen Lang, Wyatt Earp played by Kurt Russell, and Billy Clanton played by Thomas Hayden Church: George P. Cosmatos' *Tombstone* (Buena Vista, 1993).

5374

Ringo: Don't any of ya have the guts to play for blood?

Doc: I'm your huckleberry. That's just my game.

Johnny Ringo played by Michael Biehn and Doc Holliday played by Val Kilmer: George P. Cosmatos' *Tombstone* (Buena Vista, 1993).

5375

Wyatt: Are you going to do something, or just stand there and bleed?

Wyatt Earp played by Kurt Russell: George P. Cosmatos' *Tombstone* (Buena Vista, 1993).

5376

Wyatt: All right, Clanton! You called down the thunder. Well, now you got it!

Wyatt Earp played by Kurt Russell and Ike Clanton played by Stephen Lang: George P. Cosmatos' *Tombstone* (Buena Vista, 1993).

5377

Wyatt: All right, let's finish it.

Doc: Indeed, sir. The last charge of Wyatt Earp and his immortals!

Wyatt Earp played by Kurt Russell and Doc Holliday played by Val Kilmer: George P. Cosmatos' *Tombstone* (Buena Vista, 1993).

5378

Noble: You men can ride out of here ...or you can die. There's no third way!

Noble Adams played by Kris Kristofferson: John Guillermin's *The Tracker* (HBO Pictures, 1988).

5379

Mrs. Lowe: Maybe they'll give it up.

Lane: They should. They can't shoot worth a damn.

Mrs. Lowe played by Ann-Margret and Lane played by John Wayne: Burt Kennedy's *The Train Robbers* (Warner Bros., 1973).

5380

Squint: All right, you guitar-playing song-bird. If you got anything to say, say it fast. Then when you get through, I'm gonna shoot you right between the eyes. And they'll call it justifiable homicide.

Squint played by Yakima Canutt: Robert Bradbury's *Trouble in Texas* (Grand National, 1937).

5381

Marshal: You take your horse and find a position over there. And I'll be up on this side. Now, don't shoot unless I do. Now, what we want to do is get them in that dugout. I'll shoot the last man through the door and we'll have them over a barrel.

La Boeuf: You would shoot him without a call?

Marshal: Well, that will get him to know our intentions is serious. Oh well, I'll holler down after I shoot to see if any of 'em want to be taken alive.

Marshal Reuben J. "Rooster" Cogburn played by John Wayne and La Boeuf played by Glen Campbell: Henry Hathaway's *True Grit* (Paramount, 1969).

5382

Rooster: I mean to kill you in one minute, Ned, or see you hang in Fort Smith at Judge Parker's convenience. Which will it be?

Pepper: I call that bold talk from a one-eyed fat man.

Rooster: Fill your hand you son-of-a-bitch!

Marshal Reuben J. "Rooster" Cogburn played by John Wayne and "Lucky" Ned Pepper played by Robert Duvall: Henry Hathaway's *True Grit* (Paramount, 1969).

5383

Russell: Clark, you're mighty lucky to get out of this like this …outdrawing the second fastest gunman around here.

Clark: Who's the fastest?

Russell: Either me or you. Someday we'll find out!

Outlaws Robert Hightower (John Wayne), William Kearney/the Abilene Kid (Harry Carey, Jr.), and Pedro "Pete" Roca Fuerte (Pedro Armendariz) stumble on a broken-down wagon in the desert with a dying woman inside about to give birth. They promise to care for the infant and become the *3 Godfathers* (MGM, 1948) in a John Ford classic.

Bob Russell played by Wheeler Oakman and Tim Clark played by Tim McCoy: Ross Lederman's *Two Fisted Law* (Columbia, 1932).

5384

Will: All right now, I'm coming out! Any man I see out there, I'm gonna kill him. Any man takes a shot at me, I'm not only gonna kill him, but I'm gonna kill his wife …all his friends…. burn his damn house down!

William "Bill" Munny played by Clint Eastwood who also directed *Unforgiven* (Warner Bros., 1992).

5385

Allen: You're not going to give me lead for breakfast, are ya?

Dick Allen played by Robert Preston: Cecil B. DeMille's *Union Pacific* (Paramount, 1939).

5386

Jackson: I'm constantly amazed at how some people don't seem to value life.

Charley: If you're trying to intimidate me, Jackson, it's not going to work.

Jackson: Yeah, why not?

Charley: Because you're just too short, Jackson.

Jackson: I've killed taller men than you.

Charley: Yeah? I've ordered men like you to die in my place.

Jackson played by Christopher Boyer and Charley played by Dennis Gibbs: Michael Bohusz's *Uninvited* (Imperial Entertainment, 1993).

5387

Indian: If you walk away now, I'll spare your lives.

Jackson: Funny. I was about to tell you the same thing.

Jackson played by Christopher Boyer and the Indian played by Michael Bohusz who also directed *Uninvited* (Imperial Entertainment, 1993).

5388

Owen: There are some things and some people you can't run away from.

Owen Daybright played by Burt Lancaster: Richard Thorpe's *Vengeance Valley* (MGM, 1951).

5389

Virginian: Trampas, I'm trying not to have any trouble with you …just now.

Trampas: Yeah, you've been dodgin' it for five years. You've taken plenty of trouble to keep out of my way. But I got you corralled now, and I'm calling your hand.

Virginian: All right, what do you got?

Trampas: I got to believe you're a lyin' white-livered skunk. This country isn't big enough to hold the two of us. So I'm giving you to sundown to get out of town!

The Virginian played by Gary Cooper and Trampas was played by Walter Huston: Victor Fleming's *The Virginian* (Paramount, 1929).

5390

Billy: I just want to know what you're going to do. Are you going to back me or Blaisdell?

Johnny: I won't back him because you're my brother. And I won't back you because you're wrong.

Billy Gannon played by Frank Gorshin, Johnny Gannon played by Richard Widmark, and Clay Blaisdell played by Henry Fonda: Edward Dmytryk's *Warlock* (20th Century–Fox, 1959).

5391

Morgan: I'm going to tell you something, Clay.

Clay: What is it, Morg?

Morgan: I'm better than you are. I've always been better. I can beat you, Clay. Now you hit it. And you better hit it fast!

Tom Morgan played by Anthony Quinn and Clay Blaisdell played by Henry Fonda: Edward Dmytryk's *Warlock* (20th Century–Fox, 1959).

5392

John: Come on, let's take 'em!

Cole: Go ahead.

John: I mean it, Cole. I'm running out of patience!

Cole: You got to have some first, John.

Sheriff John Copperud played by Carroll O'Connor and Lewton Cole played by James Coburn: William A. Graham's *Waterhole No. 3* (Paramount, 1967).

5393

Cole: Don't make a move, Judge. I'm coming down to get ya.

Judge Bean: Come a-shootin'!

Cole Hardin played by Gary Cooper and Judge Roy Bean played by Walter Brennan: William Wyler's *The Westerner* (United Artists, 1940).

5394

Rebstock: Get your rifles, men. One man behind a rock is worth three in the open.

Barney Rebstock played by Donald Crisp: Leslie Fenton's *Whispering Smith* (Paramount, 1948).

5395

Custer: You want me as an enemy, Paddy?

Paddy: You never did give me goose bumps, Tom.

Captain Tom Custer played by Ed Lauter and Paddy Welch played by Bert Williams: J. Lee Thompson's *The White Buffalo* (United Artists, 1977).

5396

Custer: You're lookin' to wear a marble hat!

Captain Tom Custer played by Ed Lauter: J. Lee Thompson's *The White Buffalo* (United Artists, 1977).

5397

Dutch: They'll be waiting for us.

Bishop: I wouldn't have it any other way.

Dutch Engstrom played by Ernest Borgnine and Pike Bishop played by William Holden: Sam Peckinpah's *The Wild Bunch* (Warner Bros.–Seven Arts, 1969).

5398

Carter: It becomes more evident everyday that Ramsay and I must settle our little dispute with gunplay.

King Carter played by Harry Woods and Jeff Ramsay played by Dick Foran: Ford Beebe and Ray Taylor's *Winners of the West* (Universal serial, Chapter 8: "The Flaming Arsenal," 1940).

5399

Wyatt: Mr. Clements, your men respect you and I don't want to do anything to take away from that. I'm sure you've earned it. So you and your boys are welcome in Dodge City as long as you obey the law. But if you don't want to cooperate, then I'll open you up right now with this shotgun so wide your whole crew is going to see what you had for breakfast.

Wyatt Earp played by Kevin Costner: Lawrence Kasdan's *Wyatt Earp* (Warner Bros., 1994).

5400

Chavez: No, I don't know what your vision told you. But my vision told me we're headed for blood …blood like a river.

Chavez Y. Chavez played by Lou Diamond Phillips: Christopher Cain's *Young Guns* (20th Century–Fox, 1988).

5401

Billy: Reap the whirlwind, Sheriff Brady! Reap it!

William H. "Billy" Bonney played by Emilio Estevez and Sheriff Brady played by Daniel Kamin: Christopher Cain's *Young Guns* (20th Century–Fox, 1988).

Stagecoaches and Railroads

See also People; Towns

5402

[*Conversation on runaway stagecoach*]

Dixie: What do we do now?

Brisco: Well, I can swing out, get a good foothold, and climb up to the top of the stage. And then if I'm real careful, and God is on my side, I could leap onto the rear of the back horse and work my way out to the lead team …taking care not to fall beneath their thundering hoofs.

Then reach out, grab the bridle of the lead horse, and rein them in to a safe and steady stop.

Dixie: Oh my!

Brisco: Or …we can jump!

Dixie Cousins played by Kelly Rutherford and Brisco County, Jr., played by Bruce Campbell: Bryan Spicer's *Adventures of Brisco County, Jr.* (TVW, Series Premiere, 1993).

5403

Alice: Train robbers!

Hanes: That's right, miss.

Alice: Oh my goodness gracious! I simply don't know whether to be chilled or thrilled!

Alice Calhoun played by Gloria Henry and Dan Hanes played by John Ridgely: Ray Nazarro's *Al Jennings of Oklahoma* (Columbia, 1951).

5404

Taylor: I'm Hoyt Taylor, District Manager for Butterfield. We have a stage going to Lawrenceburg at noon. Just because you ran into Indians back there, doesn't mean we'll run into trouble ahead. Isn't that right?

Bill: If I know Apaches, there'll be a heap of trouble everywhere.

Hoyt Taylor played by Robert Harris and Bill Gibson played by Arthur Hunnicutt: R.G. Springsteen's *Apache Uprising* (Paramount, 1966).

5405

Toby: If that stagecoach don't leave, we are going to be in a lot of trouble. We're going to lose a lot of money.

Jess: Yeah, I know. But if those Apaches is on the warpath, I don't aim to end toes up to the sun with a lance through my gizzard for a tombstone.

Toby Jack Saunders played by DeForest Kelley and Jess Cooney played by Gene Evans: R.G. Springsteen's *Apache Uprising* (Paramount, 1966).

5406

Marshal: Unless you want to see your own gravestone on your way to hell, you'll be on the next stage. Now, that leaves here tomorrow at sundown. And you're going to like it. It crosses the desert at night. It's cooler then.

The Marshal played by Karl Swenson: Delmer Daves' *The Badlanders* (MGM, 1958).

5407

Lola: How did you know I was on that stage?

Bart: Very simple. There're posters of you from here to the Mexican border.

Lola: Is that why you chose to rob that particular stage? Because I was on it?

Bart: Well, the $10,000.00 they were carrying didn't keep me away either.

Lola Montez played by Yvonne DeCarlo and Charles E. Boles, alias Black Bart, played by Dan Duryea: George Sherman's *Black Bart* (Universal, 1948).

5408

Boles: I'll be generous about your faults if you'll be generous about mine.

Lola: Robbin' stagecoaches hardly comes under the heading of a minor vice.

Charles E. Boles, alias Black Bart, played by Dan Duryea and Lola Montez played by Yvonne DeCarlo in George Sherman's *Black Bart* (Universal, 1948).

5409

Calamity: Excitement? Why, I got more arrows in the back of that coach than a porcupine has got stickers!

Calamity Jane played by Doris Day: David Butler's *Calamity Jane* (Warner Bros., 1953).

5410

Big Jack: Rob the poor and you get a posse of outraged citizens after you. Rob a mine owner and nobody cares.

Big Jack Davis played by Raymond Massey: Andre De Toth's *Carson City* (Warner Bros., 1952).

5411

Clay: We can't hold up no train.

Cat: Why not?

Clay: Lots of reasons.

Cat: Name 'em.

Clay: We're rustlers, not train robbers.

Cat: Well, if people didn't try something new, there wouldn't be hardly any progress at all.

Clay Boone played by Michael Callan and Cat Ballou played by Jane Fonda: Elliot Silverstein's *Cat Ballou* (Columbia, 1965).

5412

Rose: We do need that railroad. The town died once before without one. But nothing comes for free, gentlemen. Call it a fee, call it a tax, call it survival. You can have part of something or all of nothing. And from where I stand, I'll take the something.

Carrey Rose played by Daphne Ashbrook: Alan J. Levi's *Dead Man's Revenge* (MCA/Universal Home Video, 1994).

5413

Zeke: That railroad is going to make a lot of changes…a lot of changes, Vance. I can remember when your daddy and I trapped the Wind River country. A man could walk a week and never see another living human …just them mountains …big, purple. It's getting so crowded a man can't draw a full breath.

Zeke Carmody played by Edgar Buchanan: Anthony Mann's *Devil's Doorway* (MGM, 1950).

5414

Dodge: Ladies and gentlemen, today a great chapter of history has been written. And we take justifiable pride in bringing this railroad to the terminal furthest west in this country. Someday, and I believe it will be in the near future, a great city will spring from this very spot upon which we now stand. A city which will represent all that the west stands for: honesty, courage, morality and culture. For all the noble virtues of civilization, I can see a great metropolis of homes, churches, schools; a fine decent city which will become the flower of the prairie.

Colonel Dodge played by Henry O'Neill: Michael Curtiz's *Dodge City* (Warner Bros., 1939).

5415

Crackel: Modoc Jim says he just wants to see how thick your [stagecoach] door is, Bill.

Bill: What business is that of his?

Crackel: Well, he says the last time he fired at you, the arrow didn't go through it. He says the next time he's going to use a heavier bow.

Bill: Take your stinking fingers off that door!

Crackel played by Elisha Cook, Jr., Bill Satterwhite played by Robert Keith, and Modoc Jim played by Frank De Kova: Delmer Daves' *Drum Beat* (Warner Bros., 1954).

5416

Earp: Mister, if I were you, I'd get back on the same train to where I'd come from.

Wyatt Earp played by Fred Ward: Piers Haggard's *Four Eyes and Six-Guns* (Turner Pictures, 1992).

5417

Zack: Where's the little man who was in there [overturned stagecoach]?

Joe: Oh, Ansel. Why, he was took dead. This sure couldn't be his money. He was too anxious to give it away.

Zack: He was just a railroad agent.

Joe: Oh, transporting for the railroad? Good! They have been over-charging me for years so I'll just consider this a rebate.

Zack Thomas was placed by Frank Sinatra and Joe Jarrett by Dean Martin: Robert Aldrich's *Four for Texas* (Warner Bros., 1964).

5418

Joe: All we want to know is, where's the train?

Quale: The train? It's out on the tracks. It seldom comes in here.

Joe Panello played by Chico Marx and S. Quentin Quale played by Groucho Marx: Edward Buzzell's *Go West* (MGM, 1940).

5419

Sims: What kind of work do you do, Bill?

Bill: Well, I'm between jobs right now.

Sims: No kidding. Well, what kind of work did you do?

Bill: I robbed stagecoaches.

Al Sims played by Don MacKay and Bill Miner played by Richard Farnsworth: Phillip Borsos' *The Grey Fox* (United Artists, 1982).

5420

Bart: We tried to rob the Three River Flier. We couldn't catch 'em. The passengers shot at us from windows for sport! It's not easy being an outlaw in times like these.

Bart Jackson played by Jim Burk: John Huston's *The Life & Times of Judge Roy Bean* (NGP, 1972).

5421

Vin: I never rode shotgun on a hearse before.

Vin played by Steve McQueen: John Sturges' *The Magnificent Seven* (United Artists, 1960).

5422

In the early West, stagecoach runs between scattered frontier towns often took two or more days, hence inns were constructed to shelter passengers overnight. Around one of those inns, called Halfway House, there was a strange story of mystery and murder — a story which began on a stagecoach …

Prologue: Philip Ford's *Marshal of Amarillo* (Republic, 1948).

5423

Nugget: This stage headed for Center City?
Driver: No.
Nugget: Ah, Channey?
Driver: No.
Nugget: You ain't lost, are ya?
Driver: No.
Nugget: Then where are you going?
Driver: Amarillo.
Nugget: Good, so am I!

Nugget Clark played by Eddy Waller and Ben, the Stagecoach Driver, played by Roy Barcroft: Philip Ford's *Marshal of Amarillo* (Republic, 1948).

5424

Ben: Sometimes I wondered if either one of us is ever going to see our money again.
Brett: Well, I'm going to see mine, Ben, because I'm going to stick with you until the train rolls in tomorrow. And if that money isn't on it, if you're not telling the truth, I can't tell you how it's going to pain me. I can tell you how it's going to pain you!

Ben Maverick played by Charles Frank and Brett Maverick played by James Garner: Hy Averback's *The New Maverick* (TVW, 1978).

5425

John Henry: Charlie, a man's got to have a goal in this life. Something to keep him going. And I've got mine. I'm going to rob a Texas train!

John Henry Lee played by Willie Nelson and Charlie Lee played by Dub Taylor: Burt Kennedy's *Once Upon a Texas Train* (TVW, 1988).

5426

Bracket: And in the meantime, all you want Johnny and me to do is pull seventy-three passengers off a moving train, in wide-open country, without being seen; and if we are seen …they'll all be killed. Is that the job?
Davenport: I told you …it can't be done.
Bracket: I didn't say that!

Hank Bracket played by Rod Taylor, Cyrus Davenport played by John McIntire, and Johnny Reach played by Dennis Cole: Douglas Heyes' *Powderkeg* (TVW, 1971).

5427

John: Thirty thousand dollars is a heap of money. Now, who would have thought of holding up a train?
Frank: Seems like a business worth considering.

John Reno played by Myron Healey and Frank Reno played by Forrest Tucker: Tim Whelan's *Rage at Dawn* (RKO, 1955).

5428

Narrator: Yes sir, that's it …the Overland Mail. San Francisco to St. Louis in 25 days. Twenty-seven hundred miles in 25 days and 25 nights …when the weather and injuns behaved. A lot farther and longer when they didn't. People said it couldn't be done. They laughed and called it the Jackass Mail.

Narration: Henry Hathaway's *Rawhide* (20th Century–Fox, 1951).

5429

Vin: I thought you took a job riding shotgun for Overland.
Chris: I quit.
Vin: How come?
Chris: My health. My doctor said to find a climate with less lead in the air.

Vin played by Robert Fuller and Chris played by Yul Brynner: Burt Kennedy's *Return of the Seven* (United Artists, 1966).

5430

Sheriff: Do you mind me asking why you are stopping trains?
Billy: I was infected with a social disease …known as bad luck.
Sheriff: The juries are beginning to take a dim view of bad luck.

Sheriff Chuck Jarvis played by Rock Hudson and Billy Massey played by Dean Martin: George Seaton's *Showdown* (Universal, 1973).

5431

Doris: What makes you think Tom's on that stage?
Tupper: Well, I sold him a one-way ticket to Phoenix myself.
Doris: He only bought one ticket?
Tupper: He's not so important that he takes two tickets to haul him.

Doris played by Julie Haydon and Tupper played

by Alan Bridge: Lloyd Nosler's *Son of the Border* (RKO, 1933).

5432

Buck: If there's anything I don't like, it's driving a stagecoach through Apache country.

Buck Rickabaugh, the Stagecoach Driver, played by Andy Devine: John Ford's *Stagecoach* (United Artists, 1939).

5433

Doc: Tombstone.
Clerk: This stage is going to Lordsburg, mister.
Doc: I know that.
Clerk: But you said …
Doc: I know what I said. I want to go to Tombstone.
Clerk: But this isn't the Tombstone stage.
Doc: Well, is there a stage that leaves Lordsburg going to Tombstone?
Clerk: Yeah.
Doc: Is it possible to get on the stage and go to Lordsburg, and get off that stage, and then go into Tombstone on another stage? Is that possible?
Clerk: Oh, you want to go to Tombstone by way of Lordsburg?
Doc: Now you got it.
Clerk: But there's a stage through here tomorrow that goes directly to Tombstone.
Doc: Well, which one gets there first? The one leaving today going to Lordsburg to Tombstone, or the one leaving tomorrow going directly to Tombstone?
Clerk: Well, that depends. A lot of things can happen: a wheel falls off, an axle breaks, horses …
Doc: Which one is supposed to get there first?
Clerk: The one through Lordsburg.
Doc: That's the one I want.
Clerk: Why didn't you say that in the first place? That will cost you fifty cents more.

Doc Holliday played by Willie Nelson and the Ticket Clerk played by Anthony Russell: Ted Post's *Stagecoach* (TVW, 1986).

5434

Guard: I ain't going.
Driver: You ain't what?
Guard: I ain't never met nobody who ran across Geronimo and lived to talk about it.
Driver: Walt, you wait just a second now. Look, Walt, I need you with me. You know that. I'll pay ya, I'll pay ya double salary out of my own pocket.
Guard: I've never yet seen a dead man give a damn about money.

The Stagecoach Guard, Walt, played by Glen

Clark and the Stagecoach Driver, Buck, played by John Schneider: Ted Post's *Stagecoach* (TVW, 1986).

5435

Dallas: I finally realized once and for all no woman is gonna find a million dollar dream in a two-dollar room.

Doc: Most women don't have a million dollar dream, Dallas.

Dallas: Every woman's got a million dollar dream. She ain't never gonna find out where she might be if she don't get away from what she already is.

Doc: You think you'll find it on that stagecoach?

Dallas: I don't know. The only thing in my life is going someplace else.

Dallas played by Elizabeth Ashley and Doc Holliday played by Willie Nelson: Ted Post's *Stagecoach* (TVW, 1986).

5436

Billy: Where are you headed?

Dallas: I knew the answer to that one when I was about fourteen. Then I hit fifteen and ran head on into that thing called reality. I've been walking with a lantern ever since.

Billy: I mean, where are you going now?

Dallas: I don't know, cowboy. Where are you going? You've been everywhere.

Billy: Nobody has been everywhere.

Dallas: Maybe you're right. It just feels like it.

Billy: Where do you want to go?

Dallas: I don't think I've ever seen it on a map.

Billy "Ringo" Williams played by Kris Kristofferson and Dallas played by Elizabeth Ashley: Ted Post's *Stagecoach* (TVW, 1986).

5437

Henry: Does anybody know why this stage has a cavalry escort?

Doc: The cavalry is here to represent our Manifest Destiny.

Henry: Our what?

Doc: To protect us from the Indians. You may have noticed that we white people have a way of taking what we want without regard to what the present owner might think about it. Some people could call that stealing. We call it Manifest Destiny.

Hatfield: You know, I'd hate to think you're calling us thieves.

Doc: What else would you call it? We come here with a gun in one hand and a jug in the other. We weaken them with the jug and then finish them off with a gun.

Henry: All I asked is why we have a cavalry escort. I didn't ask for a sermon.

Hatfield: Well, if you want it in one word, that one word is Geronimo.

Henry Gatewood played by Tony Franciosa, Doc

Holliday played by Willie Nelson, and Hatfield played by Waylon Jennings: Ted Post's *Stagecoach* (TVW, 1986).

5438

Buck: Well, they say that God protects fools and drunks. I believe we got the biggest fool in the whole southwest territory riding right here on this coach.

Marshal: Who besides me?

Buck: Well …me. Do you know anybody else that would drive a six horse team through hostile Apache territory for $8.00 a month?

Buck played by John Schneider and Marshal Curley Wilcox played by Johnny Cash: Ted Post's *Stagecoach* (TVW, 1986).

5439

Hatfield: Don't light that!

Doc: Did you say something?

Hatfield: A gentleman doesn't smoke in the presence of a lady.

Doc: I wouldn't like to think that you're implying that I am anything less. I may be, you understand. I just wouldn't want to hear you say it.

Hatfield played by Waylon Jennings and Doc Holliday played by Willie Nelson: Ted Post's *Stagecoach* (TVW, 1986).

5440

Marshal: You got a good wife.

Buck: Yeah, I know. She used to ride shotgun for me …then she said it got too hard on her ovaries.

Marshal: What's an ovary?

Buck: Well, the nearest I can tell it's, ah, you know, part of her machinery.

Marshal Curley Wilcox played by Johnny Cash and Buck played by John Schneider: Ted Post's *Stagecoach* (TVW, 1986).

5441

Dave: You know, Zeke, this is my last trip.

Zeke: Why?

Dave: Oh, Harolday won't take back what he said.

Zeke: No? What did he say?

Dave: You're fired!

Dave played by George "Gabby" Hayes, Zeke played by Raymond Hatton, and Mr. Harolday played by Don Douglas: Edwin L. Marin's *Tall in the Saddle* (RKO, 1944).

5442

Raymond: It's running a little early today. It's only two and a half hours late.

Lieutenant Raymond played by Jack Kelly: Phil Karlson's *They Rode West* (Columbia, 1954).

5443

Wade: Is the Marshal around?

Emmy: He's in the office.

Wade: Well, you tell him that the coach from Contention was held up. We

passed it on the way in. They don't have any horses. Didn't you hear what I said?

Emmy: Yeah, I heard.

Wade: Well, why don't you go tell him?

Emmy: Well, the Marshal takes his nap between one and two.

Ben Wade played by Glenn Ford and Emmy played by Felicia Farr: Delmer Daves' *3:10 to Yuma* (Columbia, 1957).

5444

Grady: Where are you going?

Lane: Where do you suppose? To rob a train!

Jesse: To rob a train?

Grady: It's something to do.

Grady played by Rod Taylor, Lane played by John Wayne, and Wil Jesse played by Ben Johnson: Burt Kennedy's *The Train Robbers* (Warner Bros., 1973).

5445

The legend of Union Pacific is the drama of a nation, young, tough, prodigal and invincible, conquering with an iron highroad the endless reaches of the West. For the West is America's Empire, and only yesterday Union Pacific was the West.

Foreword: Cecil B. DeMille's *Union Pacific* (Paramount, 1939).

5446

Monahan: There's nothing like hearing an engine whistle in the still of the night.

Monohan played by J.M. Kerrigan: Cecil B. DeMille's *Union Pacific* (Paramount, 1939).

5447

Butler: I don't believe I'll need bodyguards.

Casement: Oh, no? You'll need 'em all right.

Fiesta: You think we no good, hey?

Butler: No, it's not that. I …

Leach: We've had a lot of experience, Captain. We bodyguarded the last two troubleshooters right up to the very minute they was killed.

Jeff Butler played by Joel McCrea, General Casement played by Stanley Ridges, Fiesta played by Akim Tamiroff, and Leach Overmile played by Lynne Overman: Cecil B. DeMille's *Union Pacific* (Paramount, 1939).

5448

Lomax: What's all this got to do with me?

Taw: We're gonna take that wagon.

Lomax: We are? Have you taken a look lately at the cemetery at Emmett? There's a big bunch of cheap wooden crosses in one corner, all kind of crowded in together. That's attributed to the last fools who tried to stop the war wagon. You like facts? $1.15 for the

Taw Jackson (John Wayne) reviews plans for a gold heist with his gang: the drunk and dynamite expert, Billy Hyatt (Robert Walker, Jr.); the Indian, Levi Walking Bear (Howard Keel); the wagon driver to haul the gold away, Wes Fletcher (Keenan Wynn); and the gunfighter, Lomax (Kirk Douglas), in Burt Kennedy's *The War Wagon* (Universal, 1967).

casket, 12 cents for the crosses. Oh, Pierce foots the bill. A dollar twenty-seven seems a poor price to pay for a man's life. Especially mine!

Lomax played by Kirk Douglas and Taw Jackson played by John Wayne: Burt Kennedy's *The War Wagon* (Universal, 1967).

5449

Hank: You ain't going with us, are ya?
Correspondent: Yes, yes.
Hank: Well, I hope your hair is fastened down good!

Hank York played by Bob Burns and the Newspaper Correspondent played by Hal K. Dawson: Frank Lloyd's *Wells Fargo* (Paramount, 1937).

5450

Boone: You and me, we got about as much chance of growing old as this damn train does getting safe across Mexico!

Boone played by Jack Elam: Burt Kennedy's *Where the Hell's That Gold?!!!* (a.k.a. *Dynamite & Gold*; TVW, 1988).

5451

Pike: He gave his word.
Dutch: He gave his word to a railroad.
Pike: It's his word!
Dutch: That ain't what counts. It's who you give it to!

Pike Bishop played by William Holden and Dutch Engstrom played by Ernest Borgnine: Sam Peckinpah's *The Wild Bunch* (Warner Bros.–Seven Arts, 1969).

5452

Hartford: We'll build a railroad through Hellgate Pass and forget him.
Ramsay: We'll build a railroad all right, but I bet he'll be a hard man to forget.

John Hartford played by Edward Keane and Jeff

Ramsay played by Dick Foran: Ford Beebe and Ray Taylor's *Winners of the West* (Universal serial, Chapter 1: "Redskins Ride Again," 1940).

5453

Claire: Dad! The work train is moving!
John: They must be stealing it!
Claire: They're Indians!
John: Indians don't drive locomotives!

Claire Hartford played by Anne Nagel and John Hartford played by Edward Keane: Ford Beebe and Ray Taylor's *Winners of the West* (Universal serial, Chapter 2: "The Wreck at Red River Gorge," 1940).

5454

Raven: They'll probably blow themselves up with the bridge.
Carter: Well, just so they get the job done.

Raven played by Trevor Bardette and King Carter played by Harry Woods: Ford Beebe and Ray Taylor's *Winners of the West* (Universal serial, Chapter 3: "The Bridge of Disaster," 1940).

Towns

See also People; West

5455

Big Smith: Welcome to Sutter Creek. Five years ago, the gold ran dry. Now the Sheriff is dead, the mayor is running the brothel, and the minister is a drunk. My kind of town!

Big Smith played by M.C. Gainey: Bryan Spicer's *Adventures of Brisco County, Jr.* (TVW, series premiere, 1993).

5456

Sheriff: Donovan, this is just a half portion of a town, but we do have certain what you might call rules to live by! You don't jump another man's claim; you don't steal his wife, woman, or whiskey; you don't strike a bargain and then entertain second thoughts about the matter. Any one of these offenses could make you the exalted guest of honor at a hemp party.

Sheriff Homer McCoy played by Harry Morgan and Russell Donovan played by Bill Bixby: Norman Tokar's *The Apple Dumpling Gang* (Buena Vista, 1975).

5457

Theodore: We got to put some distance between us and this town or it's gonna be our permanent residence. And I mean permanent!

Theodore played by Don Knotts: Vincent McEvety's *The Apple Dumpling Gang Rides Again* (Buena Vista, 1979).

5458

Pete: Let's wait and see. There's no danger yet.

Smith: No danger yet? This guy is like a carrier of smallpox! Since he's arrived, this town has a fever …an infection. And it's spreading!

Pete Wirth played by John Ericson and Reno Smith played by Robert Ryan: John Sturges' *Bad Day at Black Rock* (MGM, 1955).

5459

MacReedy: You killed Komoko, Smith, and sooner or later you're gonna go up for it. Not because you killed him, but because of thinking in a town like this you could get away with it.

John J. MacReedy played by Spencer Tracy and Reno Smith played by Robert Ryan: John Sturges' *Bad Day at Black Rock* (MGM, 1955).

5460

McBain: It seems like everybody around here is stealing from everybody else.

John McBain played by Ernest Borgnine: Delmer Daves' *The Badlanders* (MGM, 1958).

5461

Paul: There's a bad element that's been drifting into town …ever since the mines opened. They ain't like us. They ain't decent. They're just tramps, Dan. And we owe it to the community to do something about it.

Dan: Go to the sheriff and volunteer as deputies without pay.

Paul: That ain't the same and you know it …you know. There's just some things the regular law can't handle. If every able-bodied man was an enforcer of the law, why, this rowdy element, they'd leave town.

Paul Carson played by Alan Young and Dan Baker played by Clint Walker: Lyman Dayton's *Baker's Hawk* (Doty/Dayton, 1976).

5462

Paul: Did you see the funeral?

Dan: Sure did.

Paul: It's going to keep on like this, you know, until that sheriff of ours clamps the lid on this town. Too many drifters.

Paul Carson played by Alan Young and Dan Baker played by Clint Walker: Lyman Dayton's *Baker's Hawk* (Doty/Dayton, 1976).

5463

Boles: What are you two doing in town?

Brady: Getting out of Texas, mostly.

Charles E. Boles, alias Black Bart, played by Dan Duryea and Jersey Brady played by Percy Kilbride: George Sherman's *Black Bart* (Universal, 1948).

5464

Clark: Are you in trouble?

Boles: In Nevada and everywhere east of there I am. Here, I'm all right .

Clark played by John McIntire and Charles E. Boles, alias Black Bart, played by Dan Duryea: George Sherman's *Black Bart* (Universal, 1948).

5465

Taggart: I know how we can run everybody out of Rock Ridge.

Lamarr: How?

Taggart: We'll kill the firstborn male child in every household!

Lamarr: Too Jewish.

Taggart played by Slim Pickens and Hedley Lamarr played by Harvey Korman: Mel Brooks' *Blazing Saddles* (Warner Bros., 1974).

5466

Canaan: What kind of town you got here? You got preachers who pack iron!

Canaan played by Armand Assante: Richard Spence's *Blind Justice* (HBO Home Video, 1994).

5467

Sheriff: You don't like this town?

Buchanan: I don't like some of its people.

Sheriff: Me included?

Buchanan: You especially.

Sheriff: Oh, you'd like to kill me, maybe?

Buchanan: I'd like to give you what you and your boys gave me.

Sheriff: Take the law into your hands, is that it?

Buchanan: No. Just you.

Sheriff Lou Agry played by Barry Kelley and Tom Buchanan played by Randolph Scott: Budd Boetticher's *Buchanan Rides Alone* (Columbia, 1958).

5468

Calamity: There comes a time in the life of every gold town when it either gets civilized or goes bust. Before it makes up its mind which, men go crazy drinking, gambling, whoring …cutting into each other's claims and shooting each other over trifles. Deadwood just happened to be in its hellfire days.

Calamity Jane played by Anjelica Huston: Rod Hardy's *Buffalo Girls* (Cabin Creek Entertainment, 1995).

5469

Bartender: Just passing through?

Jordan: I don't know. I may stick around awhile.

Bartender: Somebody like you asks my advice, I'd say keep traveling.

Jordan: I didn't ask it.

Bartender: I don't know what you're looking for, mister. But when you go hunting, you got to be sure. You got to know how much ground you're ready to cover: six hundred miles out there or six feet here.

The Bartender played by John Doucette and Trace Jordan played by Tab Hunter: Stuart Heisler's *The Burning Hills* (Warner Bros., 1956).

5470

Whitey: There's sure lot of building going on around here.

Pokey: A church, new houses, a school. I tell ya what, it's getting so civilized they'll soon tell you where to spit.

Whitey played by Frank Faylen and Pokey played

by James Burke: John Farrow's *California* (Paramount, 1946).

5471

Pete: I've never seen so many people.

John: And more are coming all the time. I tell ya, Pete, if this is the promised land, I'll take the open trail.

Pete Smith played by Raimund Harmstorf and John Thornton played by Charlton Heston: Ken Annakin's *The Call of the Wild* (MGM-UA, 1972).

5472

Griffin: You're at the wrong table, Captain …and the wrong hotel and the wrong town. And you might even be in the wrong line of business.

Griffin played by Stuart Whitman and Captain Apache played by Lee Van Cleef: Alexander Singer's *Captain Apache* (Scotia International, 1971).

5473

Zeke: This will be a different town if you put a railroad in here, you know that.

Kincaid: It could stand a little wakening up.

Zeke: I happen to like it the way it is.

Kincaid: Growing pains are always a little tough. But you can't get to be an adult without them. That goes for towns too.

Zeke: That depends on what you mean by being an adult.

Zeke Mitchell played by Don Beddoe and Silent Jeff Kincaid played by Randolph Scott: Andre De Toth's *Carson City* (Warner Bros., 1952).

5474

The town grew fast and loud. And as usual, men died faster …louder.

Prologue: Ray Nazarro's *Cripple Creek* (Columbia, 1952).

5475

Judge: Dallas will be run by Federal law …not by mob rule. We're not wild westerners. We're facing east and that's our future. We intend to build industries here, and culture. Dallas will raise people, not cows.

Hollister: If your carpetbag riffraff doesn't choke it to death in her cradle.

Judge Harper played by Will Wright and Blayde "Reb" Hollister, alias Sheriff Weatherby, played by Gary Cooper: Stuart Heisler's *Dallas* (Warner Bros., 1950).

5476

McCloud: Well, I guess Lawrence is burned to the ground.

Seton: Yeah. Well, we got a saying down in Texas: that it takes a good fire to burn down the weeds …to let the flowers grow.

Fletch McCloud played by Roy Rogers and Bob Seton played by John Wayne: Raoul Walsh's *The Dark Command* (Republic, 1940).

5477

Angus: Four killings in a week! It's got to stop!

Judge: Four? Did you say four? That's right! Four! Well, we're going to be quite a town, ain't we? I doubt that they have that many in Dodge City. No, I don't think so.

Angus: We aim to compete with any city in size …but not in lawlessness!

Angus McCloud played by Porter Hall and Judge Buckner played by Raymond Walburn: Raoul Walsh's *The Dark Command* (Republic, 1940).

5478

Scott: Hey, listen, stranger, what town is this?

Stranger: Bowie …Bowie. At least for now.

Scott: For now? Why?

Stranger: Because it's going to be hell here pretty soon!

Scott Mary played by Giuliano Gemma and the Stranger was uncredited: Tonino Valerii's *Day of Anger* (a.k.a. *Days of Wrath*; Sancrosiap/Corona Film/KG Divina Film/National General, 1967).

5479

McLean: What we got to decide right away is, do we change the name of the town or don't we? Miss Timmons?

Timmons: What? Oh yes, well, if you ask me, Mrs. McLean, I think West End is a perfect name. It means just that: the end of the west.

Mrs. McLean played by Helen Kleeb and Miss Timmons was played by Dee Carroll: Harmon Jones' *A Day of Fury* (Universal, 1956).

5480

Starrett: The trail ends in this town. There's no place to go but back.

Bruhn: The trail back is closed.

Blaise Starrett played by Robert Ryan and Jack Bruhn played by Burl Ives: Andre De Toth's *Day of the Outlaw* (United Artists, 1959).

5481

Stanek: We don't have any law in this jerkwater town. He's the law! He's passed his sentence on practically everything and everyone. The people should be the law, and will be the law, when they have the urge to get rid of Frank Patch. You see, gentlemen, what we're really deciding here is whether we move forward or backward. We either need to keep up with the times or we lose out.

Ivan Stanek played by Morgan Woodward and Marshal Frank Patch played by Richard Widmark: Allen Smithee's *Death of a Gunfighter* (Universal, 1969).

5482

Luke: There's that mayor over there drumming up a meeting with all those rich and proper jackasses …hollering and shouting around, quoting some stupid law or by-

law. Then they'll all go stomping down to the jailhouse, take a look at God Almighty [the Sheriff]. Then he'll [Sheriff] take one good look back at 'em, and they'll all wet their britches and go on home.

Lester Luke played by Carroll O'Connor: Allen Smithee's *Death of a Gunfighter* (Universal, 1969).

5483

Lucy: John, we just can't let him ride away. If it wasn't for him …

John: Yes, he changed things for everybody in town. But unfortunately, there's nothing we can do for him. I'll tell you one thing: none of us will ever forget the day that Bart Allison spent in Sundown.

Lucy Summerton played by Karen Steele and Dr. John Storrow played by John Archer: Budd Boetticher's *Decision at Sundown* (Columbia, 1957).

5484

Caroline: Mr. Booth, why don't you leave Magnolia?

McCall: Now?

Caroline: There's enough corruption in this town without you.

McCall: And what makes you think I'm corrupted.

Caroline: You're here.

Caroline was uncredited and Duell McCall, alias Henry Booth, played by Alex McArthur: E.W. Swackhamer's *Desperado: Badlands Justice* (TVW, 1989).

5485

Destry: Now you get this straight! We don't want anymore of this promiscuous shooting around here. Somebody is likely to get hurt!

Destry played by Audie Murphy: George Marshall's *Destry* (Universal, 1954).

5486

Nathaniel: If you're a coffin maker, you sure did pick a good town to settle.

Nathaniel was uncredited: Sergio Corbucci's *Django* (B.R.C./Tecisa, 1966).

5487

Wyatt: They're bad people, John.

Doc: Well, if it weren't for bad people, what would you do for a living, Marshal? Tell me about Tombstone. I mean, more than what you said in the letter.

Wyatt: It's wide open. The sheriff here, Johnny Behan, doesn't know how to organize a town. So I'm going to run against him in the election. The sheriff has got all the power here. The marshal has got a badge, and he's got some territory, but he's got no jurisdiction in the town. Gambling is heavy. There's a lot of money about town. It's wide open. So you organize the gambling. Start right here. I run the law, you run the gambling. We'll both end up rich. Very rich!

Doc: We sound like bad people, Wyatt.

Wyatt: We are, John.

Wyatt Earp played by Harris Yulin and John "Doc" Holliday played by Stacy Keach: Frank Perry's *Doc* (United Artists, 1971).

5488

Wyatt: ...and then we clean up Tombstone.

Virgil: You mean clean out Tombstone.

Wyatt Earp played by Harris Yulin and Virgil Earp played by John Bottoms: Frank Perry's *Doc* (United Artists, 1971).

5489

Dodge City, Kansas—1872. Longhorn cattle center of the world and wide-open Babylon of the American frontier—packed with settlers, thieves and gunmen.

Caption: Michael Curtiz's *Dodge City* (Warner Bros., 1939).

5490

Dodge City ...rolling in wealth from the great Texas trail-herds ...the town that knew no ethics but cash and killing.

Caption: Michael Curtiz's *Dodge City* (Warner Bros., 1939).

5491

Wade: Well, what's the news in Dodge?

Barber: Well, just about the same as always. Gamblin', drinkin', and killin'. Mostly killin'.

Wade Hatton played by Errol Flynn and Charlie the Barber played by Clem Bevans: Michael Curtiz's *Dodge City* (Warner Bros., 1939).

5492

Rusty: Well, well. So this is Dodge City, huh? Sort of smells like Fort Worth, don't it?

Wade: Oh, that's not the city you smell. That's you! We better get you to a bathtub before somebody shoots you for a buffalo.

Rusty Hart played by Alan Hale and Wade Hatton played by Errol Flynn: Michael Curtiz's *Dodge City* (Warner Bros., 1939).

5493

Dooley: I know that after all we've been through it's gonna seem kind of dumb to you, but I think I'm gonna stay here.

Cowboy: The longer I live, the more I have to reconsider what I think is dumb.

Dooley played by William Forsythe and the Cowboy played by Emilio Estevez: Gene Quintano's *Dollar for the Dead* (TVW, 1998).

5494

Arkansas: Bill, that jail ain't big. But it looks harder to get into than most jails is to get out of.

Arkansas played by Charles Kemper and Bill

Doolin played by Randolph Scott: Gordon Douglas' *The Doolins of Oklahoma* (Columbia, 1949).

5495

Malloy: Here it is, Virginia City, my kind of town.

Duchess: What constitutes your kind of town?

Malloy: Anyplace I can get rid of you.

Charlie Malloy played by Geroge Segal and Amanda Quaid, alias "Duchess," played by Goldie Hawn: Melvin Frank's *The Duchess and the Dirtwater Fox* (20th Century–Fox, 1976).

5496

Clayton: The law works fast around here.

Nacho: There is only one law in El Paso, amigo. If you want to live, you must learn to shoot ...and quick.

Clayton Fletcher played by John Payne and Nacho Vasquez played by Edwardo Noriega: Lewis Foster's *El Paso* (Paramount, 1949).

5497

Ellen: Why didn't you leave today, Ray?

Ray: Oh, I just couldn't seem to get started.

Ellen: I've heard men say that the first part of a journey is often the hardest.

Ray: Yeah, I guess it is.

Ellen: Why is that?

Ray: Oh, I don't know ...different reasons.

Ellen: Is it ever because you're afraid to start out from one place to another ...to try to change something ...even if it's bad?

Ellen Bailey played by Dorothy Green and Jim Larson, alias Ray Kincaid, played by Fred MacMurray: Paul Wendkos' *Face of a Fugitive* (Columbia, 1959).

5498

Evelyn: Oh, Johnny, why didn't we go on? Why did we settle for less than we wanted?

Evelyn played by Inger Stevens: Vincent McEveety's *Firecreek* (Warner Bros.–Seven Arts, 1968).

5499

Whittier: Nothing ever stands still. You grow or you die. And a town that collects losers will exist for their lifetimes ...no more.

Mr. Whittier played by Dean Jagger: Vincent McEveety's *Firecreek* (Warner Bros.–Seven Arts, 1968).

5500

Johnny: Mr. Whittier ...Mr. Whittier, you got a handgun here. I'll take it.

Whittier: Give it up, Johnny, it'll be a losing game.

Johnny: Come on, I want that gun!

Whittier: It's not your fight! It's not your business, Johnny!

Johnny: And that's what I've been telling myself ever since they rode in here! Well, it was my business, Mr. Whittier.

The Larkins of this world are everybody's business. And they won't disappear just by turning your head or stepping back. That boy, Arthur, is dead because I wouldn't take a stand with them in the beginning.

Whittier: I'm not watching you get yourself killed by those men!

Johnny: You say this is a town of losers. Well, how could you say that Arthur is a loser? He fought back and didn't have anything to fight back with. Now, now me a loser? Now, that's something else again! No, I'll agree with you there! The day I crossed this valley, you had the biggest loser of all times settling right here. Do you know what I saw in this place I was willing to call my home?

Whittier: I'm not giving you that gun, Johnny!

Johnny: Now, listen to me! I had my whole life ahead of me! And all I saw here was land that nobody wanted ...and ground that nobody would be challenging me for. I saw too many people die fighting over land. Well, this wasn't going to happen to me, not to Johnny Cobb. Johnny Cobb has the answer! Search for a place where there are no bruises ...and tie it up with a ribbon. And tell yourself that what's inside is the sum total of your life. And what I didn't see was: the day a man decides not to face the world is the day he better step out of it. Now, give me that gun!

Johnny Cobb played by James Stewart and Mr. Whittier played by Dean Jagger: Vincent McEveety's *Firecreek* (Warner Bros.–Seven Arts, 1968).

5501

Silvanito: We spend our time here between funerals and burials.

Stranger: Yeah, I've never saw a town as dead as this one.

Silvanito: You will never see another like it.

Stranger: What's wrong with the place?

Silvanito: We've had too many killings. You have seen the women? None of them are women. They're widows. The place is only widows. Here you can only gain respect by killing other men. So nobody works anymore.

Silvanito played by Pepe Calvo and the Stranger (Joe) played by Clint Eastwood: Sergio Leone's *A Fistful of Dollars* (United Artists, 1964; U.S. 1967).

5502

Stranger: Somebody has to run the place. Every town has a boss.

Silvanito: That's true, but when there are two around, then I would say that there is one too many.

The Stranger (Joe) played by Clint Eastwood and

Silvanito played by Pepe Calvo: Sergio Leone's *A Fistful of Dollars* (United Artists, 1964; U.S. 1967).

5503
Govern: A dead town is a pretty lonesome place.
Govern Sturges played by John Lund: Roger Corman's *Five Guns West* (American Releasing Corp., 1955).

5504
Tarry: I'm not going anywhere. I already got there.
Flaxen Tarry played by Ann Dvorak: Joseph Kane's *Flame of Barbary Coast* (Republic, 1945).

5505
Jessica: This is the last stop, Griff. The frontier is finished. There will be no more towns to break, no more men to break. It's time you started to break yourself. If a town has got to have peace, let somebody else build it on graves. You don't want the only evidence of your life's work to be bullet holes in men.
Jessica Drummond played by Barbara Stanwyck and Griff Bonnell played by Barry Sullivan: Samuel Fuller's *Forty Guns* (20th Century–Fox, 1957).

5506
Earp: Out here in Tombstone, we got a saying: don't play hero unless you got the firepower to back it up. If you don't, you'll just stir up all kind of ruckus. When that happens, I guess he's got to leave whatever he's doing and get things calmed down. Are you with me, son?
Albright: Yes sir. I wasn't trying to be a hero, sir. Earp: Next time, try not to be one even harder.
Wyatt Earp played by Fred Ward and Ernest Albright was played by Judge Reinhold: Piers Haggard's *Four Eyes and Six-Guns* (Turner Pictures, 1992).

5507
Zee: You know, I really think I've grown to like it here in Farmington.
Jesse: Well, the town looks good without gunsmoke in the air.
Zee played by Maria Pitillo and Jesse James played by Rob Lowe: Robert Boris' *Frank & Jesse* (Vidmark Entertainment, 1995).

5508
Stony: What do you think we ought to call it?
Rusty: Oh, it's so slick and pretty. Let's call it New New Hope.
Tucson: That sounds like you're stuttering.
Rusty: Well, they named another town Walla Walla.

Stony: Yeah, and another one Sing Sing.
Stony Brooke played by John Wayne, Rusty Joslin played by Raymond Hatton, and Tucson Smith played by Ray Corrigan: George Sherman's *Frontier Horizon* (a.k.a. *New Frontier*, Republic, 1939).

5509
Jones: There's a lot that goes on around here I'm not in on. That's all right with me. I got a feeling the less I know about what's going on in this town, the better I like living here.
Cash: Pretty good philosophy.
Jones: There comes a time in every man's life, though, when he's either got to be an ostrich or a man.
Cash Blackwell, alias Tex Cameron, played by Victor Mature and Peaceful Jones played by Charles Kemper in Bruce Humberstone's *Fury at Furnace Creek* (20th Century–Fox, 1948).

5510
Brady: One thing I am not is a horse thief. But that buggy looks awfully tempting though.
Burgundy: Brady, can you drive that thing?
Brady: Well, it can only go forward or backwards. Either way, we're out of this town!
Brady Hawkes played by Kenny Rogers and Burgundy Jones played by Reba McEntire: Dick Lowry's *The Gambler Returns: The Luck of the Draw* (TVW, 1991).

5511
Hotel Lady: This is the only one [room] that's unoccupied.

Clayton: Are they all like this?
Hotel Lady: There are others with women, there are others for card games, and this one is for shootin' bullets in. Sleep well.
The Hotel Lady was uncredited and Clayton played by Lee Van Cleef: Giancarlo Santi's *The Grand Duel* (Ital./Fr., 1972).

5512
Jesse: We'll make this smug Yankee town weep or we'll blow it to kingdom come!
Cole: No we ain't either, Jesse. Only a fool smokes up a town when it ain't necessary.
Jesse James played by Robert Duvall and Cole Younger played by Cliff Robertson: Philip Kaufman's *The Great Northfield, Minnesota Raid* (Universal, 1972).

5513
Ahab: Put as much distance between you and town as you can before daylight.
Ahab Jones played by Peter Whitney: Lloyd Bacon's *The Great Sioux Uprising* (Universal, 1953).

5514
Jonathan: You know, I'm kind of glad I found this town. Some of the people are even nicer than the horses.
Jonathan Westgate played by Jeff Chandler: Lloyd Bacon's *The Great Sioux Uprising* (Universal, 1953).

Cash (Victor Mature) rides to clear the name of his father in *Fury at Furnace Creek* (20th Century–Fox, 1948).

5515

Wyatt: There's no place in this town for you, Ike. The next time you ride in armed, you ride out feet first!

Wyatt Earp played by Burt Lancaster and Ike Clanton played by Lyle Bettger: John Sturges' *Gunfight at the O.K. Corral* (Paramount, 1957).

5516

Wyatt: I must go to Tombstone.

Laura: All right, go. Clean up Tombstone. There's a hundred more Tombstones on the frontier all waiting for the great Wyatt Earp. Go on, clean them all up! Go on!

Wyatt Earp played by Burt Lancaster and Laura Denbow played by Rhonda Fleming: John Sturges' *Gunfight at the O.K. Corral* (Paramount, 1957).

5517

Ringo: I'm just a stranger here myself, ma'am. But if you was to ask me, I'd say: hold off for another hour and don't do anything that might make trouble until, say, half past ten. And if he ain't gone by then, then let the Marshal go to work on him.

Pennyfeather: Shoot him down like a dog!

Ringo: Exactly, ma'am.

Pennyfeather: That sounds very sensible. What do you say, ladies?

[*Mrs. Pennyfeather was unaware that Ringo was the person she was addressing.*] Jimmy Ringo played by Gregory Peck and Mrs. Pennyfeather played by Verna Felton: Henry King's *The Gunfighter* (20th Century–Fox, 1950).

5518

Burroughs: You know, folks around here don't take to loggers.

Monty: Now look here, mister. Every place we go people are happy to see us. We spend money like water. Why, we'll put this town on the map.

Burroughs: Or take it off.

Bill Burroughs played by Paul E. Burns and Monty Walker played by Gilbert Roland: Robert D. Webb's *Guns of the Timberland* (Warner Bros., 1960).

5519

Sheriff: This is a peaceful town. Suddenly, you show up …and I got dead men everywhere.

The Sheriff played by Ross Hagen: Jim Wynorski's *Hard Bounty* (Triboro Entertainment, 1995).

5520

Stranger: How long is it gonna take you to get everybody out of your hotel?

Lewis: What?

Stranger: Everybody out. How long is it going to take?

Lewis: Why, I just can't! I mean …I got eight people living in rooms up there: my hotel. Now I just …where are they going to go?

Stranger: Out.

The Stranger played by Clint Eastwood and Lewis Belding played by Ted Hartley: Clint Eastwood's *High Plains Drifter* (Universal, 1973).

5521

Eli: It seems that what hasn't been burned down has been boarded up.

Mayor: Yeah, yeah.

Eli: I hope the church has survived.

Mayor: No, no. The church burned down, ah, about six months ago.

Eli: The church as well?

Mayor: Yeah, yeah.

Eli: Well, perhaps I can speak to your minister.

Mayor: Well, yeah, you probably passed him on your way into town.

Eli: No, all we passed was a little cemetery.

Mayor: Yeah, well, that great big gray tombstone? That was his.

Eli Bloodshy played by Jim Dale and Mayor Ragsdale played by Darren McGavin: Robert Butler's *Hot Lead and Cold Feet* (Buena Vista, 1978).

5522

Townsman: Now it's just a town of gamblin' and gunfightin', hard drinkin', and fast women.

Bloodshy: Sounds pretty good to me!

The Townsman was uncredited and Jasper Bloodshy played by Jim Dale: Robert Butler's *Hot Lead and Cold Feet* (Buena Vista, 1978).

5523

Matt: That's my mother's grave out there, Ruth. I planted them vines on the porch. I'll live here until I die …sooner or later. However, as long as I live, I'll fight the whole town for the right to die here.

Matt Weaver played by George Segal and Ruth Adams played by Janice Rule: Richard Wilson's *Invitation to a Gunfighter* (United Artists, 1964).

5524

Matt: I'm still not standing between you and something you want?

Jules: You're standing between me and the road out of town.

Matt Weaver played by George Segal and Jules Gaspard D'Estaing played by Yul Brynner: Richard Wilson's *Invitation to a Gunfighter* (United Artists, 1964).

5525

Bick: What is a factory?

Reese: Well, a factory is where a lot of people make products. You see, America is growing so fast that we got to make a lot of products for people to buy.

Bick: Well, the people that buy these products, uh, they get the money for making the products, right?

Reese: That's how it works.

Bick: How come these people don't make the products themselves and keep it? And then they won't have to go work in no factory.

Reese: Well, you can't make these products unless you have a factory.

Bickford Wanner, alias Kid Blue, played by Dennis Hopper and Reese Ford played by Warren

Oates: James Frawley's *Kid Blue* (20th Century–Fox, 1973).

5526

Hardin: Well, if you want a domicile in this town, all you got to do is find a house you like, kill whoever is in it, and drag the victim up on a sand hill and the devil pig will do the rest.

John Wesley Hardin played by Randy Quaid: Joseph Sargent's *Larry McMurtry's Streets of Laredo* (Cabin Fever Entertainment, 1995).

5527

Lisa: I hate him, Dan. I wish he was dead. I want him out of this town and out of our lives. I don't care if he goes out breathing or not!

Lisa Denton played by Angie Dickinson: Richard Thorpe's *The Last Challenge* (MGM, 1967).

5528

Riley: I always said you'd bring trouble here. That's the very reason many of us were opposed to your settling in this town from the beginning. Now when a man like Spence takes off a gun, it doesn't mean he loses the reputation or buries the legend. Trash draws flies!

Joe Riley played by Logan Ramsey: Vincent McEveety's *The Last Day* (Paramount, 1975).

5529

Bartender: What will it be, Marshal?

Morgan: Whiskey.

Bartender: Look, Marshal, it's none of my business but I would like to give you a little free advice.

Morgan: Get out of town?

Bartender: That's right.

Morgan: How much [for the whiskey]?

Bartender: It's on the house, just like the advice.

Morgan: Of course, you wouldn't know where to find him.

Bartender: If they were standing right next to you, I wouldn't tell you. I got a family, Marshal.

Morgan: I can understand that. Isn't there anybody in this town that's not afraid of Craig Belden?

Bartender: Sure, the graveyard is full of 'em!

The Bartender played by Val Avery and U.S. Marshal Matt Morgan played by Kirk Douglas: John Sturges' *Last Train from Gun Hill* (Paramount, 1959).

5530

Linda: Why don't you give up?

Morgan: You don't understand me, do you?

Linda: I understand you're going to get yourself killed. You should see those people out there, all lined up and down the street, waiting to see it happen. The human race stinks. I'm practically an authority on that subject.

Linda played by Carolyn Jones and U.S. Marshal Matt Morgan played by Kirk Douglas: John Sturges' *Last Train from Gun Hill* (Paramount, 1959).

5531

Deadwood: Well, it looks like Tombstone is where we're gonna get that lead breakfast.

Deadwood played by Raymond Hatton: Edward L. Cahn's *Law and Order* (Universal, 1932).

5532

Frame: Well, you wanted law and order and you got it. But this isn't the end. After we're gone, there will be other badmen and other towns, breaking the law and totin' guns …unless somebody has got the guts to stop 'em.

Judge: You put an end to gun totin' in Tombstone, Frame.

Frame: Tombstone's only one town.

Frame Johnson played by Walter Huston and Judge R.W. Williams played by Russell Simpson: Edward L. Cahn's *Law and Order* (Universal, 1932).

5533

Calem: This town is like a wild animal in chains, Molly. It doesn't fight back right away. It just lies there and snarls, waiting for a chance to pounce on you.

Marshal Calem Ware played by Randolph Scott and Molly Higgins played by Ruth Donnelly: Joseph H. Lewis' *A Lawless Street* (Columbia, 1955).

5534

Maddox: A man doesn't see many churches like this in a town like Sabbath.

Minister: The shape of the house of God is unimportant.

Maddox: That's not so, minister. The kind of church a man builds to pray in tells you a lot about the man. Further south, there are some fine old adobe churches. Mexican. They are cool and dark inside to give a man peace. They're made for kneeling. This one is made for standing upright.

Minister: There is no easy comfort from God.

Marshal Jared Maddox played by Burt Lancaster and the Minister played by Charles Tyner: Michael Winner's *Lawman* (United Artists, 1971).

5535

Del Rio was a town in trouble, a town with a gun in its back, plagued by crime that just wouldn't stop, and cursed with a sheriff who wore black. So, you'd think they'd be suspicious. But simple folks rarely are.

James Keach was the voice of the Lone Ranger: William A. Fraker's *The Legend of the Lone Ranger* (Universal, 1981).

5536

Gus: Well, if you was a young gal with your whole life before ya, would you want to stay in Lonesome Dove? Now, Maggie done it. Look how long she lasted.

Call: She would have died anywhere. She

just happened to die in Lonesome Dove, that's all.

Gus: My God, Woodrow! You just don't never get the point, do you? It ain't dying I'm talking about! It's living!

Gus McCrae played by Robert Duvall and Captain Woodrow F. Call played by Tommy Lee Jones: Simon Wincer's *Lonesome Dove* (TVW, 1989).

5537

So it wasn't long before a good town went bad. And the richest man in town was the undertaker.

Roger Miller was the voice of the horse, Jolly Jumper,: Terence Hill's *Lucky Luke* (Silvio Berlusconi Communications, 1991).

5538

Cronin: Listen, mister! If you expect to stay in this town, you better learn who's boss!

Mason: Is that so?

Cronin: Yeah. And Boot Hill is full of men who had to have it proved to them.

Sheriff Jud Cronin played by Leon Ames and Cliff Mason played by George O'Brien: David Howard's *The Marshal of Mesa City* (RKO, 1939).

5539

Clementine: I love your town in the morning, Marshal. The air is so clean and clear …the scent of the desert flower.

Wyatt Earp: That's me …barber.

Clementine played by Cathy Downs and Wyatt Earp played by Henry Fonda: John Ford's *My Darling Clementine* (20th Century–Fox, 1946).

5540

Wyatt: Now get out of town …and start wandering!

Wyatt Earp played by Henry Fonda: John Ford's *My Darling Clementine* (20th Century–Fox, 1946).

5541

Folsey: How long should we let Britton stay in town?

Avery: Stay? Oh, let's be generous, fellas. I'd say let him stay, ah, until as long as he lives.

Ed Folsey played by Lane Chandler, Case Britton was played by Jim Davis, and Carl Avery played by Barton MacLane: Edward L. Cahn's *Noose for a Gunman* (United Artists, 1960).

5542

Marshal: Now you just take it real easy when you ride out of town …because there're itchy trigger fingers behind most every door and window.

Marshal Tom Evans played by Walter Sande: Edward L. Cahn's *Noose for a Gunman* (United Artists, 1960).

5543

John: What's your proposition?

McCord: You go right ahead and build your town and attract settlers.

John: So you can take away their money at faro and roulette, hey?

McCord: Yeah, that's the idea. You take care of their virtues, I'll take care of their vices. That's simple, ain't it?

John Kincaid played by Hugh Sothern and Whip McCord played by Humphrey Bogart: Lloyd Bacon's *The Oklahoma Kid* (Warner Bros., 1939).

5544

Barman: You know, I don't think I'd get along in a big city. It's too full of fast men and loose women …begging your pardon, ma'am. Ah, no, now I'm too used to a quiet, simple country life.

The Barman played by Lionel Stander: Sergio Leone's *Once Upon a Time in the West* (Paramount, 1969).

5545

Bartender: Yeah, first the silver run out of the Santa Rio. Then the people run out. Then the whiskey. Then the beer run out. Well, no matter. It's good to see a high roller wander through.

Kelly the Bartender played by Matt Clark: Clint Eastwood's *The Outlaw Josey Wales* (Warner Bros., 1976).

5546

Torrance: This town is on the wrong side of ugly.

Jesse Ray Torrance played by Kris Kristofferson: Bill Corcoran's *Outlaw Justice* (TVW, 1999).

5547

Holden: What are you doing here?

Bryce: Riding through.

Holden: Yeah, well, just keep doing that.

Holden Bonney played by Sancho Gracia and Bryce played by Chad Willett: Bill Corcoran's *Outlaw Justice* (TVW, 1999).

5548

Sam: If the badge won't stop 'em, it's too late for words.

Kate: It'll take strong words from a strong man but it's not too late.

Sam: They found out they can strike fear in the town. The town will have to prove 'em wrong and run 'em out.

Sam Christy played by Jeff Chandler and Kate Miller played by Marsha Hunt: Joseph Pevney's *The Plunderers* (Allied Artists, 1960).

5549

Abilene: You boys won't have no trouble with the town folk. But just don't overlook Captain Sam.

Mule: You mean the cripple?

Abilene: Hold on now! Don't let that bad arm of his fool ya none. Folks around here, they still remember what he done in the war. They can tell ya all about Captain Sam Christy and his raiders. They still talk about him …like he was something not human. Maybe this town ain't got no fight left in it. But sometimes …just a small fire is enough to stir 'em ...to set 'em off. And Sam Christy, he's just liable to be the man to light that fire.

Abilene played by Joseph Hamilton and Mule played by Roger Torrey: Joseph Pevney's *The Plunderers* (Allied Artists, 1960).

5550

Amos: Mighty lovely place, King City. It was named after a poker hand ...where a pair of kings beat a full house.

Alice: How could a pair of kings beat a full house?

Amos: Easy! The fella with a pair of kings pulled a .45!

Amos played by David Wayne and Poker Alice Moffit played by Elizabeth Taylor: Arthur Allan Seidelman's *Poker Alice* (TVW, 1987).

5551

Amos: Now, if you care to sit a spell, I'll take you over to my house ...and I can rent ya a bed for a dollar; if you're hungry, supper will be another dollar; and if you want to wash up, that's fifty cents; and rags to dry with is a quarter.

John: You probably charge for the use of your outhouse!

Amos: Now what kind of a fella do you think I am that would charge ya for the use of his outhouse?

John: Well, something anyway.

Amos: Paper will cost ya fifty cents.

Amos played by David Wayne and John played by George Hamilton: Arthur Allan Seidelman's *Poker Alice* (TVW, 1987).

5552

The majority of black towns were destroyed, partly due to laws like the "Grandfather Clause," which kept African Americans from voting on the basis that their grandfathers as slaves had not voted.

Epilogue: Mario Van Peebles' *Posse* (Gramercy Pictures, 1993).

5553

Blind Boy: John Herod owns that house. He gets fifty cents of every dollar in this town.

Ellen: What does the town get?

Blind Boy: They get to live.

The Blind Boy played by Jerry Swindall and Ellen was played by Sharon Stone: Sam Raimi's *The Quick and the Dead* (Tristar, 1995).

5554

Herod: I'm confused. All I hear from you, you spineless cowards, is how poor you are ...how you can't afford my taxes, my protection. And yet, somehow, you've all managed to find the money to hire a professional gunfighter to kill me. Where is all this money coming from? What am I to think? If you've got so much to spare, I'm just going to have to take some more off you. Because you

clearly haven't gotten the message! This is my town! If you live to see the dawn, it is because I allow it! I'm in charge of everything! I decide who lives or who dies! Your gunfighter is dead! Old news.

John Herod played by Gene Hackman: Sam Raimi's *The Quick and the Dead* (Tristar, 1995).

5555

Markham: It makes you wonder, though, where do they all come from?

Vance: Sometimes that's an unhealthy question to ask.

Markham: Oh, I don't know. It's been a lot quieter so far than we had expected.

Vance: Well, with a mob like this, there'll be a lot of weeding out to do before Guthrie settles down to being a real town.

Colonel Markham played by Kenneth MacDonald and Vance played by Randolph Scott: Ray Enright's *Return of the Badmen* (RKO, 1948).

5556

Kirby: Nice shooting, Bladen.

Bladen: I'm glad you appreciate it, Kirby. Because I'm serving notice I like this town, and I'm not leaving until I'm ready!

Lee Kirby played by John Calvert and Bill Bladen/Durango Kid played by Charles Starrett: Derwin Abrahams' *The Return of the Durango Kid* (Columbia, 1945).

5557

Marshal: Do me a favor, friend. Stay out of Lordsburg. We don't like the smell of gunsmoke.

Marshal Will Parker played by Mort Mills: James Neilson's *Return of the Gunfighter* (TVW, 1966).

5558

Kansas: It seems to me that all cowtowns look alike.

Chito: But all cantinas have the same nice smell!

Kansas played by Tim Holt and Chito Rafferty played by Richard Martin: Lesley Selander's *Riders of the Range* (RKO, 1950).

5559

Flood: Why didn't you just leave town the way you came: in this coach ...tomorrow ...about 9 or 10 o'clock.

Dolan: Whatever is best.

Flood: 9 o'clock. It's earlier.

Alex Flood played by Dean Martin and Dolan played by George Peppard: Arnold Laven's *Rough Night in Jericho* (Universal, 1967).

5560

Rex: Well, the same thing keeps happening in all these towns. The bad guys, who are usually rich for some reason, are always taking advantage of the good guys, who are usually poor. I ride into town, join forces with the good guys to defeat the bad guys, and then I ride out ...over and over. That's my karma, I guess.

Peter: Your what?

Rex: Ah, try to get some sleep, Peter. Tomorrow is the big shootout.

Peter: Okay ...shootout?

Rex O'Herlihan played by Tom Berenger and Peter, the Town Drunk, played by G.W. Bailey: Hugh Wilson's *Rustlers' Rhapsody* (Paramount, 1985).

5561

Starr: This town is full of men who look as if they'd step on baby chicks.

Jeanne Starr played by Alexis Smith: David Butler's *San Antonio* (Warner Bros., 1945).

5562

Jeb: What do you do on Saturday night for fun here?

Kit: Well, as I remember, half of Leavenworth takes a bath and the other half gets drunk. And since there are only two bathtubs in town, things get kind of exciting around midnight.

Jeb Stuart played by Errol Flynn and "Kit Carson" Holliday played by Olivia de Havilland: Michael Curtiz's *Santa Fe Trail* (Warner Bros., 1940).

5563

Joey: Aren't you going to wear your six-shooter, Mr. Shane?

Shane: I didn't know there was any wild game in town, Joey.

Joey Starrett played by Brandon de Wilde and Shane played by Alan Ladd: George Stevens' *Shane* (Paramount, 1953).

5564

Sheriff: How long are you planning to stay?

John: Well, I don't know. I just got here. People usually let you take your hat off before they ask you to leave, Billy.

Sheriff: Well, I'm not asking you to leave, John. I'm just asking how long you figure to stay?

Sheriff Billy Wilson played by Paul Fix and John Elder played by John Wayne: Henry Hathaway's *The Sons of Katie Elder* (Paramount, 1965).

5565

Helen: I'm sure you'll be glad to know that law and order has come to Nome, Ms. Malotte.

Cherry: Yes, it'll be so much easier on the boys if the girls have to turn in their guns.

Helen Chester played by Margaret Lindsay and Cherry Malotte played by Marlene Dietrich: Ray Enright's *The Spoilers* (Universal, 1942).

5566

Mayor: When our town was tough, Horne was the kind of a man we had to have. Now he's too tough for our town.

Mayor Ted Dollar played by Allan Jones and Sheriff Horne played by Barry Sullivan: William F. Claxton's *Stage to Thunder Rock* (Paramount, 1964).

5567

Sheriff: Mike, I want to tell you something. This town is gonna bust wide open. You can tell it. Just like when you know a norther is kicking up.

Mike: It's a small town. When it rains, everybody gets wet.

Sheriff Ball played by Johnny Mack Brown and Mike played by Rod Cameron: Lesley Selander's *Stampede* (Warner Bros., 1949).

5568

Jeff: Kind of wild.

Jake: No, this is tame. Only one killing last week.

Jeff: Not too bad.

Jake: Well, that ain't good. They moved the State Capitol out today. There ain't no place for an honest man now.

Jeff: Then why do you stay here?

Jake: Oh, it comes to be known that you live in a town that can't get no worse.

Jeff Travis played by Randolph Scott and Jake Hooper played by Roscoe Ates: Andre De Toth's *The Stranger Wore a Gun* (Columbia, 1953).

5569

Prudy: What is the matter with all of you? Don't you remember how long we waited to find the man who would stand up to the Danbys? Don't you remember what this town was like before: murderers, lynching, miners shooting up the town day and night?

Fred: And aside from the few things that you mentioned, it wasn't a bad place at all!

Prudy Perkins played by Joan Hackett and Fred Johnson played by Walter Burke: Burt Kennedy's *Support Your Local Sheriff!* (United Artists, 1969).

5570

Corinne: Why the back door?

Stewart: I wanted to see the town before it saw me.

Corinne Michaels played by Jocelyn Brando and John Stewart played by Randolph Scott: Bruce Humberstone's *Ten Wanted Men* (Columbia, 1955).

5571

Jamerson: I'm not going to sit by and see this town get a reputation like Dodge City. Once we get known as a wide-open town, we'll have every gunmen, every card sharp, every piece of riffraff that can't light anywhere else moving in on us.

Henry Jamerson played by Royal Dano: Charles Marquis Warren's *Tension at Table Rock* (RKO, 1956).

5572

Luke: Dave, drag the bodies out of the street. It might give the place a bad name.

Luke Starr played by Broderick Crawford: Lesley Selander's *The Texican* (Columbia, 1966).

5573

Jess: I just don't know, Sandy. Maybe I got this whole thing figured wrong. I can't find out any information, and I can't go shooting up the town until I do.

Jess Carlin played by Audie Murphy and Sandy Adams played by Luz Marquez: Lesley Selander's *The Texican* (Columbia, 1966).

5574

Sandy: Rimrock? Mister, that's the last place you ought to be heading. Anybody who loses his saddle in open country is sure to lose his hide in Rimrock.

Sandy Adams played by Luz Marquez: Lesley Selander's *The Texican* (Columbia, 1966).

5575

Dan: The town drunk gave his life because he believed the people should be able to live in decency and peace together. Do you think I could do less?

Dan Evans played by Van Heflin: Delmer Daves' *3:10 to Yuma* (Columbia, 1957).

5576

Stony: What happened to you? Did you fall into a watering trough?

Lullaby: No, I just fell into a Saturday night!

Stony Brooke played by John Wayne and Lullaby Joslin played by Max Terhune: George Sherman's *Three Texas Steers* (Republic, 1939).

5577

Fifteen years widened trails into flourishing towns — and with them prospered good and bad alike.

Caption: Charles Barton's *Thunder Trail* (a.k.a. *Thunder Pass*; Paramount, 1937).

5578

Rosser: Well, I tamed a lot of towns, Mr. Fell. But this will be the first time I've had to go against a lawless element and a law. I always had the town behind me …and I wore a badge.

Fell: Great Plains is becoming known as a town where they kill a man every hour on the hour.

Tom Rosser played by Dana Andrews and James Fenimore Fell played by Barton MacLane: Lesley Selander's *Town Tamer* (Paramount, 1965).

5579

Masterson: This town might prove interesting.

Billy: Interesting? Well, if you find murder, robbers, and cattle rustlers interesting, you're gonna enjoy yourself here!

Bat Masterson played by Randolph Scott and Billy Burns played by George "Gabby" Hayes: Ray Enright's *Trail Street* (RKO, 1947).

5580

Dave: Hi, Mayor. Where is everybody? The town is so quiet you can hear your hair grow.

Dave played by Forrest Taylor and the Mayor played by Harry Harvey: Ray Enright's *Trail Street* (RKO, 1947).

5581

Harper: I hope that's the last of 'em.

Billy: Well, it ain't. I'm betting before you know it, this town will be hotter than a two-dollar pistol on the Fourth of July.

Allen Harper played by Robert Ryan and Billy Burns was played by George "Gabby" Hayes: Ray Enright's *Trail Street* (RKO, 1947).

5582

Virginia City, Nevada. Home of the fabulous Comstock Mines. "The richest, roughest town" on the face of the earth.

Caption: Michael Curtiz's *Virginia City* (Warner Bros., 1940).

5583

Jessie: Is this superhuman going to subdue the savage beast by the pure power of his eye, or by the menace of his six-shooter, or simply by his reputation?

Skinner: None of those, Miss Jessie. Blaisdell's only hope in Warlock is to be lead proof.

Jessie Marlow played by Dolores Michaels and Skinner played by Regis Toomey: Edward Dmytryk's *Warlock* (20th Century–Fox, 1959).

5584

Gannon: You can't stay here. Trouble and death follow you. Warlock has had enough of both.

Deputy Johnny Gannon played by Richard Widmark: Edward Dmytryk's *Warlock* (20th Century–Fox, 1959).

5585

Blue: Good morning.

Brown: Good morning.

Blue: What can we do for you?

Brown: It's the other way around. The name's Brown …from the Governor's office. Every time somebody puts a little capital into this territory, I'm called into the office and sent on my way. It don't make no difference that I suffer from rheumatism, or that I'm past the age to ride a mule back. A man who files a claim that yields, it's a town. If he finds grass, it's a town. If he digs a well, it's a town. And I have to charter them all. If the claim pitches out, the grass dies, the well dries out, everybody rides off to form up again. New territory for me to travel. Nobody fixes in this country. Everybody is blowing around with the wind. You can't bring law to a bunch of rocks. You can't make a society out of sand. Sometimes I think we're worse than the Indians. What's the name of this town?

Blue: Hard Times.

Brown: Now, you going to have to have a peace officer. You there!

Jenks: Me?

Brown: Yeah, you're the only one carrying a gun. You ever kill a man?

Jenks: Well, yes sir, I reckon I did.

Brown: Good. Here, pin that on [badge].

You are hereby sworn a Deputy Sheriff. Your salary is $25.00 a year, payable next year. Now, you'll take up a collection and build a jail. If you get a serious outlaw that ain't dead, write a letter to the capital and we'll put a circuit judge on ya. So here's the town charter, the census list forms, and a petition for statehood. Get people to sign that when you ain't busy.
Jenks: Huh …but …sir, I can't read nor write!
Brown: How about you? Can you read and write?
Jenks: Sure, he's a lawyer!
Will Blue played by Henry Fonda, Brown played by Edgar Buchanan, and Jenks played by Warren Oates: Burt Kennedy's *Welcome to Hard Times* (MGM, 1967).

5586
Zar: Ghost towns always have names full of promise. You better not let that happen when they name our town.
Blue: We'll call it what we have always called it …Hard Times.
Zar played by Keenan Wynn and Will Blue played by Henry Fonda: Burt Kennedy's *Welcome to Hard Times* (MGM, 1967).

5587
Man at Livery Stable: What do want to go to Guthrie for?

Tod Jackson: Well, I got business …
Man at Livery Stable: I wouldn't be hung in that town. I got drunk there once with an Indian and the next day I had smallpox!
The Man at Livery Stable played by Edgar Buchanan and Tod Jackson played by Randolph Scott: George Marshall's *When the Daltons Rode* (Universal, 1940).

5588
Boone: One time in Denver I ate in this restaurant that had a sign on the wall: watch your hat and coat. While I was watching 'em, somebody stole my steak!
Boone played by Jack Elam: Burt Kennedy's *Where the Hell's That Gold?!!!* (a.k.a. *Dynamite & Gold*; TVW, 1988).

5589
Johnny: Why don't you get the good citizens of the town to help you out?
Sheriff: When trouble breaks out, they're kind of hard to find.
Johnny Moon played by William Shatner and Sheriff Logan played by Joseph Cotten: Gilbert Lee Kay's *White Comanche* (International Producers Corp., 1967).

5590
Charlie: This town, I really think it's like something out of the Bible.

Wild Bill: What part of the Bible?
Charlie: The part right before God gets angry.
Charlie Prince played by John Hurt and Wild Bill Hickok played by Jeff Bridges: Walter Hill's *Wild Bill* (MGM/United Artists, 1995).

5591
Charlie: Like a city in the Old Testament, Deadwood had become a place of prophecy and vision.
Charlie Prince played by John Hurt: Walter Hill's *Wild Bill* (MGM/United Artists, 1995).

5592
Crazy Lee: They're blowing this town all to hell!
Crazy Lee played by Bo Hopkins: Sam Peckinpah's *The Wild Bunch* (Warner Bros.–Seven Arts, 1969).

5593
Thornton: What's in Agua Verde?
Coffer: Mexicans! What else?
Deke Thornton played by Robert Ryan and Coffer played by Strother Martin: Sam Peckinpah's *The Wild Bunch* (Warner Bros.–Seven Arts, 1969).

5594
Rocky: Hey, strangers! Was that you I heard shootin'?

Pike Bishop (William Holden) said, "when you side with a man, you stay with him." In this scene, comrades Tector Gorch (Ben Johnson), Lyle Gorch (Warren Oates), and Dutch Engstrom (Ernest Borgnine) join Pike in an attempt to rescue another member of *The Wild Bunch* (Warner Bros.–Seven Arts, 1969) in Sam Peckinpah's classic western.

Blair: Sure. What of it?

Rocky: As Sheriff, I could arrest you for that …but as Mayor, I welcome you to Crescent City. As President of the Council, I gave myself the afternoon off.

Rocky O'Brien played by Lew Kelly and John Blair played by John Wayne: Mack V. Wright's *Winds of the Wasteland* (Republic, 1936).

5595

Ben: What can I do for you, Mr. Behan?

Behan: I'll come straight to the point. This town isn't ready for wide sidewalks or church suppers …yet. In short, it isn't ready for law.

Ben Kane played by Robert Mitchum and John Behan played by Jack Kelly: Burt Kennedy's *Young Billy Young* (United Artists, 1969).

5596

Behan: Look, Kane, there are only two sides of the street in this town. If you're smart, you'll walk on the right one. Do you follow me?

Kane: Not very far.

John Behan played by Jack Kelly and Ben Kane played by Robert Mitchum: Burt Kennedy's *Young Billy Young* (United Artists, 1969).

West

See also People; Towns

5597

Sam: This is a great country! Why, as far as the eye can see, there ain't nothin' but country! And someday, there's gonna be more country! That's the kind of guy I am …a country guy!

Sam Spade played by Richard Pryor: Fred Williamson's *Adios Amigo* (Atlas, 1975).

5598

Farmer: Boys, it is hell on wheels. The worst damn idea in the world is to go west.

Jake: Oh, come on now.

Farmer: No, I ain't lying to you, son. We tried farming the first year and a twister wiped us out. Next year it was the cattlemen, then just pure–D rotten soil. There ain't nobody got no money excepting a few. And even if you do have, there ain't a thing worth having. It rains so much it will give ya the chilblains. A dry spell come along and you choke to death on the dust. That is if a bushwhacker don't come along and take your last damn dollar. No, I mean it boys, turn around and go on back!

The Farmer played by Charles Tyner and Jake Rumsey played by Jeff Bridges: Robert Benton's *Bad Company* (Paramount, 1972).

5599

Smith: Somebody is always looking for something in this part of the west. To the historians, it's the old west. To the book writer, it's the wild west. To the businessman, it's the undeveloped west. They say we're all poor and backward, and I guess we are. We don't even have enough water. But to us, this place is our west, and I wish they would leave us alone.

Reno Smith played by Robert Ryan: John Sturges' *Bad Day at Black Rock* (MGM, 1955).

5600

Chile: Out here we don't pry into anybody's affairs. It just ain't healthy.

Mulford: Well, if my health isn't threatened by anything more dangerous than you, I won't worry much.

Chile "Chick" Lyman played by Noah Beery Jr., and Mulford played by Douglas Walton: Lew Landers' *Bad Lands* (RKO, 1939).

5601

Rayburn: You know, when I first came out west, I heard it was a pretty dangerous place. I figured if a man took chances, he wouldn't last very long. But the more chances I took, the safer I got.

Sheriff: You know, Rayburn, I always had an idea you were a man trying to commit suicide.

Rayburn played by Addison Richards and Sheriff Bill Cummings played by Robert Barrat: Lew Landers' *Bad Lands* (RKO, 1939).

5602

Mulford: Hey, Sweet, what are the dragoons?

Sweet: For a veteran plainsman, you ain't very smart, are you?

Mulford: Oh, I've never been this far west.

Sweet: Well, they're sort of a practicing ground for the hereafter. They're supposed to be mountains, but they're really the wrong place turned inside out.

Mulford played by Douglas Walton and Billy Sweet played by Guinn "Big Boy" Williams: Lew Landers' *Bad Lands* (RKO, 1939).

5603

Rogers: Well, out here if it crawls, it'll bite ya …if it flies, it'll sting ya …and if it grows, it'll stick ya!

Captain Rogers played by Brion James: Robert M. Young's *The Ballad of Gregorio Cortez* (Embassy Pictures, 1983).

5604

Jeremy: Good country, Glyn.

Glyn: Yeah, real good country.

Jeremy: Let's hope we can keep it this way. Missouri and Kansas was like this when I first saw 'em …good, clean. It was the men who came in to steal and kill that changed things. We mustn't let it happen here.

Jeremy Baile played by Jay C. Flippen and Glyn McLyntock played by James Stewart: Anthony Mann's *Bend of the River* (Universal, 1952).

5605

McKay: If it's a fight you want, you've picked the right time for it …[*lady friend present*] …haven't you?

Leech: Yeah, I'm offering you a fight. Or ain't that a nice word back east?

McKay: You're gambling, Leech. You're gambling that if we fight, you can beat me. And you're gambling that if you beat me, Ms. Terrill will admire you for it.

Leech: Out here we leave a lady's name out of an argument.

Jim McKay played by Gregory Peck and Steve Leech played by Charlton Heston: William Wyler's *The Big Country* (United Artists, 1958).

5606

Deakins: Sure is big country. The only thing bigger is the sky.

Jim Deakins played by Kirk Douglas: Howard Hawks' *The Big Sky* (Winchester/RKO, 1952).

5607

Copeland: You know when I first came out here, the Indians was in the thousands. And the buffalo? They was in the millions. Not no more. In the beginning it was a good life. You could stand in one spot and see the same herd of buffalo go by all day long. I never saw nothing like it. It was just like the whole prairie was moving.

Copeland played by David Huddleston: Ted Kotcheff's *Billy Two Hats* (United Artists, 1973).

5608

Marshal: What's out there?

Copeland: Oh, just a lot of nothing.

Marshal Henry Gifford played by Jack Warden and Copeland played by David Huddleston: Ted Kotcheff's *Billy Two Hats* (United Artists, 1973).

5609

Jones: For a family who don't know a jackass from a mule, you sure know a lot about the west.

Gebhardt: We don't have to know about it. We …ah …we own it!

Miss Jones played by Candice Bergen and Gebhardt played by Dabney Coleman: Richard Brooks' *Bite the Bullet* (Columbia, 1975).

5610

Brandy: Something has been bothering me lately.

Lance: What's that?

Brandy: We've been run out of Kansas, Nevada, Texas, and New Mexico, and Arizona. What do we do when we run out of places?

Lance: Move further west.

Brandy: There's an ocean around here someplace.

Lance: We could start back in Kansas again. They must have a new sheriff by this time.

Jersey Brady played by Percy Kilbride and Lance Hardeen played by Jeffrey Lynn: George Sherman's *Black Bart* (Universal, 1948). *See also entry 5726.*

5611

Benj: It's a new country, a new world. Everything's changing.

Bronc: Change, just for the sake of it, ain't always good.

Benj Cartwright played by Michael Landon, Jr., and Bronc Evans played by Ben Johnson: Jerry Jameson's *Bonanza: The Return* (TVW, 1993).

5612

Tim: You can call me Missouri

Doc: Oh, Missouri! Well, that's my home state. What part are you from?

Tim: If you're from Missouri, you don't have to ask any questions about it.

Tim Ross played by Tim McCoy and Doc Shaw played by Earl Hodgins: Sam Newfield's *Border Caballero* (Puritan Pictures, 1936).

5613

Maverick: What's she doing out here?

Guthrie: I made the mistake of telling her she couldn't come.

Bret Maverick played by James Garner and Sheriff Tom Guthrie played by Ed Bruce: Stuart Margolin's *Bret Maverick: The Lazy Ace* (TVW, 1981).

5614

Running Water: Do you understand what Bronco Billy and the wild west show are all about? You can be anything you want. All you have to do is go out and become it!

Lorraine Running Water played by Sierra Pecheur and Bronco Billy played by Clint Eastwood who also directed *Bronco Billy* (Warner Bros., 1980).

5615

Pecos: There ain't no place like West Texas.

Buchanan: Then how come you're in California?

Pecos: Oh, I fiddle-footed. This country is so dang big, a man just itches to move around it. One day I got tired of watching the sun go west and I just followed it on out here. But I ain't itchin' no more. Before long I'll follow that sun right on back to where I come from.

Pecos Bill played by L.Q. Jones and Tom Buchanan played by Randolph Scott: Budd Boetticher's *Buchanan Rides Alone* (Columbia, 1958).

5616

Buck: Which way are you ridin', Preacher?

Preacher: Well, that's not exactly settled in my mind yet.

Buck: Well, you got about three possibilities.

Preacher: Oh?

Buck: North, south, or east.

Preacher: What happened to west?

Buck: We're going west.

The Preacher played by Harry Belafonte and Buck played by Sidney Poitier who also directed *Buck and the Preacher* (Columbia, 1972).

5617

Phil: Going somewhere?

Jack: Listen, Phil, there's a train leaving for the east tonight. I'm going to be on it if I have to sit on the engineer's lap.

Phil: Well, we just got here. You know what Brenda said …this place grows on ya.

Jack: Well, it'll have to grow on somebody else!

Phil played by Phil Harris and Jack played by Jack Benny: Mark Sandrich's *Buck Benny Rides Again* (Paramount, 1940).

5618

Pokey: I thought this was God's country?

Pike: Not no more it ain't!

Pokey played by James Burke and Pike played by Albert Dekker: John Farrow's *California* (Paramount, 1946).

5619

Chuck: Boy! What a place to be a cowboy!

The young lad, Chuck, played by Richard Eyer: Harmon Jones' *Canyon River* (Allied Artists, 1956).

5620

Kid: Yeah, it's all over in Dodge. Tombstone, too. Cheyenne, Deadwood, all gone, all dead and gone. Why, the last time I came through Tombstone, the big excitement there was about the new rollerskate rink that they had laid out over the O.K. Corral. I'll tell you something else. I used to work for the Buffalo Bill Wild West Show and a Congress Of Rough Riders. And I rescued many

stagecoach passengers from road agents and drunkard injuns …in the nick of time! Twice a day, three times on Saturday!

Kid Sheleen played by Lee Marvin: Elliot Silverstein's *Cat Ballou* (Columbia, 1965).

5621

Joshua: All we got here is a handful of nothing …dirt and dry mouths.

Joshua Everette played by James Whitmore: Michael Winner's *Chato's Land* (United Artists, 1972).

5622

Quincey: To you, this is so much badland: rock, scrub, desert, and then more rock. A hard land that the sun has sucked all the good out of. You can't farm it and you can't carve it out and call it your own …so you damn it to hell and it all looks the same. That's our way. To the breed, now, it's his land. He don't expect it to give him much and he don't force it none. And to him, it's almost human …a living active thing. And it will give him a good place to make his fight against us.

Quincey Whitmore played by Jack Palance and the breed, Chato, played by Charles Bronson: Michael Winner's *Chato's Land* (United Artsits, 1972).

5623

Bud: Hey, now you boys be careful! Turn your boots upside down at night, and watch where you step …and watch where you squat!

Bud played by Pruitt Taylor Vince: Paul Weiland's *City Slickers II: The Legend of Curly's Gold* (Columbia, 1994).

5624

Glen: All right, now, the sun sets in the east, right?

Mitch: No, the sun sets in the west!

Glen: That's if you're in the east. But we are way out west now, so we are past where the sun sets.

Mitch: You can't be past where the sun sets. And if you think you can, then I'm directly south of an idiot!

Glen Robbins played by Jon Lovitz and Mitch Robbins played by Billy Crystal: Paul Weiland's *City Slickers II: The Legend of Curly's Gold* (Columbia, 1994).

5625

Gabby: You know, the further west you go, the more dangerous it gets.

Gabby Whittaker played by George "Gabby" Hayes: Joseph Kane's *Colorado* (Republic, 1940).

5626

Winslow: Look at that, Julie Ann! You can see all the way into the middle of next week. A new world will be going in …that's what it is …and a start of a new life.

Fred Winslow played by Henry Hull and Julie Ann Winslow played by Dorothy Malone: Raoul Walsh's *Colorado Territory* (Warner Bros., 1949).

5627

Winslow: Are you new to this land, Mr. Rogers? The Promised Land, that's what it is. My father used to say: the sun travels west …and so does opportunity.

Fred Winslow played by Henry Hull. Wes McQueen, who was going under the alias Chet Rogers, played by Joel McCrea: Raoul Walsh's *Colorado Territory* (Warner Bros., 1949).

5628

Winslow: My boy, never buy a foot of land more than five miles from home. And not then until you've seen it, felt it, tasted it, and smelled it. And at that, you still might get bamboozled.

Fred Winslow played by Henry Hull: Raoul Walsh's *Colorado Territory* (Warner Bros., 1949).

5629

Julie Ann: Did you ever think you'd like to travel a long way off …as far and as high as the moon …forever …and stay there for good …and forget all about things down here?

Rogers: There's been plenty of times I wanted to get away from where I was.

Julie Ann: That far away?

Rogers: Yeah, that far.

Julie Ann: You never talk about yourself. I don't know anything about you at all.

Rogers: There's nothing to tell. Like you said, wanting to get far off from what you've been. This is far off.

Julie Ann Winslow played by Dorothy Malone. Wes McQueen, going under the alias Chet Rogers, played by Joel McCrea: Raoul Walsh's *Colorado Territory* (Warner Bros., 1949).

5630

Read: This is a good place.

Chief: Yes. We live here like our fathers before us and their fathers before them. We were born here …where the wind blows free and there is nothing to break the light of the sun. There are no enclosures and everyone draws a free breath.

Jim Read played by Dana Andrews and Chief Quanah Parker played by Kent Smith: George Sherman's *Comanche* (United Artists, 1956).

5631

Evie: You don't know what music is until you hear the wind in the cedars.

Evie Teele played by Katharine Ross: Reynaldo Villalobos' *Conagher* (Turner Pictures, 1991).

5632

Devlin: And speaking of politics, where we're going, there are only two parties: the quick and the dead.

John Devlin played by John Wayne: Joseph Kane's *Dakota* (Republic, 1945).

5633

Tonia: Do you know what Texas means? It's an Indian word for friends. It's a big land with room for everyone. And you could be a part of it in time.

Tonia Robles played by Ruth Roman: Stuart Heisler's *Dallas* (Warner Bros., 1950).

5634

Johnny: It's a long way to come to go back where you was.

Johnny was uncredited: Yves Simoneau's *Dead Man's Walk* (Cabin Fever Entertainment, 1996).

5635

Gale: Hey! Aren't you taking the wrong trail?

Mortimer: All trails lead out of these mountains, and right now that's my life's ambition!

Gale played by Tom Keene and Fordyce Mortimer played by Robert Cummings: James Hogan's *Desert Gold* (Paramount, 1936).

5636

Wade: William Shakespeare.

Rusty: I never heard of him. What part of Texas is he from?

Wade Hatton played by Errol Flynn and Rusty Hart played by Alan Hale: Michael Curtiz's *Dodge City* (Warner Bros., 1939).

5637

Tex: I decided to go back to Texas.

Rusty: What for?

Tex: Oh, I don't know. This place is getting too big and calm and peaceful like.

Tex Baird played by Guinn "Big Boy" Williams and Rusty Hart played by Alan Hale: Michael Curtiz's *Dodge City* (Warner Bros., 1939).

5638

Mrs. Printess: I'm so thrilled. I've never been in the west before. It's so big!

Roy Rogers: Yes, it runs all the way to the east, ma'am.

Mrs. Printess: It does?

Mrs. Printess played by Lucille Gleason and Roy Rogers played himself: John English's *Don't Fence Me In* (Republic, 1945).

5639

Van Leek: You can't ride, you can't shoot. You can't even think, boy. You're in the wrong territory!

Thomas Van Leek played by Louis Gossett, Jr.: Peter Markle's *El Diablo* (HBO Pictures, 1990).

5640

Pesky: I don't see nothin' …but nothin'. And there's plenty of that!

Pesky played by George "Gabby" Hayes: Lewis Foster's *El Paso* (Paramount, 1949).

5641

Carla: It's so quiet.

Roper: Yes, isn't it?

Carla: So completely quiet.

Roper: That's the wonderful thing about this country. Everything about it is so complete.

Carla: That's the way you want to live, isn't it? Everything complete.

Roper: Why settle for anything less?

Carla Forester played by Eleanor Parker and Captain Roper played by William Holden: John Sturges' *Escape from Fort Bravo* (MGM, 1953).

5642

Paul: For every living creature, there is a moment when reason and instinct come together and work in perfect harmony. And such a moment brings pure happiness.

Paul Weyman played by Jeff Fahey: Arnaud Selignac's *Eye of the Wolf* (Trimark Pictures/Vidmark Entertainment, 1995).

5643

Lunsford: If you own Texas, you can buy the rest.

Blair Lunsford played by David Brian: Edwin Marin's *Fort Worth* (Warner Bros., 1951).

5644

Boy: Where do you suppose everyone is?

Buck: I don't know and I don't care …as long as they stay there.

The Boy played by Damon Douglas and Buck Bowers played by Douglas V. Fowley: Frank D. Gilroy's *From Noon Till Three* (United Artists, 1976).

5645

Gatewood: We're trying to make a country here. It's hard.

Lt. Charles Gatewood played by Jason Patric: Walter Hill's *Geronimo: An American Legend* (Columbia, 1993).

5646

Joe: Rusty, I don't like the west. All that people do is kill each other. I would like the west better if it was in the east. Let's get out of here!

Joe Panello played by Chico Marx and Rusty Panello played by Harpo Marx: Edward Buzzell's *Go West* (MGM, 1940).

5647

Henry: I like it down there: Mexico. The pace suits me better …slow days and fast nights.

Henry Moon played by Jack Nicholson who also directed *Goin' South* (Paramount, 1978).

5648

Jason: I've seen a lot of it.

Britt: What's that?

Jason: Hard times. This wild country can turn good men into bad.

Jason played by Alan Shearman and Britt Johnson played by Tony Todd: Steven H. Stern's *Good Men and Bad* (TV miniseries, Cabin Fever Entertainment, 1995).

5649

Cotton: This world is moving faster all the time. You either go along with it or you get left behind. I'm going to be part of it. I'm going to help build it.

Hewey: Well, I hope you like it when you get it finished.

Cotton Calloway played by Matt Damon and Hewey Calloway played by Tommy Lee Jones who also directed *The Good Old Boys* (Turner Pictures, 1995).

5650

Undertaker: Nobody wants to work out in the west at all. There's only killin', drinkin', and playin' poker.

The Undertaker was uncredited: Giancarlo Santi's *The Grand Duel* (Ital./Fr., 1972).

5651

Sam: I've been shot five times, knifed twice, bitten in the ass by a pig's snout, stomped by a horse, and sat on by a mule. Why, once in the winter of '81, a grizzly chewed my big toe off. And I survived two avalanches, three blizzards, five Indian surprises, and seven presidential elections. But I ain't never been owned by no woman nor dog. And I've come too far down the road to let it happen to me now.

Sam Longwood played by Lee Marvin: Don Taylor's *The Great Scout and Cathouse Thursday* (American International, 1976).

5652

Yellowstone: All that is behind you now. Leave it that way. I never believed in carrying shadows into new territory.

Yellowstone Kelly played by Walter Sande: Sidney Salkow's *Gun Brothers* (United Artists, 1956).

5653

Rose: So there they are!

Chad: Yeah, the Grand Teton.

Rose: There can't be anything evil out there.

Chad: I hate to spoil your pretty picture, Rose, but some of the toughest outlaws in the west have made Jackson Hole their hideout for years.

Rose Fargo played by Ann Robinson and Chad Santee played by Buster Crabbe: Sidney Salkow's *Gun Brothers* (United Artists, 1956).

5654

Reb: The last time I saw you, you was down in Denver. Why did you leave.

Cora: Why did you?

Reb: I had a reason.

Cora: You had twelve reasons …each one 'em had a gun in his hand. I understand you got run out of Wyoming too.

Reb: Yeah.

Cora: Well, you've got a pretty good record. Texas, Arizona, Colorado, Wyoming.

Reb: I'm young yet.

Cora: You've run out of states too.

Reb: I understand there's lot of room left in Canada.

Reb Kittredge played by Audie Murphy and Cora DuFrayne played by Mary Castle: Nathan Juran's *Gunsmoke* (Universal, 1953).

5655

Captain: The west is no life for a woman.

Colonel: The west is no life for anyone. Wind, dust, Indians. I hate the wind! I hate the dust! And I hate the Indians!

Captain Paul Slater played by Jim Hutton and Colonel Thadeus Gearhart played by Burt Lancaster: John Sturges' *The Hallelujah Trail* (MGM, 1965).

5656

Billy: Son-of-a-bitch has always been a favorite expression in this country.

Billy Irvine played by John Hurt: Michael Cimino's *Heaven's Gate* (United Artists, 1980).

5657

Janet: I used to love this country. Now it seems so ugly.

Clay: It's not the country. It's some of the people who live in it.

Janet played by Felicia Farr and Clay Santell played by Audie Murphy: George Sherman's *Hell Bent for Leather* (Universal, 1960).

5658

Ira: What's the matter, boy?

Dan: I don't know. It seems kind of quiet around here.

Martha: Well, Texas is a mighty big country, son. Sound kind of gets lost in it.

Ira Hammond played by John McIntire, Dan Hammond played by Robert Ryan, and Martha Hammond played by Frances Baver: Budd Boetticher's *Horizons West* (Universal, 1952).

5659

Homer: Little by little, the look of the country changes because of the men we admire.

Homer Bannon played by Melvyn Douglas: Martin Ritt's *Hud* (Paramount, 1963).

5660

Chandler: Well, Miller certainly picked a God-forsaken country to lose himself in.

Chandler played by Kenneth Thomson and Charles Miller played by H.B. Warner: David Howard's *In Old Santa Fe* (Mascot, 1934).

5661

Briggs: I'm going to photograph the whole wild west.

Hawks: Why?

Briggs: I want everyone to see it.

Hawks: Why?

Briggs: When they see it, they'll come out here …thousands of 'em. Isn't that reason enough?

Hawks: That's reason enough to bust that camera over your head!

Briggs: Why? Don't you want to open up the west to civilization?

Hawks: Come here. Maybe you won't understand this. To me, the west is like a beautiful woman. My woman. I like her the way she is, I don't want her changed. I'm jealous. I don't want to share her with anybody. I'd hate to see her civilized.

Briggs played by Elisha Cook, Jr., and Johnny Hawks played by Kirk Douglas: Andrew De Toth's *The Indian Fighter* (United Artists, 1955).

5662

Barston: Back in the days of the old west, there were these stretches of territory that I think God and nature just plain forgot about …dark and parched and empty as all the moons of Mars. Places where sensible men never ventured …where only dreams and phantoms walked. Kind of these way-stations somewhere smack between civilization and the ninth circle of hell …the Badlands.

Barston played by Bruce Dern: Sam Pillsbury's *Into the Badlands* (TVW, 1991).

5663

Narrator: Texas territory. A big land encompassing 360,000 square miles. Bigger than the thirteen colonies combined. In 1821, it was known as Tehas and its inhabitants were known as Texians. This is the story of their fight for freedom. This is the story of Texas.

Narration by Charlton Heston: Richard Lang's *James A. Michener's Texas* (TVW, 1995).

5664

Finley: There's nothing out there.

Bowie: There's land and freedom.

Finley: A land without law is a land for the lawless.

Finley MacNab played by Daragh O'Malley and Jim Bowie played by David Keith: Richard Lang's *James A. Michener's Texas* (TVW, 1995).

5665

Clooney: I've found that a man can very often hear what he wants to hear in Texas.

Father Clooney played by Morgan Redmond: Richard Lang's *James A. Michener's Texas* (TVW, 1995).

5666

Roy: Look at this land. It's big and it's tough. The tougher the land, the bigger the man that works it. That's what makes it special.

Roy played by John Marley: Jorge Fons' *Jory* (Avco Embassy, 1972).

5667

Gernet: You know, people out here have a sort of code. They never ask questions about one's past.

Gernet Hale played by Joan Leslie: Joseph Kane's *Jubilee Trail* (Republic, 1954).

5668

Curly: You may not know it, but you are in the right place and at the right time. That's here!

Curly Bonner played by Joe Don Baker: Sam Peckinpah's *Junior Bonner* (CIN, 1972).

5669

Big Eli: And when you take a breath, it's got a clean taste to it, like nobody never used it before.

Big Eli Wakefield played by Burt Lancaster who also directed *The Kentuckian* (United Artists, 1955).

5670

Babson: You don't measure land in Texas by rod and chain. You measure by the eye. And when the eye can see no further, that's where you drive your stake. The rifle ball has not been made that can carry to a neighbor's line.

Babson played by John Litel: Burt Lancaster's *The Kentuckian* (United Artists, 1955).

There was never a dull moment scouting for a wagon train going through Indian territory for Johnny Hawks (Kirk Douglas) in Andre de Toth's *The Indian Fighter* (United Artists, 1955).

5671

Bridger: I'm going to move where a man can have a little peace and quiet. It used to be when a man heard a horse and hoofs in this country, he cocked his rifle. Now all it means is more people.

Jim Bridger played by Raymond Hatton: George B. Seitz's *Kit Carson* (United Artists, 1940).

5672

Brookshire: I'm afraid I'll blow away ...like a tumbleweed.

Ned Brookshire played by Charles Martin Smith: Joseph Sargent's *Larry McMurtry's Streets of Laredo* (Cabin Fever Entertainment, 1995).

5673

Brookshire: How far is it back?
Pea Eye: Back to where?
Brookshire: Back to where it's not like this!

Ned Brookshire played by Charles Martin Smith and Pea Eye Parker played by Sam Shepard: Joseph Sargent's *Larry McMurtry's Streets of Laredo* (Cabin Fever Entertainment, 1995).

5674

Frank: You know, that's the real west out there. You know, gold mines are all right. But if this country is going to set-tle up, people have got to plow and plant and make homes.

Frank Plummer, alias Frank Norris, played by William Elliott: Joseph Kane's *The Last Bandit* (Republic, 1949).

5675

Sheriff: Hell, there's places out there that hasn't ever seen a footprint!

Sheriff Deegan played by Kurtwood Smith: Tab Murphy's *Last of the Dogmen* (Savory Pictures, 1995).

5676

Heyward: There is a war on. How is it you are heading west?
Hawkeye: Well, we kind of faced to the north and real sudden like turned left.

Major Heyward played by Steven Waddington and Nathaniel Poe/Hawkeye played by Daniel Day-Lewis: Michael Mann's *The Last of the Mohicans* (20th Century–Fox, 1992).

5677

Mose: Lordy, Lordy! It's the end of the world!
Janet: No, Mose, it's the beginning of Wyoming!

Mose played by Fred "Snowflake" Toones and Janet Carter played by Ann Rutherford: Joseph Kane's *The Lawless Nineties* (Republic, 1936).

5678

President: Now look, when I was out here three years ago, these hills were black with buffalo. I've been here three days and haven't seen a single one. Cody, what happened to 'em?
Cody: I shot 'em!

President Ulysses S. Grant played by Jason Robards, Jr. and Buffalo Bill Cody played by Ted Flicker: William A. Fraker's *The Legend of the Lone Ranger* (Universal, 1981).

5679

Laura: I like the way you talk.
Bel-Air: You like my accent?
Laura: No, it's not your accent. It's your words. Most folks around here just grunt.

Laura Flemming played by Macha Grenon and Charles Bel-Air played by Georges Corraface: Rene Manzor's *Legends of the North* (Cinevideo Plus, 1995).

5680

Laura: There would be rivers to cross and hills to climb. But I didn't mind.

Because this was a fair land, and I rejoiced that I would see it.

Laura Ingalls played by Melissa Gilbert in Michael Landon's *Little House on the Prairie* (TVM, 1974).

5681

Governor: I expected to find you a much older man, Mr. Kilgore.

Kilgore: Oh, why?

Governor: I don't know. I suppose because of your position in these parts …your wealth, influence.

Kilgore: Well out here, Governor, you have to get a pretty fast start. You see, in these parts your chances of growing old may not always be too good.

The Governor played by Charles Meredith and Reece Kilgore played by Lyle Bettger: Stuart Heisler's *The Lone Ranger* (Warner Bros., 1956).

5682

Pea: What if I get lost?

Gus: Just head south?

Pea: South?

Gus: South, that way yonder. If you run into a polar bear, you know you went the wrong way.

Pea-Eye Parker played by Tim Scott and Gus McCrae played by Robert Duvall: Simon Wincer's *Lonesome Dove* (TVW, 1989).

5683

Jessie: Uncle Zeb, is it true it's always hot in California?

Zeb: Well now, it sure is. You know, one time out there I remember a fella who came down with the case of the chills. Well, people come from miles around just to watch him shake.

Jessie Macahan played by Vicki Schreck and Zeb Macahan played by James Arness: Bernard McEveety's *The Macahans* (TVW, 1976).

5684

Bartender: This is the Platte, gateway to the west. Summers are hotter than Hades, winters colder than a landlord's heart. The wolves are hungry and the Indians are hostile. The outlaws and renegades own the deed. Welcome, gentlemen, welcome!

The Bartender played by Cliff Emmich: Bernard McEveety's *The Macahans* (TVW, 1976).

5685

Olof: Hey, take it easy on that sky juice, stranger.

Kansas: Why? It's only water, ain't it?

Olof: Only water! Huh? Brother, let me tell you about water. When it rains out here, you get sick of the stuff. But when it don't rain, you'd wish you'd saved every drop.

Olof played by Alan Hale, Jr., and Kansas Collins played by Clancy Cooper: Felix Feist's *The Man Behind the Gun* (Warner Bros., 1952).

5686

Olof: What do you figure on doing way out in these parts? And why are you headed for Los Angeles?

Callicut: I was told when a man got this far west, nobody asked him questions.

Olof played by Alan Hale, Jr., and Major Callicut played by Randolph Scott: Felix Feist's *The Man Behind the Gun* (Warner Bros., 1952).

5687

Stoddard: I had taken Horace Greeley's advice literally: Go west, young man, go west! And seek fame, and fortune, and adventures!

Ransom Stoddard played by James Stewart: John Ford's *The Man Who Shot Liberty Valance* (Paramount, 1962).

5688

Peabody: And then with the westward march of our nation came the pioneer and the buffalo hunter …the adventurous and the bold. And the boldest of these were the cattlemen who seized the wide-open range for their own personal domain. And their law was the law of the hired gun. Now, now today have come the railroads and the people. The steady hard-working citizen, the homesteader, the shopkeeper, the builder of cities. We need roads to join those cities. Dams to store up the water of the picket wire. And we need statehood to protect the rights of every man and woman however humble.

Dutton Peabody played by Edmond O'Brien: John Ford's *The Man Who Shot Liberty Valance* (Paramount, 1962).

5689

Bat: Out here, Miss Merrick, a man in my boots is one of three things: hard, fast, or dead.

Sheriff Bat Masterson played by George Montgomery and Amy Merrick played by Nancy Gates: William Castle's *Masterson of Kansas* (Columbia, 1954).

5690

Little Tod: Damn, I don't know why they had to put Canada way the hell up here!

Little Tod played by Randy Quaid: Arthur Penn's *The Missouri Breaks* (United Artists, 1976).

5691

Jane: Why don't we just take a walk and we'll just talk about the wild west and how to get the hell out of it!

Jane Braxton played by Kathleen Lloyd: Arthur Penn's *The Missouri Breaks* (United Artists, 1976).

5692

Brett: Tell me something, Ben. You've been dreaming about the wide-open west for the better part of your life. How does it stack up for you next to the fact of the matter?

Ben: Well, it's better than a dream. And bigger.

Brett Maverick played by James Garner and Ben

Maverick played by Charles Frank: Hy Averback's *The New Maverick* (TVW, 1978).

5693

Angela: I thought by moving here, we could run away from trouble. Things don't ever change much, do they Hank? Trouble just seems to follow us around like a shadow.

Angela Cole played by Martha Hyer and Hank played by Jack Elam: Joseph Pevney's *The Night of the Grizzly* (Paramount, 1966).

5694

Preacher: In times of war, men fight and kill for what they believe in. And in these times, the west is very much like a battleground …with a constant war between good and evil.

The Preacher was uncredited: Edward L. Cahn's *Noose for a Gunman* (United Artists, 1960).

5695

Jason: Just like old times, ain't it? Us chasing after John Henry. I sure miss him …the old times, I mean.

Hayes: There never was a dull day.

Jason: Yeah, that's the trouble when you tame a land. All the fun goes out of it.

Jason Pitch played by Jack Elam, Oren Hayes played by Richard Widmark, and John Henry Lee played by Willie Nelson: Burt Kennedy's *Once Upon a Texas Train* (TVW, 1988).

5696

Bryce: You robbed banks in Mexico too?

Torrance: We had a little trouble with geography.

Bryce played by Chad Willett and Torrance played by Kris Kristofferson: Bill Corcoran's *Outlaw Justice* (TVW, 1999).

5697

Rumson: I don't care where we go as long as I stay 100 miles ahead of civilization.

Ben Rumson played by Lee Marvin: Joseph Logan's *Paint Your Wagon* (Paramount, 1969).

5698

Potter: I'm clearing out of here! I'm going back east where men may not be men, but they're not corpses either!

Painless Peter Potter played by Bob Hope: Norman Z. McLeod's *The Paleface* (Paramount, 1948).

5699

Hickok: This is a big country and trails cross …sometimes.

Wild Bill Hickok played by Gary Cooper: Cecil B. DeMille's *The Plainsman* (Paramount, 1936).

5700

Alice: You never once mentioned the desert storms, the sand fleas, the beetles …and the damn loneliness of it all!

Poker Alice Moffit played by Elizabeth Taylor: Arthur Allan Seidelman's *Poker Alice* (TVW, 1987).

5701

Ehrengard: I hate the desert. It's got no pity.

Hans Ehrengard played by Robert Ryan: Richard Brooks' *The Professionals* (Columbia, 1966).

5702

Dolworth: Nothing's harmless in this desert unless it's dead.

Bill Dolworth played by Burt Lancaster: Richard Brooks' *The Professionals* (Columbia, 1966).

5703

Cecil: Did you ever see *Cheyenne Autumn*?
Jack: Oh, yes.
Cecil: Well, in another twenty years they're going to make *Aluminum Autumn*.

Cecil Colson played by Sam Waterston and Jack McKee played by Jeff Bridges: Frank Perry's *Rancho Deluxe* (United Artists, 1975).

5704

Rick: It's miserable country! It's infested with decent citizens!

Rick Harper played by Arthur Kennedy: Rudolph Mate's *The Rawhide Years* (Universal, 1956).

5705

Jessica: You know, all my life I've been judged by who I am. Up here, it's just what I am that matters.

Jessica Harrison played by Sigrid Thornton: Geoff Burrowes' *Return to Snowy River* (Buena Vista, 1988).

5706

Rio: In this country, señora, the only sure thing about tomorrow is that it will arrive.

Rio played by Robert Taylor: John Farrow's *Ride, Vaquero!* (MGM, 1953).

5707

Ben: They're all kind of crazy, ain't they?
Matt: What's that, Ben?
Ben: The times. White men chasin' gold, Indians chasin' white men, the Army chasin' the Indians.

Ben the Merchant played by Will Wright and Matt Calder played by Robert Mitchum: Otto Preminger's *The River of No Return* (20th Century–Fox, 1954).

5708

Rooster: Everything that grows in this country will either bite ya, stab ya, or stick ya.

Rooster Cogburn played by John Wayne: Stuart Millar's *Rooster Cogburn* (Universal, 1975).

5709

Tyrel: With an education like that, what's he doing ramroding cows?
Cap: Ridin' with a secret like a lot of other men ...heading west.

Tyrel Sackett played by Jeff Osterhage and Cap Roundtree played by Ben Johnson: Robert Totten's *The Sacketts* (TVW, 1979).

5710

Orrin: No matter how far we travel, little brother, trouble always seems to follow.

Orrin Sackett played by Tom Selleck: Robert Totten's *The Sacketts* (TVW, 1979).

5711

Gabby: For a man who craves safety, you sure picked a funny place to light.

Gabby Whittaker played by George "Gabby" Hayes: Joseph Kane's *Saga of Death Valley* (Republic, 1939).

5712

Starr: Is it a western custom to push yourself in on other people?
Hardin: Yes, ma'am. That's how the west was settled.

Jeanne Starr played by Alexis Smith and Clay Hardin played by Errol Flynn: David Butler's *San Antonio* (Warner Bros., 1945).

5713

The road to Santa Fe was on iron rails to Kansas ...and pure nerve from there on.

Caption: Michael Curtiz's *Santa Fe Trail* (Warner Bros., 1940).

5714

Leavenworth, Kansas. Where the railroad and civilization ended, the Santa Fe Trail began. The old Spanish road from Mexico, now lusty with new life and a new motto—"God gets off at Leavenworth and Cyrus Holliday drives you from there to the Devil."

Caption: Michael Curtiz's *Santa Fe Trail* (Warner Bros., 1940). Cyrus Holliday played by Henry O'Neill.

5715

Cowboy: Kansas is all right for men and dogs. But it's pretty hard on women and horses.

Uncredited cowboy: Michael Curtiz's *Santa Fe Trail* (Warner Bros., 1940).

5716

Jorgensen: Someday this country is going to be a fine, good place to be. Maybe it needs our bones in the ground before that time can come.

Mrs. Jorgensen played by Olive Carey: John Ford's *The Searchers* (Warner Bros., 1956).

5717

Hennessey: Do you know how to shoot it?
Seven: Sort of. Is there some place I could try it out?
Hennessey: About 10,000 square miles of nothing out back a ways.

Sergeant Hennessey played by John McIntire and Seven Jones played by Audie Murphy: Harry Keller's *Seven Ways from Sundown* (Universal, 1960).

5718

Sakura: It is a Japanesse proverb that says when a place is deserted, it means no one there.

Sakura played by Tomas Milian: Sergio Corbucci's *Shoot First ...Ask Questions Later!* (a.k.a. *The White, the Yellow, and the Black*; Mntex Entertainment, It/Sp/Fr).

5719

Bingham: Surely, Mr. Barrabee, you don't intend to settle back in Nevada in a dinner jacket.
Barrabee: Folks out there ain't particular what kind of suit a man wears. But they're doggone particular what kind of a man is wearing it.

Rollo Bingham played by John Eldridge and John Barrabee played by Thurston Hall: Joseph Kane's *Song of Nevada* (Republic, 1944).

5720

Mary: She blamed Texas for taking her sons. Texas is a woman, she used to say ...big, wild, beautiful woman. You get a kid raised up to where he got some size, and there's Texas whispering in his ear, smiling, saying come on out with me and have some fun. It's hard enough to raise children any place, she'd say. But when you got to fight Texas, a mother hasn't a chance.

Mary Gordon played by Martha Hyer: Henry Hathaway's *The Sons of Katie Elder* (Paramount, 1965).

5721

Clint: It looks like awful lonely country.
Beale: It is ...except for Apaches. Want to go home?

Clint McDonald played by John Ireland and Edward Beale played by Rod Cameron: Ray Nazarro's *Southwest Passage* (United Artist, 1954).

5722

Stark: Is there any particular attraction in California?
Nella: No, nothing special. Just like everybody else, I'm looking for the end of the rainbow.
Stark: Rainbows aren't a matter of geography. You can find them anywhere.

Nathan Stark played by Robert Ryan and Nella Turner played by Jane Russell: Raoul Walsh's *The Tall Men* (20th Century–Fox, 1955).

5723

For many years, against tremendous odds, American civilization struggled slowly westward: 1830 — The Covered Wagons; 1840 — The Stage Coach; 1850 — The Pony Express; 1860 — The First Telegraph.

Prologue to Tenny Wright's *The Telegraph Trail* (Warner Bros., 1933).

5724

Powell: Travelers seldom die of starvation in this country but they do die of thirst. Now the desert is an unknown quantity but the river isn't.

Major John Wesley Powell played by John Beal: William Beaudine's *Ten Who Dared* (Buena Vista, 1960).

The whole town seems to get involved in a gun dispute and free for-all. In this scene, Roy Stewart (Paul Kelly) and Legare (Victor Francen) trade lead in the streets of *San Antonio* **(Warner Bros., 1945).**

5725

Powell: But how could any man describe these works of titanic art? The giant hand that carved these monuments from solid rock used only the wind and the sand …and the raindrops of unreckoned ages.

Major John Wesley Powell played by John Beal: William Beaudine's *Ten Who Dared* (Buena Vista, 1960).

5726

Tennessee: Where are you from?
Cowpoke: Arizona. Ever been there?
Tennessee: Yeah. I was run out of the Arizona territory three years ago. I was run out of New Mexico too. And Colorado, Utah, Texas, and Oregon.
Cowpoke: Well, you ought to be a bit careful here in California. I understand there is an ocean out there someplace.

Tennessee played by John Payne and Cowpoke played by Ronald Reagan: Allan Dwan's *Tennessee's Partner* (RKO, 1955). *See also entry 5610.*

5727

Tennessee: I don't know what them Texans fought so hard to get this state for. Hardest ground in the world.
Comstock: Where is it any different?
Tennessee: Why, in Cheatham County, Tennessee, the ground is so soft they use it to stuff mattresses with.

Tennessee played by Andrew Tombes and Comstock played by Edmund MacDonald: George Marshall's *Texas* (Columbia, 1941).

5728

Windy: This country ain't so big but what I won't catch up with him one of these days.

Windy Miller played by George Bancroft: George Marshall's *Texas* (Columbia, 1941).

5729

Joyce: A penny for your thoughts.
Lat: Two bits in this country.

Joyce played by Patricia Owens and Lat Evans

played by Don Murray: Richard Fleischer's *These Thousand Hills* (20th Century–Fox, 1959).

5730

Sergeant: You know, this is a fearful and unpleasant climate out here, sir. It's a deadly climate.
Doctor: Is that so? Is the death rate pretty high?
Sergeant: Well, same as it is back east …one to a person.

Sergeant Creever played by Roy Roberts and Doctor Allen Seward played by Robert Francis: Phil Karlson's *They Rode West* (Columbia, 1954).

5731

Cable: I beg your pardon, Mrs. Saunders. Out here in the hills we sometimes forget our manners.
Colt: One thing about Texas: there'll always be someone around to remind you.

Cable played by Forrest Tucker, Mrs. Lorna Hunter Saunders played by Anne Baxter, and Colt

Saunders played by Charlton Heston: Rudolph Mate's *Three Violent People* (Paramount, 1956).

5732

Lon: Do you know what it's like to run out of water in the desert? Your lips crack wide open. Your tongue swells until it's too big for your mouth. Your throat tightens until you can't breathe. If you're lucky, you'll die fast, although you're not usually that lucky.

Lon Bennett played by Jeff Chandler: Russell Rouse's *Thunder in the Sun* (Paramount, 1959).

5733

Gabrielle: Sometimes it is better to forget old customs in a new land, Louise.

Gabrielle Dauphin played by Susan Hayward and Louise Dauphin played by Blanche Yurka: Russell Rouse's *Thunder in the Sun* (Paramount, 1959).

5734

Horn: You sure come a long ways to teach school in Wyoming.

Kimmel: Well, I guess you could say I've had a romance with the West since I was old enough to read.

Tom Horn played by Steve McQueen and Glendolene Kimmel played Linda Evans: William Wiard's *Tom Horn* (Warner Bros., 1980).

5735

Hook: The dust is pretty bad out here; so is the flies this time of the year. It's best you keep your mouth closed.

Sergeant Hook played by Joel McCrea: Charles Marquis Warren's *Trooper Hook* (United Artists, 1957).

5736

Hogan: What the hell is a nun doing out here?

Hogan played by Clint Eastwood: Don Siegel's *Two Mules for Sister Sara* (Universal, 1970).

5737

Kid: Was that what it was like in the old days, Will? Everybody ridin' out, shootin', smoke all over the place, folks yellin', bullets whizzin' by?

The Schofield Kid played by Jaimz Woolvett and William "Bill" Munny played by Clint Eastwood who also directed *Unforgiven* (Warner Bros., 1992).

5738

Warrick: I expect you're wondering about me?

Ware: Out in this country, we don't ask questions.

Warrick: That's one of the reasons why I live here.

Warrick played by Sir Cedric Hardwicke and Jonathan Ware played by James Craig: George Marshall's *Valley of the Sun* (RKO, 1942).

5739

Warrick: Look out here. What do you see?

Ware: Sand, cactus, and a sun that would blister the scalp off you.

Warrick: It's what you don't see that makes it beautiful.

Ware: What?

Warrick: People.

Ware: Uh huh. There is a lot of elbow room out there, isn't there?

Warrick played by Sir Cedric Hardwicke and Jonathan Ware played by James Craig: George Marshall's *Valley of the Sun* (RKO, 1942).

5740

Honey: This country sure is getting fancy. Christening babies …importing school-marms. Pretty soon they'll be putting soda pop in the liquor. And that's when I'll be getting out!

Honey Wiggin played by Eugene Pallette: Victor Fleming's *The Virginian* (Paramount, 1929).

5741

Mr. Taylor: It don't hurry to ask a man's name out here. He says his name is Jones so you call him Jones. I guess if you knew the real name of some of 'em, you could collect a pile of money.

Mr. Taylor played by Henry O'Neill: Stuart Gilmore's *The Virginian* (Paramount, 1946).

5742

Daphne: Oh Carter, why is everything out west so western?

Daphne Brookhaven played by Lynn Wood and Carter Brookhaven played by Ivor Francis: Jack Arnold, Oscar Rudolph, Bruce Bilson, and Earl Bellamy's *The Wackiest Wagon Train in the West* (Topar Films, 1976).

5743

Wanda: Do you think we're headin' in the right direction?

Beaudray: We wouldn't be headin' in this direction if it weren't right.

Wanda Nevada played by Brooke Shields and Beaudray Demerille played by Peter Fonda who also directed *Wanda Nevada* (MGM/UA, 1979).

5744

Ezra: Not much of a country is it, Blue? If the drought or the blizzards don't get you, some devil with liquor in his soul and a gun in his claw will.

Ezra Maple played by John Anderson and Will Blue played by Henry Fonda: Burt Kennedy's *Welcome to Hard Times* (MGM, 1967).

5745

Honest John: Hey, you're a little mite polite for a native. From the east, ain't ya? Which part?

Steve: All of me.

Honest John Whitaker played by George "Gabby" Hayes and Steve Kells played by Roy Rogers: Joseph Kane's *West of the Badlands* (a.k.a. *The Border Legion*; Republic, 1940).

5746

Honest John: Miss Hurricane, where I come from chivalry is not dead.

Hurricane: Well, in this territory they got it gaspin' for breath!

Honest John Whitaker played by George "Gabby" Hayes and Hurricane Hattie played by Maude Eburne: Joseph Kane's *West of the Badlands* (a.k.a. *The Border Legion*; Republic, 1940).

5747

Emma: In this land, everyone needs the help of everyone else foolish enough to come here.

Emma Breslin played by Maureen O'Sullivan: Charles Haas' *Wild Heritage* (Universal, 1958).

5748

Callahan: Well, what will it be for you?

Constable: Information.

Callahan: That's one thing I don't sell.

Constable: I'm not buying it.

Callahan: I don't give it away either.

Callahan played by J.M. Kerrigan and Constable Pedley played by Wendell Corey: Andrew Marton's *The Wild North* (MGM, 1952).

5749

Jules: You don't mind about the weather, huh?

Constable: To tell you the truth, I never could do anything about it.

Jules Vincent played by Stewart Granger and Constable Pedley played by Wendell Corey: Andrew Marton's *The Wild North* (MGM, 1952).

5750

Wyatt: This is a harsh land, Ed. It doesn't suffer fools.

Ed: I'm no fool, Wyatt.

Wyatt: No, you're not. But you're not a deliberate man, Ed. I don't sense that about you. You're too affable.

Wyatt Earp played by Kevin Costner and Ed Masterson played by Bill Pullman: Lawrence Kasdan's *Wyatt Earp* (Warner Bros., 1994).

5751

Jerry: It was further than I thought. I didn't know there was so much United States stretched around.

Colonel: You'll find more of it as you go along.

Jerry Calhoun played by Gaylord Pendleton and Colonel Calhoun played by Wade Boteler: Joseph Kane's *Young Buffalo Bill* (Republic, 1940).

Whiskey

See also Drinking; Gambling; Saloons

5752
Major: Money, whiskey, and women …your three deities. Tell me something, Mr. Kelly. Have they made you a happy man?
Kelly: No, but not as miserable a one as you.
Major Albert Stedman played by Patrick O'Neal and Alvarez Kelly played by William Holden: Edward Dmytryk's *Alvarez Kelly* (Columbia, 1966).

5753
Jack: Me? I'll take bourbon. It kills you slower, but a lot more pleasant like.
Jack Thornton played by Clark Gable: William Wellman's *The Call of the Wild* (20th Century–Fox, 1935).

5754
Gabby: I bet your head feels bigger than an overgrown pumpkin.
Warren: Oh, it does.
Gabby: I got just the cure for it …an injun remedy. Chief Sitting Bull himself gave me the recipe for learning him how to follow a trail. It cures aches, pains, bunions, calluses, galloping consumption, and the seven year itch.
Gabby Whittaker played by George "Gabby" Hayes and Warren played by Noah Beery, Jr.: Joseph Kane's *The Carson City Kid* (Republic, 1940).

5755
Merridew: I sure hate to waste good liquor on a dead man.
Merridew played by Jeff Corey: Sam Wanamaker's *Catlow* (MGM, 1971).

5756
Nye: After your first cup, Harv, you're blind anyway. And after your second, you're darn glad you're blind!
Nye Buell played by Richard Basehart and Harvey Lansing played by William Watson: Michael Winner's *Chato's Land* (United Artists, 1972).

5757
Harley: Do you know how to make Indian whiskey, John?
John: No, Harley.
Harley: Well, you take a barrel of Missouri River water, and a couple gallons of alcohol, and some strychnine to make them crazy, and tobacco to make them sick. An Indian wouldn't figure it was whiskey unless it made him sick. Add a few bars of soap to put a head on it, and then a half-pound or so of red pepper to give it a kick. Put some tumbleweed in, boil it until it turns brown, and that's Indian whiskey.

Harley Sullivan played by Henry Fonda and John O'Hanlan played by James Stewart: Gene Kelly's *The Cheyenne Social Club* (NGP, 1970).

5758
Colonel: You reek of whiskey, Trent! Not exactly the quality one looks for in a Chief Scout.
Colonel Stuart Valois played by John Mills and Lou Trent played by James Whitmore: Gordon Douglas' *Chuka* (Paramount, 1967).

5759
Rickard: Have a drink, Wes.
Wes: Are you supposed to have that stuff?
Rickard: Oh, why not? We all got to die sometime. Me, you, and the whole cock-eyed world. It doesn't make much difference what kills us.
Dave Rickard played by Basil Ruysdael and Wes McQueen played by Joel McCrea: Raoul Walsh's *Colorado Territory* (Warner Bros., 1949).

5760
Brett: Pour yourself some backbone and shut up!
James Brett played by Zachary Scott: Edwin L. Marin's *Colt .45* (Warner Bros., 1950).

5761
Sheriff: I'll tell you what I'm gonna do, Wade. The minute I get you on the train, I'm going home and finish off a whole quart of bourbon …and go to bed. But until then, I'm gonna stay awake, sober …and nervous.
Sheriff Cauthen played by Edgar Buchanan and Brett Wade played by Rory Calhoun: George Sherman's *Dawn at Socorro* (Universal, 1954).

5762
Hostess: Here you go, honey …the best medicine there is for skunk bites.
The Saloon Hostess played by Ann Risley: Piers Haggard's *Four Eyes and Six-Guns* (Turner Pictures, 1992).

5763
Wyatt: They're temperance ladies. If they had their way, Dodge would be drier than a Texas drought.
Wyatt Earp played by Hugh O'Brian: Dick Lowry's *The Gambler Returns: The Luck of the Draw* (TVW, 1991).

5764
Tiana: You search for courage in a whiskey bottle. But the spirits you need are in-

side of you. You are the eagle, Sam. Learn to fly …and to trust your heart.
Tiana Rogers played by Devon Ericson and Sam Houston played by Sam Elliott: Peter Levin's *Gone to Texas* (a.k.a. *Houston: The Legend of Texas*; TVW, 1986).

5765
Captain: This is the most potent weapon in war. The fighting spirit is in this bottle.
The Captain was uncredited: Sergio Leone's *The Good, the Bad, and the Ugly* (United Artists, 1966; U.S. 1968).

5766
Captain: Mr. Willingham, there aren't any Indians within a hundred miles of here. Haven't you heard of the Peace Commission?
Willingham: With a cargo like this [whiskey], you got to be sure. Damn sure! With Indians, revenue agents …temperance women.
Captain Paul Slater played by Jim Hutton and Frank Willingham played by Brian Keith: John Sturges' *The Hallelujah Trail* (MGM, 1965).

5767
Orosco: My friend would like to know why you always wear your hands covered with gloves.
Florinda: Because I promised my mother I'd never touch liquor.
Don Orosco played by Frank Puglia and Florinda Grove/Julie Latour played by Vera Ralston: Joseph Kane's *Jubilee Trail* (Republic, 1954).

5768
Preacher: God gave man poppy and the coca plant to use for his benefit. Also hemp and the peyote cactus. Some say they never seen God quite so clear as when they'd been chewing cactus, brother.
Bick: Next you're going to be telling me that God gave man beer and whiskey.
Preacher: That he did, brother, that he did. And don't leave out wine.
Preacher Bob played by Peter Boyle and Bickford Wanner, alias Kid Blue, played by Dennis Hopper: James Frawley's *Kid Blue* (20th Century–Fox, 1973).

5769
Laigs: It seems like I always get it in the legs.
Brazos: I told you to spend your money for a wooden leg instead of for liquor!
Laigs played by Britt Wood and Brazos played by

Rad Robinson: Lesley Selander's *Knights of the Range* (Paramount, 1940).

5770

Elsie: What you need is some strengthening tonic. I hate to give it away but it sure looks to me like you need it.

Annie: What kind of medicine is it?

Elsie: Just general strengthening. Elegant for the nerves. I call it Pepto. A gentleman gave it to me.

Annie: How much do I take?

Myrtle: Oh, just as much as you can hold.

Elsie: You see, it kills the germs inside your nerves.

Elsie played by Gladys George, Annie played by Loretta Young, and Myrtle played by Dorothy Granger: Frank Lloyd's *Lady from Cheyenne* (Universal, 1941).

5771

Frank: You know, Major, it's possible to die from even the very best whiskey.

Major: I know, but it takes so damn long.

Frank James played by Johnny Cash and Major Edwards played by Ed Bruce: William A. Graham's *The Last Days of Frank and Jesse James* (TVW, 1986).

5772

Stokely: They say this stuff loosens a man's tongue. It seems to tighten yours.

Stokely played by Henry Hull: Alfred Werker's *The Last Posse* (Columbia, 1953).

5773

Mulligan: I'm filled to overflowing with pride.

Townsman: If that's pride, I've never smelled whiskey!

Mulligan P. Martinez played by Ward Bond and the Townsman was uncredited: Glenn Tryon's *The Law West of Tombstone* (RKO, 1938).

5774

Stewart: You know, gentleman, there's other things besides this [whiskey] that make men drunk. Yes, sir! Power does. Power makes men lie and cheat and steal …and betray their friends.

Gene Stewart played by Victor Jory: Lesley Selander's *The Light of the Western Stars* (Paramount, 1940).

5775

Hayworth: I make allowances for a whiskey-soaked brain!

Nat Hayworth played by Morris Ankrum: Lesley Selander's *The Light of the Western Stars* (Paramount, 1940).

5776

Duke: And if it hadn't been that Cliff here was too fast for 'em, we both of us would have been too full of lead to hold whiskey.

Duke Allison played by Henry Brandon and Cliff Mason played by George O'Brien: David Howard's *The Marshal of Mesa City* (RKO, 1939).

Former lawman Cliff Mason (George O'Brien) restrains Mayor Sam Bentley (Lloyd Ingraham) from going after the varmint that just murdered their marshal. The deputy (Cactus Mack) stood by and watched the killing but then dutifully reported it to the mayor in *The Marshal of Mesa City* (RKO, 1939).

5777

Jess: What do you want now, a confession?

Hogan: They say it's good for the soul.

Jess: Whiskey is better. Much better.

Jess Ryerson played by Tom Drake: Richard Bartlett's *Money, Women and Guns* (Universal, 1958).

5778

Mrs. Gideon: I hope that wasn't whiskey you were drinking!

Twillie: Ah no, dear, just a little sheep dip. Panacea for all stomach ailments.

Mrs. Gideon played by Margaret Hamilton and Cuthbert J. Twillie played by W.C. Fields: Edward F. Cline's *My Little Chickadee* (Universal, 1940).

5779

Benton: Wishing you could fill up on whiskey, Mr. Riorty?

Riorty: I told ya, whiskey doesn't make a man brave. It just helps him forget he's petrified!

Trumpeter Benton played by James Lydon and Trooper Riorty played by William Haade: Joseph Kane's *Oh! Susanna* (Republic, 1951).

5780

Charlie: Sioux? There's no Sioux around here. I got a nose for Sioux!

Calhoun: You got a nose for whiskey, Charlie!

Charlie Grass played by Charles Stevens and Captain Webb Calhoun played by Rod Cameron: Joseph Kane's *Oh! Susanna* (Republic, 1951).

5781

Dan: If you got enough whiskey, you don't have to dream about things not worth dreaming.

Dan Keats played by Don Murray: James B. Clark's *One Foot in Hell* (20th Century–Fox, 1960).

5782

Jenks: Mr. Stewart, do you want me to tell you what the fight was about?

Stewart: Not now, Jenks, I'm busy.

Broden: You better listen.

Jenks: He pushed your whiskey barrels off [of the stagecoach] to make room for a stiff.

Stewart: Well, what are you standing here for? Go back and get 'em! And the body too.

Jenks played by Fred Graham, Del Stewart played by William Bishop, and Broden played by George Eldredge: Fred F. Sears' *Overland Pacific* (United Artists, 1954).

5783

Darby: What will you have? Whiskey?

Croft: What do you got?

Darby: Whiskey.

Darby played by Victor Kilian and Art Croft played by Henry (Harry) Morgan: William Wellman's *The Ox-Bow Incident* (20th Century–Fox, 1943).

5784

Dr. Carter: Share it, by boy! Shake the hand that shook the hand of Buffalo Bill! I'm the celebrated Dr. Carter! World-renowned medicine master and inventor of Dr. Carter's celebrated Indian Remedy. A guaranteed cure all, my boy, for whatever it is that's wrong with you!

Dr. Carter played by Earle Hodgins: Carl Pierson's *Paradise Canyon* (Monogram, 1935).

5785

1st Sgt.: The trouble with that low-grade whiskey, it doesn't hit you until you try to move.

First Sergeant Emmett Bell played by Jeff Chandler: George Marshall's *Pillars of the Sky* (Universal, 1956).

5786

Vallian: Damn, what is this stuff?

Duncan: Kentucky corn liquor. 190 proof. I use it to clean the rust off my tools.

Con Vallian played by Sam Elliott and Duncan McKaskel played by Tom Conti: Richard Day's *The Quick and the Dead* (HBO Pictures, 1987).

5787

Preacher: Prepare for the vengeance of the Lord! The day of reckoning is mighty close and you'll catch a heapin' fire if you don't get to repentin' and get to it quick! Hell fire is awaitin' ya. Are you ready to meet your Maker?

Woodson: I reckon so.

Preacher: You willing to stand before the judgmency with a chaw of tobacco in your mouth? Lost souls, that's what you all are! Black with sin! Black with iniquity! The light of the Lord ain't in any of ya! Do you ever think of salvation? Do you ever think of the kingdom? No! All you ever think of is your bellies …and your corn pone and your chitlins and your corn liquor. Ah, brother, how about a swig of that jug?

The Preacher played by Victor Kilian. Frank James, who was going under the alias of Ben Woodson, played by Henry Fonda: Fritz Lang's *The Return of Frank James* (20th Century–Fox, 1940).

5788

Eula: Alcohol on an empty stomach has killed more men than outlaws' bullets.

Rooster: You don't say! Well, ma'am, my stomach ain't empty. It's full of corn dodgers, balls of hot water and corn bread, made by Chen Lee, my friend. Must be near to fifty of 'em in there.

Eula: Why are they called corn dodgers?

Rooster: Dodgin' corn whiskey in my innards, I guess.

Eula Goodnight played by Katharine Hepburn, Rooster Cogburn played by John Wayne, and Clen Lee played by Tommy Lee: Stuart Millar's *Rooster Cogburn* (Universal, 1975).

5789

Bass: Joseph Lee, if God ever made two better inventions than a pretty woman and a bottle of whiskey, I ain't heard of it.

Joe Bass played by Burt Lancaster and Joseph Winfield Lee played by Ossie Davis: Sydney Pollack's *The Scalphunters* (United Artists, 1968).

5790

Mac: That posse is in sight. Let's get going!

Kate: You still haven't told us why that posse isn't lettin' up.

Jack: Yeah, it must be that other thing.

Mac: What thing?

Jack: Well, it wasn't my fault. I was just drinking a lot of whiskey and …

Mac: Whiskey gets the blame for a lot of things you didn't do.

Mac Traven played by Tom Selleck, Kate Connery played by Katharine Ross, and Uncle Jack Traven played by Ben Johnson: Andrew V. McLaglen's *The Shadow Riders* (TVW, 1982).

5791

Smoky: There ain't nothin' like whiskey to wash the war stench out of a man's system.

Smoky Harjo played by Henry Kingi: Joseph Kane's *Smoke in the Wind* (Frontier Productions/Gamalex, 1975).

5792

Buck: If you are looking to save you some souls, preacher, right here would be a dandy place to start.

Peacock: Preacher? Goodness me no. Mother wanted me to be an actor. Father wanted me to go to hell. So I compromised. I became a whiskey salesman.

Buck played by John Schneider and the Whiskey Salesman, Trevor Peacock, played by Anthony Newley: Ted Post's *Stagecoach* (TVW, 1986).

5793

Dave: Whiskey and women. Did you ever think how much alike they are? They'll both fool ya, but you'll never figure how to do without 'em.

Dave played by George "Gabby" Hayes: Edwin L. Marin's *Tall in the Saddle* (RKO, 1944).

5794

Clint: It [whiskey] sure ain't slept in the barrel long.

Bartender: Nothing gets a chance to age in a boomtown, mister. Not even people.

Clint Allison played by Cameron Mitchell and Gus the Bartender played by Will Wright: Raoul Walsh's *The Tall Men* (20th Century–Fox, 1955).

5795

Wildcard: When the lead hits you, it'll hurt less with a little whiskey in your gut.

Trinity: Oh, yeah. Give the gentleman a double. That way you won't feel a thing.

Wildcard Hendricks was uncredited and Trinity played by Terence Hill: E.B. Clucher's (Enzo Barboni) *Trinity Is Still My Name* (West Film/Avco Embassy, 1971).

5796

Cash: Now that's Wichita whiskey, mama! It has aged about four minutes, and that ain't long enough to cure whatever they put in it.

Cash Zachary played by Audie Murphy: John Huston's *The Unforgiven* (United Artists, 1960).

5797

Judge Bean: Don't spill none of that liquor, son. It eats right into the bar.

Judge Roy Bean played by Walter Brennan. He was talking to Cole Hardin played by Gary Cooper: William Wyler's *The Westerner* (United Artists, 1940).

5798

Carl: What kind of whiskey do you prefer?

Wild Bill: Well, Carl, I prefer it in a glass. Other than that, it's all good.

Carl Mann played by Lee de Broux and Wild Bill Hickok played by Jeff Bridges: Walter Hill's *Wild Bill* (MGM/United Artists, 1995).

5799

Lottie: My pappy always said, if it burns it should be fit to drink.

Lottie Clampett played by Marie Windsor: Don Taylor's *Wild Women* (TVW, 1970).

5800

Will: How does she taste?

Blue: Damn if I know! But she sure burns a dollar's worth!

Will Penny played by Charlton Heston and Blue played by Lee Majors: Tom Gries' *Will Penny* (Paramount, 1968).

5801

Raven: I'm sorry I missed them, Mr. Carter.

Carter: That's all right, Raven. It's not the first time a bottle spoiled a man's aim.

Raven played by Trevor Bardette and King Carter played by Harry Woods: Ford Beebe's and Ray Taylor's *Winners of the West* (Universal serial, Chapter 3: "The Bridge of Disaster," 1940).

5802

Sheriff: You're drunk!

Townsman: If I ain't, I wasted a lot of good whiskey.

Sheriff McVey played by Roy Roberts and the Townsman was uncredited: Fred Sears' *Wyoming Renegades* (Columbia, 1955).

5803

Pearson: Never waste whiskey on money. Now money on whiskey, that's entirely different.

Whiskey Pearson played by Mel Welles: Fred Sears' *Wyoming Renegades* (Columbia, 1955).

Wild Women

See also Men; People; Women

5804

Rita: You ought to grow a beard too.

Marshal: When you wear a sun bonnet and apron, I'll grow a beard.

Rita: When I wear a sun bonnet and apron, I'll grow a beard.

Rita played by Ann Dvorak and Marshal Dan Mitchell played by Randolph Scott: Edwin Marin's *Abilene Town* (United Artists, 1946).

5805

Dixie: Do you like the bed? It came from France.

Brisco: Louis the Fourteenth?

Dixie: No. I think Louis was the Ninth or Tenth. But then a lady never counts.

Brisco: Oh? Then what are those notches on the bedpost?

Dixie Cousins played by Kelly Rutherford and Brisco County, Jr., played by Bruce Campbell: Bryan Spicer's *Adventures of Brisco County, Jr.* (TVW, Series Premiere, 1993).

5806

Taylor: I wonder why she hid out in a place like Apache Wells.

Henry: Well, she'll find nothing but contempt and scorn in this territory. Her reputation goes ahead of her.

Taylor: And lingers after.

Hoyt Taylor played by Robert Harris and Henry Belden played by Donald Barry: R.G. Springsteen's *Apache Uprising* (Paramount, 1966).

5807

Fanny: So if you ever get to San Francisco, Tom, look us up.

Tom: I might.

Fanny: We'll have at least a dozen ways for a man to lose his money, and enjoy the fact that he lost it.

Fanny Webson played by Glenda Farrell and Tom Herrera played by Robert Horton: Harold Kress' *Apache War Smoke* (MGM, 1952).

5808

Zack: Now don't get me wrong. I have great respect for women like you and like Miss Kitty who manage to maintain their dignity and their loneliness in a hellhole like Oblivion. I want you to know that I am here for you ...as your Marshal, as your friend, or anything you damn well need me to be.

Mattie: Zack, I haven't had sex in three years.

Zack Stone played by Richard Joseph Paul and Mattie Chase played by Jackie Swanson: Sam Irvin's *Backlash: Oblivion 2* (Full Moon Entertainment, 1996).

5809

Lawyer: Ma'am, I don't know how to tell you this, but ...

Anita: Tell me what?

Lawyer: Well, your claim is worthless without your husband alive. See for yourself ...second paragraph. Now

ma'am, I'm sorry but it's the law. Surely you understand that.

Anita: Yes, I understand that. I was worthless until I married. So now, I guess I'm worthless as a widow. Funny, I had some value as a whore.

Anita Crown played by Mary Stuart Masterson and Lawyer Jerome Lurie played by Mark Carlton: Jonathan Kaplan's *Bad Girls* (20th Century–Fox, 1994).

5810

Calamity: In them days, Janey, there was only two ways for a woman to survive out west: wifin' and whorin'. Since I weren't cut out for either one, I had to find my own way of surviving. So I lived like a man and sometimes even passed myself off as one. It got kind of sticky at times, but it gave me a kind of freedom that few women ever knew.

Calamity Jane (in a unmailed letter to her daughter) played by Anjelica Huston: Rod Hardy's *Buffalo Girls* (Cabin Fever Entertainment, 1995).

5811

Butch: I was just sort of wondering what's up there?

Bartender: Rooms. If you want to satisfy your curiosity, give her twenty bucks. She'll show you one.

Butch: I'm not that curious.

Butch Cassidy played by Tom Berenger and Jack the Bartender played by Joel Fluellen: Richard

Lester's *Butch and Sundance: The Early Days* (20th Century–Fox, 1979).

5812

Ben: I had me a quiet woman once. Outside, she was as calm as Sunday. But inside, wild like mountain scenery.

Ben played by Scott Peters: Burt Kennedy's *The Canadians* (20th Century–Fox, 1961). *See also entries 5883 and 5890.*

5813

Don Diego: There's one thing that always amazes me about you. You are the madam of a bordello house, yet you speak like the Mother Superior of a convent. But why not! All your men confess to you.

Don Diego was uncredited: Leon Klimovsky's *Challenge of the Mackennas* (Filmar Compagnia Cinematografica — Atlantida/Hemlock Enterprises, 1969).

5814

Doc: Forgive me, mademoiselle.
Guinevere: What the hell kind of talk is this?
Wyatt: Now, as I understand it, a mademoiselle is a madam who ain't quite made it yet …only younger and friskier. I'd call it a compliment.

Doc Holliday played by Arthur Kennedy, Miss Guinevere Plantagenet played by Elizabeth Allen, and Marshal Wyatt Earp played by James Stewart: John Ford's *Cheyenne Autumn* (Warner Bros., 1964).

5815

Harley: What kind of business you figure your brother left you?
John: Well, the letter don't say. But that's just like a lawyer. They don't tell you no more than it takes to confuse you. But it's a …something called the Cheyenne Social Club.

Harley Sullivan played by Henry Fonda and John O'Hanlan played by James Stewart: Gene Kelly's *The Cheyenne Social Club* (NGP, 1970).

5816

John: What's this?
Opal Ann: Just what it looks like, Johnny. D.J. always had a glass of warm milk with a raw egg in it before he went to bed. He claimed it kept his strength up, and it helped his complexion. It wasn't his complexion I cared about.

John O'Hanlan played by James Stewart and Opal Ann played by Sue Ann Langdon. D.J. O'Hanlan was John's deceased brother: Gene Kelly's *The Cheyenne Social Club* (NGP, 1970).

5817

Potter: Mr. Sullivan! Mr. Sullivan!
Opal Ann: If you're looking for Harley, he's busy right now.
Potter: Well, where is he?
Opal Ann: Well, he was with Carrie Virginia a while ago. But him and Pauline

have struck up an acquaintance now. That Harley! He's like a bad outlaw. He keeps moving from place to place.

Nathan Potter played by Richard Collier, Harley Sullivan played by Henry Fonda, Opal Ann played by Sue Ann Langdon, Carrie Virginia played by Jackie Russell, and Pauline played by Elaine Devry: Gene Kelly's *The Cheyenne Social Club* (NGP, 1970).

5818

Cisco Kid: Pancho, the first thing we do is find some señoritas and some food.
Pancho: Señoritas?
Cisco Kid: For me. Food …for you.

The Cisco Kid played by Jimmy Smits and Pancho played by Cheech Marin: Luis Valdez's *The Cisco Kid* (Turner Pictures, 1994).

5819

Columbine: Stay back, mister!
Illinois: Oh don't worry, miss. I've great respect for ladies …especially those with revolvers.

Columbine Dalton played by Penny Edwards and W.T. "Illinois" Grey played by John Russell: Reginald LeBorg's *The Dalton Girls* (United Artists, 1957).

5820

Vivien: Show too much and you can't sell it.

Vivien Skill played by Yvonne Sanson: Tonino Valerii's *Day of Anger* (a.k.a. *Days of Wrath*; Sancrosiap/Corona Film/KG Divina Film/National General, 1967).

5821

Angela: I can't charge you for crying on my sheets.
Luke: I had too much to drink.
Angela: Of course you did, lover.
Luke: Take the money.
Angela: For what? If a pipe fitter can't lay pipe, he ought to try another business.

Angela played by Amy Thomas and Luke Mills played by James Lydon: Allen Smithee's *Death of a Gunfighter* (Universal, 1969).

5822

Mona Lisa: Why aren't you out there working?
Sally: I'm on my break.
Mona Lisa: What do you girls got now …a union? Get out there!

Mona Lisa played by Gladys Knight and Sally played by Sydney Walsh: Virgil W. Vogel's *Desperado* (TVW, 1987).

5823

Sally: The kind of men that come to a place like this, they don't come here with a lot of tender feelings. In fact, me and the other girls are about the only human beings in their lives that they can get even with for all their misery. They give us their misery every night.

Sally played by Sydney Walsh: Virgil W. Vogel's *Desperado* (TVW, 1987).

5824

Cates: You always wake up in such a good mood?
Maggie: Well, I'm sorry, but the men in this place just don't bring out the best in me.
Cates: So why are you here?
Maggie: My daddy was always shouting about sin and damnation. It made me curious to see what it was all about.

Charlie Cates played by Whip Hubley and Maggie played by Debra Feuer: E.W. Swackhamer's *Desperado: The Outlaw Wars* (TVW, 1989).

5825

Destry: I bet you got a beautiful face underneath all that paint. Why don't you wipe it off someday and take a look at it. You might be surprised.

Destry played by Audie Murphy: George Marshall's *Destry* (Universal, 1954).

5826

Mayor: Where in the hell have you been?
Sheriff: At the jail taking care of my outlaw.
Mayor: I didn't make you Sheriff to take care of your outlaw but to protect my girls here [Belle's Bordello].
Sheriff: Is somebody threatening them?
Mayor: The Army is threatening them!
Stuart: The Army is threatening to move out.
Mayor: And ruin every industry in Yerkey's Hole …especially mine!
Sheriff: Why would the Army move?
Reverend: To go where the Indians are! That's what they come out west for …to fight Indians.
Mayor: What we need is a good massacre.
Sheriff: There ain't nothing but tamed Indians around here, Belle.
Mayor: Well, stir 'em up!
Sheriff: How?
Mayor: Break a treaty! Speak with a forked tongue! How the hell should I know? I never started an uprising before!

The Mayor and proprietor of Belle's Bordello played by Anna Jackson, Sheriff Hoke played by George Kennedy, Charles Stuart played by Harry Carey, Jr., and Reverend Green played by Henry Jones: Burt Kennedy's *Dirty Dingus Magee* (MGM, 1970).

5827

Sin Killer: Pearl, you're curved in the flesh of temptation. Resistance is going to be a darn sight harder for you than females protected by the shapes of sows.

The Sin Killer played by Walter Huston: King Vidor's *Duel in the Sun* (Selznick Releasing Organization, 1946).

5828

Sin Killer: Under that heathen blanket, there's a full-blossomed woman built by the devil to drive men crazy.

The Sin Killer played by Walter Huston: King Vidor's *Duel in the Sun* (Selznick Releasing Organization, 1946).

5829

Annie: I thought you were getting dressed.
Frank: Would you consider getting undressed, and help me pass the pleasant time of day?

Annie played by Dana Wheeler-Nicholson and Frank James played by Bill Paxton: Robert Boris' *Frank & Jesse* (Vidmark Entertainment, 1995).

5830

Jennie: Parties like that bring back old times for me. Those women with him? They're being paid to be there. Chippies, whores, whatever you want to call 'em. I was one once …used because I had no choice. Now I do. Three years ago, I got married to a man named John Reed. He was a hell rat like a thousand others, digging for gold. But he struck it rich. Real rich. And he married the prettiest whore in town. Suddenly, there we were, mixing with the rich, the cream of Sacramento society. Even though he needed it worse than me, John thought that I ought to take on a little polish …learn to dress and talk like a lady. So he sent me off to a St. Louis finishing school. In two years I learned everything it takes to make a whore into a lady. It wasn't easy, but I am going back a lady.
Brady: Yeah, you are.

Jennie Reed played by Lee Purcell and Brady Hawkes played by Kenny Rogers: Dick Lowry's *The Gambler* (TVW, 1980).

5831

Jenny: You weren't so eager to get rid of me last night, Jed Davis.
Jed: Come on, Jenny. There was nothing personal about it.
Jenny: Nothing personal? It'd be the first time you ever laid hands on me that it weren't personal!

Jenny, a prostitute, and Jed Davis, a townsman, were uncredited: Burt Kennedy's *The Good Guys and the Bad Guys* (Warner Bros., 1969).

5832

Marshal: Well, Billy, someday you'll learn that people don't always agree on what's good and what's bad. Now about those ladies, they were just practicing the oldest profession on earth.
Boy: I thought being Marshal was the oldest profession.
Marshal: No, that's just the second oldest.

Marshal Jim Flagg played by Robert Mitchum and the Boy was uncredited: Burt Kennedy's *The Good Guys and the Bad Guys* (Warner Bros., 1969).

5833

Tuco: I hope your mother ends up in a two-dollar whorehouse!

Tuco played by Eli Wallach: Sergio Leone's *The Good, the Bad, and the Ugly* (United Artists, 1966; U.S. 1968).

5834

Monty: Hey Jim, see if you can find some good women and bad whiskey.
Jim: How about the other way around?

Monty Walker played by Gilbert Roland and Jim Hadley played by Alan Ladd: Robert D. Webb's *Guns of the Timberland* (Warner Bros., 1960).

5835

Matt: She's a fine woman, John. I doubt you'd do any better.
John: Well now, I'm glad to hear you say that because I've been, ah, worrying a lot about her scarlet past.
Matt: Yeah, that's just what it is …past. It's what in here [heart] that counts.

Matt Dillon played by James Arness and John Parsley played by James Brolin: Jerry Jameson's *Gunsmoke: The Long Ride* (TVW, 1993).

5836

Kanning: I don't know, Donnie, I got a lot of parts on me that ain't working like they used to.
Donnie: I don't know. The only part I'm interested in seems to be working just fine.

Kanning played by Matt McCoy and Donnie played by Kelly Lebrock: Jim Wynorski's *Hard Bounty* (Triboro Entertainment, 1995).

5837

Donnie: Your time's up. Put your money on the table.
Kanning: What are you talking about?
Donnie: You heard me! If you're going to treat me like a whore, then you're going to pay me like a whore.

Donnie played by Kelly LeBrock and Kanning played by Matt McCoy: Jim Wynorski's *Hard Bounty* (Triboro Entertainment, 1995).

5838

Donnie: There's only two things I can't do. One is make love to a woman; the other one is piss up a wall. And right now, there's only one of those I regret not being able to do.

Donnie played by Kelly LeBrock: Jim Wynorski's *Hard Bounty* (Triboro Entertainment, 1995).

5839

Callie: Do you know what you are? Just trash! A bottle of whiskey for courage and the manners of a goat.
Stranger: You're the one who could use a lesson in manners.
Callie: Not from you, whiskey breath!

Callie Travers played by Mariana Hill and The Stranger played by Clint Eastwood: Clint Eastwood's *High Plains Drifter* (Universal, 1973).

5840

Mae: And don't tell me you don't [love me]. I can tell when a man wants me.

Jubal: There is a difference.
Mae: Then I'll settle for the difference.

Mae Horgan played by Valerie French and Jubal Troop played by Glenn Ford: Delmer Daves' *Jubal* (Columbia, 1956).

5841

Kehoe: Ruby, you're a danger to the whole race of men. But danger is always a fair price to pay for excitement.

Dan Kehoe played by Clark Gable and Ruby played by Jean Wiles: Raoul Walsh's *The King and Four Queens* (United Artists, 1956).

5842

Hardin: You killed our pig! What kind of a wild slut are you?

John Wesley Hardin played by Randy Quaid: Joseph Sargent's *Larry McMurtry's Streets of Laredo* (Cabin Fever Entertainment, 1995).

5843

Hardin: I don't like being in small rooms with whores who shoot pistols.

John Wesley Hardin played by Randy Quaid: Joseph Sargent's *Larry McMurtry's Streets of Laredo* (Cabin Fever Entertainment, 1995).

5844

O'Malley: That sister of yours, Stribling, was just a free drink on the house. And nobody ever went home thirsty. I mean nobody!

Brendan O'Malley played by Kirk Douglas and Dana Stribling played by Rock Hudson: Robert Aldrich's *The Last Sunset* (Universal, 1961).

5845

Hardin: There will be drinkin', tainted women, and gamblin' …and there will be trouble!

J.C. Hardin played by John McIntire: Raoul Walsh's *The Lawless Breed* (Universal, 1952).

5846

Narrator: There is nothing worse than a harlot turned respectable. A reformed anything is bad enough. But a reformed harlot is the direct wrath of the devil. It seems that those who had spent time giving pleasure for profit are all the more zealous when it comes to dealing out misery.

Narration by Tector Crites who played by Ned Beatty: John Huston's *The Life and Times of Judge Roy Bean* (NGP, 1972).

5847

Roy Bean: I understand you have taken exception to my calling you whores. I'm sorry. I apologize. I ask you to note that I did not call you callous-ass strumpets, fornicatresses, or low-born gutter-sluts. But I did say whores. There's no escaping that. And for that slip of the tongue, I apologize.

Judge Roy Bean played by Paul Newman: John

Huston's *The Life and Times of Judge Roy Bean* (NGP, 1972).

5848

Wren: I'm just a whore, Mr. Blessing.
Blessing: Well, there's worse occupations, I reckon. Politics, for example …lawyers.

Wren played by Brenda Bakke and Ned Blessing played by Brad Johnson: Jack Bender's *Lone Justice II* (Triboro Entertainment Group, 1995).

5849

Reverend: Ah, the temptations of the flesh. I fought 'em my whole life through.
Prisoner: Then how come you're in here [jail], Reverend?
Reverend: Well, I said I fought 'em. I didn't say I fought 'em off. Sometimes I lost. But believe me, it takes a lot more to tempt a preacher than it does you stumble-bums in here. When I lost, I lost big!
Prisoner: Are you a real preacher, Reverend?
Reverend: Well now, let's look at it this way. I always had the urge to preach. And if you got the urge, you're already halfway home.
Prisoner: What kept you from getting all the way?
Reverend: My temptation was women.

Reverend Hoskins played by Karl Swenson and the Prisoner played by Lalo Rios: David Miller's *Lonely Are the Brave* (Universal, 1962).

5850

Gus: I don't know why you are so down on whores, Woodrow. You've had yours as I recall.
Woodrow: Yeah, and that's the worst mistake I've ever made.
Gus: It ain't a mistake to be a human being once in your life, Woodrow. Poor little old Maggie left you a fine son before she quit this world.
Woodrow: You don't know that! That boy could be yours, or Jake's, or some damn gambler!
Gus: Yeah, but he ain't, he's yours! Now anybody with a good eye could see it. Besides, Maggie told me. We were good friends.
Woodrow: I don't know about friends. I'm sure you was a good customer though.
Gus: Well, the two can overlap you know.
Woodrow: You're the one that would know about overlapping with whores, I reckon.
Gus: You know what hurt her most? You wouldn't call her by name. You never would say Maggie. That's what hurt her most.
Woodrow: I don't know what it would have amounted to if I had.
Gus: It would have made her happy!
Woodrow: What are you talking about? She's a whore!

Gus: A whore has got heart, Woodrow, and Maggie's was the most tender I ever saw.
Woodrow: Well, why didn't you marry her then?
Gus: She didn't love me. She loved you. You should have seen how she sat in that saloon every day, watching the door …after you quit coming around.

Gus McCrae played by Robert Duvall and Captain Woodrow F. Call played by Tommy Lee Jones: Simon Wincer's *Lonesome Dove* (TVW, 1989).

5851

Dish: What's keeping you, boys? I thought you wanted a whore.
Cowboy: We don't know how much they cost.
Dish: It depends on how long you want to stay with 'em.
Newt: Long enough, I reckon. How much for that?

Dish Boggett played by D.B. Sweeney and Newt played by Ricky Schroder: Simon Wincer's *Lonesome Dove* (TVW, 1989).

5852

Cole: Good evening, ma'am.
Belle: Seems like everybody is having a real good time at this affair.
Cole: Well, I expect so. Free drinks and food and all.
Belle: How come I wasn't invited?
Cole: Because you're a whore.
Belle: Yeah, well, at least I ain't a cheap one!

Cole Younger played by David Carradine and Belle Starr played by Pamela Reed: Walter Hill's *The Long Riders* (United Artists, 1980).

5853

Belle: I just want to find out what it feels like to be respectable …for awhile anyway.
Cole: You'll never be respectable, Belle. You're a whore. You'll always be a whore. That's why I like you.

Belle Starr played by Pamela Reed and Cole Younger played by David Carradine: Walter Hill's *The Long Riders* (United Artists, 1980).

5854

Marguerita: Oh, it's been a long time since a man like you came to Chili Verde.
Hard Case: Oh, how long?
Marguerita: A week …maybe longer.

Marguerita Ventura played by Lainie Kazan and Hard Case Williams played by Geoffrey Lewis: Paul Bartel's *Lust in the Dust* (Fox Run/New World, 1985).

5855

Yancey: Mister! You! I understand you insulted the lady.
Callahan: No.
Yancey: Well, she says you did!
Callahan: That's not possible. I've never met a lady.

Yancey played by Bo Hopkins and Diego "Macho" Callahan played by David Janssen: Bernard L. Kowalski's *Macho Callahan* (Avco Embassy Pictures, 1970).

5856

Will: Is this #12 Back Street?
Lily: That's right.
Will: I'm looking for Miss Lily Fontaine.
Lily: Well, you found her.
Will: You? You're Miss Fontaine?
Lily: If you ain't the law, I am.

Will Lane played by Buddy Ebsen and Lily played by Diane Sayer: Burt Kennedy's *Mail Order Bride* (MGM, 1964).

5857

Sledge: Old man, how long has it been since you've had a hot meal, some whiskey, and a woman?
Old Man: All in one night?

Luther Sledge played by James Garner and the Old Man played by John Marley: Vic Morrow's *A Man Called Sledge* (Columbia, 1971).

5858

Billie: Goodbye, Willie. And thank you for being the only man in the Longhorn Palace that never made an indecent proposal to me.
Willie: If I had my strength, I would have.

Billie Ellis played by Julie London and Willie played by Dick Elliott: Anthony Mann's *Man of the West* (United Artists, 1958).

5859

Archer: You can have her, but you're going to have to get her some teeth.
McCabe: All right. How much for three?
Archer: Eighty dollars each.
McCabe: Eighty dollars for a chippie? You can get a damn horse for fifty!

Archer played by Tom Hill and John McCabe played by Warren Beatty: Robert Altman's *McCabe & Mrs. Miller* (Warner Bros., 1971).

5860

Mrs. Miller: Listen, Mr. McCabe, I'm a whore and I know an awful lot about whorehouses.

Mrs. Miller played by Julie Christie and John McCabe played by Warren Beatty: Robert Altman's *McCabe & Mrs. Miller* (Warner Bros., 1971).

5861

Mrs. Miller: Well, if you're so bloody smart, then you'd know that if we went ahead and bought the windows and doors for the whorehouse, we would make twice as much money.
McCabe: How come every time you talk about spending money, you say we?
Mrs. Miller: I say we, McCabe, because you think small. You think small because you're afraid to think big. I'm telling ya, you have to spend money to make money.

Hooker (Claude Akins), Ward (Dennis Weaver), and Luther Sledge (James Garner) plot to rob a gold shipment, "enough for a man to die on …more than that maybe" according to the Old Man (Johnny Marley) in *A Man Called Sledge* (Columbia, 1970).

Mrs. Miller played by Julie Christie and John McCabe played by Warren Beatty: Robert Altman's *McCabe & Mrs. Miller* (Warner Bros., 1971).

5862

Tom Logan: I couldn't get no credit at the whorehouse, so I picked up this chubby little girl off some sodbuster's outfit.

Little Tod: How was she?

Tom Logan: About like a Swiss clock …same exact movement over and over again.

Tom Logan played by Jack Nicholson and Little Tod played by Randy Quaid: Arthur Penn's *The Missouri Breaks* (United Artists, 1976).

5863

Logan: I didn't ask you. You said that you wanted it.

Jane: Well, do you?

Logan: No.

Jane: Well, then, you're not going to get it.

Logan: Good! Keep the dang thing. I don't want it.

Jane: I forgot, you do have your whores, don't you?

Logan: Sure do. Like 'em too.

Jane: Well, I'll tell you something. If you want them more than you want me …

Logan: I keep telling you, I want them a lot. I don't want you at all.

Jane: Well, why are you being so mean to me?

Logan: People have been neglecting to tell you what a nasty little bitch you are, and I'm just having to make up for their negligence!

Tom Logan played by Jack Nicholson and Jane Braxton played by Kathleen Lloyd: Arthur Penn's *The Missouri Breaks* (United Artists, 1976).

5864

Willie: Fran, you ain't nothin' but puke with lipstick!

Willie played by Scott Coffey and Fran played by

Dana Andersen: William A. Graham's *Montana* (TVW, 1990).

5865

Martine: This is our last night. I'm moving to Charlieville.

Monte: That dump!

Martine: Yeah, you're right, it's a dump. But then I work in a profession of diminishing returns. I mean, as time goes by, we all have to take the beds we can get. Perhaps one day you'll find the same applies to you.

Martine Bernard played by Jeanne Moreau and Monte Walsh played by Lee Marvin: William A. Fraker's *Monte Walsh* (NGP, 1970).

5866

Twillie: May I present my card?

Flower Belle: "Novelties and Notions." What kind of notions you got?

Cuthbert J. Twillie played by W.C. Fields and

Flower Belle Lee played by Mae West: Edward F. Cline's *My Little Chickadee* (Universal, 1940).

5867

Flower Belle: I generally avoid temptation …unless I can't resist it.

Flower Belle Lee played by Mae West: Edward F. Cline's *My Little Chickadee* (Universal, 1940).

5868

Flower Belle: Anytime you got nothing to do, and lots of time to do it, come up.

Flower Belle Lee played by Mae West: Edward F. Cline's *My Little Chickadee* (Universal, 1940).

5869

Flower Belle: Funny, every man I meet wants to protect me. I can't figure out what from.

Flower Belle Lee played by Mae West: Edward F. Cline's *My Little Chickadee* (Universal, 1940).

5870

Bowdre: During the planting season, the warden rents us out to these planters. Of course, he keeps the money. But we get the women.

Max: Yeah. How?

Bowdre: One Saturday night a month, while we're working here, he lets them come in the barracks.

Max: You mean they let the women come to the barracks?

Bowdre: Yeah, I didn't believe it myself at first.

Max: And, we get to talk to them?

Bowdre: Talk to them?

Bill Bowdre played by Arthur Kennedy and Max Sand/Nevada Smith played by Steve McQueen: Henry Hathaway's *Nevada Smith* (Paramount, 1966).

5871

Jason: There was that near-sighted gal down in Sonora town.

Hayes: Oh yeah. That was the one that went around telling everybody how much she loved ya. Everybody, that is, except her husband.

Jason: That's the one!

Hayes: And as I remember, he was that close to doing you with a shotgun.

Jason: It taught me a lesson: always check the brand to make sure you ain't driving another man's stock.

Jason Pitch played by Jack Elam and Oren Hayes played by Richard Widmark: Burt Kennedy's *Once Upon a Texas Train* (TVW, 1988).

5872

Frank: You also like to feel a man's hands all over you. You like it …even if they're the hands of the man who killed your husband.

Frank played by Henry Fonda: Sergio Leone's *Once Upon a Time in the West* (Paramount, 1969).

5873

Darby: It's my guess the married women ran her out. Oh, no tar and feathers …no rails. They just righteously made her feel uncomfortable. Not that she ever did anything, but they just couldn't get over being afraid that she might.

Darby played by Victor Kilian: William Wellman's *The Ox-Bow Incident* (20th Century–Fox, 1943).

5874

Carter: Say, what is there to do in this town, anyway?

Darby: Well, unless you want to get in line for old Drew's daughter …

Croft: We don't.

Darby: The only other unmarried woman I know is eighty-two, blind, and a Paiute. That leaves you five choices: eat, sleep, drink, play poker, or fight.

Gil Carter played by Henry Fonda, Darby played by Victor Kilian, and Art Croft played by Henry (Harry) Morgan: William Wellman's *The Ox-Bow Incident* (20th Century–Fox, 1943).

5875

Calamity: Tip your hat when you speak to a lady.

Hickok: I will …when I speak to a lady.

Calamity Jane played by Jean Arthur and Wild Bill Hickok played by Gary Cooper: Cecil B. De-Mille's *The Plainsman* (Paramount, 1936).

5876

Calamity: Bill Hickok, you ornery son-of-a-mule. You wouldn't give a bad dime to a sick kid, would ya?

Hickok: You might be right, Calamity.

Calamity: No, I ain't. I know I ain't worth a bad dime.

Calamity Jane played by Jean Arthur and Wild Bill Hickok played by Gary Cooper: Cecil B. De-Mille's *The Plainsman* (Paramount, 1936).

5877

Alice: You must be a terrible disappointment to yourself. You call me a madam. A madam is at least something! You're …you're nothing!

John: Then if I'm nothing, I have nothing to be ashamed of.

Alice: Can it be that your thinking is so warped that being nothing is a cause for pride?

Poker Alice Moffit played by Elizabeth Taylor and John played by George Hamilton: Arthur Allan Seidelman's *Poker Alice* (TVW, 1987).

5878

Dolworth: That's Chiquita. She can lick a whole regiment, but she can't dance a lick!

Bill Dolworth played by Burt Lancaster and Chiquita played by Maria Gomez: Richard Brooks' *The Professionals* (Columbia, 1966).

5879

Dolworth: Chiquita, how's your love life?

Chiquita: Terrific! You want some?

Dolworth: Don't you ever say no?

Chiquita: Never!

Dolworth: To anybody?

Chiquita: Everybody!

Bill Dolworth played by Burt Lancaster and Chiquita played by Maria Gomez: Richard Brooks' *The Professionals* (Columbia, 1966).

5880

Link: Christina, you're a whore. You've always been one. You'll always be one.

Christina: You always did know how to speak to a woman.

Link played by Charles Bronson and Christina played by Ursula Andress: Terence Young's *Red Sun* (NGP, 1971).

5881

Pepita: Hey, do you always shoot your bed partner in the morning?

Link: Well, that depends upon how good she was.

Pepita: Me?

Link: I'll let you live.

Pepita: Thanks!

Link played by Charles Bronson and Pepita played by Capucine: Terence Young's *Red Sun* (NGP, 1971).

5882

Colbee: How did I know she was married? Women aren't like cattle. They ain't got a brand on their hip to let you know when you're driving another man's stock.

Colbee played by Warren Oates: Burt Kennedy's *Return of the Seven* (United Artists, 1966). *See also entries 3936, 5871, and 5889.*

5883

Colbee: Had me a quiet woman once. Outside she was calm as Sunday. Inside she was wild like mountain scenery. I'm going to ride back that way again.

Luis: Where's that?

Colbee: Sonora town.

Luis: I was there once.

Colbee: Once? You mean you didn't go back?

Luis: What for?

Colbee: Well, there's over ten head of females for every male in Sonora, that's for what. And I ought to know. I went through over half of 'em one night. And I would have got around to the rest of 'em if I hadn't pulled a leg muscle.

Colbee played by Warren Oates and Luis played by Virgilio Texeira: Burt Kennedy's *Return of the Seven* (United Artists, 1966). *See also entries 5812 and 5890.*

5884

Sam: Lady, there's two things I don't mess around with: one is an Apache squaw and the other is the United States Government.

Sam Whiskey played by Burt Reynolds: Arnold Laven's *Sam Whiskey* (United Artists, 1969).

5885

Prostitute: See ya in a few months, lad. You won't be so fussy where you put your little pecker.

The Prostitute played by Patti Allan: Allan Kroeker's *Showdown at Williams Creek* (Republic Pictures Home Video, 1991).

5886

Boss: What happened to your money?
Quince: Gambling …women. But not necessarily in that order.

The Boss (of the gang) played by Jack Elam and Quince Drew played by Larry Hagman: Burt Kennedy's *Sidekicks* (TVW, 1974).

5887

Paden: Stella, are you "The Midnight Star"?
Stella: I am. I'm always there, but I only shine at night.

Paden played by Kevin Kline and Stella played by Linda Hunt: Lawrence Kasdan's *Silverado* (Columbia, 1985).

5888

Kaitlin: One thing I learned from prison: you get old a lot faster than you do whoring.

Kaitlin Mullane played by Crystal Bernard: Kevin G. Cremin's *Siringo* (TVW, 1994).

5889

Jesse: She said right out she loved me. She told everybody. Everybody but her husband. That taught me a lesson: always check the brand and make sure you're not driving another man's stock.

Frank Jesse played by Dan Duryea: Harry Keller's *Six Black Horses* (Universal, 1962). *See also entries 3936, 5871, and 5882.*

5890

Chink: I had me a quiet woman once. Outside, she was as calm as Sunday. But inside, wild as mountain scenery.

Chink played by Henry Silva: Budd Boetticher's *The Tall T* (Columbia, 1957). *See also entries 5812 and 5883.*

5891

Charlie: A dead whore ain't worth nothin', King!

Charlie played by Chris Cooper and Hong King played by Michale Paul Chan: Nancy Kelly's *Thousand Pieces of Gold* (Greycat Films, 1991).

5892

Hogan: Sister! This here is a cathouse!
Sister Sara: Oh no, Hogan. This is no cathouse. This is the best whorehouse in town!

Hogan played by Clint Eastwood and Sister Sara played by Shirley MacLaine: Don Siegel's *Two Mules for Sister Sara* (Universal, 1970).

5893

Alice: Just because we let them smelly fools ride us like horses, don't mean we got to let them brand us like horses. Maybe we ain't nothing but whores, but we, by God, we ain't horses!

Strawberry Alice played by Frances Fisher: Clint Eastwood's *Unforgiven* (Warner Bros., 1992).

5894

Emma: You're just going to end up on your back …under some smelly cowboy.

Emma played by Bari Buckner: Michael Bohusz's *Uninvited* (Imperial Entertainment, 1993).

5895

Charming: Exactly what are your intentions?
Handsome: To see that justice is done!
Charming: And yours?
Cactus Jack: Blow his head off! Steal the money!
Charming: And?
Cactus Jack: And I'm going to ravish you!
Charming: Handsome, you lose. What's his name has just outbid you.

Charming Jones played by Ann-Margret, Handsome Stranger played by Arnold Schwarzenegger, and Cactus Jack Slade played by Kirk Douglas: Hal Needham's *The Villain* (a.k.a. *Cactus Jack*; Columbia, 1979).

5896

Trampas: In the course of a long and varied career, I've found that no one comes out west except for one of three things: health, wealth, or …ah …bad reputation. She looks healthy and rich to me.

Trampas played by Brian Donlevy: Stuart Gilmore's *The Virginian* (Paramount, 1946).

5897

Dow: What you need here is a clean, hard-working girl. She'll work like a peasant and fuck like a lady.

Johnny Dow played by Greg Lawson: Jon Sanders' *Wicked Wicked West* (a.k.a. *Painted Angels*; Sterling Home Entertainment/Lions Gate Films, 1998).

5898

Annie: What do you know about girls, Frank? You're a pimp. You know about whores.

Annie Ryan played by Brenda Fricker and Frank McGuinn played by Bruce McFee: Jon Sanders' *Wicked Wicked West* (a.k.a. *Painted Angels*; Sterling Home Entertainment/Lions Gate Films, 1998).

5899

Jane: You can see me about as much as you want. I guess that's always been the case, ain't it?
Wild Bill: I've got to be available too. An awful lot of people want a piece of Wild Bill.

Calamity Jane played by Ellen Barkin and Wild Bill Hickok played by Jeff Bridges: Walter Hill's *Wild Bill* (MGM/United Artists, 1995).

5900

Lily: Do you know a decent man who would look twice at the likes of me?
Ben: I'm looking at you.
Lily: Out of pity.
Ben: Pity hell!
Lily: Wanting a woman is not the same. The wanting wears off. And when that happens, there's nothing left but fighting and finding fault. A man could find a lot of that …maybe in what I am.

Lily Beloit played by Angie Dickinson and Ben Kane played by Robert Mitchum: Burt Kennedy's *Young Billy Young* (United Artists, 1969).

5901

Behan: I swear, I've been working around saloons nearly all my life. It never seems to fail. A man like Kane comes along and starts playing up to one of the women …treating her like a lady. The next thing you know she's dressing in white and getting up early on Sunday.

John Behan played by Jack Kelly and Ben Kane played by Robert Mitchum: Burt Kennedy's *Young Billy Young* (United Artists, 1969).

5902

Jane: Pat, I'm going to part with a nasty secret. You used to make me hotter than a June bride sitting bare-back on a depot stove. But I don't share my bed with the law.
Pat: And I don't keep with whores no more …so ain't we both content?

Jane Greathouse played by Jenny Wright and Pat Garrett played by William Petersen: Geoff Murphy's *Young Guns II* (20th Century–Fox, 1990).

Women

See also Men; People; Wild Women

5903

Miss Kitty: Remember, the real lady is
   what's under the mask.

The voice of the cartoon character, Miss Kitty, was
that of Amy Irving: Phil Nibbelink and Simon Well's
An American Tail: Fievel Goes West (Universal, 1991).

5904

Vera: Toby Walker, you're supposed to be a
   sharpshooter and you can't even see a
   woman gal under your own nose!

Toby: I can see anything I'm aiming at.

Vera Delmar played by Pert Kelton and Toby
Walker played by Preston Foster: George Stevens'
Annie Oakley (RKO, 1935).

5905

Massai: You are very silent.

Nalinle: There are times when words come
   hard to a woman.

Massai: Not often.

Massai played by Burt Lancaster and Nalinle
played by Jean Peters: Robert Aldrich's *Apache*
(United Artists, 1954).

5906

Sally: It's kind of a pity that I only like bad
   men and want to make them good.

Sally played by Coleen Gray: Hugo Fregonese's
Apache Drums (Universal, 1951).

5907

Peso: There are two things I hate. One is a
   careless man; the other is a careful
   woman.

Peso played by Gilbert Roland: Harold Kress'
Apache War Smoke (MGM, 1952).

5908

Peso: What's a matter? You sick?

Nancy: No. Jealous. How do you fight a
   woman like that?

Peso: The same as you would fight any
   other fight. Pick your position, keep the
   wind to your back, and shoot to kill.

Peso played by Gilbert Roland and Nancy Dekker
played by Barbara Ruick: Harold Kress's *Apache
War Smoke* (MGM, 1952).

5909

Major: But after your father died, why
   didn't you go back home?

Christella: Delaware is small. It's crowded
   with too many memories.

Bart Laish, assuming the identity of Major Andrew Pepperis, played by Sterling Hayden and
Christella played by Coleen Gray: Lesley Selander's *Arrow in the Dust* (Allied Artists, 1954).

5910

Smith: She must have strained every muscle in her head to get so stupid.

Reno Smith played by Robert Ryan: John Sturges'
Bad Day at Black Rock (MGM, 1955).

5911

Fierro: Are you afraid of the dark, my dear?

Montero: The only thing she is afraid of is
   poverty.

Colonel Fierro played by Sergio Fantoni and
Montero played by James Mason. The two were
referring to Alicia, played by Gina Lollobrigida:
Gene Martin's *Bad Man's River* (Scotia International, 1971).

5912

Alicia: What do you admire most in a
   woman?

King: Well, actually, ah, all parts. What do
   you look for first in a man?

Alicia: Honesty.

King: Ah …second?

Alicia played by Gina Lollobrigida and King
played by Lee Van Cleef: Gene Martin's *Bad Man's
River* (Scotia International, 1971).

5913

Lounsberry: How much would you love
   me if I wasn't rich?

Ada: Not as much.

Lounsberry: I didn't think so.

Ada: How much would you love me if I
   weren't pretty?

Lounsberry: Well, that's a different cup of
   tea.

Ada: No it isn't. A man being rich is exactly like a girl being pretty. So there!

Cyril Lounsberry played by Kent Smith and Ada
Winton played by Claire Kelly: Delmer Daves' *The
Badlanders* (MGM, 1958).

5914

Jason: You know, they say that the admission of ignorance is the beginning of
   wisdom. I don't know a thing about
   women. I never did.

Jason Meredith played by Peter Graves: Andrew V.
McLaglen's *Ballad of Josie* (Universal, 1968).

5915

Mooney: You hardly think she could shoot
   that thing.

Jason: Ah, that woman gets crazy every so
   often.

Mooney: Yeah, they're prisoners of their
   juices.

Mooney played by Harry Carey, Jr. and Jason
Meredith played by Peter Graves: Andrew V. McLaglen's *Ballad of Josie* (Universal, 1968).

5916

Judge: Mr. Burns, I've heard you were an
   honest man and good with a gun. But I
   also heard you confessed to weakness
   for liquor, cards, and women.

Burns: Not women, your Honor. They
   ain't for the weak.

Judge Crenshaw played by Roy Roberts and Walter "Yukon" Burns played by Edgar Buchanan: Felix
Feist's *The Big Trees* (Warner Bros., 1952).

5917

Spencer: Once she gets excited, she can
   hardly speak. So I give her a whack. It
   shakes her brain box up a bit.

Spencer played by John Pearce: Ted Kotcheff's *Billy
Two Hats* (United Artists, 1973).

5918

Lance: You don't seem to be nervous traveling alone.

Lola: Should I be?

Lance: This is dangerous country for a
   woman alone.

Lola: I've never been in one that wasn't.

Lance Hardeen played by Jeffrey Lynn and Lola
Montez played by Yvonne DeCarlo: George Sherman's *Black Bart* (Universal, 1948).

5919

Ketchum: A woman ties on to a man for
   life. She shouldn't have to feel that every
   time the sun comes up she might be a
   widow.

Tom "Blackjack" Ketchum played by Howard Duff:
Earl Bellamy's *Blackjack Ketchum, Desperado* (Columbia, 1956).

5920

Choya: Posses I can dodge. Young ladies
   spitting insults I can't handle.

Choya played by Alan Ladd: Rudolph Mate's
Branded (Paramount, 1951).

5921

Lily: You may think you're pretty high and
   mighty, Trumbo. But let me tell you
   this: if I live long enough, and I will, I'm
   going to pull you down off that fancy
   horse of yours and shove your face in
   the muck …so help me!

Lily Bishop played by Barbara Stanwyck and
Jonathan Trumbo played by Ray Milland: John
Farrow's *California* (Paramount, 1946).

5922

Sam: I sure like that yellow dress. Why, you could even get hay on it and nobody would know.

Sam Mullen played by James Best: Thomas Carr's *Cast a Long Shadow* (United Artists, 1959).

5923

Billy Roy: If a woman's eyes are blue, she'll be sweet and true. But if a woman's eyes are green, she'll turn hot or cold or mean.

Billy Roy played by Solomon Sturges: Charles Marquis Warren's *Charro!* (NGP, 1969).

5924

Harley: Take Helen. She had flame red hair, pitch black eyes, ruby lips, and no teeth. But talk about a body? She could straddle two horses at the same time. I went with her until I found out she dipped snuff. There's something awful unfemale about a snuff dipper, don't you think so, John?

Harley Sullivan played by Henry Fonda: Gene Kelly's *The Cheyenne Social Club* (NGP, 1970).

5925

Yancy: Why, it'll be all over the southwest that Yancy Cravat was hiding behind a woman's petticoat!

Sabra: But you didn't! They can't say so! You shot him there nicely in the ear, darling.

Yancy: Well, you shouldn't interfere when men are having a little friendly shootin'!

Yancy Cravat played by Richard Dix and Sabra Cravat played by Irene Dunne: Wesley Ruggles' *Cimarron* (RKO, 1931).

5926

Katie: All right, mister, draw! I said, draw!

Bowie: Sorry, ma'am. Back in Louisiana when we meet any pretty ladies, we make love to them, we kiss them, spank 'em on occasion …but we never go around shootin' 'em!

Katie played by Maureen O'Hara and James Bowie played by Macdonald Carey: George Sherman's *Comanche Territory* (Universal, 1950).

5927

Seeger: She sure is a pretty girl.

Bowie: She sure is.

Seeger: Too bad she's always wearing buckskin and keeping her figure covered.

Bowie: At your age, Dan'l, you shouldn't be looking.

Seeger: At my age, there ain't much else to do!

Dan'l Seeger played by Will Geer and James Bowie played by Macdonald Carey: George Sherman's *Comanche Territory* (Universal, 1950).

5928

Regret: Am I to believe that you weighed and appraised and then selected me out of all the men on the boat?

Pilar: Do not be too conceited. It's not a very large boat.

Paul Regret played by Stuart Whitman and Pilar Graile played by Ina Balin: Michael Curtiz's *The Comancheros* (20th Century–Fox, 1961).

5929

Carter: You know, personally, I think there are only three things worth living for: fine guns, good horses, and beautiful women.

Johnny Carter played by Ray Milland: John Farrow's *Copper Canyon* (Paramount, 1950).

5930

Banner: Only a fool gives a woman a loaded gun.

John Banner played by Dale Robertson: Lewis R. Foster's *Dakota Incident* (Republic, 1956).

5931

Clarke: Just a moment ago you referred to me as a lady. In the future, please remember that I happen to be one.

Banner: No woman just happens to be a lady. There's some that work at it harder than others.

Amy Clarke played by Linda Darnell and John Banner played by Dale Robertson: Lewis R. Foster's *Dakota Incident* (Republic, 1956).

5932

Banner: You're not only pretty but you're smart too. Can you cook?

Clarke: You've got petticoat fever, haven't you?

John Banner played by Dale Robertson and Amy Clarke played by Linda Darnell: Lewis R. Foster's *Dakota Incident* (Republic, 1956).

5933

Moya: White women, squaw women …just the same …cannot tell which way they will jump.

Moya played by Larry "Buster" Crabbe: James Hogan's *Desert Gold* (Paramount, 1936).

5934

Kansas: It's talk that always gets you into trouble with a woman. They always think you mean more than you say.

Kansas played by Eddy Chandler: Cullen Lewis's (Lew Collins) *The Desert Trail* (Monogram/Lone Star, 1935).

5935

Jack: Why is it that every time you bed down with a woman she thinks she's entitled to opinions and your affairs?

Jack Cooper played by Craig Sheffer: P.J. Pesce's *The Desperate Trail* (Turner Home Entertainment, 1995).

5936

Tom: Now I bet you kind of got a lovely face under all that paint. Why don't you wipe it off some day and have a good look? And figure out how you can live up to it.

Tom Destry, Jr., played by James Stewart: George Marshall's *Destry Rides Again* (Universal, 1939).

5937

Frog: Girls are all right, but look at that! Give me a beautiful steak anytime!

Frog Millhouse played by Smiley Burnette: Joseph Santley's *Down Mexico Way* (Republic, 1941).

5938

Nancy: Johnny, I just learned something.

MacKay: Yes?

Nancy: Why women in the west seem happier than those back east.

MacKay: Red women or white?

Nancy: Both. It's knowing they're needed. If a woman's needed …if she knows she's wanted. I'm going to stay. I think I can be needed here. I hope I will be.

Nancy Meek played by Audrey Dalton and Johnny MacKay played by Alan Ladd: Delmer Daves' *Drum Beat* (Warner Bros., 1954).

5939

Roberto: Well, ah, dynamite is like a woman. It takes the right hombre to know how to make her explode.

Roberto Zamudio played by Miguel Sandoval: Peter Markle's *El Diablo* (HBO Pictures, 1990).

5940

Nacho: Just like a woman! She thinks a dinner plate to eat on is more important than a dinner plate to shoot at.

Nacho Vasquez played by Edwardo Noriega: Lewis Foster's *El Paso* (Paramount, 1949).

5941

Larkin: You don't take after your grandfather much in the way of talking. Not that I much complain when a woman keeps her mouth shut.

Evelyn: I find no complaint when a man does the same.

Bob Larkin played by Henry Fonda and Evelyn played by Inger Stevens: Vincent McEveety's *Firecreek* (Warner Bros.–Seven Arts, 1968).

5942

Larkin: You know, I've known a lot of women …been with a lot.

Evelyn: Is that supposed to excite me?

Bob Larkin played by Henry Fonda and Evelyn played by Inger Stevens: Vincent McEveety's *Firecreek* (Warner Bros.–Seven Arts, 1968).

5943

Mrs. Sawyer: Dulcie, you've no patience with the men folk.

Dulcie: Well, they come in all sizes, Mrs. Sawyer, but I've yet to find one that's worth a woman's patience.

Mrs. Sawyers was uncredited and Dulcie played by Louise Latham: Vincent McEveety's *Firecreek* (Warner Bros.–Seven Arts, 1968).

5944

Lily: Women don't usually like women who like men.

Lily Langford played by Inger Stevens: Henry Hathaway's *Five Card Stud* (Paramount, 1968).

5945

Hale: Girls are like royal flushes. It takes a little luck, a lot of savvy, and an ace up the sleeve.

Hale Clinton played by Michael "Touch" Connors: Roger Corman's *Five Guns West* (American Releasing Corp., 1955).

5946

Vinson: It doesn't take any guts to go out and shoot a lot of Apaches who are trying to kill you. That's just protecting your own skin. Real guts involve the very thing you're afraid of: a decision. Like my wife's.

Travis: Your wife's?

Vinson: I told you the Apaches murdered her and the kids. That's not exactly true. She shot the children herself rather than having them taken alive. I can't match guts like that. Can you?

Sgt. Vinson played by Joel McCrea and Travis played by John Russell: Joseph Newman's *Fort Massacre* (United Artists, 1958).

5947

Joe: You know, what I don't understand about European women is …why would you want me to be Lord and master when I offered you an equal partnership?

Max: It's because of my training, Joe: how things should be between a man and a woman. A man as a partner, I don't understand. But a master! A master …he I know how to understand.

Joe Jarrett played by Dean Martin and Maxine Richter played by Ursula Andress: Robert Aldrich's *Four for Texas* (Warner Bros., 1964).

5948

Fiske: Somebody once said, believe nothing a woman says but everything she sings.

Hooker: Who said that?

Fiske: Me!

Fiske played by Richard Widmark and Hooker played by Gary Cooper: Henry Hathaway's *Garden of Evil* (20th Century–Fox, 1954).

5949

Fiske: You know at first I thought she was one of those women who come along every so often and fascinate men without ever trying …or even knowing why.

Hooker: And now what?

Fiske: She tries …and she knows why.

Fiske played by Richard Widmark and Hooker played by Gary Cooper: Henry Hathaway's *Garden of Evil* (20th Century–Fox, 1954).

5950

Ben: I'm sorry, I didn't mean to make you cry. Forgive me.

Molly: Nonsense. There's nothing to forgive. A woman cries …she was meant to. A man can get drunk and get into fights. A woman can cry. It's good.

Ben Cutler played by Fred MacMurray and Molly Cain played by Kathryn Card: Nathan Juran's *Good Day for a Hanging* (Columbia, 1958).

5951

Bertha: A woman's job is to grin and bear it.

Aunt Bertha played by Shirley Knight: David Greene's *A Good Day to Die* (a.k.a. *Children of the Dust*; Vidmark Entertainment, 1995).

5952

Slayton: She's quite a woman, isn't she?

Jess: As far as I'm concerned, all women are alike. They just got different faces so you can tell them apart.

Slayton: To a man without taste, I suppose all things are alike. She's as different from other women as cognac is from corn liquor.

Jess: You get the same kind of headache from either one.

Frank Slayton played by Phil Carey and Jess Burgess played by Leo Gordon: Raoul Walsh's *Gun Fury* (Columbia, 1953).

5953

Davy: I've never seen a girl cry this close before. But they can't all cry as pretty as you.

Davy Hackett played by James Darren: Phil Karlson's *Gunman's Walk* (Columbia, 1958).

5954

Levi: You know, it takes a man my age to appreciate a real woman. She's worth it too.

Keno: Oh I appreciate them, Levi. Every one I've ever had. I just appreciated the hell out of 'em!

Levi Morgan played by James Whitmore and Keno played by Monte Markham: Paul Wendkos' *Guns of the Magnificent Seven* (United Artists, 1969).

5955

Colonel: Did you or did you not give that woman permission for a temperance rally?

Captain: Yes and no. That is, I had no idea it would get out of hand so to speak, sir.

Colonel: What the hell did you expect? Give a woman an acorn, the next thing you know you're up to your rump in oak trees!

Colonel Thadeus Gearhart played by Burt Lancaster and Captain Paul Slater played by Jim Hutton: John Sturges' *The Hallelujah Trail* (MGM, 1965).

5956

Cruse: You know my old lady told me that if I didn't get home early tonight, she was going to become a widow.

Al Cruse played by Mickey Shaughnessy: Michael Curtiz's *The Hangman* (Paramount, 1959).

5957

Sheriff: You're a hard woman, Hannie Caulder.

Hannie: Like the man said, there aren't any hard woman …only soft men.

The Sheriff was uncredited and Hannie Caulder played by Raquel Welch: Burt Kennedy's *Hannie Caulder* (Paramount, 1971).

5958

Lowe: You and your silly ideals. You think truth is the most important thing.

Hondo: It's a measure of a man.

Lowe: Well, not for a woman! A man can afford to have noble sentiments and poses. But a woman only has the man she marries. That's her truth. And if he's no good, that's still her truth. I married a man who was a liar, a thief, and a coward. He was a drunkard and unfaithful. He only married me to get this ranch, and then he deserted Johnny and me for good. And that's your fine truth for you. Could I bring Johnny up on that?

Hondo: No, I guess you couldn't.

Angie Lowe played by Geraldine Page and Hondo Lane played by John Wayne: John Farrow's *Hondo* (Warner Bros., 1953).

5959

Hondo: Mrs. Dow, the Apaches have a saying. They say that the nighttime is for either loving or sleeping …not talking. You better get some sleep.

Hondo Lane played by Ralph Taeger and Angie Dow played by Kathie Browne: Lee H. Katzin's *Hondo and the Apaches* (TVW, 1967).

5960

Gabby: How are you gonna argue with a female when she's made up her mind?

Gabby Whittaker played by George "Gabby" Hayes: Joseph Kane's *In Old Caliente* (Republic, 1939).

5961

Bridie: It's time your daughter saw some things close enough to know why she should keep some other things at a distance.

Bridie played by Isabella Hofmann: John Patterson's *Independence* (TVW, 1987).

5962

Vienna: A man can lie, steal, and even kill. But as long as he hangs on to his pride, he's still a man. All a woman has to do is slip …once …and she's a tramp. It must be a great comfort to you to be a man.

Vienna played by Joan Crawford: Nicholas Ray's *Johnny Guitar* (Republic, 1954).

5963
Sam: I never saw a woman who was more a man. She thinks like one, acts like one, and sometimes makes me feel like I'm not.
Sam played by Robert Osterloh: Nicholas Ray's *Johnny Guitar* (Republic, 1954).

5964
Johnny: You wouldn't shoot a man in the back.
Dancin' Kid: In front of Vienna? Why, she would never forgive such bad manners.
Johnny Guitar played by Sterling Hayden and the Dancin' Kid played by Scott Brady: Nicholas Ray's *Johnny Guitar* (Republic, 1954).

5965
Kehoe: Mrs. Sabina, you're a woman after my own heart. Tougher than wrang leather, smarter than spit, and colder than January.
Dan Kehoe played by Clark Gable and Sabina played by Eleanor Parker: Raoul Walsh's *The King and Four Queens* (United Artists, 1956).

5966
Carson: It's a funny thing about flags, ma'am. Everyone I've ever heard about was put into the hands of men by a woman.
Kit Carson played by Jon Hall: George B. Seitz's *Kit Carson* (United Artists, 1940).

5967
Annie: Do you think this hat would be better without the feather?
Elsie: Why don't you try the feather without the hat?
Annie played by Loretta Young and Elsie played by Gladys George: Frank Lloyd's *Lady from Cheyenne* (Universal, 1941).

5968
Will: You know, you're kind of hard to keep track of. First, you want to stay. Then you want to go. Now you want to stay again.
Betty: I'm a woman.
Will Spence played by Richard Widmark and Betty Spence played by Barbara Rush: Vincent McEveety's *The Last Day* (Paramount, 1975).

5969
Gates: Lady, if I was born a century too late, you were definitely born a century too early!
Lewis Gates played by Tom Berenger: Tab Murphy's *Last of the Dogmen* (Savory Pictures, 1995).

5970
Gates: I've seen this country reduce grown men to tears. It ain't no place for a woman.

Lillian: You really are a cowboy, aren't you? What is it you fellas say …we're burnin' daylight?
Lewis Gates played by Tom Berenger and Professor Lillian Sloan played by Barbara Hershey: Tab Murphy's *Last of the Dogmen* (Savory Pictures, 1995).

5971
Maria: Do you know that every time you look at me, I feel like I am running around without any clothes on?
Brad: It's gonna get mighty chilly when the sun goes down.
Maria O'Reilly played by Linda Cristal and Brad Ellison played by Jock Mahoney: George Sherman's *The Last of the Fast Guns* (Universal, 1958).

5972
Belle: To me, it always seems like it's the women who keep on living. Men kill or get killed, and women bury them. We're professional survivors.
Belle Breckenridge played by Dorothy Malone: Robert Aldrich's *The Last Sunset* (Universal, 1961).

5973
Walks Far: There is an old Blackfoot story. When Napi made man and woman, he said: you two will have to get along. And the man said, we'll get along because I'll always have the first say. And the woman smiled and said, and I'll always have the last say.
Walks Far Woman played by Raquel Welch: Mel Damski's *The Legend of Walks Far Woman* (TVW, 1982).

5974
Roy Bean: Even a bad likeness of Lillie Langtry is worth most women in the flesh.
Judge Roy Bean played by Paul Newman: John Huston's *The Life and Times of Judge Roy Bean* (NGP, 1972).

5975
Roy Bean: A man has two loves: an unattainable goddess and a mortal woman. And he loves the mortal woman twice as much for having worshiped Lillie Langtry.
Judge Roy Bean played by Paul Newman: John Huston's *The Life and Times of Judge Roy Bean* (NGP, 1972).

5976
Jerri: Believe you me, if it didn't take men to make babies, I wouldn't have anything to do with any of you!
Jerri Bondi played by Gena Rowlands: David Miller's *Lonely Are the Brave* (Universal, 1962).

5977
Riley: A killer's wife doesn't have friends. The women walked around her, and the men were afraid to talk to her. She stood it as long as she could.

Riley Wade played by Anthony Perkins: Henry Levin's *The Lonely Man* (Paramount, 1957).

5978
Gus: It's dangerous business writing two women at the same time.
Gus McCrae played by Robert Duvall: Simon Wincer's *Lonesome Dove* (TVW, 1989).

5979
Gus: Well, I can't see that you've aged that much.
Clara: Well, I have and so have you, although I doubt you'd admit it.
Gus: Well, the older the violin, the sweeter the music.
Gus McCrae played by Robert Duvall and Clara played by Anjelica Huston: Simon Wincer's *Lonesome Dove* (TVW, 1989).

5980
Lorena: I bet she has always been a lady, huh?
Gus: Well, a lady can slash your jugular as quick as a Comanche. Clara has got a sharp tongue. She's tomahawked me many a time in the past. You're like her.
Lorena Wood played by Diane Lane and Gus McCrae played by Robert Duvall: Simon Wincer's *Lonesome Dove* (TVW, 1989).

5981
Beth: Jim Younger, there are some things that a man does not ask a lady!
Jim: Well, Beth, when you're old enough to call yourself a lady, I'll keep that in mind.
Beth played by Amy Stryker and Jim Younger played by Keith Carradine: Walter Hill's *The Long Riders* (United Artists, 1980).

5982
Madron: I should have known! A female medicine man!
Sister Mary: No, no, no! Just a simple nurse, Mr. Madron.
Madron: Lady, there ain't nothin' simple about you at all!
Madron played by Richard Boone and Sister Mary played by Leslie Caron: Jerry Hopper's *Madron* (Four Star Excelsior, 1970).

5983
Kate: Hello, Alec.
Alec: Hello, Kate.
Kate: Alec?
Alec: What is it, Kate?
Kate: Oh, I just thought that sometime we would have more to say to each other than just hello.
Alec: What else is there to say?
Kate: Nothin', I guess.
Kate Canaday played by Aline MacMahon and Alec Waggoman played by Donald Crisp: Anthony Mann's *The Man from Laramie* (Columbia, 1955).

5984

Lockhart: You're just a hard, scheming old woman, aren't you?

Kate: Ugly, too!

Kate Canaday played by Aline MacMahon and Will Lockhart played by James Stewart: Anthony Mann's *The Man from Laramie* (Columbia, 1955).

5985

Billy: Well, now! If she don't look as fresh as a daisy beside an outhouse!

Billy played by Bo Hopkins: Richard C. Sarafian's *The Man Who Loved Cat Dancing* (MGM, 1973).

5986

Lapchance: I had a woman run off on me once …mailed her a suitcase.

Lapchance played by Lee J. Cobb: Richard C. Sarafian's *The Man Who Loved Cat Dancing* (MGM, 1973).

5987

Reed: How low can a man get?

Dempsey: I wouldn't know about a man. But I've just seen how low a woman will go to get what she wants.

Reed Bowman played by Jeanne Crain and Dempsey Rae played by Kirk Douglas: King Vidor's *Man Without a Star* (Universal, 1955).

5988

Lolita: Father, I was asking the Holy Mother to save me from a convent. Is that a sin?

Father: The sin, I think, would be in sending you to one.

Lolita Quintero played by Linda Darnell and Don Diego Vega/Zorro (masquerading as a Friar) played by Tyrone Power: Rouben Mamoulian's *The Mark of Zorro* (20th Century–Fox, 1940).

5989

Don Diego: But, my dear, in Spain the husbands of adorable ladies are merely background.

Don Diego Vega/Zorro played by Tyrone Power: Rouben Mamoulian's *The Mark of Zorro* (20th Century–Fox, 1940).

5990

Katherine: Are you going to stand there with that stupid look on your face while the hired help insults your wife?

McLintock: He's just ignorant. He doesn't know any better than to tell the truth.

Katherine McLintock played by Maureen O'Hara and George Washington McLintock played by John Wayne: Andrew V. McLaglen's *McLintock!* (United Artists, 1963).

5991

McLintock: Katherine, you women are always raising hell about one thing when it's something else you're really sore about! Don't you think it's about time you told me what put the burr under your saddle about me?

5992

Sam: You said she was feisty.

Jericho: Indoors, it's her say. Outdoors, it's mine.

Sam: I take it you don't get indoors much.

Sam Webster played by John Dennis Johnston and Jericho Adams played by Kris Kristofferson: Kevin James Dobson's *Miracle in the Wilderness* (TVW—1991).

5993

Sieber: You listen to me now and it'll save you grief later. The best thing a woman can be is fat. Once they're fat, they don't expect nothing. They should be sad too. A woman that ain't sad ain't worth spit. You find yourself a fat, unhappy woman and you'll be set for life.

Al Sieber played by Richard Widmark: Jack Starrett's *Mr. Horn* (TVW, 1979).

5994

Mac: Ain't you ever gonna get tired of being a widow?

Belle: If I do, I'll let the ladder down.

Mac played by Forrest Tucker and Belle Starr played by Jane Russell: Allan Dwan's *Montana Belle* (RKO, 1952).

5995

Poker Alice: Well, I'll tell you something that occurred to me some time back. It seems to me once a woman learns how to handle so-called woman's work, she never gets to handle anything else.

Poker Alice Moffit played by Susan Sullivan: Hy Averback's *The New Maverick* (TVW, 1978).

5996

Arroyo: Women are strange animals, no?

Bierce: Yeah.

Arroyo: You never know what they're thinking. Never. For they always know what a man is thinking.

Bierce: Not always. But they think they do.

General Tomas Arroyo played by Jimmy Smits and Ambrose Bierce played by Gregory Peck: Luis Puenzo's *Old Gringo* (Columbia, 1989).

5997

Cheyenne: You know, Jill, you remind me of my mother. She was the biggest whore in Alameda and the finest woman that ever lived. Whoever my father was for an hour or for a month, he must have been a happy man.

Cheyenne played by Jason Robards, Jr., and Jill McBain played by Claudia Cardinale: Sergio Leone's *Once Upon a Time in the West* (Paramount, 1969).

5998

McBain: If you want to, you could lay me over the table and amuse yourself. And even call in your men. Well, no woman

George Washington McLintock played by John Wayne and Katherine McLintock played by Maureen O'Hara: Andrew V. McLaglen's *McLintock!* (United Artists, 1963).

ever died from that. When you're finished, all I'll need will be a tub of boiling water and I'll be exactly what I was before …with just another filthy memory.

Jill McBain played by Claudia Cardinale: Sergio Leone's *Once Upon a Time in the West* (Paramount, 1969).

5999

Rio: How much for that thing on your neck there?

Vendor: This? I'm not selling that. But I'm glad you like it.

Rio: I like it $20.00 worth.

Vendor: I couldn't sell it. My husband gave it to me.

Rio: Then, I like it $30.00 worth then.

Vendor: All right.

Rio played by Marlon Brando and the Mexican Vendor played by Margarita Martin: Marlon Brando's *One-Eyed Jacks* (Paramount, 1961).

6000

Pardner: I don't know what you're talking about, Ben. Elizabeth ain't sick.

Ben: Now you listen to me. She's picked up a bad case of respectability. And in just a few days from now, that poor woman is gonna be burning up in a fever of virtue. And then, look out!

Pardner: Why?

Ben: Pardner, it's been my experience that there ain't nothing more ruthless and treacherous than a genuine good woman!

Pardner played by Clint Eastwood, Ben Rumson played by Lee Marvin, and Elizabeth Woodling played by Jean Seberg: Joseph Logan's *Paint Your Wagon* (Paramount, 1969).

6001

Hickok: Son, one of these days you're going to grow up. And you ought to know about women. You see, the thing is this. Women are …uh …well …they're, uh …well, son, I can tell ya what an Indian will do to you, but you'll never know what a woman will do.

Wild Bill Hickok played by Gary Cooper: Cecil B. DeMille's *The Plainsman* (Paramount, 1936).

6002

Hickok: It's easier sliding up Niagara Falls than it is understanding women.

Wild Bill Hickok played by Don Murray: David Lowell Rich's *The Plainsman* (Universal, 1966).

6003

Collins: May I kiss you?

Alice: I don't like men who ask.

Collins played by Tom Skerritt and Poker Alice Moffit played by Elizabeth Taylor: Arthur Allan Seidelman's *Poker Alice* (TVW, 1987).

6004

Dolworth: That's a lot of woman there: beautiful, classy, and guts. Hard enough to kill ya and soft enough to change ya.

Bill Dolworth played by Burt Lancaster: Richard Brooks' *The Professionals* (Columbia, 1966).

6005

Dolworth: She must be a lot of woman.

Fardan: Certain women have a way of changing some boys into men, and some men back into boys.

Bill Dolworth played by Burt Lancaster and Henry Rico Fardan played by Lee Marvin: Richard Brooks' *The Professionals* (Columbia, 1966).

6006

Chaney: Don't look at me! I don't want to see my shame in your eyes.

Chaney played by Dorothy Malone: Harry Keller's *Quantez* (Universal, 1957).

6007

Quigley: Lady, you are about a half a bubble off the plumb, and that's for sure and for certain.

Crazy Cora: Just because the road is rocky doesn't mean your spirit should get rocky too.

Matthew Quigley played by Tom Selleck and Crazy Cora played by Laura San Giacomo: Simon Wincer's *Quigley Down Under* (MGM-United Artists, 1990).

6008

Keane: Sometimes I like a man who doesn't believe what a woman tells him.

Altar Keane played by Marlene Dietrich: Fritz Lang's *Rancho Notorious* (RKO, 1952).

6009

Valance: You know, there are only two things more beautiful than a good gun: a Swiss watch or a woman from anywhere. You ever had a good Swiss watch?

Cherry Valance played by John Ireland: Howard Hawks' *Red River* (United Artists, 1948).

6010

Gideon: You know, I learned something in the dressmaking business. It ain't the pattern, the fabric, or the price that's important. It's the fit …and not the dress at all. It's the woman that wears it. And you sure do fit your dress!

Gideon Walker played by William Petersen: Mike Robe's *Return to Lonesome Dove* (TVW, 1993).

6011

Clara: I'm too strong for the normal man and too jealous once my feelings get riled.

Clara Allen played by Barbara Hershey: Mike Robe's *Return to Lonesome Dove* (TVW, 1993).

6012

Tessa: When Sam Teeler buys my clothes, I don't like another man to muss them up.

Tessa Milotte played by Gia Scala and Sam Teeler

A wild saloon scene with jockey Altar Keane (Marlene Dietrich) riding Deputy (Dick Wessel) in a horse race to the bar in Fritz Lang's classic *Rancho Notorious* (RKO, 1952).

played by Henry Silva: Jesse Hibbs' *Ride a Crooked Trail* (Universal, 1958).

6013

Steve: The mouth of a strange woman is a deep pit. Him that is abhorred of the Lord shall fall therein.

Steve Judd played by Joel McCrea: Sam Peckinpah's *Ride the High Country* (MGM, 1962).

6014

Rio: Whatever you say to a woman, except when you speak of love, you'll be talking to yourself.

Rio played by Robert Taylor: John Farrow's *Ride, Vaquero!* (MGM, 1953).

6015

King: Not much of a place to bring a civilized woman to, is it?
Rio: I couldn't tell you. I've never met one.

King Cameron played by Howard Keel and Rio played by Robert Taylor: John Farrow's *Ride, Vaquero!* (MGM, 1953).

6016

Esqueda: You do not wish to kill me for what I am or for what I have done, but because of a woman. I will die of many things, perhaps, but not because of a woman.

Jose Esqueda played by Anthony Quinn: John Farrow's *Ride, Vaquero!* (MGM, 1953).

6017

Lassiter: Where I was raised, a woman's word was law. I ain't quite out-growed that yet.
Tull: Meddler, we have a law here something different from a woman's whim. Take care you don't transgress it.
Lassiter: To hell with your law!

Jim Lassiter played by Ed Harris and Deacon Tull played by Norbert Weisser: Charles Haid's *Riders of the Purple Sage* (Turner Home Entertainment, 1996).

6018

Kansas: Women are funny that way.
Chito: Women are funny any way …but nice too!

Kansas played by Tim Holt and Chito Rafferty played by Richard Martin: Lesley Selander's *Riders of the Range* (RKO, 1950).

6019

Trevino: Hey, Chito, you're bleeding! How did you get that?
Chito: Oh, I got into a fight.
Trevino: Over a girl?
Chito: Well, if it was over some girl, I wouldn't mind it so much.

Captain Trevino played by Rick Vallin and Chito Rafferty played by Richard Martin: Lesley Selander's *Rio Grande Patrol* (RKO, 1950).

6020

Mark: She's beautiful, isn't she?

Matt: There's an old saying, Mark. It's only skin deep.
Mark: What is?
Matt: Beauty.
Mark: How deep should it be?
Matt: Well, ask her, son. She looks like an expert.

Mark Calder played by Tommy Rettig and Matt Calder played by Robert Mitchum: Otto Preminger's *The River of No Return* (20th Century–Fox, 1954).

6021

Mary Ann: Some women have dreams that are just dreams, don't they?

Mary Ann Neff played by Shantal Hiatt: Richard Lloyd Dewey's *Rockwell* (Imperial Entertainment, 1994).

6022

Rooster: If they ever give 'em the vote, God help us!

Rooster Cogburn played by John Wayne: Stuart Millar's *Rooster Cogburn* (Universal, 1975).

6023

Rooster: Well, I'll tell you something else that Paul said: let your women be silent in church.
Eula: How come you to know that passage?
Rooster: Well, Judge Parker is partial to it. You know, you're not the only one with a Bible. He's got a big one. It'd make two or three of yours.
Eula: It's not the size that's important, Marshal, but your knowledge of its contents.

Rooster Cogburn played by John Wayne, Eula Goodnight played by Katharine Hepburn, and Judge Parker played by John McIntire: Stuart Millar's *Rooster Cogburn* (Universal, 1975).

6024

Rooster: Well, out in the territory, we prize a dead-shot more than we do a lady's charm.
Eula: Then I've come to the right place, haven't I? You mean the men in the west do not mind if their women outshoot or outsmart them?
Rooster: If they're quiet about it. No, out here we value a spirited woman almost as much as we do a spirited horse.
Eula: Almost as much, hey?
Rooster: Yes, ma'am, almost as much. Not quite, but almost.

Rooster Cogburn played by John Wayne and Eula Goodnight played by Katharine Hepburn: Stuart Millar's *Rooster Cogburn* (Universal, 1975).

6025

McCoy: Water is like a woman: lying and fickle. You got to keep your eye on it every minute.

McCoy played by Strother Martin: Stuart Millar's *Rooster Cogburn* (Universal, 1975).

6026

McCoy: Women can no more keep their mouths shut than a yellow-tail catfish.

McCoy played by Strother Martin: Stuart Millar's *Rooster Cogburn* (Universal, 1975).

6027

Rooster: Well ma'am, I don't know much about thoroughbred horses or women. Them that I did know, I never liked. They're too nervous and spooky. They scare me. But you're one high-bred filly that don't. Of course I don't know what you're talking about half the time, but that don't matter. Being around you pleases me.

Rooster Cogburn played by John Wayne: Stuart Millar's *Rooster Cogburn* (Universal, 1975).

6028

Orrin: You know, Laura, Tyrel was right …gold hair, blue eyes, but a mite narrow between 'em.

Orrin Sackett played by Tom Selleck, Laura Pritts played by Marcy Hanson, and Tyrel Sackett played by Jeff Osterhage: Robert Totten's *The Sacketts* (TVW, 1979).

6029

Orrin: Now don't you forget what Pa used to say: the only thing more fearful than being left afoot …is a pretty gal.

Orrin Sackett played by Tom Selleck: Robert Totten's *The Sacketts* (TVW, 1979). *See also entry 6053.*

6030

Deaks: Your ma was a pretty good horse trader too. She proved that when she got rid of me.

Deaks played by Robert Wilke: Gary Nelson's *Santee* (Crown International Pictures, 1973).

6031

Grace: I've heard about you redcoats. You always get your man. Tell me, am I the first woman to your credit?
O'Rourke: Yeah, and I hope you're the last!

Grace Markey played by Shelley Winters and Sergeant Thomas O'Rourke played by Alan Ladd: Raoul Walsh's *Saskatchewan* (Universal, 1954).

6032

Charlie: It's no easy job, Sam, to take care of a woman.
Sam: No, sir.
Charlie: They expect things they never ask for. And when they don't get them, they ask you why. Sometimes they don't ask …and they just go ahead and punish you for not doing something you didn't know you were supposed to do in the first place.
Sam: What for instance, sir?
Charlie: Well, that's a very difficult question to answer, Sam. You're never quite sure. It's just that it's …sort of you might say, relative.

Sam: Relative to what, sir?

Charlie: To how they're feeling at the moment.

Sam: And how's that?

Charlie: You never know.

Sam: Well, I don't believe I really understand what you're trying to tell me, sir.

Charlie: I know, I know. I never understood it myself. I never understood it. It's just one of those things, Sam. It's around …and you just don't ever see it.

Charlie Anderson played by James Stewart and Sam played by Doug McClure: Andrew V. McLaglen's *Shenandoah* (Universal, 1965).

6033

Hannah: It's a pretty land, isn't it?

Paden: You're a pretty lady.

Hannah: A lot of men have told me that. Maybe it's true. I guess some men are slow to believe it.

Paden: Believe it.

Hannah: They're drawn to me by that, but it never lasts.

Paden: Why?

Hannah: Because they don't like what I want.

Paden: What's that?

Hannah: I want to build something. Make things grow. That takes hard work. A lifetime of it. That's not why a man comes to a pretty woman. And after awhile I won't be so pretty. But this land will be.

Hannah played by Rosanna Arquette and Paden played by Kevin Kline: Lawrence Kasdan's *Silverado* (Columbia, 1985).

6034

Lilac: We have just got to do this [social gathering] more often. I declare, it just makes life more bearable, don't it?

Beth: For some of us. Of course, we don't have the same diversion as you do.

Lilac: Meaning what?

Beth: Meaning Tom told me about you and Dell.

Lilac: Now you listen to me, Beth Poulet. I love my husband. It wasn't my idea to leave Georgia and come out here to this God-forsaken wilderness. You get through life as best you can. So I say: open season on casual contentment!

Lilac Gentry played by Wendle Meldrum and Beth Poulet played by Maria Vacratsis: Eugene Levy's *Sodbusters* (Atlantis Releasing, 1994).

6035

Cobb: When I lie down at nights, I'm thinking about a woman. And when I get up in the mornings, I'm thinking about a woman. It's been years, Baker, it's been years! I can't remember, I can't even remember what it's like.

Baker: Well, Johnny, I'll tell you what it's like. First of all…

Cobb: I don't want you to tell me! I want to do it! Now we got a deal! A Gatling gun for a woman. Now where is she?

Johnny Cobb played by Albert Salmi and Joe Baker played by Dean Martin: Andrew V. McLaglen's *something big* (NGP, 1971).

6036

Cherry: A woman doesn't run out on the man she loves. She sticks with him …win or lose.

Cherry Malotte played by Marlene Dietrich: Ray Enright's *The Spoilers* (Universal, 1942). *See also entry 6037.*

6037

Cherry: A woman doesn't run out on the man she loves. She sticks with him …win or lose.

Cherry Malotte played by Anne Baxter: Jesse Hibb's *The Spoilers* (Universal, 1955). *See also entry 6036.*

6038

(*Indian at Monastery*)

Squanto: Where are the women of your tribe?

Daniel: We have no women, Squanto. We have devoted our lives to God.

Squanto: Your tribe will die with no women.

Timothy: Squanto, we are not a tribe.

Squanto: I would never join a tribe with no women.

Squanto played by Adam Beach, Brother Daniel played by Mandy Patinkin, and Brother Timothy played by Stuart Pankin: Xavier Koller's *Squanto: A Warrior's Tale* (Buena Vista, 1994).

6039

Dave: For a man that's got a despise for women, you sure do get all snagged up with 'em!

Dave played by George "Gabby" Hayes: Edwin L. Marin's *Tall in the Saddle* (RKO, 1944).

6040

Rocklin: You might as well know right now that no woman is going to get me hog-tied and branded.

Rocklin played by John Wayne: Edwin L. Marin's *Tall in the Saddle* (RKO, 1944).

6041

Madden: What's a girl like you doing tied in with a dog like Pearlo?

Corinna: Sometimes you can get sort of attached to a dog.

Larry Madden played by Randolph Scott, Corinna Ordway Willard played by Dorothy Malone, and Cibo Pearlo played by John Baragrey: Lesley Selander's *Tall Man Riding* (Warner Bros., 1955).

6042

Allison: You know something? When a woman looks pretty at sunup, then she's really pretty!

Ben Allison played by Clark Gable: Raoul Walsh's *The Tall Men* (20th Century–Fox, 1955).

6043

Major: Lady, you're definitely much too logical for a woman!

Major Thomas Thorn played by Gary Cooper: Robert Rossen's *They Came to Cordura* (Columbia, 1959).

6044

Custer: Walking through life with you, ma'am, has been a very gracious thing.

George Armstrong Custer played by Errol Flynn: Raoul Walsh's *They Died with Their Boots On* (Warner Bros., 1941).

6045

Marie: With Lon Bennett, there are only two kinds of women: living and dead.

Marie played by Veda Ann Borg and Lon Bennett played by Jeff Chandler: Russell Rouse's *Thunder in the Sun* (Paramount, 1959).

6046

Tracey: It's an eye-opener to a girl who finds that her body can trap her decency.

Tracey Hamilton played by Luana Patten: Joseph Newman's *A Thunder of Drums* (MGM, 1961).

6047

Sarah: Whose responsibility is civilization, you tell me that.

Euphemia: Oh, I don't know.

Sarah: Women, that's who! If we left it up to the men, there would be no schools, no churches, no families …nothing that really endures. We'd just have jewels and crazy dreams and war …or politicking. That's just another piss-ant substitute for the other three.

Sarah McClure played by Dana Delany and Young Euphemia Ashby played by Tina Majorino: Karen Arthur's *True Women* (TVW, 1997).

6048

Elena: I know that many of you regard me as a degraded woman. Degraded but detached of a savage Comanche by having to live as one of them. You said, why did I not kill myself. I did not …

Gus: Go on, go on, you're doing fine.

Elena: I can't!

Gus: Well, I sure as hell can! She didn't kill herself because her religion forbids it. You know, sometimes it takes a lot more courage to live than it does to die. You would agree with that, wouldn't you Major? Yeah, I don't think any of you folks in this room have ever been to a Comanche camp. Have you, Major? No, no. I have! I usually limit my visits to three days. Three days. That's about 45 working hours for a woman in one of those camps. You know, a Comanche …he don't know when Sunday comes. And cooking is sort of the recreation for the women. And then in their spare time they chew the glue of buffalo hides so

that their man can have a nice soft pair
of moccasins. Well, you can judge for
yourself what kind of life it is by the
number of survivors we brought back.
Jim: That's right …
Gus: Now you shut up, Jim! You shut up!
And now some of you are asking why
this young lady doesn't go back. Well, it
might be interesting for you to know
that this afternoon she ask me to take
her back. Because she was treated much
better by the Comanches than she's been
treated by some of you!

Elena de la Madriaga played by Linda Cristal,
Guthrie "Gus" McCabe played by James Stewart,
and Lieutenant Jim Gary played by Richard Widmark: John Ford's *Two Rode Together* (Columbia,
1961).

6049

Diana: Chris, when I look into your eyes, I
don't see myself there.
Chris: Oh, you must be a little blind.
Diana: I see horizons, ranges of uncrossed
mountains, the unknown. You belong to
that, Chris, the way an eagle belongs to
the sky.

Diana played by Virginia Grey and Captain Christopher Holden played by Gary Cooper: Cecil B.
DeMille's *Unconquered* (Paramount, 1947).

6050

Mollie: But did you never know that flirt-
ing gets into a woman's blood like fighting gets into a man? Now, now a girl
begins coquetting to discover if she has
the power. Then she goes looking, like a
fighter after a bully for the hardest man
to conquer. But it's never the man she
wants. It's the pleasure of bringing him
to her feet.
Jeff: Until the right man comes along and
gives her the spanking she deserves.
Mollie: Ah, that's the man she dreams of!

Mollie Monahan played by Barbara Stanwyck and
Jeff Butler played by Joel McCrea: Cecil B. De-
Mille's *Union Pacific* (Paramount, 1939).

6051

Bill: There's only two ways to handle women. And nobody knows what they are!

Bill Yard played by George Cleveland: George
Marshall's *Valley of the Sun* (RKO, 1942).

6052

Menefee: What do you want? A man or a
railroad ticket?

George Menefee played by Peter Hansen: Rudolph
Mate's *The Violent Men* (Columbia, 1955).

6053

Nebraska: Baldy is always afraid every
woman he sees is gonna put a bridle on
him.
Baldy: Yeah, well, there's only two things
I'm scared of: that's a good woman and
getting set afoot.

Upon learning that his daughter has been raped and his favorite horse (Blue) stolen,
Sheriff John Copperud (Carroll O'Connor) wastes no time setting out to get Blue back
in *Waterhole #3* (Paramount, 1967).

Nebraska played by Tom Tully and Baldy played
by Vince Barnett: Stuart Gilmore's *The Virginian*
(Paramount, 1946). *See also entry 6029.*

6054

Steve: A fine way to treat a lady!
Virginian: How was I to know she was a
lady? She was with you, wasn't she?

Steve played by Sonny Tufts and the Virginian
played by Joel McCrea: Stuart Gilmore's *The Virginian* (Paramount, 1946).

6055

Cole: You're gonna have to tell me why
you named her Billee.
Sheriff: Well, her ma and me were trying
to make a boy.
Cole: Well, you didn't even come close!

Lewton Cole played by James Coburn and Sheriff
John Copperud played by Carroll O'Connor: Wil-

liam A. Graham's *Waterhole No. 3* (Paramount,
1967).

6056

(*sheriff talking to man who assaulted his
daughter*)
Sheriff: That thing with Billee. Of
course, not being there, I'll never
really know, but what was that all
about?
Cole: Just a hasty little affair. Nothing
got bruised but her pride.
Sheriff: Yeah, well, you should have stayed
to talk a bit. I always talk for about five
minutes before I run.

Sheriff John Copperud played by Carroll O'Connor and Lewton Cole played by James Coburn:
William A. Graham's *Waterhole No. 3* (Paramount, 1967).

6057

Whitman: I don't care what happens to you. It's these women I care about. You can't get them through. It can't be done with women alone.

Wyatt: Then I'll make men out of you women! Roy, when you breed cattle in that valley of yours, you kill off the weak ones. By the time we get to that valley, you'll know that the women who are left are fit stock. I'll work 'em until they're skin and bone and muscle. Once we get there, you can fatten them up.

Roy Whitman played by John McIntire and Buck Wyatt played by Robert Taylor: William Wellman's *Westward the Women* (MGM, 1952).

6058

Germany: You don't think very much of women, do you?

Cross: The hell I don't! I just don't trust 'em!

Germany played by Delta Burke and Cross played by Willie Nelson: Burt Kennedy's *Where the Hell's That Gold?!!!* (a.k.a. *Dynamite & Gold*; TVW, 1988).

6059

Tex: It's always been my experience that where there's a woman, trouble just naturally gathers like ants around a sugar bowl.

Tex Houston played by Tom Fadden: Ford Beebe's and Ray Taylor's *Winners of the West* (Universal serial, Chapter 2: "The Wreck at Red River Gorge," 1940).

6060

Tex: That gal can see trouble further and head for it faster than any critter I've ever seen!

Tex Houston played by Tom Fadden: Ford Beebe's and Ray Taylor's *Winners of the West* (Universal serial, Chapter 11: "Bullets In The Dark," 1940).

6061

Gabby: Darn persnickety women!

Gabby Whittaker played by George "Gabby" Hayes: Joseph Kane's *Young Buffalo Bill* (Republic, 1940).

6062

Martha Jane: What are you gawking at? Ain't you ever seen a pair of pants before?

Jeff: Yeah, but it ain't so much the crust that makes the pie as the filling.

Martha Jane Canary played by Barbara Mansell and Jeff Shelby played by Jody McCrea: Maury Dexter's *Young Guns of Texas* (20th Century–Fox, 1963).

6063

Hammond: She's the Black Whip!

Baxter: She couldn't be! The Black Whip has got to be a man! He's out-shot us, out-rode us, and out-fought us! He's stopped us at every turn!

Dan Hammond played by Francis McDonald and Baxter played by Hal Taliaferro/Wally Wales: Spencer Bennet and Wallace Grissell's *Zorro's Black Whip* (Republic serial, Chapter 9: "Avalanche," 1944).

Name Index

Film Index

486

Keyword and Subject Index

full circle 38
full house 1482, 5550
full of crap 4224
full of lead 5354
full of life 1150
full-blooded Indian 2811
full-blossomed woman 5828
fun 405, 1056, 1513, 2304, 3141,
  3630, 3886, 4075, 4200, 4974,
  5284, 5562, 5695, 5720
fun ride 4083
function 1322, 1722
fundament 2641
fundamental 3481
funds 2247
funeral 18, 140, 172, 174, 177,
  189, 196, 214, 223, 232, 234,
  252, 258, 279, 286, 289, 292,
  293, 941, 1549, 2060, 2070,
  3441, 3566, 3654, 3660, 3773,
  3802, 3978, 3984, 4025, 4047,
  4084, 5257, 5462, 5501
funeral march 2016
funeral procession 2427
funeral sermon 1090
funeral service 220, 311
funning 2344
funny 522, 523, 1052, 1166, 2403,
  3663, 4251, 4473, 4635, 6018
funny thing 1258, 3737, 3946,
  4299, 4717, 4965, 5966
fur 56, 4974
furniture 3535, 4801
further 5751
further and faster 6060
fury 385
fuse 5300
fuss 3579
fussy 5885
futile 2657
future 1037, 1314, 1922, 1961,
  2762, 2929, 3232, 3465, 3975,
  4176, 4541, 5475
future vs. past 5652
future vs. present 4814

gabby 163
gag 4064
gain 4181, 4864
gal 1040, 2198, 2430, 3936, 5536,
  5871, 5904, 6029, 6060
gall 4284
gallant 1445
gallant men 1759
gallantries 2310
galled 1727
gallivanted bug 4791
gallons 5757
Gallop 2281, 4718
galloping 2606
galloping consumption 5754
gallow 2139
gallows 2662
galls 4899
gals 555, 1649, 2236, 4906
gamble 1460, 1498, 1518, 1551,
  1563, 1727, 4977, 5176
gambled 1544
gambler 749, 930, 1297, 1452,

1454, 1462, 1471, 1477, 1480,
  1487, 1496, 3351, 4370, 4662,
  5850
gambler's heart 1475
gambler's widow 1470
gambles 1555
gambling 123, 1434, 1436, 1442,
  1489, 1478, 1479, 1484, 1499,
  1513, 1514, 1552, 3701, 2246,
  4118, 4133, 4479, 4974, 5102,
  5468, 5487, 5491, 5522, 5550,
  5605, 5845, 5886, 5945
gambling chance 1460
gambling hall 3361, 5100
gambling house 5101
gambling loss 1511
game 502, 644, 653, 1435, 1444,
  1448, 1456, 1458, 1467, 1468,
  1471, 1472, 1490, 1531, 1544,
  1547, 1558, 1940, 2769, 2826,
  2830, 2863, 3336, 3609, 4112,
  4448, 5146, 5236, 5374
game (cards) 785
game of chance 1512
game rooster 1204
gamely 2651
games 2854, 5065
gang 45, 64, 80, 89, 225, 628,
  3064, 3482, 3603, 3708, 3712,
  4398, 4426, 4473
gangrene 425
gangs 61, 1769
gap 4259
garbage 3361
garden 4198, 4660
Garden of Eden 4497
Garden of Evil 1586
gardens 5022
garrison 386
garrison life 1351
garter 2064
gasping 5746
gate 2814, 4948
gates of hell 2296, 5210
gateway to west 5684
gathering 4544
gathers 6059
Gatling gun 3232, 6035
gave (life) 1210
gawk 283
gawking 6062
gay 285
gaze 4319
gear 665, 3661, 3694
geared 3544
geese 2809
gem cracks 5357
gender 2451, 5120, 6063
gender thing 821
general 1383
General 437
general store 5079
general vs. specific 4170
generals 349, 409, 464, 1347
generation 3570
generations 936, 5000
generous 139, 422, 1495, 3883,
  5408, 5541
generous man 3308

genius 1992
gent 1235, 1828, 1998, 4117
genteel 2459
gentle 317
gentleman 284, 408, 415, 530,
  705, 1009, 1240, 1352, 1422,
  1445, 1655, 1657, 2217, 3336,
  3932, 4200, 4249, 4277, 4289,
  4501, 5146, 5177, 5218, 5303,
  5364, 5439
gents 3, 1093, 2265, 2280
genuine 4514
genuine good woman 6000
geography 861, 1967, 5696, 5722
geological conditions 283
Georgia 6034
germ 889, 5770
Geronimo 1243
gesture 491
get along 3991, 4598, 4749, 5973
get away 1672, 4096, 5629
get away with 3472
get away with it 5459
get even 4540
get even with 5823
get in and get out 5149
get in vs. get out 5494
get lost 4928
get out vs. get in 5494
get over it 4244
get up and go 283
getaway 2274, 4440
gets in way 5232
getting and wanting 4760
getting along 3850
getting away 662
getting into vs. out of 4725
getting out of vs. into 4725
getting up 4759
getting vs. keeping 4888
Gettysburg 379, 456, 507, 516,
  5033, 5106
ghastly 2139
ghost 469, 624, 1042, 2550,
  2830, 5268
Ghost Dance 2492, 2690, 2836
Ghost Dancer 2836
ghost sickness 2558
ghost town 5268
ghost towns 5586
ghostly 258
ghosts 2828
giant hand 5283, 5725
giant size 1391
gift 1509, 1977, 2631, 2727, 3411,
  4469, 5009, 5999
gin 5107
girl 122, 704, 821, 1276, 1277,
  1331, 1894, 3918, 3944, 3956,
  3967, 3982, 3995, 4046, 4070,
  4072, 4099, 4108,, 4818, 4974,
  5065, 5076, 5090, 5822, 5826,
  5862, 5897, 5898, 5927, 5953,
  6019, 6033, 6041, 6046, 6050,
  5945 4398
girlfriend 1331, 3934
girls and boys 5565
girls and steak 5937
give 2610

give and get 4619
give and receive 3078
give and take 1007, 4160
give a damn 51, 5434
give away 5748
give ground 4713
give it up 5379, 5500
give up 20, 616, 1722, 4435,
  4887, 5160, 5286, 5530
give vs. have 4011
give vs. take life 3275
given vs. earn 4766
giving 422
giving up 4873
gizzard 5405
glad 4111, 4806
glad heart 4111
glare 3249
glass 1041, 5107, 5798, 5816
glass windows 3789
glasses 3040, 5204, 5280
glee 1010
glorious 452
glorious west 2604
glory 435, 466, 470, 531, 1141,
  1199, 781, 1330, 1385, 1410,
  1415, 1416, 1420, 1841, 2178,
  2304, 2496, 3779, 4974, 5137
glory days 1811, 4982
glory riding 2438
gloves 5767
glow 2667
glue 6048
glum 2479
gluttons 4662
gnat 12
gnawing 4874
go and stay 5968
go along 4598, 4826, 5649
go around vs. go through 4704
go away 4928
go back 645, 5271
go on 645
go out 1199
go through vs. go around 4704
go vs. stay 6036, 6037
go west 5687
goal 1142, 1993, 3632, 5237, 5425
goal attainment 4236
goal setting 4530
goat 195, 856, 5839
God 62, 136, 181, 200, 227, 303,
  305, 409, 415, 423, 471, 530,
  554, 688, 1083, 1224, 1261,
  1614, 1663, 1692, 1693, 1829,
  1853, 1982, 2019, 2067, 2093,
  2249, 2498, 2519, 2632, 2676,
  2702, 2742, 2743, 2809, 2829,
  2892, 2900, 2912, 3118, 3121,
  3467, 3621, 3705, 3824, 4111,
  4271, 4360, 4361, 4438, 4474,
  4572, 4632, 4757, 4763, 4821,
  4846, 4949, 5021, 5060, 5184,
  5255, 5289, 5323, 5373, 5402,
  5438, 5534, 5590, 5662, 5714,
  5768, 5789, 6022, 6038
God Almighty 3289, 5151, 5188,
  5482
God fearing people 4923

"Folks, I'm afraid the party is over.
Thank you all for coming!"
— as spoken by Mrs. Waynebrook (Verna Felton)
in Francis D. Lyon's *The Oklahoman* (Warner Bros., 1957)

"Someday… somewhere…
our trails will cross again."
— as spoken by Breck Coleman (John Wayne)
in Raoul Walsh's *The Big Trail* (Fox, 1930)